EMANUEL SWEDENBORG

A CONTINUING VISION

EMANUEL SWEDENBORG

A CONTINUING VISION

A Pictorial Biography
&
Anthology of Essays & Poetry

Edited by Robin Larsen, Ph.D.
Stephen Larsen, Ph.D.; James F. Lawrence, M.A.;
William Ross Woofenden, Ph.D.

With an Introduction by
George F. Dole, Ph.D.

Swedenborg Foundation, Inc.
New York

Editor-in-Chief, Picture Editor, Archivist of the Swedenborg Image Archive:
  Robin Larsen, Ph.D.
Editors: Stephen Larsen, Ph.D.; James F. Lawrence, M.A.;
  William Ross Woofenden, Ph.D.
Consulting Editors: Virginia Branston, George F. Dole, Ph.D., Olle Hjern
Manuscript and Production Editor: Kate Davis
Designer and Production Manager: Nancy Crompton
Picture Editor: Anja Hübener
Editorial Assistant: Barbara Zucker

Produced by Chameleon Books, Inc.
211 West 20th Street
New York, NY 10011

Printed and bound in Hong Kong

Library of Congress Catalog Card Number: 87-51521

ISBN: 0-87785-136-0

First Edition

First published in the United States of America in 1988 by
Swedenborg Foundation, Inc.
139 East 23rd Street
New York, NY 10010

10 9 8 7 6 5 4 3 2 1

Affectionately dedicated
to
Virginia Branston
as a realization
of the dream she nurtured

Contents

I. Arts & Letters

II. Social Issues & Psychology

III. *The Man & His World*

Preface

THE CONCEPT OF A pictorial biography of Emanuel Swedenborg was originated in the mid-1960s when Virginia Branston acquired for the Swedenborg Foundation Dr. Marguerite Block's collection of photographs and original art prints of Swedenborgiana. At that time, the late Tomas H. Spiers was executive secretary of the foundation, and Virginia Branston was manager. While they were looking over the pictures, Mrs. Branston asked, "Now, what shall we do with this?" To which Mr. Spiers replied, "Why not publish a pictorial biography of Swedenborg?"

Soon after, Virginia Branston began to assemble other pictures from European and American sources and, in order to develop a text, conducted a series of interviews with Dr. Block, author of *New Church in the New World*, who was at that time retired from her professorship at Columbia University. These interviews continued up until Dr. Block's death in October 1974. Through the 1970s, Virginia Branston carried on the work of expanding and documenting the picture collection.

What was essential at this point was finding an editor for the volume and establishing a comprehensive resource of visual materials that could be systematically accessed in order to fill out the substance of the book. For a modern publication this bank of images should include high-quality color and black-and-white photographs as well as reproductions of eighteenth-century art illustrating the culture and environment of Swedenborg's Europe; his technological achievements; and portraits of Swedenborg's family and his associates, many of whom were historically significant.

The need for this kind of resource led to the creation of the Swedenborg Image Archive (SIA), a project funded by the Swedenborg Foundation. SIA was initiated in 1982 by Dr. Robin Larsen, an art historian and archivist, and her husband, Dr. Stephen Larsen, a psychologist and member of the foundation's Board of Directors. SIA's objective was to organize the existing collection of images and to extend it with slides and photographs to be used in publications on Swedenborgian themes as well as related areas, from history to mythology and religious symbolism.

In 1983 the Larsens traveled to England, Holland, and Sweden collecting images specifically for the biography as well as for the archive in general. Much of the visual material included in this book is an outgrowth of that work. In 1985 Dr. Robin Larsen was appointed chairperson of an editorial committee for the Swedenborg pictorial biography by the Board of Directors of the Swedenborg Foundation, and subsequently became editor-in-chief.

It was felt by the editors that a book of the scale originally conceived, however, should have depth as well as breadth, scholarly articles as well as illustrations, to show the vast reach of Swedenborg's thought and influence. This book should, if possible, be more comprehensive than any other published heretofore on the subject of Swedenborg. It should present the Swedenborgian perspective and reach beyond those already familiar with his work and into the general intellectual community.

To this end, original works were solicited from scholars of Swedenborg, essays falling into categories that might be labeled secular or academic as well as theological. The essays chosen, therefore, were selected for their treatment of particular themes or as being representative of various conceptual approaches within the broad range of contemporary Swedenborgian thought. The editorial policy of this volume, therefore, has intentionally been not to espouse a specific theological approach to Swedenborg. The objective has been to show the extent of his influence outside as well as within the religious sphere.

We thought it illuminating to include a biographical note for each of our more than forty contributing authors, detailing their educational and professional backgrounds. These biographical notes appear at the bottom of the first page of each author's essay, in the section where that writer's work first occurs in the book.

The editors faced a task of considerable difficulty, not only in presenting essays with philosophical or religious differences, but differences in style as well, especially from older sources. Where we have used articles from other sources or publications, it was to fill a particular content area deemed worthy of inclusion. These essays are preceded by prefatory remarks acknowledging and explaining the nature of their prior publication.

Inasmuch as there is some factual inconsistency in present publications on Swedenborg's life, every effort has been made to resolve these inconsistencies where possible and to represent Swedenborg's biography accurately. To do so, we have circulated materials to our editorial committee and called upon them to lend scholarly input from their various fields of expertise. However, in the case of the most complex issues—such as Swedenborg's relationship to Kant or the scanty documentation of his association with Linnaeus—our task has been simplified considerably by taking a pictorial approach and presenting an overview. For those who wish to pursue further the details of Swedenborg's life, we would refer them to the list of biographies and reference works in the Select Bibliography at the end of this book.

Wherever possible throughout the book, we have edited for nonsexist language. However, in some works previously published there may still be found masculine pronouns used generically, and even though we were sensitive to this issue, we, or the author, thought it important to reproduce the article as originally written.

Because there are many different forms of and much inconsistency in spelling of Swedish names and their English translations, the editors have decided to use original Swedish spellings from Swedenborg's day for personal names (where these could be determined) and today's current spellings for Swedish place names. Authoritative sources, including Sten Lindroth's *Svensk Lardomhistoria (Swedish Intellectual History)*; Herman Hofberg's *Svenskt Biografiskt Handlexikon (Swedish Biographical Dictionary)*; and *M·KAK Bilkartor (Swedish Automobile Association / Royal Automobile Club Atlas)*, among others, have been consulted for these spellings. For non-Swedish personal and place names we have used the preferred spellings found in *Webster's Biographical* and *Geographical Dictionaries* as well as the *Britannica Atlas*.

Quotes of Swedenborg in the text are documented by an abbreviation of the title of his work referred to, followed by paragraph, or volume and page numbers. These abbreviations correspond to those found in the key at the beginning of the Bibliography of Swedenborg's Works, at the end of this book. William Woofenden's selection for this bibliography represents a piece of scholarship in itself. There have been so many editions and translations of each work prepared that to represent them all would fill an entire volume. The works chosen for this bibliography are those cited by the various authors in the body of this book as well as those deemed worthy of inclusion by the editors and compilers. Contributing authors often refer to different editions, but the same paragraph numbers are used in most editions (see the introduction to this bibliography for more information).

In the notes following each essay, every effort has been made to provide full, scholarly reference data. Where minor omissions occur, authors may have been unable to locate or secure the needed data, but the editors feel certain that readers wishing to study further will find information sufficient to guide them in their research.

To convey the subtleties of his spiritual understanding, Swedenborg developed a specialized Latin vocabulary. In attempting to retain his original sense while rendering those terms into English, scholars have sometimes assigned specific meanings to words with a more general philosophical or theological usage. In order to identify and clarify these terms for our readers, Dr. William Woofenden, in consultation with our editorial committee and consultant Dr. George Dole, has prepared a glossary for the reference section of this book.

In addition to providing a glossary, the editors felt that it would be helpful to present an introduction to concepts essential to the understanding of Swedenborg's thought. This guide to key concepts is included in the reference section.

Full credits for artists and sources of illustrations and photographs used herein appear in a figure list at the end of the book. Accompanying each figure in the text is a caption including its title and/or a brief descriptive note where necessary. Artist's name and date of the artwork have been included in the caption only for one-of-a-kind artworks (e.g., paintings, sculptures, etc.) or limited editions of prints by major artists; most period engravings have been treated as if they were documentary photographs.

The greatest proportion of pictures used is from Swedish and other European sources. Recent photographs, which supplement images from the eighteenth century, have been contributed by a number of New Church travelers, who are credited in the figure list. For illustrating the pictorial essays, the editors have preferred to use etchings and engravings from Swedenborg's time whenever possible. Our primary criteria for choosing illustrations has been the historical relevance of their content. Most reproductions we obtained were of high quality; however, we have in a few cases included those of lesser quality when, for example, original photographs were not accessible.

This is a large book because it has a large purpose. For readers new to Swedenborg, it will provide a biographical introduction to his life and enable them to access his thought through topics with which they are already familiar. For readers well-versed in Swedenborgian ideas, it will provide an opportunity to trace his concepts in diverse fields of study, enrich their understanding, and gain further insights.

Emanuel Swedenborg's lifework probed and spanned a multiplicity of disciplines in his effort to answer the perennially vital questions of human existence. His work encompassed an extraordinary combination of depth and breadth, and it is both the reach of his imagination and the persistence of his inquiry that compels one to acknowledge the continuing relevance of Swedenborg's vision.

Acknowledgments

FROM THE BEGINNING of this project, I have been guided by Virginia Branston's original vision and continuous assistance. My gratitude is similarly extended to the Board of Directors of the Swedenborg Foundation and the Editorial and Publication Committee for their support and guidance, especially to Alice B. Skinner, John Seekamp, and George F. Dole.

For the past several years it has been my privilege to work with a competent and energetic editorial team. Each member has contributed a distinctive personal style, yet all have cooperated with mutual sensitivity and respect. Whenever the task of completing such a demanding project has seemed most overwhelming, I have always been able to rely on the creative integrity and encouragement of our editors. To Jim Lawrence, Steve Larsen, Bill Woofenden, Kate Davis, Nancy Crompton, Anja Hübener, and Barbara Zucker, I would like to say Thank you—working with you has been a rare and rewarding experience.

I wish also to thank Clayton Priestnol, Harvey Johnson, Ted Klein, and the late Richard Tafel, who were members of the initial advisory committee. Darrell Ruhl gave continual encouragement from the earliest phases of establishing the Swedenborg Image Archive, for which I am appreciative.

Donald Rose was especially helpful both as a member of the Board of Directors of the Swedenborg Foundation and for arranging contacts and finding resources at Bryn Athyn's Academy of the New Church. David Glenn, archivist at the Glencairn Museum, made available their extensive resources. Among those who assisted with research or who loaned materials are Bruce Glenn, Joyce Bellinger, Erland Brock, Bill Fehon, Morna Hyatt, Dean Morey, Aubrey Odhner, Martha Gyllenhaal, Margaret Wilde, Dennis Cooper, and Henry's Rock & Gem Store.

In addition, members of the Swedenborg Scientific Association, especially Erland Brock, Gregory Baker, William R. Woofenden, and Leon Rhodes, have supported the project in numerous ways.

At the Swedenborg School of Religion in Newton, Massachusetts, Librarian Marian Kirven made their archives available to me; after her retirement she assisted in researching poetry sources for the anthology, and initiated the process of obtaining permissions. Daniel Nielsen was especially helpful with material on the poetry of the Brownings. I would also like to thank Dr. Patricia Basu, current librarian at SSR; Louise Woofenden, archivist; Mary Bryant, who assisted with communication between our various offices; and Ethelwyn Worden and her staff at the General Convention Office at Newton.

The 1983 European research and photography trip provided essential material for the pictorial biography, and supplied us with our initial contacts with European authors. Many people assisted us in our work there, among them Olle Hjern of Stockholm, who gave us the benefit of his historical expertise, introduced us to scholars, and arranged access to private collections and public archives. The late Roy Franson of the Stockholm General Church, with his wife Britta, hosted and advised us during our stay in Stockholm. In southern Sweden, Dr. Bjorn Boyesen and Lois Boyesen directed us to significant sites.

Thanks are also extended to Gunnel Myhrberg and others at the Swedish Information Service in New York; and to Birgitta Tennander at Stockholm's Svenska Instutet; to Mr. and Mrs. von Wachenfeldt for their kind assistance; to a number of scholars at Uppsala University and Library, some of whom have also contributed essays to this book, among them most especially Gunnar Broberg; and to the helpful people at numerous Swedish museums and archives. Among the latter, special thanks are due to Eva Wallner at Uppsala's Linnémuseet; to Åke Norrgård at Tekniska Museet; to the management of Brunnsbo Kungsgård; and to Lilly Westin, who so graciously hosted us when we visited her home at Svedens Gård.

In other parts of Europe we were also assisted, guided, and made welcome by Christiaan Vonck in Antwerp; Will van Kestrin and Mr. and Mrs. Mann at Swedenborg Genootschap in The Hague; Friedemann and Hela Horn of Swedenborg Verlag in Zurich; Madeleine Waters at Swedenborg House in London. Brian and Jill Kingslake, in England, had also conceived of a pictorial archive and biography, and opened their home to our family.

For their assistance with editorial and production tasks, I would like to acknowledge Kate Davis and Eric Hughes, copy editors; Ruth Borden, proofreader; Barbara Zucker, permissions assistant and proofreader; and Anne Eberle, indexer. Gunilla Gado and Anja Hübener were indispensible consultants on Swedish culture and translators of the language.

Harvey Bellin and Tom Kieffer of the Media Group were often available with creative input from their parallel film and video projects for the foundation.

Diane Fehon, assisted by Debra Grant, photographed period documents for essay illustrations, and researched and photographed part-title still lifes of authentic objects used by Swedenborg or in his time. Many other fine photographers have contributed to the book. Especially to be thanked are Daniel Fitzpatrick of Stockholm's General Church; my husband, Stephen Larsen, who has done much of the photographing for the archive; and the many New Church travelers who have contributed their photographs and maps, among them Virginia Branston, Brian Kingslake, William R. Woofenden, Ethelwyn Worden, and Foster Freeman. Leon Rhodes, editor of *New Church Life*, also generously contributed materials from his photographic collection. John Lenz provided professional custom photoprocessing in especially difficult areas, and was always available for technical consultation.

My heartfelt thanks go to the staff of the Swedenborg Foundation, especially Kristine Jorhdahl, Lieschen Redelin, and Harriet Marasco, for communication liaison, their help with endless details, their patience and encouragement.

Introduction

George F. Dole, Ph.D.

IT WAS AN EXTRAORDINARY LIFE. It spanned some eighty-two years of intense activity with impressive achievements in a wide variety of fields, ranging from mechanical engineering to the metaphysics of spiritual experience. It included a major personal crisis, weathered in virtual solitude, and the reentry into public life of a man transformed.

Partly because it is the story of an individual who went beyond common experience, and partly because it is a story that started three centuries ago, it must be savored to be appreciated. The natural tendency is to simplify; and while there is a good deal of truth in the view that Swedenborg was a scientist whose search for the soul led him to the experience of the soul, this hardly does him justice. The depth and the breadth of his interests was extraordinary.

He was indeed a "scientist," but not in our twentieth-century sense of a university professor or a researcher for industry. Professionally, he was first an engineer and then a civil servant, and he often had to take time off from his job to follow his scientific interests. The instruments he had for research were, by modern standards, primitive. Scientific methodology was in its infancy, and the most significant writings of the era would not meet the formal criteria for a master's thesis today. In spite of this, we are still discovering his discoveries.

Nor was his progress as linear as the simplified outline suggests. There were false starts, setbacks, and dead ends. Until late in his life, he tried unsuccessfully to gain support for his method of determining longitude by observations of the moon. While his *Oeconomia Regni Animalis* was favorably received, his own judgment was that it had failed in its primary purpose—to find the soul by an exhaustive search of the body. This sense of failure was central to the personal crisis that resulted in his years of direct inner experience, recorded and evaluated with the same empirical discipline that had made his science so productive.

Wherever one looks, there is a book to be written. The overview of his life, the pictorial biography, is copiously illustrated, to help the reader view the story in its eighteenth-century context. And our volume is designed to open avenues of further exploration. The individuals who responded to his ideas with the greatest energy are often to be found in the arts, especially literature and painting, and in psychology and social issues. Essays in the first two sections of the anthology ("Arts & Letters" and "Social Issues & Psychology") introduce some notable instances. The third section ("The Man & His World") of the anthology looks at Swedenborg's time in greater detail.

It does seem, perhaps strangely, that in the two areas of his primary concern, science and religion, Swedenborg did not find his way into the mainstream of Western thought. There is a change now going on in both science and religion, however, and the climate is favorable for a fresh assessment of Swedenborg's contributions in these areas. The fourth and fifth sections of the anthology ("Religion & Philosophy" and "Theoretical & Applied Sciences") represent a beginning of this task.

The reference section is intended to enable the reader to begin to pursue particular interests that may be awakened. This is, after all, the primary purpose of the book—not to answer all possible questions, but to introduce. A life that included so many interests should be of interest to many; and it is the editors' hope that this volume may foster increased attention to the remarkable individual whose tricentennial it celebrates.

REV. DR. GEORGE F. DOLE is a minister of the General Convention (Swedenborgian church) and is professor of theology and Bible at the Swedenborg School of Religion in Newton, Massachusetts. He holds degrees from Yale, Oxford, and Harvard and served for eleven years as pastor of the Swedenborgian church in Cambridge, Massachusetts. His publications include translations of Swedenborg's *Heaven and Hell*, *The Universal Human* (extracts from *Arcana Coelestia*), as well as *Soul-Body Interaction*, *Divine Love and Wisdom*, and *An Introduction to Swedenborg's Theological Latin*. He is also the author of scripts for the films *Images of Knowing* and *The Other Side of Life*.

Emanuel Swedenborg
A Pictorial Biography

Robert H. Kirven, Ph.D. and
Robin Larsen, Ph.D.

FIG. 1. *Emanuel Swedenborg (1688-1772), 1900s*

ROBERT H. KIRVEN is professor of theology and church history at the Swedenborg School of Religion. His doctoral dissertation at Brandeis University dealt with Swedenborg's contributions to the history of ontology and epistemology.

ROBIN LARSEN is a scholar of comparative iconography, an exhibiting artist, and the archivist of the Swedenborg Image Archive of the Swedenborg Foundation. With her husband, Stephen Larsen, she presents lectures and workshops on myth and psyche. She holds an M.A. degree from New York University and a Ph.D. from the Union of Experimenting Colleges and Universities.

FIG. 2. *Emanuel Swedenborg in his nineteenth year, ca. 1707*

Ancestry & Birth

FIG. 3. *Jesper Swedberg (1653-1735)*

Although several formal portraits of Emanuel Swedenborg have come down to us, there are no pictures of Swedenborg as he lived his daily life. To visualize him as his contemporaries saw him, we must combine portraits such as the one on the facing page with sketches, paintings, and engravings from his time. We can look at pictures of places that he visited or frequented, and of people doing the kinds of things he did. We can view photographs of surviving houses and buildings that he lived in or passed through, and of objects that he touched. With a little imagination, such images can bring us closer to the man who was born three hundred years ago, the person behind the ideas and works that are discussed in this tricentennial anthology.

Emanuel Swedenborg's father, Jesper Swedberg, was thirty-five and chaplain to the court of King Karl XI when Emanuel was born. He died—doctor of theology and bishop of Skara—when Swedenborg was forty-seven. Son of a wealthy mineowner, Jesper and his older brother Peter were the first generation of the family to bear a family name instead of a patriarchal name according to the traditional Swedish practice. Jesper's father was Daniel Isaacsson, his father was Isaac Nilsson, and his was Nils Ottesson, and so on. When Daniel Isaacsson chose a family name for his sons, he called them "Swedberg," because the family farm and homestead near the great Falun Mine was called Svedens Gård, or Sveden.

FIG. 4. Sveden, *by Sigurd Erixon, 1819*

One hundred fifty miles north of Stockholm, in the heart of the mining country, the rolling wooded hills are dotted with so many lakes that the land seems like a net floating on water. There is ample timber, some farming in the short northern summer, and horse farms like Sveden. Emanuel visited here often enough to grow fond of horses and to become an excellent rider.

FIG. 5. *Guest cottage at Svedens Gård near Falun*

Wealthy mineowners and landholders like Jesper Swedberg's father maintained estates that would be comfortable today and were luxurious in their time. The spacious homestead and many of the surrounding buildings are gone, but this guest cottage still stands at Sveden.

FIG. 6. *Linnaeus's marriage room in guest cottage at Svedens Gård*

One room of the Sveden guest cottage is honored today as the room where, in June of 1739, the Swedish botanist Carolus Linnaeus married Swedenborg's cousin, Sara Elisabet Moraea. Swedenborg is known to have stayed here many times.

This handsomely crafted cabinet is an original furnishing in the Sveden guest house and bears out Sveden's tradition of excellent woodworking and cabinetry. The high quality of the remaining furniture suggests the refinement that was most likely present in the manor house as well.

This wall painting at Sveden (*The Death of Absalom*, by Berndt Svedin of Falun) suggests the level of culture at this rural estate.

FIG. 7. *Cupboard in Linnaeus's marriage room*

FIG. 8. The Death of Absalom, *by Berndt Svedin, ca. 1700*

FIG. 9. Falu Koppargruva, *view of copper mine at Falun*

The Falun mine near Sveden, one of Sweden's largest sources of copper, was the basis of much of Sweden's wealth. Both of Swedenborg's grandparents, the Swedbergs and the Behms, were stockholders in the corporation that owned and operated Falun.

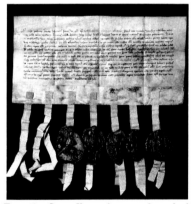

FIG. 10. *Stora Kopparberg purchase deed*

The purchase deed, dated 1288, relates to a one-eighth share in the great mine. The Stora Kopparberg (Copper Mountain Corporation) is one of the oldest corporations in the world. It provided the fortunes of many of Sweden's wealthy families, who formed the economic, social, and political backbone of the country.

The actual mining was hard and dangerous work, with few safety precautions and little mechanical assistance. Swedenborg's concern for mining and miners became evident in many of his earliest inventions, which were machines to aid in mining operations.

FIG. 11. *Miners at work in the Falun copper mine, by Pehr Hilleström, 1788*

Swedenborg's mother, Sara Behm Swedberg (1666–1696), was the daughter of Albrecht Behm, another wealthy mineowner—with a share in Stora Kopparberg and other mines—and a member (assessor) of the national Board of Mines. She was twenty when Emanuel was born, and died at the age of thirty in Uppsala when he was ten.

Emanuel Swedenborg was born in Stockholm on 29 January 1688, the third of nine children of Jesper and Sara (Behm) Swedberg. He was the second son, but his older brother, Albert, died when Emanuel was eight, leaving him the eldest surviving male in the family. Two of his sisters—Anna, who was two years older; and Hedvig, who was two years younger—remained especially close to Emanuel, each providing a home for him at different periods of his life. A younger brother, Daniel, died when Emanuel was only three; and the next brother, Eliezer, died when Swedenborg was eleven. His sister, Catharina, and brother, Jesper, both lived for seventy-seven years, but died two years before Swedenborg. He was survived by only his youngest sister, Margaretha. The birthdates of all the Swedberg children were recorded according to the Julian calendar, which was used in Sweden until 1740, when a new astronomical method was used to establish the date of Easter. If the Gregorian calendar, officially adopted by Sweden in 1753 and in use throughout the world today, were retrojected to that time, the dates would be eleven days later: Emanuel's birthday would fall on February 9.

FIG. 12. *Sara Behm Swedberg (1666-1696), 1692*

Swedenborg's Siblings

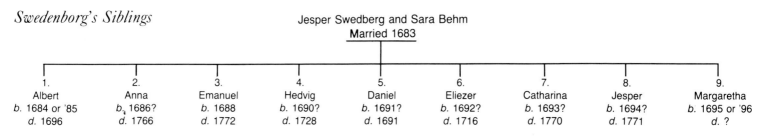

Jesper Swedberg and Sara Behm
Married 1683

| 1.
Albert
b. 1684 or '85
d. 1696 | 2.
Anna
b. 1686?
d. 1766 | 3.
Emanuel
b. 1688
d. 1772 | 4.
Hedvig
b. 1690?
d. 1728 | 5.
Daniel
b. 1691?
d. 1691 | 6.
Eliezer
b. 1692?
d. 1716 | 7.
Catharina
b. 1693?
d. 1770 | 8.
Jesper
b. 1694?
d. 1771 | 9.
Margaretha
b. 1695 or '96
d. ? |

FIG. 13. *Stockholm viewed from the west*

In 1688 as today, Stockholm was Sweden's capital and largest city. A seaport and a lakeport, the old town was a little island, connected by several bridges to the surrounding suburbs. It was the site of the royal court, government offices, and the country's largest concentration of shipping, commerce, and banking.

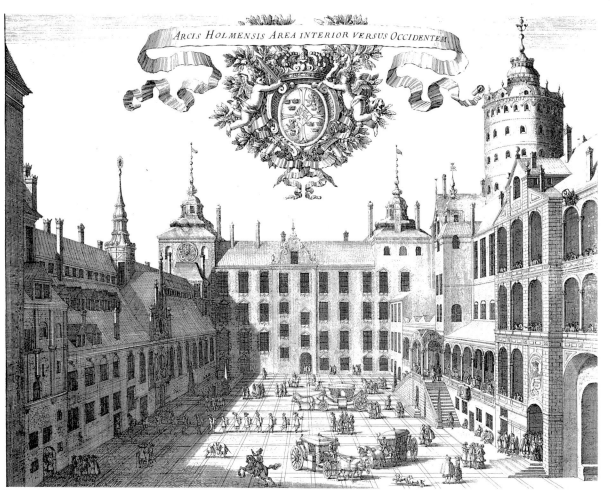

ARCIS HOLMENSIS AREA INTERIOR VERSUS OCCIDENTEM

FIG. 14. Borggården, *courtyard of Tre Kronor castle*

FIG. 15. *Chancel of Royal Chapel in Tre Kronor castle*

The old royal castle, Tre Kronor (Three Crowns), was located on the north side of the island of Gamla Stan (the Old Town). Shown here is the Borggården (Courtyard) as depicted by Erik Dahlberg, whose extensive set of engravings of Swedish historical sites and buildings was published in 1716. The present Royal Palace was built on the same site, designed by Nicodemus Tessin and completed by his son, Carl Gustav, in 1754.

Swedenborg's father preached as court chaplain in Stockholm during the first four years of Emanuel's life. The chancel of the Royal Chapel offered a magnificent pulpit for an impassioned preacher, and Jesper Swedberg used it so well that King Karl XII once warned him he had many enemies—to which Jesper replied, "A servant of the Lord is not good for much, if he has no enemies" (DOC vol. 1, p. 107).

FIG. 16. *Jakobs Kyrka*

The more modest Jakobs Kyrka in Stockholm was the site of Emanuel's baptism on 2 February, Candlemass Day, 1688. It was the same day that Princess Ulrika Eleonora, a future queen of Sweden, also was baptized.

FIG. 17. *Base of baptismal font, by Jost Schutz, 1643*

The baptismal plate and base for baptismal font shown here from Jakobs Kyrka probably are the ones used by the Reverend Matthias Wagner to baptize the infant Emanuel Swedberg, thirty-one years before he was ennobled and renamed Emanuel Swedenborg.

FIG. 18. *Baptismal plate showing Christ's baptism, by J. Jäger, 1660*

Childhood & Education at Uppsala

FIG. 19. *Uppsala Cathedral*

When Emanuel was four years old, King Karl XI appointed his father Jesper to the faculty of the University of Uppsala as professor of theology. Two years later, he was given the additional post of rector of Uppsala Cathedral, shown here as it stands today.

FIG. 20. Tidningen Uppsala *building, Swedberg residence*

In 1602 this building, at one time the office of the *Daily Uppsala*, was the residence into which the Swedberg family moved on their arrival at Uppsala. Later in his life, Swedenborg recalled this as a time when he was "constantly engaged in thoughts on God, salvation, and the spiritual sufferings of men" (L&M vol. 2, p. 696). When he was twelve, he started to "delight in conversing with clergymen about faith" (L&M vol. 2, p. 696), and experienced his first spontaneous experiments with hypoventilation, or controlled breathing, which over the years became incorporated into a meditation technique.

FIG. 21. *Näktergalen, Swedberg residence in Stora Torget*

Later, Swedenborg's family built a house they called "Näktergalen," or "the Nightingale," where they were living when Emanuel's mother died on 17 June 1696. This same year, Johan Moraeus, a cousin of Emanuel's who had been trained as a pharmacist, moved into the house as a private tutor. The next year, Jesper married again, this time to Sara Bergia, daughter of another wealthy mineowner. Emanuel became her favorite among her stepchildren. The family remained at Näktergalen until a fire destroyed the home in 1702.

Olof Rudbeck, professor of medicine and botany at Uppsala, was a friend of the family who had a great influence on Swedenborg's life. In the 1702 fire, he is credited with directing students who saved most of the books in the university library, and many of Jesper Swedberg's books, as well. He instilled a deep interest in botany and anatomy in two of his most famous students—Swedenborg and Linnaeus—and also guided them to a fascination with what today would be called comparative religions, including the religious symbols of antiquity and the visionary imagery of indigenous healers among the Lapps.

FIG. 22. *Olof Rudbeck (1630–1702), by M. Mijtens I, 1696*

FIG. 23. *Royal burial mounds with St. Lars Church*

Rudbeck supervised early archaeological digs by his students, including Swedenborg, at the site of Sweden's old royal burial grounds at Gamla Uppsala.

FIG. 24. *Uppsala, view with Fyris River and cathedral*

On 15 June 1699, the eleven-year-old Emanuel matriculated in the university at Uppsala, where he was graduated ten years later. What would today be called prep and college courses in a single curriculum were focused for him in mathematics and the natural sciences.

In spring of 1703, Jesper Swedberg moved into this house in Brunsbo, where he lived for thirty-three years as bishop of Skara. Swedenborg often visited his father here, sometimes for extended periods. During one of these visits, he installed a speaking tube into the kitchen, said to have been used for ordering coffee, a beverage of which he was especially fond.

The cellar at Brunnsbo Kungsgård probably dates from the 1200s, and the house was used as a cloister in 1404. It burned in 1712 and again in 1730, three years before Jesper's death, but it was rebuilt each time. The restoration in 1790 endures to the present day, and the building now is used as a private sanatorium. Three or four of the great old trees in the yard are said to have been planted by Jesper and Emanuel.

FIG. 25. *Brunnsbo Kungsgård, Jesper Swedberg's residence*

FIG. 26. *Erik Benzelius, the Younger (1675–1743), by J. H. Scheffel, 1723*

FIG. 27. *Anna Swedenborg Benzelius (1686?–1766), by J. H. Scheffel, n.d.*

Emanuel's older sister, Anna, married Erik Benzelius, who was librarian of Uppsala University and later professor of theology there before being appointed bishop of Linköping. When Jesper and Sara (Bergia) moved to Brunsbo, Emanuel lived with Erik and Anna for six years, until his graduation from Uppsala, and formed such a close relationship with Benzelius that he loved and revered him "as a father" (DOC vol. 1, p. 208).

Around Uppsala at that time, everyone was involved in arguments over whether to allow the freedom of inquiry, which had been encouraged by the philosopher Descartes when he taught there just before his death, or whether to maintain the old ways of teaching only what was approved by the church. In these debates, Benzelius was a Cartesian and Jesper was a leading spokesman for the conservative view. Emanuel, for much of his life, continued to be tormented by the conflict between the Cartesianism espoused by his "second father" and the obedience to faith championed by his own father, the bishop.

Student Days Abroad

FIG. 28. *Emanuel Swedenborg, ca. 1707*

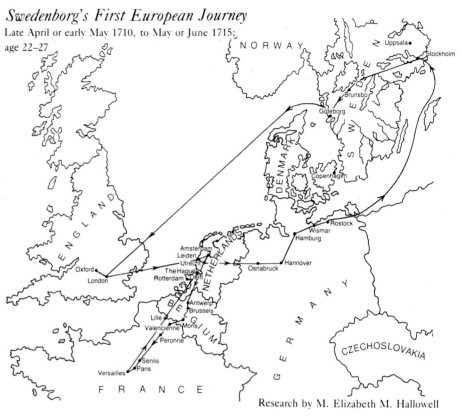

Swedenborg's First European Journey
Late April or early May 1710, to May or June 1715;
age 22–27

Research by M. Elizabeth M. Hallowell

Sweden in 1709 was an inauspicious place and time for a young man with ambitions in mechanical engineering to be leaving the university to enter the world. Sweden offered no opportunities for advanced engineering studies, and Karl XII was in the middle of his disastrous Russian campaign, which diminished the empire and depleted the treasury. Sweden was under attack from Denmark, and France was trying to blockade England, making foreign travel almost impossible; a series of crop failures brought the country close to famine; and bubonic plague would break out within months. The comfortable manse at Brunsbo offered none of the opportunities Emanuel was seeking, so during the following summer, at age twenty-two, he sailed for England in spite of the risks.

FIG. 29. Copenhagen Seen from The Sound, *warship and passenger vessels in The Sound*

The dangers of travel proved far from hypothetical, for Emanuel's life was in danger four times on the journey: once in a fog at sea, when his ship came so near a sandbank that "all considered themselves lost" (DOC vol. 2, p. 3); a second time when it was boarded by French privateers who thought the ship was British, while the passengers feared the attackers were Norwegian; a third time when it was mistaken for a French privateer and fired on, broadside, by an English warship; and a fourth time—the most serious—in London.

FIG. 30. Old East India Wharf, *at London Bridge, by Peter Monarny, 1700s*

FIG. 31. Tavern and Coffee House, *in London*

This last danger arose when the ship was quarantined outside London because of the plague in Sweden, and the impetuous youth accepted an invitation from Swedish friends in London to jump ship and land in spite of the quarantine. Arrested in London, he was threatened with hanging, and escaped death only by excellent recommendations, intervention of friends, and great good luck.

Free at last to continue his education, Emanuel pursued a two-pronged approach. Taking lodgings with a series of craftsmen, he simultaneously lived more cheaply than in conventional rooms, and learned the crafts of his hosts—watchmaking, cabinetmaking, brass instrument making, engraving, and (later in Holland) lens grinding. At the same time, he purchased books and equipment, unavailable in Sweden, to teach himself chemistry by performing Boyle's experiments. He read Newton daily, and he sought out the company of other young scientists and mathematicians to discuss the issues of the day in London's coffeehouses, like the one pictured here.

FIG. 32. Octagon Room, *Royal Greenwich Observatory*

Moving to Greenwich, he began to study astronomy in the Royal Observatory, seen here, with the great John Flamsteed, who was in the long process of making observations through this telescope for the first detailed tables of the position of the moon. Swedenborg was invited to assist him at night, making observations and recording data. Here he began thinking of his method for finding longitude at sea by means of the moon, and also conceived a dream he would cherish for years—of establishing an astronomical observatory in Sweden.

FIG. 33. *Edmund Halley (1656–1742), by R. Phillips, before 1721*

FIG. 34. *Bodleian Library, Divinity School*

After more than a year in London and Greenwich, a second allowance of money from home enabled him to move to Oxford, where he studied with the other great astronomer of the time, Sir Edmund Halley. Halley discouraged Emanuel in his longitude-finding method, based on Flamsteed's table, perhaps reflecting an apparent professional jealousy between Halley and Flamsteed.

While at Oxford, he visited the Bodleian Library to see its vast collection of books and manuscripts. He met the librarian, Dr. John Hudson, who had been corresponding with Erik Benzelius, and discussed Benzelius's literary efforts with him (L&M vol. 1, p. 35). The literary treasures of the Bodleian Library at Oxford led Emanuel to shift his focus from science for a while, and devote himself to the English poets. During this period, he wrote some Latin poetry; but his interests lay more with science than with literature, and he soon moved on to the continent of Europe.

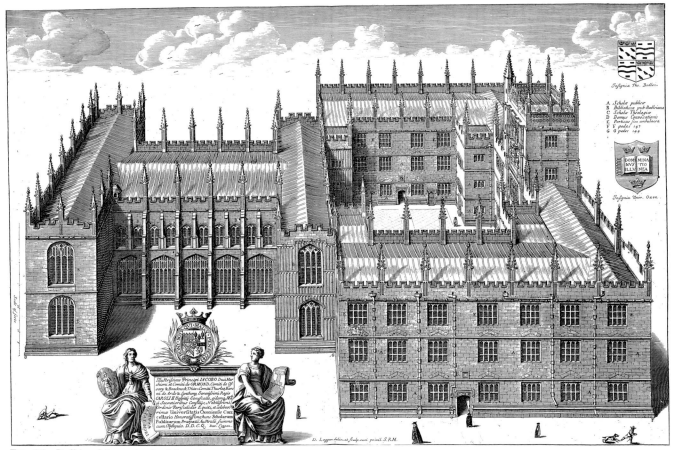

FIG. 35. *Bodleian Library in the eighteenth century*

In Leiden, Swedenborg studied science and scientific equipment at the university, taking special note of the magnificent observatory there. It is easy to picture him, walking these streets among the university buildings, some of which still remain from his time. His landlord here was a lens grinder, who taught him the techniques of that trade in exchange for assistance in the laboratory.

FIG. 36. *Leiden, eighteenth-century university buildings*

With that skill, plus the brass instrument making he had learned in London, he either made for himself (or had made under his personal direction) a microscope modeled after the instrument he had seen in van Leeuwenhoek's lab—except that van Leeuwenhoek's was 20 power, and Swedenborg's was 42. The microscope was a much-prized treasure: earlier, in London, he had written to Benzelius that he had looked at one for sale, which "I would have bought . . . if the price had not been so much higher than I could venture to pay" (DOC vol. 1, p. 224).

FIG. 37. *Swedenborg's microscope and case*

From Leiden he traveled to Utrecht, where leaders were gathered to sign an international peace treaty.

FIG. 38. City Hall in Utrecht

The 1712 Peace Congress, pictured here, was in session when Emanuel arrived, and he met with ambassadors from Sweden and other countries, such as England's Bishop John Robinson, discussing international affairs with them.

From Holland, he moved on to Paris, meeting with the leading French scientists of the time. He also visited the magnificent palace at Versailles, where he was impressed with the beauty of its gardens and marble statuary.

FIG. 39. *Utrecht Peace Congress, in City Hall*

FIG. 40. Vue du Chateau de Versailles, *by P. D. Martin, 1722*

Heading homeward after four years, he paused for several months in Rostock, passing through this very gate to enter the city—then a Swedish possession on the southern coast of the Baltic Sea—to gather his notes and drawings into something he could show for his travels.

FIG. 41. *Petritor, city gate of Rostock*

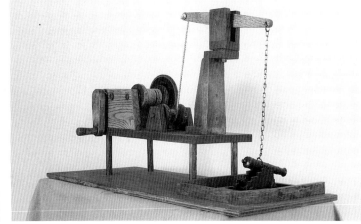

FIG. 42. *Model of Swedenborg's crane or cannon hoist*

Although most of his studies had been in chemistry, astronomy, mathematics, and poetry, his notebook was filled with practical inventions, like this crane to hoist cannons. The machines were more likely to impress his scientifically unsophisticated father and countrymen, who had little interest in the new theoretical sciences.

Several of the inventions were devices to ease the work of Swedish laborers, like this winch that would be useful in mining, smelting, and logging operations.

There were fourteen items in all, many of them inventions for use in mining, Sweden's major industry (L&M vol. 1, pp. 56ff). Mechanical hoists like this made work safer for the miners.

FIG. 43. *Model of Swedenborg's winch on wheeled carriage*

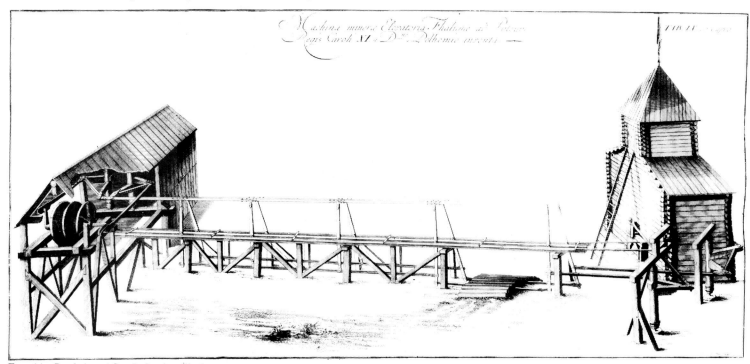

FIG. 44. *Rendering of Swedenborg's mill plan*

FIG. 45. *Model of Swedenborg's aircraft*

FIG. 46. *Aircraft model without "sail"*

Other inventions of his were more theoretical, impressive samples of a contemporary fashion among inventors, machines like this one to fly in the air.

Models of his aircraft—the first in history designed with a true airfoil wing (or "sail")—have been constructed for display in the Tekniska Museet in Stockholm and the Smithsonian Institution in Washington, D.C. The fixed wing, the cockpit for a pilot, and the landing gear were other features of the design which made it advanced for its time. Swedenborg had calculated accurately the wing surface necessary to support the craft, and recognized the need for invention of an adequate source of motive power. In the model of the aircraft shown without its "sail," the pilot is raising the flaps. Among Swedenborg's other inventions was a one-man submarine to attack enemy ships from under the sea. As he realized, these were somewhat more fanciful than the mining machines: their actual operation would require means of propulsion that were inconceivable at the time.

In November of 1714, Karl XII ended his Russian campaign by escaping from a Turkish prison and completing a heroic march to come to the defense of the Swedish outpost of Stralsund. Emanuel wrote an ode in celebration of the event, *Festivus Applausus in Caroli XII*, and set sail from the port of Rostock for home.

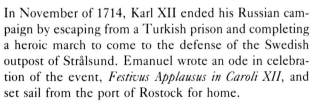

FIG. 47. *Swedenborg's notes and sketch of his aircraft*

FIG. 48. *Christopher Polhem (1661–1751), ca. 1690*

In Service to Karl XII

Christopher Polhem (1661–1751), seen here at about age thirty, was one of the most important influences on Swedenborg's life—surpassed perhaps only by Jesper Swedberg and Erik Benzelius. He was Emanuel's senior by twenty-seven years, and when Swedenborg graduated from Uppsala Polhem already was Sweden's most famous inventor, attracting visitors and students from Sweden and Europe. Emanuel had hoped to join Polhem as an apprentice at that time, but the opportunity to visit England had come first. Twenty-eight years old now, with five years' study abroad under famous teachers, and with a notebook full of inventions, Emanuel could join Polhem more as an assistant than as an apprentice.

Swedenborg spent his first six months after returning home living with his father at Starbo, one of the family estates, in central Sweden, west of Uppsala. There he prepared the first issue of his scientific journal, *Daedalus Hyperboreus,* named after Greek mythology's father of inventors. It was the first such publication in Swedish prepared for the general public. Then, after a Christmas vacation with his brother-in-law Erik Benzelius, he went to join Polhem in January of 1716. Polhem, the great inventor, living at his estate called Stjärnsund, was pleased with the new journal, *Daedalus Hyperboreus,* nearly every issue of which featured an invention of his, and he was delighted with his new assistant. He involved Emanuel in his work and soon offered him the hand of his oldest daughter, Maria.

FIG. 49. *Title page of* Daedalus Hyperboreus

FIG. 50. Stjärnsund, *in the nineteenth century*

FIG. 51. *Emerentia Polhem (1703-1760), anonymous, 1716*

Emanuel, however, preferred Maria's younger sister, Emerentia Polhem, pictured here, and employed what he called "some intrigues" to avoid marrying Maria while keeping himself in everyone's good graces. But Emerentia refused him, desiring to marry another man. Swedenborg was deeply disappointed, for Emerentia was not only beautiful but a brilliant and capable woman: after her father's death, she assumed management of the forge at Stjärnsund. In spite of his disappointment, Emanuel continued working for Polhem.

FIG. 52. Forge at Stjärnsund, *in the early eighteenth century*

Polhem had been called to the side of King Karl XII (seen here in a likeness by the great portraitist David von Krafft), who had set up a temporary headquarters at Lund in preparation for an attack on Norway. Karl commissioned Polhem to build a drydock at Karlskrona, conceived as one of the greatest in Europe, and Polhem brought his assistant, Swedenborg, with him. Swedenborg had held a low opinion of Karl but took an immediate liking to him when he met the charismatic king, and the two had many long conversations about science and mathematics. Karl admired Swedenborg's new publication, *Daedalus Hyperboreus*, and a textbook in geometry written by Polhem, which Swedenborg published. However, he took little interest in Swedenborg's *A New Method of Finding the Longitudes of Places, on Land, or at Sea, by Lunar Observations* (1721), which Swedenborg also published at this time. At Polhem's request, Karl appointed Swedenborg as special assessor (member) on Sweden's Board of Mines; this irregular appointment was resented by regular board members, who denied him a salary for over a decade.

FIG. 53. Carl XII. Werldens Hjelte (Hero of the World) *(1682-1718), by David von Krafft, 1707*

FIG. 54. *Jesper Swedberg presenting Swedish Bible to Karl XII*

FIG. 55. *Trollhättan locks today*

FIG. 56. Trollhättan Locks, *Old Sluice*

In December of 1717, his father, Jesper, joined Swedenborg and the king at Lund, to present Karl with his *Karl XII Bible* and to preach before the king three times. The following spring Jesper's second wife, Sara Bergia, died.

Karl engaged Polhem and Swedenborg to build a canal, which would have linked Stockholm with the North Sea, avoiding the strait controlled by Denmark. The whole project, complicated by steep descents over rugged mountains, was completed in its present form only in this century, and is now known as the Trollhättan Canal. Swedenborg spent the summer of 1718 working on the locks of the canal. The modern Trollhättan locks, pictured here, are within sight of the old worksite, now known as "Polhem's Sluice."

Trollhättan Canal Area

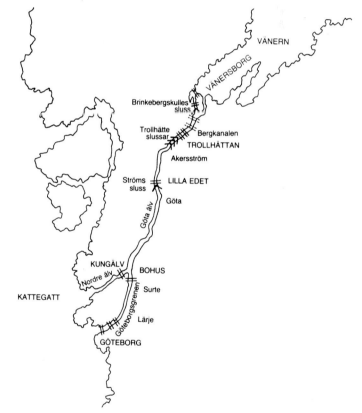

This old lithograph shows the Trollhättan locks, completed after Swedenborg's death. While working on his phase of the project, as well as the Karlskrona drydock and Sweden's first saltworks, Swedenborg also devised a method by which, under his supervision, Karl's navy moved some ships fifteen miles overland to defeat the Norwegian navy before the Norwegian stronghold of Fredrikshald, so that Karl could bring it under seige.

FIG. 57. Death of Karl XII, *by Gustaf Cederström, 1883*

In November of 1718, Karl XII was laying siege to Fredrikshald. Swedenborg had again used what he called "intrigues" (DOC vol. 1, p. 305) to avoid serving in the campaign, and appears—for that or another reason—to have fallen somewhat out of favor with the king. On November 30, however, Karl's favor suddenly became irrelevant, for he was killed by a bullet to the head. Gustaf Cederström's painting of his battlefield funeral procession is shown here. Historians have never been sure whether the shot came from a Norwegian soldier or a Swedish assassin; but Sweden was thrown into mourning—and a search for a new monarch.

FIG. 58. *Ulrika Eleonora (1688-1741), by M. Mijtens I, ca. 1730*

FIG. 59. *Swedenborg's coat of arms*

On 17 March 1719, the crown was placed on the head of Queen Ulrika Eleonora, younger sister of Karl XII—the princess who had been baptized on the same day as Emanuel Swedberg. For quite a few reasons she gained the throne in spite of the claim of another pretender—her nephew, Karl Fredrik of the Holstein-Gottorp line. One reason was that she was in the country at the time; another because her husband, Fredrik, who soon would join her on the throne, was in the trenches at the time of Karl's death and could immediately proclaim her queen and arrest Karl's prime minister (Baron Görtz, who was widely hated and later beheaded for wartime policies that greatly impoverished the country). Yet another reason was that she renounced the absolute reign enjoyed by Karl, and agreed to govern jointly with a Council of the Realm.

On 23 May 1719, Queen Ulrika Eleonora ennobled the families of Sweden's bishops. Emanuel's name changed from Swedberg to Swedenborg, and his life changed in other ways. As the eldest surviving male of the family, he was seated in the House of Nobles. Two years later the estate of his stepmother, Sara Bergia, was settled, giving him a modest independent income for life.

FIG. 60. *Lord President's Room, in Riddarhuset (House of Nobles)*

FIG. 61. *Riddarhuset assembly room; coats of arms include Swedenborg's.*

Sweden's Riddarhuset, or House of Nobles, where Swedenborg was seated after his ennoblement, was one of four houses of the Riksdag, or parliament, which governed the country. He took his seat immediately and remained an active and diligent member, attending its sessions regularly for the rest of his life, except when his travels for study and publication took him out of the country. Although he made no speeches in the House of Nobles, apparently considering himself a poor speaker because of a speech impediment, he wrote a number of papers that were published for distribution to the nobles. Many of these papers have been preserved. For the 1722-23 Riksdag, for instance, he published five pamphlets. They dealt with currency reform, balance of trade, priorities in mining noble and base metals, encouraging the production of iron, and the establishment of rolling mills. His last major contribution, an extensive paper on Swedish currency in 1771, only months before his death, reprinted the 1722 currency-reform paper and added an equal amount of new text. Swedenborg's service in the House of Nobles from 1719 to 1772 coincided almost exactly with Sweden's Age of Freedom, the more-democratic fifty-four-year interim between the autocratic reign of Karl XII and the reestablishment of absolute monarchy with Gustav III, effected by a coup on 19 August 1772.

A colleague in the House of Nobles and friend of Swedenborg's for almost thirty years was Count Fredrik Gyllenborg, who rose from being King Fredrik's chamberlain to become one of the most powerful politicians in Sweden, as well as a fellow assessor on the Board of Mines. A benevolent man, he came into financial troubles himself later in life, and died in 1769 owing twenty thousand dalers to Swedenborg.

FIG. 62. *Fredrik von Gyllenborg (1698-1759)*

Lars Benzelstierna (born Lars Benzelius in 1680, and ennobled at the same time as Swedenborg) was the brother of Emanuel's brother-in-law, Erik Benzelius, and manager of smelters on the estate of Swedenborg's mother, Sara Behm—the ironworks at Axmar, Starbo, and Skinnskatteberg.

FIG. 63. *Lars Benzelstierna (1680-1755), by Fredrik Brander, ca. 1700*

Benzelstierna married Swedenborg's younger sister Hedvig, thus becoming Swedenborg's brother-in-law. Lars and Emanuel worked in the same office for many years, and for some of those years, Hedvig and Lars provided a home for Emanuel.

FIG. 64. *Hedvig Benzelstierna (1690?-1728), J. H. Scheffel?, ca. 1707*

FIG. 65. *Starbo in the early twentieth century*

Starbo, south of Falun, was the home of Lars and Hedvig Benzelstierna on Lake Barken in Dalarna. Benzelstierna became a competitor with Swedenborg for a seat as regular assessor on the Board of Mines, and gained a salaried post two years before Emanuel. While Swedenborg was visiting Lars and Hedvig at Starbo in March of 1719, he learned that his stepmother, Sara Bergia, had died of pneumonia on March 3, leaving seven heirs and five other claimants. After a number of disputes in and out of court, the estate was settled on 12 April 1721. Lars and Emanuel each received one-seventh of Sara Bergia's estate, amounting to 4,571 dalers, and one-fifth of half of Sara Behm's. The other half went to their aunt, Brita Behm. Emanuel and Lars bought out the other shares and held joint custody of Starbo, which Lars continued to manage.

FIG. 66. *Tiled stove at Starbo*

FIG. 67. Skinnskatteberg, *view in 1854*

This tile stove at Starbo is said to have been built by Swedenborg. In 1721 he published a pamphlet on a theory of combustion and the construction of stoves. He described a stove in which fuel that normally lasts a day would burn for six days—and give more heat!

The Skinnskatteberg estate, south of Starbo, another farm and iron smelter in the Behm inheritance, was also owned jointly by Swedenborg and Benzelstierna.

The third portion of the Behm inheritance was Axmar, northward on the coast. It included the ironworks, vast forests to supply wood for the smelting, and a long stretch of coastline with its own harbor. (In 1900, this estate was valued at 20 million Swedish crowns.) The Axmar Ironworks was operated alternatively by agents of Brita Behm and agents of the minor shareholders, and disputes between these agents led to a series of lawsuits by Brita against the others. Swedenborg led the negotiations with his Aunt Brita, and suspected Benzelstierna of instigating the suits.

FIG. 68. *Axmar in the early twentieth century*

After much bureaucratic maneuvering, during which Benzelstierna and two other men received salaried posts ahead of Swedenborg, apparently because of resentment by seated members against Swedenborg's earlier appointment by Karl XII, Swedenborg eventually gained a permanent, salaried seat by 1724. He served full time as an active member for twenty-three years, until his retirement in 1747 to devote his energies to his theological writing. By that time, he had become so well accepted by the board that he was nominated for promotion from assessor to councillor on the Board of Mines. (His eulogy in 1772 was delivered by a councillor of mines.) The Board of Mines in Swedenborg's time met in a government office building at Mynttorget on the little island of Gamla Stan, the Old City of Stockholm, though the board has been relocated many times since.

FIG. 69. *Mynttorget, where the Board of Mines was located*

A later home of the board was in the Kommerscollegium (Board of Commerce) on Stockholm's Riddarholmen. It is among the buildings on the right side of the little island, seen here in a modern photograph. Some of Swedenborg's furniture still can be found in the building. To the left of the picture, across the causeway, is the Riddarhuset; behind it, the Royal Palace; and behind that, the Stor Kyrkan, or Stockholm Cathedral.

FIG. 70. *Island of Riddarholmen*

Travels & Foreign Studies
in Metallurgy

Research by M. Elizabeth M. Hallowell

Swedenborg's Second and Third European Journeys

Second Journey: May 1720 to July 1722; age 33–34 ————
Third Journey: 10 May 1733 to July 1734; age 45–46 - - - - -

Stockholm–Linköping–Sturefors–Jönköping–Ystad–Stralsund–Berlin–
Dresden–Prague–Carlsbad–Prague–Dresden–Leipzig–Halle–Blankenburg–
Braunschweig–Blankenburg–Leipzig–Kassel–Schmalkalden–Gotha–
Braunschweig–Hamburg–Stralsund–Ystad–Stockholm

After his first trip abroad, studying in England and on the continent for almost five years, Swedenborg spent the next five years in Sweden. Following the settlement of the estates of his mother and stepmother, he made two more foreign journeys—one to study mining and smelting methods in Europe and to publish his *Chemistry*, and a second in which he published his first major work, the three-volume *Philosophical and Metallurgical Works*.

FIG. 71. Copenhagen, *view of the city*

Leaving Sweden in May of 1720, on the first of these trips, he passed through Copenhagen, which, because a peace treaty was about to be signed, was now open to Swedes after being closed for several years.

FIG. 72. Hamburg, View from Harbor

He landed in Europe at the port of Hamburg, the German seaport founded by Charlemagne.

Known to be fond of the theater, Swedenborg probably attended performances in the theater at Amsterdam on several of his eleven visits to that city. During this second journey, he witnessed the signing of the peace treaty in Amsterdam between Sweden and Russia.

FIG. 73. Comédie Précédente, *in Amsterdam*

FIG. 74. *Pieterskerk, Leiden*

FIG. 75. *View of The Hague*

FIG. 76. *Aachen (Aix-la-Chapelle)*

Leiden was one of Swedenborg's favorite cities, visited on almost all of his European trips to explore its laboratories and observatories, and to renew acquaintances among its many scientists. Another favorite city was The Hague, where Swedenborg had friends among the foreign ambassadors and other officials who pursued international relations in this political center.

In his travels, he visited almost every site where he could admire the architecture of Europe, or observe the commercial and industrial methods of the different countries, such as the smelting plants in Aachen (also known as Aix-la-Chapelle). He was particularly interested in mining and smelting centers, like those in Liege, where he could enlarge his expertise in what was now his principal career interest, to increase his value to the Board of Mines.

FIG. 77. *Cologne, view with cathedral*

FIG. 78. *Cologne Cathedral, with Hohenzollern Bridge across the Rhine River*

Swedenborg not only paid attention to European methods of mining and smelting used in Sweden, but also studied industries that might be started up in Sweden—including German rolling mills near Cologne. Up until this time, all of Sweden's metals had to be exported for finishing. In this woodcut from the late-sixteenth century, we can see that Cologne was already a booming mercantile and shipping center.

Cologne Cathedral was begun in 1248 and constructed when Gothic purism was tending toward a more grandiose and ornamental style. Swedenborg enjoyed attending services in churches such as this and noted that they seemed designed to captivate the senses. In this modern picture the Hohenzollern Bridge leading to the cathedral suggests Cologne's historical importance in the steel industry.

FIG. 79. *Altenburg, tin-rolling mill*

One of the plants he visited was this stamping mill at Altenburg, which operated from the fifteenth to the eighteenth centuries, producing large revenues for the Saxon kings—money Swedenborg wanted to keep in Sweden.

FIG. 80. *Altenburg Caverns, tin mine*

In Altenburg, he also visited this tin mine, which had been in operation for some three centuries at the time.

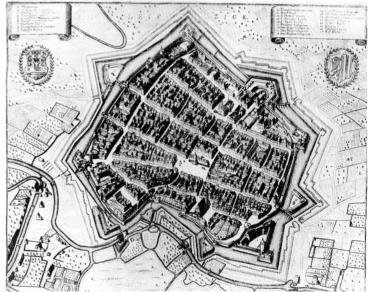

FIG. 81. *Leipzig city plan*

In addition to metallurgical industries, he was especially interested in printing, because his future plans included extensive publication. In Leipzig, he found one of the continent's premier presses, to which he returned on his next trip, when he would have a manuscript in hand ready for printing.

Author & Philosopher

FIG. 82. *Riddarhuset (House of Nobles)*

After only two years abroad, Swedenborg returned home to Stockholm and took up his life as a nobleman, bureaucrat, and author. He went to work daily at the Board of Mines, except when traveling for the board to inspect mines or smelters—often in company with Lars Benzelstierna. Whenever the Riksdag was in session, he sat in the Riddarhuset, the House of Nobles, writing detailed papers for the nobles and other houses of the Riksdag—papers like *The Balance of Trade*, and *Modest Thoughts on the Deflation and Inflation of Swedish Coinage*; and for the Board of Mines on *Noble and Base Metals*. Deeply involved in his work, he turned down an opportunity to teach at the University of Uppsala after the retirement of Nils Celsius, famous for his calibration of the centigrade thermometer.

In 1724, he helped to establish a museum of technology in Stockholm and a museum of mining at Falun. Many of the early exhibits were models of inventions by his former mentor, Christopher Polhem, and some of those models—still on display—were built by Swedenborg. An example is this cogging machine, used to shape iron or steel. In 1725 he became a mentor himself, taking under his wing the son of his brother-in-law Erik Benzelius, Jr., Erik Benzelius III, whom he instructed in physics and mathematics.

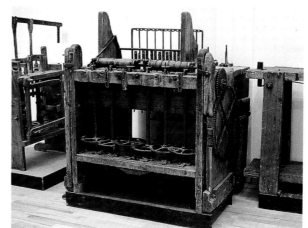

FIG. 83. *Model of Polhem's cogging machine*

FIG. 84. *Kristina Maria Steuch (1708-1739), by G. E. Schröder, ca. 1730*

FIG. 85. *Elisabet Stierncrona (1714-1769), by G. E. Schröder, ca. 1735*

During these years he courted a young woman of seventeen, Kristina Maria Steuch, daughter of the bishop of Karlstad and descended from another bishop and three archbishops. "Stina Maja," as she was called, is known to have had at least three suitors at the time—Swedenborg; a Magister Arnell, preferred by her father; and Chamberlain Cedercreutz, whom she preferred. She married Cedercreutz, and lived to age thirty. After her wedding, Swedenborg's family pointed out another eligible and pretty prospect for marriage, but he does not appear to have courted her, or anyone else.

He did have another friend, Elisabet Stierncrona, who had married his friend Count Gyllenborg in 1729, when she was fifteen and Swedenborg was forty-one. The couple remained close friends of his throughout the count's life, often visiting him in the home he later purchased on the street called Hornsgatan. Swedenborg's friendship with Elisabet continued for the ten years she lived after the death of her husband.

Instead of seeking marriage again, he rented an apartment of his own for the first time in his thirty-nine years, in Count Gyllenborg's house—the same building where Lars and Hedvig Benzelstierna also lived when in Stockholm. He hired a servant and settled into the life of a bachelor. In 1728, his sister Hedvig died, and he moved into another apartment, at 7 Stora Nygatan, in the neighborhood of streets like Prästgatan, pictured here—streets through which he walked daily to his office in the Board of Mines. His nephew, Erik Benzelius III, lived with him for part of this time and began to follow in his uncle's footsteps by studying metallurgy. Erik eventually joined his uncles Emanuel and Lars on the Board of Mines.

FIG. 86. *Gamla Stan, Prästgatan*

FIG. 87. *Berlin city plan*

After eleven years in Stockholm, during which he had established himself in the Riksdag and the Board of Mines, Emanuel completed the manuscript for his biggest work so far and traveled again in May of 1733 to Germany to see it through the press. This was the only foreign trip in which he sailed directly from Stockholm to the continent instead of traveling overland to a Swedish port closer to the continent. He traveled from Stockholm to Berlin in a week, arriving in Berlin on June 2.

FIG. 88. *Dresden, Grossen Garde*

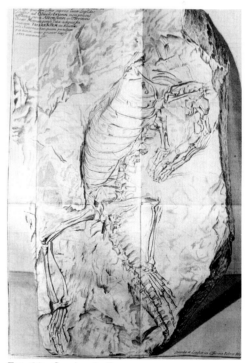

FIG. 89. *Saurian fossil*

Then he spent June, July, and August in Dresden, pictured here in a view of the handsome villas and royal gardens he so much admired. During this time he also visited Prague, putting finishing touches on his manuscript. The three-volume set was entitled *Philosophical and Metallurgical Works*, and the individual volumes were: *I. Principia*, or *First Principles of Natural Things*, *II. On Iron and Steel*, and *III. On Copper and Brass*.

The third volume of *Philosophical and Metallurgical Works* included this plate of a fossil, excavated by Swedenborg from the side of Mount Kinnekulle almost twenty years before. Discovery of the fossil had led to his hypothesis published in his 1718 work, *On the Height of Waters and the Strong Tides in the Primeval World*, claiming that the highest mountain in Sweden had once been under water. That work establishes Swedenborg as one of the earliest to publish a theory consistent with modern geology. The two mineralogical works also established Swedenborg in his own time as one of the world's leading experts in mining and smelting, the area of his professional responsibility for twenty-three years on Sweden's Board of Mines.

On 3 September 1733, he arrived in Leipzig where he turned his manuscript over to the printer who had earlier printed his 1722 work on *Chemistry*, which had been reviewed so well in the German press. Seeing the new work through the press took several months, extending into 1734. During this visit, he sat for a portrait by an engraver, which was used as the frontispiece of *Principia*.

This portrait, executed in Leipzig in the fall of 1733 for publication close to his birthday in 1734, shows Swedenborg at the end of his forty-fifth year. It shows a man sure of his place as one of the leading philosophers of his time in Europe—an estimate confirmed by the favorable German reviews of *Philosophical and Metallurgical Works*.

FIG. 90. *Leipzig, Peters Vorstadt*

FIG. 91. *Emanuel Swedenborg, engraved after a drawing from life by J. W. Stör, 1734*

About a year after Emanuel's third return to Sweden from abroad—this time having received considerable distinction from the favorable reviews in the German press of his *Philosophical and Metallurgical Works*—his father died in July of 1735. Jesper Swedberg had been bishop of Skara for thirty-three years and a doctor of theology for thirty, and was widely admired and loved, in spite of having made many enemies with his outspoken preaching and ministry. His body was laid to rest in a vault set against the outer corner of the southern side of the transept of the abbey church at Varnhem Cloister.

The funeral at Varnhem in Västergötland near Skara was held in January of 1736. The magnificent Varnhem Cloister was begun in 1150, then burned several times and rebuilt. It was reconsecrated in 1673 (the date of the buttresses and towers), and restored to its present form from 1918 to 1923. Its monumental dignity provides a fitting resting place for Jesper Swedberg, one of the leaders of the Swedish church.

Contemplating Jesper Swedberg's burial vault, it is hard to assess the impact of his death on Emanuel; but perhaps a clue can be found in a dream that Swedenborg recorded nine years later. It was early Monday morning after the spectacular night after Easter in Delft, when the Lord appeared to him for the first time; he fell asleep and dreamed that his father came to him. In the dream, he was wearing lace cuffs, and without a word his father tied the ribbons of the cuffs. Waking, Swedenborg recorded all the events of the night, concluding with this dream, noting that lace cuffs were a symbol of laity: his father tying the ribbons of them symbolized for him that his father approved of him (at last) in a life outside the clergy—because that life would now be spent in response to a direct commission from the Lord.

FIG. 92. *Varnhem Cloister, view of the apse and spire from southeast*

FIG. 93. *Varnhem Cloister, view through transept, toward altar*

FIG. 94. *Jesper Swedberg's crypt, in the northwest transept corner*

Search for the Soul

FIG. 95. *Amsterdam, view of the Old Quarter*

After two years at home, during which he published the small work *On Tremulation*, Swedenborg left for Europe again—this time for more than four years. To arrange such an extensive trip, he contributed half his salary at the Board of Mines to be distributed among three fellow members who would assume his duties in his absence. Once again, he passed through Linköping to spend a few days with Erik and Anna Benzelius, and then traveled through Copenhagen to Amsterdam.

He spent the summer in Amsterdam, where he enjoyed the atmosphere of political freedom, but disliked what he described as the prevalent attitude of greed among the people of this commercial and cosmopolitan country. He began what he planned to be a large work defining the seat of the soul—a popular effort among philosophers of his day. Working with intense concentration, aided by a technique of hypoventilation that he had used to help himself concentrate since he was ten years old, he felt assured that his thoughts were on the right track when he felt what he called "a sign": ". . . a certain cheering light and joyful flash . . . a certain mysterious radiation—I know not whence it springs—that darts through some sacred temple of the brain" (EAK 19; SD 2951). The first record of these flashes of approval when he worked were recorded during this visit to Amsterdam.

FIG. 96. *Windmill near Amsterdam*

Not all of Swedenborg's time was spent in writing and meditation, however. In the fall of 1739, he sent this table, inlaid with marble, home from Amsterdam, where he had watched the craftsman make it. His fascination with the process is recorded in a paper he wrote about it, published by the Swedish Royal Academy of Sciences in 1763 (DOC vol. 1, pp. 586–90). The table is now in the Kommerscollegium (Board of Commerce) on Riddarhdmen, which housed the Board of Mines for a short time after Swedenborg's death.

FIG. 97. *Swedenborg's inlaid table*

In the fall, he moved on to Paris. He took rooms on the rue de l'Observatoire where he could renew acquaintances with the French astronomers he had worked with on his last visit, twenty-three years before. The rooms were just a short walk from Paris's new School of Surgery and Dissection, the focus of his current interest. His new book was about the body, seen as a demonstration of the soul's operation. The findings of anatomists, who were doing their pioneering work at this time, fascinated him. He decided to rely on the dissections of others, because he anticipated that he might give undue importance to anything that he happened to discover (EAK 18), and could be more objective using the published work from other laboratories.

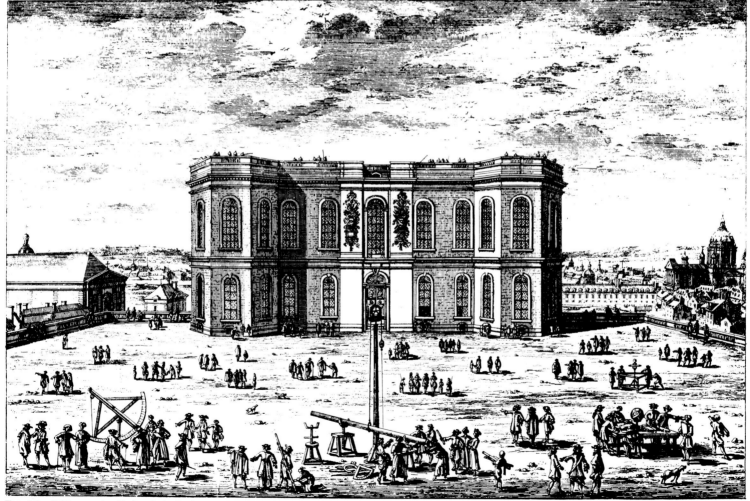

FIG. 98. *L'Observatoire Nationale in Paris*

FIG. 99. *View of Paris from Notre Dame*

While in Paris Swedenborg attended the Comédie and admired the beautiful churches, such as la Sainte-Chapelle and, shown here, the Cathedral of Notre Dame. He most likely enjoyed the view of Paris across the "leads" (roof) of the cathedral, a popular excursion for visitors to the city.

In the spring, he left Paris and traveled to Italy, arriving in Torino in time to see the parades reenacting the Passion scenes. In Italy he indulged his love of theater at the beautiful theater of Torino, pictured here.

Moving on to Milan, and then to Venice, he visited the Plaza of St. Mark's at the time of the annual celebration of the "Marriage between Venice and the Sea," pictured here. His travel diaries show that everywhere he went, he visited all the best-known architectural wonders.

FIG. 100. *Teatro Regio, in Torino*

FIG. 101. Ceremony of the Marriage of the Sea, *engraving after Canaletto, 1738?*

FIG. 102. *University of Padua*

FIG. 103. Theatrum Anatomicum

On 9 August 1738 he arrived in Padua. Again, he visited the centers of learning, such as the University of Padua. His diary suggests that he had finished at least the first draft of his *Economy of the Animal Kingdom* (*Dynamics of the Soul's Domain*), which surveyed the body as the domain of the soul, and was looking ahead to a future work on the brain.

Again, he visited one of the leading centers of dissection, the Anatomical Theater in the University of Padua, where new discoveries in the workings of the body, the brain, and the nervous system were being made.

FIG. 104. Cognoscenti in the Uffizi, *by John Zoffany, 1779*

Swedenborg was especially impressed by Florence's Uffizi Gallery, and we are fortunate to have an image of what that gallery looked like, including visitors dressed in the costumes of Swedenborg's time. This painting, John Zoffany's *Cognoscenti in the Uffizi*, is almost a candid snapshot of the gallery as Swedenborg saw it.

FIG. 105. *Colosseum, amphitheater with Arch of Constantine*

In Rome, he visited the Colosseum and all the other famous historical sites, as well as the great art galleries.

Along with the other mainstays of Roman tourism, he visited the Vatican library (where his *Philosophical and Metallurgical Works* were kept on the "Proscribed Index") and particularly admired the works of Raphael on display there. Then, journeying back through Paris to Amsterdam, he finally finished *Economy of the Animal Kingdom* and transmitted it to the printer.

FIG. 106. Vatican Library

After the press run was completed, he took some copies with him and headed for home. He spent several days in Copenhagen, studying in the libraries and visiting famous men. It may have been on this visit that he first met General and Madam Tuxen, who later entertained him so graciously on his last visit to Copenhagen in 1770.

FIG. 107. *Copenhagen, view toward the sea*

At this period of his life, Swedenborg moved in the highest circles of Swedish society. He was regularly present at the Riksdag when it was in session, and frequently in attendance at the royal court. Among his friends were men like Count Anders Johan von Höpken, who was a member from 1746 to 1761 of the executive council, which shared power with the king of Sweden. Von Höpken later claimed to have been a friend of Swedenborg's for forty-two years and a daily companion since 1756.

FIG. 108. *Anders von Höpken (1712-1789), by Fredrik Brander, 1759*

FIG. 109. *Carl Gustaf Tessin (1695-1770), by J. A. J. Aved, 1700s*

FIG. 110. *Carolus Linnaeus (1707-1778), by Alexander Roslin, 1775*

The president of the House of Nobles at this time was Count Carl Gustaf Tessin, the architect who had completed the Royal Palace in Stockholm (begun by his father, Nicodemus Tessin) and who subsequently became a member for twenty years of the executive council. Tessin and Swedenborg knew each other in government service during these years, and in 1760—after he learned that Swedenborg was the author of the theological works that were causing a stir in Stockholm—the two men held long private conversations about Swedenborg's writing. Although he never embraced Swedenborg's teachings, his respect and friendship were gratifying, and may have been useful at the time of the later "heresy trial," directed at two of Swedenborg's friends who promoted his works.

Carolus Linnaeus, often called the Father of Modern Botany, was married in the guesthouse of Swedenborg's ancestral home, Sveden, to the daughter of Johan Moraeus (Swedenborg's cousin who had tutored him as a youth). Although he and Swedenborg moved in the same circles, they both traveled extensively and were together in Stockholm only for a year in 1740–41, so they may have met only seldom. On 10 December 1740, Swedenborg was accepted into Sweden's Royal Academy of Sciences, joining Linnaeus, Tessin, and von Höpken, who had been its founding members in 1739.

On 21 July 1743 Swedenborg went abroad for the fifth time, now to publish the first two volumes of a massive work he had planned, the *Animal Kingdom*, a more detailed study of the body than *Economy of the Animal Kingdom*. The Plantin-Moretus Museum of printing, in Antwerp, Belgium, is seen here as it appeared in 1983. In Swedenborg's time, the building was the home of the Plantin Press, typical of the great printing houses of Europe that published the works of Swedenborg and other writers of the period.

This pressroom of the Plantin Press, preserved in the museum, is similar to the printing plants that produced Swedenborg's works. For all but his smallest works, Swedenborg had to travel to the continent, because Sweden had no printing facilities capable of large-scale printing jobs of the quality available in Antwerp and the presses Swedenborg is known to have used in Amsterdam, Leipzig, The Hague, and London.

FIG. 111. *Plantin-Moretus Press, courtyard*

FIG. 112. *Plantin-Moretus Press, pressroom*

The press Swedenborg chose for *Animal Kingdom* was in The Hague. This work, for which he produced first drafts of separate volumes on the brain, the fiber, the reproductive system, and other parts and systems of the human body, marked the high point of his physiological studies.

FIG. 113. *The Hague, Riddarzaal (Knights' Hall) in the Binnenhof, oldest section of the city*

The Turning Point

The Volders Gracht (Clothier's Canal), is seen here in a typical view of eighteenth-century Delft, where Swedenborg took rooms while reading proofs for *Animal Kingdom* and where he experienced the major turning point of his life.

Swedenborg almost certainly visited the Old Church in Delft to see the tomb of van Leeuwenhoek, with whom he had studied on his first trip to Holland. The Old Church containing his tomb can be seen from this tower in the New Church, frequently climbed by tourists in Swedenborg's time as today. After attending church services in Delft on Easter Sunday, 6 April 1744, he returned to his room, troubled by emotional turmoil, which had evidence in the dreams he recorded in his *Journal of Dreams* during that period.

FIG. 114. *Delft, Volders Gracht*

FIG. 115. *Delft, Oude Kerk (Old Church)*

FIG. 116. *Delft, De Groote Markt*

The towers of the New and Old churches form the backdrop to this scene of the market square in Delft. Just out of sight, the Clothier's Canal runs along the horizon behind the buildings across the center of the print. In his room in Delft, during the night after 6 April 1744, he was seized with such trembling that he fell from his bed. He then experienced a Christ vision in which he was commissioned to devote his life to theological writing in service of the Lord. It was after this vision that he fell asleep and dreamed the dream referred to in the description of Jesper Swedberg's death. After this vision, and another in London a year later in 1745, he abandoned all his studies of mathematics and physiology. Within a year he resigned at half salary from the Board of Mines in June of 1747 (when he was about to be promoted to councillor of mines), spending the remaining twenty-seven years of his life primarily in meditation, biblical study, and writing theology. He remained active in politics until the end of his life.

FIG. 117. *Swedenborg's house in Hornsgatan*

In 1745, when he was fifty-seven, Swedenborg moved from his apartment into a home he had purchased in Hornsgatan, where he lived and wrote for the rest of his life, whenever he was in Sweden. From 1749 to 1756, he published the first and biggest of his theological writings, *Arcana Coelestia*, consisting of eight large-format (quarto) Latin volumes.

FIG. 118. *Summerhouse in reconstructed garden, Skansen*

FIG. 119. *Elisabet Stierncrona (1714-1769), by Gustaf Lundberg, ca. 1750*

In the garden behind his house, he planted an herb garden and built a summerhouse where he could work in more pleasant surroundings than the crowded rooms adapted to Swedish winters.

Near the turn of our century, the summerhouse was moved to the Swedish historical park of Skansen, and in 1964 relocated again to the Skansen rose garden. An effort has been made to grow around the garden house the same herbs Swedenborg grew. Inside the garden house is the chamber organ on which Swedenborg enjoyed playing the music of Johann Sebastian Bach.

Countess Gyllenborg remained a friend of Swedenborg's after her husband's death, and there is no record that Swedenborg collected the twenty thousand dalers loan or the twelve hundred dalers interest that her husband owed him at that time. In 1751, she gave Swedenborg the manuscript of a small book she had written, *Mary's Better Part*, and he arranged to have it published anonymously. After her death in 1769, Swedenborg mentioned to a friend in the British parliament, C. A. Tulk, that he expected her to be his mate in heaven after his death.

FIG. 120. *Norra Hamngatan in Göteborg, view of canal and the former home of William Castel, now known as the Sahlgren House, to left of tower*

In the summer of 1758, Swedenborg left for Europe on his seventh trip, this time to publish *Heaven and Hell, Earths in the Universe, Last Judgment, New Jerusalem and Its Heavenly Doctrine,* and *White Horse of the Apocalypse.* On the way home, he landed at Göteborg, some three hundred miles from Stockholm on Sweden's west coast, in July of 1759.

FIG. 121. *Sahlgren House*

On the night of July 19 in Göteborg he was entertained at dinner in the home of William Castel, a prominent merchant. During the meal he became very agitated, leaving the table several times. He told the dinner guests that a great fire was raging in Stockholm at that very moment. Each time he returned to the table he described the progress of the blaze, eventually relating with great relief how the fire had been stopped close to his house but did no damage to it. Within a few days, a ship from Stockholm brought news of the fire, coinciding in every detail with Swedenborg's description. Word of his clairvoyance began circulating throughout the country.

FIG. 122. *Lovisa Ulrika (1720–1782), by Lorens Pasch, 1775*

Queen Lovisa Ulrika learned of his clairvoyance. She spoke with Swedenborg in a private audience and asked him if he could contact her brother, the recently deceased King August William of Prussia. Swedenborg agreed to try. A few days later, he returned to the court, requesting another private audience. After he spoke but a few words to the queen, she appeared shocked and exclaimed, "This no mortal could have told me!" (DOC vol. 2, p. 652). The stories of the Stockholm fire, the queen's secret, and another concerning a lost receipt, became famous throughout Europe after they were described by Immanuel Kant in a letter to a patroness, Fraulein von Knobloch, in 1763. In response to her inquiry, he had done some research into Swedenborg's character and gave an essentially favorable report.

FIG. 123. *Svindersvik, by Pehr Hilleström, late 1700s*

FIG. 124. *Johann August Ernesti (1707-1781)*

Count Tessin, described earlier as a friend of Swedenborg's, held dinner meetings of a circle of Stockholm artists and literati at his beautiful seacoast home, Svindersvik. In 1760, he invited Swedenborg to join the group. By this time, Swedenborg was known not only for his philosophical and mining publications and his telepathic powers, but also for his theological writings. Count Gustaf Bonde, a senator and past-president of the Board of Mines, now chancellor of the University of Uppsala and friend of Tessin's, had discovered the preceding January that Swedenborg was the author of the theological treatise, *Arcana Coelestia*, which had been published anonymously.

In the fall of 1760, a devastating critique of Swedenborg's theological works, which at first consisted mostly of biblical exegesis, was published in Germany by a leading biblical scholar, Professor Johann Ernesti, who mistook Swedenborg's spiritual interpretations of the Bible for the then-discredited allegorical method. In the same year, another prominent theological scholar and writer, Friedrich Christoph Oetinger, who had written favorably about Swedenborg's theological works, found himself under attack and formulated an extended defense of Swedenborg that attracted wide attention.

In 1766, the criticism that most damaged Swedenborg's reputation was published in Germany by Immanuel Kant, under the title *Dreams of a Spirit-Seer*. In the years since his 1763 letter to Fraulein von Knobloch, he had purchased and read *Arcana Coelestia* and condemned it as "eight quarto volumes full of nonsense," on the grounds that none of its data were *sense* data. He claimed that only a madman would write things that could not be proved. He explained the violence of his attack in a letter to a friend, by saying that he thought it better "to ridicule than to be ridiculed," and shortly thereafter began work on his own *Critique of Pure Reason* (published in 1781), setting forth ground rules for philosophy on an entirely different basis than Swedenborg's. Self-serving as it was, his attack on Swedenborg was so effective that for more than a generation it was impossible for any German scholar to speak favorably of Swedenborg and be taken seriously.

FIG. 125. *Immanuel Kant (1724-1804)*

FIG. 126. *Emanuel Swedenborg, with* Apocalypse Revealed, *by Pehr Krafft, the Elder, ca. 1768*

Swedenborg's theological teachings became controversial in Sweden, too. Arriving in Göteborg in 1769, after his tenth European trip, he found that two influential leaders in that city—Bishop Eric Lamberg and Dean Olof Ekebom—were heading a campaign to have his books declared heretical. They succeeded in confiscating one box of his books, and attacked two of his friends and supporters seriously enough to threaten their jobs. The two friends were Dr. Gabriel Beyer, a member of the Göteborg Consistory, and Dr. Johan Rosén, professor of eloquence and poetry at the University of Lund. Each found himself under severe pressure to renounce Swedenborgian teachings, but because of their own eloquent defense and support from various well-connected supporters of Swedenborg, neither was actually forced from his position. This portrait by Pehr Krafft, perhaps the best-known image of Swedenborg, was painted about this time.

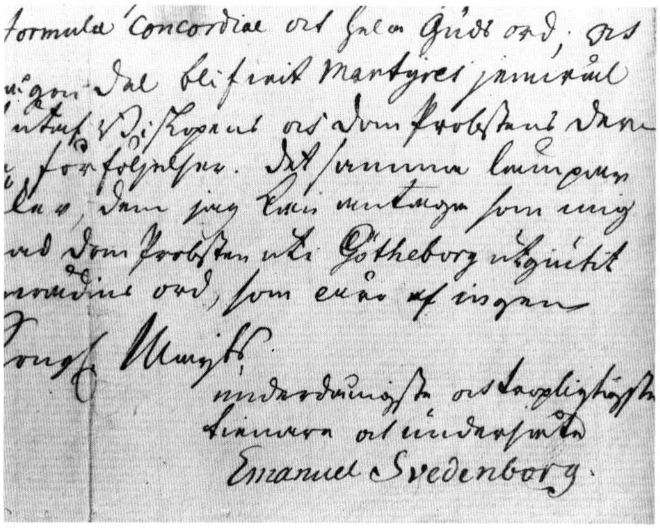

FIG. 127. *Closing paragraph of Swedenborg's letter to Adolf Fredrik*

The attacks on Swedenborg's work and reputation became so troublesome, however, that he eventually appealed to King Adolf Fredrik—husband of Queen Lovisa Ulrika, who had been impressed by Swedenborg's clairvoyance—in the letter shown here. He complained that Beyer and Rosén—and, indeed, his own works—had "become, to a certain extent, martyrs, at least so far as regards the cruel persecutions by the bishop and the dean of that town . . . sheer invectives, which do not contain a particle of truth."

FIG. 128. *Amsterdam, old harborfront with the Kantoor, and St. Nicholaaskerk with Schreierstoren (Weeping Towers) in the background*

In July of 1770, Swedenborg sailed from Sweden for the eleventh time, taking his last large manuscript to Amsterdam for publication. This was his *True Christian Religion*, the most complete summary of his theology that he had written. It was organized and formulated in a manner that addressed the concerns of Swedish Lutheranism, and so it may be considered his final reply to the heresy trial as well as the crowning statement of his theological system.

The Last Years

FIG. 129. *William Cookworthy (1705-1780)*

FIG. 130. *Swedenborg's drop-leaf table*

In August of 1771, now eighty-three years old, he returned to London. He had several good friends there, including a Quaker businessman, William Cookworthy, pictured here; an Anglican priest, the Reverend Thomas Hartley, rector of Winwick; and a physician, Dr. Messiter. Hartley had heard of the accusations of heresy in Sweden and had offered asylum should Swedenborg need it (although in fact, he had been in no personal danger).

Swedenborg took lodgings with a London wigmaker, Richard Shearsmith, and continued his meditations and his writing. The table that he worked on in his room at Shearsmith's has been preserved and is seen here with a chair belonging to an English disciple, James John Garth Wilkinson, later a good friend of Ralph Waldo Emerson's. He continued writing his manuscripts, working at all hours of the day and night, and often was heard speaking aloud—apparently to the spirits who appeared in his visions. Shortly before Christmas of 1771 he suffered a stroke, but within a month he had partially recovered his speech, and resumed his writing.

Shearsmith's maid described him as a pleasant tenant, friendly to her. She is the one who reported that he predicted the day and time of his death, and said that "he was pleased . . . as if he were going to have a holiday" (DOC vol. 2, p. 546). The maid, who subsequently became Mrs. Shearsmith, also reported that on Sunday, the twenty-ninth of March, she was sitting at his bedside, when he asked the time. When she told him it was five o'clock, "he replied, 'Dat be good, me tank you, God bless you,' . . . and about ten minutes after, he heaved a gentle sigh, and expired in the most tranquil manner" (DOC vol. 2, p. 600).

FIG. 131. *Richard Shearsmith's maid—later Mrs. Shearsmith—and Swedenborg, from the film* The Man Who Had to Know

About a fortnight before his death, Swedenborg had taken Holy Communion in his room from the Reverend Arvid Ferelius, pastor of the Swedish church in London. Reverend Ferelius conducted Swedenborg's funeral in the Swedish church on Princes Square in London. The funeral, at four o'clock on Sunday, 5 April 1772, was well attended, filling the small church. The body was laid to rest under the altar. In Sweden, a eulogy was read in the House of Nobles by Samuel Sandels, a councillor of mines.

FIG. 132. *Arvid Ferelius (1726-?)*

FIG. 133. *Swedenborg's casket leaving the Swedish Lutheran Church in London*

In 1908, when London's Swedish church was threatened with demolition, the Royal Swedish Academy of Sciences arranged to have the casket brought home to Sweden. The Swedish warship *Fylgia* sailed from England on 7 April 1908 with Swedenborg's casket lying in state on the deck.

FIG. 134. *Swedenborg's tomb in Uppsala Cathedral*

On 18 May 1908 the body was laid to rest in Uppsala Cathedral, burial place of King Gustavus Vasa and other Swedish monarchs. Swedenborg's sarcophagus is in a side chapel next to the tomb of Carolus Linnaeus.

FIG. 135. *Emanuel Swedenborg, 1771*

The last authenticated portrait of Swedenborg depicts him at age eighty-three or eighty-four, shortly before his death. Probably painted by a fashionable portraitist in London, it may have been retouched at a later date, when Swedenborg's blue eyes were mistakenly rendered as brown. Even so, the painting conveys something of the presence of this remarkably vital octogenarian, ready to embrace the next world and leave to this world the legacy of his vision.

Acknowledgments

Written by Dr. Robert H. Kirven in conjunction with picture selection by Dr. Robin Larsen and Picture Editor Anja Hübener, this biography relies heavily on earlier biographies by Cyriel Odhner Sigstedt, Signe Toksvig, and Dr. Ernst Benz, as well as on documentary evidence collected by Alfred Acton and Rudolph L. Tafel.

Swedenborg in Context
An Anthology of Essays & Poetry

Poets with Swedenborgian Connections

Compiled by Alice B. Skinner, Ph.D.

Introduction

WHAT DO Czeslaw Milosz, Elizabeth Barrett Browning, and William Butler Yeats have in common? In addition to being poets, all three were readers of Swedenborg. Poets have always been among those who found inspiration in Swedenborg, for, undismayed by scholastic prose and pedantic translations, these writers who are sensitive to the life of the spirit respond to the rich lode of imagery in his theological works. Perhaps they also feel that Swedenborg is a kindred soul, living simultaneously in this world and the spiritual world, seeking new meanings and the language to express them. As Jacques Maritain explains, "Poetic experience and mystical experience are born near one another, and near the center of the soul, in the living springs of the preconceptual and supraconceptual vitality of the spirit."[1]

This anthology selects from the works of poets with a Swedenborgian connection, writers whose interest in Swedenborg can be documented from letters or journals, biographies, or family relationships. The poets have varied associations with Swedenborg. In the late eighteenth and early nineteenth centuries, during and just after Swedenborg's lifetime, European intellectuals like Goethe and Coleridge read Swedenborg and discussed his books. That tradition persisted into the twentieth century among Europeans, like Oscar Milosz, interested in the spiritual realm. These poets were not, strictly speaking, "Swedenborgians." They read his books and expressed ideas consonant with his, perhaps because their thought already ran along similar lines. Some, like William Blake, were enthusiastic readers at some times of their lives but also practiced the theory that "opposition is true friendship," reserving the right to disagree.[2]

Some poets, like Edwin Markham, were avowed Swedenborgians who advertised the connection. Others were related to Swedenborgians and learned Swedenborgian ideas through them. Robert Frost, for example, was baptized and went to Sunday school in the San Francisco Swedenborgian church with which his mother was affiliated.

Whatever the nature of the connection, each poet has melded Swedenborgian with other influences. "Like everyone else, a creative artist inhales the surrounding world and exhales it. Whatever is taken in is given back in altered condition or transformed into matter, action, feeling, thought."[3] The poet muses on the totality of experience and from it wrestles a singular expression, fresh-minted words in poetic form which have the potential of transforming responses in others. It is unlikely that "pure" Swedenborgian thought will result from such a creative and utterly personal poetic process, even among poets who are serious students of Swedenborg's writings. But it is possible for readers to refresh their understanding of Swedenborgian perspectives by reflecting on poetic expression by kindred writers.

In this anthology the poems are grouped by themes,

ALICE BLACKMER SKINNER has served as vice-president of the Swedenborg Foundation since 1981 and is the publisher of its journal, *Chrysalis*, for which she edits thematic essays combining poetry and art. Educated at Radcliffe College (B.A., 1945), University of Minnesota (M.S.W., 1951), and Harvard University (Ph.D., 1977), Skinner is a research psychologist specializing in the study of lives. She is currently at work on a long-term study of women's decisions about life patterns and has written a biography of the Swedenborgian artist and poet Alice Archer Sewall James.

thus enabling readers to sample the varied perspectives of writers with Swedenborgian connections: poems about the processes of personal development, poems about usefulness to society, poems about correspondences, devotional poetry written by Swedenborgians, poems about life after death, and finally visionary poetry.

Marian Kirven, librarian emeritus of the Swedenborg School of Religion in Newton, Massachusetts, searched out the documentation of the poets' association with Swedenborg. Brief accounts of each poet's mode of connection, accompanied by a list of sources for further information, are given at the end of the section in which the poet's work first appears. Source notes for the specific poems cited appear at the end of each section.

The Human Process

"WHEN SOMEONE IS BECOMING a new person . . . that is, being reborn, it does not happen instantly, as some people believe, but over many years—in fact throughout our whole life . . . " (AC 4063).

Swedenborgian poets write of the process of spiritual development and the possibilities of regeneration. Robert Browning's "Rabbi Ben Ezra" describes aging in terms of "the best [which] is yet to be" and advises that we "welcome each rebuff / That turns earth's smoothness rough." The ups and downs of the process of becoming remind Paul Valéry of an "all-too-nimble bee [which] / Doubles upon its track, defeats itself, / Missing the flowerbed, hurtles at the cup." Yeats notes the vitality possible, even for "a tattered coat upon a stick" of an aged person, if "Soul clap its hands and sing" and continue to take lessons from the sages.

SELECTIONS FROM RABBI BEN EZRA

1.

GROW old along with me!
The best is yet to be,
The last of life, for which the first was made:
Our times are in His hand
Who saith, "A whole I planned,
Youth shows but half; trust God: see all, nor be afraid!"

. . .

4.

Poor vaunt of life indeed,
Were man but formed to feed
On joy, to solely seek and find and feast;
Such feasting ended, then
As sure an end to men;
Irks care the crop-full bird? Frets doubt the maw-crammed beast?

5.

Rejoice we are allied
To That which doth provide
And not partake, effect and not receive!
A spark disturbs our clod;
Nearer we hold of God
Who gives, than of His tribes that take, I must believe.

6.

Then, welcome each rebuff
That turns earth's smoothness rough,
Each sting that bids nor sit nor stand but go!
Be our joys three-parts pain!
Strive, and hold cheap the strain;
Learn, nor account the pang; dare, never grudge the throe!

7.

For thence,—a paradox
Which comforts while it mocks,—.
Shall life succeed in that it seems to fail:
What I aspired to be,
And was not, comforts me:
A brute I might have been, but would not sink i' the scale.

. . .

26.

Ay, note that Potter's wheel,
That metaphor! and feel
Why time spins fast, why passive lies our clay,—
Thou, to whom fools propound,
When the wine makes its round,
"Since life fleets, all is change; the Past gone, seize to-day!"

27.

Fool! All that is, at all,
Lasts ever, past recall;

Earth changes, but thy soul and God stand sure:
What entered into thee,
That was, is, and shall be:
Time's wheel runs back or stops: Potter and clay
    endure.

28.

He fixed thee mid this dance
Of plastic circumstance,
This Present, thou, forsooth, wouldst fain arrest:
Machinery just meant
To give thy soul its bent,
Try thee, and turn thee forth sufficiently
    impressed.

ROBERT BROWNING[1]

SPIRITUAL BEE

GOD demon demiurge or destiny
My appetite like a lively bee
Buzzes and shimmers all about the feast
Which your grace has decreed to nourish me.

Here in day's gold the muse has laid this honey:
There in the glass an elected gleam
Pure algebra and iced ambrosia
Coldly contains light out of the sky.

Carefree love of lovely understanding
Fastidious and all-too-nimble bee
Doubles upon its track, defeats itself,
Missing the flowerbed, hurtles at the cup.

This sounding point of utmost purity
Lightning-charged and crazily futile
Will it bring singular life to bear upon
The finest and most useless dream of all?

Devil in the body is God's recoil
The flame sweeps on leaving behind pure ash
A mere radiant nothing is each sun
Creating the pallor of its future dawn.

Where to place you drone of the absolute
Instant forever separate from yourself?
All that it touches is distinctly chosen
Indivisible anguish of the poem.

I love the straying that weaves a path prolonged
Within a night not miserly of worlds
Evening gleams there with its tomorrow
In the one womb of all-fruitful glooms.

PAUL VALÉRY[2]

SAILING TO BYZANTIUM

THAT is no country for old men. The young
In one another's arms, birds in the trees
(Those dying generations) at their song,
The salmon-falls, the mackerel-crowded seas,
Fish, flesh, or fowl, commend all summer long
Whatever is begotten, born, and dies.
Caught in that sensual music, all neglect
Monuments of unaging intellect.

An aged man is but a paltry thing.
A tattered coat upon a stick, unless
Soul clap its hands and sing, and louder sing
For every tatter in its mortal dress;
Nor is there singing school but studying
Monuments of its own magnificence;
And therefore I have sailed the seas and come
To the holy city of Byzantium.

O sages, standing in God's holy fire
As in the gold mosaic of a wall,
Come from the holy fire, perne in a gyre.
And be the singing-masters of my soul.
Consume my heart away—sick with desire
And fastened to a dying animal
It knows not what it is—and gather me
Into the artifice of eternity.

Once out of nature I shall never take
My bodily form from any natural thing.
But such a form as Grecian goldsmiths make
Of hammered gold and gold enamelling
To keep a drowsy emperor awake;
Or set upon a golden bough to sing
To lords and ladies of Byzantium
Of what is past, or passing, or to come.

WILLIAM BUTLER YEATS[3]

"Before anything is brought back into order, it is quite normal for it to be brought first into a kind of confusion, a virtual chaos. In this way, things that fit together badly are severed from each other; and when they have been severed, then the Lord arranges them in order" (AC 842 [3]).

Goethe reminds us that part of the human process is "to die and so to grow," enabled by a vision of a higher form of love. How scary the "desert places" (Robert Frost) of personal chaos can be, when one feels "no more / than a rock encircled by a nameless dread, / an ancient sphinx omitted from the map" (Baudelaire), as we grope to understand the implications of "Loss and Cause and all the things they teach" (A. A. S. James). The subtleties of the regeneration process, of repeated engagements with "pride of self . . . in the throes and agony of change" are represented in Anna Collier Lee's "Translation."

THE HOLY LONGING

TELL a wise person, or else keep silent,
because the massman will mock it right away.
I praise what is truly alive,
what longs to be burned to death.

In the calm water of the love-nights,
where you were begotten, where you have
　begotten,
a strange feeling comes over you
when you see the silent candle burning.

Now you are no longer caught
in the obsession with darkness,
and a desire for higher love-making
sweeps you upward.

Distance does not make you falter,
now, arriving in magic, flying,
and, finally, insane for the light,
you are the butterfly and you are gone.

And so long as you haven't experienced
this: to die and so to grow,
you are only a troubled guest
on the dark earth.

JOHANN WOLFGANG VON GOETHE[4]

DESERT PLACES

SNOW falling and night falling fast, oh, fast
In a field I looked into going past,
and the ground almost covered smooth in snow,
But a few weeds and stubble showing last.

The woods around it have it—it is theirs.
All animals are smothered in their lairs.
I am too absent-spirited to count;
The loneliness includes me unawares.

And lonely as it is, that loneliness
Will be more lonely ere it will be less—
A blanker whiteness of benighted snow
With no expression, nothing to express.

They cannot scare me with their empty spaces
Between stars—on stars where no human race is.
I have it in me so much nearer home
To scare myself with my own desert places.

ROBERT FROST[5]

SPLEEN (II)

SOUVENIRS?
More than if I had lived a thousand years!

No chest of drawers crammed with documents,
love-letters, wedding-invitations, wills,
a lock of someone's hair rolled up in a deed,
hides so many secrets as my brain.
This branching catacombs, this pyramid
contains more corpses than the potter's field:
I am a graveyard that the moon abhors,
where long worms like regrets come out to feed
most ravenously on my dearest dead.
I am an old boudoir where a rack of gowns,
perfumed by withered roses, rots to dust;
where only faint pastels and pale Bouchers
inhale the scent of long-unstoppered flasks.

Nothing is slower than the limping days
when under the heavy weather of the years
Boredom, the fruit of glum indifference,
gains the dimension of eternity . . .
Hereafter, mortal clay, you are no more
than a rock encircled by a nameless dread,
an ancient sphinx omitted from the map,
forgotten by the world, and whose fierce moods
sing only to the rays of setting suns.

CHARLES PIERRE BAUDELAIRE[6]

NOT WHOLLY ARE WE HERE

NOT wholly are we here. Some effluence
Of deeps and heights troubles the mind of each;
Our Having glimmers with the Out-of-Reach;
The wafted Real haunts us forever hence:
We grope with senses underneath the Sense
For Loss and Cause and all the things they teach;
Nor clear nor simple can we be in speech
Listening for the outlying Recompense.

Our spirits brushed by dewy vanishings
Of truths too lately with us to be seen,

Stare at their silver trains upon the floor
Moving away, while from the other door,
E'er we can see their shape or what they mean,
The Future stifles us in all its wings.

ALICE ARCHER SEWALL JAMES[7]

≈

TRANSLATION

Fragment from "The Immortal Wing-Bearer"

WHEN first the mind its ignorance discerns
And undeveloped state doth recognize,
Perception dull, and intellect asleep,
The thought is raised unto the Source of light
That shows the good in every form of truth
And wakes intelligence. And, looking back
Upon that night through which the soul hath
  passed,
There comes a little time of peace and rest.

Then onward with determination firm
To know the highest truth; but from the first
Are skilful reasonings set forth which make
The false appear the true and hide its evil;
But these once seen and recognized depart.

Then come delusions, and the pride of self
Attends these vain and subtle falsities,
And self-conceit demands obeisance.

To make one's self authority, and draw
The trusting and the unsuspicious mind
Instead of pointing to the Higher Source
Of life and light that leadeth upward,
Doth snatch away perception, and the mind
At last descendeth into utter darkness.

Then comes humiliation and despair,
And in the throes and agony of change.
A light appears, at first not clearly seen
From lack of insight and intelligence,
But when perceived, in all humility
There is acknowledgment that charity
Or love may lead the mind to know the way
And thus distinguish truth from falsity.

ANNA COLLIER LEE[8]

≈

Periods of peace and affirmation have their place in the growth experience:

> No one can know what the restful peace of the outer person is like, or the restlessness brought on by cravings and falsities, who has not experienced a state of peace. This state is so full of delight that it overflows every concept of delight. It is not just the ending of struggle, but is a life that comes from a more inward peace, moving the outer person in ways beyond description. Then truths of faith and goods of love are born that draw their life from the delight of peace. (AC 92)

The delights of peace can be experienced in terms of the permanence of "What thou lovest well," accessible to those who "Pull down thy vanity . . . Learn of the green world what can be thy place" (Ezra Pound). Alice Very draws inspiration from "Etherial voices" discovered on the mountain trails of faith.

SELECTION FROM CANTO LXXXI

WHAT thou lovest well remains,
                              the rest is dross
What thou lov'st well shall not be reft from thee
What thou lov'st well is thy true heritage
Whose world, or mine or theirs
                              or is it of none?
First came the seen, then thus the palpable
        Elysium, though it were in the halls of hell,
What thou lovest well is thy true heritage

The ant's a centaur in his dragon world.
Pull down thy vanity, it is not man
Made courage, or made order, or made grace,
        Pull down thy vanity, I say pull down.
Learn of the green world what can be thy place
In scaled invention or true artistry,
Pull down thy vanity,
                              Paquin pull down!
The green casque has outdone your elegance.

'Master thyself, then others shall thee beare'
        Pull down thy vanity
Thou art a beaten dog beneath the hail,
A swollen magpie in a fitful sun,
Half black half white
Nor knowst'ou wing from tail
Pull down thy vanity
                              How mean thy hates
Fostered in falsity,
                              Pull down thy vanity,
Rather to destroy, niggard in charity,

Pull down thy vanity,
          I say pull down.

But to have done instead of not doing
          this is not vanity
To have, with decency, knocked
That a Blunt should open
        To have gathered from the air a live tradition
or from a fine old eye the unconquered flame
This is not vanity.
        Here error is all in the not done,
all in the diffidence that faltered

EZRA POUND[9]

MOUNTAIN CLIMBING

WE walk by faith
     more than by sight;
foot feels the trail,
     hand holds tight.

Etherial voices,
     a treetop choir,

veery and whitethroat
     beside us sing;
pointing the way
     by the woodland spring
Madonna orchids
     beckon higher.

Beyond the path
     on the bare rock height
stretches uninterrupted blue.
Earth falls away
     with its blight and care
and only the light
     is everywhere.

Mountains, heaven's blazes,
     footprints of peace!
Eye can't contain
     all it takes in,
dimly discerns
     unfolding plan—
where sight leaves off
     vision begins.

ALICE VERY[10]

Connections of the Poets with Swedenborg

CHARLES PIERRE BAUDELAIRE (1821–1867) became acquainted with Swedenborg through Balzac. Baudelaire may have owned a compendium and possibly a volume or two of Swedenborg's writings, but scholars debate the extent to which poems such as "Correspondences" reflect Swedenborgian influence.

Sources (courtesy of the W. T. Bandy Center for Baudelaire Studies, Vanderbilt University)

Babuts, Nicolae. "Baudelaire et les anges de Swedenborg." *Romance Notes* 21, no. 3 (Spring 1981) pp. 309–12.

Bandy, W. T. "Trois Études Baudelairiennes," *Revue d'Histoire littéraire de la France* 53 (April–June 1953), pp. 203–5.

Jones, P. Mansell. *The Background of Modern French Poetry*. Cambridge, Eng.: Cambridge University Press, 1951, pp. 1–37.

de Jonge, Alex. *Baudelaire: Prince of Clouds*. New York, London: Paddington Press Ltd., 1976.

Juden, Brian. "Que la theorie des correspondances ne derive pas de Swedenborg." *Travaux de Linguistique et de litterature publies par le centre de litterature romanes de l'Universite de Strasbourg* 11, no. 2 (1973), pp. 33–46.

Turnell, Martin. *Baudelaire: A Study of His Poetry*. New York: New Directions, n.d.

ROBERT BROWNING'S (1812–1889) poetry includes ideas that have Swedenborgian overtones, although no records exist of his mention of Swedenborg. It is thought likely that he and his wife, Elizabeth Barrett Browning, read Swedenborg together. His references, in letters after her death, to marriage in heaven give tangible evidence of his acceptance of some Swedenborgian concepts.

Sources

Bates, Ada L. *The Influence of Swedenborg on the Brownings*. Master's thesis, Teachers College, Temple University, 1943. See especially chap. 5.

Browning, Elizabeth Barrett. *Letters to Her Sister, 1846–1859*. Edited by Leonard Huxley. New York: E. P. Dutton, 1930.

ROBERT FROST (1874–1963) was baptized by Rev. John Doughty, pastor of the Church of the New Jerusalem in San Francisco. His mother, Isabelle Moodie Frost, was originally a Presbyterian and became acquainted with Swedenborg through Emerson's essay in *Representative Men*. She joined the Swedenborgian church, took her children there to Sunday school, and taught them Swedenborgian ideas. In an interview in 1923, Frost is quoted as saying, "What's my philosophy? That's hard to say. I was brought up a Swedenborgian. I am not a Swedenborgian now. But there's a good deal of it that's left in me. I am a mystic. I believe in symbols. I believe in change and in changing symbols. Yet that doesn't take me away from the kindly contact of human beings. No, it brings me closer to them."

Sources

Feld, Rose C. "Robert Frost Relieves His Mind." *New York Times Book Review*, 21 October 1923, p. 2.

Thompson, Laurence. *Robert Frost: The Early Years, 1874–1915*. New York, Chicago, San Francisco: Holt, Rinehart and Winston, 1966. See especially pp. 11–12, 20, 70, 487–88, 499, 550.

JOHANN WOLFGANG von GOETHE (1749–1832) became acquainted with the writings of Swedenborg as a young student, through Fraulein von Klettenberg of Frankfurt, Germany. Students of Goethe's letters and poetry find evidences of his familiarity with both scientific and theological works by Swedenborg.

Sources

Peebles, Waldo. "Swedenborg's Influence upon Goethe." *New Church Review* 24, no. 4 (October 1917), pp. 507–36.

Sewall, Frank. "Swedenborg's Influence upon Goethe." *The New Philosophy* 9, no. 1 (January 1906), pp. 12–25.

ALICE ARCHER SEWALL JAMES (1870–1955), painter, poet, and teacher, was the daughter of a Swedenborgian minister, Rev. Frank Sewall. Her use of Swedenborg's ideas extended to her teaching and doctrinal writing as well as being evident in her poetry.

Sources

James, Alice Archer Sewall. *"Memoir of My Education."* Manuscript in James Archive, Swedenborg School of Religion, Newton, Mass., n.d.

Skinner, Alice B. *"Stay by Me, Roses*: A biography of Alice Archer Sewall James." Unpublished manuscript, 1985.

ANNA COLLIER LEE (1845–1908) published articles as well as poetry in New Church periodicals. She was a scholarly student of Swedenborg's writings and an active laywoman in the Boston area. Information about her is available in the archives at the Swedenborg School of Religion in Newton, Massachusetts.

EZRA POUND'S (1885–1972) references to Swedenborg in both poetry and correspondence indicate familiarity that must be based on extensive reading of Swedenborg's works.

Sources

Harmon, William. *Time in Ezra Pound's Work*. Chapel Hill, N.C.: University of North Carolina Press, 1977.

Hesse, Eva, ed. *New Approaches to Ezra Pound: A Co-ordinated Investigation of Pound's Poetry and Ideas*. Berkeley and Los Angeles: University of California Press, 1969.

Meacham, Harry M. *The Caged Panther: Ezra Pound at Saint Elizabeth's*. New York: Twayne, 1967.

Pound, Ezra. *Guide to Kulchur*. New York: New Directions, 1938.

Wilhelm, James J. *The Later Cantos of Ezra Pound*. New York: Walker, 1977.

Witemeyer, Hugh. *The Poetry of Ezra Pound: Forms and Renewal, 1908–1920*. Berkeley and Los Angeles: University of California Press, 1969.

PAUL VALÉRY (1871–1945) became interested in the question of the nature of Swedenborg's spiritual experiences after reading the biography written by Martin Lamm. Valéry wrote a lengthy essay exploring this question, concluding that Swedenborg experienced visions that had a source beyond himself but that the explanation for this phenomenon is shrouded in mystery.

Source

Valéry, Paul. *Variété V*. Paris: Librairie Gallimard, 1944.

ALICE VERY (1894–1977) was baptized and brought up in Swedenborgian

churches in Providence and Boston. In later years she was active in a Christian Science church. *Write on the Water*, the last book of poetry she published (1972), describes the influence of her father, Professor Frank W. Very, "a noted interpreter of Swedenborg's science."

WILLIAM BUTLER YEATS (1856–1939) spoke of Swedenborg in the address he delivered when awarded the Nobel Prize for literature in 1923. Yeats read extensively in Swedenborg and exhibits knowledge of Swedenborgian ideas in some of his poetry as well as in his discussions of the work of William Blake. Henry G. de Geymuller records conversations with Yeats that reveal the profundity of his understanding of Swedenborgian concepts.

Sources

Bloom, Harold. *Yeats*. New York: Oxford University Press, 1970. See especially pp. 70, 240, 408.

de Geymuller, Henry G. "William Butler Yeats." *Le Messager de la Nouvelle Eglise*. (Lausanne, Switzerland, 1925). Article translated by T. H. Spiers.

Yeats, William Butler. *The Autobiography of William Butler Yeats*. New York: Collier Books, 1965.

Notes for the Introduction

1. Jacques Maritain, *Creative Intuition in Art and Poetry* (New York: Pantheon Books, 1953), p. 235.
2. William Blake, "The Marriage of Heaven and Hell," in *The Complete Poems*, ed. Alicia Ostriker (Harmondsworth, Middlesex, England: Penguin Books, 1977), p. 192.
3. Stanley Burnshaw, *The Seamless Web* (New York: George Braziller, 1970), p. 33.

Notes for the Poems

1. Robert Browning, selections from "Rabbi Ben Ezra," in *An Introduction to the Study of Robert Browning's Poetry*, ed. Hiram Corson (Boston: D.C. Heath, 1901), pp. 286–94.

2. Paul Valéry, "Spirtual Bee," in *The Collected Works in English*, Bollingen Series XLV, vol. 2: *Poems*, trans. David Paul (Princeton, N.J.: Princeton University Press, 1971), p. 285.

3. William Butler Yeats, "Sailing to Byzantium," in *Collected Poems*, def. ed. (New York: Macmillan, 1956), p. 191–92.

4. Johann Wolfgang von Goethe, "The Holy Longing," trans. Robert Bly, in *News of the Universe*, ed. Robert Bly (San Francisco: Sierra Club Books, 1980), p. 70.

5. Robert Frost, "Desert Places," in *The Poetry of Robert Frost*, ed. Edward Connery Lathem (New York: Holt, Rinehart and Winston, 1969), p. 296.

6. Charles Pierre Baudelaire, "Spleen (II)," in *Les Fleurs du Mal*, trans. Richard Howard (Boston: David R. Godine, 1982), p. 75.

7. Alice Archer Sewall James, "Not Wholly Are We Here," in *the Morning Moon* (Philadelphia: Dorrance, 1941), p. 72.

8. Anna Collier Lee "Translation," in *Selected Verses from the Writings of Anna Collier Lee*, (privately printed, 1909), p. 44.

9. Ezra Pound, selection from "Canto LXXXI," in *Oxford Book of American Verse*, ed. F. O. Matthiessen (New York: Oxford University Press, 1950), pp. 739–40.

10. Alice Very, "Mountain Climbing," in *Write on the Water* (Boston: Branden Press, 1972).

I
Arts
&
Letters

Sunt in Cælo spirituali palatia magnifica, in quibus inter omnia fulgent lapidibus pretiosis, et decoramentis in talibus formis, ut non æquari possit aliqua pictura in Mundo, nec exprimi verbis; ars enim ibi in sua arte est, imprimis architectonica; ex illo Cælo trahunt plures artes in Mundo suas leges, et harmonias, inde pulchritudines.

❧

There are splendid palaces in the spiritual heaven, where everything glows from within with precious stones, and with ornaments so exquisitely formed that they cannot be reproduced by any painting on earth, or explained in words. Art, there is art in its own essence—especially architecture. From this heaven most of the arts in our world derive their laws, their harmonies, and therefore their beauties. (AE 831)

Spirit in American Art: The Image as Hieroglyph

Richard Silver, Ph.D.

My soul dwells in a mortal tenement and feels the influence of the elements. Still I would not live where tempests never come, for they bring beauty in their train.

—Thomas Cole, in 1831 letter to Louis Nobel

The following article has been condensed and adapted from a chapter in Dr. Silver's Ph.D. dissertation, "The Spiritual Kingdom in America: The Influence of Emanuel Swedenborg on American Society and Culture 1815–1860" (Stanford University, 1983).

BECAUSE THE CRITICAL VIEW of a painting, a piece of sculpture, or a monument depends on the perceptions and expectations of a period, the criticism or praise of a work of art provides a means of examining the cultural assumptions of a group of individuals in a historical period. In the supposedly materialist culture of the antebellum era, there were a large number of artists and critics who presented a view of artistic form, beauty, and proportion that was clearly influenced by a spiritual Platonic ideal. In presenting this aesthetic theory a number of critics and artists used Swedenborg's theories and work as both a source and an inspiration for their ideas.

During the period 1830–60 the older aesthetic notion of the proper role of art and the artist in America was challenged and ultimately revised. The Burkean vision of art as a catalog of what could be seen was rejected and replaced by an essentially spiritual view of the artist as a visionary seer, and the work of art as an ideal that inspired the viewer. And while the American paintings completed before 1820 focused on historical and classical figures, on human activity and specific time and event, most of the paintings of the 1850s emphasized atmosphere and nature to the subordination, and often the elimination, of both human figures and natural time.[1] The emphasis changed from the re-creation of nature to a concern with the message or the meaning in the depiction of nature.

The landscapes of Frederic Church exemplify this new focus. Church's *Twilight in the Wilderness* (1860), *Cotopaxi* (1863), and *Heart of the Andes* (1864) were all concerned with the effect of atmosphere on the audience. Church's massive efforts celebrated the vitality of existence and the sheer energy of the creation. Each of them presented a millennial, spiritual vision of nature. Unlike painters of the Revolutionary era, concerned with material place and a celebration of the event, Church and the artists of the 1840s and 1850s were immersed in the celebration of millennial expectations and spirituality.

This change in focus was so great that it required a shift in the American aesthetic. Archibald Alison, interpreting the Scottish Common Sense philosophy, felt that the individual's intuition was crucial for perceiving the meaning of a work of art. Because each man's mind had different experiences, the individual perception of a scene had to be different. There could be no uniform statement of sublimity or beauty. What was beautiful for one might be detestable to another. There

RICHARD SILVER is a Phi Beta Kappa graduate of Hamilton College and received his Ph.D. in history and humanities from Stanford University in 1983 for his work "The Spiritual Kingdom in America: The Influence of Emanuel Swedenborg on American Society and Culture 1815–1860." During the 1980–81 academic year he was a Mabelle McLeod Lewis Fellow and in 1981–82 he received a Whiting Fellowship. He has served as an instructor in the humanities sequence of the Western Culture program at Stanford University. Currently he is engaged in an interpretative biography of Benjamin Silliman as part of a general study that explores the relationship between theology and science in nineteenth-century America.

were, then, no absolute standards of judgment in matters of aesthetic taste. It was the viewer who determined the sublimity of the perception and the nature of the subject being viewed. The viewer, in essence, made the object.

Perhaps the best way to describe this view of art was by the Coleridgean term *esemplastic*.[2] A work of art was an organism that depended on the artist's experience and the viewer's expectations. Because there were no givens or constants, the work never remained static. It was constantly changing in form and meaning, as the knowledge and perceptions of the viewer changed. Thomas Cole, the founder of the Hudson River School, was concerned primarily not with subject matter but with the effect produced by the work on the viewer. He focused on the moral value of a work of art. As he noted, "Poetry and Painting . . . purify thought, by grouping the past, present and the future—they give the mind a foretaste of its immortality and thus prepare it for performing an exalted part amid the realities of life."[3]

Cole's later work, especially his Voyage of Life series, the *Mountain Ford* (1846) and his last painting, *The Vision* (1848), illustrate the artist's obsession with a heightened spirituality and the view of the artist as both priest and prophet. His later concerns represent nothing short of a revolution in American aesthetic theory. For Cole, nature was a veritable church. The representation of nature was a spiritual and religious act. Cole rejected the use of literature as a subject and found his Bible in nature. For Cole, there was no need to use the artifice of human creation to demonstrate piety. The immanence of God in the natural world would suffice. It was hardly an accident that Cole's Course of Empire (1844–46) series recorded not a change of landscape but a change in the human use of that landscape. The natural setting in these paintings is static, while man's use of the scene changes. Similarly, in Cole's Voyage of Life series, the natural elements remain constant, but the development, or the stage of development of the figures in the work, change and alter the viewers' perception of the landscape.

Swedenborg's writings and philosophy are the source of many of the ideas presented in America's first major art journal, *The Crayon*. William Stillman, who wrote virtually the entire first two volumes of the journal, was a Swedenborgian. At the end of his life, in his *Autobiography* (1901), he admitted that "if any one influenced me more than any other it would be Emanuel Swedenborg, who gave me a comprehension of what spiritual life was."[4]

Perhaps the best example of Stillman's use of Swedenborg can be seen in an article entitled "The Nature and Use of Beauty" (1854). In the article, Stillman presents a Swedenborgian standard of art. As he notes, "The more elevated the quality of Beauty arising from the dignity of use, the more its impression of the nature of sensation and the terms of thought. The human form contains the most perfect fitness for use and that it is the best known manifestation of Beauty."[5]

In addition to this Swedenborgian standard of use, Stillman relied on the concept of correspondences. When he discussed the means of artistic composition, he observed, "Since man is made in the image of God, it follows that every attitude of Deity has its corresponding trait in Humanity and it is evident that the visible corresponds to the different manifestations of the divine Goodness. We correspond with Nature through our likeness to God."[6] Stillman stressed that in the ideal landscape each detail should represent a spiritual truth. The arrangement of the natural objects had a particular spiritual significance, and the whole was a representation of divinity. As Stillman summarized this view, "Love is the end and wisdom the means to an appreciation of the ideal representation of the Beautiful in the details of a landscape."[7]

What is especially fascinating about these editorials is that they are nearly identical to the theory of art presented by the official Swedenborgian publication, *The New Jerusalem Magazine*. In the 1840s a series of articles written by Joseph Andrews, the Swedenborgian artist and engraver and student of John Flaxman, and Joseph Ropes, a Swedenborgian art critic and self-taught artist, examined the relationship between Swedenborgianism and art.

Ropes thought of art as a training for a higher task. As he noted in 1841, "The use of painting is but an introduction to a still higher use, the development of one of the noblest faculties of the mind, I mean the quality of perceiving exactness and beauty."[8] For Ropes, the subject of art reflected its noble end. Only the representation of an ideal justified such an exalted function, for the "artist has in his mind a standard of beauty which governs his hand and leads him only to select the highest excellence which he sees."[9]

Joseph Andrews presented a similar view of the use of art. Andrews, who was apprenticed to the great English Swedenborgian artist John Flaxman,[10] the illustrator of Dante's *Comedia*, saw that the

> use of representative art is to elevate, to refine and chasten the affections through the sense of art. It is a means of elevating and purifying the mind, of leading us to acknowledge the beneficent source of all, that of giving us power to receive the bountiful, ever sacred blessing, in all forms of beauty, which Infinite Love is continually willing to give us.[11]

For Andrews, art conveyed its meaning by means of correspondence theory. Thus, "when we regard the aspects and the object of Nature our ideas are elevated, our delight is increased and our sense of beauty is intensified."[12] As Andrews noted about *Niagara Falls*, "The general correspondence of this masterpiece is striking and instructive. As water represents truth, water in motion corresponds to truth in art or the appreciation of truth to life."[13]

When he spoke on architecture, Andrews took this theory to an extreme. He claimed:

FIG. 136. Voyage of Life: Manhood, *by Thomas Cole, 1840*

Every great change in religious faith has manifested itself by a corresponding change in architecture. It is reasonable, then, to suppose that the New Church must soon reshape architecture. [Because man] is governed by the law of correspondence, . . . there should be three parts to every church building—the lower or basement to contain rooms for instruction on a natural level, . . . the main floor—corresponding to the spiritual degree as a place of worship . . . , and . . . the higher floors corresponding to the inmost in man, where the Lord's Supper is celebrated.[14]

For the Swedenborgians, it was imperative to study nature in order to learn about God. As Andrews noted, "under orderly circumstances nature is the first means of culture."[15] But nature was not static. It changed with the viewer's perception. As such, "when the senses become cultivated, the mind begins to look into the particular to which the general character of nature owes its character. [Thus it is] our capacity to see that excites our wonder."[16]

According to the writers in the *New Jerusalem Magazine*, it was this capacity to see and appreciate nature that marked man's spiritual progress. Indeed, the Swedenborgians never tired of proclaiming that "the infinite loving kindness of the Lord is shown in man's being born in ignorance. From this, his life may be one of unceasing expression of happiness."[17]

For the Swedenborgians, nature provided man with a sense of otherness. As such its primary value was as a teaching device. The essence of the sublime was not terror, as Burke noted, or harmony, as Native American artist Washington Allston insisted, but simply the irrefutable and awesome fact of truth and revelation.

The artist's role in this type of didactic art was to represent nature so that it taught the viewer how to see correctly. Art did not merely "impart a refined pleasure to the mind," it acted to "train the mind."[18] Indeed, as Ropes observed, "Art will be found of great advantage in strengthening the conceiving power of the mind and in instructing man to arrange and express his thoughts."[19]

This Swedenborgian theory of the use and effect of art was precisely the same definition of art advanced by the noted art critic James Jackson Jarves. In Jarves's works—principally, *Art Hints* (1855), *The Art Idea* (1864), and *Art Thoughts* (1870)—art was conceived as the "spiritual representation of Love. . . . It is the instrument of the spiritual and intellectual creature," and, according to Jarves, "it is the

FIG. 137. Cotopaxi, *by Frederic Church, 1862*

FIG. 138. Twilight in the Wilderness, *by Frederic Church, 1860*

duty of the Artist to please and to teach."[20] Because, for Jarves, knowledge was valuable solely in its application, "Truth is the paramount law of Beauty."[21]

Jarves was fascinated with the spiritual dimension in art. While in Italy in the 1850s he discussed his theories of art with the members of the Browning spiritualist circle that included the Swedenborgian artist William Nelson Page and the Swedenborgian sculptor Hiram Powers.[22] Along with Page and Powers, Jarves considered art as a means to promote the appreciation of the ideal of beauty. For Jarves, art was a teaching device. It guided the spirit of man. As he insisted, "The matter is a vehicle for spirit, or the thought which gave it being. Otherwise we get only the dead form of things. . . . Matter without spirit would be inert, soulless. There would be no God in it. . . . So with art. The matter or vehicle must be impregnated with spirit."[23]

Like the Swedenborgians, for Jarves "the purpose of art was to instruct, to represent the ideal in the real and to stimulate the viewer to find that ideal in nature." The artist must begin with nature, "because without an intimate knowledge of Nature, we are incapacitated to judge of Art, because Art is but the mirror of Nature."[24] The aim of the landscapist, then, should be, "first to understand the spirit and, second, to know the details."[25]

This exalted view of the function of nature can only be appreciated if we realize that for Jarves nature "was the entire thought of God as represented in the moral and material universe."[26] Jarves, along with the Swedenborgians, saw nature as the other to man's self. In representing nature, art taught man to go beyond the self and reach out to achieve harmony with that otherness that constituted God's kingdom on earth. As Jarves proclaimed, "Knowledge is valuable solely for its application."[27]

Along with the Swedenborgians, Jarves believed that art served as a means of education, but this training of the self could occur only in perfect liberty. The individual had to choose to train the will so he could appreciate the meaning behind the landscape. Thus, for Jarves, "Art is choked by the stern case of an incipient civilization of machines. Men must work to live before they can live to enjoy the beautiful."[28] The artist and the audience must remember that the end of art, as of all study, is "the repose of mind that passeth description."[29] Idealism, then, was far more useful than mimesis. While the latter "applies itself to the portrayal of the external world, partaking more or less of copying and imitation . . . , idealism bases itself in universal truth. It deals more with emotion and ideas than fact and action."[30]

The Platonic dimension in art criticism reflected the spiritual concerns of American artists in the 1850s and 1860s. The emphasis on spirituality was not limited to the subject matter of art. It extended to the tone and the creation of an atmosphere in the painting.[31] The focus of American art, the manner in which subject and atmosphere were treated, changed drastically in the 1850s. There was a sudden concern for exotic landscapes.

As one critic has noted,[32] Frederic Church's paintings were the visible representations of Manifest Destiny. The shadings of light in works like *Cotopaxi* and *Twilight in the Wilderness* represented an apocalyptic, millennial view of the creation. The atmosphere was at once ominous yet promising, and the play of light on the canvas suggested either the end of an era or the dawn of a new age. In these paintings, Church depicted a vast cosmic drama. His attention to detail invited the viewer to see the work with his own eyes, to see what was represented on the canvas. The detail in *Heart of the Andes*, *Cotopaxi*, and *Morning in the Tropics* was too rich actually to be seen in one short viewing period. As Mark Twain said about *Heart of the Andes*, "You find a new picture every time you look at it. You seem to find nothing the second time that you saw the first."[33]

Church's works were exercises in perception. Every detail was meticulously arranged to test the viewer's sight. The longer someone looked at Church's work the more one saw. The more one trained one's perceptions, the more detail one could appreciate. In essence, Church developed an artistic expression of Manifest Destiny that enabled his audience to appreciate the potential expansiveness of sight. This effort to internalize the belief in Manifest Destiny was recognized by the Swedenborgian artist Georges Inness, who observed that "To Church the work of art was basically an abstraction. Hence his painted visions were almost hieratic presences, urging his fellow men to the glories of Manifest Destiny. His paintings were the projections of Transcendental hopes."[34]

It is important to recognize that Church's vision was primarily religious. He was familiar with Swedenborg's works, and in his letters he often referred to Swedenborg's mystical sense and the theory of correspondences between the natural and spiritual world. In his early years Church illustrated scenes from Bunyan's *Pilgrim's Progress*, and his concern for spiritual matters even led to an extended trip to Jerusalem in the 1870s. The products of this trip, principally *El Arasne* and the *New Jerusalem* were mystical combinations of light and shade that captured the public's imagination in the late 1870s.[35]

William Nelson Page was the first self-proclaimed Swedenborgian artist of national reputation.[36] Page discovered Swedenborg's writings while he was in Florence in the early 1850s. A member of the Browning circle, he attended the numerous seances held by the Brownings, spoke with the noted medium Douglas Home, and was converted to Swedenborgianism by Hiram Powers, the American sculptor, and Thomas Worcester, the minister of the Boston New Jerusalem Church, who was vacationing in Florence at the time of Page's visit.

This conversion to Swedenborgianism had a profound impact on Page's artistic theory. He had always been concerned with the influence of color on the viewer's perception of a painting, but his concern prior to the 1850s was purely technical.[37] By the 1860s Page's view of the use of color, as well as his entire theory of proportion, changed. He was no longer concerned with the technical standards of his craft. His concern was now with the content and message that accompanied this expertise. Color became a means of conveying a message. Page became obsessed with the search for a middle tone. Because, along with Church and Stillman, he believed that Swedenborg was basically a Manichaean, Page associated the color black with hell and white with heaven and sought to represent the equilibrium point, or as he found it, a midgray, as the appropriate color for the canvas of a natural painter. The precise nature of this middle tone became a point of contention between Page and the other nationally famous Swedenborgian painter, George Inness. As Inness's son recalled:

> There was only one subject that I know of that Page and my father disagreed upon; that subject was what they called "the middle tone." Now the middle tone was Page's idea. He claimed that the horizon should be a middle tone: that is, it should be half way between the lightest light and the greatest dark in the picture. Father agreed with him on that point, but what they could not agree upon was just what a middle tone really was. So Page, to explain more fully, took a strip of tin and painted it white at one end and black at the other, and then graded in stripes from both ends until it reached a gray tone in the middle. This he showed to my father and said triumphantly, "There's the true middle tone!" The next day father went to Page's studio with a similar strip of tin and declared that he had the true middle tone. When they compared the two hues, there was no resemblance between them.[38]

The point of this anecdote was not that Page and Inness differed on the precise nature of the middle tone, but that both believed in Swedenborg's equilibrium theory and, perhaps more significantly, that both saw Swedenborg as a Manichaean, who viewed the natural world as poised between the blackness of hell and the whiteness of heaven.

In an article entitled "The Measure of a Man," written for *Scribner's Monthly,* Page revealed a second debt he owed to Swedenborg.[39] Page saw in the first volume of the *Arcana Coelestia* a theory of correspondences that enabled him to develop a precise science of proportions for the human body. According to Page, when the form of the human figure was drawn in a cruciform pattern, it could be subdivided by twos until there were 144 parts to the body. These areas represented squares on a canvas, and, for Page at least, they provided a grid on which one could reproduce figures precisely in proportion to the actual human figure being represented. Precisely how this system operated remains a mys-

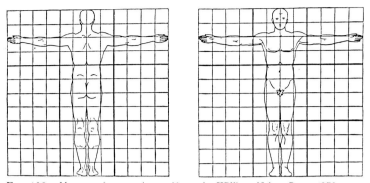

FIG. 139. *Measure of a man in cruciform, by William Nelson Page, 1879*

tery, but Page believed in its value, and for him it appeared to work quite well.

Besides these technical elements in his art, Page adopted two other Swedenborgian ideas. First, he was committed to the idea of an organic art. The viewing of a painting was a dynamic process that involved a continually changing relationship between perception and art. In effect, a painting was never complete. It was in a state of continual flux and changed with the viewer's knowledge and perception. In many ways this was similar to the theory of "art for art's sake," but what was unique about Page's idea was that it was presented by a portrait painter, an artist of the human figure. Page never painted landscapes, yet he firmly believed that a painting functioned in precisely the same way as nature functioned. It was never static. This belief may explain why the pigment in Page's work was so unstable. Page's paintings have faded and cracked with time. The bland, rather ineffectual remains of his portraits hardly do justice to his exalted theories, unless we view them as intentionally designed to age with the audience and the subject.

Finally, Page applied Swedenborg's theory of divine influx to the problem of the source of artistic inspiration. For Page, the artist had no independent role in creating a painting. He was a tool, a conduit for divine activity. Page believed that art represented the spiritual manifestation of humanity and that "true art is the feeling of one soul, through forethought and prescience, reproduced in the soul of another."[40] The painting awakened the sensibility of the viewer. The artist was only the instrument of spiritual instruction.

It was not the least of Page's accomplishments that he converted the great American landscape artist George Inness to Swedenborgianism. Inness's first contact with the belief must have come in Italy in the early 1850s when he was associated with the Browning circle, but he did not read Swedenborg until he became Page's neighbor at Eagleswood, New Jersey, in 1862. As George Inness, Jr., reported in the biography of his father:

> Page brought to my father the teachings of Emanuel Swedenborg. The philosophy came at the time of his life when

he most needed something to lift him out of himself and the limited doctrines of orthodox creeds. He threw himself into its teachings with all the fire and enthusiasm of his nature and although he did not adhere to all its tenets it led to further metaphysical research.[41]

For Inness, the most important Swedenborgian doctrine was the correspondence of the natural to the spiritual realm. As Inness revealed, "The true artist paints for values. A tree in a landscape is to him not a dark green mass, but so much color against so much sky. He studies things not for themselves, but for their relation one to another."[42] Inness believed that the canvas should represent the relationship of the natural to the spiritual realm. The controversy with Page over the nature of the middle tint emerged from this desire to establish a natural equilibrium in the canvas before the details could be added.

It was not until the last twenty years of his life that Inness reached what he considered a mature understanding of Swedenborg's ideas. His work in the 1880s and 1890s, though it

is beyond the chronological scope of this thesis, is especially fascinating because it uses a Swedenborgian view of art as a teaching device.

Before 1874 Inness experimented with Swedenborgian themes and techniques. As early as 1867 he used Swedenborgian topics as subjects for his work. The series of paintings that began with *The Valley of the Shadow of Death* and ended with *The New Jerusalem* represented a Swedenborgian version of Bunyan's *Pilgrim's Progress*. In the *True Christian Religion* Swedenborg noted that the victory of Christ on the cross lay precisely in his ability to resist the temptations of both despair and triumph. This was the subject of *The Valley of the Shadow of Death*, while *The New Jerusalem* illustrated the reward for resisting temptation. But while the theme of these paintings was Swedenborgian, the technical treatment of the theme was not. The color and tone of the paintings do not reflect their Swedenborgian content. They merely reflect the natural meaning of the painting.

By the late 1870s Inness mastered the technical aspects of his painting, and the tone and style of his work underwent

FIG. 140. The Storm, *by George Inness, 1876*

FIG. 141. Niagara Falls, *by George Inness, 1885*

a substantial change. He was no longer concerned with a conventional treatment of religious subjects. The tone and style of his work now reflected his Swedenborgian beliefs. This change can be seen in the painting *The Storm* (1877). The piece actually works in Swedenborgian terms. The storm is a common Swedenborgian metaphor for a time of trial or of a war in the soul. The sheep are Christians, natural men who seek the truth. The shepherd figure in the work can be Swedenborg or Christ, the visible manifestation of the Word. The path, the true path, leads to the light away from the storm of the soul. The apparent mist or smoke on the horizon represents spiritual truth, or the way to spiritual truth. What is especially curious about the painting is that the sheep, or at least most of the sheep, are facing the wrong way. They are looking away from the white light and toward the darkness.

The Swedenborgianism in Inness's art became even more pronounced in the 1880s. The paintings of Niagara Falls done in 1885 and 1889 are Swedenborgian. For the Swedenborgians, water always represented truth, and flowing water represented a changing truth that depended on circumstances. Niagara Falls as a subject was the perfect representative of the Swedenborgian concept of natural reality. In his 1885 painting Inness focused on man's relationship to this reality. The two figures in the painting represent Inness's Manichaean interpretation of Swedenborg's visions. The figures represent an equilibrium state between heaven and hell. They are but parts of a whole. As parts, they can only view natural truth from a single perspective—either good or evil. Despite these figures, the message of the painting is predominantly optimistic. The vapor, white and almost palpable in its intensity, rises heavenward from the water. The green of the foreground, representing natural or scientific truth, is

in contrast to the white of wisdom or truth in the water and the purer spiritual white of the clouds that almost describe figures from the Swedenborgian apocalypse.

In contrast to this depiction of the falls, the 1889 painting merges the falls, the sky, and the earth in a continual haze of white. It is as if Inness now accepts Swedenborg's doctrine of the coexistence of earth, spirit, and the celestial realm. The earth brown supports the green and white haze. It also serves as a contrast to these lighter colors. Significantly, it supports the other colors: it does not pull them down. As in Swedenborg's doctrine, there is no "discrete degree" [see Glossary] where brown becomes green and green becomes white. The whole is a continual mass of color. The painting pulsates with life. It is in continual motion that points upward toward the whiteness of the upper canvas, toward the spiritual and celestial truth that should be a person's destiny.

Inness's use of Swedenborg's theories reached its culmination in the 1893 painting *Moonlight*. In this last great work, there is no longer any distinction of tone. The whole painting is done in a thick haze, a single abnormal impenetrable mist that envelopes everything and threatens to destroy the individuality of discrete objects. The only light in the work comes from an orange half-moon that is about to be obscured by dark clouds. Indeed, the only color in the work is a dull orange hue that, as Swedenborg notes, represents an equilibrium state between the love of the world and the love of God.

In *Moonlight* the haze is so thick that objects have no clear relationship to each other. Instead, they merely exist somewhere in space and time. It is as if Inness is representing the spiritual realm of Swedenborg's universe where objects have no temporal relationship to each other and their spatial relations are based on accidental contiguity rather than a logical functional relationship.

The dark haze that dominated all of the canvases in the 1890s corresponded to Inness's own dark vision of the natural human. The natural human could not see clearly. One simply could not see face to face. One could only see the truth as in a mist, could only catch glimpses of light that revealed spiritual truth. In the paintings of the 1890s Inness was at once depicting the condition of the natural human, especially the inability to see clearly, and urging one to see further. By recognizing one's own lack of spiritual vision, the natural human would be encouraged to use his or her natural sight to its fullest ability.

Unlike Page, who incorporated Swedenborgian thought into his artistic theories, Inness used Swedenborg for technique, message, and content. It would be a mistake to see Inness only as an American impressionist, for he was a unique artist who integrated his religious faith into his art and provided his audience with a lesson in Swedenborgian ethics.

The other nineteenth-century American artist who was a professed Swedenborgian was the California painter William Keith.[43] Unlike Inness and Page, Keith's career lies entirely outside the chronological limits of this work. However, because no one has adequately examined the link between Keith's painting and his Swedenborgianism, it might be useful to explore briefly the connections.

Keith had a long-standing friendship with Joseph Worcester, the minister of San Francisco's Swedenborgian church, but Worcester succeeded in converting Keith only after the death of Keith's wife in 1882. From that date there was an obvious change in Keith's work. Before 1882 Keith was a colorist, virtually indistinguishable from a host of California painters. His work was picturesque, light, and generally inoffensive. But after 1882 something happened to Keith's work. It became darker, more ominous, yet more profound. A thick haze replaced the bright detail of the 1870s. Objects were no longer distinct. Colors were no longer prominent. Instead, they merged, blended, seemed to surface for a time and then blended again. While space and time were not obliterated in the paintings, most of the work was not place-specific. The objects were in their naturally correct places but they could have been located anywhere in space or time. It was not the object that was important for Keith, it was the handling of the object in space and the viewer's reaction to it that were significant.

Perhaps the most representative painting of this late period

is *Evening*. In this painting a haze dominates the scene. Reds, greens, and browns merge in the foreground and highlight the blue of the pond that is at the center of the canvas. The oak trees, standing erect, frame the clear water and reach upward toward the white of the sky. The female figure at the left is an unobtrusive visitor to the natural scene. She is there merely to add human interest to the view. The whole scene, the blending of the colors of truth and love, the erect oaks and the figure of justice and grace, all point to the central image of the pond, representing truth.

The significance of the Swedenborgianism in the work of Church, Page, Inness, and Keith was that it was part of a larger spiritual school of American art. This spiritual school was Platonic in its inspiration. It rejected the Lockean aesthetic of Burke in favor of the exaltation of the ideal. It was consciously didactic, yet its didacticism did not become a rigid pedagogy. Its works challenged the viewer. They were intended to stimulate the viewer's imagination. The audience had to create the painting. The viewer had to give the work meaning, and that meaning changed as the viewer's own understanding and knowledge changed.

The Swedenborgian artists created an art that was organic. It was in continual flux. The painting, in itself, meant nothing. Its meaning was provided by the viewer. As such, each painting was an exercise in self-education. The viewer of an art piece had to train his mind to appreciate the spiritual realm that coexisted with the natural world.

Art, then, was a means of self-education. It was an effort to force the viewer to see the kernel of truth that existed in the natural world. To accomplish this, the Swedenborgians Inness, Page, and Keith, used a correspondence theory that included the use of color for effect, the derangement of normal temporal and spatial arrangements, and the masking of details behind an obscure haze. Church and the other spiritual artists aimed at the same end as the Swedenborgians. Where Church and his colleagues differed from Page, Inness, and Keith was in their looser interpretation of how they would achieve their end. None of these artists adhered to a scientific theory of correspondence, nor did any of them aim at a deliberate derangement of the senses. But all of them intended to project in their art a spiritual attitude toward life. The material world was not everything. Nature was not an end in itself. It was a type, a representation of an inner truth. And the great inner truth that these artists sought to portray was the reality of the human soul.

Notes

1. For an examination of this change, see Barbara Novak, *American Painting of the Nineteenth Century* (New York: Praeger, 1969), chaps. 1–4, pp. 15–91.

2. Coleridge's term initially applied to poetry, specifically to the nature of language. However, it can easily be applied to any of the creative arts. See I. A. Richards, *Coleridge on the Imagination* (Indianapolis: University of Indiana Press, 1969); and M. H. Abrams, *The Mirror and the Lamp* (New York: Oxford University Press, 1953).

3. Thomas Cole, "Essay on American Scenery," in John McCoubrey, ed., *American Art: Essays and Sources* (New York: George Braziller, 1965), p. 106.

4. William Stillman, *The Autobiography of a Journalist* (Boston: Houghton Miffin, 1903), p. 418. Stillman was a student of Frederic Church, who gave up painting in the late 1850s. He was sole editor of *The Crayon* for its first two years, but had to resign after the third volume was issued. Later in life, Stillman served as United States consul in Crete and wrote for the New York dailies.

5. William Stillman, "The Nature and Uses of Beauty," *The Crayon* 2 (1856), p. 34.

6. Ibid., p. 66.

7. Ibid., p. 191.

8. Joseph Ropes, "Lectures on Painting," *The New Jerusalem Magazine* 13 (April 1841), p. 84.

9. Ibid.

10. For a biography of Flaxman, see W. G. Constable, *John Flaxman: 1756–1826* (London: University of London, 1927). Flaxman was best known in the United States for his illustrations of Dante's *Divine Comedy*.

11. Joseph Andrews, "Lectures on Art," *The New Jerusalem Magazine* 13 (April 1841), p. 284.

12. Ibid., p. 286.

13. Joseph Andrews, "Nature as a Means of Culture," *The New Jerusalem Magazine* 37 (December 1868), p. 600.

14. Joseph Andrews, "On Architecture," *The New Jerusalem Magazine* 13 (December 1841), pp. 413, 414.

15. Ibid.

16. Andrews, "Nature as a Means of Culture," p. 509.

17. Ibid., p. 510.

18. Ropes, p. 88.

19. Ibid., p. 90.

20. James Jackson Jarves, *Art Hints: Architecture, Sculpture and Painting* (New York, Harper and Brothers, 1855) p. 138. The only biography of Jarves is by Francis Steegmuller, *The Two Lives of James Jackson Jarves* (New Haven, Conn.: Yale University Press, 1951).

21. Jarves, *Art Hints*, p. 98.

22. Powers was the most important Swedenborgian sculptor. He was a member of the Cincinnati New Church founded by his father-in-law, Frederick Eckstein. But because all his great work was done in Florence and Europe, he was not really an American artist. Therefore, I have not discussed his work in this chapter. For a biography of Powers, see Sylvia Crane, *White Silence: Greenough, Powers and Crawford: American Sculptors in Nineteenth Century Italy* (Miami: University of Miami, 1972).

23. James Jackson Jarves, *Art Thoughts: The Experience and Observations of an American Amateur in Europe* (New York: Hurd and Houghton, 1870). pp. 8–9.

24. Jarves, *Art Hints*, p. 98.

25. Ibid.

26. Ibid., p. 15.

27. Ibid., p. 69.

28. Jarves, *The Art Idea: Part Second of Confessions of an Inquirer* (New York: Hurd and Houghton, 1864), p. 16.

29. Ibid.

30. Jarves, *Art Hints*, p. 68.

31. Barbara Novak examines the influence of the spiritual on the composition and structure of American art in her works: *American Painting of the Nineteenth Century;* and *Nature and Culture: American Landscape and Painting: 1825–75* (New York: Oxford University Press, 1980). According to Novak, a distinctive luminist tradition, represented in the words of Church and his colleagues, developed in the 1850s. This tradition was distinguished by a planar, horizontal design, an ideational order, the absence of stroke, and cool, hard, almost-palpable treatment of light.

32. See David Huntington, *The Landscapes of Frederic Church* (New York: George Braziller, 1966).

33. Quoted in Huntington, p. 67.

34. George Inness, Jr., *The Life and Letters of George Inness* (New York: Century, 1917), p. 66.

35. See Huntington, chap. 6.

36. The best account of Page's life and work is Joshua Taylor, *William Nelson Page: The American Titian* (Chicago: University of Chicago Press, 1959). It includes an excellent discussion of Page's religious beliefs and their influence on his art.

37. William Nelson Page, "The Art of the Use of Color in Imitation and Painting," *Broadway Journal* (8 February–29 March 1846).

38. George Inness, Jr., *Life and Letters of Inness*, p. 119.

39. William Nelson Page, "The Measure of a Man," *Scribner's Monthly* (1879), p. 832.

40. Quoted in Taylor, p. 67.

41. George Cikovsky has noted that religion was central to Inness's art and that his work after the 1860s reflected his religious beliefs. Aside from Cikovsky's conjectures, no critic has examined how closely Inness's work was shaped by his Swedenborgianism. See George Cikovsky, *The Life and Work of George Inness* (Cambridge, Mass.: Harvard University Press, 1965).

42. George Inness, "Letter on Impressionism" (1884), in John McCoubrey, ed., *American Art: Essays and Sources* (New York: George Braziller, 1965), p. 51.

43. The best studies of Keith are by Brother Cornelius, *William Keith: Old Master of California* (New York: 1942); and Eugene Neuhaus, *William Keith: The Man and the Artist* (Berkeley, Calif.: University of California Press, 1938). There are also a number of exhibition catalogs, among them *The Watercolors of William Keith* (Oakland, Calif.: Oakland Museum, 1979).

The Influence of Swedenborg on the Music of Richard Yardumian

Ethelwyn Worden

> Only that music has a future that has been inspired by a noble
> love to grow into the wisdom of the spiritual.
> —Richard Yardumian

IN THE SUCCESSION of New Church [Swedenborgian; see Glossary] hymnals, and in the choral files of quite a number of Swedenborgian churches, is a large and glorious collection of music written or arranged by a variety of composers from within the church. Of these, some attained local or national standing through aspects of their musicianship other than composition, though their names have become familiar to Swedenborgian churchgoers in the context of hymns, liturgy, or special works.

George James Webb, J. B. Dykes, John Worcester, William Wallace Gilchrist, Rollo F. Maitland, Clarence and Mary Lathbury, Frank and Maude Sewall, Brian Kingslake, and other musicians have over time created a firm basis for New Church worship. Only a few became known as composers outside of New Church circles.

One composer who was notably influenced by the theology of Emanuel Swedenborg, and whose music gained international recognition, was Richard Yardumian, a highly active and energetic member of The Lord's New Church in Bryn Athyn, Pennsylvania, until his death in August 1985 at the age of sixty-eight.

Born of Armenian parents in Philadelphia in 1917, Richard, the youngest of ten children, grew up within a powerful musical heritage full of the history and rich, dark sounds of the Russo-Turkish areas north of the Middle East. His fa-

ther, the Reverent Haig Yardumian, had fled Turkey when Armenian leaders and intellectuals were persecuted. Richard began to play and compose music of his own at an early age. It was based largely on Armenian melodies and forms, and influenced by the musicianship of an older brother, a pianist. He later studied form, theory, and composition on his own, at the Philadelphia Free Library, and under such notable teachers as José Iturbi, Alexander Matthews, and George Boyle, with encouragement and guidance from Leopold Stokowski.

That his music was of world-class quality was obvious from the beginning. His orchestral piece *Desolate City* was premiered by Eugene Ormandy and the Philadelphia Orchestra when Richard was twenty-eight, thus beginning a long association between the composer and that outstanding orchestra. The earlier *Armenian Suite*, written when he was nineteen, was also well received, and it remains a joyful part of many an orchestral program in this country and abroad.

As a young man, Richard questioned his Armenian Apostolic heritage and a variety of religious philosophies in searching for something relevant to his life, mind, and music. Introduced to the works of Emanuel Swedenborg by the woman who became his wife, 'Ruth Seckelmann, Yardumian's quest for a compatible source of spiritual direction was answered.

ETHELWYN WORDEN, a Philadelphia native, spent her early youth in China, Italy, and Eastern Shore, Maryland. She studied singing as an undergraduate at Temple University, and music history and literature at the graduate level at Temple University and the University of Maine at Orono. For twelve years she taught choral and vocal music and music history at Wesley College in Delaware. She is currently director of the Central Office of the General Convention of Swedenborgian Churches, as well as a professional singer and performer in the Boston area.

During the New Church Music Festival in Bryn Athyn, Pennsylvania, in June 1986, Ruth Yardumian was the keynote speaker, discussing her husband and his music. What follows are extended excerpts of that speech:

When I first met Richard Yardumian in 1935, he played some Beethoven and some Schumann for me and a few short pieces of his own that he called "Waves." Clearly he was trying to express feelings from quite deep within himself. One day I told Richard I knew of something that would give his music the spiritual light and a direction he was looking for. When I told him of the New Church and about the Second Coming of the Lord, like a man hungering and athirst, he partook of the study of the "new revelation," and his life, too, was changed. His life and his profession began a new song.

Suffice it to say that during his lifetime, beginning with his world debut with the Philadelphia Orchestra and Eugene Ormandy, his music has become played and known worldwide. Ormandy and the Philadelphia Orchestra gave about a hundred performances, including ten world premieres, all of which were recorded. So far, seven different record companies in the United States and England have released Yardumian works, and all editions have been sold out. Orchestral works, piano solos, organ and choral music, and much more have been published.

He had more commissions for solo pieces, ensemble works, concertos, and so on than he could fulfill, as well as music he wanted to write.

But having music published, performed, recorded, and played by radio stations does not make music great or make the composer a great writer. To be great—truly great for all time, not momentarily lauded as exemplifying a current musical fad—there must be a song so moving, so full of grace to the listeners' inner ears that they, too, feel the composer's message and love his musical language and are moved, changed in some way.

Richard's lifework was dedicated to the Lord as given in the works of Emanuel Swedenborg. I could easily list his works and show the intimate inspiration for each piece and its details, but that is not the subject. That his music touched so many is what is important.

His musical language is of some importance because it was the means, the form, through which Richard's religious beliefs were set down. While it is absolutely unique, it is totally pleasing to listeners and, at the same time, communicates the delights of spirituality. Richard will someday (as the study of his system enters the music schools and conservatories) become identified as the discoverer and codifier of the interrelation of all the ancient and medieval modes, and the composer who breathed life into them when he developed his polymodal system and his quadradic harmony.

Of the innumerable critiques worldwide, nearly all of them were favorable; many were genuinely appreciative and a few were perceptive. One critic who had the opportunity to review multiple performances and most of the recordings, consistently compared Yardumian to Bach—in quality of means and nobility of message. Many reviewers shared this response to Richard's music.

A New York critic said of the Second Symphony (*Psalms*) that it is essentially an act of worship in which the composer invites the audience to join him.

When the Jesuits of Fordham University wanted to commission a new mass in English, they telephoned Richard, explaining that the quality of spirituality they heard in his music was what they wanted to have enter into their church.

The Primate of the Armenian Apostolic Church in America often called on Richard to speak to such gatherings as choir conferences, for instance, because, while others could speak eloquently of technique, it was Richard Yardumian whose music and life inspired a spirit of genuine worship of the Lord through music.

When Iceland's leading musician, Arni Kristjansson, a fine pianist, was in America as a judge for the first Van Cliburn competition, he was asked if there was anything special he would like to do or see. His only request was to meet the great American composer Richard Yardumian. He had heard performances of Richard's work in Iceland by the symphony orchestra in Reykjavik and he knew the recordings. He loved the music, he said, and then added that he and his wife, Ani, were the only New Church people in Iceland.

Richard often wrote messages to himself around the edges of his scores. Some are directly quoted from [Swedenborg's] *Arcana Coelestia* and *True Christian Religion*, for instance, and these are very revealing; but there are so many, I'll only take time to read one: "Only that music has a future that has been inspired by a noble love to grow into the wisdom of the spiritual."[1]

Yardumian's melodies soar, coming out of the modes—those early seven-note scales whose names and characteristics are familiar to students of early and folk music. Students today learn them by noting where the beginning tones fall on the white keys of a piano: D for Dorian, E for Phrygian, and so on.

The modes were the scales of the chants of the Catholic church, codified by St. Ambrose (Milan) and Pope Gregory (Rome—and hence "Gregorian chant"). They were named by the ancient Greeks, who also attributed moods and mystical powers to them. Before that they were the melodies of the chants of the Hebrews and other Middle Eastern worshipers. I like to think they evolved as a natural outgrowth of speech, from the basic need of the human soul to address the focus of its worship in the loveliest and most continuous sounds its physical body could muster—a gift of one's breath and being to the original giver of life and breath.

The modes have strong pivotal intervals, the distances between notes. These are the fourth and fifth (e.g., between C and F, and between C and G on a piano), which became the earliest forms of harmony permitted in the Western church. Music with the fourth, particularly, is also characteristic of oriental music. Scientifically, these intervals are among the first few steps of the harmonic (overtone) series discovered by Pythagoras, out of which have also grown our modern scales and our knowledge of music theory.

Yardumian's work, then, carries the full burden of Western music history as well as the expansion of the modal system he devised, in polymodality (simultaneous use of more than one mode) and quadradic harmony. The former was common in masses and sacred works from the 1300s through the early 1600s. More recent examples, though in modern keys and not modes, are in some of Charles Ives's polytonal music.

For quadradic harmony, in which the basic chord has four tones (quadrad—do me so te) instead of the usual three (triad—do mi so), Yardumian developed what he referred to as his own grammar and syntax. His polyphonic style was derived from the old style of the early Renaissance, where each voice or instrumental line was an independent melody, with the rhythm and harmony just emerging as the voices sounded together. As the musical Renaissance moved to its end and into the early baroque styles, the modes gradually gave way to two strong modes that became the modern major and minor scales. The free polyphony, with its subtle internal impetus or rhythm, moved into the more squarely measured rhythmic patterns of meter and into the more schooled forms such as canons and fugues.

Yardumian, while working within the framework of modern meter (4/4, 3/4, etc.) and with the instruments of a modern orchestra and its full-bodied sonority, reached back to the early modes and their horizontality and developed his quadradic system. In an essay on his musical idiom and style, he writes:

> The fundament or the governing procedure within my compositions are what I term "quadrads" with their syntax. This term should imply a parallel to the "triad" and as well suggest that the "quadrad" is an evolution out of centuries of composition arising from the common triad and all that it generates.
>
> Historically, there were two main approaches to the quadrad and its use in my works. The first, characteristic of compositions written before 1954, I will call a chromatic, twelve-note organization, mainly homophonic [vertical, or chordal]; while the other approach within most of the writings after 1954 is a modal seven-note organization of the quadrad involving a mutation of the quadradic.
>
> In the understanding of either approach, a particular configuration should be kept in sight: that is the keyboard, which has a natural form that lends itself specifically to the forming or creating of quadrads in both its chromatic and modal contexts.
>
> Out of this natural form of the keyboard originates the train of thought. This is an alternating succession of black and white (or white and black) keys—except at E-F and B-C, where two white notes are in succession. This is applied to

FIG. 142. *Richard Yardumian (1917-1985)*

> thirds, the backbone of tonal music, in the following way: starting at C, a series of thirds in black and white (or white and black), alternating in succession are C E♭ G B♭ D F# A C# E (or E#) G# B (or B#).
>
> In still keeping to this black-and-white configuration are formed four-note chords called "quadrads" (in order to distinguish them from sevenths, which by tradition relate to a triadic context and function): on the first degree, or C, is C E♭ G B♭; on the second degree, or C#, is C# E (or E#) G# (or B#); and so are formed quadrads with this configuration on each of the twelve degrees.
>
> Keeping to this same configuration are ninths, elevenths, thirteenths, and so on.
>
> Most all of the major and smaller works written before 1954 have absolute derivation from this chromatic-quadradic principle, including my *Violin Concerto*.
>
> After 1954 a mutation took place changing the chromatic or twelve-note organization of the quadrad to a modal or seven-note organization. A series of thirds (still in the keyboard black-and-white configuration or train of thought), the Dorian mode on F (or F#) is thus realized: F A♭ C E♭ G B♭ D (having a three-flat signature); F# A C# E G# B D# having a four-sharp signature. This transposition of the Dorian mode to F and F# makes all the other modes available in the quadradic context by simply moving the final accordingly.
>
> Governing both approaches from the very beginning has been the philosophy or rationale, old as it is, of music as a living language, whose evolution brings freedom for the thought and feeling rather than inhibiting it.
>
> From this philosophy there was also perceptible, as from an innate sense of direction, that the quadratic context or syntax indeed does have roots and is a further evolution as from the golden thread; that it is a continuity from an interaction with conscious mental processes of old masters (of music) from every major period, that both the centripetal and the centrifugal forces with the quadradic syntax give to it a sound of inevitability in common with those same forces of

its ancestor, the common triad.

Frequently used are polymodal passages, again generated by the inherent potentials of the quadradic syntax. For example, two-thirds of the way through the "Kyrie" of my *Mass: Come, Creator Spirit*, four melodies, each in a different mode, are in polymodal counterpoint:

1. An original melody
2. "Holy, Holy"—from the Armenian Liturgy
3. "Christmas Eve"—English traditional carol
4. "Veni, Creator Spiritus"—*Liber Usualis*

Their harmony and their entrance points are characteristically quadradic.

But also of greatest importance, and from very early on, was an inspiration to formalize a kind of polyphony invoked by a passage from Emanuel Swedenborg's *True Christian Religion*: "I looked up and lo! the whole heaven above me was resplendent with light, and from the east to the west I heard a long continued glorification by the angels of the eastern and western heavens [and] from the northern and southern heavens there was heard a gentle murmur" (TCR 625).

Striving to clothe such a beautiful image in valid musical form was and is a strong motivation for mastering the polyphonic art.[2]

Richard Yardumian's musical output is considerable and in a variety of forms from a simple four-voice chorale to organ and piano works, string quartets, symphonies, a mass, and a major oratorio (*The Story of Abraham*). *Abraham* uses a full orchestra, large choir, soloists, and a special film "painted on light" in transparent, Chagallian colors, by the late French artist André Girard.

In the program notes for *Abraham*, the writer touches on the several levels always present in Yardumian's work:

For those audiences who are especially seeking a musical experience, Yardumian has provided another major sacred score to rank next to his *Mass*. The novelty of the film projection seems to be no more than the illustrative material included in the publication of a fine book—interesting, but hardly vital to its success or failure as a work of art.

As with many of the scriptural narratives, the story of Abraham has an inner meaning, and proves to be an allegory of the spiritual regeneration of Everyman.

As he has visualized his musical forces for the allegory, the composer chose the orchestra to be the aural canvas on which to paint his characters. The choir thereupon represents the voices of angels—who directly express the words of Jehovah. And his general musical style? "Polyphony itself is a community of individuals in harmony." The spiritual and artistic community is an important part of Judaism, of Christianity, and specifically of Swedenborgianism as well.[3]

In spite of world renown; friendships with major musical figures including Jean Sibelius, whose work parallels Yardumian's in feeling; and the constant need to meet deadlines for commissions and publication, Yardumian found time for over thirty years to serve as music director of his church. This job entailed, among many other things, writing the liturgical music and a book of hymns in chorale style, and training the entire congregation to sing in four-part harmony in Hebrew, Latin, and English.

A service at The Lord's New Church is a moving experience, beginning with the quiet meditation of looking through the clear arched window into tree branches and sky. For a first-time visitor used to fairly reticent congregations, the total involvement of everyone in a four-part reading of liturgical chants or hymns is both a shock and a thrill. Yardumian, standing with his wife and various members of his large family, would boom out a strong bass, giving a solid foundation to the chorale.

Dr. Lucy E. Carroll, in a memorial article on Yardumian for *The Choral Journal*, writes:

The casual observer of the chorales will find what appear to be non-related seventh chords, but the music is actually written in a unique quadradic system. As Bach's chorales were a microcosm of his harmony, so Yardumian's chorales are a perfect synthesis or miniature of his compositional technique. He told me that they were very dear to him; he was as concerned with each chorale as with his larger works—perhaps more so, for they are a vocal statement of faith from a deeply religious man. What he told me of the chorales is true of all his music: each part is an independent line, even in seemingly homophonic sections. Voice leading, he said, was the most important aspect in performing his works. Yet there was an underlying consideration as well. "The music," he insisted, "must communicate: a listener's reaction to the music is important. Every note is meaningful within its context, every word of text important. The academic analysis is secondary."[4]

The spirituality in Yardumian's music is unmistakable. Not just in the natural reaction of the listener or in chorales derived from chant, spirituality is obvious in the use of biblical texts from the book of Genesis as an influence in the development of his Symphony no. 1, in the direct use of psalms sung by a contralto soloist in the Symphony no. 2, and in the notes and references he wrote for himself in the margins of his working scores.

He was always ready to discuss his music, to have one read through a new chorale at the piano in his spacious studio, to chuckle at comments that one of his "signature motifs" had shown up again in a new piece, or to refer to his ever-present *Liber Usualis* for a chant on which a chorale was based, in order to show its original source. He was just as ready to settle into a good discussion of the theology and philosophy of Emanuel Swedenborg, ideas that permeated every aspect of his life.

Yardumian's life centered on his family—his wife and thirteen children (all of whom inherited musical and artistic talents from both parents), and on the larger family of good friends and more distant relatives. For all of them he was lavish with his time, energy, support, and love, and from them he drew energy and inspiration for his work.

The implications of Richard Yardumian's music are on many levels. Most obvious is the fact that his music, while clearly of the twentieth century, seems to be of an older, more familiar style, and is comfortable to listen to. It speaks to the listener's inner self and evokes much more than a casual response. On the next inner level the music raises questions about its making. Since music is full of tension and resolution, where does this line or chord resolve? How can a chord resolve to a seventh? Maybe if it isn't treated as a seventh . . . , and so on, as the music asks the listener to think about the substructure of what is heard. For some this will result in the meaningful discovery of Yardumian's quadradic system and use of modes.

On a yet more internal level the listener realizes he or she is being moved at the gut level and wonders why. A look at the text or at program notes will give a clue to the innate spirituality of the music and to the sincere intent of the composer. It will tell us why this modern, "today" music seems to evolve out of our own deepest historic roots, giving us a connection to the timeless and legendary "music of the spheres."

Yardumian has combined his influences and resources into a powerful body of music that can appeal to us intellectually; but it is the music itself that moves us, that makes us say, "Yes, this composer has truly spoken to me in the universal language of music, and I understand and respond to it."

Richard Yardumian's Music[5]

Choral Music:
Anthem: *Create in Me a Clean Heart*
Eleven Easter Chorales
Magnificat
Six Christmas Chorales
Twelve Chorales for General Use
Mass: Come, Creator Spirit
Oratorio: *The Story of Abraham*

Voice:
"To Mary in Heaven" (Robert Burns Poem for Voice and Orchestra)

Piano Solo:
Chromatic Sonata
Danse
Prelude and Chorale
Songs and Dances from *Armenian Suite*
Three Preludes: "Wind," "Sea," "Sky"

Organ Solo:
Chorale Fantasy: "Ee Kerezman"
Chorale Prelude: "Jesu, Meine Freude"
Chorale Prelude: "My God, My God, Why Hast Thou Forsaken Me?"

Instrumental Solo:
Epigram: William M. Kincaid (flute & piano)
Monologue (Violin Solo)

Chamber Ensembles:
Cantus Animae et Cordis (String Orchestra or String Quartet)

Orchestral:
Armenian Suite
Chorale Prelude: "Veni Sancte Spiritus"
Concerto for Violin and Orchestra
Desolate City

Ee Kerezman (*Resurrection*)
Epigram: William M. Kincaid
Passacaglia, Recitative, and Fugue (Concerto for Piano and Orchestra)
Symphonic Suite
Symphony no. 1 (*The Story of Noah*)
Symphony no. 2 (*Psalms*) (for Voice and Orchestra)
Three Pictographs
Three Preludes for Orchestra
"To Mary in Heaven"
Two Chorale Preludes for Orchestra

Discography
(Many of these are currently out of print)
Armenian Suite (Columbia, EMI)
Cantus Animae et Cordis (Columbia, EMI)
Chorale Prelude: "Veni, Sancte Spiritus" (Columbia)
Chromatic Sonata (EMI)
Concerto for Violin and Orchestra (Columbia)
Danse (EMI)
Desolate City (Columbia)
Mass: Come, Creator Spirit (CRI, previously RCA)
Passacaglia, Recitative, and Fugue (Columbia, RCA, EMI)
Prelude and Chorale (EMI)
Psalm 130 (Columbia)
Symphony no. 1 (Columbia, EMI)
Symphony no. 2 (Columbia, Varese-Sarabande)
Three Preludes (EMI, Musical Heritage Society)

Acknowledgments

Thanks to Vera R. and Dara Yardumian, of Hyannis, Massachusetts, for having provided valuable material on and recordings of their father's work.

Notes

1. Ruth S. Yardumian, keynote speech at New Church Music Festival, Bryn Athyn, Pa., June 1986. Extracts printed with permission.
2. Richard Yardumian, "Essay on the Musical Idiom, Style, and Method of Composition of Richard Yardumian," unpublished.
3. Anonymous, notes from the program book of the Philadelphia premiere of *The Story of Abraham*, 1973.
4. Dr. Lucy E. Carroll, "Remembering Composer Richard Yardumian, *The Choral Journal* (March 1986).
5. Published works in the Elkan-Vogel catalog (Bryn Mawr, Pa.: Theodore Presser).

The Human Face of God

Kathleen Raine, D.Litt.

The "Human Face of God" was presented first as a lecture at L'Universite St. Jean de Jerusalem, May 1985, on the occasion of an annual conference established by Henry Corbin. In 1984 it was published by the Swedenborg Foundation in *Blake & Swedenborg: Opposition Is True Friendship*, edited by Harvey Bellin and Darrell Ruhl. The article that follows has been enlarged by several illustrations, and some pictures first published in black and white appear here in color. A key to abbreviations of works from which quotes by Blake are taken can be found at the beginning of the Notes section following this essay.

Dr. Raine wrote of Swedenborg's contribution to Blake's *Songs of Innocence* and *Experience* in *Blake and Tradition* (Bollingen Series, Princeton University Press, 1962). She expanded this theme to include Swedenborg's continued influence on Blake's later works in her 1982 book, *The Human Face of God* (Thames and Hudson, 1982), a study of Blake's 1823–26 *Job* engravings.

> Fortunately a valuable record exists (apart that is from his own writings) of some of Blake's most deeply held convictions, faithfully set down by Crabb Robinson, Wordsworth's friend and diarist. . . . [Blake] told Crabb Robinson that Swedenborg was "a divine teacher"—an important record since it is evidence of Blake's continued admiration for Swedenborg to the end of his life. . . . In fact Blake's "system" which has bewildered so many is in essence the Doctrine of Swedenborg's Church of the New Jerusalem. . . .
>
> No Blake scholar has yet done justice to the extent and importance of Swedenborg's influence on Blake. . . . Scholars have been misled by Blake's strictures on Swedenborg in *The Marriage of Heaven and Hell* in which he says Swedenborg has taught, no "one new truth," but "all the old falsehoods." . . .
>
> It is tempting to conclude from these intemperate words that Swedenborg had little or no influence on Blake's later writings. This is not the case. . . . Swedenborg's "leading doctrines" are in fact the ground of Blake's own unusual form of Christianity which has puzzled so many who have deplored its heresy or admired its originality. He uses Swe-

denborg's terms and adheres to his doctrines throughout the Prophetic Books, and a late work, *The Everlasting Gospel*, is an impassioned summary of the most distinctive and controversial of Swedenborg's leading doctrines.

In the following text of her 1985 Paris lecture "The Human Face of God," Dr. Raine expands on her thesis that "the influence of Swedenborg, if anything, is clearer in the last works [of Blake] than in the first." (See also Harvey Bellin's essay "Opposition Is True Friendship," elsewhere in this anthology.)

I WILL BEGIN BY PRESENTING a poem, perhaps known to many of you. It is entitled "The Divine Image," and comes from *Songs of Innocence*, a collection of poems written for children and published in 1789, when its author, the poet William Blake, was thirty-two years old. No one, of whatever place, time, or religion, could fail to understand and to assent to the simple directness of its message:

> *To Mercy, Pity, Peace and Love*
> *All pray in their distress;*
> *And to these virtues of delight*
> *Return their thankfulness.*
>
> *For Mercy, Pity, Peace, and Love*
> *Is God, our father dear,*
> *And Mercy, Pity, Peace, and Love,*
> *Is Man, his child and care.*
>
> *For Mercy has a human heart,*
> *Pity a human face,*
> *And Love, the Human form divine,*
> *And Peace, the human dress.*

KATHLEEN RAINE, poet and critic, was born in 1908 and educated at Girton College, Cambridge, England. In 1961 she delivered the Andrew Mellon Lectures, which were published in 1962 as *Blake and Tradition*, by Princeton University Press (Bollingen Series XXXV, vol. 2); a shorter version was later published in paperback as *Blake and Antiquity* (1968). Dr. Raine has published a number of books, including a volume of criticism, *Defending Ancient Springs* (1967); her popular book about Blake as an artist, *William Blake* (Thames and Hudson, 1970); and a study of Blake's Book of Job engravings, *The Human Face of God* (1982). She has edited with George Mills Harper *Selected Writings of Thomas Taylor* (1969) and edits the journal *Temenos*, a review of the arts of the imagination. She lives in London.

FIG. 143. The Divine Image, *from* Songs of Innocence and Experience, *1789*

Then every man, of every clime,
That prays in his distress,
Prays to the human form divine,
Love, Mercy, Pity, Peace.

And all must love the human form,
In heathen, turk or jew;
Where Mercy, Love, & Pity dwell
There God is dwelling too.

For all the apparent simplicity of this poem, the depth of its resonance leads us into deep eschatological mystery. At first sight it might appear to be a simple statement of the Christian doctrine of the Incarnation, but there is much in the poem that might be unacceptable to the Apostolic church, Catholic and Protestant alike; for Blake is not writing of the historical Jesus but of "the human form in heathen, turk or jew"—a comprehensive phrase which embraces all the races and religions of mankind without exception.

How did it come about that Blake was able to make, with such luminous simplicity, this affirmation which goes far beyond any conventional declaration of faith in Jesus Christ? He was a mystic, to be sure, but mystics are of their time and place. He was a reader of the Bible, and in the first chapter of Genesis it is written that God said, "Let us make man in our image, after our likeness. . . . So God created man in his own image, in the image of God created he him."[1] But these words have been variously interpreted. According to the Gospel of St. John, the first-created man who was "in the beginning with God" "was made flesh and dwelt amongst us" in the person of Jesus Christ, but not otherwise. There have been certain mystics—Eckhardt, for example—who have understood the mystery of the Incarnation in a more universal sense, but these have generally been frowned upon. At the end of the eighteenth century Blake spoke openly of a realization which had hitherto been the secret knowledge of a few. He was—and knew himself to be—prophetically inspired, and "The Divine Image" is the quintessence of his prophetic message—that God is "in the form of a man" and that the Incarnation is not particular but universal. Such is the power and certainty of Blake's genius that in simple words he cuts through all theological tangles to the mysterious heart of the Christian revelation. When Jesus affirmed "I and the father are one" and "he who has seen me has seen the father," his words were deemed blasphemous and led to his condemnation. Blake's religion, as he constantly declared, is "the religion of Jesus" (by which he does not necessarily mean as taught by the Christian church) and under the guise of "poetic license" the radical, not to say revolutionary content of his affirmation passes unnoticed. Such poems as "The Divine Image" win the assent of the heart before their doctrinal implications become apparent. "Knowledge is not by deduction, but Immediate by Perception or Sense at once. Christ addresses himself to the Man, not to his Reason."[2] In Blake's terms, Jesus, "the true man," is the Imagination present in all. That innate Imagination assents to Blake's words as being as self-evident as the light of day.

Yet they embody the spirit of a new age, a new apprehension of the Christian revelation. But when in *The Marriage of Heaven and Hell* Blake wrote that "a new heaven is begun" he spoke not on his own authority but as a follower of Emanuel Swedenborg, as a member of the Swedenborgian Church of the New Jerusalem. Wonderful as are Blake's poems, his visionary paintings, his aphorisms, it is, in essence, the doctrines of Swedenborg that Blake's works embody and to which they lend poetry and eloquence. So, unawares, the teachings of Swedenborg's Church of the New Jerusalem have permeated the spiritual sensibility of the English nation, through Blake. Few of the ever-growing numbers who regard Blake as a prophet of the New Age are aware that the coherent and revolutionary interpretation of the Christian mysteries which underlies Blake's prophecies is that of Swedenborg.

The writings of Swedenborg, stilted and voluminous, written in Latin at a time when Latin was ceasing to be the common language of the learned, have nonetheless had a profound influence throughout Protestant Europe and beyond; Henry Corbin himself saw the seminal significance of Swedenborg, whom he went so far as to describe as "the Buddha of the west." He was by profession neither philosopher nor theologian but a man of science, assessor of minerals to the Swedish government. He spent much time in London, where he had a small but devoted following, and might even have been seen by Blake as a boy, for Swedenborg died in London in 1772, when Blake was fifteen. Doubtless Swedenborg had predecessors in the millennial tradition, stemming from Joachim of Flora; but we must accept Swedenborg's word that his extraordinary prophetic insight came to him not by study but by what he described as an "opening" of his consciousness which revealed to him the inner worlds which he calls the "heavens" and the "hells"; and which those who follow the terminology introduced by Henry Corbin would call the *mundus imaginalis*; worlds not in space, but in mankind's inner universe. In his visions it was shown to Swedenborg that a "new church" had been established in the heavens, following a "Last Judgment" passed on the Apostolic church, which was to be superseded by the "Church of the New Jerusalem," the last and perfect revelation of the nature of Jesus Christ as the "Divine Humanity"; a mystery which had hitherto been imperfectly understood, but which was, in the New Church [see Glossary], to be fully revealed in the epiphany of the "Divine Human." This New Church, of which Swedenborg's writings are the scriptures, is to be the last in the six thousand years of the world's history from the creation to the end of days and the coming of the kingdom. There have already been, according to Swedenborg, twenty-six such churches,* from the time of Adam, through a succession of prophetic revelations made to the patriarchs, to Noah, Abraham, Moses, Solomon, and within the Christian era the churches of Paul, Constantine, Charlemagne, and Luther; each of these representing some new realization—or revelation—which is to reach its term and perfect fulfillment in a total affirmation of the humanity of God and the divinity of man, their unity and identity. In his setting

out of the leading doctrines of the Church of the New Jerusalem Swedenborg declares: "The Lord is God from eternity" and the Divine Human is not merely the Son of God but God himself. "God and man, in the Lord . . . are not two, but one person, yea, altogether one . . . He is the God of heaven and earth." The Divine Humanity is almighty; or, as Blake simply says, "God is Jesus" (LAOC; K 777). Since in this teaching the oneness of the human and the divine is total, it follows that the Christian revelation can go no farther, man and God being one, not only in the historic person of Jesus Christ but totally for the Christ within the whole human race.

Jung has written in criticism of the Christian church that, if not in principle, at all events in practice, the Divine Being has been envisaged as outside man and the Redemption (in the doctrine of the Atonement) also as an occurrence outside man, occurring once only in history. It is true that the Mass is held to be not a commemoration of that event, but a timeless reenactment; but even so, that mystery, as commonly taught and understood, is an external and historical event. Jesus Christ, moreover, is an exceptional being, virtually a demigod in the pagan sense, not fully human. Jung in his remarkable work *Answer to Job*, admired by Henry Corbin,[3] and expressing the mature thought of a lifetime on the meaning of Christianity, writes that

> Christ, by his descent, conception and birth, is a half-god in the classical sense. He is virginally begotten by the Holy Ghost and, as he is not a creaturely human being, has no inclination to sin. The infection of evil was in his case precluded by the preparations for the Incarnation. He therefore stands more on the divine than on the human level.[4]

The same is true of the Virgin Mary: "As a consequence of her immaculate conception Mary is already different from other mortals, and this fact is confirmed by her assumption."[5] Thus salvation is available to humankind through the external intervention of these superhuman personages. In making this criticism of Christianity, Jung makes no mention of Swedenborg's teachings (he had in fact read Swedenborg early in his life), which did raise and respond to many of his own criticisms, in calling for an interiorization of the Christian mysteries of the Incarnation, Passion, and Resurrection. Swedenborg gives an actual date—1757 (which was, incidentally, the date of Blake's birth)—when a "Last Judgment" had been passed on the Apostolic church "in the heavens"—that is to say, in mankind's inner worlds—to be followed by an epiphany of the Divine Humanity in his full glory in the inner worlds or "heavens." With this inner event a new kind of realization, a new kind of consciousness, began to dawn within Christendom, following the interiorization of the Apostolic teaching. This Last Judgment was not an outer event, in time and in history, but an inner event, which

---

*Swedenborg's standard scheme identifies five stages, or "dispensations," which he defines in terms of churches—the Most Ancient Church (antediluvian), the Ancient Church (pre-Decalogue), the Jewish Church, the Christian Church, and the New Christian Church (New Jerusalem). Blake seems to have derived his model of twenty-seven churches by adding up the substages which Swedenborg identified, but did not total. (See "Churches" in Glossary.)—The editors.

would, not dramatically, but gradually, make itself apparent also in the outer world of history. A new church is thus a new consciousness. Without invoking the idea of "evolution" (as understood by materialist science), we are to understand Swedenborg's concept of the twenty-seven churches as a progressive revelation in time and history. This is entirely in keeping with the linear view of time common to all the Abrahamic religions (Judaism, Christianity, and Islam) and indeed without such a conception time and history become meaningless. Blake indeed saw the twenty-seven churches as cyclic rather than linear, a progressive darkening of the paradisal vision from Adam to Jesus Christ, followed by a progressive recovery to be fulfilled in the "second coming" in the inner worlds. This event completes the cycle which leads humankind back to the paradisal state from which we have fallen.

What is under consideration is not in its nature an event to be pinned down like an event in history to a certain date, but is rather a subtle change of awareness. It seems that such a change in the understanding of the nature of spiritual events did begin to manifest itself at that time, which has continued to grow like a plant from a small seed. Swedenborg's seed fell on fertile ground in the spirit of William Blake; and our presence here at the University of St. John of Jerusalem, dedicated to an understanding of the imaginal universe, the inner universe, is an expression—one amongst others—of this new understanding, in a world where the old foundations seem inadequate. It may well be that in the future our own time will be seen not as the age of the triumph of materialist science but as the breakdown of that phase and the beginning of just such an "opening" of humanity's inner worlds as Swedenborg prophetically experienced and foresaw.

This theme is a central one for Jung, who in his *Answer to Job* sets forth at length a view of the Bible in which, from Job to the Incarnation of Jesus Christ, there is what he calls "a tendency for God to become man." This tendency is already implicit in Genesis, when by a special act of creation Jahweh created man, who was the image of God. Jung is, of course, using the terms not of theology but of psychology and is therefore writing of changes in human consciousness of the Divine Being, and not of changes in God himself in an absolute sense. Jung writes:

> In omniscience, there had existed from all eternity a knowledge of the human nature of God or of the divine nature of man. That is why, long before Genesis was written, we find corresponding testimonies in ancient Egyptian records. Preparations, however, are not in themselves creative events, but only stages in the process of becoming conscious. It was only quite late that we realized (or rather, are beginning to realize) that God is Reality itself and therefore—last but not least—man. This realization is a millennial process.[6]

Jung sees this process foreshadowed in the story of Job—the type of the human encounter with the divine. The God of the Book of Job is so totally other that Job seems to himself to be insignificant, powerless, without recourse— except to God himself; and Jung is in agreement with theologians who have seen in Job's words, "I know that my redeemer liveth, and that he shall stand in the latter day upon the earth . . . yet in my flesh shall I see God,"[7] a foreshadowing of the Incarnation:

> The life of Christ is just what it had to be if it is the life of a god and a man at the same time. It is a *symbolus*, a bringing together of heterogenous natures, rather as if Job and Yahweh were combined in a single personality. Yahweh's intention to become man, which resulted from his collision with Job, is fulfilled in Christ's life and suffering.[8]

On the way to this realization, Jung points out, we have Ezekiel's vision of the "Son of Man," which reappears in the Book of Daniel, and later (about 100 B.C.) in the Book of Enoch. Ezekiel is himself addressed as "Son of Man"— the man on the throne whom he beheld in his vision; and hence a prefiguration of the much later revelation in Christ. Daniel had a vision of the "Ancient of Days," to whom "with the clouds of heaven there came one like the son of man." Here the "son of man" is no longer the prophet himself but a son of the "Ancient of Days" in his own right.

I suggest that the power of Swedenborg's revelation, and of Blake's prophetic writings lies in the reality of what they describe, a growing inner awareness on which we cannot go back. Jung and even Freud were aware of this process of interiorization of the mysteries, but they were not the first to challenge the externalized consciousness of post-Cartesian science; "The Divine is not in Space," Swedenborg affirmed, "although the Divine is omnipresent with every man in this world, and with every angel in heaven" (DLW 7). This, it may be said, has always been so and is implicit in every religious tradition; yet as a fact of the history of two thousand years of Christendom, the realization has been progressive and come but slowly. Seen in another way, Swedenborg's teaching can be seen as a return to a lost traditional norm at the height of the age of Deism or "natural religion" as a philosophic creed, whose effects in every sphere of life are still dominant in our own world. Materialist science has identified "reality" as the natural order, conceived to be an autonomous mechanism external to mind; and in his denial of this view of the "real," Swedenborg, it might be said—and Blake no less—restored a lost norm which understands that mind is not in space but space in mind.

The divine (Swedenborg declared) is everywhere, yet not in space; and insists that these things cannot be comprehended by a natural idea because there is space in that idea; for it is formed out of such things as are in the world; and in each and all these things, which strike the eye, there is space. Everything great and small is of space; everything, broad and high there is of space; in short every measure, figure and form there is of space. (DLW 7)

Swedenborg strove to remove the identification of reality with an external material order. Space is a function of the natural body, but the human spirit is capable of the omnipresence of the nonspatial.

Furthermore, it is not God who is omnipresent spirit while man exists in space; because "God is Very Man" (DLW 289) the human universe is likewise boundless spirit, as God is. He writes:

> In all the heavens there is no other idea of God than the idea of a man; the reason is, that heaven as a whole, and in every part is in form as a man and the Divine, which is with the angels, constitutes heaven; and thought proceeds according to the form of heaven; wherefore it is impossible for the angels to think of God otherwise. Hence it is that all those in the world who are conjoined with heaven (that is with the inner worlds) when they think interiorly in themselves, that is, in their spirit, think of God in a like manner. For this cause that God is a Man. . . . The form of heaven affects this, which in its greatest and in its least things is like itself. (DLW 11)

Heaven in its whole and in every part is "in form as a man"; and because man was created "after the image and likeness of God," "the ancients, from the wise to the simple"—from Abraham to the primitive Africans—thought of God as a man. This is not anthropomorphism in the sense in which the word is currently understood, as a projection of the human image upon the divine mystery, but rather the reverse, a recognition of the divine image imprinted on the inner nature of humankind, as "the Divine Human," to use Swedenborg's term. "All is Human, Mighty, Divine," Blake writes; and summarizes the Swedenborgian teaching in a quatrain:

> *God Appears & God is Light*
> *To those poor Souls who dwell in Night,*
> *But does a Human Form Display*
> *To those who dwell in Realms of day.*
> (AI; K 434)

These lines are the reversal of the "enlightened" view that we cease to see God in human form as we learn more about "the universe" as natural fact. The ultimate knowledge, according to Blake and Swedenborg, is that the universe is contained in mind—a view to be found also in the Gnostic writings, in the Vedas, and in other spiritually profound cosmologies of the East, but long forgotten in the West with its preoccupation with externality.

Thus we are given a conception of man totally other than that of a materialist science: Man in his spiritual being is boundless and contains not a part of his universe but its wholeness and infinitude. The "body" of the Divine Human is not contained in natural space but contains all things in itself. Swedenborg writes, "His human body cannot be thought of as great or small, or of any stature, because this also attributes space; and hence He is the same in the first things as the last and in the greatest things and the least; and moreover the Human is the innermost of every created thing, but apart from space" (DLW 285).

Swedenborg uses a strange but cogent argument for the humanity of the Divine: that the attributes of God would be inconceivable except in human terms; and since God is knowable only in human terms, He must therefore possess human attributes:

> That God could not have created the universe and all things thereof, unless He were a Man, may be very clearly comprehended by an intelligent person from this ground that . . . in God there is love and wisdom, there is mercy and clemency, and also there is absolute Goodness and Truth, because these things are from Him. And because he cannot deny these things, neither can he deny that God is a Man: for not one of these things is possible abstracted from man: man is their subject, and to separate them from their subject is to say that they are not. Think of wisdom and place it outside man. Is there anything? . . . It must be wisdom in a form such as man has, it must be in all his form, not one thing can be wanting for wisdom to be in it. In a word, the form of wisdom is a man; and because man is the form of wisdom, he is also the form of love, mercy, clemency, good, and truth, because these make one with wisdom. (DLW 286)

It is for these reasons, Swedenborg argues, that man is said to be created in the image of God, that is, into the form of love and wisdom. It cannot be that man invented God in his own image, since that image is already imprinted in us in our very being. The argument is a subtle one; and although it could be asked, could not God have created beings and universes other than man, the same argument would in every case apply: whatever their attributes these too would bear the image and imprint of their creator and source. Blake, who had read and annotated Swedenborg's *Divine Love and Wisdom* with evident delight might, when he wrote his poem "To Mercy, Pity, Peace and Love," have been thinking of this very passage.

Swedenborg dismisses the idea of those who think of God as other than as a man, and "of the divine attributes otherwise then as God as a man; because separated from man they are figments of the mind. God is very Man, from whom every Man is a man according to his reception of love and wisdom" (DLW 289).

So it is that:

FIG. 144. Glad Day, *or* The Dance of Albion, *1800–1803*

> . . . *Mercy has the human heart,*
> *Pity a human face,*
> *And Love, the human form divine,*
> *And Peace, the human dress.*

"The human form divine" is not the natural body idolatrously glorified, but the spiritual form of our human nature.

In understanding that when he wrote these words, so luminously simple, Blake is propounding Swedenborgian doctrine, it becomes perfectly clear that no humanism is implicit in his assigning the human attributes to God, the source and author of our humanity. Swedenborg wrote that "*in all forms and uses there is a certain image of man,*" and that "all uses from primes to ultimates, from ultimates to primes, have relation to all things of man and correspondences with him, and therefore man in a certain image is a universe; and conversely the universe viewed as to its uses is man in an image" (DLW 317). Swedenborg draws the conclusion that it is for this reason that man is called a microcosm, since the universe is totally present in all its parts. Or again, in Blake's words, "One thought fills immensity." What Swedenborg is saying

in his stilted style, and Blake is repeating in what to his contemporaries seemed "wild" poetic ravings, is in fact of extreme subtlety and great profundity—that human consciousness contains its universe. This is a return to the ancient teaching, as found, for example, in the *Hermetica*, that mind is not in space, but all spaces and whatever these contain, in mind, "Nothing is more capacious than the incorporeal." To have reaffirmed this realization in the eighteenth century attests to an insight so extraordinary that it can only be described—and Swedenborg did so describe it—as a prophetic revelation.

But if for Swedenborg the true man is not the natural body, he nevertheless insists in great detail on the minutiae of the spiritual anatomy:

> Because God is a Man, He has a body, and everything belonging to the body; consequently He has a face, a breast, an abdomen, loins, feet; for apart from these he would not be a Man. And having these, he has also eyes, ears, nostrils, mouth, tongue; and further the organs that are within a man, as the heart and lungs, and the parts which depend on these . . . but in God Man they are Infinite. (DLW 21)

He insists "that the angelic spirits are in every respect human . . . they have faces, eyes, ears, hearts, arms, heads and feet; they see, hear and converse with one another and, in a word, that no external attribute of man is wanting, except the material body" (HH 75). In describing realities of the imaginal world Swedenborg insists on the clarity and distinctness of the spirits: "I have seen them in their own light, which exceeds by many degrees the light of the world, and in that light I have observed all parts of their faces more distinctly and clearly then ever I did the faces of men on earth" (HH 75).

It is hard to know whether Blake possessed this faculty or if he is paraphrasing Swedenborg, so closely do their accounts tally:

> A Spirit and a Vision are not, as the modern philosophy supposes, a cloudy vapour, or a nothing: they are organized and minutely articulated beyond all that the mortal and perishing nature can produce. He who does not imagine in stronger and better lineaments, and in stronger and better light than his perishing, and mortal eye can see, does not imagine at all. The painter of this work asserts that all his imaginations appear to him infinitely more perfect and more minutely organized than any thing seen by his mortal eye. Spirits are organized men. (DC; K 576–77)

This is pure Swedenborg; but it may be that we also have to conclude that those gifted with the clear vision of the imaginal world are in essential agreement because describing the same reality.

To return to Swedenborg, he affirms continually that the universal heaven is in the form of a man, and "each society in heaven, be it large or small, is so likewise; hence also an angel is a man, for an angel is heaven in its least form" (HH 52, 53). Thus every part down to the smallest "heaven in its least form" is infinite, and the Divine Human an infinite whole made up of infinite wholes, and "the universal heaven consists of myriads of myriads of angels" (DP 63). (Here it must be said that Swedenborg's angels are also men, but discarnate. The word *angel*, as he uses it, is not to be understood in the sense of the Near Eastern religions, or indeed of the Christian fathers and Dionysius the Areopagite's celestial hierarchies.)

The human form is present throughout the universe alike in its greatest and in its least parts. Swedenborg writes that "in God Man infinite things are distinctly one. It is well known that God is Infinite, for he is called the Infinite. He is not infinite by this alone, that He is very Esse and Existere in Himself, but because there are Infinite things in Him" (DLW 17). The "vision of light" Blake described in a letter to a friend is purely Swedenborgian; every infinitesimal part of nature is human—and this is his answer to Newton's theory that light is made of "particles":

> *In particles bright*
> *The jewels of Light*
> *Distinct shown & clear.*
> *Amaz'd & in fear*
> *I each particle gazed,*
> *Astonish'd, Amazed;*
> *For each was a Man*
> *Human-form'd. Swift I ran,*
> *for they beckon'd to me*
> *Remote by the Sea,*
> *Saying: Each grain of Sand,*
> *Every Stone on the Land,*
> *Each rock & each hill,*
> *Each fountain & rill,*
> *Each herb & each tree,*
> *Mountain, hill, earth & sea,*
> *Cloud, Meteor & Star,*
> *Are Men Seen Afar.*[9]

Swedenborg's Grand Man [see Glossary] of the Heavens is a concept of great splendor. In this Divine Man or Human Divine all lives are contained, individually and as angelic societies within the one life of the Divine Humanity; and so down to every inhabitant of heaven who is "every one in his own heaven" and the whole is reflected in each. "The Lord leads all in the universal heaven as if they were one angel" and in the same way "an angelic society sometimes appears as one man in the form of an angel" (HH 51). So "when the Lord himself appears in the midst of the angels, he does not appear encompassed by a multitude but as one in an angelic form" (HH 52). "I have seen," he writes of a visionary society, that "when at a distance it appears as one, and on its approach, as a multitude" (HH 62). And again it is hard to know whether Blake is describing his own vision or paraphrasing Swedenborg when he writes: "The various States I have seen in my imagination; when distant they appear as One Man but as you approach they appear multitudes of nations" (VLJ; K 609). Blake summarizes the essence of the Swedenborgian vision of the Grand Man in a passage several times repeated in the Prophetic Books:

> *Then those in Great Eternity met in the Council of God*
> *As one man. . . .*
>
> *As One Man all the Universal Family; & that One Man*
> *They call Jesus the Christ, & they in him & he in them*
> *Live in Perfect harmony, in Eden the land of life.*
> (FZ; K 277)

Eden the land of life is the *Mundus imaginalis*, the "bosom of God," our native place and state. [See also in this anthology, "The Subtle Realm: Corbin, Sufism, and Swedenborg" by Roberts Avens.]

In affirming the humanity of God, Swedenborg is nevertheless remote from what is now called "humanism"; for man is (in Blake's words) only "a form and organ of life" and the life of every individual, or every community, of the whole creation, is "from the Lord." No man's life belongs to himself, each is a recipient of the one life. Thus, whereas Blake wrote that "God is Man & exists in us & we in him,"[10] this is no more nor less than the teaching of St. John's Gospel and the words of Jesus, "as thou, Father, art in me, and I in thee, that they also may be one in us."[11] Created beings and men exist by virtue of what Swedenborg calls the "influx" of the one divine life. This influx is through the inner worlds; the outer world of natural appearances is the mirror of spiritual realities, but has itself no substance. (This is, of course, the teaching of Plotinus on nature, and of other Platonic writers.) But the outer form—whether of human being or animal, plant, or mineral—is the "correspondence" of their living nature. Nothing in nature is, as for materialist science, a self-existent physical entity subject to natural causes; indeed, for Swedenborg there is no such thing as a natural cause, all causes being spiritual and "nature" the lowest effect. Again Blake is giving expression to this doctrine when he writes that "every Natural Effect has a Spiritual Cause, and Not a Natural; for a Natural Cause only seems: it is a Delusion of Ulro & a ratio of the perishing Vegetable Memory" (M 27; K 513). The realities mirrored in nature belong to the imaginal world—in Blake's terms, the Imagination.

> This world of Imagination is the world of Eternity; it is the divine bosom into which we shall all go after the death of the Vegetated body. This World of Imagination is Infinite

and Eternal, whereas the world of Generation, or Vegetation, is Finite & Temporal. There Exist in that Eternal World the Permanent Realities of Every Thing which we see reflected in this Vegetable Glass of Nature. All Things are comprehended in their Eternal Forms in the divine body of the Saviour, the True Vine of Eternity, the Human Imagination (VLJ; K 605–6)

Blake insists that the imaginal world is a plenitude of forms, and in the same work writes:

Many suppose that before the Creation All was Solitude & Chaos. This is the most pernicious Idea that can enter the Mind, as it . . . Limits All Existence to Creation & to Chaos, to the Time & Space fixed by the Corporeal Vegetative Eye . . . Eternity Exists & all things in Eternity, Independent of Creation. (VLJ; K 614)

While Blake's account of the imaginal world bears a more Platonic stamp than does Swedenborg's, with his emphasis on the inner forms of the Imagination as the originals of which the natural forms are images or copies, yet it is evident that Swedenborg's accounts of heavenly scenery are describing the same imaginal reality. The destination of the discarnate soul is not an empty *nirvana* but comparable to the Far Eastern paradises which await the discarnate soul after death, and the similar paradises and hells of the Near and Middle Eastern religions. In *Divine Love and Wisdom* Swedenborg writes:

The spiritual world in external appearance is quite similar to the natural world. Lands appear there, mountains, hills, valleys, planes, fields, lakes, rivers, springs of water, as in the natural world. . . . Paradises also appear there, gardens, groves, woods, and in them trees and shrubs of all kinds bearing fruit and seeds; also plants, flowers, herbs and grasses. . . . Animals appear there, birds and fish of every kind. (DLW 321)

Thus in his systematic manner Swedenborg spells out the presence in the "heavens" of the mineral, vegetable, and animal kingdoms. In Swedenborg's "heavens" and Blake's Imagination, which both call the Divine Human, [in Latin *Homo Maximus*] the whole universe is contained in its infinite variety as the diversification of the single being of the Divine Humanity. In an early work, *Vala*, or *The Four Zoas*, Blake describes the whole natural creation striving—"groaning and travailing," in the words of St. Paul[12] to bring forth the human:

. . . *Man looks out in tree & herb & fish & bird & beast*
Collecting up the scatter'd portions of his immortal body
Into the Elemental forms of every thing that grows.
. . . .
In pain he sighs, in pain he labours in his universe
Screaming in birds over the deep, & howling in the wolf
Over the slain, & moaning in the cattle & in the winds

. . . .
And in the cries of birth & in the groans of death his voice
Is heard throughout the Universe: wherever a grass grows
Or a leaf buds, The Eternal Man is seen, is heard, is felt
And all his sorrows, till he reassumes his ancient bliss.

(FZ; K 355)

Humanity, the immortal body "distributed," as the Platonist would say, in the "many," must be reassumed into the "one," the bosom of God, the human Imagination. In that universe microcosm and macrocosm are one.

I mentioned earlier C. G. Jung's highly significant criticisms of the Christian church for its conversion of the figures of Jesus Christ, and in the Catholic church the Virgin Mary likewise, into what have been to all intents and purposes pagan demigods. Jung's criticisms of Christianity have indeed been cogent, and he has played a significant part in calling for an interiorization of the Christian mysteries. In the introduction to his work on *Psychology and Alchemy* he writes:

We can accuse Christianity of arrested development if we are determined to excuse our own shortcomings. In speaking therefore not of the deepest and best understanding of Christianity but of the superficialities and disastrous misunderstandings that are plain to see. The demand made by the *imitatio Christi*—that we should follow the ideal and seek to become like it—ought logically to have the result of developing and exalting the inner man. In actual fact, however, the ideal has been turned into an external object of worship, and it is precisely this veneration for the object that prevents it from reaching down into the depths of the soul and transforming it into a wholeness in keeping with the ideal. Accordingly the divine mediator stands outside as an image, while man remains fragmentary and untouched in the deepest part of him.[13]

—and later in the same work:

It may easily happen, therefore, that a Christian who believes in all the sacred figures is still undeveloped and unchanged in his innermost soul because be has "all God outside" and does not experience him in the soul. . . . Yes, everything is to be found outside—in image and in word, in Church and Bible—but never inside. . . . Too few people have experienced the divine image as the innermost possession of their own souls. Christ only meets them from without, never from within the soul.[14]

This summons to our time to discover the God within may be seen as perhaps Jung's greatest contribution—and a very great one it is. But Jung seems not to have been aware of Swedenborg as a predecessor and prophet of just such a transformation of consciousness as he himself wished to see. Swedenborg, on his part, would have seen Jung as one fulfillment of his prophecy, his vision of a Last Judgment in the heavens passed on the Apostolic church, to be followed by the appearance of the Lord in the inner heavens. Jung writes of the "God-image," the divine signature or archetype, imprinted in every soul. Accused by theologians of "psychologism" for making his appeal to this God-image (whose presence is testified nevertheless in the first chapter of Genesis) and thereby of "deifying the soul," Jung replied, "When I say as a psychologist that God is an archetype, I mean by that the 'type' in the psyche. The word 'type' is, as we know, derived from τυπος 'blow' or 'imprint'; thus an archetype presupposes an imprinter."[15] The argument is very close to that of Swedenborg, that human qualities must mirror divine qualities. In this respect Henry Corbin, in the review already cited, defends Jung, he himself being deeply concerned with defining and discovering the "imaginal" world.

> True, C.G. Jung chooses not to speak otherwise than as a psychologist, and deals only with psychology; he does not claim to be a theologian or even a philosopher of religion. But having said "Only a psychologist, only psychology" one has the sudden sense of having committed a grave injustice, of associating oneself by that way of speaking with all those who, mistrusting for one reason or another the implications of Jung's works, close the matter after each one with the comment "it is *nothing but* psychology." But one may well ask oneself what they have done with their *soul*, with their *Psyche* to dismiss it in this way and to dare to speak of it in terms of being "nothing but that." So why when one has shown that there are psychological factors which correspond to divine figures, do some people find it necessary to cry blasphemy as if all were lost and those figures devaluated?[16]

Swedenborg too had insisted that the imprint of the infinite and eternal is within every form; and moreover, that the infinite and eternal is present in the infinite variety of things, "in that no substance, state or thing in the created universe can ever be the same or identical with any other." So that in none of the things that fill the universe can any sameness be produced to all eternity. This (he continues) is perspicuously evident in the variety of faces of all human beings; "not one face exists in the whole world which is the same as another, neither can exist in all eternity; nor therefore one mind for the face is the type of the mind" (DLW 315). Here Swedenborg is using the word *type*—imprint—in exactly Jung's sense. Yet by influx all these are forms of the divine image, in Blake's words:

> . . . *the Divine—*
> *Humanity who is the Only General and Universal Form*
> *To which all Lineaments tend & seek with love & sympathy.*
> (J; K 672)

There is not one image or face of God but an infinity of images, an infinity of faces. The implications are overwhelming, for it follows that every human face in the world is,

insofar as it is open to the divine influx, one of the myriad faces of God. Was it not this mystery that Jesus himself sought to impart in the parable which tells how the "Son of Man" says to the Just, "I was an hungered and ye gave me meat, I was thirsty and ye gave me drink; I was a stranger and ye took me in, naked and ye clothed me: I was in prison and ye came unto me."[17] The Just ask,

> Lord, when saw we thee an hungered, and fed thee? Or thirsty and we gave thee drink? When saw we thee a stranger and took thee in? Or naked, and clothed thee? . . . and the King shall answer and say unto them . . . inasmuch as ye have done it unto one of the least of these my brethren, ye have done it unto me.[18]

and so with the Unjust, who have rejected in all these the "Son of Man." Whereas the conventional reading may be that to serve the hungry and thirsty, strangers and prisoners, is equivalent to serving the Lord in person, the plain reading of the text is that it actually *is* the Divine Humanity who is present in all these.

Swedenborg claimed for his Church of the New Jerusalem that it is to be the ultimate Christian revelation and understanding of the Son of God in his Divine Humanity; and indeed it is not possible to conceive a closer union of God and Man than in this universal influx of divinity in all creation and in all humankind.

To turn once again to Jung's remarkable diagnosis of our present situation, *Answer to Job*: He describes the gradual emergence, in the Bible, of the idea of God as man, becoming ever clearer from Job to Ezekiel to Daniel, to the Book of Enoch, and finally to the Incarnation of Jesus Christ. But Jung, like Swedenborg, does not see the gradual realization as ending there. As Swedenborg in the symbol of his twenty-seven churches sees, from the time of Jesus, not one but several successive churches emerging and falling into decay, so does Jung see the Christian Revelation as incomplete. As a psychologist he had witnessed, over a long lifetime, the pressure within the human soul itself toward some further understanding. Whereas Swedenborg saw the awaited completion as a perfected understanding of the nature of Jesus Christ as omnipresent in all, Jung saw it as an awaited incarnation within poor imperfect earthly humankind; which indeed was what Swedenborg himself understood by his New Church but saw it as already accomplished. Jung points out that Jesus himself in sending to his disciples "the spirit of truth," the Holy Ghost, envisages a continuing realization of God in his children, which amounts to a continuance of the Incarnation. He reminds his disciples that he had told them that they were "gods." The believers or the chosen ones are children of God, all "fellow-heirs with Christ." Of this teaching the fourth Gospel is full:

"The indwelling of the Holy Ghost" means nothing less than an approximation of the believer to the status of God's son. One can therefore understand what is meant by the remark "you are gods." The deifying effect of the Holy Ghost is naturally assisted by the *imago Dei* stamped on the elect. God, in the shape of the Holy Ghost, puts up his tent in man, for he is obviously minded to realize himself continually not only in Adam's descendants, but in an indefinitely large number of believers, and possibly in mankind as a whole.[19]

Only in suffering the limitations of the "empirical human being," Jung insists, can God truly suffer the human condition, for in a Christ exempt from sin he could not do so. Jung points out that throughout the history of the church, both Catholic and Protestant, whereas the worship of the Son has been practiced and encouraged, the presence of the Holy Spirit within the soul has been played down, to say the least. Jung cites the instance of the banning of the writings of Eckhart on account of certain passages in which this teaching is made too clear for the liking of the apostolic hierarchy. Again Corbin supports Jung, commenting:

the action of the Paraclete, metaphysically so important, is wholly undesirable for the good organisation of the Church, for it eludes all control. In consequence there was to be energetic affirmation of the uniqueness of the event of the Incarnation, and the progressive indwelling of the Holy Spirit in man either discouraged or ignored. Whoever felt himself to be inspired by the Holy Spirit to "deviations" was a heretic, his extirpation and extermination both necessary and in accordance with Satan's liking.[20]

This is the Protestant point of view, shared by Jung, son of a Lutheran pastor, by Henry Corbin, by Swedenborg, and by William Blake. It is at the heart of the great and unresolved division within Christendom.

The millennial prophesies of Joachim of Flora have echoed throughout subsequent history his foretelling of a third phase of Christendom which he called the Age of the Holy Spirit, which was to follow the ages of the Father and of the Son. Within this tradition Swedenborg and Blake are situated, and indeed so is Jung himself. Jung writes on the sending of the Paraclete:

Since he is the Third Person of the Deity, this is as much as to say that *God will be begotten in creaturely man.* This implies a tremendous change in man's status, for he is now raised to sonship, and almost to the position of a man-god. With this the prefiguration in Ezekiel and Enoch, where, as we saw, the title "Son of Man" was already conferred on the creaturely man, is fulfilled. But that puts man, despite his continuing sinfulness, in the position of the mediator, the unifier of God and creature. Christ probably had this incalculable possibility in mind when he said, ". . . he who believes in me, will also do the works I do," and referring to the sixth verse of the Eighty-second Psalm, "I say, 'You are gods, sons of the Most High, all of you,' " he added, "and scripture cannot be broken."[21]

I have quoted Jung at length because his understanding of Christianity as a progressive revelation stands within the mystical mainstream represented by Joachim of Flora, Eckhart, Swedenborg, and Blake; even though Jung seems to have known little of the latter two, who certainly had no direct influence on Jung's own conclusions.

In some respects Swedenborg's Christianity lies within the mainstream of orthodoxy; he believed, for example, that Jesus Christ alone among humankind was resurrected in the natural body. Blake indeed reproached Swedenborg because he had not in fact taught anything new. In *The Marriage of Heaven and Hell* Blake writes: "Now hear a plain fact: Swedenborg has not written one new truth. Now hear another: he has written all the old falsehoods" (MHH; K 157). What Blake chiefly held against Swedenborg was that he laid excessive stress on moral virtue, placing the virtuous in the heavens and the evildoers in the hells. Blake himself saw Divine Humanity as embracing the wholeness of life, both heaven and hell, reason and energy, the darkness and the light in a holiness and a wholeness beyond what humankind calls good and evil in terms of the moral laws of this world. Like Jung, Blake understood that there can be no completeness if any part of the totality of the Divine Human is excluded. It is probable that Blake did not, either, share Swedenborg's view of the unique and exceptional nature of the historical Jesus Christ. He does profess "the religion of Jesus," but by this he may not have meant Apostolic Christianity but the religion that Jesus himself practiced. Blake's view is that "Jesus, the Imagination," the Divine Human, is born, lives, and dies in every life, and the Resurrection is not of, but from, the carnal body. God is born in every birth, not one only; when Jehovah

> . . . *stood in the Gates of the Victim, & he appeared*
> *A weeping Infant in the Gates of Birth in the midst of Heaven.*

—he is born not in one but in all:

> . . . *a little weeping Infant pale reflected*
> *Multitudinous in the Looking Glass of Enitharmon* . . .
> (J 63; K 697)

—that is, in the "mirror" of the natural world. The one Babe of the eternal Incarnation is reflected not in one, but in multitudes of births, in every birth. For Blake's Divine Humanity says,

> . . . *in Me all Eternity*
> *Must pass thro' condemnation and awake beyond the grave.*
> (K 662)

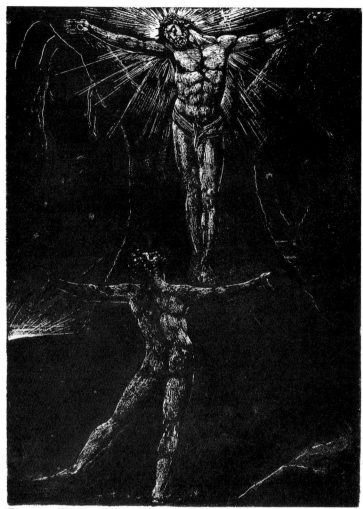

FIG. 145. The Crucifixion, *from* Jerusalem, *1804-20*

Man is not once but continually redeemed in "the Body of Jesus"—that is, in the Divine Humanity in whom all participate; and the "Divine Similitude"—the face of God—is seen

> *In loves and tears of brothers, sisters, sons, fathers and friends*
> *Which if Man ceases to behold, he ceases to exist.*
>
> (K 664)

The "Divine Family" is "as one Man"

> *. . . and they were One in Him. A Human Vision!*
> *Human Divine, Jesus the Saviour, Blessed for ever and ever.*
>
> (K 667)

Thus the "Divine Humanity" is not a single individual, but a family; and Blake goes so far as to condemn explicitly the teaching that the Lord, or any of the "eternal states" which constitute the human universe is or ever could be represented by any single individual. In this Blake certainly goes beyond Swedenborg, at least in relation to the Jesus Christ of history. How strongly Blake held this view is clear from these lines from *Jerusalem*:

> *Los cries: "No Individual ought to appropriate to Himself*
> *"Or to his Emanation [his feminine counterpart] any of the*
> *   Universal Characteristics*
> *"Of David or of Eve, of the Woman or of the Lord,*
> *"Of Reuben or of Benjamin, of Joseph or Judah or Levi.*
> *"Those who dare appropriate to themselves Universal Attributes*
> *"Are the Blasphemous Selfhoods, & must be broken asunder.*
> *"A Vegetated Christ & a Virgin Eve are the Hermaphroditic*
> *"Blasphemy, by his Maternal Birth he is that Evil-One*
> *"And his Maternal Humanity must be put off Eternally,*
> *"Lest the Sexual Generation swallow up Regeneration.*
>
> (J 90; K 736)

—and the passage ends with the invocation,

> *"Come, Lord Jesus, take on thee the Satanic Body of Holiness."*

The Divine Humanity is invoked to put on a generated body in order to transcend his natural humanity, transmitted by the mother. To Blake mortal generation is a binding of an immortal spirit into the cruel bondage of mortality:

> *Thou, Mother of my Mortal part,*
> *With cruelty didst mould my Heart,*
> *And with false self-deceiving tears*
> *Didst bind my Nostrils, Eyes, & Ears:*
> *Didst close my Tongue in senseless clay,*
> *And me to Mortal Life betray.*
> *The Death of Jesus set me free.*
> *Then what have I to do with thee?*
>
> (SE; K 220)

This poem from *Songs of Experience* is far indeed from those Christmas lullabies of the Nativity to which we are accustomed, but is a concise summary of Swedenborg's teaching. Readers unfamiliar with Swedenborg's view of the place of the mother in the mystery of the Incarnation must find Blake's treatment of the Incarnation in this and other passages extremely puzzling. But the Leading Doctrines of the Church of the New Jerusalem, far from supporting the view of the Immaculate Conception of the Virgin Mary, see the mother as the means through which Jesus Christ took on sin. Both Swedenborg and Blake had confronted the question which was later to present itself to Jung, of how the not-quite-human son of a mother herself born without sin could experience the human condition. If, as Swedenborg taught, Jesus came to "glorify his human" by overcoming the successive temptations "admitted into his human from the mother" in order to "put on a human from the Divine within him, which is the Divine Human, and the Son of God" (FD 4, 64), then the mother is indeed, as in Blake's poem, "cruel" and the source of evil, not of good. Swedenborg is quite categorical in his insistence that the natural humanity inherited by Jesus Christ from his earthly mother "cannot be transmuted into the Divine Essence nor can it be commixed with it . . . thus it follows that the Lord put off the human from the mother which, in itself, was like the human of another man, and thus material, and put on the human from the Father, which, in itself, was like His Divine, and thus substantial; and from which the Human was also made divine" (FD 77)—not, be it understood, by the elevation of what Blake calls "a Vegetated Christ" but, on the contrary, by putting off his natural humanity. Blake summarizes the Swedenborgian teaching when he writes, of Jesus,

> He took on Sin in the Virgin's Womb,
> And put it off on the Cross & Tomb.*
> (EG; K 749)

Thus in his doctrine that "the Lord put off the human from the Mother, and put on the Human from the Divine in himself which is called the father" Swedenborg anticipated and resolved Jung's later question as to the incompleteness of the Incarnation. What Jung saw as a future possibility Swedenborg and Blake saw as already accomplished in the mystery of the Incarnation, which had not hitherto been properly understood. The two lines just quoted are taken from a late poem by Blake entitled *The Everlasting Gospel,* a series of fragments which are in fact all expositions of Swedenborg's Leading Doctrines; which fact entirely confutes the often-propounded view of Blake scholars that Swedenborg's influence is to be found only in Blake's early works. This is by no means the case; the influence of Swedenborg, if anything, is clearer in the last works than in the first. One fragment expands at length the necessity that the mother of Jesus should be a vehicle of sins and not "a Virgin pure / With narrow Soul & looks demure." He comes very close indeed to Jung when he writes

> Or what was it, which he took on
> That he might bring salvation?
> A body subject to be tempted
> From neither pain or grief Exempted?
> Or such a body as might not feel
> The passions that with sinners deal?
> (EG)

Yet in affirming the indwelling of the Divine Human in mankind, and the total humanity of Jesus in taking on a fully human, fully sinful inheritance, how far are Swedenborg, and Blake, and Jung also for that matter, from any humanistic intent of exalting the natural humanity—the mortal selfhood—to a godlike status, usurping the name of humanity from the divine principle in man and affirming the supremacy of the natural man. Swedenborg insists that it is only through putting off his natural humanity through temptations overcome, and finally on the cross, that Jesus glorified the Divine Humanity of the Father. Blake, who saw the divine image

---

*Blake concludes this passage with the line: "To be worship'd by the church of Rome." He is in this sense right that the Roman church specifically teaches the resurrection of the physical body and that the natural man ascends to heaven.

FIG. 146. When the Morning Stars Sang Together..., 1805-10

in every human face, wrote:

The Spirit of Jesus is continual forgiveness of Sin: he who waits to be righteous before he enters into the Saviour's kingdom, the Divine Body, will never enter there. I am perhaps the most sinful of men. I pretend not to holiness: Yet I pretend to love, to see, to converse with daily as man with man, & the more to have an interest in the Friend of Sinners. (K 621)

And finally Jung, who has most powerfully carried into our own day the mystery of the divine presence in every man, concludes his *Answer to Job* with these words, on the paradox of the divine presence that indwells "the ordinary mortal who is not free from original sin": "Even the enlightened person remains what he is, and is never more than his limited ego before the One who dwells within him, whose form has no knowable boundaries, who encompasses him on all sides, fathomless as the abysms of the earth and vast as the sky."

Abbreviations

Quotations from Blake's works are taken from *The Complete Writings of William Blake*, edited by Geoffrey Keynes (London and New York: Nonesuch Press, 1957; Oxford: Oxford University Press, 1966). References in the text are cited by abbreviations for Blake's works (see below), sometimes including line or page numbers, followed by "K" and Keynes's page number. References to letters are included in the endnotes.

AI   "Auguries of Innocence," from the Pickering Manuscript (c. 1803)
DC   *A Descriptive Catalogue* (1809)
EG   *"The Everlasting Gospel"* (c. 1818)
FZ   *Vala*, or *The Four Zoas* (1795–1804)
J   *Jerusalem* (1804–20)
LAOC   *Laocoön* plate (c. 1820)
M   *Milton, a Poem in 2 Books* (1804-08)
MHH   *The Marriage of Heaven and Hell* (c. 1790-93)
VLJ   *A Vision of the Last Judgment* (1810)

Notes

1. Genesis 1:26.
2. Annotations to Berkeley's *Siris;* K 774.
3. Henry Corbin, review of Jung's *Answer to Job*, in *La Revue de Culture Européen*, no. 5 (1953).
4. Carl G. Jung, *Answer to Job*, trans. R. F. C. Hull, Bollingen Series XX, *The Collected Works of C. G. Jung*, vol. 11 (Princeton, N.J.: Princeton University Press, 1969), p. 669.
5. Ibid., 669n.
6. Ibid., p. 402, para. 631.
7. Job 19:25–26.
8. Jung, *Answer to Job*, p. 409, para. 648.
9. Blake's letter to Thomas Butts, 2 October 1800; K 804–5.
10. "On Berkeley"; K 775.
11. John 17:21.
12. Romans 8:22.
13. Carl G. Jung, *Psychology and Alchemy*, trans. R. F. C. Hull, Bollingen Series XX, *The Collected Works of C. G. Jung*, vol. 12 (Princeton, N.J.: Princeton University Press, 1968), p. 7, para. 7.
14. Ibid., pp. 11–12, para. 12.
15. Ibid., p. 14, para. 15.
16. Corbin, review in *Culture Européen*, p. 14. See also Jung, *Psychology and Alchemy*, p. 21, para. 24.
17. Matthew 25:35–37.
18. Matthew 25:37–40.
19. Jung, *Answer to Job*, para. 656.
20. Corbin, p. 29.
21. Jung, *Answer to Job*, para. 692.

"Opposition Is True Friendship"
Swedenborg's Influences on William Blake

Harvey F. Bellin

The following article was previously published by the Swedenborg Foundation in the anthology *Blake and Swedenborg: Opposition Is True Friendship*, edited by Harvey Bellin and Darrell Ruhl (1984). We reprint it here, altered slightly, as we feel it presents a valuable contribution to the study of Blake's relationship to Swedenborg and, ultimately, to the understanding of the subtle dynamic of the influence and diffusion of Swedenborg's ideas among visionary artists following Blake. A key to abbreviations of works from which quotes by Blake are taken can be found at the beginning of the Notes section following this essay.

"The End of a Golden String"

> Father O Father what do we here
> In this Land of unbelief & fear
> The Land of Dreams is better far
> Above the light of the Morning Star
>   (LD 17–20; E 486–87)

LONDON, 1772

IN A STERILE ABATTOIR of bone-white, plaster-cast, dismembered bodies, William Blake (1757–1827) spent the last years of his childhood. For five years he had copied copies of life—ossified heads, hands, and feet from classical sculptures; eyes, ears, and noses from Renaissance engravings. His white-wigged instructors, wielding sharp compasses and dividers, dissected and trisected the fragments, reducing them to the circles, squares, triangles, and solid geometrical forms of which logical art was made. Thus the fiery-haired boy of fourteen, his Imagination pulsing with vivid pictures and poems, had been taught "art" at the Pars School of Drawing.

Blake was coming of age in the Age of Reason, an era enamored of its new goddess Science, and her handmaiden Mathematics. It was an age that built its churches and synagogues in the mathematical form and likeness of classical temples, and built its philosophies upon the mathematical formulations of its patron saint Sir Isaac Newton. In the irrefutable logic-language of numbers, Newton had revealed universal laws governing everything from the orbit of planets to the fall of apples. Henceforth, all matters—cosmic and pedestrian, sacred and secular—were expected to yield their dark secrets to the Enlightenment and her vanguard of scientists.

Blake's psyche, however, had not evolved the appropriate wheels and gears to mesh with this new mathematical logic. He was a creature of another time, an anachronism, like a rough-hewn Gothic gargoyle in an age of polished steam engines. His eyes were not adapted to the clear light of Reason; they perceived more in the tinted, stained-glass light of the "Land of Dreams." They saw visions—a specter of God peered into his window, and sent him screaming; a tree on the fields of Peckham Rye blossomed with angels, "bright angelic wings bespangling every bough like stars."[1]

Upon completing his training at the Pars School, as he and his father searched London for a master engraver with whom young William could apprentice, Blake was perhaps seeking a mentor of another sort—one who had mastered the hidden

A graduate of Yale College with high honors in the history of art, and of the Yale School of Drama with an M.F.A. in directing, HARVEY F. BELLIN is a motion-picture and television writer/director/producer. In partnership with Tom Kieffer, he produced the PBS national television series "The Shakespeare Hour Hosted by Walter Matthau," and other programs about culture and religions around the world. Their award-winning television programs for the Swedenborg Foundation include: *Blake: The Marriage of Heaven and Hell*, a docu-drama starring Anne Baxter and George Rose; *Swedenborg: The Man Who Had to Know*, a docu-drama featuring Lillian Gish; *Johnny Appleseed and the Frontier Within*, about the Swedenborgian frontier-missionary Johnny "Appleseed" Chapman; *Images of Knowing*, narrated by Anne Baxter; and *The Other Side of Life*, narrated by George Rose. At the time of publication, they are producing a television program on Swedenborg's scientific career.

knowledge of the "Land of Dreams."

Around the same time, in the same city, in rented rooms above a wigmaker's shop, an octogenarian Swedish scientist, Emanuel Swedenborg, informed his English maid that several matters required his immediate attention because he would be dying in three weeks' time at five o'clock in the afternoon. The maid, Elizabeth Reynolds, later recalled: "He was as pleased as if he were going to have a holiday, and go to some merrymaking" (DOC vol. 2, p. 546).

Swedenborg was not a man who despised his life or his times; on the contrary, he had partaken of the fruits of the Age of Reason with great delight. He was an accomplished scientist and inventor, and author of many thick volumes of refined Latin prose on science, philosophy, psychology, and· theology. Despite a recent stroke, he remained actively involved in the theological writings to which he had devoted his past twenty-eight years. He simply had no fear of death, of which he had written: "Death is not an extinction, but a continuation of life . . . merely a transition from one state to another" (TCR 792).

Three weeks later, on 29 March 1772, at 5:00 P.M., Swedenborg asked Elizabeth Reynolds the time. Upon hearing her answer, he replied, "That is good, I thank you. God bless you." He then died peacefully (DOC vol. 2, p. 546).

Two days before his death, he was visited by a resident pastor of the Swedish church, the Reverend Arvid Ferelius, who advised him to recant the new theological ideas set forth in Swedenborg's books—writings some clergy had branded as heretical. Swedenborg rose up from his sickbed, smiled at the pastor, and replied, "As truly as you see me before your eyes, so true is everything I have written. . . . When you enter eternity, you will see everything; and then you and I shall have much to talk about" (DOC vol. 2, pp. 557–58).

Swedenborg's writings did give others in London "much to talk about." Shortly after his death, his books, such as *Heaven and Hell, Divine Love and Wisdom, Divine Providence,* and *Universal Theology* (*True Christian Religion*) were widely known and discussed, and were in the personal libraries of many progressive thinkers, including a young engraver, William Blake.

LONDON, 13 APRIL 1789

Although Swedenborg had never initiated the formation of a new religious denomination, a number of his English and Continental followers gathered in a chapel in Great East Cheap, London, on 13 April 1789, to convene a General Conference for establishing a sectarian church founded upon "the truths contained in the Theological Writings of the honorable Emanual Swedenborg."[2] Among those signing the register of the General Conference were William Blake and his young wife, Catherine.

The church was to be called the New Jerusalem, an image cited in Revelation, which Swedenborg saw as his emblem for a new age of spiritual liberation. When William and Catherine Blake entered the New Jerusalem chapel, they passed through a portal with a sign proclaiming the motto of the new church: NUNC LICET—NOW IT IS ALLOWABLE. Swedenborg had seen this phrase in a vision, inscribed over the door of a crystal-walled church; and he interpreted it to mean "Now it is allowable to enter intelligently into the mysteries of faith" (TCR 508).

Blake's Imagination would pass through a portal proclaiming "Now it is allowable" time and again in future years. In the frontispiece of his most ambitious illuminated poem, aptly titled *Jerusalem,* Blake portrays himself as the mythic poet Los, entering such a portal with a bright lantern.

Where does this gateway lead? To the New Jerusalem? To the "mysteries of faith"? To the subconscious realm, the "Land of Dreams"? To the wellsprings of art? To the worlds beyond the grave? Or to a world very much like our own?

For both Blake and his spiritual predecessor Swedenborg, all these are synonymous. The essence of spiritual liberation,

FIG. 147. *Frontispiece from* Jerusalem, *1804–20*

the substrata of visions and dreams, the imagery of deeply moving works of art, the shapes of the afterlife, and the living forms of nature are all intertwined—are each threads of a "golden string" leading back to a single source:

> I give you the end of a golden string,
> Only wind it into a ball,
> It will lead you in at Heaven's Gate,
> Built in Jerusalem's Wall.
>
> (J 77:1–4; E 231)

Blake would not find "Heaven's Gate" immured within the formal doctrines and prescribed rituals of the New Jerusalem Church; for he felt that "The whole of the New Church is in the Active Life and not in Ceremonies at all."[3] He quickly broke with the fledgling church and never returned.[4] He had, however, found the "end of a golden string" in Swedenborg's writings, which addressed many of Blake's own inner conflicts and doubts.

Blake's early engraved books of pictures and designs, *Songs of Innocence* and *The Book of Thel*, both created around the time of the 1789 General Conference, brim with Swedenborgian metaphor and message.[5] Despite his leaving the New Jerusalem church, Blake maintained close friendships with prominent Swedenborgians, such as the sculptor John Flaxman and the legislator C. A. Tulk,[6] till the end of his life.

Presumably, Blake never met Swedenborg;[7] it was the legacy of Swedenborg's writings, their articulate affirmation of much of what Blake had himself intuited, that created the "golden string" linking Blake to the Swedish scientist-theologian. But even a golden string can break; and it did so, resoundingly, in a book Blake created in the early 1790s which contained this warning:

> The man who never alters his opinion is like
> standing water, & breeds reptiles of the mind.
>
> (MHH 19; E 42)

LONDON, 1793

By 1793 Blake had completed an anonymous book, which he'd written, illustrated, engraved, and printed in his home workshop. He titled it *The Marriage of Heaven and Hell*—a clear satire of Swedenborg's *Heaven and its Wonders, and Hell*.

In this social-political-religious allegorical romp through the fires of hell, Blake exalts Energy and Poetic Genius, and seems to permanently damn Swedenborg into the "Satanic" pantheon of intellectual malfeasants into which Blake had cast Newton, Locke, and other shapers of the Age of Reason. Swedenborg's influences, however, would re-emerge as a dominant force throughout Blake's career. [For a discussion of the Swedenborgian basis of Blake's late, mature works, see Kathleen Raine's essay "The Human Face of God," elsewhere in this anthology.]

Blake left an intriguing clue to his own "reptilian" change

of opinion about Swedenborg in a paradoxical line he engraved beneath a scaly Leviathan on plate 20 of *The Marriage of Heaven and Hell*. In the chapter where this plate appears (MHH 17–20; E 41–42), Blake challenges an angel-follower of Swedenborg to "shew me my eternal lot . . . and see whether your lot or mine is most desirable." They fight a conjurer's duel, materializing the bestiaries lurking within each other's psyches. The angel casts Blake's lot between rows of vast black and white spiders who prey upon "the most terrific shapes of animals sprung from corruption." Blake counters, casting the angel into a deep pit beneath a church on Saturn, where they enter a charnel house of cannibalistic simians, and exit carrying the "skeleton of a corpse"—Swedenborg's books, transformed into Aristotle's dry *Analytics*.

In the midst of this duel, from out of a "cataract of blood mixed with fire," the giant Leviathan emerges. Engraved beneath this "reptile of the mind," partially obscured by Blake's thick patina of watercolor pigments in several copies of this hand-painted book, is Blake's final comment on his battle with Swedenborg's angelic alter ego: "Opposition is True Friendship" (MHH 20; E 42).

FIG. 148. Leviathan, *facsimile drawing from* The Marriage of Heaven and Hell, *1790-93*

When is opposition true friendship? It is when a young man discovers his own unique mission, declares his independence, and leaves his father's house without ever losing the legacy of his roots. In a similar way Blake declared his artistic independence in the early 1790s. Shouting loud "opposition" to his former "true friendship" with Swedenborg's theological writings, he departed; but the imprint remained—so deeply ingrained that Blake assimilated much of Swedenborg's vision and made it his own.

Others influenced Blake's thoughts—Jakob Böhme, in particular—and Blake never resolved his differences with some of the theological propositions he had read in the pious, transliterated, early editions of Swedenborg's books. Nonetheless, in large measure, the essence that Swedenborg articulated in measured Latin prose formed a golden string that Blake would continue to weave in handmade books of pictures and poems. Both men had been shaped by profound visionary experiences, and each dedicated his energy, wealth, and talents to promulgating the inner realities he had come to know.

Much of their shared vision is represented in Blake's engraving of a caterpillar and sleeping human-faced chrysalis, titled *What is Man*!

What is human existence—nothing more than the course of a mouth-first caterpillar, a "mortal worm," eating its path along a darkened leaf of vegetable nature? Or is there more—a promise of metamorphosis, a flight on radiant wings, in the dreams of the sleeping chrysalis? Will the chrysalis waken from its occluded cocoon, forget its dreams, and simply procreate another round of mortal worms?

Blake left the answer to the viewer, as he indicated in a couplet engraved beneath the emblematic insects:

> *What is Man!*
> *The Suns Light when he unfolds it*
> *Depends on the Organ that beholds it.*
> (GP frontispiece; E 260)

In a later work, Blake again considered the "Organ that beholds," and concluded, "Mental things are alone real" (VLJ 94; E 565).

Over half a century earlier, Swedenborg had reached similar conclusions, but he had arrived there along a very different route. He began as a most reasonable product of a most reasonable age, who beheld "the Organ that beholds" in the clear light of the Enlightenment.

Emanuel Swedenborg (1688–1772)—The Man Who Had to Know

> If the mind is truly connected with the organs of the senses, in other words, if man is truly rational, he is perpetually aspiring after wisdom. . . . The means which are especially conductive to a truly philosophical knowledge are three in number—EXPERIENCE, GEOMETRY, and the FACULTY OF REASONING.
>
> —Swedenborg (PRIN vol. 1, p.1)

Thus began Swedenborg's theoretical scientific tome, *Principia*,[8] or *the First Principles of Natural Things, Being New Attempts Toward a Philosophical Explanation of the Elementary World*, which he published in 1734.

Had Blake read *Principia*, he would have railed loudly at Swedenborg's evocation of the terrific trinity: Experience (experimental facts), Geometry (measurement), and the Faculty of Reasoning. Blake had little faith in these three muses of the scientific age: "He who sees the Infinite in all things, sees God. He who sees the Ratio only, see himself only. If it were not for the Poetic or Prophetic character the Philo-

FIG. 149. *Frontispiece from* For the Sexes: The Gates of Paradise, *ca. 1818*

sophic & Experimental would soon be at the ratio of all things & stand still, unable to do other than repeat the same dull round over again" (NNR; E 3).

Blake was yet to be born, however, when *Principia* was written, and Swedenborg was in the midst of a brilliant scientific career, which seems to have earned him the distinction of having been the last man on earth to master all the knowledge of his times.

In an era when science and philosophy had become trendy salon amusements of the idle rich, Swedenborg, himself a well-heeled aristocrat, was a true scientist in every respect. In books such as *Motion and Position of the Earth and Planets* (pub. 1719), *Principles of Chemistry* (pub. 1721), and *Philosophical and Mineralogical Works* (3 vols., pub. 1734), all of which he published at his own expense, Swedenborg articulated his theories and discoveries in exquisite mathematical minutiae, honoring the three muses: Experience, Geometry, and the Faculty of Reasoning.

In these books of meticulous Latin prose and mathematical formulations, Swedenborg was addressing a pan-European intelligentsia that deified science and reason and relegated the biblical deity to the role of "cosmic mechanic" or vestige of an unenlightened, superstitious past. To these "enlightened" persons, Swedenborg boldly proclaimed that his science was predicated on very different assumptions:

Possibly there may be innumerable other spheres, and innumerable other heavens similar to those we behold . . . yet being but finite, and consequently having their bounds, [they] do not amount to a point in comparison with the infinite. Consequently, if all the heavenly hosts are not even a point in respect to the infinite; if the whole visible expanse, which to our eye appears so immense, is only a point in relation to the finite universe; if our solar vortex forms only a part of this expanse, and our own world only a small part of the solar vortex; truly we may ask, *What is Man?*

. . . Behold and see how small a speck thou art in the system of heaven and earth; and in thy contemplations remember this, that if thou wouldst be great, thy greatness must consist in this—in learning to adore Him who is Himself the Greatest and the Infinite. (emphasis Bellin's; PRIN vol. 2, pp. 238–39)

Swedenborg's metaphor has a familiar ring, strangely similar to the imagery of scientific and sci-fi literature and motion pictures of our own times. His underlying religious message, however, might seem out of place for a scientist-philosopher, and possibly seemed old-fashioned to his own contemporaries, especially when he stated, "True philosophy and contempt of the Deity are two opposites. Veneration for the Infinite Being can never be separated from philosophy; for he who fancies himself wise, while his wisdom does not teach him to acknowledge a Divine and Infinite Being . . . he has not a particle of wisdom" (PRIN vol. 1, p. 35).

In his refutation of the learned advocates of a mechanistic, Newtonian universe, Swedenborg is strikingly similar to a later scientist who shattered the Newtonian model of nature—Albert Einstein:

You will hardly find one among the profounder sort of scientific minds without a religious feeling of his own. . . . His religious feeling takes the form of a rapturous amazement at this harmony of natural law, which reveals an intelligence of such superiority that, compared with it, all systemic thinking of human beings is utterly insignificant reflection. . . .

The ancients knew something we seem to have forgotten. All means prove but a blunt instrument, if they have not behind them a living spirit . . . science without religion is lame, religion without science is blind.[9]

Swedenborg, as he approached his fiftieth year, continued to envision a literal link between physical science and the "living spirit" of religion and sought to apply his science to

extricating the reality of that living spirit. He narrowed the focus of his research, concentrating on anatomy and physiology, with but one intention: "I have pursued this anatomy with the single purpose of searching out the soul" (RP intro.). "[For] she is represented in the body, as in a mirror" (AK intro.).

While pursuing this spiritual intention, Swedenborg made several significant physical discoveries, including the function of the endocrine glands. He drafted extensive research on the blood, respiratory system, gastrointestinal tract, the skin, senses, and procreative organs, and published many of his findings. He continued on relentlessly: "I am resolved to allow myself no respite. . . . I shall open all the doors that lead to her, and at length, contemplate the soul herself" (AK intro.).

He then narrowed in even further, concentrating his search for the seat of the soul on a single organ: "I am determined . . . for the sake of a closer approach to examine her very brain, where the soul has disposed her first organs" (AK intro.).

In 1743–44, Swedenborg compiled a staggering four-volume treatise *The Brain*. In it, he was the first to discover the functions of the cerebellum, pituitary gland and spinal fluid, the localization of thinking and memory in the cerebral cortex, and the integrative action of the nervous system.

But he did not find the soul lurking between the synapses of the cerebral cortex. He had pushed objective science to the limits, and failed. His three muses—Experience, Geometry, and the Faculty of Reasoning—had gone mute. He would not meet the soul *in vitro*, in the flayed tissues or corpses or in cold calculations; if she was to be discovered, she must be seen *in vivo*.

As he continued his anatomical studies, a new muse began to emerge, sending seismic shock waves to the very core of this objective man of the Age of Reason. The process started with a series of disturbing dreams, which he carefully recorded in a private journal:

. . . Stood beside a machine, that was set in motion by a wheel. The spokes entangled me more and more and carried me up so that it was impossible to escape. . . . Wakened.

Freely and boldly I descended a great staircase. Below there was a hole leading down into a great abyss. It was difficult to reach the other side without falling in. On the other side were people to whom I reached out my hand, to help me over. . . . Wakened. . . . Signifies my danger of falling into the abyss, if I do not get help. (JD 18, 20)[10]

Where could he "get help" to understand the process unfolding within himself? Alone, in temporary rooms rented during his frequent overseas travels, in the mid-eighteenth century, Swedenborg tried to decipher the hidden meanings of dreams. He need no longer pursue the soul from the outside in; she was beginning to speak to him in her own language, from the inside out. Her message, however, was not clear, was not phrased in logical terms. Her language consisted of bizarre, disjointed images; her tone was disconcerting. She remained distant, appearing only in the night, in the darkened mirror of dreams.

Then, with horrific power, she began to manifest herself in waking visions:

> I was in London and dined rather late one night. . . . Towards the end of the meal I noticed a dimness before my eyes; this became denser, and then I saw the floor covered with horrid crawling reptiles. . . .
>
> I was amazed; for I was perfectly conscious, and my thoughts were clear. (DOC vol. 1, p. 35)

As Blake would later warn, "The man who never alters his opinion is like standing water, & breeds reptiles of the mind" (MHH 19; E 42).

Swedenborg's opinions began to alter. He realized that he could no longer rely on his intellect alone; he would need other, more intuitive ways of knowing. He was now at great risk, his sanity was at stake; but his long quest seemed to be nearing fruition.

His life was rushing toward a crucial turning point. He was about to experience the meaning of one of Blake's *Gates of Paradise* engravings, titled, "At length for hatching ripe he breaks the shell" (GP 6; E 262).

FIG. 150. At length for hatching ripe. . ., *from* For the Sexes: The Gates of Paradise, *ca. 1818*

"A Theatre Representative of the Lord's Kingdom" (*Swedenborg's Theology*)

> Divine Providence has ruled the acts of my life since my youth . . . so that by means of the knowledge of natural things [through science] I might be able to understand the things which lie deeply concealed in the Word of God, and thus serve as an instrument for laying them bare.
>
> —Swedenborg (WE 2532)

Whatever force had been emerging within the fifty-six-year-old Swedenborg became "for hatching ripe" on the night after Easter, 6–7 April 1744.

He had been reading about the miracles Moses performed, and was questioning the logic of the mechanisms involved. He smiled to himself and noted in his journal that "angels and God reveal themselves to shepherds, but never to the philosopher" (JD 49), such as himself, who is so easily ensnared in his own intellectual minutiae. He then went to sleep and ". . . At about 12:00, 1:00 or 2:00 in the night a strong shuddering came over me from head to foot, with a thundering noise as if many winds beat together, and shook me. . . . I found that something holy was upon me . . ." (JD 51, 52).

He found himself prostrate, his hands clasped in prayer. He experienced a vision of Jesus, instructing him to redirect the course of his life. It was a compelling event: "From that day I gave up the study of all worldly science, and laboured in spiritual things. . . . The Lord opened my eyes . . . so that in the middle of the day I could see into the other world, and in a state of perfect wakefulness converse with angels and spirits" (DOC vol. 1, pp. 35–36).

Swedenborg devoted the rest of his life, over a quarter century, to "spiritual things," writing volume upon volume of visionary theology. He published in Latin, at his own expense, signing most of the books simply, "A Servant of the Lord." Throughout, he maintained the methodical, analytical approach that had been the hallmark of his "worldly science."

What is to be made, however, of Swedenborg's transformation experience? Had this disciplined scientist simply gone too far, and fallen victim to his own delusions?

Swedenborg recognized the magnitude of his claims: "I am well aware that many will say that no one can talk to spirits and angels . . . that it is a fantasy, that I invent it to gain credence for my writings. . . . But by all this I am not deterred; for I have seen, I have heard, and I have felt" (AC 68).

An important insight into what Swedenborg "saw," "heard" and "felt" occurs in the writings of the late psychologist, Dr. Carl G. Jung, who was quite familiar with Swedenborg's career: "I admire Swedenborg as a great scientist and a great mystic at the same time. His life and work has always been of great interest to me, and I read seven fat volumes of his writings when I was a medical student."[11]

In another context, Jung proposed that visionary experiences (such as those of Swedenborg and Blake) are not to be automatically dismissed as symptoms of insanity, for they can be remarkable breakthroughs to the deepest strata of human awareness:

Too few people have experienced the divine image as the innermost possession of their own souls. Christ only meets them from without, never from within the soul . . . [for] they cannot see to what extent the equivalent images are lying dormant in their own unconscious.

The believer should not boggle at the fact that there are *somnia a Deo missa* (dreams sent by God) and illuminations of the soul which cannot be traced back to external causes. . . . The soul must contain in itself the faculty of relationship to God, i.e., a *correspondence*, otherwise a connection could never come about. *This* correspondence *is, in psychological terms, the archetype of the God-image.* (extra emphases Bellin's)[12]

It was precisely this concept of "correspondence," the powerful links inherent in the "images lying dormant in the unconsicous," that gave Swedenborg his key to the soul and formed the core of his theological writings. What he had not found by peeling back the tissues of cadavers, he would now discover, wondrously alive, by peeling back the layers of his own psyche.

In seeking the meanings of his dreams, Swedenborg had noticed that literal, physical images seemed to have deeper psychological meanings. For example, when he was approaching a crisis and dreamt of being in danger of falling into a deep abyss, it was his mental balance, not his physical agility, that was being represented. He began to recognize that his inner awareness, his soul, was writing these dramas to tell him something of importance. She was communicating in her own powerful image-language, with a vocabulary so bizarre that it defied rational analysis, yet seemed to convey its meanings at a deeper, more direct level of awareness.

Swedenborg set out to understand this image-language and how it worked.

He gained direct access to this image-language of "correspondences," this "stuff as dreams are made on," in the visions he continued to experience until the end of his life. Most occurred while he was fully awake, others in a hypnagogic state midway between sleep and wakefulness. Some were out-of-body experiences, in which his perceptions were "more acutely sensitive than ever in physical wakefulness" (HH 440). He had discovered an inner arena, where transient external thoughts are stilled, and the deepest levels of the psyche can unfold themselves; and where, as Swedenborg noted, "angels and spirits can be seen . . . heard, and remarkably, touched" (HH 440).

Drawing open the curtain of the psyche, he set free her *dramatis personae*. He saw, heard, and felt their living presence; and discovered that "all the world's a stage" in this mental proscenium—that the realities of the physical world are recast by the psyche into their corresponding spiritual roles: "*The visible universe is nothing else than a theatre representative of the Lord's Kingdom*" (AC 3483). To which Blake would later add, "*There Exist in that Eternal World the Permanent Realities of Every Thing we see reflected in this Vegetable Glass of Nature*" (VLJ 69; E 555).

Swedenborg spent years compiling lexicons of the image-language of the "Eternal World," tracing the correspondences between the "Permanent Realities" of the soul and their reflections in "this Vegetable Glass of Nature." Swedenborg would now apply his former zeal for studying natural phenomena to spiritual phenomena by deciphering "correspondences"—"representations of spiritual and heavenly things in natural things" (TCR 204).

Swedenborg proposed that correspondences operate through built-in channels within the psyche, which react to our perceptions of the physical world. Every aspect of creation—sun and stars, earth and air, fire and water, minerals and plants, birds, beasts, creeping things, and other people—each of these triggers a specific resonance somewhere deep within us, beneath the surface of ordinary awareness. Through these correspondences the natural world strikes specific keys, which pluck specific strings, which play emotionally charged notes within the chambers of the mind.

The music plays on, usually at a volume below perception, but affecting the tempo and rhythm of our actions. It reveals itself when the noisy chatter of the intellect is stilled—in dreams and visions, and in seemingly inexplicable responses to nature: a rapturous sensation when we witness the flight of a butterfly or a richly hued sunset; a sense of loathing triggered by a crawling cockroach or winter darkness. We respond to each of these quite differently, almost out of reflex, as if they corresponded to different parts of ourselves.

The composer and conductor of this inner symphony is the human imagination (i.e., the image-making faculty), which links each individual to all of creation through correspondences. Swedenborg's writings translated the scores of these symphonies of the imagination into more accessible formats, and as such they have been magnets to artists and writers such as Blake. The 1980 Nobel Laureate poet, Czeslaw Milosz, heralded Swedenborg's unique contribution to artists:

In effect, his system constitutes a kind of "meta-aesthetics." . . . If Swedenborg did not glorify art, he nonetheless effected a shift from object to subject, whereby the role of the artist became exalted, something readily seized upon by Blake.

[For Swedenborg] the visible world is merely a reflection of the spiritual world, everything perceived on Earth by the five senses is a "correspondence," an equivalent of a given state in the spiritual realm. . . . That some flowers, beasts, trees, landscapes, human faces are beautiful and others ugly derives from the fact that they are spiritual values. . . . Here Swedenborg is heir to the medieval, Platonic-inspired axiom, "as above, so below," which held that *the whole of creation was one of the two languages in which God spoke to man—the other was Holy Writ.* (emphasis Bellin's)[13]

"Holy Writ," the Bible—that was the arena for Swedenborg's theological triumph. He had studied the Bible since childhood; and, as he noted on the night of his transformative vision, the literal text of the Bible often seemed illogical, unrealistic, only acceptable by an act of faith. For example, how could God separate light from dark before he created the sun and other sources of illumination? If this compendium of Judeo-Christian beliefs is truly the Word of God, ought it not to make sense? His intellect could never resolve this puzzle.

After he "gave up the study of all worldly science," Swedenborg began to reread the Bible in his visionary state. He then recognized that many passages are written in an image-language similar to that of dreams and visions—that the Bible contains a spiritual subtext, written in correspondences:

> The spiritual sense of the Word is not that meaning which shines forth from the literal text when one is studying and explaining the Word to confirm some dogma of the church. . . . The Spiritual sense does not appear in the literal text; it is within it, as the soul is within the body, as thought is in the eyes, and as love is in the face. (SS 5)

> Since the Word interiorly is spiritual and celestial, therefore it is written in pure correspondences. . . . It is holy in every sentence, in every word, sometimes in the very letters. Therefore the Word conjoins man to the Lord and opens heaven. (SS 8, 3)

Swedenborg is making a subtle, but important distinction: The holiness of the Bible—which he devoutly believed to be the Word of God—is in neither its literal narrative nor its moral lessons but in the very nature of its imagery. Like the soul-revealing imagery of dreams, the words and images of the Bible are correspondences—representations of inner development which trigger direct channels into the subconscious. As such, the Bible is truly a transcultural, spiritual guide, which "conjoins man to the Lord and opens" the heavens within each individual psyche.

Swedenborg was not alone in this belief. For centuries Jewish Cabalism has viewed the Torah (Five Books of Moses) as an outward vessel of history and law housing an inner flame that illuminates the bridge between human consciousness and its divine origins. The Torah, therefore, is sacred down to the very shape and number of its flame-crowned, Hebrew letters. There is a similar sense of exegesis in the Epistle to the Hebrews, and, as Milosz noted, in the Neoplatonic tradition.

One must turn to the writings of Blake, however, to find the clearest reflection of Swedenborg's thoughts:

> Why is the Bible more Entertaining & Instructive than any other book. Is it not because (it is) addressed to the Imagination, which is the Spiritual Sensation. . . .[14]

> The Hebrew Bible & the Gospel of Jesus are not Allegory but Eternal Vision or Imagination of All that Exists . . . . Fable or Allegory are a totally distinct & inferior kind of Poetry. Vision or Imagination is a representation of what Eternally Exists. Really & Unchangeably. (VLJ 68; E 554)

Blake was convinced that "The Old and New Testaments are the Great Code of Art" (LAOC; E 274), and strove to incorporate a biblical style of correspondences in his own "prophetic books." For Swedenborg, the Bible was the great code of the art of living. In seeking its hidden meanings, he created his own monumental legacy of writings, including *Arcana Coelestia* (1749–56), his eight-volume study of correspondences in Genesis and Exodus, and his detailed exegesis of the Book of Revelation, *Apocalypse Explained* (1757–59), and *Apocalypse Revealed* (1766).

As he continued to explore "the things which lie deeply concealed in the word of God" (WE 2532), Swedenborg began to realize that the channels of correspondences can operate as two-way streets. Just as particular images from the physical world can trigger specific responses deep within the psyche, so too, deeply felt images within the psyche can trigger our responses to, and perceptions of, the physical world. Or, as quoted earlier, in Blake's terms, "The Suns Light when he unfolds it / Depends on the Organ that beholds it."

Swedenborg recognized to what a large extent we each live in a mind-made universe of our own; how our deeply felt needs and beliefs color and fill in the details of the world we each experience: "Everything that happens or emerges in the outer, or natural, person, happens or emerges from the inner, or spiritual. . . . For whatever a person earnestly gives his mental attention becomes, so to speak, present to him" (HH 92, 196).

This recognition of how inner needs can create perceived outer realities helped Swedenborg address the question of an afterlife. He could not accept the mechanistic model of eternity advocated by his Christian contemporaries: a Day of Judgment, when the deceased are assembled like scientific specimens, their moral balance-sheets weighed and measured, and their souls dispatched to either devilish tormentors or angelic choirs.

Through his understanding of correspondences, Swedenborg saw how people will often create their own living heaven or hell by projecting into their environment their own personal angels or demons. In Swedenborg's holistic vision of existence, these psychological realities persist after death: "When a person dies, he simply crosses from one world to another. . . . All of his intentions and loves remain with him after death. . . . He leaves nothing behind except his physical body" (HH 445, 461, 547).

Swedenborg envisioned the afterlife not as an end product, but as a process—a process of psychological clarification and self-discovery. The external circumstances and social masks worn on earth disappear, and each person is freed to create new circumstances that can best fulfill his or her deepest inner needs. Inner and outer realities continue to correspond, but in much more precise ways:

> Once a spirit is in the state proper to his inward concerns . . . he is acting on the basis of what really belongs to him. If he was inwardly involved in something good in the world, he then behaves wisely—more wisely, in fact, than he did in the world, because he is released from his ties with a body and therefore from those things that darken and, so to speak, cloud things over.
>
> On the other hand, if he was involved in something wicked in the world, he then behaves crazily—more crazily, in fact, than he did in the world, because he is in freedom and is not repressed. (HH 505)

Swedenborg described these resulting conditions—the state of heightened wisdom, and that of profound insanity—in the traditional terms, "heaven" and "hell." These are not physical places, however, they are *states*, outer circumstances that are the crystallizations of corresponding inner needs.

For example, someone who has been driven by a lifelong need for ego satisfaction will "behave crazily," like a starved cur in a butcher shop, once freed of all social and legal restraints. In the totally psychological medium of the afterlife, these inner needs continue to project outward, creating a mental environment in which to enact their ends. This is the state Swedenborg called "hell." It is a mind-made hell, born of oneself, rather than of divine judgment: "The evil within a person is hell within him. . . . And after death, his greatest desire is to be where his own evil is. . . . Consequently, the person himself, not the Lord, casts himself into hell" (HH 547).

The hell Swedenborg visualized is somewhat akin to a prison for the criminally insane without guards or supervisors. Each of the inmates is free to act upon his or her prevailing drives. In the economy of this state, no devils are needed, since the perpetrators are each other's victims. This hell is not simply a Dante's *Inferno* minus its cloven-hoofed demons; it is a mind-made reality, the collective projection of like-minded people.

This hell corresponds to the psycho-logics of daily realities: it is a hell because it is a state of endless striving after meaningless, selfish goals, and never attaining them. It is a hell of mutually thwarting, unchecked egos. It is a hell, the worst hell, because it is the state of ultimate aloneness, of being cut off, wanting no one and being unwanted.

Swedenborg envisioned heaven as an opposite, but comparable correspondence to mind-made realities. He did not share his contemporaries' image of a dull and pious heaven, populated with android Christian angels forever recycling top hits from the hymnals of their favorite earthly churches. Swedenborg saw heaven as an active state of affirmation, a magnifying mirror of the earthly joys of exchanging love, sharing wisdom, and exercising one's most cherished talents through useful deeds.

"There is no happiness in life apart from activity," Swedenborg wrote; "praising and honoring God is not the right kind of active life, for God has no need of praise and honor. He rather wants people to perform useful deeds" (HH 403–4).

This focus on "useful deeds" over formal worship is central to Swedenborg's theology. The need to perform useful acts for others, rather than the need to perform prescribed church rituals, is the truest correspondence to the state of heaven: "Heaven is in people, and people who have heaven in themselves come into heaven. . . . It includes all people who live in the good of charity in accord with their own religious persuasion" (HH 319, 328).

This "heaven," this state experienced by "all who live in the good of charity in accord with their own religious persuasion," is predicated on transcultural psychological realities rather than on religious doctrine, and is decidedly pluralistic. It is a conceptual cousin of another, "self-evident Truth" born of the Age of Reason—" that all men are created equal, that they are endowed by their Creator with certain inalienable Rights . . . Life, Liberty, and the Pursuit of Happiness." Swedenborg's vision of heaven is a similar celebration of individual freedom, of the inalienable right of each individual to shape his or her own destiny; and because all outward forms in this mind-made heaven correspond to their inward meanings, Swedenborg visualized a composite representation of heaven in the form of a "Maximus Homo" [Universal Human; see Glossary], an emblem of his conviction that "God is very man" (DLW 11).

"God became as we are that we may be as he is," (NNR ii; E 3) Blake echoed in the pages of the first "illuminated" books he created with his own hands. This refrain continued throughout his works, and into the verses of his late, unfinished *Everlasting Gospel*:

> *Thou art a Man   God is no more*
> *Thy own humanity learn to adore.*
> (EG k:71–72; E 520)

Or, in Swedenborg's words, "Love is the life of Man . . . and the Lord, because he is Life itself, is Love itself" (DLW 1, 4).

In 1825, the critic, Henry Crabb Robinson, to whom Blake had acknowledged his debt to Swedenborg as a "divine teacher," asked Blake to define the divinity of Jesus. "He is the only God," Blake replied, then added, "And so am I, and so are you."[16]

"God is very man." Perhaps that is Swedenborg's and Blake's shared answer to the question "What is Man!" which Blake had posed beneath his engraving of a sleeping, human-faced chrysalis.

Swedenborg's recorded answers to this question reflect his transformation from the days when he was a young scientist, and wrote, "What is man? . . . Behold and see how small a speck thou art in the system of heaven and earth" (PRIN vol. 2, p. 239). After his many years of visionary experiences, Swedenborg reversed this cosmology: "Man is both a heaven and an earth in microcosm" (HH 90). Experience can bring wisdom, but it has its price. . . .

"The Price of Experience" (Swedenborg's Final Years)

What is the price of Experience
 do men buy it for a song
Or wisdom for a dance in the street?
 No it is bought with the price
Of all that a man hath . . .

(FZ II:11–13; E 325)[17]

The last years of Swedenborg's life had a curious twist. After reaching the age of seventy, Swedenborg was thrust into public attention because of several demonstrations of his clairvoyant talents, such as his vision of the Stockholm Fire of 1759, while he was hundreds of miles away in Göteborg.[18] As a result of this attention, people began to identify this clairvoyant Swede as the author of certain anonymous books of visionary theology; and fame brought its price.

When Swedenborg's books became better known in Sweden, a group of conservative local clergymen condemned his ideas as heresy, and demanded a trial. They made him an object of public ridicule, and conspired to confine him to a mental asylum. Upon their insistence, the Swedish Royal Council issued a decree on 26 April 1770, in which it "totally condemned, rejected, and forbade the theological doctrines in the writings of Swedenborg," and prohibited the import of his books.[19]

So much for the Age of Reason in Sweden.

Swedenborg left his homeland, but continued writing and publishing abroad. In September 1772 he arrived in London, where young William Blake was copying plaster-cast fragments of classical sculptures at the Pars School. Six months

later Swedenborg saw a vision of his own death, and the vision came true.

Blake probably was unaware of this precognitive vision until several years later. His own link with Swedenborg, however, was to be reinforced by another of Swedenborg's visions—one that was not of death, but, instead, concerned the year of Blake's own birth.

William Blake (1757–1827)—A "Blake-smith" Who Would Forge a New Jerusalem

The Eternal Female groan[e]d! it was heard over all the Earth . . . .
In her trembling hands she took the new born terror howling. . . .
The fire, the fire, is falling!
Look up! look up! O citizen of London.

("A Song of Liberty," MHH 25; E 44)

"The new born terror," William Blake, entered the mortal world as the son of a London hosier, James Blake, on 28 November 1757.

In that same year, a "New Jerusalem" was born in the visions of Emanuel Swedenborg. Several times in 1757 he experienced powerful visions of cosmic events—a reordering of the heavens, and a dawning of a new age of spiritual liberty—happenings that mirrored the visions of John in Revelation:

And I saw a new heaven and a new earth. . . . And I, John, saw the holy city, the New Jerusalem, descending from God out of heaven, prepared as a bride adorned for her husband. . . .
And he that sat on the throne said: Behold, I make all things new.[20]

Swedenborg adopted the image of a "New Jerusalem" as emblematic of a new age of spiritual liberation from the mind-limiting dogmas of the past:

The state of the world will be precisely what it was before . . . as to outward form . . . but men of the church will be in a freer state of thinking on matters of faith. . . . Because spiritual liberty has been restored. . . . He can better perceive inner truth, if he so desires. (LJ 73–74)

Now it is allowable to enter intelligently into the mysteries of faith. (TCR 508)

Blake, who was well acquainted with Swedenborg's writings concerning 1757,[21] and who was endowed with a singular affinity for the miraculous, no doubt felt a strong identification with this new age of spiritual/psychological awakening, which, like himself, was born in 1757. Blake possibly saw in Swedenborg's 1757 visions something quite real, which is not readily apparent at first glance.

It would be logical to dismiss Swedenborg's 1757 New

FIG. 151. William, *Blake's self-portrait, from* Milton, a Poem in 2 Books, *1804–08*

Jerusalem visions as his own deeply felt personal experience, which he projected out of all proportion and claimed to signify the advent of a new age. Historical evidence points to few cosmic changes occurring in 1757, other than the Vatican's lifting its ban on books about the rotation of the earth. If anything, history would indicate a source of Swedenborg's apocalpytic visions in the famed 1755 earthquake which destroyed Lisbon and claimed upward of forty thousand lives in the ensuing tidal wave, week-long fires, and panic. Because the earthquake occurred on All Saints Day while most of the population was attending church, and because its rumblings were felt from Scotland to Asia Minor, it was seen by many as the beginning of a Last Judgment. Even that most reasonable man Voltaire wrote his pessimistic satire *Candide* in response to the Lisbon cataclysm.

Swedenborg's 1757 visions, however, dealt with something far more subtle and far-reaching. In his own words: "The state of the world will be precisely what it was before . . . as to outward form" (LJ 73). According to his paradigm of correspondences, the outward manifestations will result from their germination in human thoughts and desires. The new age he saw unfolding was a psychological process. In 1757, percolating within the minds of intellectual giants and commonfolk, were the seeds of the great political, social, industrial, commercial, scientific, and artistic revolutions of the late-eighteenth century. When these thoughts later became physical realities, such as the American and French revolutions, they did, in fact, initiate a new age of liberty by dramatically changing the institutions of the past. These apocalyptic changes had existed in the preceding decades as antecedent thoughts in the minds of those bold enough to "enter intelligently into the mysteries of faith." It was almost as if Swedenborg had tapped into the collective psychology of 1757 and had seen its essence represented, through the psychological image-language of correspondences, in the form of apocalyptic events re-ordering the heavens.

Blake, in the late 1780s, saw many of these revolutionary outward manifestations taking place before his eyes. He seized upon the meaning of Swedenborg's New Jerusalem visions at a critical point in his own life. During this period of his most intense direct ties with Swedenborg's writings and Swedenborgian circles, Blake formulated his own life mission—to become a champion of this new age as a spiritual artist. He determined his own "great task": "to open the Eternal Worlds, to open the immortal Eyes / of Man inwards" (J 5:17–19; E 147); and, as he later explained, he felt himself to be properly qualified for fulfilling this "great task":

> The Thing I have most at Heart! more than life or all That seems to make life comfortable without, Is the Interest of True Religion and Science. . . .[22]

> I am not ashamed afraid or adverse to tell you what Ought to be Told. That I am under the direction of Messengers from Heaven Daily & Nightly. . . .
>
>   If we fear to do the dictates of our Angels & tremble at the Tasks set before us. If we refuse to do Spiritual Acts because of Natural Fears and Natural Desires! Who can describe the dismal torments of such a state!—I too well remember the threats I have heard!—If you who are organized by Divine Providence for Spiritual communion Refuse & Bury your Talent in Earth even tho you should want Natural Bread, Sorrow & Desperation pursues you thro life! & after death shame and confusion of face to Eternity.[23]

Such threats of "Sorrow & Desperation," "shame and confusion," delivered by his messengers from heaven, would, no doubt, spur Blake on to the great task assigned him by Divine Providence. His mission, however, might have been a response to a more gentle prodding from Swedenborg's writings. The New Jerusalem of Swedenborg's visions was a potential energy existing in a spiritual/psychological dimension; to further her manifestations as kinetic energy in the world of men would require the active intervention by:

". . . A man, who is not only able to receive these teachings in his understanding, but is also able to publish them by the press" (TCR 779).

Swedenborg met this task, writing and publishing many thick volumes of these new age teachings, at his own expense. Blake would have followed this pattern gladly, but he faced a significant obstacle. Like Swedenborg, Blake would find no help from the established publishers and would have to become his own publisher; but unlike the independently wealthy Swedenborg, Blake was rarely in possession of discretionary funds. He and his wife were often at the brink of absolute poverty and survived through the benevolence of a few patrons, such as the middle-level civil servant, Thomas Butts, to whom the preceding letter was written.

It was clear to Blake that "I must create a System, or be enslav'd by another Man's" (J 10:20; E 153). Around 1788 he devised an ingenious appropriate technology that freed him from the publishers' monopoly of letterpress equipment. Using acid-resistant varnish, he painted the words and designs of his illuminated poems directly onto copper printing plates, in mirror-image. He poured acid onto the plates, etching away the unpainted areas. The result was a relief-plate with raised-up areas where he had painted the words and designs. Unlike intaglio engraved plates, which require the pressure of a heavy press to lift ink out of the incised lines and onto printing paper, Blake's relief-plates could be printed on the simple wooden proofing-press in his home workshop. He had created a medium for combining poetry and visual art that would last him a lifetime.[24]

Perhaps Blake's new system had been born of necessity; Blake, himself, attributed the discovery to the spirit of his departed brother Robert, who "in a vision of the night . . . stood before him, and revealed the wished-for secret."[25] It is significant, nonetheless, that Blake devised this system during his formative period of greatest involvement with Swedenborg's writings, and that the early works he created with this system are deeply Swedenborgian in both intent and imagery.[26] In many ways Blake's discovery of both the mission and method of his life's work seem to answer the call for a man who could receive the teachings of a New Jerusalem and "publish them by the press."

In the early 1790s, after Blake broke with the New Jerusalem Church, his printing method assumed a new metaphor. In *The Marriage of Heaven and Hell*, he proclaimed ironically, "I was in a Printing House in Hell & saw the method in which knowledge is transmitted from generation to generation . . . [by] fire raging around & melting the metals into living fluids" (MHH 15; E 40). He deemed his fiery, acid-etching process "the infernal method," and mythologized it as a kind of alchemy—a physical transformation by purifying fires, which yields a spiritual transformation:

. . . This I shall do, by printing in the infernal method, with corrosives, which in Hell are salutary and medicinal, melting apparent surfaces away, and revealing the infinite which was hid.

If the doors of perception were cleansed everything would appear to man as it is: infinite. For man has closed himself up, till he sees all things thro' narrow chinks in his cavern. (MHH 14; E 39)

Even in this context, Blake seems to echo Swedenborg, who wrote of "realities that exist in the spiritual world that . . . can be seen by man when his internal sight is opened" (AC 1966); but, because of external concerns and dogmatic thinking,

there is no opening, for they obstruct and close the door, which cannot be opened by the Lord, but only by the man himself. . . .The Lord continually entreats man to open the door to Him, as is plain from the Lord's words in Apocalypse (III:20): "Behold I stand at the door and knock; if any hear my voice and open the door, I will come in to him." (DP 119)

After *The Marriage of Heaven and Hell*, Blake's references to Swedenborg are few, and are generally quite positive [see Kathleen Raine's essay "The Human Face of God," elsewhere in this anthology].[27] The self-appointed mission Blake has assumed before declaring "opposition" to Swedenborg's writings continued as a strong undercurrent in his prophetic books of the 1790s [see the following section of this essay, "Bright Sculptures of Los's Halls"], and resurfaced in his nineteenth-century works. In the preface to his 1804–8 *Milton, a Poem in 2 Books*, Blake states, "When the new age is at leisure to Pronounce, all will be set right." He then reaffirms his own role in bringing about this new age:

> I will not cease from Mental fight,
> Nor shall my Sword sleep in my hand:
> Till we have built Jerusalem,
> In England's green & pleasant Land
>
> (M 1:13–16; E 95–96)

The mental fight to build Jerusalem in "England's green & pleasant Land" is told in the greatest work created by Blake's infernal method, titled *Jerusalem: The Emanation of the Giant Albion* (1804–20).

Jerusalem is depicted on the bottom of the title page of this book in the form of a butterfly-winged woman, a prophetic fulfillment of the sleeping human-faced chrysalis of Blake's earlier "What is Man!" engraving. She too is asleep, because, like the New Jerusalem of Swedenborg's visions, she remains a dormant, radiant-winged essence not yet "for hatching ripe" into the mortal realm without active intervention. Her direct kinship with Swedenborg's New Jeru-

FIG. 152. *Title page from* Jerusalem, *1804–20*

salem, the age in which "spiritual liberty has been restored," is clearly indicated in Blake's definitions of his butterfly-winged Jerusalem:

> *JERUSALEM IS NAMED LIBERTY*
> *AMONG THE SONS OF ALBION*
>
> (J 26; E 171)
>
> *The form is the Divine Vision. . .*
> *This is Jerusalem in every Man. . .*
> *And Jerusalem is called Liberty among*
> *the Children of Albion*
>
> (J 54:2,3,5; E 203)[28]

In Blake's mythos, Jerusalem, the not-so-distant avatar of Swedenborg's new Jerusalem, becomes the "Emanation" (anima) of Albion,[29] a primordial Giant whose name was synonymous with England, the island he conquered. Blake gives Albion an additional meaning, that of the Universal Man. Albion is like Adam Kadmon, the "Universal Man" of the Cabala, as Blake noted in a chapter of the poem addressed "To The Jews": "You have a tradition, that Man

contained anciently in his mighty limbs all things in Heaven & Earth" (J 27: E 171). Blake does not acknowledge the other source of his Universal Man—Swedenborg's image of the "Universal Human," "the microcosm of heaven and earth" (HH 90).

These Swedenborgian connections unfold in the central drama of the poem—the struggle to awaken Jerusalem and unite her with Albion, in other words, to bring about the era of the New Jerusalem in "England's green & pleasant Land." Albion, however, has himself fallen into a "sleep of death":

> *England! awake! awake! awake!*
> *Jerusalem thy Sister calls!*
> *Why wilt thou sleep the sleep of death!*
> *And close her from thy ancient walls.*
>
> (J 77b:1–4; E 233)
>
> *Awake! Awake Jerusalem! O lovely Emanation of Albion*
> *Awake and overspread all Nations as in Ancient Time*
> *For lo! the Night of Death is past and the Eternal Day*
> *Appears upon our Hills; Awake Jerusalem, and come away.*
>
> (J 97:1–4; E 256)

Despite these calls, Albion cannot awaken to receive his Emanation, his spiritual liberation, because his "doors of perception" have been locked by Locke, Newton, and Bacon, the materialistic propagators of the Age of Reason:

> *. . . O Divine Spirit sustain me on thy wings!*
> *That I may awaken Albion from his long & cold respose.*
> *For Bacon & Newton sheathed in dismal steel their terrors hang*
> *Like iron scourges over Albion. . . .*
>
> *I turn my eyes to the Schools and Universities of Europe*
> *And there behold the Loom of Locke whose Woof rages dire*
> *Washd by the Water-wheels of Newton, black the cloth*
> *In heavy wreaths folds over every Nation; cruel Works*
> *Of many Wheels I view, wheel without wheel, with cogs tyrannic*
> *Moving by compulsion each other: . . .*
>
> (J 15:9–12, 14–19; E 159)

"Cruel Works / Of many Wheels . . . with cogs tyrannic / Moving by compulsion each other"—the hardware of the Industrial Revolution and its birth in the software of the Age of Reason, enfolding Europe in deadly sleep under heavy wreaths of black cloth. The image is reminiscent of Swedenborg's dream about a "machine set in motion by a wheel," with spokes that entangled him and carried him up until "it was impossible to escape" (JD 18). As Swedenborg warned at the height of his scientific career: "the intelligence of the soul is not mechanical . . . he who thinks he can possess any wisdom without a knowledge and veneration of the deity has not even a particle of wisdom" (PRIN vol. 1, pp. 28, 35).

Both Swedenborg and Blake know that the places to gain this wisdom, the sources of spiritual/psychological awakening, are not to be found in either material progress or in church dogma, but within the recesses of one's own psyche (within Albion, the Universal Man), for here is contained a reflection of the Eternal World.

Who is to be the champion, the standard-bearer of the New Jerusalem, able to enter this Eternal World to rescue the dormant Jerusalem and restore her to Albion? Who can kindle a light bright enough to awaken Albion from his own deadly sleep—a light bright enough to re-enlighten the men of the Enlightenment?

In the frontispiece of *Jerusalem*, Blake depicts this hero carrying a bright lantern into a Gothic portal (as shown earlier). He is "Los," the blacksmith, the archetypal poet-artist, and Blake's personification of the Imagination. This light-bearing champion's name seems to be an anagram of "sol" (the sun); and because he is portrayed wearing Blake's own hat and coat, one might detect an autobiographical pun in that Los, the blacksmith, is very much a "Blake-smith."[30]

Blake's self-portrait as Los represents the poet-blacksmith entering a dark portal into the "interiors of Albion's Bosom" (the universal subconscious) to restore Albion's Emanation, Jerusalem (spiritual liberty); for as was proclaimed over the portal of the New Jerusalem church that Blake himself entered in 1789; "Now it is allowable to enter intelligently into the mysteries of faith." Thus, Los began his quest:

> *Fearing that Albion should turn his back against the Divine Vision*
> *Los took his globe of fire to search the interiors of Albion's Bosom. . . .*
> *The articulations of a mans soul.*
>
> (J 45:2–3,10; E 194)

Los's "globe of fire" can illuminate "the articulations of a mans soul" because Los is the Imagination, the image-making faculty; and as such, Los is the master of correspondences. He is the intuitive center of consciousness, conversant in the psyche's own language—the image-language of correspondences. He is the poet-artist, guided by this same image-language in "the great Code of Art" (LAOC; E 274), the Old and New Testaments. He is the blacksmith-alchemist, smelting the crude ore of perceived realities, and reworking the purified essence on his anvil into Eternal Realities through the medium of correspondences. As he searches "the interiors of Albion's Bosom" (the universal subconscious) Los forges pathways of correspondences to the angels of the brightest heavens, and to the most terrifying creature of the mind-made hells—the Spectre, each person's own black and opaque inner demon.

As master of correspondences, Los, the Imagination, is the human faculty most qualified to awaken Albion and to forge the new age of Albion's dormant Emanation, Jerusalem. Los can find the way through the "articulations of a mans soul" because within the chambers of Los's own halls, in the "Eternal World of Imagination," are the "Permanent

FIG. 153. *Los at forge with a spectre, from* Jerusalem, *1804-20*

Realities [correspondences] of Every Thing we see reflected in This Vegetable Glass of Nature" (VLJ 69; E 555).

> *All things acted on Earth are seen in the bright Sculptures of*
> *Los's Halls & every Age renews its powers from these Works*
> *With every pathetic story possible to happen from Hate or*
> *Wayward Love & every sorrow & distress is carved here*
> *Every Affinity of Parents Marriages & Friendships are here*
> *In all their various combinations wrought with wondrous Art*
> *All that can happen to Man in his pilgrimage of seventy years*
> *Such is the Divine Written Law of Horeb & Sinai:*
> *And such the Holy Gospel of Mount Olivet & Calvary.*
>
> (J 16:61–69; E 161)

Such is the redeeming power of imagination, custodian of the archetypal images from which art is made.

The "bright Sculptures of Los's Halls" are the poetic reincarnation of Swedenborg's paradigm of correspondences—particularly because both the authors define the content of these psychological repositories as both "all things acted on Earth" and all things of "Divine Written Law (&) The Holy Gospel" (Old and New Testaments). Los's halls are the seat of the soul, which Swedenborg had sought for so many years; and they are the *sanctum sanctorium*, the "awful cave," in which Blake learned the "wond'rous art of writing."

"Bright Sculptures of Los's Halls" (Blake's Visionary Arts)

> *Reader! lover of books! lover of heaven,*
> *And of that God from who all books are given,*
> *Who in mysterious Sinais awful cave*
> *To Man the wond'rous art of writing gave,*

Again he speaks in thunder and fire!
Thunder of Thought, & flames of fierce desire:
Even from the depths of Hell his voice I hear,
Within the unfathomed caverns of my Ear.
Therefore I print; nor vain my types shall be:
Heaven, Earth & Hell, henceforth shall live in harmony.

(J 3:1–10; E 145)

William Blake's poetic and visual imagery has an uncanny impact; it "speaks in thunder and fire," even when its meanings elude rational understanding. It resonates "within the unfathomed caverns of [the] Ear" because it is patterned on the "bright Sculptures of Los's Halls"—the archetypal imagery of correspondences. Blake's unique gift was his ability to think, write, and draw in correspondences, the medium of the imagination—a spiritual medium for conveying spiritual truths directly into the spiritual receptors of the reader or viewer.

Like Swedenborg, Blake gained direct access to this imagery through visions, and many of Blake's works seem very much like visions or dreams. It is often difficult to follow his story-lines, precisely because his stories are not linear; nor is his time sequential, nor his space geometrical. Cosmic phenomena, political events, and Blake's personal concerns shift abruptly from one to another. Characters change form, molt, merge, split, evolve, and devolve. Everything seems to exist in a universe of liquid time, space, and event; however, as Blake asserted in the introduction to his poem *Jerusalem*, there is nothing random or arbitrary in his art: "*Every word and every letter is studied and put into its fit place: the terrific numbers are reserved for the terrific parts—the mild & gentle, for the mild and gentle parts . . . all are necessary to each other*" (J 3; E 146).

"Every word and letter . . . in its fit place," as a vehicle for its inner meanings—this is precisely how Swedenborg described correspondences in the Bible: "Such is the style of the Word that it is holy in every sentence, in every word, and sometimes in the very letters. Therefore the Word conjoins man to the Lord and opens heaven" (SS 3).

Creating an art form that could mirror the Bible's power to "conjoin man to the Lord and open heaven," was the consuming passion of William Blake, a man who subtitled his poem, *Milton: To Justify the Ways of God to Men* (E 95). Blake saw himself as the artist-missionary of a new age and was audacious enough to attempt the creation of its new illuminated bible, beginning with his "prophetic books" of the 1790s. His *The (First) Book of Urizen, The Book of Los,* and *The Book of Ahania* not only echo the narratives of the Book of Genesis and Book of Exodus, but even explicitly copy the two-column format of printed Bibles from Blake's era.

Swedenborg's influences on the evolution of these prophetic books has been overlooked to a large extent by schol-ars who have focused on the Swedenborgian roots of Blake's works from earlier and later periods. Just as Blake had found a new poetic metaphor for his early engraved poems in Swedenborg's lexicons of correspondences, so too would he draw upon Swedenborg in creating a new poetic medium for his prophetic books.

Blake seems to have recognized a core achievement in Swedenborg's visions of heaven and hell, which could serve as a model for a mythic new testament. To see this core, one must subject Swedenborg's heaven and hell to Blake's alchemical "infernal method," "to reveal the infinite which was hid." Dissolve Swedenborg's theology in fiery acid. Melt away all conventional terms, such as heaven and hell, good and evil. Etch down even further, melting away all references to the Lord and his holy Word. What precipitates out in adamant crystals is Swedenborg's finely detailed, kinetic sculptures of the human psyche, set in a high-relief landscape of a totally psychological universe.

Swedenborg himself was quite clear in defining his angels, heaven and hell as representations of the psyche, the spirit within a person:

> The inside of a man, his spirit, is essentially an angel. . . . An angel is a perfect human form. (HH 314, 373)

> In common with angels, man's inward elements are patterned after heaven. . . . Heaven, taken as a single whole, reflects a single person. . . . In Revelation 21:17, this is described: "he measured the wall of holy Jerusalem, 144 cubits, the measure of a man—that is, of an angel." (HH 57, 73)

Swedenborg's multihundred-page descriptions of the daily life of heaven and hell are descriptions of the daily workings of mind. They form a vital almanac of the time, space, seasons, cosmology and geology, flora and fauna, and human inhabitants of a totally psychological universe. If a person is heaven in microcosm—in fine print—then heaven and hell are the human mind spelled out in uppercase bold type.

Blake easily adapted Swedenborg's almanac of the afterlife into a medium for his prophetic books—a totally psychological art, based on the logic of the psyche. Within this new medium, Blake made his own unique achievement: the creation of a mythology for a new age. He peopled his psychological universe with mythic personifications of the functions of mind, archetypal beings called "Giant Forms." As Blake later explained about the figures of Moses and Abraham in one of his paintings, "The Persons Moses and Abraham are not meant here but the states signified by those names[,] the individuals being but representatives or Visions of those States" (VLJ 76; E 556).

Blake's "Giant Forms"—Tharmas, Urizen, Luvah, Los (Urthona); their Emanations: Enion, Ahania, Vala, and Enitharmon; and all their myriad offspring and hybrid mutations—these creatures do not exist in any lexicon of mythology, rather they are themselves the mythic lexicons of human existence. They are the "bright Sculptures of Los's Halls," and the distillates of biblical figures and inhabitants of Swedenborg's heaven and hell, filtered through the permeable membranes of Blake's Imagination.

In fashioning his epics of the Mental Wars of liberation waged by his Giant Forms, Blake drew upon Swedenborg as a textbook of the nonphysical physics in a dimension created by and for psychological beings. The angels of Swedenborg's heaven exist in a universe where "Mental things are alone real," where psychological states are the building blocks of external environments:

> [Angels'] outward elements correspond to their inward ones. . . . The states of different things visible to their sight change . . . and choose a form that accords with the things within them. (HH 173, 156)

> [For example,] when angels are at the peak of love, they are in light and warmth . . . surrounded by radiance. When they are at the bottom of the scale, they are in shade and cold. (HH 155)

It is this quality of mind-made light which illuminates Blake's illuminated poems. Like Swedenborg's angels, Blake's characters transform according to their inner states—they brighten into their lovely Emanations, or darken into their terrific Spectres. Their dramas unfold in the tinted gothic light of the "Land of Dreams"; in fact, some of Blake's figures are delineated with such thick lines around their musculature, that they themselves appear to be made of leaded elements from a stained-glass window. Here again, "outward elements correspond to their inward ones."

The master of these correspondences, and hero of Blake's prophetic books is Los, the poet-blacksmith. In Blake's mythology, Los is one of the Four Zoas,[31] eternal beings who correspond to the fundamental aspects of man: Tharmas (Body), Urizen (Reason), Luvah (Emotions), and Los or Urthona (Imagination). The Zoas represent the cardinal points of the universe within Albion (the Universal Man) and Los sits in the northern, ruling position. Mental War erupts within Albion when the other Zoas try to usurp the rightful throne of Los (Imagination).

Blake usually portrays Los as a flame-enshrouded, red-haired,* naked youth, often armed with blacksmith's tools. On first impression, Blake seems to have cast Los in the outward form of a devil, yet Los is just the opposite: he represents the redeeming, spiritual faculty, Imagination.

This apparent paradox is resolved by viewing Los from

*Los, Albion, and Los's son Orc (the fiery spirit of Revolution) all tend to resemble each other and to resemble their red-haired creator, William Blake, in idealized form. Perhaps they each represent Blake's self-image at various stages in his career, as he was creating many books in which these figures are depicted.

FIG. 154. *Los (detail), from* The (First) Book of Urizen, *1794*

the perspective of correspondences. His flames are not hell-fire, they are an external manifestation of the "light and radiance" of his inner nature—like the auras depicted around Jesus, the Buddha, and other "enlightened" beings. And, as such, Los's attributes are patterned on Swedenborg's descriptions of the photodynamics and thermodynamics of a mind-made heaven. "Heaven's light is not a natural light . . . it is a spiritual one" (HH 127). "Heaven's Light is the Divine-True. . . . This light varies according to [an angel's] acceptance of the Divine Truth from the Lord. . . . Light among angels corresponds to their intelligence and wisdom" (HH 127, 128, 131).

Los, the Imagination, is the human faculty singularly adapted to perceiving "Divine Truth" and is therefore engulfed in light. Because he is the inner (spiritual) core of the psyche, Los is the embodiment of the innermost core of Swedenborg's heaven, the "celestial kingdom," and he is enshrouded with its special kind of "fiery" light. "The light in the celestial kingdom [highest or innermost heaven] looks fiery, since the angels there accept light directly from the Lord as the sun" (HH 128).

Similarly, Los's flames and blacksmith's forge embody the psycho-logics of Swedenborg's heavenly thermodynamics—they correspond to the fiery intensity of Los's mission: "A person is kindled and warmed in proportion to the extent and quality of his love. . . . That is why love and warmth in heaven correspond to each other" (HH 134, 135). "Heaven's warmth constitutes the life of an angel's intending, since heaven's warmth is the . . . Divine love" (HH 134, 135, 136).

"Heaven's warmth constitutes . . . intending." Throughout Blake's poems, the artist-poet (in the form of Blake, or the blacksmith, Los) invokes the fiery implements of his spiritual "intention":

> *Bring me my Bow of burning gold:*
> *Bring me my Arrows of desire:*
> *Bring me my Spear: O clouds unfold!*
> *Bring me my Chariot of fire!*
>
> (M 1:9–12; E 95)

And, in the next stanza, Blake clearly states the goal of his fiery intention:

> *I will not cease from Mental Fight,*
> *Nor shall my Sword sleep in my hand:*
> *Till we have built Jerusalem*
> *In Englands green & pleasant Land.*
>
> (M 1:13–16)

Because Los, the Imagination, is the most appropriate "mental warrior" to champion the New Jerusalem, he is clad in the armour of this crusade: he is light-enveloped and totally naked, as are the angels of Swedenborg's inmost heaven:

FIG. 155. *Jerusalem and Vala, from* Jerusalem, *1804–20*

"The clothes angels wear correspond to their intelligence. . . . The most intelligent have clothes that gleam as if aflame. The angels of the inmost heaven, though, are naked" (HH 178). "The angels of the inmost heaven," the living powers at the core of the psyche, are naked truths. Blake concurred: "Art can never exist without Naked Beauty displayed. . . . The Eternal Body of Man is The Imagination (Los)" (LAOC; E 273–74).

Similarly, Blake depicted Jerusalem, that innermost of the inmost aspects of the psyche, as a lovely naked figure (sometimes with butterfly wings), and defined her in terms strikingly parallel to Swedenborg's vision of the gleaming light which clothes the angels in enlightenment.

> *In Great Eternity, every particular Form gives forth or Emanates*
> *Its own peculiar Light, & the Form is the Divine Vision*
> *And the Light is his Garment   This is Jerusalem in every Man.*
>
> (J 54:1–3; E 203)

In contrast, Blake's earth goddess, Vala, is depicted veiled, because she is emblematic of those natural realities which can be an occluding veil over spiritual truths—a shell which is shattered on Los's forge, so that the inner light of correspondences can be revealed.

Jerusalem's champion, Los, plays a unique role in this cosmic scheme. He is Imagination, the ultimate power in a mind-made universe. As such, he can boast, *"Both time and space obey my will"* (M 22:17, E 117).

Time and space obey Los's will in Blake's poems according to the principle governing heaven and hell in Swedenborg's vision: "Outward elements correspond to their inward ones" (HH 173).

Both Blake and Swedenborg had confirmed this principle through their visionary experiences. The space they entered did not conform to any present Cartesian grids; for in a psychological universe, space is organic.

> *The Microscope knows not of this nor the Telescope. They alter*
> *The ratio of the Spectators Organs but leave Objects untouched*
> *For every Space larger than a red Globule of Mans blood*
> *Is visionary: and is created by the Hammer of Los*
> *And every Space smaller than a Globule of Mans blood opens*
> *Into Eternity of which this vegetable Earth is but a shadow.*
>
> (M 29:17–22; E 127)

Psychological space is fluid; it warps to correspond to its mental prototypes: "This can be understood more clearly by considering a man's thoughts, in that spaces do not exist for them. For whatever a person earnestly gives his mental attention to becomes, so to speak, present to him" (HH 196).

This is the space that Swedenborg experienced in his visions of heaven: "Angels have no concept of place or space. . . . There are no spaces in heaven except states that correspond to inner ones" (HH 191, 193). Under these circumstances, the paranormal becomes the normal, and psychokinesis or mental teleportation are common occurrences: "All journeys in the spiritual world are simply changes of state . . . nearnesses are similarities, and distances, dissimilarities. . . . Consequently, people who are in dissimilar states are far apart" (HH 192–93).

With devastating poetic flair, Blake applied Swedenborg's model to the spaces of his own narrative of eternal happenings: When Blake's Giant Forms argue, their "dissimilarities" of opinion cause a corresponding rending apart in the mountains of Eternity—a great hemorrhage in the visionary "Globule of Mans blood":

> Rage, fury, intense indignation
> In cataracts of fire blood and gall
> In whirlwinds of sulphurous smoke. . . .
> Sund'ring, dark'ning, thund'ring!
> Rent away with a terrible crash
> Eternity roll'd wide apart
> Wide asunder rolling
> Mountains all around
> Departing; departing; departing;
> Leaving ruinous fragments of life
> Hanging frowning cliffs & all between
> An ocean of voidness unfathomable.
>
> (UR 4:45–5:11; E 72–73)[32]

In the mind-shaped spaces of Blake's prophetic books and Swedenborg's heaven, thoughts can and do move mountains; "for whatever a person earnestly gives his mental attention to, becomes . . . present to him" (HH 196).

Psychological time is also a function of internal states; as Los declared: "Both Time and Space obey my Will."

Swedenborg showed that common sense demonstrates the mechanisms of mind-made time. "People are aware that time originates in states, because times . . . seem short when people are engaged in happy or pleasant affections, long when they are engaged in unpleasant or disagreeable ones" (HH 168). The same principle applies in the afterlife, but in a more pervasive manner: "Angels do not know what time is. . . . there are no years or days in heaven, but changes of state" (HH 163). In the eternal, timeless realm of heaven, the ticking of the clock corresponds to the tempo of the heart—time slows or quickens as feelings drop or rise.

Blake's alter ego, Los, is an extension of Swedenborg's paradigm of the heavenly pendulum: When Los is exercising his true talents, performing useful deeds as a spiritual poet-artist, time corresponds to his inner state of heaven, and his great task is accomplished in a densely packed instant—the creative flash:

> Every Time less than a pulsation of the artery
> Is equal in its period & value to Six Thousand Years.
> For in this Period the Poets Work is Done: and all Great

> Events of Time start forth & are conceivd in such a Period
> Within a Moment: a Pulsation of the Artery.
>
> (M 28:62–29:3; E 127)

When Los's arteries pulse to a different beat, time will assume a correspondingly altered tempo. In *The Book of Urizen*, when Los has captured his enemy Urizen (Reason) and bound him in chains, Los is suddenly overcome with pity: "He saw Urizen deadly black / In his chains bound, & Pity began" (13:50–51). As the space about them freezes into an image of Los's inner state, Los stands transfixed in time:

> Ages on ages rolld over them
> Cut off from life & light frozen
> Into horrible forms of deformity
>
> (UR 13:41–43; E 77)

Los is no longer master of time and space. His inner state, "Cut off from life & light," no longer corresponds to heaven. His inward realities externalize, "frozen into horrible forms of deformity," indicative of a state Swedenborg called "hell"—the psychological domain of Los's arch-foe, Urizen.

Urizen, whose name seems to be a pun on "Your Reason,"[33] haunted Blake's life. He was probably that terrifying face of God that set the four-year-old Blake screaming after his first visionary experience.[34] He was among the most pervasive images in Blake's art, from his sketchy prototype in Blake's first relief-engraved book[35] till his apotheosis in the last painting Blake completed before his death.[36] The myth of Urizen and his mental wars with Los was the focus of Blake's 1784 *Book of Urizen*, and remained a dominant theme in subsequent narrative poems.

On first impression, Urizen, unlike the fiery Los, seems a goodly, if not godly, sort. Venerable, white bearded, and white robed, he looks like a Sunday school picture of God—and it was precisely that mistaken image of God that Blake was refuting with this figure. Urizen is Reason; unfeeling, law-bound Reason. He is the deity of the materialistic philosophers of the Age of Reason, and is the impotent, aging icon of those churches Swedenborg condemned for teaching people that they "are sanctified if only they fold their hands and look upwards, and utter some customary form of prayer" (AR 263).

Urizen is not a philosophical metaphor, he is a living psychological reality. He is that aspect of mind that sets limits and draws boundaries. His razor-edged mental matrices slice life into tiny fragments, to be weighed, measured, and evaluated according to a ledger of his own design, while the living essence escapes his notice. He formulates the doctrines, codes, and laws that impose a thick, occluding veil over naked truths. He darkens what is bright, chills what is warm.

Urizen is not inherently evil, however: Reason is an indispensable function of mind, one of the fundamental Four

FIG. 156. *Title page from* The (First) Book of Urizen, *1794*

Zoas. Urizen becomes dangerous and destructive when individuals or societies elevate him to the throne of the one true god, as was done in the Age of Reason (and, to a large extent, in our own century).

As supreme deity, as ruler of consciousness, Urizen creates those "-isms" that close the doors of perception and enslave people into myopic "-ists." Then Urizen (Reason) will trample creativity and Imagination (Los), ban his books, censor his thoughts, and bind his aspirations

> *In chains of the mind locked up*
> *Like fetters of ice shrinking together.*

> (UR 10:25–26; E 75)

This is dramatized in Blake's myth when Urizen appears before Los, and "Thus Urizen spoke collected in himself in awful pride":

> *Obey my voice young Demon*
> *I am God from eternity to eternity*

> (FZ I, 12:22–23; E 307)[37]

Urizen (Reason) deified will invert the positions of heaven

and hell, casting the Spiritual Faculty (Los) into the role of a rebellious "Demon." In trying to reshape reality to his matrix, Urizen's own demonic "awful pride" creates a living hell, as he was warned by the Daughters of Albion:

> *O Urizen! Creator of Men! Mistaken demon of Heaven:*
> *Thy joys are tears! thy labour vain, to form men in thine image.*

> (VDA 5:3–4; E 48)

Their cries seem an echo of Swedenborg's similar cautioning about the dangers of losing sight of inner (spiritual) realities, and vainly attempting to "form men in [the] image" of a religion predicated on Reason alone:

> Intellectual faith . . . is to see falsities for truths and evils for goods. The fire that kindles that light is the love of self and the conceit therefrom of one's own intelligence.
>
> So far as one excels in ingenuity, he is able to rationalize anything he wants. . . . This is especially so when any given dogma is assumed as the very truth . . . and confirmed to be so only by *reasonings*. . . . A man who looks at all the dogmas of his religion this way may assume whatever principle he wants, and by the light of confirmation make it appear to be a truth from heaven, although it is *a falsity from hell.* (emphases Bellin's; AE 846)

The deified Urizen is also the high priest of his own religion founded on the "falsities of hell" (i.e., on dogmas that do not correspond to psychological realities). He is that demonic holy man who sets the impetus for holy wars and Inquisitions; that Satanic architect of vast prisons for those who do not conform to the religious, racial, or political norms of his codes. Blake's *Book of Urizen* is "the dark vision of torment . . . of the primeval Priests assum'd power (UR 2:7, 1; E 70).

Blake's "dark vision" seems to parallel another of Swedenborg's cautionings: "Priests ought not to claim for themselves any power over the souls of men. Still less ought they to claim the powers of opening and shutting heaven."[38]

It is the state of hell, rather than that of heaven, that opens in Blake's depiction of Urizen's empire. It is a seemingly paradoxical hell, however: Rather than a glowing scorching landscape of fire and brimstone, hotter than the hinges of hell, Urizen's realm is a "ninefold darkness" (UR 3:9) . . . "where winter beats incessant" (BA 2:23–24). Here Urizen assembles his icy intellectual powers:

> *His cold horrors silent, dark Urizen*
> *Prepar'd. . . .*
> *In his hills of stor'd snow; in his mountains*
> *Of hail & ice; voices of terror*
> *Are heard. . . .*

> (UR 3:27–33; E 71)

Such are the seasons of Urizen, which could be a page from Swedenborg's almanac of the mind-made seasons of

Eternity, where ". . . Anything temporal in phenomenon on a man's level are changed into a concept of state. . . . Spring and morning are changed into a concept of love and wisdom as in the first state of angels . . . *night and winter* to a concept of *conditions prevailing in hell*" (emphases Bellin's; HH 166).

"Night and winter," the "conditions prevailing in hell," become the "ninefold darkness" . . . "where winter beats incessant" in the mind-made hell of Urizen. Just as Blake seems to have patterned the bright and fiery state of his hero Los, on the psycho-logics of Swedenborg's vision of heaven, so too he seems to have derived the dark and wintery state of his mythic villain Urizen from Swedenborg's vision of hell.

From the top of his snowy-white mane to the hem of the quasi-biblical white robe, which almost invariably covers his nakedness, Urizen seems to correspond to Swedenborg's vision of persons in hell who "run away from heaven's light and plunge into their own light" (HH 553). Urizen is cut off from heaven's light (psychological truths). In his cavern of wintery darkness, he tries to discover truths through his own light—through his own "infernal method," the scientific method of Experience, Geometry, and (his own) Faculty of Reasoning:

> *He form'd a line & a plummet*
> *To divide the abyss beneath.*
> *He form'd a dividing rule:*
> *He formed scales to weight;*
> *He formed massy weights;*
> *He formed a brazen quadrant;*
> *He formed golden compasses*
> *And began to explore the Abyss.*

(UR 20:33–40; E 80–81)

Despite his many cleverly fashioned probes, Urizen (Reason) cannot pierce the ninefold darkness of his abyss, for his wintery hall lacks the fiery light of the "celestial kingdom," which illuminates the realm of Los (Imagination). Filtered through the cold metallic glow of Reason, the fiery light of Divine Truths (spiritual-psychological realities) becomes distorted or invisible. Reason can only discern those literal, quantifiable facts (natural realities) which are visible to the silicon eyes of binary logic in the cold glow of a computer screen. As Swedenborg explained:

> True things outside heaven are not radiant the way things within the heavens are. True things outside the heavens have *a cold radiance*, like something *snow-white* without warmth. This is because they do not draw their essential substance from what is good [loving] the way true elements within heaven do. (emphases Bellin's; HH 132]

Blake's snow-white Urizen embodies, corresponds to, this loveless knowledge of "true things outside heaven"; yet he will not be dissuaded from his myopic quest to impose himself as "God from Eternity to Eternity." The fire that burns

FIG. 157. The Ancient of Days *(Urizen), frontispiece from* Europe a Prophecy, *1794*

within Urizen's icy bosom, unlike the divinely inspired flames that warm Los's forge, rages from a demonic need to elevate himself at the expense of others. Urizen's fire corresponds to what Swedenborg deemed "hellfire":

> There is warmth in the hells, too. . . . Warmth in heaven is what is meant by "holy and heavenly fire," while warmth of hell is what is meant by "hellfire." Each one refers to love— heavenly fire to love for the Lord and love toward one's neighbor . . . while *hellfire refers to love of self* and love of the world. (emphasis Bellin's; HH 134)

The "hellfire" within Urizen leads to that "vision of dark torment" that is his myth. "The Lord does not cast anyone into hell, each individual casts himself in," Swedenborg explains (HH 548). Swedenborg's hell corresponds to a torment that is born of love of self—that torment of an ego that never can be satisfied, which becomes a self-enclosed horror, cut off from others, alone, unnurtured. It is precisely this sort of self-made "Demon" that Urizen has become at the beginning of Blake's *Book of Urizen*:

Lo, a shadow of horror is risen
In Eternity! Unknown, unprolific!
Self-clos'd, all-repelling: what Demon
Hath form'd this abominable void
This soul-shudd'ring vacuum!—Some said
"It is Urizen", But unknown, abstracted
Brooding secret, the dark power hid.

(UR 3:1–7; E 70)

Blake's Urizen, a dark "shadow of horror," is also a very clear mirror of Swedenborg's vision of the self-made demons of hell, a state in which

. . . all of them are reflections of their own hell. . . . Each is a model of his own evil quality . . . they are forms of contempt for other people and menace for people who do not pay them homage . . . their faces are frightful . . . their bodies grotesque . . . All of them [correspond to] forms of self-love and love of the world. (HH 553–54)

The psychological monsters born of Urizen's self-love take form, and he codifies them into a book of laws written in metal—the new bible of his self-made hell. With consummate pride, he announces to all Eternity:

Here alone I in books form'd of metals
Have written the secrets of wisdom
The secrets of dark contemplation
By fightings and conflicts dire,
With terrible monsters Sin-bred:
Which the bosoms of all inhabit;
Seven deadly sins of the soul.

Lo! I unfold my darkness: and on
This rock, place with strong hand the Book
Of eternal brass, written in my solitude.

(UR 4:24–33; E 72)

FIG. 158. *Urizen as skeleton, from* The (First) Book of Urizen, *1794*

Urizen's bible, that "dark contemplation" written in "eternal brass" and placed on rock (Mt. Sinai) by the "strong hand" of Urizen, is what Swedenborg had termed "a picture written in dark colors on a black stone" (TCR 441)—a beknighted religious creed without any basis in spiritual (psychological) realities.

All Eternity recoils when Urizen reveals his metal laws, with their artificial hell of "monsters Sin-bred" and their absurd litany of egocentricity guised as monotheism:

One command, one joy, one desire,
One curse, one weight, one measure
One King, one God, one Law"

(UR 4:38–40; E 72)

As the mountains of Eternity are rent asunder, whirlwinds of Eternal Truths pour down upon Urizen in "cataracts of fire blood & gall (UR 4:46; E 72); and Urizen reacts exactly like those self-condemned to a state of hell in Swedenborg's visions—he flees "in howlings & pangs & fierce madness" (UR 5:24; E 73).

Urizen crumbles, "hoary, age-broke, and aged" (UR 5:26; E 73), and his inward realities materialize about him in corresponding outward form:

And a roof, vast petrific around
On all sides He fram'd: like a womb;
. . . & like a black globe
View'd by sons of Eternity, standing
On the shore of the infinite ocean
Like a human heart struggling & beating
The vast world of Urizen appear'd

(UR 5:28–29, 33–37; E 73)

This image of the "vast world of Urizen, . . . a black globe . . . like a womb," seems to echo Swedenborg's image of "A faith that is like a sterile seed . . . like an egg without a prolific principle" (TCR 441)—a characterization of the sterile moral code of Urizen, which materialized "like a black globe" about this "age-broke" body.

In a grotesque rewriting of Genesis, Los helps the gestating Urizen evolve within his "black globe," until, at length for hatching ripe, Urizen breaks the shell. Urizen awakes and explores his dens. He finds a world teeming with

Portions of life; similitudes
Of a foot, or a hand, or a head
Or a heart, or an eye

(UR 23:4–6; E 81)

like the fragmentary similitudes of life young William Blake had copied at the Urizenic Pars School of Drawing. And like Blake's subsequent art, these fragments coalesced into living forms—the children of Urizen. But Urizen

curs'd
Both sons & daughters; for he saw
That no flesh nor spirit could keep
His iron laws one moment

(UR 23:23–26)

Urizen departed, wandering the heavens "in weeping & pain & woe"; but he left his offspring a dark legacy, born from "the sorrows of Urizens soul":

A cold shadow follow'd behind him
Like a spider's web, moist, cold & dim
Drawing out from his sorrowing soul
The dungeon-like heaven dividing. . . .

Till a Web dark & cold, throughout all
The tormented element stretch'd
From the sorrows of Urizen's soul
And the Web is a Female in embrio
None could break the Web, no wings of fire.

So twisted the cords, & so knotted
The meshes: twisted like to the human brain.

And all call'd it, The Net of Religion.

(UR 25:9–10, 15–22; E 82)

Curiously, Urizen's attempts to create a theology ended where Swedenborg's had begun—at the threshold of the knotted, twisted cords of the human brain. Unlike the threshold of Swedenborg's visionary New Jerusalem, which beckons all with a sign proclaiming NOW IT IS ALLOWABLE, Urizen's Net of Religion closes the threshold of the brain with a "Web dark & cold," which signifies "Thou Shalt not!"—do not enter![39]
Swedenborg's legacy, as reworked by Blake on Los's forge, was intended to "conjoin man to the Lord and open heaven." Urizen's legacy—which remains a reality, and not simply a metaphor—is intended to fetter man to the earth with "mind-forged manacles," by obscuring and closing the channels of correspondences and hiding away the ever-present Jerusalem from the children of Urizen:

No more could they rise at will
In the infinite void, but bound down
To earth by their narrowing perceptions

They lived a period of years
Then left a noisom body
To the jaws of devouring darkness

(UR 25:45–28:3; E 83)

The legacy of Reason-made beliefs is that of a dark and hopeless, mind-made hell.

FIG. 159. *Albion on a hill, from* Jerusalem, *1804–20*

"The Dark Religions Are Departed"

Awake! awake O sleeper of the land of shadows, wake! expand!
I am in you and you in me, mutual in love divine. . . .

(J 4:6–7; E 146)

Blake's myth did not end with the children of Urizen permanently ensnared in his Net of Religion until each died into the "jaws of devouring darkness." Blake reworked the myth for many years, and late in his life he was able to portray a resolution to the struggle between Reason and Imagination within the Universal Man, who awakens in psychological wholeness to restore his Divine Vision, Jerusalem.

Perhaps somewhere within Blake there was a similar Jerusalem, a hidden bright Emanation he had found in his youth, when he had needed her most. Despite the occasional "opposition" he voiced against her, the richly hued patterns of her wings seem to have cast their colors brightly across the pages of his books throughout his adult life.

Ultimately, the degree to which Swedenborg had influenced Blake is less important than the degree to which their individual visions and missions had corresponded. Each, without support or affirmation from any secular or religious power, without any expectation of reward, chose to devote his life, talents, and wealth to a revolutionary and revelatory "great task." Perhaps in our own Age of Reason there remains something to be learned from a Swedish scientist who saw angels, and a British poet-artist who saw every species of visionary creature. Perhaps in our own all-too-infrequent moments of inward attention, after the noise is temporarily stilled, we too can sense dim reflections of something they had seen glowing bright with promise.

At the height of his scientific career, Swedenborg wrote, "If the principles I have advocated have more truth in them than those which are advocated by others . . . I shall gain the assent of those who are able to distinguish what is true from what is untrue; if not in the present, then in some future age" (PRIN vol. 2, Appendix; pp. 365–66).

It is therefore fitting that Swedenborg made one of the most eloquent summaries of his life's work to a representative of a future age—a child. After he became famous for his visionary experiences of heaven and hell, a neighbor's daughter repeatedly asked Swedenborg to teach her how to see angels. He finally consented. Swedenborg brought her into his garden to a small cottage that housed his library, and requested that she stand before a curtain drawn across a wall. "Now you shall see an angel," Swedenborg proclaimed, as he drew aside the curtain. Behind the curtain was a mirror in which the girl saw herself reflected (DOC vol. 2, pp. 724–25).[40]

Blake too knew the redeeming powers of Imagination in drawing aside curtains. At the end of an immense epic poem written in his private notebook, Blake evoked Urthona (the "earth-owner"),[41] the ultimate creative power of Imagination, of whom Los is but a spectre, to arise in "the golden armour of science / For intellectual War,"[42] as a new age dawns:

The Sun has left his blackness and found a fresher morning
And the mild moon rejoices in a clear & cloudless night
And Man walks forth from midst of the fires the evil is all consumd

. . . & one Sun
Each morning like a New born Man issues with songs & Joy

. . . & Urthona rises from the ruinous walls
In all his ancient strength to form the golden armour of science
For intellectual War The War of swords departed now
The dark Religions are departed & sweet Science reigns.

End of the Dream

(FZ 138:20–28, 139:7–10; E 406–7)[43]

Perhaps Swedenborg was evoking that same "sweet Science" at the conclusion of his own book on heaven and hell: "Anything which is loved brings light with it into the mind's concepts—especially when what is true is loved, for everything true is in the light" (HH 603).

"If not in the present, then in some future age. . . ."

Abbreviations

Quotations from Blake's writings are taken from *The Complete Poetry and Prose of William Blake*, ed. David V. Erdman, rev. ed. (Garden City, N.Y.: Anchor Books, 1982), which was first published by Doubleday in 1965 under the title *Poetry and Prose of William Blake*. References are cited by plate number and line (for engraved poems) or page number and line (for manuscripts and letterpress books), followed by the letter *E* and Erdman's page number. Titles of Blake's works are abbreviated according to the following list:

BA   *The Book of Ahania* (1795)
EG   *The Everlasting Gospel* (c. 1818)
FZ   *Vala, or The Four Zoas* (1795–1804)
GP   *For the Sexes: The Gates of Paradise* (c. 1818)
J   *Jerusalem* (1804–20)
LAOC   *Laocoön plate* (c. 1820)
LD   *The Land of Dreams* (c. 1800–04)
M   *Milton, a Poem in 2 Books* (1804–08)
MHH   *The Marriage of Heaven and Hell* (c. 1790–93)
NNR   *There is No Natural Religion* and *All Religions are One* (c. 1788)
UR   *The (First) Book of Urizen* (1794)
VDA   *Visions of the Daughters of Albion* (1793)
VLJ   *A Vision of the Last Judgment* (1810)

Notes

1. As described by Blake's Victorian biographer, Alexander Gilchrist, in *The Life of William Blake*, 2 vols. (London and Cambridge: Macmillan, 1863), vol. 1, p. 7.

2. For an account of the 1789 General Conference and the theological propositions adopted by its participants, please see the excerpt from Hindmarsh's *Rise and Progress of the New Jerusalem Church* reprinted in the "Historical Contexts" section of Harvey F. Bellin and Darrell Ruhl, eds., *Blake and Swedenborg: Opposition Is True Friendship* (New York: Swedenborg Foundation, 1985).

3. From Blake's annotations to DLW 220 (E 605).

4. For a complete discussion of Blake's changing relationship to Swedenborg's writings and to the early New Jerusalem Church, please see Paley's "A New Heaven Is Begun: Blake and Swedenborgianism" in Bellin and Ruhl; reprinted from *Blake: An Illustrated Quarterly* 12 (1979), no. 2, pp. 64–90.

5. For a detailed analysis of Swedenborg's influences on Blake's early works, please see Raine's "The Swedenborgian Songs" in Bellin and Ruhl.

6. Please see Deck's "New Light on C. A. Tulk, Blake's 19th Century Patron" in Bellin and Ruhl.

7. Please see Gilchrist's excerpt in the "Historical Contexts" section of Bellin and Ruhl for an amusing speculation about Blake and Swedenborg having "met unwittingly in London streets."

8. *Principia* is volume one of Swedenborg's three-volume *Opera Philisophica et Mineralia*, a wide-ranging philosophical/scientific study of solar and stellar vortices, mechanisms of magnetism, origins of planetary systems, fire, and so forth, which he published in Dresden and Leipzig in 1734. Quotations from *Principia* are taken from Rev. Augustus Clissold's translation (London, 1846), as reprinted by the Swedenborg Scientific Association (Bryn Athyn, Pa., 1976).

9. Reprinted from Albert Einstein's *Ideas and Opinions*, ed. Carl Seeling (New York: Dell, 1973), pp. 49–50, 53, 55, by permission of The Crown Publishing Group; copyright © 1954, Crown Publishing, Inc.

10. Swedenborg, *Journal of Dreams*, trans. J. J. G. Wilkinson (1860), ed. William Ross Woofenden (New York: Swedenborg Foundation, 1977), pp. 5, 6. This private journal of 104 pages, which Swedenborg wrote in Swedish during his critical transitional period of 1743–44, was never intended for the public and had remained unknown until the Royal Library in Stockholm purchased the original manuscript in October 1858. Paragraph num-

bers cited in this essay are for the 1977 edition.

11. C. G. Jung, as quoted in *Tribute to Emanuel Swedenborg*, ed. Howard Miller, 2nd. ed. (Boston: New Church Union, 1980), p. 6.

12. Reprinted by permission of the publisher from *The Collected Works of C. G. Jung*, trans. R. F. C. Hull, Bollingen Series XX, vol. 12, *Psychology and Alchemy* (Princeton, N.J.: Princeton University Press, 1968), pp. 10–13. Copyright © 1953 by Princeton University Press.

13. Reprinted by permission of the publisher from Czeslaw Milosz's *The Land of Ulro*, trans. Louis Iribarne (New York: Farrar, Straus and Giroux, 1981, 1984).

14. From Blake's letter of August 23, 1799, to Rev. Dr. Trusler (E 702).

15. From the Declaration of Independence, adopted by the Continental Congress of the United States of America on July 4, 1776.

16. From the diaries of Henry Crabb Robinson, reprinted in G. E. Bentley, Jr., *Blake Records* (Oxford: Clarendon, 1969); also cited in Michael Davis, *William Blake, A New Kind of Man* (Berkeley and Los Angeles: University of California Press, 1977), pp. 158–59, and elsewhere.

17. Citing specific quotations from Blake's unpublished, much-reworked manuscript *Vala, or The Four Zoas* is, as always, a complex Urizenic tangle. As is the case in the other Blake quotation cited herein, this is taken from Erdman's 1982 edition of *Complete Poetry*, in which these lines represent "Night the Second" (II), page 35, lines 11–13, as reprinted on page 325 of Erdman (E 325). These same lines in the *Blake Concordance* of 1968 and in the various editions of Keynes (K) represent "Night the Third," lines 397–99 (III, 397–99) in the pagination scheme used by Keynes in his many anthologies of Blake's works.

18. Cyriel Odhner Sigstedt, *The Swedenborg Epic* (London: Swedenborg Society, 1981), pp. 269–70.

19. As reported in Tafel's *Documents*, and retold in Cyriel Odhner Sigstedt's classic biography, *The Swedenborg Epic* (London: Swedenborg Society, 1981), pp. 387–409.

20. Revelation 21: 1–2, 5.

21. As evidenced in MHH 3: "As a new heaven is begun, and it is not thirty-three years since its advent." Please see Paley, "A New Heaven Is Begun: Blake and Swedenborgianism," in Bellin and Ruhl, and in *Blake: An Illustrated Quarterly*.

22. "Science" in this context is not that materialistic pursuit of the Newtonian Age, which

Blake so frequently condemned; rather it is that "sweet Science" (FZ IX, 139:10; E 407) of essential wisdom, as derived from the Latin root *scientia*, "to know." Please see S. Foster Damon, *A Blake Dictionary* (Boulder, Col.: Shambala, 1979), pp. 359–60, for an exposition of Blake's two contrary meanings of the word *science*.

23. Letter to T. Butts. Although Blake has himself dated this letter "Jan. 10, 1802," Erdman's *Complete Poetry* (E 723–24) dates the letter as Jan. 10, 180*3*, based on evidence in E. B. Murray's "A Suggested Redating of a Blake Letter to Thomas Butts," in *Blake: An Illustrated Quarterly* 13 (1979–80), pp. 148–51.

24. For an excellent study of Blake's graphic arts techniques, please see Robert N. Essick's *William Blake, Printmaker* (Princeton, N.J.: Princeton University Press, 1980).

25. As described by Gilchrist, vol. 1, p. 69.

26. Please see Raine, "The Swedenborgian Songs," in Bellin and Ruhl.

27. Please see also Paley, "A New Heaven Is Begun," in Bellin and Ruhl.

28. See also J 26; E 171. Quotations from *Jerusalem* are taken from Erdman's *Complete Poetry* (1982 edition), and follow the pagination of chapter 2 in copies A, C, and F of *Jerusalem*, which differs from the arrangement in the text of Geoffrey Keynes, based on copies D and E. (Various copies of *Jerusalem* in different collections and museums are designated by the letters *A* to *F*.)

29. *Jerusalem*'s relationship to Albion in Blake's mythos is fairly complex. Generally, in the poem that bears her name she is seen as Albion's Emanation (his bright female portion; or in Jungian terms, his "anima"). However, when Albion fell into self-division, his wife Brittannia "divided into Jerusalem and Vala" (the earth goddess) (J 36:26). In Blake's unpublished poem *Vala, or The Four Zoas*, she is the daughter of Albion and Brittannia. She is also the chosen wife of Jesus, as foretold in Revelation 21; and in this context, Albion takes Vala as his wife (J 20:40, 63:7, 64:19, 65:71; K). When Albion falls into his deadly sleep, he hides Jerusalem away from Jesus and loses his own Divine Vision (J 4:33). The drama of the poem *Jerusalem* is the struggle to restore her.

For a more complete discussion of these complex relationships, please see Damon, pp. 9–13, 206–13.

30. Ibid., pp. 246–53, for a detailed definition of Los, the hero of Blake's mythos.

31. Blake's term *Zoa* seems to derive from a Greek plural word used to describe the four beings

seen in John's apocalyptic vision (Revelation 4:6), and in Ezekiel's vision by the river Chebar (Ezekiel 1:5 ff). *Zoas* is often translated as "beasts," but a more appropriate choice would be "living creatures." In this context Blake uses the term to describe the four essential aspects of man, in a manner foreshadowing the writings of Jung. For a full discussion of the Four Zoas and their meanings, please see Damon, pp. 458–60.

32. Blake's 1794 *The (First) Book of Urizen*, was republished under the title *The Book of Urizen*, after he had found alternate titles for his books that continued the Urizen myth.

33. For definitions of Urizen's name and details of his myth, please see Damon, pp. 419–26.

34. According to a Feb. 2, 1852, entry in Henry Crabb Robinson's *Reminiscences* (London, 1869), Blake's wife, Catherine, said to Blake: "You know dear, the first time you saw God was when you were four years old, and he put his head to the window and set you a'screaming."

35. A compass-wielding, crawling, proto-Urizenic figure appears on the "Application" page of Blake's *There is No Natural Religion*, which together with his *All Religions are One*, constituted Blake's first use of his relief-printing process (c. 1788).

36. Shortly before his death, the bedridden Blake painted one last print of "The Ancient of Days," the frontispiece of his book, *Europe, a Prophecy*, which depicts Urizen measuring the heavens with a giant metal compass. As reported by Gilchrist (vol. 1, pp. 359–60), this image was "a singular favorite with Blake and one it was always a happiness to him to copy."

37. This quotation is i:319–20 in Keynes.

38. Compressed from Swedenborg's AC 10, 789, as reprinted in *A Compendium of Swedenborg's Theological Writings*, ed. Samuel M. Warren (New York: Swedenborg Foundation, 1974 reprinting of 1875 edition), p. 431.

39. In his *Song of Experience*, "The Garden of Love," Blake writes of a chapel built in his garden where he used to "play on the green. / And the gates of this Chapel were shut, / And Thou Shalt not. writ over the door" (SE 44:4–6; E 26).

40. This anecdote about Swedenborg's young neighbor Greta Askbom, was related by historian Anders Fryxell.

41. For a definition of Urthona, please see Damon, pp. 426–27.

42. Please see note 19, concerning Blake's definitions of "science."

43. These lines are equivalent to FZ ix:25–33 and 52–55 in Keynes.

Psyche in Stone
The Influence of Swedenborg on Funerary Art

H. W. Janson, Ph.D.

FIG. 160. Thine Is the Kingdom, *by John Flaxman, early 1800s*

Professor H. S. JANSON (1913–1982) received his M.A. from Harvard University in 1938 and his Ph.D. in 1942. From 1949 to 1975 he was chairman of the Department of Fine Arts at New York University as well as Professor Emeritus from 1972 to 1982. Janson was also professor at the Institute of Fine Arts. His *Key Monuments of the History of Art* (1959) and *History of Art* (1962; extensively revised in 1969) are university standards.

This essay was originally presented as a slide lecture, "The Influence of Swedenborg on Funerary Art," at the annual meeting of the Swedenborg Foundation, 10 May 1982. It subsequently appeared in abbreviated form—transcribed and edited by Robin Larsen and Kate Davis—as "Psyche in Stone" in the introductory issue (Winter 1985) of *Chrysalis*, the journal of the Swedenborg Foundation. The lecture is printed here in its entirety by the gracious permission of Mrs. Janson, and with the assistance of the Department of Fine Arts of New York University and the Institute of Fine Arts.

I CANNOT TELL YOU what a pleasure it is for me to speak on this subject, namely, the influence of Swedenborg's doctrine on funerary art, to an audience that does not require me to tell them who Swedenborg was and what his thoughts on many spiritual matters were. I can take all this for granted. What I cannot take for granted, of course, is your familiarity with the particular monuments that I shall discuss. And while the main subject of my talk will be those funerary monuments that are based on Swedenborgian ideas, I feel I should give you a bit of background to serve as perspective on the problem of the human soul—not, of course, the theological problems, as I am not equipped to discuss that, but as a problem of visual representation.

How has the human soul been represented in art and when did the influence of Swedenborg make itself felt in this particular domain? Now we could carry this subject all the way back to the ancient Egyptians, when the earliest images of the human soul arose. I will content myself with telling you that the Egyptians visualized the soul as images of two kinds: either as a human-headed bird or as a shadow; that is, as simply a two-dimensional projection of the human figure of the deceased, life-sized without internal design and, of course, without any three-dimensional existence.

Let me begin rather at a somewhat later time, with the Greeks and the Romans, because our civilization owes a great deal to the heritage of the Greeks and the Romans. How did they visualize the human soul? In the *Prometheus Sarcophagus* we have a characteristic example of a Roman sarcophagus. The Romans practiced both inhumation—meaning they buried the bodies in strong containers known as sarcophagi—and cremation, which does not concern us at the moment. What is interesting for us is the way the Romans visualized the human soul. Down in the bottom center of this relief you see a nude man stretched out. That is the deceased, and from him there rises a lightly clad young lady with butterfly wings, who has been taken in hand by a deity, namely Mercury. This young lady with butterfly wings is the soul of the dead man who lies on the ground. The standard image of the soul among the later Greeks and the Romans sometimes is seen abbreviated simply to a butterfly, but more often is a young lady with butterfly wings, because the Greeks and Romans were very fond of personifications. What distinguished this human being as a personification are the butterfly wings, which are specifically attributes of the soul.

If we look at early examples of Christian art, that is, those examples that are still influenced by the pagan heritage of the Greeks and the Romans, we find that this classical image of soul is taken over. An example of this can be found in a Venetian mosaic presentation of the *Animation of Adam*. The Lord has already created Adam, but in this particular image he is animating him. He does so by pushing a smaller but-

FIG. 161. Prometheus Sarcophagus, *drawing after Roman relief*

FIG. 162. Animation of Adam, *drawing after Venetian mosaic*

FIG. 163. Dormition, *the death of Mary, drawing after Byzantine ivory relief*

FIG. 164. The Burial of Count d'Orgaz, *by El Greco, 1586–88*

terfly-wing replica of Adam against the body of Adam, and as the smaller image (which represents the soul) is absorbed by the larger one, Adam comes to life.

This was not a tradition that was acceptable to later Christian art, however, because the four wings implied an independent mobility on the part of the soul. In medieval art, the standard image of the soul is simply a kind of homunculus, that is, a miniature human being that often really looks like a swaddled child. There are medieval tombs about which you can say quite literally that the deceased "gives up the ghost," the ghost being the same as the soul. In a Byzantine *Dormition,* you see it coming out of the mouth, a tiny figure welcomed and physically seized by angels that have descended for this very purpose from on high. If this had been an evil person, then it would be devils who would immediately take the soul off to hell. There are literally thousands of these homunculus representations of the soul in medieval art, always a "babylike image taken to heaven by one or two angels." No one, of course, would want a tomb with the soul being seized by devils, and such a tomb could not have existed on holy ground, so you simply do not see such a one, although theoretically that could be the case. The point is that in the medieval Christian period, the soul does not move

on its own volition; it has to be moved either by angels or devils. And there is no attempt to personalize the soul, to make it look like the deceased. It is always simply an infant or a baby or a kind of a miniature human being with no individual features.

The Burial of Count D'Orgaz, by El Greco, painted about 1586, is probably the last example of the medieval baby-soul image, because by then it had completely gone out of fashion. By the standards of Renaissance art, the idea of showing the soul as a baby or a homunculus seemed incongruous, so it took very extraordinary circumstances to produce such an image at the end of the sixteenth century. One can, of course, say that El Greco was working in Toledo, in Spain, and that he was maybe just being old-fashioned. He did all this on purpose. He knew that Count D'Orgaz had actually been buried in the fourteenth century, two hundred years before the painting was done, and I think he realized that in those days souls were represented by infants. And, as a matter of fact, he has done something quite extraordinary. In the center of the painting is an angel rising from along the crowd of people assembled in the lower half of the picture, where the actual burial takes place. The angel is carrying something up toward heaven that looks like a kind of cloud, but actually

FIG. 165. *Papal tomb design, drawing by B. Bandinelli, early 1500s*

FIG. 166. *Tomb of Mrs. Engelbach, by Landolin Ohmacht, 1796*

is a baby-shaped cloud, or if you prefer, a baby made out of cloud matter, and that is indeed the soul of Count D'Orgaz. You see, El Greco has very cleverly painted not an ordinary baby, but a baby made out of cloud matter, in order to show that it is without substance, that it is a spiritual entity.

But no one followed in his tracks. Instead, the Renaissance tried to invent a new image of the human soul. An early example is the drawing from the early sixteenth century by an Italian sculptor, a proposal for a papal tomb in which the artist tries to launch a new type of image for the human soul, namely, an ideally beautiful nude youth who is full-sized rather than reduced in size, as in the medieval images. At the bottom of the drawing there is the reclining effigy of the body of the Pope, and above him is the standing nude youth in a kind of gloriole, being carried upward to heaven by angels. But this image did not catch on. The tomb was never built, and there are no other images of this sort, apparently because the image of the ideally beautiful nude youth was not sufficiently distinctive: it could be confused with an image of Apollo, or what have you. Actually in the sixteenth, seventeenth, and most of the eighteenth centuries, there is no standard image of the human soul; you can look through all the tombs done during these centuries and see all kinds of interesting things going on in them, but the one thing that did not exist was an image of the human soul.

But all of a sudden, at the end of the eighteenth century, things began to change. First, very briefly, we had a revival of the ancient notion of the butterfly as an image of the soul. In a late-eighteenth-century tomb, quite a pretty one, by a German sculptor for a Mrs. Engelbach, the mother has just died and is reclining in a chair, and her soul, in the shape of a butterfly, has escaped from her mouth and is fluttering in the air. The two little children, who do not understand what is going on, are really trying to catch this butterfly. It is a charming notion in its own way but obviously not something that could very well become a standard image for the human soul at this time: the butterfly is not a sufficiently monumental creature for such purposes.

The tomb by the English sculptor John Flaxman, made in 1784 as a memorial for Mrs. Morley is, on the other hand, something that we have not seen before, ever. She is not actually buried there, because she died at sea during childbirth, returning from India; so both she and her child were buried at sea. What Mr. Flaxman chose to represent here was Mrs. Morley rising from the waves, being welcomed by heavenly spirits. This, I think, is the first tomb based on the Swedenborgian conception of the human soul. Because, as I hardly need to tell you, according to Swedenborg, the soul has a shape, and the shape is simply that of the human body. Just as our earthly clothes conform to the shape of the body underneath, so the body, being the garment of the soul, must conform to the shape of the soul. So here you have the

FIG. 167. *Tomb of Sarah Morley, by John Flaxman, 1784*

"Swedenborgian soul" of Mrs. Morley rising from the waves and being welcomed by heavenly spirits.

There are, of course, a great many advantages to this image, because not only did it seem a lot more natural but the whole conception of the soul as laid down in Swedenborg's writings was terribly attractive to the Age of Enlightenment. It seemed eminently more reasonable than what anyone else had said about the soul before. And the endless theological discussions about the soul, which you find in the Middle Ages and the Renaissance, all seemed resolved in the very logical kind of structure that Swedenborg presents in discussing the soul. Not only does he define the fate of the soul, but he also says what the attributes of the soul are, in other words, what aspects of the living person belong to the soul rather than the body. He is the first to tell us, for instance, that all capacity for sense experience belongs to the soul rather than the body and therefore goes along with the soul when the body and soul separate at the moment of death.

Now you might well ask, Why does this idea first make its appearance in England? Well, there is a very good reason: in the eighteenth century, Sweden was not very tolerant in matters religious. Lutheranism was the state religion, and Swedenborg found it impossible to publish his writings in Sweden, so he did so in Holland and London, where they almost immediately attracted the attention of people like William Blake, who was a great friend of John Flaxman. Flaxman, in turn, even illustrated some of Swedenborg's writings, so they were both immediate enthusiasts for the new taste, so to speak.

In fact, during the late years of the eighteenth and the early years of the nineteenth centuries, Swedenborgian societies, or churches, were established throughout the old and the new world. One of the most important American sculptors of the second quarter of the nineteenth century, Hiram Powers, was a Swedenborgian. I myself became acquainted with the writings of Swedenborg by working in the library of the Swedenborgian Society in Zürich, Switzerland, which owns the writings of Swedenborg in at least a dozen different languages (so I had my choice). And they are all beautifully indexed, as you know, so I was able in a comparatively short time to read everything that Swedenborg has to say about the soul simply by looking up the appropriate passages according to available indexes.

Mrs. Morley's tomb was only the first of a long series of very beautiful tombs that John Flaxman made on the same pattern. The next one dates from the late 1790s and is in Chichester Cathedral. In the tomb of another young woman, Agnes Cromwell, she has been taken upward by celestial spirits who have no wings but who are nevertheless clearly

FIG. 168. Deliver Us from Evil, *by John Flaxman, early 1800s*

FIG. 169. *Tomb of Ann Neufville and F. Dwarris, by John Bacon, 1798*

FIG. 170. *Memorial to Admiral Richard Kempenfelt, by John Bacon, 1782*

characterized as celestial spirits. [The same theme is depicted in the bas-relief by Flaxman shown on the first page of this essay. That relief and *Deliver Us from Evil*, shown here, form a pair illustrating angelic and demonic struggles for the soul.] If we have any doubts as to the meaning of these images, we need only point to Flaxman's own drawings, which make the matter very plain indeed. Among a number of similar tomb designs, we find a theme repeated; for example, there is one with the body of the mother on her deathbed, already enshrouded; at one end of the bed her husband is mourning her demise; at the other end are the children. But suddenly an angel materializes pointing upward, and at the very bottom of the drawing, in Flaxman's own handwriting and in quotes, you get the words of the angel: "She is not here, but risen." Now these are almost exactly the same words that according to the Gospels the angel says to the Marys who come on Easter morning to the tomb of Christ. And because, in this case, the body is in plain view, it is obviously the soul that has risen, and in a form that resembles the body because it is a "Swedenborgian soul."

It is surprising how quickly this idea spread to other British sculptors. An interesting example is the tomb of Ann Neufville and F. Dwarris from Kingston, Jamaica. The wealthy planters in Jamaica at the end of the eighteenth century had quite enough money to import the most fashionable tomb monuments from England. This one has a special interest to us because it is a double tomb of a young woman and a middle-aged man. I will not bother you with the names, but you can see that the two souls are very clearly distinguished as to age and sex, because the appearance of the souls has correspondence to the appearance of the bodies.

The memorial in Westminster Abbey, to a British admiral by the name of Kempenfelt, tells with almost mathematical precision the exact moment the division of body and soul occurred. You can see that the admiral went down with his ship, but the ship has not yet hit bottom, because part of it is still above the horizon. Nevertheless, the admiral has already died: you can see him, minus his uniform, making his way upward in the direction of the heavenly spirits that are about to work on him.

Perhaps the most theatrical and elaborate of all these tombs is in St. George's Chapel in Windsor. This very dramatic performance appears in a monument to Princess Charlotte Augusta, who died in childbirth. Because she was a royal princess, very special treatment was called for. The relief depicts her, or rather her soul, making its way upward without angelic assistance. The angels are rather occupied with the child, which is not yet capable of unaided locomotion. The body is merely a shrouded entity in the center, and other shrouded figures are the mourners. The tomb was first exhibited at the Royal Academy in London before it was installed in St. George's Chapel, and we have heard elaborate accounts of thousands of people being moved to tears by this spectacle. Today we tend perhaps to be impressed more by the tremendous display of marble drapery than anything else.

The tomb dated 1871 and made for a Mrs. Montagu is a more modest but also rather later example and shows that the tradition goes right on into the late-nineteenth century. She obviously was not young but middle-aged, and the artist was very careful to characterize her as being exactly the age she was at the time of her death.

The English, then, started this new type of tomb. But within less than twenty years it had established itself on the continent as well. An engraving for the tomb of an Austrian lady by the name of Mrs. Rottman is probably the earliest example on the continent. The great Italian sculptor Canova must have gotten the idea from Flaxman, either directly or indirectly. In any event, Mrs. Rottman is pictured leaving the earth, which is represented by a dark marble sphere; she is made of white marble. Only a few years later, we find the

FIG. 171. *Tomb of Mrs. Montagu, by Edgar Boehm, 1871*

same idea in the Cloisters attached to the Munster at Basel, Switzerland, in the tomb of Suzanna Forcart by an anonymous artist, who nevertheless has done a rather touching job in showing a young mother who obviously died while giving birth to twins. She too is about to lift off from a sphere that represents this earth.

By the middle of the century, the soul often takes flight in an extraordinarily energetic fashion, as in the case with this tomb in the Church of Santa Croce in Florence. Those of you that have been to Florence and have seen the interior of Santa Croce will not remember the tomb, because it has

FIG. 172. *Tomb of Susanna Forcart, anonymous, 1820s*

FIG. 173. *Tomb of Louise Faureau, by F. de Fauveau, 1858*

been banished to the basement. I myself had a very difficult time locating it, but it is actually still there. It is the tomb of a young lady, a French woman by the name of Faureau, and you can see her rising above a view of Florence with extraordinary energy, you might say.

The male counterpart to this soul flight can be seen in a tomb in Florence, for a member of the Poniatowski family, Stanislao Poniatowski, whose flamboyant soul, with some angelic assistance, rises heavenward in a similarly dramatic fashion.

But the man who really popularized this image in Italy was the great Danish sculptor Thorvaldsen. He spent most of his adult life in Rome, where he had a tremendous studio open to all comers and where the original plaster models of all his works were on view. These included a number of "Swedenborgian" tombs, such as the relief on the monument for the Baroness Chandoir. The soul of the deceased clutching a little cross, a sign of her Christianity, is independently rising toward the spheres, while down in the corner the pagan genius of death with his upended torch witnesses her ascent. You can compare this relief with that of an Italian sculptor in the great cemetery at Bologna. In the Colognesi tomb the Italian clearly has derived the main outlines of his image from Thorvaldsen, but he has omitted the pagan genius because it was not compatible with Catholicism.

You might very well ask, Were all these people Swedenborgians? Were they even aware of the fact that this image was invented on the basis of Swedenborg's conception of the soul? The answer obviously is no. In fact, Thorvaldsen was not a Swedenborgian; he was a staunch Lutheran, the only Lutheran sculptor who was ever commissioned to make a papal tomb for St. Peter's. (Of course, the Italian sculptors bitterly resented this for financial as well as religious reasons.) I think apart from the earliest examples, we can say that the image perpetuated itself because of its own internal appeal and not because the people were aware of the Swedenborgian origins of the idea. And this is how it happened that Italian cemeteries are full of images of this sort. They were extremely popular, but we can be equally sure that if it had been known that these were Swedenborgian images, the church would have stepped in immediately and forbidden them. This, however, was not the case.

Sometimes, as in the Ruffa family tomb, you see the image of the deceased hovering over the tomb but with no upward movement at the same time. The artist has managed, rather impressively, to suspend this image of a mother, who again must have died in childbirth, above the sarcophagus. This tomb is also in Bologna.

I must add at this point that there had been a great revolution in what you might call "cemetery sculpture" in the late years of the eighteenth and the early years of the nineteenth centuries, at least on the European continent, and within a few decades, also in this country. Until the late-

FIG. 175. *Tomb of Angela Colognesi, anonymous, 1864*

eighteenth century, people were buried either in the church, that is, under the floor of the church, or in a tiny graveyard attached to the church. But with the expansion of the cities and the increasing prosperity that the Industrial Revolution brought about, the available space simply became insufficient. And people had to be dug up every few years in order to make room for others. Eternal rest could be guaranteed for no more than five years, in most cemeteries. After that, the bones were collected and put together in ossuaries, where they took very much less room. In many cities, such as Paris, it came to a real crisis: the main cemetery in the middle of Paris started polluting the water supply, and at that point the government had to crack down and say no more burials within city limits. So new cemeteries had to be established outside city limits, usually a convenient carriage ride of twenty minutes or so away. By now these cemeteries have all been absorbed because the cities have grown so much since the late-eighteenth century. But because they were not attached

FIG. 176. *Tomb of Ruffa family, anonymous, 1800s*

FIG. 177. *Monument to G. Solari, by F. Fabiani, 1901*

FIG. 178. *Tomb of Giuseppe Benedetto Badaracco, by G. Moreno, 1878*

to churches but laid out as cemeteries on a very large scale, there was much more space than before. And because more people were prosperous and could afford to erect monuments to themselves, the demand for space for such monuments also mounted tremendously, and that accounts for the sheer numerical explosion in cemetery sculpture during the nineteenth century.

But let's get back to some of these Italian cemeteries. On some of these monuments, you can see an angel actually carrying the soul. But mostly the soul manages to make her way upward without such assistance. To create a more dramatic image, the Italian sculptor of the Solari monument has pretended that the soul has cast open the lid of the sarcophagus. Actually, as the photo shows, the sarcophagus is securely closed, but there is a false lid attached to the real lid. If you stand on the floor, where you get a different perspective of the tomb, you should not be able to see that. Instead, it would seem as though the soul had exploded out

of the sarcophagus and is now making her way upward. And what is peculiar here is that the portrait of the deceased, on the side of the sarcophagus, shows clearly a middle-aged gentleman. So his soul does not match his physical appearance. As I said before, because these people really did not know where this whole idea of what you might call the "full-bodied soul" came from, the sculptor probably did not even worry too much about this. The word for *soul* in those Western languages that have genders is always feminine: the personifications and allegories are apt also to be feminine, and anyway, it is more fun to have in this role a lightly clad young lady than an elderly gentleman. There are examples of male souls in Italian cemeteries, such as the Badaracco tomb. You can see that, try as he might, the sculptor has not been able to endow this image with the same kind of sensuous charm that the lightly clad female souls have. So Italian sculptors usually stuck to the female form of the soul and emphasized its miraculous escape from the tightly closed crypt, the way

FIG. 179. *Crypt of Gnecco-Garibaldi, by A. Rota, 1882*

FIG. 180. *Tomb of J. M. Pelton, anonymous, late 1800s or early 1900s*

FIG. 181. *Soul guided by angel, anonymous relief, late 1800s or early 1900s*

the soul sort of oozes between the bronze doors that close the Gnecco-Garibaldi crypt while the family looks on.

Now Italy in the nineteenth century was a great exporter of both sculpture and sculptors, and it was Italian sculptors who carried this Swedenborgian soul image into places it might not have reached by itself. The Pelton tomb is a very nice example from one of the cemeteries in New Orleans. The interesting thing here is that it was not made on the spot: it is actually a cast-iron monument cast in Philadelphia, as the manufacturer's mark down at the bottom will reveal. But the design was surely by an Italian, because it matches very closely the examples we have seen in marble in Italy. Even in small towns in modest cemeteries such as Natchez, Tennessee, you will find the image. Here is a young woman who has died in childbirth and is being guided by an angel, who has taken charge of the infant and is leading the soul of the mother to a heavenly sphere.

In conclusion, I present you a pair of tombs from 1848

and 1849 respectively, in the Wall Street Cemetery in New Haven. The first is the tomb of the Trowbridge twins. Mrs. Trowbridge gave birth to twins, who died at the age of a year and a half. And you see in the main relief how an angel has taken charge of the twins and is comfortably settling them on the little bank of a cloud. Unfortunately, a year later Mrs. Trowbridge herself died, giving birth to another child, and the relief shown in the next figure is her own tomb. An angel guides Mrs. Trowbridge toward heaven, where she is expected by three little children—the twins, bigger because they were born earlier, and the newborn one right in the middle.

These are not necessarily great works of art, but they do tell us a little about the sentiment that motivates this funerary art. The whole tradition is entirely restricted to the nineteenth century; as soon as we hit the years close to 1900 it simply disappeared. The demand disappeared because somehow the reality of the human soul itself had come to be doubted. As soon as that happens then the hope for a life after death tends to collapse; as a result you no longer have monuments of this kind. But during the 120 years or so that this type of tomb can be encountered, in thousands upon thousands of examples both on American and European soils, a Swedenborgian idea has made its way into a very essential place in the imagination of practically everyone, whether or not they had ever heard of Swedenborg.

FIG. 182. *Tomb of Trowbridge twins, anonymous, 1849*

FIG. 183. *Tomb of Jane Trowbridge, anonymous, 1850*

Emerson:
The Swedenborgian and
Transcendentalist Connection

Eugene Taylor

RALPH WALDO EMERSON, son of a long line of New England preachers, was born in a parsonage in Boston, 1803, and grew up in an urban setting still rural enough to walk his mother's cow each morning to graze on the Boston Common. Emerson's father, the Reverend William Emerson, although not well off, was a force in the local intellectual community as a founder of the Boston Athenaeum, member of the Massachusetts Historical Society, and participant in the Physiological Society at the home of Dr. James Jackson. He died in 1811, leaving Mrs. Emerson and her six children bereft of financial support. Despite these limitations, Waldo, as he was then called, successfully passed through Boston Latin School and, with the help of his grandfather, the Reverend Ezra Ripley of Concord, entered Harvard College in 1817. Not so well off as the other students, Emerson had to wait tables in the student dining hall, and he had the added duty of "President's Freshman," a position in which he was responsible for communicating messages from President Kirkland to the first-year students. It was Emerson who was also required to call those duly summoned for infractions. In exchange for these tasks, he received his meals, and lodging in the form of a room over President Kirkland's study.[1]

While time-consuming, these activities put Emerson in contact with every member of his class, and he was soon known throughout the college. Not yet having decided upon a definite vocation, he pursued the regular course of studies, but in a somewhat lackluster fashion. His biographers tell us that he liked to spend most of his time thinking, taking walks, and composing poetry. Oliver Wendell Holmes's brother, John, later remembered Emerson as quiet, unobtrusive, only a fair scholar, but every inch a king in his dominion.

During Emerson's freshman year, a Swedenborgian study group flourished among a few Harvard students who were his acquaintances and who were destined to play a role in providing what was perhaps the first literary impulse to Emerson's career. Chief among these were Sampson Reed and Thomas Worcester. Reed, born in Bridgewater, Massachusetts, June 10, 1800, son of Reverend John Reed, was raised on his father's farm and entered Harvard in 1814. During his first year at college, he met Thomas Worcester, because Reed's father was a mutual friend of the Reverend Pitt Clark, to whom Worcester had previously been apprenticed. As freshmen, Worcester and Reed occupied rooms in the same private residence near President Kirkland's house, and they became college roommates the following year, despite a difference in ages—Worcester was nineteen and Reed five years his junior. Both were impoverished students and most of their expenses were paid for by waiting tables at the dining hall, which, by their senior year, put them in contact with Emerson, also working at the same occupation. Like Emerson, they, too, taught school during the winter vacation in order to make ends meet.[2]

Reed was most diligent in his college studies, while Worcester's principal activity was in reading Swedenborg's *Heavenly Doctrines*[3] and in transmitting their content to his fellow Harvard students. A set of Swedenborg's writings had been deposited in the college library in 1794 by the Reverend William Hill, and Worcester had contrived by ingenious means to get his hands on the complete collection. He kept these volumes on his mantel with the permission of President Kirkland for the four years he was a student, and his room quickly became the center of many student discussions and conferences. In addition to Sampson Reed, this circle included

EUGENE TAYLOR is currently associate in psychiatry at Harvard Medical School, consultant in the history of psychiatry at the Massachusetts General Hospital, and author of *William James on Exceptional Mental States* (New York: Scribner's, 1982).

Thomas B. Hayward, John H. Wilkins, Nathaniel Hobart, Caleb Reed, Warren Goddard, and Theophilus Parsons. Reed and Worcester graduated in the class of 1818, when Emerson was beginning his sophomore year. Both immediately enrolled in the theological school, which at that time had not yet attained an independent status from the college. One merely stayed on in the capacity of what was called a "Resident Graduate," to read for the ministry.

It was also at this time that the nucleus of the first Boston Swedenborgian Society was formed in Cambridge at the boardinghouse of Mrs. Thomazine E. Minot, who had set up housekeeping in hopes of furthering the work of the church among Harvard students. Worcester, Reed, and others found it a congenial home and religious center while pursuing their ministerial studies. Other interested persons also gathered there to read Swedenborg's works, and out of these meetings twelve people constituted the original founding body of the First Swedenborgian Church in Boston, still situated downtown on Bowdoin Street. In 1821 this society officially asked Thomas Worcester to become their pastor, and he accepted. Worcester married that same year, and Mrs. Minot, seeing that her work in Cambridge had come to an end, moved her home to Boston, which then provided living facilities for the new parson and his new wife. Sampson Reed and his classmate, John H. Wilkins, left their theological studies to join the activities of the new church. Reed became a teacher for a short time, while Wilkins published a small book on astronomy, the success of which soon led him into the book business.

The previous August, 1821, Reed had received a Master of Arts degree at Harvard, and at that time, he delivered a speech at the commencement ceremonies entitled "Oration on Genius." Emerson, just completing his Bachelor of Arts degree, participated in the ceremony as Class Day Poet, after seven before him had declined the invitation. He was present in the audience when Reed gave his oration and was greatly pleased by the speech. The commencement audience found it tedious, because, as one auditor put it, it was so "miserably delivered," but Emerson later referred to it as "native gold," and after the presentation, prevailed upon his brother, William, who was in Reed's class, to borrow the manuscript. Emerson "copied the whole of it and kept it as a treasure."[4] He referred to the work frequently in his journals, and the oration was passed around and discussed freely among Emerson's family.[5] As Perry Miller has described it:

> It was the first admonitory indictment of formalism in the liberal church and pointed the way for an appeal from institutional legalities to a fresh and creative approach to nature; it insinuated that the first requirement would be a rejection of Locke. And then it took as its subject "genius"—with the implication that all who turned to nature could be geniuses. It excited the expectation of a new day, and it did so in an

oracular, cryptic style, such as had not been heard in New England before, no accent of which was lost on the delighted eighteen year old Waldo Emerson.[6]

Love, Reed said in this oration, is the very life of man. The brute depends on physical strength; while the great man depends on society, particularly the state of its arts and sciences. But the spiritual man knows that love and wisdom are from no other source than the Divine. Great men are not more like God than others. But because we believe the opposite, we fall into worshiping other men, rather than the Divine. Divinity shines through man. When we see this, we should rejoice in the truth itself and not rejoice in the mere fact that we have found it. There is an ambition that hurries a man after truth, and takes away the power of attaining it. Genius in this regard may carry the seed of its own destruction. Genius is divine not when man thinks he is God, but when he sees his powers are from God. So it is true of the arts, for feelings of all kinds will discover themselves in music, in painting, in poetry, but it is only when the heart is purified from every selfish and worldly passion that they are created in real beauty, for in their origin they too are Divine.

Science, however, is more fixed; its laws according to which natural things are fixed are either true or false. Because God is love, nature exists. Science becomes sterile without according nature its true divine origin. After all, man may see the light, but he does not make it. In nature both the sciences and the arts exist embodied. Only when the heart is purified from all selfishness and worldly affections will the genius of the mind descend to unite with all nature. Only then will a new age of science dawn as surely as we ask, "Watchman, what of the night?" and he saith, "The morning cometh."[7]

It was a remarkable spiritual document that would later become the basis for Reed's *Growth of the Mind*. But by 1822, his finances strained, Reed turned from teacher to apothecary's apprentice, and this finally became his principal trade. That same year, Emerson entered the theology school, and while not enrolled as a regular student, he began studying under William Ellery Channing. The impression is left that Emerson continued to pursue his own interests. We hear, for instance, that because his eyes had troubled him, he had not taken notes for his lectures and so was excused from examinations. He had begun keeping his journals the year before, and in December 1824 he made his first reference to the Swedenborgians, classifying them as a quiet little sect like the Quakers.[8]

After three years of independent study, Emerson was approbated to preach by the Middlesex Association of Ministers. He later said of this rite of passage, "If they had examined me they probably would not let me preach at all."[9] Meanwhile, by 1825 Sampson Reed had opened his own wholesale drug business on Hanover Street, taken an assistant, and immediately found time to write. He prepared a short article based on his 1821 oration for the *North American Review*, which the editor recommended be published as a book. The article was praised by one reader as "some essential poetry of high order." It was duly enlarged and published in August 1826, under the title *Growth of the Mind*, brought out by the book company his classmate John H. Wilkins worked for.[10]

Emerson's reading of Reed confirmed the doctrine of self-reliance, the reality of the World Spirit; and the feebleness of the arts and sciences when divorced from their true source. From it Emerson also confirmed the importance of the genuine man, as opposed to the merely great man, and he saw in it both the harmony of philosophy and religion and a nearly unshakable optimism in the future. And as we shall see in his own book, *Nature*, foremost was the Swedenborgian idea of correspondences.

On September 10, 1826, Emerson hailed Reed's little book as a "revelation."[11] Three days later he wrote to his brother, William, that it was one of the best books he had ever seen.[12] On September 29, he again wrote to his brother mentioning Reed's book, saying that it was a rich work, comparable to Plato, and that its author should have the chair of philosophy then recently vacated at Harvard by Professor Levi Frisbie. Emerson was amused, however, that this great work had been composed in a drugstore.[13]

He lost no time in sending a copy to Aunt Mary Moody Emerson. He wrote to her, "Has any modern hand touched the harp of great nature so rarely? Has any looked so shrewdly into the subtle and concealed connection of man and nature, of heaven and earth?"[14] Aunt Mary's response to the book was that she found in it "triteness, obscurity," and "Swedenishness." And she thought its rarer parts were culled from Wordsworth, who was no Swedenborg.[15]

Nevertheless, Reed's ideas entered into Emerson's sermons and journal passages with renewed vigor. In 1827, for instance, Emerson wrote "Peculiarities of the Present Age." Under "Transcendentalism," he listed Reed as the best American representative and Swedenborg as the best "from Germany" [*sic*].[16] This, by the way, was Emerson's first use of the word *transcendentalism* in his journals. He referred to Reed as a spiritual rather than secular teacher and he regarded him as one of a number of personal acquaintances who had enriched his life. His journals into the 1830s recount several conversations with Reed and Worcester.[17] By 1827 Reed had helped launch a new magazine, *The Swedenborgian Messenger*, and from further references in Emerson's journals it is evident that he examined succeeding issues of this publication and read Reed's many articles. In 1832, for instance, Emerson quoted Swedenborg, who "considered the visible world and the relation of its parts as the dial plate of the invisible

FIG. 184. *Ralph Waldo Emerson (1803–1882)*

one."[18] Was this the origin of the name for the later transcendentalist publication, *The Dial?*

In the latter part of 1833 Emerson returned from his first European trip. It was an uncertain time for him, as he had then recently lost both his first wife and his brother and resigned his pulpit in Boston after his congregation had refused to allow him to give up administering communion, which, he said, he no longer believed in. He lived first in Boston, then in Newton during this period, and to his surprise, he found, upon mounting the public lecture platform, that he could get people to listen to religious subjects on Wednesday evening to which their ears were absolutely closed on Sunday morning. Curiously enough, his first lectures as a secular prophet were on scientific topics before the Boston Society for Natural History. He did not give up preaching entirely, however. At one point he traveled to New Bedford to deliver a guest sermon and recorded in his journals with pleasure the comment of a Swedenborgian minister friend, Dr. Artemas Stebbins, who said that he felt excused from preaching while Emerson was in the vicinity because the people were receiving from him as much of the New Church doctrine as they could bear.[19]

On May 14, 1834, Emerson first wrote to his new friend, Thomas Carlyle. With his letter he sent a volume of Webster's speeches, which Emerson put "with a little book of my Swedenborgian druggist, of whom I told you."[20] It was, of course, *Growth of the Mind*. Carlyle replied on August 12, "I have read both your books at leisure times, and now nearly finished the smaller one. He is a faithful thinker, that Swedenborgian Druggist of yours, with really deep ideas, who makes me pause and think, were it only to consider what manner of man *he* must be. 'Through the smallest window look well, and you can look out into the infinite.' "[21] Emerson responded November 20, 1834: "I am glad you like Sampson Reed, and that he has inspired some curiosity respecting his church. Swedenborgianism, if you should be fortunate in your first meetings, has many points of attraction for you."[22] He went on to mention the natural world as a symbol of the spiritual, the animals as incarnations of certain affections, and the use of all figurative language as statements of spiritual fact. The Swedenborgian theory of social relations, Emerson wrote was most philosophical and, while at variance with popular theology, self-evident. Emerson objected to the descriptive theism of the Swedenborgians, to the accounts of what he called "their drollest heaven," and to certain of their autocratic decrees of God. "In general too," he said, "they receive the fable instead of the moral of their Aesop. They are to me, however, deeply interesting, as a sect which I think must contribute more than all other sects to the new faith which must arise out of all."[23]

Emerson, then, introduced Carlyle to Swedenborg through Reed's work. Evidence for this comes from a letter Carlyle wrote, August 2, 1838, to Dr. James John Garth Wilkinson, English physician and translator of Swedenborg's pretheological writings. Wilkinson asked Carlyle if he had read Swedenborg, to which Carlyle replied:

> Hitherto I have known nearly nothing of Swedenborg; or indeed, I might say less than nothing, having been wont to picture him as an amiable but insane visionary, with affections quite out of proportion to his insight; from whom nothing at all was to be learned. It is so we judge of extraordinary men. But I have been rebuked already. A little book, by one Sampson Reed, of Boston, in New England, which some friend [Emerson] sent hither, taught me that a Swedenborgian might have thoughts of the calmest kind on the deepest things; that, in short, I did *not* know Swedenborg, and ought to be ready to know him.[24]

This was the beginning of an important relationship between Carlyle and Wilkinson, which would eventually lead Wilkinson into a friendship with Emerson himself.

Emerson, meanwhile, in his journals recorded that on January 6, 1835, he visited the Swedenborgian Chapel for the first time. He later told Reed, "The sermon was in its style severely simple and in method and manner [was] much [like] a problem in geometry, wholly uncolored and impassioned. . . . With the exception of one passage [it] might have been preached without exciting surprise in any church."[25]

In late February 1836, while preparing the last two chapters of *Nature*, Emerson referred to Reed in his journals as "my early oracle" and again quoted from Reed's "Oration on Genius." He wrote to his brother, William, June 28: "My little book is nearly done. Its title is 'Nature.' Its contents will not exceed in bulk Sampson Reed's 'Growth of the

Mind.' My design is to follow it with another essay, 'Spirit,' and the two shall make a decent volume."[26]

In early September 1836, *Nature* appeared anonymously. There are mixed accounts of its sales, but all agree that five hundred copies were produced. One account said they were all gone in a month. Before the second American edition appeared in 1849, there were at least six unauthorized pirate editions printed in Britain. Up to 1844, some five to six thousand of these had been sold. Francis Bowen at Harvard called it "a contradiction." Oliver Wendell Holmes said that "certain passages . . . [were] as exalted as the language of one who is just coming to himself after having been etherized."[27] It gave Carlyle "true satisfaction." He called it "the foundation and ground-plan." Alcott said it was "a gem throughout."[28]

Emerson's main theme, of course, was that the highest use of nature is to draw forth the latent energies of the soul and lead men away from self-love. This, you will remember, was Swedenborg's definition of correspondence. Listen to these passages from *Nature*:

> Before Nature, all mean egotism vanishes. I become a transparent eyeball. . . . The currents of universal being circulate through me.

> When a thinker, resolute to detach every object from personal relations, and see it in the light of thought, shall, at the same time kindle science with the holiest of affections, then will God go forth anew.

> If the Reason be stimulated to more earnest vision, outlines and surfaces become transparent, and are no longer seen; causes and spirits are seen through them. The best moments of life are these delicious awakenings of the higher powers, and the reverential withdrawing of Nature before its God.

> The moral influence of Nature upon every individual is that amount of truth which it illustrates to him. This is the unspeakable but intelligible and practicable meaning of the world conveyed to man, the immortal pupil, in every object of sense. To this one end of Discipline all parts of nature conspire.[29]

This was no literal interpretation of Swedenborg, however, for Emerson rejected as too absolute the so-called Swedenborgian dictionary of correspondences, which required the reader to accept as gospel the exact spiritual meaning Swedenborg himself had placed on each object in nature. Rather, Emerson preferred to adopt the general law to his personal purposes, and as later commentators have shown, he never tired of collecting specific instances of his own.[30]

In this, we see the seeds of what was soon to become a dark cloud forming in the relation between Reed and Emerson. On October 29, 1836, Emerson wrote again in his journals:

I have always distinguished Sampson Reed's Oration on Genius, and Collin's Ode on the Passions, and all of Shakespeare as being works of genius, inasmuch as I read them with extreme pleasure and see no clue to guide me to their origin, whilst Moore's poetry or Scott's was much more comprehensible a subject to me. But as I become more acquainted with Sampson Reed's books and lectures, the miracle is somewhat lessened in the same manner as I once found Burke's was. As we advance, shall every man of genius turn to us the axis of his mind, then shall he be transparent, retaining, however, always the prerogative of an original [thinker].[31]

The rift between Reed and Emerson over their different interpretations of Swedenborg became evident when in 1838 Reed brought out a new edition of *Growth of the Mind*. In a preface, he flatly called the transcendentalists unoriginal and parasitic for their appropriation and distortion of Swedenborgian ideas. Emerson retaliated shortly thereafter by confiding in his journals that it was not impossible for him to know "SR" because he had become "entrenched *in another Man's mind*" (emphasis Emerson's). He wrote, "You feel as if you had conversed with a spy . . . and you have not the satisfaction of a good deliverance yourself because of the malign influences of this immense arrogancy and subtle bigotry of his church."[32]

Nevertheless, Emerson continued to mention Swedenborg favorably in public; in his Phi Beta Kappa address on the American scholar in 1837, in his Harvard Divinity School address in 1838, for instance, and despite their controversy, Reed's work was given an honored place among the transcendentalists when Elizabeth Peabody published the "Oration on Genius" in her *Aesthetic Papers* in 1849, along with articles by Thoreau, Emerson, Alcott, and James John Garth Wilkinson.

Then, in 1842, an entirely new chapter opened in Emerson's relation to Swedenborgian ideas when he met the eccentric philosopher of religion, Henry James, Sr., in New York City. It was on the occasion of a public lecture that Emerson gave in March of that year. Henry James, Sr., later left us a vivid picture of that first impression:

His demeanor upon the platform . . . was modesty itself; not the mere absence of display, but the presence of a positive personal grace. His deferential entrance upon the scene, his look of inquiry at the desk and the chair, his resolute rummaging among his embarrassed papers, the air of sudden recollection with which he would suddenly plunge into his pockets for what he must have known had never been put there, his uncertainty and irresolution as he rose to speak, his deep relieved inspiration as he got well from under the burning glass of his auditor's eyes, and addressed himself at length to their docile ears instead: no maiden ever appealed more potently to your enamoured and admiring sympathy. And then when he looked over the heads of his audience into the dim mysterious distance, his weird monotone began to reverberate in your bosom's depths, and his words flowed on, now with a river's volume, grand, majestic, free, and anon diminished themselves to the fitful cadence of a brook, impeded in its course, and returning in melodious coquetry upon itself, and you saw the clear eye eloquent with nature's purity, and beheld the musing countenance turned within, as it were, and harkening to the rumor of a far-off but on-coming world: how intensely personal, how exquisitely characteristic it all was![33]

James the Elder went home after that first night and immediately wrote to Emerson, extending to him an invitation "to share in his love of truth," finding Emerson a man earnestly like himself, one who sought the inner reality of things. James recounted in his letter something of his own lonely search, and after pouring out his soul, said, "You have become a sort of confidant between me and myself . . . in a manner bound to promote harmony there."[34] He wrote that he felt he may have overstepped his bounds in expressing himself so confidently, but felt sure Emerson's cordial response would vindicate him.

Emerson accepted the invitation. On his first visit he met the little babe, William, "the young philosopher-to-be," as James called him. Emerson gave the famous blessing over William's crib, which subsequent events show Emerson to be what might be called William's godfather (immediately before this episode, Emerson's own son, Waldo, had just died). Thereafter, Emerson and James launched correspondence and visits that went on for forty years, while Emerson established important relationships with James's children as well. Just after they first met, James helped arrange lectures for Emerson in the New York area, and Emerson always stayed with the James family in what came to be known as "Emerson's room." The lecture circuit, Emerson said, mortified his delicate constitution, and he wrote in his journals that it would "soon become intolerable if it were not for a few friends, who, like women, tempered the acrid mass. Henry James Senior," Emerson wrote, "was a true comfort,—wise, gentle, polished, with heroic manners, and a serenity like the sun."[35] Henry, Junior, the novelist, later in his life recalled one of these visits, where he saw in his mind "the winter firelight of our back parlor at dusk and the great Emerson—I knew he was great, greater than any of our friends—sitting in between my parents . . . as an apparition, sinuously, and I held, elegantly slim, benevolently alien, to any we heard round about."[36]

And what did Henry James, the Elder, see in Emerson? He anticipated from the very first that Emerson was the living embodiment of the Divine Natural Humanity—the perfect man, completely lacking in egotism and sin. But after their first meeting, James was sorely disappointed in his expectations. He quickly discovered that Emerson had no idea how he had gotten the way he was; and had no well-worked-out logical system for achieving such a condition, as he knew of it only intuitively. Moreover, Emerson was functionally incapable of entering into any argument or debate about his philosophy, thus robbing James of the most pregnant opportunity for refutation and verification. "Oh Emerson," he once wrote, "you man without a handle," and in another letter began with, "Dear invisible Emerson; Henceforth I commit the visible Emerson to my wife for her repose—and mine in leisure hours . . . but it is to the real, the hidden Emerson that I now write."[37] But to no avail. Emerson's letters made no reply to James's plea for an intellectual system. Emerson only acknowledged the admiration he personally felt because James was so interested in his work.

In fact, Emerson was quite eager to introduce James to all his friends. He sent a letter to James by way of Henry David Thoreau, asking for some contribution to *The Dial*. Thoreau returned with a good impression saying, "He is a man and takes his own way, or stands still in his own place. I know of no one so patient to have the good of you. . . . He actually reproaches you by his respect for your poor words. I had three hours' solid talk with him, and he asks me to make free use of his home."[38] Margaret Fuller came to visit just before the Jameses left for England. James thought of her as a "dear and noble woman." Theodore Parker was a frequent guest, and so was Bronson Alcott. Alcott and James had personalities and philosophies that made them simultaneously attractive and repulsive to each other. Unable to tolerate James's translation of Alcott's own idealism into common sense, or James's constant attacks on the pretensions of civilized morality, Alcott at one time called James "a sinner to all eternity . . . , damaged goods." James, thinking Alcott had left out the practical application of ideas, and that he was a man of understanding who lacked will, called Alcott "an egg, half hatched."[39]

Henry James, Sr., in turn, fueled the transcendentalist fires with ideas from the local social reformers, among them, his friends Horace Greeley and Albert Brisbane, two of America's foremost spokesmen for the utopian ideas of Charles Fourier. It was Greeley and Brisbane, we learn from the recent Emerson biography by Gay Wilson Allen, who first introduced James the Elder to Emerson.[40] James was a member and financial backer of the local Fourierist Association, and his cousin, Edmund Tweedy, was the official treasurer. We know that Fourierist ideas were of interest to the transcendentalists, as they appeared in essays throughout the pages of *The Dial*.

In 1844, with his wife and two newborn sons, William and Henry, who were a year in age apart, Henry James, Sr., made plans to sail for England. On the eve of his departure, Emerson wrote: "I hear of your plans of traveling with a kind of selfish alarm, as we do the engagement of beautiful women who shall now shine no more on us. We talked along so comfortably together, and the madness (is it?) you find in my logic made such good antagonism, that New York looked greatly nearer and warmer to me for your inhabitation."[41]

When Henry James, Sr., set sail with his family, he went armed with a letter from Emerson to Thomas Carlyle and John Sterling. James was immediately admitted to Carlyle's English literary circle, which included John Stewart Mill, Alfred Lord Tennyson, George Lewes, Frederick Denison Maurice (noted clergyman and Christian socialist of the Church of England), Alexander Bain, and, later, James John Garth Wilkinson.

Before he was there many months, ensconced in suitable accommodations with his family, and while sitting at the table one night after dinner alone by himself, James experienced a spiritual crisis of such proportions as to have been reduced to an utter emotional wreck. His visit with local physicians was to no avail, because there did not appear to be anything organically wrong; their only prescription for him was to frequent the baths, take the water cure, and hope that purgatives would cure his problem. While attending one of these local resorts, in absolute despair he confided in a Mrs. Chichester the depths and blackness of his recent experience—his whole being now adrift in a dark sea—and his complete uncomprehension as to what must have happened. To his surprise, she gave the first sensible explanation he had heard, saying that what he had experienced was what Swedenborg called a "vastation," or complete emptying out of the contents of selfhood in preparation for receiving true spiritual sight. After her somewhat superficial sketch of Swedenborg's system, as he later recounted it, he rushed out and purchased *Divine Love and Wisdom* and *True Christian Religion*. Devouring them immediately, he declared himself a convert.

It was not long after this that, probably through Carlyle, Henry James, Sr., met James John Garth Wilkinson. Wilkinson, in effect, became the equivalent of a pastoral psychiatrist, first to James the Elder, and later to members of James's family. In appreciation for Wilkinson's aid at this crucial time, James named one of his sons Garth Wilkinson James, to honor his new friend. Wilkinson reciprocated by naming his own daughter, Mary, after James's wife. Then, we know that from 1846 to 1860 James financed Wilkinson's translations of Swedenborg; he arranged for Wilkinson to become a foreign correspondent for the *New York Tribune* and a contributor to the Fourierist publication, *The Harbinger*. James also introduced Wilkinson to his American friends, Longfellow, Dana, and Hawthorne; and he launched Wilkinson on the public-lecture circuit by introducing Wilkinson's works to the New Church in America. It was James who suggested that Wilkinson turn to the practice of homeopathic medicine, and again it may have been James who helped

Wilkinson, already a member of the Royal College of Surgeons, to get a degree from the Philadelphia College of Homeopathic Medicine. When Emerson went abroad in 1855, he met Wilkinson for the first time through James and the exchange that took place led to copies of Wilkinson's books in Emerson's personal library.[42]

The most notable influence of Henry James, Sr., and James Wilkinson on Emerson in the late 1840s can be found in the pages of Emerson's *Representative Men* (1850).[43] In 1845, the year James returned from abroad, Emerson began lecturing to public audiences on Swedenborg. It was the same lecture, polished over time with each repetition, until 1850, when it appeared as chapter 3, "Swedenborg, the Mystic," in Emerson's collection of distinguished portraits. Great men, Emerson said there, are a window onto humanity. When they die, there is no replacing them, for their class dies with them. Their achievement, however, is in the awakening of humanity to the possibilities they inspire, for once seen, even the meanest of us now know that the pinnacle can be reached. Swedenborg was our example of the genius who was inwardly oriented and who, in his writings, gave us a vision of our spiritual interiors.

While the members of the Swedenborgian church objected strenuously to Emerson's characterization of Swedenborg as a mystic, Emerson maintained that his use of the term meant Swedenborg stood for all those who look within, because no other such personality type was represented in the remaining men of his book. Swedenborg's life, he said, was one worthy to be held up as a window into the world soul. Significantly, the details of Swedenborg's life Emerson culled exclusively from Wilkinson's then-recent biography of the Swedish seer, and much of the content of Swedenborg's books reported on by Emerson was taken from Wilkinson's translations of those works.

As for his assessment, while he exalted Swedenborg's life, Emerson was also equally critical of it. He was naturally attracted to the self-taught, intensely inner nature of Swedenborg's accomplishments. But, Emerson said, as he had elsewhere, that Swedenborg erred in assigning a fixed ecclesiastical meaning to each object. "The slippery," says Emerson, "is not so easily caught. In nature each individual symbol plays innumerable parts . . . , Nature is no literalist . . . , and she avenges herself on hard pedantry that would chain her waves." Swedenborg's "theological bias thus fatally narrowed his interpretation of nature, and the [great] dictionary of symbols is yet to be written. But the interpreter whom mankind still expects will find no precursor who has approached so near the true problem."

And finally, Emerson said:

> My concern is with the universal truth of Swedenborg's sentences, not at all with the circumstances or vocabulary. To seek too much of that were low and gossiping. He may and

must speak to his circumstance and the way of events and belief around him, to Christendom or Islamism as his birth befell; he may speak of angels or Jews, or gods or Lutherans or gypsies, or whatever figures come next to hand; I can readily enough translate his rhetoric into mine.[44]

Naturally, then, the diffusion of Swedenborgian ideas throughout the transcendentalist community radiated from the personality of Emerson himself. At Emerson's behest, members of the loose-knit Transcendentalist Club in Concord made a careful study of Swedenborg's major theological works, including *True Christian Religion, Heaven and Hell*, and *Conjugial Love*.[45] Thereafter, Swedenborg would occasionally come up, for instance, as a topic in Bronson Alcott's famous conversations. Once, when Alcott contended that dark-skinned people were demonic, and blue-eyed blonds closest to God, someone in the audience reminded him that Swedenborg had said that Negroes are the most beloved of all the races of heaven.[46] Alcott, we also know, had read the works of Sampson Reed and discussed Swedenborg with Emerson, after which he attempted to apply Reed to the educational classroom environment in his *Observations and Conversations with Children on the Gospels* (1836). Alcott's other major work, *Orphic Sayings* (1841–42), borrowed in part from Swedenborg's *True Christian Religion* and *Heaven and Hell*. His doctrine of the "Lapse from Grace" was also taken from Swedenborg.[47]

Thoreau and Parker read Swedenborg more lightly, if at all. Canby, in his biography of Thoreau, for instance, quotes a passage from Thoreau's journals, where Thoreau wished to record "the perfect correspondence of Nature to man, so that he is at home in her," but Canby surmises that Thoreau was not adhering to a strict Swedenborgian meaning of correspondence.[48] Harding and Meyer state that Thoreau was probably most familiar with Swedenborg through conversations with Emerson, and they quote a letter that Thoreau wrote to B. B. Wiley, December 12, 1856, in which Thoreau states, "I cannot say that Swedenborg has been directly and practically valuable to me."[49]

James Freeman Clarke, who was also conversant in Swedenborg's works, went so far as to hire the Swedenborg Chapel in Boston, January 1841, in his attempt to form a new congregation of his own. Despite competing services held nearby by William Ellery Channing, Clarke spoke to a full house.[50] Another member of Emerson's circle, James Elliot Cabot, who, with Emerson and Parker, launched the *Massachusetts Quarterly Review* in 1847, in an opening statement boldly declared that one of the burning questions of the day was to settle Swedenborg's reputation. Frederick Henry Hedge, the German scholar of the group, had published an article on Swedenborg in the *Christian Examiner* as early as 1832, later claiming that it was one of the earliest published pieces to lean in the direction of transcendentalism.[51]

FIG. 185. Brook Farm, *by J. Wolcott, ca. 1844*

Julia Ward Howe, returning by ship from a holiday in Rome in 1851, on a month's voyage, occupied herself with, among other books, Swedenborg's *Divine Love and Wisdom*, and later described the dawn of her new attitude toward Christianity as deriving from an understanding of Swedenborg's theory of the divine man, Parker's preaching, ideas discussed at the Boston Radical Club, and F. Ellingwood Abbott's comparison of Jesus with Socrates. These influences led her to conceive of Christ, she said, as "a Heavenly being whose presence was beneficence, whose word was judgement, whose brief career on earth through the body of Jesus ended in a sacrifice, whose purity and pathos have had much to do with the redemption of the human race from barbarism and the rule of the animal passions."[52] Lydia Maria Child, another member of the Concord circle, was actually a member of the Boston Swedenborg Society beginning in 1821, but by 1840 had become somewhat disappointed that the New Church did not take a more active part in social reform.[53]

In addition, Van Wyck Brooks recounts that William Dean Howells's father, of Welsh and Pennsylvania Dutch descent, was an ardent Swedenborgian, printer, and antislavery man, who sympathized with Robert Dale Owen, was a friend of President Garfield, and often read aloud from Swedenborg's *Arcana*. Howells encouraged his son in a career of letters and had the kind of spiritual personality that understood well the daydreams of young William, toiling over a type case, spontaneously composing stories as he went along setting them up in print.[54]

The transcendentalists, in short, took up Swedenborg avidly and adapted him to their own individual purposes. They saw him as comparable to other great mystical writers, such as Plotinus and Jakob Böhme, and believed him worthy of the same recognition as Kant, Schelling, Coleridge, and Channing. They took him partly by way of protest against the prevailing secular materialism as well as the pretensions of ecclesiastical orthodoxy, and partly as an affirmation of the divinity within each person. They saw in him a vast suggestiveness, and his ideas became part of the major reform movements of the times.

Nowhere is this spirit of reform more evident than in the Swedenborgian influence on Brook Farm, that idyllic experiment of a "perfected earth that shall at last bear on her bosom a race of men worthy of the name,"[55] whose great motto was "leisure to live in all faculties of the soul."[56] Brook Farm, of course was the transcendentalist utopian experiment that lived and died on twenty-one acres of land in West Roxbury, Massachusetts, between 1841 and 1847. Born as the brainchild of George Ripley, a disaffected Unitarian minister and confidant of Emerson's inner circle, Brook Farm boasted such illustrious personalities in its heyday as Charles Anderson Dana, George William and James Burrill Curtis, John Sullivan Dwight, and Nathaniel Hawthorne (who shoveled manure in the mornings so he could "buy time to write" in the afternoons). Emerson, Fuller, Alcott, W. H. Channing, Brownson, Parker, and Cranch were among its distinguished visitors.[57]

As contemporary scholarship has it, the Brook Farm community began as a communal experiment to establish a heaven on earth of harmonious labor and intellect, the practical application of transcendentalist principles that sought to equalize the status of all tasks in society, while at the same time preserving the integrity of individual minds. It was later characterized as succeeding in spiritual vigor but failing because of economic ineptitude. While transcendentalist idealism sustained it in the beginning, some overall structure was eventually sought, and in 1843, the community became an organized Fourierist phalanx. It was a remedy that one commentator has said eventually led to its ruin.

Two stages, then, can be identified with its formal period of operation, but a look at their main publication, *The Harbinger*, during the full eight years of its operation, I would submit, suggests a third phase, namely, Swedenborgian. While Swedenborgian ideas occasionally appeared in the literary output of *The Harbinger* during its first six years of operation, it became more evident when, after the community closed in 1847 because of a major fire, *The Harbinger* moved to New York City and continued under the direction of Henry James, Sr., until 1849.[58]

A year later, in 1850, Emerson published his *Representative Men*, which brought to a close the forty-year era of his most extensive references to Swedenborg.[59] The saturation of transcendentalist thought with Swedenborgian ideas had by that time been accomplished, and its next phase would be a further diffusion throughout New England culture. One sure sign was the acquisition of Swedenborg's works by the Concord Public Library, all editions of which date from 1850 to 1900. Meanwhile, Swedenborgian churches flourished throughout the region and were supported by the wealth of famous New England families. When Harvard Divinity School declined funds to endow a chair in Swedenborgian studies, the Swedenborg School of Religion was founded in 1889 in Cambridge for the preparation of New Church ministers.

The aging Thomas Worcester was its first president. Swedenborgian interest in homeopathy was widespread in Massachusetts by that time, and in the 1890s, influential church members, such as Dr. Samuel Worcester, a Harvard Medical School graduate, prevailed upon the Massachusetts legislature to grant public tax money to open Westboro State Hospital, the first homeopathic insane asylum in the state.[60] By far, however, the greater diffusion of Swedenborgian ideas took place outside the institutional church, especially through the writings of the younger transcendentalists and in the practices of the American mental healers, who were the principal inheritors of an intuitive psychology of character formation that had been summarily abandoned by the scientific psychologists returning to America in droves from German universities in the closing decades of the nineteenth century.

Entwined as the Swedenborgian and transcendentalist impulses were, it is no wonder, with the passing of the Golden Age in Concord, that public interest in Swedenborg would also go into eclipse. Strange as it may seem, though the name of Swedenborg was so well known at the time, barely one hundred years later, in our own day, if any man or woman were asked, it is likely that fewer than one in a thousand would have ever even heard the name. Emerson, at least, fares a little better. Nevertheless, through a process that might be called the naturalization of ideas—in which specific intellectual influences have now become part of the flow of common culture, both Swedenborgian and transcendentalist thought survive as integral, albeit hidden, strands of the fabric that defines present-day folk consciousness in America.

Acknowledgments

Acknowledgments are gratefully extended to Mrs. Marsha Moss, archivist at the Concord Public Library, Concord, Massachusetts; Mrs. Marian Kirven, librarian at the Swedenborg School of Religion, Newton, Massachusetts (now retired), and to Professor Michael Meyer and the staff at the Thoreau Lyceum, Concord, for their invaluable help in locating material. Dr. Gay Wilson Allen has provided important clues through his correspondence, and Dr. William Woofenden at the Swedenborg School of Religion gave much-needed information on secondary sources. The late Dick Davison and David Belise, both modern-day transcendentalists, delivered up many penetrating insights at important moments of the research, while Dr. Raymond Deck, Brandeis University, was my guide through the trunk containing Henry James's annotated Swedenborg collection.

Notes

1. The biographical material here and following has been adapted from Oliver Wendell Holmes, *Ralph Waldo Emerson: A Memoir* (Boston: Houghton Mifflin, 1884); James Elliot Cabot, *A Memoir of Ralph Waldo Emerson*, 2 vols. (Boston: Houghton Mifflin, 1888); and Gay Wilson Allen, *Waldo Emerson: A Biography* (New York: Viking Press, 1981).
2. Sampson Reed, *A Biological Sketch of Thomas Worcester, D.D.* (Boston: Massachusetts New Church Union, 1880).
3. Reed quotes Worcester on the title, probably *Arcana Coelestia*.
4. Ralph Waldo Emerson, *Letters*, ed. Ralph Rusk, 6 vols. (New York: Columbia University Press, 1939), vol. 3, p. 74.
5. Ibid., vol. 1, p. 306.
6. Perry Miller, *The Transcendentalists: An Anthology* (Cambridge: Harvard University Press, 1950), p. 50.
7. Sampson Reed, "Oration on Genius," in Elizabeth Palmer Peabody, ed., *Aesthetic Papers* (New York: G. P. Putnam, 1849), pp. 58–63.
8. Ralph Waldo Emerson, *Journals*, ed. E. W. Emerson and W. E. Forbes, 10 vols. (Boston: Houghton Mifflin, 1909), vol. 2, p. 25.
9. Holmes, *Emerson*, p. 41.
10. Sampson Reed, *Observations on the Growth of the Mind*, with a biographical preface by James Reed (Boston: Houghton Mifflin, 1886; first published, 1826).
11. Emerson, *Journals*, vol. 2, pp. 116–17.
12. Emerson, *Letters*, vol. 1, p. 173.
13. Ibid., p. 176.
14. Emerson, *Journals*, vol. 2, p. 124.
15. Emerson, *Letters*, vol. 1, p. 273, n. 21.
16. Emerson, *Journals*, vol. 2, p. 164.
17. Ibid., pp. 455–56, for instance.
18. Ibid., pp. 500–501.
19. Ibid., p. 266.
20. Ralph Waldo Emerson to Thomas Carlyle, 14 May 1834, in *The Correspondence of Thomas Carlyle and Ralph Waldo Emerson, 1834–1872,*

2 vols. (Boston: Houghton Mifflin, 1883), pp. 16–17.

21. Carlyle to Emerson, 12 August 1834, *ibid.*, vol. 1, p. 19.

22. Emerson to Carlyle, 20 November 1834, *ibid.*, p. 32.

23. Ibid.

24. Reed, *Growth of the Mind* (1886), p. ix.

25. Emerson, *Journals*, vol. 3, p. 432.

26. Cabot, *A Memoir*, vol. 1, p. 259.

27. Holmes, *Emerson*, vol. 1, p. 93.

28. Ibid., pp. 79–81. See also the introduction to Emerson's *Nature, Addresses, Lectures*, ed. R. E. Spiller and A. R. Ferguson (Cambridge: Harvard University Press, 1979), pp. ix–6; and M. R. Konvitz, ed., *The Recognition of Ralph Waldo Emerson: Selected Criticism Since 1837* (Ann Arbor: University of Michigan Press, 1972), pp. ix–xiii.

29. Culled at random from Emerson, *Nature*.

30. See, for instance, Paul F. Boller, Jr., *American Transcendentalism, 1830–1860: An Intellectual Inquiry* (New York: G. P. Putnam, 1974), which has a discussion on Emerson's use of the term *correspondence*.

31. Emerson, *Journals*, vol. 4, pp. 36–38, 131–32.

32. Emerson, *Letters*, vol. 1, p. 173, ed. n. 21.

33. Henry James, Sr., "Emerson," *The Atlantic Monthly*, no. 96 (1904), p. 741.

34. Quoted in Ralph Barton Perry, *The Thought and Character of William James* (Boston: Little, Brown, 1931), vol. 1, pp. 39–41.

35. Austin Warren, *Henry James The Elder* (New York: Macmillan, 1934), p. 43.

36. Ibid.

37. Warren, *Henry James*, pp. 44–45.

38. Ibid., p. 47.

39. Ibid., p. 48.

40. Allen, *Waldo Emerson*, p. 401.

41. Warren, *Henry James*, p. 46.

42. See, for instance, only a partial listing in Walter Harding, *Emerson's Library* (Charlottesville, Va.: University of Virginia Press, 1967), p. 301; and a more complete list of references in R. K. Silver, "The Spiritual Kingdom in America: The Influence of Emanuel Swedenborg on American Society and Culture, 1816–1860," Ph.D. diss. (Stanford, 1983; Ann Arbor, Mich.: University Microfilms).

43. Ralph Waldo Emerson, *Representative Men: Seven Lectures* (Boston: Houghton Mifflin, 1887; originally published, 1850).

44. Quoted in Clarence Paul Hotson, "Sampson Reed, a Teacher of Emerson," *New England Quarterly* 2, no. 2 (April 1929), p. 272.

45. Silver, "Spiritual Kingdom," p. 88.

46. Martha Saxton, *Louisa May: A Modern Biography of Louisa May Alcott* (Boston: Houghton Mifflin, 1977), p. 122.

47. Silver, "Spiritual Kingdom," p. 101. Silver also said that Margaret Fuller reported a number of conversations with Emerson and Alcott on the subject of Swedenborg. Fuller was familiar with some of Swedenborg's books as well as articles about him, and many of her critical pieces in *The Dial* borrowed from Swedenborg's ideas of correspondences and universal order. The Concord poet Christopher Cranch also borrowed his ideas of analogy and correspondences from Swedenborg. Cranch had read parts of the *Arcana* and used the correspondence theory to write poetry for *The Dial*. Silver, "Spiritual Kingdom," p. 99.

48. Henry S. Canby, *Thoreau* (Boston: Houghton Mifflin, 1939), p. 421.

49. W. Harding and M. Meyer, *The New Thoreau Handbook* (New York: New York University Press, 1980), p. 98.

50. Hale, E. E., ed., *James Freeman Clarke: Autobiography, Diary, and Correspondence* (Boston: Houghton Mifflin, 1891), pp. 156–57.

51. G. W. Cooke, *An Historical and Biographical Introduction to Accompany "The Dial,"* 2 vols. (New York: Russell & Russell, 1961), vol. 1, p. 191; vol. 2, p. 73.

52. Julia Ward Howe, *Reminiscences, 1819–1899* (Boston: Houghton Mifflin, 1899), pp. 204, 208.

53. Cooke, *Historical and Biographical Introduction*, pp. 166–67. Cooke also reports that William Henry Channing, in his publication *The Present*, wrote several articles on Swedenborg.

54. Van Wyck Brooks, *New England Indian Summer, 1865–1915* (New York: Dutton, 1940), pp. 40–41.

55. Lindsay Swift, *Brook Farm: Its Members, Scholars, and Visitors* (Secaucus, N. J.: Citadel Press, 1973; first published in 1900).

56. Ibid.

57. Ibid.

58. The most notable convert who actually took part in the utopian experiment was, of course, Warren Burton, a Harvard classmate of Emerson's and Unitarian minister in East Cambridge, who joined Brook Farm in 1841, and, as a result of interest among its members in Swedenborg's writings, switched denominations and joined the New Church. Swift, *Brook Farm*, pp. 194–98.

59. Scattered references to Swedenborg do occur in Emerson's journals after 1850, mainly comparing him to other writers on the nature of inner experience who appealed to Emerson.

60. For more on the diffusion of the Swedenborgian influence in the late nineteenth century, but with emphasis on the growth of the Swedenborgian church, see Marguerite Block, *New Church in the New World* (New York: Swedenborg Foundation, 1978).

Strindberg and Swedenborg

Göran Stockenström, Ph.D.

The following article previously appeared in an anthology edited by Marilyn John Blackwell, *Structures of Influence: A Comparative Approach to August Strindberg*, published by the University of North Carolina Press at Chapel Hill (1981). Originally titled "The Symbiosis of 'Spirits' in *Inferno*: Strindberg and Swedenborg," the version of the essay included here has been rewritten and expanded by the author and illustrated with sketches from Strindberg's diary and photographs from productions of his plays.

STARTED WRITING BREVIARY. ["Breviarium"]

Got out Swedenborg's *Heaven and Hell* at dinner time; when I'd read about hell and its eternity for a while, the room turned pitch dark so that I could no longer read. This was repeated once more. The sky had been brilliantly clear all day, and became so again until evening. Immediately afterwards I saw Swedenborg's face in the floral pattern of the sofa cover. He had only one eye and half his face was black; Klemming appeared next to him in a German student cap.

FIG. 186. *Sketch of G. E. Klemming, from Strindberg's diary*

My calendar fell down and came apart right up to [27th?] 30th December.

Portents of death today and yesterday; my watch stopped during the night of 24th–25th at 2.35; the door opened of its own accord. Alf is very ill.

When I was taking my afternoon nap I was woken by my own cry of "Death!"[1]

Have you read Swedenborg?

You do not read Swedenborg, you are receptive (*undfår*) to him, or you are not receptive to him. You can only understand him if you have experienced the same as he.[2]

FEIF: . . . It certainly is strange that the King has surrounded himself with one-eyed people these last few years!

SWEDENBORG: Oh no!

FEIF: Yes, indeed! Frölich, Müllern, Grothusen, and Görtz see only with one eye!

SWEDENBORG: It would be amusing if there were not a hidden meaning in it!

FEIF: Bah! Pure chance!

SWEDENBORG: No, Feif . . . but that you'll never understand. . . .

FEIF: Dreams, Swedenborg, I don't understand![3]

Toward a Spiritual Understanding of the Natural World

IN THE ANNALS of Swedish science, Emanuel Swedenborg is exceeded only by Carolus Linnaeus [Carl von Linné] in the number of significant contributions to various fields of scientific inquiry. Swedenborg was a natural scientist, a visionary, and a theologian, though, perhaps, above all else he was a poet who portrayed his visions of a supernatural realm with a gripping concreteness. For both Linnaeus and Swed-

GÖRAN STOCKENSTRÖM is a professor in the Department of Scandinavian Studies at the University of Minnesota, and has been its chairman from 1978 to 1985. He previously taught at the University of Uppsala in Sweden and at the University of Oslo, Norway. Presently he is director of the Alrik and Cleyonne Gustafson Strindberg Collection and the Tell G. Dahllöf Collection of Swedish-Americana at the University of Minnesota Library. His teaching includes dramaturgy, drama, film, literature, and Scandinavian immigrant history. Recipient of a number of research grants and awards, his publications include *Ismael i öknen: Strindberg som mystiker* (*Ishmael in the Desert: Strindberg as a Mystic*) (1972); *Strindberg's Dramaturgy*, forthcoming from the University of Minnesota Press (1988); and coauthored with Karin Petherick a scholarly edition of August Strindberg, *The Occult Diary 1896–1908*, forthcoming from the University of Minnesota Press. He has also published a great number of articles on various aspects—dramaturgical, ideological, comparative—relevant to modern drama and theater, as well as articles on the acculturation of Swedes in America. Swedenborg has been a central theme in his research on Strindberg in the context of nineteenth-century art and culture.

enborg, the rigorous language of natural science ultimately did not suffice to evoke the inner truth that was concealed beyond the visible forms of nature. Strindberg also entertained the twin ambitions of being a physical scientist and a metaphysical poet, so it is not surprising that he should have compared himself to Linnaeus and Swedenborg in letters written during 1896: "Swedenborg was a mineralogist, rooted in the bowels of the earth, but also in the world of the spirit! . . . I am a naturalist-occultist, like my great teacher Linné. First physics, then metaphysics. I want to see with my outer eye first and then with the inner eye."[4]

Swedenborg's *Spiritual Diary*, Linnaeus's *Nemesis Divina*, and Strindberg's *En blå bok* (*A Blue Book*, 1907)—each document incorporates a similar shift from adherence to a scientific explanation of the human and the world to an explanation apparently grounded in some manner of religious experience. In spite of the general parallels among Swedenborg, Linnaeus, and Strindberg, the important differences in their individual processes of spiritual development cannot be overlooked. The task of describing these spiritual processes for each individual, let alone seeking mutual impact and influence, has caused tremendous problems for literary scholars. Strindberg offered the following description of his own altered viewpoint in a letter to Anders Eliasson dated 28 October 1896:

> In any case, Elias, don't you think that life at our age begins to appear otherwise than before; that a certain intervening hand is disclosed from time to time, and that even behind the so-called natural explanations, there are others to be found?
>
> For a year, I have taken note of everything and kept both a diary and a nocturnal book of dreams, and, as you know, I have become a mystic. I approve of the natural explanations as exoteric accounts for the public, but behind these lie the esoteric truths.[5]

During the spring and fall of 1896, Swedenborg first began to play a meaningful role in the crucial period in Strindberg's life, which has been named the Inferno crisis after the novel of the same name. This essay is an examination of the relationship between Swedenborg and Strindberg, as well as the diverse critical judgments that have been made regarding the issue of influence.

Into the Heart of Strindberg's Spiritual Universe

The attempt to determine one author's influence on another author is an extraordinarily hazardous enterprise. When it concerns Strindberg and Swedenborg, the task certainly does not become any easier. The period of influence can be limited in time to the so-called post-Inferno production (1896–1912). Swedenborg's importance for the later works of Strindberg can be supported by a host of the author's own statements found in letters, diaries, and the literary works themselves. The number of direct references to Swedenborg's spiritual doctrines in Strindberg's prose is strikingly large. In the literary portrayal of the author's conversion found in *Inferno* (1897), *Legender* (*Legends*, 1898), and *Jakob brottas* (*Jacob Wrestles*, 1898), it was Swedenborg who saved Strindberg from madness. In a highly idiosyncratic interpretation of Swedenborg's spiritual teachings, Strindberg imagined that he had found an explanation for all the horrors and scourges that had afflicted him as well as his brothers-in-misfortune in Lund and Paris. In *Ockulta dagboken* (*The Occult Diary*, 1896–1908) exceedingly diverse phenomena are interpreted as symbolic signs according to Swedenborg's doctrine of correspondences. In this way, all these fearful experiences could be given a "natural" explanation. The spirit world, which Swedenborg assigned to a supernatural sphere of existence, was for Strindberg transposed to the here and now.

In Strindberg's rich post-1900 production, *A Blue Book* occupies a central position. The origins of the work extend back to studies in natural philosophy that the author began in the mid-1890s. His stated purpose then had been to investigate "the infinite order in the great chaos," while in 1907 his aim had become to prove "the axiom of God's existence." The plans to construct and write a work of occult natural philosophy—"This is an occidental hermeticism that is intended to annul Mme. Blavatsky's *Secret Doctrine*"[6]—were realized in 1903 as a projected sequel to "Världshistoriens mystik" ("The Mysticism of World History"). At this point, Strindberg applied his own "philosophy of history" to humankind and the world in a series of "Colloquier," with Martin Luther's *Colloquia* serving as the formal model.

In the relatively complete drafts of the following year, the syncretistic religious ideas have moved into the foreground. This work in progress now had the working title "Breviarium," the manuscript for which is quite close to the final version, which was published in 1907 under the title *En blå bok*.

In the finished work the breviary form has been outwardly abandoned and a certain amount of systematization has taken place. This is true primarily for the natural scientific materials, which have been combined into longer sections. The interesting manuscript of 1906 is described by Strindberg as a "Swedenborgian fugue with preludes."[7] By this term the author was probably referring to the themes from the master, which are repeated and varied at regular intervals throughout the manuscript. This radical formal principle was modified somewhat at the time of publication because of a request of the publisher. Both the reactions of his contemporaries and the findings of later research indicate that Strindberg's artistic intentions were not effective means for producing the desired goal. It scarcely helped that he later sought to defend "the magic chaos" by referring to the example of "Swedenborg's quarry-books."[8] The choice of a musical principle of form must be understood as a manifestation of his experimental interest in music. But such a form did not fit well for a work that Strindberg wanted to advertise as a revivalist tract for the people. To this end, Strindberg had offered to subsidize a popular edition at the rate of one crown per book, and he considered establishing a foundation of "Christians, Theosophists, and Swedenborgians."[9] Although these plans were not realized, the book that was produced was characterized by the author now as "my life's synthesis," now as "my testament to mankind." Afterward, he referred all inquiries about his beliefs and world view to "*A Blue Book*, where the subject is treated conclusively."[10]

Although it is not possible in this context to give a detailed account of the complex origins of *A Blue Book*, a brief look at the genesis of the work will permit us to draw a few important conclusions. During the first decade of this century, Strindberg had time and again entertained plans to summarize his religious opinions in a more systematic form. The appearance of "The Mysticism of World History," or "God in History," as it was originally called, should be seen as a step in the same direction. The dedication of *A Blue Book* reads, "To Emanuel Swedenborg / Teacher and Leader / Is dedicated this Book / by the Disciple." In *The History of "A Blue Book*," a supplement to *A Blue Book*, Strindberg sought to interpret the genesis of his work in terms of divine inspiration, a calling analogous to Swedenborg's own conversion and self-understanding.[11] The sum of Strindberg's devotion to Swedenborg is gathered in *A Blue Book* and therefore the work must be said to occupy a decisive position in any attempt to determine the influence between the two.

There has as yet been no systematic investigation of *A Blue Book* or the author's post-1900 religious opinions. Although there is a striking sense of continuity in Strindberg's *interpretation* of many of Swedenborg's ideas, there are nevertheless important shifts in emphasis in his views, especially with regard to the problem of reconciliation or atonement. Nor has there been a coherent and complete survey of the material in *The Occult Diary*, 1896–1908. Even if the author's complete picture of reality cannot be reconstructed on the basis of the diary, it is nonetheless evident that it has great importance for illuminating the author's interpretation of reality and thus indirectly his world view. Whether or not the term *world view*, with its implication of systematic thought, is applicable at all in this case is a central problem that is extremely difficult to resolve. The scholarly descriptions of Strindberg's opinions during the nineties differ considerably, and the varying choice of terminology betrays important differences in points of departure.

In some reflections on Swedenborg as a source of literary inspiration, Inge Jonsson points out that no systematic study of Swedenborg's influence has yet been carried out.[12] Those studies that do exist are limited to certain specific periods or individual authorships, for example, Schelling, Goethe, Balzac, Baudelaire, Blake, Emerson, and Yeats. Among Swedish literary figures Atterbom, Almquist, and Strindberg have received some critical attention, while authors such as Ekelund, Lagerkvist, and Gyllensten are yet untreated. Just how different scholarly results can be, and the great extent to which they are determined by the scholar's point of departure itself, is illustrated by two modern studies of the literature and cultural milieu of France during the 1890s: Phillipe Van Tieghem, *Les influences étrangéres sur la littérature française* (*Foreign Influences on French Literature*, 1961), and Anna Balakian, *The Symbolist Movement* (1967). In the former work Swedenborg is only incidentally mentioned in connection with Balzac, whereas in the latter study he becomes one of the more prominent figures of the period.

The same situation of contrary judgments prevails in the

FIG. 187. *August Strindberg, by Edvard Munch, 1896. In this portrait, Munch has positioned the figure of a nude woman on the right side; her flowing hair encircles the suffering poet in both a seductive and a threatening way (wavy lines and zig-zag pattern). This perpetual motion of dualistic opposites in Munch's composition characterizes Strindberg's captive spirit.*

question of Swedenborg's influence on Strindberg. In this case, the evaluations are clearly dependent on the points of departure. On the one hand, there are scholars who emphasize the continuity in Strindberg's authorship and consequently assume Swedenborg's influence to be of only secondary importance. This is especially true of scholars such as Torsten Eklund, Gunnar Brandell, and Guy Vogelweith, who proceed from the viewpoint of an individualistic psychology of one type or another.[13] They tend to see the Inferno crisis primarily as one in a long line of similar crises extending all the way back to the author's youth. The author's early childhood experiences become crucially significant for an understanding of his subsequent development. On this basis the scholars proceed to describe a collection of ideas and impressions engendered by the experiences of recurring religious crises. In the eyes of this "school," these ideas do not comprise a coherent outlook or philosophy of life. Moreover, the new literary production after the Inferno is regarded as the result of projections emanating from a mind suffering from neurotic anxiety.

On the other hand, Swedenborg is considered to be of primary significance by those scholars whose research stresses the novel elements that appear in the growth of a new systematic religious viewpoint during the last phase of the Inferno crisis. This is to a large extent true of scholars who approach the subject in terms of intellectual history, for example, Axel Herrlin, Martin Lamm, Karl-Åke Kärnell, and Göran Stockenström.[14] To varying degrees they accept the conclusion that the development of a systematic religious position did occur during these years. To be sure, these scholars recognize the roots of Strindberg's religious ideas in his past, but they believe the ideas were formulated differently from before. The new view of life is seen as the basis for the innovative aspects of the later authorship.

Each scholar cited above uses his own terminology. In reality it is a question of complementary approaches, and one cannot speak of an absolute dialectical opposition. None of the scholars employs one or another methodology exclusively; rather, it is as always a question of nuances and accents. We will have reason to return to the arguments sketched above. Irrespective of the answer to the question of Swedenborg's influence, several other equally difficult questions remain: How much of what we attribute to Swedenborg was really his own, and how much was in general intellectual circulation? For the period of the nineties, at least, we can speak of Strindberg's direct contact with Swedenborg's writings, as well as indirect influence via the spiritistic movement and a large number of the French occultists. How much in Strindberg's work is based on the reading of Swedenborg's writings? How much must be assigned to other sources contemporary with the Inferno crisis? How much is time-bound interpretation? To what degree is it a question of older,

subjective reinterpretations? What is it that basically happens when one great mind is inspired by another? How shall we be able to determine and describe such a process scientifically?

The Symbiosis of "Spirits" in Inferno

The first known contact between Strindberg and the works of Swedenborg dates from the middle of the 1870s. Strindberg borrowed the compilation of Swedenborg's ideas entitled *Tankar och syner i andliga ämnen* (*Thoughts and Visions on Spiritual Subjects*, 1858) from the Royal Library in 1875 and again the following year. The book was actually a translation of D'Aillant de la Touche's *Abrégé des ouvrages d'Emanuel Swedenborg* (*Summary of the Works of Emanuel Swedenborg*, 1788), a scattered, rambling summary of Swedenborg's system based mainly on *Vera Christiana Religio*.

The loan records from the Royal Library confirm that Strindberg pursued fairly comprehensive studies of occult literature during the seventies. He borrowed, among other things, Plancy's *Dictionnaire infernal* (*Infernal Dictionary*, 1818), the Leymaire edition of *Procès des spirites* (*Trial of the Spirits*, 1875), and Maximilian Perty's *Die Realität magischer Kräfte* (*The Reality of Magic Powers*, 1863). The last work was borrowed no fewer than five times.[15] Strindberg's studies in this literature can be partially understood against the background of the time. Ever since the mid-1850s modern spiritism had spread out from America to Europe in wave after wave. By the 1870s the movement had found its way into Sweden, where one of its leading figures was Strindberg's supervisor and mentor at the Royal Library, Gustaf Edvard Klemming.

In the above-cited vision from 1906, which occurred in connection with the beginning of the final manuscript for *A Blue Book*, Strindberg had envisioned Klemming's spirit as well as Swedenborg's. The association was in and of itself quite natural, for it was Klemming who edited the first edition of *Swedenborgs drömmar 1744* (*Swedenborg's Dreams 1744* [*Journal of Dreams*]) in 1858. It is at least plausible to suspect that impulses from Klemming inspired Strindberg's first contact with Swedenborg. In both *The Occult Diary* and *A Blue Book*, we catch glimpses of Klemming, who is described on several occasions as the author's benevolent guardian spirit.

FIG. 188. *Sketch of G. E. Klemming "in a cloud," from Strindberg's diary*

In an autobiographical note from 1909 Strindberg wrote of his former supervisor: "I have treated the issue of Klemming and his influence on my career in several places, always with reverence and thankfulness, but in veiled terms."[16] At his request, Strindberg wrote the article "Djefvul" ("Devil") in the first edition of the encyclopedia *Nordisk familjebok* (*Nordic Family Book*), published in 1880. In that case, as well as in the letters of his youth and in his later authorship, it is striking how often he identifies himself with demonic representations.

According to Torsten Eklund, Strindberg formulated a neurotic attitude toward life in his early years, and this in turn gave rise to a fatalistic belief "that he was one of those chosen by providence or fate for a great, global mission or, more often, a conviction that he was not only doomed to be cast down himself, but even to draw others with him into unparalleled suffering; condemned to bring ruin on himself and others."[17]

In this manner, Strindberg's paranoia, megalomania, and superstition are explained for us. Eklund, like Lamm and even later like Brandell, wants to trace these and similar notions to the early years of the author's life. From the perspective of source criticism, however, the problem of documentation is extraordinarily complex. For this study of the early years researchers are almost totally dependent on Strindberg's autobiography, lacking supplementary corroborating materials.

Many of the elements of thought that were original and important in Strindberg's religious speculations of the seventies became current again in the cultural milieu of fin-de-siècle Paris. There is, therefore, no reason to attach much importance to Strindberg's critical judgments of Swedenborg from the eighties, as these only represent the author's rationalistic standpoint at that moment. In *Inferno*, when Strindberg wanted to summarize his view of Swedenborg at an earlier phase, he wrote: "a charlatan, a fool with a dissolute imagination."[18] Strindberg's opinions from the mid-eighties were in accord with the negative and ironic critique of the visionary extending back to Kant's *Träume eines Geistersehers* (*Dreams of a Spiritualist*, 1766). This attitude had been manifested during the Swedish Enlightenment in the struggle for "*sans och vett*" (reason and common sense). The classic expression of antagonism toward the seer from that period is found in Johan Henric Kellgren's poem "*Man äger ej snille för det man är galen*" ("One Does Not Possess Genius Simply Because One Is Crazy").

In May 1896 Strindberg wrote a letter to the theosophist Torsten Hedlund that reflects some of the moods and impressions from the two years he had lived in Paris: "Swedenborg is very important here. He is reckoned as the first theosophist in modern times, before Allan Kardec. I often get to read that I am from the homeland of Swedenborg, etc. Thus, I

read *Séraphita* by Balzac. How great and wonderful it is!"[19] In this case, Strindberg is alluding to an article in the March 1896 number of *L'Initiation* in which Paul Sédir had paid homage to Strindberg as a fellow countryman of Swedenborg and mentioned Balzac's "Swedenborg-book" (*Séraphita*, 1879). Strindberg was himself a collaborator on *L'Initiation*, and he described the policy of the journal in a June 1896 letter to Fredrik Ulrik Wrangel: ". . . scientific occultism, continuing the work of Charcot, Ribot, DuPrel, Crooke, and others. If G. E. Klemming were alive, he would have procured it for the Royal Library."[20]

The investigations of hypnotism and related phenomena conducted during the eighties became the most important breeding ground for the occult world of the nineties. With the support of the authorities mentioned above, a psychological point of view with markedly mystical features evolved in Strindberg's thinking during the closing years of the 1880s. If the Swedenborgianism and raising of spirits of the eighteenth century in one way be seen as a reaction against a prevailing image of the rationalistic world, so can the stream of occult ideas in the 1890s be explained in part as a reaction against the scientific positivism of the nineteenth century. In certain respects, however, it is probably a question of a surviving tradition. Strindberg himself has stressed the continuity in the evolution of ideas during the preceding decades that led to *Inferno*:

> Do you remember how we anticipated all this current fin-de-sièclism and even Satanism out there on Kymmendö? Do you remember "Strindberg's Religion" of Satan as the Prince of the World! We were Buddhas out there; experiencing amidst loneliness, cold, and punch-fumes premonitions of what would happen to the world, and we had gone much farther then than Huysmans has now.[21]

Strindberg also alluded to this continuity in the playlet *De Creatione et Sententia Vera Mundi* included in *Efterspelet till Mäster Olof* (*The Epilogue to "Master Olof,"* 1877). In revised form and with the new title *Coram Populo*, this work was used to introduce the French edition of *Inferno* (1898), subtitled *Mystère* (*Mystery*). Before the French public, Strindberg found it necessary both to assert his priority relative to French occultists such as Huysmans, and at the same time to point out the continuity in his personal evolution. With the same purpose in mind, Strindberg included in the text of *Inferno* several scientific studies of a mystical character in order to indicate the necessary stages from positivism via occultism to religion.

Swedenborg's works had been translated and circulated in France since the end of the eighteenth century. It was first under the auspices of the Swedenborg Society of Avignon founded by Pernety, and later of the Parisian branch of this group that the work of spreading Swedenborgian teachings was conducted. Strindberg visited the Paris society in May 1896:

> There is a Swedenborgian Society here with a chapel, a library, a reading room, and a publishing house. I visited there the other day and saw two portraits of the Theosopher. But they are only casings and tell me nothing, except that our souls are thrust into holsters that don't fit, and thus, we feel no more comfortable here on earth than we do in clothes that don't fit. . . . Therefore I have read *Séraphita* by Balzac. How great and wonderful it is! It is set in Norway, deals with a Swede, a descendant of Swedenborg. And this Swede is like Swedenborg's angels—androgynous. She has revelations. . . .[22]

Balzac was indeed among the number of Swedenborg devotees in France, and it was through him that a powerful current emanated that struck such innovative figures in modern literature as Baudelaire and Strindberg.

For the author of *Inferno*, who was haunted by a fear of persecution and constant anxiety, the story of Séraphita's transformation from an earthly creature to an angel served to illustrate the possibility of redemption from suffering. It was this evangelical idea of reconciliation in the novel that gripped Strindberg so strongly. Furthermore, the author saw Balzac's hero as a translation of Nietzsche's *Übermensch* ideal into a Christian ideal of superman as mystic. Balzac, in fact, shaped the androgynous character of Séraphita-Séraphitus out of a very freely interpreted understanding of Swedenborg's dualistic psychology. Balzac ignores Swedenborg's central notion of the dynamic internal struggle between the forces of heaven and hell. From the outset of the story, Séraphita is basically an *"esprit angélique"* and hence she cultivates only one of the life alternatives in the Swedenborgian pattern.

Strindberg encountered the same idea of reconciliation in *Louis Lambert* (1832), which he read at Christmastime 1896. The novel is an idealized portrait of a precocious youth growing up, with many features drawn from Balzac's own life. Louis incarnates an ideal of a Christian superman and he professes his faith in Swedenborg's theology as the synthesis of all the religions of the world. The book was of great importance for the development of Strindberg's own religious syncretism, and he began to plan a study in naturalistic mysticism with the following title: "Swedenborg, the Buddha of the North, interpreted by Balzac."[23] It was Balzac's reinterpretation that captivated Strindberg in 1896, and this version can scarcely be said to be identical to Swedenborg's actual system. However, it did bring about a new rationalization that allowed the author to evade a confrontation with the strong feelings of guilt that drove him to the brink of insanity.

A contrast in viewpoints is also strikingly apparent whenever Strindberg came into contact with Swedenborg's own texts. "Here I have come into contact with Swedenborg's

FIG. 189. *August Strindberg (1849–1912). This photo was taken during Strindberg's stay with his friend Dr. Anders Eliasson, to whom he had turned for help during the height of his crisis in July–August 1896.*

writings for the first time. There are wonderful things in them,"[24] Strindberg wrote in a letter to Torsten Hedlund in September 1896. At that time the author found himself in Austria, where he had gone in hope of a reunion with his wife and child. A period of relative calm had commenced after the flight from Paris and the stay with Dr. Anders Eliasson in Ystad. In Austria, his mother-in-law, Marie Uhl, and her twin sister Melanie Samek, whom Strindberg described as adherents of a religious occultism based on Catholicism and Swedenborgianism, presented him with a book entitled *Emanuel Swedenborgs theologische Werke oder dessen Lehre von Gott, der Welt, den Himmel, der Hölle, der Geisterwelt und dem zukünftigen Leben* (*Emanuel Swedenborg's Theological Works, or His Teachings on God, the World, Heaven, Hell, the World of Spirits, and the Life to Come*, 1789). It was once again a question of D'Aillant de la Touche's compilation of Swedenborg, which, moreover, also served as Balzac's primary source. This time the author's impressions were of a wholly different nature than before. This is attested to by the detailed excerpts in *The Occult Diary* (8 Sept. 1896) under the heading "Swedenborg's Description of Hell." In contrast to *Séraphita*, Strindberg had now discovered a depiction of the torments of the damned in multiple hells, at once fascinating and terrifying in its concreteness. When his fear of persecution was intensified anew in October and November, Strindberg summarized his impressions:

> The view of existence that has evolved in me is almost like that of Pythagoras, which Origen later adopted: We are in hell for sins committed in a previous existence. Therefore,

do not pray for anything other than resignation! Desire nothing, absolutely nothing from life. If possible, be glad in adversity, for each misfortune that happens, an entry in the "deficit column" is struck out. Swedenborg's description of Hell is close to earthly life without his having meant it, so exact that I am convinced.[25]

This citation is an excellent illustration of a recurring dilemma in the comparative approach to the history of ideas. The idea that earth is really hell, that human beings are reincarnated creatures, and that suffering itself is atonement was seen by the author as the essence of a world view with its roots in Pythagoras and Origen. In the context of Strindberg's life, it is a reinterpretation that allows him to continue playing the game of hide-and-seek with his personal guilt. Even if Swedenborg's image of hell did serve as a new argument, Strindberg's interpretation itself cannot be supported by Swedenborg's doctrines. One of Strindberg's earlier masters, namely, Schopenhauer, could more justifiably be adduced as the source of this thought. In the latter's works the world is consistently described as the true hell, human beings as creatures of torment, and life as guilt.[26] There is no doubt that these conceptions are of central importance to Strindberg. They are among the most prominent elements of the world view that grew out of the Inferno crisis. In terms of the history of ideas, this complex of opinions can be traced back in Strindberg's life long before his acquaintance with Schopenhauer. What we have in all likelihood is a largely original personal conception of humankind and the world, which Strindberg later was able to confirm in the writing of numerous learned authorities.

The fear of persecution and anxiety retained its hold on Strindberg after his return to Lund at the end of 1896 and long into the following year. The belief that various people were trying to persecute him was still an urgent matter. An alternative view of his condition, which Strindberg considered, was that he was suffering from authentic paranoia, in other words, insanity. A third possibility was that he was being tortured through the agency of higher powers, though Strindberg did not know if they were good or evil. Under the circumstances, it seemed more likely to him that they were malignant: "I am alone again; moved into two rooms where I hear no sound, only my heart beating. I have struggled with God and Fate; have sought the dear Lord, and found the evil One. What does that mean?"[27] Unable to resolve his dilemma, Strindberg began to keep scrupulous notes in his diary about the visitations. In this way he felt he could better study and understand their hidden meaning. He also sought guidance in renewed studies of occult literature during the first half of 1897. Swedenborg's works occupied a clearly dominant position in these studies. In attempting to determine the extent of Swedenborg's influence on Strindberg, we must distinguish between at least two areas

where this influence could have had profound effects. On the one hand, there is the role that Swedenborg played directly in the course of the crisis itself, and thereby indirectly in the evolution of a religious orientation in the widest sense. On the other hand, there is the question of artistic impulses in the form of ideas and structures that the author successively assimilated and used in his own writing.

It was the mother of Bengt Lidforss, herself a Swedenborgian, who lent Strindberg the first four parts of the Swedish edition of *Arcana Coelestia* (1861–73) and the complete Swedish edition of *Apocalypsis Revelata*, volumes 1–3 (1839–1858). *Arcana* and *Apocalypsis* contain Swedenborg's allegorical interpretation of the Pentateuch and Book of Revelation respectively. The *Arcana*, moreover, contains a running account of Swedenborg's visions and teachings. In February Strindberg purchased Klemming's edition of *Swedenborg's drömmar 1744* (*Journal of Dreams*, 2nd ed., 1860) at Tullstorp's bookshop in Lund. In March he came across Abbé Pernetty's two-volume French translation (1782) of *De Coelo et Ejus Mirabilibus et de Inferno ex Auditis et Visis* [*Heaven and Hell*] and *De Telluribus in Mundo Nostro Solari* [*Earths in the Universe*]: *Les merveilles de ciel et de L'enfer et des terres planétaires et astrales*, volumes 1 and 2 (1789). The former is among the most widespread of Swedenborg's works. It has had a tremendous impact on the spiritistic movement, the basic concepts of which can be traced back to that work. Swedenborg's *Journal of Dreams* and *De Telluribus* became of special importance to Strindberg in connection with the so-called March experience. In May and June, Strindberg was able, through Axel Herrlin, to borrow that remarkable work on marital love from Swedenborg's old age, *Delitiae Sapientia De Amore Conjugiali . . .* [*Conjugial Love*]. In addition to these texts, Strindberg also read a number of adaptations, for example, the monographs on Swedenborg written by Beskow and Atterbom, the result of which is a relatively comprehensive, if unsystematic, reading of Swedenborg concentrated within the space of a few months.[28]

In connection with Strindberg's study of Swedenborg, Axel Herrlin deserves special mention. His significance in this matter is attested to by many letters in which Strindberg has written of their joint venture in "*deschiffering av makternas kilskrifter*" (deciphering the cuneiform of the powers). The author also pondered the possibility of leaving the manuscript of *The Occult Diary* to Herrlin or Torsten Hedlund, who were the two who had been closest to him during the Inferno crisis: "The explanation of this diary is found in letters to Torsten Hedlund and in conversations with Docent Herrlin. After my death this diary should go to Torsten Hedlund or Axel Herrlin or both. The only ones who understand it!"[29] Later, Strindberg suggested as a third alternative depositing the diary with the Swedenborgian congregation in Stockholm at Nya Kyrkan (The New Church).

Docent Herrlin later became a professor in psychology and pedagogy. In addition to articles on Swedenborg, he published the first two studies on the subconscious in Swedish, *Själslifvets underjordiska psykologi* (*The Subterranean Psychology of the Mind*, 1901) and *Snille och själssjukdom* (*Genius and Mental Illness*, 1903). In *Legender*, Strindberg described his friend's suffering at the hands of the Swedenborgian disciplinary spirits so candidly that Herrlin obtained the proofs from Gernandt's and vigorously revised the legend about "the precocious prodigy."[30]

Herrlin has played an important role in Strindberg research because of his study of the Inferno crisis. He placed the crisis in the context of the metaphysical ideas and natural philosophy of the time. Herrlin chose Spencerian evolutionary theory as the point of departure and key to the dominant existential outlook of the eighties. Despite the fact that Strindberg disputed the idea that the universe conformed to laws, he had difficult freeing himself from the Christian teleological concept of a purpose and an order in the universe. His goal became to discover the hidden order behind the apparent chaos of nature. Incorporating impulses from Swedenborg, the Christian doctrine of providence, and his perception of earlier religious crises, he developed a coherent world view during the last phases of the crisis. Herrlin saw a marked parallel to Swedenborg in Strindberg's exaggerated manner of interpreting various situations in everyday reality. Both Swedenborg and Strindberg perceived a reality controlled by invisible spirits and forces.

Herrlin's insights had the effect of bringing about a dramatic change in Martin Lamm's Strindberg research, notably in his study *Strindberg och makterna* (*Strindberg and the Powers*, 1936). In contrast to *Strindbergs dramer II* (*Strindberg's Plays, II*; 1926), Lamm now showed a much greater understanding of the personal characteristics in Strindberg's crisis of religious conversion. In light of the author's inclination to trace uncanny relationships in everyday life, even Lamm had to compare him with Swedenborg and point to the parallel evolution in a mystical direction, which had been noticeable in Strindberg's scientific research ever since the end of the 1880s. Lamm also emphasized the vital importance of *The Occult Diary* and *A Blue Book* for the later Strindberg ideas, but he was not inclined to ascribe the character of a coherent system to a series of notions and impressions that originated in the personal religious crisis of the Inferno period.

All subsequent research on the Inferno crisis proceeds in one or another respect from Lamm's *Strindberg och makterna*. Herrlin's basic view is found in the research of Kärnell and Stockenström, whereas Eklund and Brandell proceed from John Landquist's criticism of Lamm's work. Lamm was sharply criticized in a review by Landquist (*Aftonbladet*, 15 May 1936) for underestimating the role of guilt feelings as the central component in the religious crisis. Moreover, according to Landquist, Lamm failed to pay sufficient attention to the importance of external factors, such as the author's isolation and poverty during the years in Paris. For Landquist the poetic value of Strindberg's later writing was incompatible with a thoroughgoing conversion to superstition. Instead, he interpreted it as a symbol for a deeper and more coherent process: ethical conversion.

It was, above all, Swedenborg's depictions of the spirit world and the multiple hells that captured Strindberg's attention. He interpreted this material in a highly personal way with direct reference to his own circumstances. In a letter to Marie Uhl he communicated his first impressions: "Am now reading Swedenborg's *Arcana Coelestia* and am terrified. It all appears to be true to me, and still, too cruel from a God of love. So I prefer *Séraphita*."[31] Strindberg's guilt feelings were still so strong that he could not accept the thought of guilt and punishment in any form. Consequently, he characterized Swedenborg's moralism as a personal scourge in which he almost dared not believe. In the face of the terrifying prospect, the idea of reconciliation from *Séraphita* and *Louis Lambert* was revived: "And Grandma should receive *Séraphita* as medicine for Mama Frida. Because the earth forsakes us we have heaven remaining. And when you have absorbed *Séraphita*, you can muse over *Louis Lambert* by Balzac as well."[32] In another letter we find Strindberg repeating the familiar ideas that had been engendered by his religious crisis: "Read your Swedenborg and behold how he depicts hell. Exactly like life on earth. So we are already there, and should delight in sorrow, for every sorrow is a partial payment for sin."[33]

The Swedenborgian hell is transposed to earthly life and transformed into a purgatory where crimes from the present or some past existence are expiated. In this Strindbergian reinterpretation any sense of personal guilt and responsibility is explained away, but this rationalization has no basis of support in Swedenborg's own teachings.

Swedenborg's *Journal of Dreams*, in which Swedenborg recorded his dreams from March to October 1744, had an even greater significance for the development of the author's crisis. Swedenborg's agitated state of mind during the critical period of transition prior to the onset of the real visions is reflected in this day-by-day account. A condition of severe anxiety, marked by a trembling and shuddering so violent that he was often thrown to the ground, portended nightly revelations by spirits to Swedenborg. This was naturally of great interest to Strindberg, who had experienced so many nocturnal anxiety attacks himself. Strindberg eventually described the course of the attacks in terms nearly identical to Swedenborg. Of special interest to the author was the dramatic account of the vision of Christ that occurred on Easter 1744. Strindberg was able to follow the course of a crisis analogous to his own in Swedenborg's dream diary. There he read how Swedenborg became ever more intensely aware of the existence of spirits and how, with the aid of the doctrine of correspondences, he could interpret their true meaning. The parallel to Strindberg's own situation was obvious, but in spite of that he did not think he had found a satisfying explanation for suffering.

The author continued his intensive investigations of the seer's writings in the hope of an answer that would deliver him from his wretched situation. He scrutinized one text after another until March of 1897, when he began to read a work that would differ in important respects for him from his earlier reading of Swedenborg. The work in question is *De Telluribus* [EU], which depicts the philosopher's visits to the other planets of our solar system through a series of "interiors" that capture the imagination. Besides *De Cultu et Amore Dei*, *De Telluribus* is one of Swedenborg's most engaging works from a literary point of view. To a great extent this charm is dependent on the contrast between existence on the other planets and life in this world. When Swedenborg depicts the different societies of spirits, he applies the same system that he did earlier, but with a decisive difference. The spirits represent different degrees of innocence that no longer exist elsewhere. The contrast between that world and earthly life logically concludes in a stinging criticism. Swedenborg tries to examine the origin of languages and the sciences from the same perspective. What fascinated Strindberg more than anything else was the graphic description of the spirits' daily life in the different societies, as well as their presence and intervention in human life. From his own experience, he imagined he recognized the pale teaching spirits, the sparking and smoldering spirits of contradiction, and the brown-clad chimney sweeps. Strindberg's fanciful associations are reflected in the diary, and he had long before proclaimed the existence of "human shapes who possess reality in the form of hallucinations, fantasies, and dreams."[34]

As he read about the spirits on Jupiter, Strindberg had finally found a passage that seemed to offer an acceptable causal explanation for his own suffering. The passage involved a detailed description of how the disciplinary spirits torment the inhabitants of Jupiter for the sake of their moral improvement. The relatively long account was noted in the author's diary on 21 March 1897, accompanied by the following commentary:

> Read yesterday and today in Swedenborg about the spirits on Jupiter and was enlightened in respect of many wonderful things which have happened to me this past year.
>
> For instance about Espirits censeurs et correcteurs which torment man from evil to good by means of pains in the hand (N.B.! my hand disease) in the foot (see 19th March [earlier entry]) or in the epigastrium region (stomach catarrh 1883–84.) Outre la douleur des membres ils emploient un serrement douloureux vers le nombril comme causé par une *cein-*

ture piquante; des étouffements de poitrine de temps à autre (angina pectoris) poussés jusqu'aux *angiosses*; des *dégouts* pour tout autre aliment que le pain, pendant quelques jours. [There were besides pain of the joints, a painful constriction also around the middle of the belly, which is felt as a compression by a sharp girdle. And then there was a taking away of the breath at intervals even to distress; and also the prohibition from eating anything but bread for a time.] (It all fits!)[35]

All of it seemed to agree point by point with his own suffering. The psoriasis on his hands had worsened during the last years and had led to a stay in St. Louis Hospital in January 1895. The troubles were not yet over, as this note from his diary for March 20 indicates: "Arrived back home '*excremented.*' (N.B.! The backs of my hands are torn and bleeding from the pores.)" The diary entry for March 19 shows that another event could now be explained: "Saw a skull with a monk's cowl in the fire in my tiled stove. Something pierced my right heel when I went out, so that I had to take off my boot. (Swedenborg: Lorsqu'ils voient quelque mauvaise action ou intention a mal faire ils l'en punissent par une douleur au pied, à la main ou autour de la région epigastrique. [If they find that he has done evil, or thought evil, they reprove him, and also chastise him with pain of the joints, and of the feet or hands, or with a pain about the epigastric region.])" Even the stomach pains of the *Giftas* (*Married*) prosecution period (1884–85) now appeared in their true light. The sharp, stinging girdle of pain led Strindberg's thoughts back to all the "electrical assassination attempts" that he believed he had been exposed to in the past. Feelings of suffocation and symptoms of paralysis were regular features of his own attacks of paranoia, nor was aversion to food unknown to him—"It all fits!"

Despite these obvious points of identification, the explanation for Strindberg's insight and relief lies elsewhere. Rather, it was the confirmation of the existence of a benevolent providence that had a liberating effect on him. The notions that the disciplinary spirits were well-meaning and, consequently, that suffering was an atonement had long loomed in the author's mind. Only now were these notions definitely confirmed for the first time in Swedenborg's own writings. Through the belief that the power of evil was relatively limited and the denial of eternal damnation, it became possible for Strindberg to hope that he could atone for himself by carefully policing his thoughts and actions from that time onward. As a motto for the frontispiece of the diary, the author wrote, "Ne fais plus cela!" (Do so no more!), the standard warning of the disciplinary spirits to the sinner (EU 75). By so doing, Strindberg codifies his own conversion as central to an understanding of his own existential soul journal. As earlier, however, Strindberg's interpretation does not have a basis of support in Swedenborg, because the ideal society of the innocent spirits on Jupiter can in no way be analogous to the human situation on earth. In the Swedenborgian texts that he had read previously, there was no possible basis for the type of liberal reinterpretation Strindberg desired. It was for that reason that Strindberg had earlier reacted in a consistently negative way: "Swedenborg is so horrible that everything about him bothers me. Isn't my own hell enough? Should there be others as well?"[36]

The impulses toward a mystical interpretation of reality had long been present, but it now seemed that these tendencies could be legitimized by the Swedenborgian teachings about spirits and the spirit world. The older notions of a meaningful and coherent universe could be gathered around a new dramatic pattern. In spite of everything, he was not insane. The strange events of the preceding years were part of reality. They had been the handiwork neither of human persecutors nor of evil spirits. It was the Swedenborgian disciplinary spirits who had tortured the author on the orders of the Eternal One.

On the psychological level, the implication of the March experience seems to be that the feelings of guilt were again pushed into the background. Strindberg repeated the same experience as before in a letter to Carlheim-Gyllensköld in April 1896:

> As far as the apparent harshness of people is concerned, I have personally become resigned, but only through an attempt, like that of Pythagoras, to assume preexistence and reincarnation. I now believe that the assumption has since been confirmed by experience and observation. The explanation that my own fate seems so painful to me lies without a doubt in crimes committed in preexistence. I am so keenly convinced that we find ourselves in the Inferno, especially after finding earthly life represented in detail in Swedenborg's descriptions of hell.[37]

Thus it is evident that we cannot speak of an ethical conversion, which implies an acknowledgment of guilt.

In literary terms, the experience finally made it possible to articulate an interpretation of the events of recent years in *Inferno*, written May–June 1897. It is first in *Inferno* that the author can be said to have made an effort to recognize his own guilt and responsibility. Nevertheless, the symptoms of crisis had not ceased. Strindberg was still held in the grip of mental agitation and paranoia. If the situation is seen as a whole, it could most nearly be described as a successive abatement of the mental crisis distinguished by reversals and a condition of anxiety. During the summer Strindberg did subject himself to moral self-examination, and in *Inferno* we can trace the more reconciled frame of mind and greater measure of resignation that were the result: "If I can offer solace and peace of soul on the other hand, then I am ready, because hate and revenge do not live with me anymore, as earlier, ever since I discovered that man is not responsible

for his fate and that our sins are assigned to us as punishment."[38]

The importance of the March experience is confirmed by the simultaneous increase in the number of entries in the diary. The increased number of entries mainly involved mystical interpretations of reality, and there developed a relatively firm pattern in the author's associations and interpretations. Sometimes the formulations are paraphrases of Swedenborg, as when he writes the following entries in his diary:

> Met an old woman with a cadaverous face. Strolled down to the asylum; felt this compression of the chest which I've called the electric girdle. . . .
>
> At 5 p.m. Papus was in my room but invisible. In all probability he's reading my manuscript at this moment. Malaise; pressure in my chest; occasional constriction in my back; occasional heat in my rib cage.[39]

All physical ailments were construed as manifestations of the activity of spirits. From that time on Strindberg kept a record in *The Occult Diary* of the scourges the disciplinary spirits visited on himself and others. Visions and dreams assume an ever greater importance and sometimes reflect a genuine expectation of revelations on a par with those reported by Swedenborg. When he thought that he had recognized Frida Uhl on a street in Lund on July 10, 1897, a question made its appearance in his diary: "Met Frida in the street in Lund; she was dressed in brown. As I turned my head she disappeared, but there was no entrance, no alleyway. Was it a vision?" One morning in a state between dream and waking, Strindberg suddenly saw Herrlin:

> Friday. When I woke this morning I saw Herrlin. Seen in perspective he sat as it were next to the tiled stove; visible as through a veil; faintly yellow over white; he looked solemn; wore a pince-nez and every now and then he looked towards me, as though he were watching over an invalid. It was 6.30 a.m. (Herrlin told me that he was ill when he woke up this morning.)
> This is the first vision I've had. It now remains to be seen if something has happened to Herrlin!!![40]

In order to describe the author's thinking, scholars have employed different conceptions according to their own particular points of departure. Herrlin, for example, spoke from a psychological viewpoint about "*förtolkningar av verklighetssituationer*" (reinterpretations of everyday situations), whereas Lamm spoke from a religious perspective about the relationship between Strindberg and "*makterna*" (the powers). This last term was Strindberg's favorite expression. It was used for the first time in the spring of 1897, in connection with the idea of the Eternal One and his disciplinary spirits as upholders of the moral order of the universe. The term *makterna*, it should be noted, has a more neutral connotation than *andar* (spirits), which is the usual conceptual term found in the private diary entries. I have myself used the term *mysticism*, but not in the conventional sense of *unio mystica*, that is, the experienced ascent and absorption into the godhead. It is used instead in reference to the other main current within mysticism, namely, the intellectual-speculative tradition, as defined by, for example, Joseph Maréchat in his *Études sur la psychologie des mystiques* (1937–38).

The Vastation of the Soul on the Road to Damascus

Count Max explains in *Götiska rummen* (*The Gothic Rooms*, 1904): "You do not read Swedenborg, you are receptive to him. . . . You can only understand him if you have experienced the same as he."[41] This viewpoint became decisive for Strindberg's interpretation of the conversion motif in the autobiographical confessional writings and penitential dramas. If reality could have been defined earlier in positivistic terms, then it now seemed like "something half-real, a series of visions, conjured by someone and with a conscious purpose."[42] If this half-reality was staged by spirits, then neither actions in the usual sense nor human relationships can be explained in terms of any logical, causal connections. The new writing, itself a creative force, should be understood first of all in light of the spiritually inspired world view that was the result of the March experience. Within the framework of this world view, Strindberg could draw upon the ideas and structures of the Swedenborgian spirit world that had stimulated him as a writer. In order to incorporate this whole complex of ideas, Strindberg himself used the Swedenborgian term *ödeläggelsen* (vastation [see Glossary]). The author intended by this his own subjective version of the course of events. The fact that this distinguishes him from Swedenborg scarcely needs to be pointed out. When the term *ödeläggelsen-vastation* is used below, it is in the Strindbergian sense in order to describe a central motif complex in the later authorship.

To this complex belong motifs that already had a pronounced literary character when they were originally used by Swedenborg. A representative scene from *Arcana* follows:

> Those who in the life of the body had for their end mere sensual pleasures, and loved only to indulge their propensity and to live in luxury and festivity, caring for themselves and the world alone, holding Divine things as of no account, being without faith and charity, are after death introduced first into a life similar to that which they lived in the world. There is a place in front, to the left, at some depth, where there is nothing but sensual pleasures, sports, dancing, feasting, and frivolous talk. Such spirits are brought to this place and then they do not know otherwise than that they are in the world.

> But the scene is changed; after some tarry here they are brought down into a hell under the buttocks which is merely excrementitious; for such pleasure, which is merely corporeal, is turned into what is excrementitious in the other life. I have seen them there bearing dung and bewailing their lot." (AC 943)[43]

By analogy with the Swedenborgian doctrine of correspondences, the inner life of human beings is projected in external reality. In this way the transformation becomes a vehicle for visualizing the difference between appearance and reality in the metaphysical sense. Strindberg's excerpts from Swedenborg are filled with such observations:

> Fires of Hell: awaken passions which are never satisfied, flare up anew; sinful lusts are kindled in order to be frustrated and punished. When the heavenly light reaches lost souls an icy chill flows through their veins and their blood coagulates.
>
> Lost souls resemble the passions: hate, envy, contempt for others, cruelty. In each others' eyes they appear human in form, but in the light of heaven they have a horribly cadaverous appearance.
>
> Some of them black, others like burning fires, others with warts and boils; some a tuft of hair on their face, others with bones without skin, others only one row of teeth. Fighting, quarrelling, rough voices.
>
> Seekers of sensual delight, honor and riches. Which are indeed obtained, only to be lost again. They wander around lonely and gloomy, they hunger and have nothing to eat; they enter the hovels and ask for work, but when they have been given it, they leave and are tormented with dissatisfaction. Once indoors, the door is locked and they have to toil for food and clothing; given a *whore* for company.
>
> Despair, hatred of goodness and God.[44]

It was in this way that Strindberg learned to know "Swedenborg's correspondences," which he often cited as "the key to my method." The authentic meaning of the doctrine of correspondences in the Swedenborgian system, where everything natural is a shadow image of something spiritual and spiritual reality only the reflected image of the original ideal in heaven, was something that did not overly concern Strindberg. To try to relate Strindberg's conception to the abstract speculation behind the doctrine of correspondences is futile. The connection between Baudelaire's "universal analogies" and Swedenborg's system is equally tenuous, although the doctrine of correspondences was a departure point. What remains of the doctrine after its transformation for poetic purposes by Strindberg and Baudelaire is the conviction that the world and humanity reflect spiritual reality.

The difference between the two is nevertheless considerable. For Baudelaire and the symbolists the idea of correspondences remained abstract and general, while Strindberg forged his mystical vision of man and the world out of actual experience and in close dependence on concrete reality. In his art it resulted in a brand of symbolism peculiarly his own with no direct counterpart regardless of the many obvious parallels to the fin-de-siècle literature. The decisive difference has to do with the Inferno crisis and the part it played in Strindberg's personal and artistic development. It was an evolution on scientific and religious lines in many ways parallel to that of Swedenborg. For both, a spiritual universe opened up beyond the visible forms of nature, which made new forms of expression possible. If Baudelaire's version in the sonnet "Correspondances" is stamped by poetic mysticism in the spirit of the fin-de-siècle, then Strindberg's version is more concrete and dramatically effective. Witness, for example, the following lines from the sketch "Huru man blir Swedenborgare" ("How to become a Swedenborgian"):

> Well, Swedenborg has in his Hell a disrobing chamber into which the deceased are conducted immediately after their death. There they lay aside the dress they have had to wear in society and in the family. Then the Angels see at once whom they have before them.

. . . sin and evil leave traces behind them, but that these are not apparent in the human face until old age. Subsequently, in the disrobing room on the other side, they look as if they had been thrown through a magnifying glass on a white screen.

. . . a great man, the nation's greatest son, is instructed to step into the throne room (the stripping room). Dressed in his doctor's frock and bedecked with the medals of his orders, the newcomer is called upon to occupy his place under the throne-sky. Then the nation comes to greet him with speeches; the great one is invested with crown and mantle and with the sound of drums and trumpets he is proclaimed a king. Then the scene begins to alter itself. The crown becomes a saucepan, the royal mantle a white sheet, the laurel wreath is thrown into the beef stew like bay leaves, the orders become contrary signs. The nation evaporates before his eyes and the great one sits alone in a solitary closet.[45]

The transformation scenes in the post-Inferno dramas became metaphysical unmaskings of the spiritual essence of the material world. If we compare the dinner scene in *Lycko-*

FIG. 190. *The Stranger and the Doctor in the inn scene, from part II of Bergman's adaptation of* To Damascus. *In the nightmarish atmosphere of the inn, the Doctor takes on the mission of destroying the unrepentant heart of the by-now-paralyzed sinner. The terrifying shadow figures in the background reincarnate memories from the Stranger's sins and crimes. The Dominican stands above, holding the crucifix to signify the Damascus motif of conversion.*

Pers resa (*Lucky Per's Journey*, 1882) with the alchemist's banquet in *Till Damaskus II* (*To Damascus II*, 1898), the contrast is striking indeed, from theatrical spectacle to spiritual revelation. The motif of unmasking occupies a pivotal position in the Swedenborgian spirit world, and Strindberg often used the expression "*afklädningsrummet*" (the stripping room) to characterize the world of spirits. As a title for the unmasking process itself, Strindberg referred to the Swedenborgian *vastation*. He perceived vastation to be analogous to the scourges visited on him by the disciplinary spirits during the Inferno crisis and interpreted the process as one of moral purification, to which he had been exposed through the Eternal One and his "powers":

> This feeling of woebegoneness often occurs about the fortieth or fiftieth year. It is the balancing of books at the solstice. The whole past is summed up, and the debit-side shows a plus which makes one despair. Scenes of an earlier life pass by like a panorama, seen in a new light; long-forgotten incidents reappear even in their smallest details. The opening of the sealed Book of Life, spoken of in Revelation, is a veritable reality. . . . Swedenborg calls this natural process the "vastation"—of the Evil.[46]

Like many authors before and after him, Strindberg was fascinated by the scenes from Swedenborg's spirit world. According to Swedenborg's doctrine, the dead are gathered in a realm between heaven and hell, the so-called spirit world, where at the outset they retain their individuality and have no idea that they are dead. The souls have been freed through death from their material bodies, which are subsequently replaced with spiritual bodies. To that extent they continue to appear in human shape, and on the strength of the doctrine of correspondences Swedenborg could equip the world of spirits with the same profusion of concrete details as in earthly life. This fusion of natural and supernatural clearly facilitated the poetic transposition of spiritual reality to the world of here and now.

According to these beliefs, human beings determine their own doom in this life, depending on whether they choose good or evil. God does not condemn anyone to hell, because the wicked ones themselves desire to go where they may freely cultivate their vices. Those who are thoroughly evil are dispatched to a hell that corresponds to their particular style of evil. Concomitantly, the righteous win entry to a heavenly society that corresponds to their particular degree and manner of goodness.

For the greater number of people, however, it is a different matter. They are neither thoroughly good, nor utterly evil, but evince various mixtures of the two essential tendencies. These different shadings are hardly noticed in life because human beings can disguise themselves—a capacity that is lost in the spirit world. According to Swedenborg, there are two heavenly angels and two satanic spirits constantly at work inside every person. These spirits are in turn influenced by other spirits and, finally, all of these "powers" (*makter*) are ruled by God. In this way, a human being becomes a center for a host of angels and spirits who can directly affect an individual's thoughts and feelings. The idea of a fundamental conflict between opposed forces carries with it an inherently dualistic concept of personality by which the person is divided into inner and outer selves. The heavenly light penetrates into the former, whereas in the latter the desires and passions of the flesh exert their influences.

The sojourn in the spirit world serves to remove the disparity between the inner and outer selves, that is, between appearance and reality in the metaphysical sense. It is this process which Swedenborg called "vastation." If the good outweighs the evil in a person, then the wicked element is "vastated" and replaced by truth. If the evil is preponderant, then the element of truth is vastated and replaced by falsehood. The final goal of this purgation is to have the good and evil voluntarily join the society in heaven or hell that corresponds to their respective true selves.

By analogy with the optimistic theodicy of the March experience, Strindberg used the term *vastation* exclusively in the first sense mentioned, that is, as a stage in the process of moral purification, to which he had been exposed through the agency of the disciplinary spirits. Thus, in a note to a draft Strindberg equated vastation and awakening: "*Ödeläggelsen = Väckelsen*" (Vastation = Awakening).[47]

Vastation in the spirit world could occur through a successive chain of events in which the deceased could no longer conceal their thoughts, and, correspondingly, their physical appearances became mirrors of their true selves. This could also occur through a more dramatic series of actions, as was especially the case for those who refused to acknowledge their crimes. The completely unrepentant were unmasked by angels who would scrutinize their eyes and read from the so-called Book of Life, where all thoughts and actions were inscribed from inner memory:

> These exposures were made as suddenly as when a scene bursts upon the sight, and sometimes continued for hours together. There was one who had made light of the evil of backbiting. I heard his backbitings and defamations recited word for word and the names of the persons about whom and before whom they were uttered; all this was reproduced to the very life, though everything had been studiously concealed by him while he lived in the world. Another person, who had deprived a relative of his inheritance by a fraudulent pretext, was judged and convicted in the same way, and, wonderful to relate, the letters and papers which had passed between them were read in my hearing, and I was told that not a word was wanting. The same person, also, shortly before his death, secretly murdered his neighbor by poison; and this crime was brought to light as follows. He was seen to dig a

hole under his feet, out of which a man came forth like one coming out of a grave, and cried to him, "What has thou done to me?" Every detail was then revealed; how the murderer talked with him in a friendly manner and offered the cup; also what he thought beforehand, and what happened afterwards. After these disclosures he was condemned to hell. In a word, all evils, villainies, robberies, artifices, and deceits are so clearly exhibited to evil spirits, and brought forth from their own memory, that they stand convicted; nor is there any room for denial, because every detail is disclosed. (HH 462, 463)[48]

The preceding paragraph is summarized in the margin of the author's copy with the words "*Lifvet drar förbi*" (Life draws past).[49] Strindberg had immediately associated it with the so-called life review, that is, the panoramic overview of the past that is observed in the moments prior to death. In Swedenborg, however, this process is more closely associated with the biblical "Doomsday Book"—a conception, moreover, which is found in similar form in many religions. Strindberg has captured better than anyone else the intrinsic dramatic potential of these scenes by characterizing them as a *skamdefilering* (procession of shame). In the vastation scenes of the post-Inferno dramas, the procession, or defilement, of shame is among the most constant elements, occurring in many different forms. Perhaps the most spectacular variant of this dramatic phenomenon is the asylum scene in *Till Damaskus I* (*To Damascus I*, 1898).[50] It can be used by way of conclusion to illustrate some of the problems presented by literary comparison.

In *To Damascus* life has the character of a dream. The core experience of the protagonist in *To Damascus* is directly referred to as "a bad feverish dream": ". . . I lay there and saw—like a panorama—my whole life unroll before me, from childhood through youth and all the way up to . . . and when the roll ended, it began all over again. . . . And all the time I could hear a millwheel turning and the millstone grinding. . . . And I can still hear it . . . I can even hear it now."[51] The meaning of the Stranger's nightmare is explained by the Mother with reference to on the one hand the functioning of pangs of conscience, on the other to punishment in the hands of the Invisible One and his serving spirits.

This haunting dream is re-created in the most spectacular scene of the play, with the asylum scene positioned as the turning point in the circular composition of the drama. In terms of the religious symbolism, the asylum scene is a dramatization of the religious awakening, alluded to in the title *To Damascus*, that is, Saul's conversion and transformation to Paul, midway on the road from Jerusalem to Damascus. The idea of an "asylum" or prison refers to those who, like the Stranger, are mad or, in religious terms, obsessed by evil. Scenically this is allegorized by a painting representing Michael slaying the Evil One. Whenever the protagonist tries

to avert his eyes from the horrifying images out of the past, which surround him, his glance is ineluctably riveted to the face of the Archangel. In line with this religious setup, the asylum is at the same time described as a cloister named "The Good Help," alluding to Christ's act of atonement. The same motif is illustrated by the Stranger's inability to accept even the slightest token of mercy and emphasized prior to that through the news about his attempt to tear down the cross of Christ.

The characteristics of vastation are stressed in Strindberg's stage directions:

> At a long dining table to the left THE STRANGER is sitting alone, dressed in a white hospital gown, and with a bowl in front of him. At the table to the right are sitting the PALL-BEARERS IN BROWN from the first act; THE BEGGAR; A WOMAN IN MOURNING with two children; A MAN who resembles the Doctor but is not he; THE MADMAN'S DOUBLE; DOUBLES OF THE FATHER AND THE MOTHER; THE BROTHER'S DOUBLE; THE PARENTS of the "prodigal son," and others. All are dressed in white but over their white gowns they are wearing gauze costumes in various colors. Their faces are waxen and deathly white. Their whole appearance and their gestures are ghostlike."[52]

With the help of costuming, makeup, and gestures the dramatist indicates that the participants in this ghost-supper are those already dead and the doubles of those still living. All these specters from the past are materializations of guilt from the protagonist's point of view and parade before him as in a nightmare. The coloring, the movements, and the use of gauze accentuate the dreamlike quality and remind us of similar annotations of dreams in *The Occult Diary*. The Stranger imagines that he sees them as in a mirror and does not know if it is visions out of a dream or reality. To his question concerning their nature, the Abbess answers: "If you mean are they real—yes they're terrifyingly true."[53] It is this inner reality of crime and guilt that Strindberg fashioned into visual concrete dramatic form. One by one the ghosts in this scene mirror the past crimes of the protagonist. The unconscious fear and anxiety of the Stranger is expressed in scenic symbols, which assume the characteristics of a haunting dream. Even when an inner reality is suggested in a dreamlike fashion, Strindberg never loses his realistic focus and becomes abstract.

It becomes clearly evident in what follows that the asylum scene originated in Swedenborg's spirit world. The Confessor steps into the role of a disciplinary angel and reads aloud the voluminous content of the Stranger's Book of Sins. One after another, the guilt-laden images step forward and confront the impenitent sinner. The course of events is musically accompanied by the requiem "Dies irae, dies illa." In the chant the idea of a book of sins is introduced:

FIG. 191. *The Confessor and the Stranger in the asylum scene, from Ingmar Bergman's adaptation of parts I and II of Strindberg's* To Damascus, *at the Royal Dramatic Theater in Stockholm, 1974. The Confessor, in the role of correctional spirit, is reading from the Stranger's Book of Sins at the moment of spiritual awakening on the road to Damascus. In the background, soup-eating participants in the ghostly supper serve to materialize the protagonist's sins and crimes.*

Quantus tremor est futurus	What trembling there will be
Quando judex est venturus	When the Judge comes
Cuncta stricte discussurus,	To make stringent examination of all things.
Tuba mirum spargens sonum	The trumpet scattering awesome sound
Per sepulchra regionum	Through the tombs of the earth's regions
Coget omnes ante thronum.	Will herd all men before His throne.
Mors stupebit et natura,	Death and nature will stand aghast
Cum resurget creatura	When creation rises again.
Liber scriptus proferetur	The written Book will be brought forth
In quo totum continetur	In which everything is contained
Unde mundus judicetur.	From which the world will be judged.
Judex ergo cum sedebit	Thus when the judge is seated,
Quidquid latet apparebit	There will emerge manifest anything that lies hidden;
Nil inultum remanebit.[54]	Nothing will be left unpunished.

Crime after crime is unveiled in the metaphysical unmasking of the protagonist, which culminates with the reading of the Deuteronomic curse to the unrepentant sinner. At the same time the total burden of guilt is represented by the Stranger's victims, who form a chorus repeating: "Cursed shalt thou be!"[55] In religious language the scene concludes with the moment of awakening, affirmed by the protagonist's question about the possibility of salvation.

It is striking how closely Strindberg followed Swedenborg when, with a sovereign dramatic instinct, he sought to realize the artistic intentions of the prototype, and orchestrated image, character, movement, and word into a unified metaphor for the stage. The aesthetic structure of the "procession of shame" is built on the technique of repetition. The psychological point of departure is the function of pangs of conscience in consciousness. In Swedenborg the vastation is shaped along metaphysical lines alone. In Strindberg's drama the protagonist's insight into his own evil becomes the beginning of his rebirth. This rebirth is effected through the Stranger's transformation from one who projects his evil and destructiveness onto the world about him into a religious seeker in the latter part of the play. The central position of the scene in the structure of the drama is stressed by the dramatist:

Yes, it is no doubt a poem with a terrifying half-reality behind it. The art lies in the composition, which symbolizes the Repetition (Gentagelsen) Kierkegaard speaks about; the action unfolds toward the Asylum; there it strikes the point and kicks back, the pilgrimage, the repeated lessons, the repeated swallowings. So the game begins anew in the same place where it ends and where it had begun. Perhaps, you didn't notice how the scenes coil up backward from the asylum like the back of a book which closes itself and encloses the action. Or like a serpent that bites itself in the tail.[56]

Strindberg's description, "a poem of terrifying half-reality," refers to the roots of the play in his religious crisis and, as a consequence of that, his changed interpretation of reality. The transformation of its very basis made him reflect on the half-real nature of existence, and out of this follows the parallel to the dream, conscious or unconscious, in the text. Strindberg substantiates that the circular composition and the inversion of the scenes are to be understood as a structural expression of its theme. The dramatist also stresses the unique position of the asylum scene as the point of departure for his dramatization of the religious core experience, alluded to in the title of his play. To characterize the structure and principle of composition, he refers us to the concept of Repetition, "Gentagelsen" in Kierkegaard. Is it then possible to find the solution in the latter's philosophy?

Nils Åke Sjöstedt, in his study of Kierkegaard's influence on Swedish literature, rejects any connection with the religious and ethical categories in Kierkegaard's concept of "Gjentagelse" and points, instead, to the "unfolding of the past," which is what is specifically Strindbergian in the concept.[57] In the latter sense it is also used by Strindberg synonymously to "ödeläggelse" (vastation), for example, "Helvetet eller Paradiset: Ödeläggelsen = Gentagelsen: Weltmühle (Hell or Paradise: Vastation = Repetition: World Mill)."[58] The last item in the equation refers to the mill in Sólarljöö or the Song of the Sun, which stands at the entrance to the kingdom of the damned and grinds the evil ones into smithereens of black matter. This concept of the World Mill goes back among others to Viktor Rydberg's Undersökningar i germanisk mythologi, 1–2 (Investigations into Germanic Mythology, vols. 1–2, 1886–89), and emerges for the first time in Strindberg's Inferno.[59] There it functions as an alternative designation for the Swedenborgian vastation in Strindberg's interpretation. It is associatively linked with the latter through the procession of shame motif, analogous to the repetition of guilt of the nightmare. The Danish term gjentagelse (repetition) seems to incorporate this meaning better than any corresponding Swedish term. Does Swedenborg offer any more insight than Kierkegaard, or is it rather an example of how freely Strindberg appropriates ideas for his own artistic purposes?

The dramatic principle of To Damascus and, in particular, the asylum scene, is summarized in the following annotation from his working drafts in the form of a "reminder": "vastation: the past takes place again but now."[60] On the one hand, Strindberg asserted that the circular composition and the inversion of the scenes in the drama is an expression of the drama's central idea. On the other hand, he declared

that the asylum scene holds a unique position in relation to the remaining scenes. In other words, does the Swedenborg-inspired pattern in the asylum scene also have implications for the drama's form and technique in a wider sense?

We can scarcely investigate this complicated relationship under the present circumstances, but raising this comparatively important question can lead to a few hypothetical reflections. In general terms, the asylum scene is without a doubt the point of departure for Strindberg's dramatization of the central religious experience alluded to in the title. The asylum scene differs stylistically from the remaining scenes in the sense that Strindberg had indicated to the audience that the characters are materializations of the protagonist's guilt. The scene also functions as a summation of the scenes of the first half of the drama, because it has been indicated to the audience earlier that the Stranger bears a burden of guilt toward these ghosts from his past. The asylum scene follows the Swedenborgian pattern closely insofar as the protagonist's guilt is totally revealed. In the spirit world, situations and actions are resurrected to the slightest detail, whereas in Strindberg's play, the Confessor cites all the particulars of the accusations. The motivation behind this correlation is seen in the fact that Strindberg had already produced a corresponding dramatization of the guilt material in the individual scenes of the first half of the play.

In terms of technique, each of these scenes has been constructed so as to repeat and dramatically represent the protagonist's guilt in the present. From this perspective, the figures of the drama are seen to function consciously or unconsciously as doppelgänger in relation to the Stranger. This is true to an equal extent with respect to the reflection of physical reality: the notes from the funeral march, the withering Christmas rose, the sound from the deathwatch beetle and the rumbling mill, the cloud formations and the chilling wind, the profile of the werewolf in the flowers on the wallpaper, the pattern in the tablecloth or the rocks in the ravine. The Stranger asks himself time and time again:

> What's going on? Who's persecuting me? You tell me your husband is sympathetic toward me, and I'm sure he is, but he can't open his mouth without torturing me. Every word he spoke stabbed me like a needle. —God, there's that funeral march again! I can really hear it! . . . And there's the Christmas rose again. . . . Why does everything have to keep coming back and back again? Corpses and beggars and fools and madmen and whole lives and childhood memories. . . .[61]

In this manner Strindberg succeeds to mirror the guilt of the protagonist and project it in the world around him. The "procession of shame" of the asylum scene is from that viewpoint only a spectacular summation of the "ghosts" from the earlier scenes of the play. This relation could be described as that of a Chinese box, where the asylum scene encloses, so to speak, the lesser boxes. The visionary character of the asylum scene is indicated and it is apparent to an audience that the characters embody the Stranger's crimes.

The strange experiences of the protagonist make him continuously question the nature of existence. Is it a "fairy tale" or something he has "read" or "dreamt"? The terrifying dreams of night transform during day to the panorama of his life forever unrolling before his eyes. The Stranger has visions and hallucinations but for most of the time he feels persecuted by "little recurring events."[62] The protagonist ponders if life is a dream or the dreams themselves reality. The Stranger draws in the sand with his cane the name of a Lady he has just christened and whose identity he has created. He draws again and this time a new doppelgänger appears in the shape of a Beggar repeating his philosophy word for word. He writes in the sand a third time, and this time the buried corpse incorporating his own life story is introduced by the Pallbearers in brown.

That appearances are deceptive is confirmed by their answer to his question concerning the color of their dress: "To us in our ignorance we are in black. But if you, Sir, insist, then it's brown for you."[63] Material existence is subjective and transforms for the beholder in the manner of dreams. For the eyes of the Stranger the Christmas rose, a symbol of salvation, is changed into its opposite—a mandragora, the flower of evil. The sunlit rose room transforms to an ice cellar and the view of the beautiful countryside changes likewise to a dismal poorhouse with a crazy old woman. Screams, darkness, and trembling trees reflect the fall of the Stranger and the Lady. Physical nature itself is produced and created from spiritual sources, and the evil of the protagonist is constantly projected in the world around him. When he demands cadavers, the Doctor immediately produces a leg and an arm. Asking for ghosts, the madman Caesar appears, mirroring the Stranger's perverse ambition to change the universe and incarnating parts of his past life. Characters and physical settings change from the first to the second half in correspondence with the transformation of the protagonist. Characters double and multiply. The Stranger mirrors himself in the beggar and soon thereafter he is himself transformed into a beggar. When the two meet again, missions reversed, the Beggar steps into the role of Christ and the Stranger into that of Saul.

The "modernistic" idea of conceiving of a play as a dream structurally is also present in To Damascus. Strindberg writes: "Time can only be defined by before and after; 'now' is undefinable; 'now' can possibly be said to be the boundary between or the synthesis of the past and the coming."[64] In To Damascus Strindberg has used a symbolic frame to define the "now" of the dramatic action. In the opening and closing scene of To Damascus the Stranger sits on a bench drawing in the sand with his cane. In the final instance, the repetition of the same action receives the following commentary: "(The Lady entering). What are you doing? / The Stranger. Writing in the sand. (Still at it.)"[65] By means of scenic repetition and careful placement and use of the word *still*, Strindberg establishes the journey of the play within the mind of his protagonist. All that has transpired during the undefinable "now" was the Stranger's own drawings in the sand.

The suggestion of a similar conception of time can also be found in To Damascus II.[66] In this case the protagonist is sitting in the Rose Chamber waiting for a child about to be born. He is still sitting in the same place when he receives the newborn baby in the final scene. Everything that happens in the drama is placed inside the frame of this present time, and from this perspective the protagonist's terrifying experiences appear to be anguished dreams.

Strindberg started with a similar scenic metaphor in an early version of Carl XII (Charles XII, 1901), in which the king was presented on a camp bed outside the Fredriksten fortress watching the flames in a fire. The king was still staring into the fire in the final act, until he finally rose to set off on the fateful final tour of the trenches. Through this theatrical setting, the tableaux of the drama would be comprehended as dreamlike images passing before consciousness in the moment before it is extinguished in death. This bold formal stroke was never executed, although a few recollections of it do remain in the drama.[67]

This technique was developed with sovereign skill in A Dream Play (1901), where the frame symbol is the chrysanthemum on the roof on the growing castle. At the outset the flower is on the verge of blooming, and this process develops fully only at the conclusion. Thus, it seems that all that occurs from the opening to the close of the play happens between these two instants in the blooming of the flower. Inside the frame of this "now" the panorama of life, both that of the individual and the world, is presented. The characterization of To Damascus as "my earlier dream play"[68] is more apt than comparison first seems to indicate. The point of departure is a conception of reality that lies at the heart of the action in To Damascus and that takes its aesthetic inspiration from the vastations of the Swedenborgian spirit world.

In this connection, the course of action in the earlier and later halves of To Damascus can be compared to their corresponding Swedenborgian prototypes. Swedenborg's vastation process consists of two distinct stages. First, the defilement of shame and annihilation of evil occurs, as in the first part of Strindberg's opus. The second state involves the reestablishment of truth and goodness in order to facilitate entry into a heavenly society. Here again there are a striking number of parallels between the author's works and the Swedenborgian prototype. The procession of shame in the asylum scene transforms the protagonist into a religious seeker.

In Christian terms, this would be the moment of awakening. The "reborn" protagonist is tested in scene after scene in Strindberg's play. The testing scenes are constructed according to the same mirror-technique as in the first half, but now the intention is to confront the Stranger with his old and corrupt attitude toward life. With the repetition of the drama's scenes in inverted order, the author brings about an effective contrast between the Stranger's view of the world from the first to the second half of the play. The artistic gain with this mirror effect lies in the possibilities of contrasting damnation and rebirth. Together, the two sides of the process amount to vastation, or conversion. If people and things in the first half mirror the protagonist's evil projections, the second half is marked by a successive harmonization analogous to the Stranger's conversion and newly won faith. The Mother is altered, the Beggar steps into the role of Christ, and the Stranger is reunited with the Lady. The Christian symbolism assumes an ever-more-prominent significance, and the journey is concluded by the church door in expectation of "new songs." The outer movement of the action has its thematic analogue in the three stages—illusion, unmasking, resignation—which are passed through in the conversion process. The scenic composition of the play is certainly an attempt on the part of the dramatist to give a structural expression of its central theme.

In existing dramatic criticism there are a number of attempts to describe the structure of the play from different points of departure. It is safe to say that Strindberg, through the compositional arrangement and mirror inversion of the scenes, attempted a direct structural expression of the process of conversion itself. The Stranger's retrocession of the steps of his journey to the asylum in the second half of the play is analogous in meaning to the recapitulation of crime and guilt in the first half: "My son: you have left Jerusalem and you are on the way to Damascus. Go there! The same way you came here. And plant a cross at each station, but stop at the seventh. You don't have fourteen as He had."[69] The conversion of Saul to Paul midway on the road from Jerusalem to Damascus is used to interpret on the level of myth the inner journey and transformation of the protagonist. A structural analogy is established in the way in which the succession of scenes retraces the fourteen Stations of the Cross with the asylum [X] as the turning point and the return in the beginning and final scene [0] as the circular frame of the action, graphically depicted in this figure:

$$1,2,3,4,5,6,7,$$
$$0 \quad \rightleftarrows \quad X$$
$$1,2,3,4,5,6,7,$$

For Strindberg, this compositional arrangement was a direct expression of the process of conversion, which was central to the drama and derived from the prototype of the Swedenborgian vastation pattern. The Swedenborgian pattern for the last reckoning with existence is transposed from the spiritual world to human existence. This was in and of itself consistent with the dramatist's view: "Human beings are reincarnations, and life on earth a purgatory or inferno. Swedenborg's depiction of hell is identical to life on earth."[70]

It is the boldness of raising dead people and regretted crimes onto the same plane as the present that gives the half-real quality of vision and dream to scenes such as the one from the asylum. In this and similar unmasking scenes Strindberg could draw upon ideas and structures from the Swedenborgian spirit world, which had stimulated him as a writer. The Swedenborgian concept of vastation is used in his own subjective interpretation to incorporate these structures and ideas. Given the basic assumption that each dramatist has a vision that he or she seeks to concretize in terms of language, the playwright cannot simply rely on language and dialogue but must also employ existing scenic means of expression, for example, setting, properties, lighting, music, sound effects, groupings, the actor's individual expression, mime, gestures, movements, hairstyle, makeup, costume, and tone of voice. The asylum scene has served to illustrate this basic relationship between vision and dramatic metaphor, its technique of unmasking being directly related to Strindberg's interpretation of the vastation theme. In the course of action it was seen to be the crystallizing moment drawing upon a number of scenic elements repeated earlier in the play. The different scenic means of expression were fused together to create a stratified scenic image charged with thematic significance. It did not consist of spoken dialogue alone. The haunting setting of the asylum was there with the Stranger as its focal point, the stage properties in constant interaction with his changing perceptions. Costuming, makeup, gestures, movements, and the use of the ghosts as a chorus all contributed to the impact of this central dramatic metaphor. In the post-Inferno dramas the unmasking, the transformation, and procession-of-shame motifs become vehicles to visualize the difference between appearance and reality from a metaphysical viewpoint.

For *To Damascus*, the vastation motif undoubtedly has implications for both the technique and the structure of the play. The style in the asylum scene is representative for a number of similar scenes in the post-Inferno plays, characterized in general as "expressionistic" and related in its historical importance to many developments in the theater in our century. The term coined by Strindberg, "*hexscener*" (witch scenes),[71] is an excellent evocation of their style, real and surreal at the same time. Sometimes the dramatist indicates their nature to an audience by means of the setting or by defining them as haunting dreams in the dialogue.

To describe and differentiate this surreal quality of nature,

Strindberg employs time and again the concept of half-reality. At times comparing it to the Swedenborgian visionary states—"that half-real state that is not vision or hallucination, but corresponds to what Swedenborg calls transported by the spirit"—on other occasions referring it to the occultist ideas about somnambulism, reincarnation, and the astral plane.[72] The following reflection from the same time period as *To Damascus* is elucidating: "It is evident that the powers become stricter in questions of morality. And how modern they have become. No dreams or visions, since people don't pay attention to such things. No, instead of these are whole stage-productions of complete realism, things spread out for observation, and where you don't get very far with a discussion."[73] In *To Damascus* the Stranger also emphasizes that it is not hallucinations but "little, recurring events, real ones," that persecute him. It was this sense of concreteness in Strindberg's understanding of reality, its fundamentally half-real nature notwithstanding, that distinguished him from the German expressionists and many others. An epigram from the Talmud, often quoted by the dramatist, expresses this attitude: "If you wish to get to know the invisible, observe the visible with an open gaze."[74]

Kurt Aspelin offers the following commentary to our discussion of the vastation motif in *To Damascus*:

> The poet's Swedenborgian doctrine of correspondences presupposed a conception of reality, where all existing things corresponded to profound spiritual realities and apart from that could serve as signs for the moral and religious education of the ego. In plays such as *A Dream Play* and *The Great Highway* (1909) such a vision of the world is created in dramatic metaphors, where the physical and the spiritual can be translated in one another's language in ever new, ever more complicated symbol relationships. These symbols' possible interpretation is, indeed, "fathomless" since no *definitive* interpretation can strictly speaking ever be established.[75]

In Strindberg's theater an experimental paradigm of supernatural origin is displaced to a natural frame of reference and reconstituted within traditional experience. In this process of reinterpretation Strindberg developed radically new modes of organizing experience, new ways of seeing the outer world, and a new set of relations of the individual to himself, to nature, to history, and to his fellowmen. Many of the distinctive and recurrent elements in Strindberg's vision of man and the world derive from Swedenborgian ideas and concepts. As such these structures are constantly mirrored in his art. An analysis of Strindberg's mystical vision, or in general terms, his ideas, is thus necessary in order to formulate a corresponding synthesis concerning his dramatic art. Aspelin cautions any critic attempting to describe Strindberg's theatrical aesthetics regardless of approach or method against mistaking his or her traditional ways of organizing

experience for the conditions of reality applicable to Strindberg's post-Inferno plays. His theater aesthetics during this symbolistic period violated the accepted rules governing the relationship between the stage and the audience to such an extent that it should take a gifted person of the theater like Reinhardt to prove in the 1910s the extraordinary possibilities of Strindberg's "dream plays" and chamber plays.

Swedenborg and the Bible

Strindberg's Swedenborg studies certainly continued after the spring of 1897, but from the perspective of his ideas these impulses are of limited interest. For example, he read Swedenborg's *Vera Christiana Religio* in a French edition in early 1898, but he was again repelled by the aspect of rigorous moralism. Subsequently, he always insisted that "in certain ways, I am a Swedenborgian, but not according to *Vera Christiana religio*, where the theology starts again."[76]

During his studies of occult natural philosophy, he consulted Swedenborg's scientific works on several different occasions.[77] In the following years he first read Swedenborg's allegorical commentary on a motif in the book of Revelation, *Du cheval blanc* [WH].[78] He consulted *Spiritual Diary* in the preparation of his historical dramas, (*Gustavus Adolphus* (*Gustav Adolf*, 1900), and *Charles XII*,[79] and read Swedenborg's epic of creation, *De Cultu et Amore Dei*, in 1904. The reading of Kardec, Maeterlinck, Goethe, and Emerson brought Swedenborg to the fore by various turns, and the same could be said for his spiritual studies after 1904. In the personal library Strindberg left behind, there is a large and often well-annotated collection of Swedenborgian texts and commentaries, in all thirty-nine volumes, that he had purchased through the years.[80] He also subscribed to the Swedenborgian publications *Nunc Licet*, edited by Albert Björck, and *Nya Kyrkans Tidning* (*New Church Bulletin*).[81]

Strindberg's relationship to Swedenborg is of an intensely personal and at the same time subjective nature. The "dream structure" in *To Damascus* reflects in many ways reality as he perceived it and was, after all, secondary to him. Bearing this in mind it was, however, thanks to the very same extreme subjectivism that Strindberg became the first modernist in the theater. The psycho-expressionism in *To Damascus*; the existential closed stage-room of *Dödsdansen I* (*Dance of Death I*, 1900); the radical mise-en-scène of *A Dream Play*; and the distortion of reality toward the grotesque in *Spöksonaten* (*The Ghost Sonata*, 1907) are examples of elements in Strindberg's dramas that have influenced important developments within the theater in our century among different schools of drama, such as the expressionists, the existentialists, and the absurdists.[82]

In *The Occult Diary*, 1896–1908, exceedingly diverse phenomena are interpreted as symbolic signs, and in this way all the fearful experiences could be given a "natural" explanation. The spirit world, which Swedenborg assigned to a supernatural sphere of existence, continued for Strindberg to be transposed to the here and now. Even in Strindberg's social realistic novels *The Gothic Rooms* and *Svarta Fanor* (*Black Banners*, 1907), the same theme is analyzed from a historical perspective, again with reference to the same central ideas from Swedenborg. The new writing, itself a creative force, should be understood in light of the spiritistically inspired view of the world, which was the end product of the Inferno crisis. If reality seemed like a dream, half-real in nature and at times staged and manipulated by spiritual forces, then neither actions nor human relationships could any longer be defined in positivistic terms and be explained by ordinary cause-effect relationships.

Strindberg's religious philosophy appears in more systematic form in *A Blue Book* (1907), which occupies a central position in his rich twentieth-century production. Its existence in several earlier versions gives ample evidence that this plan had been entertained from the mid-1890s. Its dedication to Emanuel Swedenborg by the "disciple" refers to the central themes from his "teacher and leader," which are reflected in this work, described by Strindberg as his "testament to mankind."[83] *A Blue Book* was to be followed by *En ny blå bok* (*A New Blue Book*) and *En blå bok, avdelning III* (*A Blue Book, Part III*) in 1908, finally concluded in 1912 by *En blå bok, avdelning IV* (*A Blue Book, Part IV*). These colloquia, or breviaries, contain the synthesis of Strindberg's religious thinking in the spirit of Swedenborg.

Through his conversion Strindberg came to incarnate many of the radical changes that occurred at the turn of the century. In his case the transformation of the very basis of reality during the Inferno crisis, the perception of its half-real nature, and, in essence, its spiritual character put him in line with similar developments in the art and literature of the period, all in various degrees and ways representing what might be termed a dissolution of the very perception of reality.

For the impressionistic painters, for example, reality tended to become fleeting impressions on the retina of the eye, but it proved difficult at times to differentiate between sensation and illusion. To the symbolists of a later era, on the other hand, only the self was real, while the external world appeared as a continuous stream of dreamlike impressions emanating from the soul. In a similar vein many schools of philosophy asserted that what is termed reality only exists to us and that the world is in fact only an idea in our consciousness. Schopenhauer, for example, insisted that it was a projection of our will, by that referring to our blind urge for survival. Reality in itself, if it ever existed, was for time eternal hidden behind a veil. Many physicists contributed through their atomic theories in a similar manner to undermine the popular belief concerning the actual nature of real-

ity. The study of the unconscious mind eventually led into different types of occultism and transcendental mysticism, whereby the contact with "true" reality was established not through observation but through intuition, contemplation, or ecstasy.

Strindberg lived a number of years in Paris at the height of the symbolist school and knew several of its prominent representatives, painters, writers, occultists, and so on. There are a number of indications on his part of an awareness and understanding of the symbolist principle of artistic creation, not in imitation of but rather in defiance of reality. Even if any direct influence has been hard to prove, a number of examples are found in Brandell, among others Gauguin, who offers the following aesthetic prescription in letters to a friend in 1888:

> Do not copy too much from nature, art is an abstraction; take away from nature by weaving in dreams and consider your imagination. . . . By arranging lines and colours I achieve a symphony, a harmony that does not correspond to anything real in the true sense of that very word. They do not express anything directly but they shall make you think of music without the help of ideas or images, quite simply through the mystical correspondence between our thought and such compositions in lines and colours.[84]

It is seldom, if ever, possible to analyze the complicated web of causes and effects that determine in its entirety what is often called the "Zeitgeist." Neither is it an easy task to define the vision of the individual, nor the complex relationships between the individual and his time.

In conclusion, it can be asserted that, despite his extensive reading, Strindberg's devotion to Swedenborg rested on a narrow and subjective basis of understanding. He never achieved a thorough understanding of the system of Swedenborg's theology. Nonetheless, the encounter of the two "spirits" during the final phase of the Inferno crisis did lead to a symbiosis, which engendered rich literary fruits. Even in the spring of 1910 he could still confess to his friend Nils Andersson: "It is only Swedenborg and the Bible that give me courage. It seems hopeless here in hell. As Origen understood, the world was created for the mortification of the wicked, who should torment each other forward to the cross, and, therefore, life cannot be otherwise than it is. Therefore we deportees are still recruited."[85]

In his one literary representation of Swedenborg,[86] Strindberg had him appear as the dreamer and the seer, who knew best how to decipher the riddles of existence. In his physical suffering during the last years of his life, Strindberg reaffirms again and again his profound debt to his guiding spirit, Emanuel Swedenborg: "Is the end approaching? That I do not know but I have a presentiment. Life forces me out, it seems, or persecutes me, and I have long ago set my hope to 'the other side,' to which I am connected like Swedenborg."[87]

Notes

1. *Ockulta dagboken* (The occult diary, 1896–1908; hereafter *O. D.*), 25 June 1906, Nordiska Museets Strindbergssamling (hereafter SgNM: file 72) in deposition at Kungliga Biblioteket (hereafter K. B.), Stockholm. Translations out of *O. D.* are from a forthcoming scholarly edition by Karin Petherick and Göran Stockenström, *The Occult Diary 1896–1908* (Minneapolis: University of Minnesota Press).

2. August Strindberg, *Götiska rummen* (The gothic rooms) in John Landquist, ed., *Samlade Skrifter av August Strindberg* (Collected works of August Strindberg; hereafter *S. S.*) 55 vols. (Stockholm: Bonniers, 1920–25), vol. 40, p. 259.

3. *Carl XII* in *S. S.*, vol. 35, p. 212; translation from August Strindberg, *Queen Christina, Charles XII, Gustav III*, ed. Walter Jonson (Seattle: University of Washington Press, 1955), pp. 159–60.

4. Letters to T. Hedlund, 15 February and 21 June 1896, in *August Strindbergs Brev* (hereafter *Brev*), ed. Torsten Eklund (Stockholm: Bonniers, 1948–76), vol. 11, pp. 132, 219.

5. Letter to A. Eliasson, 28 October 1896, in *Brev*, vol. 11, p. 369.

6. Letter to G. af Geijerstam, 4 December 1897, in *Brev*, vol. 12, p. 230.

7. Letter to E. Schering, 24 November 1906, in Bonniers Arkiv (Bonniers Archive), (hereafter B. A.), Stockholm.

8. Letter to K. Börjesson, 14 September 1907 (SgNM), K. B.

9. Ibid. 2 September 1907 (SgNM), K. B.

10. Quote 1: Letter to E. Schering, 25 June 1908, B. A.; quote 2: Letter to R. Bergh, 1 November 1907, (SgNM), K. B.; quote 3: *O. D.*, 22 August 1906 (SgNM: 72), K. B.

11. *S. S.*, vol. 46, pp. 404–15.

12. Inge Jonsson and Olle Hjern, *Swedenborg, sökaren i naturens och andens världar: hans verk och efterföljd* (Swedenborg, the explorer of the worlds of nature and spirit: His work and influence) (Stockholm: Proprius, 1976), pp. 81–102.

13. See Torsten Eklund, *Tjänstekvinnans son: En psykologisk Strindbergsstudie* (The son of a servant: A study in Strindberg's psychology) (Stockholm: Bonniers, 1948); Gunnar Brandell, *Strindbergs Infernokris* (*Strindberg in Inferno*) (Stockholm: Bonniers, 1950; Cambridge: Harvard University Press, 1974); Guy Vogelweith, *Le Psychothéâtre de Strindberg: Un Auteur en quête de métamorphose* (Strindberg's psychotheater: An author in search of transformation) (Paris: Librairie C. Klincksieck, 1972).

14. See Axel Herrlin, "Bengt Lidforss och August Strindberg: En studie över deras tankegemenskap och förhållande till samtida naturfilosofiska och metafysiska idéströmningar" (Bengt Lidforss and August Strindberg: A study of their ideological connection and relation to contemporary ideas in natural philosophy and metaphysics) in *Bengt Lidforss: En minnesskrift* (Bengt Lidforss: A memorial publication), ed. Einar Sjövall, (Malmö: Framtiden, 1923), pp. 53–86; Martin Lamm, *Strindberg och makterna* (Strindberg and the powers) (Stockholm & Uppsala: Svenska Kyrkans Diakonistyrelses, 1936); Karl-Åke Kärnell, *Strindbergs bildspråk: en studie i prosastil* (Strindberg's imagery: A study in prose style) (Uppsala: Almqvist & Wiksell, 1962), pp. 242–87; Göran Stockenström, *Ismael i öknen: Strindberg som mystiker* (Ishmael in the desert: Strindberg as a mystic) (Uppsala: Almqvist & Wiksell, 1972).

15. Hans Lindström, *Hjärnornas kamp: psykologiska idéer och motiv i Strindbergs åttiotalsdiktning* (The struggle of the brains: Psychological ideas and motives in Strindberg's fiction from the 1880s) (Uppsala: Appelbergs, 1952), pp. 223–24.

16. *S. S.*, vol. 54, p. 471.

17. Eklund, pp. 267–68.

18. *S. S.*, vol. 28, p. 55. Cf. *S. S.*, vol. 7, p. 24 and *S. S.*, vol. 8, pp. 345–46.

19. Letter to T. Hedlund, 15 May 1896, *Brev*, vol. 11, p. 192.

20. Letter to F. U. Wrangel, 7 June 1896, *Brev*, vol. 11, p. 206.

21. Letter to L. Littmansson, 17 July 1894, *Brev*, vol. 10, p. 140.

22. Letter to T. Hedlund, 15 May 1896, *Brev*, vol. 11, p. 192.

23. Letter to K. Staff, 24 January 1897, *Brev*, vol. 12, p. 47.

24. Letter to T. Hedlund, 7 September 1896, *Brev*, vol. 11, p. 317.

25. Ibid., 31 October 1896, *Brev*, vol. 11, p. 376.

26. See Eklund, pp. 286ff. and Brandell, p. 99.

27. Letter to M. Uhl, 5 February 1897, *Brev*, vol. 12, p. 62.

28. Pehr Daniel Amadeus Atterbom, *Svenska siare och skalder* (Swedish visionaries and poets) (Örebro: 1862), vol. 1; and Bernhard von Beskow, *Minne öfver Swedenborg* (Swedenborg in memoriam) (Stockholm: 1860). Cf. Stockenström, p. 75.

29. *O. D.*, frontispiece, 1896. Cf. Stockenström, pp. 72–73.

30. Cf. Stockenström, pp. 228–29.

31. Letter to M. Uhl, 17 December 1896, *Brev*, vol. 12, p. 21.

32. Letter to Kerstin Strindberg, 26 December 1896, *Brev*, vol. 12, p. 28.

33. Letter to M. Uhl, 14 January 1897, *Brev*, vol. 12, p. 39.

34. *S. S.*, vol. 28, pp. 45–46, cf. pp. 59–60.

35. *O. D.*, 21 March 1897 (SgNM: 72), K. B. [. . .] indicates later addition to the text of *O. D.* Translations (*O. D.* 19 and 21 March 1897) from *The Heavenly Arcana Disclosed*, Rotch ed. (Boston & New York: Houghton Mifflin, 1907) vol. 22, pp. 46–47. Cf. Stockenström, pp. 86–109.

36. Letter to M. Uhl, 17 December 1896, *Brev*, vol. 12, p. 21.

37. Letter to V. Carlheim-Gyllensköld, 12 April 1897, *Brev*, vol. 12, p. 102.

38. Letter to M. Uhl, 25 July 1897, *Brev*, vol. 12, pp. 133–34.

39. *O. D.*, (SgNM: 72), K. B., quote 1: 29 April 1897, and quote 2: 28 August 1897.

40. *O. D.*, (SgNM: 72), K. B., 29 June 1897.

41. *S. S.*, vol. 40, p. 259.

42. *S. S.*, vol. 28, p. 235.

43. Translation from *The Heavenly Arcana Disclosed*, vol. 2, p. 96. Cf. Stockenström, pp. 154–57.

44. *O. D.* (SgNM: 72), K. B., 8 September 1896. Strindberg's quotes are gathered from *Emanuel Swedenborgs theologische Werke oder dessen Lehre von Gott, der Welt, der Himmel, der Hölle, der Geisterwelt und der zukünftigen Leben* (Leipzig: 1789), pp. 144–46. Cf. Stockenström, pp. 56–57.

45. Quote 1: *S. S.*, vol. 46, pp. 49–50, cf. p. 60. Quote 2: p. 130; translations from August Strindberg, *Zones of the Spirit* (New York & London: G. P. Putnam's Sons, 1913), Claud Field's translation of the religious essays in *A Blue Book* (1907). Quote 3: "Huru man blir Swedenborgare" (How to become a Swedenborgian), (SgNM: file 11), K. B. Strindberg refers to the Swedish explorer, Sven Hedin.

46. *S. S.*, vol. 46, p. 33–34, translation from Strindberg, *Zones of the Spirit*, pp. 40–41.

47. "Swedenborg: alpha" (SgNM: file 9), K. B. Cf. Stockenström, pp. 83–84, 96–97, 143–44.

48. Translation by F. Bayley in *Heaven and Its Wonders and Hell* (New York: Dutton, 1909), p. 239.

49. Annotation in Strindberg's copy of E. Swedenborg, *Les merveilles de ciel et de l'enfer et des terres planétaires et astrales*, ed. A. J. Pernetty (Berlin: 1782), vol. 2, p. 35. Strindberg's library is in the Strindberg Museum in Stockholm. Cf. Stockenström, pp. 82–84.

50. Cf. Göran Stockenström, " 'His Former Dream Play To Damascus' " in *Strindbergs Dramen im Lichte neuerer Methodendiskussionen* (Strindberg's plays in light of recent discussions of methodology), ed. O. Bandle, W. Baumgartner, and J. Glauser (Basel & Frankfurt am Main: Helbing & Lichtenhahn Verlag AG, 1981), pp. 211–35.

51. Evert Sprinchorn, *The Genius of the Scandinavian Theater* (New York: New American Library, 1964), pp. 339 and 340.
52. Ibid., p. 332.
53. Ibid., p. 333.
54. Ibid., p. 335.
55. Ibid., p. 336.
56. Letter to G. af Geijerstam, 13 March 1898, *Brev*, vol. 12, pp. 279–80.
57. Nils Åke Sjöstedt, *Søren Kirkegaard och svensk litteratur: Från Frederika Bremer till Hjalmar Söderberg* (Soren Kirkegaard and Swedish literature: From Frederika Bremer to Hjalmar Söderberg) (Göteborg: Wettergren & Kerber, 1950), pp. 248–50. Cf. Stockenström, *Ismael i öknen*, pp. 96–97, 190–91, 308–10.
58. "Legendes de ma vie" (Legends of my life) (SgNM: 9: 3), K. B.
59. Viktor Rydberg, *Undersökningar i germanisk mythologi* (Investigations into Germanic mythology), vol. 1, pp. 425–27. Cf. Stockenström, *Ismael i öknen*, pp. 176–78.
60. "Page from Notebook" (SgNM: 9: 3), K. B.
61. Sprinchorn, p. 305.
62. Ibid., p. 302.
63. Ibid., p. 294.
64. "Tid och Rum" (Time and room), (SgNM: 3: 2), K. B.
65. Sprinchorn, p. 359.
66. Cf. Stockenström, *Ismael i öknen*, pp. 348–84.
67. Cf. *Göran Stockenström*, "Charles XII as Dream Play" in *Strindberg's Dramaturgy*, ed. Göran Stockenström, forthcoming (Minneapolis: University of Minnesota Press, 1988).
68. "Preface to A Dream Play," in *Six Plays by August Strindberg*, ed. Elizabeth Sprigge (New York: Anchor Books, 1955), p. 193.
69. Sprinchorn, p. 345.
70. Strindberg, *Zones of the Spirit*, pp. 68–69.
71. Letter to G. af Geijerstam, 15 November 1897, *Brev*, vol. 12, p. 212.
72. Ibid. Strindberg is citing from Swedenborg's *Arcana Coelestia*: 1882–85. Cf. *The Heavenly Arcana Disclosed*, vol. 3, pp. 317–19.
73. *S. S.*, vol. 28, p. 285.
74. *O. D.*, frontispiece, 1896 (SgNM: 72), K. B.
75. Kurt Aspelin, *Teaterarbete* (Theater work) (Stockholm: PAN/Norstedt, 1977), pp. 327–28.
76. Letter to C. W. Palmgren, 27 September 1910, (SgNM), K. B. Cf. Stockenström, *Ismael i öknen*, pp. 208–20, 256–58.
77. Strindberg borrowed from the University Library in Lund the following books by Swedenborg (title 1 and 2 on 13 May 1898; title 3 on 8 July 1898): *Opera Philosophica et Mineralia* (Leipzig & Dresden: 1734), vol. I–III; *The Principia or First Principles of Natural Things* (London: Newbery, 1846), vol. I–II; and *Regnum Animale, Anatomice, Physice, et Philosophice Perlustratum* (The Hague and London: 1744–45), vol. I–III.
78. E. Swedenborg, *Du cheval blanc dans l'apocalypse* (White horse of the apocalypse) (Paris: 1850).
79. Cf. Göran Stockenström, "Strindberg och historiens Karl XII" (Strindberg and the historical Charles XII), in *Meddelanden från Strindbergssällskapet* (Notes from the Strindberg society), nos. 47–48 (1971), pp. 35–36.
80. See Hans Lindström, *Strindberg och böckerna*, (Strindberg and the books) (Uppsala: Almqvist & Wiksell, 1977), pp. 84, 85, 94, 96, 100, 101, 102, 104, 105, 108, 118, 190, 191, 195, 203.
81. Ibid., p. 102.
82. Cf. Göran Stockenström, " 'The Journey from the Isle of Death': The Idea of Reconciliation in 'The Ghost Sonata,' " in *Scandinavian Studies* 50, no. 2 (1978), pp. 133–50.
83. *S. S.*, vol. 46, title page.
84. Letter to E. Shuffenecker, 14 August 1888, in *Lettres de Gauguin à sa femme et à ses amis*, ed. M. Malingue (Paris: B. Grasset, 1946), p. 134. Cf. *Gunnar Brandell*, pp. 204–30.
85. Letter to N. Andersson, 23 May 1910, B. A.
86. See *Carl XII, in S. S.*, vol. 35, translation by Walter Johnson in *Queen Christina, Charles XII, Gustav III* (Seattle: University of Washington Press, 1955). Cf. Stockenström, "Charles XII as Historical Drama" and "Charles XII as Dream Play" in *Strindberg's Dramaturgy*.
87. Letter to E. Schering, 2 April 1907, *Brev*, vol. 15, p. 356.

Dostoevsky and Swedenborg

Czeslaw Milosz

Translated by Louis Iribarne

"Dostoevsky and Swedenborg" was published previously as chapter 9 of Czeslaw Milosz's 1980 Nobel Prize–winning book *Emperor of the Earth* (University of California Press, 1977). While the wording remains the same as in the original, both the text and notes are reproduced here with only slight typographical changes.

VERY FEW BOOKS AND STUDIES on Dostoevsky appeared in the first two decades after his death. The year 1900 may be chosen as the turning point; after that date the number of publications, first in Russian and then in other languages, increased steadily. By the middle of our century the canon of Dostoevsky scholarship was well established, so that hardly any new departures seemed to be possible. Today, whether our attention is focused on Dostoevsky's opinions or upon the stylistic devices and structures of his novels, we note that practically every method of approach has already been tried by at least one of our predecessors. Thus Dostoevsky, not unlike Nietzsche, was discovered and appropriated by the first half of the twentieth century. It was then that he grew to the stature he now possesses, and it was then that he was recognized as a forerunner of new trends in European literature and philosophy.

Seen from the present, as the past recedes in time, it is quite normal for the perspective to change and for some habits of thought once accepted as universal to reveal their conventional character. These habits explain certain blind spots or unintentional omissions, while new questions arise concerning Dostoevsky's significance as a historical phenomenon. This essay toys with some interpretations of Dostoevsky which may be applied in the future, when the present transitional stage is over. It introduces the name of Emanuel Swedenborg as a useful catalyst.

Swedenborg may be linked with Dostoevsky in two ways. First, Russia's cultural lag left the Russian intelligentsia open to a sudden onslaught of Western scientific thinking, with centuries compressed into a few decades. That is why Dostoevsky the religious thinker is similar in many respects to religious thinkers in the West who earlier resisted the corroding impact of scientific innovations. Not infrequently, he resembles and even sounds like Pascal. In the seventeenth century Pascal was, after all, the most representative of those writers engaged in the defense of the faith against the skeptics. Also the Age of Reason, as personified by Voltaire, oppressed Dostoevsky, as did nineteenth-century science,

CZESLAW MILOSZ has emerged as a preeminent voice of conscience for the twentieth century. A Lithuanian-born poet, novelist, essayist, translator, critic, and literary scholar who writes in Polish, Milosz received the Nobel Prize for literature in 1980 and the Neustadt International Prize for literature in 1978.

He is best known for the poetic articulation of his experience of World War II, the Holocaust, and the devastation of Warsaw. Milosz is considered as a founder of the catastrophist school of Polish poetry. In his acceptance speech for the Nobel Prize, however, he remarked that contemporary poetry—including his own—"was not prepared to cope with those catastrophes" of the twentieth century that "by their death-bearing range surpassed all natural disasters known to us." After the war, he dedicated himself to the Polish diplomatic service from 1946 to 1950, but he reluctantly exiled himself to Paris in 1951. In 1960, he moved to Berkeley, California, to join the faculty at the University of California. He is now an American citizen and Professor Emeritus of Slavic languages and literatures there.

His work shows a strong propensity for spiritual themes as well as a deep admiration for those visionaries who lift the level of perception to salvatory realms of sanity. He claims his most important sources of inspiration are Swedenborg, Simone Weil, Dostoevsky, Blake, and his own distant cousin, Oscar V. de L. Milosz.

personified for him by Claude Bernard ("Bernardy" in *The Brothers Karamazov*). As a theologian confronted with the rationalistic science of the day, Swedenborg had recourse to an aggressive exegesis of Christianity, and an analogous tendency can be distinguished in Dostoevsky.

A second link is provided by Dostoevsky's borrowings from Swedenborg. To affirm that they exist is not farfetched, for even the books in Dostoevsky's library supply a sort of material proof. The catalog of Dostoevsky's library, published in 1922 by Leonid Grossman,[1] lists three such books. These are, all in Russian, the following: A. N. Aksakov, *The Gospel According to Swedenborg: Five Chapters of the Gospel of John with an Exposition and a Discussion of Their Spiritual Meaning According to the Teaching on Correspondences* (Leipzig, 1864); A. N. Aksakov, *On Heaven, the World of Spirits and on Hell, as They Were Seen and Heard by Swedenborg*, translation from the Latin (Leipzig, 1863); A. N. Aksakov, *The Rationalism of Swedenborg: A Critical Analysis of His Teaching on the Holy Writ* (Leipzig, 1870). A. N. Aksakov was in Russia a chief proponent of spiritism or, as we would say today, parapsychology—an interest which was treated unkindly by Dostoevsky in *The Diary of a Writer*. He became acquainted with Swedenborg, however, thanks to Aksakov's essays and translations and he took from these books what suited his purpose.

Swedenborg in the First Half of the Twentieth Century

During the first half of our century much attention was paid to so-called symbolism in poetry. It seems strange that, in spite of this preoccupation, Swedenborg was little known. After all, Baudelaire's sonnet "Les Correspondances"—a poem crucial to symbolist poetics—took its title and its contents from Swedenborg. Curiosity alone should have directed critics to explore the original concept, not just its derivatives. The truth is that every epoch has dusty storage rooms of its own where disreputable relics of the past are preserved. Swedenborg was left there together with the quacks, miracle workers, and clairvoyants so typical of the not-so-reasonable Age of Reason—people such as Count Cagliostro, the legendary Count Saint-Germain, and an initiator of the "mystical lodges" in France, Martinez Pasqualis. The risk of taking Swedenborg seriously was too great; besides, nobody seemed to know what to think of him.

Neither his contemporaries nor posterity ought to be blamed too much for this neglect. Swedenborg's destiny was extraordinary. A scientist of wide reputation who pursued researches in various disciplines from geology to anatomy, a member of the Royal Mining Commission in Sweden, he had a sudden moment of illumination, abandoned his scientific pursuits, and produced a voluminous *oeuvre* in which he described his travels through heaven and hell and his conversations with

spirits. He continued to frequent the high society to which he belonged as a royal counselor, and even though he claimed to move simultaneously in the other world, his congeniality and humor disarmed those who would have been ready to call him a madman. After his death in 1772 his works, translated into English, made several converts who organized themselves into the Swedenborgian Church of the New Jerusalem. Romanticism in its turn made use of Swedenborg, adapting him to its own needs. For its adherents an ethereal, spiritual world opposed to the world of matter was almost alluring: it was this they saw, albeit not quite correctly, in Swedenborg's teachings. Balzac's *Séraphita* is typical of such a Romantic misinterpretation.

Swedenborg's legend was still alive at the time of Balzac and Baudelaire, but gradually it waned during subsequent decades. In the period which interests us, namely, the first half of the twentieth century, Swedenborg was at best an enigma attracting explorers of mental abnormality. It will suffice here to mention two major names which exemplify an attitude of uncertainty, if not of actual helplessness.

The first name is that of Karl Jaspers, who published a study of schizophrenia in 1922; he chose Strindberg, Van Gogh, Swedenborg, and Hölderlin as cases of famous schizophrenics. The second name is that of Paul Valéry, whose 1936 essay on Swedenborg is quite curious. Valéry was once at the center of the symbolist movement; moreover, as a brilliant essayist he dominated the French literary scene for several decades. He confesses that Swedenborg has always been for him no more than a literary myth and leaves one wondering whether he has ever read the author with whom he is dealing. Valéry's essay was written as an introduction to the French translation of a book on Swedenborg by the Swedish scholar Martin Lamm. The book does not provide any answer to the question which preoccupies Valéry, namely: "How is a Swedenborg possible?" so he looks for a solution of his own, rejecting the most common hypotheses, those of charlatanism and of insanity. But his own, psychological, explanation sounds even less convincing than Jaspers's diagnosis of mental illness and betrays Valéry's positivistic bias. His rather weak essay on Swedenborg offers us an insight into the positivistic background of French symbolism, into its basic duality. Swedenborg's visions were, according to Valéry, a kind of daydreaming—they occurred in a state between sleep and wakefulness. Perhaps we would not be guilty of insolence if we read into that statement, precisely because it lacks Valéry's usual sharpness, an avowal of his skepticism regarding creations of the human mind. He is very tactful and voices his respect for the "real" reality of nature and of human society; another reality, that of the artist, of the visionary, is autonomous, a separate area where veracity and delusion are on an equal footing.

Swedenborg was not the only writer who was something

of a nuisance then. Another was William Blake. The question of Blake's mental illness was debated quite seriously at the beginning of our century, and though his admirers rejected it as nonsense, their studies published in the thirties and in the forties were known to relatively few people. The fact that Blake today has become a major figure of English literature is one of the signs indicating a serious change in attitude. And, of course, an acquaintance with Blake must awaken interest in Swedenborg, not only because Blake was influenced by him, but also because Swedenborg can best be understood when approached using Blake's own criteria.

Let us pose a simplistic question: Did Swedenborg really travel through heaven and hell and did his conversations with spirits really take place? The most obvious answer is no, not really. He only believed that he had access to the other world at any time, for instance, when attending a party or walking in his garden. Everything happened only in his mind. This amounts to conceding that Jaspers was right when he pronounced his verdict: schizophrenia. We should note that romanticism had already treated Swedenborg in a way no different from the way positivistic psychiatry did later on, namely, a split into the material (that is, real) and the spiritual (that is, illusory) had been accepted, but with a plus sign, not a minus, added to the phantoms of our mind. If, however, William Blake's help is enlisted in reading Swedenborg, the picture changes radically. The question asked and the answer given would be rejected by Blake as absurd. Blake read Swedenborg exactly as he read Dante: these were for him works of the supreme human faculty, Imagination, thanks to which all men will one day be united in Divine Humanity. Through Imagination spiritual truths are transformed into visible forms. While opposing Swedenborg on certain crucial matters, Blake felt much closer to his system than to the system of Dante, whom he accused of atheism. Blake's *The Marriage of Heaven and Hell* is modeled upon Swedenborg, and he would have been amused by an inquiry into whether he had "really" seen the devils and angels which he describes. The crux of the problem—and a serious challenge to the mind—is Blake's respect for both the imagination of Dante, who was a poet, and the imagination of Swedenborg, whose works are written in quite pedestrian Latin prose. Dante was regarded by his contemporaries as a man who had visited the other world. Yet Jaspers would not have called him a schizophrenic, because the right of the poet to invent— that is, to lie—was recognized in Jaspers's lifetime as something obvious. It is not easy to grasp the consequences of the aesthetic theories which have emerged as the flotsam and jetsam of the scientific and technological revolution. The pressure of habit still forces us to exclaim: "Well, then, Swedenborg wrote fiction and he was aware it was no more than fiction!" But, tempting as it is, the statement would be false. Neither Swedenborg nor Blake were aestheticians; they did

FIG. 192. *Fedor Dostoevsky (1821-1881)*

not enclose the spiritual within the domain of art and poetry and oppose it to the material. At the risk of simplifying the issue by using a definition, let us say rather that they both were primarily concerned with the *energy* which reveals itself in a constant interaction of Imagination with the things perceived by our five senses.

Swedenborgian Elements in Crime and Punishment

The doctrine of correspondences is treated at length in Swedenborg's *Heaven and Hell*, which Dostoevsky may have purchased or read in Aksakov's translation during his stay in Germany in 1865. Let us note the place of publication, Leipzig, and the date, 1863. *Crime and Punishment* was begun in Wiesbaden in 1865. That Baudelaire in his *Flowers of Evil* was indebted to Swedenborg is well known, but there are, in my opinion, strong traces of Swedenborg's influence in *Crime and Punishment* also. A big phantasmagoric city, whether it be Paris, literally called by Baudelaire *la cité infernale,* or St. Petersburg, where Raskolnikov is beset by nightmares, already seems to be the modern form of a Dantesque hell; a description of it may refer implicitly to the doctrine of correspondences. To sound convincing, one ought to quote numerous passages from Swedenborg. However, this is beyond the scope of a brief essay and I shall limit myself to a few sentences.

"What a correspondence is, is not known at the present day"—says Swedenborg—"for several reasons, the chief of which is that man [a human; see Glossary] has withdrawn himself from heaven by the love of self and love of the world" (HH 87). That lost vision embraced creation as a unity, because "the whole natural world corresponds to the spiritual world, and not merely the natural world in general, but also every particular of it; and, as a consequence, everything in the natural world that springs from the spiritual is called correspondent" (HH 89). Man by virtue of his mind is part of the spiritual world and therefore "whatever effects are produced in the body, whether in the face, in speech, or in bodily movements, are called correspondences" (HH 91). Perhaps the gist of Swedenborg's teaching resides in his carrying the anthropocentric vision implied by Christianity to an extreme. The maxim "As above, so below" has always been invoked by hermetic Christian movements with their system of mirrors, for, according to them, the macrocosm was reflected in the microcosm and thus correspondences are to be found in the whole tradition of alchemy and in Jakob Böhme. But Swedenborg went one step further: for him the whole universe in its only valid essence, celestial and spiritual or infernal, had a human shape: "It has been shown that the entire heaven reflects a single man, and that it is in image a man and is therefore called the Greatest Man [Universal Human, see Glossary]" (HH 94). As a consequence, everything human acquires an extraordinary importance, for this entire world to which we apply physics and chemistry exists so as to provide *human* imagination with archetypes and human language with signs.[2] Any man may live in a constant relationship with the Greatest, Cosmic, Man—in other words, live in heaven—but he may also avoid it and keep company with the Cosmic Evil Man—in other words, live in hell. When he dies, he finds himself in one of the innumerable heavens or hells which are nothing other than societies composed of people of the same inclination. Every heaven or hell is a precise reproduction of the states of mind a given man experienced when on earth and it appears accordingly— as beautiful gardens, groves, or the slums of a big city. Thus everything on earth perceived by the five senses will accompany a man as a source of joy or of suffering much as the alphabet, once learned, may be composed into comforting or depressing books. In the eighteenth century Swedenborg was not alone in discovering this strange dimension: the dimension of human inwardness. Others as well searched for a counterbalance to the world of scientists, which was conceived as a mechanism seen *from the outside*. Different as they are from each other, in many ways several thinkers have in common this search for *the inside*: Berkeley with his *esse est percipi*—to be is to be perceived—Kant with his categories of the mind, and, of course, Blake. Swedenborg's choice of states of mind and images as the foundation of his system

was to appeal to romantic and symbolist poets for obvious reasons. Yet by shifting the emphasis they obtained the opposite of the original idea. Correspondences are not symbols to be arbitrarily chosen by a poet or a novelist. If the word *symbol* applies here, they are "objective symbols," preordained by God and determined by the very structure of nature and of human imagination. A visionary, a prophet unveils them, and Swedenborg, who assigned himself a prophetic role, deciphered with their help the hidden spiritual meaning of the Bible. All this had little to do with literature, at least as far as he was concerned. It was not destined to become a basis for legitimizing uncontrolled subjectivity or for establishing a democratic equality of subjective symbols and metaphors. It is true, some poets have noticed that not all symbols are of equal power and they have valued the most those which have their roots in archetypes. But this is a separate issue, alien to Dostoevsky, at least on a conscious level.

In *Crime and Punishment* the streets of St. Petersburg, the dust, the water of the canals, the stairs of tenement houses are described as seen by Raskolnikov; thus they acquire the quality of his feverish states. His dreams, his coffinlike room, and the city itself are woven into the rich symbolic texture of the novel. All this is not unfamiliar to a reader of the early Dostoevsky, and seems only to intensify the devices already used in *The Double* or in *The Landlady*. There is, however, one character who displays too much kinship with the spirits of Swedenborg for his direct descent from the book *Heaven and Hell* to be doubted. This is Svidrigailov. We will grant that he has captivated many readers and scholars who sensed in him a somewhat exotic element previously unencountered in Dostoevsky's novels. While a good deal of symbolism is involved in the name, appearance, and behavior of Sonya, we feel in Svidrigailov still another dimension, as though he had just arrived from and were returning to the beyond, in spite of his palpable presence and his presumed biography. Everything about him—the way he visits Raskolnikov for the first time, his physical features, his gestures, his speech, and his dreams—qualify as Swedenborgian correspondences; viewed from that angle, he is, though alive, a melancholy inhabitant of hell. In parenthesis, the strong identification of Dostoevsky with Svidrigailov has been noted by critics, but nobody to my knowledge has pointed to the origin of that hero's name to back the assumption. Dostoevsky was not indifferent to the past of his family and he liked to refer to his ancestors, nobles who had owned an estate, Dostoevo, in the Grand Duchy of Lithuania. One of the Lithuanian rulers of the fifteenth century was Duke Svidrigaila, a well-known historical figure. No other character of Dostoevsky's is endowed with a Lithuanian name.

But unraveling the author's little secrets is more or less an idle game. What is important is that love of self, as a central theme, appears in *Crime and Punishment* in two forms: the one represented by Raskolnikov, who gradually becomes aware of its power, the other by his double, Svidrigailov, who has nothing to learn for he knows his evil nature and has a feeling of eternal damnation. Love of self, according to Swedenborg, characterizes all the inhabitants of the infernal realm, which remains, however, infinitely differentiated. To quote:

> Every evil, as well as every good, is of infinite variety. That this is true is beyond the comprehension of those who have only a simple idea regarding every evil, such as contempt, enmity, hatred, revenge, deceit, and other like evils. But let them know that each one of these evils contains so many specific differences, and each of these again so many instances of particular differences, that a volume would not suffice to enumerate them. The hells are so distinctly arranged in accordance with the differences of every evil that nothing could be more perfectly ordered or more distinct. Evidently, then, the hells are innumerable. (HH 588)

Raskolnikov is an intellectual of the nineteenth century who has rejected heaven and hell as depicted in Christian iconography and rejected immortality along with them. The conversation between him and Svidrigailov on that subject is one of the strangest in world literature:

> "I don't believe in a future life," said Raskolnikov.
> Svidrigailov sat lost in thought.
> "And what if there are only spiders there, or something of that sort," he said suddenly.
> "He is a madman," thought Raskolnikov.
> "We always imagine eternity as something beyond our conception, something vast, vast! But why must it be vast? Instead of all that, what if it's one little room, like a bathhouse in the country, black and grimy and spiders in every corner, and that's all eternity is? I sometimes fancy it like that."
> "Can it be you can imagine nothing juster and more comforting than that?" Raskolnikov cried, with a feeling of anguish.
> "Juster? And how can we tell, perhaps that is just, and do you know it's what I would certainly have made it," answered Svidrigailov, with a vague smile.
> This horrible answer sent a cold chill through Raskolnikov.

How could we assume that this image of a private hell does not come straight from Swedenborg? Spiders, tarantulas, scorpions as symbols of evil return so persistently in Dostoevsky's late works that they deserve the appellation of correspondences. A passage from Swedenborg enlightens us sufficiently as to the hells which are built out of correspondences to things perceived by the senses:

> Some hells present an appearance like the ruins of houses and cities after conflagrations, in which infernal spirits dwell and hide themselves. In the milder hells there is an appearance of rude huts, in some cases contiguous in the form of a city with lanes and streets, and within the houses are infernal spirits engaged in unceasing quarrels, enmities, fightings, and brutalities; while in the streets and lanes robberies and depredations are committed. (HH 586)

Of course, in view of the infinite variety of hells, there is room also for a country bathhouse with spiders.[3]

Svidrigailov suffers from the systematic visits of specters, but he does not dismiss them as delusions. He is inclined to think that "ghosts are, as it were, shreds and fragments of other worlds, the beginning of them." The dreams he has shortly before his suicide are so vivid that they resemble visions more than sequences of blurred images loosely bound together by an oneiric logic. Their horror surpasses even Raskolnikov's dream after the murder. One would not be far wrong in considering *Crime and Punishment* a novel that deals with Raskolnikov's self-will on one level only, while on a deeper level there is another crime and another punishment: Svidrigailov's rape of a child and his suicide. But is there any reason to think that Svidrigailov had really committed that crime? Not necessarily. The coffin in which a fourteen-year-old girl lies among flowers, like Shakespeare's Ophelia, may lead us to believe that he had debauched an adolescent, who then committed suicide. If so, he is a very sensitive devil indeed, for in the next dream the victim changes into a five-year-old child and he is terrified when suddenly she opens her eyes and looks at him with "a glowing, shameless glance." Faced with Svidrigailov's presumed misdeeds the reader is more or less in the position of Dostoevsky's biographers, aware of his obsession and uncertain whether he had in fact once raped a little girl.

Just as in *Crime and Punishment* the very core of evil had to do with the rape of a child, so in *The Possessed* Stavrogin, though he harbors in himself all the devils of Russia, accuses himself in his *Confession* of precisely the same sin. Yet his conversation with Tikhon leaves the reader perplexed. It is impossible to be certain that Stavrogin once behaved as he says he did. The purpose of his confession, reflected in the ugliness of its style, is noted by Tikhon: This is an act of defiance by Stavrogin, not of contrition; he does not ask for forgiveness, but tries to provoke hatred and scorn. If this applies to the style, it may apply to the content as well and the whole story of the rape might have been invented. It seems as if Dostoevsky's feelings of guilt were constantly searching for expression through one symbolic event which returns again and again as a fixed correspondence. That symbolic reality has the same substance as do Swedenborg's hells; it resides beyond commonly accepted notions of the existing and the imaginary, the objective and the subjective.

A literary parentage going back to Gogol and E. T. A. Hoffmann is sufficient to explain the fantastic elements in the young Dostoevsky's fiction, for instance, the pranks of Golyadkin Jr. in *The Double*, which are still explained away in a rational manner by Golyadkin Sr.'s mental illness. Beginning with *Crime and Punishment,* the rational cover for these extraordinary, bizarre occurrences grows very thin and thus they are elevated above mere phantoms. A rational explanation is contrived in the form of a state between dreaming and wakefulness, as experienced by Svidrigailov on the night before his suicide; of a confession written by Stavrogin; of falling asleep in *The Dream of a Ridiculous Man,* though his travel through time into the remote past of mankind has nothing dreamy about it; or, in *The Brothers Karamazov,* of the sober, psychiatric title of a chapter: "The Devil. Ivan's Nightmare"—while neither Ivan nor the reader is convinced that the Devil was merely a product of Ivan's sick brain.

Dostoevsky as a Heresiarch

It is more than likely that Dostoevsky read Swedenborg when working on *Crime and Punishment* and that he was emboldened by a theology which assigns such a prominent place to the imagination. Whether and precisely what he borrowed from Swedenborg remains uncertain, with the possible exception of Svidrigailov's bathhouse full of spiders. But Dostoevsky's strategy as a religious thinker is of more consequence than possible borrowings of details, and Swedenborg's writings may offer some clues in this respect.

Anna Akhmatova used to call Dostoevsky and Tolstoy "heresiarchs," as we learn from Nadezhda Mandelstam's memoirs.[4] This is true enough. Their extraordinary minds, their fervor, and the gigantic stakes they played for did not save them from preaching fuzzy or even wild doctrines. Although basically dissimilar, they were alike in their efforts to adapt Christianity to what they believed to be the needs of modern man. Yet Tolstoy's "true" Christianity, diluted by Rousseauism, resembled more and more a nontheistic Buddhism, as Solovyov noted. In Tolstoy's copious output as a sermonizer, the metaphysical meaning of the Gospels evaporated and only the moral meaning remained. It would hardly be an exaggeration to say that Tolstoy ended where Dostoevsky started, and to locate the latter's point of departure during his Fourierist phase, at the time when he belonged to the Petrashevsky circle.

The Christian vocabulary of utopian socialism should be kept in mind, whether its spokesman be Saint-Simon, Fourier, or George Sand. In its rejection of Christian churches and in placing itself under the sign of the Gospels, utopian socialism was to some degree the inheritor of such populist Christian movements of the past as the Hussites or the Anabaptists, who had proclaimed a return to the original purity of the early Christian communes. Yet the vocabulary veiled a profound change in belief, a result of the eighteenth-century *Lumières.* A social utopia now occupied the first place, not Christ: he was admired only as its announcer, as the most

sublime teacher and reformer. Dostoevsky, as we know, was shocked by Belinsky's derogatory and scornful words about Christ. When he joined the Petrashevsky circle, it was different; discussions on Fourier or Considérant did not threaten his personal attachment to the figure of Jesus as a moral ideal, for the precise reason that they focused upon the Kingdom of God on earth as something not very remote but easily attainable. Subsequently Dostoevsky's whole life, beginning with his stay in the penal colony of Omsk, would be marked by the incessant struggle in his mind between two images of Christ; one, a model of perfection never equaled by anyone else, yet still a mortal man and thus subject to the law of death; the second, a God-Man triumphant over death. A contradiction, overlooked by the humanists and socialists of the Petrashevsky circle, gradually was to take shape in Dostoevsky's work, up to its most poignant presentation in *The Legend of the Grand Inquisitor.* For the argument of the Grand Inquisitor with Christ is nothing more and nothing less than that of a utopian socialist with his supposed leader who refuses to serve as such and, what is worse, shows that his disciple had misunderstood him. Christ says in fact that his Kingdom of God is not of this world—and the freedom he offers man does not lead to any perfect society. No one but the God-Man intending to lift man up to his own divine level can ask for acceptance of this freedom. The utopian in Dostoevsky yearned so much for the Kingdom of God on earth that he sided with the Grand Inquisitor; it is this that explains the forceful speech the author, himself internally divided, puts into the mouth of his tragic old man. The divine nature of Christ appears as a major obstacle to human happiness on earth and therefore should be denied. But, by a dialectical countermovement, as soon as the earthly happiness of man is chosen as a goal it becomes obvious that it can be attained only at the price of the total annihilation of human freedom. Thus the argument expresses Dostoevsky's despair at the thought of the erosion of Christian faith—in himself, in the Russian intelligentsia, and in Western Europe. And it was this that forced him to resort to arbitrary and unrealistic remedies. In that big either/or—either a Christian civilization or the totalitarian society of Shigalev and of the Grand Inquisitor—he paradoxically hoped to find a third way, and clung to his "Holy Russia" with the peasant below and the tsar above as the only possible mainstay of Christianity and consequently human freedom.

The Human and the Divine

The problem of the two natures of Christ underlies Dostoevsky's whole work, and it also determines his journey from a socialist utopia to a nationalistic one. To say that at some given moment he became an atheist (whatever that word may mean) under Belinsky's influence is not truly relevant, for he was haunted by the figure of Christ the teacher perhaps no less in the forties than later on, when in the penal colony. Yet undoubtedly he underwent a change of heart in Omsk, in the sense that now the necessity of an act of faith became clear. His much-quoted letter of 1854 to Fonvizina, written upon his release from the prison camp, contains the nucleus of those internal contradictions which torment his major heroes:

> I will tell you regarding myself that I am a child of the age, that I have been a child of unbelief and doubt up till now and will be even (I know it) until my coffin closes. What terrible torments this thirst to believe has cost and still does cost me, becoming the stronger in my soul the more there is in me of contrary reasonings. And yet sometimes God sends me moments when I am utterly at peace; in those moments I have constructed for myself a symbol of faith in which everything is clear and sacred to me. This symbol is very simple: to believe that there is nothing more beautiful, more profound, more sympathetic, wiser, braver, or more perfect than Christ; and not only is there nothing, but, as I tell myself with jealous love, there *could not* be anything. Even more: if somebody proved to me that Christ is outside the truth, and if it were *a fact* that the truth excludes Christ, I would rather remain with Christ than with the truth.

This last sentence is potentially that of a "heresiarch." Who could *prove* to Dostoevsky that Christ was beyond the truth? A scientist, a philosopher, for whom everything is submitted to deterministic laws and who would shrug at the story of Christ rising from the dead as an offense to our reason? That sort of proof, through the universal order of nature, is accepted by those characters of Dostoevsky's who are, more or less, the spokesmen for his "intellectual part"— Ippolit in *The Idiot*, Kirillov in *The Possessed*, and Ivan Karamazov. "And if Christ be not risen, then is our preaching vain, and your faith is also vain," says Saint Paul.[5] Ippolit, Kirillov, Ivan, and the Grand Inquisitor have their negative proofs that it is really so, but they also realize that if it is so, if Christ deluded himself in foretelling his resurrection, then the world is a devil's farce. Dostoevsky himself, or the part of him which turns against his skeptical characters, "would rather remain with Christ than with the truth" and thus yields the field in reality to the so-called scientific Weltanschauung. The opposition of faith to reason has behind it an old tradition, but the opposition of faith to truth is a desperate novelty and dangerously favors any self-imposed deception.[6]

There is perhaps also a second layer of meaning in that enigmatic sentence. Because the Gospels are not a treatise on ethics and their message is often self-contradictory, many Christian mystics counseled clinging to the person of Christ as opposed to norms or values. A well-founded counsel— but at the same time a precept cherished by every sectarian, for it authorizes transforming the image of Christ as suits a given man or community. The suspicion arises whether "the Russian Christ" of Dostoevsky is not connected with such an exalted arbitrariness.

The Onslaught of Philosophy—and of Gnosticism

A brief digression is necessary here. Christianity has in modern times, beginning with the Renaissance, been forced to renew its quarrel with philosophic thought. At one time, in the Roman Empire, it had been Greek philosophy; assimilated and tamed by the church, it tended nevertheless to recover its autonomy and at last—thanks to so-called humanism—it grew in strength, inspiring modern science. Or to be more precise, one side of Greek thought was now taken over and turned against the other, which had been fused with the Jewish heritage. Quite symptomatic was the revival in the sixteenth century of the Anti-Trinitarian heresy also known as Arianism, though Arius had been condemned by the Council of Nicaea long before, in A.D. 325. Perhaps one should call it *the* heresy and trace it down through the history of Christianity in its various contradictory guises. At first sight the "luminous" rationalistic trend in the Renaissance (and undoubtedly Arianism, with its dislike of incomprehensible dogma, belongs here) had nothing to do with its contemporary "dark," more esoteric counterpart. Yet the two were just the two sides of the same philosophic coin, much as they had been before in the Hellenistic world. The origins of attacks upon the Trinity should be traced back to Gnosticism, which had already by the second century A.D. introduced a duality, a separation between Christ on the one hand and the God of the Old Testament on the other. The very dogma of the Trinity—of the three *hypostases* designated the Father, the Son, and the Holy Ghost—was elaborated as the response of the early church to that Gnostic cleavage which broke the continuity of the Revelation through history. From its birth the Gnostic heresy, in its various ratiocinations, had at its core a resentment of the evil world: a God responsible for such evil could not be a supreme being, while Christ was—or represented—the true deity.[7] Then the Manichaeans stepped in and followed a well-blazed trail. Ever since, Christology has been a territory for which heretics have had a predilection; they have tended to oppose Redemption to Creation, the Savior to Jehovah, or even to exult in the human nature of Christ, who, through *kenosis*, "emptied himself" of his divine attributes. In Dostoevsky's major novels all these problems are present implicitly or explicitly.

The theology of Swedenborg, who was both a modern Christian and a scientist, was a major attempt at wrestling with the dogma of the Trinity as recognized by all three branches of Christianity: Roman Catholic, Orthodox, and Protestant. He accused them all of teaching the faithful to imagine three gods, and thus disguising polytheism under a formula incomprehensible to the human mind. At the same time, however, he disapproved of the solution offered by the Arians, for whom Christ was not of the same nature as the Father and for a large number of whom he was merely a man. Swedenborg's system is dominated by a Christ who is *the only God*, not in spite of his having been born a man, but precisely because he was born a man. Absolutely Christocentric, Swedenborg's system is also absolutely anthropocentric. Its most sacred books are the Gospel of Saint John and the Apocalypse; by coincidence these were also the most sacred books for Dostoevsky. Swedenborg's credo is embodied in the exclamation of Thomas the Apostle when he touched Christ's wounds: "My Lord and my God." Man was created in the image and semblance of God, for Our Father in heaven is man; heaven, as I have already quoted, is according to Swedenborg the Greatest Man [Universal Human].

To compare Dante and Swedenborg as writers would be hazardous, but their respective visions of "the other shore" constitute two decisive testimonies to the imaginative life of our civilization. Dante's cosmology is medieval and his theology is based upon Thomas Aquinas, in whose syllogisms Greek philosophy was put to a Catholic use. The importance of man, created and redeemed by God, is guaranteed in Dante by the Earth's central place in the universe. But by Swedenborg's time the universe is resolved into a motion of whirling planets and stars. If it were not for one man, Christ, God incarnated, mankind would dwindle into a speck of dust, into an accident in the incomprehensible mechanical order of things. Perhaps for that reason Swedenborg emphasizes God-Man as preexisting, the Creator and Redeemer in one person. It would be incorrect to classify Swedenborg as an Anti-Trinitarian, for all he wanted was to propose a new concept of the Trinity. Yet his disciple William Blake, occasionally a rebel against his master, hardly modified the Swedenborgian doctrine when he chose the Human Form Divine as the key to all the secrets of existence. And, unlike in Swedenborg, gnostic affinities are obvious in Blake's multiple reversals of religious concepts: God the lawgiver equated with Satan, Elohim with inferior demiurges. The creation of the world, presented by Blake as an act of divine mercy *after* the Fall has already taken place (or simultaneously with it, which is the same where there is no time), is purely Manichaean. In the teachings of Mani (d. A.D. 277), the founder of Manichaeism, after the Kingdom of Light was contaminated by the Kingdom of Darkness, the Kingdom of Light allowed an inferior demiurge to create the world in that zone so that it might be purified through the action of time.

Swedenborg (and Blake) humanized or *hominized* God and the universe to such an extent that everything, from the smallest particle of matter to planets and stars, was given but one goal: to serve as a fount of signs for human language.

Man's imagination, expressing itself through language and identical in its highest attainments with the Holy Ghost, was now to rule over and redeem all things by bringing about the era of the New Jerusalem. Man was again at the center, even though his Earth and his galaxy were not. The Christian strategy of Swedenborg (and Blake) perhaps parallels that of Thomas Aquinas, who felt that philosophy (or at least Aristotle, *the* philosopher) must be absorbed by Christian thought. In the eighteenth century the Christian strategist was confronted with a more difficult task: philosophy was to be absorbed in its two derivatives, in the rationalistic trend and in the more somber heretical tradition of duality, of a chasm between Creation and Redemption. It was made possible by affirming that the divine is eternally human and that the human is potentially divine.

But Swedenborg (and Blake) teetered on the very edge, where the equilibrium between Christian faith and its anti-Christian denial was constantly threatened. The divinization of man was already in the offing, accompanied by the advent of "European nihilism" as foretold by Friedrich Nietzsche. Our era, the second half of the twentieth century, is marked by a tragicomic escapism, namely, a "death of God" theology which proceeds from the idea of divine humanity and subjects it to an imperceptible alteration, so that it changes into its opposite. It is enough to read a book on Blake by one of the chief "death of God" theologians[8] to observe how this can be accomplished—obviously by enlisting the help of Hegel. To Dostoevsky's credit, let us recall here that, while the dialectics of God-Man and Man-God were present in his novels, he desperately struggled against blurring the basic antinomy between the two.

Dostoevsky's Attempts to Solve the Problem

When describing the books in Dostoevsky's library, Leonid Grossman admits the probability of Swedenborg's influence upon what we may consider Dostoevsky's last word in religious matter, namely, upon the discourses of Father Zosima on prayer, love, hell, and contact with other worlds.[9] Grossman's hint has not, to my knowledge, been taken by anybody, and a study of the subject is lacking. Father Zosima in many of his pronouncements indeed sounds like Swedenborg, particularly in his talk on eternal damnation. A man's life, according to Zosima, is "a moment of *active living* love" and is given to him as a gift of time and space, where love can be exercised. The drama of eternal life resides precisely in the brevity of this encounter with time and space, which soon are no more and then everything one has lived through becomes part of his interior states. The flames of hell are within the damned and correspond to the quality of their love on earth: "For them hell is voluntary and they cannot have enough of it. . . . They cannot behold the living God without hatred and demand that there be no God of life, that God destroy himself and all his creation."[10]

In Father Zosima's thinking, a Manichaean hatred of creation is characteristic of the damned. Yet Dostoevsky, like Swedenborg and Blake before him, tried hard to absorb the heresy and integrate it into a Christology of his own. In a novel this is, however, more difficult than in theology and poetry. Dostoevsky seems to say: If the concept of God-Man free from sin is to have any validity, then human nature should allow us at least an inkling as to how it might be possible. That is why Dostoevsky spent so much energy striving to create a perfect good man as a hero of fiction. And he failed. Prince Myshkin is a living negative proof, for his acts show to what extent love of self is at the root of human nature and how insufficiently human someone is who lacks it. Myshkin, who is completely selfless, devoid of aggression and sexual drive, is no less a monster of emptiness than is Stavrogin with his excess of self-love. Father Zosima comes straight from the lives of the saints and eludes our questioning, for he is protected by his prestige as a repentant sinner. As for Alyosha, he is convincing only as one of the Karamazovs, united by their dark, violent blood. His missionary activities among schoolboys and the resulting brotherhood are, to be frank, melodramatic and outright schmaltz. Artistic falsity reveals here the falsity of Dostoevsky's self-imposed collectivistic belief, his heresy which he propagated especially in his journalism. Alyosha, a Christlike leader, suggests the future Russian Christ and is surrounded by twelve children-disciples, but by a strange twist of stylistic fate (there are stylistic fates), the presumed church changes into a Boy Scout unit. It is a doubtful proposition that one can achieve the Kingdom of God on earth by converting mankind into boy scouts, and that is why those chapters of *The Brothers Karamazov* read like an unintended parody. Shatov in *The Possessed*, who loves the Christlike Russian people but does not believe in God, might, however, have been a sarcastic jab intentionally directed by Dostoevsky against himself.

In the history of the rebellion of man against God and against the order of nature, Swedenborg stands out as a healer who wanted to break the seals on the sacred books and thus make the rebellion unnecessary. By revealing that God is man he was convinced that he had fulfilled Christ's promise to one day send a comforter, the spirit of truth; that spirit spoke through him. Swedenborg's serene Christology may help in elucidating Dostoevsky's tormented and tortuous Christology. At the same time such a study would uncover some Blakean elements in Dostoevsky, who never heard of Blake.

Dostoevsky's rebels are invested with a false, exaggerated moral sensitivity: the order of the world should be rejected because it offends man's moral judgment; this world is full of the suffering and agony of creatures tormenting one another. The ideal man, Jesus [Divine Human; see Glossary], must stand in opposition to that natural order; unfortunately, he was for the rebels merely a man and his mistakes had to be corrected; hence the only logical conclusion was to postulate the advent of a Man-God. But Dostoevsky's "positive" heroes fare no better. His failures in drawing them probably testify to his utopian (Fourierist) vision of the ideal man as perfectly meek, perfectly humble, and deprived of selfhood. William Blake knew better: he distinguished between Imagination enslaved by the Spectre—by the self—and Imagination making use of the Spectre, which is a permanent component of human nature. Such an appraisal of human faculties is more realistic. But Dostoevsky's failures, even more than his successes, pay tribute to the permanence of the dilemma which, some eighteen centuries ago, emerged in the guise of a quarrel between the early Christian churches and the Gnostics. The divinization of man, when one abhors the order of the world as essentially evil, is a risky and self-contradictory venture.

Notes

1. L. P. Grossman, *Seminarii po Dostoevskomu* (Seminar on Dostoevsky) (Gosudarstvennoe Izdatel'stvo, 1922; reprint, Great Britain: Prideaux Press, 1972).

2. In this respect an English metaphysical poet, Thomas Traherne, is Swedenborg's predecessor, as, for instance, in the following stanza:

   This made me present evermore
   With whatsoere I saw.
   An object, if it were before
   My Ey, was by Dame Natures Law,
   Within my Soul. Her Store
   Was all at once within me: all her Treasures
   Were my imediat and Internal Pleasures,
   Substantial Joys, which did inform my Mind.

   with all she wraught,
   My Soul was fraught,
   And evry Object in my Heart a Thought
   Begot, or was; I could not tell,
   Whether the Things did there
   Themselves appear,
   Which in my Spirit truly seemd to dwell;
   Or whether my conforming Mind
   were not even all that therin shind.

   From "My Spirit," in *The Poetical Works of Thomas Traherne* (New York: 1965).

3. In Swedenborg's system there are no angels and devils except the saved and the damned humans. To this Dostoevsky refers in his notebook of 1875–76: "Are there devils? I could never imagine what satan's would be like. Job. Mephistopheles. Swedenborg: bad people . . . about Swedenborg." From *The Unpublished Dostoevsky*, ed. Carl R. Proffer (Ann Arbor, Mich.: Ardis, 1975), vol. 2.

4. Nadezhda Mandelstam, *Vtoraya kniga* (Second book) (Paris: YMCA Press, 1972).

5. 1 Corinthians 15:14.

6. Here Dostoevsky comes close to Kierkegaard, but the dichotomy is resolved by Kierkegaard, who tips the scales in favor of "inwardness," "subjectivity," and thus identifies faith with truth: "The truth is precisely the venture which chooses an objective uncertainty with the passion of the infinite." "But

the above definition of truth is an equivalent expression for faith." "Faith is precisely the contradiction between the infinite passion of the individual's inwardness and the objective uncertainty." From Kierkegaard, *Concluding Unscientific Postscript* (Princeton, N.J.: Princeton University Press, 1971), p. 182. A saying of Meister Eckhart's may be recalled here: "If God were able to backslide from truth I would fain cling to truth and let God go."

7. "The following may be noted as the main points in the Gnostic conception of the several parts of the *regula fidei:*

a) The difference between the supreme God and the creator of the world, and therewith the opposing of redemption and creation, and therefore the separation of the Mediator of revelation from the Mediator of creation.

b) The separation of the supreme God from the God of the Old Testament, and therewith the rejection of the Old Testament, or the assertion that the Old Testament contains no revelations of the supreme God, or at least only in certain parts.

c) The doctrine of the independence and eternity of matter.

d) The assertion that the present world sprang from a fall of man, or from an undertaking hostile to God, and is therefore the product of an evil or intermediate being.

e) The doctrine that evil is inherent in matter and therefore is a physical potence [*sic!*].

f) The assumption of Aeons, that is, real powers and heavenly persons in whom is unfolded the absoluteness of the Godhead.

g) The assertion that Christ revealed a God hitherto unknown."

From Adolph Harnack, *History of Dogma* (New York: Dover, 1961), vol. 1, pp. 257–59. Harnack also lists other, additional points.

8. Thomas J. Altizer, *The New Apocalypse: The Radical Christian Vision of William Blake* (Ann Arbor, Mich.: University of Michigan Press, 1967).

9. Grossman.

10. Grossman.

Singing Masters of the Soul
Swedenborg's and Blake's Influence on William Butler Yeats

Jennifer L. Leonard, Ph.D.

SAILING TO BYZANTIUM

I

That is no country for old men. The young
In one another's arms, birds in the trees
—Those dying generations—at their song,
The salmon-falls, the mackerel-crowded seas,
Fish, flesh, or fowl, commend all summer long
Whatever is begotten, born, and dies.
Caught in that sensual music all neglect
Monuments of unageing intellect.

II

An aged man is but a paltry thing,
A tattered coat upon a stick, unless
Soul clap its hands and sing, and louder sing
For every tatter in its mortal dress,
Nor is there singing school but studying
Monuments of its own magnificence;
And therefore I have sailed the seas and come
To the holy city of Byzantium.

III

O sages standing in God's holy fire
As in the gold mosaic of a wall,
Come from the holy fire, perne in a gyre,
And be the singing-masters of my soul.
Consume my heart away; sick with desire
And fastened to a dying animal
It knows not what it is; and gather me
Into the artifice of eternity.

IV

Once out of nature I shall never take
My bodily form from any natural thing,
But such a form as Grecian goldsmiths make
Of hammered gold and gold enamelling
To keep a drowsy Emperor awake;
Or set upon a golden bough to sing
To lords and ladies of Byzantium
Of what is past, or passing, or to come.

(W. B. Yeats, 1927; collected in *The Tower*, 1928)[1]

JENNIFER L. LEONARD is a writer and teacher and currently the resource editor for *Chrysalis* magazine. She holds a Ph.D. in English from Tufts University, an M.A. in English from Vanderbilt University, and an undergraduate degree in philosophy from Goucher College. Her area of expertise is the Neoplatonic tradition in Western philosophy, religion, and art and its presence in modern literature. Her research has led to publications and presentations about the writing of Lawrence Durrell, Paul Scott, and Anthony Powell. She lives in Cambridge, Massachusetts, with her husband and grows roses in a small garden.

WILLIAM BUTLER YEATS fired his magnificent poetry in the alembic of magic and inspiration from the hermetic tradition.* His was a lifelong study of the spirit through psychical research, theosophy, and astrology; he pursued his interest by membership in the Order of the Golden Dawn, the Dublin Hermetic Society, and the Esoteric Section of the Theosophical Society. In a recent article on Yeats, Denis Donoghue writes that these studies ". . . gave him access to a religious tradition, heterodox with reference to Christianity but—the names of Plotinus, Henry More, Thomas Taylor, Böhme, Swedenborg and Blake are enough to make the point."[2] The point being that while this tradition is outside the church, one should perceive it as the esoteric equivalent of the church's exoteric teachings.

That Blake was inspired by Emanuel Swedenborg has been made clear in the fine book, *Blake and Swedenborg,* a series of scholarly essays exploring the sources of Blake's art in the writings of Swedenborg.[3] The importance of Blake for Yeats is equally as strong as Swedenborg for Blake and confirms Yeats in the visionary, spiritual tradition. Kathleen Raine, the eminent Blake scholar, finds evidence for such a relation in her major study, *Blake and Tradition.* In her introduction she writes, ". . . of all his commentators Ellis and Yeats (or was it above all Yeats?) most nearly shared Blake's essential premises."[4]

The commentary Miss Raine refers to is the 1893 volume in which Yeats edited the collected works of Blake with Edwin J. Ellis. To evidence the importance of magic—a word Yeats used as a rubric for his hermetic studies—we have an explicit connection in Yeats's words: "If I had not made magic my constant study I could not have written a word of my Blake book. . . . The mystical life is the center of all that I do & all that I think & all that I write."[5]

Yeats shared with Swedenborg and Blake, as indeed with all the adepts of this tradition, an understanding of love as the medium of spiritual insight. In his study, *Symbolism in Painting,* he writes that to perceive with love, with *agape,* one then liberates oneself and the object of perception from the illusion of separateness, the bonds and motives and their actions, causes, and effects. Then, perceiving with love alone, the "object" "will change under your eyes, and become a symbol of an infinite emotion, a part of the Divine Essence."[6]

*This tradition supports an enormous amount of knowledge gathered into a body of works attributed to Hermes Trismegistus, hence the name *hermetic.* The tradition goes from this partially understood current of Egyptian occult and philosophical ideas down through Plato, Plotinus, Iamblichus. During the Italian Renaissance writers like Ficino and Nicholas of Cusa translated hermetic and Neoplatonic texts and the tradition became fixed in Western civilization, infusing the writings of Paracelsus and Böhme, Swedenborg and Blake, and so to the current novels of Lawrence Durrell and Anthony Powell. The major thrust of the tradition was to discover the interconnections between human life, the *anima mundi,* and the divine world.

Yeats is here in full agreement with Swedenborg, who taught that the heart of being is love. To participate in love, which gives access to divine unity, is predicated on a liberated imagination. Yeats wrote that when the imagination enters experience and turns it into symbol, releasing the mind from its domination, ". . . that is to say, when Christ is born of Mary, he puts on, through his maternally derived portion, a body for the express purpose of taking it off."[7] The symbol of the Human-God and the paradox embodied therein is the key to imaginative perception, and thereby, redemption. The tragedy of modern humanity, as Czeslaw Milosz writes in *The Land of Ulro,* was the age of reason, which identified humanity as separated individuals. The modern age is depicted by spiritual vacancy, isolation of the individual, and "the minatory character of civilization as a whole. . . . But the underground tradition endured, thanks to Martinez Pasqualis, Saint Martin and Swedenborg"[8]— and, I would add, Blake and Yeats. These visionaries believed the soul's resurrection occurs now, in this world, through an act of imagination.

Before incarceration in the body, the soul, according to this spiritual tradition, was baptized in Lethe's waters, and she has forgotten her divine origin. She lives trapped in the physical world, suffering in a realm of transience and decay—wrapped in sensual music amid dying generations. Something must shake her from lethargy if she is to begin her ascent to the Divine where she can reunite with her Creator. The imagination can touch the soul, rouse her to awareness, and in her contemplation of truth as it is found embodied in art, she gains strength, emerging from physical slumber, awakened by the Muses. Yeats describes the awakening and the ascent of the soul in a way understood by hermeticists. Beginning with Plato, he gives us evidence of the soul's experience of release and purgation in the magnificent poem, "Sailing to Byzantium." The poem has several laminations, as it is first a description of the journey of the soul, and second a work of art itself, the purpose of which is to stir the soul of the reader in that initial rousing, the beginning of the journey.

The pattern for the soul's rise, traditionally, follows a fourfold expression.[9] The history of the four-fold pattern can be traced to Plato's *Phaedro* and *Symposium,* where Plato speaks of a kind of initiatory frenzy or delirium. Denis de Rougemont writes about this extraordinary state Plato described, saying that it

> is neither conceived nor born in a man's soul except by the inspiration of heaven. It is alien to us, its spell is wrought from without, it is a transport, an infinite rapture away from reason and natural sense. It is therefore to be called enthusiasm, a word which actually means, "possessed by god," for the frenzy not only is of heavenly origin, but culminates at its highest in a new attainment of the divine. . . . Love is

the way that ascends by degrees of ecstasy to the one source of all that exists, remote from bodies and matter, remote from what divides and distinguishes.[10]

Plato described four different kinds of enthusiasm. Later, during the Renaissance, mystics and philosophers such as the scholiast Hermeas, Giordano Bruno, Ficino, and Cornelius Agrippa arranged these enthusiasms in a specific hierarchical order and related them, as Plato did not, to corresponding cosmic and imaginative hierarchies. Thus by being associated with enthusiasm and powerful animating experiences, the distinct imaginative levels of insight became symbolic stages denoting rising spiritual energies, while at the same time each stage could be artistically treated as a reality in itself, with attributes peculiar to its cosmic position, either near the base of earthly confusion or close to the ultimate godhead.

The first enthusiasm, associated with poetry, and in a more general sense with all of the arts, was represented by the Muses, who stirred the soul from its somnolence by way of the imagination. The next enthusiasm, the telestic, brought the soul to a consciousness of the wide range of spiritual experience. In the mystical animation of this state the soul is relieved of diabolical fantasy and becomes sane. This enthusiasm was associated with Dionysus, for example as where one encountered the Dionysian experience of rending apart and rejuvenation. The prophetic third level was attributed to Apollo and known simply as Apollonian. Those who attained this level perceived the entirety of the natural world. The fourth level was described as the realm of love, Eros-Agape. Hermeas explains that it is the last stage, the final cause, which in a sense determines the whole movement, because all creative enthusiasm is directed ultimately toward the final object of love, the soul's desire.

Before reading "Sailing to Byzantium" for its hermetic paradigm, outwardly signaled by the four stanzas of the poem, it will be illuminating to understand what Byzantium meant to Yeats. In his volume *A Vision*, the poet writes,

I think if I could be given a month of Antiquity and leave to spend it where I chose, I would spend it in Byzantium a little before Justinian opened St. Sophia and closed the Academy of Plato. I think I could find in some little wine-shop some philosophical worker in mosaic who could answer all my questions, the supernatural descending nearer to him than to Plotinus even, for the pride of his delicate skill would make what was an instrument of power to princes and clerics, a murderous madness in the mob, show as lovely flexible presence like that of a perfect human body.

I think that in early Byzantium, maybe never before or since in recorded history, religious, aesthetic and practical life were one, that architect and artificers . . . spoke to the multitude and few alike. The painter, the mosaic worker,

FIG. 193. Voyage of the Magi, *Byzantine mosaic*

the worker in gold and silver, the illuminator of sacred books, were almost impersonal, perhaps without the consciousness of individual design, absorbed in their subject-matter and that the vision of a whole people. They could copy out of old Gospel books those pictures that seemed as sacred as the text, and yet weave all into a vast design, the work of many that seemed the work of one, that made building, picture, pattern, metal-work of rail and lamp, seem but a single image. . . .[11]

Byzantium is a city of the soul, and "Sailing to Byzantium" is a poetic expression for the soul's awakening to her saving enthusiasms. Yeats's first stanza describes the sensual world of physical engendering; the birds in this stanza are as intent on the sensual music as Chaucer's birds in the Prologue to the *Canterbury Tales*:

> . . . smale foweles maken melodye,
> *That slepen al the nyght with open yë*
> (So priketh hem nature in hir corages)."[12]

The engendering of species brings them to life only to die in the charnel house of the physical world, yet paradoxically, this is not a country for old men, as they have lost their lust. The old men are in the figure of the *senex amans*, the old man, the fallen Adam.

In the second stanza, the felicitous image of the soul clapping its hands, singing, might have come from Blake, who witnessed his brother Robert's death and watched his soul depart its body, singing and clapping its hands.[13] In terms of the paradigm for the soul's release, singing suggests the inspiration of the Muses, which rouse the soul and lift it to the first level of salvation. And then Yeats tells us that singing school is the study of the soul's "monuments of its own magnificence," meaning the perception of art that awakens the imagination, that key to the kingdom. The poet sails to Byzantium, where "religious, aesthetic and practical life were one" and the artists wove their work into a vast design that seemed the work of one.

The Dionysian element enters the third stanza: sick with the desires of the flesh the poet entreats the sages, standing in the gold mosaic, to purify him, consume his heart, thereby purging him of his dying flesh, freeing him from the body that does not know what it is, and gathering him "into the artifice of eternity." Remembering that the creation is God's work of art explains the use of the word *artifice* here.

This stanza shimmers like a luminous palimpsest. The poet in the creation of the poem imagines himself in the ideal city of Byzantium. He looks into a mosaic representing sages standing in holy fire and entreats them to come from this static design and perne in a gyre,* revealing the eternal, which Yeats called Divine Essence, taking him to themselves in the "artifice of eternity." According to the hermetic tradition, the Dionysian enthusiasm frees through the very violence of its destruction; it precipitates a purgation and a

rejuvenation, in this case, allowing the soul to rise to a level where it becomes aware of itself in the context of eternity.

In the fourth stanza, the poet, once out of nature, will take on a created form not biologically engendered but artistically created. It is through art that thought, meditation, and an understanding of harmony come together to lift the soul to the third, Apollonian, level of its rise. In Hermeas's words, "The Apollonian mania converts and coexcites all the multiplied powers, and the whole of the soul, to *the one* of it."[14] The hermeticists thought that once the Apollonian level has been reached, the soul perceives reality as one, it is aware of the simultaneity of time, "of what is past, or passing, or to come."

Yeats does not discuss the fourth enthusiasm in this poem, as it is a statement of process, sailing. But it should be said that artists, according to Hermeas, in their concern with revealing eternal truth, attempt to show the way, to reveal the pattern by which the soul moves toward the final realization of its desire, the perfect union in God's love.

Yeats schooled himself to art and its truth therein. He chose to be one of the Byzantine craftsmen, one whose work would be woven into a vast design, becoming a part of the Divine Essence, the true mystic reality. That he succeeded may be witnessed by this poetic tribute to the soul's magnificence. "Sailing to Byzantium," standing in the mystic tradition as it does, can be read as a hymn honoring William Blake and Emanuel Swedenborg.

---

*To "perne" is to rise. Yeats's use of the word *gyre* here carries a meaning similar to one Swedenborg meant when he wrote, "There are gyres into which newly arrived Spirits must be inaugurated, to the intent that they may be able to be in the company of others, so as to speak and to think together with them. In the other life there must be an agreement and unanimity of all, as one . . ." (AC 5182). The gyre would seem to be the place for Swedenborg and Yeats where the initiate learns perennial truth.

Notes

1. William Butler Yeats, "Sailing to Byzantium," in *The Collected Poems of W. B. Yeats* (New York: Macmillan, 1956), p. 124.
2. Denis Donoghue, "The Young Yeats," *New York Review of Books* 33, no. 17 (14 July 1986), p. 15.
3. Harvey F. Bellin and Darrell Ruhl, eds., *Blake and Swedenborg: Opposition Is True Friendship* (New York: Swedenborg Foundation, 1985).
4. Kathleen Raine, *Blake and Tradition*, Bollingen Series XXXV, 2 vols. (Princeton, N.J.: Princeton University Press, 1968), vol. 1., p. xxv.
5. Donoghue, p. 15.
6. Ibid., p. 16.
7. Ibid.
8. Czeslaw Milosz, *The Land of Ulro*, trans. Louis Iribarne (New York: Farrar, Straus, Giroux, 1981), p. 193.
9. The significance of the tetrad or fourfold configuration is well-established. It appears again and again in art, literature, and music of the Western tradition. It is documented in *The Land of Ulro* where Milosz discusses the pattern as found in Swedenborg, Blake, and Carl Jung (ibid., pp. 166 and 185). It is described by Kathleen Raine, who has said, "The total cosmology of Platonism presumes four worlds. . . ." along with other remarks on the importance of the formation of fours in a published interview with Brian Keeble from *Lindisfarne Letter*, no. 9 (1979) (Lindisfarne Press, R.D. 2, West Stockbridge, MA).
10. Denis de Rougemont, *Love in the Western World*, trans. Montgomery Belgion (New York: Random House, 1966), p. 61.
11. W. B. Yeats, *A Vision* (New York: Collier Books, 1986), pp. 279–80.
12. F. N. Robinson, ed., *Chaucer: Canterbury Tales* (Cambridge, Mass.: Riverside Press, 1957), p. 17, ll. 9–11.
13. T. R. Henn documents this anecdote about Blake in his study of Yeats, *The Lonely Tower* (London: Methuen, 1966), p. 225n.
14. Hermeas's *Scholia on the Phaedrus*, cited extensively as a note by Thomas Taylor in his translation and edition of Iamblichus, *On the Mysteries of the Egyptians, Chaldeans, and Assyrians* (London: Reeves and Turner, 1895), p. 354n.

Poets with Swedenborgian Connections

Compiled by Alice B. Skinner, Ph.D.

Visions of Potentialities

NOWADAYS quite a few people have verbal revelations apart from any perception, even people who are not involved in anything good, especially through dreams or visions. . . . But since these people lack perception, they are only verbal or visual revelations without any perception of their meaning. Genuine perceptiveness arises through heaven from the Lord, and influences a person's intellect spiritually, leading it observably toward thinking in accord with reality, with an inner agreement from some unidentified source. It seems to be inherent in the person, but it is an inner voice through heaven from the Lord flowing into the deeper levels of thought, concerned with matters that transcend the natural and the sensory—that is matters involving the spiritual world and heaven. (AC 5121 [2])

Like Swedenborg, some poets are visionaries, tuned to a voice that "flow[s] into the deeper levels of thought" and connects with spiritual realities. From this perspective everyday life is transposed into heavenly terms, revealing the world intended by the Creator, a world infused with love and potentialities and dependent on humans to transform it. These poets emphasize God's design, as did Swedenborg:

> The reason we are in God through a life in accord with [his] design is that God is present everywhere in the universe, in its each and every detail: he is in its inmost things, since these are in accord with [his] design. In things that are not in accord with the design . . . God is everywhere present through a ceaseless struggle against them, and through a ceaseless effort to bring them back into the design. For this reason, insofar as we let ourselves be brought back into the design, God is omnipresent in our whole being; and therefore God is in us and we are in God. God's absence from us is no more possible than is

the absence of the sun from earth through its warmth and light. (TCR 70 [2])

In the following selections, Vachel Lindsay and Edwin Markham envision a world of opportunity in which people, including "slave[s] of the wheels of labor," are able to develop their potential as befits the "handiwork [of] God." William Blake, sounding like an Old Testament prophet, deplores restrictions on the power of Love and calls upon society (England) to awaken to Jesus, the "bright Preacher of Life," and heal the disease of denial of the spiritual realm. Recognizing that "the old world waits the time to be renewed," Elizabeth Barrett Browning writes of life that "develops from within" and depends on the "poet's individualism / To work your universal . . . , [to quicken] hearts in individual growth." Vachel Lindsay celebrates the Master at rest on the seventh day, singing of the newly built Holy City "gleam[ing] in the murmuring plain."

THE LEADEN-EYED

LET not young souls be smothered out before
They do quaint deeds and fully flaunt their pride.
It is the world's one crime its babes grow dull,
Its poor are ox-like, limp and leaden-eyed.

Not that they starve, but starve so dreamlessly,
Not that they sow, but that they seldom reap,
Not that they serve, but have no gods to serve,
Not that they die, but that they die like sheep.

VACHEL LINDSAY[1]

A NET TO SNARE THE MOONLIGHT

(WHAT THE MAN OF FAITH SAID)

THE dew, the rain and moonlight
All prove our Father's mind.
The dew, the rain and moonlight
Descend to bless mankind.

Come, let us see that all men
Have land to catch the rain,
Have grass to snare the spheres of dew
And fields spread for the grain.

Yea, we would give to each poor man
Ripe wheat and poppies red,—
A peaceful place at evening
With the stars just overhead:

A net to snare the moonlight,
A sod spread to the sun,
A place of toil by daytime,
Of dreams when toil is done.

VACHEL LINDSEY[2]

THE MAN WITH THE HOE

(*Written after seeing Millet's world-famous painting*)

BOWED by the weight of centuries he leans
Upon his hoe and gazes on the ground,
The emptiness of ages in his face,
And on his back the burden of the world.
Who made him dead to rapture and despair,
A thing that grieves not and that never hopes,
Stolid and stunned, a brother to the ox?
Who loosened and let down this brutal jaw?
Whose was the hand that slanted back this brow?
Whose breath blew out the light within this brain?

Is this the Thing the Lord God made and gave
To have dominion over sea and land;
To trace the stars and search the heavens for
    power;
To feel the passion of Eternity?
Is this the dream He dreamed who shaped the
    suns
And marked their ways upon the ancient deep?
Down all the caverns of Hell to their last gulf
There is no shape more terrible than this—
More tongued with censure of the world's blind
    greed—
More filled with signs and portents for the soul—
More packt with danger to the universe.

What gulfs between him and the seraphim!
Slave of the wheel of labor, what to him
Are Plato and the swing of Pleiades?
What the long reaches of the peaks of song,
The rift of dawn, the reddening of the rose?
Through this dread shape the suffering ages look;
Time's tragedy is in that aching stoop;
Through this dread shape humanity betrayed,
Plundered, profaned, and disinherited,
Cries protest to the Judges of the World,
A protest that is also prophecy.

O masters, lords and rulers in all lands,
Is this the handiwork you give to God,
This monstrous thing distorted and soul-quenched?
How will you ever straighten up this shape;
Touch it again with immortality;
Give back the upward looking and the light;
Rebuild in it the music and the dream;
Make right the immemorial infamies,
Perfidious wrongs, immedicable woes?

O masters, lords and rulers in all lands,
How will the Future reckon with this man?
How answer his brute question in that hour
When whirlwinds of rebellion shake all shores?
How will it be with kingdoms and with kings—
With those who shaped him to the thing he is—
When this dumb terror shall rise to judge the
    world,
After the silence of the centuries?

EDWIN MARKHAM[3]

THE GARDEN OF LOVE

I WENT to the garden of Love.
And saw what I never had seen:
A Chapel was built in the midst,
Where I used to play on the green.

And the gates of this Chapel were shut,
And Thou shalt not. writ over the door;
So I turn'd to the Garden of Love,
That so many sweet flowers bore.

And I saw it was filled with graves,
And tomb-stones where flowers should be:
And Priests in black gowns, were walking their
    rounds,
And binding with briars, my joys & desires.

WILLIAM BLAKE[4]

SELECTIONS FROM *JERUSALEM*

READER! [*lover*] of books! [*lover*] of heaven,
And of that God from whom [*all books are given,*]
Who in mysterious Sinais awful cave
To Man the wond'rous art of writing gave,
Again he speaks in thunder and in fire!
Thunder of Thought, & flames of fierce desire:
Even from the depths of Hell his voice I hear,
Within the unfathomd caverns of my Ear.
Therefore I print; nor vain my types shall be:
Heaven, Earth & Hell, henceforth shall live in
    harmony

Of the Measure, in which
    the following Poem is written

    We who dwell on Earth can do nothing of
    ourselves, every thing is conducted by Spirits,
    no less than Digestion or Sleep.

• • •

Trembling I sit day and night, my friends are
    astonish'd at me.
Yet they forgive my wanderings, I rest not from
    my great task!
To open the Eternal Worlds, to open the immortal
    Eyes
Of Man inwards into the Worlds of Thought: into
    Eternity
Ever expanding in the Bosom of God, the Human
    Imagination
O Saviour pour upon me thy Spirit of meekness &
    love:
Annihilate the Selfhood in me, be thou all my life!
Guide thou my hand which trembles exceedingly
    upon the rock of ages.

• • •

I see the Four-fold Man. The Humanity in
    deadly sleep
And its fallen Emanation. The Spectre & its cruel
    Shadow.
I see the Past, Present & Future, existing all at once
Before me; O Divine Spirit sustain me on thy wings!
That I may awake Albion from his long & cold repose.
For Bacon & Newton sheathed in dismal steel,
    their terrors hang
Like iron scourges over Albion.

• • •

Let every Christian as much as in him lies engage
himself openly & publicly before all the World in
some Mental pursuit for the Building up of Jerusalem

I stood among my valleys of the south
And saw a flame of fire, even as a Wheel
Of fire surrounding all the heavens: it went
From west to east against the current of
Creation and devourd all things in its loud
Fury & thundering course round heaven & earth
By it the Sun was rolld into an orb:
By it the Moon faded into a globe,
Travelling thro the night: for from its dire
And restless fury, Man himself shrunk up
Into a little root a fathom long.
And I asked a Watcher & a Holy-One
Its Name? he answerd. It is the Wheel of Religion
I wept & said. Is this the law of Jesus
This terrible devouring sword turning every way
He answerd; Jesus died because he strove
Against the current of this Wheel: its Name
Is Caiaphas, the dark Preacher of Death
Of sin, of sorrow, & of punishment;
Opposing Nature! It is Natural Religion
But Jesus is the bright Preacher of Life
Creating Nature from this fiery Law,
By self-denial & forgiveness of Sin.
Go therefore, cast out devils in Christs name
Heal thou the sick of spiritual disease
Pity the evil, for thou art not sent
To smite with terror & with punishments
Those that are sick, like to the Pharisees
Crucifying & encompassing sea & land
For proselytes to tyranny & wrath.
But to the Publicans & Harlots go!
Teach them True Happiness, but let no curse
Go forth out of thy mouth to blight their peace
For Hell is opend to Heaven; thine eyes beheld
The dungeons burst & the Prisoners set free.

———————

England! awake! awake! awake!
    Jerusalem thy Sister calls!
Why wilt thou sleep the sleep of death?
    And close her from thy ancient walls.

    Thy hills & valleys felt her feet,
        Gently upon their bosoms move:
    Thy gates beheld sweet Zions ways;
        Then was a time of joy and love.

    And now the time returns again:
        Our souls exult & Londons towers,
    Receive the Lamb of God to dwell
        In Englands green & pleasant bowers.

WILLIAM BLAKE[5]

SELECTIONS FROM AURORA LEIGH

". . . 'YOU will not compass your poor ends
Of barley-feeding and material ease,
Without the poet's individualism
To work your universal. It takes a soul,
To move a body,—it takes a high-souled man,
To move the masses, even to a cleaner stye:
It takes the ideal, to blow an inch inside
The dust of the actual: and your Fouriers failed,
Because not poets enough to understand
That life develops from within.'

• • •

. . . Art's a service,—mark:
A silver key is given to thy clasp,
And thou shalt stand unwearied, night and day
And fix it in the hard, slow-turning wards,
To open, so, that intermediate door
Betwixt the different planes of sensuous form
And form insensuous, that inferior men
May learn to feel on still through these to those,
And bless thy ministration. The world waits
For help. Beloved, let us love so well,
Our work shall still be better for our love,
And still our love be sweeter for our work,
And both commended, for the sake of each,
By all true workers and true lovers born.
Now press the clarion on thy woman's lip
(Love's holy kiss shall still keep consecrate)
And breathe thy fine keen breath along the brass,
And blow all class-walls level as Jericho's
Past Jordan,—crying from the top of souls,
To souls, that, here assembled on earth's flats
They get them to some purer eminence
Than any hitherto beheld for clouds!
What height we know not,—but the way we know,
And how by mounting ever, we attain,
And so climb on. It is the hour for souls,
That bodies, leavened by the will and love,
Be lightened to redemption. The world's old,
But the old world waits the time to be renewed,
Toward which, new hearts in individual growth
Must quicken, and increase to multitude
In new dynasties of the race of men;
Developed whence, shall grow spontaneously
New churches, new œconomies, new laws
Admitting freedom, new societies
Excluding falsehood: He shall make all new."

ELIZABETH BARRETT BROWNING[6]

I HEARD IMMANUEL SINGING

The poem shows the Master with his work done, singing to free his heart in Heaven.

This poem is intended to be half said, half sung, very softly, to the well-known tune:

"Last night I lay a-sleeping,
There came a dream so fair,
I stood in Old Jerusalem
Beside the temple there,"—etc.

Yet this tune is not to be fitted on, arbitrarily. It is here given to suggest the manner of handling rather than determine it.

I HEARD Immanuel singing   *To be sung.*
Within his own good lands;
I saw him bend above his harp.
I watched his wandering hands
Lost amid the harp-strings;
Sweet, sweet I heard him play.
His wounds were altogether healed.
Old things had passed away.

All things were new, but music.
The blood of David ran
Within the Son of David,
Our God, the Son of Man.
He was ruddy like a shepherd.
His bold young face, how fair.
Apollo of the silver bow
Had not such flowing hair.

I saw Immanuel singing   *To be read.*
On a tree-girdled hill.   *very softly,*
The glad remembering branches   *but in*
Dimly echoed still   *spirited*
The grand new song proclaiming   *response.*
The Lamb that had been slain.
New–built, the Holy City
Gleamed in the murmuring plain.

The crowning hours were over.
The pageants all were past.
Within the many mansions
The hosts, grown still at last,
In homes of holy mystery
Slept long by crooning springs
Or waked to peaceful glory,
A universe of Kings.

He left his people happy.   *To be sung.*
He wandered free to sigh
Alone in lowly friendship
With the green grass and the sky.
He murmured ancient music
His red heart burned to sing
Because his perfect conquest
Had grown a weary thing.

No chant of gilded triumph—
His lonely song was made
Of Art's deliberate freedom;
Of minor chords arrayed
In soft and shadowy colors
That once were radiant flowers:—
The Rose of Sharon, bleeding
In Olive-shadowed bowers:—

And all the other roses
In the songs of East and West
Of love and war and worshipping,
And every shield and crest
Of thistle or of lotus
Or sacred lily wrought
In creeds and psalms and palaces
And temples of white thought:—

All these he sang, half smiling   *To be read*
And weeping as he smiled,   *very softly*
Laughing, talking to his harp   *yet in*
As to a new-born child:—   *spirited*
As though the arts forgotten   *response.*
But bloomed to prophecy
These careless, fearless harp-strings,
New-crying in the sky.

"When this his hour of sorrow   *To be sung.*
For flowers and Arts of men
Has passed in ghostly music,"
I asked my wild heart then—
What will he sing to-morrow,
What wonder, all his own
Alone, set free, rejoicing
With a green hill for his throne?
What will he sing to-morrow,
What wonder all his own
Alone, set free, rejoicing,
With a green hill for his throne?

VACHEL LINDSAY[7]

❧

Doubters find it difficult to understand how visionaries gain access to knowledge about the spirit world. Oscar Milosz describes a process of knowing, noting that "By degrees to climb until you feel yourself penetrated by the very matter of pure space / Is not to know; it is still to record phenomena of manifestation." Moving through doubt and prayer, acknowledging a desire to know, Oscar Milosz describes receiving a stone "in which he [Father of the Ancients] was utterly and at the same instant I was given the crown of light."

CANTICLE OF KNOWLEDGE

THE teaching of the sunlit hour of the nights of the Divine.

For those, who, having asked, have received and know already.

For those whom prayer has led to meditation on the origin of language.

Others, thieves of joy and pain, knowledge and love, will understand nothing of these things.

To understand them, it is needful to know the objects designated by certain essential words

Such as bread, salt, blood, sun, earth, water, light, darkness, as well as the names of metals.

For these names are neither brothers, nor sons, but truly fathers of sensible objects.

With these objects and the prince of their substance they were hurled from the motionless world of archetypes into the abyss of the turmoil of time.

Only the spirit of things has a name. Their substance is nameless.

The power to name sensible objects absolutely impenetrable to spiritual being

Comes to us from knowledge of archetypes which, being of the same nature as our spirit, is like it situated in the consciousness of the solar egg.

Everything described by means of ancient metaphors exists in a situated place; of all places of the infinite the only one situated.

These metaphors which language still imposes on us today as soon as we question our spirit's mystery

Are vestiges of the pure language of times of faith and knowledge.

God's poets saw the world of archetypes and described it reverently by means of the precise and luminous terms of the language of knowledge.

The decline of faith shows itself in the world of art and science by a coarsening of language.

Nature poets sing the sensible world's beauty in the old sacred mode.

Yet, struck by the secret discord between the mode of expression and its object,

And powerless to lift themselves up to the only situated place, I mean Patmos, earth of the vision of archetypes,

They imagined in the night of their ignorance an intermediary world, floating and sterile, the world of symbols.

All the words whose magical gathering has formed this song are names of visible substances

Which, by grace of Love, the author has seen in the two worlds of blessedness and desolation.

I speak only to those who have recognized prayer as the first of man's duties.

The highest virtues, charity, chastity, sacrifice, knowledge, the Father's love itself,

Will be granted only to those who, by their own movement, have recognized the absolute necessity of humility in prayer.

Yet concerning the arcana of language I shall only reveal what the infamy and madness of this time allow me to reveal.

Now I can freely sing the canticle of the sunlit hour of the nights of God

And, proclaiming the wisdom of the two worlds opened to my sight,

Speak of the lost knowledge of blood and gold

Within limits imposed by the companion in service.

I have seen. He who has seen stops thinking and feeling. He can only describe what he has seen.

Here is the key to the world of light. From the magic of the words I gather here

The sensible world's gold draws its secret value.

For it is not its physical virtues that have made it king of spirits.

Truth is that in relation to which the Limitless is situated.

But truth does not make sacred language lie: for it is also the visible sun of the substantial world, of the motionless universe.

From this sun, earthly gold draws its substance and color; the man of light his knowledge.

Truth's language regained has nothing new to offer. It only awakens remembrance in the memory of the one who prays.

Do you feel the most ancient of your memories awakening in you?

I reveal to you here the holy origins of your love of gold.

Seven times has madness blown upon knowledge's golden candlestick.

The words of the Aaronites' language are profaned by lying children and ignorant poets

And the candlestick's gold, seized by the darkness of ignorance, has become the father of negation, theft, adultery, and massacre.

This is the key to the two worlds of darkness and light. O companion in service!

For love of this sunlit hour of our nights,

For the safety of the secret between you and me,

Whisper to me the sun-enveloped word, the thunder-charged word of this dangerous time.

I have named you! Here you are in the first ray in the womb of the fixed cloud, mute as lead.

In the leap and wind of the fiery mass,

In the appearance of the virginal spirit of gold,

In the passage from the egg to the sphere,

In the tremendous halt and the holy descent, when you look at a man between his two eyebrows,

In the immobility of the infinite cloud, of a single prayer, the work of the jewellers of the kingdom,

In the return to desolation wedded to Time,

In the compassionate whispering accompanying it.

But holy knowledge's golden key has stayed in my heart.

It will still re-open the world of light for me. By degrees to climb until you feel yourself penetrated by the very matter of pure space

Is not to know; it is still to record phenomena of manifestation.

The path leading from little to much is not holy science's.

I have just described the ascent towards knowledge. You must rise to the solar Place

Where by omnipotence of affirmation you become—what?—what you affirm.

Thus myriad spiritual bodies reveal themselves to virtuous senses.

First climb up! Sacrilegiously! To the craziest affirmations!

Then descend, rung by rung, regretless, tearless, with a joyous confidence, a regal patience,

To that mud which already contains everything with such terrible obviousness and by a necessity so holy! By a necessity so holy, holy, truly holy! Alleluia!

Who speaks here of surprise? There is still surprise in the unexpected sight, through shadows of an ancient city gate,

Of a far view of the sea with its holy lights and blessed sails.

But in the birth of a new sense, a sense which will serve the spirit of true science, there are no more surprises.

It is the custom on our heights to embrace every novelty like a spouse regained after time and forever.

In this manner the relation of the solar egg to the soul of earthly gold was revealed to me.

And this is the efficacious prayer into which the operative must plunge himself:

Sustain in me love of this metal that colors your gaze, knowledge of this gold that is the world of archetype's mirror

So that I might measurelessly expend my whole heart in this solar game of affirmation and sacrifice.

Receive me in the archangelic light that slumbers
thousands of years in funerary wheat, there sustaining
life's hidden fire.

For the grain of ancient tombs, split in the furrow,
lights up like a heart with its own charity

And it is no mortal sun that gives to the harvest its
immutable hue of wisdom.

Such is the key to the world of light. To whoever
handles it with a sure and pious hand it also opens—
the other region.

I have visited the two worlds. Love led me to being's
utter depth.

I have carried the weight of the night on my chest, my
brow has distilled the walls' sweat.

I have turned the wheel of horror of those who go and
return. In many places all that remains of me is a
circle of gold in a handful of dust.

I have explored gropingly the raging world's hideous
labyrinths and my strange homelands slumber
beneath great waters.

I said nothing. I waited only for my king's madness to
seize me by the throat. Your hand, O my king, is on
my throat! That is the sign, this is the moment. I
shall speak.

You had me born in a world that no longer knew you,
on a naked, cold planet of iron and clay.

Amid a murmer of thieves sunk in contemplation of
their sex.

The stench of massacre there is followed by the idiotic
flattery of the deceivers of peoples.

And yet, son of mud and blindness, I have no words to
describe

The iniquitous precipices of this other All, this other
Limitlessness

Created by your own omnipotent negation.

This separated place, different, hideous, this immense,
delirious, Luciferic brain

Where for eternity I suffered trials of the multiplication
of great lightning-flashes, those barren systems.

At the zenith was the worst, and I saw it as from a
black sun's precipice.

Ah! Infinite sacrilege, beside which the holy cosmos,
the one revealed before our lowly world,

Is like a square of hoarfrost lit up for the Nativity and
ready to melt at the Child's breath.

For you are He who is. You are both above yourself and
the absolute necessity by which you are.

That is why, Affirmer, total negation is in you, the
freedom to pray and not to pray. It is also why you
make affirmers pass great trials of negation.

For you tossed me into the blackest heat of this eternity

of horror where one feels seized

By the jaw by the fiery harpoon and hung in the folly of
perfect emptiness,

In this eternity where darkness is absence of the other
sun, extinction of the joyous golden ellipse;

Where lights are fury. Where all is marrow of iniquity.

Where thinking's operation is one and endless,
beginning in doubt and ending in nothing.

Where a person is not solitary but solitude, not
destitute but destitution, not damned but damnation.

I was a traveller in these lands of nocturnal din

Where, among physical things, only

Mad love and the lepra of the face bathe their damned
roots.

There like a blind worm I measured the meanderings of
a line of your hand. That country of night, thick as a
stone,

That world of the other morning star, of the other sun,
the other prince, was your closed hand. The hand
opened and here I am in the light.

One must have seen Him, the Other, to understand
why it is written that he comes like a thief. He is
farther away than the first cry at birth, he hardly is,
he is not. The space of a grain of sand, here he is,
whole in you, he, the other, the prince seated mutely
in eternal blindness.

You in the solar egg, you, immense, innocent, you
know yourself. But the two infinites of your
affirmation and your negation do not know each
other, will never know each other, for eternity is but
the flight of the one before the other.

All the hideous, mortal melancholy of space and time is
only the distance from a yes to a no and the measure
of their irremediable separation.

This is the key to the world of darkness.

The man in whom this song has awakened not a
thought, not an emotion, but a memory, a most
ancient memory, from now on will seek love with
love.

For this is what it is to love, this is what it is to love: to
seek love with love.

I sought like a sterile woman, furiously, with anguish. I
found. What? Who? The dominator, the possessor,
the dispensor of the two lepras.

I have returned to communicate my knowledge. Woe
unto him who goes and does not return.

Do not pity me for having gone and seen. Do not weep
for me:

Drowned in the blessedness of ascension, dazzled by
the solar egg, hurled into the madness of the black
eternity beside me, limbs bound about with algae of

darkness, I am always in the same place, being in place itself, the only one situated.

Learn from me that all sickness is a confession of the body.

True evil is hidden evil; but once the body has confessed it takes very little to bring the spirit itself, the preparer of secret poisons, into submission.

Like all sicknesses of the body, lepra portends the end of spiritual captivity

Spirit and body struggle for forty years: this is the famous critical age of which their science, that sterile woman, speaks.

Has evil opened a door in your face? Melchizedek, the messenger of peace, will enter by this door and it will close behind him again and his beautiful coat of tears. But repeat after me: *Pater Noster.*

See, the Father of the Ancients, of those who speak pure language, played with me as a father with his child. Only we, who are his little children, know this sacred game, this holy dance, this happy floating between worst darkness and best light.

You must prostrate yourself, full of doubt, and pray. I complained I did not know him at all; a stone came down into my hand in which he was utterly and at the same instant I was given the crown of light.

Look at me! Surrounded by snares I no longer fear anything.

From the dark of conception to the dark of death a thread of catacombs runs through my fingers in dark life.

And yet, who was I? A cloacal worm, blind and fat, with a pointed tail. A man created by God and in revolt against his Creator.

"Whatever its excellence and beauty, the future will never equal non-being in perfection." Such was my sole certainty, my secret thought: a sterile woman's poor, poor thought.

Like all nature poets I was sunk in profound ignorance. For I believed that I loved beautiful flowers, beautiful views and even beautiful faces for their beauty alone.

I was questioning the eyes and faces of the blind: like all courtesans of sensuality I was threatened by physical blindness. This too is a teaching from the sunlit hours of the Divine.

Until the day when, noticing I had stopped before a mirror, I looked behind me. The source of lights and forms was there, the world of profound, wise, chaste archetypes.

Then this woman who was in me died. For a tomb I gave her all her kingdom, nature. I buried her in the most secret spot in the deceitful garden, where the gaze of the moon, the eternal promiser, divides in the leafage and descends upon the sleeping woman in myriad degrees of sweetness.

Thus I learned that in its depths man's body encloses a remedy for all ills and that the knowledge of gold is also knowledge of light and blood.

O unique One! Do not take from me the memory of these sufferings on that day when you cleanse me of my evil as of my good and have me clothed in the sun by your own, the smiling ones. *Amen.*

OSCAR V. de L. MILOSZ[8]

Connections of the Poets with Swedenborg

WILLIAM BLAKE (1757–1827) signed a declaration of belief in the doctrines of Swedenborg in 1789 but did not join the New Church. His poetry reflects both criticism of Swedenborg (as in *The Marriage of Heaven and Hell*) and adherence to Swedenborgian ideas (as in *Songs of Innocence*).

Sources

Bellin, Harvey, and Ruhl, Darrell, eds. *Blake and Swedenborg: Opposition Is True Friendship.* New York: Swedenborg Foundation, 1985.

Bindman, David. *William Blake: His Art and Times.* London: Thames and Hudson, 1982.

ELIZABETH BARRETT BROWNING (1806–1861) was introduced to the works of Swedenborg in 1951 by a friend from London, Miss E. F. Haworth. Her letters to friends include references to her reading of Swedenborg and discussions of his ideas. In a letter to her sister Henrietta in 1857, Browning called herself "a Swedenborgian."

Sources

Bates, Ada L. *The Influence of Swedenborg on the Brownings.* Master's thesis, Teachers College, Temple University, 1943. See especially chap. 5.

Browning, Elizabeth Barrett. *Letters to Her Sister, 1846–1859.* Edited by Leonard Huxley. New York: E. P. Dutton.

VACHEL LINDSAY grew up in Springfield, Illinois, where he was acquainted with a group of Swedenborgians. Through them he became familiar with some of Swedenborg's ideas, which he incorporated into the ecumenical and reformative world view evident in much of his poetry.

Sources

Massa, Ann. *Vachel Lindsay: Fieldworker for the American Dream.* Bloomington, Ind.: Indiana University Press, 1970.

Chenetier, Mark. *Letters of Vachel Lindsay.* New York: Burt Franklin, 1979.

Masters, Edgar Lee. *Vachel Lindsay: A Poet in America.* New York, London: Charles Scribner's Sons, 1953.

EDWIN MARKHAM (1852–1940) listed Swedenborg's *Heaven and Hell* among thirteen books he would choose for his library on a desert island. He lectured and wrote about Swedenborg, including a poem for the dedication of a bust of Swedenborg made by Adolph Jonsson and placed in Lincoln Park, Chicago, Illinois. The archives at the Swedenborg School of Religion in Newton, Massachusetts, contain Markham's articles and lectures about Swedenborg.

Source

Stidger, William L. *Edwin Markham.* New York, Cincinnati, Chicago: Abingdon Press, 1933. See especially pp. 98, 205, 222–25, 234.

OSCAR V. de L. MILOSZ (1877–1939) considered Swedenborg to be one of his spiritual guides. In 1924 he wrote, "The best years of my life I have spent in my solitude, getting drunk on the Holy Scriptures and nourishing myself on them, first with my teacher Eugene Ledrain, then with some of my spiritual guides. Goethe, Swedenborg, Martinez de Pasqually, Claude de Saint Martin." Milosz' reading of Swedenborg is especially evident in the "Epistle to Storge," the first section of "Ars Magna" (1924).

Sources

O. V. de L. MILOSZ. *The Noble Traveller: The Life and Writings of O. V. de L. Milosz,* Edited and selected by Christopher Bamford. West Stockbridge, Mass.: Lindisfarne Press. 1985. See especially pp. 465, 467.

Notes for the Poems

1. Vachel Lindsay, "The Leaden-Eyed," in *Collected Poems* (New York: Macmillan, 1925), pp. 69–70.
2. Vachel Lindsay, "A Net to Snare the Moonlight," in ibid., pp. 52–53.
3. Edwin Markham, "The Man with the Hoe," in *Modern American Poetry,* 6th rev. ed., ed. Louis Untermeyer (New York: Harcourt Brace, 1942), pp. 111–12.
4. William Blake, "The Garden of Love," in *The Complete Poems,* ed. Alicia Ostriker, (Harmondsworth, England: Penguin Books, 1977), p. 127.
5. William Blake, selections from *Jerusalem,* in ibid., pp. 636, 650, 661, 798, 799.
6. Elizabeth Barrett Browning, selections from "Aurora Leigh," in *Poetical Works* (New York: Dodd, Mead, 1899), vol. 5, pp. 328, 390, 391.
7. Vachel Lindsay, "I Heard Immanuel Singing," in *Collected Poems,* pp. 369–72.
8. O. V. de L. Milosz, "Canticle of Knowledge" (selection from "The Confessions of Lemuel") in *The Noble Traveller,* ed. and trans. Christopher Bamford (West Stockbridge, Mass.: Lindisfarne Press, 1985), pp. 171–83.

II
Social Issues
&
Psychology

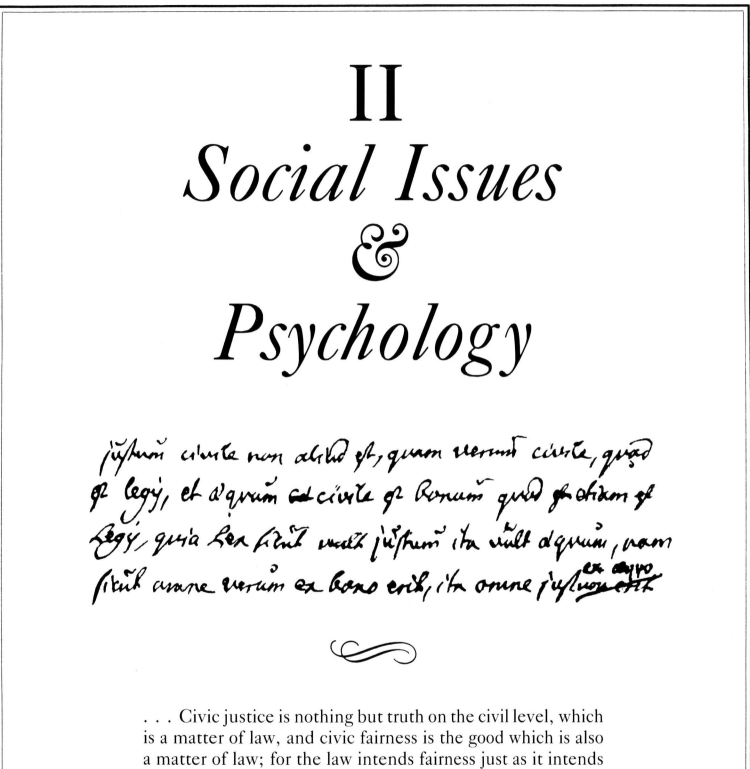

. . . Civic justice is nothing but truth on the civil level, which is a matter of law, and civic fairness is the good which is also a matter of law; for the law intends fairness just as it intends justice. As everything true must come from what is good, so everything just must come from what is fair. . . . (AE 1112)

Swedenborg and the Visionary Tradition

Stephen Larsen, Ph.D.

The two parts of the following essay were first presented to the annual meeting of the Society for the Scientific Study of Religion, San Antonio, in 1980. Subsequently they were published as a single piece in *Studia Swedenborgiana* 3, no. 4 (June 1980).

Herein the article has been divided into two parts. The first represents a positive statement on Swedenborg's mental health, which the editors felt especially necessary to include because over the years various psychiatric writers have tried to psychoanalyze Swedenborg *ex post facto* with a negative approach and diagnosis, that is, assuming that his visionary experiences were the result of pathology. This kind of approach has undoubtably done Swedenborg damage for many general readers unacquainted either with his biography or the great internal coherence of his work.

The second essay, using transpersonal psychology as a reference, shows in precisely what ways Swedenborg's unusual experiences should be perceived not as abnormal but as part of what the author refers to as the "visionary tradition." Like the "perennial philosophy," to which it has made a substantial contribution, the tradition shows us spiritual truths about the human condition that transcend time and culture. The thesis is that Swedenborg should be considered a major Western contributor to this tradition.

Part 1
Swedenborg's Mental Health

AT ABOUT THE AGE of fifty-five Emanuel Swedenborg began to experience a series of visions in which he felt as if his "inner sight" were being opened; and he beheld a spiritual dimension intimately but invisibly connected to this world. It was characteristic of Swedenborg to write of his inner experiences in meticulous detail, with the same scholarly care he had given to his numerous scientific treatises. Thus, he left one of the most complete psychological journals ever written. His visionary revelations caused considerable controversy in his own time as well as after. As is often true of inspirational material, there was conflict with established thought. Theologians who had no trouble preaching the existence of the transcendental reality portrayed in the scriptures had more difficulty with a contemporary who claimed to have entered the realm experientially.

Subsequent opinion on Swedenborg's life and work would

STEPHEN LARSEN received his B.A. and M.A. from Columbia University and his Ph.D. from the Union Graduate School. A teacher and practicing psychotherapist, he has been active in helping to develop the emergent discipline of transpersonal psychology (psychology with a spiritual side) in the United States and abroad. He is on the board of directors of the Swedenborg Foundation in New York City. His published writings include *The Shaman's Doorway* (Harper & Row, 1976) and the introduction to the volume on Swedenborg in the Paulist Press series Classics of Western Spirituality, as well as numerous articles and papers.

vary from seeing him as the avatar of a planetary "New Church" [see Glossary], to believing him mad and his visions suitable mainly for psychoanalysis.

It is the purpose of this essay to move into the space between these opposites. The scientifically and psychologically sophisticated modern reader requires an introduction to Swedenborg that starts from a premise neither unilaterally critical nor credulous. Contemporary perspectives in the social sciences need to be taken into account. More specifically, I feel it is important to portray the human dimension of Swedenborg, and to look at his visions not as aberrations, but as particularly unique and valuable instances of what is, in fact, a universal human capacity. The recorded annals of this capacity are what I refer to as "the visionary tradition." It is a tradition shown by anthropologists to have roots as far back as Paleolithic times. Shamanism in particular shows visionary activity to be the genesis of healing, psychology, and art. There is a great deal of difference between the visions of the madman and those of the shaman.

In psychology, the emerging field called "the psychology of consciousness" establishes the visionary capacity as available to all humanity, and the allure to enter "inner space" as powerful a human urge as exploration of the outer world. In respect to this quest Swedenborg is indeed an exemplary preceptor and guide, helping us to establish both the scope of the quest and its potential values as well as dangerous pitfalls. For a society that ranges as far as India and Tibet for guides to inner space, perhaps a guide culturally "closer to home" will seem a welcome relief. And as we shall see, many of the inner conflicts Swedenborg experienced and worked on in his visionary process—such as that between science and religion—are also core conflicts for Western society in the current age. Fortunately, there are excellent biographies that do provide sensitive and penetrating insights into the nature of the man without discrediting his creative and human stature.[1] Details of his life abound, from well-documented and reliable sources, as Swedenborg both traveled widely and mixed freely with people of all social classes. Evidently he was a singular enough person to have stimulated people to write about him, both during his life and afterward.

Immanuel Kant, for example, during Swedenborg's lifetime, was impressed and disturbed enough by the rumors of his spiritual visions to have sent a distinguished and trustworthy emissary, the English merchant Joseph Green, who reported to Kant "a reasonable, polite, and open-hearted man."[2] The majority of personal experiences of Swedenborg agree with this account, obliging the sensitive reader to question the credibility of the various psychotic and neurotic diagnoses generated for him *a posteriori* by an intellectual generation with different cultural assumptions. The problem, it seems, with some psychohistorical treatments of lives long past is a failure to see the individual embedded in his

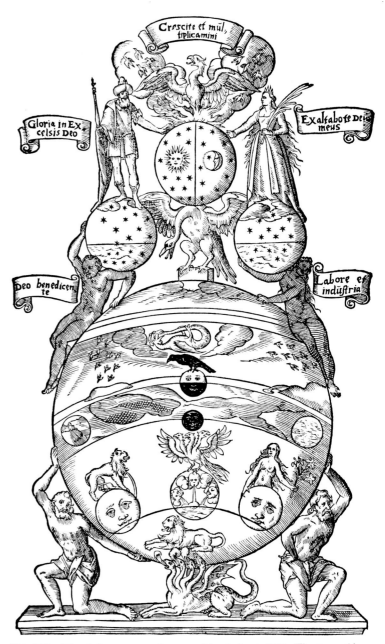

FIG. 194. *Libavius's monument, from an alchemical text, 1606. The stages of inner transformation are shown as an alchemical process. The alchemists knew that integration and disintegration were stages of the evolving soul rather than pathology.*

own time (not Freud's), and a failure to free psychoanalytic interpretations from their own sociohistorical biases.

On the other hand, the modern scholar of Swedenborg meets with the Swedenborgians, whose literature, being that of religious believers, may be suspected by the more "objective" scientist of another kind of bias. Yet belief has not deterred many Swedenborgian authors from meticulous scholarship and an ethical dedication to "telling the truth,"[3] even about one's special spiritual patron. In this spirit are the Woofenden-Klemming-Wilkinson edition of the *Journal of Dreams*, and the new edition of the *Journal* with commentary by Wilson Van Dusen (see Bibliography), which (fortunately) do not omit, as did earlier editions, nor translate into Latin the sexual aspects of some of Swedenborg's dreams. These are quite explicit, rather than cunningly disguised with "defense mechanisms," and healthy enough for a person of Swedenborg's bachelor status. They add, in fact, a rich human and emotional dimension to experiences that often seem too theological and abstract.

While the present essay is psychological in orientation, let me clarify that its primary purpose is not to "psychologize" in the way of an analysis or exposition according to any one school of thought within psychology. Rather I propose to call attention to patterns in Swedenborg's life and experiences that resemble patterns found in the general social science framework far beyond the limiting models of psychopathology. I draw on material from history, anthropology, and mythology as well as psychology. The attempt is not to "explain away" the mysterious and provocative data surrounding this unusual man, but to amplify, call attention to, and compare.

In the process we may lay to rest the myth of his "mental illness" which seems to me an error in epistemology and interpretation rather than any kind of valid diagnosis. The visionary tradition reveals a pattern of human psychological experience of a more than personal, or "transpersonal," nature. Swedenborg's visions arose not from personal pathology (the psychoanalytic assumption) but from an experiental plunge into a transpersonal level of the human psyche. The phenomenology and stages of this level are by now rather well known, having appeared similarly in many human psyches, despite a bewildering variety of personal, cultural, and historical settings.[4] This is not to say that Swedenborg did not bring personal-historical and cultural assumptions to his experiences. These are, in fact, abundantly evident as we follow his journey within to the luminous core of his transpersonal experience.

These three dimensions will be found as areas of special importance in the understanding of a visionary (or any individual who penetrates more deeply into the inner regions of the self):

1. *The personal formula* includes (a) genetic heritage and (b) learning history. This forms the total pattern of the "personality" (or all those factors some psychologists try to exclude as "individual differences").
2. *The sociocultural formula* consists of a collective sharing of symbols: language, belief systems, folklore. This composite is introjected to greater or lesser extent by the participant.[5]
3. *The transpersonal level* contains patterns that are transcultural as well: death and rebirth, the hero journey, the "feminine," the "masculine," God, or "the sacred." These patterns not only are encountered by all human beings but have proliferated into the many human mythologies that nonetheless all have a similar basic or archetypal substructure.[6]

The mystic, as he or she seeks God, or ultimate meaning, penetrates toward the core—but never without personal and cultural expectations.[7] The vision itself is the core's reply, never really predictable, because "other," but ultimately to be formulated in the same vocabulary of symbols as the question was asked. This includes a shaping by both personal and sociocultural formulas. (E.g., Zen Buddhists practicing Zazen get *kensho*, or *satori*, not exactly the same as the Christian's *unio mystica* with Christ.) However, there are, to be sure, common elements enough in mystic experience to make the "perennial philosophy" a very viable concept.[8]

There is much rich and deep perennial philosophy in Swedenborg, truths of a luminous and universal kind; but we shall find the other levels represented as well. Personal, cultural, and mythic-transpersonal elements each play their role.

The sharing of a vision by a community is an important factor, as I have elsewhere described.[9] Madmen are visionaries with no one with whom to share their visions. It is as if the transpersonal levels of energy are too powerful for a single individual and must be diffused into a group. And we may well ask, even at the inception, when the visionary first opens himself or herself to vision, with whom, how, and for what is it to be shared when it comes? I have come to feel, as a student of mythological and visionary data, that the end is somehow as important as the means. The visionaries in traditional societies are healers, diviners, celebrants of ritual. The "power" of their vision flows through them to their people. Their dark brothers are the institutionalized modern visionaries, out of synchronization with their community, burst by a vision of power with nowhere to go. Tranquilized and maintained by a (not so) benevolent state, such people are like empty pods stripped of life.

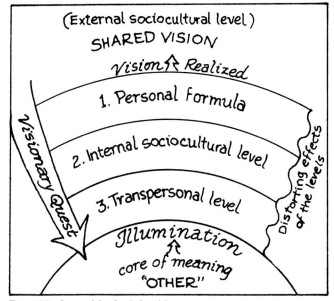

FIG. 195. *Internal levels of the vision quest*

The only alternative for the shaman in modern society would seem to be the creative life: to write, paint, sing, somehow share the vision. This satisfies the mythic formula and creates a "community" of souls, united by a common experience. That Swedenborg has such a community is evident. This simple fact alone may enable us to discern that he is far closer to the shaman than the madman.

Psychology and the Issue of "Mental Illness"

Psychology is largely a "school" science in that there is as yet no universal consensus but rather a variety of approaches, both to special areas and to problems. Behaviorism, for example, might have little of use to say about a man who was so thoroughly steeped in inner experiences.* While Freudians have found much of interest in Swedenborg, the material seems to me far richer for a Jungian. One might look for the affectional and human dimensions proposed by Erich Fromm[10]; and Abraham Maslow[11] would have had an intriguing pattern of self-actualization to decipher. Julian Jaynes's "Bicameral Mind" theory seems tailor-made to the "hallucinatory" aspect of Swedenborg's visions.[12] (He hears voices and sees visions, indeed, but Swedenborg did not assume they were the *vox Dei*, nor simply obey them—he questioned, dialogued, even scolded those with faulty opinions.)

Perhaps more productive for this inquiry than any of the aforementioned are the special areas of the psychology of consciousness, and transpersonal psychology; two still embryonic but promising disciplines. These schools are revitalizing William James's hundred-year-old dictum that psychology must include the study of "altered states of consciousness": "No account of the universe in its totality can be final," he says, "that leaves these other forms of consciousness quite disregarded.[13]

A study of altered states of consciousness leads us to different descriptions of reality. One of these recurring descriptions portrays the world in its essence, as "sacred." The phenomenology of this description is basically what constitutes transpersonal psychology. Included within its purview are the "technologies of the sacred"—spiritual disciplines such as yoga, meditation, philosophy, but also the study of ecstatic states, visionary narratives, mythology, ritual, archetypal elements in dreams, healing, and ESP.

Swedenborg anticipated this field in his own study; Emerson wrote of him in *Representative Men* that he began in his own life "what phenomenology and introspection would later

do." We will also see yogic practices, shamanistic visionary elements, dream incubation and interpretation, and some rather well-documented ESP.[14]

But first we must consider, and hopefully lay to rest, the issue of psychopathology or Swedenborg's "mental illness." In the early days of psychoanalysis it was perhaps permissible to apply the dazzling new theory to all dimensions of culture. As is the case with such imaginative juxtapositions of system with data, rich harvests of insight were collected. Psychoanalysis itself experienced a kind of polymorphous perversity, feeling (some would say groping) its way into the as-yet-virgin territory of literature and literary criticism, art, anthropology, history, and religion. Psychohistory became acceptable to scholars of psychoanalysis (but to few historians), and when well done, to the general public; Erik Erikson's evocative study of Luther is a case in point.[15]

Serious scholars of their respective disciplines, however, especially social scientists, began to resent the epistemological intrusion (some called it violation). Often ignoring the standard ground rules and methodology of an established discipline, psychoanalysts were as likely as not to leap right in and begin interpreting the life of some historical figure. The neo-Freudians tempered this naïve tendency in the area of culture and personality,[16] making anthropology's point that even such seemingly universal (to Freud) structures as the Oedipus complex are subject to the laws of cultural relativity. Adler and Jung each left the Psychoanalytic Association, taking off into whole psychological areas that Freud ignored or explained as merely derivative from "the sexual libido." Each founded a discipline to study the neglected areas of "the power urge" and "the religious impulse" in man.

These observations should certainly make it less defensible to adjudge someone "mentally ill" based on the assumptions of a particular "school" or psychological system. The "issue of normality" is, in fact, an extremely complex one, as any textbook of abnormal psychology will show. The two most frequently cited "models" for normality are (1) the sociocultural model (How well does the individual integrate within his or her local social group?) and (2) the personal adjustment model (How successfully does the individual function with relative freedom from anxiety and psychogenic discomforts?) (A third, the medical model, uses the term *illness* for all psychological dysfunction, a labeling many psychologists find unacceptable, as it seems to render all psychology into psychiatry, i.e., medicine.)

The question of Swedenborg's sanity, then, must be considered within the sociocultural climate of his times and must include evaluations of his personal happiness, productivity, and freedom from anxiety. Swedenborg was never adjudged insane, nor institutionalized. It was only later that psychiatrists would *ex post facto* judge him insane. Karl Jaspers di-

---

*Although John Watson tried hard to exclude inner experience from "the science of human behavior," it recurs, paradoxically, in behavior modification in the use of fantasy techniques in desensitization process. John Watson was the founder of the American school of experimental psychology called *behaviorism*, originally inspired by the ideas of Ivan Pavlov, in the early twentieth century.

agnosed him as schizophrenic (in a study comparing Swedenborg to Strindberg, Van Gogh, and Holderlin).[17] Lagerborg, a Finnish scholar, believed the diagnosis to be paranoia, marked by regression.[18] Von Winterstein postulated an inverted Oedipal attachment to his father with repressed homosexuality.[19] Emil Kleen's diagnosis was *paranoia tardiva expansiva religiosa*," presumably a rare subspecies of paranoia.[20] The paranoid is "delusional" because he believes unusual or grandiose things to be true: Swedenborg's "appointment by the Lord" to reveal the inner sense of the scriptures has been construed in this way. The "special mission" syndrome is in fact known to many clinical consulting rooms.

However it must be pointed out that belief in "the Lord" and a literal heaven filled with winged angels above, and Satan's pit yawning beneath was the commonplace belief system of the day. Swedenborg differed from the cultural norm only in that he claimed to visit and experience visitants from those worlds. Of his "hallucinations" or extrasensory experiences, Swedenborg was clearly able to distinguish his visions from waking consciousness. He sought solitude when the visionary world became dominant. Only on a few noteworthy occasions, such as his clairvoyant seeing of the Stockholm fire hundreds of miles away, did visions disrupt his ordinary social composure. His social persona is described in different places as "polite," "gallant," "kind," "open-hearted."

Swedenborg went through a heroic struggle to reconcile his visions with this ingrained Christian belief system. At his time, in Sweden, witches were still burned. The biblical injunction, "You shall not permit a sorceress to live,"[21] was a death knell to the still proliferating visionary tradition in Europe. Shamans, druids, and *wicca* (wise women) had been the official "technicians of the sacred" only a few centuries before. Then came massive politically enforced as well as spontaneous conversions to the new Middle Eastern religion. But it seems hard to shut the experiental doors to that invisible realm once they are open for a people. Even within the close-mesh net of official Christian dogma, visionaries surfaced, delivered their message, and were either burned or canonized, depending upon its reception.[22]

According to William James, Protestantism especially disowned the visionary tradition:

It is odd that Protestantism, especially evangelical Protestantism, should have abandoned everything methodical in this line. . . . Protestant mystical experience appears to have been almost exclusively sporadic. It has been left to our mind-curers to introduce methodical meditation into our religious life.[23]

I have personally spent considerable time with those strange wounded modern visionaries called "paranoid schizophrenics." At best they are filled with a burning intensity of purpose and belief. At worst, and far more often, they are boring and exasperating. They harangue one with their monomyth to exhaustion. They ignore the satisfying give-and-take of human communication; often, in fact, belaboring the mythic and ignoring the human. There is a "blaming" aspect, in which the world and its deficiencies are responsible for their own shortcomings. There is an emphasis on others' evil and a literally projected "devil."

We see none of this in portraits of Swedenborg. If he even spoke of his visions it usually was at another's request. In ordinary social discourse he was a reasonable and urbane man. He could discuss politics, economics, his travels without intruding his visionary insights. Lacking a culture with which to share these, he wrote—for whoever would read. There was no coercion, no bombast. For over fifteen years he published his visionary writings anonymously. He blamed no one for his "predicament." His image of the devil is, in fact, psychological—the principle of exclusive self-love in each of us. His devil (or Jungian "shadow") not only is not projected but is considerably more sophisticated and *less* paranoid than that of his contemporaries:

All the hells are this kind of community. So at heart, every individual in them nurses hatred against his fellow citizen, and as a result of this hatred, breaks out into cruelty insofar as he is strong enough. It is these bursts of cruelty and the resulting torments that are meant by hellish fire, for these are the results of cravings. (HH 573)

Swedenborg's hell resembles the psychologically sophisticated desire-hells of the Buddhists far more than the literalistic punishment-and-torment hells of his Christian contemporaries.

We do not, in fact, have a word for what might be called "positive paranoia." We know well the phenomenology of the negative breakthrough where the sick soul blames the world for his or her misfortunes. These have been abundantly described in psychopathology. William James says in *Varieties of Religious Experience*:

In delusional insanity, paranoia as they sometimes call it, we may have a *diabolical* mysticism, a sort of religious mysticism, turned upside down. The same sense of ineffable importance in the smallest events, the same texts and words coming with new meanings, the same voices and visions and leading and missions, the same controlling by extraneous powers; only the emotion is pessimistic: instead of consolations we have desolations; the meanings are dreadful; and the powers are enemies of life.[24]

But what of the breakthrough in the opposite direction, in which the mystic (Jakob Böhme) says:

I knew and saw in myself all three worlds, the external and visible world being of a procreation or extern[al] birth from both the internal and spiritual worlds; and I saw and knew the whole working essence . . . and how the fruitful bearing womb of eternity brought forth.[25]

Or this from Swedenborg:

I . . . lay awake but as in a vision . . . yet in the spirit there was an inward and sensible gladness shed over the whole body; seemed as if it were shown in a consummate manner how it all issued and ended. [My spirit] flew up . . . and hid itself in an infinitude, as a center. (JD 87)

These certainly would be instances of "positive paranoia," in which the universe becomes intensely meaningful, in a benevolent and not a baleful way. And the images of metaphors for the universe are positive versions of depression's emptiness and meaninglessness. There are profound insights into "the workings of things" that are part of the *perennial philosophy*.

James uses the emerging world view of the visionary as a diagnostic of the authenticity of the vision.

It is evident that from the point of view of their psychological mechanism, the classic mysticism and these lower mysticisms spring from the same mental level, from that great subliminal or transmarginal region of which science is beginning to admit the existence, but of which so little is really known. That region contains every kind of matter: "seraph and snake" abide here side by side. To come from thence is no infallible credential. What comes must be sifted and tested, and run the gauntlet of confrontation with the total context of experience, just like what comes from the outer world of sense.[26]

The criterion of bringing the vision into relationship with the world of common sense seems to me at the highest level of responsible relationship to the inner world. What Hegel called "dialectical process" and what Jung called "the transcendent function" both involve this give-and-take, a *dialogue*, which I have elsewhere described as the fifth and highest stage of relationship with the mythic imagination.[27] This procedure has seemed to me the essence of sanity,

while insanity lies at stage 1, "Mythic Identity," total absorption in the psychic world of images and desires. It is not the *presence* of unconscious materials that determines insanity, but how the ego relates to them.

Swedenborg did not confuse himself with the contents he experienced at the transpersonal levels. He described these as *other*. They range through hierarchies of spiritual beings to the Lord himself, the transpersonal Core of the Universe. In his *Spiritual Diary* [see Bibliography] especially, Swedenborg describes his dialogues with the inhabitants of the world of spirits.

Wilson Van Dusen, a contemporary clinical psychologist, has reported dialogues he entered with spiritual entities he felt were inhabiting his patients. Some he called "lower order," which were not open to real dialogue, but repetitive, of low intelligence and malicious (not unlike "poltergeists"[28]). A higher order appeared less frequently, but in noninterfering ways, it showed itself open to dialogue and provided meaningful inner guidance for the patient. (Jung and Freud had, in fact, disagreed over the higher order, but not the lower; Jung postulating an "anagogic" or guiding attribute to the unconscious, which personified itself in positive inner figures.) Van Dusen credits Swedenborg with opening his understanding to the implications of the two orders. Exclusive self-interest and lack of an ethical viewpoint opens the psyche to possession by the lower order, which Swedenborg describes as "insanity." Selfless motives, compassion, and religious impulse open the psyche to the higher order, and what he describes as "the good" and "the true."[29] The sane man stands in between two hierarchies of spiritual forces, not just the simple instrument of, but willing host to, whichever he will choose.

How tiresome and anachronistic to view all breakthroughs in consciousness as pathological. As we will see in part 2 of this essay, in the traditions of shamanism and yoga these ontological breakthroughs are among the highest and most sought-after human experiences.

Notes

1. Of the more recent biographies, particularly good are Signe Toksvig, *Emanuel Swedenborg: Scientist and Mystic* (New Haven, Conn.: Yale University Press, 1948); and Cyriel Odhner Sigstedt, *The Swedenborg Epic: The Life and Works of Emanuel Swedenborg* (New York: Bookman, 1952). For a less favorable presentation, see Inge Jonsson, *Emanuel Swedenborg*, trans. (from Swedish) Catherine Djurklou (New York: Twayne, 1971).

2. Joseph Green was a man Kant often entrusted with criticizing his own manuscripts.

See Sigstedt, pp. 303, 304, 341, or Toksvig, p. 185.

3. Swedenborg is one of the most thoroughly cross-referenced authors in the world. Generations of Swedenborgian scholars have translated, edited, and interpreted his voluminous work. See, e.g., Rev. John Faulkner Potts, comp., ed., trans., *The Swedenborg Concordance: A Complete Work of Reference to the Theological Writings of Emanuel Swedenborg: Based on the Original Latin Writings of the Author*, 6 vols. (London: Swedenborg Society,

1888 and 1976).

4. Joseph Campbell, *The Hero with a Thousand Faces* (New York: Meridian, 1970); also see William James, *The Varieties of Religious Experience: A Study in Human Nature, Being the Gifford Lectures on Natural Religion Delivered at Edinburgh in 1901–1902* (New York: Modern Library, 1902, 1929).

5. Horney's social concept of "introjection"; Karen Horney, *The Neurotic Personality of Our Time* (New York: W. W. Norton, 1937).

6. C. G. Jung, *The Archetypes and the Collective*

Unconscious, vol. 9-1 of *The Collected Works of C. G. Jung*, trans. R. F. C. Hull, Bollingen Series XX (Princeton, N.J.: Princeton University Press, 1959).

7. Laski's "overbelief"; see Marghanita Laski, *Ecstasy: A Study of Some Secular and Religious Experiences* (New York: Greenwood Press, 1968).

8. Aldous Huxley, *The Perennial Philosophy* (New York and London: Harper Brothers, 1945).

9. See Stephen Larsen, *The Shaman's Doorway: Opening the Mythic Imagination to Contemporary Consciousness* (New York: Harper & Row, 1966), particularly "The Enactment of Vision," chap. 2.

10. Erich Fromm, *Psychoanalysis and Religion* (New Haven, Conn.: Yale University Press, 1950).

11. Abraham Maslow, *The Farther Reaches of Human Nature* (New York: Viking Press, 1971).

12. For Jaynes, the right hemisphere (controlling the left side of the body) is the source of hallucinated voices read as divine proclamations. See Julian Jaynes, *The Origin of Consciousness in the Breakdown of the Bicameral Mind* (Boston: Houghton Mifflin, 1976).

13. James, *Varieties*, p. 379.

14. Swedenborg's ESP was well documented in interviews with witnesses. See discussions of his psychic abilities in Toksvig, Sigstedt, and Jonsson.

15. Erik Humburger Erikson, *Young Man Luther: A Study in Psychoanalysis and History* (New York: W. W. Norton, 1958).

16. See Horney, and Erikson.

17. Karl Jaspers, *Strindberg and Van Gogh* (Berlin: Springer, 1926).

18. R. Lagerborg, *Finsk Tidsskrift* (1923), p. 281 as cited in Toksvig, p. 162, n. 13. Lagerborg also cites E. Hitschman, a German scholar, to confirm the diagnosis of paranoia.

19. Von Winterstein discussed in Toksvig, p. 163, n. 14.

20. Emil A. G. Kleen, *Swedenborg* (Stockholm: 1917, 1920).

21. Exodus 22:18. See also Deuteronomy 18:10: "Anyone who practices divination, a soothsayer, or an augur or a sorcerer, or a charmer, or a medium, or a wizard, or a necromancer. For whosoever does these things is an abomination to the Lord, and because of these abominable practices the Lord your God is driving them out before you." (This covers the whole visionary tradition rather well.)

22. See Margaret Murray, *The God of the Witches* (Garden City, N.Y.: Doubleday, 1960).

23. James, *Varieties*, p. 397.

24. Ibid., p. 417.

25. Ibid., p. 402n; James quotes Jakob Böhme.

26. Ibid., pp. 417–18.

27. Larsen, *Shaman's Doorway*, pp. 33–45.

28. "Poltergeists," or noisy ghosts, are usually agreed to be malicious, mischievous, repetitive, childlike. See Sacheverell Sitwell, *Poltergeists: An Introduction and Examination* (New York: University Books, 1959).

29. Wilson Van Dusen, *The Presence of Spirits in Madness* (New York: Swedenborg Foundation, 1972); or see the chapter by the same name (chap. 6) in Van Dusen, *The Presence of Other Worlds: The Psychological/Spiritual Findings of Emanuel Swedenborg* (New York: Harper & Row, 1974).

Part 2
The Visionary Tradition

The seer is pure vision. Though pure, he looks out through the vesture of the mind.

—Patanjali, *Yoga Sutras*[1]

IN THIS PART we shall explore analogies between Swedenborg's experiences and those of other classes of visionaries, particularly yogis and shamans. While Swedenborgian scholars have emphasized the unbidden nature of Swedenborg's revelation, especially that it occurred at the Lord's instigation, not Swedenborg's own, it must be pointed out that there were aspects of Swedenborg's life that made him the ideal recipient for such a revelation: his already formidably disciplined mind, his periods of solitude, his penchant for writing.

In addition, as we shall see, Swedenborg practiced some of the classical psychophysical techniques of the inward explorer, including special breathing, concentration, and visualization. These reveal a far-from-passive attitude toward his experiences, rather, a collaborative, active involvement. Swedenborg should not be seen simply as a "mouthpiece" for divine revelation, notwithstanding his own assertion that something like this was so. The biographical data show him more the participant, even a highly trained spiritual athlete who realized how much his own "condition" affected the visionary process. As Patanjali says so well, "The association of seer with things seen is the cause of the realizing of the nature of things seen and also of the realizing of the nature of the seer."[2]

The Yogic Comparison

Swedenborg had begun in early childhood to experiment with respiration. He noticed that thought synchronizes with breathing; in fact, thoughts "flow in," as does the air in breathing. Thus he discovered at an early age the "stream of consciousness" as it later came to be known in Western literature. The naïve view of consciousness is that we "think our own thoughts," but a few moments of attentive introspection reveals that they "flow by themselves" like a stream. Directed thinking is only a portion of mental life, in which the stream is redirected to our own intentional channels. But abandon the effort of control for a moment, and the flow resumes its spontaneous quality, carrying unpredictable flotsam and jetsam of experience, memory, intuition, never ceasing.

Now to paraphrase the classical definition of yoga from the *Sutras* of Patanjali, it is the intentional stopping of the involuntary movements of the mind-substance. The "mind substance" (*cittavṛtti*) is the subtle "substance" of the stream of consciousness, also called "psychomental flux." The goal of this practice, which may take many years, or a lifetime, is "cosmic consciousness" (*samādhi*). "When the perturbations of the psychic nature have all been stilled, then the consciousness, like a pure crystal, takes the color of what it rests on, whether that be the perceiver, perceiving or the thing perceived."

Swedenborg, without any instruction, nor reference to the whole metaphysical structure of yoga, had begun the quest for cosmic consciousness, using one of the fundamental yogic techniques, *prāṇāyāma*. He writes:

> . . . for instance, when in childhood I wished to hold my breath purposely, when they prayed in the morning and evening [presumably his parents]; also, when I wished the times of the respiration to agree with those of the heart, and so observed that then the understanding almost began to vanish as it were; then afterwards, when I wrote in imagination, that I had observed that I held my respiration as if it were tacit. (SD 3320; see also 3464)

Young Emanuel, a prodigy of the inner quest, quietly practiced yogic *prāṇāyāma* while his parents were at prayers. He also visualized what would be his life's work: "writing in imagination," an act that would seem to require eidetic (lifelike, vivid) imagery and would train his inner perception.

Patanjali's classic *Yoga Sutras* devotes three chapters to *prāṇāyāma*, a practice that begins with slowing, and concludes with suspension, of the breath.

Eliade notes:

> By making his respiration rhythmical and progressively slower, the yogin can "penetrate"—that is he can experience, in perfect lucidity—certain states of consciousness that are inaccessible in a waking state. . . . The yogin, without re-

nouncing his lucidity, penetrates the states of consciousness that accompany sleep.[4]

Eliade draws a relationship between Brahmanic Sacrifice and the sacrifice of breath in *prāṇāyāma*. It is an act of religious opening and devotion, which appears in shamanism, Chinese Taoism, and Sufism. One may well wonder where young Emanual learned this technique; however, later on he credits spiritual instructors, mentioning in *Spiritual Diary* that he was taught some breathing techniques by spirits from the Indies who "induced a like respiration upon me that I might know this from experience" (SD 402).

Because there was little or no literature on yoga in Swedenborg's day, what are we to make of this? Yogins also mention "listening to the heart" and attaining *samādhi*, through the precise technique of heart and breath synchronization.[5] But yoga is not the only source of contemplative techniques using breathing. Compare the following from Eastern Christian mysticism—the eighteenth-century monks of Mt. Athos:

WHY THE BREATH MUST BE HELD DURING PRAYER

Since your mind or the act of your mind is from childhood accustomed to disperse and scatter itself among the sensible things of the outer world, therefore, when you say this prayer, breathe not constantly, after the manner of nature, but hold your breath a little until the inner word has once spoken the prayer. . . . Through this momentary holding of the breath the hard and tough heart becomes thin, and the humidity of the heart being properly compressed and warmed, becomes tender, sensitive, humble, and more disposed to compunction and to shedding tears freely. . . .[6]

FIG. 196. *Yogasana with chakras. The interlocking spirals of kundalini yoga,* idā *and* pingalā, *lunar and solar energies (respectively, left and right), coil around the central* suśumnā *(see also the discussion of spirals in the last section of this essay, and especially the figure of the caduceus).*

The Hesychasts, a Greco-Byzantine monastic sect, had practiced "quietness" (Gk.; *hēsychia*) through prayer and breathing, since at least the thirteenth century. St. John Climacus writes, "Let the remembrance of Jesus be present with each breath and then you will know the value of the *hēsychia.*"[7] Though Catholicism had retained a few traditions like this, and the Roman Catholic *Exercitia* of St. Ignatius, it was unusual for a solitary little Swedish boy to begin practicing sophisticated contemplative exercises.

Swedenborg also discovered "subtle breathing," a technique utilized in Chinese *tai chi* as well as in the Hindu *prāṇāyāmas.* One "visualizes breathing" at the same time as physically breathing. The "breath" may be sent around the body, or imagined "filling the belly," for example. Swedenborg observed that subtle breathing pervaded his body, and in fact worked on the organs of his body: "There were also shown to me other varieties of respirations; for instance, abdominal respirations pertaining to the region of the genitals and loins; then also that there is a respiration of the left side, and not at the same time of the right side" (SD 3325).

Certain yogic *prāṇāyāmas* are directed through subtle channels, alternately to the left and right side of the body (*idā* and *pingalā*) to "purify" them. Yogis also heal organs by directing the breath through them to "soften" them.[8]

But other correspondences between Swedenborg's spontaneous inner practices and the systematic techniques of yoga are worth noting. *Ashtanga,* eight-limbed yoga, a "complete" form of yoga, consists of: (1) *yama* (restraints), (2) *niyama* (disciplines), (3) *āsana* (postures), (4) *prāṇāyāma* (rhythm of respiration), (5) *pratyāhāra* (withdrawal of senses), (6) *dhāraṇā* (concentration), (7) *dhyāna* (yogic absorption), (8) *samādhi* (union, ecstasy).[9]

Swedenborg practiced: (1) sexual restraint, (despite his natural endowment with a healthy sexuality),* dietary restrictions, often doing without food, or subsisting on coffee and milk; (2) disciplines—the yoga texts mention especially "cleanliness, serenity, asceticism (*tapas*)." After his key vision in which he felt the Lord had told him, "Eat not so much," Swedenborg practiced asceticism and restraint in diet and other personal habits. We read that Swedenborg often spent twelve to thirteen hours in bed; though he probably practiced only (3) the *āsana* called *śavāsana,* "sleep of the dead." This is likely to produce deep trances and out-of-the-body experiences. Swedenborg says, "It has happened to me, that I sometimes forgot that I was in the body . . ." (SD 2542). Swedenborg used (4) respiration to control thought (*prāṇāyāma* meditation). "Thus the thoughts have their play in every act of respiration; therefore when evil thoughts en-

---

*Swedenborg frequently mentions that his "love of the sex," or continual interest in women, is one of his major life themes. He didn't seem to feel anything was "wrong" with this, but suggested it could be sublimated to a spiritual level of love.

tered, the only thing to do was to draw to oneself the breath, so the evil thought vanished" (JD 111). As to (5) withdrawal of senses (*pratyāhāra*), Swedenborg might isolate himself in his rooms for several days, leaving word not to be disturbed. He would become absorbed in (6) mystical contemplation: "I was thus during many years, from the period of childhood, introduced into such respirations, especially by means of absorbing speculations, in which the breathing seems to become quiescent, as otherwise the intense study of truth is scarcely possible" (SD 3464).

What was the nature of these "speculations" that led him within?

(7) Absorption (*dhyāna*): He wrote to his friend Dr. Beyer, "From my fourth to my tenth year I was constantly engaged in thought upon God, salvation and the spiritual sufferings of men; and several times I revealed things at which my father and mother wondered, saying that angels must be speaking through me."[10]

Yoga texts mention that the yogi must make the Lord (*Īśvara*) the motive of all one's actions. Swedenborg says, "'Thy will be done; I am thine, and not mine'; and as I have given myself from myself to our Lord; so let him do with me according to his good pleasure." [As he notes his own reaction to this inner declaration:] "In the body there was a certain dissatisfaction; but in the spirit, gladness thereat" (JD 117). He also notes that "in ecstasy or trance the man holds his breath; at this time the thoughts are, in a manner of speaking, away" (JD 112). (8) As for union: while Swedenborg did not even have the concept *samādhi* in his cultural experience, he wrote,

> [My spirit] flew up . . . and hid itself in an infinitude as a center. There was love itself. And it seems as though it extended around therefrom, and then down again; thus, by an incomprehensible circle, from the center which was love, around and so thither again. (JD 87)

In the terms of yoga philosophy, he circles the *Ātman-Brahman*, sentient core of the self, and of the universe. The love (*bhakti*) that he feels also matches the descriptions of *samādhi* as sexual in a spiritual sense: "This love, in a mortal body, whereof I then was full, was like the joy that a chaste man has at the very time when he is in actual love and in the very act with his mate; such extreme pleasantness was suffused over the whole of my body" (JD 88).

While such a description might jar conventional Protestant sensibilities, in which religion and sexuality are strictly segregated, Swedenborg is closer in spirit here to the yogic or tantric mystics and to ecstatics of the Western tradition, such as St. Theresa.[11]

Whoever has seen the outside of a Hindu temple, like the one at Khajurāho, knows the erotic may cloak the spiritual, as a vibrant metaphor: "The frieze of *maithunas* of men and women in erotic embrace . . . in their ecstasy typify the ultimate union of the soul with the divine."[12]

Swedenborg is the inverse of Freud. While Freud insists spirituality is a sublimation of sexuality, Swedenborg reads his sexual feelings as spiritual events. After a dream in which he has explicit sex with a mysterious woman, he says, "This denotes the uttermost love for the holy; for all love has its origin therefrom; is a series; in the body it consists in its actuality in the projection of the seed; when the whole . . . is there, and is pure it then means the love for wisdom" (JD 172).

Swedenborg later had the wholesomeness to envision marriage in the spiritual world and in heaven—a concept that scandalized the puritanical clergy of his day and caused John Wesley to denounce him and his "Mahometan Heaven."[13]

The Shamanistic Dimension

Much as the previous discussion may help us to understand the preparation of Swedenborg as a visionary, such preparations are merely necessary but not sufficient conditions to explain his crisis and psychospiritual transformation. In fact, though Swedenborg had already practiced techniques of introversion since childhood, these alone certainly did not occasion his spiritual breakthrough. (They may, however, have aided the strong intuitive and introspective clarity he brought to his scientific treatises.)

But something qualitatively different began to happen to him in his middle fifties. As we have it from his *Journal of Dreams*, mainly from the year 1744, this was an event of psychic upheaval that threw the formidably disciplined mind of the scientist into personal chaos.* Several times he mentions "fragmentation of his thoughts" as occurring, for example:

> During the whole night, for about 11 hours, I was neither asleep nor awake, in a strange trance: knew all that I dreamed; my thoughts were held bound up, which made me sometimes sweat. The state of this sleep I cannot at all describe; but through it my double thoughts were in a manner severed or split asunder. (JD 174)

It is perhaps the hasty interpretation of passages like this that has led to the diagnosis of schizophrenia or psychosis.† But the mistake is in making "symptoms" of a supposedly permanent nature of them, rather than seeing them as teleological stages in a time-honored and archetypal human

---

*The fact that Swedenborg kept a journal during this troubled period is a tribute to his willingness to understand the unsought psychic upheaval. Journal keeping itself is a type of "dream incubation," like that of the Asclepius cult of the classical world.

†It would seem that one phenomenologically able to notice his own "split thoughts" already possesses a perspective that can lead to reintegration.

experience: the hero journey, the dark night of the soul, death and rebirth.

"Psychotic" images did indeed appear to Swedenborg at this time; nightmares of monsters, animals, huge machines, *vagina dentata*; visions of storms fraught with thunder and wind, images of Jesus crucified, androgynous figures. He experienced frequent "tremors" and seizures. He described being "thrown about" his rooms, often landing flat on his face. He had evident mood swings, from despair to ecstasy and back again.

Living in Amsterdam by himself, when in these states, Swedenborg kept to his rooms; in public he appeared normal. Occasionally someone would hear him in his rooms talking to his "spirits" or crying aloud. Here we may ask, as does Lili Tomlin, Why is it that when we talk to God it's called prayer, but when he talks to us it's called schizophrenia?[14] The response from the "other" is always beyond expectation and comes to us from within, sometimes accompanied by profound personality disorganization.

But we find remarkable analogies to this stage in the world of the preliterate traditional societies. Among the primitive and ancient reindeer hunters of Siberia, for example, the soul in a crisis of this sort is seen as being in the initial stages of the genesis of a "greater shaman"—an individual who is undergoing a spiritual transformation into a healer, and a spiritual leader for the community. "Lesser shamans" are initiated by the human community, for reasons hereditary or social. "Greater shamans," however, are chosen by the spirits in a spontaneous vocation. Swedenborg clearly belongs to the "greater" class of visionary. Despite the preparation attained in his practices, he experienced his crisis and subsequent revelation as unsought.

Siberians call the early time of personality disorganization "the first indwelling of the spirits." The human medium is being "opened from within" to transpersonal powers. He is called *amurakh*, "temporarily mad." At this point, according to Eliade, senior shamans are called in to guide the ensuing psychic dismemberment and reconstitution. Their role is really less that of initiators than a type of psychic midwife, officiating at a supernaturally ordained rebirth process.[15]

Swedenborg, of course, had no "senior shamans" to help him through the transformation; so he asked for guidance from within. But he insisted that it be from no lesser spirit than the Lord himself. Swedenborg was a Christian before a shaman and insisted that his visions be consistent with his deepest belief. He wished to go beyond intermediaries to the luminous core of meaning itself.* This intensity of inner purpose served him as a valuable sea-anchor in the storms that followed. We take ship with him now for a while in turbulent waters—but alert for the beacons that offer guid-

*Monotheism seems to me to polarize the personality in a rather strong way, leading to a firm standpoint on good and evil, and ethics in general.

FIG. 197. *Initiation on a mountaintop, after an alchemical text, 1600s. Hermes the mystagogue is a guide to the king's son (also called spirit and soul).*

ance, and using some ancient but still serviceable maps.

In what St. John of the Cross called "the dark night of the soul" or what we may call "the death experience," there is a terrible loss of direction and meaning. Swedenborg dreamed, "I saw hideous specters, without life horribly shrouded and moving in their shrouds; together with a beast that attacked me, but not the child" (JD 15).

The soul is deprived of its inner source of life, and the fragmentary part-selves we normally identify with are seen as empty specters. The ego is a dying beast that "attacks"— but not the "child" (the symbolic potential for rebirth).

Swedenborg felt hopeless about his ability to save himself.

> It seemed I lay on a mountain with a gulf under it: there were knolls upon it; I lay there and tried to help myself up, holding by a knoll, without foothold; a gulf was below. It signifies, that I myself wish to help myself from the abyss of hell, which is not possible to be done. (JD 16)

The Swedish word *harg*, "rocky hill" or "knoll," also means "sacred ground" or "place of sacrifice."[16] Swedenborg here is hanging, like Christ on the cross; Prometheus, helper of men, on his rock; or his own mythic "countryman" Odin, the ancient Norse god of wisdom, questing for the runes of power:

> *I know I hung*
> *on the windswept tree,*
> *through nine days and nights.*
> *I was struck with a spear*
> *and given to Odin*
> *myself given to myself.*[17]

Swedenborg, too, was questing for the "runes of power," his hermeneutic calling, to find the meaning within the sacred scriptures.

Facing his own death and helplessness, the shaman, the

human hero, has no recourse but to submit to the sacrifice, "himself to himself" and place his trust in the transpersonal power behind the process.[18]

At this point it seems annihilation is imminent. The Siberian shamans have a particularly grisly description of the dismemberment process. A Samoyed shaman reports the following visionary initiation experience. He enters a hole in a mountain and finds a naked man with a huge caldron. The naked man sees him and seizes him with tongs:

> The novice had time to think "I am dead!" The man cut off his head, chopped his body into bits, and put everything into the caldron. There he boiled his body for three years. There were also three anvils, and the naked man forged the candidate's head on the third. . . . Then he threw the head into one of three pots that stood there.[19]

Later the "naked man" initiates him and teaches him a healing divination using the temperature of the water in the ritual pot.

Compare the following dream from Swedenborg in the midst of his initiation: "Hideous dreams: how the executioner roasted the head he had struck off; and laid one roast head after the other in an empty oven that never got full. It was said that it was his meat. He was a great big woman; smiled, had a little girl with him" (JD 136).

The "empty oven that never got full" resembles the inexhaustible caldron of Norse and Celtic mythology. It is the vessel of transformation. The "head," or guiding principle, is what needs to be renewed. The "naked man" or the "executioner" is the negative aspect of the positive spiritual principle that is, in fact, behind the initiatory ordeal. We find a mystery here: death is the precondition of new life, dismemberment the key to regeneration. The executioner "smiles" and is revealed as an androgyne, a man who changes into a woman with a little girl. The monster of the dismemberment process contains a feminine element and thus the key to rebirth.*

Swedenborg here is in the depths of his psychic journey: "I seemed to myself in the lower parts to be enveloped in lamellated strata that in various ways were twined about me" (JD 143).

He is in need of a guide, and because of his openness, and the rightness of his quest, one comes: "There was a very good natured dog, dark brown, that followed me; when any reptile or vermin came, he rose up; when there was water, he went there in order to know the depth" (JD144).

The dog is the well-known and appreciated guide to the underworld traveler. His nose and instinct help him to find

FIG. 198. *The king revived by the wolf, or dog, after an alchemical text, 1687. The animal then becomes a substitute for the king, assisting in his rebirth out of the alchemical fire.*

the paths through the "sightless realms." He is an instinctive guardian. Here he helps by guarding Swedenborg and testing the depth of the water. Eliade writes, "The Shaman encounters the funerary dog in the course of his descent to the underworld, as it is encountered by the deceased or by heroes undergoing an initiatory ordeal."[20]

The animal may menace or keep out the unauthorized underworld visitor; but when he appears as here in the guise of "the helping animal" (a mythologem that shows up universally in the wonder tale), his presence affirms the appropriateness of the hero's quest and his acceptability to his own hidden instinctive life. Swedenborg mentions dogs no fewer than ten times in the crisis period of the *Journal of Dreams*. One of the dogs startles him by licking his neck; shamans may be awakened from trance by dogs licking them (compare the alchemical drawing here).

Alchemical images, studied by Jung as a metaphor for the process of psychic transformation, show up frequently in Swedenborg, enough to merit a whole separate study.[21] The "king," who is the subject of the transformative process, appears six times (personified as actual kings with whom Swedenborg had associated or knew of); water, fire, and darkness appear and disappear. At one point he dreams of "some who endeavored as it were to make gold; but they saw that they must climb up; but this they could not do, and without it, it was impracticable to make gold" (JD 114).

Swedenborg here, like Jung, recognized that personal transcendence and transformation is the real goal of the alchemical process. He equated gold with God's grace.

"What is good ought to be effected, and . . . the gold lies therein" (JD 114). Jung hypothesizes that the quest for inner transformation never left the European imagination, but because of persecution by the church, it had to go underground

---

*The androgyne is a frequent motif for rebirth, or wholeness, as in the alchemical tradition. Shamans often wear women's clothing and enact androgynous roles, as in the Siouxan Wintkes, or the Chukchee "soft men."

disguised in the chemical operations of the alchemists. Swedenborg fits very well into this tradition. A burning spiritual quest was hidden within his "science."

Symbols of Transformation

The alchemists also depict the transformative process as an awakening of the androgynous, bisexual nature of the initiate. He must encounter the feminine within. We are not surprised then to find that Swedenborg's other inner guide is feminine. The women that appear in his dreams and visions seldom are identified. They resemble the "unidentified woman" Carl Jung describes as the "anima." For the male visionary she represents his own soul and the principle of the creative unconscious that leads him to his "gnosis." She occurs in various disguises in *Journal of Dreams*, no fewer than twenty-two times, an important guide for his spiritual crisis. The index of *Journal of Dreams* notes her: dressed in black, with teeth (*vagina dentata*), hidden, fighting, conceiving, spying, married, unmarried, with fine property, fat and red, with a magical book, pregnant. Jung observes that the anima is a nixie, noting that her abode is the "living water" of the unconscious psyche: "She changes into all sorts of shapes like a witch, and in general displays an unbearable independence that does not seem at all proper in a psychic content."[22]

Eliade notes her important role in the shaman journey:

> A large number of myths and legends show the essential role played by a fairy, a nymph, or a semidivine woman in the adventures of heroes; it is she who teaches them, helps them in their difficulties (which are often initiatory ordeals), and shows them how to gain possession of the symbol of im-

mortality or long life (the miraculous herb, the magical apples, the fountain of youth). . . . It is always a feminine being who helps the hero to conquer immortality or to emerge victorious from his initiatory ordeals.[23]

Wilson Van Dusen in his insightful study of Swedenborg, *The Presence of Other Worlds*, points out that before his crisis, Swedenborg's relation to his feeling dimension was atrophied (compared to his intellectual hypertrophy). To become more whole he had to meet with a feeling, feminine, earthly dimension. Van Dusen notes that the "Disting Fair" of which Swedenborg dreamed (JD 281) "was a festival dedicated to female deities."[24] The fair is rather surprisingly held upstairs in the parlor of his father's house "at Uppsala," which could be interpreted as representing the patriarchal Judeo-Christian tradition. Here a feminine pagan rite is celebrated in the midst of his paternal zone.

He is being introduced to the world of female deities: the unconscious, Faust's "realm of the Mothers." Van Dusen writes:

> It seems that it only gradually dawned on Swedenborg that his quest for God demanded that he change internally. The early Swedenborg could only see God as a rather remote, cold intellectual theology. To truly see God the whole inwardness of Swedenborg had to be opened and intensified. He had to be instructed in the inner subtle, rich language of feeling-image-symbolism. The whole feeling side of him had to be awakened and take a position superior to intellect.[25]

At one point in Swedenborg's dream life his anima revealed herself to him overtly in her creative aspect:

> There came to hand a little letter, for which I paid nine stivers. When I opened it there lay within it a great book

FIG. 199. The Crowned Hermaphrodite, *after an alchemical text, 1550*

FIG. 200. (right) *The anima as a fairy or nixie, from Andrew Lang's* The Yellow Fairy Book, *1894*

FIG. 201. *The anima as mystical guide, after an alchemical text, 1617. Maria Prophetissa points to the mystical union of the "above" with what is "below"; the two streams of water can also be interpreted as the union of spiritual and natural truth.*

containing clear blank paper. . . . There sat a woman on the left hand; then she removed to the right and turned over the leaves, and then drawings or designs came forth. (JD 195)

Here she is depicted as his creative muse, who moves him from "left" (the unconscious, intuitive side, whose vocabulary is images) to the "right" (the verbal, linear, more conscious side). Swedenborg will eventually be able to dialogue with his previously "unconscious" inner images consciously. His anima is playful and sensuous as well as creative. Swedenborg describes her as with a broad bust and "on both sides down to the lower parts quite bare; the skin, shining as if it were polished; and on the thumb a miniature painting" (JD 195). But let us follow for a while the development of his relationship to the inner woman as his dreams depict it.

In the early stages, before the transformative process is complete, Swedenborg had dreams of *vagina dentata*: "Lay with one that was by no means pretty, but still I liked her. She was made like others; I touched her there, but found that at the entrance it was set with teeth. It seemed that it was Archenholtz [a politician] in the guise of a woman" (JD 120).

He didn't know what to make of this. "What it means I do not know; either that I am to have no commerce with women; or that in politics lies that which bites; or something else" (JD 120). But his dream would seem in our developmental interpretation to point to a premature attempt at *mysterium conjunctionis* (sacred union) with the inner feminine, before he is ready to penetrate such a mystery. In fact, the mysterious woman had appeared to him earlier as a queen, disappointed because jewels she had received were not "the best": "She asked me to come in again; but I excused myself on the ground of being so shabbily dressed, and having no wig" (JD 23).

Swedenborg felt unprepared for such an encounter. Indeed in this stage of the process the ego is a pauper while the anima possesses the full riches and royalty of the creative psyche. The *vagina dentata* is the perilous entrance to the other world, which is often described as "clashing rocks," such as the Symplegades, or a dangerous gate. Here the threat is expressly to the procreative capacity.

Later Swedenborg would succeed in the *hieros gamos* (sacred marriage, or visionary union) with the mysterious woman, "*en merveille*" as he said; and with the feeling that she would conceive. With the remarkable consistency of the visionary world, we are not then surprised to find her appearing, five months later in September, quite pregnant; dressed in "very white clothes" offering him wine to drink (JD 239).

Having not encountered this curious mystery of "spiritual pregnancy" before, I was struck by the following comparative example when I came across it in the LSD visions of a professional therapist undergoing a personal rebirth experience.[26] S. had a series of visions in which he, like Swed-

enborg, was learning to accept his own feminine dimension. At the end of an unsatisfactory first LSD experience filled with painful transformation symbols (he had a total of four guided sessions), he heard guttural voices saying something in Dutch like, "*Die mutter's schevi*," which he translated as "your mother's heavy." He did not at the time understand what this meant.

Our subject's second session, however, culminated in a lovely vision of a feminine body:

. . . the moon . . . rising from behind great billowy clouds. It is indescribably lovely and thrilling. . . . [Then] the moon and a great cloud are seen as mother's buttocks and I am staring at them from between and within them. Floating from darkness into strong pale white light, I exclaim out loud, "Mother, I'm almost there!"

The spiritual rebirth motif here presented itself with breathtaking unexpectedness. And S. was looking from the viewpoint of the spiritual "child." His third session was filled with earthly images, which he gradually had to learn to accept. But in his fourth there was finally a wonderful culminating scene in which he became a woman, and in the throes of giving birth. He writes:

Celestial trumpets and choirs of angels proclaimed this wonderful birth; lightning flashed and comets arched through the heavens, giant sunrises and sunbursts pulsed through the universe. . . . I reached down and pulled my baby up to my face and glory of glories . . . it was me! But a transformed, almost spotless, perfected me.

Thus the mysterious process of transformation by which a man may "give birth to himself." And something like this must have been happening to Swedenborg. As he wrote in the next-to-last paragraph in the *Journal of Dreams*: "It seemed that a rocket burst over me spreading a number of sparkles of lovely fire. Love for what is high, perhaps."

After his rebirth Swedenborg was to be let far more deeply into that fire and that light: "I have been elevated into the light, which sparkled like the light radiating from diamonds; and while I was kept in it I seemed to myself to be withdrawn from corporeal ideas, and to be let into spiritual ideas" (AC 4413).

We don't have to stretch our metaphor much to see in the visionary "light" the "enlightenment" of the philosophical systems, with their "awakenings" to, and "dawnings" of, knowledge. With the light comes power and mystical sight, prized by visionaries from shamans to Zen Buddhists, to Christian mystics. Eliade writes of the Eskimo *angakoq* that it is

. . . a mysterious light which the shaman suddenly feels in his body, inside his head within the brain, an inexplicable searchlight, a luminous fire, which enables him to see in dark, both literally and metaphorically speaking, for he can now, even with closed eyes, see through darkness and perceive things and coming events which are hidden from others; Thus they look into the future and the secrets of others.[27]

We think of the *antar jyotih* (inner light) of the Upanishads, described as the essence of the indwelling *Atman*; also of the "white light" of the *Bardo Thodol*, the Tibetan Book of the Dead.

Raymond Moody, writing of near-death experiences in his book *Life After Life*, quotes some luminous visions by those "in the vestibule." A woman who had been in a coma for a week writes:

I felt as though I were lifted right up, just as though I didn't have a physical body at all. A brilliant white light appeared to me. The light was so bright that I could not see through it, but going into its presence was so calming and so wonderful. In the presence of the light the thoughts or words came into my mind: "Do you want to die?"[28]

The following more lighthearted example is from a man at death's door:

I looked up and saw a beautiful polished door, with no knob. Around the edges of the door I could see a really brilliant white light, with rays just streaming like everybody was so happy in there and reeling around. It seemed like it was awfully busy in there. I looked up and said, "Lord here I am. If you want me, take me." Boy, he shot me back so fast it felt like I almost lost my breath.[29]

But this light appears not only in ecstasy or at death; Swedenborg saw it often as he was thinking or meditating. Signe Toksvig, in her excellent biography, mentions that Swedenborg believed light to attend men of science, and that ". . . after a long course of reasoning [they] make a discovery of the truth; straightway there is a certain cheering light, and joyful confirmatory brightness, that plays around the sphere of their mind."[30]

This practice of attuning to confirmatory light called *photism* has also been cultivated by many other kinds of intuitives and mystics as well.

A few years later Swedenborg wrote:

A flame appeared to me so often and, indeed, in different sizes with a diversity of color and splendor, that during some months when I was writing a certain work, hardly a day passed in which a flame did not appear, as vividly as the flame of a household hearth. It was then a sign of approval, and this was prior to the time when spirits began to speak with me viva voce. (WE 6905)

Swedenborg's feminine personification and inner light, then, serve as most important symbols of transformation. They are his guides through the labyrinth within to a uniquely open state to the spiritual dimension.

Swedenborg as Visionary Pathfinder

The concluding section of this study evaluates the relevance of Emanuel Swedenborg to the visionary quest of our modern world. In an age that has embraced a remarkable import cargo of spiritual practices, from yoga to Sun Myung Moon's totalistic communities, from Gurdjieff to Nichiren Shoshu Buddhism, from Subhud to Jonestown, it seems important for us all to understand the religious urge in human life. The same quest that can vitalize the psyche and bestow a translucent meaning upon and within it, can also lead to fanaticism and blind destructive action. It is foolish to avoid or disbelieve the two-edged, ambivalent nature of spiritual power.

Because of this, it seems to me crucial to have an interface of psychology and religion. And in psychology's scientific study of the visionary individual, who is at the core of all religious process, biography must play a most important role. Partisans of one religious doctrine or another may harangue each other to exhaustion without proving whether there is one God or three, nor even considering whether the issue is worth debating. But in the details of an individual's life, and in his or her relationships to the immediate physical, social, and historical factors surrounding, we have a story any human of sensibility can understand. This story, or "life myth" of an individual, should function as a context for understanding his or her revelation. We can understand mysteries, doctrines, and dogmas better in the context of human life. For instance, the ethical principles included in most religious systems are enlivened by example in the life of the visionary-founder. Contrarily, we feel uncomfortable when someone "preaches one thing and practices another."

From my own modest look into both the life and theological works of Emanuel Swedenborg, I feel he has excellent credentials as a New Age visionary. Ethically, he seems to me impeccable. A man with his insight and clairvoyant powers could have negotiated for power (and loved) like Rasputin, could have organized people around him like Gurdjieff at Fontainbleau.[31] But Swedenborg lived modestly and mostly alone. People enjoyed his kindly ways and sense of humor; he paid promptly and well those who lodged and served him. He was affectionate with children, a devoted gardener, skillful with living things. He did not, like Aleister Crowley, the magician-mountaineer, leave a wake of human debris behind him, the wreckage of the lives so often attracted to and left behind by spiritual charismatics.[32] There are those among us who must ask, unable to help ourselves, What worth have all the magical discoveries, high transpersonal principles and doctrines, if a person does not live them?

The New Age visionary should embody the salient themes

of human growth for the current time. He or she should partake of both mythic and sociocultural symbols of the age. On the mythic level, Swedenborg's astrological birth sign (sun sign) Aquarius also corresponds with the New Age astrological mythologies, which speak of an "Aquarian age." Edward Whitmont, a Jungian scholar, reads the sign Aquarius as the symbol of "dialogue" of the human dimension (the ego) with the realm of the spirit (the unconscious).[33] Aquarius is also more classically "the water bearer," the human truthseeker who, after completing his or her own spiritual quest, then pours out the healing message of subsequent discovery to the human race for their sustenance. (For Swedenborg also, water represents "truth.") Both of these mythologems correspond well to Swedenborg's life-myth: his dialogue with the spirit, which we have followed now a bit, and his pouring out of his "truth" to the world (his writings).

In this last section I briefly (but I hope provocatively) investigate a few of Swedenborg's visionary findings, also called his "theological doctrines." These will be discussed in a nontheological way, however. We shall be concerned with practical and empirical referents for the transpersonal doctrines, inquiring, wherever possible, Where are the roots of this idea in Swedenborg's life? and, Does it find echo in the perennial philosophy, thus meriting "transpersonal status"? May we not also begin to think of a "perennial psychology," in which concepts and structures from the many psychological systems are included on the basis of their usefulness and applicability to a broad range of human experience, rather than elaborate theoretical justifications of one system over another? Is the human psyche not large enough to contain some of Freud's "defense mechanisms" and Jung's "archetypes" as well, Piaget's early developmental stages and their later culmination in Maslow's "self actualization"? When such concepts are understood as heuristic devices, not literal "things" in the psyche, they enrich remarkably our understanding of human behavior.[34] While they are hard to test empirically, perhaps their inclusion in everyday vocabularies and use in practical psychology is an empirical test of a different sort.

Swedenborg's thought is full of concepts of this kind. While he describes them as spiritual principles, we can often find their commonsense psychology. Consider, for example, his concept of "ruling love": men or women develop an inner motivational and affectional system based on what they are drawn to most. Their continuing choices and involvement cause the "ruling love" to become dominant in the hierarchy of their motives; it becomes autonomous and "rules" them. Other motives, or "reinforcements," become secondary while this becomes primary. Eventually, for Swedenborg, this "desire-body" not only affects one's physical life, but survives the transition through death and determines membership in heaven or hell. "Like is drawn to like" and the spirit realms are communities of those alike in "ruling love."

> Man is able to know, think and understand many things; but when he is left to himself he rejects these things which are not in agreement with his love; and he also rejects them after the life of the body, when he is in his spirit; for that only remains in the spirit of a man which has entered into his love. (NJHD 113)

> That which anyone does from love remains inscribed on his heart; for love is the fire of life, and thus is the life of everyone. Hence such as the love is, such is the life; and such as the life is—thus such as the love is—such is the whole man as to the soul and as to the body. (AC 10740)

It seems to me there are profound implications for practical psychology in this concept. One man's "reinforcement" is clearly not another's. And, as any good behaviorist knows, the secrets of behavior-change lie in the manipulation of those reinforcements that work for the particular individual. Swedenborg places an important emphasis on the power and autonomy of motivational structures. Selfish loves become dead ends because they further competition with other beings rather than cooperation. Also selfish loves usually gratify our part-selves, not the integrative self. If one tries to attain complete happiness through eating or sex or personal power or even orderliness, the result is a lopsided catastrophe. Yet we do not have to look far to find fellow humans caught up totally in such futile enterprises, and eventually unable to abandon them, even when the destructive consequences are all too apparent.

Swedenborg was especially outspoken on the issue of "love of power" or domination:

> All who give themselves up to these loves have regard for themselves alone in and for whose existence all others have their being. Such have no pity, no fear of God, no love of the neighbor and consequently are unmerciful, inhuman and cruel. They have an infernal covetous lust of plunder and robbery. . . . If men were not restrained by fear of punishment inflicted by law . . . the whole human race would be destroyed. (TCR 498)

Freud would probably have agreed with this last. But besides legal penalties there is another more psychologically subtle coping mechanism for such destructive one-sided passions in human life. Through a gradual awakening of the spirit, the person learns to value the reality of other people. At the same time a realization dawns of the incredible subjectivity of the self and of exclusively selfish needs. Turning one's "ruling love" to unselfish ends, a process Swedenborg calls "regeneration" [see Glossary] sets in. Regeneration is a process parallel to Jung's "individuation," or other developmental schemes of the mature psyche. These models, buttressed now by the universally accepted facts of children's cognitive development, show a "childhood of the spirit" continuing for the individual even in mature years. Jung was the modern genius who played Piaget's games of imagination with adults as well as children, eliciting their transformation symbols in mandalas, dreams, and life-myths. The psyche must, it seems, forever undo its egocentricity, which places the ego (Swedenborg's "proprium" [see Glossary]) at the center of the universe. Piaget has brilliantly described naïve egocentricity in childhood and its gradual replacement by the moral stages necessary for life in the social environment. The adult must gradually come to accept all those other centers-of-the-universe too.

Cognitive psychologist Lawrence Kohlberg puts the "universal ethical principle stage" at the top of Piaget's fully operational ladder.[35] The human psyche may grow beyond the zone of legal penalties into a full moral consciousness—which automatically considers others as no less important than oneself. Swedenborg calls this, somewhat archaically, "love for the neighbor." Alfred Adler, too, some centuries later, would see "love for the neighbor" as the antidote to the power principle.[36]

It seems to me that the highest form this ethic may take is in a spontaneous feeling response, which need not even mentally debate the ethical issues concerned. The other is spiritually felt to be equal to oneself. We think of yoga's *tat tvam asi* (thou art that) or the Hindu greeting *namasté* (I greet the God within you), Christ's "Golden Rule" or Buber's "I-thou." Orthodox religion seems to have missed the point—that these ethics are descriptions of spontaneous feeling states, rather than rules to be legislated. Being "forced" to "love one's neighbor," one may never learn to do it spontaneously. Lower developmental stages never succeed in "legislating" higher ones. Christ's exhortation is probably rather a call to transformation through growth; the only way to reach the next stage. This growth then is a primary task of the regeneration process.

Regeneration, says Swedenborg, is accomplished from within, through the mysterious process of *influx* [see Glossary]. This is a concept as much cosmological as psychological. It resembles Gurdjieff and Ouspensky's "ray of creation" that extends from a hypothesized source of life in the universe (God) through several orders, or "degrees," of creation.[37]

In both systems, human life as well as organic life on the planet are intermediate stages in a process of energy transformation: from the spiritual Sun to the natural sun, to organic life on earth. (For Gurdjieff the last stage is the moon, evoking the mythologies that portray the moon as the last abode of souls.)

Swedenborg says:

There is a continual influx from the spiritual world into the natural. He who does not know that there is a spiritual world and that it is distinct from the natural world . . . can know

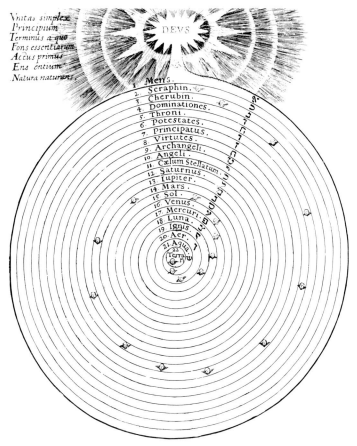

FIG. 202. *The soul's descent and regeneration, illustrating the "ray of creation," from an alchemical text, 1617*

nothing of this influx. . . . It is the spiritual principle which derives its origin from the sun wherein the Lord is, and proceeds to the ultimates of nature, that produces the forms of the vegetables and animals, and exhibits the wonders that are in both; and it clothes them with material substances from the earth that these forms may be fixed and enduring. (DLW 340)

The human being, while partaking in organic life, also rises above the rest of creation in being a conscious or mental recipient of direct spiritual influx (Gurdjieff's "three-brained beings"). The influx through man's higher faculties is considered by Swedenborg to come from the Lord. The lower comes through the domain of nature and is like the "libidinous" desire of Freud's *id*, and the natural egocentricity we have discussed as each human child's birthright. Swedenborg sees "the natural" and "the spiritual" as actual intertwined spirals of energy; curiously anticipatory of the double helix of DNA.

[Individuals] . . . are actually born animals, but become people.

The natural mind is curved into spirals from right to left, while the spiritual mind is curved into spirals from left to right, so that the two minds are turned against each other, in reverse. This is a clue that evil dwells in the natural mind,

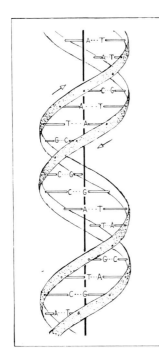

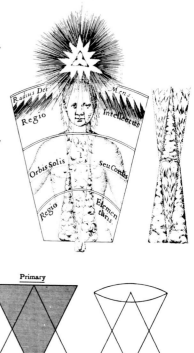

FIG. 203. (left) *Deoxyribonucleic acid (DNA) schematicized in the double-helix model proposed by James D. Watson and F. H. C. Crick in 1953*

FIG. 204. (below) *Swedenborg's vision of left and right spirals, suggesting the movement of the DNA double helix (also reflected in figures on the facing page)*

FIG. 205. (below right) *Yeats's interlocking cones of life vectors, described in* A Vision. *In* Divine Love and Wisdom *Swedenborg describes left and right spiral movements of his vision.*

FIG. 206. (right) *An alchemical image of influx from spiritual to natural, 1617. Seen as interlocking cones, here they achieve perfect equilibrium in the Universal Human.*

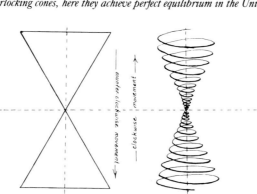

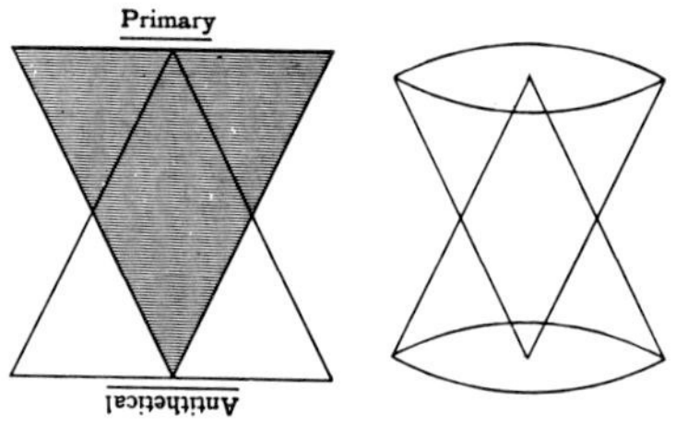

and works from that base against the spiritual mind. Further, spiraling from right to left is downward and therefore toward hell, while spiraling from left to right moves upward, and therefore toward heaven.

The following experience has enabled me to see the truth of this. Evil spirits cannot turn their bodies from left to right, only from right to left, while good spirits have great difficulty turning their bodies from right to left, but easily turn them from left to right. The turning follows the flow of the more inward elements of the mind. (DLW 270)

We think of the gnostic dualisms of spirit and matter, of Enkidu and Gilgamesh, Esau and Jacob, Evnissyen and Nissyen (from *The Mabinogion*)—the motif of the dark brother. The alternative to the fratricide that so naturally befell these two is the redemption motif. As Gilgamesh tried to save Enkidu, as Jesus redeemed John the Baptist, there must be a piercing of the cloud of unknowing that causes spirit and matter to regard each other as the enemy. At the end of *Parsival*, in Wolfram von Eschenbach's admittedly psychological and deep rendering, Parsival embraces Fierfies, the dark brother. The opposites are united.

While Swedenborg was raised in a society far more absolutist than our own in its understanding of good and evil, and to some extent he shared in its naïveté, he also went far in his concept of regeneration to show the process of human spiritual growth to be a dialogue—between the faculties of will (feeling) and understanding (cognition), between natural and spiritual, between human beings and God: "For man thinks and wills as if from himself, and this 'as if from himself' is the reciprocal of conjunction; for there can be no conjunction without a reciprocal" (SBI, Influx 14).

William Butler Yeats was to see the human psyche as two interlocking cones or spirals.[38] Between these spirals play the pairs of opposites of *will* and *mask, creative mind* and *body of fate*. Yeats's rendering is closer to the less dualistic Celtic tradition, which has always tended to portray life as a dialogue of a spiritual dimension with human nature.[39] The yogic *kundalini* serpent, like the natural spiral, lies coiled around her phallus at the base of the spine (and the *nadis, idā* and *pingalā*, coil around the *suśumnā*).[40] The caduceus of healing, inherited from classical time, also shows the "serpents" intertwined around a staff. The iconic message to the human sufferer is clear: holistic health includes both serpents, both spirals.

Carl Jung, like Swedenborg, was a Protestant pastor's son. Both men were raised in a home with a powerful patriarch who knew what good and evil were all about. Both were also to come to their own unique ethical stance on this issue, but through the attainment of the universal ethical principles, not through a legalistic imitation of the family patriarch. Jung would later write his *Answer to Job*,[41] and develop the technique of "embracing the dark brother" in the dialogue with the shadow. He conceived of this as the starting work of the individuation process (the masterwork being the dialogue with the anima). (We have already followed some of these stages in Swedenborg's own life.) Jung's concept of individuation bespeaks the same slow process of moral transformation as Swedenborg's concept of regeneration, and may have been influenced by it.[42]

Both men agree that man is a "receptacle" for transpersonal forces (Jung's *archetypes*, Swedenborg's *spirit world*). Jung writes:

FIG. 207. *The Seal of Solomon, or Srī Yantra (of Indian Tantra), and the yin-yang of the Far East. Like the helix and the spiral, both are images of the relationship of the spiritual and the natural in the universe.*

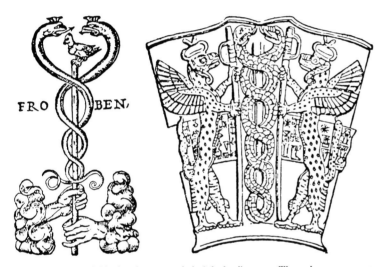

FIG. 208. (above left) *A caduceus, symbol of the healing arts. The caduceus represents the life energy in left and right spirals coiled 3½ times around the central staff (c.f. kundalini-yoga image earlier in this essay).*

FIG. 209. (above right) *The Cup of King Gudea of Lagash, ca. 2025 B.C., depicting intertwined serpents forming a double helix*

FIG. 210. *Opposing left and right spirals on the threshold stone at New Grange, Ireland. Such patterns appear commonly at Neolithic tomb or shrine entrances, suggesting that the symbolic connections of right-left, life-death, divine-human, or spiritual-natural may be very ancient and widespread.*

The religions should therefore constantly recall to us the origin and original character of spirit, lest man should forget what he is drawing into himself and with what he is filling his consciousness. He himself did not create the spirit, rather the spirit makes *him* creative, always spurring him on, giving him lucky ideas, staying power, "enthusiasm" and "inspiration." So much, indeed does it permeate his whole being that he is in the gravest danger of thinking that he actually created the spirit and that he "has" it. In reality, however, the primordial phenomenon of the spirit takes possession of *him*, and while appearing to be the willing object of human intentions it binds his freedom . . . becomes an obsessive *idée force*. Spirit threatens the naïve minded man with inflation. . . .[43]

And for Swedenborg, knowledge of man is that of

merely vessels or recipients, and that too of a rude, yea, of the rudest kind, into which are poured from the Lord those things which they were designed to contain. . . . (SD 1935)

Every man as to his spirit, although he does not know it, is in society with spirits while he lives in the body. Through them a good man is in an angelic society and an evil man in an infernal society. (HH 438)

While these ideas may seem archaic to the modern skeptic, skirting all too close to primitive "animism," they are in fact ideas so widespread as to merit inclusion in the perennial psychology. Among the teeming nontechnological societies of the world, divination, exorcism, possessed oracles, and spirit healers are still rather commonplace. It is only among the "scientifically socialized" that such things are viewed as unusual. Swedenborgianism is, in fact, highly successful in Africa, where the people have no problem at all with the concept of "the spirit world."

But while we may feel we "understand" the spiritual in these cultural contexts, perhaps we grow less comfortable with the "spiritualists" closer to home (even, in our phobia, like Harry Houdini), becoming obsessed with proving them frauds. This has often been the response to Swedenborg, but this kind of apotropaic behavior toward a human capacity as traditional as spirit-seeing seems to me made more of fear than wisdom. The concept of the spirit world is itself numinous, and as such, threatens the so newly won safety of our secular world view. Busy denying its existence, we forget to study its phenomenology.

In search of a modern visionary who had experiences similar to Swedenborg, I identified Robert Monroe, a modern businessman who began spontaneously to have out-of-body experiences. As I reviewed Monroe's experiences I found there were many parallels to Swedenborg, as well as discrepancies. Remember, though, the formula for vision includes personal and cultural, as well as transpersonal, elements. Considering the cultural and personal differences

FIG. 211. Mirror of Virginal Nature, *from an alchemical text, 1617. The World Soul is in service to the Divine and directs the action of the natural world.*

between Monroe and Swedenborg, the similarities are striking. Both men describe a "spiritual world" separate from but connected to this one. Both describe a "lower" and a "higher" order of spiritual forces. The lower are obsessive and dangerous while the higher leave one in freedom but offer guidance. Both agree that spirits often will try to fool you, shapeshift and appear in disguise. Thought is equivalent to movement in the spirit dimension.

Monroe says, "The automatic navigational system . . . works by what and of whom you think. Let one small stray thought emerge dominantly for just one microsecond, and your cause is deviated. . . ."[44]

Swedenborg observed that those who think alike are drawn together and that affections are like a binding force. Monroe experienced the same "vibrations" as Swedenborg did (and as do shamans) when "entering or leaving the body." While he attentively described his experiences and the beings he

met, Monroe's view of the spirit world was far more secular and less theological than Swedenborg's. In this way it may approximate modern sensibilities more closely. Of the two, however, Swedenborg's account is phenomenally more detailed and much more specific about the operation of principles and laws of the psyche and spirit world.

Perhaps the most important question for any modern follower of Swedenborg is this: Does one do as he said, or do as he did? The former leads to Swedenborgianism, the latter to a type of shamanism (Christian monotheist shamanism, albeit). The orthodox Swedenborgian would wholeheartedly reject the latter option. Swedenborg's election is divine. The Lord himself opened Swedenborg's psyche, and his alone, for the revelation of the New Jerusalem. One does not voluntarily emulate his life; to do so would be presumptuous indeed, not to mention inviting spirit possession and madness. Swedenborg himself, in no uncertain terms, discouraged his readers against dabbling in spiritualism. Yet it might be observed that in the temper of our times, the latter quest holds more meaning. The psychologically and culturally sophisticated pilgrim of today is not seeking a new doctrine or dogma so much as experience. Experience is the key concept of the entire "human potentials movement," and the lure that beguiles many contemporary Christians from their proper intellectual worship to experience of the fiery tongues of the Pentecostal movement, or to involvement in totally other traditions. In the midst of perhaps the most extroverted society in human history—contemporary America—the inward quest in its various forms has in the last decade peopled the land with lamas, yogis, sannyasins, mysterious Zens, and Korean messiahs. The inward quest is at least a major national pastime and shows no signs of diminishing.

Such a movement of collective consciousness cannot fail to have its uncontrollable, dangerous side, and this follows from lack of established cultural guidelines for the journey. Many street-corner shamans of today have peeked into the spaces Swedenborg saw, and that they are indeed vast and terrifying is witnessed by the casualties. It is dangerous to see too far, to know too much too soon. The visionary who has no audience, who performs no communal ritual, who enacts no service of healing nor work of art, is often driven mad by the power of the vision.

Swedenborg may prove an examplary guide for the modern inward seeker first in the modesty of his approach to the visionary state. Like a "greater shaman" the vision sought him; he used no chemical aids. He was an early participant in what Jean Houston has called the "psychenaut" program—the inner space equivalent of the astronaut's push into outer space. He combined the mythologems of science and religion, following science religiously and explaining religion scientifically. He leaped bravely into the chasm between Western religion's "God outside" (or *totaliter aliter*, totally other) and Eastern religion's "God within" (the *Atman*, or Jung's "self"). All of these factors make Swedenborg's writings worth reading for the modern phenomenologists of inner space. In him we may see a coincidence of much that is ancient in human psychology with much that is modern, West with East, Neoplatonism along with yoga, shamanism, and Buddhism. His is an especially bright star in that succession of luminous beings we call visionaries, always trying to let a little more light into our dark, forgetful world.

Notes

Full details for the shortened form of some references can be found in notes to part 1 of "Swedenborg and the Visionary Tradition."

1. Patanjali, *Yoga Sutras*, interpretation by Charles Johnson (London: John M. Watkins, 1964), bk. 2, p. 39, n. 19.
2. Ibid., bk. 2, p. 40, n. 23.
3. Ibid., bk. 1, p. 24, n. 41.
4. Mircea Eliade, *Yoga: Immortality and Freedom*, trans. Willard R. Trask, Bollingen Series LVI (Princeton, N.J.: Princeton University Press, 1969), p. 56.
5. Ibid., index: respiration, heart.
6. From the *Encheiridion* of Nicodemus the Hagiorite, quoted in ibid., p. 64.
7. Hesychasts: *Encyclopedia Britannica*, 15th ed., (Chicago: University of Chicago Press, 1979), vol. 5, p. 19.
8. Eliade, *Yoga*, p. 61.
9. Ibid., p. 49.
10. Swedenborg: letter to Beyer, 14 November 1769.
11. See chapter on sexual aspects of ecstasy in Marghanita Laski, *Ecstasy: A Study of Some Secular and Religious Experiences* (N.Y.: Greenwood Press, 1968).
12. Benjamin Rowland, *The Pelican History of Art*, 3rd. ed. (Baltimore, Md.: Penguin Books, 1970) p. 289.
13. See Toksvig, Sigstedt, and Jonsson; see also Ormond Odhner, "Swedenborg and Wesley," *New Church Life* (February 1958).
14. Paraphrased from *Lili Tomlin Live*.
15. Mircea Eliade, *Shamanism: Archaic Techniques of Ecstasy*, trans. Willard R. Trask, Bollingen Series LXXVI (Princeton, N.J.: Princeton University Press, 1970).
16. Peter Andreas Munch, *Norse Mythology: Legends of Gods and Heroes* (New York: American-Scandinavian Foundation, 1963.)
17. H. R. Ellis Davidson, *Gods and Myths of Northern Europe* (Middlesex, Eng., and Baltimore, Md.: Penguin Books, 1964).
18. See Stanislav Grof, *Realms of the Human Unconscious* (New York: E. P. Dutton, 1976).
19. Eliade, *Shamanism*, p. 41.
20. Ibid., pp. 466–67.
21. See C. G. Jung, *Psychology and Alchemy*, vol. 12 of *The Collected Words of C. G. Jung*, trans. R. F. C. Hull, Bollingen Series XX (Princeton, N.J.: Princeton University Press, 1953); and Jung, *Alchemical Studies*, vol. 13 of ibid. (1968).
22. Jung, *Archetypes and Collective Unconscious*, p. 25.
23. Eliade, *Shamanism*, p. 78.
24. Van Dusen, *Presence*, p. 50.
25. Ibid., pp. 52–53.
26. Research based on professional volunteer sessions conducted at Maryland Psychiatric Research Center, particularly by Stanislav Grof (see his *Realms of Human Unconscious*). Full account of S.'s journey in Stephen Larsen, *Myth and Consciousness: An Enquiry into the Phenomenology of Mythological Experience and Contemporary Consciousness* (Ann Arbor, Mich.: University Microfilms, 1975) chap. 5, 3a, p. 449. All quotes from Larsen's personal files.
27. Eliade, *Shamanism*, p. 88.
28. Raymond Moody, *Life After Life* (New York: Bantam Books, 1976), p. 75.
29. Ibid., p. 76.
30. From *Journal of Dreams*, as quoted in Toksvig, p. 127.
31. See René Fulop-Miller, *Rasputin: The Holy Devil*, trans. (from German) F. S. Flint and D. F. Tait (Garden City, N.Y.: Garden City Publishing, 1927, 1928); and J. G. Bennett, *Gurdjieff: Making a New World* (New York: Harper & Row, 1973).
32. Symonds and Grant, *The Confessions of Aleister Crowley* (New York: Hill and Wang, 1969).
33. Edward C. Whitmont, lecture presented at C. G. Jung Foundation for Analytical Psychology, New York City, 1966; see also Whitmont, *The Symbolic Quest* (New York: G. P. Putnam's for Jung Foundation, 1969).
34. As in J. Piaget, *The Moral Judgment of the Child* (New York: Free Press, 1948); or A. Maslow, *The Farther Reaches of Human Nature* (New York: Viking Press, 1971).
35. L. Kohlberg, "The Development of Chil-

dren's Orientations Toward a Moral Order," *Vita Hum.* 6 (Basel, Switzerland, 1964).

36. Alfred Adler, *Superiority and Social Interest* (Evanston, Ill.: Northwestern University Press, 1964 and 1970).

37. See P. D. Ouspensky, *In Search of the Miraculous: Fragments of an Unknown Teaching* (New York: Harcourt Brace and World, 1949).

38. W. B. Yeats, *A Vision* (New York: Collier Books/Macmillan, 1965).

39. See W. B. Yeats, *Essays and Introduction* (New York: Macmillan, 1961), specifically parts on the Celtic imagination.

40. Arthur Avalon, *The Serpent Power* (Madras, India: Ganesh, 1964); see parts on kundalini yoga.

41. C. G. Jung, *Answer to Job* (1952), in *Psychology and Religion: West and East*, in *The Collected Works of C. G. Jung*, trans. R. F. C. Hull, Bollingen Series XX, vol. 11 (Princeton, N.J.: Princeton University Press).

42. C. G. Jung, *Symbols of Transformation*, in ibid., vol. 5 (1956); or Jung, *Archetypes and Collective Unconscious*, index: shadow.

43. Jung, *Archetypes and Collective Unconscious*, p. 213.

44. Robert Monroe, *Journeys Out of the Body* (New York: Doubleday/Anchor, 1973).

Swedenborg, Transpersonal Psychology, and Wholeness

Rachel Martin

This essay was originally published under the title "Transpersonalism, Healing and Swedenborg" in *Studia Swedenborgiana*, vol. 5, no. 1 (June 1983), an academic journal published by the Swedenborg School of Religion. For this anthology it has been sharply edited in places in order to focus more closely on the inherent similarities between Swedenborgian thought and transpersonal psychology.

SWEDENBORG PROCLAIMS THE COMING of a new age. This new age, he says, will be a time of gaining a clearer understanding of the part God plays in each of our everyday lives. In a famous passage, he declares, "Now it is permitted to enter intellectually into the mysteries of faith" (TCR 508[3]). Through this increased understanding, individuals will have greater potential for actively manifesting the love of God in the world. From a nontheological vantage point, transpersonal psychology envisions the same end. By examining the actual processes and assumptions involved in the healing and growth cycles of the Swedenborgian system specifically and the transpersonal psychological system generally, it can be seen that Swedenborg's insights are surprisingly modern.

The Fourth Wave: Transpersonal Psychology

Transpersonal psychology has emerged in the eighties as the fourth major school of psychology—that young and volatile child of the twentieth century. The Freudian school, the behaviorist school, and the humanistic school, in historical order, still reign in various quarters, and there is no clear consensus among scholars or practitioners regarding the relative superiority of any of the schools of theory and method. The behaviorist school, in particular, is still strong, and it would be difficult to deny that it is by far the most influential of the four movements, controlling as it does virtually the entire American educational system, especially and including the huge majority of universities and colleges.

Nevertheless, a striking coalition of important thinkers have broken rank with these schools and have articulated a spiritual understanding of the nature of both humanity and the universe. This new school, the movement known as transpersonal psychology, grew mainly out of the humanistic school. While retaining many of the affirmative principles of humanistic psychology—notably the belief that psychology is best defined through study of healthy individuals, rather than an exclusive obsession with the sick—transpersonal psychology has taken its field of inquiry far beyond the domain of humanistic psychology to explore realms hitherto left to religion.

Both East and West have entered prominently into the creative search in the transpersonal community. From the West, Carl Jung and William James are most often cited for their articulation of a spiritual philosophy that is as broad and far-reaching as advocates of transpersonal psychology believe psychology needs to be. It is in this company that Swedenborgianism is most at home, and it is of no small import that transpersonal thinkers nearly always regard Swedenborg's teachings positively. Via William James and the transcendentalists [for a full discussion of this subject, see Eu-

RACHEL MARTIN is a pastoral psychotherapist and an ordained parish minister. She received a B.A. in humanistic psychology from Sonoma State University in California and an M.A. in transpersonal counseling from Beacon College in Boston. She is a graduate from the Swedenborg School of Religion in Newton, Massachusetts. She has had private practices in the greater metropolitan areas of Boston and St. Louis. She is currently a pastoral psychotherapist and minister at the Hillside Community Church (Swedenborgian) in El Cerrito, California.

gene Taylor's essay "Emerson: The Swedenborgian and Transcendentalist Connection," elsewhere in this anthology] a compelling case can be made that Swedenborg contributed quietly to laying the groundwork that has made the emergence of transpersonal psychology possible.

TRANSPERSONAL PSYCHOLOGY DESCRIBED

Transpersonal psychology can be defined as the inquiry into the nature of consciousness.[1] Significantly, there is not one transpersonal psychology, but rather many transpersonal psychologies. Each utilizes different methods and each describes different passages, but all strive for a realization of the upper reaches of psychological development.[2] To this end, transpersonal psychologies recognize the necessity of modifying human consciousness and of allowing and evoking transcendental experience and identity.[3]

Primary to most, if not all, transpersonal psychologies (hereafter to be called transpersonal psychology) are the beliefs that life is an orderly process of unfoldment; that the ego is ultimately servant to a higher Self;* that each individual life's meaning and purpose fit into humanity's meaning and purpose; that personality is just one aspect of a person's psychological nature. Transpersonal psychology stresses that the ultimate oneness and universality of reality is alive in each unique part; that alternate ways of perfection are available; that consciousness affects material reality.[4]

Much is being written these days regarding the confluence of the "new physics" and spirituality [for a full discussion of this subject, see Michael Talbot's essay "Swedenborg and the Holographic Paradigm," elsewhere in this anthology]. Transpersonal psychology believes, in accordance with modern physics, that physical reality is actually motion, or energy. Human beings, then, can also be seen as primarily energy forms, with the "possibility of direct contact between one human being and another, contact between the spiritual essence of each that is not limited by the physical properties of the nervous system."[5] Love may be understood as an energy or reality that actually bridges the gap between people.

Similarly, transpersonal psychology affirms emphatically that the human being is nourished and maintained by non-physical sources as well as by physical sources.[6] In fact, transpersonal psychology suggests that different levels of being (physical, emotional, mental, spiritual) may be thought of separately, but are operationally inseparable. Relative to this, some psychologists (e.g., Abraham Maslow[7]) hold that they cannot conceive of an experiment as "controlled" simply because they have properly manipulated physical factors. Each level of reality, of being, affects all other levels. No

*_Self_ is capitalized in this essay when referring to one's higher, more complete and integrated sense of being, as opposed to one's normally limited sense of I-ness.

act can be purely physical, separated from its emotional, mental, and spiritual features.

A confirmation of this postulate comes from scientific experimentation itself. The Heisenberg Uncertainty Principle (1925) has become a centerpiece of modern physics. It states that the smallest particles of matter, which appear to be units of energy, cannot be observed, because the effects of the observer alter their motion. When left unobserved, the smallest units of matter are waves. Once they are observed, however, they become particles. There is something about the act of observation that causes a wave to collapse into a particle.[8] Or put another way, there is something emanating from the human consciousness, whether at the mental or spiritual level, that affects and alters physical reality. The notion of the aloof and detached scientific observer is a myth!

Transpersonal psychology also incorporates the concept of holography, which, simply stated, means that each part of a total reality not only influences every other part, but that each part is also actually the container of every other part.[9] Let's take an analogy. In photography, if a negative of a picture of an apple were cut up, each piece of the negative, when projected, would picture one part of the apple. One would need to put all the pieces of the negative back together to be able to see the whole apple. If, however, a holographic plate picturing an apple were shattered, projection of any piece of the shattered plate would display a picture of the entire apple. Each part, down to the most minuscule chip, contains the whole. This concept of the whole being fully resident in each part is revolutionizing both brain research and theoretical science describing the nature of the universe,[10] and is central to the transpersonal perspective. Holography, as we shall see, also has profound implications for understanding ourselves as spiritual beings.

In addition, transpersonal psychology describes the universe as caring and responsive.[11] All life interconnects within a universal order. What has usually been called "coincidence" is now recognized as a meaningful occurrence within the universal order. Things do not happen "by chance" or "by accident." Though the causes for the synchronicity of such events may be inexplicable by outer circumstances, the connection may be powerfully cogent when viewed from an inner state.

Transpersonal psychology is committed to exploring how individuals can live more in harmony within the universal order via a person's higher nature. For example, it may appear to be a selfish act to turn inward in search of one's higher Self, yet paradoxically, to be uniquely and truly oneself is to be doing one's part in serving humanity. It is when one is cut off from the true sense of Self, when the ego is alienated and feeling lost and separated that, through fear and ignorance and a desire for power, one feels, thinks, and acts antagonistically toward the environment.

While the goal for other psychologies has been ego control, transpersonal psychology seeks to aid people in listening to their higher Selves—that is, transcendence of the ego. Right relationship to one's higher Self may be seen as the core goal of transpersonal psychology. The humanistic psychology dictum, "Do your own thing," taken at the ego level, could mean havoc and selfish disregard. Transpersonal psychology urges one "do your own thing truly," not on a surface level, but with the ego as servant to the higher Self.

To help people awaken to a deeper and more complete sense of Self, transpersonal psychology explores ways of sensing and experiencing that draw heavily upon Eastern traditions of spirituality. Accustomed to trusting the five senses solely and to orienting attention toward outer reality rather than inner reality, the Western mind does not generally value intuition. Convinced of the intrinsic merit of intuition, however, transpersonal psychology pursues skill-building in meditation, intuition, dreamwork, guided imagery, and other inward-turning methods, in hopes of expanding one's awareness of reality and discovering one's fuller potential.

Humanistic psychology states that "we are our bodies." Transpersonal psychology says not only that we are our bodies, but we are also the chair we are sitting on, the house we inhabit, the people we are talking to, our thoughts, our feelings, and on and on. At the same time, transpersonal psychology suggests that we are none of these; we are, instead, pure self-consciousness.[12] The paradox is lively and productive: we are everything and we are nothing.

Because we are connected to everything and are the container of all levels of reality, we can "tune in" and become aware of different "frequencies" along the band of consciousness. When one tunes in at the ego band, for example, one perceives reality with a certain set of assumptions. When one tunes in at the existential band, one perceives reality in a different way with a different set of assumptions about "how things are."[13]

Healing Prayer

In order to see the fertile interplay between the Swedenborgian and the transpersonal psychological ways of understanding reality, it is helpful to discuss how they might operate in practice in a specific area. Healing prayer is an avenue appropriate to this discussion. This writer uses "healing prayer" to mean a conscious act whereby one turns toward love while seeking the best for another. This usage allows for either a theological or a nontheological perspective on the process of healing. For a theologian, the love one turns toward is God. Yet, love can also be conceived of nontheologically as the natural healing force in life.

Prayer is a religious word. In Charles Tart's extensive anthology of transpersonal psychologies, the term *prayer* is only used in the section "Christian Mysticism" and once in the introductory section. Tart writes, ". . . the universe is very responsive to 'prayer,' in the sense that what you want sets up nonphysical forces that tend to bring things about physically."[14]

Healing through prayer does not require any communication or contact, in the usual sense, between the healer and the one being healed. What it does require is a genuine moving into the same "spiritual space." Healing prayer, as such, provides a good example for the exploration of the transpersonal tenet that the nonphysical impacts the physical plane.

The terms *healing* and *growth* can be looked at as describing the same process. Healing, or growth, is a movement from fragmentation and separation toward wholeness and integration. This movement, however, is not one steady, linear progression; it is, rather, a cyclical process. The high point of the cyclical process may be described as a restoring of order, balance, and right relationship between the one being healed and the universe. The cyclical process continuously provides the opportunity to integrate on greater levels of wholeness. The following illustration presents a two-dimensional picture of the healing and growth cycle; it is complemented by the suggestion of natural cycles of days and seasons.

THE HEALING PROCESS

When one feels separated from a real sense of Self, it is difficult to open to that higher sense of Self and direct its intentionality. At such times, healing prayers can offer the one who needs healing an opportunity to draw upon the vision of harmony and wholeness, as well as the support of love and care. Transpersonal healers use differing symbols and language to describe their experiences in healing. Lawrence LeShan has found that regardless which symbols of thought or imagery are used, the commonality among transpersonal healers may be summed up as:

- withdrawal from the ordinary, consensual state of being into an altered state of consciousness, where time and space, the separation between people, and other usual boundaries do not exist

- actively caring for the person undergoing the healing process. This can be by praying for the best for that person. It can be by invoking spirits to assist in the caring for the person. It can be by imaging unity with the person, or being with them as separate notes in the same symphony, thus stimulating that person's own self-healing mechanism within him- or herself.[15]

What LeShan has discovered phenomenologically is identical to what Ken Wilber describes theoretically in his definitive and landmark study, "Psychologia Perennis: The Spectrum of Consciousness."[16] The reader familiar with

The Healing/Growth Cycle

From a to b: noon; summer
　　　　 harmony
　　　　 a sense of peace and well-being
　　　　 unity between one's thoughts and feelings and
　　　　　　 actions
　　　　 ego serving the Self

From b to c: evening into night; autumn
　　　　 feeling that something is not quite right
　　　　 discontent; pain
　　　　 incongruity; disorientation
　　　　 agitation; tension; conflict
　　　　 sense of alienation beginning; disquiet
　　　　 split between ego and Self
　　　　 disintegration

From c to d: darkest hour; winter
　　　　 hopeless
　　　　 loneliness and fear
　　　　 depressed; staring into the depths of darkness
　　　　 deep pain; sadness; despair
　　　　 separation; alienation
　　　　 little or no sense of Self
　　　　 incubating seeds of hidden potential, within and
　　　　　　 without

From d.to a: dawn; spring
　　　　 calm; acceptance
　　　　 recuperation; release from a state of fear
　　　　 new sense of meaning and purpose and direction
　　　　 self-acceptance; deliverance
　　　　 feeling hopeful; feeling more on top of life
　　　　 ego realigning with Self
　　　　 deeper sense of who one is; "seeing the light"
　　　　 reintegration at a higher level than before

Swedenborg will recognize the above characteristics. Swedenborg also writes of the subjectivity of time and space in the spiritual world and of the flexibility of these boundaries, which are generally perceived as fixed (HH 129–31, 195–98). He stresses, too, the often unrecognized interconnectedness among people, as well as the importance of one's uniqueness as an individual.

Central to transpersonal healing is the belief that the power to change is not inherent in material reality. According to transpersonal psychology, material processes are products of consciousness.[17] This is contrary to the usual belief that consciousness is a product of and at the mercy of material reality.

Transpersonal psychology posits the belief that life goes far deeper than the material plane. Human beings are not just so many more cogs in the mechanistic wheel; rather, human beings are relatively free co-creators acting from a deep rooting in spiritual reality and can thus act positively and effectively in bringing about their own well-being.

Likewise, Swedenborg teaches that the spiritual world is the realm of causes, and the natural world is the realm of effects. Whatever one wills, whatever one intends, makes a difference. These capacities of will and understanding, or intentionality and discrimination, have potential power. By using the will to focus on a loving act, to the best of one's understanding, a person is opened to the spiritual realm, allowing the Lord's love to flow in. Experiencing the love and truth of God relaxes one's fearful hold on trying to live from one's self (little "s"). Letting in God's love and truth is progressing toward ultimate well-being.

Primary to all forms of transpersonal healing is the loving intention within a focused act. In terms of healing prayer, a focused act consciously brings all of one's thought and intention together for a single purpose. Concurrently, the one seeking the healing may assist the process by either moving into a state of inner quiet or by using their own images to open up to a state of loving transformation.

According to the tenets of transpersonal psychology, the healthy state of well-being is the natural state. As blocks are removed or dissolved, healing and growth occur; the natural state is restored. The single most common—and effective—block to health is the belief that one is alone. In such a mental state, a person is turned away from the source of life. It is precisely in this condition that healing prayer can facilitate growth.

TRANSPERSONAL PSYCHOLOGICAL PERSPECTIVE ON HEALING

In times of hurt and pain, how can one person's prayer potentially aid another person in the healing process? As the very name of this movement suggests, people are seen to be constantly influencing each other in a multitude of ways. One person's thoughts, beliefs, feelings, and expectations affect another person's state of being. This happens whether one is consciously aware of it or not. It can be plainly seen how people affect each other in physical ways. There are readily identifiable cause-effect relationships in one person feeding another, in a doctor binding up a wound, in one boy knocking another one down. When moving into the inner reaches of being, cause-effect relationships are less readily perceived but are held to be potent nonetheless.

Just as a person can aid in the healing process by providing quiet, comfort, the cleansing of wounds, nurturing food, so also can that person aid the healing process by offering to another a quieter, lighter, more peaceful, loving, and supportive psychic environment. Just as a person's actions and well-being are affected by their state of mind, one's state of mind is affected by the state of mind of others. All of this comprises the psychic, or spiritual, climate. From the transpersonal perspective, both physical and spiritual ways of offering healing affect the person being healed and are important to their well-being. Therefore, a key assumption in transpersonal psychology holds that reality and human consciousness are multidimensional. In this framework, people have the ability to affect each other in more than the conventionally conceived ways.

How can one consciously put this effect to good use in helping a healing take place? The answer seems to be the conscious focusing of loving intentionality. Lawrence LeShan has specifically researched the meditative state in relation to the psychic intent of one person's aiding in another person's healing. In the meditative state one moves from the world of the many to the world of the one. Seeing *all* as part of the *one* is one of the common denominators LeShan has found to be present in transpersonal healing systems.[18] Practice in the art of meditation strengthens the ability to focus one's intentionality.[19]

One result of a sustained meditation practice is an increased ability to disidentify with the disharmony one experiences, both within and without oneself. Simultaneously one increasingly feels more compassionate toward oneself and others who are in states of disharmony and disease. LeShan underscores the utility of these benefits as assets for those consciously participating in the healing and growth process.

Within the transpersonal psychological perspective the healer's role creates an environment of love, acceptance, and clarity for the purpose of healing a split, awakening a vision, and promoting order in another person's psyche. "From a transpersonal viewpoint every client is seen as having the capacity for self-healing. In other words, the therapist does not cure an ailment for a patient, but enables a client to tap inner resources and allow the natural healing or growth to occur."[20]

The goal of the healer is not to make the person being healed whole on the spot, double-time. Rather, the healer seeks to facilitate a natural healing process that will be appropriate for the person in question. Results are therefore not to be gauged through external indicators alone. For example, that the person begins to feel better does not necessarily mean that the growth process is moving forward (see Swedenborg's "vastation of state"—e.g., AC 1106ff). Perhaps the person in question needs to descend into more darkness before being ready to emerge into the light. Emerging into the light prematurely may stunt the healing and growth process instead of contribute to it. Transpersonal psychology stresses that the healer (or therapist) does not know what the eventual healthy state of the person needing healing (client) will look like. LeShan warns of trying to heal too specifically—a posture presuming that the healer knows what is right—but suggests it is best to leave it up to the innate self-healing ability of the one undergoing the process. The healer nurtures the self-healing mechanism in the other person and is therefore in the same relation to the healing process that a midwife is to a physical birth.

Transpersonal psychology affirms the declaration of William James (reared, interestingly enough, in a vigorous Swedenborgian household) that human beings operate far below his or her full potential. The transpersonal healing process is designed to help the person being healed draw upon more of his or her latent potential. As transpersonal psychology posits a stronger connection between human beings than is ordinarily believed in or consciously acted upon, the therapist can aid the client with a nurturing spiritual environment in which to tap inner resources.

Therefore, the role of the person in need of healing (in a specific transpersonal healing experience, when a healer is praying for the other's well-being) is simply to receive. If healing and growth are seen as states of wholeness, then disease can be thought of as a state of separateness. Fear and loneliness usually accompany a dis-easeful state, contracting and paralyzing the inner spirituality of the person. According to the perspective of transpersonal psychology, the primary cause of fear is the perception of duality. In light of this understanding, the healer images the person, through prayer, as whole, well, and surrounded by a harmonious love. In this context, the person may find the courage to move through the dark state of fear and separation into the light on the other side.

SWEDENBORGIAN PERSPECTIVE ON HEALING

Well-being from a Swedenborgian perspective can be described as growing in love and understanding, and actively manifesting this in the world. This is how one moves into a heavenly state and closer to God. God is the source of all life. God is eternally and fully present everywhere. "To move closer to God" is an adage meaning to recognize God more fully in our lives. Creation itself is the manifestation of God's love. Human beings were created to participate and share in the joy of God's love. A human being is a soul clothed with a body. Each human being is a unique expression of God's love. Swedenborg uses the image of the Universal Human ("*Maximus Homo*")—an integrated society of which everyone is a part—to illustrate the unity of creation. In this spiritual society all work together for a common good, and each person has one's own function and purpose. Because all are a part of the Universal Human, each affects all others. Coming at the same reality from the other side of the coin, Swedenborg also declares that each individual is a heaven in miniature.

The modern science of holography provides a helpful corollary by which to explain this Swedenborgian concept. In holography, the whole is seen to be contained in each of its parts. In the holographic model a small fragment of a holographic plate will produce the complete image (as discussed earlier), but the more complete the holographic plate, the more clear and sharply detailed the resulting picture. So it is with Swedenborg's concept of heaven: the more whole and complete an individual, the more fully is God's life and nature resident in that person. Each individual person mirrors the entire creation. These twin Swedenborgian concepts give us a rich and dynamic idea of what it means to be human: each person not only mirrors the entire creation, but each person affects all others.

Swedenborg states that there is a relationship between the outer world, the realm of nature, and the inner world of the mind and spirit of a person, describing this relationship as correspondential. Every physical object, act, or event is anchored in a spiritual reality.

At the same time, Swedenborg emphasizes that the spiritual is the realm of causes, and the natural is the realm of effects. Without a spiritual correspondence, nothing has life or existence: the spiritual within the natural is life itself. In *Rational Psychology*, Swedenborg writes, "It is the soul which sensates, that is, which hears, sees, perceives, thinks, judges, wills . . ." (RP 113). It is through the understanding of correspondences that one can see the spiritual within the natural.

Spiritual love and understanding from the Lord flow into a person's intentionality and discrimination. A person's natural body, in turn, exists and is sustained by one's intentionality and discrimination. This is another way of saying that physical reality is an effect of consciousness. Note that it is not "mind over matter," as it is usually understood, for it refers to a cause resulting from a spiritual state rather than an exertion on the part of the ego.

Healthiness is the inherent state of being. All persons are created for heavenly life and for intimate fellowship with the Lord. As one moves through the process of healing and growth (synonymous with Swedenborg's term *regeneration* [see Glossary])—which necessarily includes times of dis-ease (mental or physical)—one moves toward this ultimate state of spiritual wholeness and well-being. In a sense, the battle being fought is a battle between heaven and hell. For Swedenborg, heaven holds everything together in connection and health through the medium of mutual love. The Lord is the absolute source of cohesiveness and order in heaven (AC 5713, 5718). Hell, being a state of denying the Lord, destroys health and well-being.

Direct medical intervention (medicine, surgery, a splint, stitches, etc.) can serve as agents of healing, according to Swedenborg, but it is the spiritual correspondence within these natural means that is the cause of the healing. As everyone is a part of the intradependent Universal Human; as human beings inhabit both the physical and spiritual worlds; and as effects result from spiritual causes, individuals have the potential for affecting one another through spiritual means.

People are affecting one another whether they are consciously aware of it or not. Healing through prayer is one means of consciously moving into a spiritual state and focusing one's intentionality for the well-being of another person. One's perceptions are enlightened in a spiritual state, and since this is the level of causation, one's loving intent is the channel for a potentially powerful effect. Swedenborg writes, ". . . the sight appears as though it were in the eye, yet we see when the eye is closed, and the more the eye is closed the more the internal sight and imagination is perfected, and indeed, so perfected that the external sight is rather an obstruction to the internal" (RP 508).

While in a spiritual state and seeing with an internal sight, by imaging a person in the presence of God (see LeShan's common denominators for transpersonal healers in "The Healing Process" section earlier in this essay) one is offering another person a spiritual environment where the person can be safe and comforted and can thereby relax his or her fears. This allows for the "self-healing mechanism" of the person to function more freely. In a Swedenborgian conceptual framework, the self-healing mechanism can be described as the divine reality of God's love that is ever present yet infinitely patient, and that is always flowing through a person's heart and mind and out into the body.

Swedenborg teaches that God is always with a person, but that during times of struggles an individual will feel especially separate, alienated, and alone (see the healing and growth cycle described and diagrammed earlier). In the process of growing closer to God, people are confronted with distortions of God's love and truth, thus engaged by evils and falsities. It is a real battle to learn how to recognize and choose what is right and good. Disease can be a manifestation of one of these battles. These distortions can arise from one's personal life, from being a part of the Universal Human, or from a confluence of the two. As the Swedenborgian perspective maintains all causes to be ultimately spiritual, whether from one's own personal sphere or as part of a larger sphere, the physical manifestations correspond to a deeper inner state, to some distortion or split or breakdown on a spiritual level. It is important to underscore that such spiritual stresses may be originating in the larger social matrix rather than in the individual's personal spirituality. (For example, when 30 percent of an asbestos factory's employees are stricken with cancer, the largest stress factor—high levels of exposure to a known carcinogen—seems obviously more prominent than the anxiety levels or health habits of those stricken.)

To be in a diseased state does not imply that an individual is an evil person, but rather is evidence that somewhere a battle is being fought. Confronted with a disorderly (diseased) state, the person has an opportunity for reordering and reintegration (again, see the healing and growth cycle). Ebbs are a natural part of the growth process, and there is a great deal to be realized at this stage.

The search for health involves trying to understand the causes of the specific disease. To what might this situation be corresponding? To what might it possibly awaken the person? Whether the disease is manifesting a more personal spiritual need for reintegration at a higher level, or a broader need for social reform, will influence the character and experience of the healing and growth process. It is instructive to sense where a disease is leading (i.e., its purpose), as well as where it came from (i.e., its cause).

Concluding Remarks

Seen through the examples of healing prayer and the growth cycle, Swedenborgian theology and practice is compatible with the emerging and rapidly growing school of transpersonal psychology. Swedenborgian theology describes a reality comprised of an active and positive force permeating life, and it provides a clear outline for relationship (prayer) with this active healing force (God). The transpersonal movement offers methods—Eastern, Western, and modern—for guiding the development of the skills necessary for spiritual development. While offering an admittedly eclectic belief system, this movement's chief tenet is to use only that which proves truly useful—a pragmatic philosophy present in Swedenborgianism, also. It is always a challenge to retranslate ideas across centuries and cultures, but it is clear to this writer that Swedenborg presented forcefully the core concepts that make up the important new coalition of movements known as transpersonal psychology, albeit from a much more theological and Christological perspective. The rearticulation of traditional religious concepts in the transpersonal psychology movement is an important event, if valuable spiritual concepts are to be made accessible to a much greater number and variety of people in the waning decades of the twentieth century.

Notes

1. John Welwood, ed. *The Meeting of the Ways: Explorations in East/West Psychology* (New York: Schocken Books, 1979), p. 3.
2. Roger N. Walsh and Frances Vaughan, eds. *Beyond Ego: Transpersonal Dimensions in Psychology* (Los Angeles: J. P. Tarcher, 1980), p. 18.
3. Ibid., p. 16.
4. Charles T. Tart, ed., *Transpersonal Psychologies* (New York: Harper & Row, 1975), pp. 61–111.
5. Tart, p. 74.
6. Ibid.
7. A. H. Maslow, *Psychology of Science*. (New York: Harper & Row, 1966).
8. Gary Zukav, *The Dancing Wu Li Masters: An Overview of the New Physics* (New York: Bantam Books, 1979), pp. 111–14.
9. Walsh, p. 226.
10. George Leonard, *The Silent Pulse* (New York: E. P. Dutton, 1978; reprint, New York: Bantam Books, 1981), pp. 70–71, 141–50.
11. Tart, p. 76.
12. Ken Wilber, *No Boundary: Eastern and Western Approaches to Personal Growth* (Boulder and London: Shambala, 1981).
13. Ken Wilber, "Psychologia Perennis: The Spectrum of Consciousness," *Journal of Transpersonal Psychology* 7, no. 2 (1975), pp. 105–32.
14. Tart, p. 9.
15. Lawrence LeShan, Lecture given at Interface in Newton, Mass., September 1981.
16. Wilber, "Psychologia Perennis," pp. 105–32.
17. Walsh and Vaughan, p. 77.
18. LeShan.
19. Ibid.
20. Frances Vaughan, "Transpersonal Psychotherapy: Context, Content, and Process," *Journal of Transpersonal Psychology* 2, no. 2 (1979), p. 102.

A Mystic Looks at Swedenborg

Wilson Van Dusen, Ph.D.

> The doctrines simply are not much use to me unless I know what
> it is in my own experience that they are talking about.
>
> —George Dole, from *Messenger* review of *Arcana Coelestia*

> . . . There is the closest relation between the mode of apprehen-
> sion and the thing apprehended.
>
> —Gabriel Marcel, from *Creative Fidelity*

The Nature of Mysticism

I USE THE WORD *mystic* in its simplest and most basic sense. A mystic is one who experiences God. There are other associated meanings and very complex analyses in religious encyclopedias, but they all rest in this—the experience of God. Some might ask, "Don't all people experience God?" And I would answer yes, but many are not aware of it. The mystic is aware of it.

Perhaps I need to underline the verb *experience*. It is quite a bit more than simply thinking about God or addressing God. God becomes manifest, obvious. And by using the present tense I also mean to imply that the experience tends to be ongoing. Having experienced God once, one acquires a taste for it. The mystic learns how to find his or her way back into that communion.

In this essay I'll cite my own experience merely because it is handy for me, with some reference to the experience of others. My aim is to make the spiritual experience familiar enough to be recognizable to the reader. After establishing this base we will then see how this is reflected in Swedenborg. The parallel is not simply in the fact that Swedenborg talks about God. Most theological writing concerns God, but most also seems quite flat and unmystical to me. On the other hand, certain music, literature, paintings, and other art forms easily bring me back to the experience of the Divine. The relevance of mystical experience to Swedenborg's own has more to do with a mode of experiencing than with mere content matter.

If someone asked when I first became aware that I was a mystic, I would date it to early adolescence. We lived on the top floor of several flats, and I soon discovered I could climb a ladder to the roof. In the crowded world of San Francisco I found that the rooftop offered me an expansive private world. The dusk of evening was always the nicest time. Lights were dimming and my thoughts soared. I came back repeatedly to the feeling of the oneness of things. All the city lights, all the dusky shapes, all the sounds were One Life. I knew also I was this One Life looking at and admiring the One Life. The basic feeling was awe or reverence. No matter what the difficulties of the day, in the evening, under the stars, it was indeed wonder-full.

WILSON VAN DUSEN is a natural scholar with wide interests, but his central focus is on the internals of religious experience. He explored the psychology side of this interest by taking a Ph.D. in clinical psychology and by working for many years with the mentally ill. His approach to the religious side includes personal practice and wide reading in the world's religions. He discovered Swedenborg in 1952, and he has gradually gained recognition as one who can throw light on Swedenborg's experience. He is the author of two widely popular books, *The Natural Depth in Man* and *The Presence of Other Worlds*. He has also drawn useful practices out of Swedenborg's religious works with essays such as "Uses," published as a pamphlet by the Swedenborg Foundation. He is now busily retired with his artist wife in a small town, writing and, of all things, teaching in nautical sciences. He hopes to focus more on the internals of religious experience in worlds to come.

On the front of the roof was a curved decoration. It was high enough so that I could lean on it and safely look down on the street. I remember lovingly touching the tar paper with awe. The very reality of substance seemed miraculous. I heard the sound of a distant dog bark. I was in such a sense of oneness that it was as though I heard my own life. I remember hearing a screen door squeak and slam shut somewhere, and with that simple sound I knew the design of creation. I remember swearing to myself that no matter what happens in life, I would always come back to the peace of evening. And, in a real sense, by writing of it I am back to that peace. I was so awestruck by the wonder of existence. There was also no sense of ego—no me versus it. Me and it were one.

Reverence is the term that would come to me now to describe the experience, but it would not have then. I had yet to learn that religion and God really existed. My father was an atheist and my mother disdained all religion, even though she was raised a Catholic. She had had a hard life. She had said many times, "If there was a God, he would be unspeakably horrible." I had heard church services on the radio, but they didn't impress me. The preachers sounded like pompous salesmen, selling the Word instead of cars.

At that time my experience was nameless. I can remember the book that first suggested to me I was not alone, that there were others out there with similar experiences. My first five-cent book purchase was Thomas Troward's *Edinburgh Lectures in Mental Science.*[1] I was struck by the wonder of money, if it could buy treasures like that. Thomas Troward was a member of the New Thought Movement. For the first time I saw echoes of my experience in print: "But because the universal personalness is the root of all individual personalities, it finds its highest expression in response to those who realize its personal nature."[2] Yes, that's it. A spiritual moment is immensely personal. I didn't hear any of the religious radio programs say that. "He must realize that the whole process is that of bringing the universal within the grasp of the individual by raising the individual to the level of the universal, and not vice-versa."[3] Yes, yes! So when I see the design of all in the sound of a screen door, it is the universal. Everything I saw, heard, or touched spoke of the universal. It was a great comfort to discover, at last, that I was not alone. Others have realized the same thing.

But, in a way, the experience was frustrating. It was like standing on the edge of a vast sea of mystery, feeling that it was all here, yet I wanted something specific. I'd ask the universal for guidance in my life, and then chide it for its lack of specificity. All wasn't enough; I wanted something more!

But the idea of the oneness of all things took firm root. It found countless echoes later, in the ecologist's concern for life, in the universality of humanity, for examples. When I

was young one of my favorite fantasies was that I was making speeches to the world on peace and the fellowship of humanity. I had a whole binder of what seemed, at the time, like very inspired lectures. In later years I burned them as a bit too adolescent to keep. But it still happens that the theme of the universality of life can easily bring tears to my eyes. It is something I feel so strongly that my reason has to stand aside. I know I'm me and you're you, and that much separates and distinguishes us. But that's the job of reason, to cut things up and set them apart. It doesn't matter. I've experienced the oneness of All. It became apparent to me that life could either be taken apart or experienced as a one. The experience of oneness was the more fundamental, satisfying, and powerful. It was the truth. All this taking apart is secondary, flat, and trivial in comparison.

You might wonder what the mystical experience does to personal identity. Sensing the All, would I not be greater than most who don't do this? Not in the least. Sensing the All, I am the equal of all—the equal of tar paper, a dog's bark, and stars. I would say the experience relaxes the personal identity down to the point where it doesn't matter. Later I was impressed by the Greek expression *En to Pan,* "the One is the All."

Over the years it gradually dawned on me that my experience was religious and that the Universal One was another name for God. You see, I had these kinds of experiences before names, even before speech or words. Though I began this essay with an account from adolescence, I can recall an experience all the way back in infancy, when I was still in a crib, possibly around the age of one. I lay there with my head turned to the side. Sunlight was streaming though the window. Motes of dust floated and turned in the beam of sunlight. Fixing on them I saw endless rainbows of color. The feeling was of ecstasy and awe. Later I learned in my study of psychoanalysis that this identification with everything is common in children—that it was a childish quality I'd apparently failed to outgrow! Be that as it may, I found the roots of mystical experience can exist before words, concepts, religious training, before all the obscuring machinations of the world. I suspect these experiential roots are pretty much universal; they occur in all people. But in various ways our education and acculturation can obscure them. The center can be forgotten.

In some way my memory was turned around. My experience of the All became my foundation. Later, people were surprised when I said I could far more easily doubt my own existence than I could doubt God's. My own existence seems variable, hard to grasp, doubtful, and really trivial. The All is everything. Perhaps by some bit of luck (another term is *God's grace*) I retained the memory of what others also knew and misplaced or forgot. In some way I feel obliged to describe the mystical experience so that others may recover it.

So here I will describe my adult way of returning to it, which may also work for you. I've been in and out of mystical experiences so often that it has finally become clear how to find my way back. It can be done anywhere, at any time. But there are certain necessities. I cannot be rushed nor in pain. The mood is one of no hurry, endless time. I feel very open. I'll accept whatever is given. It is the opposite of making demands on God. The mood is one of openness and play. Just for the fun I feel like stopping here and admiring the flowers. Long ago I discovered it is the heart of aesthetic experience. How best to appreciate what is before you but by stopping, looking, being open to what is suggested?

I had a group of alcoholic women contend that this could not be done within the bare walls of an institution. So I had them dwell intensely on the floor. One noticed a crack in the cement, and in describing what it suggested to her, she came to a tearful description of her life pattern. Everything reveals if we are patient with it.

The whole of existence is like looking at a painting. I am regarding Van Gogh's second self-portrait. At first I take in the obvious details: his face is angular and bearded; his clothes are rude, those of a peasant; the blue background swirls around his head with areas of chaos. There's a remarkable, quiet intensity in the face. Though closed-mouthed and mute, the intensity is almost wild, brooding. And this is the center of the man. He has painted his very nature. I empathize with the power of his struggle. In the mystical mood I allow all there is to speak, to affect me. If I had to train mystics I would certainly consider using art appreciation as a first step. For in it is the foundation of letting things reveal themselves to you.

But you may say this is merely aesthetic and not religious. The aesthetic is a step into the doorway of the religious. Its basic attitude is one of appreciation. It leads to awe and respect. It is the practice of openness to what is here. Like the aesthetic person, the mystic is in an appreciation of things as they are. This moment is perfect. It is all here, all there is.

There is a tremendous nowness to the mystical experience. It is as though all there ever was passes through this present into all there ever will be. One rests in such a moment. Questions have no place. Doubts are absent. Here, thus, it *is*. I once asked God for a sign of his existence. God answers in direct knowing, beyond words. His answer was in effect, "Is not the whole of existence sign enough?" Well, yes, that's a pretty good one: existence—yes, I'd call that a substantial sign!

My existence is among these signs. So sometimes I just look at and admire my hand. Interesting form. Skin a little wrinkled because I'm aging. A real marvel how it is animated. Look at it writing here. Marvelous. I wonder what words are and how my hand works. I am mystery, looking at mystery, appreciating mystery. The very essence of mystical experience is to appreciate this fully—what is. Does it plague me that I am a mystery? No. I appreciate it. How far this is from egotism or Swedenborg's term *proprium* [see Glossary]. No egotism, because I know beyond my understanding that the same life animates the pine tree in my backyard that animates me. What a delightfully pervasive mystery. What an honor to be an equal to pine trees, grass, and clouds.

I've described the mood and attitude that leads to mystical experience—taking the time to be open and thoroughly appreciate what is before you. But there are also deeper hallmarks of the mystical experience. Meaning is given, "noetic." You suddenly realize something that is prior to thought, before any reasoning. You might just *know* that God is present. If someone asks how or where, you would have nothing to point to. This knowing can vary from a gentle suggestion to an absolute certainty. Outside that experience the subject himself can doubt it. "Was God really present?" But during the noetic givenness of knowing, doubt or questioning is not possible. I've even formulated my biggest questions and written them down, only to find my own sheet of questions rather ridiculous during the experience of God. One of the reasons I've written for many years and barely said anything of this experience is that it is sacred and beyond doubt.

I recall a woman who had a sudden, unexpected experience of God lasting probably less than five seconds. She described it to a nun, who remarked, "You probably just had a digestive upset." The woman spent decades studying mysticism and trying to return to the experience, but after the nun's rejection she rarely told anyone of it. She now trains priests in the deeper aspects of religious experience. The mystical experience is so characterized by direct knowing that I'd call into question an experience where God talks aloud to a person.

The experience is up through the core of one's being. Words are not necessary. I once saw an angelic figure with wings crossed in front as though to conceal something. I wondered what was concealed. Suddenly the answer came flooding in, but not in words. I was just given to know. The hidden secret was that there is no death. Nowhere in the whole of existence is there death. You are struck with not only the words but also the full ramifications of them. People think of death as real. The angel revealed the deeper truth; no one ever dies. And like waves and ripples the full ramifications play on the consciousness. In Raymond Moody's cases of people who "died" on the operating table and later were revived, many reported meeting a radiant figure who communicated by direct mind-to-mind knowing.[4] A parallel in ordinary experience is the way lovers sense so much before anything is said. In sharp contrast, when people who are hallucinating meet demons of hell, they *talk* endlessly but they say little! The more powerful the feeling that goes with direct knowing, the more I'd suspect it is just plain truth. Often in these experiences symbols are given, and at the same time the meanings of the symbols are given. A meaning can be so nonverbal that the person receiving it may have difficulty putting it into words. In these cases I'd say it is therapeutic and useful to draw what was seen and attempt to extract and put into words all the information. Otherwise the ordinary consciousness may later look at what was given and translate it into something much less significant than it was at the time (e.g., "I saw an angel and I guess it meant so and so"). But going back to the experience, one finds it packed with meaning. I was once given a simple hand gesture of two fingers extended and its meaning. I was thrilled years later to see it in an old painting in the Eastern Orthodox Church.

William James writes about the noetic:

> Although so similar to states of feeling, mystical states seem to those who experience them to also be states of knowledge. They are states of insight into depths of knowledge. They are states of insight into depths of truth unplumbed by the discursive intellect. They are illuminations, revelations, full of significance and importance, all inarticulate though they remain; and as a rule they carry with them a curious sense of authority for aftertime.[5]

William James also describes the mystical experience as "ineffable," or impossible to describe in words. I would not go so far as to say this. With care one can describe the state. It's just that one can't fully convey the state in words because, as he says, it is more like states of feeling than intellect.

The Several Paths Are One Path

Having experienced a remarkable state, I was naturally curious to look at what the world's literature had to say of it. There are a number of scholarly compilations—collections and commentaries on what mystics have to say. Other than a few touching quotes from real mystics, these commentaries fall quite flat for me. Those writing them often draw conclusions that are just untrue, possibly because they haven't had the experience. They also tend to make a basically simple and direct experience quite complex, constructing stages, and stages within stages of the experience. Yet the real experience is terribly simple and straightforward.

In great contrast, the work of actual mystics often soars for me. Among these I'd list Plotinus, Khalil Gibran, Saint Theresa of Lisieux, Jakob Böhme, the Zen Buddhists, some Hindu works, and Omar Khayyám. Notice that this listing ranges across several religions. Mystics are dealing with universal truth revealed in most, and perhaps all, religions. Even though the content of these authors seems different—Gibran is in verse; Saint Theresa describes her relationship to Christ;

Plotinus the Greek, like Jakob Böhme, presents a soaring intellectual understanding—they have the power of one who has been there.

In my experience mystics have no difficulty recognizing other mystics. Because their eye is on the universal they see beyond historical and doctrinal differences. I've often been asked by individuals whether their experience of God was true. Let me cite an unusual case to illustrate the process. I was at a Christian church gathering at a camp in the mountains. A minister's wife indicated she wanted to speak to me. As a practiced clinical psychologist I could see that great feeling was involved. She hesitated to speak. Finally I got her to tell her story.

One day a friend came to see her, bearing the message that her deceased father loved her. Suddenly the situation opened up for her. She knew beyond doubt that this man, in the body of a known friend, was actually God, and God came to repair the relationship with her father. She had been emotionally alienated from her father. She asked me if this was a true experience of God, even though inwardly she knew beyond doubt it was. I felt a tremendous impact in her story. We both struggled unsuccessfully with tears. My response was that her story had the ring of truth to it, though I had never before seen the form of her experience—God coming in the body of a friend. God is able to come in any form, even the form of a friend. The incident essentially did good: it brought her into loving relationship with her father.

The woman's story had all of the hallmarks I look for in a genuine experience of God. The people hesitate to speak. What they have to say is powerfully sacred to them. It is the opposite of bragging: they would rather say nothing happened then to have the sacred rejected. The experience is linked to powerful feeling, which indicates to me that it comes from beyond mere intellect, from beyond the manipulations of consciousness. It is as though the very source of life is touched and shaken. Finally I ask whether the experience does good. If so, I believe it is from God. I affirmed, as she already inwardly felt, that the experience was quite genuine.

What you often find, as was true of her, is that the mystical experience can be so powerful and otherworldly that the subject is somewhat at a loss as to what to do with it. I saw she was having difficulty integrating the experience. She said she went to the bishop of her church afterward and he so discredited the experience that she swore to herself never to speak again of religious feeling in church! I took the opposite tack. Given that God was trying to repair the bond between her and her father, I asked that she prayerfully dwell on the love between them. I reinforce the trend in the experience. I try to act in concert with the tendencies shown by God. Countless bishops and psychotherapists could not kill the inner life of her experience. But in a few moments

I could strike a sentient chord merely by recognizing and reinforcing the quality of the experience given her.

I relate this incident to illustrate several things. I believe mystics can easily see and empathize with genuine experience in others regardless of religious differences, no matter how unusual the form. I also think it something of a crime for someone to invalidate the depth of experience in others. It would have been far better if the bishop had said, "I don't know if your experience was really of God," for actually he didn't know.

Would I call this woman a mystic? Potentially, yes. She had had only one experience, but treating this one in a positive way would encourage her to open to others. She was just at the entrance of the house; she had yet to move in and become comfortable in the house. This woman's story also illustrates that the mystical experience is not totally ineffable, beyond description. Difficult to convey, yes; impossible, no. Moreover, in attempting to do so, others who hear of it might rethink their own sacred experiences and renew their belief in the wonders that have been given to them.

Follow, if you will, a fantasy of mine. Suppose I am able to encourage many people to describe their sacred experiences. I compile and publish a newsletter of these and we convene to discuss them. In these meetings the mood is one of acceptance of and respect for even the tiniest traces of sacredness in each other's experience. Because one describes, others recognize similar experiences in themselves. Because we accept and express and share these, new experiences arise and are shared. Mystical experience becomes common and we are able to explore the length and breadth of it. A fantasy? Not entirely.

I've seen Teen Challenge sessions in which a similar situation occurred. All of the members present had been drug addicts picked up while down and out on the street. Because the group had expectations that the experience of Christ would occur, it did frequently. I recall one addict saying he watched in amazement as his hands poured heroin down the toilet. In that moment he knew that Christ controlled him.

I have also seen Teen Challenge members speak to religious groups and frighten them. Most people's experience of religion is cool, rational, controlled. These people really believe, and they frighten people of a cool religion. For a similar reason in the history of mysticism it was fairly common for mystics to write anonymously (as did Swedenborg at first) or to come into conflict with the church (Teilhard de Chardin), or to write their experiences in a partly disguised form ("The Rubáiyát" of Omar Khayyám).

So let me alter my fantasy above. Only mystics (of any religion) may enter our circle, and we share with each other only. But the underlying theme of my fantasy is that we share and respect experiences of God and thereby encourage others to recognize it in their life. In this day and age, I find that what is missing from and repressed in many people's lives is the sacred, not sexuality, as some maintain.

Why? At first, one might suggest we tend to hold back a sacred experience because we don't want others to scoff at it. The bishop's put-down of the woman discussed previously is a good example. The experience is particularly delicate if one has had only one or a few experiences. This is a partial reason for repressing the sacred. But there is another reason that has to do with the inward nature of the experience. What opens up in the person is the deepest root of life itself. It *is* one's life. Would we hand a scalpel to a passing stranger to perform surgery on us? The experience is our life, our very life. It often repels even the skeptical probing of the subjects themselves. That is, the experience can seem alien and incredible to even the person who has it. There is a great difference between the person who is moved in one sacred moment and the same person in the workaday world. In the light of day, that transcendent experience can be questioned and doubted by the subject who had it. Did it really happen? Was that God, or digestive upset? It is uncomfortable to doubt it. It is like pinching oneself unnecessarily. So an uneasy peace settles.

I believe that in the most inward sense there is a natural protection around the sacred. At the very worst the experience will totally disappear from memory rather than leave the sacred to be permanently questioned. So the barriers to assault on it are both internal and external. I don't want it to be laughed at so I won't tell others. It is somehow wrong even for me to question it, so I'll not do so. It takes respect for the sacred by one person to open it up to expression in another. The woman who reacted to the bishop's put-down wasn't simply a petulant woman. The sacred protects itself, so she resolved never to expose real religious feeling in church again. I don't fully understand how the sacred protects itself. But I suspect if we could see its full ramifications we'd be surprised at its artful, in-depth protection. I am so convinced that the sacred is the very root and source of life itself that I'm sure some have died rather than expose it (e.g., the early Christian martyrs). The doubts of others are rather easy to fend off: simply keep quiet about it. Internal doubt is another matter.

I would not be at all surprised to learn that one day madness itself comes from turning against the early budding of mystical experience in a person. Why do I say this? Because in madness I often see a strange tangle of essentially religious elements turned back on itself. It would be better not to have the experience of God than to harm it in any way. At the very least the person who has it would be better off to leave the possibility of its reality open and seek out its possible good than to turn away.

There are several other hallmarks of the mystical experience. One is a strong sense of the familiar, no matter how unusual the outer situation. Once I was watching a play. An actor said, "I've returned as I promised." Suddenly the play opened up. I felt that God spoke through the actor, and I was in tears that God had returned. I've walked in ruined churches that I'd not seen before and suddenly had an overwhelming feeling of the familiar. In the ruins of a monks' abbey I was suddenly familiar with the monks and their devoted labor of building the church. Sometimes when interviewing a person it also occurs that suddenly, again, there is the familiar God in them. The feeling is very pleasant, like coming home after a long trip. It often comes to me when I'm with people talking about sharing with others or about universal humanity. The full mystical experience leaves a very broad signature on the inner life that then finds itself expressed in many ways. The sense of familiarity is so consistent that I would question whether the experience of *déjà vu* might not be a part of mysticism. I would encourage those with *déjà vu* to reflect deeply on what they recognize in the experience. Try to bring up and examine all the feelings. It may be a tiny precurser to the mystical. I was once talking to a neurotic woman. There was something in her very preened formality. Suddenly I felt the essence of Egyptian religion. It is difficult to describe, but it has to do with reaching and preserving the contact with the Eternal. The changeless is close to the sacred—so it was necessary to preserve the body. A religion that seemed foreign to me was suddenly familiar. It revered the changeless, which is an approach to the Eternal.

There is another aspect of the mystical experience that seems to be consistently misunderstood. It is as though we must die to ourselves in order to see God. This leads to all sorts of efforts to overcome the self. This is an impossible paradox, for the one struggling against the self turns out to be simply the self. In a way, the self is actually intensified by the effort to get rid of it. The truth is that in a mystical experience there is an expansion of the self—quite the opposite. It is as though God is always present and is the root and source of our very life. God need only expand our awareness to come into consciousness. The relaxed openness is part of allowing this to happen, allowing the source to speak. The love of God calls forth the experience.

There is another related problem. I've wondered if I should tell you of my great visions. Readers might compare their little visions to my great ones and conclude that they have not yet reached the same level. This is a kind of spiritual nonsense. Like Swedenborg,[6] we become disappointed if our vision doesn't knock us clear out of bed. It is the doubting little self that demands miracles, lightning to strike this very instant. What is wrong is that this competitive race for the biggest vision overlooks all the tiny ones. It is loving appreciation of the tiny ones that may (God willing) prepare us for a bigger vision. A key to understanding here is that we really can't (repeat, *can't*) make God come give us a giant experience. This is a presumption against the very nature of the spiritual. Learn to appreciate the absolute wonder that you already have. We breathe, don't we? Isn't it a marvelous process that we take in and expel the world regularly, whether we think of it or not? I wonder if there is meaning beyond oxygenating the blood. The Hindus have described a way to God that includes principally focusing on breathing. Earlier I described a mystical experience in simply looking at and wondering at the life that cleverly moves my hands, I know not how. Looking at and enjoying the wonder of nature is a universal experience of humankind. Beware of asking God for big visions, just to prove he exists. Having had one vision, you may tend to doubt it and ask for one more bigger one, and so on. Finally you will die, and it is hoped that the vision you have then will at last be big enough!

Both the effort to overcome the self and the demand for big visions are common spiritual traps. God comes by expanding your present awareness. Learn to see the miracles here all the time. The very essence of the mystical experience is to appreciate what is here now. That is becoming a child again—finding amazingly beautiful something as small as a dried-up leaf that fell from a tree.

Some may conclude that the mystical can be sensed in the beautiful things in life (i.e., nature) but not in the ugly things. Not so. I have reflected on rubbish and garbage heaps and found wonders in them. Some put a big boundary between the things made by God (i.e., nature) and those made by human beings. In this dichotomy human creations are low and nature's high. This seems foolish to me. I am so aware that God designed the people who make things, that I am most anxious to watch science's discoveries and the unfolding of clever electronic gadgets. If you look for God, he may be found anywhere.

It would be fair to ask what the mystic ultimately discovers. Swedenborg's writings contain some of the better descriptions.

Swedenborg's Mysticism

I cannot but open up those things of the Word that are called mystical, that is, its interior things. . . .

—Emanuel Swedenborg (AC 4923)

It came as a considerable surprise to me to learn that there is a tradition among students of Swedenborg's religious writings that Swedenborg is not a mystic. It is only too apparent to a mystic that his works are a major contribution to this literature, and mystics have freely referred to him as one of their own. Swedenborg's spiritual writings define mysticism in a way that inescapably makes Swedenborg a mystic. How is it, then, that some of his followers say, with earnest conviction, that he is not a mystic? We will look at what mysticism precisely is and how this error arose. We will also see how his religious works define mysticism and how this compares with the current accepted meaning. This is not a mere quibble over a term. At its least it implies a misunderstanding of mysticism. At its worst it may involve a misunderstanding of the very nature of Swedenborg's writings themselves.

The definition of mysticism has two conflicting currents. One, which we will call the scholarly definition, reflects the actual experience of mystics. The other, which we will call the layperson's definition, stands outside the experience and basically says it doesn't make sense. This confusion of opposing definitions is quite old and extends back before Swedenborg's time. Many dictionaries will reflect both views. The core of the scholarly definitions is the experience of union with the Divine. The core of the layperson's definitions is whatever is occult, mysterious, unclear, or involved with spirits.

Followers who use the layperson's definition are more than happy to say Swedenborg wasn't interested in the occult, which is true, and hence not a mystic. The very rationality and clarity of his spiritual writings would seem to militate against their being mystical. Let us look at the dictionary definitions. The closer the dictionary is to the popular mind, the more likely it will reflect the unprofessional layperson's definition as well as the scholarly. Scholarly religious dictionaries tend to drop the popular misconception altogether and deal only with the real internal meaning of the experience. The following reflects more of the popular misconception:

> Mystical, 1. mystic; occult. 2. of or pertaining to mystics or mysticism: mystical writings. 3. spiritually symbolic. 4. rare: obscure in meaning; mysterious.[7]

Swedenborg's own definition was the third one above—"spiritually symbolic." This same dictionary, reflecting the popular conception, says of the word *mystic*: "known only to the initiated; of occult power or significance; of obscure or mysterious character. . . ." It is from this aspect that followers of Swedenborg's religious writings wanted to dissociate themselves, for these works are eminently rational and clear. Another dictionary almost overlooks this popular misconception:

> Mystical 1: having a spiritual meaning or reality, or the like, neither apparent to the senses nor obvious to the intelligence; symbolical; as, the church is the mystical body of Christ. 2: of, resulting from, or manifesting an individual's direct communion with God, through contemplation, vision, an inner light, or the like; as, mystical rapture. 3. now rare: unintelligible; cryptic.[8]

Notice that the definitions, "obscure in meaning, mysterious" and "cryptic" are now seen as rare.

It is through communion with the Divine that direct spiritual understanding is given, which is often symbolic and difficult to translate into ordinary terms for others. The difficulty of conveying the internal experience to others has made it seem obscure to outsiders. Then, to add to the confusion, there have been the pseudomystics who use the term for self-aggrandizement, as though to say, "This is mystical and too deep for your understanding, but of course I understand it!"

The very authoritative *Hastings Encyclopedia of Religion and Ethics* goes to the heart of the matter:

> MYSTICISM—"Mysticism," in common speech-usage, is a word of very uncertain connotation. It has in recent times been used as an equivalent for two characteristically different German words: *Mystizismus*, which stands for the cult of the supernatural, for theosophical pursuits, for a spiritualistic exploitation of physical research; and *Mystik*, which stands for immediate experience of a divine-human intercourse and relationship. The word "mysticism" has, furthermore, been commonly used to cover both (1) the first-hand experience of direct intercourse with God and (2) the theologico-metaphysical doctrine of the soul's possible union with Absolute Reality, i.e., with God. It would be conducive to clarity to restrict the word "mysticism" to the latter significance, namely, as an equivalent for the German word *Mystik*, and as designating the historic doctrine of the relationship and potential union of the human soul with Ultimate Reality, and to use the term "mystical experience" for direct intercourse with God.
>
> First-hand, or mystical, experience is primarily a psychological question; the doctrine of mysticism is essentially a metaphysical problem. Mystical experience is as old as humanity, is not confined to any one racial stock, is undoubtedly one of the original grounds of personal religion, and does not stand or fall with the truth or falsity of the metaphysically formulated doctrine of mysticism. Mystical experience is marked by the emergence of a type of consciousness.[9]

The more than twenty pages of tiny print make no further reference to the layperson's definition. In spite of what the author, Rufus Jones, a noted scholar of mysticism, would like to see, the term *mysticism* is used most often for the experience. The literature on the qualities of the experience is vast; that on the doctrinal aspects is relatively scant. In fact Swedenborg's spiritual writings are an unusual combination of the experiential and the doctrinal aspects of mysticism. In brief, then, the most accepted definition of mysticism refers to all aspects of the experience of conjunction or union with the Divine and secondarily to doctrines about this. This is the sense in which I use the term.

It is relatively easy to demonstrate that all those who have said Swedenborg was not a mystic used the now-rare and not really acceptable layperson's definition. None of them were trying to say that his writings do not deal with the experience of the Divine—the core of the accepted meaning of mysticism. My sources are not complete, but a couple of references will illustrate the point.

Herbert C. Small in 1929 did one of the more impressive antimystical articles. A few quotes will show he is using the layperson's definition: "Mysticism is the main cause of all religious superstition and phantasy. . . . These experiences run the entire gamut of magic, spiritism, occultism, Holy Ghostism, theosophy . . . and what not. . . . [Swedenborg] sought no occult source, and employed none."[10] Small's complete argument can't be put down so easily. Basically he says that mystics are led by their own intuition, which becomes an authority higher than the Word. This is simply not true. There are countless mystics who revere the Word because they have experienced something of its inner sense. But his is the view of the one outside the experience. Indeed, he feels those who have the experience are incompetent to judge it; only one outside it can be a proper judge! "It is quite useless in most cases to rely on definitions of mysticism as given by its devotees, for they have no knowledge of its true nature."[11] Standing outside the experience, he links it to all excesses of self leading and falling into occult and mysterious falsities. If, for his use of the term, one substitutes the now-accepted meaning of the term—the experience of the Divine—then all his arguments would fail; for he could not say the one who has *no* experience of the Divine is better able to judge the worth of the experience than one who *has known* God. There would be no linking to "spiritism," for the experience of God is not the experience of spirits. He emphasized Swedenborg the scientist, collecting and analyzing facts, but he had to admit Swedenborg was led of the Lord, which is precisely what the now-accepted definition of mysticism means.

In a recent example Brian Kingslake also disclaims Swedenborg as a mystic.[12] Though he finds many similarities between Swedenborg's life and that of other prominent mystics, he sees a difference in that Swedenborg's religious works are rational. Mysticism is nonrational; this is again from the layperson's definition. As a matter of fact, mystical writings vary across the whole spectrum of clarity and rationality. Basically, mysticism, or the experience of God, is irrational to those outside the experience. It is rational, true, and clear to those in the experience. It informs reason of higher truths. If Swedenborg had not clarified his experience beyond the *Spiritual Diary* he would appear to have been very irrational. The experience of God makes a higher sense. Seen in the whole of the world's mystical literature, Swedenborg's spiritual writings are perhaps near average for clarity or rationality. When you go to the heart of the meaning of mysticism—the experience of God—and substitute this for the

word *mysticism*, then most of the arguments that Swedenborg was no mystic fall. He obviously had much experience of God and tried to teach us of this, which is precisely what being a mystic means. Some will find it clear and rational and others will not. The closer one is to a similar experience of the Divine, the clearer and more rational these works of Swedenborg will seem. For example, by comparison, Christ's teachings are perhaps even clearer and much of Böhme's works less clear.

The only perceptive use of mysticism I was able to find in the collateral literature was in Block's conclusion to her historical survey. Two quotes might entice some readers to review the whole chapter:

> The New Church in general has ignored the mystical side of religion, though it is absolutely inherent in the doctrine of influx—the entrance of God into the individual soul, as well as in the doctrine of perception, or interior reception of spiritual truth.[13]

> Perhaps after all the issue in the New Church is not the simple and obvious one between "fundamentalism" and "modernism," but the more ancient one between literalism and mysticism which has appeared in almost all the world's religions at various times.[14]

I suspect Block has her finger on the difficulty. I fear that there are natural and fundamentally different approaches to reality and human experience reflected in her literalism versus mysticism, that even if Swedenborg were a classic mystic the literalists would not be able to discover this. But this is another whole large issue, whether any amount of doctrine can ever get us to break out of the shell of our inherent approach to reality.

The following will clarify the contrasting definitions of mysticism:

MYSTICISM

The outsider's position, layperson's rare meaning	*The inside experience, scholarly accepted definition*
Being led by every emotional whim	Being led by God
Concerned with spirits and other powers	Concerned with God alone
Irrational and mysterious	Rational, a higher understanding
Seen as contrary to the authority of Swedenborg's religious writings	Seen as reinforcing the authority of Swedenborg's religious writings
Each is a law unto himself	God rules all

What do Swedenborg's religious writings themselves say of mysticism? It is disturbing to me to think of all those who claim to stand on the authority of his writings and choose to overlook what they say of mysticism. Swedenborg uses the term *mystical* (*mysticus*) rarely, only fourteen times that I count in his work. In the Latin it means what is hidden or secret. He uses it in several related senses, which include both the layperson's and the scholarly uses.

Sometimes he uses it to disparage the pretentiously obscure (AC 5223, 7296), or the irrational, such as the mystic dogma of the trinity (TCR 169) or when he refers to the mystical and enigmatical faith of present-day theology (TCR 351).

At other times he uses it to mean the sacred that is not understood and appreciated and hence rejected. Speaking of the science of representations and correspondences, which is often rejected, he writes:

> . . . Hardly anyone is willing to believe that it exists, and they who do believe this, merely called it something mystical that is of no use. (AC 2763)

> And if what is internal or spiritual is merely mentioned, they either ridicule it or call it mystical, consequently, all conjunction between them is broken, and when this is broken, the spiritual man suffers grievously among the merely natural. (AC 5022)

> But what is meant thereby, Christianity (now-a-days) does not enquire because it places the celestial and spiritual things of the Word in its literal sense, and calls its interior things mystical for which it does not care. (AC 9688)

But these are his peripheral uses of the word *mystical*. In his strongest and most unambiguous uses he refers to the interior spiritual and celestial sense of the Word. Note the power of these statements:

> I cannot but open up to those things of the Word that are called mystical, that is, its interior things, which are the spiritual and celestial things of the Lord's kingdom. (AC 4923)

> The mystical things which some seek in the Word, are nothing else than the spiritual and celestial senses. (DV 21)

> The arcana of wisdom of the three heavens contained in [the Word] are the mystical things of which many have spoken. (AE 1079)

> "I am in the Father, and the Father in Me." This is the mystical union of which many speak. (AC 2004)

Paragraph 4923 of *Arcana Coelestia* is worth reading in its entirety. Very clearly Swedenborg says the holy and the mystical that many felt existed in the Word, and for which they search, is nothing other than the interior of the Word, which he describes.

Does Swedenborg's definition of the mystical as the internal of the Word accord with the present-day scholarly definition? It is fully in accord if you are careful of what is meant. If one said "the experience of the internal sense," then there would be no doubt. The internal of the Word is the life of God. Experience of this internal sense is the experience of the Divine. I make this proviso so that one does not mistakenly think a mere knowledge of this internal sense brings one into the spiritual and celestial, which is the internal of the Word. Some kind of living involvement in the internal sense is necessary, and involvement that leads to uses and charity. To me, one of my more significant discoveries was the way Swedenborg personally invested himself in his study of the Bible.[15] This went beyond "knowledge of" to entering into the "life of" the internal. If one is thinking of a living participation in the internal sense of the Word, then Swedenborg's definition of the mystical accords with the modern scholarly meaning of mysticism. Can we then say that the person who "cannot but open up those things of the Word that are called mystical" is not a mystic?

There is a larger sense in which Swedenborg was clearly a mystic, a sense that breaks out of the limitations of a single word he actually didn't use very often. In the accepted positive scholarly sense, the mystic is simply one who has direct experience of the Divine. I doubt that any follower of Swedenborg's spiritual writings would say Swedenborg did not have direct experience of the Divine. Then he was a mystic. Mystics who write attempt to share their experience and its subsequent understandings with others. Contrary to the ideas of some that mysticism is irrational, most mystics who have written have produced quite rational works. In only a few places did Swedenborg say it was more than could be told or that it was not permitted yet to reveal. He made an eminent attempt to convey his direct experience and his consequent understandings. Have other mystics attempted to make as clear or rational a presentation? Indeed, yes. To those who want to pursue further the positive side of mysticism, I commend the works of Evelyn Underhill, especially her *Practical Mysticism*.[16] Her big volume *Mysticism*[17] leads one to the larger body of world literature on the subject.

Is there more mysticism in Swedenborg's religious writings than one man sharing his experience and findings of the Divine? I believe so, but this point cannot be proven in a limited space. If the mysticism of his writing lies preeminently in the internal sense of the Word, why is this sense presented to us? Is it to satisfy our curiosity, so we bystanders can look in at the dynamics of the life of God? I don't believe this is its purpose at all. Instead I submit that this was presented so we might come into the kingdom. If I had to describe Swedenborg's spiritual writings and their fundamental purpose in one line, it would be this: the writings are a clear presentation meant to be used by individuals to lead them into the life of God—as an actual part of their experience. His writings are rational, but that is their style, not preeminently their nature. Their nature and overwhelming purpose is to lead to God, which accounts for many aspects of their structure. So in this sense, not only are his writings the work of a mystic, they are meant to help create mystics, that is, to lead others to the Divine. I am quite in accord with the position of some regarding the sacredness and authority of Swedenborg's writings.

Perhaps a few words on the general nature of mysticism in organized religion may help those to whom the connection of mysticism and Swedenborg's religious writings is new. Mystics, those who have contact with the Divine, have sprung up in all religions, all cultures, and all times. They express themselves variously in the forms and uses of their time, culture, and religion. Contrary to the outsider's idea that they may depart on any wild whim or intuition, persons with the experience of the Divine tend to be able to recognize this in others even across the barriers of time and circumstances. It is as though having touched the universal they can recognize others who have also done so. They tend to be socially useful, and in fact their uses may be the only outer expression of their experience of the Divine. Like Swedenborg, they tend to support *the old religious forms* but give them deeper meaning. It is not appropriate to rank them as to which is the greater mystic, for they are in no contest with each other. Rather we can say, "This one touches me and that one doesn't," which describes our own uniqueness. It is characteristic of mystics that they speak from experience rather than from speculation and past authority. It is often their lot to be seen as a threat to conventional religious authority, which may not dare claim an experience of God. Are mystics rare? Not really. Probably all persons have the experience of the Divine, often in childhood, but people differ in how conscious and ruling this experience is. Included in the scholarly definition is nature mysticism—the feeling of God present in nature—which must be a universal experience.

What is the evidence in Swedenborg's writings that he came into the experience of God? There is an even more critical interior question: What in his writings can lead you to God? To a mystic the signs of Swedenborg's contact with God are too legion to catalog, but I'll deal with the most general first. Throughout his writings Swedenborg is saying, "I have experienced. . . ." This is not said in an aggrandizing way. The whole *Spiritual Diary* contains his experiences. The "memorable relations" scattered through all of his religious writings are experiences. He makes practically no reference to other scholars or theologians. On a few occasions he says the internal sense of the Bible was revealed by the Lord alone. No angels or spirits led him in this. Does he mean the Lord dictated the *Arcana Coelestia* word for word? I don't believe so. It was a noetic, direct-knowing experience. The experience has very pleasant inner verities, so one knows beyond doubt the real author. I am reminded of the phrase somewhere in the Bible that the sheep know their master. I picture a shepherd who lives all day with his sheep and sleeps with them at night. They know his very footsteps and smell. It is that kind of interior familiarity that exists in Swedenborg's writing.

Secondly, his writings not only come from experience but their real substance deals primarily with *human* experience. It is not as though the Divine and the human are two contents; there is but one content: the Divine/human. Swedenborg's is an immensely human view of theology. This may not be apparent to everyone. *Heaven and Hell* deals with angels, spirits, and demons. If they are human, don't they at least seem a bit removed from our world of humans? Not so. We have each experienced something of heaven and hell in this world. While we are in this life we each participate in societies of heaven and hell. That is, by our very nature, choices, or uses, we are intimately related to aspects of heaven and hell. Moreover I am struck how heaven and hell can also be understood as deeper aspects of mind. We not only exist by influx through the spiritual worlds, but also our interior design is in their form. For me, it has been a useful clarification to think how acts of mine and others may be heavenly or hellish.

The interior human aspect is throughout his writings. "Evidently it is these delights that rule the man's thoughts, and the thoughts are nothing apart from them; yet they seem to him to be nothing but thoughts; when in fact, thoughts are nothing but affections so composed into forms by his life's love as to be presented in light" (DP 199). It took a good deal of close observation to see that thoughts are formed of affections or feelings. The whole of the twelve-volume *Arcana Coelestia* has to do with the Lord's glorification, which is the model for the individual's spiritual development. But Swedenborg isn't merely dealing with the psychology of persons. His is a unique psychology thoroughly pervaded and informed by his spiritual experience. In two words it is a spiritual psychology. Because he is dealing with the very stuff of human existence, what he has to say is ultimately open to empirical test. I don't quite mean it is open to scientific test, because science can only deal with what is external. But I do mean it is open to test and confirmation by individuals. My pamphlet on *Uses*[18] is an example of bringing one of Swedenborg's core doctrines into personal experience, where the individual can see for oneself if it is true.

How is it that a boy's early experiences of wonder could eventually teach him to respect Swedenborg? For me the whole of religion is like a single tree. Religions are branches and the sects are leaves. We can concentrate on the leaves—how this one is different from that one, this finer than that. Or we can look to the one life of the tree. If we concentrate on differences, the whole is impossibly complex and confusing. As a boy, and now as a man, I badly need to understand the one life of the tree. This brings me the peace of heaven. I find myself in profound accord with a man born three centuries ago, a man who walked in silver buckled shoes and me in Adidas sneakers. He put words to what used to be nameless for me:

> Hence it is plain that the church of the Lord is not here, nor there, but that it is everywhere, both within those kingdoms where the church is, and outside them, where men live according to the precepts of charity. Hence it is that the church of the Lord is scattered through the whole world, and yet it is one; for when life makes the church and not doctrine separate them from life, then the church is one, but when doctrine makes the church, then there are many. (AC 8152)

I have difficulty in answering the question of what religion I belong to. If the questioner is reflective I answer with surprise, "Do you honestly mean there is more than one?" But to others I answer simply, "I belong to all religions."

Some will think it must be a life of constant highs to be a mystic. Not so. Much of the time I grumble at my fate and God kicks me. It is sometimes that way with lovers. But it is a respite to wander among Swedenborg's words, touched here and there, and shot through with a wonderful light.

Notes

1. Thomas Troward, *Edinburgh Lectures in Mental Science* (New York: Dodd, Mead, 1909).
2. Ibid., p. 50.
3. Ibid., p. 54.
4. Raymond Moody, *Life After Life* (Atlanta, Ga.: Mockingbird Books, 1975).
5. William James, *The Varieties of Religious Experience* (New York: Modern Library, 1902), p. 371.
6. Wilson Van Dusen, *Swedenborg's Journal of Dreams* (New York: Swedenborg Foundation, 1986).
7. *Random House Dictionary of the English Language* (New York: Random House, 1966).
8. *Webster's Collegiate Dictionary* (Springfield, Mass.: Merriman, 1942).
9. *Hastings Encyclopedia of Religion and Ethics* (New York: Scribners, 1961).
10. Herbert Small, "What Is a Mystic?" *The Messenger* (1929), p. 340.
11. Ibid.
12. Brian Kingslake, "Was Swedenborg a Mystic?" *New Church Magazine* (1977); pp. 52ff.
13. Marguerite Block, *The New Church in the New World* (New York: Octagon, 1968), p. 393.
14. Ibid., p. 400.
15. Wilson Van Dusen, "Another Key to Swedenborg's Development," *New Church Life* (1975), pp. 316–19.
16. Evelyn Underhill, *Practical Mysticism* (New York: Dutton, 1915).
17. Evelyn Underhill, *Mysticism* (New York: Dutton, 1961).
18. Wilson Van Dusen, *Uses* (New York: Swedenborg Foundation, 1981).

Swedenborg's Journal of Dreams and Divine Knowledge

Lars Bergquist

Translated by Veronica Royston

This essay was originally presented in Swedish as a lecture to the Swedenborg Society in Stockholm, at the Tegnerlunden Church in the summer of 1985. It appears here in its entirety with a few amplifications and with reference notes added by the author.

THE NIGHT BETWEEN 14 and 15 April 1744, Swedenborg is at The Hague to supervise the printing of his great work *Regnum Animale* (*Animal Kingdom*). He writes in his dream book (*Journal of Dreams*), "I have slept supernaturally long and well, for twelve hours" (JD p. 1).[1] A week earlier, he has been deeply shaken by a religious revelation in the course of which he has spoken with Christ and has sat in his bosom. After this vision he feels continually burdened down by his sins. He feels he has received a call, without as yet knowing to what. The result is anxiety, strange and wild dreams:

It seemed as if I were racing down a stairway; I touched each step only a little, and came safely down all the way without danger. There came a voice from my dear father: "You are making such a racket, Emanuel!" It was said he was angry, but it would pass over. This means that I made use of the

cross too boldly, yesterday, but by the grace of God I came through without danger.

I climbed up on a shelf, and broke off the neck of a bottle, from which some thick fluid came forth and covered the floor and then flowed down, I believe. [This means] that yesterday, by the grace of God and not by my own power, a mass of evil was eradicated from my thoughts. . . .

I heard a bear growling but I did not see him. Dared not remain in the upper story, for there was a carcass there which he might scent.

Several more dreams and interpretations follow. But the above quotations, I believe, give an adequate picture of his state of mind. He is truly making an outcry, is anxious, troubled, noisy. Yet this turmoil and confusion subsides. Gradually a discernible pattern appears in his jottings, a pattern typical not only of Swedenborg but also of the time in which he was living.

The diary, which mainly covers rather more than seven months of his life, can be approached as an autobiographical document. It is exceptionally candid, strictly private. It gives

LARS BERGQUIST was born in Stockholm, Sweden, in 1930. He took his Fil. kand. (B.A.) degree in 1953, and after receiving his law degree, Jur. kand., in 1956 he studied further at Yale Law School until 1957. From 1958 to 1960 he was a member of the editorial staff of the *Dagens Nyheter*. He has had a long and varied career in the Swedish foreign service, first serving as press attaché at the Swedish embassy in Paris 1960–63, then in the prime minister's office 1963–65. In 1965 Bergquist became first secretary at the Swedish embassy in Moscow until 1968, and from there served the same post in Warsaw for five years. From 1973 to 1976 he was head of the East European Section at the Swedish Foreign Ministry, and then, until 1977, minister councillor of the Swedish embassy in London. For the next five years he was minister councillor of the Swedish embassy in Paris and was also director of the Swedish Cultural Center. Since 1982 he has been the Swedish ambassador in Beijing, China. Lars Bergquist has published three novels and two diaries. The last book, which appeared in 1982, consisted of translations of the French poet René Char. A book about Swedenborg's dream journal will be published in January 1988.

us a picture of Emanuel Swedenborg the human being—his strength, his weaknesses, his social role, the company he kept, his social standing.

The diary may also be read as documenting a shipwreck, a catastrophe, precipitated more immediately by his unreasonably overambitious research program, by the excessive demands he placed on his own capacities. A prerequisite for this approach to his diary, however, is a familiarity with his earlier research, his studies, with what he had read and with the company he had been keeping. This is the approach adopted by Martin Lamm in his biography, and by Inge Jonsson in his study of Swedenborg's *Worship and Love of God*.[2]

A third approach to the diary is one that focuses on its religious element, concentrating our attention on the religious thought to which these jottings bear witness, on the theological trends of his century, examining especially the links between the diary and Swedenborg's extensive output subsequent to the crisis. A record such as his *Journal of Dreams*, full of dreams, visions, interpretations, and private reflections on crucial issues, should after all be able to help us to arrive at a better understanding of the specific components that went to make up Swedenborg's religious attitudes and of the various lines that connect different parts of his great system.

This way of looking at it is not so very different from the one that focuses on his philosophical and scientific development, but the questions are posed differently. Here I shall attempt to suggest the possibilities offered by the latter "religious" perspective.

Taking the *Journal of Dreams* as a point of departure does not mean that this period in any way marks a religious conversion on its author's part. As far as we know, during the years previous to the journal, Swedenborg never questioned Lutheran doctrine, at least not in its main features. We have, however, reason to believe that he always shared his father's negative opinion of the then-often-professed belief in salvation through "faith alone." "*Sola fide*" was, both for the father and his son, never enough. Charity was as important for salvation as faith.

Atheism was an unusual stance for the sixteenth- and seventeenth-century intellectuals. This was, after all, an age of "natural theology," a mode of thought based on God's self-revelation in nature. St. Paul's Epistle to the Romans contains an idea that both Swedenborg and Linnaeus made their own: "Because that which may be known of God is manifest in them; for God hath shown it unto them. For the invisible things of Him from the Creation of the world are clearly seen, being understood by the things that are made, even His eternal power and Godhead."[3]

Swedenborg's teacher Polhem, the much-admired Newton, and the great Dutch anatomists all seem in one way or another to have been believers. And, in general, we may presume that religious notions, Christian thinking, and Christian associations of ideas were far closer to people's minds in Swedenborg's day and age, and far more often discussed, than nowadays. The art of that age, in all its manifestations, stands as clear proof of such a "presence."

Yet up to the summer of 1743, when his diary commenced, it seems as if, for Swedenborg, the Christian philosophy of life had in all essentials been only one element in the great equation he had been trying to put together during the 1730s and early 1740s. His aim was to try to describe the nature of the human soul—thereby to discover the workings of the relationship between God and humans. For his own part he does not seem to have been religiously involved in a fully personal way. And it is here that his journal marks a change.

My first point is basic. It has to do with Swedenborg's view of humanity's relationship to God.

We know the background. He had grown up in an environment where each day and each waking hour were marked by a belief in God's presence. His father, the bishop, was a deeply religious man, whose morning, noon, and night were staked out by prayers, singing, and Bible readings. He was by no means a pietist, but he emphasized one of the pietists' most important tenets—that religion is a question of the individual's subjective relations to God. The quality of this relation depended on the intensity of his or her worship, intensity of faith. This stress on the intimacy of our links with the divine may seem natural for us. But we must remember that Swedenborg's young days occurred during the period of Lutheran orthodoxy, where the state tried to channel religion through the church and its servants. Doctrinally, the bishop represented the Lutheran view, to which the ideas of people being children of God and of forgiveness were fundamental. Added to this was an emphasis, typical both of Swedberg and Swedenborg, on the importance of good deeds, of action, to man's justification. Faith alone was not enough.

In his scientific works from the 1730s and 1740s Swedenborg had already laid down the general outlines of a theology to transcend the nucleus of his father's faith. His reflections did not conflict with it, but his doctrine was more intellectualized. Furthermore, it was conceived from other starting points. The main point is that during the 1730s Swedenborg's entire philosophy had become increasingly dynamic, organic. He saw everything, arranged everything so that it fit into a course of events whose ultimate goal was an ongoing realization of the kingdom of God. The world, the universe, was in constant motion. No one factor could be understood except as part of this overall process.

Jesper Swedberg, we know, like several others among Swedenborg's contemporaries, also saw the world in this way.

But few if any were so consistent as Emanuel. Almost none were so dominated by the same thirst for knowledge; and hardly anyone possessed his tremendous energy.

With Swedenborg's point of departure—that we are all fulfilling God's plan for his Creation—two questions logically ensue. The first concerns our attitude: What can we do with our lives to further the realization of this plan? Like other Christians, Swedenborg directs us to the Ten Commandments and the Gospels. The second question, although perhaps not strictly necessary, is nevertheless warranted: What appears to be the nature of this plan and of this Creation? Swedenborg replies that knowledge of this is granted to us to the extent that we subordinate ourselves to God's will and, in our relationship to him, seek the answers to these questions. That is to say, to be a child of God is not only a goal in itself, but also a starting point for all knowledge.

Here we may reasonably see St. Paul as having provided the basis for Swedenborg's theology. Emanuel's collection of excerpts not only shows that he had studied the apostle in detail, but also that in the First Epistle to the Corinthians, in particular, he had found support for his theory of the parallels between the human body and the kingdom of God. Presumably, St. Paul also reflected on thoughts about knowledge. The famous words in the First Epistle to the Corinthians concerning the feebleness of our vision and "knowing in part" must have directly appealed to Swedenborg, always busy as he was widening his knowledge.

I am not at this point going to dwell on the background of Swedenborg's theory of knowledge, because its philosophical and scientific aspects have already been so thoroughly analyzed by Martin Lamm and Inge Jonsson. But I should like to emphasize that nowhere is the epistemological aspect of Swedenborg's religious attitude so clearly expressed as in his *Journal of Dreams*. In fact its prime theme is how to acquire knowledge—most obviously knowledge in the sense of guidance for the scientific work he was occupied with during his crisis. But it is also concerned with knowledge and insight in a wider sense. After the night between 12 and 13 October Swedenborg wrote:

> I saw also in a vision that beautiful loaves of bread were presented to me on a plate. This was a premonition that the Lord Himself will instruct me, since I have now first come into such a state that I know nothing, and that all preconceived opinions have been taken away from me, which is the beginning of learning, viz., that one must first become a child, and then be wet-nursed into knowledge, as is now taking place with me.

He is to be "wet-nursed into" (the expression *ammas upp uti* is ambiguous, and could almost equally well be translated "breast-fed on") knowledge. This is one of the most important aspects of the Swedenborgian relationship to God—the one that entitles us to call his doctrine a "theosophy,"

in the true sense of the word, that is, a knowledge of and wisdom concerning God.

This theory of knowledge he had already formulated in works dating back to the years before his *Journal of Dreams* crisis. It may also be found in *Animal Kingdom*, the work he was writing contemporaneously with *Journal of Dreams*.

Very briefly, then, Swedenborg believed that human beings through their souls have been granted a possibility of direct communication with goodness, with God. But our will to goodness is disturbed when influences from the lower world of the senses become too strong. If earthly temptations—greed for renown, acquisitiveness, overindulgence of all kinds—are allowed to gain the upper hand, one loses one's contact with goodness. And not merely with goodness but also with true knowledge.

Seen in this way, knowledge is inherent in all of us, but hidden. It is a question of what Goethe called "evident secrets." The closer we come to the divine, the more we see. A relationship to God is dynamic, an element in an ongoing process of creation.

Much later on, in *True Christian Religion*, Swedenborg gives his own account of what happens. Just as blood, flowing into all the limbs of our body, fills them with life, so faith enters into all the various parts of a theological system.

So much for his doctrinal edifice. What happens at this point is that Swedenborg existentially flings himself body and soul into experiencing the implications of his own doctrine. During the seven months and a little more that his crisis lasts, we can follow, day by day, the scientist and philosopher being gradually turned into a theosopher, in the sense just indicated.

Here I shall raise some crucial points, not in order to belittle Swedenborg's achievement but rather to stress that his writings belong in a major Christian tradition with roots in antiquity, a tradition that had already had important forerunners during the European baroque.

The first point has to do with knowledge, as such. As I have mentioned, Swedenborg sees facts and events in a dynamic perspective, in terms of which everything has a purpose and each end harmonizes with all the others. Everything conspires to realize a single goal, namely, the ongoing expansion of the divine Creation. Built into this view of the world is, of course, an analysis of its origin, its cause. In all his observations the scientist and theosopher finds himself confronted with a triptych: phenomena must be examined as contingency, as cause and as effect. It is an outlook we encounter in the theosophical tradition from Plotinus, in antiquity, through Böhme and Malebranche. Swedenborg applies it systematically to the scientific work he is doing during his *Journal* crisis, an anatomical investigation that stresses the various organs' roles and functions.

At times, sometimes day by day, *Journal of Dreams* mirrors his attempts in *Soul's Domain* to explain the bodily functions. Dream images and sequences become symbolic keys to the doors he is trying to unlock.

It is a way of thinking in parallels, by analogy. Swedenborg was not fond of classical thought processes, based on deduction. To his mind, its deductions, in a world where everything is purposive and in a state of development, become too private and specific. Inge Jonsson has shown how the theory of correspondences is dependent on Swedenborg's doctrine of series and degrees [see Glossary] and its connection to the contemporary baroque system of emblems—its proclivity to symbolism—in art and literature.[4] The matter may also be seen from a religious, theosophical viewpoint. A doctrine of correspondences of the kind he advocated is, after all, a vital element in all theosophy, as it is as well for all who stand for the idea that the godhead is the fountainhead of all truth: Fludd, Böhme, Dippel, Malebranche, and Oetinger, to mention only a few. Seen from this point of view it is in fact completely self-evident. Implicit in the idea that God is the source of all truth is that thanks to our relationship with God we recover within ourselves a knowledge hitherto concealed from us. Man is the object of such knowledge. And as our nature is structured, so is the world's.

Visions in dreams, symbols: in *Journal of Dreams* we encounter the first practical application of Swedenborg's doctrine of correspondences, which appears in all his subsequent writings. Concepts are endowed with several fixed layers of meaning. For instance, a palace, a beautiful house, denotes a view of life or a doctrine. A room stands for a part of the palace, a scientific task, or a state of mind. Dogs stand for impurity. China bowls, then as later, are symbols for receptables of truth and beauty; gardens, for paradise. Phenomena of light signify truth.

Even so, at the time when he was writing his journal, Swedenborg was still only on the threshold of his prophetic period. Implicit in his concept of knowledge is that the closer we come to the heavenly light, the more continuously our knowledge develops.

Swedenborg's doctrine of correspondences achieves its theological apotheosis, as we know, in the work that took him so many years to write, *Arcana Coelestia*. The Pentateuch was, in Swedenborg's view, entirely made up of symbols. It is certainly no coincidence that he was reading the books of Moses while writing his *Journal of Dreams*. In the last passages of this diary he records a revelation: he is to write what he calls "a sacred book on the worship of God and His divine wisdom" (JD p. 250). To the extent that he completed it, this work is a paraphrase of the Creation story. In writing this work he is in good company: any number of philosophers and scientists were interpreting and writing commentaries on the same text during the two centuries spanned by Swed-

enborg's lifetime. This is as true of his teacher Polhem as of Jakob Böhme. As it happens, Böhme's perhaps most famous book, *The Great Secret*, also takes the first book of the Pentateuch as its starting point.[5]

After the night of 13–14 October 1744, Swedenborg notes the following: "Among other things, it was said to me that since the last fortnight I had begun to look much more handsome, and to be like an angel. God grant that this be so. May God stand by me in this and not take his grace from me" (JD p. 268).

This observation and his prayer, made just before ending his *Journal of Dreams*, is one of the many entries indicating that Swedenborg, through his faith in God and consequent increasing knowledge, finds that he is undergoing a physical transformation. In another jotting we read that his sight has become keener (JD p. 260); further, that his handwriting has improved, and that his "penetration"—his capacity for analysis and understanding in depth—has grown (JD p. 282).

In what concerns his sense of being physically affected by the Divinity, the *Journal of Dreams* is one starting point for his later writings. The closer he comes to God, the more he is conscious of his task in the drama where he is playing his role, and this lucidity also manifests itself physically. In the works he has before him at the time of the crisis he tells us on several occasions that higher powers are guiding his hand as he writes. Later it seems to him he can discern in himself, in his own body, powers or elements from another world.

A digression into other domains of culture may throw light on this interrelation between the divine and the human. Swedenborg lived at a time when stylistic elements of the baroque were still appearing in art, architecture, and literature. In baroque painting, and above all in the theater, men and women were often depicted as coactors in a divine drama: the temporal was united with the celestial, the theater stage was connected by its side battens and painted ceilings with the divine. In the Jesuits' celebrated theatrical performances, with which they intended to counteract the Reformation, the human being is, precisely, a figure whose acting and mime form part of the divine comedia. We are all elements in a celestial context and must play our part.

We meet this integration of the spiritual and the human in the *Journal of Dreams* as well as in Swedenborg's later works. It is a distinguishing feature in his doctrine of spirits. Here I am referring to the idea that we live on after our deaths, albeit in a rarified state that corresponds to the kind of love that has dominated us during our lifetime. Each of us has within himself or herself one's own potential heaven and hell. This is one aspect of Swedenborg's doctrine of spirits. The other consists in the idea that during our earthly

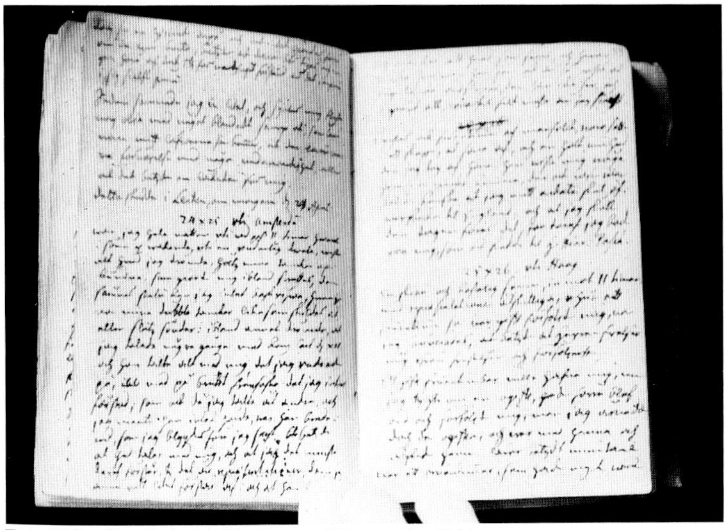

FIG. 212. *Swedenborg's* Drommar (Dreams), *1744*

lives we are under the influence of these spirits, that is, of the departed, or of angels who themselves have once been human beings.

The first line of thought—that we live on in a form corresponding to our earthly lives—is already to be found in Swedenborg's thinking before the crisis. The second, however, appears only much later. In its conception we may, again, trace an influence from the bishop. The pious father found himself living in a world where spirits of all kinds, good and bad, lived in constant coexistence with human beings, and he often referred to his "guardian angel," or "servant angel." Judging from his autobiography he took these beings for granted, without discussion of their origin.[6]

In Swedenborg's dreams we encounter several of his still-living contemporaries: Erland Broman, for instance, who was court marshal of the palace of Fredrik I of Sweden; the Francophile politician Henning Gyllenborg, as well as several close relatives. In his interpretations Swedenborg is always making these figures stand for something—Broman for sensuality, Gyllenborg for social life, vanity, conceit. The dead, chiefly his own father, a protective angelic figure, also appear in his dreams.

At the same time as these characters stray in and out of his dreams, he is night after night, day by day struggling against temptations, evil thoughts, which, he says, are "like roving Poles and hussars" (JD p. 64). He soon comes to recognize his evil spirits. He greets them, he says, frightens them, and accuses them.

But sometimes he does not know what attitude to adopt toward them: obviously his uncertainty is particularly great when it is a question of thoughts connected with his scientific work. In October 1744, when his dream life after several months of diminished intensity and relative uncertainty is again rising in a crescendo, he notes a circumstance to which he will several times return: "A number of times I have noticed that there are spirits of various kinds. The one spirit, which is the spirit of Christ, is the only one who has with him all beatitude. The others try in a thousand ways to make one join them, but unhappy he who does so" (JD p. 247).

Prior to this, in connection with his great Easter vision in April of the same year, he had recalled a passage from the First Epistle of John, where the apostle warns against false prophets: "Beloved, believe not every spirit, but try the spirits, whether they are of God; because many false prophets are gone out into the world. Hereby know ye the spirit of God: Every spirit that confesseth that Jesus Christ is come in the flesh is of God."[7] That is to say, he has by now noticed their different characters. That same month he says he understands that the other spirits, who must be tested, appear in the guise of loves, *amores*. That is to say, it is our loves—what we human beings desire and yearn for—that need to be put to the test. And the test is simple: Is the love in question compatible with Christ's message and mission?

We can thus discern a pattern. People appear in dreams, where they symbolize a way of life or a direction taken by the dreamer's will. At the same time Swedenborg is learning to recognize and associate with his own thoughts, thoughts he is gradually coming to see as *amores*—loves or preferences. From this is it no great step to the fusion, which we later come across in his religious writings, of *amores* with people. Once the spirits have been identified as desires or loves, Swedenborg, with his strong determination to discover a cause for and the purpose of each phenomenon that will fit into God's all-embracing plan, sees an influence from figures in other phases of his life. Thoughts, spirits, which are loves, are after all clearly discernible, recurrent. In Emanuel's dreams, Erland Broman, the court marshal, who was still alive at the time, came to stand for sensuality (JD pp. 21, 41), as mentioned earlier. In a waking or half-waking state, the thoughts he embodies do not necessarily refer to any particular individual. But Swedenborg's thinking is always associative. He had been brought up in a world where people believed everything to be animated, and where supernatural spirits were an everyday reality. It was natural for him to see each particular love and the actions it was conducive to as resulting from a concurrence between, on the one hand, a person's own will, and on the other, a power corresponding to the dominant love from a figure who once, when he was alive, had desired the same thing.

It is the element which is unique to Swedenborg's theosophy, where he goes further than any other mystic or theosopher. No one, he says on several occasions, has the same capacity or knowledge as he.

Divinely inspired knowledge, the world as a sign, human beings as actors in God's all-embracing drama—these are a few of the spheres of thought Swedenborg actively tested out during his *Journal of Dreams* period and which are later to imbue like watermarks the pages of his subsequent purely religious writings. Now aged fifty-six, he is on the way to discovering his mission.

We can distinguish two primary components of Swedenborg's position and message. If we follow his scientific work up to the *Journal of Dreams* crisis, we find that he, like everybody else, is a child of his time, working with the philosophical and scientific questions that were being discussed at European universities and by the age's literature.

But this would not suffice. Swedenborg's own particular way of looking at things, his choice of problems and manner of tackling them, must be seen in their religious context. It is only here that his individuality and greatness assume their true proportions.

In an entry from 25–26 April 1744, he indirectly raises this particular question:

> It was a woman who owned a very beautiful estate in which we walked about and I was to marry her. She signified *pietas*, and also, I believe, *sapientia*, which owned these possessions. I was also with her, loved her in the usual way, which seemed to stand for the actual marriage. . . . So also in a certain way it was represented to me that I ought not to contaminate myself by other books, treating of theology and such subjects because this I have in the Word of God and from the Holy Spirit. (JD p. 179)

That is to say, he is not to study theological literature. In the final entry of his diary, dated 26–27 October he pursues this thought. Already at the beginning of that month he has been told in a vision to put aside his scientific work and devote himself instead to the Creation paraphrases about the worship of God and his divine love. Now, during the last night covered by his *Journal of Dreams*, he dreams that beautiful porcelain bowls are placed in a hall both inside and outside his own room. This, he writes, means "that I must take nothing of anyone else's goods, only my own, as they were in my parlor I had rented, and my chamber" (JD p. 278).

Perfectly clear instructions. The fact that no other quotations from any other theologian are to be found anywhere throughout his considerable collection of excerpts, only from St. Augustine, seems to confirm the matter.

But of course it was not quite so simple. As I have said, Swedenborg's whole environment and the age he lived in—the Stockholm of the early 1740s—were permeated by religious notions, indeed, to the extent that it has been called a veritable hothouse. It is safe to assume that in his final phase, Swedenborg acted on his own words in his *Journal of Dreams*, that is, left aside the age's ample output of theological literature. Naturally, this did not mean he was unaware of the mainstreams of its religious thought. As I have tried to demonstrate elsewhere,[8] he was, during the period covered by the *Journal of Dreams*, under the influence of the thoughts and worship of the Moravian Brethren and their founder, Count Nikolaus Ludwig von Zinzendorf.

But Swedenborg's teachings bear his own, very characteristic hallmark. It is, in fact, only when we see his thought in the context of his times that we can truly appreciate his originality. He had indeed studied the world outside himself, the thought of his times. In the *Journal of Dreams*, we find him discovering the world within himself, the unique personal component that sets his work apart.

Notes

1. The edition referred to is Emanuel Swedenborg, *Journal of Dreams*, trans. C. Th. Odhner (Bryn Athyn, Pa.: Academy of the New Church, 1918).
2. Martin Lamm, *Swedenborg. En studie över hans utveckling till mystiker och andeskådare* (Swedenborg: A study of his development as mystic and visionary) (Stockholm: Gebers, 1915); Inge Jonsson, *Swedenborgs skapelsdrama "De cultu et amore Dei." En studie av motiv och intellecktuell miljö* (Swedenborg's creation drama "Worship and Love of God": A study of motif and intellectual milieu), with a summary in English (Stockholm: Natur och Kultur, 1961).
3. Paul's Epistle to the Romans 1:19–20.
4. Inge Jonsson, *Swedenborgs korrespondeslära* (Swedenborg's doctrine of correspondences), with a summary in English (Stockholm: Acta Universitatis Stockholmiensis, 1969).
5. Jakob Böhme, *Mysterium magnus* (The great secret), in *Sämtliche Schriften* (Complete works), vols. 7–8 (Stuttgart: 1955–60).
6. Henry Tottie, *Jesper Svedbergs lif och verksamhet* (Jesper Swedberg's life and work) diss., Uppsala University, 1885–86; Jesper Swedberg, *Festum magnum* (The great feast day) (Skara, Sweden: 1724), pp. 180, 186.
7. First Epistle of John 4:1–2.
8. Lars Bergquist, *The Joy and the Agony: A Study of Swedenborg's Journal of Dreams* (Stockholm: Norstedt, 1988).

Substance and Form
The Swedenborgian Vision
in Architecture

Leon S. Rhodes and
James F. Lawrence

FIG. 213. *Ezekiel Tower of Bryn Athyn Cathedral, with Raymond Pitcairn and Billy Johnson at base of lancet windows*

For a biography of LEON S. RHODES, please see the following essay, "Reports on Eternal Life."

JAMES F. LAWRENCE received a B.A. in economics from the University of Texas at Austin and is a graduate of the Swedenborg School of Religion in Newton, Massachusetts. He is currently the editor of *The Messenger*, the national magazine for the General Convention of Swedenborgian Churches, and is a minister of the San Francisco Society of Swedenborgian Churches.

FIG. 214. *West porch under construction*

As BEFITS SWEDENBORG'S THEOLOGY, his followers have believed that outward form should reflect inner substance. They have therefore taken extraordinary care in creating houses of worship that would at least *approach* the holiness of the doctrines that inspired them. Oftentimes, highly acclaimed architects have been called into service (Cass Gilbert in St. Paul, Bernard Maybeck in San Francisco, Lloyd Wright in the greater Los Angeles area); on other occasions the vision of the congregation has given rise to notable achievements (in Tuscon, in the greater Chicago area, in St. Louis, among other places). There have been numerous outstanding traditional efforts, as well. Bryn Athyn Cathedral in Pennsylvania is the most prominent of these, and other examples can be found in Philadelphia; Washington, D.C.; Boston; and several in England. Gaining even more notice, however, has been the Swedenborgian flair for a contemporary architecture celebrating nature, particularly in Wright's masterpiece Wayfarers Chapel, and in the Worcester-Maybeck church in San Francisco.

We have chosen to present here two inspiring churches: the Bryn Athyn Cathedral embodies the traditional spirit, and the Wayfarers Chapel illuminates the contemporary.

The splendid cathedral church in Bryn Athyn, Pennsylvania, appears similar to other Gothic/Romanesque churches, but is unique in many features, including architectural "refinements" and examples of craftsmanship that have made it a popular visitors' attraction for thousands annually.

The Bryn Athyn Cathedral was started in 1913 and built in a manner comparable to the ancient guild system. The original architect was Ralph Adams Cram, but it was designed primarily by Raymond Pitcairn, son of John Pitcairn. The cathedral's style departs from modern building practices by deliberate use of curved lines and much-admired irregularities.

The stained glass of the cathedral, designed by Winfred Hyatt (who also designed the whole west portal area), represents the rediscovery of the lost art of pot-metal glass with

FIG. 215. *Aerial view of Bryn Athyn Cathedral, showing the central tower and Ezekial Tower*

FIG. 216. *Metalwork on door of west porch, detail*

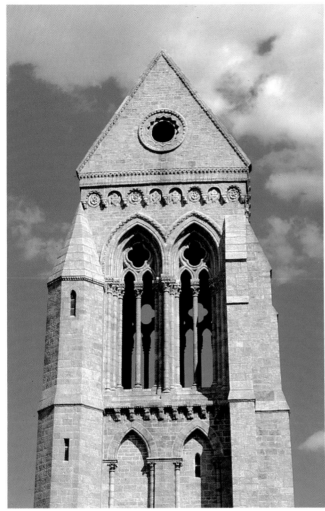

FIG. 217. *Ezekiel Tower, south wing*

qualities previously unduplicated in six hundred years. All the glass was produced at the cathedral site after painstaking research and experimentation.

The metalwork of the cathedral is done from a natural alloy, "Monel" metal, in what may well be a unique artform, with striking examples among the finest wrought-metal achieved in modern times.

FIG. 218. *The west window, depicting the "Five Churches"*

FIG. 219. *The crossing, chancel, and sanctuary*

FIG. 220. *Bryn Athyn Cathedral, view of the 150-ft. central tower*

FIG. 221. *Glencairn, view from the south lawn*

The magnificent fine arts center of the Academy of the New Church was built as a private home between 1929 and 1939 by Raymond Pitcairn. This Romanesque, castlelike structure includes the notable Glencairn Museum, which attracts visitors from far and wide.

The Academy of the New Church in Bryn Athyn has grown since its beginning in Philadelphia in 1876 and its move to new buildings at the turn of the century. The growing campus now includes more than a dozen buildings providing New Church education from kindergarten through college and theology school. It serves some seven hundred students annually, many of them from foreign countries. Cairncrest, the office center of the General Church of the New Jerusalem, houses publications and printing facilities, a book center, mailing center, and television equipment. The new Swedenborg Library of the Academy of the New Church was dedicated in June 1987 and opened in September. Its extensive collection of Swedenborgian literature serves not only the academy students but other research scholars as well.

FIG. 222. *Aerial view of the Academy of the New Church campus, showing secondary-school buildings (lower center), cathedral (to the left, or west), college (right of cathedral), Glencairn (north of cathedral). The new Swedenborg Library, not yet built at the time of this photo, is now situated near the college buildings (in direction of Glencairn).*

FIG. 223. *Wayfarers Chapel and belltower, overlooking Abalone Cove*

The striking "Glass Chapel" in Rancho Palos Verdes at Portuguese Bend, California, is the Wayfarers Chapel, designed by Lloyd Wright and dedicated to Emanuel Swedenborg. Completed in 1951, its uplifting contemporary architecture features glass walls, triangular roof panels, and a tall stone belltower. Within its sun-filled interior, one is inspired by the natural stone altar and baptismal font, as well as by the feeling of oneness with the natural world. Its transparent walls seem to bring in the surrounding greenery and to open on to a view of nearby Abalone Cove on the Pacific Coast, and giving one the sense that this place of worship is a living thing. The chapel embodies the description of a temple in the spiritual world, of which Swedenborg wrote in *Arcana Coelestia:* "The light of their sun is let in through the openings between branches and everywhere transmitted through crystals. . . ."

FIG. 224. *Entrance to Wayfarers Chapel, designed by Lloyd Wright*

FIG. 225. *The 50-ft.-tall belltower, completed in 1954, called by Wright the "Hallelujah Tower"*

In *Heaven and Hell* Swedenborg wrote, "I have seen palaces of heaven so noble as to defy description. . . . The designs of heaven's buildings are so perfect that you would say they represent the very essence of the art; and small wonder, since the art of architecture comes from heaven" (HH 185). With a faith that this is manifestly so, Swedenborgians will continue to pursue architectures that call into being the most powerful expressions of higher spirituality possible. As the notion of "church" continues to undergo clarification and redirection, however, one cannot anticipate what future forms may be manifested. But the perspective of Swedenborgian theology will provide the necessary imagination.

FIG. 226. *Baptismal font of local rock, designed to represent a mountain stream*

FIG. 227. *Wayfarers Chapel, interior*

Swedenborg and the Near-Death Experience

In this section we have included a major article by Leon S. Rhodes, a lifelong scholar of Swedenborg and a founding member of the International Association for Near-Death Studies (IANDS), as well as a list of similarities between Swedenborg's descriptions and those recorded in near-death experiences (NDEs), prepared by Rev. Wendel Barnett.

Other excerpts are taken, with the author's and the publisher's permissions, from Dr. Kenneth Ring's book *Heading Toward Omega*. The longer passages selected are striking because they contain reference, in the vision of several NDEers, to what Swedenborg described as "The New Jerusalem," a spiritual city of lights like that in the visions of St. John described in the book of Revelation, descending out of heaven. The accounts are more striking because the experiencers seem to have been unacquainted with the importance of the New Jerusalem in Swedenborgian thought.

The section ends with some pertinent quotes on the afterlife from Swedenborg himself.

Part 1
Reports on Eternal Life

Leon S. Rhodes

WHEN DR. RAYMOND MOODY'S BOOK, *Life After Life*[1] leaped to the best-seller list and was reprinted by the *Reader's Digest*, the impact could hardly have been predicted, and Dr. Moody himself was among the most surprised. This unpretentious paperback recounted his own discoveries of patients who had "died" but recovered with vivid memories of another realm of consciousness, and gave them the name *near-death experiences*, now known as NDEs.

Since its publication in 1975, Moody's book has been followed by an avalanche of articles, books, media programs, and seminars, so that today NDEs are well known, but what . is more important, the message of these brief glimpses into a nonphysical world has profoundly affected public attitudes.

Moody reported a modest number of experiences that had come to his personal attention. The most compelling aspect of the accounts was that while they reflected amazing variety, the experiences included similarities that could not be explained, similarities that, indeed, could be considered "evidence" of the reality of the NDE. How would you react if you happened to have a vivid dream some night and told friends about it and then learned that literally thousands of people had the same dream? Further, while dreams usually

A lifelong Swedenborgian, LEON RHODES followed his father's footsteps in becoming a writer, but primarily a writer of scripts for technical and information motion pictures. Much of his writing has been related to New Church [Swedenborgian; see Glossary] subjects, including editing church newsletters, which brought him into contact with a variety of subjects, including his association with the primary investigators studying the "near-death experience." He has been a director of the International Association for Near-Death Studies (IANDS) since 1980 and has lectured on the subject.

don't make immediate sense to us, and they usually fade, so that few can really recall a dream after time has passed, the NDE by contrast remains unforgettable and a powerful influence on the experiencer's life.

Moody wondered if in the past others had reported such experiences, and he undertook a modest "research" effort to find historical examples in agreement with those of his own patients. In an Atlanta library he found interesting material in both the Eygptian and Tibetan Books of the Dead,[2] but he also came upon Swedenborg's *Compendium*,[3] which contained descriptions about life after death. Moody included a few selections in his book, although they represented only a fraction of the explanations contained in Swedenborg's writings.

It was soon evident that the significance of the NDE phenomenon was more than Moody had expected, and as the topic came into public prominence, the message of the NDE became more and more influential. Not only did the number of NDEs become enormous, but it was soon clear that these experiences had involved an astonishing variety of cases—women in childbirth, patients on the operating table; victims of drug overdose, automobile accidents, drowning, suicides; with children and adults of every age represented; nonreligious people and of all denominations; and reports accumulated from around the globe. Many of the NDE accounts were not current; often experiencers had kept a profound secret in the heart rather than expose it to possible ridicule.

The noted pollster Dr. George Gallup produced seemingly incredible statistics in *Adventures in Immortality* indicating that *eight million* experiencers and approximately one-third of those patients who are declared "clinically dead" and then survive will have had an experience of another level of consciousness—even those who do not actually recall an NDE.[4]

Psychologist Dr. Kenneth Ring, of the University of Connecticut, began to study how common the NDE is and found that "approximately 35% of those who come close to death have such experiences."[5]

The classical features of the NDE—sometimes called the "core experience"—can be outlined as follows. Some parts may not occur and the sequence might differ, but a significant majority will describe several of the features. In one example of countless settings, one would find the hospital staff responding to the emergency code, watching the cardiac monitor, as the highly qualified and experienced physician fails to detect the pulse and declares that this patient has ceased living.

1. Even in distressing and traumatic conditions, the person becomes aware of a peacefulness, freedom from pains, and an indescribable bliss.
2. The person is able to be an observer, floating above the unconscious body, able to describe the activities and conversations of doctors and friends, often in astonishingly

accurate and verifiable detail.
3. There is a sensation of traveling through a dark tunnel—floating or at high speed—and an awareness of a distant bright light.
4. Approaching the "light," which is indescribably bright yet not painful to the eyes, one may sense an identity or personality, feeling that the light has come to convey the message that the person has died.
5. One finds oneself in a beautiful new realm with magnificent colors, never before seen, with preternatural beauties.
6. Other people may then be encountered—a few or a great many—and frequently it is possible to recognize friends that are known to have already died.
7. There may be communication with these people, but usually not in verbal language so much as thought transfer of a profound nature.
8. The person encounters or is told about a sort of *border* that may not be passed beyond because "it is not yet time," or may feel there is something still to be accomplished on earth. Frequently one also reports a reviewing of one's own life, a "book of life," in great detail.
9. With a feeling of family obligations or unfinished work, the experiencer finally chooses to return and is abruptly back in the body, conscious of the surroundings.[6]

Whatever may be the variations in this sequence of experiences, it is almost universally said of the encounter that it is "ineffable," beautiful beyond words, full of love, peace, and joy, and that the near-death experience almost always leaves the person without a fear of death.

Such dramatic experiences, each with its very special character and personality, quite naturally found an eager audience and, sure enough, once the first examples had been made known, thousands of new experiences "came out of the closet." But the need for serious analysis and thought was undeniable. Challenges and questions, theories and explanations were inevitable. The most comprehensive evaluation was undertaken by the group that formed the International Association for Near-Death Studies, under the leadership of Dr. Kenneth Ring. IANDS was then headquartered at the University of Connecticut Psychology Department, with participants in widely scattered places and consultants from many fields of expertise, including Dr. Elisabeth Kübler-Ross, Raymond Moody, and Wilson Van Dusen; I have been a member of the IANDS board since 1979.

While IANDS continued to collect individual NDEs and to establish contact with thousands of experiencers, it also organized the studies of a large number of researchers and scholars, and set up programs, seminars, and surveys to explore the many aspects of the experience from a "scientific perspective." Cardiologist Michael Sabom made a detailed account of 116 victims of heart arrest, adding to the IANDS studies.[7] Bruce Greyson, assistant professor of psychiatry at the University of Michigan, teamed with Dr. Ring and S. Franklin on a study, "NDE and Attempted Suicides,"[8] and coauthored a book with Dr. Charles P. Flynn, associate professor of sociology, Miami University, Oxford, Ohio—*Problems, Prospects, and Perspectives of the NDE.*[9] Numerous books, papers, and lectures were promoted "to enrich our understanding of the nature and scope of human consciousness and its relationship to the life process," as the IANDS brochure states,[10] but the role of IANDS soon passed beyond the theoretical to practical applications.

The experiencers themselves frequently were confused and distressed after their recovery, encountering problems with their friends and families. Counseling was often needed, and IANDS worked to bring experiencers together to share their ideas. In addition, the organization found that descriptions of the NDE offered comfort and reassurance to the bereaved as well as to the terminally ill. Any life-threatening illness could be ameliorated by the clear message that the long-dreaded process of death was not "just more suffering," but a deeply beautiful and meaningful release. It is striking how many bedside accounts of the last moments report a remarkable change when the moment of death arrives. IANDS chapters and other groups were established in widely scattered locations, and learning about the near-death experience increasingly changed the attitude of people about the subject of dying and the prospects beyond death.

Within a decade, the subject of the NDE has so permeated the thinking of our time that people have begun to talk freely about survival after death in ways that have profoundly influenced what may very well be a "spiritual revolution." It became acceptable to speculate about a higher level of consciousness, of surviving the death of the body, and of looking forward to a new, pain-free existence in idyllic surroundings. Though there is a powerful religious implication to this type of thinking, there was no direct association with religious denominations. Many survivors interviewed simply said that they "became more religious," but in an inner, spiritual way, and many "stopped attending church services,"[11] feeling that the spiritual approach to living was not the same as formal religion.

In much of the exploration of the NDE the name of Emanuel Swedenborg kept recurring.[12] The striking agreement of "the experience" with what Swedenborg had described two centuries earlier enriched the NDE and provided explanations not to be found in other ways. An article of mine, "The NDE Enlarged by Swedenborg's Vision" in the IANDS journal *Anabiosis*,[13] was reprinted and widely distributed, and Swedenborg's teachings were frequently quoted in discussing the idea of life beyond the grave.

In 1985 a series of thirteen half-hour television programs, "Death, Dying, and Beyond" with Rev. Wendel Barnett interviewing NDE reporters and then citing parallels with Swedenborg's descriptions of the spiritual world, attracted wide response in repeated broadcasts and in seminar programs.[14] Other TV and radio broadcasts, lectures, and discussions resulted in the collection of no less than one hundred comparisons between the reports of experiencers and passages in Swedenborg's writings. The following are a few examples from Wendel Barnett's long list of passages in Swedenborg that seem similar or identical to NDE reports:

> Angelic speech expresses in a single word thousands of ideas: HH 239, 269
> The heavenly scenes indescribable: HH 411
> Delights of heaven ineffable and innumerable: HH 314, 398
> Spirits tell newcomer that he or she has died: HH 450; AC 185
> Welcoming spirits assist the newly arrived spirit: AC 314
> Thought continues even after the body appears dead: HH 433
> Feeling of peace and serenity: HH 284
> "Dark tunnel" experiences and bright light seen: HH 171; AC 186; CL 500 [4, 5]
> Out-of-body sensation: HH 440, 441, 499; TCR 157
> Encountering spirits in new realm: HH 495
> Being of Light: HH 170, 171; AC 185; TCR 25 [1]

Followers of the doctrines given through Swedenborg are well aware that the near-death experience is but a brief glimpse into far deeper spiritual levels. His descriptions of the careful and orderly progression after the spirit awakens into the spiritual world go far beyond the fragments of "things seen and heard" (the subtitle of *Heaven and Hell*) by those who have come close to physical death. Even the indescribable beauty, love, and order experienced can be considered no more than a brief view through the portal that awaits us all.

In my involvement with NDE studies, I have been associated with many programs about the NDE that included "experiencers" who were familiar with Swedenborg's accounts. Their accounts are similar to the general pattern, but may have an additional pertinence when coupled with an existing acceptance of a life after death. A most interesting account came from a lady who was a Swedenborgian who had an NDE during which she saw a group of people who she knew had died previously. She also heard the reassuring voice of a woman *behind her*, but did not turn to see the woman because she somehow recognized the voice of her mother *who had died giving her birth*! Another Swedenborgian lady recognized her sister among the angels who came to comfort her during her difficult childbirth—the sister who had died several years earlier. An elderly man whose son, John, had died several years before, had been in a coma as death approached and had no signs of life, but in the last moments he sat up and declared cheerfully, "Why, there's

John!" These experiencers who well knew the descriptions in Swedenborg's writings found them to be confirmations of what they had been taught.

But it is increasingly evident that the emergence of the NDE subject has opened up understanding and provided an exciting introduction into the vast realm that Swedenborg explored in order to broaden all aspects of human consciousness. During his transition period, when Swedenborg was first becoming conscious of the spiritual world, he kept a remarkable journal, a private record of experiences that he recognized to be far more than mere dreams. On the night of 29 September 1744, he saw a vision of "the most beautiful palace that could possibly be seen; glory like the sun upon it. It was said to me that I should be a member that was immortal, which [note the wording] no one previously had been, *except those who had been dead and had lived again. Others said there were several!*" (emphasis Rhodes's; JD p.76, no. 243) "Those who had been dead and lived again" had seen

such glorious visions. During an NDE?

It can be inferred that the books published by Swedenborg dated from 1745 until his death were unacceptable to many because the honored scientist had entered a realm beyond that considered to encompass the orderly facts of nature; things measurable, provable. In this area, forbidden in the "Age of Reason," even the most rational concepts were held suspect, for who could give credence to a scientist who spoke with angels for twenty-seven years? But today, in an age when incomprehensibly vast knowledge of physical laws and scientific facts can leave humanity with a feeling of frustration and bewilderment, is it not possible that we are again starting to raise our vision higher? Is this moment in our history of profound importance because it marks a radically new idea of what constitutes human life? Will we change our behavior and our attitudes because we have the testimony of people who have died, rather than the "evidence" of physicians and instruments that life has ended?

Notes

1. Dr. Raymond Moody, Jr., *Life After Life* (Atlanta, Ga.: Mockingbird Books, 1975).

2. W. E. Evans-Wentz, ed., trans., and comp., *The Tibetan Book of the Dead* (London: Oxford University Press, 1960).

3. *Compendium of Theological and Spiritual Writings of Emanuel Swedenborg* (Boston: Crosby and Nichols, 1853).

4. Dr. George Gallup, Jr., *Adventures in Immortality* (New York: McGraw-Hill, 1982).

5. Dr. Kenneth Ring, *Heading Toward Omega* (New York: William Morrow, 1984), p. 34.

6. Dr. Kenneth Ring, *Life at Death* (New York: Coward, McCann and Geoghan, 1980).

7. Michael Sabom, *Recollections of Death* (New York: Harper & Row, 1982).

8. Bruce Greyson, Kenneth Ring, and S. Franklin, "NDE and Attempted Suicides."

9. Bruce Greyson and Dr. Charles P. Flynn, *Problems, Prospects, and Perspectives of the NDE* (Charles Thomas, 1984).

10. International Association for Near Death Studies, c/o Dr. Bruce Greyson, Research Director, The University of Connecticut Health Center, Farmington, CT 06032, or c/o Dr. Elisabeth Fenske, President, 3310 Baring St., Philadelphia, PA 19104.

11. Gallup, chap. 3.

12. See, for instance, Moody; Martin A. Larson, *New Thought*; and David Lorimer, *Survival*.

13. Leon S. Rhodes, "The NDE Enlarged by Swedenborg's Vision," *Anabiosis* 2, no. 1 (June 1982), pp. 15–35.

14. Wendel Barnett, "Death, Dying, and Beyond," television program made by the Gill Cable, channel 2-B, San Jose, Calif. Barnett's tapes are in the General Church Video Library, Box 278, Bryn Athyn, PA 19009.

Part 2
Excerpts from
Heading Toward Omega

Kenneth Ring, Ph.D.

THERE IS GOOD EVIDENCE that the near-death experience has occurred to millions of people and has indirectly touched the lives of other millions. Probably one in every twenty people will undergo an NDE. Those who have done so testify that the appearance of death is not at all like the experience of death. The following list describes some of the frequently occurring characteristics of the NDE:

1. Journey through a tunnel; may hear buzzing or windlike sounds
2. May feel one is viewing one's body from another location (OBE)
3. Mental state of clarity and alertness; "nothing like a dream"
4. Life review of major experiences
5. Peacefulness; a sense of well-being; removal from pain or any other bodily sensations
6. Encounters with people who have died before, often loved ones
7. A meeting with a spiritual "being of light" who may communicate mentally
8. "A feeling like you are in a kind of eternity"
9. The spiritual core of the NDE is so awesome and overwhelming that the person is thrust into an entirely new mode of being
10. Once the decision is made by the person to return, then the experience ends abruptly
11. People often avoid reporting experience to others for fear of misunderstanding or ridicule
12. Universality—experiences seem similar throughout many cultures
13. No seeming demographic differences—class, age, marital status, education
14. No essential difference because of religious beliefs or lack thereof
15. Manner of "death" has no evident effect; once the NDE begins, it unfolds in a similar pattern[1]

Those who have had a near-death experience go on to describe their emotions of love encountered, radiant colors, quality of timelessness, brilliant light, instant communication, God's forgiveness, and the essence of life itself. Here are a few of those accounts, in the words of people who have nearly "died."

> I cannot begin to describe in human terms the feeling I had at what I saw. It was a giant infinite world of calm, and love, and energy and beauty. It was as though human life was unimportant [but] the importance of life [was]. . . . Death [is] a means to a better, different life.[2]

> At first I became aware of beautiful colors which were all the colors of the rainbow. They were magnified in crystallized light and beamed with a brilliance in every direction . . . [like] a prism made by a most beautiful and purified diamond. . . . I was in a heavenly pasture with flowers. . . . My ears were filled with a music so beautiful no composer could ever duplicate it. It was soothing, gentle, and warm and seemed to come from a source deep within me.[3]

> I became aware of colors that were far beyond the spectrum of the rainbow known to the human eye.[4]

> Time meant nothing. Just being. Love. Pure love. . . . The Light was Yellow . . . in, around and through everything. . . . It is God made visible. In, around, and through everything. One who has not experienced it cannot know its feeling.[5]

> You have a feeling of absolute, pure love . . . the warmest feeling [but] don't confuse it with warm in temperature. . . . It's a perfect temperature. . . . You realize that you are suddenly in communication with absolute, total knowledge. It's hard to describe. . . . You can think of a question . . . and *immediately* know the answer to it. As simple as that.[6]

KENNETH RING, Ph.D., is professor of psychology at the University of Connecticut, past president of the International Association for Near-Death Studies, and author of *Life at Death* and *Heading Toward Omega*.

I mentioned the golden light. It should be Golden light and you ask if it burned my eyes. No, it did not. Fact being, I gained strength gazing upon it. There was a transformation of a higher power, knowledge, understanding, and the "oneness of everything."[7]

It is so bright, so brilliant . . . it is *brighter* than a light that would immediately blind you, but this *absolutely* does not hurt your eyes at all. . . . Events take place . . . within a millisecond. . . . The light communicates to you. . . . This communication is what you might call telepathic. It's absolutely instant, absolutely clear. It wouldn't even matter if a different language was being spoken . . . it would be instant and absolutely clear. . . . Never a doubtful statement made.[8]

When I communicated . . . with the light, there wasn't a transfer of words. . . . It's like thinking a thought and having them know it and answer it immediately.[9]

As the light came toward me, it became a person—yet it wasn't a person. It was a being that radiated. And inside this radiant luminous light which had a silver tint to it—white with silver—[was] what looked like a man.[10]

When he took hold of my hand, I immediately knew him to be the greatest friend I had. . . . The thrill of his touch of hands exceeds anything I have ever experienced on earth.[11]

It was like I knew everything that was stored in my brain. Everything I'd ever known from the beginning of my life I immediately knew about. And also what was kind of scary was that everybody else in the room knew I knew it and that there was no hiding anything. . . . Every single thing that you do in your life is recorded and . . . even though you pass it by not thinking at the time, it always comes up later.[12]

You are shown your life—and you do the judging. . . . Can you forgive yourself? This is the judgment.[13]

I felt inside my being [God's] forgiveness for the things in my life I was ashamed of, as though they were not of great importance. I was asked . . . "What had I done to benefit or advance the human race?"[14]

City of Lights

The following descriptions from NDEs of a "city of lights" bear striking similarity to the New Jerusalem about which Swedenborg wrote.

. . . I moved closer to the lights and realized they were cities—the cities were built of light. At the moment I realized what it was . . . we were there. There was no more traveling or floating along this path.

I stood in the square of a brilliant, beautiful city and I will describe the city. The building I went in was a cathedral. It was built like St. Mark's or the Sistine Chapel, but the bricks or blocks appeared to be made of Plexiglas. They were square, they had dimension to 'em, except you could see through 'em and in the center of each one of these was this gold and

silver light. And you could see the building—and yet could not for the radiance. . . . Now, this cathedral was literally *built* of knowledge. This was a place of learning I had come to. I could sense it. 'Cause literally all information—I began to be bombarded with data. Information was coming at me from every direction. It was almost as if I was stickin' my head in a stream and each drop of water was a piece of information and it was flowing past me as if my head was under it.

Other core experiencers have described such cities in even more detail. For example, there is the following word picture painted by a forty-one-year-old woman I met at a conference on near-death experiences in March 1981. At the workshop I was conducting—in North Carolina, by the way—Stella (a pseudonym) had been asked by the conference organizers to share her NDE with my audience. As usually happens on these occasions, we went out afterward to talk further, and eventually Stella, too, came north to the Near-Death Hotel for a couple of extended visits. During one of them, we tape-recorded her narration of her NDE in which she spoke of her experience in a city of light.

Her NDE itself occurred as a result of massive hemorrhaging following surgery in June 1977.

. . . suddenly there was this tremendous burst of light and, uh, I was turned . . . to the light. I saw at a great distance a city. . . . It's not like you'd look out of an airplane and see the layout of a city. . . . Even at tremendous distance, I realized that it was *immense*! It all seemed to have the same dimensions and there seemed to be nothing supporting it and no *need* for anything to support it. And then I began to realize that the light was coming from within this city and there just seemed to be a laser beam of light and in the midst of that, that was directed to me. And I just rode that laser beam of light through a vastness, being aware that there were other life forms going by [this aspect was also independently mentioned by two others], but this was only a minor part of this experience. The main thrust of my attention was where I was headed. [Did you have a sense of your speed?] Oh, tremendous speed, tremendous speed. [Any change in speed?] I think that as I got closer to it, there was an acceleration to a point. It was almost as though this light was not an arc, but it had that feeling to it; that I was going to the top of what I saw. It's hard to conceive that so much could happen so quickly. And yet, the intensity of it had more depth than anything I've known before or since. Then I got to a point where I was almost looking down. I suddenly thought, "I guess I blew it!" [laughs] Because I was going so fast, I thought I was going on by. And almost at the same instant—it must have been the perfect point—I just went right down into it. I don't know how to explain that. It wasn't as though it was lowering, but I just went from the perfect point above it into this city.

The first thing that I saw was this street. And it had such a clarity. The only thing I can relate it to in this life was a look of gold, but it was clear, it was transparent. . . . Everything there had a purity and clarity. . . . The difference (between things here and there) was also—you think of gold as something hard and brittle; this had a smoothness and softness. Not a giving softness, but almost a blending. . . . Everything was very defined, on the one hand, but it also had a blending with everything else. The flowers and the flower buds by that street—the intensity, the vibrant colors, like pebbles that have been polished in a running stream, but they were all like precious stones, rubies and diamonds and sapphires. One that I remember in particular had a yellow color to it and yet I would relate it to a diamond . . . all these things were just around flowers. [What did the flowers look like?] They looked like . . . tulips . . . and yet they had the fragrance of roses. Strong fragrance of roses. And I started to walk further on this street and . . . then I saw, as I was looking down, walking, I saw the feet, just the toes, of this man's feet and the bottom of his garment in my path. And I wasn't allowed to go any further. And I could hear *languages*. All languages. Languages that I had never heard before and I could understand them. I wanted to be allowed to go on. I knew there was so much more there and I wanted to be able to experience it, to see it. . . . There was the knowledge that was beyond anything that I could possibly describe to you. I began to realize that I was going to have to leave and I didn't want to leave [begins to cry].

Jayne also reports perceptions very much like Stella's, although Jayne did not describe the city as one of lights. Nevertheless, the parallels are evident. In this portion of her experience, just following, it seems, her sense that she was "an infinite being in perfection" and that, indeed, *all* was perfect, she relates:

. . . after I had been in that for whatever infinite time this was, I suddenly found myself on a green plain. And I had a body again. I was aware of a body. And this was a beautiful green meadow, with beautiful flowers, beautiful flowers, lit again with this glorious radiant light, like no light we've ever seen, but there was sky, grass, flowers that had colors that I'd never seen before. And I remember so well looking at them and thinking, "I have never seen some of these colors!" Just utter glory in color. And I walked along and I saw that there were people up on a little rise in front of me. So I started walking toward the rise to talk with these people and when I had just gotten up there, I could see a city.

I intend to sum up this set of NDEs by drawing on a narrative account that comes from the pen of Rev. Carol Parrish-Harra. This woman, who is both a minister and a

healer, and I started corresponding in 1980 and finally had a chance to meet briefly in April 1982. During that time Carol was writing a book on death and dying, which included an account of her own NDE. This took place in 1958, when she had an allergic reaction to a drug while giving birth. I will quote from the prepublication draft of the chapter in which she describes her experience. I cite it here not only because Carol expresses her encounter with a "being of light" so well, but especially because of her ability to state in general terms the way in which transcendental knowledge is transmitted during these experiences and the form it takes. Carol writes:

By my side there was a Being with a magnificent presence. I could not see an exact form, but instead, a radiation of light that lit up everything about me and spoke with a voice that held the deepest tenderness one can ever imagine. . . . as this loving yet powerful Being spoke to me, I understood vast meanings, much beyond my ability to explain. I understood life and death, and instantly, any fear I had, ended. There was a totality, a completeness in the realization that I could continue to experience and that there was absolutely no reason to continue my frantic struggle to exist.

For what seemed to be endless time, I experienced this Presence. The Light Being, pure, powerful, all-expansive, was without a form and it could be said that great waves of awareness flowed to me and into my mind.

As I responded to these revelations, I knew them to be so. Of course, it didn't matter if one lived or died, it was all so clear. There was a complete trust and greater understanding of what these words meant.

It seemed whole *Truths* revealed themselves to me. Waves of thought—ideas greater and purer than I had ever tried to figure out came to me. Thoughts, clear without effort revealed themselves in total wholeness, although not in logical sequence. I, of course, being in that magnificent Presence, understood it all. I realized that consciousness is life. We will live in and through much, but this consciousness we know that is behind our personality will continue. I knew now that the purpose of life does not depend on me; it has its own purpose. I realized that the flow of it will continue even as I will continue. New serenity entered my being.

As this occurred, an intensity of feeling rushed through me, as if the light that surrounded that Being was bathing me, penetrating every part of me. As I absorbed the energy, I sensed what I can only describe as bliss. That is such a little word, but the feeling was dynamic, rolling, magnificent, expanding, ecstatic—*Bliss.*[15]

Notes

1. List paraphrased from Kenneth Ring, *Heading Toward Omega* (New York: William Morrow, 1984), pp. 36–52.
2. Ibid., pp. 54–55.
3. Ibid., p. 64.
4. Ibid., p. 65.
5. Ibid., pp. 55–56.
6. Ibid., p. 58.
7. Ibid., p. 88.
8. Ibid., pp. 57–58.
9. Ibid., p. 60.
10. Ibid., p. 71.
11. Ibid., p. 77.
12. Ibid., pp. 68–69.
13. Ibid., p. 70.
14. Ibid., p. 67.
15. City of lights accounts: ibid., pp. 72–75.

Part 3
Three States of Afterlife

Compiled by Stephen Larsen, Ph.D.

AS SWEDENBORG SAID he had been permitted by the Lord to experience the deeper reaches of these regions reported by those "in the vestibule" of the spiritual world, it seems appropriate to conclude this section with some of his observations of this realm.[1]

> We undergo three states after death, before entering either heaven or hell. The first state is of more outward things; the second is a state of more inward things, and the third state of preparation. We undergo these states in the world of spirits. . . .
>
> As to the first state, the state of more outward things, we enter this immediately after death. We all have, as to our spirits, more outward and more inward aspects. The more outward aspects of spirit are the ones by which it adjusts the human body to [conditions] in the world, especially our face, speech, and actions, for getting along with other people. The more inward aspects of spirit are the matters of our actual intent and its consequent thought, which are rarely obvious in face, speech, or act. From infancy, we have accustomed ourselves to showing friendship, good will, and sincerity, and concealing what our actual intent is thinking. So we habitually carry around a life that is civilly and morally acceptable, no matter what we are like inside. . . .
>
> Our first state after death is like this state in the world, because we are at that point similarly involved in external concerns. Face, speech, and personality are similar, and so therefore are moral and civil behavior. . . . So the one is carried over into the other, and death is only a crossing. (HH 491f)
>
> Our second state after death is called a state of more inward things, because we are then let into the deeper workings of our minds, or of our intentionality and thinking, and the more outward concerns we were involved in during the first state go to sleep. . . .
>
> When spirits are let into the state of their more inward workings, then it can be clearly seen what kind of people they were in the world, because they are acting from their genuine selves. People who were inwardly good in the world behave rationally and wisely—more wisely than in the world, in fact, because they have been freed from their connection with a physical body, and therefore with those earthly things that darken and, so to speak, becloud. People who were inwardly evil in the world, on the other hand, behave grossly and crazily—more crazily than in the world, in fact, because they are now in freedom and not constrained. . . . Hidden things are thus opened and secrets laid bare. . . . (HH 499ff)
>
> Every evil bears its own punishment with it; they are united. So the person who is involved in an evil is also involved in the punishment of that evil. Still, no one after death undergoes punishment for evils done in the world, but only for evils done then and there. But it boils down to the same thing . . . since everyone returns to his or her own life after death, and therefore returns to similar evils. (HH 509)
>
> Our third state after death, or the third state of our spirit, is a state of instruction. This state is appropriate to people who are entering heaven and becoming angels, but not for people who are entering hell, because these latter cannot be taught anything. So their second state is also their third, and ends by their turning completely toward their own love and therefore toward the hellish community that is in the same love. . . . But good people are brought through from the second state into a third, which is a state of their preparation for heaven through instruction. The only way anyone can be prepared for heaven is by insights into what is good and true, therefore only through being taught. For no one can know what is spiritually good and true, and what is evil and false. . . . without being taught. (HH 512)

Note

1. Swedenborg's *Heaven and Hell* excerpts from George F. Dole. ed. and trans., *A View from Within: A Compendium of Swedenborg's Thought* (New York: Swedenborg Foundation, 1985).

For biographical information, see Stephen Larsen's other essay in this anthology, "Swedenborg and the Visionary Tradition."

An Iconography of City Planning: The Chicago City Plan

Irving D. Fisher, Ph.D.

ANYONE WHO SETS ABOUT TO PLAN a city reveals whatever propensities he or she may possess as an artist, technician, and ideologue. The emphasis of these talents varies with the intent, intelligence, knowledge, and experience of the planner. Unless a planner is playing games with lines and boxes (no matter how seriously the person takes the game) and unless employed by a client whose sole motive is speculation, city planners link their plans to the manner in which people behave or to the manner in which they believe people ought to behave. The planner is a social engineer. Some intrinsic frame of reference that gives form to the planner's design emerges in the final product. Some planners, clearly aware of their references and intentions, broadcast the relationship of ideology to the technical aspects of their plans. With some planners the ideological referents emerge unconsciously. In other cases a planner, while consciously aware of the controlling ideology that pervades his design, deliberately withholds that information from his patron or his public. Daniel Burnham fits this latter category: he revealed to no one that his great *Plan of Chicago* was meant to be the earthly embodiment (i.e., the correspondent form) of Emanuel Swedenborg's heavenly city.

In 1909 Daniel H. Burnham offered his *Plan of Chicago* to the Commercial Club, his sponsor, and to the people of Chicago; he offered it to his home city as his consummate effort in city planning. Already he was the famous and wealthy head of a renowned architectural firm; his Chicago Plan was a culmination and a refinement of his exercises in formulating plans for Washington, D.C., Manila and Baguio in the Philippines, and San Francisco.

The Chicago Plan is historically significant. It has had a profound influence in stimulating the course of city planning in the United States. The Chicago Plan heralded the modern city planning movement. The design was the first comprehensive city plan that encompassed a metropolitan region. In its emphasis upon monumental architectural symmetry and beauty and an interconnected system of parks and recreational areas, Burnham's plan gave impetus and ideality to the City Beautiful movement. Burnham averred that the "American city, and Chicago preeminently, is a center of industry and traffic."[1] Thus the Chicago Plan gives primary considerations to the improvement of commercial facilities and to the transportation of persons and goods. Burnham aimed for a well-ordered, convenient, and unified city ostensibly to promote the "material advancement" of the business interests of Chicago.[2]

In his plan for Chicago, Burnham's appeal to the business community is apparent. He concurred in the prevailing values of businessmen. Indeed, he grounded the success of his architectural firm on the kinds of entrepreneurial skills that characterized the contemporary businessman. In pressing the business of his firm and in his dealings with clients, Burnham had the reputation of being "a tough and hard-headed businessman."[3] Louis Sullivan, who knew Burnham, described him as one who made masterful use of methods and men and as "an enthusiastic promoter of great construction en-

IRVING D. FISHER is professor of political science at the University of Southern Maine in Portland, Maine. Born in Hartford, Connecticut, he was educated at the University of Connecticut and took his Ph.D. in political philosophy at Columbia University. He has taught at Brooklyn College of the City University of New York, at Columbia University, and at Bowdoin College. He initiated his study of Daniel Burnham's *Plan of Chicago* while a Fellow in the National Endowment for the Humanities Seminar at Columbia University. Fisher has been director of the Robert A. Taft Institute of Government Seminar at the University of Southern Maine since 1979. He is the author of the book *Frederick Law Olmsted and the City Planning Movement in the United States*, published in 1986.

terprises," and "a colossal merchandiser" who merged into the prevailing ethic of "bigness, organization, delegation, and intense commercialism."[4] He was also, by all reports, a kind, generous, civic-minded, charitable, loyal person.

In other words, Burnham, an architect, was a successful businessman who knew how to appeal to the outstanding businessmen of the nation. Burnham stated that his aim was "to direct the development of the city towards an end that must seem ideal, but is practical."[5] His purpose was not "to invent novel problems for solution, but to take up the pressing needs of today and to find the best methods of meeting those requirements. . . ."[6] He succeeded in gaining the wholehearted support of the Commercial Club, a group of conservative Chicago businessmen who included Burnham. The roster of the Commercial Club was comprised of such tycoons as George Pullman; Philip D. Armour; Marshall Field; Cyrus McCormick; James W. Ellsworth, president of the Illinois Central Railroad; Charles H. Thorne, president of Montgomery Ward; and Charles H. Wacker, wealthy brewer. The club gave financial and organizational support to the formulation and promotion of Burnham's plan.

Under cover of a plan whose rhetoric purported to renovate and organize Chicago's transportation systems, create a harmonious, ordered, convenient city, and to beautify Chicago, Burnham devised a plan for Chicago whose contours he deliberately based upon the heavenly city described in *Heaven and its Wonders and Hell*—a work of the eighteenth-century scientist, theologian, and mystic Emanuel Swedenborg. Fundamentally, Burnham's *Plan of Chicago* is a massive blueprint for the ideal city derived from the eschatological writings of Swedenborg. No critic has discerned this paradox, least of all the "practical" businessmen of Chicago who supported and financed Burnham's design. Only one other person besides Burnham understood Burnham's method—his assistant, Edward H. Bennett. In his diary, Bennett gives us the following clue:

> We went to see Dr. Worcester, Swedenborgian minister of San Francisco, a life-long friend. Mr. Burnham always acknowledged his influence. "He has always kept a hand on my shoulder" was the way he put it. *The laws of spiritual correspondence were often in his mind and one evening at the bungalow on Twin Peaks [San Francisco] he interested himself in tracing the correspondence of spiritual powers and the municipal powers as indicated in the physical lay-out of the centre of the city.* I had proposed a system of concentric rings or circuits surrounding the ideal Centre of Government.[7] [emphasis Fisher's]

There are other entries in Bennett's diary that reveal Burnham's attachment to Swedenborg's doctrine. On one of his visits with Burnham, Bennett writes, "We talked of Swedenborg, or rather I listened to his discourse on the subject, and came away strengthened in purpose."[8]

Had the members of the Commercial Club known of the spiritual mysticism that underlie the foundation of the plan that they were sponsoring, Burnham's reputation notwithstanding, one can imagine a profound skepticism, even alarm, pervading the members. The hardy entrepreneurs of the club might even have prided themselves on being deeply religious, but their materialism would have made them shy of establishing a religious utopia in the city of Chicago. The values of these powerful captains of business were hardly likely to comport with the aspirations of a religious mystic.

Daniel Burnham—Formative Years

Daniel Burnham was born in 1846 into a family firmly devoted to Swedenborgian Christianity. Burnham's maternal grandfather, the Reverend Holland Weeks, was a graduate of Dartmouth College and an ordained Congregationalist minister. Weeks was an early convert to Swedenborgianism. He began preaching New Church doctrines in his congregation in Abington, Massachusetts. He was tried for heresy and excommunicated from his church in 1820. He moved to Henderson, New York, where he established a congregation of the Church of the New Jerusalem and continued his missionary activities for the New Church. Edwin Burnham joined Weeks's congregation and married the reverend's daughter. Daniel Burnham was an offspring of this union. Daniel's mother and father carried on the missionary work of the Reverend Weeks. They aided in organizing New Church activities in Detroit, western New York, and Chicago. Thomas Hines, Burnham's most recent biographer, describes the Burnham family in this fashion: "Spiritually, ethically, intellectually and socially, the Swedenborgian faith pervaded the Burnham household."[9]

Daniel attended Snow's Swedenborgian Academy in Chicago, but later switched to the public school system. In 1863 Daniel was sent to the New Church School in Waltham, Massachusetts, to prepare for entrance to Harvard. The school was kept by the Reverend Joseph Worcester, a Swedenborgian minister with whom Daniel formed a lifelong friendship. Two years later Daniel was in Bridgewater, Massachusetts, for more intensive training for the Harvard entrance examination. Again his tutor was a Swedenborgian minister and scholar, the Reverend Tilly Brown Hayward. Burnham never made it to Harvard nor to his second choice, Yale. He failed the entrance examinations and returned to Chicago.

While in Massachusetts, however, his interest in architecture had been whetted. In Chicago he began training as an apprentice draftsman under the tutelege of the innovative engineer and architect William Le Baron Jenney. After a year's apprenticeship Burnham departed Chicago for the West. He was enticed by the possibilities of making his fortune in mining. He failed in this venture and returned once more to Chicago in 1870 to a career in architecture.

In 1872 Burnham found employment as a trainee in the architectural office of Carter, Drake, and Wright. Here he met John Wellborn Root, a fellow employee and an adherent of the religious principles of Swedenborg.[10] Root possessed a facile, creative mind. He was intellectually curious and his interests were wide-ranging. He joined Burnham in a fruitful and harmonious partnership that endured for eighteen years— until Root's death in 1891. The originality of Root's designs and the success of his experiments in building construction marked the beginnings of the Chicago school of architecture.

In 1872, Burnham and Root initiated their partnership. They intended to take advantage of the opportunities occasioned by the disastrous Chicago Fire of 1871. Mayer and Wade state that in an area of about 1,688 acres the fire destroyed property worth $200 million. The business section of Chicago was almost entirely gutted. Of the heterogeneous population of three hundred thousand persons, nearly one-third of them found themselves homeless as a result of the fire.[11]

Chicago's recovery from the great fire was rapid and exuberant. The Chicagoans, spurred by their entrepreneurial impetus, speedily rebuilt their wasted city. Without changing the gridiron pattern of the old street system, merchants, industrialists, and real estate speculators reconstructed the commercial blocks of Chicago's core. In the process of reconstruction the architects and engineers established the roots of an impressive aesthetic and functional architectural style that became the model for the development of modern architecture.

The Need for Comprehensive City Planning

Creative and impressive though the commercial and industrial rebuilding may have been, there was little regard for cohesive, organic city planning. As a result of the fire the Chicago City Council passed an ordinance prohibiting construction of wooden buildings in the downtown section of the city, but regard for housing, sanitation, adequate garbage collection, and civic amenities were neglected.

An evident opportunity for the city of Chicago to offer and implement a comprehensive plan that would accomplish physical and social welfare reform passed without acknowledgment. No plan was offered, no plan was implemented. The merchants and industrialists disregarded a need for a plan that would anticipate and relieve the growing city of the congestions, filth, pollution, slums, traffic chaos, and garbage that blighted Chicago before the fire. They continued their neglect during the period of restoration and commercial expansion.

No heed was paid to the counsel that Frederick Law Olmsted, the renowned landscape architect, had offered in 1868. Referring to the Great Fire of London in 1666—a disaster similar in its devastation to the Chicago Fire—Olmsted urged that no opportunity be lost to engage in comprehensive city planning.

Olmsted asserted that the failure of the London merchants and landowners to implement the city plan of the renowned architect Christopher Wren resulted in the inconveniences of crowding and confinement, chaos, disease, and pauperism. Instead of a rational plan for rebuilding the burnt-out area, the shortsighted, self-seeking businessmen, "each man for himself," began to rebuild as fast as possible with no thought to future requirements.[12] Olmsted's criticism would have applied *pari passu* to the Chicago Fire in 1871. Burnham used the same example to support comprehensive city planning.[13]

The neglect to provide for the welfare and the amenities of civic life led to shocking social conditions in Chicago. In the wake of the fire almost one hundred thousand of the working class had to scuffle for housing in the crowded wooden cottages surrounding the business center.[14] The influx of unskilled immigrants from eastern Europe and southern Italy exacerbated the problems of slum life.[15] By the turn of the century, "many residential districts near downtown continued to be overcrowded, with too many people for every room, too many families for every house, too many buildings for every block."[16]

Between 1880 and 1890 Chicago's population swelled by annexation of surrounding towns and by in-migration, from 505,185 in 1880 to more than 1,000,000 in 1890.[17] With its heterogeneous mix of immigrants, Chicago had become the nation's second city after New York. In 1890 the city's foreign-born population was almost as numerous as its whole population in 1880.[18]

By the 1890s an estimated 162,000 persons were living in Chicago's slums. Only New York City had a greater number of slum dwellers. The slum district, as defined in the 1893 report of the U.S. Department of Labor, included the area between Halsted Street on the west and State Street on the east, Polk Street on the north and Twelfth Street (now Roosevelt Road) on the south. According to Agnes Sinclair Holbrook, a resident social worker of Hull House:

> Rear tenements and alleys form the core of the district, and it is there that the densest crowds of the most wretched and destitute congregate. Little idea can be given of the filthy and rotten tenements, the dingy courts and tumble-down sheds, the foul stables and dilapidated outhouses, the broken sewer pipes, the piles of garbage fairly alive with diseased odors, and of the numbers of children filling every nook, working and playing in every room. . . . It is customary for the lower floor of the rear house to be used as a stable and outhouse, while the upper rooms serve entire families as a place for eating, sleeping, being born and dying. Where there are alleys the refuse and manure are sometimes removed;

where there are none, it would seem they accumulate undisturbed. In front of each house stand garbage-receivers—wooden boxes repulsive to every sense, even when as clean as their office will permit, shocking to both mind and instinct when rotten, overfilled, and broken, as they often are.[19]

By the 1890s Chicago demonstrated not only its economic and social consolidation, but its cultural aspirations as well. The buildings of the Chicago school of architecture were already models for emulation. In 1891 Theodore Thomas established the Chicago Symphony Orchestra, and in 1892 the University of Chicago opened its doors. For all this, Carl W. Condit points out:

> The city was unbelievably dirty. . . . The smoke from the high-sulfer Illinois bituminous coal poured daily out of thousands of homes, skyscrapers, factories, and locomotives. Soot and cinders in the air, sewage far beyond the oxidation point in the Sanitary Canal, the excrement of horses covering the streets, ashes and rubbish around the rail yards and engineer terminals, the junk accumulating from abandoned machines, containers and other metal objects—these features characterized the whole working city, and if some progress was made in getting rid of them, there were other forms of ugliness and dirt to take its place.[20]

With the demographic, physical, and commercial growth the needs and demands for costly public works such as railroad services, water, gas, electricity, trolleys, telephones, sanitation, and garbage-collecting services became imperative. When Julia C. Lathrop, a member of the Illinois State Board of Charities, inquired what provisions were made "to meet sickness, accident, non-employment, old age and that inevitable accident, death," she found that the city of Chicago provided none of such social services.[21] Cook County, with the aid of private charity, was the provider. However, Lathrop wrote, "County aid was reluctantly sought. Even the poorest of the slum-dwellers turned to county aid as a last resort." Whatever services the county offered, Lathrop declared to be woefully inadequate. The inadequate personnel who dealt with the poor, the insane, the elderly, and the sick were untrained, brutal, patronage appointees whose employment depended upon the political climate.[22]

The extraordinary, rapid increase in population and territory of the city of Chicago called for the reform and extension of the governmental structure and functions. Like most city charters of the period, Chicago's charter reflected a governmental instrument fit for small-town, rural America. Again, like most governmental units of the nineteenth century, and especially municipal governments, the *laissez-faire* doctrine was controlling. With social Darwinism in vogue, attention to human welfare needs was scarcely considered by public agencies. Both idealogically and functionally the city government of Chicago was not responsibly attuned to attend to the human problems of its dense, destitute population.

In regard to taxation and administration the city of Chicago was hardly a consolidated governmental unit. The towns that Chicago had annexed still operated as quasi-independent units. In addition to twelve towns, the city had to contend with overlapping state and county agencies as well as special bodies such as school, library, three park boards, and a sanitary district—each of which possessed some degree of jurisdictional independence and taxing power. All these agencies operated in the Chicago area.[23] Such chronic administrative chaos resulted in the failure of responsible public action. The confusion provided opportunities for fraud in letting licenses, franchises, and contracts for public works and services.[24]

Rudyard Kipling visited Chicago in the 1890s. He found Chicago to be a filthy city "inhabited by savages." After his exploration of the city he averred, "I urgently desire never to see it again."[25]

The White City—Precursor to the Chicago Plan

To show the world that the city of Chicago was something more than a hive of industry and commerce the World's Columbian Exposition Corporation undertook the construction of a great world's fair. The corporation, a group of civic-minded Chicago citizens who had government support, appointed Daniel H. Burnham to be director of works to supervise the entire project. On the shore of Lake Michigan, Frederick Law Olmsted designated a barren site for the Chicago World's Fair of 1893.

In the spring of 1891, when he initiated construction, Burnham, at the age of forty-three, was the senior member of the architectural firm of Burnham and Root. The foremost architectural firm in Chicago, well known and successful, they had by 1890 "built in the neighborhood of $40 million worth of buildings."[26] Burnham and Root pioneered the construction of commercial skyscraper buildings—the hallmark of the Chicago school of architecture. Before Root's death in 1891 the firm had designed, in the Chicago-school idiom, the Montauk Building (1860), the Rookery (1888), the Rand-McNally Building (1890), the Masonic Temple (1892), and the Monadnock Building (1892). In the years following the World's Fair, Burnham's eminence as an architect and organizer brought his firm commissions to design such multistoried commercial structures as the Flatiron Building (1903), New York's first skyscraper, and the Selfridge Department Store (1906) in London.

As the general supervisor of all construction work of the fair, Burnham chose the architects, artists, sculptors, and engineers to design the buildings. To give the fair a national purview he included along with the midwestern architects three renowned eastern architectural firms from New York and two from Boston. He agreed to the judgment of the

FIG. 228. *Rookery, Chicago, 1888*

FIG. 229. *Masonic Temple, Chicago, 1892*

FIG. 230. *Monadnock Building, Chicago, 1892*

FIG. 231. *Flatiron Building, New York City, 1903*

FIG. 232. *White City, at the Chicago World's Fair of 1893*

eastern architects that the design of the buildings should be in the neoclassical style of the École des Beaux-Arts of Paris. Burnham unilaterally decided that the dominant color of the fair's buildings be white.[27] It was this *mise-en-scène* that gave the fair the designation of the "White City." Burnham and the staff of the fair orchestrated the administrative, social, aesthetic, and intellectual sensibilities of the fair's visitors. The fair was an archetype of a municipal government. The White City was a comprehensively planned city, albeit a temporary, "make-believe" city. Efforts were made to provide for the convenience, safety, and security of the 27.5 million transients who would attend the fair. Sanitary engineers introduced an innovative filtering system to provide an abundance of pure drinking water. The cleanliness of the White City was ensured by a sophisticated sewage system. Street cleaners removed the debris and litter of the day's activities. Public toilets were maintained, and medical and emergency hospital services were available. The fair had its

own electrical power system for the extensive use of lighting and its electric railway. A department of professionally trained personnel provided fire protection. The so-called guards or policemen of the White City were required not only to maintain order but to be solicitous, as William Dean Howells reports, of the "pleasure as well as the welfare of the people."[28] Burnham's vision evoked a planned micro-city that manifested and provided for beauty, convenience, amenity, space, and order for the fair's visitors. "He wanted space for compositional effects and for large numbers of people, and he wanted visual unity. . . ."[29] The White City was a vivid contrast to the chaotic, slum-infected, unsanitary conditions that prevailed in nineteenth-century American cities.

Transient though the Columbian Exposition was, Bessie Louise Pierce notes, "It marked, in fact, a new epoch in the aesthetic growth not only of Chicago but of the nation." The White City had opened the eyes of millions of visiting Americans "to the possibilities of transforming some of the ugliness and unsightliness of their own abodes, the real cities of the country, into a more lasting beauty."[30]

But the White City was particularly the antithesis of Chicago—the germinator of the fair itself. Visitors to the fair viewed the dreamlike, artificial city as the ideal urban community. The beauty, symmetry, grandeur, planned unity, and the probity of its administration—all so wanting in the nation's cities—induced among the visitors the sense that they were within the precincts of Utopia.

To some, the glittering White City was the secular, physical embodiment, or at least a symbol, of God's heavenly kingdom. To Howells, the fair city was a "bit of Altruria," Howells's utopia. In its "grandeur of design and freedom of expression" it seemed to the Altrurian visitor that the capitalists of America had "put themselves into the hands of artists" and in so doing offered a "foretaste of heaven."[31]

The White City became a metaphor for the city laid up in heaven. The Chicago World's Fair of 1893 called forth the Puritan longing to create the ideal community—the "city on the hill"—which would be the model for all to emulate. It was, indeed, a manifestation of the radical Augustinian view: the city of heaven was established on earth and stood side by side with its antithesis—Chicago—the city of man.

The ordered beauty so entranced some idealistic writers that they viewed the White City as "the Celestial City," the "model of an earthly heaven," and the "New Jerusalem."[32] For Daniel Burnham, that is precisely what he later intended the city of Chicago to be—the corresponding earthly embodiment of the visionary heavenly city described in Emanuel Swedenborg's visionary writings.

Hines states that the Chicago World's Fair was a turning point in Burnham's life. It "was the pivotal moment in Burnham's career. . . . It dominated his thought for the rest of his life."[33] Burnham came to regard the White City as the spring from which flowed the auspicious, comprehensive plans that marked the movement toward modern city planning. Burnham's management and the popular success of the fair enhanced his reputation as an administrator and architect. His architectural achievements in Chicago and in the West had brought him distinction and affluence. For directing the White City he acquired national renown. In 1894, Yale, Harvard, and Northwestern University endowed Burnham with honorary degrees. The American Institute of Architects elected him its president.

At the turn of the century the United States was attaining the stature of a world power. Indeed, the grandeur of the Chicago World's Fair was a symbolic manifestation of just such a posture. In keeping with such an awareness, official Washington turned its attention to rehabilitating the national capitol. The centenary commemoration in 1900 of the removal of the seat of government from Philadelphia to Washington, D.C., was the occasion for the revival of the L'Enfant design for the na-

tion's capitol and the improvement and renewal of the District. Under the aegis of Senator James McMillan, chairman of the Senate Committee on the District of Columbia, the Senate Park Commission was established with Daniel Burnham as its chairman. The other members of the commission were Charles F. McKim, the New York architect; Augustus St. Gaudens, sculptor; and Frederick Law Olmsted, Jr., landscape architect. All the commission members, including the younger Olmsted, had participated in the formulation of the Chicago fair. Though the commission revived the original L'Enfant plan and added their own revisions to meet the needs of a modern city, their 1902 plan for Washington carried the imprint of the neoclassicism of the White City. The national acclaim that greeted the work of the Washington planners inspired emulation by other cities.

Burnham's experience in planning the Chicago fair and Washington served to amplify his reputation as a city planner. He was called to chair the Group Plan Commission for the city of Cleveland. Burnham with the New York architects John Carrère and Arnold Brunner issued their Cleveland Plan of 1903. At the behest of Secretary of War William H. Taft, Burnham sailed to the Philippines to make master plans for the cities of Manila and Baguio. He completed these plans in 1905. In the same year, Burnham presented his ambitious design for the city of San Francisco to the members of the Association for the Improvement and Adornment of San Francisco.

All these plans, avers Mel Scott, were "minor productions" compared with Burnham's great achievement—his 1909 *Plan of Chicago*. Scott declared the Chicago Plan "the greatest of the City Beautiful plans."[34] It was the first regional plan for the modern metropolitan city. It was comprehensive in outlook; it encompassed a metropolitan region of four thousand square miles. It linked the urban core and the suburbs of Chicago. What Burnham had achieved in the White City he desired to attain and extend in his plan for Chicago. He asserted that "the origin of the plan of Chicago can be traced directly to the Worlds Columbian Exposition. The World's Fair of 1893 was the beginning, in our day and in this country, of the orderly arrangement of extensive public grounds and buildings."[35]

The Chicago Plan was Burnham's last creative public work and his masterwork in city planning. The plan for Chicago was a culmination of Burnham's art, skill, and experience as a city planner. The plan manifested Burnham's love for Chicago and his sense of commitment to civic duty. According to Charles Moore, Burnham found satisfaction in this effort; he regarded the plan as the "supreme effort of his life."[36] In all his engagements in city planning Burnham generously offered his services without compensation.

With his plan, Burnham intended to surmount the pervasive deficiencies that the people of Chicago endured. In stating his objectives Burnham declared that, because Chicago is preeminently a center of industry and traffic, his plan gives attention to

> the betterment of commercial facilities; to methods of transportation for persons and for goods; to removing the obstacles which prevent or obstruct circulation; and to the increase of convenience. It is realized also, that good workmanship requires a large degree of comfort on the part of the workers in their homes and their surroundings, and ample opportunity for that rest and recreation without which all work becomes drudgery. Then, too, the city has a dignity to be maintained, and good order is essential to material advancement.[37]

In his plan, Burnham delineated consolidated systems for freight and passenger railways that would rationalize traffic circulation. He would mitigate traffic congestion in Chicago's urban core with a network of streets, avenues, and boulevards facilitating the circulation of people and traffic in the business district.

A distinctive feature of Burnham's plan was in the grouping of monumental buildings that were "united by a common purpose."[38] He designated inner-city locales as centers of uses, such as civic-governmental, commercial, cultural, and educational.

Burnham was an avid supporter of the contemporary vogue of building urban parks. His plan for Chicago reflected the current "back to nature" sentiment of the late-nineteenth century. The *Plan of Chicago* envisages recreational parks in inner-city neighborhoods and at Chicago's lakefront, large urban landscaped parks, and great forest preserves. The proposed total acreage encircling urban-suburban park area would comprise fifty thousand acres.

The plan embodies two aspects of aesthetics—the beauty of nature and the beauty of architectural design. Burnham believed that urban landscaped parks and wild forest preserves are necessary for the "health and pleasure of the great body of workers." He claimed that city life is physically and mentally debilitating. Human nature, Burnham held, requires the restorative of wild nature to prevent vice and disease and to maintain morals, health, and sanity.[39] Burnham claimed, "When a citizen is made to feel the beauty of nature, when he is lifted up by her to any degree above the usual life of his thought and feelings, the state of which he is a part is benefited thereby."[40]

Burnham assumed that there is not only a human compulsion to commune with nature there is also an equal craving for civic beauty.[41] To give Chicago "dignity" Burnham formulated a comprehensive plan that is aesthetically harmonious. It manifests symmetry, grand vistas, visual order, and organic functionalism. He pictured an inner-city core of uniform, majestic public buildings in the neoclassical mode. Burnham joined the beauty of nature and the beauty of civic art into a total aesthetic environment. He assumed that this would "appeal to the higher emotions of the human mind."[42] He believed that an aesthetic experience would have a beneficial psychological effect.

The notion that the contemplation of nature would enhance moral behavior and cultivate and refine the public taste was widely regarded. The writings of John Ruskin and Ralph Waldo Emerson were influential in expressing this view. It was Frederick Law Olmsted with Calvert Vaux whose landscaped urban parks gave the impetus and rationale to the movement to provide recreative oases of urban beauty for the free use of the public. The landscaped parks were the transitional element in the movement to beautify the urban environment. Olmsted creatively fused art with nature to produce a work of artistic beauty. His purpose was not only sanative; he believed that the parks inspired an aesthetic impulse that acted as an effective vehicle for moral education.

The concept of extending aesthetic education to include architectural art with the landscaped park was realized in the White City of the 1893 world's fair. With the association of Olmsted, Burnham engineered a fusion that resulted in a totally planned aesthetic environment. Olmsted's design along Chicago's lakefront was the setting for the architectural symmetry of the impressive white, neoclassical buildings and the accompanying sculptural effects. The beauty of the White City was an exemplar of what a planned urban environment might be. Advocates of city beautification contended that exposure to an environment of beauty would produce in the public an aesthetic impulse that would have an ennobling effect. In such a milieu the aesthetic drive would encourage a psychological transformation that would redeem the individual from sordidness, specialization, and monotony and would achieve a realization of a full, multifaceted personality—a Neoplatonic conception.

Swedenborgian Doctrines Employed

To understand the iconography of the *Plan of Chicago* one must consider the religious doctrines of Swedenborg and Burnham's adherence to Swedenborg's religious tenets. In his Chicago Plan Burnham prominently employed two doctrines in Swedenborg's system—the doctrine of series and degrees and the doctrine of correspondences. Swedenborg carried over both doctrines from his intensive scientific studies to his later visionary phase.

Swedenborg developed the theory of series and degrees in his attempt to realize a dynamic, universal order in which all things in the universe belong to a series. In each series there are three discrete degrees which are interrelated through correspondence as end, cause, and effect. These three are subordinate and coordinate elements in a progressive chain that extends to God. According to Swedenborg there are three great series in nature—the mineral, the plant, and the animal realms. Each of these three realms of earth corresponds to each of the three heavens revealed to Swedenborg—the natural, the spiritual, and the celestial heavens. Within the three realms and their correspondents are subordinate series that progress from the simplest elements to complex compounds. Swedenborg explained the manner in which the discrete degrees progress to form a composite or series thus: "every muscle in the human body consists of minute fibers [fibrils] and these put together into little bundles form fibers, called motor fibers, and groups of these form the compound called a muscle" (DLW, 190). The same system of discrete degrees holds true, according to Swedenborg, for all the organs and viscera of the body. Swedenborg predicated his universal system in terms of a threefold progression or a "trine."

A second essential element in Swedenborg's scientific and visionary system which figures in Burnham's plan is the doctrine of correspondences. Swedenborg declared that there exists a network of correspondences between the material and spiritual realms. In his scientific work *Animal Kingdom* Swedenborg explains, "In our Doctrine of Representations and Correspondences, we shall treat of both these symbolical and typical representations, and of the astonishing things which occur, I will not say in the living body only, but throughout nature, and which correspond so entirely to supreme and spiritual things, that one would swear that the physical world was purely symbolical of the spiritual world" (AK 451).[43]

In his visionary phase the doctrine of correspondences became a basis for Swedenborg's anagogic analysis of scripture. He perceived an exquisitely precious correspondence of all things in the physical universe with heaven. In Swedenborg's cosmos the visible world of appearances is symbolic of the world of spirit, all of which has a divine origin.

Swedenborg stated that his visits to the divine sphere in heaven and his discussions with the spirits and angels there revealed to him the nature of life after death. Swedenborg gives a vivid description of the spiritual universe in his book, *Heaven and its Wonders, and Hell from Things Heard and Seen.* In Swedenborg's spiritual system the heaven he described is the sphere of being that forms the living core of the material universe; it is the realm of causes whose effects are material phenomena. For Swedenborg the world of nature and the spiritual world form a dynamic unity. The spiritual life, he claimed, is neither merely the future life nor life after death. He held that "every man in respect to his spirit, even while he is living in the body, is in some society with spirits, although he does not know it" (HH 438).

The heavenly region revealed to Swedenborg consists of three great parts—heaven, the world of spirits, and hell. (Because Burnham modeled his Chicago Plan on the divisions of heaven and the world of spirits, I have omitted in this essay the description of hell.) The heavenly region itself, which Swedenborg claimed to have witnessed and where he conversed with angels, is an ordered and hierarchical organism. In its external appearance the spiritual world is altogether like the natural world. It contains all the elements of the three categories of mineral, vegetable, animal. The landscape is varied with mountains, hills, valleys, plains, fields, lakes, and rivers. There are forests, groves of trees, shrubs, gardens, and flowers of every kind. Animals, birds, and fishes abound. And "man there is an angel or spirit" (DLW 321).

It must be immediately realized that Swedenborg was a celestial urbanist. In pursuit of scientific knowledge he traveled extensively. His residences in trade and governmental capitals of Europe, such as Copenhagen, Leipzig, Hanover, Amsterdam, Rome, Paris, and especially London, gave him a strong urban orientation. Like Jean Calvin of Geneva, Swedenborg developed a theological system that recognized the urbanization of European society. Swedenborg's vision of heaven was that of a complex, dynamic city. His heavenly city displays the governmental, economic, social, cultural, and recreational institutions and appurtenances that characterize the great cities of the eighteenth century. The city of heaven is entirely a correspondent, spiritual homology of the earthly city of man. Swedenborg expressed the sophistication of the heavenly city in his citations of the varieties of agencies and activities that he stated he found there. The celestial citizens are engaged in civic ecclesiastical, educational, charitable, domestic, and nutritive affairs and services (HH 388). From his visits to the heavenly city Swedenborg reported that he observed administrative offices, ministries, businesses, courts of justice, colleges, libraries, museums, works of art, auditoriums, gymnasiums, and even stables for horses. He walked through the avenues, streets, and public squares of heaven and entered the sumptuous homes of the married angels (CL 76, 207). He noted that beautiful, landscaped parks were located specifically on the south side of the heavenly municipality and that magnificent palaces dotted the city. The impressive buildings of heaven prompted him to write, "Such is the architecture of heaven that you would say that art there is in its art; and no wonder, because the art is itself from heaven" (HH 185).

Salient to the master plan of heaven, indeed of the cosmos, is the centrality of the essence of the Lord. "He is the common center, the source of all direction and determination . . . both in the heavens and on the earths" (HH 124). The Lord is the spiritual sun of heaven and the source of life. From the east God constantly irradiates heaven by the infinite attributes of divine love—the heat of heaven—and divine truth—the light of heaven. The spiritual sun is the prototype of the corresponding inanimate sun—the source of heat and light of the natural world. Though God appears to the angels as a sun above them, he may, at times, appear in their midst in "an angelic form" (HH 52).

In *Heaven and Hell* Swedenborg described the physical design that was revealed to him in his heavenly visits. Extending outward from the godhead in the east in graded descent are a series of three heavens that reflect the angelic social structure. It should be noted that Swedenborg believed that perfection consisted in the unity of three parts. He writes, "in order that anything may be perfect, there must be a trine in just order, one under another, and a communication between, and that this trine must make a one."[44]

Each of the three heavens are subdivisions of the general plan of heaven. The three heavens are designated respectively as follows—the celestial, the spiritual, and the celestial-spiritual-natural. Each heaven corresponds to the relationship of the heavenly residents to the Lord.

The angels of the third and inmost circuit—the celestial heaven—are the most intimately associated with the godhead. They have manifested in their natural life a continuous love of God. The wisdom of the angels of the third degree far surpasses the wisdom of the angels of the lower two heavens. Their insights into divine truth is "seemingly instinctive or inborn." They are most accessible by influx to the warmth of God's love and the light of his wisdom. With the knowledge gained from his heavenly informants Swedenborg promised that those persons who lived their earthly life in divine love of the Lord would succeed in an elegant spiritual life in the celestial heaven. As angels they will live in a separate heavenly subdivision on what appeared to Swedenborg to be mountains. By virtue of their exclusive, elite status the celestial angels will reside on estates in palaces overlooking grainfields and vineyards (HH 31–33, 189, 270, 489).

The angels of the second degree inhabit the spiritual or intermediate heaven. While the celestial angels seem to perceive divine truths instinctively and think in terms of ends, the spiritual angels use their intelligence to arrive at divine truths rationally. They think in terms of causes. The angels of the second degree are those who have devoted themselves to intellectual pursuits. They are adept in the sciences (DLW 202, 275). The spiritual angels live on hills amidst gardens and landscaped parks. Because the angels of the second degree are skilled in symbolic representation, they will understand that gardens, flower beds, grass plots, and trees correspond to the sciences and knowledge (HH 11, 176, 489).

At the lowest level of the angelic hierarchy are the angels of the first degree, the celestial-spiritual-natural angels. They are gathered in the circuit farthest removed from the godhead. The angels of the first degree represent the effects of having lived a moral life in accordance with the divine will. However, they have lived so from obedience and duty. They have manifested faith based upon belief. To the angels of

this outmost heaven divine truths are somewhat obscure (HH 31–33, 227, 271). These angels dwell in a subdivision that appears, according to Swedenborg's observation, to be in a valley on a stone ledge at the lowest level of heaven. They are content to live in the sector of the city where the angelic population is the most dense. Their apartments are spacious and exquisitely furnished. Where the angels live together "their houses are near each other, arranged one next to the other in the form of a city with avenues, streets, and public squares, exactly like cities on earth." Gardens and lawns surround the dwellings (HH 184, 188).

While curvilinear boulevards mark off the boundaries of each of the heavens, the streets within each heaven are platted in a rectangular pattern. This can be deduced from the following: in a scriptural quotation from Revelation Swedenborg described the holy city of the New Jerusalem as "foursquare"—equal in breadth, height, and length (HH 307). The seer declared that foursquare, or quadrangular, signifies justice (AE 1314). Further, Swedenborg explained that straight streets symbolize doctrinal truths whereas crooked streets signify deviations from truths. Natural man and the spirits who inhabit hell may take the crooked paths, but the perceptive angels find their way unswervingly on the broad, straight boulevards of divine truth (AE 352).

The angelic society that appeared to Swedenborg is paternalistic and rigidly class-stratified. The angels are clothed, fed, and housed gratuitously by the Lord (HH 181, 190, 266). The separation of the angelic classes and subdivisions is fixed by curvilinear boundaries. There is neither inter-heavenly companionship nor communication among the different classes. Neither is there ascending nor descending social mobility. As will be shown presently, the entire heavenly community that Swedenborg envisaged was functionally organic, united by the downward flowing irradiation (i.e., influx) immediately of the Lord and mediately from the higher heaven to the lower (HH 37, 207–9).

In the course of his visitations to the heavenly city Swedenborg observed an adjoining suburb at the perimeter of the heavenly municipality. The suburb is in the nature of a supernal depot for the spirits of deceased men and women. Swedenborg explained that this neighborhood is not purgatory. In the transmutation from mortal life to the spiritual condition that follows death, men and women enter an intermediate state and place. In this condition the conduct and conscience of each spirit's earthly behavior is revealed, assignments to the heavenly city or to hell are determined, and instruction given to those spirits destined to join the company of angels of heaven (HH 421–22, 427–30).

The faubourg of instruction comprises a wide semicircular swath of territory at the border of the heavenly city. This area is spread out from east to west in length and from north to south in breadth (HH 514). At the conclusion of preparatory instruction the Lord leads each spirit who has lived a good life from the outer region to his or her proper angelic circle in one of the three subdivisions in the core of the heavenly city (HH 519, 520).

In his portrayal Swedenborg gave both form and content to the heavenly city and its angelic society. He asserted that the whole heaven "reflects a single man, and is a Divine spiritual man in the largest form, even in figure" (HH 65). The Lord himself, Swedenborg averred, gives human form to the heavenly city. All parts of the master plan of the city of angels are ultimately joined in a universal unit, which the seer labeled the Universal Human (*Maximus Homo* [see Glossary]). In its entire complex the city of heaven is an archetype of the natural world and also corresponds to natural man. The correspondence is "not only with each of the members, organs, and viscera of the body in general," but also in the minutest detail to every element of the body—including the series of fibers, nerves, glands, and blood vessels (HH 63, 418). "The whole heaven is in this image," Swedenborg held, "because God is a Human" (DLW 287).

Swedenborg's use of symbolism is pervasive. For example, each of the three heavens corresponds to parts of the Universal Human. The third and most elite heaven—that of the celestial angels—corresponds to the head; the second or middle heaven corresponds to the bodily area of breast to the knees; the first or lowest heaven forms the feet to the soles. According to Swedenborg's system of correspondences the various parts of the Universal Human are symbols of human thought, feeling, and action. The head represents intelligence and wisdom; the eyes give understanding; the ears analogize obedience; the nostrils provide perception; the organs of generation symbolize marriage love; the kidneys represent the search, reparation, and correction of truth; the liver, pancreas, and spleen purify good and truth.

Within the heavenly city Swedenborg saw a dynamic, interrelated, functioning social order. He ridiculed the belief that heaven is populated by winged angels who spend their time in placid idleness solely in praising God. Such a life, Swedenborg held, "would stupefy all the powers of life; and everyone ought to know that without activity of life there can be no happiness of life (HH 403, 404). The Lord's kingdom, Swedenborg declared, is a kingdom of uses (i.e., vocation or employment). After death and upon admittance to the heavenly city each angel comes into his or her own occupation or service corresponding to the angel's occupation in just the same condition of life as in the worldly existence.

Because heaven is a spiritual counterpart of the mundane world, there is a similar complexity in function and division of labor. To perform the innumerable tasks of society the angels are separated by uses into societies or work groups that coincide with their vocations. Angels of similar interests are grouped together into societies of varying sizes. Some societies consist of a few angels; some larger societies have an aggregate of hundreds of thousands.

In the seer's organicist formulation each of the multitude of angelic societies are bodily parts of the Universal Human. Thus within the Universal Human the bodily organs represent centers of civil governance and administration, business, cultural and scientific study, welfare, recreation, worship, and all the varied activities of the complex heavenly society. Each angel, performing his or her calling within their work groups, is a minute particle contributing to the good of the vast society of the city of heaven. In its dynamics the aggregate reflects the integration of the single will of the Lord. Swedenborg has presented us with a visionary ecology with his intricate doctrine of correspondences.

Swedenborg's use of symbolism and his world view have made him particularly attractive to writers in the field of belles lettres, for example the English poet William Blake,[45] Honoré de Balzac,[46] Charles Baudelaire,[47] August Strindberg,[48] and William Butler Yeats.[49] In the United States Swedenborg's writings had a profound effect upon a number of both secular and religious intellectuals, such as Ralph Waldo Emerson, Henry James, Sr., Helen Keller, recent winner of the Nobel Prize for literature Czeslaw Milosz,[50] poets Edwin Markham and Vachel Lindsay,[51] and Robert Frost.

It also seems that Swedenborgianism resonated among a few of the genitors of the new architecture of the Chicago school. It has already been noted that John Welborn Root, Burnham's partner, entertained Swedenborg's notions. What is not well known is that Louis Sullivan, one of the most renowned of America's architects, incorporated Swedenborgian principles into the ideological structure of his system of architectural ornamentation and in his tall office buildings.[52]

It was left to Daniel Burnham, deeply inbred with the religious ideology of Emanuel Swedenborg, instilled by his evangelizing parents, to carry the seer's vision of heaven into modern city planning with a regional plan for Chicago.

The Master Plan—Blueprint for an Ideal City

Burnham and Bennett developed a master plan that comprised the elements of seventeenth- and eighteenth-century aesthetics. Mathematical symmetry; formal, in-city, model parks; axiality; and balanced diagonal boulevards are prominent components of the plan. Although Burnham made some concessions toward romanticism in his advocacy of regional forest preserves that would fringe Chicago, his design is essentially a manifestation of the baroque style of city planning.

It is possible to trace the linkage of Burnham's propensity for the baroque style from the philosophical method of René Descartes (1596–1650) to Burnham via Emanuel Swedenborg. Descartes declared that universal, immutable laws govern nature. He believed that such laws could be stated in mathematical language. Such a view assumes an ordered universe. The Cartesians maintained that if nature can be perceived as a mathematical construct, art—the mirror of nature—must also be subject to the laws similar to the natural sciences. This aesthetic theory presupposes a harmony between science and art in terms of exact and universal rules that govern a God-given order. This mathematical orientation resulted, architecturally, in the precision and the balanced formalism of neoclassicism.

It is granted that Burnham's observation of the capital cities of Europe influenced his conception of city design. However, of greater significance is the profound religious influence of Swedenborgianism upon Burnham's psyche. Swedenborg was an avowed disciple of Descartes. He also professed an immoderate desire for mathematics.[53] The Cartesian philosophic method is pervasive in Swedenborg's scientific and visionary literature. The Cartesian-Swedenborgian stream of thought conduced to the layered symbolism in the master plan that Burnham and his assistant, Bennett, formulated for Chicago. The plan is first a representation of an ordered universe. But more immediately it is, through the doctrine of correspondence, an earthly symbol of Swedenborg's vision of the organically structured heavenly city. From Bennett's diary entries we are reminded that Burnham delineated the symbolism of municipal powers to spiritual powers and related both of these to the physical arrangement of the core of the city. An examination of the *Plan of Chicago* will reveal that correspondence.

In his plan for Chicago Burnham conceived a comprehensive system of arterials that included the following considerations: efficient circulation of traffic to and from the center of Chicago; relation of all functions to each other; the separation of local residential traffic from throughway traffic; and the pleasurable effect of symmetry, order, and variety. He specified three separate interrelated arterial systems for the core of the city. In doing so Burnham created three vital areas in the core. Each area corresponds in a given order directly to each of the three heavens Swedenborg depicted in *Heaven and Hell.* The outmost of the three street systems forms a perimeter enclosing the two inner street systems. The second system encloses the third and inmost system. The first circuit extends southward from Chicago Avenue along Michigan Avenue to Cermak Road (formerly Twenty-second Street). The route turns westward along Cermak Road to Halsted Street; thence diagonally in a northwesterly direction to the juncture of Ashland Avenue and Roosevelt Road (formerly Twelfth Street). The circuit proceeds north on Ashland Avenue to Union Park (at Ogden Avenue and Randolph Street); runs diagonally from Union Park in a northeasterly direction to the corner of Chicago Avenue and Halsted Street; thence east on Chicago Avenue to Lake Michigan.[54]

The intermediate or second circuit originates at Lake Shore Drive (formerly Lincoln Park Boulevard) and Chicago Avenue. It proceeds westward on Chicago Avenue, thence, at the juncture of Chicago Avenue and Michigan Avenue, southwestward on a diagonal to the meeting of Milwaukee Avenue and Canal Street. The route runs southerly to the intersection of Canal Street and Washington Street and again turns southwestward on a diagonal to the Civic Center Plaza at Halsted and Congress streets. From this point the circuit turns southeastward on a diagonal back to Canal Street where it meets Roosevelt Road (formerly Twelfth Street). The route continues southeastward on a diagonal to Sixteenth Street where it crosses the Chicago River; proceeds in the same direction to the intersection of Archer Avenue, State Street, and Cottage Grove Avenue; extends along Cottage Grove Avenue to Cermak Road. It then follows Cermak Road directly east to Lake Michigan. This circuit, Burnham explained, passes around the business center of the city.[55]

The inmost or third circuit begins at Washington Street and Michigan Avenue. It runs south along Michigan Avenue to Roosevelt Road where it turns west at Roosevelt Road. The route transverses Roosevelt Road to the juncture of Canal Street. At this point the circuit utilizes the diagonals of the intermediate circuit and follows a northwestward path to the Civic Plaza at Halsted and Congress streets. From the Plaza the circuit turns northeastward on the diagonal to the intersection of Canal and Washington streets. The route then proceeds directly east on Washington Street to Lake Michigan.[56]

The three partitions created by the systems of arterials analogize and symbolize the three heavens of the celestial city.

The area contained by Burnham's first and second arterial systems corresponds to the first and, hierarchically and geographically, the lowest of the three heavens of Swedenborg's empyrean. Swedenborg found this heaven the most distantly removed from the godhead, the largest in area, and the most dense in population. The resident angels of this heavenly sector are of the third degree. They manifest neither the transcendence of the celestial angels nor the rationality of the spiritual angels in perceiving divine truths. They are moral by virtue of obligation and belief. When Burnham was preparing his plan, the population center of Chicago lay in the outmost residential area of the city's core. This division lies outside but surrounds the government, business, finance, science, and art centers of Chicago.

The second arterial system forms the intermediate enclave with the third or inmost system. The purpose of the circuit is to divert traffic whose destination is outside the center from having to transverse the city streets. Of precious consideration for Burnham, however, is the inclusion of Grant Park in this middle sector of his master plan. Amid the green

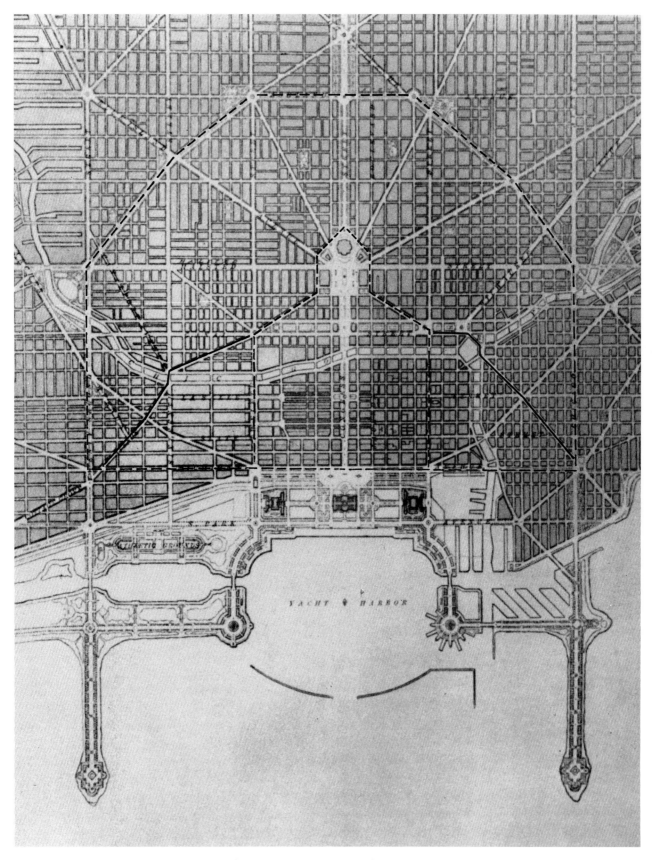

FIG. 233. *City center plan, the Chicago Plan. Burnham's three street systems correspond to the three heavens depicted by Swedenborg in* Heaven and Hell.

FIG. 234. *Burnham's drawing for the proposed Field Museum, 1908*

lawns, parterres, and trees of Grant Park, Burnham planned the development of the "intellectual center of Chicago."[57] In his projection for Grant Park Burnham detailed a threefold grouping of monumental buildings devoted to literature, science, and art.[58] When Burnham prepared his design, the Chicago Art Institute was already established in Grant Park and arrangements for the construction of the Field Museum of Natural History had been consummated. Burnham declared that the Field Museum (designed by D. H. Burnham and Co.) would "gather under one roof the records of civilization culled from every portion of the globe and representing man's struggle through the ages for advancement.[59] With its anthropology, botany, geology, and zoology collection the museum would become a mecca for the curious and the studious. Burnham expected that the construction of the new Crerar Library in Grant Park would attract students in the social, physical, natural, and applied sciences. He wished, too, that the Chicago Public Library would relocate to the park. Grant Park would become, Burnham averred, "a center of letters, similar to the Sorbonne in Paris."[60] Burnham anticipated that Grant Park would become a meeting center for the scientific societies of the West.

The plan for Grant Park did not come to fruition precisely as Burnham had planned; neither the Crerar nor the public libraries relocated to Grant Park. However, with the addi-

tions of the Buckingham Fountain (1927), the Shedd Aquarium (1929), and the Adler Planetarium (1930), Grant Park has become the impressive cultural center that Burnham intended.

Burnham's concern to include Grant Park—a scientific and intellectual center—in his second sector was to realize correspondence with the middle heaven Swedenborg pictured. In *Heaven and Hell* Swedenborg explained that the second heavenly subdivision is the quarters for the spiritual angels—those angels of the second degree dedicated to the sciences and the pursuit of knowledge during their natural and heavenly lives. They arrived at divine truth rationally. They lived in a landscaped gardenlike setting, because floral and sylvan life symbolize science and knowledge (HH 176). Burnham meant to express this symbolism in his representation of Grant Park as a center of knowledge and culture.

The third circuit forms the inmost area of the Chicago Plan. It is the "Heart of Chicago."[61] Burnham gave this sector such a designation because it contained within its precincts the offices of the banking, financial, and corporate elite. He asserted that this section of the city will become increasingly valuable by virtue of its business and commercial uses.[62] The spiritual correspondent of Burnham's inmost "Heart of Chicago" is, according to Swedenborg, the third and ultimate heaven to which the Lord assigns the elite angels. The ce-

FIG. 235. *Field Museum of Natural History, Chicago, 1920*

FIG. 236. *Pentagonal Civic Center Plaza*

lestial angels are the privileged of all the heavenly angels. They are the angels of the third degree. In their love of God and their wisdom they far exceed the angels of the two lower heavens. They are the beneficiaries of the most intimate relationship with God. It is these celestial angels who would be the spiritual archetypes to the business and financial elite of Chicago. Moreover, in his portrayal of his representation of the third heaven, Burnham positioned his representational earthly elite in immediate proximity to the symbolic godhead—the governmental center at the Civic Plaza.

The apex of Burnham's grand design on the east-west axis is the civic center—a pentagonal plaza on which would be erected three groups of buildings. Each of the three groups were to be occupied respectively by the administrative staffs of a level of government—the national, the county, and the city (a state level is not mentioned). In its totality the civic center manifests the authority and legitimacy of political power. Burnham envisioned the city hall as a monumental structure in the classical style with a dome so impressive as to rival "the dome of St. Peter's at Rome."[63] It is "to be seen and felt by the people, to whom it should stand as the symbol of order and unity."[64] The civic center is Burnham's earthly analogue of the celestial godhead. It is symbolic of the divine presence of the Lord.

Burnham designed the civic center to be the "center of gravity . . . of all the radial arteries entering Chicago."[65] He intended the arterial system of circulation to unite the city with the surrounding country. The center is the unifying "keystone" of the Chicago Plan. It is the culminating point at which the system both converges and radiates.[66]

At the Civic Center Plaza Burnham designed a fanlike configuration of ten diverging arterial radials. Four of these thoroughfares radiate on the cardinal points of the compass, six on the ordinal. Burnham declared that the radial arteries are necessary in heavily populated cities with a rectilinear street pattern such as Chicago's. Symbolically the radials are the means of communication to admit the influx of official government decisions from the civic center—the focal point of political power—to all sections of the city. In tracing the correspondence of spiritual powers to municipal powers, evidently Burnham perceived the mayor of Chicago, sitting in the domed, civic cathedral, as the worldly analogue of the heavenly godhead.

Burnham viewed the city as an organism in which the city's vital functions relate to one another to form a unity. He planned to achieve the interrelation in his master plan through his complete plan of street circulation. His proposed arterial system consisted of circuits and radials which he imposed upon an existing rectilinear street pattern. The practical purpose of Burnham's plan of roadways was to relieve traffic congestion and to permit the easy movement of traffic to and from various functional centers. Complementary to his circulatory system is Burnham's advocacy of grouping buildings of common purpose into centers.[67] His system integrated the centers—whether commercial, educational, cultural, recreational, transportive, or governmental—into an organic whole. In delineating the details of his plan Burnham resorted to the organicist model that Swedenborg employed in describing the city of heaven as having the configuration of the Universal Human. In Swedenborg's portrayal each of the innumerable centers of uses or functions corresponds to a bodily organ—all of which are nourished by the blood of the arterial system. Burnham adopted this motif. The city corresponds to the human body whose organs (i.e., centers of use) are sustained through the arterial systems stemming from the "Heart of Chicago."

With the demarcation of the three earthly "heavens" for Chicago's core, Burnham, following Swedenborg's frame of reference, delineated a fourth section that encloses the three core circuits. The boulevard system that Burnham labeled the "grand circuit" encloses a great swath of suburban territory between the outmost of the three core circuits. This area is Burnham's terrestrial correspondent to the fourth heavenly space Swedenborg observed in his visits to the city of heaven. In Swedenborg's spiritual cosmos the area is a suburb surrounding the city of the angels. It is a place where the spirits of the recently dead await judgment concerning their eternal destiny in heaven or hell. It is also a place of instruction and preparation for the spirits who will be angels.

In Burnham's master plan the great circuit begins at Lake Shore Drive at Lake Michigan. The route extends westward to the juncture of Irving Park Road (formerly Graceland Avenue) and Western Avenue. The thoroughfare continues in a grand, sweeping arc to the meeting of Elston Avenue, Addison Street, and Kedzie Avenue. The circuit continues

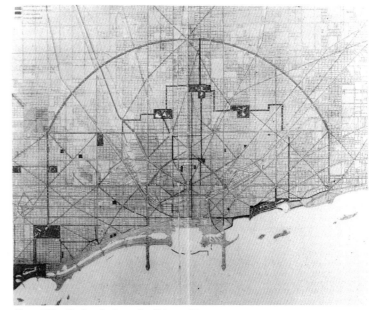

FIG. 237. *Regional plan, the Chicago Plan*

to the southwest, crossing the intersection at Diversey Avenue and Pulaski Road. Then it goes to North Avenue at Cicero Avenue. The boulevard reaches its farthest distance from the "Heart of Chicago" at Congress Street and Laramie Avenue. From this point the arc touches Thirty-first Street at Cicero Avenue and continues in its southeasterly direction to the juncture of Forty-seventh Street, Archer Avenue, and Central Park Avenue. The arc ends at Western Avenue and Garfield Boulevard. The route follows Garfield straightaway in an easterly direction to Michigan Avenue. The course turns to the north on Michigan Avenue and continues to its origin at Irving Park Road. According to Burnham the route covered a distance of nearly thirty miles within the city limits of Chicago.[68]

In Burnham's planning, Swedenborg's theory of series and degrees held a significant place. In the seer's formulation reciprocal phenomenalistic forms ascend in a tripartite progression from simples to compounds. Burnham adapted and incorporated the doctrine throughout his master plan.

In his arterial system Burnham distinguished streets in an ascending order of importance in accordance with the doctrine of series and degrees. His threefold classification included the street for local traffic serving residential neighborhoods, the avenue for express thoroughfare traffic, and the landscaped boulevard or parkway.[69] Burnham identified three types of street patterns—the rectilinear, the circle, and the round point. As with the streets, each of these forms represents a position in an ascending order. Burnham's concern with the motion of traffic is resonant of Swedenborg's attention to the origin and analysis of motion.

Before the visionary period of his life Swedenborg attempted to determine scientifically the form of motion. He developed a theory of forms based upon Cartesian natural philosophy. The theory regarded matter as particulate and motion as vortical. In his visionary writings Swedenborg's doctrine of forms evolved into the doctrine of series and degrees. In the theory, matter possessed three forms—the angular or linear, the circular or spherical, and the spiral or vortical. The angular is the lowest of the natural forms. Angular forms are inert and passive. The circular form is the principal form of motion. The spiral, or gyrational, form is the third stage in an ascending scale, and this third, vortical stage comprises not only active forces but "conatus," or effort (EAK 261–273a [Acton translation]).

Burnham applied this trine of street forms in his system of thoroughfares. The rectangular grid was the original street pattern of the town of Chicago. As the town spread over the surrounding flatlands the gridiron pattern prevailed. Chicago was described by a nineteenth-century observer as "the most right-angle city in the United States."[70] The national government's Ordinance of 1785 mandated division of the new territory into one-mile square sections. This reinforced the use of the gridiron pattern.[71] The fixation of the rectilinear street system, Burnham stated, comported with the line of the Lake Michigan front. It was an orderly arrangement of streets that wasted a minimum of ground space. Besides these practical attributes Burnham noted a behavioral dimension in the grid pattern. He observed that the extended linearity offered vistas that stimulated the aesthetic sense.[72] Finally, Burnham believed in an inherent moral quality in the rectangular system. He declared that "it certainly accords with the ideas of *rightness* inherent in the human mind."[73] In other words there is a conformance with justice in that which is rectangular. The symbolism is consonant with Swedenborg's doctrine of correspondences. In *Apocalypse Explained* Swedenborg assents, "What is quadrangular or foursquare signifies what is just" (AE 1314).

Burnham's second mode—the circle—corresponds to the second stage or degree in the doctrine of degrees. Burnham declared that the ideal form for the city circuits is the continuous curve. He attempted to achieve his ideal in the semicircular parkway of his "grand circuit." The continuous curve expresses "in an ideal manner," Burnham stated, "what is aimed at by all inner circuits" for central Chicago.[74] The constraints of the existing street pattern precluded Burnham from making the three inner circuits circumferential. He chose to attain a resemblance of circularity with diagonals. He claimed that the continuous curve for the inner circuits would fail to develop the necessary articulation with the existing important streets of the rectangular system. Moreover, Burnham said, the cost would be prohibitive.[75] Burnham's concern with circularity in his arterial systems relates to two of Swedenborg's conceptions. First, as the principal form of motion, the circle has relevance to Burnham's regard for the free movement of vehicular traffic. Second, with the heavenly city as his model, Burnham attempted to simulate circular boundaries for each of the city sectors. Swedenborg's angelic heavens were separated by circular perimeters.

The third form that appears in Burnham's plan is the vortical, or gyrational, form of motion. The traffic device that expresses this form is the round point—traffic circle. Burnham used it for traffic control at the intersections of main thoroughfares.[76] He adopted the gyrational, or whirlpool, device to preclude vehicular gridlock at intersectional points. He insisted that the movement of vehicles "similar to that of a whirlpool" would avoid congestions at the juncture of thoroughfares. Each vehicle entering the traffic circle would be required to move around the circumference until it reached its particular street. Burnham regarded each vehicle as a particle in a vortical or "continuous gyratory motion."[77]

There is other evidence besides the street system that Burnham utilized the doctrine of degrees. The most prominent use in this respect is, of course, the tripartition of central Chicago into three earthly "heavens"—each heaven correlative and symbolic of each of the successively superior spiritual heavens. When Burnham addressed the problem of railroad trackage for the transfer and carriage of freight, he proposed a circumferential system of four graduated, interconnecting loops, three of which he located within the city. The fourth loop lay outside the city limits.[78] He favored the construction of three passenger railroad terminals between State Street and the South Branch of the Chicago River at Roosevelt Road. To keep the business center of Chicago convenient to the terminals, Burnham designed a threefold system of streetcar circuits. The circuits are layered in the following manner: the first is an elevated, overhead circuit; the second is a surface streetcar circuit; the third is an underground subway system.[79] At Grant Park he envisioned "three great groups of buildings devoted to the intellectual and aesthetic cravings of man. . . ."[80] The doctrine of the trine appears at the civic center with the provision of separate governmental administrative office buildings for each tier of government—the city of Chicago, Cook County, and the national government. There is no explanation why the state of Illinois would have no public business in Chicago and a place in the civic center.

Burnham has deservedly earned universal praise for his *Plan of Chicago*. However, at least one aspect of his design has puzzled city planners and architectural critics—his advocacy of a uniform cornice height for buildings.[81] Burnham was one of the originators of the Chicago school of architecture. He was among the earliest architects to design the individualistic, soaring skyscraper. So his proposal for uniformity in the height of buildings is an anomaly. Jules Guer-

in's panoramic paintings express Burnham's vision of the new Chicago. The paintings depict a city of buildings whose unvarying height would be in sharp contrast to the existent jagged skyline of Chicago. It was a skyline to which Burnham had contributed his own designs for towering office buildings.

Burnham explained that he sought neither formality nor large-scale uniformity in the design of buildings. He wanted, he said, to achieve an artistic harmony. He undoubtedly envisioned the harmonious, visual unity for Chicago that he had achieved at the World's Columbian Exposition of 1893. He cited the cities of Europe as architectural models for Chicago. There is, however, a hidden agendum in Burnham's desire for architectural symmetry and uniformity of cornice line. That agendum Burnham derived from Swedenborg's doctrine of correspondences.

In *Heaven and Hell* Swedenborg quotes the following from Revelation in the *New Testament*: "I saw a new heaven and a new earth, for the first heaven and the first earth had passed away. . . . And I saw the holy city New Jerusalem coming down from god out of heaven. . . . The city was foursquare . . . the length, the breadth, and the *height of it are equal* (emphasis Fisher's; HH 197, 307). In his anagogic exegesis of this passage Swedenborg prefigured a new earthly heaven, the descent upon the new earth of the holy city of Jerusalem "in all its dimensions," the emergence of a new church, and the revelation of the Lord's heavenly doctrine (HH 197, 307). Correspondingly, Burnham's *Plan of Chicago* would herald the new Chicago—the New Jerusalem—the city whose model is Swedenborg's heavenly city.

Notes

1. Daniel H. Burnham and Edward H. Bennett, *Plan of Chicago*, ed. Charles Moore (New York: Da Capo Press, 1970), p. 4.
2. Ibid., p. 4.
3. Thomas S. Hines, *Burnham of Chicago, Architect and Planner* (New York: Oxford University Press, 1974), pp. xviii–xix.
4. Louis H. Sullivan, *Autobiography of an Idea* (New York: Press of the American Institute of Architects, 1924), pp. 286, 291, 314, 321.
5. Burnham and Bennett, p. 2.
6. Ibid., p. 4.
7. Charles Moore, *Daniel H. Burnham, Architect Planner of Cities* (New York: Da Capo Press, 1968; reprint, 2 vols. in 1, Boston: Houghton Mifflin, 1921) vol. 2, p. 170.
8. Ibid., vol. 2, p. 174.
9. Hines, p. 5.
10. Harriet Monroe, *John Wellborn Root, A Study of His Life and Work* (Boston: Houghton Mifflin, 1896; reprint, Park Forest, Ill.: Prairie School Press, 1966), pp. 41–42.

11. Harold M. Mayer and Richard C. Wade, *Chicago: Growth of a Metropolis* (Chicago: University of Chicago Press, 1969), pp. 109, 117.
12. Frederick Law Olmsted and Calvert Vaux, "Report of the Landscape Architects Superintendents, 1 January 1868," *Annual Reports of the Brooklyn Park Commissioners, 1861–1873.* (January 1873), pp. 181–82.
13. Burnham and Bennett, pp. 21, 32.
14. Mayer and Wade, pp. 122, 144–45.
15. Ibid., pp. 152–54, 160.
16. Ibid., p. 252.
17. Carl W. Condit, *Chicago, 1910–1929: Building, Planning, and Urban Technology* (Chicago: University of Chicago Press, 1973), p. 301.
18. Arthur Meier Schlesinger, *The Rise of the City, 1878–1898* (New York: Macmillan, 1933), p. 65. Mayer and Wade, pp. 176–78.
19. Agnes Sinclair Holbrook, "Map Notes and Comments," in *Hull House Maps and Papers: A Presentation of Nationalities and Wages in a Congested District of Chicago Together with Com-*

ments and Essays on Problems Growing out of the Social Conditions* (New York: Thomas Y. Crowell, 1895; reprint, New York: Arno Press, 1970), pp. 3, 5, 6. See also Bessie Louise Pierce, *The Rise of a Modern City, 1871–1893*, vol. 3 of *A History of Chicago* (Chicago: University of Chicago Press, 1957), pp. 320–23.
20. Condit, pp. 89–90.
21. Julia C. Lathrop, "The Cook County Charities," in *Hull House Maps and Papers*, pp. 143–44.
22. Ibid., pp. 147, 153, 157, 160–61.
23. Pierce, vol. 3, pp. 318, 336, 338–39. Samuel Edwin Sparling, "Municipal History and Present Organization of the City of Chicago," *Bulletin of the University of Wisconsin*, Economics, Political Science, and History Series 2, no. 2, pp. 106–8, 140–42, 158, 164.
24. Sparling, pp. 78, 109–12, 116. Pierce, pp. 347–51.
25. Rudyard Kipling, "How I Struck Chicago and How Chicago Struck Me," in *The Amer-*

ican City: A Sourcebook of Urban Imagery, ed. Anselm L. Strauss (Chicago: Aldine, 1968), p. 41.

26. Moore, vol. 1, p. 34.
27. Moore, vol. 1, p. 50.
28. William D. Howells, *The Altrurian Romances* (Bloomington, Ind.: Indiana University Press, 1968), p. 203.
29. Condit, p. 60.
30. Pierce, vol. 3, pp. 511–12.
31. Howells, pp. 199–202 passim.
32. David F. Burg, Chicago's White City of 1893 (Lexington, Ky.: University Press of Kentucky, 1976), pp. 291–93. Reid Badger, "The Great American Fair," in *The World's Columbian Exposition and American Culture* (Chicago: Nelson Hall, 1979), p. 126.
33. Hines, p. 124.
34. Mel Scott, *American City Planning Since 1890* (Berkeley and Los Angeles: University of California Press, 1969), p. 101.
35. Burnham and Bennett, p. 4.
36. Moore, vol. 2, p. 147.
37. Burnham and Bennett, p. 4.
38. Ibid., p. 80.
39. Ibid., pp. 44–48, 53, 58.
40. Moore, vol. 2, p. 101.
41. Burnham and Bennett, p. 30.
42. Ibid.

43. Quoted in Inge Jonsson, *Emanuel Swedenborg*, trans. Catherine Djurklou (New York: Twayne, 1971), p. 107.
44. Emanuel Swedenborg, *Posthumous Theological Works*, ed. and trans. John Whitehead, 2 vols. (New York: Swedenborg Foundation, 1961), vol. 1, pp. 39–40, n. 17.
45. Jonsson, p. 186.
46. Ibid., pp. 17, 190.
47. Ibid., pp. 190–92.
48. Ibid., pp. 192–94.
49. William Butler Yeats, *The Autobiography of William Butler Yeats* (New York: Macmillan, 1938), pp. 141, 218, 453. See also William Butler Yeats, *If I Were Four-and-Twenty* (Dublin, Ireland: Cuala Press, 1940), pp. 21ff.
50. Czeslaw Milosz, *The Land of Ulro*, trans. Louis Iribarne (New York: Farrar, Strauss and Giroux, 1984), chaps. 26–29 passim.
51. Vachel Lindsay, *Collected Poems*, rev. ed. (New York: Macmillan, 1925), pp. xx–xxiii. Edwin Markham, "Swedenborg," *The New Church Review* (January and April 1925).
52. Narciso G. Menocal, *Architecture as Nature: The Transcendentalist Idea of Louis Sullivan* (Madison, Wis.: University of Wisconsin Press, 1981) pp. 24–34, 62–63.
53. Jonsson, p. 21.
54. Burnham and Bennett, p. 96.

55. Ibid., p. 92.
56. Ibid., p. 96.
57. Ibid., p. 112.
58. Ibid., pl. CXXIV.
59. Ibid., p. 110.
60. Ibid.
61. Ibid., pp. 99, 100.
62. Ibid., p. 99.
63. Ibid., p. 116, pls. CXXX, CXXXI.
64. Ibid., p. 116.
65. Ibid., p. 115.
66. Ibid., p. 117.
67. Ibid., p. 80.
68. Ibid., p. 95.
69. Ibid., p. 82.
70. Quoted in Mayer and Wade, p. 12.
71. Ibid., pp. 16, 21.
72. Burnham and Bennett, p. 90.
73. Ibid., p. 89.
74. Ibid., p. 96.
75. Ibid.
76. Ibid., p. 88.
77. Ibid., p. 89; caption at pl. XCVI.
78. Ibid., p. 66; pl. LXXIII.
79. Ibid., p. 73.
80. Ibid., p. 112.
81. Ibid., p. 86.

Poets with Swedenborgian Connections

Compiled by Alice B. Skinner, Ph.D.

Caring in Action

"TRUE WORSHIP consists of fulfilling uses and therefore in expressing caring in action" (AC 7038).

Lives led in this spirit "minister . . . unto the weal Of *all* his [God's] creatures" (Mary Hume).

SELECTION FROM *NORMITON*

WE but hold in trust,
God-given, all good gifts of heart and mind,
No less than more external blessings lent
To minister therewith unto the weal
Of *all* his creatures; and, as faithful stewards,
Must seek to turn them to the best account—
Perfect them to the utmost; must join hands
With those who in our efforts best may aid,
Helping us to be better than we are,
That so we may the better worship God
In serving man. If for the sake of *one*
(Ah! subtle plea,—say rather for our own!)
We peril our possession of the gifts
Entrusted to us, risk our powers of use,
Out spirit's peace and health, Heaven's choicest boons,
We are unfaithful stewards, and justly then
May be deemd selfish: and should surely miss
Ev'n that we aimed at.

MARY CATHERINE HUME[1]

The essence of worship, as Swedenborg sees it, is a daily life in which personal talents are dedicated to practical purposes. This orientation of the spirit leads to a focus on usefulness and a life tinged with joy.

Some people believe that it is hard to live the life that leads to heaven, which is called a spiritual life, because they have heard that you have to renounce the world and give up the desires people associate with the body and the flesh, and "live spiritually." All they understand by this is rejecting worldly concerns (especially concerns with money and prestige) and going around in constant devout meditation about God, salvation, and eternal life, spending one's life in prayer and in reading the Word and devotional books. . . . But people who renounce the world and live by the spirit in this way acquire a mournful life, one that is not receptive of heavenly joy. . . . Rather, in order to be receptive of heaven's life, we should by all means live in the world and be involved in its duties and business. In this way, through a moral and civic life we accept a spiritual life. There is no other way spiritual life can take shape in us, no other way our spirits can be prepared for heaven. (HH 528)

Some Swedenborgian poets, such as Edwin Markham, write about people whose lives illustrate caring in action, such as Abraham Lincoln "Pouring his splendid strength through every blow."

LINCOLN, THE MAN OF THE PEOPLE

WHEN the Norn Mother saw the Whirlwind Hour
Greatening and darkening as it hurried on,
She left the Heaven of Heroes and came down
To make a man to meet the mortal need.
She took the tired clay of the common road—
Clay warm yet with the genial heat of earth,
Dasht through it all a strain of prophecy;
Tempered the heap with thrill of human tears;
Then mixt a laughter with the serious stuff.

Into the shape she breathed a flame to light
That tender, tragic, ever-changing face;
And laid on him a sense of the Mystic Powers,
Moving—all husht—behind the mortal veil.
Here was a man to hold against the world,
A man to match the mountains and the sea.

The color of the ground was in him, the red earth;
The smack and tang of elemental things:
The rectitude and patience of the cliff;
The good-will of the rain that loves all leaves;
The friendly welcome of the wayside well;
The courage of the bird that dares the sea;
The gladness of the wind that shakes the corn;
The pity of the snow that hides all scars;
The secrecy of streams that make their way
Under the mountain to the rifted rock;
The tolerance and equity of light
That gives as freely to the shrinking flower
As to the great oak flaring to the wind—
To the grave's low hill as to the Matterhorn
That shoulders out the sky. Sprung from the West,
He drank the valorous youth of a new world.
The strength of virgin forests braced his mind,
The hush of spacious prairies stilled his soul.
His words were oaks in acorns; and his thoughts
Were roots that firmly gript the granite truth.

Up from log cabin to the Capitol,
One fire was on his spirit, one resolve—
To send the keen ax to the root of wrong,
Clearing a free way for the feet of God,
The eyes of conscience testing every stroke,
To make his deed the measure of a man.
He built the rail-pile as he built the State,
Pouring his splendid strength through every blow:
The grip that swung the ax in Illinois
Was on the pen that set a people free.

So came the Captain with the mighty heart.
And when the judgment thunders split the house,
Wrenching the rafters from their ancient rest,
He held the ridgepole up, and spiked again
The rafters of the Home. He held his place—
Held the long purpose like a growing tree—
Held on through blame and faltered not at praise.
And when he fell in whirlwind, he went down
As when a lordly cedar, green with boughs,
Goes down with a great shout upon the hills,
And leaves a lonesome place against the sky.

EDWIN MARKHAM[2]

People dedicated to the use of their unique talents sometimes lead singular lives expressive of their own "inner
drummers." Vachel Lindsay celebrates Johnny Appleseed, a Swedenborgian missionary, as such a dedicated
man.

THE APPLE-BARREL OF JOHNNY APPLESEED

ON the mountain peak, called 'Going-To-The-Sun,'
I saw gray Johnny Appleseed at prayer
Just as the sunset made the old earth fair.
Then darkness came; in an instant, like great smoke,
The sun fell down as though its great hoops broke
And dark rich apples, poured from the dim flame
Where the sun set, came rolling toward the peak,
A storm of fruit, a mighty cider-reek,
The perfume of the orchards of the world,
From apple-shadows: red and russet domes
That turned to clouds of glory and strange homes
Above the mountain tops for cloud-born souls:—
Reproofs for men who build the world like moles,
Models for men, if they would build the world
As Johnny Appleseed would have it done—
Praying, and reading the books of Swedenborg
On the mountain top called 'Going-To-The-Sun.'

VACHEL LINDSAY[3]

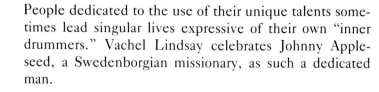

A life of personal usefulness is oriented toward others,
toward the "neighbor": ". . . the neighbor is not just the
individual person, but also people in the collective sense.
It is the community, smaller or larger, it is the nation, it
is the church; it is the Lord's kingdom, and above all it
is the Lord" (NJHD 91). The personal contribution involves cooperation and can be seen as "a grain of sand /
To enlarge the sum of human action used / For carrying
out God's end" (E. B. Browning). The work of cooperation on behalf of the community extends beyond its founders, requiring generations of "Lincoln-hearted" people
(Vachel Lindsay).

SELECTION FROM AURORA LEIGH

". . . BE sure, no earnest work
Of any honest creature, howbeit weak,
Imperfect, ill-adapted, fails so much,
It is not gathered as a grain of sand
To enlarge the sum of human action used
For carrying out God's end. No creature works

So ill, observe, that therefore he's cashiered.
The honest, earnest man must stand and work.
The woman also,—otherwise she drops
At once below the dignity of man,
Accepting serfdom. Free men freely work.
Whoever fears God, fears to sit at ease."

He cried, "True. After Adam, work was curse;
The natural creature labours, sweats, and frets.
But, after Christ, work turns to privilege,
And henceforth, one with our humanity,
The Six-day Worker working still in us,
Has called us freely to work on with Him
In high companionship. So, happiest!
I count that Heaven itself is only work
To a surer issue. Let us work, indeed,
But no more work as Adam,—nor as Leigh
Erewhile, as if the only man on earth,
Responsible for all the thistles blown
And tigers couchant, struggling in amaze
Against disease and winter, snarling on
Forever, that the world's not paradise.
Oh, cousin, let us be content, in work,
To do the thing we can, and not presume
To fret because it's little! 'T will employ
Seven men, they say, to make a perfect pin;
Who makes the head, content to miss the point;
Who makes the point, agreed to leave the join:
And if a man should cry, 'I want a pin,
And I must make it straightway, head and point',
His wisdom is not worth the pin he wants.
Seven men to a pin,—and not a man too much!
Seven generations, haply, to this world,
To right it visibly a finger's breadth,
And mend its rents a little. . . ."

ELIZABETH BARRETT BROWNING[4]

ON THE BUILDING OF SPRINGFIELD

LET not our town be large, remembering
That little Athens was the Muses' home,
That Oxford rules the heart of London still,
That Florence gave the Renaissance to Rome.

Record it for the grandson of your son—
A city is not builded in a day:
Our little town cannot complete her soul
Till countless generations pass away.

Now let each child be joined as to a church
To her perpetual hopes, each man ordained:

Let every street be made a reverent aisle
Where Music grows and Beauty is unchained.

Let Science and Machinery and Trade
Be slaves of her, and make her all in all,
Building against our blatant, restless time
An unseen, skilful, medieval wall.

Let every citizen be rich toward God,
Let Christ the beggar, teach divinity.
Let no man rule who holds his money dear.
Let this, our city, be our luxury.

We should build parks that students from afar
Would choose to starve in, rather than go home,
Fair little squares, with Phidian ornament,
Food for the spirit, milk and honeycomb.

Songs shall be sung by us in that good day,
Songs we have written, blood within the rhyme,
Beating as when Old England still was glad,—
The purple, rich Elizabethan time.

• • •

Say, is my prophecy too fair and far?
I only know, unless her faith be high,
The soul of this, our Nineveh, is doomed,
Our little Babylon will surely die.

Some city on the breast of Illinois
No wiser and no better at the start
By faith shall rise redeemed, by faith shall rise
Bearing the western glory in her heart.

The genius of the Maple, Elm and Oak,
The secret hidden in each grain of corn,
The glory that the prairie angels sing
At night when sons of Life and Love are born,

Born but to struggle, squalid and alone,
Broken and wandering in their early years.
When will they make our dusty streets their goal,
Within our attics hide their sacred tears?

When will they start our vulgar blood athrill
With living language, words that set us free?
When will they make a path of beauty clear
Between our riches and our liberty?

We must have many Lincoln-hearted men.
A city is not builded in a day.
And they must do their work, and come and go,
While countless generations pass away.

VACHEL LINDSAY[5]

Connections of the Poets with Swedenborg

(See earlier sections for information on Markham, Lindsay, and E. B. Browning.)

MARY CATHERINE HUME (1824–1885) studied Swedenborg's writings with Charles Augustus Tulk, a friend of her father and one of the founders of the New Church in England. She wrote poetry and pamphlets that reflected her Swedenborgian convictions.

Source

Hume, Mary Catherine. *A Brief Sketch of the Life, Character, and Religious Opinions of Charles Augustus Tulk* (with a short introductory chapter or historical outline of the author's life by Charles Pooley), 2nd ed. (London: James Spiers, 1890).

Notes for the Poems

1. Mary C. Hume, selection from *Normiton: A Dramatic Poem in Two Parts. With Other Miscellaneous Pieces* (London: John W. Parker and Son, 1857).
2. Edwin Markham, "Lincoln, the Man of the People," in *Modern American Poetry*, 6th rev. ed., ed. Louis Untermeyer (New York: Harcourt Brace, 1942), pp. 112–13.
3. Vachel Lindsay, "The Apple Barrel of Johnny Appleseed," in *Going to the Sun*, ed. F. O. Matthiessen (New York: E. P. Dutton, Hawthorne, 1923).
4. Elizabeth Barrett Browning, selection from "Aurora Leigh," in *Poetical Works* (New York: Dodd, Mead, 1899), vol. 5, pp. 338–39.
5. Vachel Lindsay, "On the Building of Springfield," in *The Winged Horse Anthology*, ed. Joseph Auslander and Frank Ernest Hill (Garden City, N.Y.: Doubleday, Doran, 1943), pp. 616–17.

III
The Man
&
His World

I have often experienced being withheld and so to speak borne upward—that is, toward more inward things—and thereby into the company of the good, and thus withheld from evil spirits. I have perceived and sensed that given a little leave, the evil spirits would flood [me] with their persuasive false and evil principles. I have also perceived and sensed that they did rush in to the extent that leave was given. 1749 9 Mar. Thurs. (SD 4165)

Swedenborg's Sweden

Robert H. Kirven, Ph.D.

FIG. 238. Violin Player, *by Pehr Hilleström, 1700s*

For biographical information, see Kirven's and Larsen's pictorial biography of Emanuel Swedenborg, earlier in this book.

FIG. 239. *Storage building at Julita Gård*

FIG. 240. *Wall painting in the farmhouse at Julita Gård*

IN EMANUEL SWEDENBORG'S TIME, in Sweden as in Europe and even colonial America, the activities of a typical day were not in themselves different from our modern routines: people dressed, ate, kept house or went to work, shopped, socialized with a few friends, or attended public functions. But the details of such activities differed considerably, mostly in ways that took more time and more effort and restricted an individual's possibilities.

But, though most of us would find it harder to live under those conditions than our own, it would be a mistake to feel sorry for Swedenborg or his compatriots. They lived life as they found it, as it had been lived for centuries before them, and as it was for almost two centuries after them. Indeed, homes without plumbing, electricity, or telephones, where life differed little from life in Swedenborg's time, were not uncommon at the end of the first quarter of this century in America. Among the rural poor, and in remote regions, many features of such a way of life continue today. In eighteenth-century Sweden, few people imagined anything easier, and most lived productive and rewarding lives in conditions that might seem difficult to us.

Julita Gård is an entire farmstead that was removed from Dalarna in central Sweden to the Skansen outdoor museum in Djurgården, Stockholm. The interior of the log farmhouse displays wall paintings characteristic of the region, revealing a colorful and pleasant way of life. Also typical of Dalarna are the distinctively shaped storage buildings with canti-levered upper story. Swedenborg's ancestral home, Sveden, or Svedens Gård, was near Falun in Dalarna. The main room of the guesthouse can still be seen, with its painted walls and fine furnishings representative of a genteel country life. The murals, unlike the more usual decorative work at Julita Gård, depict biblical scenes.

Candles and oil lamps were both less convenient and less effective than electric lights, so activities were regulated more strictly by sunrise and sunset than they are today. During summers in Stockholm, work and social commerce began before four o'clock in the morning and lasted until late, but in the winter the active day was much shorter.

Fireplaces and wood stoves afforded less comfort than modern central heating, so most people lived in smaller rooms. Swedenborg built himself a summerhouse, in order to have a more spacious and comfortable place to work when freed from the constraints of winter heating.

Travel between houses was less common at night than it is for us, particularly in the winter, when such travel was seriously life-threatening in rural areas. Even in Stockholm, people are known to have frozen to death walking from house to house at night. Large landholders, aristocrats, and others who could afford, like royalty, not to walk, traveled in coaches like the one preserved at the old bishop's residence of Brunnsbo-Kungsgård—a coach known to have been used by Swedenborg's father, Bishop Jesper Swedberg.

FIG. 241. *Bishop's coach at Brunnsbo-Kungsgård*

FIG. 242. *Midsummer pole at Svedens Gård*

Most pictures from the period show summertime activities, suggesting that in winter everything that could be postponed, including painting, was put off until the climate grew more hospitable.

Midsummer's Eve was celebrated at the Monk's Bridge (Munkbron) in Stockholm, and throughout Sweden. There was a midsummer pole in the square, with dancing, entertainment for children, and a midsummer market where birch branches were sold for decorating houses. At Sveden, in

Swedenborg's time and today, young girls on white horses ride around the colorful midsummer pole on June 21, one of the most festive nights of the year.

Sveden's midsummer pole was placed on the lawn between the guest cottage and the barn. Perhaps the farm's oldest surviving structure, the barn was built with bricks of fired clay from the Stora Kopparberg pit at Falun, and shows the slightly iridescent blue-green and "Falun red" color of Kopparberg brick.

FIG. 243. Midsummer Eve at Munkbron in Stockholm, *by Elias Martin, 1700s*

FIG. 244. *View of farm at Julita Gård*

The majority of Sweden's population lived outside of Stockholm and the other cities. Seventy-five percent of the people were farmers, and the 8.5 percent involved in production were divided between city craftsmen and the many laborers in Sweden's copper and iron mines.

To judge from the restorations and authentic recreations of farmsteads in the Skansen historical park, many Dalarna farm homes were substantial enough to house large extended families in a fair degree of comfort; most, however, in Dalarna and other parts of Sweden were small and rustic.

The home of a mine master in the Swedish mining country shows that, whether mineowners or owners' agents, the masters were the aristocracy of the region. By contrast to the masters' estates, the houses of the miners ranged from simple to primitive. Swedenborg later expressed concern over the living conditions of the miners, describing some of their homes as hovels.

The details of life in all of these settings, however, were primitive compared to modern living. In country houses, homemakers went outdoors in good weather and bad to wells

FIG. 245. *Eighteenth-century mine manager's house and grounds*

FIG. 246. *Eighteenth-century miner's cottage*

FIG. 247. Stockholm from Kungsholmen, *by Elias Martin, 1700s*

for their water. In the city, water was delivered daily in carts filled from public waterways, which were shared by the horse that pulled the watercart and, from time to time nearby, other flotsam.

In the finest of homes, food was prepared with few of the conveniences of a modern kitchen; and even where a mangle was available to iron the sheets, its operation demanded a lot of muscle (presumably, the maid seldom received the assistance of a man in fancy dress—in this case, Carl Bellman, an entertainer from the royal court).

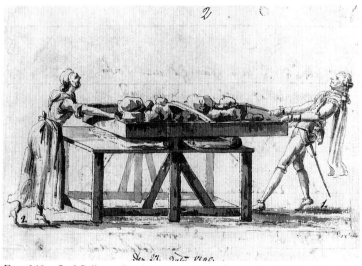

FIG. 248. *Carl Bellman drawing a mangle, by Johann Gottlob Bruselle, 1700s*

FIG. 249. Grinding Coffee, *by Pehr Hilleström, 1778*

Much further down the scale of convenience, sailors from a ship at anchor in the harbor—where on-board fires were forbidden—prepared meals on open fires at the water's edge.

Many aspects of daily life in the workplace, too, differed little from today. The carpenter's plane, and the grindstone where he sharpened its blade, were essentially the same as those in a modern shop, or those of a Roman carpenter at the time of Christ. The scythe, the rake, and the split-rail fence in a common farmyard also resembled their counterparts in many rural areas of the world today.

In the deep Swedish forests, woodsmen felled trees with axes that, although homemade at that time, were basically identical to the hand tools of a modern woodsman. They dragged their logs as logs have been hauled out of woods ever since—although more often now by tractors or logskidders—to rivers like the Dalälven, which then provided the only means of long-distance transit of timber, as they still provide the cheapest in many parts of the world.

Sweden's biggest industry in Swedenborg's time was mining, the area of his government service. In the early part of his career, copper was the country's richest export, much of

FIG. 251. Carpenter in His Workshop, *by Pehr Hilleström, 1700s*

FIG. 250. Sailors, *by Elias Martin, 1700s*

FIG. 252. Harvest, *by Pehr Hilleström, 1778*

it coming from the great mines of Falun. Open pit mines of the day were hand dug, offering more spectacular, and more dangerous, scenes than modern open pits scraped level by earth-moving machinery. Underground mines were shored up by structures that have remained unchanged to the present day, but included arduous and life-threatening features that have been replaced in modern mining. Workmen, and engineers like Swedenborg, descended to the ore by way of perilous structures that have now been replaced by safer elevators, and they performed in the mine many jobs that since have been moved outside. Cave-ins—miners' greatest fear in the eighteenth century as today—trapped workmen at Falun and other mines, as depleted ore led them farther and farther into the earth.

As copper mines neared depletion, iron moved to the first place among Sweden's mineral exports during Swedenborg's period of service with the Board of Mines. Rods and bars were moved by river barges from smelters and mills near the mines to the port at Stockholm, where they were weighed and taxed before being loaded onto ships for Europe.

FIG. 253. Open Pit Mine, *by C. G. Gillberg, early 1800s*

FIG. 255. Iron Weigh-house, *by Elias Martin, 1700s*

FIG. 254. *Miners at work in the Falun copper mine, by Pehr Hilleström, 1781*

FIG. 256. *Olof Rudbeck and his musical family, 1680s*

In Swedenborg's day, as now, music was very much a part of Swedish life at all levels of society, both in public and private gatherings. Among the privileged, entertainment featured the harpsichord—fairly new on the musical scene—as well as the older woodwinds and strings. Many people formed their own choral groups or came together to sing, as did the family of Olof Rudbeck, one of Swedenborg's teachers at Uppsala.

In both upper and lower classes, people also gathered for quiet games of cards, for dancing on festive occasions, and in taverns for drinking.

Much of the day-to-day social life centered around the marketplace, such as the one near Munkbron (shown earlier), and in the streets, where people met as they walked to their various activities.

Festive occasions drew large crowds to such events as this one in the Djurgården—the unveiling of a statue of the poet and entertainer Carl Bellman—or to political events.

FIG. 257. *Musical group in eighteenth-century salon, by Pehr Hilleström, 1776*

FIG. 258. Cardgame at State Secretary Schröderheim's Home, *by Pehr Hilleström, ca. 1782*

FIG. 259. *Ball at Gröna Lund amusement park*

FIG. 260. *Celebration at unveiling of monument to Carl Bellman*

The great Drottningholm Castle, home of Swedish royalty during Swedenborg's time, was the scene of the biggest parties and the most prestigious theatrical events. The castle contained an ornate theater, which was the special pride of Gustav III, prince regent during much of Swedenborg's adult life. Swedenborg was a great lover of the theater, but it is not known whether he attended performances at Drottningholm.

Gustav's reign, which began two years before Swedenborg's death, ended with his assassination in that theater. The engraving of his death scene shows well the dress of men and women of the court, gathered for what was to have been a festive occasion.

FIG. 261. *Drottningholm Theater, one of the oldest preserved theaters in Europe*

FIG. 262. *Assassination of Gustav III*

Swedenborg and Uppsala

Gunnar Broberg, Ph.D.

Translated by Gunilla Stenman Gado

UPPSALA OCCUPIES A CENTRAL PLACE in the multifaceted life of Emanuel Swedenborg. Among Swedish locales, only Skara, Falun, and Stockholm are comparable to it; among foreign cities, only London. It could scarcely be otherwise. Uppsala was and is the home of Sweden's oldest university, and it is from the same city that the Swedish church is governed. Jesper Swedberg was active as professor of theology in Uppsala from 1692 to his appointment as bishop of Skara in 1703. In order to acquire the necessary academic education, his son remained in Uppsala under the protection of Erik Benzelius, his brother-in-law. As Benzelius's protégé, Swedenborg was to be introduced not only to humanistic disciplines but also to the new natural science. Even after he left the university, he maintained these ties. During his travel abroad in 1710–14, Swedenborg acted as a liaison between the scientists on the Continent and the scholars in Uppsala, and he entertained the hope of gaining a seat at his old university.

Superficially, Uppsala at this time was by no means an especially remarkable place. In addition to a population of six hundred to eight hundred students, perhaps about four thousand to five thousand inhabitants lived in the city. The houses spread along the ground and were mostly wooden, making them vulnerable at any moment to the threat of fire. A few elegantly built stone buildings surrounded the Main Square. Over everything towered the thirteenth-century cathedral, its spires seeming to rise still higher because of the flatness of the land that stretched outward from the city. Beside it was the low "Peasant Church" designated for the city's humble population (which also included the students). Up on the ridge there was the castle, an imposing but never

completed construction from the middle of the sixteenth century. Among the academic buildings, Academia Gustaviana—which housed the university library and lecture rooms as well as the exercise hall for physical development—deserves special mention. The city had two centers: one, for the burgeoisie, at the Main Square; the other, for the university and the church, around the cathedral. The river Fyris—broad and fast-running in the spring but no more than a sewage ditch in the summer—could be said to divide the city into two halves, one bourgeois and the other academic, which mostly produced screech and clatter when they came together. Life in the city was gazed down upon by the castle, the seat of worldly power, which on important occasions was visited by members of the royal family and otherwise served as the year-round residence of the governor. If ever the basic division of society into four estates, so fundamental in Swedish history—nobility, clergy, burghers, and peasants—was made manifest through the plan of a city, it was in Uppsala. The peasants lived on the fertile clay plain that surrounded the city and they visited the "*Disting*," a market with roots in the heathen era. The city was rich in history, but it was also fraught with social tensions evident every day. Last but not least, Uppsala was also a center of intellectual force, a living cultural environment seemingly far removed from wars on land or sea.

The streets around the cathedral run crisscross and uphill. There, poor students and the sons of the wealthy bumped shoulders with venerable professors. To the traditional role of the university as a school for clergy, the nobility added, in the seventeenth century, their demand for a secular ed-

GUNNAR BROBERG was born in 1942 and received his Ph.D. from Uppsala University in 1976. He has taught and carried out research both in Lund, Sweden, and in Berkeley, California. Currently he is an associate professor at Uppsala University. Broberg's published works include *Homo sapiens L. Studier i Carl von Linnés naturuppfattning och människolára* (*Homo sapiens L: Studies of Carolus Linnaeus's Concept of Nature and Anthropology*) (1975) and a commentary of Olof Rudbeck the younger's *Book of Birds* (1986). He is editor of the *Annual of the Swedish Linnaeus Society* and the *Annals of the Royal Academy of Arts and Sciences of Uppsala*. He is preparing a comprehensive textbook on the Swedish history of ideas, which is due to appear in the near future. Among his current research projects is the history of eugenics in Scandinavia.

ucation that would be useful on the Continent in connection with the country's political affairs. Academia Gustaviana had been built on a grander scale for the sake of the young noblemen, and an exercise hall was designed for their riding and fencing training. Rhetoric and politics were to be taught by prominent imported scholars. In the streets, one heard greetings and observed encounters conducted according to a strict protocol based on rank.

Someone sweeps by in an especially magisterial manner. It is Olof Rudbeck, the strong man of the university since the middle of the century, a universal genius who had gained an international reputation with his discovery of the lymphatic system. His colleague on the faculty of medicine, Lars Roberg, has assumed the mantle of academic eccentric. He is badly dressed, without a wig even, but each man is brilliant in his own way in his field. The hustle and bustle is striking, particularly because the end of the spring semester is nearing. It is at this time that the disputations [the defense of doctoral theses] take place—exercises that offer quite some drama for the initiated. This is the culmination of academic life, the goal and meaning of all the studies. The conferring of degrees, elevating the recipient to the rank of master or doctor, takes place on formal occasions when the learned scholar rises to Parnassus.

Uppsala University, founded in 1477 and thereby the oldest university in the north, was thus not just any seat of learning. There were four other universities within the Swedish empire: in Åbo, Greifswald, Dorpat, and Lund—the latter two having been created as part of a campaign to make newly won territories Swedish. In itself, this fact indicates that higher education, far from being just schooling exclusively for clergymen, also had a secular aim. At the same time, it must also be emphasized that the university had the character of an independent corporation in society, a heritage from the Middle Ages that had diminished over the years. However, the university had its own board of directors, with the Rector Magnificus as president of the consistory, the collective body of academic teachers (the duty rotated among the professors each semester). The duty of the consistory was to govern the academy as well as to pass judgment on delinquent students, either sentencing them to punishment by the academy's own police or—in the case of more serious crimes—forwarding them to the city authorities. The records of the consistory proceedings from this time are wonderfully informative documents regarding the morality—or, rather, mostly the immorality—of the time. The sentences may often seem harsh, but it is still clear that the academic fathers supported their students. The deans for the four faculties (in theology, law, medicine, and philosophy) acted as *censores* [overseers of the examinations] for the multitude of dissertations that were produced continuously. Difficult cases were brought to the consistory, which demanded corrections or

proscription. With its own government and jail, the university had the aspect of a complete society.

In this society, the chancellor represented secular power; always one of the most prominent men in the country, he had the responsibility to see to it that scholarly discussions did not develop into quarrels. Equally important was the fact that the treasurer, fiscally responsible for the university, also was appointed by the king. The prochancellor—that is, the archbishop—was constantly present and constituted the tie with the church. It is noteworthy that the employees of the university were considered part of the clerical estate as long as Sweden remained a society of four estates—that is, up to 1866.

It would be wrong, however, to regard the secular and ecclesiastical powers as pitted against each other as enemies; that is not how they were viewed. The Swedish church was and still is a state church. Nevertheless, from a historical perspective, frictions can be discerned. How typical seem the events around the great celebration of the Uppsala Concord (1593), when Jesper Swedberg was Rector Magnificus, and the king, Karl XI, visited the academy with his entire court. In his autobiography, Swedberg proudly describes his role in the festivities, how he expatiated on the proper qualities of a scholar: to be learned and willing to learn; to live right and be prepared for suffering. Learn, Live, Suffer [*Lära, Leva, Lida* in Swedish] are the three "L's" an academic should strive for. The last L means that he is to "raise his voice like a trumpet" when so required.[1] Having said this, Swedberg goes on to express his outrage at the students who, at a disputation before the king, discussed whether the king's power is conferred by the grace of God or created by man—in other words, they were dealing with very current problems concerning natural rights. First, the question was not to be discussed, because the Bible stated that all authority derives from God, and second, such talk before such an audience was impudent.

Jesper Swedberg was inspector of Västmanland-Dala Nation, a position to which he succeeded after it had been occupied by none other than Olof Rudbeck. The system of student "nations" needs explaining. Their international background can be traced to the medieval student organizations; in Paris, for example, the Scandinavian students were said to belong to the "Dacian nation." The Swedish academic nations, to which students with a common geographic origin belonged, were founded some decades after the reestablishment of Uppsala University at the beginning of the seventeenth century. Poor students far from home thus found a second home. But the nations were also a tool for the university to hold wild spirits in check. To this end was established the office of inspector, a position that was to be held by a professor from the same region. The appointment has long been sought after as a position of honor in Uppsala. By the middle of the century, the nation system had become formally established and had become an indispensable part of student life. During this early period, they led a peripatetic existence; they met in rented cellars or at the home of the inspector. The senior members of the nation were to take care of the younger ones; the younger ones were to assist the seniors. Fagging existed, but it was prohibited by a royal decree of 1691. The youngest students were called *recentiores*; thereafter followed juniors and seniors; thus the nation—as well as the university—reflected the class distinctions in society. At their meetings, the students practiced the art of formal disputing with preses, respondents, and opponents. Jesper Swedberg was an energetic promoter of this type of scholarly exercise.

Västmanland-Dala Nation was one of the large nations. A bill, preserved from a party in 1689, reveals the consumption of great quantities of Rhine wine and beer, as well as the procurement of two hundred lemons, imported from somewhere, plenty of tobacco, seven dozen clay pipes, walnuts, salmon, roast meat, butter, and bread. The bill also specifies roses on the table, borrowed portraits to decorate the walls, and honoraria for shawm players. Expenses also mounted because of all the things that were broken—some 130 beer glasses, for example. The students' partying and the subsequent disorder in the dark of the night remained a problem for the university, but this type of concentrated excess disappeared toward the turn of the century when political tensions prevailed. Furthermore, society was undergoing the great civilization process that made proper citizens out of a people who previously were barbarians. Jesper Swedberg, who held his nation in firm hands, was very popular. The earliest preserved bylaws for the nation date back to his time; they were signed by him and 166 other members of the nation, one of whom was his son Emanuel.

Classic and Christian ideas were indissolubly joined in the education offered at the university. Lutheran doctrine was explained with the help of Aristotelian logic; moral philosophy and politics were taught as much through reading of the classic writers as through the Gospels. But even though, at first glance, everything might seem stable and fully established, several shifts had taken place during the seventeenth century. Actually, the university had gone through one of the most heartrending academic disputes in its history—the Cartesian battles that took place toward the end of the century. Other life-and-death issues concerned the soundness of Rudbeck's theories, and, further, the question of the principles of worldly power or of "natural rights"—which Swedberg had regarded as such a sensitive subject. Religious orthodoxy was at the height of its power, but it knew where the enemy was. The new English experimental philosophy posed the major challenge. This was imported through the students' travels abroad, necessary for gaining

FIG. 263. *Olof Rudbeck (1630-1702), frontispiece from* Atlantica, *1675*

higher learning and language proficiency, but also exposing impressionable young minds to dangerous notions. Thus Cartesian philosophy was brought home from France and Holland.

The absolute resistance Cartesianism encountered in some places is explained by the fact that "tolerance" was not a positive concept for the orthodox [see Lenhammar's essay "Toleration and Doctrinal Unity," elsewhere in this anthology]. Multiplicity meant weakness; oneness, strength—this also in accordance with the demands of the political autocracy. Students of medicine had brought Cartesian philosophy to Uppsala in the mid-1660s, when the first heated discussions were conducted. Among others, Rudbeck was the driving force in the camp. Twenty years later, the second Cartesian battle erupted, this time led by Petrus Hoffwenius in medicine and Johan Bilberg, professor of philosophy. The opponents argued for proscription in long memoranda and were also successful in blocking a dissertation by Nils Celsius on the Cartesian idea of the world. Since Joshua 10:12–13 states that the sun stood still in Gibeon, it would be ungodly to maintain that the earth moved around the sun. Every introduction of an allegorical interpretation of the Bible, as well as the thought that the Bible could accommodate "two truths," was exceptionally dangerous, especially now that the "higher" truth evidently could be searched out by philosophers and medical scholars. To a large extent, the Cartesian battles represented a territorial dispute. Medical scholars and philosophers ought to keep to their field, which was not to be expanded. The Cartesian postulate that everything—with the exception of man's soul—literally consists of matter in motion was too expansive. Thereby, not only was an insurrection mounted against traditional knowledge, but such optimism regarding the possibilities of learning was also presumptuous and a manifestation of hubris. Another fundamental element in the battle was the confusion of language that threatened when the old scholastic terminology was about to founder. Entire libraries of learned texts seemed on the way to becoming useless. For some years, the battle engulfed the university, with lampoons issuing from both sides. When the chancellor failed to unite the opposing sides, a royal decree was delivered that both sides could interpret as a victory.

And perhaps it was. The battle was suspended, and each side was to keep to itself. But now scholars in medicine and physics are no longer restrained from advancing the mechanistic theory of the world, which was maintained by all concerned. Yet no one should suppose that the church and theology had lost their footing. For several decades at the close of the seventeenth and the beginning of the eighteenth centuries, the strongest demonstration of power ever by Swedish orthodoxy was evinced in the form of a new church law (1686), a new hymnal (1693), a new translation of the Bible (1702), a new catechism (1689), and, finally, in the Conventicle Act—an ordinance against the inclusion of guests in religious services held in the home. Unity afforded the strength that Sweden needed at a moment when the wolves were gathering on the borders.

It may seem paradoxical to find Olof Rudbeck among the supporters of the subversive Cartesianism. But Rudbeck was also the central figure with the Gothic school of ideas with its roots in classical literature, in Tacitus and the sixth-century Roman historian Jordanes. Through the great patriotic work of the brothers Johannes and Olaus Magnus, the Gothic school influenced the Swedish view of society from the Renaissance on. Its climax was reached with Rudbeck and his *Atland eller Manhem* (*Atlantica*), a monumental but unfinished work published in four volumes. His essential idea can quickly be summarized: The Swedes were not only the old tribe of the Goths that once had overthrown the classic culture; no, the Goths were also the inhabitants of Atlantis, the island that sank not in the Atlantic Ocean or somewhere else, but in the sea of oblivion! Rudbeck proved his thesis by, among

other devices, producing innumerable etymologies that traced everything in such a way as to fit the scheme. For example, the apples of the Hesperides: these were letters or runes that had ripened in the land of the midnight sun and later reached the peoples of southern lands. By virtue of its seniority, the north was superior to other nations. Europe was rightly to be conquered again, this time through Karl X and Karl XI. Although Rudbeck did not state this proposition directly, it could be inferred from his many words. In addition to all his exaggerated patriotism and questionable inebriation with words, Rudbeck also had a visionary and utopian streak. Large parts of the *Atlantica* contain very interesting interpretations of myths in which his ability to synthesize must impress the reader. Furthermore, there was also a rich measure of empirical studies in the spirit of Bacon. For example, the excavations in Old Uppsala, where Rudbeck searched for the heathen temple of Viking culture—which, of course, he found—were a pioneering contribution. His genius rejects every simple summary; it was all-embracing, expansive, of its time, yet looking to the future, speculative and yet realistic. No one in Uppsala could escape his influence.

But it was not only single individuals who gave the university its character. Without an insight into the role that family connections played, the picture of the scholarly life remains without a frame. People married within a fixed set of established combinations. Carolus Linnaeus's (Carl von Linné) much-sung story of his love for the daughter of the Falun doctor, Johan Moraeus, becomes less romantic once one considers that the expectation of eventually succeeding to the father-in-law's post was implicitly part of the marital contract. Swedenborg's relationship with Christopher Polhem's daughter Emerentia remains unclear, but their union must have been quite convenient for similar reasons. Not only did everybody know everybody else at the university, but, for the most part, they were also related. One example is the kinship between the Swedenborg-Benzelius and the Rudbeck families: Anna Swedenborg married Erik Benzelius, Jr., at about the time Olof Rudbeck entered into his third marriage, with Anna Schöldström, who was related to the Swedbergs along various fairly complicated lines. The Hiorter, Strömer, and Elvius families were particularly interrelated. The appointments in astronomy alternated among them. The Celsius family was another scholarly family interested in astronomy: Nils, who was previously mentioned, and Anders Celsius, who, as the inventor of the centigrade thermometer, became the most famous. The importance of family identification for gaining appointments is obvious. The Benzelius family furnishes an extreme example of how posts were passed on: not only did Erik Benzelius, Sr., attain the position of archbishop, but so, too, did three of his sons. There were also several other high church dignitaries within the family. It can thus be said that the Swedish academic families in a way constituted an aristocracy, a circle within which members knew how to keep academic power to themselves. Throughout his life, Emanuel Swedenborg everywhere met relatives who were called by the general appellations "cousin" or "brother." He explained his protected position in Swedish society in a late letter to Pernethy in 1769, which precisely referred to his family connections with the Swedish clergy. Another reason he was respected was that he was known for keeping company with angels.

More closely regarding Emanuel Swedenborg's time in Uppsala, it must be said that source material is surprisingly limited. Letters from or to Swedenborg are missing. Jesper Swedberg, in his voluminous autobiography, is remarkably silent regarding his son—although not much is said about the other children, either. However, we do have a frame into which to put him. We can immediately see that he was an unusually privileged student in that he resided in a good home and found the road into the world of the university already marked. Unlike the majority of students, he did not have to gnaw on the piece of salt meat brought from home. It is also not likely that he participated in his nation's bacchanalian rites in order to gain friends. Yet he bore the burden of the many and great expectations others had of him. We can only guess as to what inner forces drove him.

In another late letter—this one to Gabriel Beyer in 1769—Swedenborg remembers how, between the ages of four and ten, he often pondered religious questions, and how, from his sixth to twelfth year his "delight was discovery with clergymen concerning Faith" (L&M vol. 2, p. 696). There was his father, professor of theology, so imposing and forceful, yet he had his limitations. No one has doubted his good heart, and his deep influence on his son is obvious. One example is his criticism of "great faith." "Fie, you ugly great faith,"[2] he writes, referring to the orthodox belief that only faith, and not deeds, was needed for salvation. But Jesper Swedberg had less to give in philosophical matters; neither Aristotle nor Descartes seems to have worried him much. As every reader of his extensive authorship realizes, his view of the world was basically old-fashioned, full of superstition of one kind or another, and, from the perspective of our time, almost exotic. Nobody knows anything concrete about the generation gap between father and son, but Emanuel oriented himself toward the most modern learning of the age. Perhaps his tutor during his early years, Johan Moraeus—his relative and, later, Linnaeus's father-in-law—helped him. In any case, Moraeus later professed adherence to the modern mechanistic school of medicine.

The years around 1700 were full of change for young Emanuel. His mother died in 1696, and his father entered into a new marriage the following year. The family lived in its house on the Main Square, right next to that of Olof Rudbeck. Inevitably, Emanuel must have run into "Olof Storkopf" [the epithet, a combination of Swedish and German words, translates as "Bighead"]. Perhaps he received from him some encouraging words, perhaps an admonition not to throw snowballs at old gentlemen. Then, in 1702, all of Uppsala burned. All the houses east of the Fyris River turned to ashes, but, thanks to well-built brick walls, Rudbeck's collections were miraculously saved. The Gustavianum, containing the university library, also escaped destruction, but the cathedral was razed. This terrible day must have etched itself into young minds. A few weeks later, the aged Rudbeck died, and everybody understood that an era was drawing to a close. Abroad in Europe, Karl XII had just won his astonishing victory at Narva, but his luck in war was soon to turn against him. On May 15, 1699, Emanuel had been registered as a student at the Västmanland-Dala Nation; at the age of eleven, his childhood was over and preparations for adulthood were in full swing. Finally, in 1703, Jesper Swedberg was appointed bishop of Skara and left Uppsala.

Emanuel then moved in with his brother-in-law, Erik Benzelius, Jr., who had newly been appointed librarian and was in relatively good economic circumstances. Recently returned home from his European study tour and barely thirty years old, Benzelius must have been a great intellectual stimulus. The availability of books was above normal in the Benzelius home. The university collections were within reach, of course, but because they were available only to academic teachers, it is doubtful that such a young, inexperienced scholar as Emanuel was able to enjoy them. But there was Benzelius's own library—about three thousand volumes, one of the best in the city. It contained the classic writers and, as time passed, quite a lot of natural science. Benzelius improved book acquisition at the university; he was a successful teacher and researcher. As a linguist and Orientalist, he worked on editions of Philo Judaeus and Ulfilas's Bible—the "Silver Bible" [Codex Argentus], written in the otherwise-lost Gothic language and the greatest treasure of the university. It is not hard to understand where Swedenborg got his early interest in Eastern languages. In Benzelius's house, situated on the west side of the Fyris River close to the Iceland Bridge, the atmosphere is said to have been free—almost ungodly, according to Andreas Norrelius, Benzelius's successor as librarian. Opinions regarding Benzelius tended in that direction, but one also senses jealousy behind them; in the case of Norrelius, anger over his bad relationship with his wife—and Benzelius's daughter—Greta. In *Spiritual Diary*, Benzelius is characterized as showing a proud exterior, but being a truly good man inside. It is evident from late correspondence that he embraced Emanuel with true friendship. It must have been a privilege to spend one's student days in Benzelius's home.

Swedenborg is mentioned in the nation's roster as being

"*optimae indolis*" ("of the best inborn quality"), a very promising young man. That his father was inspector during his first years of study scarcely worked to his disadvantage. In some instances, Emanuel appears in the records in connection with his nation's exercises in the academic art of disputation. In 1704, he appears as the opponent in a dispute over God's providence (*De Providentia Dei*). A couple of years later, he was the opponent at the defense of a dissertation on natural law, and in 1708 he nominated himself as preses for a similar work. But that would not do; the seniors of the nation vetoed the notion that a junior should receive such an honor. Swedenborg obviously acted out of youthful hubris, and the inspector of the nation, the Orientalist and theologian Johan Palmroth, did not allow any departure from tradition.

Swedenborg's own public defense of his dissertation, dealing with a number of quotations from Seneca and the Syrian Mimus ("L. Annaei Seneca et Pub. Syri Mimi Selectae Sententia cum annatationibus Erasmi et Graeca versione Jos. Scaliger" ["Selected Sentences from L. Annaeus Seneca and Publius Syrus Mimus with Annotations by Erasmus and Greek Version by Joseph Scaliger"]), was presented in 1709 before the professor of theoretical philosophy, Fabian Törner. Evidently, Swedenborg had formulated his thesis himself, which hardly was customary. One must remember that, first and foremost, the disputations were exercises in verbal attack and defense, not proofs of a research talent. Indeed, the presiding professor often wrote the document, thereby earning a little extra something for himself. When the respondent wrote the dissertation, it rather suggested certain ambitions. Thus this scholarly dissertation stands as evidence that the time with Benzelius had not been spent in vain. The presentation of the argument—a combination of philology and classical philosophy—was scarcely original; even so, one could think that Swedenborg had demonstrated the requisite competence. Jesper Swedberg sat among others in the audience at the disputation, which took place in the Auditorium Majus in the Gustavianum. He must have felt fatherly pride on that day in June, but we do not know what his views were in his opposition *extra ordinem*. The son had dedicated his work to him in the hope of in time coming to resemble his father "in writing as well as in mind." This brought Swedenborg's academic studies to an end.

Despite having proceeded for ten years, these studies did not lead to a degree. But a degree was not regarded as immediately called for. It is conceivable that Swedenborg had chosen the wrong preses: a letter to Benzelius written soon afterward tells us that the professor of rhetoric, Johan Upmark, had been unfavorably disposed toward him; had Upmark been an ally, he would have provided stronger support for the possibility of a continued academic career for Swedenborg. And indeed, it is probable that Swedenborg had

entertained such plans. But first he had to see Europe. This scholarly peregrination was expected of all serious academics. His father and Erik Benzelius had traveled extensively throughout educated Europe. Despite the wars, differences in religion, and language problems, they were able to get out and, normally, also to return.

His departure was delayed by the Danish fleet's encirclement of Göteborg, the port of embarkation, so Swedenborg had to wait in the family home at Brunsbo. In 1710, he finally could set out on his journey, which lasted four whole years (and went far beyond the scope of this article). The contacts with Uppsala were very intense from time to time in the form of numerous and informative letters to Benzelius. Swedenborg also purchased books for the library and instruments for the departments of the university. He also was to sound the depths of the new currents within science and philosophy. Several professors wanted answers to their questions—for instance, the astronomer Pehr Elvius about the new Newtonian mechanics—and Swedenborg could provide knowledgeable answers. Because of the Collegium Curiosorum, which had been established in Uppsala in 1710 as the first Swedish scientific academy and of which Benzelius was its driving force, Swedenborg's letters home increasingly spoke of matters concerning natural science and technology. Swedenborg knew everyone in that circle, and the ambitions at work there were identical to his. Through the new technology, particularly well developed in England, and the native genius of Polhem, Sweden would grow in glory and prosperity.

The long stay abroad and the tumultuous state of affairs in an increasingly war-torn country weakened his ties to Uppsala. Swedenborg made inquiries to Karl XII himself about the prospects of obtaining a state commission. The king's great interest in mathematics and Swedenborg's visionary belief in technology could have led to something great had the political game not intervened. Coupled with Polhem, Swedenborg really had something to contribute to the nation. With an optimism unique in those dark times, he founded *Daedalus Hyperboreus* (*Northern Inventor*), the first number of which appeared in 1716. This remarkable journal, the first scholarly one in Sweden, was actually published in Swedish, with contributions mainly by Polhem, but also by Swedenborg (among other things, the essay on "tremulation," the extreme consequence of the Cartesian mechanistic physiology). The framework for *Daedalus Hyperboreus* was the Collegium Curiosorum, but it was Swedenborg who alone carried the workload as well as the expenses. He therefore had to get back to Uppsala to discuss with Werner, the printer, matters of design that because of meager resources were complicated, especially regarding the illustrations. But once again, those with whom he was involved at the university had to recognize Swedenborg's competence.

Several times it has been suggested that Swedenborg actually sought an academic career. And, in fact, nothing would have been more natural: with rows of bishops and professors in the family, he belonged to the nation's upper academic echelon. The question of an appointment at the university appears several times in his correspondence with Benzelius, who constantly promises him his support. We may think that an important credential was missing: a master's or doctor's degree. On one such occasion, at one point in the correspondence with Benzelius, he is spoken of as "the student" Swedenborg. But, obviously, the degree was not always necessary for a professorship. Among others, Anders Spole, the well-known astronomer, had been appointed without any formal titles. Instead, Swedenborg's study tours had earned him an unquestionable credential. Benzelius had been appointed to his position as librarian immediately upon returning home from his peregrination. Personal contacts, book learning, and language proficiency were best acquired abroad: the age believed that the academic world should literally be international. The first time Swedenborg expressed an interest in an appointment was in 1715, when the chair of rhetoric occupied by Professor Upmark was expected to become vacant. Though he could not count on getting that very chair, he could presume, given the policy of promotion from within the university, that the appointment of another to Upmark's chair would create a vacancy somewhere else in this relatively closed system and that this vacancy might be filled by him. But this did not happen: for good reasons, a rhetorician from Lund was summoned. By then, however, Swedenborg had already had time to develop his thoughts of a professorship in technology at the university. His motives were at once patriotic and personal; the prospect of an acceptable salary was a primary concern, but because these expectations exceeded the wages paid tenured professors, his hopes were hardly realistic. Some time later, however, Swedenborg would be appointed assessor in the Board of Mines which would change the course of his career. But in 1724, the thought of an academic position for him was still alive. At that time, Benzelius informed Swedenborg of the death of Nils Celsius, the professor of astronomy, and advised his protégé as to the salary he could ask. If nowhere else, lodgings were available on the Main Square, where Swedberg's house had been rebuilt after the fire.

Among Swedenborg's many interesting plans was one to improve Uppsala University in respect to education in science and technology. In a memorandum from 1716 he argues for locating the observatory in one of the towers of the castle—actually an obvious idea that was much discussed without leading to anything. He also wanted to move the mechanical laboratory, Christopher Polhem's creation, from Falun to Uppsala, where it would be placed under the supervision of a mathematical society. The notion seems to have been to manufacture, under its auspices, Polhem's inventions on a larger scale. The profits were to be divided among the society, Polhem, and Swedenborg himself: there were not many others from whom to choose. They were to concentrate on mechanics, on machines for use in manufactures, in shipbuilding, in artillery, and in mining. Such a proposal would have meant a tremendous change in the university. It does seem difficult to imagine practical instruction in shipbuilding in the narrow Fyris River, but anything seemed possible at the time. There were several visionary project makers in the country: Anders Gabriel Duhre, connected with agricultural education at Ultuna outside Uppsala; Mårten Triewald, who introduced the steam engine in the mining business at Dannemora; and Anders Bachmansson-Nordencrantz, a writer on economics whose extensive production seemed to offer solutions to all of society's problems. Throughout, the influences from the debate in England are evident. One notes that Swedenborg was influenced by the Royal Society of London in his academy proposal, and when he and Polhem wanted to spread information about useful knowledge to the common public, London's Gresham College is discernible as the model. The professors there were expected to give public lectures every week for the commonweal of society.

What would have happened to the university in Uppsala if Emanuel Swedenborg had become a professor there? He would have replaced the traditional book learning of 1720 with practical exercises, and he would have worked for a radical modernization. We can only speculate over this and many other things. The fact remains that Swedenborg's life did not follow any humanly predictable course.

The reverse of the question—How did Uppsala influence Swedenborg?—can be answered with greater certainty. His father introduced him to the world of the university, and Erik Benzelius became his guide and his support in his classical studies. More than anyone else, he was Swedenborg's mentor—though several other teachers could be mentioned. Cartesianism was strong among the scientists who did not yet want to accept Newton. Among the philosophers, an ever-growing number professed an eclectic concept of knowledge, and in the 1720s, Wolffian rationalism would make its entrance. In broad terms, the philosophy of the university consisted not in a single system, but in an expanding framework that increasingly accommodated current social questions. During the eighteenth century, the university was to become secularized—in the sense of being tied to promoting the benefit of society—and this development is already noticeable in Swedenborg's time. A strong patriotic undertone is evident in all the features mentioned above, but it is also evident in him—which, considering his later international work, may be paradoxical.

In addition, if any single person warrants recognition as his inspiration, it must be Olof Rudbeck. His multifaceted work provides many connections to Swedenborg. In medicine, as mentioned, there is a connection to the new mechanistic philosophy. We might remind ourselves that Rudbeck taught mechanics in order to modernize Swedish mining in the 1660s and 1670s. He was an architect and inventor who actually built central parts of academic Uppsala himself. Like young Swedenborg, he avoided theology, at least in writing, in order to approach poetry and mythology instead.

Among the great variety of learned investigations in Rudbeck's *Atlantica*, there are a number of insightful interpretations of myths, characterized by great ability to synthesize, comparable to Swedenborg's *De Cultu et Amore Dei* (1745). Swedenborg was also to explain his theory *Motion and Position of the Earth and Planets* (written in 1718) in conjunction with Rudbeck's theories: previously, they claimed, an eternal spring prevailed everywhere on earth. Rudbeck is his reference for the paradisical existence of that age, as well as for the migration of the Goths and their colonization of Europe. Swedenborg's reliance on this historiography is not surprising; his teacher Fabian Törner, for example, interpreted the old Scandinavian *Edda* literature in the same spirit in a series of dissertations. One can observe that it persisted long after Rudbeck's death, disappearing only with the fall of the Swedish empire. It might be possible to make the argument that, for Swedenborg, this Gothic vision of paradise was temporarily an expression of the religious interest that would become manifest much later. One small item ties Swedenborg directly to the empirical side of Rudbeck the archeologist—namely, a lost and never-published manuscript on how to calculate the volume of burial mounds; we must imagine

that, like Rudbeck, he measured and dug at Old Uppsala, the holy place of the Goths. Last but not least there is a correspondence between Rudbeck and Swedenborg in the ambitiousness of the tasks they set for themselves. Rudbeck had established the standard by which a research project would be measured. His *Atlantica* has its counterpart in Swedenborg's *Principia Rerum Naturalium* [1734]. We can also point to Carolus Linnaeus's *Systema Naturae* (1735) as a similar boundless effort to investigate all creatures on earth. In these writings the authors do not doubt that they will explain and describe literally everything. Swedenborg belonged to a generation of multitalented men, for whom, in some instances, nothing but the universal was enough.

Thus, Uppsala may not have been a big town during the decades around 1700. Judged by international standards, its academy was relatively modest, but it fostered some truly universal university men. Despite Rudbeck's efforts, Uppsala was not and had never been Atlantis, of course, but science and the humanities—and, soon, Linnaeus's natural history—began to flourish. Without a doubt, more was now being accomplished than the admired but more barbaric Goths had brought about. Swedenborg's contribution to this breakthrough in Swedish scholarship was considerable, but Uppsala's role in his own development is just as remarkable. From our perspective, Swedenborg and the town are inextricably linked. He should be remembered as walking the street with his fellow students to an academic disputation—perhaps on the new natural philosophy and its philosophical, theological, and religious implications.

Notes

1. Jesper Swedberg, *Lefwernes beskrifning* (An account of life) published by Gunnar Wetterberg (Lund, Sweden: Society for Science in Lund, 1941), vol. 25:1, pp. 173–74.
2. Ibid., pp. 487ff.

Academic Uppsala

Anja Hübener

FIG. 264. *St. Erik's Square, with Uppsala Cathedral in the background*

ANJA HÜBENER is a Swedish writer living in New York City. She has written extensively on art and culture for a variety of Scandinavian and American magazines. Ms. Hübener is a graduate from the University of Lund, Sweden, in film theory and journalism, and is a member of the editorial staff of this anthology.

A SMALL, STILL-PROVINCIAL town, Uppsala was in Swedenborg's time dominated by the castle, the cathedral, and the university. Little has changed. The university has grown many times its size since the eighteenth century, but the academic atmosphere remains unchanged. The cathedral still stands, as it has for over seven hundred years, as the hub of Swedish religious life. Only the old castle has lost its importance, leaving behind a ruin as a reminder of its glorious past.

During the eighteenth century Uppsala saw extensive development. After a devastating fire in 1702, a great part of the town was left in ashes, and very little of the Uppsala from the sixteenth and seventeenth centuries could be saved. A large part of the population had to be evacuated, and the town suffered financially for a long time. However, considering the remoteness of much of the work force and the stronger building regulations handed down by the town council, the recovery was swift. Rebuilding and renovating began almost immediately. One of the new rules stated that only stone buildings were allowed around the cathedral and the university. All of these buildings can still be seen. The major part of the eighteenth-century official buildings in Uppsala were designed by the distinguished Swedish architect Carl Hårleman. As a result the old part of the town, with the cathedral as its center, is a beautifully laid out, coherent example of Swedish architecture in the early- to mid-1700s.

This was a great time in history for Uppsala University. An interest in expanded knowledge and minute research was part of the liberal ideal. New theories and radical ideas made their way into the minds of students and faculty, sometimes struggling against the defenses and ignorance of extreme patriotism and religious orthodoxy. Because of their achievements, world-renowned scientists, such as Carolus Linnaeus, Anders Celsius, and Torbern Bergman, helped turn Uppsala University into an internationally acclaimed institution.

For over five hundred years Uppsala University has been the center of academic life and thought in Sweden, challenged only by the two-centuries-younger University of Lund. In the early days students were mainly guided in subjects required for the priesthood. But as the nobility slowly acquired a desire for higher education, the university had to accommodate the needs for a more secular curriculum. Academia Carolina was the oldest university building. It was restored after the fire, but subsequently torn down.

Emanuel Swedenborg was a member of the Västmanland-Dala Nation [or fraternity; see Broberg's essay "Swedenborg and Uppsala," elsewhere in this anthology, for more on student "nations"], where his father held for some time the honorary post of inspector. At the beginning of the eighteenth century, the nation did not have its own building but rented space for meetings in a house near Stora Torget. After Swedenborg's time, the nation had acquired its own quarters.

FIG. 265. *View of Uppsala: the cathedral, the university, and the castle*

FIG. 266. *Academia Carolina*

FIG. 267. *Stora Torget (the Great Square)*

FIG. 268. *An eighteenth-century student in fashionable dress*

The students came from a quite homogeneous background in Swedenborg's time. Education was something only the upper classes could afford. As an effort to reach the less fortunate, gifted young men (women were at this point not even considered for higher education) were offered scholarships. A number of disputes between the sober theology students and the new groups of aristocratic youths have been recorded. One of them concerned proper clothing. The fashion of the day, with an abundance of lace and curls, was seen by some as unsuitable for serious and devoted scholars.

Dormitories did not exist, and lodging was usually with a family or an older person. A lucky few were able to stay with relatives or friends of the family, who could help introduce them to Uppsala and to their new academic life. A typical student room was small, equipped with desk, bookshelves, and a bed. The entrance hall and reading room of the Västmanland-Dala Nation in 1918 was still probably quite similar to the eighteenth-century student meeting places. The portrait between the windows is of Swedenborg, the bust is of Svedelius, both distinguished alumni.

FIG. 269. *Entrance hall of the Västmanland-Dala nation, photographed in 1918*

FIG. 270. *Academia Gustaviana*

Academia Gustaviana was the former administration building. It was originally designed by Olof Rudbeck, and after its restoration was again considered one of the major university buildings. Under its roof the famous Anatomical Theater can be found, as well as the university library and the auditorium.

The Consistorium was built in the mid-1700s. That a major building would be erected for administration offices was a sign of the times and an indication of the university's increasing independence. Originally, the offices were located on the upper floors, while the ground floor housed shops,

the city's fire equipment, and the university penitentiary. At one time secondary-school exams were held there, and today the building still goes under the name of "Kuggis" (the Flunk).

The building housing the Observatorium was bought by the astronomer and physicist Anders Celsius, who subsequently converted it into an observatory. The most eye-catching addition was the tower, with its high windows for the telescopes. It can be seen as a landmark high above the rooftops on views of old Uppsala. Here Celsius invented the 100-degree thermometer named after him.

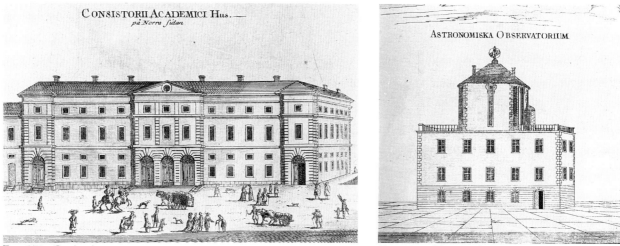

FIG. 271. *Consistorium*

FIG. 272. *Observatorium*

FIG. 273. *Laboratorium Chemicum*

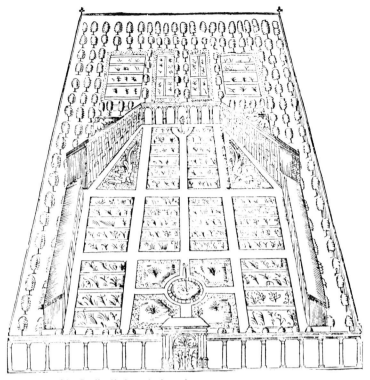

FIG. 274. *Olof Rudbeck's botanical garden*

FIG. 275. *Exercitiegården (lit., exercise court)*

FIG. 276. *Seventeenth-century houses in Uppsala. The library of the Academy of Sciences is on the left.*

On the other side of the town, situated in an area where many professors and city officials had their large houses and gardens, is the Laboratorium Chemicum.

The botanical garden of Olof Rudbeck, Sr., was planned and developed in the late-seventeenth century. It is here that he built his house and resided. The garden rapidly became a first-class source for observation and experimentation, serving students of medicine and botany. Later, following Olof Rudbeck, Jr., as chairman of the department, Linnaeus took charge of the garden, and today it is known as the Linnaeus Garden and Museum. The university's new botanical garden is situated in the former palace garden.

The Exercitiegården was built under the motto "*Mens sana in corpore sana*" (A Healthy Mind in a Healthy Body), and held sufficient space for equipment for the students' exercises. Most popular were the aristocratic sports riding and fencing.

In the mid-seventeenth century a little house (on the left of the figure) was erected as a working studio for one of the university's professors. Its architect was Olof Rudbeck. After a many-faceted history this pretty building now houses the library of the Academy of Science. Even after the 1702 fire the majority of houses in Uppsala were built of wood, painted in red or gray, and often with sod roofs. They gave a very picturesque, provincial look to the town. The Italian traveler Magalotti wrote about these houses, "When they are green in the spring and summer, it looks like a meadow, and is beautiful to the eye."[1]

FIG. 277. *Uppsala Castle, with cathedral in background*

Uppsala Castle, beautifully situated on a hill overlooking the town, dates back to the sixteenth century. It was razed in the fire of 1702, and due to the extensive damages, was not restored. Parts of the still-standing walls were torn down, and the brick was used for other buildings. But in 1744 Prince Adolf Fredrik initiated a restoration of the castle, arguing its historical value. The architect entrusted with this major renovation was Carl Hårleman. Because of financial difficulties the construction had to be halted several times, until it was finally discontinued in 1762.

The foundation stones for Uppsala Cathedral were laid in the thirteenth century. It was considered a bold enterprise in its day, and the cathedral is still the largest in Scandinavia. The erection itself took more than 150 years, and it was not until 1435 that the cathedral could be consecrated. In the 1702 fire the high spires of the towers fell down, and the greater part of the medieval interior was destroyed. The church was restored, and the "Hårleman hoods" replaced the earlier spires (as can be seen in the first figure of this essay). In spite of numerous renovations and remodelings, it is still considered the most noteworthy example of medieval architecture in Sweden.

FIG. 278. *Uppsala Cathedral, with earlier spires, before 1702 fire*

Note

1. Nils Taube et al., *Uppsala i Närbild* (Uppsala in close-up) (Stockholm: Wahlström & Widstrand, 1948), p. 44.

A Rationale for Swedenborg's Writing Sequence, 1745–1771

George F. Dole, Ph.D.

WE KEEP TRYING TO MAKE sense out of our lives, and to some extent, we seem to succeed. Certainly, at least, our retrospective view is normally tidier than our current experience. This suggests to me that one dimension of the art of biography is the re-creation of uncertainty—the telling of the story as though one did not know what was going to happen next. Life's issues tend to be more uncertain while we are involved in them than when we look back on them.

In the specific case of Swedenborg, his own retrospective judgment that the Lord had been guiding him toward his call ought not to be retrojected into his youth and early maturity. We must, I believe, assume that he did not take his post with the Board of Mines in order to accomplish some particular phase of preparation for illumination. His own life would testify to the fact that "we are allowed to see divine providence after the fact and not before" (DP 187), because "if we were to see divine providence openly, we would intrude ourselves into the sequence and tendency of its process" (DP 180).

The section of *Divine Providence* immediately following these citations begins with the statement, "Our own prudence is nothing. It only seems to exist; and further, it should seem to exist; but divine providence covers everything because it is so detailed" (DP 181). In this essay, then, I will to some extent be dealing with a nothing that does and should seem to exist, namely Swedenborg's own prudence, as it relates to his theological works. On the assumption that we should not retroject his final view of this phase of his life into its beginning, I want to try to reconstruct, from the evidence, an image of how it all happened to and for him. He was setting out into uncharted territory, on an unplanned task; and the Lord's guidance, under the laws of providence, would have taken the form of providing resources for decision making instead of or in addition to the form of ready-made decisions.

Let me begin, then, with the retrospective view, primarily because it is the most familiar. We are indebted to Carl Robsahm for relaying Swedenborg's account of the pivotal event in the London inn, which is traditionally dated April 1745. I would call attention particularly to the following words in that account: "He (that is, the Lord) then said that He was the Lord God, the Creator of the world, and the Redeemer, and that He had chosen me to unfold to men the spiritual sense of the scripture, and that He Himself would show to me what I should expect to write."[1]

Swedenborg himself was elderly when he described this event to Robsahm, and the present version was written down in 1782. This does not mean that it is necessarily inaccurate, but simply that it represents an understanding of the call in the light of subsequent events. Why, for example, if the deity identified himself by name as "the Lord God," did Swedenborg use the name "God Messiah" throughout his first effort to "unfold . . . the spiritual sense of the scripture," *Word Explained*? More to the point, there is evidence to suggest that this definition of his task proved too narrow, and it is this evidence that I will be presenting and exploring. The evidence is primarily of what he did in fact do and write, and its pertinence rests in the assumption that he was constant in his effort to heed his call as his understanding of it developed.

More or less in the course of his call, he wrote *Worship and Love of God*, publishing only part of it. It begins "Walking once alone in a pleasant grove to dispel my disturbing thoughts, and seeing that the trees were shedding their foliage . . . ," and develops into an account of his musings on the seasons of the human race. As far as I am aware, it contains no explicit references either to his own otherworld experiences or to scripture, though the vision of the center of dazzling light (WLG 112) is suggestive of the one, and the choice of Adam and Eve as protagonists rests clearly in the other. To me, it looks very much as though he was making use of an accepted literary device to begin to communicate his newfound and

---

For biographical information on Dr. Dole, see his Introduction, at the beginning of this book.

growing meaning, and was as yet not ready to "lay it on the line." There is a posthumous, third-hand report that he said of it, "It was certainly founded on truth, but somewhat of egotism had introduced itself, as he had made a playful use of the Latin language, on account of his having been ridiculed for the simplicity of his Latin style in later years" (DOC vol. 2, pp. 709ff).

His next major undertakings we presume began after his call—the so-called *Spiritual Diary*, and a very substantial *Bible Index*. These were to serve as basic resources for his later writing; but the present issue is how they related to each other as he began to compile them. The *Index* clearly relates to *Word Explained*, a major undertaking in its own right. He carried this work through the Pentateuch, and extended it by treating Isaiah and fifty of the fifty-two chapters of Jeremiah, at which point he apparently stopped. His intent was apparently to write a commentary on the whole of scripture.

The manuscript itself may have been intended for the printer. While the handwriting does vary, there is a minimum of deletion, and it was not in the two-column format that he later used for first drafts.

There is also evidence that the "diary" material was intended for publication. J. Durban Odhner[2] has assembled some persuasive evidence that Swedenborg was thinking of a volume to be entitled "Spiritual Experiences." There is also the internal evidence, beginning early in the manuscript, of such "addresses to the reader" as "To relate all the cases of experience would be prolix" (SD 153), as well as the fact that Latin was Swedenborg's language for publication, while Swedish (cf. *Journal of Dreams*) was his normal "diary language." The format of the manuscript is, however, not up to his usual standard for submission to a printer, and his notes to himself (SD 153) indicate that he had in mind considerable editorial work. He eventually indexed it, and drew on it quite freely for other works.

Now, there is in fact a close connection between Swedenborg's spiritual experiences and his understanding of the Word. I may cite two rather different examples of this connection. First, suggesting that his spiritual experiences contributed to his understanding of the Word, there are such passages as ". . . in the natural sense, earth is earth, but in the spiritual sense it is the church, because they who are in the spiritual sense, that is, who are spiritual, as the angels are, when 'the earth' is named in the Word, do not understand the earth itself, but the nation which is there, and its Divine worship . . ." (LJ 3). Second, suggesting that his study of the Word contributed to his spiritual experience, there are such passages as the following, where, after describing an encounter with a spirit, he writes, "While this was taking place, I was reading the first chapter of Deuteronomy" (AC 1769). Swedenborg states the connection clearly in such statements as "Man, being born for both lives, can,

while in the world, be also in Heaven, through the Word, which is for both worlds" (AC 2588[6]).

Notwithstanding this connection, however, these two foci of attention—scripture exegesis and spiritual experience—remained distinguishable. As late as 1770, Swedenborg could write, "As the Lord has opened to me the spiritual sense of the Word, and as it has been granted me to be together with angels and spirits in their world as one of them . . ." (TCR 776). We can therefore see Swedenborg immediately after his call following two related but quite distinct tracks and devoting a good deal of time and energy to each. Odhner cites evidence that Swedenborg was working consciously on this dichotomy. Speaking of *Word Explained*, he writes:

> In the course of writing this "unfolding" of the Old Testament text, Swedenborg began to indent certain paragraphs concerned with his own spiritual experiences. In addition, he was annotating a number of experiences together on the final pages of the volume in which he was working. During the early part of this phase, he was aware of some need to keep them separate, and had doubts about inserting them in the work *Explicatio*, the publication of which he at that time thought to be the goal toward which God Messiah was leading. Toward the end of this phase, however, he was clearly aware that these volumes contained two different works, i.e. an explanation of the Old Testament on the one hand, and the record of his spiritual experiences on the other, which latter he actually referred to by the collective title, "Experiences."[3]

As we know, scripture exegesis came to the fore, to the extent that the years 1749–56 saw the publiction of the eight volumes of *Arcana Coelestia*, a commentary on the books of Genesis and Exodus. One factor in this turn of events was Swedenborg's own strong Lutheran background. The heart and soul of Lutheranism was its insistence on the Bible—not the church, tradition, or "natural theology"—as the sole source of revealed truth. Swedenborg can state this quite strongly: "When those who are in enlightenment are reading the Word, they see the Lord. . . . This takes place solely in the Word, and not in any other writing" (AC 9411).

There is evidence in *Arcana Coelestia* itself that Swedenborg planned to continue it well beyond Exodus. He makes occasional reference to his intent, God willing, to give further information on one topic or another when he gets to Leviticus, Joshua, or Judges.

The *Arcana* itself, however, almost immediately presents a duality. At the close of its second chapter, Swedenborg appends an account of his experience of dying, and as the volume proceeds, he uses the interchapter spaces to present material on the spiritual world. It had been my own untested assumption that he did this to relieve the monotony of sustained exegesis, but I now believe that this is the direct descendant of the indented paragraphs in *Word Explained*, and represents a kind of latent agenda. That is, while his best conscious judgment is that his primary task is the exposition of spiritual meaning in scripture, the urgency and import of his spiritual experiences is too strong to be repressed. Or to put it another way, his spiritual experiences were too intimately connected to his understanding of scripture to allow intelligible treatment of the latter without mention of the former.

As the work drew to a close, evidence of still another agenda began to emerge. The closing chapters of Exodus tell the story of the building of the tabernacle in terms virtually identical to the earlier narration of God's commandments for its building. In those closing chapters, Swedenborg simply referred the reader to his treatment of the parallel material and used the "space" this created for consecutive presentation on a number of doctrinal topics.

By the end of *Arcana Coelestia*, then, we have three basic modes of presentation: the scripture exegesis, which he regards as his divinely ordained task; the narration of spiritual experience; and the delineation of a theological system. It might be noted, incidentally, that Lutheranism historically expressed open hostility to reasoned theology, tracing the downfall of Christianity to the insidious influence of pagan (i.e., Greek) philosophy. This did not prevent the emergence of a number of Lutheran theologians; but they were scrupulously careful to base their theological premises on "the Word."

Within two years after the publication of the last volume of the *Arcana*, no less than five separate works were written and published, all drawing heavily on the *Arcana*. *White Horse of the Apocalypse* is a treatise on the nature of the Word, with copious *Arcana* references. *New Jerusalem and Its Heavenly Doctrine* is a kind of theological glossary, with extensive *Arcana* extracts appended to each brief chapter. *Earths in the Universe* is lightly edited from interchapter material, while *Last Judgment* and *Heaven and Hell* are expanded treatments of subjects introduced in the same way.

The latter three works also rest heavily on Swedenborg's spiritual experiences. Material that was secondary in the *Arcana* now takes center stage for a while. The former two works (*White Horse* and *New Jerusalem and Its Heavenly Doctrine*) show a clear theological orientation. Material that was scattered through the exegesis of Genesis and Exodus is now gathered together and is arranged topically. The same concern for topical rather than scriptural ordering is of course represented in Swedenborg's two indexes to the *Arcana*. The three modes of presentation have emerged in separate works.

As the five works just mentioned came off the press, Swedenborg turned back to scripture. It is immediately evident that he had abandoned any thought of writing a commentary on the whole Word. Now, having published on the first two books, he turned to the last, the book of Revelation, and began writing *Apocalypse Explained*.

This is the only work of Swedenborg's for which we have both a rough draft and a "fair copy"—the latter being written with particular care for submission to a printer. He got about halfway through the nineteenth chapter (out of twenty-two), and then laid it aside. The fair copy, incidentally, stops only a couple of paragraphs short of the rough draft. It is a substantial work, comprising six volumes in English translation; and there have been various opinions as to his reasons for dropping it.

I would suggest that the main reason can be seen in the nature of the work itself. Through much of it, Swedenborg sticks quite close to his exegetical task. Now, however—aided no doubt by his extensive *Bible Index* and prompted at least in part by the awareness that he was not going to do a consecutive commentary on the whole of scripture—he gathers and comments on passages from other parts of scripture quite copiously. As a result, *Apocalypse Explained* proceeds much more slowly through Revelation than the *Arcana* did through Genesis and Exodus. The *Arcana* averages about nine Bible chapters per volume, while *Apocalypse Explained* averages about three (Standard Edition).

Early in his treatment of Revelation 15, however, Swedenborg begins to attend to another task. Whereas in the *Arcana* he had inserted material between chapters, he now appends material to each (numbered) paragraph. At paragraph 932, he begins with a discussion of "The Goods of Charity," pursuing it at paragraph 933 with the heading "*Continuatio*"; and he continues this procedure to the end of his work. It is particularly noteworthy that this "secondary" material gradually grows in scope, and that the exegetical material becomes more and more cursory. The scriptural focus is being replaced, this time not by an experiential focus, but by one on topical or systematic theology.

The result is awkward. Suppose you are involved in reading two books concurrently. It is one thing to read a chapter of one and then a chapter of the other. It is quite another thing to read a paragraph of one and then a paragraph of the other. Consecutive reading toward the close of *Apocalypse Explained* requires one to make this kind of shift on virtually every page. It simply does not work; and I doubt that we need look any further for Swedenborg's reason for laying the work aside.

It is estimated that he did so in 1759. In 1763, he published no less than six books—the four doctrines (*Doctrine of the Lord, of Sacred Scripture, of Life,* and *of Faith*), *Continuation on the Last Judgment,* and *Divine Love and Wisdom;* and in 1764 he published *Divine Providence.* Much of this material is clearly foreshadowed in the "continuations" in *Apocalypse Explained.*

Now, however, there is a new dimension to the shift of focus. Swedenborg's preface to the first of these 1763 works, *Doctrine of the Lord,* reads in part as follows:

Some years ago there were published the following five little works:

1. On Heaven and Hell
2. The Doctrine of the New Jerusalem
3. On the Last Judgment
4. On the White Horse
5. On the Planets and other Earths in the Universe.

In these works many things were set forth that have hitherto been unknown.

Now, *by command of the Lord* [emphasis Dole's], who has been revealed to me, the following are to be published:

The Doctrine of the New Jerusalem concerning the Lord

The Doctrine of the New Jerusalem concerning the Holy Scripture

The Doctrine of Life for the New Jerusalem from the Ten Commandments

The Doctrine of the New Jerusalem concerning Faith

A Continuation concerning the Last Judgment

Angelic Wisdom concerning the Divine Providence

Angelic Wisdom concerning the Divine Omnipotence, Omnipresence, Omniscience, Infinity, and Eternity

Angelic Wisdom concerning the Divine Love and Wisdom

Angelic Wisdom concerning Life

Swedenborg was reasonably obedient to this command, publishing seven of the nine works stated, and in fact covering all the topics involved. It is worth particular note that in the four doctrines he is as concerned to present their biblical foundations as to explain them systematically, and that in sharp contrast to this, there is very little biblical material in *Divine Love and Wisdom*. He seems deliberately to be keeping his agendas separate.

At this point, we can gain a clearer view of the process. If we put the nature of *Apocalypse Explained* together with the command of *Doctrine of the Lord*, then the "continuations" can be seen as a kind of pre-echo of the command. They are evidence that Swedenborg was beginning to pick up a message concerning the specific direction his work should take, a direction different from the biblical one that was foremost in his consciousness. Providence and prudence were on divergent courses.

It is particularly significant in this context that while Swedenborg seems to have heard the command quite explicitly, in the form of nine specific titles, his own prudence had the freedom to follow the listing in principle rather than in complete detail. While there is no evidence of his having worked on either of the neglected titles as a separate book, when Dr. Gabriel Beyer questioned him about this, he replied (in February of 1767) as follows:

About the promised treatise on infinity, omnipotence, and omnipresence. Answer: There are many things on these subjects interspersed throughout the *Angelic Wisdom concerning the Divine Providence*, paras. 46–54 and 157; also in the *Angelic Wis-*

dom concerning the Divine Love and Wisdom, paras. 4, 17, 19, 21, 44, 69, 72, 106, 156, 318; and in *The Apocalypse Revealed*; these subjects will be further treated of in the arcana of *Angelic Wisdom concerning Conjugial Love*; for to write a separate treatise on these Divine attributes, without the assistance of something to support them, would cause too great an elevation of the thoughts; wherefore these subjects have been treated in a series of other things which fall within the understanding. (DOC vol. 2, p. 261)

It is also worth special note that in listing the works already published, Swedenborg did not mention the *Arcana*—a rather substantial omission, since at that time it represented about two-thirds of his published theology. I could ask for no clearer indication that he regarded the 1763–64 works as being in the same "special category" as the 1758 works, quite distinct from his "explicit" task of scripture exegesis.

When *Divine Providence* was published in 1764, then, Swedenborg evidently felt both free and commissioned to return to the Book of Revelation. The freedom is witnessed by his singleminded and efficient exegesis: the twenty-two chapters are covered in two volumes (Standard Edition). The commission was apparently quite explicit. At the close of a "Memorable Relation" (undated) in *Marriage Love*, he says, "Then I heard a voice from heaven, 'Go into your room, close the door, and get down to the work you started on the *Apocalypse*. Carry it to completion within two years' " (CL 521ff). The *Apocalypse Revealed* was in fact published in 1766, two years after the publication of *Divine Providence*.

On 8 April 1766, Swedenborg sent eight copies of *Apocalypse Revealed* to Beyer from Amsterdam. The next day, Swedenborg received a letter from Beyer which is of particular interest here because of the following sentence: "Another wish I have besides—to see the subject of marriage fully treated which, among those who have delicate feelings, awakens embarrassing questions of conscience, and by the generality of men is not well understood, and still less properly explained."[4]

Swedenborg had apparently started work on *Marriage Love* when he received this letter. Though it was not among those listed as commanded in *Doctrine of the Lord*, he mentioned a projected book *On Marriage* in *Doctrine of Life* (LIFE 74, 77). If, however, he was working on it at the time of Beyer's suggestion, it is very strange indeed that he made no mention of it in his prompt reply to Beyer, especially because he did respond specifically to a question about the status of the Epistles. A year later, he was certainly working on *Marriage Love*. The letter to Beyer already cited, dated February 1767, makes explicit mention of it as a projected publication, though not under its final title. The bibliography at the end of *Posthumous Theological Works*, volume 2, incidentally, dates the first draft of *De Conjugio* (*On Marriage*) as 1767.

There is then a strong possibility that Beyer's suggestion at least precipitated the final draft of *Marriage Love*. This might account in part for some of its unusual features. It was the first of his theological works to bear his name on its title page, even though the secret had been out for at least eight years, during which seven works were published. He himself described it as "not a theological work, but mostly a book of morals" (DOC vol. 2, p. 306), and no other work keeps such an insistent focus, in its expository sections, on human behavior and circumstances. No other work has such a high proportion of narrative to exposition. Swedenborg entitled the work "Delights of Wisdom concerning . . ." in preference to "Angelic Wisdom concerning. . . ." Further, the device of opening with an extended "Memorable Relation," especially one that borders on the slapstick, is quite without precedent in his other works. It may also be pertinent to note that the topic of marriage receives only passing mention in the otherwise compendious *True Christian Religion*.

Marriage Love was published in 1768. Swedenborg was then eighty years old. His age itself must have militated against undertaking another major exegetical task, and circumstances began to press him in another direction. Since the time when his authorship became known, criticism of his theology began to be addressed more directly to him, and there were the beginnings of "official" Lutheran opposition. Now his few followers were meeting the established church's opposition that would culminate in the Göteborg heresy trial, which began that fall.

It may come as no surprise, then, that we find Swedenborg suddenly occupied with the study of standard Christian doctrine. For example, his working manuscripts now deal with such topics as "Justification and Good Works," "A Conversation with Calvin," and "Remission of Sins." In 1769 he addressed directly the relationship of the new theology to the old in *Brief Exposition*. In sharp contrast, *Soul-Body Interaction*, published in the same year, is quite exclusively "philosophical," dealing with none of the issues raised at the heresy trial. This may represent another instance of his deliberately keeping his agendas separate.

It is, in a way, a short step from *Brief Exposition* to *True Christian Religion*. Dr. Robert H. Kirven has on occasion suggested that this latter work is modeled on traditional systematic theologies. I suspect that this is quite true, and that it was precipitated by the theological issues that led ultimately to the heresy trial. Hitherto Swedenborg had not tried to give an overall survey of the new theology. He had followed the course of scripture, he had shared his spiritual experi-

ences, and he had dealt with specific and timely topics. I would suggest that he was convinced of the need to address the growing opposition from orthodox Lutheranism more directly.

To do so, he needed to rely on authorities that the Lutheran Church regarded as valid. His compiling of "Scripture Confirmations" was a deliberate step in preparation. This surely illustrates his determination to present the new theology as biblically based; and the extensive quotations from the Epistles, which he regarded as noncanonical and had previously cited only sparingly, demonstrate his willingness to meet his opponents on their own grounds. I suspect that this purpose of *True Christian Religion* is inconspicuous because he had exercised such polemical spirit as he had in *Brief Exposition* and realized that it would not contribute to a constructive outcome.

Further, the work is organized around Lutheran theological constructs. Swedenborg's own theology would not have prompted separate chapters in the three persons of the trinity or on imputation, and would presumably have prompted chapters on heaven, hell, the world of spirits, and marriage. In short, the work seems best understood not as a final summary of this theology but as a proposal for the rethinking of Lutheran theology. In a way, it tries to bridge the gap between the metaphysical concepts of *Divine Love and Wisdom* and traditional Christian beliefs. It is Swedenborg's demonstration that the encounter with the transcendent requires a complete rethinking of orthodox concepts, not necessarily contradicting them verbally, but seeing radically new meaning in familiar words.

To summarize the whole process, then, we begin with a person profoundly committed to a Lutheran view of the exclusive centrality of scripture. We find him encountering meaning in quite unexpected forms, particularly in direct, intense, and enlightening spiritual experience. We find a distinct tension at this level, issuing in uncertainty as to the best means of fulfilling his mission. This uncertainty is resolved by a kind of alternation between exegetical, experiential, and topical presentation; and in this alternation we can see the interactive effects of his own conscious judgment, his own deeper sense of urgency, his circumstances, and divine mandates.

I would regard this whole "rationale" as no more than the direction in which the evidence seems to point, and would acknowledge that the evidence is slender. I do however believe that the slender indications seem to be pointing toward a coherent and believable process.

Notes

1. Benjamin Worcester, *The Life and Mission of Emanuel Swedenborg* (Boston: Little Brown, 1907), p. 204.

2. Emanuel Swedenborg, *Experientiae Spirituales*, ed. J. Durban Odhner (Bryn Athyn, Pa.: Academy of the New Church, 1980), pp. xiff.

3. Ibid.

4. Cyriel Sigstedt, *The Swedenborg Epic* (New York: Bookman, 1952), p. 324.

Swedenborg's London

Dennis Duckworth

Adapted by William Ross Woofenden, Ph.D.

FIG. 279. East View of the City of Westminster, *in the early nineteenth century*

Rev. DENNIS DUCKWORTH was ordained in 1939 by the British Conference of the New Church. He has served many of the British societies during his long years in the ministry, and even now in retirement continues to be active in the churches in the London area. In addition to his ministerial skills, he is also an artist. An exhibit of his drawings was a part of the worldwide celebration of Swedenborgians held in London in 1970.

FIG. 280. A Bird's-Eye View of London, *in the eighteenth century*

This article has been adapted from a booklet compiled by Dennis Duckworth entitled, *A Newchurchman's Guide to London*.[1] The original booklet was designed to be used as an actual tour guide for visitors to London. In this article we shall simulate the original intent by tracing the proposed tours on a map made especially for this publication, combining features of contemporary London and features of the London of Swedenborg's time, even though a number of the latter places and streets no longer exist. In the three tours outlined in the essay, the intent is to seek out and identify places associated with Swedenborg in London and also places of special importance to the history of organized Swedenborgianism.

LONDON, A WONDERFUL CITY two thousand years old, is also rich in associations for the devotee of Swedenborgiana.

Swedenborg came to London a dozen times, sometimes staying in the city for extended periods. Here his most ambitious theological work, *Arcana Coelestia*, was published. It was here that Robert Hindmarsh, the first Swedenborgian, lived. Swedenborg died in London. Here the organized New Church [Swedenborgian; see Glossary] began when Hindmarsh first called together the earliest receivers of Swedenborg's religious writings. Here the first church for worship by Swedenborgians was built, the little chapel off what was then Great Eastcheap, now called Cannon Street.

Modern London remains a center of New Church activity. The Swedenborg Society, the major publisher of Swedenborg's works in the United Kingdom, has its headquarters at Swedenborg House, 20 Bloomsbury Way. This is also the home office of the British Conference of the New Church.

London is big—very big: thirty miles across. It has grown rapidly during the past two centuries. It is many times larger than the London Swedenborg knew. In 1750 London stretched from Marble Arch to just beyond the Tower, in an east-to-west direction; and from roughly the present locale of Swedenborg House to The Elephant and Castle in a north-to-south direction. All beyond was open country. If we were to compare modern London in size to a large mailing envelope, Swedenborg's London was about the size of a postage stamp!

In his work *Continuation on the Last Judgment* Swedenborg wrote of "the noble English nation." He loved England for its spirit of freedom, and the consequent "interior intellectual light" of its people. He was not blind to the insularity of the British, as when he noted the readiness "to contract intimacy with friends of their own nation, and rarely with others. Englishmen," he said, "are lovers of their country and zealous for its glory, but regard foreigners much as a person looking through a telescope from the roof of a house regards those outside the city." But he added, "They are kind in relieving each others necessities, and are lovers of sincerity" (CLJ 39–41; TCR 808).

It was because of the freedom of the English press that Swedenborg could publish his works in London without interference—a privilege denied to him in his own country. It is hoped that those who visit London today will still find, in the historic streets of this great city, a love of freedom, a little intellectual light, sincerity, and a general spirit of friendliness and helpfulness.

The London of Swedenborg's Day

Emanuel Swedenborg first visited London as a young man of twenty-two, a graduate of Uppsala University, getting to know the world. This was in 1710. At this time, before the ennoblement of the family, his name was Swedberg. He came with the scant approval of his father, Bishop Jesper Swedberg.

The voyage from Göteborg to London was adventurous. The ship was boarded by the crew of a Danish privateer, by mistake was fired on by an English guard ship, and was becalmed on a sandbank in a dense fog. The vessel finally anchored in the Thames, just off Wapping Old (or Dock) Stairs, east of the Tower of London. It is a district where, not many years ago, men carried knuckle-dusters [brass knuckles] in their pockets, and policemen walked about in twos and threes.

Near Wapping Old Stairs, in Swedenborg's time, stood an inn, to which pirates were brought, made insensible with gin, and hanged. Swedenborg narrowly missed being hanged—not for piracy, but for ignoring quarantine regulations—a serious offense. The plague had broken out in Sweden, and all on board ship were commanded to stay there for six weeks. Swedenborg's youthful impatience got the better of him: he left the ship, was caught, and severely reprimanded—probably escaping the gallows only because he was the son of a distinguished bishop. His first letter home, dated "London, October 13, 1710," is apologetic in tone, and reveals a certain homesickness.

London was a fair and flourishing city. The Augustan age of art and literature had dawned, and genius was abroad. Queen Anne was on the throne, to be followed by the first four Georges. London was newly built after the Great Fire (1666), and Swedenborg, in a letter to Benzelius, his brother-in-law, writes, "The magnificent temple of St. Paul was finished . . . a few days ago" (L&M vol. 1, p. 13). In Westminster Abbey he kissed the tomb of Casaubon (at the corner of the nave and south transept). Isaac Casaubon, a Swiss theologian, translator, and critic, had been dead nearly a hundred years. He was a great Latinist; and Swedenborg, fresh from college, seems to have had a veneration for him.

It is not known where, or with whom, Swedenborg stayed on his first visit to London. He moved from place to place, staying with those from whom he could learn a craft. "I put my lodgings to some use" (L & M vol. 1, p. 21), he wrote to Benzelius. He was certainly not the first, or the last, Scandinavian to do this. "I study Newton daily" (L & M vol. 1, p. 21), he wrote again. He made the acquaintance of Flamsteed, the astronomer royal, of Halley, and other members of the Royal Society—possibly at the headquarters of that society in Crane Court, off Fleet Street.

Swedenborg had, to use his own words, "an immoderate desire" for knowledge; and he bought books, both for himself and for libraries in Sweden, in Paternoster Row. He was therefore "short of cash," and complained to Benzelius that his father was not sufficiently mindful of the needs of a young student. He visited Sion College Library in London Wall (now Victoria Embankment), which whetted his appetite to see the Bodleian at Oxford.

These few facts can be given, but little else can be said with certainty about Swedenborg's first visit to London. But he was to return again and again in later years, and to record his activities more precisely.

Before beginning our tours of London a visit to Swedenborg House would be in order. The fine premises of the Swedenborg Society are situated in the heart of London. Just off the great artery of New Oxford Street, and fringing one of the famous old squares of Bloomsbury, they stand in a district noted for its intellectual and artistic life. Nearby is the British Museum. Many large publishing houses are near neighbors. This is the bookman's London. Many a visitor, strolling along Bloomsbury Way, has paused before a certain bookshop window, and caught his first sight of the name "Swedenborg." It is also the traveler's London, for Bloomsbury abounds with hotels and boardinghouses, large and small.

Swedenborg House Locale

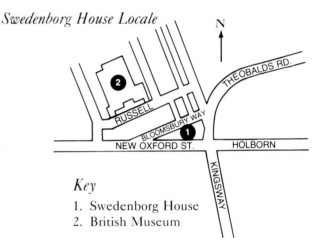

Key

1. Swedenborg House
2. British Museum

FIG. 281. *Swedenborg House, offices of the Swedenborg Society*

Tours Through London

These tours are planned so that you may wander along from place to place without fatigue.

Take the bus to Ludgate Circus, and you are in the heart of Swedenborg's London. Travel west along Fleet Street, north toward Clerkenwell Road, or east to St. Paul's and the City, and you tread the ground that Swedenborg once trod. You are, moreover, in the cradle of the infant Swedenborgian church organization. If you take with you a modern street map, realize that such a map cannot be a true guide to the London Swedenborg knew; for the topography of a great city is continually changing. You will need to leap about—mentally, of course—from date to date, for it will be impossible to follow a time sequence as you go exploring. The London pavements are hard, so take the simple straightforward way, and let the dates take care of themselves.

Starting from Ludgate Circus, walk up Ludgate Hill toward St. Paul's. The Church of St. Martin-Within-Ludgate is on the left. This marks the position of the city gate, built—according to popular tradition—in 66 B.C. by King Lud, who is said to have built the city's first walls. Adjoining the church is Ye Olde London public house. This was *The London Coffee House*, where, in 1783, Robert Hindmarsh called the first meeting of "receivers of the Heavenly Doctrines."[2] Five people attended, and they immediately adjourned to the Queen's Arms Tavern, St. Paul's Churchyard, "and drank tea together"!

Describing this first New Church meeting, Hindmarsh says, "To hear the story of each other's first reception of the doctrines, and to observe the animation that sparkled in the eye and brightened up the countenance of each speaker, as

FIG. 282. *St. Paul's Cathedral, south porch*

Route No. 1
Key

1. Church of St. Martin-Within Ludgate
2. Ye Olde London public house
3. St. Paul's Cathedral
4. Paternoster Row, site of Lewis's print-shop, the Bible and Dove
5. Church of St. Mary-le-Bow
6. Mansion House
7. Royal Exchange
8. Bank of England
9. The Monument
10. Site of Maidenhead Court and the Great Eastcheap Chapel
11. The Tower of London
12. Royal Mint
13. Wellclose Square
14. Swedenborg Square, site of old Swedish church

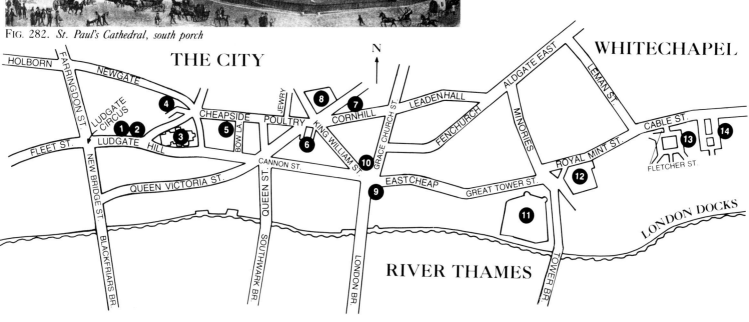

it came his turn to relate the particulars of that never-to-be-forgotten event, was itself a little heaven."[3]

Sir Christopher Wren's masterpiece, St. Paul's Cathedral, stands before you. Blackened by the smoke of a million chimneys (until it was recently cleaned) it was, in Swedenborg's day, white and fresh. A climb up to the Whispering Gallery, the Stone Gallery, the Upper Gallery, and the Ball will be rewarding for those with energy and a steady head; while in the Crypt may be seen the tombs of great Englishmen—including Wren's, with its famous inscription: "*Lector, si monumentum requiris, circumspice*" (Reader, if you seek his monument, look around you).

Leaving the cathedral, make your way to the northeast corner of St. Paul's Churchyard, to Paternoster Row—just behind Nicholson's draper's shop. (Until recently Paternoster Row was a ruin. Now it has been rebuilt as a garage.) Before World War II it was a narrow thoroughfare lined with bookshops—a real gem of old London. It had been a publishers' and booksellers' lair for hundreds of years, and its printers' signs, hung above the doors and windows, were lore for the antiquarian. In the mid-eighteenth century, at no. 1, under the sign THE BIBLE AND DOVE, was the shop of John Lewis, publisher of that largest of the theological and expository works of Swedenborg, *Arcana Coelestia*. Swedenborg came many times to this shop during the years of its publication (1749–56). On Horwood's 1799 *Map of the City of London*,[4] no. 1 Paternoster is shown as being on the right-hand side, a few paces down from Cheapside.

Walk along Cheapside (site of the Great Market of London in medieval times), past the Church of St. Mary-le-Bow (of Bow Bells fame), and, unsuspectingly, you are in Poultry. At the house of Thomas Wright, watchmaker to the king, no. 6 Poultry, a meeting was held on Tuesday, 31 July 1787, that may be regarded as "the commencement of the New Church in its external and visible form."[5] The sacrament of the holy supper was administered to eleven persons, and five others were baptized into the faith of the New Church. The communion cup used on this occasion is still in regular use by the congregation, which until very recently met on Gainsborough Road, North Finchley district—now moved to new quarters (177 Leicester Rd.) in the Greenhill neighborhood, New Barnet district, North London. On Horwood's map, no. 6 Poultry is shown as being on the right, just beyond Bucklersbury, and almost opposite Old Jewry.

A few steps will bring you to the hub of the City of London—to the Mansion House (on the right), the official residence of the lord mayor, the Royal Exchange (straight ahead), and the Bank of England (on the left).

Speaking of the English in the spiritual world, Swedenborg describes "two large cities like London, into which most of the English enter after death. I was permitted to see them, and also to walk through them. The middle of the first city

FIG. 283. *The Royal Exchange*

answers to that part of London, England, where the merchants meet, called the Exchange" (CLJ 42).

Just beyond the Mansion House, turn right into King William Street, which runs south to the Monument and London Bridge. At its junction with Cannon Street (this portion of which was previously named Great Eastcheap) stood Maidenhead Court, in which was the Great Eastcheap Chapel—the first ever used for New Church worship. The origin of the chapel is involved in much obscurity. The chapel was occupied by the Baptists until 1760, when the lease expired, and later by the Swedenborgians, and then the German Lutherans, until its demolition in 1820. Hindmarsh mentions that it was rented for thirty pounds per annum, and that "at the end of the passage, in the street that led to the place of worship, was placed a painted board, on which was inscribed, 'The New Jerusalem Church'; and over the entrance of the chapel was the inscription, 'Now it is allowable,' in conformity to the memorable relation in *True Christian Religion* 508."[6]

Maidenhead Court is shown on old maps of the city. The first Swedenborgian society occupied the Great Eastcheap Chapel for six years—from 27 January 1788, to the end of the year 1793. The first five meetings of the Swedenborgian British Conference were held here, and the first New Church ordinations were performed within its halls.

Continue now along Eastcheap and Great Tower Street to the Tower of London. Keep to the north of the Tower, and enter Royal Mint Street, crossing the Minories (where Swedenborg once lodged) and Leman Street. Continue on an easterly direction along Cable Street—a narrow street, gloomy and, at first sight, forbidding. A very mixed population lives here: Jewish, Negro, Indian, Asiatic, and Scandinavian—on the fringe of dockland. This was Scandinavian London in Swedenborg's time; and names such as Thollander, Carlson, and Svenne are still to be seen. The second turning on the right (Fletcher Street) leads into Wellclose

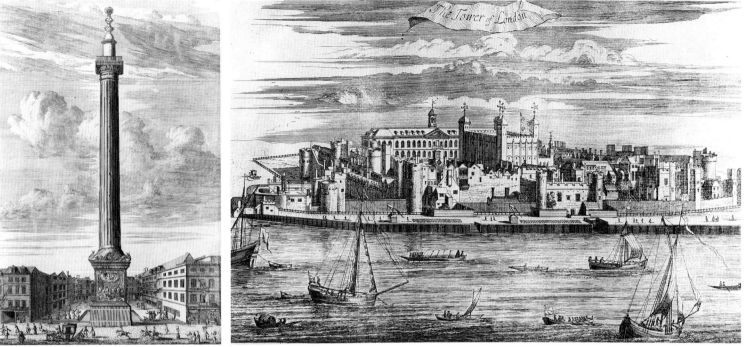

FIG. 284. *The Monument*

FIG. 285. The Tower of London

Square. Here Swedenborg once lodged for ten weeks with his friend Eric Bergstrom, landlord of the King's Arms Tavern; and it is probable that he stayed here at other times too.

Return to Cable Street, and the fourth opening on the right leads into what was until recently Swedenborg Square, formerly Prince's Square, in which stood the old Swedish church. Swedenborg worshiped here, his funeral was here, and he was buried in a vault beneath the altar at the east end of the church. In 1908 his remains were removed to Sweden and placed in a handsome red marble sarcophagus in Uppsala Cathedral. The old Swedish church was demolished and the ground on which it stood made into a garden. Until recently, Swedenborg Square was a delight to visit on

a warm, sunny day. The garden was neat, well kept, and full of flowers. Wooden seats surrounded a small pond, and little children played on swings and merry-go-rounds. Now, however, the square has been much developed and accordingly has lost much of its old charm. In fact, it is but a tired relic of former days, one of those quaint spots of historic association hidden in the heart of London. But Swedenborg's name, at least, is still commemorated here in the East End, with its teeming populace from all over the world, in a drab tenement development named "Swedenborg Gardens."

Return to Cable Street, turning left, and then right along Leman Street, to Aldgate East, where you will find buses running to most parts of London.

FIG. 286. *The Old Swedish Church*

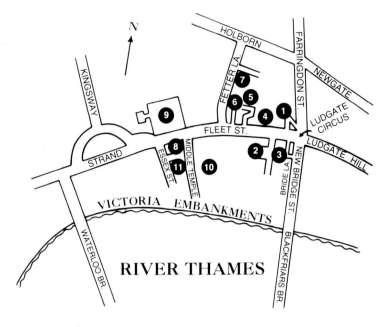

Route No. 2
Key

1. Poppin's Court
2. Salisbury Court
3. St. Bridget's (St. Bride's) Church
4. Ye Olde Cheshire Cheese restaurant
5. Gough Square
6. Crane Court, site of Royal Society headquarters
7. Neville's Court, site of Moravian Chapel
8. Temple Bar
9. Royal Courts of Justice
10. The Temple
11. New Court, site of New Church meetings

FIG. 287. Fleet Street near Temple Bar

ROUTE NO. 2

This will be a shorter route, but one packed with interest. The starting place, again, is Ludgate Circus. (As before, take a bus there from Swedenborg House.)

Under the railway bridge, on the south wall, is an inscription: "In a house near this site was published, in 1702, the Daily Courant, first London Daily Newspaper." Thus was the ball set rolling! Look west, along Fleet Street, the home of the great British newspaper industry; for this is the way we go. The birth of the New Church was possible only where "freedom of the press" existed; and it existed in England in 1749, when the first volume of the *Arcana* was published by John Lewis and printed by John Hart of Poppins Court, Fleet Street.

Poppins Court is the first on the right in Fleet Street, going west. It is likely that Mr. Hart's home and printing shop was down the alley to the left, on the site now occupied by the London *Standard* newspaper. Swedenborg spent many evenings with the Hart family, when the *Arcana* was being printed; and it is interesting to note that at this time, in Gough Square nearby, Dr. Johnson, "the great lexicographer," was busy. Samuel Richardson, on the other side of Fleet Street, was writing and publishing his novels *Clarissa* and *Pamela*, with Oliver Goldsmith as proofreader. And not far away, in the Inner Temple, William Cowper and Edmund Burke were sucking pens in the uncongenial environment of a solicitor's office. Maybe Swedenborg rubbed shoulders with these "giants" in the busy neighborhood of "Grub Street"—as Fleet Street was nicknamed.

Salisbury Court, off Fleet Street (the second opening on the left) is associated with an earlier visit of Swedenborg. In 1744 he traveled to London from Holland with a certain John Seniff, "a pious shoemaker," and a member of the Moravian Church. Seniff introduced him to Paul John Brockmer, a gold-watch chaser, of Salisbury Court, with whom he lodged for two months. This part of London is still the home of goldsmiths, silversmiths, and jewelers. Swedenborg thus lived almost next door to one of the most beautiful of Wren's churches, St. Bridget's (St. Bride's); and in the shadow of the notorious Bridewell House of Detention.

Walk along Fleet Street, past the newspaper offices. Note Ye Olde Cheshire Cheese restaurant, the haunt of Dr. Johnson. We know that Swedenborg was accustomed to dining at an inn in Fleet Street; was it this? See also Johnson's house in Gough Square, a fine example of a house of Swedenborg's day. Crane Court (the last on the right before Fetter Lane) is probably where Swedenborg met Flamsteed, Halley, and other members of the Royal Society, at the society's headquarters.

Turn the corner and walk a little way up Fetter Lane, to see the site of the old Moravian Chapel, where Swedenborg worshiped for a short time while staying with Brockmer. He

FIG. 288. *Crane Court*

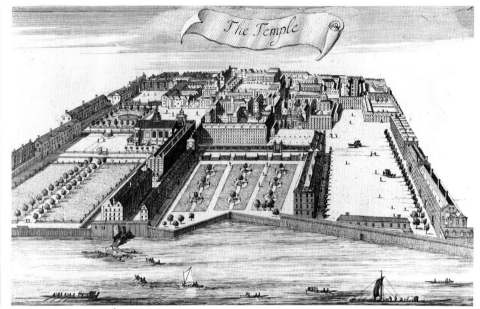

FIG. 289. The Temple

was attracted by the Moravian simplicity of life, but was repelled, at length, by their theological beliefs. Their chapel in Fetter Lane, until completely destroyed by bombing in the last war, was one of the small historic chapels of London. Built in the reign of James I, it escaped the Great Fire and survived many a religious riot. John Wesley resigned from membership of the Fetter Lane Chapel four years before Swedenborg's attendance. The chapel was entered at no. 32 Fetter Lane, and also from Nevill's Court (or Alley)—the third opening on the right.

Return to Fleet Street, and walk on a little way to Temple Bar. To the right lie the Royal Courts of Justice, and to the left lies the Temple. The Temple, before the war wrought havoc there, had not altered much in two hundred years. It is still one of the most charming spots in London, combining as it does antiquarian interest and rural quiet. It is a collection of courts, lanes, squares, gardens, and passageways, where barristers have their rooms and legal men their chambers. The Temple is of particular interest to the Swedenborgian because it was the first domicile of the infant New Church.

Hindmarsh, after describing the Queen's Arms Tavern meeting, says:

> In the course of the following week we engaged chambers in the Inner Temple, near Fleet Street; and to make our next meeting more public, we caused an advertisement to be inserted in some of the newspapers, stating the objects we had in view, and giving a general invitation to all the readers of Emanual Swedenborg's Writings, in London or elsewhere, to join our standard.[7]

We do not know where these chambers were; but Hindmarsh goes on to say that after meeting two or three times in them, he and his friends took more convenient rooms in the New Court, Middle Temple. New Court lies between Middle Temple Lane and Essex Street, and "contains only one large house, which occupies the entire west side."[8]

The meetings in New Court were attended by many persons of reputation and talent, including James Glen of Demerara, who took the new doctrines to America; F. H. Bathelemon, the royal musician; John Flaxman, sculptor; Lieutenant General Rainsford, governor of Gibraltar; possibly William Blake and his father; and others destined to play an important part in the growth of the New Church organization.

The Temple takes its name from Solomon's Temple in Jerusalem; and it is more than interesting that the New Jerusalem Church should have its foundation here.

Essex Street, just to the west of the Temple, is of interest because at no. 31, the home of George Prichard (two-thirds of the way down, on the left), on 26 February 1810, was held the first meeting of the London Printing Society—now the Swedenborg Society.

ROUTE NO. 3

Again the start is Ludgate Circus, reached by bus from Swedenborg House. Before traveling north, you might wish to make a slight sojourn south to Blackfriars, the site of an ancient Dominican monastery. From Ludgate Circus, walk up Ludgate Hill, turn right down Creed Lane, and right along Carter Lane. The first narrow street on the left is Blackfriars Lane, at the bottom of which, on the left, is Hutchinson House—a publisher's depot. This is certainly the site—and possibly the actual building—of the Friars Street New Church Society, which commenced in 1792 under the leadership of the Reverend Manoah Sibly, as an offshoot of

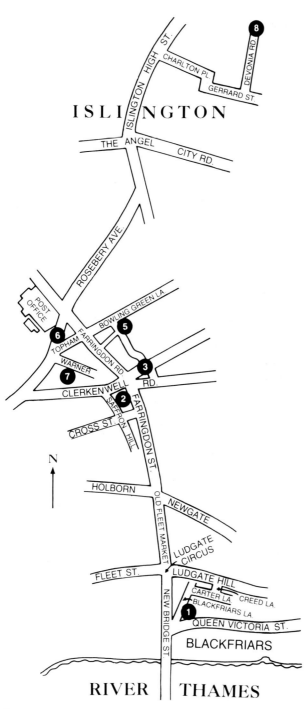

Route No. 3

Key

1. Hutchinson House, site of Friars Street
   New Church Society
2. Site of Cross Street, Hatton Garden Church
3. Clerkenwell Green
4. Clerkenwell Close
5. Hindmarsh's house
6. Site of Cold Bath Square and Shearsmith's house
7. Site of Red Lion
8. Former Site of New Church College,
   now Polish Catholic church

the Great Eastcheap Society. On Horwood's map, the chapel is shown on this spot.

Return to Ludgate Circus, and walk in a northerly direction along Farringdon Street—not one of the most attractive of London's highways. Look out for Cross Street, as it is known today—about the seventh opening on the left. This is the locale where the old Cross Street, Hatton Garden Church used to be. Hindmarsh says:

> The remnant of the society formerly meeting in Great East Cheap, ever since their removal from that place of worship, entertained the design of erecting a more convenient building. This offered itself in the year 1796, in Cross Street, Hatton Garden, when three individuals of the society, viz., Mr. Ralph Hill, of Cheapside, Mr. Richard Thompson, of Snow Hill, and myself, entered into a negotiation with the proprietor to purchase the freehold estate, called *Hatton House*.9

The purchase, the building of the church, and the opening ceremonies, are described in detail—followed by an account of the society's rather precarious early history. In time the society settled down and continued here for nearly eighty years. The name ever associated with the Cross Street, Hatton Garden Church is that of the Reverend Samuel Noble, author of the famous *Appeal* on behalf of the New Church, and brilliant advocate of its teachings throughout his long ministry. It is said that William Blake composed his poem "The Divine Image," in one of the pews of the church; and the baptismal register contains the name of Richard D'Oyly Carte (1844–1901), famed for his production of the Gilbert and Sullivan operas.

Continue along Farringdon Street (here called Farringdon Road) to its junction with Clerkenwell Road, turn right, and immediately left, into Clerkenwell Green—a bit of real old London. Clerkenwell Close leads out of the green—a narrow winding road through some rather "down-at-the-heel" property. No. 32, the home of Robert Hindmarsh, "Printer to His Royal Highness, the Prince of Wales," seems to be the only house demolished during the war. The small, bombed site is on a corner. Horwood's map shows this spot as no. 32, and the numbering is unchanged today. Here, then, lived Hindmarsh, and here he had his Sunday morning meetings (when Swedenborg's writings were read in Latin), before ever the New Church as an organization was thought of.

Walk on past the site of Hindmarsh's house, and take the first turning left—Bowling Green Lane; this will bring you again into Farringdon Road. Cross the road and walk a few steps north, to find Topham Street, formerly Great Bath Street. *Omnia mutantor*—how the times and the customs and the situations change! This little collection of prefabs, surrounded by tall and ugly tenement flats, was once a fine square of desirable suburban residences—Cold Bath Square, with its spring of medicinal waters. Swedenborg took lodgings at no. 26 Great Bath Street, the house of Richard Shearsmith, a wigmaker; here Swedenborg had a "paralytic stroke," just before Christmas 1771; and here he died on Sunday, 29 March 1772.

The house—and, indeed, the whole street—was destroyed in the "blitz," and there is some little doubt as to just where no. 26 stood. The entire area was rebuilt in the last century, and the numbering of the houses was altered. Horwood's map does not show a no. 26 at all. However, the Swedenborg Society has photographs of a house *thought* to be the one (or on the site of the one) in which Swedenborg lodged.[10]

Swedenborg also lodged at one time in Warner Street (at a right angle with Topham Street), with "a Mrs. Carr, next to the Red Lion."[11] The site of the Red Lion is still to be seen.

Now, for one last look, come out into the busy thoroughfare of Rosebery Avenue and take a bus to "the Angel," Islington. Walk north on Islington High Street and turn into Charlton Place, on the right. This will lead you to the top of Gerrard Street, down which the first opening on the left is Devonia Road (previously Devonshire Street). The large Polish Catholic church that you see there was, until 1931, the New Church College, Devonshire Street, Islington. Today the college is located in the north of England, in Manchester, far away from the historic scene that was once Swedenborg's London.

FIG. 290. *Site of Richard Shearsmith's house*

Notes

1. Dennis Duckworth, *A Newchurchman's Guide to London* (London: Finchley, 1956). Available from the Swedenborg Society, Inc., 20 Bloomsbury Way, London WC1, England.
2. Robert Hindmarsh, *Rise and Progress of the New Church* (London: Hodson & Son, 1861), p. 14.
3. Ibid., p. 16.
4. The introduction of *The A to Z of Regency London* (London: Guildhall Library, 1985 reprint) notes in part: "Richard Horwood's plan, here adapted and reproduced in its third edition of 1813 at approximately half the original scale, is one of the most richly detailed maps of London ever produced."
5. Hindmarsh, p. 58.
6. Ibid., pp. 59, 61.
7. Ibid., p. 17.
8. Ibid., p. 23.
9. Ibid., p. 169.
10. See *New Church Life* (June 1929), p. 321, and *New Church Herald* (November 1950), p. 189, for interesting information.
11. Cyriel Odhner Sigstedt, *The Swedenborg Epic* (London: Swedenborg Society, 1981), p. 459, n. 289.

Swedenborg: The Man Who Had to Publish

William Ross Woofenden, Ph.D.

CELEBRATING THE INVENTION OF TYPOGRAPHY, LEIPZIG, 1740*

*As learned Leipzig again tends to the praise of that art which forms words
not by mouth, but in [movable] bronze type,
I too would celebrate the praises of the inventor, but I lack the measures
I know he deserves.
"Who was it?" you ask. Not a Frenchman, nor a Belgian nor an
Englishman—it was, if you believe the evidence, a German!
Fust taught Schoeffer, but before either of them, it was from Gutenberg
that printing presses flowered into service.
He was born from those banks whence flow the Palladian spring; and
from those presses and that source may the spring continue to flow.*

—Emanuel Swedenborg

EMANUEL SWEDENBORG BEGAN TO WRITE and publish at the age of twelve. He continued to do so for seventy years. If hereditary tendencies have any reality, one way of explaining this extraordinary lifelong fascination with writing and publishing might be to take a glimpse at the publishing penchant of his father, Bishop Jesper Swedberg. From this we learn that Swedberg found time, in addition to his episcopal activities, for a literary production of a scope which puts in the shade everything of which even the other theologians of that century were capable (drunk as they seemed to be with writing).

Jesper attributed his bent for writing to an interpretation of his Christian name, which in Hebrew was said to mean "he shall write." He said of himself that ten carts could hardly hold everything he had written and printed. "And yet," he added, "there is much; yes, just as much not yet printed."[1] (One could say nearly the same of his son Emanuel.)

The printing press which was set up at Brunsbo at Swedberg's behest served in great part for the publication of his works. Although I have found no direct evidence to verify it, it seems likely that Emanuel's first literary production in 1700, a poem of a dozen verses to mark the wedding of

---

*In June 1740 the printers in Leipzig celebrated the 300th anniversary of the invention of movable type by Gutenberg. Among the printers was Swedenborg's friend and publisher of his *Principia* Friedrich Hekel, who probably asked Emanuel to contribute to a festal volume being prepared for the celebration. He obliged with a ten-line poem in Latin—here freely translated into English.

Rev. WILLIAM ROSS WOOFENDEN, Ph.D., is professor of theology and philosophy at the Swedenborg School of Religion in Newton, Massachusetts. He is editor of the school's journal, *Studia Swedenborgiana*. He has had pastorates in New York, Detroit, Chicago, St. Louis, and Bridgewater, Massachusetts. In July 1979 and July 1980 he lectured at several universities in Australia on Swedenborgian ideas. He is a director of the Swedenborg Scientific Association. His M.A. thesis, *Swedenborg's Concept of Love in Action*, 1969, was published in 1971. His Ph.D. thesis, *Swedenborg's Philosophy of Causality*, 1970, is available from University Microfilms, Ann Arbor, Michigan. He and his wife, Louise Dole Woofenden, have eight children and twelve grandchildren and live in Sharon, Massachusetts.

Johannes Kolmodin and Beata Hessalia, may have been printed there. Part of the last stanza of this Swedish poem, rendered freely into English, reads:

> *Grant that these twain may, in a happy life,*
> *Angelically live as man and wife.* (OP p. 3)

By the time of this composition Emanuel was already enrolled as a student at Uppsala University. His graduation ten years later also marked his next publishing effort, the printing of his "master's thesis," which dealt with some maxims from Roman ethics.

Then, as one biographer put it, "in spite of war and pestilence, he succeeded in reaching the objective he had early set for himself, namely, a period of study abroad."[2] His travels during the next five or six years took him to England, Holland, France, and Germany, and no doubt he learned, among other things, where the major publishing centers of Europe were located. His only press production during these years was a collection of his Latin poems, which he published at the coastal town of Greifswald (in what was then Pomerania, almost due south of Sweden across the Baltic Sea). It should be noted that "anybody who was anybody" in those days was expected to be capable of writing Latin verse, and the *sine qua non* of the burgeoning scholar was to publish such a volume.

Swedenborg's real interests, however, lay in mathematics and mechanics, and his first claim to fame resulted from his next publishing effort, a short-lived periodical he called *Daedalus Hyperboreus*, or "Northern Inventor," after the Greek hero supposed to have been the world's first inventor. Only six issues appeared, from 1716 to 1718. And although the sixth and final issue of *Daedalus* was dated "April, May, June 1717," Swedenborg did not in fact publish it till October 1718. The reason for this delay was given as "lack of means."

Daedalus is noteworthy as the first scientific journal to be published in Sweden. Swedenborg decided that this magazine should be patterned after the journals of foreign societies and be in the native language, Swedish, instead of the scholarly Latin. However, curiously, due to pressure from the king, the fifth issue was printed in both Swedish and Latin on facing pages (L&M vol. 1, pp. 67–68). It was hoped that this publication would serve as a basis for continuing scholarly efforts in the country, which indeed it did, as it is regarded by the present Society of Sciences of Uppsala as the first of its *Proceedings*.

After the death of his patron Karl XII in 1718, Swedenborg complained bitterly of the change of political climate, which included an apparently complete lack of understanding of the importance of scientific research. The king's death not only was the probable cause of the sudden end of *Daedalus*, it also meant the end of a number of Swedenborg's pet projects: a canal to open an inland waterway from the center

FIG. 291. *Heinrich Keyser printshop in Stockholm.* "Nine of these presses are now running in my printshop."

of Sweden to the Atlantic seaboard, and an astronomical observatory, to name just two. Further, his proposal of marriage to Polhem's daughter was refused around this time. (For possibly more reasons than this, he remained a bachelor all his life.) And although he published four significant studies from 1718 to 1722, this was followed by a twelve-year silence.

The four noteworthy publications just referred to were (1) a first Swedish textbook on algebra, published in Uppsala; (2) a short work on the motion and position of planets, published at Skara; (3) an extensive collection of scientific studies, known in English simply as *Chemistry*, published at Amsterdam; and (4) a volume called *Miscellaneous Observations*, published at Leipzig. During these same years, after being refused the title of a regular official of the Board of Mines (which he had served as a sort of extra employee under the aegis of Karl XII), Swedenborg absented himself for four years from meetings of the board, pending his later recognition as a bona fide "assessor."

Swedenborg the publisher next emerges in 1734. During that year he put through the press at Dresden and Leipzig four large and diverse works, a three-volume set totaling some 1,370 folio (large-size) pages, and a shorter work of 270 octavo (normal-size) pages. Not only had the author asked for nine months leave of absence to see the large work through the press, it also seems to be the case that he wrote the latter work in something less than a month while overseeing the printing work of the others in Leipzig.

Of these, only volume 1 of the large work has been translated into English and kept in print, the work known as *Principia*, and the smaller work—with a long title—*The Infinite and the Final Cause of Creation, also concerning the Mech-*

anism of the Operation of the Soul and Body. The other two works in the large set were technical treatises, principally on the mining of iron and copper.*

At this point one might state with great confidence and only a modicum of exaggeration that from this time to the end of his long life it would seem that Swedenborg seldom was without a pen in hand, busily writing away. One present-day scholar is convinced that Swedenborg was ambidextrous and that when his right hand tired he simply transferred the pen to his left hand and kept on writing! There is much to commend this theory to one's reason, for the prodigious output of literary work that poured from his pen from now on simply boggles the mind. Much of what he wrote he left unpublished. But the works that he did publish during his lifetime, translated for the most part into English and bound in standard-size volumes, need about a six-foot shelf to hold them. If you add to that the posthumously published works, add another shelf!

In light of the above observation, the reader might easily surmise that to continue laboriously to identify and describe in detail the many works to follow and the facts of their publication would get tedious indeed. So let us get on to what I hope will be more interesting things.

It should be noted that Swedenborg continued writing and publishing through the year 1745 in what became a more and more ornate Latin style. However, about that time a major upheaval occurred in his life—call it a transition or a conversion or even (as some have claimed) an excursion into insanity—and three or four years passed in which actual publishing on his part ground to a halt. But these were anything but years of inactivity; rather, they involved an almost feverish reassessment of his life goals, based on what he was firmly convinced was a "call" he had received from the Lord to abandon his career as scholar and bon vivant and enter on a serious and sure-to-be-misunderstood new life as a revelator.

What we *do* know for sure is that during those few years he did indeed abandon his scientific studies and writing and instead embarked on a crash course in Bible study, compiling his own extensive Bible indexes, and he also wrote a very long and tentative work of scripture interpretation. There is some evidence of an intent to publish this work, but eventually he left it incomplete and in manuscript, and a century passed before his followers published it in Latin. It was not until the present century that an English version appeared, titled *Word Explained*, in a ten-volume set.

But then, in 1749, a London printer named John Lewis, of Paternoster Row, announced the publication of a large anonymous work being offered to the public, a work that promised to be a multivolume set of considerable importance. The price unbound was to be six shillings per volume, and the entire proceeds from the sale of the work was to be given to the Society for the Propagation of the Gospel in Foreign Parts. Let me quote briefly from Lewis's advertisement for volume 2:

> This author has struck out a new path through the deep abyss of sacred scripture, which no man ever trod before. He neither meddles with any other commentators nor does he copy them. His thoughts are all his own. But the *Arcana* is not a book to be understood with a slight and cursory reading. The thoughts of this author are sublime and deep. Let the reader peruse them over and over and they will yield a noble repast to a pious mind.[3]

Whatever the hopes may have been, sales were dismally slow. In a note in his *Spiritual Diary* Swedenborg wrote in part, "I received letters informing me that not more than four copies had been sold in two months" (SD 4422). Whether this was a determining factor for his next step is not clear, but he did decide to do an unusual thing with volume 2: he not only instructed the printer to issue the next volume in six sections of one chapter each, he also commissioned a friend of his, John Merchant, to translate the volume into English, and the English sections were issued at the same time as the Latin sections. (These English sections, by the way, have become exceedingly rare and are now collectors' items.)

By the time volume 3 appeared in 1751, our author, for whatever the reason, had abandoned his two-language publishing and, so far as I know, only once again—some eighteen years later—did he publish any of his works in English. That was in 1769, when he published his *Summaria Expositio Doctrinae Novae Ecclesiae.* He commissioned the same man who had translated volume 2 of the *Arcana*, John Merchant (or Marchant—it seems he may have spelled his name either way), to prepare an English translation of this work, which was published the same year in London as *A Brief Exposition of the Doctrine of the New Church.*

One or two other curious facts about this phase of Swedenborg's publishing career are worth mentioning. He obviously and radically altered his way of writing Latin. Instead of the rococo style he had developed by 1745,* he now adopted a spare and simple form, so radically different from

---

*It should be noted that a chapter of the work on iron, dealing with the converting of iron into steel, was translated into French and printed in Strasbourg in 1737. Then in 1762 the whole of part 1 of this work was translated into French and published in Paris. More recently, in 1923, the whole of the work on iron was translated into Swedish and published in Stockholm. Finally, in collaboration with the British Non-Ferrous Metals Research Association, in 1938 the London Swedenborg Society published an English translation of the entire work on copper in a limited duplicated typescript edition. All of these are out of print.

---

*See, e.g., *Regnum Animale* (in either Latin or English) where he writes in part, "There the lymphatics joyfully receive their new guests, beset them with their lips, load them with kisses . . ." (AK 292).

his earlier writing that at least one Latin expert (not a Swedenborgian) that I asked to look at samples of the writing from the two periods swore that the same person could not have written both!

A second fact of interest is that although our author had from time to time published anonymously in his earlier years, his identity was usually quickly discovered. Now, however, he published anonymously for nearly twenty years and, so far as I know, managed to keep his secret—this time prompted by his modest assumption that because what he now wrote was largely based on his revelations, he felt he did not deserve personal credit or fame for the works.

He at last broke the silence in 1768 when he published his book *Marriage Love* and put on the title page, "by Emanuel Swedenborg, a Swede." His countrymen "rewarded" him for this by instituting a heresy trial, the brunt of which fell on two of his most ardent advocates, Dr. Gabriel Beyer and Dr. Johan Rosén. (Both were eventually exonerated, as were Swedenborg's writings.)

His next short work, published the next year, was signed the same way. Later that same year he printed and distributed privately (instead of "publishing" in the usual way) a work we know in English as *Soul-Body Interaction*. We may well applaud the simplicity of this title: the first English edition, published by some of Swedenborg's followers in 1770 was titled *A Theosophic Lucubration on the Nature of the Influx, as it respects the Communication and Operations of Soul and Body* (I'm serious!).

Swedenborg's final published work, datelined Amsterdam 1771, *True Christian Religion*, has on the title page, by "Emanuel Swedenborg, Servant of the Lord Jesus Christ." (Publishers of English editions of some of Swedenborg's other works have tended to identify the author in this same way, even though it is the only instance in which he so designated himself.) One of his biographers, Benjamin Worcester, makes this provocative statement about the fact of its place of publication: "The author had a desire to publish it in Paris, but obtaining permission from the censor *only on the condition that it should bear the false imprint of London or Amsterdam*, he scorned the evasion and published it in Amsterdam" (emphasis Woofenden's).[4]

And with this testimonial to the candid and forthright nature of our "man who had to publish" we have found an appropriate keynote on which to end.

Notes

1. Cited in Ernst Benz, *Emanuel Swedenborg, Naturforscher und Seher* (Emanuel Swedenborg: Natural scientist and seer), 2nd rev. ed. (Zürich: Swedenborg Verlag, 1969), p. 13.

2. Inge Jonsson, *Emanuel Swedenborg* (New York: Twayne Publishing, 1971), p. 20.

3. Cited in full in William White, *Emanuel Swedenborg*, 2 vols. (London: Simpkin, Marshall, 1867), vol. 1, pp. 311–19.

4. Benjamin Worcester, *The Life and Mission of Emanuel Swedenborg* (Boston: Little, Brown, 1907), pp. 315–16.

Toleration and Doctrinal Unity
A Study in Swedish Swedenborgianism, 1765–1795

Harry Lenhammar, Theol.D.

Translated by D. A. H. Evans

The following article by Harry Lenhammar was completed more than twenty years ago as a precis of his doctoral dissertation, published by Uppsala University Press. Inasmuch as Swedenborg had opened a new way of approaching the Christian experience for his readers, there was an inevitable collision with the more conservative elements in Swedish Lutheranism. In the case of academics who taught his theological ideas, or preachers who incorporated them into sermons, there were even heresy trials. Swedenborg, who was a profoundly sympathetic and humane man, during his latter years took an intense interest in the Swedish followers of his ideas who were exposed to such persecution. It was felt by the editors of this volume that this paper should be included to introduce the reader to some of the theological and political issues surrounding Swedenborg in his own time.

Introduction

THE QUESTION OF WHETHER and how far the state should tolerate religious dissent became a live issue in Sweden with the arrival there of Swedenborgianism in the second half of the eighteenth century. Swedenborgianism involved not only certain theological modifications of the church's teaching and central doctrines of orthodoxy but an entirely new way of apprehending the world of the spirit.

In *Arcana Coelestia, Apocalypsis Revelata*, and *Vera Christiana Religio*, Swedenborg's severely critical view of orthodoxy emerges clearly. The orthodox doctrine of the Atonement constitutes, in his view, a danger to morality and also leads to a false notion of the Trinity. Swedenborg lays stress on a person's own responsibility for his or her actions. And the truth of Swedenborg's doctrine of "correspondences"—the basis of his theology—was confirmed, he held, by visions he had and by direct contact with the world of heaven.

Swedenborg's theology could be seen as a development of both that of Pietism and of the Enlightenment. In Radical Pietism and the so-called Wurtemberg Pietism, for examples, orthodoxy was transformed to such an extent that the individual's own religious experience and inner conviction replaced external credos and the authority of the church. Private religious experience was also strongly emphasized in Moravianism, which was very active in Sweden from the middle of the eighteenth century.

But the inhabitants of Sweden were obliged to adhere to the interpretation of scripture as laid down in the articles of the Lutheran faith. This interpretation was protected by laws and ordinances of the Swedish state, while new laws were promulgated as occasion arose to defend the received faith against the recurrent threat of heresy. These heresies could also be regarded from a social and political viewpoint as a threat to the stability of society.

In the eighteenth century the judicial application of the religious laws—both those related to religious freedom in general and those related to freedom of publication—was transferred to a secular court, testimony that it was the interest of society, rather than the purity of doctrine, that was regarded as of primary importance.

Public censorship existed in Sweden until 1766. After that

HARRY LENHAMMAR was born in 1930 in Lenhovda, South Sweden, and was educated in Uppsala, where he studied history, philosophy, and religion. He served as a teacher and in 1967 became doctor of theology. From that year he served as assisting professor in church history at the University of Uppsala, and since 1985 he holds, as professor, the chair of the Department of Church History at the university. Dr. Lenhammer has written the textbook *One Thousand Years of Scandinavian Church History*. Other books of his are *Religion and Freedom of the Press in Sweden, 1809–1940; The General Assembly of the Church of Sweden, 1908–1973;* and *With Trowel and Sword: 250 Years of Freemasonry in Sweden*—all written in Swedish.

religious censorship remained and was not abolished until 1810. Imported books were subject to censorship, and special rules applied to periodicals. The censorship was in the hands of the cathedral chapters, who had a decisive influence in the application of religious laws. It was they who decided what was to be regarded as in conflict with the true faith. Instead of providing a theological consensus for the whole country, the official theological attitude could vary not only from one age to another but from one chapter to another depending on the opinions held by the doctors in the different chapters.

In 1765 certain lecturers and members of the Göteborg Cathedral Chapter attached themselves to Swedenborgianism, and this made the question of faith and dissent a matter of immediate concern to the authorities of church and state.

This study seeks to illustrate the relation between the demand for toleration of dissent and the demand for doctrinal unity and to elucidate the authorities' position in the matter.

Swedenborgianism in Göteborg

GÖTEBORG—COMMERCIAL CENTER AND DIOCESAN CAPITAL

In the eighteenth century Göteborg developed into a flourishing seaport, which gave the town a marked cosmopolitan air. Its vigorous mercantile activity created an influential merchant class, some of whose members were of foreign stock, a fact of some significance for the religious climate of the town. Englishmen and Germans formed their own congregations. The German influence also manifested itself in Moravianism, which created considerable interest, especially among the humbler members of the merchant class.

The merchants were ready to give a sympathetic hearing to the ideas of the Enlightenment with its leaning, both in politics and in religion, to common sense and utility. Their religious concerns expressed themselves in philanthropic and charitable activities, while on the other hand they had no interest in questions of dogma, which they regarded as belonging to a past epoch. Rather, the cultural activities to which they devoted themselves were conditioned by this air of the Enlightenment, affecting their newspapers and their social club life. The lecturers who taught at the diocesan theological training college participated keenly in all this activity. Some of them traveled to England to further their intellectual interests and were well versed in foreign scholarship. The leading figure in this group was Johan Rosén, who lectured in Latin, while his colleague Gabriel Beyer, who taught Greek, concerned himself rather with biblical scholarship.

Old and new ways of thinking, as well as old and new social patterns, were brought face to face in the cathedral chapter, which was composed of the lecturers together with the bishop and dean. It was the chapter's task to ensure that no heretical doctrines circulated in the diocese.

THE DISPUTE BEGINS

Swedenborg often passed through Göteborg on his journeys and thus came to know some of the lecturers and merchants, who became interested in his ideas. Beyer and Rosén were particularly interested, and in a letter to Swedenborg, Beyer asked him a number of questions about his theology, especially his interpretations of scripture. A collection of Beyer's sermons, published in 1767–68, exhibits a cautious adherence to Swedenborg's theology. Swedenborgianism is used by Beyer to stress the need for a religion that is practical and useful, but Beyer did not employ it as an instrument of polemic against the doctrines of the Lutheran church. As for Rosén, he showed his favorable interest in Swedenborgianism in a review of *Apocalypse Revealed* in his journal.

At the convocation of diocesan clergy in 1768 the teachings of Swedenborg became the object of criticism. This arose from a treatise, published in connection with the convocation, in which the doctrine of the Atonement was explained along the lines of Johann Dippel and Swedenborg. The treatise had been approved by Bishop Eric Lamberg. The clergy called on the chapter to pronounce on Swedenborg's works. Beyer wanted to refer the matter to the Crown, while Dean Olof Ekebom urged the orthodox view, that is, that the clergy themselves should handle the matter, and the dean's arguments prevailed. The chapter therefore referred the matter to the Estate of Clergy in the Swedish Parliament. Because, in the Period of Liberty, Parliament exercised supreme power in the state, the Estate of Clergy enjoyed great influence in church affairs. Thus, in the spring of 1769, the question of Swedenborgianism was passed to the Estate of Clergy for consideration, and in its deliberations the bishop of Göteborg participated, though this did not prevent the chapter in Göteborg from continuing to discuss the matter. The debate now became particularly intense, partly because Swedenborg himself arrived to participate in it and defend his visionary theology, and partly because this defense became a public document after Beyer had seen to it that Swedenborg's letter was included in the official report of the proceedings.

A layman of orthodox views, A. J. Aurell, who had earlier fallen out with the chapter, took care to see that the purity of the faith should not suffer through the mutual loyalties of the members of the chapter or their wish to avoid doctrinal disputes. He demanded to be informed whether the chapter recognized the censor's stamp of approval that Beyer's volume of sermons had, according to the printed copy, received from the chapter. The approval was formally incorrect—the chapter had not decided to give the approval—but was in accordance with the common practice, and it was recognized by the chapter. Small publications were given approval through the president only.

THE DISPUTE WIDENS

A letter from Swedenborg came to play an important part in the subsequent course of events. This letter had taken the matter beyond the sphere of law and dogma into Beyer's own personal religious life. In the autumn of 1769 Beyer's wife had died, and on her deathbed she apparently disso-ciated herself from Swedenborgianism. Thereupon Swed-enborg wrote a letter in which he explained her action as the work of evil spirits, and added some strongly worded criticism of the doctrines of the church. This letter, which Beyer had caused to be printed, created much stir, and the dean set an investigation in motion. While this investigation was taking place, the matter came to the notice of Parliament; the bishop of Göteborg sought, by letter, to calm the local disquiet and sent instructions as to the further handling of the affair. Having himself had no share in the course of events, he now had, with the publication of Swedenborg's letter, an oppor-tunity to appear publicly as the defender of the purity of the faith. Aurell continued his attacks and, on the publication of the letter, commenced legal proceedings against Beyer and also approached directly the speaker of the Estate of Clergy to inform him of Swedenborgianism in Göteborg. In the prevailing atmosphere of tolerance and enlightenment, however, the Estate of Clergy was reluctant to appear as the defender of the pure faith, and the clergy in Parliament therefore resolved to act with extreme caution in challenging Swedenborgianism. They turned the whole matter from a theological affair into a legal one: smuggling written matter into Sweden. By so doing they had managed to pass the question over to a secular official, namely the attorney gen-eral, a functionary whose task it was to see that law was observed and to initiate court proceedings in religious cases. Thus the view of the church as an organ of the state had prevailed in the Estate of Clergy. The Estate of Clergy de-clined a proposal from the Uppsala Cathedral Chapter to publish a refutation of Swedenborgianism; they wished to avoid drawing public attention to the matter.

THE CHAPTER AND THE CROWN

The attorney general for his part showed no reluctance to lay down theological pronouncements. He declared that Swedenborgianism was a heresy causing public disturbance and therefore required the intervention of society. He pro-posed that the Göteborg chapter should be asked to submit a statement on Swedenborgianism and should be called upon to supervise properly the application of the censorship reg-ulations. This was also the decision taken by the Council of the Realm. Most of the members of the chapter found the teachings of Swedenborg to be in conflict with the articles

of the Lutheran faith and the Word of God. Beyer, however, asserted that the teachings were in accordance with the Word of God, which, he said, was superior to the articles of the faith. Swedenborg's biblical exegesis was, he maintained, the full development of ideas that other men had earlier only glimpsed.

Rosén too defended Swedenborg's views, saying that the enlightenment of the age should not be affronted by holy writ's receiving just treatment. The bishop made his dissent from Swedenborgianism plain in the same terms as the ma-jority of the chapter. He defended the convocation treatise (mentioned earlier) on the ground that it was addressed to an educated public capable of judging for itself such ques-tions.

The Council of the Realm was unable to regard the state-ments of Beyer and Rosén as constituting a rejection of Swed-enborgianism, and, though a minority of the council urged a strict application of the religious laws, which would have meant a prosecution, the majority decided to give the two men one more chance to clarify their position. The majority felt it was important not to attract public attention; a trial would only increase general interest and give further cur-rency to the heresies. At the same time the Council of the Realm condemned Swedenborgianism in stronger terms than before.

Analogous action was taken on the administrative level. Beyer and Rosén were debarred from all theological teaching duties. Further measures, too, were taken by the bishop and chapter in the defense of the purity of the faith, in an effort to meet diocesan opinion, which demanded sterner action against the false doctrines. Beyer and Rosén for their part tried to overcome their isolation by demonstrating that the bishop and members of the chapter had themselves some share in the alleged heresies.

THE ESTABLISHMENT VIEW PREVAILS

The government's aim was to try to resolve the dispute that had arisen in the church by eliciting a statement from the two lecturers in acceptable theological terms and thereafter permitting them to retain their positions. This brought up the whole problem of the integrity of the individual's reli-gious views versus the demand of authority for official ad-herence to publicly received doctrine. The two men refused to renounce their inner convictions, and they could take up this attitude with all the greater force in that they had en-lightened opinion on their side.

Beyer and Rosén's new statements were not found ac-ceptable by the Council of the Realm, which now referred the matter to the courts. The justification for this was that the heretics, so far from heeding the warning they had re-ceived, had persisted in their errors and left the authorities with no alternative to court action. This step also prevented the Estate of Clergy from taking up the matter once more. In court, however, the argument for toleration made itself felt, and, as it could not be shown that Swedenborgianism had given rise to public disturbance, that case was overridden. On the other hand, toleration could not be taken so far that existing laws were nullified; the chapter followed the orthodox line, and the two accused were debarred from promotion, while the restrictions already imposed on them were confirmed. In 1778 Beyer gave up his position as lecturer, and with that the matter was written off.

The attitude taken to Swedenborgianism in Göteborg shows that society was threatened; it was not concerned to act in defense of the purity of the faith for its own sake. That was left to the chapter to defend, with such means as were at its disposal. For the followers of Swedenborg the events in Göteborg showed that the age of toleration had not yet arrived; caution was still necessary.

The Swedenborgianism of Beyer and Rosén was known to later Swedenborgians through the statements they submitted to the court, of which copies were distributed among sympathizers, and through a number of catechism documents, of which some were later printed. Here we see reflected the markedly rationalistic note of their brand of Swedenborgianism. Beyer and Rosén also became known to later Swedenborgians as translators of Swedenborg's writings.

Swedenborgianism in Skara
THE LEADERSHIP OF THE DIOCESE AND UNITY OF CREED

In Göteborg, Swedenborgianism acquired its special character from the mercantile culture of the town and from the dual participation of the lecturers in that culture and in the cathedral chapter. In Skara, on the other hand, the background was quite different; here, the emergence of Swedenborgianism was preceded by vigorous Pietist activity. While in Göteborg it was the lecturers who brought to a head the question of toleration, in Skara it was the diocesan clergy around whom the issue centered. In addition there was the fact that the dean of Skara was none other than the powerful and very important theologian Andreas Knös. After a Moravian past, Knös, under the influence of Bible Pietism, had renounced Moravianism and dissociated himself from orthodoxy. Christianity ought to be a religion of works, he maintained, with its creed taken direct from holy writ.

The diocesan leadership showed in a number of cases what limits it set to freedom of doctrine. Frequently it adopted the method of preserving tranquillity in religious affairs by dampening down doctrinal arguments. In the discussions the rural deans were often brought in to participate, so that in Skara a greater degree of cooperation existed between the clergy and their leaders than was the case in Göteborg.

THE PROBLEM EMERGES

A case arose in Skara of a clergyman who, in a Swedenborgian vein, had proclaimed a subjective view of the Atonement. He was summoned to examination, but the matter was written off after the chapter had found itself able to accept the explanation he had given. In another case, Swedenborg's writings were explicitly adduced, and this case was only settled after it had come to court and the accused had there renounced his heresies. In these two cases the chapter had managed to preserve unity of doctrine by proceeding cautiously.

At the convocation of diocesan clergy in 1773 Swedenborgianism was condemned as heretical, and some criticism was also voiced of Knös's Bible Pietist theology. Knös's attitude to Swedenborgianism at the beginning of the 1770s does not emerge from the official material, but in a private letter he expresses himself favorably, though cautiously, about the teachings of Swedenborg, especially because he had made the Bible the foundation of his doctrine.

THE DISPUTE INTENSIFIES

In the mid-1770s unity of doctrine in the diocese was put to a severe test. At the convocation of diocesan clergy in 1775 the treatise published for the occasion aroused fierce discussion because a note of Bible Pietism characterized its exposition. On the same occasion the bishop again uttered a warning against Swedenborgianism, which was also the subject of some individual representations to the chapter.

The vigilance of the chapter increased. A candidate for ordination received a warning for holding Swedenborgian sentiments, and the chapter also sent a circular letter to all the clergy of the diocese to urge them to be on their guard. This letter particularly singled out for condemnation Swedenborg's false teachings about the Trinity and the Atonement. At the following convocation the bishop managed to keep the peace by curbing arguments about doctrine. A critical attack on Swedenborg's teachings was not permitted to be published, while theological disagreements were subdued by the fact that that year's treatise dealt with an uncontroversial subject.

Yet another case arose in which the chapter had to decide what attitude to adopt toward an individual clergyman, in this instance one who had previously been warned because of his Swedenborgian sympathies. On that occasion he had renounced them, but this time he was dismissed from his post. This served as a warning to all clergy with Swedenborgian leanings. The increased vigilance against heresy also manifested itself in the censor's treatment of a volume of dogmatics composed by Knös. In this work, written in Swedish, Knös expressed strong criticism of the church's teaching on the Trinity, the Atonement, and other aspects of doctrine.

Permission to print the work was given only after the author had made certain alterations.

OPEN WAR

The unstable balance of forces in ecclesiastical politics, manifested in the royal toleration policies and the ever-more-open questioning of the church's doctrines on the diocesan level, aroused a strong orthodox reaction to Knös's Swedish work on dogmatics. This orthodox reaction reached its climax at the convocation of 1780. At the very start the formulation of the subject for that year's treatise (on the Atonement) awoke disputes in the chapter. The bishop now held to the orthodox line and did not wish to blur the sharpness of disagreement at the expense of the purity of the faith. When the treatise was presented to the meeting by a clergyman well known for the strength of his hostility to Swedenborgianism, a fierce debate took place. The foremost critic was Dean Knös, whose views the Swedenborgians of Stockholm were also eager to notice; his Bible Pietist theology could be used by them as a screen for their own views. The dispute continued after the convocation was over, especially in connection with the chapter's attitude to censoring a number of orthodox sermons. Uppsala Cathedral Chapter gave permission for the printing of a work strongly critical of Knös.

In Stockholm the new age again made itself felt; questions of theological doctrine were no longer the concern merely of the clergy but were the subject of public debate. In the leading newspaper of the capital a discussion of theological censorship was carried on, taking as its starting point the state of affairs in Skara. In this newspaper debate the orthodox demand for the application of the existing laws for the protection of religion was confronted by the opposing argument that stressed the anachronistic character of theological censorship in the midst of the century of toleration.

As far as theological questions were concerned, Knös tried, in a large work on dogmatics, to counter his opponents. This work occasioned a prolonged censorship struggle in the chapter. Knös's opponents maintained that in a number of points his theology was contrary to the articles of the Lutheran faith, to which the clergy were bound by oath. Knös's reply was that his theology was well in accord with holy writ, whose authority was superior to that of the articles; therefore his theology could not be heretical. Only after certain alterations, and with much hesitation, did Knös receive the censor's approval. The opposition to his theology had intensified in the chapter.

Knös for his part looked for support in the more tolerant view of doctrinal disputes taken by the secular authorities. While the bishop was away in Parliament and with Knös as chairman of the chapter, the chapter referred the case of a Swedenborgian clergyman to the courts, hoping that the matter would be written off. The chapter's course of action was not approved, however, because the accused had never been warned. At a further hearing with the bishop in the chair, a sterner line was taken, which looked for support to the greater sympathy that Gustav III's policies showed for the viewpoint of the church since the Parliament of 1786. This time too, however, it was found possible, with the court's help, to dismiss the case, which was one of purity of doctrine alone: no social disturbance had been caused.

In Skara, Swedenborgianism enjoyed strong support from Dean Knös and his family, from the household of Lars Lindström, a merchant, and from many clergymen's households. The movement was more strongly supported among the clergy in Skara than in Göteborg.

In Skara the chapter had managed to handle Swedenborgianism as a private affair of the diocese. It was the bishop, the chapter, and the convocation, not the Crown, that controlled events.

Swedenborgianism in Stockholm

Swedenborgianism in Stockholm developed in a cultural climate of greater tolerance than its adherents in Göteborg and Skara enjoyed. The Edict of Toleration of 1781 was taken as a sign that the age of toleration had arrived, and the king himself saw to it that the religious laws were applied in a very liberal spirit.

The Swedenborgians could benefit from the interest in mysticism, which found expression in the various "orders" or secret societies of the day (of whom the Freemasons were the best known), from occult activities of a more private kind, practiced by educated and uneducated alike, and also from the tradition of scientific speculation, which went back to Böhme and Paracelsus. Around 1780 the brothers August and Carl Fredric Nordenskiöld emerged as leading figures among the Swedenborgians in Stockholm; they tried to establish contact with their fellow believers both in Sweden and abroad, and around them a little group of courtiers and others gathered.

UNDER THE CENSORSHIP

The Swedenborgians were vigorously active in trying to spread their doctrines through translations, reprints, and original compositions. They talked of creating a society to promote this activity, though this was not realized: they did not succeed in getting anything actually printed except for a dictionary of dreams, and there Swedenborg's ideas were so confusedly presented that some Swedenborgians dissociated themselves from the volume. An attempt was made with only partial success to exploit as an instrument of Swedenborgian propaganda a newly founded newspaper to advance the king's policies. It was indeed supported, to start with, by a recommendation from the cathedral chapter, but when matter directly translated from Swedenborg himself appeared in its columns the recommendation was withdrawn.

Theological censorship was the subject of keen debate in the press, but this same censorship was employed by the chapter to prevent the advocates of freedom from presenting their case in full. The Swedenborgians made an attempt to have their translations printed in Copenhagen and raised a fund to this end, with contributions from the king and from sympathizers in various parts of Sweden. However, this plan failed: theological censorship existed in Denmark too. A little Swedenborgian tract by Christian Johansén was printed in Skara through the agency of the wife of Dean Knös, but led to a trial in which the printer was found guilty. Thus, the censorship laws constituted an effective hindrance to Swedenborgian activity.

IN THE PROTECTION OF THE RELIGIOUS LAWS

Swedenborgianism in Stockholm became involved with many other beliefs, for instance alchemy. In the 1780s August Nordenskiöld was engaged in alchemist pursuits under royal protection. He drew parallels between Swedenborgianism and alchemy, between the transformation of the soul and that of gold. The patrons of this activity were Lieutenant Governor Axel von Axelson and, at Drottningholm, Deputy Lieutenant Governor Adolf Fredrik Munck, a favorite of the king and a prominent figure among the occultists and theosophists. One of their protégés was Court Chaplain, Peter Fredell, who had studied in Skara and knew Dean Knös well. In 1780 Fredell delivered before the king in Stockholm a celebrated sermon, whose substance deviated considerably from the doctrines of the church and was marked by Radical Pietism and Quietism. Fredell's large library contained a great many writers, such as Böhme, Paracelsus, the Petersens, Hohburg, Gyon, Arnold, Dippel, cabalistic authors, and so on. He belonged to a Radical Pietist group, the New Sect, which attracted a good deal of attention in the early 1780s. The king protected them against the religious laws. Fredell himself enjoyed the king's favor, as a number of official appointments show, but at last a breach arose between him and the court; Fredell was forced to give up his offices, and he died in poverty. The obscurity of Fredell's mysticism led some Swedenborgians, among them those of Skara, to refuse to cooperate with him.

Swedenborgianism's association with popular beliefs about demoniacal possession appears in Johan Tybeck, a clergyman from the neighborhood of Strängnäs, who was also familiar with Knös and his theology. His acquaintance with a girl who was thought to be possessed by evil spirits convinced him of the truth of Swedenborg's teachings about the connection between men and spirits. Tybeck tried to persuade Knös to adopt a more active policy in promoting Swedenborgianism, but Knös remained steadfastly attached to caution: the im-

portant thing was to practice one's religion, not to alter the formulation of doctrine.

This cautious attitude also characterized another of the leading Swedenborgians in the Stockholm district, the previously mentioned Christian Johansén. A manufacturer from Eskilstuna, he had known Swedenborg personally and had been won over early to his teachings. He was approached by many with queries about Swedenborg's doctrines, and his information and replies were marked by a cautious Swedenborgianism expounded without any criticism of the doctrine of the church. The religious laws were not employed either against him or against Fredell or Tybeck; their Swedenborgianism was expressed in such a way that it would have presented a difficult target in proceedings to uphold the purity of the faith, when a tolerant king was on the throne.

Swedenborgianism's Growth and Decline

THE EXEGETIC AND PHILANTHROPIC SOCIETY

After the Parliament of 1786, Gustav III showed greater consideration to the interests of the clergy and their demand for legal protection for the doctrines of the church. But although the climate had become less favorable, the Swedenborgians grew steadily more active, and on November 1, 1786, the Exegetic and Philanthropic Society was founded. Its primary aim was, on the English model, to work for the publication of Swedenborg's writings. Swedenborgians all over the country joined the society, though many chose to keep their membership a secret. The society won powerful patrons at court, chief among them Duke Karl, the king's own brother.

To begin with, only brief works were printed, translated excerpts from Swedenborg's writings. These appeared under the common title of *Samlingar for Philantroper* (*The Philanthropists' Library*). These publications aroused critical notice from two quarters, first from the adherents and essayists of the Enlightenment, who in *Stockholms Posten* made repeated assaults on mysticism in all its forms and whose attacks were answered in a series of articles by Tybeck criticizing his opponents' materialist viewpoint; and second from the chapter which declared that the printing of these writings was in breach of the censorship laws, and they instituted proceedings.

The subsequent activities of the society were considerably involved in magnetism, a way to cure the sick by sitting together and holding hands. The members believed Swedenborg's doctrine about spirits provided an explanation and they gave it in their practical exercises. This gave the critics a new angle of attack, and the Swedenborgians were now described as lawbreakers and cranks who constituted a danger to society. Both the men of the Enlightenment and the clergy received support for their actions from the king, while the Swedenborgians sought in vain to extract any privileges from him. The religion established by law won the day. With the aid of the censorship laws the chapter stopped the Swedenborgian contributions to the press debate, while the men of the Enlightenment heaped ridicule on Swedenborgianism.

THE DECLINE OF SWEDENBORGIANISM IN SWEDEN

In different quarters Swedenborgians tried to defend themselves by adroitly taking advantage of any opportunities presented themselves. But the involvement of the movement in magnetism had opened the way for criticism of the more purely theological aspects of Swedenborgianism. In a publication that won the recommendation of the Estate of Clergy, Swedenborg's doctrines were subjected for the first time to a detailed examination. The refutation that the Estate of Clergy had not ventured to have published on the occasion of the Göteborg case, for fear of giving the movement gratuitous publicity, could now be printed, because Swedenborgianism was now so heavily compromised that public opinion would support the clergy in condemning it. It was no longer a question of lack of toleration or a dispute about irrelevant theological doctrines.

The Swedenborgians had difficulty in defending their position. Various works were printed in Copenhagen and smuggled into Sweden. In this way a number of translations of Swedenborg's own writings were printed, among them *Vera Christiana Religio*.

Under the combined impact of the loss of support from the king and the outbreak of the French Revolution, the movement took on an increasing color of political radicalism. The changed state of affairs after the king's death in 1792 brought with it no change in their own situation. Enthusiasm for the Exegetic and Philanthropic Society cooled among its members; interest in Swedenborgianism took other outlets. They zealously pursued magnetism, which they endowed with an extremely religious character, and followed with eagerness accounts of popular visions and revelations. These they regarded as a sign that the last days were now at hand.

The increasingly occult tone of the movement aroused criticism from certain of the Swedenborgians themselves, who were more interested in pleading for a Swedenborgi-

anism of the inner way. In a document from the 1790s Dean Knös utters some favorable observations about Swedenborg, who understood the inner world. An outward separation, such as the English Swedenborgians worked for, interested neither Knös nor the movement's other supporters in Sweden. They worked for a Swedenborgianism in which the chief stress was laid on enactment of faith in a person's mode of life. That was where the inner life of faith should be seen, rather than in connection with public business out in the world. Christian Johansén came more and more to assume the leadership of this brand of Swedenborgianism, and as an instrument of making it better known, his followers managed to have several publications printed in Copenhagen, among them sermons and catechisms.

Our inquiry has shown that Swedenborgianism developed in different forms. The type that appeared in Göteborg and Skara was essentially theological, constituting a relaxation—conditioned by Pietism, mysticism, and the Enlightenment—of certain central points in the church's doctrines, such as the doctrines of the Atonement and the Trinity. This theological form of Swedenborgianism was able to fuse itself with the official doctrine of the church, until the orthodox interests succeeded in obtaining political backing for their demand for action. One should distinguish from this form of Swedenborgianism the occult type, associated with magnetism and scientific speculation. There were certain personal links between these two branches, though not such as to allow one to speak of mixed forms. This second type of Swedenborgianism spread widely in certain circles in Stockholm in the tolerant climate that lasted for most of Gustav III's reign. But this led to the collapse of Swedenborgianism and to the end of the climate of toleration, because the critics of the Enlightenment made no distinction between theological and mystical Swedenborgianism. Both were condemned. The interests of society required a judicious adjustment between the demand for toleration and compulsory adherence to the state church. It was only when the stability of society was threatened that intervention appeared necessary. But in the next century, during the period of Romanticism and liberalism, the freedom became greater.

Swedenborg in Stockholm

Olle Hjern

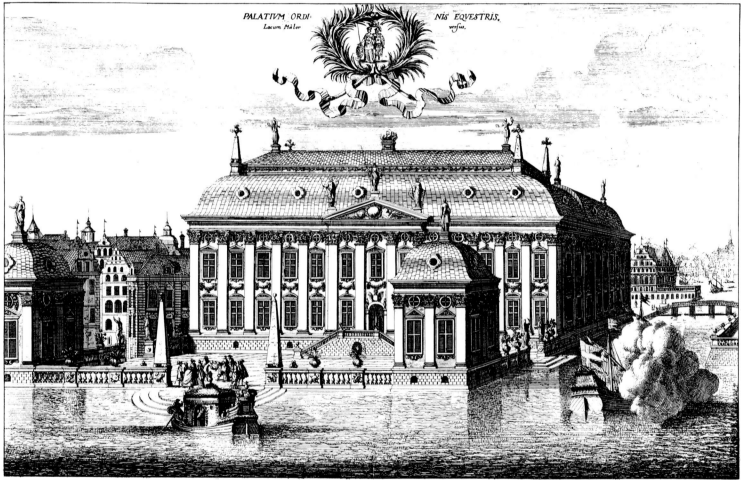

PALATIVM ORDI-
Lacum Mäler

NIS EQVESTRIS,
versus.

FIG. 292. *Riddarhuset (House of Nobles)*

OLLE HJERN was born on 21 February 1926 at Jönköping, Sweden, and is a minister of the New Church (Nova Hierosolyma) and pastor of the church in Stockholm. He holds B.Th. Swedish university degrees in Semitic languages, Latin, and comparative religion from Lund, Uppsala, and Stockholm universities, and has taught at the Theological School of the Lord's New Church in Bryn Athyn, Pennsylvania. Olle Hjern has been editor of *Nya Kyrkans Tidning* from 1958 to 1983 and 1987, and in 1978 was chairman of Skandinaviska Swedenborgs Sällskapet. He has authored several publications and articles, including, with Inge Jonsson, *Swedenborg: Hans verk och efterföljd* (*Swedenborg: His Work and Influence*), published in 1976 by Proprius Publishers of Stockholm.

FIG. 293. *Emanuel Swedenborg, bas-relief on Järnkontoret*

WE KNOW THAT EMANUEL SWEDENBORG spent much of his time traveling in countries outside of Sweden, and that he spent the last part of his life in England. But it is quite clear that the place where he worked the most and to which he always returned was Stockholm, the same place where he was born. Of course this city has changed quite a bit since he lived there, but still the whole structure of the central parts, where he is said to have been seen quite often, is much the same as during his lifetime.

According to the "Old Style" calendar,"* Emanuel Swedenborg was born on 29 January 1688, in Stockholm in Jakobs Kyrka (Church of St. James), at 18 Regeringsgatan in the present center of the city. His father then served as a royal court and army chaplain, and the distance from there to the old Royal Palace was quite short. The records of the baptism of the infant Emanuel Swedberg in the parish church are still preserved.[1] Nearby is the park Kungsträdgården (the King's Garden), and we also have accounts of how, later on, the adult Emanuel met with people in this central Stockholm park. Facing the park is the present-day Järnkontoret, the "Iron Office," which today incorporates some functions of the eighteenth-century Board of Mines. The Board of Mines was dissolved in the mid-nineteenth century, but its activity was continued by the Kommerscollegium (Board of Commerce) and by the Järnkontoret, both existing earlier.

One can see on the outside corner of the Järnkontoret building a large portrait medallion of Emanuel in profile, with several other prominent Swedish scientists. Around 1950, when I myself was a young man and new in the New Church, we used to investigate the old buildings at Regeringsgatan in order to find out how much was left of the house where Swedenborg was born. Clearly part of the house was still there, but some years after that, all the old buildings around the Church of St. James were leveled to the ground, and now there are only recently built buildings.

Just about the same seems to apply to the house where Swedenborg had his first permanent Stockholm residence as an adult, near the now-almost-disappeared Brunkeberg Square. Only when he had arrived at the mature age of thirty-six and had secured a position as full assessor in the Board of Mines (15 July 1724) did he rent his own rooms in Count Gyllenborg's house within the parish of Santa Clara, not far from the present central railway station. During his stay in this patrician house he is said to have employed a manservant, called Olof. He also at that time was in close, though perhaps not always cordial, association with Lars Benzelstierna, to whom his sister Hedvig was married, and who lived in the same house.[2]

The island of Gamla Stan (the Old Town), is the very central part of Stockholm, and for a long time Emanuel worked and resided there. The Board of Mines was in Swedenborg's time situated at Mynttorget in Gamla Stan, in a building that until recently was used by the central Swedish government. When the Board of Mines was moved from Mynttorget, pieces of Swedenborg's furniture were moved to the building occupied by the present Kommerscollegium at Riddarholmen.

The Kommerscollegium is close to Riddarholmskyrkan, the royal funeral church, where all his royal friends are entombed. Quite nearby is Riddarhuset (the House of Nobles), where, as the representative of his family, he was quite active as a member of the Swedish Diet from 1719 until his last years. During Emanuel's childhood the old Royal Palace,

*In 1753, Sweden adopted the Gregorian ("New Style") calendar, which reflected an eleven-day difference in dates from the previous Julian ("Old Style") calendar.

FIG. 294. *Jakobs Kyrka*

FIG. 295. *Entrance to present-day Järnkontoret*

Island of Gamla Stan, Stockholm

FIG. 296. *Riddarhuset in 1983*

Key

1. Stora Nygatan #7
2. Kommerskollegium
3. Riddarholmskyrkan
4. Riddarhuset
5. Mynttorget
6. Royal Palace
7. Räntmästarehuset
8. Hornsgatan

FIG. 297. *#7 Stora Nygatan*

also in this same area, was destroyed by a fire, and during his adult life the new one that can be seen today was built by the great Swedish architect Nicodemus Tessin and finished by his son, Carl Gustaf Tessin, a close friend of Swedenborg's.

In 1728, Swedenborg's sister Hedvig died, and shortly afterward he moved from the northern part of the central city to Gamla Stan. He then took quarters at Stora Nygatan, now no. 7, on the corner of Stora Nygatan and Göran Helsings Gränd. The residence was very close to the Board of Mines, now situated at Mynttorget, and during his five years here he finished his three-volume work *Opera Philosophica et Mineralia*. He recorded a remarkable vision from Stora Nygatan in his *Spiritual Diary*:

The interior sight was opened to me, and I looked into that street of Stockholm called Stora Nygatan and then I saw many people walking about there. I was afterwards brought into that street, and there were angels with me who said that in the houses round about there was not anyone alive, but all were dead, that is, spiritually, so that they were horrified and did not want to go any further. When they are dead in the houses there, there appear no windows in the houses, but holes within which all is dark; but when they are alive, windows appear, and men within them. I was next led through the little new street [Lilla Nygatan]. It was said that some few there were living. After this I was conducted back towards the coast, at the market-place. There along the shop-houses scarcely anyone was living, that is, some were. Likewise at the other side of the bridge, where the life-saving houses were. In the market-place there were not anyone who was living, except in the old house at the corner. None, moreover, in the large house there. Next to that, I was conducted to the long street [Långgatan, Västra Långgatan] out of the market-place, next to that, to the chemist's shop and no one was alive, but I did not look far within. Nor was there anything from the market-place towards the sea and so on. (SD 5711)

Swedenborg's experience, in the spiritual world, of the judgment of the people of this district in Stockholm, provides quite an exact picture of this district today. The same streets—Stora Nygatan, Lilla Nygatan, and Långgatan—are still there, as is the marketplace near the water, Kornhamnstorg.

When Swedenborg returned from his fourth journey abroad in October 1740, he left this street and rented a flat vacated by his relative the great scientist Carl von Linné, generally known in English books as Carolus Linnaeus. It was the so-called Räntmästarehuset, on the corner of Slussplan and Skeppsbron, in the southern part Gamla Stan, near the water that separates this part of Stockholm from the southern central part, Södermalm. The old buildings there remain more or less as they were in Swedenborg's time.[3]

FIG. 298. *Old houses at Stortorget, in original city center*

FIG. 299. *Räntmästarehuset in the early twentieth century*

FIG. 300. *The old Academy of Sciences*

FIG. 301. *Interior of the old Academy of Sciences*

In November 1740, Linnaeus invited Swedenborg to become a member of the then recently organized Academy of Sciences, and they must have known each other quite well. While still a student of medicine, Swedenborg's elder cousin, Johan Moraeus, served as Emanuel's private tutor in his home.[4] He and his wife took over the family estate of Sveden, near Falun in the province of Dalarna, and this is the reason why Linnaeus was married there to Moraeus's daughter, Sara Elisabet Moraea. During the years 1738–40 Linnaeus had been active as a physician in Gamla Stan, and held very popular public lectures there.[5] Swedenborg and Linnaeus

simply cannot have avoided meeting each other. It is far more likely that they saw each other almost daily.

An original copy of the work *Heaven and Hell*, donated by Swedenborg to Linnaeus, has been preserved in the library of the Swedish Academy of Sciences and is now in the Stockholm University Library.

Swedenborg was quite frequently abroad, as he was between 1743 and 1745, but during that time he had apartments arranged for himself in Stockholm. In 1745 he resumed residence in Räntmästarehuset. Frans G. Lindh, the main researcher of Swedenborg's places in Stockholm, thus describes this residence:

> According to the taxation list, the apartment was on the first floor and facing south because, as is well-known, Swedenborg preferred to have his residence in rooms with sun from the south. Downstairs there was a coffeehouse, which surely was visited by the coffee-loving Swedenborg and which was owned by a shopkeeper by the Danish-sounding name of Finn Holsten Hobel.[6]

From an account by a Swedish clergyman, we also know that Emanuel Swedenborg could be seen now and then at the tavern Gyldene Freden, the "Golden Peace," a restaurant from that time, which still exists in Gamla Stan. In the eighteenth century this place was especially connected with the appearance of the Swedish national poet Carl Michael Bellman, famous also as a singer and musician, younger than Swedenborg but partially contemporary. Evidently, both of them had very good contacts with the family of the Dutch ambassador, de Marteville, and both of them had problems in connection with the same bishop, Petrus Filenius.[7] They had resided near each other in the south of Stockholm,[8] and it is likely that Bellman and Swedenborg, two well-known Stockholm characters from the same country, saw each other now and then.

The name of the clergyman who gave us this information was Carl Nyrén, who has written:

FIG. 302. *Interior of the restaurant Gyldene Freden (now called Gyllene Freden)*

To arrange his installation party the week after that, Bishop Filenius asked me to serve as marshal on the same occasion and to go around in a rented car inviting guests to the inn Gyllende Freden, where they would be honestly treated. Among other acquaintances I then also had that of Assessor Swedenborg, whom some people deeply venerated while others treated him with ridicule. But he was not very talkative, and he went away after the first toasts had been drunk.[9]

Not too far from central Stockholm is the estate Svindersvik and the Palace of Drottningholm, both of them well kept, well preserved, and regularly shown to the public. At Svindersvik Swedenborg took part in social evenings, arranged by his friend Carl Gustaf Tessin. And on one occasion, in September 1760, it is mentioned that, instead of taking part in the usual billiard playing, the guests remained seated for a long time listening to Swedenborg give an account of his ideas.[10] This is evidently the year when Swedenborg's function as a seer and prophet and as the author of his anonymously published religious works became generally known.

The name of Drottningholm refers to the *Drottning*, the "queen," and in Sweden we especially connect this place with Queen Lovisa Ulrika, powerful, intelligent, but controversial. She had received the palace as a personal gift, even though it had been named for an earlier queen. She sent for Swedenborg, asking about her deceased brother, who was in the other world. Swedenborg must have impressed her intensely, and several times he must have visited Drottningholm (DOC vol. 2, pp. 647–66). He told C. C. Gjörwell in August 1764 that he had just given books recently printed in England to the king and the queen at Drottningholm and had been well received.[11] I have seen one of these volumes, with the beautiful mark of the queen, in the collection of the present Royal Library in Stockholm. Several other volumes of this kind evidently once belonged to this library, but as the library did possess double copies some

FIG. 303. *Aerial view of Drottningholm Palace today*

were sold at auctions there in the nineteenth century, probably to libraries and private people in England and America.

At present the Palace of Drottningholm with its wonderful park is a permanent residence for the royal family, and it is also well known for its most interesting Royal Theater, where operas and ballets from the eighteenth century are regularly performed in summer. The theater dates from Swedenborg's time, and then was only for royal guests. One might wonder whether Emanuel had ever been there.

In 1743, Swedenborg bought part of the block "the Mole" at Södermalm, and later on he took his residence there on the street Hornsgatan (now no. 41–43).

The southern part of the present central city, Södermalm, has changed quite a bit, and in the biographies of Swedenborg we are reminded of large and destructive fires within this district, especially the one that he saw clairvoyantly from Göteborg in 1759.[12] Nevertheless, the streets and lots of

FIG. 304. *Drottningholm Palace seen from the east in Swedenborg's time*

FIG. 305. *Maria Magdalena Church*

FIG. 306. *Mariatorget, where Swedenborg Park is located*

buildings there remind us of Swedenborg's time. In Hornsgatan is Maria Magdalena Church, occasionally attended by Swedenborg; it was badly damaged by fire but restored again. There, in 1751, Swedenborg had a well-known conversation with Christopher Polhem at Polhem's funeral, when Polhem expressed his astonishment at the minister's talk concerning Polhem's future resurrection, as he was already resurrected and fully alive (SD 4752). Near this church one can still find an old square, now called Mariatorget (Maria Square), formerly Adolf Fredrik's Square. During his later years, Swedenborg lived close to this square, and it is not long ago that the Stockholm city authorities honored Swedenborg by establishing Swedenborg Park and placing in it a bust of him by the Stockholm sculptor Gustav Nordahl. At its base is a relief showing Swedenborg in his nearby garden introducing an angel to a little girl by letting her look into a mirror.[13]

Maria Square is close to the present Swedenborg Street, and, consequently, to the place of his former estate. In the part of the block where Swedenborg lived, "the Mole," in Krukmakargatan, is a recently built house where the architect Nils Orento has tried to restore parts of Swedenborg's garden. The gate to this garden, in art metalwork, was made by the young Stockholm artist-metalsmith Annika Söderström, and on it are figures of plants from Swedenborg's garden. Among these plants is the pea, which, among other seeds, had evidently been imported from America, where the Swedberg-Swedenborg family had so many contacts.[14]

We don't know exactly when he moved to his own house, but we know that he lived there in 1747 when, at his own request, he obtained permission from the king to take leave of his office at the Board of Mines.[15] At last he now had his own house, surrounded by a large and beautiful garden with "summerhouses" where in quiet harmony he could open his mind to the divine revelations he experienced and which he felt a duty to communicate to the world. Rev. C. J. N. Manby, pastor of the New Church in Stockholm until his death in 1920, writes in a pamphlet:

We will never forget our deep-felt spiritual reverence when, about 1865, we entered for the first time the place where Swedenborg had his home during the last decades of his life, in Hornsgatan, Stockholm. The house was still in good condition. The garden was quite large and left a free space around the house. A gate or latticework door formed the entrance to a long walk, at the end of which was situated the well-known summerhouse. We entered his house and noticed how a gentleman in the eighteenth century lived. We also climbed the stairs to the upper story. His summerhouse was quite well preserved. We wrote our names in a register that was kept there for that purpose. We also climbed into the loft of the summerhouse. All was so new to us. It was a lovely summer's day. No wonder our feelings were subject to holy awe.[16]

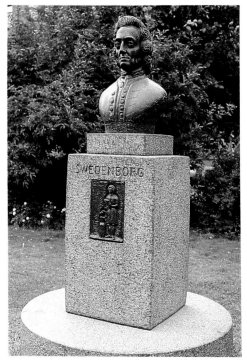

FIG. 307. *Bust of Emanuel Swedenborg, by Gustav Nordahl, mid-1900s*

In her biography, Cyriel Sigstedt quotes a description of Swedenborg's summerhouse from an 1867 article in the English *Intellectual Repository*:

At the end of the walk are two poplars; behind them is the summer-house, which looks down the garden walk between the trees. It occupies the middle of the end of the garden and is about fourteen feet square. There are three stone steps up to the doorsill, a double door, on each side a window; a vine gathers over them and the top of the door, and clambers partly over the roof. On the two sides are external traces, and the shutters, of windows which are now obliterated inside. In the room is another door opposite the entrance; it opens into a lobby, a pace wide, on the right of which is a cupboard, on the left the bricked-up doorway, which formerly led to the covered way; a part of it remains between the summer-house and the long side of the garden, away from the street. From that angle to within a few yards of the house the covered way has been removed. It appears as if it originally ran down the length of the garden, and served as a protected path to the summer-house—pleasant in bad weather or at night. Like the house, the summer-house or study is built of logs, raised on a granite foundation about a couple of feet from the ground. It is as gay in color as the house—dark red lines on yellow ground, with white window frames and a black roof, all well contrasted with the bright green of the vine. The roof does not go up to a ridge or gable, but is broken through by a short vertical portion, in which are long narrow windows, serving to light the loft over the room. This, in turn, is roofed with hip rafters. On the two points of the ridge is a ball ornament, on which is perched a little golden star. A chair which belonged to Swedenborg remains in the summer-house. His organ lately stood there, but has passed into the possession of Mr. Hammer, in whose museum, in Byström's Villa, it may be seen.[17]

Christian Hammer, the former owner of the organ, was a well-known Stockholm jeweller and art collector, and was very interested in Swedenborg. As a point of interest, he was the model for "the wealthy blind man" in August Strindberg's *Dream Play*. Nordiska Museet and Skansen bought the organ from his estate.[18]

F. G. Lindh writes about Swedenborg's home in his article "Swedenborg som Söderbo":

Only farmhouses were facing on to Hornsgatan; in the western corner of the grounds was a coachhouse with appurtenant storeroom for garden implements, and in the eastern corner was a stable and cattleshed, which, facing the yard, was semi-detached with a small timber house containing three large rooms; on the ground floor were two rooms, one of which was, no doubt, a spacious kitchen, and on the first floor one room; most likely his gardener with family lived there. They also looked after his horse and the cows. It could be taken for granted that he did not let the buildings, equipped for the animals, stand empty, in particular as it is known that Swedenborg liked to mix in society, in the city as well as in the country, and therefore needed means to move about in a comfortable way, the distances being long and roads and streets being beneath contempt. Thus, he probably kept a horse and a carriage. It is also known for certain that Stockholmers of that period generally kept cows that grazed in the daytime on the commons outside the city and in the evenings were driven home to their cattle sheds by special so-called cowherds. Swedenborg's diet also included milk as an important foodstuff, if not the most essential one. The fact that he lived so far out at Södermalm was, to be sure, also an advantage for him in that respect, as his cows did not have so far to go to and from the pasture outside the city. At the back of the gardener's house, facing the grounds, there was a small garden with flowerbeds and shrubs of box, cut in the Dutch fashion in the shape of birds, pots, and all sorts of other figures. On the other side of this little planted yard, opposite the gardener's house, Swedenborg's own dwelling was situated, a half-timbered brick house, with paneled outside and inside. Swedenborg's house was painted yellow and the gardener's house red; both of them rested on solid stone foundations. On the ground floor Swedenborg had two large rooms and one small room; one of the two large ones was probably used as a reception room or drawing room, the other as a study, and the small room was probably used as a bedroom. The upper floor, on top of the dwelling rooms, was

FIG. 308. *Stockholm viewed from the east*

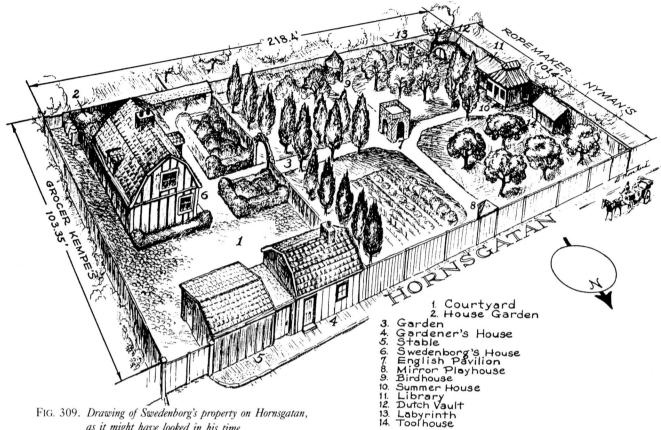

FIG. 309. *Drawing of Swedenborg's property on Hornsgatan, as it might have looked in his time*

1. Courtyard
2. House Garden
3. Garden
4. Gardener's House
5. Stable
6. Swedenborg's House
7. English Pavilion
8. Mirror Playhouse
9. Birdhouse
10. Summer House
11. Library
12. Dutch Vault
13. Labyrinth
14. Toolhouse

arranged as a sort of greenhouse, probably with a glass wall facing south and with a brick floor; the greenhouse and the dwelling rooms underneath were all equipped with tile stoves; evidently the house was warm and cozy also in the severe wintry cold; in the study Swedenborg used to have a continuously burning log fire. One might feel chilly from sitting writing all day long; and the fact that Swedenborg suffered from indigestion and had to live almost exclusively on a milk diet was probably due to the sedentary life he led. On the other hand, it is known that he did not admit a log fire in his bedroom, but had instead so many more blankets or quilts during the night. This was a habit he had picked up on his journeys abroad, in England and France in particular, where, as you know, there is no fire in the bedrooms.[19]

Swedenborg was always very interested in trees, flowers, and shrubs and, as did the men he has described as those of the Most Ancient Church [see Glossary], no doubt he experienced these growing things as representing and signifying spiritual realities. Now, in this home, during several years and with a tremendous industry, he wrote all the volumes that contain what he saw as the Lord's revelation to the New Church. Outwardly he seems to have lived a quiet and retired life, though he was always willing to receive those who cared to visit him. As of 1760 he had three female servants, and some years later, we hear, for the first time, that a family took care of his garden and had the benefit of its income. More or less accurate anecdotes all testify to the

very deep affection the serving or employed people felt for their master, Emanuel Swedenborg.[20]

Swedenborg's close friend Carl Robsahm, who lived at another estate in Stockholm near Swedenborg's, tells us in his *Memoirs of Swedenborg* how anxious the gardener and his wife were when during certain nights Swedenborg appeared to be in a state of great disturbance and desperation (DOC vol. 1, pp. 30–51).[21] From his room they could hear words such as, "Lord, help me! Oh Lord, my God, do not forsake me!" But when they approached him then, he calmly assured them that everything was fine with him and that whatever happened to him, happened by the permission of the Lord. The gardener's wife had also told Robsahm how shocked she was when once she had opened the door to Swedenborg's room and seen his "burning eyes." But Swedenborg then told her, "Do not be afraid, the Lord has opened my bodily eyes, and I have seen in the spirit [*in spiritu*], but in a little while I shall be restored again, and this does not hurt me" (DOC vol. 1, p. 40). After half an hour, she told Robsahm, this appearance as if of a fire had disappeared.

The garden is especially mentioned in connection with another incident from the year 1769 when from the Estate of Clergy in the Swedish Diet an action had been started to put Emanuel Swedenborg into a mental hospital—a very popular method for treating religious dissenters in Sweden at that time. A friend of his in the diet had heard of the plans and sent him a message with the advice that he should immediately leave the country. But Swedenborg stayed. Rob-sahm tells us, "Swedenborg was then very grieved but soon he went out into his garden, there he kneeled down praying to the Lord in tears, asking what he should do now? And he then got the consoling conviction that nothing evil would happen to him" (DOC vol. 1, p. 47). The plans were not carried out; after all, at that time Swedenborg had quite powerful supporters of high standing within the country.

The orthodoxy was hard and condemning, but some important clergymen had been somewhat softened by the influence of the writing of the philosopher Christian Wolff, whose philosophy had been a matter of interest also to Swedenborg himself.[22] One of these men was Andreas Knös, who might have helped Swedenborg in the difficult situation. Concerning this, I would like to quote from a well-informed booklet by the Swedish physician H. I. Carlson:

> When, at the 1769 Diet within the Estate of the Clergy, the writings of Swedenborg were discussed for the purpose of having their author declared insane and if possible put into an institution, it was commissioned to one of the most learned and orthodox members of the Estate, Dean Andreas Knös, to give a verdict concerning the matter, and this man who was too conscientious not to judge what he did not closely know, started a serious and impartial study of all these large works, the consequence of which was that he finally found himself convinced concerning their truth. The Estate then decided not to proceed further, and the issue was silent.[23]

Andreas Knös died in 1799 as a fully convinced New Church believer.[24]

We have a description of a visit to Swedenborg's garden in the book *Notes in Swedish History* by Carl Christopher Gjörwell, printed in Stockholm in 1786. As a librarian of the Royal Library in Stockholm, Gjörwell paid a visit to Swedenborg on 28 August 1764 in order to get his recently published books for the library and also to investigate his ideas on religion. After his visit there, Gjörwell wrote:

> A little while ago I came from Assessor Emanuel Swedenborg, whom, on behalf of the Royal Library, I asked for his last works published in Holland. I met him in the garden, which he has beside his house at Södermalm and in Hornsgatan, taking care of his plants and attired in simple garments. His residence was a wooden house, low, and looked like a garden pavilion, and also the windows were toward the garden. Without knowing me or without knowing my commission he told me with a smiling face: "You are going to take a walk here in the garden." I then answered him that I wanted to have the honor of visiting him, and on behalf of the Royal Library, of asking for some of his most recent works from him that we might have a full set of his works, as we already possessed the earlier volumes which he had handed over to the Royal Secretary, Mr. Wilde. "Yes, with the greatest pleasures," was his answer. "I had also already intended to send them there,"

FIG. 310. *Summerhouse at present site in the Swedenborg rose garden, Skansen*

FIG. 311. *Roses in the reconstructed Swedenborg garden*

he added, "as the reason for my publishing them has been that they should be generally known and come into the possession of intelligent people." I thanked him for his kindness, and he showed the books to me, and after that we walked around together in the garden. In spite of the fact that he is an old man and that the gray hairs protruded everywhere under his wig, he walked briskly, talked with pleasure and with a special cheerfulness. His face was indeed thin and meager, but cheerful and smiling. Soon he started, of his own accord, to talk about his ideas, and as in reality it was my second purpose to hear them by my own ears, I listened most eagerly to what he said, did not contradict his doctrines, but only asked questions, as it were for my own enlightenment.[25]

The recounting of another remarkable visit to Swedenborg's garden can be found in the book *Tessin and Memorabilia*, published in Stockholm in 1819 and containing extracts from Carl Gustaf Tessin's diaries and manuscripts. Like Gjörwell, Tessin went there in order to find out more about Swedenborg's visions and his doctrinal teachings. He was very well received, and Tessin mentions his happy cheerfulness, his friendly, jovial, and open attitude. Generously, he gave Tessin information and promised to send him a copy of *Heaven and Hell*. This visit took place in March 1760.[26]

Robsahm mentions three summerhouses in Swedenborg's garden, one with quite strange doors, a labyrinth ("only to amuse honest people . . . and especially their children"), a blind gate, which could be opened and, by applying a mirror inside, give an illusion of a far larger garden. This of course was the gate that he opened when he wanted to show an angel to the young girl Greta Askbom in the quite authentic anecdote. All stories about the man testify to a cheerful mind, a playfulness, and a great love for children.

It has also been claimed that Swedenborg's *real* house was destroyed shortly after Swedenborg's death because of fear of ghosts there.[27] But there is little doubt that Rev. C. J. N. Manby visited the right house, the house where Emanuel

FIG. 312. *Swedenborg and Greta Askbom, bas-relief by Gustav Nordahl, 1970s*

lived and worked regularly. This house had a passage, a corridor, to the still-preserved summerhouse. It is said that when he was working, he was mainly surrounded by Bible texts in Latin and in the original languages, dictionaries, and his own indexes and excerpts from the Bible, and probably also by his record of his own spiritual experience. When it was not too cold he must have worked quite often in the summerhouse.

As servants Swedenborg often used married couples. Then the husband evidently took care of the horses, cows, and the garden, from which he generally enjoyed some profit, and the wife took care of Swedenborg's housekeeping, when necessary. Sometimes they had children, who often surrounded Swedenborg. F. G. Lindh has remarked—and his sources were the census records for the city of Stockholm— that when retired, these servants were remarkably well-off. When Swedenborg finally moved into his house in Hornsgatan, the serving couple had their three girls, between ten and fifteen years of age, living with them.[28]

Different stories have been told about Swedenborg's life during his later years in the south of Stockholm. From these years we have an account concerning his hesitancy to take the Lord's Supper in his residential parish, the parish of Maria Magdalena. It should be mentioned that for a long time the regular taking of this sacrament was regarded as a national duty in the state Church of Sweden. Two bishops are said to have approached him about the matter. Swedenborg claimed that his living connection with the Lord and the spiritual world was enough for him, and he could not stand the sermons of the parson. But he agreed to take the sacrament from his curate, with whom he felt a greater spiritual friendship (DOC vol. 1, pp. 36, 37).[29]

From Swedenborg's very last years we have accounts of visits by quite young men, all seriously interested in spiritual matters. One of them was evidently the visionary "Skara boy," whom Swedenborg's friend Gabriel Beyer in Göteborg thought would be able to reveal healing cures from the spiritual world. Swedenborg admitted that the boy's experiences testified to contacts with the spiritual world, but at the same time he stressed his immaturity, both as to age and spiritual experience. Nevertheless, he was very much interested in the boy, asked that he might be sent to him in Stockholm, and promised to arrange that he be taken care of properly.[30]

An oral, but quite probable, tradition says that Swedenborg was visited by the young Jonas Pehrson Odhner, who had been a private tutor in one of the first New Church families in Sweden, the Lars Lindström family, who was well and personally acquainted with Swedenborg. In 1795 in Copenhagen, Odhner published the first translation into Swedish of *True Christian Religion*. He became one of the Swedenborgian clergymen of the Church of Sweden.[31]

Two rather well-known clergymen in Sweden were also

among Swedenborg's visitors at Hornsgatan. Both of them were probably rather far from Lutheran orthodoxy. Yet both of them seem to have been in quite good spiritual agreement with Swedenborg at the time of their visits. One was Nicolas Collin, for a long time active within the Swedish Church in America, which had been entirely stamped by Jesper Swedberg and his many "heresies." When he visited, Nicolas Collin at first evidently wanted information concerning his recently deceased brother. Swedenborg did not give him any such information, but he did invite him to have coffee in the house, and there the two gentlemen discussed the problem of the human soul and the concept of the spiritual world. Among other things, they considered the ideas in Nicolaus Wallerius's *Psychologia Empirica*, published in Stockholm in 1755 (DOC vol. 2, pp. 417–24, 1158).[32] The other clergyman to be mentioned is Anders Rutström, author of hymns, leader of schools, and at that time the central person of the Moravians in Sweden. For several years this man was exiled because of his heresies and died in jail in Sweden in 1772. Swedenborg had told Carl Robsahm that "This Rutström saw every thing, but his life and deeds showed that his Moravian sect was dearest to him, in which he had long ago confirmed himself, even to persuasion" (DOC vol. 1, pp. 37, 627).

In Swedenborg's biographies are recorded oral traditions about personal contacts between Swedenborg and the most remarkable central person of the early Swedish New Church movement, Christian Johansén, a pious and devoted man, and a true spiritual leader. His correspondence concerning spiritual matters formed much of the early New Church movement in Sweden. Copies of his letters were widely distributed, and large collections of copied letters from him exist in some Swedish archives. He started his studies of Swedenborg in 1767, at the young age of twenty-one. He also became a pioneer of Swedish technology and the iron industry. The great day of his life, hardly at all mentioned in his many letters but recently found recorded in a preserved personal diary, was a beautiful winter's day in Stockholm, with light snow falling all day long. On 3 January 1770, Swedenborg received him in his home. The meeting seems to have given Johansén quite renewed strength as a New Church believer. It is possible that they also discussed the work *De Cultu et Amore Dei* that day. It has often been said in the New Church tradition that Swedenborg told Johansén that this work was of less value than the later works. But Johansén must have felt it was nevertheless of great value, for he soon started to translate it into Swedish. His translation manuscript is preserved in the Royal Library in Stockholm (DOC vol. 2, pp. 709, 710).[33]

The Swedish author Carl-Göran Ekerwald writes in a new article on Swedenborg:

> One of Swedenborg's younger friends was the chemist Carl Wilhelm Scheele, the discoverer of oxygen. When Swedenborg set out on his last journey—I think it was in 1770, to Holland and England—he had decided that the remaining chattels in Hornsgatan were to go to Scheele, who was at that time working at the chemist's shop with the name "Korpen" [the Raven].[34]

However, Swedenborg had at the same time provided that a marble table with inlays of playing cards, and five small pictures with inlaid bird motifs were to be handed over to his former place of work at Mynttorget in Stockholm; they still can be seen in the premises of the Swedish Kommerscollegium (Board of Commerce). In 1763, Swedenborg had written a paper "Huru inläggningar ske uti marmor-skifvor, til bord eller annan hus-zirat" ("How Inlays Should Be Made in Marble Plates, for Tables or Other House Ornaments"), published in that year's volume of documents from the Royal Swedish Academy of Sciences. Evidently, the marble table

FIG. 313. *Swedenborg's table with marble inlay*

FIG. 314. *Summerhouse, interior with chamber organ*

FIG. 315. *Summerhouse photographed at its original site, ca. 1880*

FIG. 316. *Summerhouse being moved to the present site, at Skansen*

and the other objects with inlays were not made by Swedenborg himself but had been ordered by him in Holland and then manufactured there under his supervision.[35]

After his death, Swedenborg's estate in the south of Stockholm must have undergone many changes. Some parts of the estate were pulled down or moved, other parts soon deteriorated. By the 1880s, there was some uncertainty as to what was genuinely "Swedenborgian."[36] The one part that was unquestionably authentic was the small *lusthus* (the summerhouse). At the bicentenary of Swedenborg's birth, in 1888, the new house at Hornsgatan was already built; between the buildings standing on the grounds where Swedenborg's house and garden once were situated, members of the New Church in Sweden and in other countries put up a cast-iron plaque with Swedenborg's image in a gilded medallion. On the plaque are engraved the following words: "*Venturum est tempus quando illustratio*" (A time is coming when there will be enlightenment) (AC 4402).[37] As of October 1986, advanced plans are being made for restoring the whole garden with the summerhouse.

The island of Djurgården, at the eastern part of the present central Stockholm, was in Swedenborg's time a popular place for relaxation, excursions, picnics, and entertainment, and has remained so to the present day. No doubt Swedenborg visited the place often. Around 1890, energetic attempts were undertaken to make the island of Djurgården a center for Swedish folk culture, and for this purpose the large open-air museum, Skansen, was founded. Its founder, Arthur Hazelius, the son of a New Churchman, decided in cooperation with the New Church societies to move the old summerhouse—then the last remaining part of Swedenborg's estate—to the new open-air museum. This took place in 1896.[38]

In 1960, the Skansen authorities relocated the summerhouse again, creating around it a rose garden that was supposed to have as much similarity to Swedenborg's garden at his original estate as possible. But more and more the house needed repairs, and financial assistance for this was then provided by the Scandinavian Swedenborg Society, founded in 1978, in cooperation with New Church and Swedenborgian organizations in America and England. In September 1985, Swedenborg's chamber organ, used by him for private meditative playing, was also repaired. Now we can listen to a concert with music from Swedenborg's time, played by the organ conservator himself, Mads Kjersgaard. Kjersgaard conjectures that this organ had been made by young journeymen at one of the organ workshops situated near Swedenborg's residence in Hornsgatan.

At the end of July 1770, "after having generously provided for his both servants," as F. G. Lindh puts it, he left Stockholm for Holland and England, especially to publish his work *True Christian Religion*. Thus, he left this world not in the city where he was born but in London, on 29 March 1772.[39] But from these quiet corners in the Swedish capital, the most important spiritual impulses had already gone out to the whole world, and this process is certainly still continuing.

FIG. 317. *Hornsgatan House, photographed at its original site, ca. 1880*

Printed Circular Letter from Stockholm, 1875

The property which EMANUEL SWEDENBORG owned at Stockholm for sale.[40]

It is a great pleasure to us to know that our brethren in England are taking the warmest interest in the spiritual welfare both of EMANUEL SWEDENBORG'S fatherland and of our City, where the great Revelator lived on his property, Hornsgatan No. 43, during the most memorable part of his life! Having had much evidence of this warmhearted interest of our English New Church brethren, we hope that it is not in vain to ask them and other friends abroad to assist us with means to purchase EMANUEL SWEDENBORG'S former property, which he owned until his death and which now is for sale. This property has in itself so many remembrances dear to us that is is very desirable that it come into the possession of the New Church.

But to these remembrances we wish very much to add another: A common New Church Library containing all kinds of New Church literature, and to complete this we should like to receive, with great thankfulness, grants both of money and of books.

Thinking that many wish to be shareholders in the property, so dear to us because of its remembrances, we have on the lists of subscription suggested one rubric for donations and one for shareholders. One share should amount to 100 crowns or about £6, and the subscribers should get legal security in the property. All the lists of subscription will be bound and kept for future times.

Additionally, each subscriber will get a receipt showing the name of the bearer, and we will always consider this receipt to be a letter of recommendation.

The sum needed to purchase the property is 25,000 crowns, or about £1,389, and to put the property in suitable condition, we need another 5,000 crowns, or about £278.

As our principal aim is to build a New Church society in our city, and being in want of the material means to carry out this purpose, we suggest also one rubric for those of our brethren who would kindly like to assist us with a certain sum either yearly or otherwise.

It is desirable if the lists could be returned to the Treasurer of the Society, Mr. Z. Falk, Regeringsgatan 82, before October this year.

Recommending us to the good will of our brethren, we bring them our most hearty salutations and our best wishes.
Stockholm 26 May 1875.
In behalf of the New Church society

A. T. BOYESEN
Chairman

EDV. ABRAHMSEN
Secretary

Notes

1. Frans G. Lindh, "Swedenborgs födelseort och dap" (Swedenborg's place of birth and his baptism), *Nya Kyrkans Tidning* (1914), p. 138.
2. F. G. Lindh, "Swedenborgs som äktenskapskandidat" (Swedenborg as a candidate for marriage), *Nya Kyrkans Tidning* (1917), pp. 41–43.
3. F. G. Lindh, "Swedenborg som Söderbo" (Swedenborg as resident of Södermalm), *Nya Kyrkans Tidning* (1921), p. 137.
4. Cyriel Sigstedt, *The Swedenborg Epic* (London: Swedenborg Society, 1981), pp. 97, 162.
5. Carl Forsstrand, *Linné i Stockholm* (Linnaeus in Stockholm) (Stockholm: Hugo Gebers, 1915), p. 58–151.
6. Lindh, "Swedenborg som Söderbo," p. 138.
7. P. D. A. Atterbom, *Svenska siare och skalder* (Swedish prophets and poets) (Örebro, Sweden: N. M. Lindh, 1863), vol. 1, pp. 13, 48.
8. Arne Munthe, *Västra Södermalm intill mitten av 1800-talet* (West Sodermalm until the mid-nineteenth century) (Stockholm: Församlingshistoriekommittén i Sancta Maria Magdalena och Högalids församlingar, 1959), p. 313.
9. Quoted from ms. in Fredrik Böök, *Svensk vardag* (Swedish daily life) (Stockholm: P. A. Norstedt & Söners, 1922). p. 85.
10. Sigstedt, p. 276.
11. C. G. Gjörwell, *Anmärkningar i Swenska historien* (Notes in Swedish history), (Stockholm: N.J. Nordström, 1786), sect. 26, pp. 220–24.
12. The oldest account of the Göteborg fire is in a letter by Immanuel Kant, published in English as an appendix to the Goerwitz-Sewall translation of *Dreams of a Spirit-Seer* (London: New Church Press, 1899, 1915).
13. The story was originally told in a letter from her grandson Anders Fryxell, printed in Bernhard von Beskow, *Minne öfver assessoren i Bergs-kollegium Emanuel Swedenborg* (Memory of the assessor in the Board of Mines Emanuel Swedenborg) (Stockholm: P. A. Norstedt & Söners, 1860), p. 108.
14. Kerstin Wickman, "Jobb for en droppsbyggare" (Work for a bodybuilder), *Stockholms Tidningen* (24 February 1982).
15. Lindh, "Swedenborg som Söderbo," pp. 138–40.
16. C. J. N. Manby, *Swedenborg och Nya Kyrkan* (Swedenborg and the New Church) (Stock-

holm: Nykyrkliga Bokförlaget, 1906), p. 38.

17. Sigstedt, p. 492.

18. Carl-Göran Ekerwald, "Lusthus för andes-kådare" (Summerhouse for mystics), *Vi* 43 (23 October 1986), p. 13.

19. Lindh, "Swedenborg som Söderbo," pp. 145, 146.

20. Henrik Alm, *Emanuel Swedenborgs hus och trädgård* (Emanuel Swedenborg's house and garden), *Samfundet Sankt Eriks Årsbok 1938* (Yearbook of the Association of St. Erik 1938) (Stockholm: Wahlström & Widstrand, 1938), p. 162.

21. Carl Robsahm, "Robsahms memoirer öfver Swedenborg" (Robsahm's memoirs of Swedenborg), *Skandinavisk Nykyrktidning* (1876), pp. 60, 74, 91, 105, 122, 137, 153, 170. Also published in Tafel's *Documents* (DOC).

22. Tore Frängsmyr, "Wolffianismens genombrott i Uppsala" (The breakthrough of Wolfianism in Uppsala), *Skrifter rörande Uppsala universitet. C. Organisation och historia* (Papers concerning Uppsala University: Organization and history) (Uppsala: Uppsala Universitet, 1972), vol. 26, p. 136.

23. H. I. Carlson, *Anmärkningar vid Herr Professor And. Fryxells skildring af Emanuel Swedenborg* (Notes on Professor And. Fryxells account of Emanuel Swedenborg (Stockholm: Nya Kyrkans Bekännares förlag, 1876), p. 2.

24. Harry Lenhammar, "Tolerans och bekännelsetvång" (Toleration and doctrinal unity), thesis (Uppsala: Uppsala University, 1966), p. 315.

25. Gjörwell, pp. 220–24.

26. *Tessin och Tessiniana: Biographie med anecdoter och reflexioner, samlade utur framledne Risk-Rådet m.m. Grefve C. G. Tessins egenhändiga manuscripter* (Tessin and memorabilia: Biography with anecdotes and felexions compiled from the letter councillor Count D. G. Tessin's own manuscripts) (Stockholm: Johan Imnelius, 1819), pp. 555, 556.

27. Alm, p. 165.

28. Lindh, "Swedenborg som Söderbo," pp. 171, 172.

29. Alfred Stroh, *Den Nya Kyrkan i Norden* (The New Church in Scandinavia) (Copenhagen: Alfred Stroh, 1913), p. 9. Also see Robsahm, p. 91.

30. *Samlingar för Philantroper. I. Utdrag af några bref från Emanuel Swedenborg til åtskillige des vänner* (Collections for philanthropists. Vol. 1. Excerpts from some letters by Emanuel Swedenborg to several of his friends), letter 10 (Stockholm: Exegetiska och philantropiska sällskapet, and A. J. Nordström, 1787).

31. Hjalmar Kylén, *En Swedenborgsreformation i Sverige under 1800-talets första decennier* (A Swedenborgian reformation in Sweden during the first decades of the nineteenth century) (Stockholm: F. C. Askebergs, 1910).

32. Sigstedt, pp. 346–48. Jesper Swedberg, *America illuminata* (Illustrated America), trans. and with an intro. by Robert Murray (Stockholm: 1985), passim. A copy of Wallerius's *Psychologia Empirica* can be found in the New Church Library, 4 Banérgatan, Stockholm.

33. Inge Jonsson, *Swedenborgs skapelsedrama "Du Cultu et Amore Dei"* (Swedenborg's drama of creation, *"Worship and love of God"*) (Stockholm: Natur och Kultur, 1961), pp. 23, 24. Lenhammar, pp. 256, 380, and passim. Bror-Erik Ohlsson, *Eskilstuna fristad* (Eskiltuna, a free state), Historiska skrifter (Historical writings) (Eskilstuna, Sweden: Eskilstuna kommun III, 1971), p. 104. Olle Hjern, "Christian Johansén," *Gnosis* 1-2 (1986), p. 55.

34. Ekerwald, p. 13.

35. Alm, pp. 167, 168.

36. Ibid., p. 166.

37. "Den 29 januari 1888," *Skandinavisk Nykyrktidning* (1888), p. 29.

38. The move is described by Alm, p. 171.

39. Lindh, "Swedenborg som Söderbo," p. 171.

40. The attempt to purchase the property failed. Now a new appeal for the restoration of the garden has been made.

The Pivotal Change in Swedenborg's Life

Donald L. Rose

NO ONE BOTHERS TO GUESS whether the disciples of Jesus were good at their initial job of catching fish. St. Peter's cathedral in Rome would not have an additional pinnacle or even an additional brick if Peter had won a reputation as one of history's most accomplished fishermen. Those men of Galilee had two parts to their lives: they were fishermen; they became disciples. Swedenborg's multifaceted life also had two parts. The *Shorter Oxford Dictionary* describes him in the briefest dichotomous phrase, as a Swedish scientific and religious writer. At a certain time the scientist turned to religious writing. From that time the product of his pen was theology, the testimony of religious visions. He wrote of heaven and hell, the scriptures, the Lord.

Although Swedenborg himself did compare the two aspects of his life to the life of the disciples (and we will later be looking at his comparison) we see much difference. Swedenborg's claim to fame is arguably that he was very good at a number of things. The Ripley "Believe It Or Not" blurb devoted to him would hardly be less impressive if the religious element were removed; thirty-eight occupations follow Ripley's heading: "He was a . . ." Only two of them have to do with religion! Swedenborg's name got into the *Guinness Book of Records* by virtue of his estimated IQ and his early conception of an airship. Otherwise he would not have qualified.

A change there was, however, in Swedenborg's life, and virtually every written account of his life undertakes in one way or another to describe that change.[1] The Ripley item we have just mentioned has been printed over and over again, and encompasses an account of Swedenborg's life in three crisp paragraphs. The pivotal change is handled in this single sentence: "At the age of 56 he gave up the study of worldly science and became a seer and theological revelator."[2]

Swedenborg turned away from one pursuit and devoted himself to another. The most widely read biography of Swedenborg calls this "a great change" and "a revolutionary change in the order of his life":

> It was not until 1743 that he began to have direct intimation of the great change that was about to come over him. When in the early part of that year he made application to the Board of Mines for leave of absence to go abroad and publish his *Regnum Animale*, it is evident that he had no thought of such a revolutionary change in the order of his life.[3]

Another durable biography, addressed to younger readers, refers to "the great change," "a remarkable change in his life and work," something that "completely changed the whole character of his life."[4]

The twenty-page biographical sketch by Dr. Sig Synnestvedt puts it this way: "Swedenborg came to believe that God had called him to bring a new revelation to the world, and from 1745 until his death twenty-seven years later he spent the bulk of his time adding theological works to his already lengthy scientific and philosophic writings."[5]

How does the observer of Swedenborg's life regard this change? One might on the one hand view it with regret, lamenting that a scientist of so much promise should have

DONALD L. ROSE has studied Swedenborg's works for thirty-five years. Among the fruits of his studies is a booklet about the religious works produced for the 1970 New Church World Assembly, which Mr. Rose helped to organize in London. Mr. Rose also published in 1980 a hundred-page companion booklet for the six-volume *Swedenborg Concordance* by J. F. Potts. Mr. Rose attended the University of Grenoble in France and received his B.A. from the Academy of the New Church in Bryn Athyn, Pennsylvania. After ordination in 1957 he has served pastorates, either resident or visiting, in Australia, New Zealand, Holland, France, England, and the United States. He is now a department editor of *Chrysalis* magazine and edits the monthly journal *New Church Life*, which has been devoted to the religious works of Swedenborg for more than a century.

gone off into the doubtful world of religious vision. One might on the other hand view it with the religious zeal of one eager to proclaim the importance of new theological doctrines. Considering the possible shades of perspective on this, it seems best to concentrate on how Swedenborg himself seemed to regard the change, leaving readers to make their own evaluations. In doing this we would make a distinction between Swedenborg's comments on the subject a quarter of a century later and his immediate comments when the change was taking place. But let us first ask briefly what *happened* to change the focus of Swedenborg's life.

It is natural to crave to pinpoint a specific happening as the historic event initiating Swedenborg's change of focus. This is probably why a certain document has been so attractive to those who would tell the story of Swedenborg's life. The document itself consists of some twenty pages of handwriting (in Swedish) dated March 29, 1782. Just ten years after Swedenborg's death an old gentleman by the name of Carl Robsahm was asked to write down what he could remember of Emanuel Swedenborg, because he had been personally acquainted with him during the latter part of his life. A generalization scholars make about what Robsahm then recorded is that it is far more reliable when dealing with Swedenborg's final years than when dealing with the earlier part of his life (to illustrate this generalization, see DOC vol. 1, p. 620, n. 19).

When Robsahm wrote about the last time he set eyes on Swedenborg he was recalling something that had happened twelve years previous. Robsahm's habit is to recall what Swedenborg said as if he were quoting verbatim. He has Swedenborg using the following words in his farewell upon leaving Stockholm:

> The Lord has promised me, that I shall not die, until I shall have received from the press this work (*True Christian Religion*), which is now ready to be printed and for the sake of which I now undertake this journey; but if we do not meet again in the body we shall meet again in the presence of the Lord, provided we live in this world according to His will and not according to our own. (DOC vol. 1, p. 39)

Having recalled the above as if quoting Swedenborg's actual words, Robsahm reports: "He then took leave of me in as blithe and cheerful a frame of mind, as if he had been a man in his best years" (DOC vol. 1, p. 39). Swedenborg was then eighty-two.

One presumes that this is pretty close to what Swedenborg actually did say in his final conversation with Robsahm, even though it was written down twelve years after the event. Other instances in which Robsahm seems to give direct quotes are suspect not only because of the limitations of Robsahm's memory but also because of the possibility that Robsahm may not have gotten the story right when he first heard it. Signe Toksvig suggests that Swedenborg himself had the story mixed up when at some time in the 1760s he told Robsahm about a divine commission that had occurred presumably in the spring of 1745. She writes: "The human memory is a great dramatist, and it loves the unities of time and place, especially when, instructed by overwhelming need, it selects the incidents to be combined."[6]

We cannot with confidence rely upon the description of the event of Swedenborg's commission. We would agree with Cyriel Sigstedt that it is "strange" that we do not have a description directly from Swedenborg about this divine commission. But we doubt that Sigstedt ought to have used the phrase "verbatim account" in her biography: "It is strange that our knowledge of this momentous event derives not from Swedenborg himself, at first hand, but from a verbatim account written down by a friend."[7]

The "friend," of course, is Robsahm. In his document Swedenborg says that God appeared to him and said that, "He had chosen me to declare to men the spiritual contents of Scripture; and that He Himself would declare to me what I should write on this subject."[8]

Sigstedt rightly says that we should compare Robsahm's account with that of Dr. Gabriel Beyer. Beyer wrote a letter in 1776, four years after Swedenborg's death, in which he says that he remembers what Swedenborg told him at a dinner party (which took place eleven years earlier, in the summer of 1765). Beyer's letter (dated 23 March 1776) says:

> The information respecting the Lord's personal appearance before the Assessor, who saw Him, in imperial purple and majestic light, seated near his bed, while He gave Assessor Swedenborg his commission, I had from his own lips at a dinner-party in the house of Dr. Rosen, where I saw the old gentleman for the first time. I remember that I asked him, how long this lasted; whereupon he answered, About a quarter of an hour: also, whether the strong light did not affect his eyes; when he said, No. (DOC vol 2, p. 426)

Beyer assigns no date to this event, and scholars have wondered whether it may have been related to something Swedenborg himself describes in the *Journal of Dreams* as occurring in April of 1744. This was in Holland a year previous to the commission Robsahm describes as having taken place in London. The *Journal of Dreams* entry has with good reason been quoted many times in biographies of Swedenborg. In quickly written Swedish Swedenborg noted (not for publication) that he beheld the Lord Jesus Christ face to face and that he understood the phrase, "Well, then, do," to mean, "Do what thou hast promised" (JD 54).

What had Swedenborg promised prior to April of 1744, more than a year before the date often given for his "commission"? We do not know. Indeed the point that we offer here is that we just do not know the particulars of Swedenborg's call, at least not in the sense of an incident that we can pinpoint or describe in detail. What is obvious is that

Swedenborg did make a change of focus in his mid-fifties and that more than one incident played a part in his eventual determination toward spiritual studies and writing. A comparison helpful in clarifying this is that of the already mentioned change in the disciples of Jesus. What happened to change Simon Peter from a fisherman to an apostle? It is clear that there was a series of incidents and yet that there are important particulars we do not know.

Consider this sequence: One assumes that the first time Simon encountered Jesus was the day Jesus "looked at him" and gave him his nickname.[9] There must have been things that Jesus said to the first disciples that disposed them to respond on a later occasion when he called them from their fishing boats. He spent most of a day in a house with two of them,[10] and a handful of them had been in the company of Jesus for a considerable period well before the time he called them and said, "Come after Me, and I will make you become fishers of men."[11] Peter then followed him, and Jesus spent the night in Peter's house before the incident in which he said to Peter, "From now on you will catch men."[12] Later Jesus selected twelve of his followers to become apostles.[13] Much later than that he would give Peter a commission in the words, "Feed my lambs. . . . Tend my sheep."[14] And it was subsequent to that that Peter and the other disciples were given the famous commission to go forth into all nations.[15]

We shall refer again to Swedenborg's own comparison of his calling to that of the fishermen of Galilee. One of the great differences is that we have an abundance of direct evidence about Swedenborg's attitude and reaction to the pivotal change in his life.

Swedenborg's Attitude and Reaction

We will begin with Swedenborg's references in the last few years of his life. These are quite direct and are relatively few in number. Then we will refer to more immediate references made by Swedenborg around the time when the change in his life was taking place.

It is interesting that Swedenborg's references to his own childhood generally were made during his final years on earth. He was well nigh the age of eighty-two when he confided in a letter (dated 17 Nov. 1769) to Dr. Beyer that from the age of four to the age of ten he was frequently engaged in thought about God and salvation and that his parents wondered at him, "saying that angels must be speaking through me" (DOC vol. 2, p. 279).

He was eighty-three when he wrote in *Invitation to the New Church,* "It has pleased the Lord to prepare me from my earliest youth to perceive the Word, and He has introduced me into the spiritual world, and has enlightened me . . ." (INV 55).

He was approaching the age of eighty-four when he wrote to a German duke describing his life's mission and saying that the Lord "prepared me for this from my childhood." This letter, written in Amsterdam in Latin, includes the following:

> The Lord our Saviour foretold that He would come again . . . But as He cannot come again into the world in person, it was necessary that He should do it by means of a man, who should not only receive the doctrine . . . by his understanding, but also publish it by means of the press; and as the Lord had prepared me for this from my childhood, He manifested Himself in person before me, His servant, and sent me to do this work. This took place in the year 1743; and afterwards He opened the sight of my spirit, and thus introduced me into the spiritual world, granting me to see the heavens and many wonderful things there, and also the hells, and to speak with angels and spirits, and this continually for twenty-seven years. I declare in truth, that this is so. (DOC vol. 2, p. 387)

We would mention two more letters written by Swedenborg in his old age. In a letter to Friedrich Oetinger he said that "spiritual truths have a correspondence with natural truths, because in these they terminate, and upon these they rest. . . . For this reason I was introduced by the Lord first into the natural sciences, and thus prepared; and indeed, from the year 1710 to 1744, when heaven was opened to me" (DOC vol. 2, p. 257).

The final example of Swedenborg's reference in his old age to the calling that had changed his life has come down to us thanks to the Reverend Thomas Hartley of England. In August of 1769 Hartley had written to Swedenborg urging him to write an account of his life. The old man responded, "After reflecting on this, I have been led to yield to your friendly advice, and will now communicate to you some particulars of my life, which are briefly as follows." Then after sixty-four lines about his worldly connections and accomplishments he says:

> But all that I have thus far related, I consider of comparatively little importance; for it is far exceeded by the circumstance, that I have been called to a holy office by the Lord Himself, who most mercifully appeared before me, His servant, in the year 1743; when He opened my sight into the spiritual world, and enabled me to converse with spirits and angels, in which state I have continued up to the present day. From that time I began to print and publish the various arcana that were seen by me or revealed to me, concerning Heaven and Hell, the state of man after death, the true worship of God, the spiritual sense of the Word, besides many other most important matters conducive to salvation and wisdom. (DOC vol. 1, p. 9)

Such was Swedenborg's view in his old age of the change that had taken place a quarter of a century earlier. Toksvig, whose biography has a good share of reserve and skepticism, says flatly, "That he came to believe firmly in the commission we know."[16] But she also notes, as I mentioned earlier, that "the human memory is a great dramatist . . . especially when, instructed by overwhelming need, it selects the incidents to be combined"[17] Toksvig observes that Swedenborg expresses uncertainty months after the commission had supposedly taken place. Hesitating on things he has written concerning a verse of scripture, he says, "Therefore, if God grants, they must be amended at some other time, and this in such a way that I can then seem to myself to speak things absolutely true" (WE 541). Noting this, Toksvig asks: "Eight months or so after he was supposed to have received a divine commission to reinterpret the Bible, could he write such a confession of uncertainty?"[18]

What Swedenborg said during the time of the change in his life is more complex than were the brief descriptions he gave in his old age. And whereas the latter were addressed to others, the former were written down mostly for himself.

When we look at what Swedenborg was saying during the time the change was taking place, we can sometimes identify in particular the things that he said in retrospect many years later. For example, in Swedenborg's older years he wrote in a letter to a friend, "I was forbidden to read writers on dogmatic and systematic theology, before heaven was opened to me . . ." (DOC vol 2, p. 260). One might speculate long on the question of when this prohibition took place and what form it may have taken. Some have wondered whether Swedenborg was so forbidden when he was a youth. But it would not have made sense to him unless it occurred near the time when he was beginning to see that he had a special mission. We do find that when he was fifty-six years old he noted the following in the *Journal of Dreams*: "It was also represented to me in a certain way that I ought not to contaminate myself by reading other books, treating of theology and such subjects" (JD 180).

Take the matter of Swedenborg's study of the Hebrew language. Why would a man at the age of fifty-six interrupt his scientific pursuits with this kind of discipline? Obviously this was to prepare him for the work of unfolding the scriptures. But what specifically caused him to begin the study of Hebrew? Again we have a reference in his later years. He writes to his friend Dr. Beyer, in retrospect saying, "when heaven was opened to me, I had first to learn the Hebrew language" (DOC vol. 2, p. 261). We can find no reference near the time when he undertook the study of Hebrew saying that he was instructed or was determined to do so. We simply have the obvious fact that he studied Hebrew.[19] This particular point illustrates the general change in Swedenborg's life. We have the obvious—that he turned from one thing to another. We have the sayings toward the end of his life and certain testimonial statements in his religious works themselves. We have some evidence of what seems to be a sequence of invitations, so to speak, to undertake a new mission. (And we seem to know very little about such invitations.) But we do have the things that Swedenborg wrote down during the time of change.

FIG. 318. *"I will make you . . . fishers of men."*

Swedenborg's Writings During the Change

Three works in particular that Swedenborg wrote between 1744 and 1747 give insight on what the change in his life meant to him at that time. In them we find Swedenborg seeming to talk to himself occasionally about the implications of the change that was taking place. He did not publish any of these three, but in the case of the longest it is evident that he thought he was writing the first draft of something that would eventually be published. The three are *The Journal of Dreams, Messiah About to Come*, and the extensive one (2,102 manuscript pages), the *Word Explained*. A work he wrote for publication at that time, *The Worship and Love of God* has rightly been regarded as a kind of transition work. The only observation I would make on it here is that Swedenborg stopped writing this work in mid-sentence and that we next find him writing *Messiah About to Come*.

Of the three items mentioned the one that has received the least attention by scholars is *Messiah About to Come*. The reason for this is obvious. The *Journal of Dreams*, a set of private handwritten notations, did not come to light until almost a century after Swedenborg's death. It gives a unique insight into Swedenborg's thoughts over the period of a few months. *Word Explained* is a massive document in which a persistent student can find intriguing personal statements by Swedenborg. *Messiah About to Come*, on the other hand, contains no personal statements or comments of any kind. It consists primarily of scriptural quotations. A reader might glance over it quickly and feel that he or she grasped its contents. But in 1975 Dr. Wilson Van Dusen approached the little document in a manner that amounted to something of a breakthrough in considering the change in Swedenborg's life. Van Dusen's study is entitled, "Another Key to Swedenborg's Development." Among the things he brings out are the following:

Several things occur to the reader who uses this work to feel his way back into Swedenborg's life. For one, the Lord often speaks directly to the reader in the first person. It is no academic exercise. . . . Why did Swedenborg choose some passages and not others? . . . My guess is that he chose passages which spoke most clearly and intimately to him. This is in accord with his underlining certain passages and his comments. Swedenborg's approach seems to have been intimate and spiritual rather than an academic exercise. . . . We have to feel our way back into Swedenborg's situation. . . . One such passage has two such notations. The passage has to do with Jova raising up a prophet into whose mouth the Lord's words will be put. This theme of the servant of God through whom the Lord will speak, Swedenborg notes several times. . . . The combination of Swedenborg's choice of passages, his underlining, his N. B. and his comments leads to the conclusion that he experienced these passages as the living Lord speaking to him. . . . The Lord is speaking to his servant who will have the word of God issue from his mouth and lead his people to the New Jerusalem.[20]

Van Dusen's study concludes with the words, "*The Messiah About to Come* is a lovely, significant, unnoticed gem among Swedenborg's works."[21]

In the introductory issue of the Swedenborg Foundation's magazine *Chrysalis*, Dr. Van Dusen refers to *Messiah About to Come* as a "pivotal work" of Swedenborg, and he comments, "It is strange that Swedenborgian scholars have missed the importance of this gem."[22]

Van Dusen's approach gives one a fascinating perspective on this little work of scarcely more than a hundred pages. Swedenborg is writing down phrases that may have been immensely significant to him. For example, he writes on one page, "Jesus Christ our Saviour is the Messiah about to come. . . . The time is now at hand, and is to come shortly. . . . The signs which were foretold have been and are to be made now in the present century" (MES 13).

Swedenborg the scientist may have been turning over in his mind the thought of Swedenborg the potential seer or prophet when on the final page he quoted from the book of Samuel, "He who today is called a prophet, of old was called a seer."[23] On the same page he quoted from the Book of Numbers:

> If one of you be a prophet of Jova, I will make myself known unto him by visions and will speak with him in dreams. But not so with my servant Moses, whose faith is accounted the faith of my whole house. But I will speak to him in his presence, being present before him, and without dark sayings or an image.[24]

Swedenborg arranged this work under fourteen headings. One of the shortest entries is under the heading "The Tree of Life." Here is the sparse wording that this man—so steeped in knowledge—wrote under this heading: "The Tree of Knowledge leading to the Tree of Life. Science is the key

of natural things whereby things heavenly are opened up (MES 104).

The *Journal of Dreams* (written before *Messiah About to Come*) comes to about a hundred pages in English translation.[25] The *Word Explained* (written after *Messiah About to Come*) comes to almost four thousand pages. Following Van Dusen's example in trying to sense Swedenborg's situation, a reader gains insight into Swedenborg's view of the change in his life's work.

Swedenborg speaks in the *Journal of Dreams* of bursting into tears of joy "that our Lord has been willing to show such great grace to so unworthy a sinner" (JD 71). His pride surfaces when he later comments that sometimes when people did not show him respect he thought to himself, "If you only knew what grace I am enjoying you would act otherwise" (JD 75). This "grace" seems to include a sense of being selected and prepared for a task of historic importance. Did he see himself at the threshold of doing something for the human race without precedent in history? "While the thought occurred to me, as it often does, if it should happen that anyone took me for a holy man, and therefore made much of me; nay, as is done by some simple-minded folks, if they were not only to venerate me but even adore me as a supposed saint; I then perceived that in the zeal in which I then was, I would be willing to inflict upon him every evil . . ." (JD 72). The thought of being idolized was repugnant to Swedenborg, as he seemed to realize his name would go down in history. Toward the end of one of his last theological pieces (written twenty-eight years after the *Journal of Dreams*) Swedenborg alluded to a unique place in history: "We do not read anywhere in history that such intercourse with angels and spirits has been granted from the creation of the world. For I am daily with angels there, even as I am in the world with men; and this now for twenty-seven years. Evidence of this intercourse are the books which I have published" (INV 43). Perplexed hesitation often came upon Swedenborg at the time when he was making his entries in his journal of dreams, but even in hesitation he seems to have been contemplating a mission more important than anything he had faced before.

> I came into a state of hesitation. . . . There came a mass of involved reasonings . . . but I gathered courage and experience and perceived that I had come here in order to do the very best and to promote the glory of God, that I had received talent, that everything had helped to this purpose; that the spirit had been with me from my youth unto this end. I considered myself unworthy to live if I had gone otherwise than the right way, and thus I laughed at the other seductive thoughts. Thus as to pleasure, wealth, high position, which I had pursued, I perceived that all was vanity. . . . By the help of God I came to a resolution. May God help me! (JD 164, 165)

Many months passed. In the spring and summer of 1744

he is writing the *Journal of Dreams*. In the summer of 1745 he is writing *Messiah About to Come*. And then toward the end of 1745 and throughout 1746 he is writing the *Word Explained*, and is *still* not clear exactly what he will do! The following few quotations in sequence give a hint of the alternating states of conviction Swedenborg continued to experience.

> I could at last plainly see that the tenor of Divine Providence has ruled the acts of my life from my very youth, and has so governed them that I might finally come to the present end; that thus, by means of the knowledges of natural things, I might be able to understand those things which lie more interiorly within the Word of God Messiah, and so, of the divine mercy of God Messiah, might serve as an instrument for opening them. Thus, those things now become clear which up to the present have not been clear. (WE 2532)

But then later he writes, "Up to now the labor has been in vain. . . . I know nothing as to whither I shall go" (WE 2755, 2756). Swedenborg wonders whether what he has written should be inserted eventually in a printed form. "As to whether these should be inserted, if leave be given by God Messiah, this as yet I do not know. I await" (WE 5588). He makes notes on how deceptive spirits can be, and he wonders how he should convey this, making the following notation: "But see as to how this should be set forth; it is to be told prudently—for I know not whether those spirits to whom it was granted to do this were good spirits; also lest men may thereby doubt concerning the visions referred to above" (WE 6155).

A note made on 22 July 1746 shows Swedenborg's dismay: "These things are as yet most obscure to me, and I can by no means understand them. Therefore I pass them by, for I have never been so disturbed, and disturbed in so perplexing a way" (WE 6657).

None of the quotations just above were published by Swedenborg. It was not until the year 1749 that he first published a theological work, *Arcana Coelestia*. From that time onward he published a series of books (e.g., *Heaven and Hell*, *Divine Providence*, *Conjugial Love*), and when the last had appeared in print (*True Christian Religion*, in 1771) he wrote that the evidence of his experience in the world of the spirit are "the books which I have published" (INV 43). One of those published books contained the following in its final paragraph:

> I was once asked how from a philosopher I became a theologian; and I answered, In the same manner that fishermen were made disciples and apostles by the Lord; and that I also from early youth had been a spiritual fisherman. On hearing this the inquirer asked, What is a spiritual fisherman? I replied that a fisherman in the spiritual sense of the Word, signifies a man who investigates and teaches natural truths, and afterwards spiritual truths rationally. . . .
>
> My interrogator said, Now I can understand why the Lord called and chose fishermen to be His disciples, and therefore I do not wonder that He has also called and chosen you, since, as you have said, you were from early youth a fisherman in the spiritual sense, that is, an investigator of natural truths; that you are now an investigator of spiritual truths, is because these are founded on the former. (SBI 20)

Swedenborg saw himself as a fisherman called to a task to which he devoted himself for the last thirty years of his life. And he records at the end of his last published work an encounter with angels in which he told them that the task was completed. Their response was uplifting: "The angels rejoiced that it had pleased the Lord to disclose such things, so that man might no longer from ignorance be in doubt respecting his immortality" (TCR 846).

Notes

1. There are at least one hundred biographies or biographical sketches of Swedenborg, more than sixty of which are in the English language. See William R. Woofenden, *Swedenborg's Concept of Love in Action* (Boston: Massachusetts New Church Union, 1971), p. 9.
2. Robert Ripley, "Believe It or Not" newspaper column series. Reproduced by the Swedenborg Foundation by special permission of Robert Ripley.
3. George Trobridge, *Swedenborg: Life and Teachings* (New York: Swedenborg Foundation, 1969), p. 84. This biography was first published in 1907 by the Swedenborg Society in London and is now being published in a modern, revised edition by the Swedenborg Foundation in New York.
4. Eric A. Sutton, *The Happy Isles* (London: Dent & Sons, 1938), pp. 69–71.
5. Sig Synnestvedt, *The Essential Swedenborg* (New York: Swedenborg Foundation, 1970). The biographical sketch in this book is now also published as a separate pamphlet.
6. Signe Toksvig, *Emanuel Swedenborg: Scientist and Mystic* (New Haven, Conn.: Yale University Press, 1948), p. 154.
7. Cyriel O. Sigstedt, *The Swedenborg Epic* (London: Swedenborg Society, 1952), p. 198.
8. Ibid.
9. John 1:42.
10. John 1:39.
11. Mark 1:17.
12. Luke 5:10.
13. Matthew 10.
14. John 21.
15. Matthew 28:19.
16. Toksvig, p. 154.
17. Ibid.
18. Ibid.
19. Sigstedt, pp. 215 and 224.
20. Wilson Van Dusen, "Another Key to Swedenborg's Development," *New Church Life*, 95, no. 7 (1975), p. 316.
21. Ibid.
22. Wilson Van Dusen, "Now You See It, Now You Don't: The Soul," *Chrysalis: Journal of the Swedenborg Foundation*, introductory issue (Winter 1985), p. 24.
23. I Samuel 9:9.
24. Numbers 12:6–8.
25. The Swedenborg Foundation has published a full commentary by Dr. Wilson Van Dusen on *Swedenborg's Journal of Dreams, 1743–1744* (New York: Swedenborg Foundation, 1986).

Poets with Swedenborgian Connections

Compiled by Alice B. Skinner, Ph.D.

Expressions of Spirituality

NOT MANY PEOPLE know what representations and correspondences are, and there is no way they can know unless they are aware that there is a spiritual world distinguishable from the natural world. For correspondences occur between spiritual and natural things, and the things that occur in natural phenomena as a result of spiritual ones are representations. We call them correspondences because they are completely responsive, and representations because they portray. (AC 2987)

Spiritual messages shining through the natural world are expressed by poets who are alert to basic truths made available through everyday experiences. Anna Collier Lee writes of the "upward path" opened by the language of symbols, and Baudelaire of the "forests of symbols" provided by nature, ever watchful for opportunities to communicate.

SONNET

WHAT is a symbol? That which doth appear
To outward sense in Nature's varied forms;
In stone and tree, in mountains, winds and storms,
In man, in beast and bird, and times of year,
In human smile or frown, and falling tear,
In any use which man or beast performs
Behold the body which the soul transforms
And shows to illumined minds the meaning clear,
Not by mere fancy may it be discerned;
Know well both root and branch, for in the seed
Is stored the message that the symbol brings;
From God it came, to him may be returned;
And he who finds this upward path may read,
Perceive and know whereof the poet sings.

ANNA COLLIER LEE[1]

CORRESPONDENCES

NATURE is a temple from which living pillars
Now and then allow disordered phrases to emerge;
Man comes there among forests of symbols
Who observe him as if familiar.

Like long echoes that mingle from afar
In a profound and tenebrous unity,
Vast as night and radiance,
So perfumes, colors, sounds correspond.

There are perfumes fresh as the flesh of infants,
Sweet as oboes, green as prairies,
——And others, corrupt, rich, and triumphant,

Expansive as infinite things:
Amber, bergamot, incense, and musk,
Singing the rapture of spirit and senses.

CHARLES PIERRE BAUDELAIRE[2]

"I have been taught by a great deal of experience that there is nothing whatever in the natural world and its three kingdoms that does not portray something in the spiritual world, or that does not have something there to which it corresponds" (AC2992).

"Earth's crammed with heaven, / And every common bush afire with God," (Elizabeth Barrett Browning) is a poetic expression of the omnipresence of the spiritual realm.

SELECTIONS FROM AURORA LEIGH

WITHOUT the spiritual, observe,
The natural's impossible,—no form,
No motion: without sensuous, spiritual
Is inappreciable,—no beauty or power:
And in this twofold sphere the twofold man
(For still the artist is intensely a man)
Holds firmly by the natural, to reach
The spiritual beyond it,—fixes still
The type with mortal vision, to pierce through,
With eyes immortal, to the antetype
Some call the ideal,—better called the real,
And certain to be called so presently
When things shall have their names.

・ ・ ・

But man, the twofold creature, apprehends
The twofold manner, in and outwardly,
And nothing in the world comes single to him,
A mere itself,—cup, column, or candlestick,
All patterns of what shall be in the Mount;
The whole temporal show related royally,
And built up to eterne significance
Through the open arms of God. "There's
   nothing great
Nor small," has said a poet of our day,
Whose voice will ring beyond the curfew of eve
And not be thrown out by the matin's bell:
And truly, I reiterate, nothing's small!
No lily-muffled hum of a summer-bee,
But finds some coupling with the spinning stars;
No pebble at your foot, but proves a sphere;
No chaffinch, but implies the cherubim;
And (glancing on my own thin, veinëd wrist),
In such a little tremour of the blood
The whole strong clamour of a vehement soul
Doth utter itself distinct. Earth's crammed
   with heaven,
And every common bush afire with God;
But only he who sees, takes off his shoes,
The rest sit round it and pluck blackberries,
And daub their natural faces unaware
More and more from the first similitude.

ELIZABETH BARRETT BROWNING[3]

❦

Access to understanding of correspondences depends upon an understanding of levels:

A knowledge of levels is like a key for unlocking the causes of things and entering into them. Without this knowledge, one can know hardly anything about the causes of things. In fact, the objects and subjects of each world seem straightforward, as though nothing more were involved than the eye can observe. Yet this, relative to what lies within, is only a minute fraction—most minute. The deeper matters that are not visible cannot be unveiled without a knowledge of levels. We progress from more outward to more inward things, and through these to the inmost, by levels—not by a continuous slope [lit., "continuous levels"] but by quantum leaps [lit., "discrete levels"]. (DLW 184)

Seeing into the depths seems unnecessary to those "too grossly apt / To hold the natural, as dogs a bone." Elizabeth Barrett Browning considers it the poet's task to raise the sights of humans so they may recognize in every "flower of spring" its alliance "by issue and symbol, by significance / And correspondence, to that spirit-world / Outside the limits of our space and time, / Whereto we are bound." Surely if humans properly understood "The hieroglyphic of material," the result would be "reverence [for] fish and fowl, the bull, the tree, / And even his very body as a man."

SELECTIONS FROM AURORA LEIGH

AND verily many thinkers of this age,
Ay, many Christian teachers, half in heaven,
Are wrong in just my sense who understood
Our natural world too insularly, as if
No spiritual counterpart completed it
Consummating its meaning, rounding all
To justice and perfection, line by line,
Form by form, nothing single nor alone,
The great below clenched by the great above,
Shade here authenticating substance there,
The body proving spirit, as the effect
The cause: we meantime being too grossly apt
To hold the natural, as dogs a bone
(Though reason and nature beat us in the face),
So obstinately, that we'll break our teeth
Or ever we let go.

・ ・ ・

See the earth.
The body of our body, the green earth,
Indubitably human like this flesh
And these articulated veins through which
Our heart drives blood. There's not a flower
   of spring
That dies ere June, but vaunts itself allied
By issue and symbol, by significance
And correspondence, to that spirit-world

Outside the limits of our space and time,
Whereto we are bound. Let poets give it voice
With human meanings,—else they miss
   the thought,
And henceforth step down lower, stand confessed
Instructed poorly for interpreters,
Thrown out by an easy cowslip in the text.

· · ·

           Art's the witness of what Is
Behind this show. If this world's show were all,
Then imitation would be all in Art;
There, Jove's hand gripes us!—For we stand
   here, we,
If genuine artists, witnessing for God's
Complete, consummate, undivided work;
—That every natural flower which grows on earth
Implies a flower upon the spiritual side,
Substantial, archetypal, all a-glow
With blossoming causes,—not so far away,
But we, whose spirit-sense is somewhat cleared,
May catch at something of the bloom and
   breath,—
Too vaguely apprehended, though indeed
Still apprehended, consciously or not,
And still transferred to picture, music, verse,
For thrilling audient and beholding souls
By signs and touches which are known to souls.
How known, they know not,—why, they
   cannot find,
So straight call out on genius, say, "A man,
Produced this," when much rather they should say,
" 'T is insight and he saw this."
                  Thus is Art
Self-magnified in magnifying a truth
Which, fully recognized, would change the world
And shift its morals. If a man could feel,
Not one day, in the artist's ecstasy,
But every day, feast, fast, or working-day,
The spiritual significance burn through
The hieroglyphic of material shows,
Henceforward he would paint the globe with wings,
And reverence fish and fowl, the bull, the tree,
And even his very body as a man.

ELIZABETH BARRETT BROWNING[4]

∽

Swedenborg is explicit about correspondences, showing how it is possible to learn about the spiritual world from natural processes. For example:

A person who is being reborn, like a tree, begins from a seed; so "seed" is used in the Word to refer to the true that comes from the good. Then just like a tree, the individual produces leaves and then flowers and eventually fruit. The person produces elements of understanding which are referred to in the Word as "leaves," and then elements of wisdom. These are referred to as "flowers." Finally the person brings forth elements of life, namely good things of love and charity in act, which in the word are referred to as "fruits." This kind of pictorial resemblance between a fruit tree and a person who is being regenerated is so complete that one can learn from a tree how regeneration works, given only some prior knowledge of what is spiritually good and true. (AC 5115[2])

Poems release essences of nature, as in two poems about trees. Vachel Lindsay compares his lady to the "youngest woodland sapling / Swaying, singing in the wind." Valéry finds in a palm tree "ever-living hopefulness" and "roots of eagerness / That put the deserts to work."

MY LADY IS COMPARED TO A YOUNG TREE

WHEN I see a young tree
In its white beginning,
With white leaves
And white buds
Barely tipped with green,
In the April weather,
In the weeping sunshine—
Then I see my lady,
My democratic queen,
Standing free and equal
With the youngest woodland sapling
Swaying, singing in the wind,
Delicate and white:
Soul so near to blossom,
Fragile, strong as death;
A kiss from far-off Eden,
A flash of Judgment's trumpet—
April's breath.

VACHEL LINDSAY[5]

PALM

To Jeannie

OF his formidable grace
Scarcely veiling the glory,
An angel lays on my table
Tender bread, smooth milk;
With his eyelid he makes

Me the sign of a prayer
That speaks to my seeing:
—Calm, calm, still be calm!
Know the weightiness of a palm
Bearing its profusion.

For as much as it may bend
Under its treasured abundance,
Its form is fulfilled,
Its heavy fruits are its bond.
Wonder at how it sways,
And how a gradual sinew
Dividing a moment of time
Unpretendingly apportions
The attraction of the ground
And the weight of the firmament!

Lovely mobile arbiter
Between the shadow and the sun,
It simulates the wisdom
And the slumber of a sibyl.
Still about the same place
The ample palm tree never tires
Of summonses and farewells. . . .
How noble it is, and tender,
How worthy to await
Only the hands of gods!

The frail gold it murmurs
Rings on the air's artless finger,
And with a silky armor
Invests the soul of the desert.
An imperishable voice
Which it gives to the sandy wind
Sprinkling it with its grains,
Serves as its own oracle,
Soothing itself with the miracle
The griefs sing to themselves.

Self-oblivious the while
Between heaven and the sand,
Every day as it still shines
Compounds another mite of honey.
This sweetness is measured out
By the divine durability
That is not counted in days
But rather disguises them
In a juice where accumulates
All the aroma of the loves.

If at times there is despair,
If the adorable strictness,
For all your tears only labors
Under the guise of languors,

Do not accuse of miserliness
Her Wisdom as it prepares
So much gold and so much power:
Through the sap's funereal pace
An ever-living hopefulness
Mounts towards its ripening.

These days that seem to you void
And wasted for the universe,
Have their roots of eagerness
That put the deserts to work.
That dense and hairy mass
Allotted to the shades
Never can arrest itself,
Into the world's entrails
Pursuing water in the depths
To satisfy the treetop.

Endurance, endurance,
Endurance, in the sky's blue!
Every atom of silence
Is a chance of ripened fruit!
There will come the happy shock:
A dove, a breath of wind,
An imperceptibly gentle shake,
The touch of a woman as she leans
Will release that fall of rain
That sends us down on our knees!

Let a whole people now fall,
Palm tree!...irresistibly!
Let them wallow in the dust
On the fruits of the firmament!
For you those hours were no loss
Now you are left so light
After such lovely yieldings:
Image of a thinking mind
Where the spirit spends itself
To be increased by what it gives.

PAUL VALÉRY[6]

～～～

To have perceptiveness in spiritual matters, we need to be absorbed in an affection for what is true, an affection whose source is good, and we need a constant longing to know what is true. This brings enlightenment to our ability to discern, and when this ability is enlightened, we are granted the ability to see profoundly into the intrinsic nature of things. (AC 5937[3])

Poetry aids in seeing into the "intrinsic nature of things." Yeats reflects on the significance of water and swan found in his homeplace, Ballylee, and nearby Coole Park, the home of his colleague in the Irish Renaissance, Lady Gregory. Robert Frost, a "Slave to a springtime passion for the earth," finds love in the process of sowing seed and watching for the new beginning "Shouldering its way and shedding the earth crumbs," and Coleridge sees his daughter as a spirit, shining "through her body visibly."

COOLE AND BALLYLEE, 1931

UNDER my window-ledge the waters race,
Otters below and moor-hens on the top,
Run for a mile undimmed in Heaven's face
Then darkening through "dark" Raftery's
    "cellar" drop,
Run underground, rise in a rocky place
In Coole demesne, and there to finish up
Spread to a lake and drop into a hole.
What's water but the generated soul?

Upon the border of that lake's a wood
Now all dry sticks under a wintry sun,
And in a copse of beeches there I stood,
For Nature's pulled her tragic buskin on
And all the rant's a mirror of my mood:
At sudden thunder of the mounting swan
I turned about and looked where branches break
The glittering reaches of the flooded lake.

Another emblem there! That stormy white
But seems a concentration of the sky;
And, like the soul, it sails into the sight
And in the morning's gone, no man knows why;
And is so lovely that it sets to right
What knowledge or its lack had set awry,
So arrogantly pure, a child might think
It can be murdered with a spot of ink.

Sound of a stick upon the floor, a sound
From somebody that toils from chair to chair;
Beloved books that famous hands have bound,
Old marble heads, old pictures everywhere;
Great rooms where travelled men and
    children found
Content or joy; a last inheritor
Where none has reigned that lacked a name
    and fame
Or out of folly into folly came.

A spot whereon the founders lived and died
Seemed once more dear than life; ancestral trees,
Or gardens rich in memory glorified

Marriages, alliances, and families,
And every bride's ambition satisfied.
Where fashion or mere fantasy decrees
Man shifts about—all that great glory spent—
Like some poor Arab tribesman and his tent.

We were the last romantics—chose for theme
Traditional sanctity and loveliness;
Whatever's written in what poets name
The book of the people; whatever most can bless
The mind of man or elevate a rhyme;
But all is changed, that high horse riderless,
Though mounted in that saddle Homer rode
Where the swan drifts upon a darkening flood.

WILLIAM BUTLER YEATS[7]

PUTTING IN THE SEED

YOU come to fetch me from my work tonight
When supper's on the table, and we'll see
If I can leave off burying the white
Soft petals fallen from the apple tree
(Soft petals, yes, but not so barren quite,
Mingled with these, smooth bean and wrinkled pea),
And go along with you ere you lose sight
Of what you came for and become like me,
Slave to a springtime passion for the earth.
How Love burns through the Putting in the Seed
On through the watching for that early birth
When, just as the soil tarnishes with weed,
The sturdy seedling with arched body comes
Shouldering its way and shedding the earth crumbs.

ROBERT FROST[8]

PHANTOM

ALL look and likeness caught from earth
All accident of kin and birth,
Had pass'd away. There was no trace
Of aught on that illumined face,

Uprais'd beneath the rifted stone
But of one spirit all her own;—
She, she herself, and only she,
Shone through her body visibly.

SAMUEL TAYLOR COLERIDGE[9]

Connections of the Poets with Swedenborg

(See earlier sections for information on Lee, Baudelaire, E. B. Browning, Lindsay, Valéry, Yeats, and Frost.)

SAMUEL TAYLOR COLERIDGE (1772–1834) made no public statement about Swedenborg, but his correspondence with early New Church members and annotations in his copies of a number of Swedenborg's philosophical and theological volumes indicate his interest in Swedenborg's ideas.

Sources

Edmiston, Leonard Martin. *Coleridge's Commentary on Swedenborg*. Ph.D. diss., University of Missouri, 1954.

Kirven, Robert H. *Emanuel Swedenborg and the Revolt Against Deism*. Ph.D. diss. Brandeis University, 1965.

Notes for the Poems

1. Anna Collier Lee, "Sonnet," in *Selected Verses from the Writings of Anna Collier Lee* (privately printed, 1909), p. 8.
2. Charles Pierre Baudelaire, "Correspondences," trans. Robin Larsen (unpublished).
3. Elizabeth Barrett Browning, selections from "Aurora Leigh," in *Poetical Works* (New York: Dodd, Mead, 1899), vol. 5, pp. 294–95.
4. Ibid., pp. 335, 119.
5. Vachel Lindsay, "My Lady Compared to a Young Tree" in *Collected Poems* (New York: Macmillan, 1925), pp. 288–89.
6. Paul Valéry, "Palm," in *The Collected Works in English*, Bollingen Series XLV, vol. 2: *Poems*, trans. David Paul (Princeton, N.J.: Princeton University Press, 1971), pp. 229–35.
7. William Butler Yeats, "Coole and Ballylee, 1931" in *Collected Poems*, def. ed. (New York: Macmillan, 1956), pp. 239–40.
8. Robert Frost, "Putting in the Seed," in *Mountain Interval* (New York: Holt, Rinenehart and Winston, 1969).
9. Samuel Taylor Coleridge, "Phantom," in hart and Winston, 1969).
mondsworth, England: Penguin Books, 1957), pp. 100–1.

IV
Religion
&
Philosophy

*Praeterea omnis religio pro fine habet
vitam, docet enim mala quae fugienda
sunt, ac bona quae facienda, religio quae
pro fine non habet vitam, non
dici potest religio*

❦

Further, all religion has life for its end:
it teaches what evils are to be avoided
and what good things are to be done. Any
religion that does not have life as its end
cannot be called a religion. . . . (AE 847)

Testimony to the Invisible

Jorge Luis Borges

Translated by Catherine Rodriguez-Nieto

A longtime friend of the Swedenborg Foundation, Jorge Luis Borges had agreed to write an essay for this anthology in which he would contrast the three salvatory schemas proposed by Christ, Swedenborg, and Blake. His sudden passing in the spring of 1986 while in Switzerland came before he had actually composed any of his promised essay. We were fortunate, however, to have already in our possession an essay in Spanish that he dictated to his secretary, which was used for a prologue to a Spanish edition of Sig Synnestedt's *The Essential Swedenborg*. This essay addresses the overall theme of this anthology perhaps more directly than the proposed essay that was never written.

In "Testimony to the Invisible," one of the twentieth century's greatest writers testifies to the inspiration that he received from Swedenborg's work, showing from many angles why Swedenborg's religious vision is compelling to a poet and short-story master.

IN HIS ADMIRABLE LECTURE of 1845, Ralph Waldo Emerson cited Emanuel Swedenborg as a classic example of the mystic. This word, while it is extremely accurate, runs the risk of suggesting a man apart, a man who instinctively removes himself from the circumstances and urgencies we call, though I will never know why, reality. No one is further from that image than Emanuel Swedenborg, who journeyed, lucid and laborious, through this and all other worlds. No one accepted life more fully, no one investigated it with a passion so great, with the same intellectual love, or with such impatience to learn about it. No one was less like a monk than that sanguine Scandinavian who went much farther than Eric the Red.

Like the Buddha, Swedenborg rejected asceticism, which impoverishes men and can diminish them. Within the boundaries of heaven he saw a hermit who had set out to gain admittance there, and had voluntarily spent his mortal life in the solitude of the desert. Having reached his goal, the blessed one discovers that he is unable to follow the conversation of the angels or fathom the complexities of Paradise. He is finally permitted to project around himself a hallucinatory image of the wilderness. There he remains, as he did on earth, engaged in self-denial and prayer, but without the hope of reaching heaven.

Jesper Swedberg, Emanuel's father, was an eminent Lutheran bishop, in whom fervor and tolerance existed in rare conjunction. Emanuel was born in Stockholm near the beginning of 1688. From early childhood, he thought about God and actively sought conversation with the clerics who frequented his father's house. It is not insignificant that he placed above salvation through faith, the cornerstone of the reform preached by Luther, salvation through good works, which is irrefutable evidence of the former. This peerless, solitary man was many men. He did not scorn craftsmanship; as a youth in London he practiced the manual arts as bookbinder, cabinetmaker, optician, watchmaker, manufacturer of scientific instruments, and engraver of maps for globes. All of this he accomplished without neglecting the discipline

JORGE LUIS BORGES has been a perennial candidate for the Nobel Prize in literature. Born of Spanish, English, Portuguese, and Jewish descent, Borges was reared in an educated and sheltered environment. As a young man in post–World War I Spain, Borges found a spiritual home with the Ultraist movement, among young writers who criticized the established writers as decadent and self-consciously artistic. Borges helped to forge a reaction to the reigning paradigm in fiction by creating a modality of free verse and a liberal use of metaphor and absurd humor. He returned to his native Buenos Aires in 1921, which was to become his base for the rest of his life. Immediately, he found himself as the spiritual founder and leader of the Ultraist values for all of South America.

At first primarily a poet, he later became best known for his short stories. His most famous stories were written in the forties and fifties after a near-fatal bout with blood poisoning in 1938. Upon recovering, he found himself obsessed by a fear of having lost his creative powers. He

(Continued on the next page)

of the various natural sciences, algebra, and the new astronomy of Newton, with whom he would have liked to converse but whom he never met. His application was always inventive; he anticipated the nebular theory of Laplace and Kant [for a detailed discussion of this issue, see Steve Koke's essay "In Search of a Religious Cosmology," elsewhere in this anthology], and designed a craft capable of flight and another, for military purposes, that could navigate below the surface of the ocean. We are indebted to him for a personal method of fixing longitudes and a treatise on the diameter of the moon. Toward 1716 he began publication in Uppsala of a scientific journal beautifully titled *Daedalus Hyperboreus*, which would continue to appear for two years. His aversion to purely speculative endeavor caused him, in 1717, to refuse the chair in astronomy offered him by the king. During the reckless and quasi-mythical wars waged by Karl XII, he served as a military engineer. He conceived and constructed a device to move boats over a stretch of land more than fourteen miles long. In 1734 his three-volume *Opera Philosophica et Mineralia* appeared in Saxony. He wrote good Latin hexameters, and was interested in English literature—Spenser, Shakespeare, Cowley, Milton, and Dryden—because of its imaginative power. Even had he not consecrated himself to mysticism, his name would be illustrious in the annals of science. Like Descartes, he was interested in the problem of the precise point at which the soul is connected to the body. Anatomy, physics, algebra, and chemistry inspired the many works he wrote, following the custom of his time, in Latin. In Holland he was struck by the faith and well-being of the inhabitants; he attributed them to the country's being a republic, because in kingdoms the people, accustomed to adulating the king, also adulate God, a servile characteristic which cannot please him. We should note in passing that, during his journeys, Swedenborg visited schools, universities, poor neighborhoods, and factories, and was fond of music, particularly opera. He served as assessor to the Royal Board of Mines and sat in the House of Nobles [of the Riksdag]. He always preferred the study of sacred scripture to that of dogmatic theology. Latin translations were not good enough for him; he studied the original texts in Hebrew and Greek. In a private diary he accuses himself of monstrous pride; while leafing through the volumes that lined the shelves of a book-store, it occurred to him that he could, without much effort, improve on them, and then understood that the Lord has a thousand ways of touching the human heart and that there is no such thing as a useless book. Pliny the Younger had written that no book is so bad there is nothing good in it, an opinion Cervantes would recall.

The most important event of Swedenborg's human life took place in London, one night in April 1745. He himself called it the "discrete degree" [see Glossary] or the "degree of separation." It was preceded by dreams, prayer, periods of doubt, fasting, and—much more surprisingly—by diligent scientific and philosophical work. A stranger who had silently followed him through the streets of London, and about whose looks nothing is known, suddenly appeared in his room and told him that he was the Lord.* He immediately entrusted to Swedenborg the mission of revealing to men, by then sunk in atheism, error, and sin, the true, lost faith of Jesus. He announced to him that his spirit would travel through heavens and hells and that he would be able to converse with the dead, with demons, and with angels.

The chosen one was then fifty-seven years old; during nearly thirty years more he led the life of a visionary, which he recorded in closely reasoned treatises written in clear, unequivocal prose. Unlike other mystics, he eschewed metaphor, exaltation, and vague, fiery hyperbole.

The explanation is obvious. The use of any word whatsoever presupposes a shared experience, for which the word is the symbol. If someone speaks to us about the flavor of coffee, it is because we have already tasted it; if about the color yellow, because we have already seen lemons, gold, wheat, and sunsets. To suggest the ineffable union of man's soul with the divine being, the Sufis of Islam found themselves obliged to resort to prodigious analogies, to images of roses, intoxication, or carnal love; Swedenborg was able to abstain from this kind of rhetorical artifice because his subject matter was not the ecstasy of a rapt and fainting soul, but rather the accurate description of regions that, though ultra-

---

*[So far as can be ascertained, Borges's account of a man following Swedenborg around the streets of London and then appearing to him as the Lord is a totally original one. See Donald L. Rose's essay "The Pivotal Change in Swedenborg's Life" elsewhere in this anthology, for further discussion of this period of Swedenborg's life.]

---

decided to write a short story, reasoning that failure in a genre for which he was less known would be less humiliating. The result was "Pierre Menard, Author of Don Quijote," one of his greatest works. He had discovered his most powerful medium.

For the next twenty years, Jorge Luis Borges forged an art form for fiction in Latin America. His metaphysical themes and stylistic innovations have inspired younger generations to explore the realities of their rapidly evolving societies with far greater concern for universal and aesthetic values than did their predecessors. Introducing imagination as the chief fictional ingredient, Borges delivered Latin American literature from dry, documentary realism. In doing so, he gave birth to a new genre of literature.

terrestrial, were clearly defined. In order for us to imagine, or to begin to imagine, the lowest depth of hell, Milton speaks to us of "No light, but rather darkness visible." Swedenborg prefers the rigor and—why not say it?—possible wordiness of the explorer or geographer who is recording unknown kingdoms.

As I dictate these lines, I feel the reader's incredulity holding me back like a high, bronze wall, buttressed by two assumptions: deliberate imposture on the part of the man who wrote such strange things, or the influence of sudden or progressive madness. The first is inadmissible. Had Emanuel Swedenborg intended to deceive, he would not have resorted to anonymous publication of a good part of his work, as he did for the nine volumes of his *Arcana Coelestia*, which do not avail themselves of the authority conferred by his already illustrious name.* We know that he was not proselytizing in the dialogue. Like Emerson and Walt Whitman, he believed that arguments persuade no one, and that stating a truth is sufficient for its acceptance by those who hear it. He always shunned polemic. There is not one syllogism in his entire work, only terse, tranquil affirmations. I am referring, of course, to his mystical treatises.

The hypothesis of madness is equally unfounded. If the writer of *Daedalus Hyperboreus* and *Prodromus Principiorum Rerum Naturalium* had gone mad, we would not owe to his tenacious pen the thousands of methodical pages he wrote during the following thirty years or so, pages that have nothing at all to do with frenzy.

Let us consider now his coherent multiple visions, which certainly contain much that is miraculous. William White† has observed with acuity that we docilely surrender our faith to the visions of the ancients, while tending to reject or ridicule those of the moderns. We believe in Ezekiel because he is exalted by remoteness in time and space; we believe in Saint John of the Cross because he is an integral part of Spanish literature; but we do not believe in William Blake, Swedenborg's rebellious disciple, or in his master, still near to us in time. Gibbon said the same of miracles. Exactly when did true visions cease and apocryphal ones begin?

Swedenborg devoted two years to the study of Hebrew in order to examine scripture directly. I personally believe— and it must be understood that this is the opinion, doubtless heterodox, of a mere man of letters and not a researcher or theologian—that Swedenborg, like Spinoza or Francis Bacon, was a thinker in his own right who made an awkward mistake when he decided to adapt his ideas to the framework

of the two Testaments. This had happened to the Hebrew Cabalists, who were essentially Neoplatonists when they invoked the authority of the verses, words, and even letters and transpositions of letters in Genesis to justify their system.

It is not my intent to expound the doctrine of the New Jerusalem revealed by Swedenborg, but I do want to dwell on two points. The first is his extremely original concept of heaven and hell, which he explains at length in the best-known and most beautiful of his treatises, *De Coelo et Inferno*, published in Amsterdam in 1758. Blake repeats it and Bernard Shaw vividly summarized it in the third act of *Man and Superman* (1903), in the narration of John Tanner's dream. Shaw never, so far as I know, spoke of Swedenborg; it might be supposed that he wrote under the stimulus of Blake, whom he mentions frequently and with respect; nor is it impossible to believe that he arrived at the same ideas independently.

In a famous letter to Cangrande Della Scala, Dante Alighieri points out that his *Commedia*, like sacred scripture, can be read four different ways, of which the literal way is only one. But the reader, in the thrall of the splendid poetry, forms an indelible impression that the nine circles of hell, the nine terraces of purgatory, and the nine heavens of paradise correspond to three establishments: one whose nature is penal, one penitential, and another—if the neologism is allowable—premial. Passages such as "*Lasciate ogni speranza, voi ch'entrate*" (All hope abandon, ye who enter here) reinforce the topographical conviction created through art. Nothing is farther from the ultraterrestrial destinations of Swedenborg. The heaven and hell of his doctrine are not places, even though the souls of the dead who inhabit and, in a way, create them perceive them as being situated in space. They are conditions of the soul, determined by its former life. Heaven is forbidden to no one, hell imposed on no one. The doors, so to speak, are open. People who have died but fail to realize they are dead* project, for an indefinite period of time, an illusory image of their customary ambiance and of the people who surrounded them. At the end of that period, strangers approach them. The wicked dead find the looks and manner of demons to be agreeable, and quickly join them; the righteous choose angels. For the blessed, the diabolical sphere is a region full of swamps, caves, burning huts, ruins, brothels, and taverns. The damned are faceless or their features are mutilated, atrocious (in the eyes of the righteous), but they believe themselves to be beautiful. For them, happiness lies in the exercise of power and in mutual hatred. They devote their lives to politics, in the most South American sense of the word; that is, they live to scheme, to lie, and to impose their will on others. Swedenborg recounts that a ray of celestial light once fell into the depths of hell;

---

*[Swedenborg published all of his religious works anonymously until he brought out *Conjugial Love* in 1768 with his by-line.]

†[William White was a nineteenth-century biographer of Swedenborg who published his account of Swedenborg's life in two volumes—the first adulatory and the second critical.]

*In England, popular superstition has it that we will know we have died only when we see that the mirror no longer reflects our image.

the damned perceived it as stench, as an ulcerated wound, and as darkness.

Hell is the other face of heaven. Its exact opposite is necessary for the balance of creation. The Lord rules over it as he does over heaven. Balance between the two spheres is required for free will, which must unceasingly choose between good, which emanates from heaven, and evil, which emanates from hell. Every day, every instant of every day, man is shaping his eternal damnation or his salvation. We will be what we are. The terrors or anxieties of agony, which usually occur when a dying person is frightened and confused, are of little importance. Whether we believe in the immortality of the soul or not, we must recognize that the doctrine revealed by Swedenborg is more moral and reasonable than one that postulates a mysterious gift gotten, almost by chance, at the eleventh hour. To begin with, it leads us to the practice of virtue in our lives.

Innumerable heavens constitute the heaven Swedenborg saw, innumerable angels constitute each heaven and each angel is, individually, a heaven. All are ruled by an ardent love of God and neighbor. The overall shape of heaven (and of the heavens) is the shape of a man* or, what amounts to the same thing, that of an angel, because angels are not a separate species. Angels, like demons, are the dead who have passed into the angelic or demonic sphere. A curious stroke, suggesting the fourth dimension contemplated by Henry More: angels, wherever they may be, are always directly facing the Lord. In the spiritual sphere, the sun is the visible image of God. Space and time exist only as illusions; if one person thinks of another, the second is immediately at the side of the first. The angels converse like men, through spoken words that are enunciated and heard, but the language they use is natural and need not be learned. It is common to all the angelic spheres. The art of writing is not unknown in heaven; more than once, Swedenborg received divine communications that seemed to be handwritten or printed, but that he was unable to descipher completely because the Lord prefers direct, oral instruction. Regardless of baptism, regardless of the religion professed by their parents, all children go to heaven, where they are taught by the angels. Neither riches, nor happiness, nor luxury, nor worldly life are barriers to entering heaven; to be poor has no merit. It is no virtue, any more than is the suffering of misfortune. Good will and the love of God are essential; external circumstances are not. We have already seen the case of the hermit who, through self-mortification and solitude, made himself unfit for heaven and was obliged to forgo its delights.

In his treatise on conjugial love, which appeared in 1768, Swedenborg says that marriage is never perfect on earth, because understanding predominates in men and will predominates in women. In the celestial state, a man and woman who have loved one another will form a single angel.

In the Apocalypse, one of the canonical books of the New Testament, Saint John of Patmos speaks of a heavenly Jerusalem; Swedenborg extends this idea to other great cities. Thus, in *Vera Christiana Religio* (1771), he writes that there are two ultraterrestrial Londons. When men die, they do not lose their character. The English preserve the intimate light of their intellect and their respect for authority; the Dutch continue to engage in commerce; Germans are usually loaded down with books, and when someone asks them a question, they consult the appropriate volume before answering. Moslems present the most curious case of all. Because the concepts of Mohammed and religion are inextricably intertwined in their souls, God provides them with an angel to teach them who pretends to be Mohammed. This is not always the same angel. The real Mohammed emerged once before the community of the faithful just long enough to say the words, "I am your Mohammed," before turning back and sinking back into hell.

There are no hypocrites in the spiritual sphere; each person is what he is. An evil spirit ordered Swedenborg to write that it is the delight of demons to commit adultery, robbery, and fraud, and to lie; and they also delight in the stench of excrement and dead bodies. I am abridging this episode; the curious may consult the last page of the treatise *Sapientia Angelica de Divina Providentia* (1764).

Unlike the heaven referred to by other visionaries, Swedenborg's heaven is more precise than earth. Shapes, objects, structures, and colors are more complex and vivid. In the Gospels, salvation is an ethical process. Righteousness is fundamental; humility, misery, and misfortune are also exalted. To the requirement of righteousness, Swedenborg adds another, never before mentioned by any theologian: intelligence. Let us again remember the ascetic, who was forced to recognize that he was unworthy of the theological conversation of the angels. (The incalculable heavens of Swedenborg are full of love and theology.) When Blake writes, "The fool shall not enter into Glory, no matter how holy he may be," [*El tonto no entrará en la Gloria, por santo que sea*] or "Strip yourselves of sanctity and clothe yourselves in intelligence," [*Despojáos de santidad y cubríos de inteligencia*], he is doing nothing more than minting laconic epigrams from the discursive thought of Swedenborg. Blake also affirms that the salvation of man demands a third requirement: that he be an artist. Jesus Christ was an artist, because he taught through parables and metaphor rather than abstract reasoning.

It is not without misgiving that I turn now to outline, albeit partially and in a rudimentary fashion, the doctrine of correspondences, which for many is central to the subject we are studying. In the Middle Ages it was thought that the Lord had written two books, one of which we call the Bible and the other of which we call the universe. It was our duty

---

*By analogy, the overall shape of hell is a demon.

to interpret them. I suspect that Swedenborg began with the exegesis of the first. He conjectured that each word of scripture has a spiritual sense, and eventually prepared a vast system of hidden meanings. Stones, for example, represent natural truths; precious stones, spiritual truths; stars, divine knowledge; the horse, a correct understanding of scripture, but also its distortion through sophistry; the abomination of desolation, the Trinity; the abyss, God or hell; et cetera.[1]

From a symbolic reading of the Bible, Swedenborg would have gone on to a symbolic reading of the universe and of human beings. The sun in the sky is an image of the spiritual sun, which is in turn an image of God; there is not a single creature on earth that does not owe its continued existence to the constant influence of the Divine Being. De Quincey, who was a reader of Swedenborg's works, writes that the smallest things are secret mirrors of the greatest. Carlyle says that universal history is a text we must continually read and write, and in which we are also written. The disturbing suspicion that we are ciphers and symbols in a divine cryptography whose true meaning we do not know abounds in the volumes of Leon Bloy, and the Jewish Cabalists knew of it.

The doctrine of correspondences has brought me to mention the Cabala. No one whom I know of or remember has yet investigated its intimate affinity. In the first chapter of scripture we read that God created man according to his own image and likeness. This affirmation implies that God has the shape of a man. The Cabalists who compiled the *Book of Creation* declare that the ten emanations, or *sefiroth*, whose source is the ineffable divinity, can be conceived under the species of a tree or of a Man; the primordial man, the Adam Kadmon. If all things are in God, all things will be in man, who is his earthly reflection. Thus, Swedenborg and the Cabala both arrive at the concept of the microcosm, that is to say, man as the mirror or compendium of the universe. According to Swedenborg, hell and heaven are in man, as well as plants, mountains, seas, continents, minerals, trees, flowers, thistles, fish, tools, cities, and buildings.

In 1758, Swedenborg announced that the previous year he had witnessed the Last Judgment, which had taken place in the world of the spirits on the exact date when faith was extinguished in all the churches. The decline began when the church of Rome was founded. The reform undertaken by Luther and prefigured by Wycliffe was imperfect and often heretical. Another Last Judgment takes place at the moment of each man's death; it is the consequence of his entire former life.

On 29 March 1772, Emanuel Swedenborg died in London, the city he so loved, the city in which God had one night entrusted to him the mission that would make him unique among men. Some testimonials remain of his last days, of his ancient black velvet suit and of a sword with a strangely shaped hilt.

His way of life was austere during his last years; his nourishment consisted of only coffee, milk, and bread. The servants could hear him at any hour of the day or night walking to and fro in his bedroom, conversing with his angels.

Sometime around 1970, I wrote this sonnet:

EMANUEL SWEDENBORG

Taller than the others, this man
Walked among them, at a distance,
Now and then calling the angels
By their secret names. He would see
That which earthly eyes do not see:
The fierce geometry, the crystal
Labyrinth of God and the sordid
Milling of infernal delights.
He knew that Glory and Hell too
Are in your soul, with all their myths;
He knew, like the Greek, that the days
Of time are Eternity's mirrors.
In dry Latin he went on listing
The unconditional Last Things.[2]

Notes

1. Anyone wishing to pursue this study may examine *A Dictionary of Bible Imagery* by Alice Spiers Sechrist (New York: Swedenborg Foundation, Inc., 1973), which analyzes over five thousand words from the sacred texts.
2. Sonnet translated by Richard Howard and Cesar Rennert.

The Relevance of Emanuel Swedenborg's Theological Concepts for the New Age as It Is Envisioned Today

Michael W. Stanley, Ph.D.

SWEDENBORG'S THEOLOGICAL AND BIBLICAL WRITINGS are sometimes considered to sound old-fashioned and ponderous. Currently we have seen the sprouting of New Age groups of all sorts, often weird and wonderful-looking, each into their own thing, or trying out the latest psychic or psychological fad or fancy. So what has Swedenborg got to do with the New Age? Beneath the surface, a great deal indeed. And in fact, it is typical of the New Age approach at its best to look beneath the surface of everything and everyone.

As it has turned out, it is Blake, not Swedenborg, who has been given the title "Father of the New Age," wearing the more modern dress of exotic symbolic imagery and leaving us exuberantly expressionist etchings. One could be forgiven for mistaking Swedenborg's writings at first sight as those of a dry, unfeeling eighteenth-century recluse. But you would be mistaken. There had to be some good reason why the key religious concepts of Blake's later works were drawn from Swedenborg, and why he referred to Swedenborg as a "divine teacher." In fact, on examination, it is Swedenborg (or rather his teachings) who should be seen as the Father of the New Age.

The wisdom in his writings is such as to encompass the very fundamentals of human thought and life, including those of the New Age prophets and teachers. Yet his voluminous writings are colored by the theological, philosophical, and psychological thought forms and jargon of the eighteenth century.

It is my purpose in this essay to point briefly to the main ideas fundamental to both Swedenborg and New Age philosophy, in the hope that this may help lead to a renewed interest in Swedenborg as a vitally relevant source for evaluating and understanding the many forms of New Age consciousness.

The New Age

What exactly is meant by the term *New Age*? Because of the inherent diffuseness of New Age forms and practices, there is great difficulty in defining it or pointing to its outward manifestation. Additionally, it is a leading characteristic of the New Age to give special value not to any particular forms but to form in general as a vehicle of spiritual content. Any created form is seen as potentially able to manifest what is holy or divine.

Following Swedenborg and Blake, further prophets of a new spiritual era began to emerge—Madam Blavatsky, Rudolph Steiner, Alice Bailey, Edgar Cayce, and David Spangler being perhaps the best known and most influential.

Originally trained as a physicist (with papers on the nature of defects in the crystalline lattice structure of metals, semiconductors, and quartz) Dr. MICHAEL W. STANLEY's interests turned more deeply toward the spiritual nature of life and people's spiritual needs. He became ordained as a minister into the New Jerusalem Church (Swedenborgian) in 1971, and having studied philosophy, psychology, comparative religion, and the spiritual symbolic meaning of sacred scriptures and having led church societies in Mauritius and England, he was in 1976 appointed principal of the New Church College (Swedenborgian) in Manchester, England. While in this post, in addition to teaching full-time students, he gives public lectures on Swedenborg's teachings and the New Age and leads several spiritual growth groups, which use a number of new psychospiritual techniques that he is currently developing.

Their visions were in terms of a renewal of a spiritual knowledge, perception, and awareness—an "ancient wisdom," as they called it—that had once flowered in the East long before Christ, in fact before the dawn of recorded history. For Swedenborg this was the "wisdom of the ancients" centered on an "ancient Word" from which the early chapters of Genesis derive. The problem is to extract the true ancient wisdom from accretions of misunderstanding, distortion, fancy, and sensualizing, picked up while reading countless less perceptive and worldly authors. Swedenborg's delineation of the true ancient wisdom is both clear and compelling, showing of what the profundity and truth of ancient thought and perception really consists.

But the first real signs of the emergence of a new generation affected by a new consciousness and attitude was not until the 1960s, when it manifested in the hippie phenomenon. Anti-intellectual, anti–all authorities, it caught the attention of the West by rallying the intelligent children of the wealthy, and by practical emphasis on love in action, above all else. Now twenty years later, the hippies' naïvely expressed philosophy has sprouted many mystical, esoteric, and psychological branches and blossomed in numerous colorful ways.

To grasp the essence of what makes up the New Age, we need to look to fundamentals, to key principles of thought and attitudes of mind. And it is in such areas that the influence and importance of Swedenborg's thought becomes apparent. In the following sections I shall take in turn several key principles that characterize the New Age, and correlate them with those corresponding aspects of Swedenborg's teachings that provide an overall philosophical, theological, and psychological framework to unite and ground them. However, it should be borne in mind that these principles are new only as regards the form in which they are expressed. Eternal principles of truth or reality tend to become distorted or lost, and reemerge periodically at the birth and flowering of a new age, wearing a very new dress that reflects the further development and increased complexity of man's thought and life.

Oneness of All Life

There is and can only be one life, which is necessarily in all created forms for them to maintain their existence. This one life has been given many names—the Source, the Infinite, the Absolute, the Divine, God, Brahma, Allah, and so on. Although essentially invisible, it manifests in infinitely many ways. A human's "fall," or fundamental mistake, is to see and regard oneself as separate from nature, other persons, and God—a sense of separation constantly reinforced by "Old Age" Christian teaching, and neo-orthodox teaching of God as "wholly other" than human.

According to Swedenborg, oneness is not a simplistic undifferentiation but, through love, a harmony and interpenetration of many distinctive "parts": "A form makes one the more perfectly in proportion as the things which enter into the form are distinctly different and yet united" (DP 4[4]). The heaven of united spirits is one because "there is only one influx which is received by every individual according to his peculiar quality . . . and although the influx is only one, yet all things obey and follow as a one because of the mutual love in which they are" (AC 1285[2]).

Swedenborg expresses the New Age view very beautifully by his concept of the Divine Human and Universal (or Greatest) Human. The invisible (because infinite) Divine constantly manifests itself through the human form, or forms related to aspects of the human form. By "human form" Swedenborg means the perfect patterning and functioning of the human mind or spirit, so that a tree, for example, manifests correspondentially the growth, branching out, and bearing fruit of developing thought. The Divine inflows perpetually into the human, maintaining distinction *without* separation (across what Swedenborg terms a "discrete degree" [see Glossary]). The perfect manifestation of this eternal process is the Divine Human [see Glossary], termed the "Body of Christ" in the New Testament. The physiological body mirrors this mystic body perfectly, being made in its image.

> As God is a Man [human; see Glossary], the universal angelic heaven in the complex relates to one Man which is distinguished into regions and provinces according to the members, viscera, and organs of man. (DLW 288)

> The head of this Man is constituted of the highest heaven, its breast and the middle region of the body constitute the second and lowest heavens, and its loins and feet constitute the Church on earth. The Lord himself is the soul and life of this whole Man. (TCR 119)

Whereas the Old Age theology had separated the one Divine into three co-equal persons, each effectively having a different personality, Swedenborg set forth clearly the universal trine, or trinity, in the Divine as well as in all forms: (1) an invisible inflowing life, (2) a visible form or vessel, and (3) an outflowing life, colored by the quality of the vessel, like colored glass transmitting a partial and modified facet of the pure incident white light. The Christ is the perfect humanity perfectly transmitting the invisible divinity as the Holy Spirit.

> For anything to be perfect there must be a trine . . . and this trine must make a one. (COR 17)

> The Divine Trinity in one Person is to be understood as soul, body and proceeding operation which together constitute one essence. . . . There is a similar trinity in every individual

man which together constitutes one person, namely, the soul, the body and proceeding operation. But in man this trinity is finite . . . whereas in the Lord the Trinity is infinite. (9Q 6)

Cosmic (Universal) Christ or Buddha

In New Age thought, the Christ or Buddha concept is a universal, eternal one. The Christ nature is within every human form, though frequently buried and lost beneath delusions and distortions of all kinds. So the Divine itself (the Father) and the Christ (the Son) are necessarily at the center of everyone, and each person in essence is a part of that universal Christ. For Swedenborg every spirit is essentially a part or function within the Universal Human or Body of Christ: "In the Lord's view the whole human race is as one Man . . . It is not the men who thus appear together but their uses. Those appear together as a perfect and beautiful man who are of good use" (DLDW 17). The Christ story of the Gospels, spiritually understood, is the emergence of the Christ spirit in each individual: "When a person receives the Lord by acknowledging Him as his Creator, Redeemer and Saviour, then is His first Coming" (TCR 766).

Holistic Approach and Networking

In New Age holistic thinking, all of creation is a unitary whole, and yet also a complete network of interrelationships, with reality lying not in objective units, but in dynamic functions or patterns of life, each interacting ultimately on all others. In Swedenborg's Universal Human, encompassing all God's creation in its order and perfection, the one whole can be viewed as manifesting countless interrelated functions exactly mirrored by all the various functions of the physical body, so that human physiology presents a correspondential picture of the collective world of spirit infilled with the Divine.

From this the concepts of unity in variety and universal religion follow, implying the need for many varied forms of religion and spirituality, yet all serving the one divine life of unity in love. So in Swedenborg's heaven we find doctrine and worship indefinitely diverse, with each society of spirits reflecting divine love and wisdom in their own unique way.

> The perfection of heaven is the result of variety in worship[;] for unity[,] to be perfect, must be formed from various parts. Every unity has its existence from diversity. . . . That this is the origin of all perfection is evident from all the beauty, pleasantness and delight that affect the senses as well as the mind. For these exist and flow from no other source than the concept and harmony of many concordant and harmonious parts, either coexisting in order or following in order. (HH 56)

Balance of Right and Left Brain Modes of Thought

Swedenborg's insight into the different functions of the two halves of the brain went completely unnoticed in his own time and is generally not known even today. According to Swedenborg, "the left side of the brain corresponds to rational or intellectual things, and the right side corresponds to the affections or things of the will" (AC 3884). He was well aware of the extreme imbalance in his day in favor of coldly rational and argumentative disputes, and taught that the two aspects "head" and "heart" need to be balanced. Recent brain research indicates that the right brain is associated with intuitive, holistic, synthesizing thought as opposed to the analytical, logical thought associated with the left brain. In New Age circles the intuitive right brain mode is given a very high place, though sometimes at the expense of intellectual rationality. Generally though, the need for harmonizing complementaries or polarities is recognized and stressed.

The most common method of tapping the intuitive mode is that of meditation, a technique used regularly by Swedenborg, who refers even to angels practicing spiritual meditation (TCR 767).

Swedenborg mainly used the Bible as a focus for his meditation, allowing his mind to be guided into an awareness of its spiritual significance by the Lord or Source within. This path to enlightenment is the one most recommended by Swedenborg, superior indeed, in his view, to that of receiving communication from angels. However he also stressed the importance of a true and rational doctrinal framework as a safeguard against having ingrained spiritual fallacies and falsities reflected back to the meditator.

Even though the meditation mode is a hallmark of Eastern religious practice, and objective scientific observation and deduction that of modern Western practice, Swedenborg's thought shows the powerful effect of combining and balancing the two approaches. (See also the section "Masculine and Feminine," in the following pages of this essay.)

Esoteric Significance of Sacred Texts

The ancient esoteric mode of expressing spiritual realities through the medium of myth, fable, and parable was reinstated by Swedenborg, along with the universal key to reopen the door on correspondential or symbolic insight and awareness. So the New Age approach instinctively looks beyond literal meanings to the facets or aspects of the soul mirrored in the sacred stories. Swedenborg provides a spiritual language, in terms of degrees and facets of love and wisdom and their opposites, with which to grasp intellectually as well as intuitively the esoteric correspondential meaning of the sacred scriptures and the elements of nature that form their colorful backdrop. Thus the spiritual is always mirrored in the natural forms and images, not through any random, arbitrary use of symbols, but by a universal divine process in which all outer natural forms are created as correspondential uses or functions of the spiritual forms from which they originate. "From the things which come forth in the natural world can be seen as in a mirror the things which are in the spiritual world" (HH 56). "The Divine truths of the Word . . . are like mirrors in which the Lord's face is seen" (AR 938[2]). Sacred texts (including ancient myths and legends) make use of this principle to express dynamic processes and developments in the human psyche, so that they are in effect profound psychospiritual studies powerfully expressed in the ancient mode.

The principle on which correspondence between inner and outer (or spiritual and natural) rests is that of use or function. So, for example, spiritual light serves the same function in the spirit as natural light does in the world, namely, to show up what is there so that it can be seen and identified. This rational principle, illustrated countless times in Swedenborg's writings, combines wonderfully with the openness of meditation, to provide illuminating insights into one's inner psyche, its dynamics, and the divine love at the heart of life.

Power of Inner Belief

The powerful effect (beneficial or destructive) of one's inner belief system (which is often unconscious) on one's spiritual state is becoming recognized, as is just how much this belief system may be at variance with one's overt conscious beliefs. The latter, when it is merely an intellectual set of beliefs is, in Swedenborg's terms, "dead," having no power to save one from the spiritual ill effects of a separated, self-centered inner life. "Saving faith" is for Swedenborg an effect of the desire to love and serve others, and so stems from an inner belief system based on love as the only reality and source of true happiness.

> Belief on the Lord brings about conjunction with Him and consequently salvation. To believe on Him is to have confidence that He saves, and since no one can have this confidence except one who lives a good life, therefore this is also understood by believing on Him. (TCR 2)

> The faith which is the internal of the Church is that which is of or from love and charity. . . . He who has the life of charity knows all things of faith. (AC 1798)

> Faith is the eye of love, for by love through faith the Lord is seen, and love is the life of faith. (AC 3863[12])

> Love is like a fire . . . and faith is like the light from that fire. (AC 9434[2])

This true or living faith, which may not at first be coupled with an overt faith in God or some religion, *has* real power to change one's life from within so that the spirit is enabled to receive inner peace, love, and joy; though the process should be accelerated with the aid of a suitable outer faith also.

> Faith is a complex of truths shining in the mind of man. . . . Faith without truths is like seed deprived of its inside substance . . . whereas faith from truths is like good grain. . . . But truths do not actually live until they are in deeds. (TCR 347)

> True faith by an abundance of truths cohering as it were in a bundle, becomes more enlightened, perceptible, evident and clear, and more unitable with goodness of charity. . . . Especially does it become more powerful against evils and falsities, and so more and more living and saving. (TCR 352)

This accounts for why some New Age groups are not overtly religious, offering "self-realization" or "holistic health" in place of salvation, though insofar as these are sought for increasing one's power to affect others beneficially, they are ways of opening the interiors to the flow of divine love and spirit from the Source.

Free Will and Responsibility

Great stress is placed in New Age thought on personal choice and responsibility for one's choices. The stifling effect on spiritual growth of reliance on external authority of any kind is made clear. The only true authority is the internal one of conscience, the inner Teacher, the Christ within. So too in Swedenborg we find this vital though unpopular doctrine made central. Self-examination, the seeking of enlightenment from meditating on the scriptures, and the decision of the will are essential for regeneration or spiritual growth: "It is the part of a wise man to know the purposes that are in him. . . . He must pay attention to the various states in which he is, for they greatly vary his perception. . . . How important it is to explore and know from what origin the affections are" (AC 3796[3–4]).

Heaven or hell after death are not placements made on the basis of external obedience to church or Bible, but are states of life freely chosen from within and for which we take full responsibility. So Swedenborg frees us from the authority of any religious dogma (even his own teachings!).

> It is not the part of a wise man to confirm a dogma, but to see whether it is true before it is confirmed. (HD 257)

> Those who are in the spiritual affection of truth do not see the Word when they read it from the doctrine of the Church in which they were born, but see it as if they were separated from that doctrine, because they desire to be enlightened

and to see truths inwardly in themselves and not from others. Those who are in such a state are enlightened by the Lord, and it is granted them to form for themselves doctrine from the truths which they themselves see. (AE 190)

In our freedom we must accept responsibility for the inner voice of authority, after rationally considering the truths we can see, or are guided to see, revealed in the scriptures and nature.

Nonexistence of Chance

Because man has inner freedom of choice and rational responsibility, all that happens to him is never by chance—even, Swedenborg cites, the fall of dice or the dealing of cards.

> Who can do anything against fortune if it opposes him? . . . When you shake the dice and shuffle the cards does it not seem to know and dispose the twists and turns of the hand and wrist to favour one player more than another from some definite cause? Can the cause have any other source than the Divine Providence in ultimates, where by means of things constant and changing it works in a wonderful way along with human prudence, and at the same time conceals itself? . . . Fortune is not an illusion of the mind, nor a sport of nature, nor something without a cause, for this has no reality. But it is ocular evidence that the Divine Providence is in the most individual things of man's thought and action. (DP 212)

All happenings are provided or permitted as opportunities for vital soul experience and spiritual growth. So too, the New Age approach is to take a positive attitude to everything that occurs to us and treat it as a good learning experience. Hence we can take the positive attitude that "nothing really bad can ever befall me, though I can still respond foolishly to circumstances, and suffer as a consequence." Every failure is another learning experience on the path of soul development. On this basis we can begin to develop a real trust in life, or God's providence. So we have the teaching that all is governed by universal and eternal spiritual laws, which lead inevitably to difficulties when ignored or broken. Swedenborg's works abound with insights into such laws and their essential rationality or rightness, such as:

> Goodness has in itself its own reward, thus heaven, and evil has in itself its own punishment, thus hell. The former law is from the Lord, because the Lord wills good to all. But the latter is not so, because the Lord wills evil to no one. Nevertheless it so happens, not from the Lord, but from the man who is in evil, consequently from evil. (AC 9033)

Linking with the Higher Self

New Age thought presents us with the importance of recognizing our Higher Self (or Christ within), and choosing to be linked or united with it. Swedenborg distinguishes between this and the Divine Creator as follows: "The Infinite and Eternal *in* itself is the Divine Itself, or the Lord in Himself. But the Infinite and Eternal *from* itself is the Divine Proceeding, that is, the Lord in others created from Himself, thus in men and angels" (DP 55). This union involves rejecting the lower self, or ego, as being not what we really are because it is not what we choose to be. In Swedenborg it is the need actively to "repent," that is, turn from ego (self-centered "proprium" [see Glossary] in Swedenborg) and its evil as our center, to the Lord with his love as our only true Center.

> After repentance the good a man does is a full good, open from the Lord Himself. It is lovely, innocent, pleasing, heavenly. There is the Lord and heaven in it; there is good itself in it. It is alive. . . . With every breath it puts away itself and its proprium, thus putting away evil. Its form is like the form of a lovely and beautifully coloured flower, shining out brilliantly under the sun's rays. (CHAR 207[7])

This turning that constitutes repentance will need to be made again and again, because the ego constantly endeavors to turn us away from God. So we need to keep on reaffirming that we do not accept any evil we may discover in our lives, but only the love from God through the Higher Christ Self or Lord within.

Spiritual Transformation and Growth

Unlike Western orthodox Christianity, which stresses a person's weakness, guilt, and sinfulness, the New Age affirms one's potentialities for spiritual development. Because one is essentially linked to God, his or her potential, drawing on the power of God within, can be developed limitlessly, though within certain personal constraints. What is needed is to discover the inner blocks inhibiting growth and to seek guidance and practice in removing them. Through truly believing in the Divine goodness and power, a person opens the way to becoming an ever greater channel for the flow of that power.

Much of Swedenborg's theology is concerned with this in the form of what he terms "regeneration" [see Glossary], which is an ongoing transformation of spirit from within so long as "evils" present in the motivations are brought to light and rejected.

> The regenerated are not regenerated at one time, but continually through the whole life, and also in the other life. (AC 3200)

The man who is in good is being reborn every moment from earliest infancy to . . . eternity. (AC 5202[4])

Man can never be so regenerated that he can be said to be perfect in any way, for there are things indefinite in number which are to be regenerated. (AC 5122[3])

This regeneration is also effectively the same as becoming united to God: "Conjunction with the Lord and regeneration are one thing, for in proportion as anyone has been conjoined with the Lord, in the same proportion he has been regenerated" (DP 92). This gradual transformation into the Divine image and likeness is built upon the foundation of God-given angelic experiences called "remnant states," which every person receives from infancy onward. These are chiefly experiences of love and its reality, such as tender mother love, for example. But the growth process is not linear but cyclic or, better, upwardly spiral, taking place through alternating states of enlightenment and "temptation combat," which are dark emergences into consciousness of hidden or buried selfish desires or motivations.

Throughout regeneration there is an alternation between no life and real life. (AC 933[2])

The man who is being regenerated . . . undergoes variations of states [of] love and faith by elevation towards interior things and by depression [towards] exterior ones. (AC 10134[6])

The hidden evils are like poisons that on breaking forth as open sores can then be healed (or removed) by spiritual truths and love. Thus the growth process according to Swedenborg also involves the concept of spiritual healing, which is central to much New Age practice and is mirrored correspondentially in the outward healing miracles of the Gospels. Swedenborg also links the spiritually healthy mind to the desire to be useful: "A man is not of a healthy mind unless use is his affection or occupation" (DLDW 46).

Masculine and Feminine

In the New Age the importance of the feminine has re-emerged after millenia of suppression. This involves the nurturing and intuitive functions now being associated with right-brain activity. Masculine and feminine are seen as complementary and both vital to each other to maintain a balance, because they have emerged from a oneness in the Divine itself.

Swedenborg makes a major contribution to this subject in his concept and teaching on the "conjugial relationship," which provides the foundation for understanding the basic polarity of male and female aspects at all levels down to physical sexual expression. The reuniting of these two separated-out elements is seen as one of the most basic processes involved in spiritual regeneration. The masculine principle alone develops the objective structuring (left brain) side of the mind, and the feminine principle alone develops the intuitive, personal, feeling (right brain) side. As a conjugial pair, each person has the formerly undeveloped side stimulated, developed, and integrated by the matching side of the partner. So each partner shapes one side of inner life with the other, and the two are then described by Swedenborg as being effectively, one human.

Love truly conjugial is the union of two as to their interiors which are of thought and will, that is, of truth and goodness . . . for he who is in love truly conjugial loves what the other thinks and what the other wills. So he also loves to think and will as the other, and so be united to the other and to become as one man. (AC 10169)

In this relationship is mirrored the union of goodness and truth, which makes the heavenly condition: "Conjugial love is the fundamental love of all loves, for it descends from the marriage of goodness and truth in the heavens . . . and is therefore heaven itself in a man" (AC 9961[3]).

Here Swedenborg throws a clear light on the ancient ideas of alchemy (or fusion of the masculine and feminine), long before the spiritual psychologist Jung performed a valuable service in extracting a truly spiritual clothing out of the dross (the modern search for making actual gold out of base metals) that had all but smothered the older more spiritual science.

The New Age teaching is thus seen to be the ancient wisdom in modern dress adapted to a natural scientific age, coming in the wake of the historical, incarnational Christ.

The Second Coming of Christ

New Age movements influenced more specifically from Christian sources see the new spirituality and awareness of the New Age as a new and triumphant revelation of the inner Christ, and this consciousness or revelation becomes his prophesied descent or "coming at the end of the age." This view is presented very fully and centrally in Swedenborg's teachings in the form of an inner coming in the spirit and an opening up of the inner esoteric meaning of the sacred scriptures, revealing to modern man the glory of the risen Christ within the "clouds" of the outer literal level.

By the Lord's advent is not meant His appearance in the clouds, but the acknowledgment of Him in hearts by love and faith. It also means His appearance in the Word whose inmost sense treats of Him alone. (AC 6895[2])

The coming of the Lord is not according to the literal sense, that He would again appear in the world; but it is his presence in each one, which takes place as often as the gospel is preached, and its holiness is thought about. (AC 3900[9])

Thus the New Age is to be seen as the manifestation of

Christ's "Second Coming" in the emergence of a renewed inner spirituality and awareness lost since the end of the original primitive era in Christianity.

Life After Death

Belief in man as an immortal spirit is universal in New Age thinking, though controversy continues to rage over whether or not the spirit lives through cycles of physical birth and death before reuniting with its Divine Source. The ability of discarnate spirits to communicate spiritual truth to incarnate spirits in a variety of ways and levels, is widely recognized, and in fact much New Age thought is claimed to have come from relatively recent sources of this nature (e.g., David Spangler's "John").

Swedenborg casts a wealth of light on not only the nature of the spiritual world but also the fundamental principles governing it. Interestingly, the reincarnation debate continues "unsettled" even among the discarnate, but Swedenborg's teachings on spiritual evolution and development in the spiritual world remove any need to invoke what many see as such a problem-riddled theory.

Swedenborg describes the naturalness and widespread nature of angelic communications with people in humankind's first or "most ancient" period on earth. In course of time spiritual degeneration set in, and humans generally lost the ability to receive such highly spiritual messages. He also warns of the danger of being too influenced by communications from lesser spirits, ignorant or malicious, who key in with one's less pure desires. With the coming of the New Age, however, more truly angelic communication will become possible.

> Man has been created by the Lord in such a manner that while he lives in the body, he is capable of conversing with spirits and angels, as indeed occurred in the most ancient times, for he is one with them, being a spirit clothed in a body. But because in course of time mankind immersed themselves in corporeal and worldly things to such a degree as to care for almost nothing else, the way to effect this communication became closed. As soon however as the bodily things in which man has been immersed are removed, the way is again opened, and then man is among spirits and associates with them. (AC 69)

> It is granted to no one to speak with angels and spirits as a spirit and angel unless he is such that he can be consociated with them as to faith and love. Neither can he be consociated unless his faith is directed to the Lord and unless his love is love to the Lord. . . . And when he has been conjoined with

Him, he is safe against any assault of the evil spirits who are from hell. (AC 9438 [2])

Angelic Help

In many of the New Age movements angels are regarded not only as intermediaries or guides in the process of revelation, but also as very present helpers to people (i.e., channels of divine qualities of love and goodness). Swedenborg provides a fundamental framework of teaching on the flow of both light and life from the Infinite down through various spiritual levels or degrees and into a human's spirit, providing intuitive perception and those essential impulses to loving creation: "Man of himself cannot possibly do what is good and turn towards the Lord except by the ministry of angels; neither can the angels except from the Lord alone" (AC 233[2]). "It is the Lord who fights [falsities in man] by means of the angels that are adjoined to the man" (AC 653). So the use of angels as intermediaries by the Divine is not to place anything between humans and the saving action of the Lord, for the angels are essentially the body of Christ, infilled by Christ, and therefore Christ in action: "All in heaven are said to be 'in the Lord's body' " (AC 6135[5]). "Heaven constitutes the Lord's body. Therefore to be in His body is to be in heaven" (TCR 719).

Conclusion

Swedenborg stands at the threshold of the New Age. In fact, as we have seen, he claims that the spiritual revelations in his writings (particularly the teachings that aid in the opening up of the spiritual sense of the Bible) usher in the new spiritual epoch he calls the Age of the New Church; and through them the triumphant nature and glory of the Christ are manifested and form his "Second Coming."

Both his teachings and much of subsequent New Age writing can be said to be a fresh revelation of the ancient universal truth in a form suited to modern scientific man living in the aftermath of the historical incarnation of the Christ. Though the form of Swedenborg's spiritual writings looks far from "New Age," their essential content is expressed in the key New Age ideas, and I find that his teachings are a vital aid in understanding clearly what the New Age is about, how to evaluate its many varied forms and distinguish its darker side, and how to place the New Age in proper relation to the spiritual ages preceding it. Swedenborg's teachings should come to form a basic reference point of evaluation for the New Age, particularly when their truth and universalism are more clearly recognized.

Swedenborg's Contributions to the History of Ideas

Robert H. Kirven, Ph.D.

EMANUEL SWEDENBORG MADE SIGNIFICANT contributions to the history of ideas in at least three fields: philosophy, science, and theology. Several of his contributions create a previously unseen alternative between two positions that had been in conflict for a long time. It was characteristic of him to say "both . . . and" where many others had seen only "either . . . or." His place in the history of ideas can be seen in the development of philosophy, science, and theology, viewed from a perspective that highlights the significance of his contributions to them.

Philosophy

ONTOLOGY

Probably his most significant contribution to the history of ideas lies in two areas of philosophy: ontology and epistemology. Ontology is the study of reality. Every time we question or affirm the possibility of the existence of anything ("Can it *be*?" "Yes, it really *is*!") we engage in ontology. But when professionals talk to each other about these matters, ordinary little words such as *is*, *being*, and *real* become terms of highly specialized definitions.

Along with this specialized use of common words, ontology employs several highly uncommon terms, such as *ontology* itself, from the Greek *on*, meaning "reality," and *logos*, meaning "words about," or "knowledge of." These terminological definitions have been sufficient over the centuries to keep the topic in the rather exclusive playground of a kind of academic elite. A victim of this exclusivity, Swedenborg is a major contributor to ontology who has received little of the historical attention he deserves.

The following brief history shows the importance of his work and how, through an accident in academic history and one man's career-building schemes, it got buried in the foundations of modern philosophy.

THE BEGINNING: THALES

General agreement among philosophers and historians place the beginnings of philosophy in Western thought early in the sixth century B.C. with the work of Thales. It was he who first asked *the* ontological question: "What is?" What makes Thales' question so brilliant is that, while its answer is verifiable by definition, twenty-four centuries of concentrated effort, including the work of some of history's greatest minds, failed to produce an answer that received acceptance by consensus.

DOMINATING THE FIELD: PLATO AND ARISTOTLE

At least a dozen of the early attempts to answer this ontological question were cogent enough to attract the attention of historians and a few philosophers, but it was almost the beginning of the fourth century before an answer appeared that is still taken seriously today. After people had suggested that maybe *change* is all there is, or *infinity*, or *earth, fire, air, and water*, or equally unsatisfactory answers, two major and enduring answers were offered by Plato and his student Aristotle. Their two answers to the basic ontological question have satisfied more people than any others; and in addition, they formulated most of the other "good questions" that have occupied philosophers ever since, and their answers to many of those questions remain serious contenders for universal consensus. Their answers to the basic ontological question "What is?," in particular, were such good answers that over two millennia passed before anybody offered a viable third alternative.

Plato's answer to "What is?" was "Ideas." Ideas of things are real, perfect, and eternal. Things themselves are illusory, imperfect, and ephemeral reflections of ideas. He elaborated at least four levels of reality, with archetypal ideas of the good and the true being most real; next are ideas that we think; physical things are still less real; and reflections or

---

For biographical information, see Kirven's and Larsen's pictorial biography of Emanuel Swedenborg, earlier in this book.

images of things are the least real.

It should be noted that Plato did not say that things—such as trees and tables—are *not* real, only that they are less real than the universal idea of a tree, or the idea in a carpenter's mind when he made the table. Later thinkers, developing this kind of ontology (called "idealism"), formulated more extreme and limiting positions. For instance, seventeenth-century English idealist George Berkeley said that only ideas are real: the only reality to the chair that holds up my idea of a body is my idea of the chair; and when I go out of the room and forget about it, the chair ceases to exist—except that it continues to exist as an idea in the mind of God. Plato's idealism was not so narrow. Until the dawn of scientific thinking of the Enlightenment of the sixteenth century, Platonic idealism was the most commonly accepted ontology.

The next most popular answer throughout those centuries was the one proposed by Plato's student Aristotle. That answer is called "materialism," because Aristotle insisted that only material things—things that can be touched and seen—are real; ideas are our minds' reaction to things and have no independent reality. Aristotelian materialism always had a kind of commonsense appeal (the chair I sit on certainly *seems* real) and also was more consistent with scientific inquiry to many thinkers after the Renaissance.

TWO ALTERNATIVES: DESCARTES AND SPINOZA

In the seventeenth century, René Descartes came up with a new ontology, a third alternative to idealism's and materialism's answer to Thales' question. Descartes's answer was called "dualism" because he maintained that *both* ideas and things are equally real, but said that they exist in different realms of reality that have almost nothing to do with each other. Things are real in a realm of "extended reality" where their extension in space can be measured as dimensions, and their extension in time can be measured as their endurance between formation and dissolution.

Ideas exist in "nonextended reality," obeying a different set of natural laws, occupying no space and being in some sense eternal after their conception. The worlds of extension and nonextension function quite independently of each other most of the time. The only exceptions occur when, for instance, my sitting on a chair in the world of extension provides the "occasion" for my thinking of a chair in the nonextended world of ideas. The apparent frequency of these occasions should not suggest that the two worlds of extension and nonextension actually influence each other. They do not.

Gottfried Leibniz, who also developed a Cartesian kind of dualism, commented on the fact that we think (in the nonextended realm) of the idea of noon when the clock in the extended realm strikes twelve, by observing that if a master clockmaker winds and sets two perfect clocks at the same time, we should not be surprised, or suppose some covert influence of one on the other, if both of them chime simultaneously.

A fourth alternative was the idea of Benedict Spinoza, who was convinced that everything that exists was created by God out of himself. Therefore, everything from ideas to rocks, from generated things such as people and horses to human-made things such as tables and houses, from abstract ideas such as God and the good, to human thoughts and concepts, are all equally real; and all are part of God. For Spinoza, whose ontology is called "monism," there was no problem of communication between different realms of reality, because there was only one realm. The problem that his critics found was a difficulty in differentiating categories within the one divine creation. They warned him to be careful when he walked barefoot through the mud (squishing God between his toes!).

SWEDENBORG'S RESOLUTION: HOLISM

By this time, four answers had been proposed to the fundamental ontological question "What is?," and these seemed to exhaust the logical possibilities.

Graphically, the four might be presented on a rosette:

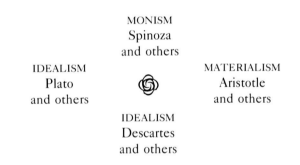

MONISM
Spinoza
and others

IDEALISM
Plato
and others

MATERIALISM
Aristotle
and others

IDEALISM
Descartes
and others

The long-standing dichotomy (left-right in the diagram) between idealism and materialism—"ideas are real and things are only reflections of them" versus "things are real and ideas are only responses to them"—now had company. Dualism claimed that "both ideas and things are real, but there's almost no connection between them," and monism claimed that "both ideas and things are real and there is no difference between them." None of the four positions could claim a consensus, but among them they seemed to cover the entire range of logical possibilities.

Emanuel Swedenborg's contribution to this effort was developed over a period of years in the middle of the eighteenth century. Although he did not name it, and it received little discussion in academic circles, it has many of the characteristics of an ontology suggested about a century later by a minor philosopher, Jan Christian Smuts, and again in our century by a biologist, Edmund Sinnot, and a psychologist, Ira Progoff. Borrowing their term, I have called it "holism."[1]

Swedenborg's holism is an assertion that all four of the major ontological positions are correct in their assertions, erring only in what they deny about reality. Ideas are real, substantial, and enduring, as the Platonists thought. They are part of the reality that Swedenborg called the "spiritual world," which includes ideas, thoughts, feelings, motives, and values. The spiritual world is populated by angels in heaven, evil spirits in hell, and human spirits enveloped in physical bodies.

Things are real, as the Aristotelians thought. They are part of Swedenborg's physical or natural world, which contains all manufactured and natural things, including the bodies that envelop spirits to make human beings.

So both ideas and things are real, as the dualists thought, but they are not disconnected. Rather, they are interrelated at every point in a pattern that Swedenborg called "correspondences": everything in the universe—however small or large, however simple or complex—corresponds to something in the spiritual world, so that all reality comprises a coherent whole.

And everything is equally real, as the monists thought, but not in the same, undifferentiated way. Spiritual and material things are unmistakably different—spiritual things are not extended in space and time, while material things are extended, just as the dualists said—along with their inherent interrelationships.

In Swedenborg's analogical model of this ontology, the differences are external, vertical, and discrete; the connections are internal, horizontal, and continuous. Spiritual things are higher than and discretely different from material things, but inside every material thing there is something spiritual, and there is a continuous range of distinctions between the outer matter and the inner spirit.

This formulation solved so many of the ancient problems of ontological thought that it attracted intense interest from Immanuel Kant, who was emerging in history as a leading thinker. Kant found many similarities to his own ontological thinking, but then realized that, in Swedenborg's system and his own, the existence of a spiritual reality in close interconnection with material reality could not be proved by traditional logic, and therefore was subject to endless attack on epistemological grounds (which we will discuss presently).

Deciding that, in his words, "it is better to ridicule than to be ridiculed," he separated himself from Swedenborg's ontology in a viciously satirical essay, *Dreams of a Spirit-Seer, Illustrated by Dreams of Metaphysics*. This work, Kant's last before the logically unassailable series of *Critiques*, enjoyed such wide circulation in Germany and all of Europe, and its satire was so effective, that for many years it barred Swedenborg from the bibliography of any professional philosopher who hoped to be taken seriously by his academic colleagues.

Today, when an ontology of very similar structure is emerging from the confluence of thought represented by such thinkers as physicist David Bohm, biologist Rupert Sheldrake, psychologist Karl Pribram, and philosopher Reneé Weber, among others, Swedenborg's holism is remembered by few as a pioneering synthesis in the same direction.

His contribution was not entirely unnoticed, of course, and appeared without attribution in the work of several European philosophers of the late-eighteenth and nineteenth centuries; but its origin and its integrity as a theory were obscured as a result of Kant's attack—and by the foolish attempts of Swedenborgians to respond to that attack by trying to prove Kant incompetent. As a result, the development of a characteristically modern ontology was delayed by a century or two.

EPISTEMOLOGY

If a prize were offered for the Best Question of All Time, it would be given, by a plain consensus of philosophers through the ages, to Thales for his "What is?" question. The second prize in the same competition would be for "How do you know?" Philosophers call this *the* epistemological question, credited to the Greeks and derived from *epistēmē* ("knowledge") and *logos* ("words about," or "knowledge of"). The fundamental ontological and epistemological questions never get separated for long because we cannot know anything that is not real and if there is anything real that nobody knows . . . well, nobody knows about that.

Plato found reality in ideas and knowledge in the mind. Aristotle found reality in things and knowledge in experience. Consequently, Platonists said that knowledge is what we find in our minds from the perception of reality and use to understand our experience, and Aristotelians said that knowledge is what we put into our minds from our experience and use to define reality. Neither Platonists nor Aristotelians ever convinced each other, but they divided the field between them, leaving no logical alternatives.

After a few centuries, the history of ideas became the history of Christian thought. Early Christian epistemology tended to be Platonic, because revelation provided the mind with unquestionable certainty. Powerfully persuasive thinkers from Augustine to Thomas Aquinas were convinced—and convinced everybody else—that it was necessary to believe (i.e., accept revelation) in order to understand the world of our experience.

But Copernicus and Galileo were able to know the stars better (i.e., predict their positions more accurately) by paying attention to experience (i.e., by using charts based on observation) than had ever been possible by revelation or contemplation, and Aristotle was the favorite philosopher of Thomas Aquinas, so Aristotelian epistemology enjoyed a resurgence in the Renaissance. Finally, Francis Bacon established the Aristotelian epistemology of science as the major alternative to the Platonic epistemology of religion by proclaiming that "knowledge is power." What the mind learned from experience in the world, it could use scientifically to change the world; and because knowledge that works is self-evidently true, this perspective on knowledge became the dominant one.

By the seventeenth century, Aristotelian epistemology—which by then was called "empirical epistemology" because it was derived from experience—was so highly regarded that even theologians began developing empirical arguments to validate knowledge that had been revealed in the Bible. When books such as Matthew Tindal's *Christianity as Old as the Creation: or, The Gospel a Republication of the Religion of Nature* became best sellers in both religious and scientific circles, it appeared as if the controversy between Platonic and Aristotelian epistemologies had been resolved in a marriage between science and religion.

That merger turned out to be a fatal one for Platonic epistemology, however. When the certainty of religious ideas depended on validation by empirical evidence, then science was recognized as the primary authority. The mind's innate knowledge, and knowledge afforded by revelation, could be analyzed and debated to infinity by academics in their ivory towers, while empirical scientists got on with the business of the world. There still were only two views of knowledge, but one was the scientific view, which worked and explained new things about the world almost every day, and the other one didn't really matter.

Proponents of a Platonic epistemology that gave authority and honor to the Bible and personal revelation got tired of seeming to lose arguments with their Aristotelian opponents, and withdrew behind the position that their epistemological claims were not subject to discussion.

Theologians in the Aristotelian camp developed views of God commonly called "deism," which seemed to provide scientific reasons for believing in the existence of God, but described that God as a kind of retired watchmaker sitting back and watching his creation tick. The Platonic theologians were grouped into "Pietists," who emphasized the authority of personal revelation and inner illumination along with that of the Bible, and the academicians of the main-line Reformation, whose sole epistemological authorities were faith alone and the scriptures alone.

Emanuel Swedenborg grew up right in the middle of this hotly contested debate. The son of a Swedish bishop of radically Pietist leanings, he went to the University of Uppsala at the height of the excitement over the discovery of Cartesian philosophy—which included the empirical epistemology that had given rise to deism. His early writings were unmistakably deistic in outlook, but a midlife crisis brought personal conflicts into simultaneous confrontation with the great epistemological struggle of his time. He emerged from that crisis with an original epistemology as distinctively creative as his ontology.

He used this theory without expounding it or giving it a name, so I have called it "empirical revelation."[2] As in his ontology, Swedenborg assimilated the assertions about knowledge that characterize both poles of the field, rejecting only the denials of both positions. He continued to rely on empirical data as he had in earlier deistic-oriented scientific works, but he expanded his conception of knowledge in two significant respects. For one thing, he made room for affection as well as perception in the process of knowing, linking perception and reason to value and intention. For another, he gave data from his own psychic experiences equal significance with data from experiments and other experiences. From his psychic experiences, he came to recognize multiple levels of meaning in the Bible and insisted that all of them had absolute authority as truth because of the Bible's origin as divine revelation.

He not only gave equal weight to information from both kinds of sources, but he also intermingled them. He used observations from nature to validate revealed truth, called on biblical evidence to reinforce rational deductions, and employed accounts of his own spiritual experiences to support biblical interpretations and systematic constructions. It was this comprehensive concept of knowledge which enabled him to see reality as an all-encompassing whole in his ontology and allowed him to authenticate it with a systematic coherence that eluded his nemesis, Kant.

In the last great work of his career, *True Christian Religion*, published two years before his death in 1772, he recorded a psychic experience in which he encountered a temple in the spiritual world. Inscribed over the door of the temple were the Latin words for "Now it is permitted," which he took as a sign that "now it is permitted to enter with understanding into mysteries of faith." No longer did he have to choose between the empirical certainties of an Aristotelian epistemology and the inner authority of a Platonic one. He had merged the two concepts of knowledge into a workable whole. The marriage of science and religion, dreamed of in the seventeenth century by the English *virtuosi* and the French *philosophes* who started the Enlightenment, had indeed been achieved.

It was a marriage on different terms than had been envisioned by those who had longed for it, because, while neither side surrendered anything, neither reigned supreme. Swedenborg's epistemology gave equal status to the insights the Platonists loved and the data dear to Aristotelians, and accorded the highest certainty to knowledge in which the two kinds of knowing intersect.

Science

Swedenborg also had a distinguished career as a scientist, even though most of his scientific work was avocational while he worked for Sweden's Board of Mines. He filled a notebook with designs for inventions, including a plan for an airplane. Engineers at the Smithsonian Institution who built a model according to his plans said that it would have flown had he known how to build a motor light and powerful enough. Later, working for the Board of Mines, he designed some devices to help the mining industry; and once, to meet a military emergency, he engineered the movement of navy ships eighteen miles across a peninsula.[3]

The accomplishments that deserve a place in the history of ideas, however, were achieved while he was practicing scientific investigation as a hobby—a popular hobby among intellectuals of the seventeenth and eighteenth centuries.

COSMOLOGY

His first accomplishment of real significance was a cosmological theory that, though founded entirely on speculation, explained much astronomical data and actually had a place in the evolution of our cosmological understanding. The theory appears in his *Principia* of 1734. It includes a hypothesis for the formation of matter out of energy (a kind of primitive precursor to atomic theory) in which pure energy localizes into "points," which then cluster into "first finites," and finally coalesce with other first finites to form matter.

Beyond that, the theory explains the formation of the solar system by hypothesizing particles spinning off from the sun and coalescing into planets. This part of the theory is of particular importance in the history of science because it was appropriated and elaborated by an English astronomer named Thomas Wright, of Durham (several Thomas Wrights published about this period), and Wright's work provided the basis for the further work of Immanuel Kant, the *General History of Nature and Theory of the Heavens*. Kant's work, in turn, was incorporated into Laplace's 1792 publication of what is now called the "Kant-Laplace nebular hypothesis." Laplace's work is often called the origin of modern cosmology.[4]

Work that is principally a footnote to a hypothesis that is itself by now only a footnote to modern cosmological theory does not occupy a significant niche in the history of ideas. Swedenborg's nebular hypothesis does not find a place in most history books. It is mentioned here for two reasons, however. One is that Swedenborg's publication on the solar system in 1734 relates to an aspect of his theology discussed later in this article. A second reason is that his nebular theory is one of several remarkably accurate theories that preceded recognized scientific discoveries by 50 to 150 years. Two of these ideas follow.

NEUROLOGY AND PSYCHOLOGY

In the manuscript for *Brain* (published posthumously), he localized the thinking processes to the cortex of the cerebellum and identified what later were called the "pyramid cells" as being linked with each other and with various body parts to function as sensation receptors and motor directors half a century before this became commonly accepted in the medical community.[5] A few years later, in *Arcana Coelestia*, he observed in several contexts that the left and right hemispheres of the brain perform distinct and specialized functions, the left being involved with rational and intellectual processes, and the right with affection and intention (AC 3884 and elsewhere).

Another manuscript from the early 1740s, *Rational Psychology* (also published posthumously), described a *mens*, which is conscious and thinking. The *mens* is in communication with—but distinct from—the "animus," which involves physical sensations and motor control, and the "anima," which is concerned with affections and motives. Although it does not equate precisely with Freud's schema of id, ego, and superego, this structure anticipates by almost 150 years Freud's epochal distinction between the conscious and unconscious minds.

SUMMARY

It must be recognized that this catalog of discoveries places Swedenborg no closer than the periphery of world-class scientific discovery. If in his own time he had published *Brain* or *Rational Psychology* and if he had confirmed his speculations with experimental evidence, the story might have been different. As it is, Swedenborg's place in the history of ideas depends on what may be concluded about indirect influence and on his work in metaphysics—ontology and epistemology—and on his contributions to theology.

Theology

Emanuel Swedenborg's best-known contributions to the history of ideas, of course, were in theology. Although he was in his middle fifties before he began writing on theological subjects, his output in that field far exceeded the volume of his scientific writing. Although Kant, Herder, and Goethe commented mainly on his ontological and epistemological stance, the theological works attracted international reaction from such notable figures as Ernesti, Oetinger, Balzac, and Hugo. His theological writing defined what his contemporaries meant by "Swedenborgianism," and it provided the basis for his heresy trial and gained him a following of disciples who eventually formed the Swedenborgian church.

By his own perception and that of his contemporaries, the primary differences between his theological thought and the teachings of his day lay in his interpretation of the Bible, the Trinity, and his spiritualization of the human environment and experience. A fourth distinction—his incorporation of the Copernican revolution into his theological system—was his most radical contribution, having no direct precedent in theological thought.

SCRIPTURE INTERPRETATION

Because Swedenborg's first clearly theological publication was devoted mostly to scripture interpretation (the massive *Arcana Coelestia*), that was the aspect of his theology first criticized. Oetinger, whose own ontology had marked similarities to Swedenborg's—especially regarding the reality of spiritual beings—agreed with most of his theological positions, but found his biblical interpretations, or "hermeneutics" [see Glossary], to be a stumbling block. Ernesti, however, was so upset by Swedenborg's use of the Bible that he could not see anything else. The grounds for these objections, particularly Ernesti's, and the essential novelty of Swedenborg's position can only be seen in the light of the history of Christian use of the Bible.

The earliest Christian exegesis was based on recollection of the original meaning of scriptural passages and its application to current situations. This rabbinical methodology built on earlier hermeneutical formulations as often as it returned to original sources.

An alternative tradition, called the "allegorical method," was pioneered by Philo, who was attempting a synthesis between the Hebrew scriptures and Greek philosophy. Philo took biblical figures, places, and events to be *types* of philosophical concepts. This enabled him to construct a characteristically Jewish system, based on scripture but using the terms and methods of Hellenic thought. This new, interpreted meaning was the allegory, and the method tended to treat the Bible as an anthology of "proof texts" rather than a whole revelation.

Christian hermeneutics readily adopted Philo's methods, and no significant advances were made in hermeneutical theory during the Dark Ages or the Renaissance. The first dawn of the movement that would become the Reformation began with a reaction against the allegorical tradition—a tradition that by then had degenerated into a habit of claiming that scripture "really meant" almost anything the interpreter wanted it to mean.

Although the new hermeneutic had no conscious base in rabbinical tradition, it nevertheless shared with the older discipline an important characteristic. For both, the original text is the primary authority and any new interpretation depends for its validity on conformity to the text. This interest in scriptural origins led to renewed interest in Greek and Hebrew, so that the text could be studied in its original form. The next development was an interest in more scientific translation, so that the original intent could be carried with maximum accuracy into the modern languages.

Ernesti was one of the pioneering translators, striving toward an ideal of "one word, one meaning," which would allow only one translation, with no alternatives, for each word of the original Hebrew or Greek. Pursuing this ideal as a means to better living through better interpretation of the Bible, Ernesti was utterly horrified to see Swedenborg—who already had some reputation as a scientist—seemingly defying every principle of scientific hermeneutics with his doctrine of correspondences. This approach to reading the Bible, which appeared to allow for a whole new level of translation—from Hebrew (or Greek) to Latin and then to "Correspondentia" (if there were such a tongue), seemed to Ernesti a wilder aberration from allowable interpretation than ever the allegorists had attempted. It was a radical retreat from every hermeneutical advance since the Renaissance, and fit only for ridicule.

In fact, though, Swedenborg's doctrine of correspondences opposed the allegorical tradition as much as it did Ernesti's "one word, one meaning" ideal. Whereas allegory imposed few limitations on the range of types that could be assigned to any particular biblical image, correspondential interpretation was tied tightly to the created nature of things used as biblical symbols.

Before Swedenborg used correspondence as a principle of biblical interpretation, he had developed it in connection with his cosmology. In that system, where spiritual realities were created first and material things came into being as correspondents of spiritual forms, every spiritual truth would lie open to the investigator who knew the true correspondences of natural things. God, who had created all things with this built-in correspondential relationship, guided the biblical writers so that their every word carried spiritual meaning in addition to its natural sense by means of that relationship. Therefore, correspondential interpretation permits no latitude except for context (water, for instance, means one thing to a person in danger of dying of thirst and something quite different to someone threatened by drowning).

So, in the long dispute between limited interpretation on the one hand (first in the rabbinical tradition, then in the "scientific" approach of the early Reformation) and free or allegorical interpretation on the other, Swedenborg once more offered a third alternative that preserves values from each side of the controversy. The correspondential method roots all biblical interpretation firmly in the images of the text itself, and at the same time allows for full expression of the larger reality that is both spiritual and natural.

From Swedenborg's perception, this approach to scripture recognizes its holy origin. He saw the new, "scientific" interpreters as denigrating the Bible by treating it like any other piece of literature because they found nothing holy in it as interpreted by traditional allegorism. His approach, honoring both the letter of the original text and the spiritual reality symbolized by it, overcame the whole range of errors that both sides in the long dispute had been combating, and made the full scope of biblical truth available for the first time.

TRINITY

The dispute over a correct understanding of the Holy Trinity arose from the fact that the Bible speaks of a Father, a Son, and a Holy Spirit without giving any precise idea of the relationship among them. Specifically, it speaks of Jesus the Christ as being the Son of God, as having existed "in the beginning with God," and as being one with the Father. This ambiguity did not bother early theologians. Origen, for instance, embraced it and wrote theology that was quoted later by opponents on both sides of the argument over whether Jesus was fully divine but less than fully human, or fully human and less than fully divine.

At first, a majority of writers identified Jesus as one with God, but a significant minority was ready to accept a teaching that he really was human like other people, with certain divine characteristics. When that teaching was proclaimed heretical, and Jesus' divinity was once again recognized by the whole church, another viewpoint appeared. This one, originated by a theologian named Arius, accorded to Jesus the Christ all the attributes of God except one: Arius said that the Christ came into being when God already was. This idea upset the church because it made the Christ so little different from God that it could not be defeated by appeal to previous judgments against other humanizing tendencies, yet it still made the Son in some way less than God the Father.

The dispute over the nature of the Son was threatening a split in the church just at a time when the emperor Constantine wanted the church to appear unified, so in 325 he called the bishops to Nicaea to resolve the problem. The council produced a creed, similar in form to the baptismal creeds that had been used in local churches, but this one was supposed to rule out any kind of Arian subordinationism. The bishops agreed on the wording of the creed, but some began to disown it even before they got home again, and it took another council, in Constantinople in 381, to get it finally adopted. Still called the Nicene Creed and still intended to establish the equal divinity of all three elements of the Godhead, the creed described the Son as of the "same substance" as the Father. It called Him "begotten, not made," to distinguish Him from the creation; and "eternally begotten" to exclude the Arian position. Equal divinity was maintained.

But the conflict did not stay resolved. Some thought they could keep the consensus but make the Son less than fully divine by changing "same substance" to "similar substance" (changing the Greek *homoousion* to *homoiousion*). Others tinkered with it in other ways, such as by saying that the Holy Spirit proceeded from the Father *and from the Son* (instead of just "from the Father"), to create a three-tiered hierarchy. The argument got mixed up with regional politics, and the Eastern church used "similar substance" and "and from the Son" as reasons for separation from the Western church. This was the first crack in the solidity of the Holy Roman Empire, prompting the historian Gibbon to call it "the only empire ever destroyed by a diphthong" (referring to *homoiousion*).

It took until 451 for the Council of Chalcedon to forge a stable settlement—and that only in the West—to the issue that Constantine ordered resolved in 325. Using the language of the Nicene Creed, enriched by language from Augustine's elegantly reasoned discussion of the Trinity, the Chalcedon Creed spoke of the Son as *homoousion*, "begotten before all ages." Father, Son, and Holy Spirit each was a "person" (from the Greek *prosōpon*, Latin *persona*, the mask worn in Greek and Roman drama), but the Godhead was "one person" and "one essence" (hypostasis). Once again the matter seemed resolved, with the equal divinity of each element and the unity of the Godhead both forcefully maintained.

The settlement did last for a while, at least in part because the fall of the Holy Roman Empire ushered in the Dark Ages, when the best thought and energy of the church were fully occupied with survival in a lawless and marauding environment, and with copying the Bible and other texts that had been preserved before the destruction of once-great libraries. However, such fine-tuned resolutions, based on minutely careful distinctions, tend to deteriorate over time if they are not actively polished and advanced. By the beginning of the Reformation "three persons" was understood as something dangerously close to "three people" in popular thinking and some professional theology, and Trinitarian monotheism had degenerated almost into tritheism.

By the time Swedenborg appeared on the scene, he saw tritheism as a present danger (if not an existing heresy) and set about to correct the situation. His first target was the word *person*. Instead of *person*, he used the parallel term from the Chalcedonian formula, *essential*, to describe each of the elements. "Three Essentials of the One God" seemed to him to leave no room for polytheistic misunderstanding.

Two centuries of trinitarian debate have tended to validate Swedenborg's criticism. Mainstream trinitarian language, although continuing to use *person*, conveys fewer tritheistic implications. Nevertheless, trinitarian formulations remain problematic, especially now that Eastern churches are once again becoming involved in worldwide ecumenical discussions. Because Swedenborg's trinitarian formulations do not seem in basic conflict with mainline Catholic, Protestant, or

Orthodox positions, his contributions may yet form a basis for ecumenical resolution.

REALITY AND PRESENCE OF SPIRIT

In Swedenborg's time as in our own, the debate over the "soul-body problem," arguing the reality and presence of a spiritual aspect to human existence, was the theological flank of the much older ontological struggle over the possibility of spirit or any nonmaterial reality. Swedenborg's contribution to the metaphysical dimension of this conflict has been described, but he had more to add in a specifically theological context.

As already mentioned, his doctrine of correspondences allowed him to detail a spiritual sense enveloped within the literal sense of the Bible, just as he saw the human spirit enveloped within the physical human body. Further, he described the spiritual world—consisting of heaven, hell, and the world of spirits—in such minute detail that the description almost became an effective validation that the world really exists; and he developed a psychology that included spiritual influence as a dominant component of human personality.

Together, Swedenborg's emphasis on the holiness of the Bible in its multiple levels of meaning, the unity of the triune Godhead, and the spiritual and material wholeness of life constitute a significant influence in eighteenth-century theology. It was essentially a reforming influence on aspects that were deviating from the Apostolic ideal.

INCORPORATING THE COPERNICAN REVOLUTION

It was not appreciated by his contemporaries and was scarcely noticed by later commentators who took it for granted, but Emanuel Swedenborg was the first theologian in history to incorporate the Copernican revolution into a theological system.

When Nicolaus Copernicus completed his manuscript of *On Revolutions* in the sixteenth century, the concept of a flat earth surrounded by water and situated beneath a domed sky on which the stars pursued their courses was so widely accepted that it was assumed to be the image of the creation described in the first chapter of Genesis, so it had the authority both of consensus and revelation. *On Revolutions*'s mathematical calculations contradicted this view, however, substituting one in which the sun was the center of a plane on which the earth and other planets moved in annual revolutions. The calculations were validated by Copernicus's ability to indicate where a particular star would appear in the sky more accurately than astronomers using the Ptolemaic system.

Copernicus was already an old man, and publication of his work actually was posthumous. His bishop, who wanted to see the work published but was disturbed by the way it contradicted both popular consensus and the doctrine of the church, added a preface to it, which he claimed had been suggested by Copernicus on his deathbed. The preface explained that the earth really was the center of the universe, but for some unknown reason that must be regarded as a mystery of faith, astronomical calculations are more accurate if they are based on the assumption that the sun is at the center. So, for over half a century astronomers used Copernicus's formulas without anybody's being upset by the possibility that perhaps the universe was not the way it looked.

This convenient detour, by which faith avoided a confrontation with contrary physical evidence, was destroyed by the work of Galileo Galilei, who argued in a highly convincing work, *Dialogue concerning the Two Great World Systems*, that Copernican calculations were more accurate than Ptolemaic ones for the simple reason that the earth *did* in fact revolve around the sun. In addition, Galileo popularized the use of the telescope so that more people got into the act of testing astronomical theories by actual observation. Before long, most astronomers accepted that the earth revolved around the sun and that the sun itself revolved in a larger galactic orbit.

Galileo convinced the astronomers but not the hierarchy of the church. The church forced him to recant his teaching and continued to support a Ptolemaic universe as the correct view for the faithful to hold.

Theologians of the Reformation were too much involved with earthly problems to care what the astronomers said revolved around what, and their successors—both Catholic and Reformed—perpetuated the old tradition of pursuing theological discussions as if the Ptolemaic universe was the one in which we actually live. To incorporate the Copernican revolution into a theological system involved dealing with a couple of difficult problems, and by a consensus that probably was unconscious, theologians agreed not to face them.

Both of those problems involved the Incarnation. For one thing, if the earth is not the center of the universe, and not necessarily the only abode of human beings, what does it mean that God became incarnate *here*? Did God's supreme act of revelation and salvation affect only the inhabitants of our planet, or was it one of many incarnations on many planets? If the first option is adopted, furthermore, the question remains, Why did the Incarnation occur here and not somewhere else? The second option leaves the question, Are the Gospels in error (and, thus, is all divine revelation called into question) by exaggerating the cosmic significance of the Incarnation by depicting it as a unique act? The problems were formidable, but their very weight weakens the coherence of any theological system that ignores them by clinging to the fiction expounded by Copernicus's bishop.

Swedenborg, a scientist who had written on astronomical issues before beginning his theological work, had no doubt about either the accuracy of the Copernican calculations or their theological validity. Neither did he seem awed by the obstacles that his theological predecessors had avoided.

He stated flatly—and almost in passing, as if everyone already knew it—that the Incarnation was a unique event, occurring only on this earth, even though the earth is not the center of the universe. It happened here because, in effect, this was the worst place in the universe, where divine intervention was most urgently needed. In spite of its local occurrence, however, its saving consequences were equally effective for the populations of every planet in every galaxy. Throughout the universe, it is known that the Lord became incarnate on the planet Earth; and the spiritual effect of the Lord's life here is influential throughout the universe without regard to space or time.

This understanding, which appears in scattered passages in *Arcana Coelestia* and is fully developed in *Earths in the Universe*, makes Swedenborg's the first theological system in history to incorporate the Copernican revolution. Whereas Swedenborg's other contributions to the history of theology were reformative in nature, this one was purely original, and appears in line with the new theories of morphogenesis, formulated by Rupert Sheldrake.[6]

ADDENDA

Another of Swedenborg's original contributions to the history of theology also went unnoticed until very recently, and that is his recognition of the dipolar nature of God. It had been regarded as a twentieth-century discovery of the Anglo-American philosopher Alfred North Whitehead that God had two natures, one absolute and the other contingent. The hypothesis is an important one, for it resolves many of the dilemmas posed by a synthesis of the classical philosophical tradition begun by Plato and Aristotle with the theology based on the Judeo-Christian scriptures. For one thing, the God of the philosophers was eternal, absolute, unmoved, and unchanging; while the God of the Bible was alternately pleased by people's offerings and angered by their sins—that is, his state was contingent on the actions of others. He himself took action to change his relationship with human beings, and incorporated into himself the experience of a lifetime as a human being. Beyond this, from a philosophical perspective, God is the ground of reality and all reality is characterized equally by both endurance and change.

To deal with these and other problems of philosophy, Whitehead hypothesized that God is both eternally permanent and continually changing, both absolute and contingent. The notion was part of an entire system of thought that has come to be known as "process philosophy" or "process theology." Its name derives from the fact that, along with the idea of a dipolar God, it is characterized by an idea of all reality being a process. From the viewpoint of process philosophy, Thales' ontological question was the wrong one.

Instead of asking, "What is?," he should have asked, "What's happening?" The process answer to the fundamental ontological question thus avoids the whole rosette of alternatives that faced Swedenborg in the eighteenth century and, instead, sees reality as a continuing series of moments in which material and spiritual entities and influences interact in the present, and impacts on the future, participating in a continuing flow of process. The complete system of thought, with all its ramifications, forms what appears to be the leading edge of philosophical and theological work in this latter part of the twentieth century.

At the same time that he was formulating his comprehensive resolution to the spirit-matter dilemma, as described earlier, Swedenborg was also positing a dipolar God and a viewpoint that placed process at the center of the reality of all human experience. In both *Divine Love and Wisdom* and *True Christian Religion*, he described God as being both *esse* itself and *existere* itself. His precise intent in the two Latin words is not easily translated into English, but he was talking about something like "reality" and "presence," or "being" and "manifestation." The first term of either pair suggests eternity and immutability and the second implies process. Swedenborg describes the two mutually exclusive qualities as being "distinguishably one" in God, 150 years ahead of Whitehead's process philosophy.

His thought parallels Whitehead's and the later process philosophers and theologians in other ways, too: He viewed human life as a process from nature-centered to spirit-centered, he saw the Incarnation as a process, and he did not differ in any fundamental way from the principal thrusts of process thought. Because he did not develop the dipolarity of God outside of a few paragraphs that were conspicuously positioned but very tightly worded, and because the process aspects of his system were not widely noticed, his work cannot be demonstrated to have exerted any influence on the later developments in process philosophy. Rather, as in the case of his contributions to the history of science, he contributed an original idea that went undeveloped, only to emerge independently later as a significant influence on intellectual history.

Of course, it is impossible to prove or disprove that such later contributions were really independent, or were the product of indirect Swedenborgian influence. While it cannot be demonstrated in every case that the authors of parallel positions had read Swedenborg, it is hard to deny that they were influenced in some way by Blake or Coleridge, Oetinger or Lavater, Herder or Goethe, Schelling or K. C. F. Krause, Balzac or Hugo, Emerson, the elder Henry James, or C. S. Peirce.

Conclusions

Emanuel Swedenborg wrote in the middle of the eighteenth century, a period that includes the line drawn by most historians who separate modern philosophy from earlier periods. He appears as the first of the modern thinkers, or the last of the classicals. He dealt with many of the issues that had concerned thinkers from Plato through Kant—questions of reality, knowledge, and human nature, or substance and form, matter and spirit—and also exhibited many characteristically modern philosophical viewpoints, such as phenomenology, existentialism, and process philosophy.

His contributions to the history of ideas were characterized by a careful continuity with a broad spectrum of existing knowledge, and also by an originality that was coherent with his total system of thought. He managed to synthesize resolutions to dilemmas that had plagued generations before him—matter and spirit, experience and revelation—as well as problems that were not even recognized until decades after his death—the Incarnation in a Copernican universe, and the dipolar nature of God.

For a variety of reasons, including both his own decision not to publish many of his works and his decision not to be their personal advocate, as well as powerful opposition from Immanuel Kant (which appears to have had more to do with personal motives than with either stated or implied intellectual opposition), many of Swedenborg's contributions seem to have been unknown or ignored in his time, only to have reappeared later from sources that appear to be independent but may be linked by indirect influence.

Notes

1. See my *Emanuel Swedenborg and the Revolt against Deism* (Ann Arbor, Mich.: University Microfilms, 1965).
2. Ibid.
3. G. Berggren, "Emanuel Swedenborg and the Transportation of Galleys from Strömstad to Iddefjord," *New Philosophy* 29, no. 1 (January 1926), pp. 6–12.
4. Theodore F. Wright and Magnus Nyren, "Swedenborg and the Nebular Hypothesis," *The New Church Review* (July 1897), pp. 361–79. [For a full discussion of the similarity and dissimilarity of Laplace's and Swedenborg's nebular hypotheses of the formation of our solar system, see Steve Koke's essay "In Search of a Religious Cosmology" in this anthology.]
5. Erik Nordenskiöld, *The History of Biology* (New York: Alfred A. Knopf, 1928), p. 188.
6. Rupert Sheldrake, *A New Science of Life: The Hypothesis of Formative Causation* (London: Blond & Briggs, 1981).

Swedenborg and the Bible

Dorothea Harvey, Ph.D.

BORN IN 1772, Swedenborg was brought up and remained a committed Christian. A natural scientist by bent and education, he was a productive contributor to the physical and biological sciences of his day, both in theory and also in practical application to such areas as mining engineering and metallurgy. When his search for the soul in the human body led him inward to his own psychological process, he recorded his dreams and inner experience with the precision of a scientist. A psychic from childhood, he moved from his own inner work to direct religious experience and then to regular contact with angels and spirits in the spiritual world. Finally, a mystic with experience in some ways similar to that of Böhme and the German nature philosophers, he found in every natural object the presence and power of an infinite wisdom. When, after his religious experience, Swedenborg devoted years to study of the Bible as a major focus of his mission, his approach to the Bible brought together all four of these sides of the man.

As a Christian, he understood the Bible as divinely inspired and therefore holy. The question he wanted to investigate was not whether it contained God's revelation, but where its divinity resided. He found this most clearly in its manner of expression. "The style of the Word is the Divine style itself . . . such that there is a holiness in every sentence and in every word, and even in some places in the very letters, and thereby the Word conjoins man with the Lord and opens heaven" (TCR 191).

As God "spoke the Word through Moses and the prophets," so Jesus, the Word made flesh, "spoke the Word in the Gospels, much of it by His own mouth, and the rest of it by the breath of His mouth, which is the Holy Spirit, through His twelve disciples" (TCR 190). The revelation is not limited to the words of the Bible, then, but is present equally in the life of Jesus that he lived in this world. For Swedenborg, the Bible and the life of Jesus were both the "Word of the Lord."

Swedenborg's conclusion on where the holiness resided in the Bible paralleled the results of his search for the soul. The holiness is not in the words themselves taken literally, but in the spirit or internal sense contained within them. Just as the physical body is not the person, but is dead without its soul or life, without understanding in the eyes and affection in the face, so the words are an envelope for the Word of life. Those who read the words with the desire to find divine truth and to apply the truth to their lives do find it (TCR 192, 194). Words, of course, are regularly understood as symbols of meaning, and this is particularly true in the parables of the Bible or in poetry. To read of a lamb or sheep or goat in Jesus' parables without a sense of symbol would be to miss the meaning. The immediate and obvious power of the Twenty-third Psalm would be lost if the reader tried to take "The Lord is my shepherd" literally.

For Swedenborg the whole Bible has this poetic or parable dimension, or, as he called it, correspondence. Swedenborg found a consistent and easily apparent range of meanings throughout the Bible in words such as *lamb, shepherd, mountain, water,* or *earth.* But he found meaning also in more unexpected words, such as *stone* or *shoulder* or *Egypt* or *Assyria.* For him all the elements had meaning and the history of Israel recorded in the Bible was not only the actual history of a people, but also an image of the spiritual growth of every human being, from leaving the garden, being redeemed from Egypt, and wandering in the wilderness, to finding a home in Canaan, a place in Jerusalem. The Bible as a whole, and not only the parables of Jesus, could function as a series of psychodramas leading to spiritual awareness.

For him, these specific correspondences were not allegorical. He approached his study of the Bible with his scientist's

---

Dr. DOROTHEA HARVEY is a 1943 graduate of Wellesley College. She received her M.Div. at Union Theological Seminary with a major in the Old Testament, and her Ph.D. in literature of religion at Columbia University. She has taught at Wellesley College, Milwaukee-Downer College, and Lawrence University, and has been professor of religion at Urbana University since 1968. Ordained in 1975, she is the minister of the Church of the New Jerusalem in Urbana, Ohio, with special concern in her ministry for spiritual and personal growth.

respect for the actual, physical event or object. Land and water, invasions by Assyrians, or migrations into or out of Egypt were physically, historically real, to be taken seriously with all the scientist's tools of investigation. They were not mental symbols only, from an imagination concerned with presenting an idea. Swedenborg was a natural scientist who found the whole natural order of biology, geology, or magnetism, or anything else, full of the wisdom of God, giving insight after insight into the harmony of God's creation. For him it was true that "each and all things in nature correspond to spiritual things," as all ancient peoples, including the tellers of Greek myths, understood (TCR 201–2). The meaning was not so much allegorical as archetypal. The two sides of reality belonged together.

As a Christian and as a scientist, Swedenborg saw a consistent universe of lawful and meaningful operation. As a psychic, he again was aware of two sides of reality. When traveling in Europe, seeing different and intriguing architecture, he would find himself in contact with the mind of the architect. When reading the Bible, he would find himself in the spiritual world. "I have been permitted to learn through much experience, that man has communication with heaven through the Word. While reading the Word . . . a clear perception was given me that each verse communicated with some society of heaven, and thus the whole Word with the entire heaven" (TCR 272). He found that the Bible was not just for this world, but for "all the heavens" as a source of angelic wisdom (TCR 240). He once recounted his experience of seeing the Bible in the shrines of temples in the spiritual world shining "before the eyes of the angels like a great star, sometimes like a sun" with a "bright radiance" and "most beautiful rainbows" around it, so much as to make any hands or clothing that rubbed it also shine (TCR 209).

Swedenborg's Christian, scientific, and psychic experience were all important in his approach to the Bible, but perhaps the most important was his particular kind of practical mysticism. Harvey Bellin comments that Swedenborg saw the holiness of the Bible in the "nature of its imagery," in images like those of dreams, "representations of inner development which trigger direct channels into the subconscious." Bellin goes on to speak of Jewish Cabalism as taking a similar approach.[1] Swedenborg himself describes these "correspondences" as "representations of things spiritual and celestial in the natural" (TCR 204). A correspondence was an actual presence with power. Divine truth was present in the physical, literal words of the Bible "in its fulness, its holiness, and its power" (TCR 214).

Swedenborg saw every existing entity as a form of love itself, the ultimate reality and reason for all that is. The form love takes in any entity is governed by wisdom, the "instrumental cause" of all that is. The particular existing entity gives love and wisdom a practical reality, an actual "complex, containant, and base," to such an extent "that all things of love and all things of wisdom are actually in it; it is where they are all simultaneously present" (DLW 213). This is the kind of mysticism that led Buber to see the whole of reality in a tree, or Blake "the universe in a grain of sand," or in Swedenborg's words, to see love and wisdom, and so efficient power in "each and everything created . . . even sand" (DLW 172).

Swedenborg saw the text of the Bible as just such an entity in which "there is an inner sense which is spiritual, and in this an inmost sense which is celestial; and thus the outmost sense, which is natural and is called the sense of the letter, is the containant, and thus the basis and support of the two interior senses" (TCR 212). The "celestial and spiritual senses of the Word [the celestial the dimension of love, the spiritual of wisdom] exist simultaneously" in the natural sense of the Bible (TCR 214).

The actual words of the Bible and their connection with the history of a people who existed in the world are essential to the inner meaning. "In fact, the Word without the sense of its letter would be like the human body without its coverings which are called skins, and without its supports which are called bones. With both of these absent all its inner parts would fall asunder" (TCR 213). The Bible, with an almost celestial meaning "like a gentle flame that enkindles," and an intermediate spiritual meaning "like a light that enlightens," is "like a transparent object receiving both the flame and the light," a gemstone shining (TCR 216). The Bible is a reality on two levels, then. Its literal content available to human reason is necessary for study and for arriving at doctrine for a religious body. Its inner level, divine truth, is available to those who seek to live the truth, turning to God's help, "who are in enlightenment from the Lord," not to put into words for others, but as a power and direction in their lives (TCR 225).

And so the Bible, through the nature of its imagery, can really be God's Word, God's revelation to human beings, divine truth touching finite minds. This is not true if we quote its words as words of God, attempting to catch the infinite in words available to our reason. God's Word is not contained in human sentences. It is true if we see its images as images, striking us with a new awareness of the natural as we open ourselves to a reality beyond our definition, partly within our experience and partly mystery. Then each of us, letting the image affect us, can reach the depths within. Swedenborg speaks of the "inexpressible power of the Word," a power of truth, not "a statement uttered by someone in authority, which ought for that reason to be obeyed," but truth, the kind of truth that created heaven and earth (TCR 224).

This power pervades the images in the Bible. I think no Christian can read in the Book of Revelation of the one who sat upon the white horse, whose "eyes are like a flame of fire, and on his head are many diadems; and he has a name inscribed which no one knows but himself. He is clad in a robe dipped with blood, and the name by which he is called is The Word of God," and not know that this is the Christ, the Christ we know, and also that there is more here than we know (19:12–13). Biblical images are not boxed in by what we understand at any point. Each time we let them touch us, they move us to new depths or heights and always to new awareness that there is more beyond. Swedenborg says this is as true of angels in heaven as it is of us. "In short the power of the Lord proceeding from the Word is infinite" (TCR 209). It is the Word of God.

Note

1. Harvey F. Bellin and Darrell Ruhl, eds., *Blake and Swedenborg: Opposition Is True Friendship* (New York: Swedenborg Foundation, 1985), p. 46.

An Image of God in a Mirror

George F. Dole, Ph.D.

> Every created thing . . . is by nature recipient of God . . . ; it is suitable because it was created in God by God; and because it was created in this way, it is an analogue, and . . . is like an image of God in a mirror.
>
> —Emanuel Swedenberg (DLW 56)

THERE IS, I BELIEVE, a level of Swedenborg's thought that is only now becoming accessible to people who have not had extensive suprasensory experience. The statement just quoted is a prime example. In terms of our normal consciousness, it is perhaps best taken as a kind of poetic suggestion of the quality of our highest sensitivity. If, however, we take seriously the characteristics of the hologram, it becomes a trenchant and almost literal description of a radically significant fact. Every part of the universe is an image of the whole.

I want to explore several dimensions of this in the following pages. First is the general matter of our use of physical models for our understanding of things unseen. Second is the holographic model in specific, which involves the wave properties of matter and relates to the Swedenborgian concept of inflow. Further, there are corollaries that concern learning and communication, as well as consciousness and boundaries (including ego boundaries). This finally suggests an ethic for both individual and societal levels of human interaction.

Physical Models of the Unseen

As I write, there is a spate of interest in the phenomenon of stress and in its effects on human well-being. The basis of this interest must be the usefulness of the concept: it must be helping people in ways they want to be helped, otherwise it would not have the popularity it presently enjoys. It is the basis of this usefulness that intrigues me.

Measurable stress is a matter of Newtonian physics, involving the (continued) application of force to a body that has a certain amount of inherent resistance. To speak of psychological stress is to speak in an image, using something

we can observe by sensory means or measure. It is not literal description; it is more like pragmatic poetry.

In an interview published in *Psychology Today*, the neuropsychologist Karl Pribram made the following observation: "We'd been searching for some organizational principle that would allow for the basic facts of perceptual constancy, transfer of learning, and the elusiveness of memory in the brain. Suddenly, this principle was presented to us in the hologram."[1]

In similar fashion, the phenomenon of physical stress provides an organizational principle that allows us to organize basic facts that might otherwise seem unconnected or elusive. The apostle Paul was no stranger to these "basic facts" of human experience, but because his sensory experience was structured differently, his image was a very different one:

> So take up God's armor now! Then when the evil day comes, you will be able to resist the enemy's attacks, and after fighting to the end, you will still hold your ground. So stand ready: have truth for a belt tight around your waist; put on righteousness for your breastplate, and the readiness to announce the Good News of peace as shoes for your feet. At all times carry faith as a shield; with it you will be able to put out all the burning arrows shot by the Evil One. And accept salvation for a helmet, and the word of God as the sword that the Spirit gives you.[2]

Probably because Newtonian physics is such a powerful force in our physical lives, it has become a rich source of images for the understanding of our unseen processes. We speak of tension, friction, action and reaction, checks and balances, and pressure without any apparent sense of the

---

For biographical information on Dr. Dole, see his Introduction, at the beginning of this book.

way in which we are transferring meaning from one realm to another.

There are liabilities, though, to this lack of awareness. In general, these images are selective: they tend to focus our attention on particular common aspects of the human process, while other equally common aspects may go unheeded. There will be examples of this subsequently. In particular, Newtonian physics is the study of the interaction of forces; so the courses of action it suggests tend to involve the application of force, and therefore tend to legitimize violence.

Still, we are left with sensory images as apparently necessary means to observing our unseen structures and processes and to communicating our discoveries to each other. Understanding this function of sensory experience is fundamental to understanding Swedenborg's theology. His position is concisely stated at the close of *Arcana Coelestia*:

> The reason the way things are in this world is so like the way they are in heaven (with the difference that in the world there are sequential states of time, while in heaven there are states of life) is that all the things that exist in this world have been created as images of things in heaven; for natural things come into being from spiritual ones as effects from their causes. As a result, there is a correspondence of all things in this world with things in heaven, and the natural universe is therefore a theater that portrays the Lord's kingdom. (AC 8812)

It is no coincidence that physical events can be used as models for understanding spiritual events. There is an ontological relationship between them, the physical events being results of the spiritual ones. This principle provides Swedenborg with the basis of a highly developed epistemology, which will figure in the following pages.

THE HOLOGRAPHIC MODEL

A holographic plate is a photographic recording of the interference pattern of two sets of light waves. A laser is used as the single source of light. Its beam is split by the use of a half-silvered mirror and spread by lenses in such a way that half of it reaches the plate unaltered—as coherent light—while half of it is reflected to the plate by some object.

The "image" on the plate bears no visible resemblance to the object being recorded. It has been compared to the pattern one sees on the surface of water when ripples from two points of impact overlap each other. However, when this plate is properly illuminated, it alters the light rays passing through it in such a way that a three-dimensional image of the original object appears.

In some apparently paradoxical way, this whole image can be re-created from any portion of the plate. The main stricture is that the smaller the portion of the plate used, the less overall detail there is in the image. It also happens that the smaller the portion, the more critical it is that it be properly

How a Hologram Is Made

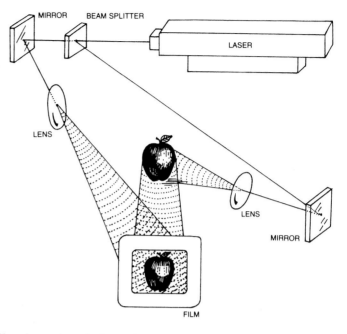

illuminated and viewed.

This strange feature, of the whole image being present in every segment of the plate, was critical in Dr. Pribram's application of the holographic model to the functioning of the brain:

> Sir John Eccles mentioned in an article several years ago that "synaptic potentials"—the electrical exchanges between brain cells—don't occur alone. Every nerve branches, and when the electrical message goes down the branches, a ripple, or a wave front, is formed. When other wave fronts come to the same location from other directions, the wave fronts intersect and set up an interference pattern. . . .

> It seemed plausible to me that if there are interfering wave fronts in the brain, those fronts might have the same properties as a hologram. Both holograms and brain tissue can be cut up without removing their image-processing capabilities. Holograms are resistant to damage—like memory in the brain. The persistent puzzle of a distributed memory might be solved. The brain had to behave, in part, like a hologram.[3]

In itself, this observation involves an analogy between two physical systems. However, Dr. Pribram shows a vivid awareness of some metaphysical implications: "In the frequency domain [that is, the domain of waves as opposed to particles], time and space become collapsed. In a sense, everything is happening all at once, synchronously. But one can read out what is happening into a variety of coordinates of which space and time are the most helpful in bringing us into the ordinary human domain of appearances."[4]

And to the interviewer's later comment, "In some metaphysical systems, that domain corresponds to the definition of God," Pribram responded:

That's right. Leibnitz talked about "monads," and a windowless, indivisible entity that is the basic unit of the universe and a microcosm of it. God, said Leibnitz, was a monad. Leibnitz was the inventor of the calculus, the same mathematics that Gabor used to invent the hologram. I would change one word in the monadology. Instead of calling it windowless, I prefer to call monads lensless. In a monadic organization, the part contains the whole—as in a hologram. "Man was made in the image of God." Spiritual insights fit the descriptions of this domain. They're made perfectly plausible by the invention of the hologram.[5]

With this bridge between the physical and the spiritual, including even the divine, we may turn to explicit consideration of some aspects of Swedenborg's metaphysics.

Wave Properties and Inflow

We may begin with what I should like to call the intersective nature of our reality. There are many places in Swedenborg's theological corpus where this is presented, the following being characteristic:

> Further, in regard to the union of heaven with the human race, it should be realized that the Lord himself is flowing into every individual according to heaven's design—into the individual's most inward and most outward [aspects] alike. . . . The former inflow of the Lord is called direct inflow, while the other inflow, which happens by means of spirits, is called indirect inflow. . . . This divine inflow is constant, and is accepted in what is good in good people, but not in evil ones. These latter either reject it, stifle it, or corrupt it. (HH 297)

We may take this as an application to the human situation of an even more general principle: "There are always two forces which hold anything together in its coherence and in its form—a force acting from the outside, and a force acting from within. Where they meet is the thing that is being held together . . ." (AC 3628[3].

It is possible but not particularly profitable to take these images in a Newtonian, mechanical way, visualizing one discrete unit impinging on another for their mutual definition. Swedenborg's own experiences of influx, however, indicate that we should conceive of influx as primarily a wave phenomenon rather than as a particle one.

> Since I have been in the company of spirits and angels constantly for nine years now, I have very carefully observed how it is with influx. When I thought, I could see solid concepts of thought as though they were surrounded by a kind of wave, and I noticed that this wave was nothing other than the kinds of thing associated with the matter in my memory, and that in this way spirits could see the full thought. But nothing reaches [normal] human sensation except what is in the middle and seems to be solid. I have compared this surrounding wave to spiritual wings by which the object of thought is lifted out of the memory. This is what brings it to our attention.

> I was able to determine that there was a great deal of associated matter in that surrounding wave-substance from the fact that spirits in a subtler sphere knew from it all that I had ever known about the subject, drawing out and absorbing in this way everything proper to a person. The genii who are sensitive only to desires and affections draw out things proper to one's loves. For example, when I was thinking about someone I knew, then his image appeared in the middle as he looked when he was named in human presence; but all around, like something flowing in waves, was everything I had known and thought about him from boyhood. So that whole man, as he existed in my thought and affection, was instantly visible among the spirits. Again, when I thought about a particular city, then the spirits knew instantly from the surrounding sphere of waves everything I had seen and knew. The same holds true for matters of knowledge. (AC 6200)

If we put these images together, the resemblance to the hologram is striking. We are constituted by the intersection of two flows—one direct, from the divine, and one indirect, from the divine via our environment. We can view ourselves as interference patterns, because the inflow is a wave phenomenon, and we are where the waves meet. We are regions in a total field where direct and indirect influx intersect or overlap.

This may help us to give due attention to an everyday situation that mechanical models tend to obscure, namely that our responsibility is both real and limited. There are schools of thought that see the criminal, for example, as simply a victim of society, and schools of thought that see the criminal as totally responsible. Yet if any individual feels either totally enslaved by circumstances or totally unconditioned by them, we begin to think in terms of psychosis. The vastly predominant weight of human experience indicates that our behavior is shaped *both* by our own inner intentions *and* by the impingement of circumstance, and not by either to the exclusion of the other. We are defined not by either the direct or the indirect inflow alone, but by the way they intersect.

The more general statement of the active-passive principle (AC 3628[3] sup.) may seem irrelevant to solid matter, but contemporary science suggests otherwise. To quote Pribram again: "We make images of objects, but at another level of analysis, quantum physics tells us that the universe is composed of wave forms that interact to form particles—or vice versa."[6]

That is, what we experience as solid matter in discrete units is at a subtler level a similar confluence. It does under some conditions have particle properties, which are undeniably significant. It is perhaps more important to realize that it also has wave properties, because these are at least equally significant and are relatively unknown. Still, the indications are that we should take a both/and stance rather than an either/or one.

Further, Pribram's sense of a connection between the frequency domain (the domain of wave properties) and the divine involves ideas central to Swedenborgian theology. In regard to the collapse of space and time, Swedenborg made statements such as the following:

> The future and the present are the same to the Lord. The future is present, or, what will happen has happened. (AC 730)

> The divine fills all space of the universe without [being bound by] space. (DLW 69)

> The divine is in all time without [being bound by] time. (DLW 73)

> Banish space, and absolutely rule out a vacuum, and then think about divine love and wisdom as actual essence once space is denied and vacuum ruled out. Then think spatially, and you will perceive that the divine is the same in the largest and the smallest [segments] of space. (DLW 81)

We have then two basic ways of viewing ourselves. On the one hand, in the Newtonian or particle model, we are discrete individuals, with clear boundaries and definable contents, progressing through measurable space and time. We interact with other individuals, giving and receiving, helping and harming, teaching and learning. On the other hand, in the quantum or wave model, we are identifiable areas of intersection in a total field of flow. Our whole life, both within and beyond time and space, is present to the Lord all at once. What we call "our own" is simply what flows into our consciousness.

While Swedenborg does often use particle models, I am presently concerned to call attention to his use of wave models. In regard to our concepts of ourselves, the following may suffice:

> If only people believed the way things really are, that everything good is from the Lord and everything evil from hell, then they would not make the good in themselves a matter of merit, nor would they ascribe evil to themselves. For in everything good they thought and did they would focus on the Lord; and everything evil that flowed in they would cast back into the hell it came from. But since people do not believe in any inflow from heaven and from hell, and therefore think that everything they think and intend is in themselves and therefore from themselves, they therefore make the evil their own, and pollute the inflowing good with a sense of merit. (HH 302)

> To the extent that we are in the form of heaven . . . we are involved in intelligence and wisdom. In fact . . . all the thinking of our discernment and all the affection of our intentionality reach out into heaven on all sides, according to its form, and communicate marvelously with the communities there, and they with us.

> There are people who believe that thoughts and affections do not really reach out around them, but occur within them, because they see their thought processes inside themselves, and not as remote from them; but they are quite wrong. As eyesight has an outreach to remote objects, and is influenced by the pattern of things seen "out there," so too that inner sight which is discernment has an outreach in the spiritual world, even though we do not perceive it.

> There was a spirit who believed that he thought independently—that is, without any outreach beyond himself and consequent communication with outside communities. To let him know that he was wrong, he was deprived of communication with his neighboring communities. As a result, he not only lost [the power of] thought, he even collapsed, virtually lifeless—just able to flail his arms about like a newborn infant. After a while, the communication was restored to him, and bit by bit as it was restored, he returned to his thinking state. (HH 203)

> To the extent that anyone is in the form of heaven, he or she is in heaven; in fact, he or she is a heaven in miniature. (HH 203)

> Before we say anything about the inflow and working of the soul into the body, it must be clearly recognized that the inner person is formed in the image of heaven and the outer in the image of the world, even to the point that the inner person is a heaven in miniature and the outer a world in miniature—a microcosm. (AC 6057)

Quantum physics in general and the holographic model in particular suggest that we should take these descriptions quite seriously, and if we do, they give sudden significance to a number of quite common experiences. There is, for example, the intimate interrelatedness of our understanding of ourselves and our understanding of our world. Discoveries in either "area" alter our view of the other. There is the phenomenon of discovery itself, the nature of "recognition of new truth." When this happens, there is normally a sense of familiarity: "It was there all the time, but I couldn't identify it. I knew it, and yet I didn't know it." There is the fact that "giving information" to someone else does not deprive the giver of the information, but actually strengthens the giver's retention of it. If you want to learn something thoroughly, try teaching it. There is the fact that knowledge seems to have no boundaries. To understand a single grain of sand absolutely, one would have to know all chemistry and physics to begin with, and then know what has happened since the Big Bang to bring oneself and the grain of sand together. There is the impossibility of distinguishing what is "ours" from what is "others'" in the realm of our thoughts.

I quote Pribram and Swedenborg, using a language I learned from others, to say things that are still somehow distinctively enough "mine" that I must hold myself accountable for them.

In the holographic model, these are quite normal and natural situations. Because we are miniature worlds, of course our understandings of things inside and things outside are intimately related. They are different views of the same structures and processes. Of course new knowledge has an aura of familiarity. It has been there all the time. Of course I do not lose information by teaching: I am not giving any *thing* that was not there. Of course knowledge has no boundaries. All meaning is present everywhere. And how can I call anything exclusively "mine" if I am in fact a confluence of inner and outer flows?

In fact, Swedenborg enables us to be a little more precise about the nature of this confluence:

> Since the soul is spiritual substance, and by reason of order is more pure, more primary, and more inward, while the body is material and therefore more crude, more secondary, and more outward, and since it is in keeping with order for the more pure to flow into the more crude, the more primary into the more secondary, and the more inward into the more outward, it is therefore in keeping with order for the spiritual to flow into the material, and not the reverse. This means that the thinking mind flows into the sight, subject to the state imposed on the eyes by the things that are being seen— a state which that mind, further, organizes at will. In the same way, the perceiving mind flows into the hearing, subject to the state imposed on the ears by words. (SBI 1)

To state this in other terms, under this construction there is no such thing as purely subjective or purely objective perception. Consciousness itself is an intersection of subjective and objective flows, so that Heisenberg's indeterminacy principle, insisting that the observer affects the observation, comes as no surprise. We should expect in every area the same kind of selectivity we find in our everyday consciousness—a tendency to focus on what we think is significant.

That is, the direct inflow is primary not just in a general or broadly ontological sense, but quite particularly and personally for each individual. What is most distinctively "mine," what I "have" or perceive that you do not, is whatever is flowing into me directly from within. In theological terms, it is whatever the Lord chooses to give me. Paradoxically, then, given the divine constancy, what is most profoundly "mine" is exactly the same as what is most profoundly "yours."

> It does seem as though the divine were not the same in one person as in another—that it were different, for example, in a wise person than in a simple one, different in an elderly person than in an infant. But this appearance is deceptive. The person is a recipient, and the recipient or recipient vessel may vary. A wise person is a recipient of divine love and divine wisdom more aptly and therefore more fully than a simple person, and an elderly person who is also wise more than an infant or child. Still, the divine is the same in the one as it is in the other. . . . (DLW 78)

Consciousness and Boundaries

The image of "solid concepts of thought . . . surrounded by a wave" (AC 6200, sup.) suggests one of the central features of the wave properties of human phenomena, namely that they have no ontological boundaries. The "solid concept" is best regarded as having boundaries drawn by Swedenborg's own focus of attention, by his own consciousness. Spirits with a (deeper and therefore) wider focus "saw" a larger field, which included related information that Swedenborg knew, but of which he was not conscious at that time.

It is physically true of us that we can focus on only a minute fraction of the information that our senses are supplying at any given moment. For example, the fovea of the eye is the only area of the retina where the photosensitive cells are densely enough packed to allow the discrimination of detail, and the fovea comprises only one-forty-thousandth of the total area of the retina. You can test this by looking directly at one word on this page and observing how many words you can read without shifting that focus. Again, careful attention to one set of signals tends to render us oblivious to other sets, so that, for example, fascination with a speaker's mannerisms makes it very difficult to attend to the speaker's meaning.

Yet all these signals are reaching all our senses in a ceaseless stream, a stream without intrinsic boundaries. We are apparently incapable of handling this level of complexity, so we "make meaning" by selection and by simplification. We draw boundaries in the flow, as indeed we must.

> There are also communities . . . which believe that if they gaze into the Infinite and worship a hidden God they can be in a love for him; yet they are not unless they make that infinite finite by means of some concept or make the hidden God visible among themselves by limited intellectual concepts. Otherwise they would be gazing into blackness. . . . (AC 4075[3])

> . . . for angels are finite, and the finite cannot have any concept of the infinite. (AC 7211[2])

That is, our finiteness consists less in our having absolute boundaries than in our inability to function without boundaries. We realize when we listen to an unknown foreign language that the spoken sound stream is a continuum, yet when we hear our native language, we hear discrete "words." When a person in brown clothing is sitting in a brown armchair, we effortlessly distinguish the person from the chair in spite of the fact that the color contrast is far less than that between the clothing and the face. Human perception is a constant process of interpretation, of deciding which boundaries are significant, or, more precisely, which frequency shifts need to be regarded as boundaries. This, I suspect, accounts for our fascination with those line drawings in which various familiar objects are "hidden."

A paragraph from *Heaven and Hell* indicates that this boundary-drawing function of consciousness may be more central than it has seemed.

> I may add to this that every individual, as long as he or she is living in the body, is as to spirit in a community with spirits without knowing it—good people in an angelic community and evil people in a hellish community—and that each one arrives in that same community after death. People who are arriving among spirits after death are often told and shown this. People are not visible in this community as spirits while they are living in this world because then they are thinking naturally; but people who are thinking withdrawn from the body, being then in the spirit, are sometimes visible in their communities. When they are visible, they can be readily distinguished from the spirits who are there because they move along lost in thought, silently. They do not look at others: it is as though they did not see them. And the moment any spirit talks to them, they vanish. (HH 438)

What Swedenborg is saying is clear, simple, and startling. We are present in the spiritual world at all times, but visible only as our consciousness moves to that level. It seems that it is our consciousness that draws the boundaries around us that make us distinguishable from "the general landscape"—from the rest of the ontologically seamless field of reality.

This may not seem to be true of us as physical beings, but both science and doctrine indicate that it is. On the simplest physical level, we are constantly taking in new matter and discarding old. On the quantum level, we are areas in the total energy field, and there is no particular reason to draw physical boundaries around us. Even in terms of Newtonian physics, we are always factors in some kind of balance of forces. Doctrinally, ". . . nothing unconnected ever occurs, and anything unconnected would instantly perish" (AC 2556).

We do experience our physical bodies as discrete entities, nevertheless, and Swedenborg suggests a reason for this. He states, ". . . the divine-true that emanates directly from the divine-good flows in by stages, and in its course, or at each new stage, it becomes more general and therefore coarser and hazier, and it becomes slower, and therefore more viscous and colder" (AC 7270).

Matter, then, is not discrete and solid, it is simply viscous. It is our consciousness that is keeping our bodies distinct from the rest of the landscape, but matter reacts to spirit so sluggishly that after our consciousness departs, it will be quite a while before our bodies become indistinguishable from the earth in which they are interred. In similar fashion,

FIG. 319. The Days of Creation *(the Sixth), by Edward Burne-Jones, 1875–76*

it often takes years for self-defeating attitudes to have a marked effect on our physical health, but eventually they do.

The tendency of our consciousness to draw boundaries around ourselves plays an important role in our spiritual histories.

> Our state when we are involved in our self-image [*in proprio*], or when we think we live on our own, has been compared to a deep sleep. . . . I have been allowed to know better than others how things are with the human self-image for a number of years now, [discovering] that I did not think anything at all from my own resources, and being shown that every single concept of my thought was flowing in—sometimes even seeing how it was flowing in. So people who think they do live on their own are involved in falsity, and by believing that they love on their own, appropriate all kinds of evil and falsity to themselves, which they would never do if they believed the way things really are. (AC 150)

We "are" what we "appropriate"—what we call our own, what we include within the boundaries our consciousness draws around ourselves. The implications of this are extensive; and within the confines of the present exploration we can raise only one further point. To believe the way things really are, that everything is flowing in, and that it is our consciousness that is drawing boundaries around us, is not to lose our identity and merge with the totality. Quite the contrary, because the wave/particle paradox is a constant, letting go of the effort to bound ourselves leads to a more intense sense of identity. "The more nearly we are united to the Lord, the more distinctly we seem to be our own, and the more obvious it is to us that we are the Lord's" (DP 42).

Ethical Implications of the Holographic Model

The central implication of the holographic model in the area of ethics is both simple and radical. If I am a microcosm of the whole, this has consequences for my entire concept of the self-other relationship. The only "you" I know is the "you" within my consciousness. I do indeed love my neighbor *as I love myself,* and vice versa, because my neighbor participates in my being.

In *Divine Love and Wisdom*, Swedenborg offers the following definition of love: "Love consists of having what is one's own belong to another, and feeling another's joy as joy in oneself—that is loving" (DLW 47). Now either this is total unrealism, total disregard of the facts, or "what is one's own" *does* belong to another, and the other's joy *is* joy in oneself. The notion of love as self-sacrifice, of altruism as behavior that brings no benefit whatever to the actor, misses the point completely.

Once this is said, however, we must immediately remember that as finite creatures, we need boundaries. We are not equipped simply to identify totally with everything. We can, however, maintain an awareness of the connection between the need and the boundaries. We can recognize that they are not ontological, but "convenient," and that they are not to be perpetuated beyond the limits of their appropriateness.

So I may recognize that my consciousness expands and contracts, that what is "mine" changes. I may also recognize that to call anything "mine" is not to deny that it also belongs to "others." This boundary is more appropriate for my accountability than for my privilege.

Centrally, however, I am to realize that I perceive nothing in others that is not in myself. The image of nuclear holocaust is simply my own desire for the removal of the inconvenient, blown up to a global scale. It is a vivid and inescapable expression of the fundamental quality of the wish that disquieting people would go away and stay away.

Further, every polarity that occurs in my world exists within me. I have a pacifist mind and a military mind, a totalitarian mind and an anarchistic mind, a capitalistic mind and a communist mind. I "have" them, at least, to the extent that I understand what pacifism is, what militarism is, and so on. The task, both internally and externally, is not to eradicate them but to see their appropriate limits and relationships. Swedenborg is quite unequivocal about the evil nature of "the love of self," yet he writes, "People who are involved in the good of charity and faith also love themselves and the world, but only as means to an end. For them, the love of self comes to a focus in love to the Lord, since they love themselves as means to the end of service to the Lord . . ." (AC 7819).

There are major implications of the holographic model concerning the nature of evil, which at this point I would only suggest. The passage just cited concurs with many others in the assumption that "evil" is good out of order, lesser good elevated above greater. This lends credence to the idea that in order to deal with the "enemy out there," I must discover the meaning of the corresponding enemy within myself. This will often involve struggle, demanding that I call and rely upon my "military mind." But there are limits to the appropriateness of that mind. It is to control only, not to destroy the enemy. Once control is established, then it is the task of the peacemaking mind to discern, foster, and appreciate its use in the whole. The only peace that has a chance is the one that converts the enemy to an ally, not the one that would annihilate the enemy. This conversion must respect the actual nature of the other, not forcing it into a mold but providing it with a wholly suitable domain of activity.

In the holographic model, doing this on the personal scale and doing it on the global scale are inseparable. If one asks which must come first, then the answer is simply "The one that lies immediately to hand." Once the relationship is seen and felt, the personal nurtures the global and vice versa. Swedenborg writes in *Divine Providence* " . . . all wars, on whatever scale, are representative of states of the church and are responsive to them. This was the nature of the wars described in the Word, and is also the nature of all wars in our own times" (DP 251[3]). The issues that divide us in communities, within our nation, and on a global scale, are issues we are to come to grips with within ourselves. Any radical separation between the "out there" and the "in here" is dangerously misleading.

Summary

Attention to the wave properties of matter, and to the holographic model in particular, highlights elements of Swedenborg's theology that have often hitherto seemed elusive, and which therefore have not been brought to bear effectively on the situations in which we commonly find ourselves. As a model from the realm of physics, it would seem to be most immediately applicable to our physical natures; but it seems singularly apt to more spiritual phenomena. An initial exploration indicates that it calls attention to aspects of our inner and outer relationships that we normally ignore and that offer promise of progress toward a peaceful way of living on all scales, from the very private to the global.

In this light, there is particular forcefulness to the following summary:

The union of angelic communities into a single heaven rests in these laws.
1. Every unity in the heavens arises as a form of many elements joined together according to a heavenly concord.
2. Love is spiritual union, the source of heavenly concord.
3. There must be a universal bond if the specifics are to be kept united.
4. The universal bond flows into specific bonds and constitutes them.
5. The universal bond is the Lord, therefore love from him and a consequent love for him.
6. The specific bonds are secondary, and are mutual love or charity toward the neighbor. (AC 9613)

Notes

1. See Karl Pribram's articles in *Psychology Today*, February 1979, pp. 71ff.
2. Ephesians 6:13ff., Today's English Version.
3. Pribram, p. 72.
4. Ibid., p. 84.
5. Ibid.
6. Ibid., p. 83.

The Subtle Realm:
Corbin, Sufism, and Swedenborg

Roberts Avens, Ph.D.

Excerpted and Compiled by Kate Davis

This essay has been compiled from two articles by Roberts Avens: "The Idea of Subtle Embodiment in Henry Corbin," previously published in *Hamdard Islamicus* (Karachi, Pakistan); and "The World of Emanuel Swedenborg," previously published in abridged form as "The Concept of the Soul Protected," in *Chrysalis*, the journal of the Swedenborg Foundation (Winter 1985).

Western Dualism and Reality of the Soul

THE CONTEMPORARY FRENCH PHILOSOPHER Gilbert Durand has stated that classical spirituality is a "pseudospirituality": by separating spirit from matter—and thereby mind from body—it denies concrete reality to the soul.[1] The archetypal psychologist James Hillman has appropriately called this Cartesian dualistic attitude the "double curse of our Western myth—the spirit's vision of perfection and matter's fundamental limitation, two archetypal fictions."[2] In this view there is no third way between the unlimited and the limited, the eternal and the temporal, spirit and matter. It is always the case of either matter tending to absorb spirit or spirit swallowing up matter. In its final formulation, matter (*res extensa*) and spirit (*res cogitans*) are conceived as two completely separate realities, which, thanks to divine ordination, come together at only one point—the human brain. The final outcome of the Cartesian dualistic fantasy is that the material world is automatically deprived of any spiritual content, while the spirit, for its part, is reduced to the status of an abstract counterpart of the material reality.

Swedenborg, together with the Islamic scholar and mystic Henry Corbin (d. 1978), belongs to the tradition of *sophia perennis* (perennial wisdom), whose proponents have undertaken the difficult and unpopular task of resuscitating the soul as the third realm between matter and spirit. For these "protectors" of the soul, the third realm is the proper "place" of all spiritual or visionary events, which, in turn, must be seen as events of the soul.

In Swedenborg and Corbin (as well as in Jung and Hillman), the soul is real; it represents the coming together and resolution of the polarities of the spiritual and the physical, the divine and the human, the universal and the concrete. What is meant here by the word *soul* is far removed from some vaporous, ghostly substance (refined matter) inside the body. For these thinkers, the soul is not something purely spiritual standing in opposition to matter, but a microcosmic reality, a compendium of nature reflecting the macrocosm. Clearly, in such a perspective the question of "inner" and "outer," subjective and objective, spirit and matter, simply does not arise. All events whatsoever take place in the soul, or rather they are transfigured in the light of the soul, which is the same as saying that they are first imagined then perceived. Imagination and perception are two gnoseologically and ontologically distinct "faculties" or powers.

Swedenborg possessed what in mystical literature is known as "dual vision"—the ability to perceive things in at least two ways simultaneously. In Paul Valéry's words, he was capable of "an effortless coming and going between two worlds."[3] There was no confusion in his mind between ordinary reality (the world of precepts) and the world of visions or images. Swedenborg could imagine and perceive concurrently.

ROBERTS AVENS is a professor of religious studies at Iona College, New Rochelle, New York. Born in Latvia, he received his B.A. and M.A. in humanities from the University of Brussels, and an M.A. and Ph.D. in theology and the phenomenology of religion from Fordham University. Dr. Avens is the author of *Imagination Is Reality* (Spring Publications, 1980), *The Imaginal Body* (University Press of America, 1982), and *The New Gnosis* (Spring Publications, 1984), as well as numerous articles.

Psychic Reality and Archetypal Images

For Swedenborg, "spirit" (the soul) is quite real in its own right. In this sense, his system is consonant with Jung's idea of psychic reality. Jung describes the status that must be ascribed to the psyche as follows:

> It is characteristic of the Western man that he has split apart the physical and the spiritual for epistemological purposes. But these opposites exist together in the psyche. . . . "Psychic" means physical *and* spiritual. . . . This "indeterminate" world seems unclear and confused because the concept of psychic reality is not yet current among us, although it expresses life as it actually is. Without soul, spirit is as dead as matter, because both are artificial abstractions; whereas man originally regarded spirit as a volatile body, and matter as not lacking in soul.[4]

Jungian psychology has experienced an important creative development in the form of archetypal psychology, founded by James Hillman.[5] Hillman's work constitutes a daring attempt to restore the soul to its central place not only in psychology, but in human and cosmic life as a whole—to "re-soul" the world. In archetypal psychology the Jungian archetypes, the patterns of the psyche, are no longer noumenal (unknowable), but always phenomenal. Archetypes are simply images, infinitely ambiguous in character, multivalent, and polysemous (capable of having a variety of meanings). Our psychic essence is "imaginal," and, as such, fully accessible to imaginative exploration. Psyche *is* image and imagination.

The Imaginal Realm

Henry Corbin has assisted in fathering archetypal psychology by his insight that the world of archetypes (the Sufi *ālam al-mithāl*) is identical with *mundus imaginalis*, a distinct field of "imaginal" realities requiring a *sui generis* mode of perception. The adjective *imaginal* is used by Corbin in order to distinguish it from the derogatory connotation that often accompanies the word *imaginary*. He proposed the term *imaginal*, as well as the Latin locution *mundus imaginalis*, as pointing to an order of reality that is ontologically no less real than what we call physical reality, on the one hand, and spiritual or intellectual reality, on the other. The characteristic faculty of perception within the *mundus imaginalis* is imaginative power, which noetically is on a par with the power of the senses or the intellect. In short, imagination, and by the same token the soul, is a structured reality and functions as an intermediary (the Platonic *metaxy*) between the sensible world and the intellectual world.[6]

Corbin's main body of writings is devoted to Sufism, to pre-Islamic, Islamic, and Persian philosophy and to Ismailian Shī'ism, areas in which he has uncovered vistas of thought previously unknown to or underestimated by Westerners. His thinking, nurtured by early interest in Böhme, Swedenborg, and Heidegger, emphasizes the inner, visionary pursuit of truth.

According to Corbin, the realm of creative imagination encompasses the "suprasensible world which is neither the empirical world of the senses nor the abstract world of the intellect."[7] It is the "angelic world," or the *mundus archetypalis*, the place of visionary events that are witnessed by each human soul at the time of its exit from this world of astronomical time and space. The forms and figures of the imaginal realm subsist on an ontological plane above the concrete and opaque density of the material things and below the intelligible world of pure ideas; they are more immaterial than the first and less immaterial than the second.

We thus have a threefold universe (corresponding to the tripartite human of archetypal psychology): the earthly human or sensible world (the object of ordinary sensory perception); the intermediary world of archetypal or visionary imagination—known in Sufism as *ālam mithālī*, or *Malakūt*, the world of the soul (the object of imaginative perception); and the world of intellectual forms, of pure cherubic intelligences (the object of intelligible knowledge). The function of *mundus imaginalis* is defined by its median and mediating situation between the intellectual and the sensible worlds. The faculty of perception corresponding to this intermediary world is archetypal imagination, whose "specialty" is to effect a complete and immediate realization of the imagined contents. In Corbin's words, imagination on the visionary plane "posits real being."[8]

Imagination is not only the human faculty par excellence but also the primordial power of the universe; in a sense, it is reality itself.

Let me also add, by way of anticipation, that Corbin's concept of imagination escapes the pseudodilemma of myth versus history, real versus unreal. The events taking place in the *mundus imaginalis* are neither myth nor history in the ordinary sense of these words. Rather, it is history of the *Malakūt*—imaginal or visionary history. Similarly the places and countries of this history constitute imaginal or visionary geography. Access to these imaginal realms is opened for us by the kind of hermeneutic denoted by the Arabic word *ta'wil*, literally to "reconduct something to its source, to its archetypal image, to its true reality." According to Corbin, *ta'wil* is a "symbolic understanding, the transmutation of everything visible into symbols, the intuition of an essence or person in an Image which partakes neither of universal logic nor of sense perception. . . ."[9] *Ta'wil* is a theophanic method of discourse, based on the ancient principle "only the like knows the like." It is in this sense that *mundus imaginalis* becomes accessible only by generating in oneself a minimum of visionary power. Put simply, the imaginal world is to be known only by imagination.

In Sufism the organ that is said to be responsible for the creation of *mundus imaginalis* is called *himma*, "creative power of the heart," connoting the notions of meditation, projection, intention, desire, force of will, faith. The creativity of *himma* is ontological in the sense that it produces changes in the so-called outside world: the object on which the "heart" concentrates its creative power, its imaginative meditation, appears as an outward, extrapsychic reality perceivable by others who have reached an equivalent degree of visionary power. These "objects," however, are not separate from the imaginer's imagination; they are "out there" and yet no other than the person who imagines them. One could say, their "outness" is only an index of the microcosm that is a human being insofar as he or she reflects the macrocosm. It is because people are compendiums of spirit and nature, that their imaginative power is capable of "placing" them exactly where they want to be. In these realms seeing is not only believing, but also being. In Corbin's terms, the creative function of archetypal imagination (*himma*) consists in "initiation to vision." Visions, in contrast to rational demonstrations and sensual perceptions, are "in themselves *penetrations* into the world they see."[10]

The imaginal world is also called by Islamic authors the "eighth clime" (subsisting beyond the seven climes of the sensible world of space) or the "climate of the Soul." It is a *concrete* spiritual world of apparitional forms, a country of nowhere that can only be reached by going inward (*ta'wil*) that is, from the external, literal, and exoteric to the hidden, inward, and esoteric. In the language of gnosis it is a movement from macrocosm into microcosm. However, when this journey is completed, the microcosm (the infinitely small) turns out to be a reflection of the macrocosm (the infinitely great). The inner reality now envelops, surrounds, and contains the outer and the visible reality. As a result of this "internalization," the spiritual reality itself *is* the "place" of all things, meaning that it is not located anywhere *in* sensory space; in relation to the latter, the "where" of the imaginal reality, "its *ubi* is an *ubique*,"[11] a "ubiquitous place."

The ubiquity of the imaginal space is the very opposite of the quantitative scientific space conceived as an infinite, lifeless, cold void. The quantitative space is the "satanic space" of William Blake, the blank, unfeeling stage on which matter plays its aimless, random acts without regard for the human. The person who inhabits this space is, as Pascal has it, only an accidental reed, liable to be crushed at any moment by the forces of a blind, indifferent universe. "Cast into the infinite immensity of spaces of which I am ignorant, and which know me not, I am frightened."[12] To be a "thinking reed" may well be a special privilege but it also adds to a person's essential loneliness in the midst of an unthinking nature.

In contrast to the quantitative space of modern cosmologies, the real imaginal space for Corbin is a field of unframed relationships, evoked by myth, dream, and religious vision, in which the figures and events seem free-floating in an environment without clear-cut boundaries. Like the chariot of Ezekiel, the bodies in this qualitative space move through no spatiality external to themselves. Each body has its own world, or rather, creates its own world, and, in Swedenborg's terminology, according to its "ruling love."

In view of the above it should not be insuperably difficult for us to assert with the Sufi masters that the imaginal world refers to the archetypal images of *individual* and *singular* things; that it possesses extension and dimension, figures and colors. Indeed, everything in this world has shape, size, color, and other qualities that the material objects of our world have; as in Swedenborg it has a scenery like that of the earth, human forms, grotesque or beautiful, senses that know pleasure and pain.

The eighth clime of the Sufi gnosis is a real imaginal place, fully accessible to imagination: there are heavens and earths, animals, plants, minerals, cities, towns, and forests. The physical things of our terrestrial earth are reflections of the celestial earth, the world of the soul. Or again, as Corbin observes in another variation of this theme, the celestial earth and all things belonging to it represents the phenomenon of the earth in its absolute state, that is, "absolved from the empirical appearance displayed to the senses. . . . Here all reality exists in a state of Images and these Images are *a priori*, or archetypal."[13] In other words, it is a realm of absolute or pure psychic activity. Or, if you prefer, the *mundus imaginalis* is a world composed of absolute matter, that is, free from the determinations that are peculiar to the dense and corruptible matter of the sublunar world. Absolute matter is a kind of prematerial, or primal matter, which is fully transparent to its own forms. Like anything in an artwork, it is pure apparition, a purely visionary thing, an image pure and simple.

It is important to emphasize that the figures and objects of the eighth clime, even though they are the exact replicas of everything existing in the sensible world, cannot be perceived by the senses. They are images, or the essences, of the sensible corporeal things, having different causal properties from those of the physical world. But this is far from saying that these images are identical to Platonic Ideas or, for that matter, to the unknown and unknowable archetypes of Jung. According to Corbin, the contrast between celestial (subtle) matter and the earthly visible matter must not be reduced to a Platonic dualism between idea and matter or between the universal and the particular. For "the state of infirmity, of lesser being and darkness represented by the present condition of the material world, results not from its material condition as such but from the fact that it is the zone invaded by the demonic Contrary Powers, the arena of struggle and also of the prize."[14]

In contrast to the universal and immaterial character of the Platonic Ideas, the beings of the world of archetypal images are conceived by Sufi meditators as "*particular* forms that are separate from matter, but by no means from all material envelopes."[15] They are personal presences, individual and unique, having a corporeality and spatiality of their own, an "immaterial" materiality, or what the Cambridge Platonist Henry More called *spissitudo spiritualis,* a kind of "spiritual extendedness." In the median world of theophanic space, the soul, instead of being bound to spatial coordinates, as in the quantitative space of science, is *situative* (creates its own space).

It is also for this reason that in the Sufi gnosis the question that is consistently asked is not about the essences (whatness) of things, but about their "personality" as, for example, *Who* is the earth? *Who* are the waters, the plants, the mountains? The *mundus imaginalis,* or the "eighth clime," is a fully personified cosmos, a presence in which the essence of a thing is fully manifested in its existence. As in a painting or a poem, in these environs the content is inseparable from the form; things mean exactly what they are, and are what they mean. As Swedenborg would have it, in the world of spirits, the masks drop off.

The Image of God in a Mirror

The key to Swedenborg's visionary universe is his doctrine of "correspondences," which he shares with Neoplatonism, the hermetic, alchemical, Gnostic, and cabalistic traditions. The principle of correspondences is succinctly expressed in the hermetic dictum "As above, so below; as below, so above"; it embodies the insight that "there is always a correspondence (harmony) between the laws and phenomena of the various planes of being and life"[16]—inorganic, plant, animal, human, spiritual. In psychological terms, correspondence is similar to the Jungian "synchronicity"—a meaningful connection among physical and psychic planes of events. According to Swedenborg, everything we perceive in our visible or material world has a counterpart in or symbolizes with the invisible or the spiritual world. The spiritual world is a duplicate, in more noble form, of the visible world, and the correspondence between the two extends to the most minute details.

Another central idea in Swedenborg is that of "influx." All things exist by divine influx: "Every created thing . . . is a recipient of God," that is, "an image of God in a mirror" (DLW 560). It is important to note that the divine influx, or the divine life, is received according to the capacity of the recipient and thus presents infinite variety (AC 2888, 3484). This, however, should not be construed as pantheism, for "the created universe is not God, but is from God; and since it is from God, there is in it an image of Him like the image of man in a mirror, wherein indeed the man appears, but still there is nothing of man in it" (DLW 58).

The Sufi seers have tried to convey this idea by saying that the subtle body (human as microcosm) is a mode of being that constitutes its own matter. The most frequent comparison, used by Suhrawardi, is the mode in which images appear and subsist in a mirror. Images are like forms seen in a mirror: the mirror is the place of the apparition of images, but images themselves are "in suspense"; they are neither like material things in a place nor like an accident in its substratum. The expression *in suspense* indicates that the image or the subtle body is "independent of the substratum in which it would be immanent in the manner of an accident (e.g., like the color black subsisting through the black object in which it is immanent)."[17]

To illustrate Suhrawardi's statement, Corbin invites us to imagine the form of a statue in its pure state, liberated from the marble, the wood, or the bronze. Corbin's comparison of the subtle body with the pure form of a statue is certainly helpful provided we do not confuse the latter with the ideal forms of Plato, relegating the statue itself to a "phantasmic" and shadowy piece of artistry (and so twice removed from the ideal form). In the Sufi view, the bronze or the wood would have to be wholly in the statue, just as in Hillman's view images are wholly in the modes of their manifestation. For it is precisely the artist's task to transform the crude "material" matter into subtle or spiritual matter in such a way that the former disappears or, rather, is fulfilled in the latter. It is in this sense that we may say with Suhrawardi that the statue—as an image—is independent from its substratum, the bronze. The bronze is only used, like the alchemist uses vulgar metals, to create a new thing, which, *as created,* is independent from and ontologically prior to the material substance. The "new thing" (the statue or the subtle body) exists "in suspense" because its status is that of a median and intermediate reality. It is a visionary thing, which, in order to be seen, demands a corresponding visionary ability in us.

Everything in the universe is a mirror reflecting the supreme light (*Maximus Homo*), and all the mirrors reflect in such a way that each one of them reflects all the rest of the mirrors. There is a mutual interpenetration among all things and events, a kind of circumincession, which makes Swedenborg's view of reality pansymbolic rather than pantheistic. This, however, far from dissolving the individual into a mushily selfless condition, establishes him as a unique embodiment of the universal reality.

The Universal Human

In Swedenborg, as in Sufism, the status of the human being is that of an intermediary reality or a subtle body. Each person is a potential angel (potentially divine) or a potential demon, but never "just a person" in a flat humanistic sense. A human is essentially "ek-static," a being that is always beyond itself, outside its simple ontic presentness. Humans are not simply "localable," not confined to a fixed, predetermined place in the scheme of things, but participate in all the strata of the universe. For, according to Swedenborg, besides the correspondences that exist between the outward creation and spiritual world, there is also an intimate (symbolic) relation between the nature (*physis* in the pre-Socratic sense) and the "spirit" (soul) of a person. There is a correspondence of all things in a person with all things in the physical universe. There is a spiritual (imaginal) heaven and earth, spiritual sun, moon, and stars; there are mountains, hills, valleys, and plains of the soul; there are spiritual (imaginal) trees, flowers, and tender herbs. All these living multitudes have correspondences in the soul of what Swedenborg calls *Maximus Homo*, the Universal Human. The universe is a living organism (Platonic *anima mundi*). Expressed in religious language, a human is a microcosm in the image of God not only in the spiritual sense, but also in the corporeal sense. A person is a gestalt, an image, the whole of which is more than the sum of its parts. In the human, God himself is present and spiritually perceptible.

Swedenborg repeatedly stresses that "God is the essential person. The only concept of God throughout all the heavens is the concept of a Person. This is because heaven, overall and in its parts, is like a person in form, and the divine which is among angels constitutes heaven" (DLW 11).

Swedenborg's idea of a cosmic or divine person has nothing to do with a simplistic anthromorphism; rather what is meant here is that humanity is the norm of the creation and that knowledge of the cosmic human is to be the realization of true humanity.

Swedenborg distinguishes between the divine being (*Esse Infinitum*, which he rather incongruously also calls Jehovah) and divine existence (*Existere*) or manifestation (the Lord or the Divine Human).[18] Jehovah or *Esse* is beyond all thought and every conceivable thing, hence it is in vain to seek or learn the nature of God in his *esse*. It is enough to know him according to created things in the bosom of which he exists in an external form. The Divine Human, then, is the "face of Jehovah," the first manifestation of God in "the form of an angel" (AC 1057). God manifested in this form prior to his historical incarnation in Jesus the Christ (the latter, according to Swedenborg, became necessary when humanity turned away from God in his first "incarnation" as the Divine Human).

Swedenborg's Universal Human is homologous to the Adam Kadmon of Cabala, the Logos of St. John's gospel, Prajapati or Purusha of Hinduism, the Iliaster of Paracelsus, the *filius philosophorum* or the *anthropos photeinos* (the man of light), Metatron in the Zohar, the Buddha, and to the intellectual intuition or the *nous* in the emanationist scheme of Plotinus. The Universal Human is also *sophia* (at once Mary and Eve), which functions as the intermediary between the divine abyss (*sunyata*) and the world of *maya* (Sufi *Hi jab*).

In Böhme's theosophy, *sophia* is the "body" or the "housing" of God through which the corporeal manifestation of God takes place. She is the supreme veil (illusion, fiction) and also the supreme theophany, or the "first step toward the inception of the path of God whose end is corporeality."[19] Islam ascribes the same function to the "Divine Mercy" (*rahmah*) whose "breath," symbolizing the nostalgia of God to be known, existentiates the world. According to the famous tradition of the Prophet, "I was a hidden treasure, I desired to be known, hence I created the world in order to be known" (*Hadith Qudsi*). In all cases the basic idea is that God, out of the innermost dark depths of his being, presses toward self-revelation, toward the manifestation of his essence in a bodily form. The world is God's self-disclosure.

Active Intelligence

Swedenborg traces the "oblivion" of the Divine Human to pre-historical times. For him, this oblivion has been the result of a general deterioration of human affairs on the terrestrial plane. A fascinating parallel seems to exist between, on one hand, these speculations by Swedenborg on the oblivion of the Divine Human and the consequent necessity of a second incarnation; and on the other hand, the loss in Western philosophy of the "Active Intelligence"—a loss that Corbin sees as being the root cause of man's alienation from the cosmos. Corbin identifies Active Intelligence with archetypal imagination, or "agent imagination." According to him, the Active Intelligence (*nous poietkos*, creative imagination) prior to Latin Averroism and Aristotelian Thomism was a quasi-cosmic reality constituting what is highest, most powerful, and most worthy in the essence of both man and nature. Beginning with Averroes, in the twelfth century, however, this power is severed from the individual soul; the latter receives its individuality and uniqueness no longer from the Active Intellect but only through the fact of its union with the body. In this way, says Corbin, "the individual is identified with the perishable; what can become eternal in the individual pertains exclusively to the *separate and unique intelligence*."[20]

From Averroes onward, the Active Intelligence was regarded by the Western rationalistic orthodoxy as heretical, or, at best, was accorded the status of a secondary faculty that "secretes nothing but the imaginary, that is, the unreal, the mystic, the marvelous, the fictive, etc."[21] The tragedy, the "metaphysical catastrophe," is that in the course of this development the official philosophy of the West came to admit only two sources of knowledge—sense perception, providing so-called empirical data, and the concepts of understanding that order and govern empirical experience.

As a consequence, what must be called "spiritual events" are deprived of a *situs* of their own and are assigned either to the realm of history and chronological time or—when explanation through historical causality fails—to the realm of myth (see the earlier section "The Imaginal Realm").

The proper place of the ultimate kind of imagining is, according to Corbin, " 'the place of apparition' of spiritual beings, Angels and Spirits."[22] The *situs* of these archetypal figures is "an intermediate universe 'where the spiritual takes body and the body becomes spiritual,' a world consisting of real matter and real extension though by comparison to sensible, corruptible matter these are subtle and immaterial."[23] In this realm there is no gap between reality and appearance, for what "appears" or presents itself as an image is from the very outset radically multiperspectival and metaphorical.

The same must be said of another pair of opposites—being and thinking: in the world of vision, being and thought coincide. Thought is creative in the sense that whatever we will or desire tends to be brought about. Of course it is not at all the case that every whim, every fleeting fancy of ours is always in some mechanical way immediately fulfilled; that would be sheer chaos, a madman's world. What is meant by the creative character of thought is that "in the long run" a person is as he or she thinks. To put it as does the ancient Greek sage Heraclitus, as well as the Lord Buddha, "character is destiny." In states of archetypal imagination there is no wavering between conflicting desires; we desire what we are and are what we desire. As Swedenborg portrays it, we invariably get what we love.

Angels and Spirits

An angel is a human in whom the inner and the outer, the material and the spiritual, perfectly correspond to each other, that is, a person in the state of completed self-expression (Jung's individuation) or in the state of fully realized divine image. An angel's face, far from being an idealized stereotype, is a true image of a spiritual state. In Swedenborg's words:

> When angels present themselves to the sight, all their interior affections appear clearly and shine forth from the face so that the face is an external form and representative image of them. It is not permitted in heaven to have any other face than that of one's affections. Those who simulate another face are cast out from the society. From this it is evident that the face

corresponds to all the interiors in general, both to man's affections and to his thoughts. (HH 479)

Swedenborg's conception of angels stands in sharp contrast to that of the traditional Christian theology, where angels are imagined as higher types of created spirits (spiritual substances) not bound up with a body. In this way they are distinguished from the human soul, which is assumed to be unable to function without the aid of a physical body. To circumvent the fact that in the scriptures angels occasionally do appear to men in bodily form (for example to Abraham and Lot), Mortimer Adler, representing the Thomistic view, suggests that these bodies must be merely "assumed bodies." The angels take them on not for their own sake, but for ours, in order to perform their ministry to us. "Strictly speaking [for this view], they would be like masks, which are not real visages but deceptive counterfeits of faces."[24]

In Swedenborg's eschatology, angels, far from being special creations, are men and women in perfect (imaginal) form: "There is not a single angel in the universal heaven who was originally created as such, nor any devil in hell who was created an angel of light and afterwards cast down thither, but all, both in heaven and in hell, are from the human race" (HH 311; see also 73, 75, 77).

Swedenborg's spirits and angels do not exist in astronomical time and space. Space is given to them not as something which is without, but as a flowing, placeless medium. This is to say that spiritual and angelic space is of the nature of a state rather than of a place. There is direction, but not in the sense of "from somewhere to somewhere." As in music, it is direction from one state to another, from an "everywhere" to another "everywhere" (as in the hall of mirrors).[25] The motion of spirits is not a change of place or position but a change of state. The spirit is where it acts or "where the action is." In Swedenborg's words:

> All changes of place in the spiritual world are affected by changes of state of the interiors, which means that change of place is nothing else than change of state. . . . Such are all movements of the angels; and in consequence they have no distances, and having no distances they have no spaces, but in place of spaces they have states and their changes. (HH 192; see also AC 5846, 5848–52)

Spirits are visible to one another when they are in accord, and they vanish when in discord, for their distance from one another depends on their state of affections:

> . . . Approaches are likenesses of state of the interiors, and separations are unlikenesses; and for this reason those are near each other who are in like states, and those are at distance who are in unlike states; and spaces in heaven are simply the external conditions corresponding to the internal states. (HH 193; see also DLW 7)

When a spirit desires the presence of another spirit he immediately sees him appear before his eyes: "Whenever anyone . . . thinks about another he brings his face before him in thought, and at the same time many things of his life; and when he does this the other becomes present, as if he had been sent for or called" (HH 494; see also 194, 196).

In a similar way, everything that spirits and angels see around them are correspondences of their dominant interior state or their "ruling love" (see HH 527; see also 58, 479). Things are representations of the feelings and thoughts of the angels; they are real or "substantial" appearances in that all things existing in the natural world subsist in the spiritual world in a more perfect form. To a spirit who asked Swedenborg if the differences between "substantial" and "material" (spiritual and natural) is not a simple question of degree, the latter replied:

> Such is not the distinction. By no subtilization can the natural so approximate the spiritual as to become the spiritual; for the distinction is like that between the prior and the posterior. . . . For the prior is in the posterior as a cause in its effect; and the posterior is from the prior as an effect is from its cause. Therefore the one is not visible to the other. (TCR 280; see also 38)

The Swedenborgian psychologist Wilson Van Dusen puts it as follows: "Essentially, spirits are affections or feelings, the inner or essential aspects of mind that underlie thought or memory."[26]

The idea that people in heaven appear in their "true colors" should be taken literally. The inner human possesses a colorful aura, which at death becomes visible in the spiritual world: ". . . A man or a soul in the other life is known among angels from his sphere, and . . . this sphere . . . is represented by colors like those of the rainbow, in variety according to the state of each person relatively . . . to the goods and truths of faith" (AC 1053; see also 1626, 1627, and HH 178, 183, 186). Angels are literally colorful; they are the colorful faces of the deity, and our earthly faces are but pale reflections of the rainbow of the heavenly colors. According to Ernst Benz, colors constitute essential elements and characterizations of the spiritual corporeality of the heavenly world itself.[27] They are not a "chimera" of the creation, but belong to the essence of the divine self-revelation, whose goal is corporeality. Instead of being a diminution and distortion of the pure spirituality of God, corporeality in the theosophic tradition of Christian mysticism "belongs to the consummate nature of God. God is the *ens manifestativum sui*, the being who presses towards self-revelation, towards self-realization . . . and this self-revelation presses towards corporeality."[28]

Angelomorphosis

The Swedenborgian view of the angelic condition closely parallels the speculations about angels in the Islamic gnosis. According to Corbin, the human soul is individuated not through the union with a physical body (as in Aristotle) but by becoming a perfectly polished mirror of its angel in a strictly one-to-one relation. We realize our virtual angelicity through a progressive illumination attained on earth; we are called, by right of our origin and if we consent, to an *angelomorphosis*.[29]

Instead of speaking about human nature in general, Corbin raises the problem of "specific individuality," that is, of an individuality that is "no longer subordinated to species but is itself its species, its archetype."[30] The virtual angelicity of the human soul postulates "not only numerical individuation within the same species, but an individuality specific in itself."[31] This is achieved by the natural desire that exists between the human souls and the angelic archetypes. In Corbin's phrasing, individuation of the soul means that it is "to hear and obey a *verde was du bist*" (become what thou art).[32]

For the Gnostics and Swedenborg as well, "mystical experience" is not necessarily a matter of attaining union with an undifferentiated Godhead or the Divine Essence. What a human being is destined to attain is the "Angel," the "Face of the Divine" which is also one's own original "Face" or "the celestial pole" of one's being.[33] As a Sufi saying has it, "He who knows himself [his angel] knows his Lord."

In view of these considerations, the process we described earlier as "dropping of the mask" is in effect an angelomorphosis, a *reductio ad modum angelicum*, or a transformation of the human into angel. Swedenborg's world of spirits and angels is nothing more nor less than a further theophanic manifestation, an ever more irresistible desire on the part of the Infinite to disperse itself in singular things so as to enable each thing to mirror the whole, to be a "world."

Spatializing: Creating Sacred Space

It might be possible to understand the structure of imaginal space more adequately by relating it to what Martin Heidegger calls a human being's essential tendency to remove distance (*Ent-fernung*), to bring close, to "situate."[34] Humans exercise a spatializing function by giving things that they frequently use their place according to the importance they have in life. The various places of space that arise in this way have no relation to geometric space: their hierarchy is determined by the necessity they have for the work to be done. Thus what is "nearest" to us is hardly ever that which has the least distance from us but is rather something that is "within reach" and available for our preoccupied grasp. Heidegger uses the comparison between our "closeness" to a friend approaching us on the sidewalk, and the sidewalk itself. Objectively speaking, the sidewalk is closer to us than the friend; yet we are not aware of our closeness to the sidewalk at all. This observation, trivial in itself, has far-reaching implications. It seems that a human, instead of being a world-less spirit, is necessarily bound up with existence in space or, more primordially, is *already* in a world. Space, therefore, is neither subjective nor objective, but rather the result of a person's spatializing activity; it is a mode of one's existence in the world.

Now once we accept the ontological status of the imaginal world, there is nothing that prevents us from applying it to the kind of spatializing activity that in principle is not different from the one occurring in the "secular" world of humans. Just as humans spatialize in everyday concernful dealing with things, so do they spatialize "in" the *mundus imaginalis*, in accordance with the directions of their "ruling love." It is only that in the latter case their spatializing is, so to speak, more thorough and consistent than usually; there is no possibility of falling back into the geometrical space. One does not return from the *mundus imaginalis* to this world to wait for another chance, as in the reincarnationalist hypothesis.

It is also significant that the traveler in the ubiquitous soul-space is said to be unable to indicate the road to others. One can only describe where he or she has been, but cannot *show* the road to anyone who does not share the "mentality" of the traveler himself. Roads can be shown only because there is distance between the traveler and the traveler's destination, whereas in the celestial landscape, as Swedenborg said, "all progressions . . . are effected by the changes in the state of interiors" (HH 193), that is, by the "ruling love" of the traveler. The soul itself spatializes, converting geographical destination into her destiny, terrestrial geography into "visionary geography."

The Sufi *illuminatus* Shaikhi Kermānī points out that a human's essential body is fashioned according to the extent of one's knowledge, to one's capacity to understand, to one's spiritual consciousness and moral conduct. The more developed one's spirituality, the subtler also will be one's essential body. We create for ourselves a dwelling place in proportion to the capacity of our spiritual energy. Just as we create the places of our dreams, so is our environment in the "other" world created by human imagination. Indeed it is only in the imaginal realm that we create the kind of environment that is fully and literally our own (fully human). In Kermānī's somber and liberating words, "Nobody can ever escape from himself, get out of himself; nobody becomes someone other than himself; nothing becomes other than itself."[35]

The Center

The great historian and phenomenologist of religion Mircea Eliade has described what he calls the sacred or hierophanic space of archaic religions in terms that seem to corroborate Corbin's interpretation of Sufi cosmology. According to Eliade, the deepest meaning of sacred space is revealed in the symbolism of the "Center." The Center has no geographic implications, but is rather part of what Corbin calls visionary geography.[36] Every inhabited region may have several centers, each of which is called "the center of the world"; it can be associated with sacred trees, rivers, mountains, and sanctuaries and is thought to be the meeting point of three cosmic regions—heaven, earth, and hell. Eliade believes that the multiplication of such centers betrays the nostalgia to be as often as possible near the archetype. Every person tends, even unconsciously (or, to be exact, imaginatively), toward a center, where that person can find sacredness *or* "reality." It is "the desire to find *oneself always and without effort* in the Center of the World, at the heart of reality, and by a short cut and in a *natural manner* (i.e., *in concreto* or in a bodily form) to transcend the human condition. . . ."[37]

To use Eliade's conceptual framework, in the world of imagination we are always at the center of the universe, for our center is where the "ruling love" is. In terms of St. Augustine's memorable maxim, *amor meus pondus meum* ("my love is my gravity"). We get what we love, because our love is a space-maker, constantly reorganizing and refining the circumstances and the environment of our body. Put differently, each soul is not only *at* the center of the universe, but is a universe in itself.

In the visionary geography of Iranian Sufism, the hierophanic space bestows a center, which is none other than the spatializing and situative soul. The soul, by being a spatializing agency, is also a centering power. "Hierophanies take place in the *soul*, not in things. And it is the event of the soul that situates, qualifies, and sacralizes the space in which it is imagined."[38] The mountaintops of the visionary earth are the mountaintops of the soul. The images of the earth and the images of the soul correspond to one another; as the soul projects the earth, so each physical structure discloses the mode of psychospiritual activity. Put simply: on the visionary plane, spirit and nature are reciprocal realities because the substance of the soul is made of the celestial earth and the celestial earth is made of the substance of the soul. Thus there is far less difference between the "living" and the "dead" than we are accustomed to suppose.

Death

In the traditional Sufi narratives the question is often asked, Where are the faithful believers *post mortem*? The answer is always the same: They are in bodies that are in the likeness of their material bodies.

Swedenborg's conception of death is summarized by the great philosopher of German romanticism F. W. Schelling in his theology of corporeality. To Schelling death is not so much a separation as an "essentification," destroying the contingent and preserving the essential, the most truly human, which is far more real *than* the fragile physical body. He therefore defends St. Paul's view of resurrection against all "merely rational and sterile doctrines of immortality"[39] and maintains that spiritual corporeality is already present in our material corporeality. Swedenborg points out that the appearance of things in the world of the dead are plastic to the states of mind of the spirits. The spirits are not "fixed and dead," but are, like images, ever-changing.

Swedenborg teaches that in the physical body of a human there is contained a subtle organism that is extended but lacks the mechanical properties (inertia and weight) characteristic of ordinary matter. This subtle organism—called *limbus* or *nexus*—forms the link between body and soul; it persists after death and is one's bodily substance in the postmortem state.[40] *Limbus* is the intermediate zone between the physical organism and the suprasensory soul, an organizing mold or formative agent serving as the vehicle (Proclus's *okhema*) of forces, which Swedenborg sees as rigorously conditioned by the soul. At death a person sheds the external or the less refined components of his or her physical nature, which become one's "containants." One must be careful not to confuse the *limbus* with the "spiritual body." *Limbus* itself lacks substantial unity; it is entirely plastic and protean and hence neutral in the formative sense.

Having in itself no particular form (amorphous), the limbus has the potential of assuming any form conceived (imagined) by the soul. The morphological human aspect of the *limbus* derives from the human soul and its power of imagination. In the last analysis, it is imagination that creates for the soul a corporeal vehicle, a spiritual body that in the postmortem states constitutes the whole person. The organic form of a human is the soul itself as it becomes concrete through the tangible matter, which it structures.

To fail to realize one's divine image is to die as only a soul can die—by losing one's potential angelicity, one's ultimate archetypal form.

The dead exist in the world of archetypal images. They pass through our world, but we do not see them *with* our bodily eyes. The *mundus imaginalis* is beyond our world, but it is also invisibly in our world; it is "a description of the outer things which are the *apparentiae reales* [archetypal im-

ages, or real imaginal bodies] of inner states."[41]

The figures and events of the *mundus imaginalis* are not what we perceive with our bodily eyes; rather they themselves are the eyes through which we see the world. In a sense, it is the "dead" who enable us to be alive.

Heaven and Hell

All things in the archetypal world are outer manifestations of a person's inner being. "The Paradise of each one is absolutely proper to him. It consists of man's works and actions, which in the other world will appear to him in the form of *houris* (voluptuously beautiful women), castles, and verdant trees."[42] Each person is inside his or her own paradise or, alternatively, inside one's own hell. A Shaikhi saying echoes this fundamental thesis: "The paradise of the faithful gnostic is his very body and the hell of the man without faith or knowledge is likewise his body itself."[43]

Hell is essentially a condition of sleep (unconsciousness) in which the person is ignorant of the true nature of sensory perceptions. One is passively subjected to them as though they were material, objective, and unalterable. It is a complete subservience to data (empirical, historical, etc.), to a fact-mongering mentality, and ultimately to the enslaving objectivizations of reason (the "idiot questioner" of William Blake).

The Irish poet W. B. Yeats, in an essay on Swedenborg, says, "So heaven and hell are built always anew and in the hell or heaven . . . all are surrounded by scenes and circumstances which are the expression of their natures and the creation of their thought."[44]

Within the Swedenborgian frame of reference, heaven and hell are not *just* states of mind but places or spaces created by the mind, or, rather, by imagination. A human being naturally gravitates in the direction of his or her most basic affections and thereby creates the kind of space that corresponds to these affections: "The activity of love is what gives the sense of delight; in heaven its activity is with wisdom, and in hell with insanity, but in both cases the activity produces the delight in its subjects. . . . If, therefore, you know what delight is, you know what heaven and hell are, and their nature" (TCR 570).

Like Gautama Buddha, Swedenborg maintains that man builds his own heaven and hell out of the knowledge and experience he obtained here on earth. Every least thing that we have thought, willed, spoken, done, or even heard and seen is engraved in our souls and can never be erased. Physical death in itself, therefore, does not change the human personality. It simply reveals and brings out into the light of open day what we really are in our innermost being.

The Swedenborgian heaven and hell are fully imaginal states inhabited by real people—real as only images can be real—

subtle bodies in which the inner and the outer exactly correspond to each other. It is a dream-world peopled by real dream-bodies, a world of shadows containing the seed forms (archetypal images) of our empirical existence. As a Kalahari Bushman once said: "There is a dream dreaming us." Indeed, it is not only we who imagine our dead relatives and friends in dreams; they too dream and imagine us. We are all dreaming one another's dreams and are parts of a dream dreaming us.

Notes

1. Gilbert Durand, "Exploration of the Imaginal," *Temenos* 1 (1981), p. 17.

2. James Hillman, *Healing Fiction* (Barrytown, N.Y.: Station Hill Press, 1983), p. 97.

3. Paul Valéry, *Masters and Friends*, trans. Martin Turnell (Princeton, N.J.: Princeton University Press, 1968), p. 119.

4. C. G. Jung, *The Collected Works of C. G. Jung*, trans. R. F. C. Hull, Bollingen Series XX (Princeton, N.J.: Princeton University Press, 1967), vol. 13, p. 51, n. 2.

5. James Hillman's main works initiating a departure from Jungian orthodoxy are: *The Myth of Analysis: Three Essays in Archetypal Psychology* (New York: Harper & Row, 1972); *Re-Visioning Psychology* (New York: Harper & Row, 1975); *The Dream and the Underworld* (New York: Harper & Row, 1979). See also Roberts Avens, *Imagination Is Reality: Western Nirvana in Jung, Hillman, Cassirer, and Barfield* (Irving, Tex.: Spring Publications, 1980); *Imaginal Body: Para-Jungian Reflections on Soul, Imagination, and Death* (Washington, D.C.: University Press of America, 1982).

6. Henry Corbin, "*Mundus Imaginalis* or The Imaginary and the Imaginal," *Spring* (1972), p. 15; see also p. 7. See also Henry Corbin, "Theophanic Imagination and Creativity of the Heart," in *Creative Imagination in the Sūfism of Ibn 'Arabi*, trans. R. Manheim (Princeton, N.J.: Princeton University Press, 1969), chap. 4. The other works of Corbin, available in English translation, are: *Spiritual Body and Celestial Earth: From Mazdean Iran to Shī'ite Iran*, trans. Nancy Pearson (Princeton, N.J.: Princeton University Press, 1977); *Avicenna and the Visionary Recital* (Irving, Tex.: Spring Publications, 1980); *The Man of Light in Iranian Sufism* (Boulder, Col.: Shambala, 1978).

7. Henry Corbin, "Towards a Chart of the Imaginal," *Temenos* 1 (1981), p. 23.

8. Corbin, *Creative Imagination*, p. 180.

9. Ibid., p. 13. In archetypal psychology too, the soul has its own *logos*, which operates in the poetic and metaphorical mode rather than "logically." The logic of the soul is based on the Platonic insight that the cosmos, no less than man, is a soul-permeated magnitude. From this universal kinship the ancient thinkers derived the postulate that the like is apprehended by the like. Probably it is best expressed in Plotinus (*Ennead* 1.6.9): "For one must come to the light with a seeing power akin and like to what is seen. No eye ever saw the sun without becoming sun-like, nor can a soul see beauty without becoming beautiful."

10. Corbin, *Creative Imagination*, p. 93.

11. Corbin, "*Mundus Imaginalis*," p. 12.

12. Blaise Pascal, Pensées, ed. Brunschvig, fr. 203.

13. Corbin, *Spiritual Body and Celestial Earth*, p. 82.

14. Henry Corbin, "Cyclical time in Mazdaism and Ismailism," in *Man and Time, Papers from the Eranos Yearbooks* 3, Bollingen Series XXX (Princeton, N.J.: Princeton University Press, 1957), vol. 3, p. 118.

15. Corbin, *Spiritual Body and Celestial Earth*, p. 174.

16. *The Kybalion* (Chicago: Yogi Publication Society, 1940), p. 28.

17. Corbin, *Spiritual Body and Celestial Earth*, p. 83; see also pp. 80–81, 87–88, 127.

18. Henry Corbin, "Hermeneutique spirituelle comparée (I. Swedenborg–II. Ismaelienne)," *Eranos Jahrbuch* 1964, XXXIII, (Zürich: Rhein Verlag, 1965), pp. 85ff.

19. Ernst Benz, "Color in Christian Visionary Experience," in *Color Symbolism*, Eranos Excerpts (Zürich: Spring Publications, 1971), p. 115.

20. Corbin, *Creative Imagination*, p. 12. See also Aristotle, *Nicomachean Ethics*, sec. 117a, pp. 14–20.

21. Corbin, "Towards a Chart of the Imaginal," p. 23.

22. Corbin, *Creative Imagination*, p. 4. See also Corbin, *Spiritual Body and Celestial Earth*, p. 102.

23. Corbin, *Creative Imagination*, p. 4.

24. Mortimer J. Adler, *The Angels and Us* (New York: Macmillan, 1982), p. 72.

25. Victor Zuckerhandl, *Sound and Symbol: Music and the External World*, trans. Willard R. Trask (Princeton, N.J.: Princeton University Press, 1956), pp. 309, 336, 338, 339.

26. Wilson Van Dusen, *The Presence of Other Worlds: The Findings of Emanuel Swedenborg* (New York: Harper & Row, 1974), p. 77.

27. Benz, "Color in Christian Visionary Experience," p. 84.

28. Ibid., pp. 114–15; see also pp. 97, 98.

29. Henry Corbin, "Divine Epiphany and Spiritual Birth in Ismaelian Gnosis," in *Man and Transformation, Papers from the Eranos Yearbooks* 5, Bollingen Series XXX (Princeton, N.J.: Princeton University Press, 1964), pp. 70–71; cf. *En Islam iranien* (Paris: Galimard, 1971), vol. 1, p. xix.

30. Corbin, *Creative Imagination*, p. 4.

31. Corbin, "*Mundus Imaginalis*," p. 7.

32. Ibid., p. 8.

33. Ibid., pp. 10, 11.

34. Martin Heidegger, *Being and Time*, trans. John Macquarrie and Edward Robinson (New York: Harper & Row, 1962), sec. 22–24.

35. Corbin, *Spiritual Body and Celestial Earth*, p. 225.

36. Ibid., p. 30.

37. Mircea Eliade, *Images and Symbols*, trans. Philip Mairet (New York: Sheed and Ward, 1961), p. 55.

38. Corbin, *Spiritual Body and Celestial Earth*, p. 23.

39. F. W. Schelling, *Philosophie der Offenbarung*, in S. W., XIV, 207, trans. Ernst Benz, "Theogony and Transformation in Schelling," in *Man and Transformation, Papers from the Eranos Yearbooks* 5, Bollingen Series XXX (Princeton, N.J.: Princeton University Press, 1964), vol. 5, p. 234.

40. Hugo Lj. Odhner, *The Spiritual World* (Bryn Athyn, Pa.: Academy Publication Committee, 1968), pp. 32–55.

41. Corbin, *Spiritual Body and Celestial Earth*, p. 330, n. 16; see also pp. 255–56.

42. Ibid., p. 233.

43. Ibid., p. 102; see also pp. 187, 227.

44. W. B. Yeats, "On Swedenborg, Mediums and the Desolate Places," Yeats's Appendix to Lady Gregory's *Visions and Beliefs* (1920), vol. 2, p. 303.

Swedenborg and the Egyptian Hieroglyphs

Horand K. Gutfeldt, Ph.D.

GREAT WISDOM WAS ATTRIBUTED to the Egyptians by the ancients. For instance, Plato[1] quotes approvingly an old Egyptian priest in one of his more important dialogues, referring to the Greeks as children "unaware of age-old wisdom." (Considering that great thinkers in modern times have repeatedly referred to all subsequent philosophy as nothing but footnotes to Plato, this is no small praise.) The accomplishments in building the pyramids underscores the fact that the ancient Egyptians possessed a remarkable wisdom. The Great Pyramid of Khufu covers thirteen acres and is described in the *Encyclopaedia Britannica* as "a masterpiece of technical skill and engineering ability."[2] It is still today the greatest single building ever erected, containing over two million blocks weighing up to 16 tons (average $2\frac{1}{2}$ tons each), hewn with such precision that it is not possible, after thousands of years have passed, to push a knife blade between contiguous blocks.

For thousands of years, the writing of that time, the famed hieroglyphics, could not be deciphered. Great expectations were in the air when the key was finally discovered by the French scholar J. F. Champollion in 1821.* With eagerness, now scholars collected, transcribed, and translated every piece of ancient Egyptian writing extant. The dry climate of the country has preserved many of the ancient documents, and the Egyptians left many colossal monuments with line upon line of beautifully carved inscriptions. Researchers cataloged the voluminous inscriptions found in the pyramids, beginning with the last king of the Fifth Dynasty, Unas (ca. 2340 B.C.), which were recognized as the oldest religious documents on earth.[3] Later the "Coffin Texts" were developed,[4] as was the Egyptian Book of the Dead. These consist largely of invocations to deities, fragments of myths, and adulations for the owner of the tomb.

As the literature was brought together, however, an increasing disappointment prevailed. Most of the inscriptions appeared trivial and superstitious by modern standards. Where was the great wisdom? Were all of these traditions nothing more than products of an essentially primitive culture that was later romanticized?

The feeling of mystery within the hieroglyphs remains alive. Even on the American dollar bill we see a pyramid with an eye on top. Many have claimed amazing insights and interpretations, yet in most cases there is not enough solid and consistent evidence in the existing texts to be convincing. Consequently, serious scholars almost unanimously have rejected most of these conjectures (e.g., *Secrets of the Great Pyramid*[5]).

A New School of Scholarship

In the beginning of this century the French Egyptologist Etienne Drioton made a strange discovery in the Louvre in

*Jean François Champollion, after careful study of related languages and the Rosetta stone (hieroglyphic, demotic, and Greek inscriptions, now in the British Museum), pieced items together and made the decisive breakthrough by intuitively recognizing the function of determinatives in hieroglyphic script. With his discovery, the phonetic reading of the Egyptian script became possible.

Rev. HORAND K. GUTFELDT was born in Latvia. He studied theology at the University of Marburg, Germany, in the early 1950s with Paul Tillich, Rudolf Bultmann, and Ernst Benz. In 1955 he obtained his Ed.M. from Harvard University. While in Cambridge, Massachusetts, he also graduated from the Swedenborg School of Religion, which was at that time adjacent to the Harvard campus. He later took his Ph.D. from the University of Vienna, Austria, in philosophy with a strong minor in Egyptology. He has been professor of behavioral science and college chaplain at Urbana University, Urbana, Ohio, and later an adjunct faculty member at J. F. Kennedy University in Orinda, California. Currently he is on the ministerial staff at the Hillside Community Church (Swedenborgian) in El Cerrito, California, and is president of the Berkeley Area Interfaith Council.

Paris. (The Louvre possesses some of the most splendid exhibits in the world of Egyptian works of art.[6]) Drioton discovered that a stela, or gravestone, from Egypt could be read in two entirely different ways. In one way of deciphering, the stela described the funerary ceremonies employed at that time for the dead. In another mode of interpretation, it rendered the story of the life of the person in question.[7]

This surprising discovery led him to a number of inquiries into similar double meanings among various ancient Egyptian inscriptions and documents. The hieroglyphs often contain in most cases various letter values and can thus be read phonetically. A partial lettering is often added to image-words for greater clarity—the so-called phonetic complement. Evidently, these writings said something to the general reader, but to the initiated, something else was resident in the symbols, adding another level of meaning. Following the lead of Drioton, a number of other scholars have made similar discoveries, and an international science of Egyptian cryptology has developed from these endeavors. Some inscriptions even showed one encoded text written above and another decoded one below.[8]

In connection with different levels and shades of hidden meanings in ancient literature, it is worth noting that various forms of allegories and symbolic allusions have been used to convey difficult or metaphysical truths. "Allegorical layers of meaning were used extensively in the Hindu and Buddhist scriptures and in ancient Persian and Arabian heroic legends."[9] It could be added that in certain cases the additional aspects of meaning are rather apparent, while in other cases they may be hidden and only known to initiates.

This brings us to the assertions of Emanuel Swedenborg. In his treatment of biblical texts, he makes some specific and far-reaching claims regarding inner levels of meaning. He gave convincing evidence that a number of the books of the Old and New Testaments contain, beyond the literal language, several levels of previously unknown but totally coherent messages of spiritual significance. In his crowning work, *True Christian Religion*, he states, "In the Word, there is a spiritual sense hitherto unknown" (TCR 139). [For a discussion of Swedenborg's interpretation of scripture, see Dorothea Harvey's essay "Swedenborg and the Bible," elsewhere in this anthology.]

Swedenborg declares that there was once a very ancient civilization on the earth that possessed a natural and intuitive understanding of the spiritual and interior correspondences of the physical and exterior world. Their manner of communication carried multiple meanings effortlessly, for such was the nature of their comprehension of reality. He makes the startling assertion that the ancient Egyptian hieroglyphs are a remnant of this ancient culture, and that the symbols portrayed in the hieroglyphs are to be fathomed only through an understanding of their correspondential meanings. He

refers often to Egypt, even titling one manuscript (not published until 1984) *Hieroglyphic Key*. This manuscript does not provide the material suggested by the title, but it does suggest that the hieroglyphs can be deciphered in a similar manner by which he treated the scriptures (KEY 193).

There have been other writers in historical Christendom who have made claims for some manner of mystical interpretation of the Judeo-Christian scriptures. The most famous one is, interestingly enough, an Egyptian, the third-century A.D. early church father of the Greek Church, Origen. Origenes Adamantius (ca. 185–254) propounded a well-known, three-tiered internal system of meaning in the scriptures, which was accepted without question for a time but is now widely disregarded. He wrote, "The spirit has mingled not a few things by which the historical order of the narrative is interrupted and broken, with the object of turning and calling the attention of the reader, by the impossibility of the literal sense, to an examination of the inner meaning."[10]

Swedenborg's method of revealing inner levels of meaning contrasts sharply, however, with Origen's allegorical method and with all other mystical interpretations. His doctrine of correspondences is completely unique in the history of scriptural interpretation. In brief, Swedenborg employed his well-honed scientific capacity for detail in his treatment of the scriptures, and he was able to produce thousands of pages of consistent demonstrations of inner levels of meaning by applying the correspondential method of interpreting symbols in the scriptures, which, he says, was shown to him by a special enlightenment. A rock in one place does not mean something else in another place in the scriptures. The figure Isaac does not mean something in one context and something else in another. Swedenborg gives the inner meanings verse by verse of the first two books of the Bible to demonstrate to readers that he is not simply devising a clever schema.

From a scholarly and scientific aspect, investigation of various levels of meaning in ancient writings is a formidable task. It is extremely difficult, if not impossible, to prove or disprove shades of meaning beyond any doubt, and this is the reason that so many shy away from this research. Especially in the Anglo-Saxon countries, where linguistic research and exact scientific pursuit is in the foreground, there is hardly any room given for other possibilities. In continental Europe, however, even cautious and thorough scholars, such as Helmut Brunner in his concise *Outline of a History of Egyptian Literature*, declare that strong evidence exists for a second meaning in many texts.[11]

Ancient Egyptian writing combines various forms of symbols. The "alphabet" is neither a pure system of pictures (as many have believed), nor is it a collection of sound signs (phonetic symbols), as are most letters in modern languages. Combinations of various possibilities provide a margin for differing interpretations.

Perhaps because of religious beliefs, this fairly complicated combination schema was maintained over thousands of years, even though its interpretation seems to have undergone a number of changes. The advance of Greek culture expedited abandonment of the hieroglyphs, though they were partially adopted into the Coptic script. Later, the hieroglyphs were simply forgotten, waiting for a rediscovery by later scholarship.

Findings of the Viennese School

Much research has been under way in continental Europe to recover more of the fullness of meanings, but these efforts have escaped attention in America. Most of the important discoveries were made shortly before, during, and immediately after World War II. The findings most consonant with Swedenborg's view are the observations put together by three successive Viennese scholars, who were directors of the institute, professors H. Junker, W. Czermak, and Gertrud Thausing.

The present director of the Institute of Egyptology at the University of Vienna, Thausing,[12] points out that up to seven different layers of meaning and connotation can be recognized. They can be identified by context, allegations, and cues. This is called in German *gestaffelter Sinn,* or "stratification of meanings." An often questionable late authority on the hieroglyphs, Horapollo, describes in his sixteenth-century work *Hieroglyphica* four levels of meaning: literal, figurative, allegorical, and analogical.[13] Swedenborg mentions three and sometimes four, frequently referring for corroboration to the Old Testament.

Let us look more closely at the levels of interpretation discerned in the work of the Viennese scholars. The first level is the immediate and surface literal sense. A second level refers to history and contains historical references. A third level refers to the traditional journey of the deceased through different stages of the necropolis and cemeteries, which are again full of symbolic allusions and rites. This is often referred to, in a shortened form, as the journey from "Buto to Hermopolis"—the two cities that played the key roles in funeral ceremonies.

A fourth level is related to the rites used at coronations, initiations, and the Sed festival. They are also related to previous symbolic patterns and have their origin in ancient spiritual significance. They symbolize the transition to a new stage of life, as well as the end of a former phase. In the fifth level, this becomes even more pronounced, for the fifth level refers to the spiritual development of the soul. This process as depicted by the Egyptians seems to parallel strongly several other spiritual traditions, such as the medieval tradition known as the "Via Mystica,"[14] and the yoga path in Hinduism. Characteristic of these processes is a three-step way: purification, illumination, and union (with the Divine).

Swedenborg also posits a three-step process of spiritual regeneration (repentance, reformation, and regeneration), which he sees reflected symbolically in many cycles of Hebrew scripture.

The sixth level refers to the way of the soul in the other world, more specifically described in the Book of the Gates and the Am-Duat, two of the main Egyptian treatises on the subject, again reflected in ceremonies. The seventh level traces a cosmogonic framework, describing the origin of the world in terms of a road from "Chaos" to "Cosmos" (order).

This far have the Viennese scholars recognized various levels or degrees of meaning, which interpenetrate in the texts as we have them today. They explain further that sometimes one level and sometimes another stands in the foreground, yet together they constitute a wholeness that cannot be completely separated. In this way, the discovered pattern is fundamentally different from pure allegory or an encoded text, whose surface level can be discarded once the inner meaning is separated out. Rather, the stratified levels of meaning, each with its own internal integrity, bears strong resemblance to both the consistent claims of Swedenborg concerning the documents that have become the basis of Judaism and Christianity, and Swedenborg's several allusions to the Egyptian hieroglyphs themselves.

Even though the Viennese school of Egyptological research is a respected academic cadre, their findings are accepted by only a small minority of experts. A much greater number of Egyptologists, primarily with linguistic backgrounds, reject all such claims of multiple levels of meaning; they refer them to the realm of fantasy. They also laugh off Plutarch's belief, recorded in his book *On Isis and Osiris*: "If anyone should assume . . . all these things [the myths] had really happened, one would have to spit out and cleanse the mouth. . . . this view is godless and crude . . . these legends contain an education about tribulations and sufferings."[15]

Could it be that the internal levels of meaning referred to by Swedenborg are more deeply hidden than anyone assumed? Certainly, a number of divergent views were once in existence, as witnessed by the newly discovered Gnostic library in Egypt.[16] Swedenborg asserts, "The Internal Sense . . . its veriest life . . . is never evident from the sense of the letter (AC 64). Manfred Lurker suggests, "The entire symbolization is built upon an assumed correspondence of things, an intuitively perceived . . . connection between Microcosm and Macrocosm that is ultimately a fact."[17]

To this one may add that Swedenborg's system and principle of correspondence is shown by him to be a universal law of reality and all causation, going in many ways beyond Lurker's "Microcosm and Macrocosm," and involving archetypes that find expression in all human language. For example, all facets of expression are based upon a correspondence of consciousness that manifests in many ways: in the body, in the mode of thought, in speech, and in actions. Every word expresses feelings and ideas of the speaker or writer that become encoded in many ways. The choice of words, the tone of voice, the style, the syntax are all encoded with subtle communicative signs conveying aspects of feeling and meaning, which the receiver interprets and understands instinctively and without reflection.

In the case of ancient Egypt, we are justified in inferring interpretations from the existing written material regarding the ideas and attitudes of the people who made the hieroglyphs. We are also on strong footing that the written word was believed to include magical powers. The term *hieroglyph* itself means "holy carving." Of course, what can be discovered and reconstructed today can only be a part of the original complexes of meaning and expressions, but already this fragment is fascinating and full of surprises. Many unexpected discoveries have been made and are still in progress, especially by those scholars who have penetrated the ancient texts directly with an open mind. Let us examine some aspects of the hieroglyphs in greater detail.

The Soul and Afterlife in Ancient Egypt

Ideas regarding the soul and its fate have been relatively overlooked in modern Christianity, or at least treated in a simplistic manner, while in Egypt the entire civilization seemed to accept a complex of metaphysical beliefs concerning the soul and its afterlife as a central organizing factor of life.

In Egypt, descriptions of the "Other World" have been found in prominent places, such as on coffins of a number of kings. These offer a considerably more detailed view than what most other great religions and civilizations have produced, as observed by Egyptologist E. A. Wallis Budge in his work *The Egyptian Heaven and Hell*,[18] which bears some striking resemblances to Swedenborg's own work *Heaven and Hell*. Budge investigates two of the central documents, the so-called Am-Duat and the Book of the Gates. He tries to accomplish something that was not done in antiquity, namely, to establish a synopsis or combination of essentials between the two similar texts.

Budge summarizes a number of characteristics of the afterlife in the following manner:

> In the abode of the blessed he [the soul of the deceased] was free to go wherever he pleased, to travel from one place to another, to visit his friends, to eat, to drink, to enjoy the society of wives and women of pleasure, and to rejoice in a family life which was only the glorified duplicate of what he had known on earth. [This other world is basically] divided into twelve portions, some of which are called . . . "Field" . . . others "city," etc.[19]

A similar picture was given by professor Erik Hornung, of the University of Basel, Switzerland, in a widely publicized lecture at the University of California at Berkeley, in 1978.[20]

There seem to be strange parallels to Swedenborg's basic division of two main kingdoms and three degrees in each of them, as well as with Swedenborg's consistent contention that "people are after death such as their lives had been in the world" (HH 20–40, 470). Swedenborg's descriptions are generally much more tightly reasoned and orderly. The Egyptian book is composed of authoritative declarations that seem to be spoken for eternity, but they are clearly derivative of visionary experiences of priests, which are interpreted in an extremely literal way. For example, it is described how the bark of the Sun God goes through the Other World lighting different areas. While this is very close to Swedenborg's descriptions of the Lord appearing as the sun in the other realm, one can see that there is much more room in Swedenborg's presentation of metaphorical meaning. Another strong parallel to the visions of Swedenborg is the monotheistic reform movement of Pharaoh Ikhnaton. In the hymn of this king, similar in many ways to Psalm 104, it is evident that there is a spiritual, as well as a material, idea regarding the sun, indicating a unified source of divine essence, just as Swedenborg describes.[21]

In the Egyptian tradition, very physical images are often introduced. Budge has tried to pin all things down to one spatial image of location, leading eventually to a number of contradictions and paradoxical superstitions. Superstitious beliefs seem to have already crept in at an early age of the Egyptian civilization. In later times especially, one finds in the graves terracotta *ushebti*, figures of slaves. The name is derived from the word for "answerer," and the figures were supposed to answer magically, instead of the soul, when there was a call for service in the afterlife. Days of service for projects of the state and the king were a common part of Egyptian life, a kind of corvée necessary for payment of taxes in societies with little cash. Again, it is conceivable that ideas regarding afterlife originally merged with magical concepts and a wish for greater power over one's destiny. Budge documents the development of these beliefs in his book *Egyptian Magic*.[22]

A good case can be made for the intermingling of material and immaterial concepts of the soul in the hieroglyphs. Two main designations appear for the soul: *ka* and *ba*. While appearing as separate terms and symbols, each seems to be related to a specific complex of meanings. At the same time, each one represents something of the essentials of the person whose soul is in need of ministry. The *ba* is written with a hieroglyph that shows a bird with a human head,[23] often preceded by a bowl of incense with smoke (or a flame) rising from it, as a sacred connection. Instead of this may appear the drawing of a human heart, pictured as a vessel. The fire

FIG. 320. *Symbol of the soul, probably from the Middle Kingdom period. Ba, a bird with a human face, represents the soul, and in particular its spiritual energies. In this figure, the* ba *wears the eye makeup customary in ancient Egypt. The beard identifies it with Osiris, god of the underworld. In Egyptian hieroglyphs, birds are often used to denote spiritual powers. The human face indicates belief in immortality.*

may point toward life, and in a coffin text it is said, "My *ba* does not burn with the body." Birds generally point to spiritual qualities in the hieroglyphic system; a certain type of bird, the crested ibis, means "spirit" or "spirit-like nature."[24] The meaning can be extended to designate some spiritual energy or power, resembling Swedenborg's correspondence for the heart as the dominant love of the person. From another angle, the heart is the symbol of a vessel, the receiver of higher energy from the Divine.*

---

*"A bird signifies spiritual love . . . successive varieties of spiritual life as to intelligence" (AC 8910); "The heart corresponds to the affection which is of love, thus to the will [intentionality]" (AC 9377); "The Divine of the Lord [His energy] . . . can flow . . . into a humble heart" (AC 1832); Spiritual things form their vessels or recipients in man (AC 1832); Men are vessels (SD 3759).

The other symbol for the soul, the *ka*, puts the individuality and cognitive faculties of the person into the foreground. The design of *ka* is a pair of outstretched arms, picturing a common attitude of worship.[25]

Many have inferred from these two designations that the Egyptians believed in two separate souls, each with different qualities. How the two could be regarded as one becomes a problem in many respects, although we can discriminate different parts in ourselves that may seem "in dialogue" with each other. The question of an essential unity comprised of diversity has long occupied philosophers and psychologists. Swedenborg observed that there may have been very ancient traditions that referred to the two main aspects of the soul, the cognitive and the affective functions, which make an inseparable unit, belonging together like substance and form. ("Thoughts, perceptions and affections are substances and forms" [DLW 42].) Swedenborg relies on this essential unity of distinguishable functions throughout his entire theological corpus. Love and wisdom, good and truth, will and understanding always make a whole, although they can be differentiated from each other for purposes of observation and analysis.

Another paradox regarding the soul appears often in the ancient texts. The Egyptians seem to have held the view that the soul is spiritual and immortal, while at the same time somehow influenced by the physical remains of the body. In the Pyramid texts it is said, "The corpse of King Unas goes to the earth, his soul goes to heaven" (spell no. 273).[26] Nevertheless, a great deal of care was given to embalm the body and conserve it as a basis for some form of life in the future. Many funeral cults performed sacrifices for the dead, especially libations (pouring of oil, wine, etc.), which were thought to have a magical effect upon the departed soul. Again, one may hypothesize that at the beginning there may have been some idea of a spiritual body that retained a connection with earthly life if, with love and care, a visionary priest made the proper provisions.

The Judgment of the Dead

In the Book of the Dead, of which at least excerpts were placed in every coffin, one chapter stands out. The heart of the deceased (or a corresponding symbol) in the form of a vessel is weighed against a feather (the symbol of Maat, the goddess of truth and justice) before Osiris. It is a scene of judgment. Maat is sometimes pictured in entirety and at other times is declared more as an abstract principle. Champollion has recognized that all inscriptions surrounding these judgment scenes contain hieroglyphs with special and unusual values, which others have called "enigmatic writing" (Goodwin, Budge), evidently pointing toward realms of higher meaning. This central chapter (no. 125) of the Book of the

Dead contains declarations of innocence and good deeds, some of which would have a place in any moral framework of today. "I have given bread to the hungry and water to the thirsty" is a typical sentence of this chapter.

Many details in the Egyptian tradition parallel those in the famed Tibetan Books of the Dead, which also describes scenes in the afterlife. Both contain doctrines and allusions concerning heaven and hell; both describe a judgment scene in which a balance is established between the good and bad of a life before a great god; both describe a jury of deities looking on; the mirror of karma in the Tibetan book corresponds nicely with the record book held by the god Thoth in the Egyptian tradition.[27]

A considerable list of parallels struck the first translator, W. E. Evans-Wentz, who literally sat at the feet of a Tibetan lama for years. Later scholars, Detlef Lauf among them, have concurred. Lauf made extensive intercultural comparisons in his book *Secret Doctrines of the Tibetan Books of the Dead*. Among many observations, he notes similarities in animal-shaped deities that picture manifestations of the human intellect.[28] He also notes that in both the Tibetan and Egyptian traditions the dead person enters into the "full light of day" immediately after death. These are just a few of the indicators supporting Swedenborg's claim that in the early stages of humanity there existed a common religious tradition that covered much of the earth. He called this epoch the "Most Ancient Church" [see Glossary] and partially "Ancient Church," referring often to Egypt (AC 280 and elsewhere). This broadly shared tradition became fragmented and distorted, according to Swedenborg, degenerating into superstitious and magical practices in later times. Furthermore, the clearest traces of this ancient tradition, according to Swedenborg, existed in Egypt (AC 5223). For corroboration, let us look at several myths crossing many cultures, all of them present in the ancient Egyptian texts.

Myths of a Great Flood

We have in the Old Testament the story of Noah.[29] The Mesopotamian texts contain close parallels, as do the Vedic hymns of India, the myths of Greece, and a smattering of accounts in as diverse places as New Guinea, Southern Asia, and ancient America.[30] Generally, these accounts tell of a small remnant surviving a gigantic flood. This story is also told in an Egyptian papyrus. It is not evident that such a deluge has ever occurred, one covering the entire earth, but there are traces of a massive flood in Mesopotamia. It is more than plausible that the truth is best approached through a spiritual interpretation. Swedenborg provides a very detailed spiritual exegesis of the story of the flood in his mammoth *Arcana Coelestia* (AC 1060–1104).

The Golden Age

Swedenborg also elaborated upon a version of the "Golden Age" theme that appears so often in esoteric and spiritual literature. He provides consistent substantiation for the prospect that such an age—the Most Ancient Church—had its day on earth, and he likens it to the innocence of childhood.* It was the childhood of the dawning of humanity before our rational capabilities were fully established.

Versions of some golden era are present in the Greek traditions, as related by Hesiod,[31] in Persian sources,[32] and in Egyptian sources, where descriptions abound of an age when the Sun God reigned on earth, the oldest period of Egyptian "legendary" history.[33] Is there any hard evidence at all for these wistful legends?

The eminent British archaeologist Sir Flinders Petrie (1853–1942) may well have provided the foundational research in his minutely conscientious scientific methods of excavation. In his book *Prehistoric Egypt*,[34] he describes evidential remnants of a civilization existing circa 8,000–10,000 B.C., whose traces were discovered near El Badari.

> The prehistoric civilization seems to have been so well organized and unified that the same tastes, ideas, patterns and material prevailed throughout. This shows that there were not isolated and warring tribes . . . but rather a peaceful, if not united rule over all Egypt and Nubia. . . . There was a firm belief in a future life, shown by fine and valuable objects placed in the grave.[35]

This is confirmed by Hayes in *The Sceptre of Egypt*, which describes the Badarian culture: "An agricultural and pastoral people, their unwarlike nature is attested by the complete absence from their graves and settlements of any save hunting weapons."[36]

These landmark archaeological findings seem to counter the prevailing modern notion that progress has been one long linear development from primitive times to today. Leading Egyptologists such as E. A. Wallis Budge and James H. Breasted[37] have ignored these findings, asserting instead that everything, including moral consciousness, has developed from less perfect original conditions. Scholars who have shed the blinders of such a dogma present a more differentiated and comprehensive view, involving cycles in the history of the world, as advocated by the doyen of historians, Arnold Toynbee,[38] and the Harvard sociologist Pitirim Sorokin.[39] In a similar way, Swedenborg describes great cycles of rise and decay of world religions that apparently swept over entire human cultures and describes four religious epochs, or "churches" (AC 231; TCR 760 and elsewhere).

---

*"The Golden Age was the time of the Most Ancient Church" (AC 1551). "When there was innocence and integrity, and when everyone did good from good, and justice from justice" (AC 5658).

Although such a thesis is doubted by certain scholars, they seem to apply especially to Egypt, which gives strong evidence of great creative capabilities in its earliest phases and later shows a slow decline with increasing crude imitations and repetitions. In the theory of linear evolution, an early belief in one central deity is utterly improbable, yet there are strong indications that it existed in ancient Egypt.[40] Furthermore, how does one explain that the greatest period for the pyramids is in the very early stages of that culture?* In the later stages, one observes a tendency toward indiscriminate borrowing from other traditions. This coincides with Swedenborg's claim that "memory knowledge," or knowledge by tradition instead of real experience, was chief among the factors leading to the decline of that culture's once-exalted position.† There is no doubt whatever that the later funeral texts claim increasingly that knowledge and/or possession of the magic texts is the key to salvation.[41]

The Opening of the Mouth Ceremony and the Symbol of Peace

A great ritual that stood at the threshold of transition from this world to the next is the "Opening of the Mouth" ceremony. This rite was very prominent during the early period. It was performed three days after the death of a person, whose body was wrapped in a temporary way before mummification. Detailed descriptions, as well as kits of the set of symbolic instruments, are shown in museums today.[42] (Again, a similarity appears in the Tibetan culture, before Buddhism made its appearance.[43]) A specially designated priest opened the eyes, the ears, and the mouth of the corpse in a figurative way, thus symbolizing, in the presence of bereaved relatives, the deceased person's resurrection to eternal life. In later times, this appears to have been interpreted as a magical procedure, supposedly effecting a vivification. Originally, it was likely intended to be a comforting visualization, such as others described by Swedenborg, who also states that the resurrection is completed generally on the third day after death (HH 452).

A related example is the so-called "Cannibal Hymn" from the Pyramid texts. It speaks of an "Eating of the Gods" (spell no. 273 in the Sethe collection). This must either be an indication of a primitive mind-set, as many take it to be,

or it may point to a more spiritual conception, referring to an eternal bliss that comes from receiving wisdom. Just as Swedenborg exalted love and wisdom as the two fundamental aspects of God, the initiates may well have understood the "Cannibal Hymn" in a like manner, as the names of the two most important deities refer to qualities of love and wisdom. A solemn communal eating of sacrifices harks back to early antiquity, and is continued in Christianity in the Eucharist or Holy Communion. Swedenborg gives a fascinating overview of the development of sacrificial worship,* and its significance and decline into superstition.

A specific example in the Egyptian texts demonstrating a connection between sacrifice and worship is the symbol of peace. The hieroglyphic system presents the concept of being at peace and rest through a picture of a loaf of bread sitting upon a reed mat in a sacrificial manner.[44] It does not seem problematic to interpret this offering of sacrifice as being at peace with higher powers. This may well have been clear when the sign was originally conceived, combining a symbol with a corresponding idea and feeling. The same sign is used for "altar" and "to be pleased." Harmony and happiness are apparently involved in this sacrifice. Swedenborg writes that in ancient times sacrifices signified "worship from love to the Lord" (AC 7857). This brings us to a short treatment of ideas and representations of deities in general in ancient Egypt.

The Deity and Divine Beings

The oldest texts of wisdom do not speak of many gods, as do later documents. There are many indications that in the earliest known period there was a belief in one god. Some scholars have found convincing evidence for this amazing possibility.[45] A specific European anthropological school has produced a wide range of linguistic analyses. In Egypt, no single original name has been discovered for a central high god, yet probably "The Great God" (*ntr aa*) seems to have been a designation. The broad range of later male and female deities, numbering in the hundreds, is preceded by some of the earliest names, which are all epithets, or names of divine qualities: "Horus" means "the remote" or "transcendent one"; "Maat," the wife of Thoth, means "truth and justice"; "Sia" means "wisdom"; "Ra" means "the spiritual and physical sun"; "Amun" means "the hidden one," which can also be connected to a root *mn*, meaning "to be permanent."

Each male god had a female counterpart, and there were many trinities and trinities of trinities that were also regarded as one. It is different with Osiris, the god of eternal life and resurrection. Alone among all the gods to have been born a man on the earth, he combines divine and human qualities. He redeemed humanity from ignorance and evil. The myth

---

*A survey of Egyptian history shows the greatest pyramids were built under the Fourth Dynasty, ca. 2613–2494 B.C. The invention of the hieroglyphs etc. is also very early in Egyptian history. Until the Persian conquest there were twenty-six dynasties.

†"Egypt . . . the knowledge of natural truths . . . or human wisdom" (AC 1462); also called "scientifics" by Swedenborg, in a different sense from its present use, for he says, "Doctrinal things, so long as they are solely in the memory, are only scientific truths" [the most external, typical to Egypt] (AC 6525).

*"Sacrifices . . . were the chief representatives of worship" (AC 2180); ". . . derived from the Ancients" (AC 2177).

FIG. 321. Judgment of the Soul in the Other World, *replicas assembled in the Rosicrucian Museum, San Jose, California, resembling an Egyptian tomb of the Middle Kingdom. The wall painting to the left shows the Judgment Scene before Osiris. In it, the heart of the deceased is portrayed in the form of a vessel and weighed against* *a feather, the symbol of Maat, goddess of truth. Also in the scene, the protective god Anubis escorts the deceased to judgment. Anubis is carrying the ankh, the sign of life. Thoth, keeper of the divine archives, is looking at a list of deeds from the life of the deceased.*

reported by Plutarch describes Osiris as a great king and teacher who taught Egypt wisdom and industry. He was killed by the evil deity, Seth, and was resurrected through the love and magical wisdom of his wife, Isis. Everyone rising from the dead is identified with him.[46] Osiris was worshiped as the main deity in many respects, together with his sister/wife, Isis. Thus, the Osiris-Isis myth emphasizes marriage and family, expressing the idea of redemption through the integration of love and wisdom, a core concept in Swedenborgian salvation.

There are other, more remote parallels to the Greek myth of Hercules. It had been prophesied that a human being would bring victory in a final struggle of the Olympian gods against the Titans. After many violent struggles, including a trip to the underworld, Hercules was received among the gods, becoming the protector of all education and a major figure for cleansing and redemption.

The Egyptian deities that are depicted together with the kings, in an often affectionate embrace, exhibit in many cases the same size and body features as humans. They frequently have the heads of animals—in one case that of a scarab beetle. Could it be that the animal features point to the supernatural, stressing some specific quality that the Egyptians

saw represented in the animal? The name of the scarab, for instance, is a frequently employed symbol identified with becoming and evolving. The word for *becoming* is always written with the sign of the beetle.

The most general hieroglyph for *deity* is a flag, "a cloth wound on a pole,"[47] which also designates anything divine and holy (e.g., a cemetery). Swedenborg mentions a banner as sometimes signifying divine meaning for gathering (AC 8624), and in the oldest existing religion, Hinduism, a flag indicates the place or house having an altar for a deity.

Conclusion

These brief examples give at least an idea of the wide range of symbolic connotation within the hieroglyphs. Most Egyptologists still hold to a purely linguistic scientific orientation, but at least they appear to be puzzled by some of the gaps in their excruciatingly narrow theory. The leading Egyptian grammarian, Sir Alan Gardiner, says, for instance, that "for unknown reasons" the sign for the giraffe signifies "to foretell."[48] Who does not perceive that the farsighted animal that can see beyond the human range of vision could become the emblem of foretelling? The head of a leopard indicates "strength";[49] a ram's head has become the representative for "worth, dignity."[50] One of the signs, again "for unknown reasons," means "good."[51] The image rendered in this emblem has been identified as a heart[52] and has the letter value of *nfr* (as in Nefertiti).

Here, Swedenborg's comprehensive system of correspondential relationships between different degrees, or planes, of reality offers a consistent and meaningful methodology of interpretation. He points, in his own correspondential analysis of the Bible, to an ontological interconnection of meanings that occur with symbols naturally, whether the user is consciously aware of them or not. Those scholars devoted to the fixed assumption that all ancient Egyptian writing is literal and phonetic will remain skeptical, but for those who suspect that a far greater wisdom pervaded ancient Egypt, as Swedenborg did, the symbolic interconnections are irresistible. Further application of symbolical analysis may hasten the understanding of an ancient wisdom that has become lost and obscured.

Notes

1. In the treatise Timaeus, dealing with cosmology, physics, and biology, he swallows any Greek pride and describes a discourse of Solon (who was regarded as the wisest of the Athenians) with an old Egyptian priest (III.21C). Solon declares ignorance about the most ancient origins (III.22A). From German translation of the series Rowohlts Klassiker der Literatur und Wissenschaft, Griechische Philosophie, vol. 5 (Leck/Schleswig, Ger.: Clausen & Bosse, 1959), p. 148.

2. *Encyclopaedia Britannica* (Chicago: Encyclopaedia Britannica, 1968), vol. 18, p. 895. It is mentioned here that St. Peter's at Rome, the cathedrals of Florence and Milan, Westminster Abbey, and St. Paul's Cathedral could all be grouped inside that area of the pyramid. A system of ventilation ducts keeps always a circulation of fresh air inside.

3. Among the leading scholars, Karl Sethe and James Breasted acknowledge that these are traditions from prehistoric times, while others (Kees, Scharff) believe that they are younger. S. Mercer, *Literary Criticism of the Pyramid Texts* (London: 1956), p. 42.

4. The "Coffin Texts" is a specific branch of Egyptian literature, representing an entire phase of literary legacy. See A. de Buck, *The Egyptian Coffin Texts*, 3 vols. (Chicago: University of Chicago, Oriental Institute Publications, 1935–47).

5. Peter Tompkins, *Secrets of the Great Pyramid* (New York: Harper & Row, 1971). With an open yet critical mind, one has to declare that by far the greatest part of the conjectures is fantastic and not hard to refute, although a few assertions may merit more investigation.

6. See *The Louvre, Paris*, 12th printing, in the series Great Museums of the World (New York: Newsweek, 1980), pp. 18–33, "Egypt."

7. Etienne Drioton, "Essai sur la cryptographie de la fin de la XVII dynastie," in *Revue de l'Egyptologie* 1, nos. 1, 2 (Paris: Librairie E. Leroux, 1933): "Egypte a possédée . . . une tradition cryptographique." In a number of other publications, Drioton has stated his findings, which have been corroborated by other scholars, among them Alexandre Piankoff in *Le Livre du jour et de la nuit* (Cairo: French Institute of Archaeology, 1942).

8. Professor Erich Winter (of Vienna and Mainz), "Die Rolle der Kryptographie in der Altägyptischen Hieroglyphenschrift," in the series of booklets Symposion über alte Sprachen und Schriftsysteme, edited by Neudorf, vol. 8, May 1966 (Graz, Austria: Akademische Druck-und Verlagsanstalt), pp. 7–10. Winter especially documents hidden theological implications, p. 9. He also describes parallels between funeral rituals and the biography of the deceased.

9. *Encyclopaedia Britannica*, vol. 1, p. 641. Here also allegories in the Christian scriptures are mentioned, according to some occurring in several levels of meaning.

10. Origenes, *On First Principles* (New York: Harper Torchbooks, 1966), p. 287.

11. Professor Dr. Helmut Brunner, *Grundzüge einer Geschichte der Altägyptischen Literatur* (Outline of a history of Egyptian literature) (Darmstadt, Ger.: Wissenschaftliche Buchgesellschaft, 1966), p. 18. "One has proved in the teachings of Ptahotep . . . convincingly that under the clear and simple principal meaning (*Obersinn*) there is a deeper and hidden one, which comes forth, if the words are heard differently. . . . Referring to the Judgment of the Dead . . . there is an avenging justice in the other world."

12. Professor Gertrud Thausing is almost completely unknown in America. A very comprehensive book of hers is *Sein und Werden: Versuch einer Ganzheitsschau der Religion des Pharaonenreiches*, in the series Acta Ethnologica et Linguistica, ed. and pub. Engelbert Stiegelmayr, trans. Horand Gutfeldt (Vienna: 1971). Some of the main research in this direction was done by the former director of the Vienna Institute, Wilhelm Czermak, "*Zur Gliederung des 1. Kapitels des Ägyptischen Totenbuches*" (About the structure of the first chapter of the book of the dead), in Zeitschrift für die Ägyptische Sprache und Altertumskunde, ed. Walter Wolf (Leipzig: J. C. Heinrichs Verlag, 1940), vol. 76, pp. 9–23.

13. Horapollo, *Hieroglyphica* (The Hieroglyphics of Horapollo) trans. George Boas (New York: Pantheon Books, 1950).

14. The medieval mystical tradition is influenced by Gnostic and Neoplatonic sources, mainly represented by (Pseudo) Dionysius Areopagita, who "became of decisive importance for the theology and spirituality of Eastern Orthodoxy and Western Catholicism (*Encyclopaedia Britannica*, vol. 7, p. 464). Among others, the ascent of the soul to the immediate vision of God in ecstasy is described, stripping away the senses as a consequence of a negative theology.

15. Plutarch, *On Isis and Osiris*, German translation by Th. Hopfner, with commentary (Prague: Oriental Institute, 1940), vol. 1, p. 20. See also his pronouncement on Osiris, chap. 45. There is evidence that Plutarch obtained firsthand information about the Egyptian mysteries and was able to describe some of this knowledge. He explains all the deities of the Egyptian pantheon as abstract principles and energies. Plutarch influenced Shakespeare, and is available in a number of English translations (G. Lindskog and K. Ziegler, eds., and by B. Perrin in the Loeb series, 1914–39). He is less known at the present time.

16. James Robinson, ed., *The Nag Hammadi Library* (New York: Harper & Row, 1981). A number of different gospels and creation stories are recorded here.

17. Manfred Lurker, *Symbole der Alten Agypter* (Weilheim, Oberbayern: O. W. Barth Verlag, 1964), p. 9. Lurker is coeditor of a group of scholars on a comprehensive bibliography of symbolism (*Bibliographie zur Symbolkunde* [Baden-Baden]).

18. A reprint appeared in paperback (La Salle, Ill.: Open Court Publishing, 1974). The

analysis on pp. 87–88 is noteworthy in that no word in our language does full justice to the central concept of the "Other World," in Egyptian *Duat* (Budge transliterates *Tuat*). Although Budge's research is impeccable and a large amount of documentation is quoted, including Egyptian illustrations, there is always the problem of avoiding present theological concepts in interpreting ancient texts.

19. Ibid., p. 74.

20. In the yearly endowed Foerster lecture on the immortality of the soul; "Ancient Egyptian Ideas on the Reunion of Soul and Body," Berkeley, Calif., University of California, 27 February 1978. The lecture presented the ideas of ancient Egypt in a comprehensive survey.

21. See Eleonore Bille-De Mot, *The Age of Akhenaten* (New York: McGraw-Hill, 1966). The Amarna epoch is well described. Afterward, under Tutankhamen, the country reverted again to polytheism.

22. E. A. Wallis Budge, *Egyptian Magic* (London: Kegan Paul, 1901; reprinted New York: Dover Publications, 1971, and Secaucus, N.J.: Citadel Press, 1978). In the Dover edition, the explanation is in chap. 3, "Magical Figures," pp. 65–73. In the story of the "Eloquent Peasant" is also an episode where a magical power is desired to fulfill an unjust craving, bringing this close to black magic.

23. Sir Alan Gardiner, *Egyptian Grammar*, 3rd. ed. (London: Oxford University Press, 1964)—the leading book on the topic—p. 473, sign G53 (bird with human head), preceded by R7 (flame). This was the way "soul" was signified beginning with the Eighteenth Dynasty. (The use of hieroglyphs has changed during Egyptian history.)

24. Ibid., p. 470, sign G25; another bird sign for the soul is G29, the jabiru bird, with the phonetic value *ba*.

25. Ibid., p. 453, sign D28, the sign for soul and spirit can be combined with a standard and signifies then the soul as of divine nature, D29. It can also contain a notion of uniting, D30.

26. The Pyramid texts (*Die Altägyptischen Pyramidentexte*) were collected and compared for parallels by the German Egyptologist Dr. Karl Sethe (of Göttingen) and edited in 4 vols. (Leipzig: 1908–9). A commentary and translation by Sethe appeared posthumously in Glückstadt, Hamburg. There is an English edition translated by S. Mercer.

27. W. E. Evans-Wentz, *The Tibetan Book of the Dead* (London: Oxford University Press, 1960), p. 36 and elsewhere. He also calls attention to parallels in Plato's *Republic*. He points out further that main deities appear in trinities, that the entire book was in the beginning a guide for life, and that there are parallels to the so-called purgatory.

28. Detlef Ingo Lauf, *Secret Doctrines of the Tibetan Books of the Dead* (Boulder, Col., and London: Shambala Publications, 1977) calls attention to the fact that there is an entire literature closely related, thus many books of the dead. Chap. 5 offers comparisons with ideas about death and the afterlife in other cultures, India, Persia, Egypt (pp. 194ff), and also in Western schools of thought, especially in the last scenes of Goethe's *Faust*, which contains sections from Swedenborg's Memorable Relations, as investigated by Professor Gollwitzer (of Stuttgart), who gave lectures in Vienna in the Urania center in the 1960s. See published account "Rosensegen und Hollenbrauch," in *Forum*, no. 123 (March 1964), pp. 147–51.

29. Genesis 6, 7, 8, 9.

30. See article in *Encyclopaedia Britannica*, vol. 9, p. 456, comparing the biblical account, the Mesopotamian texts, especially the Gilgamesh epic, Greek mythology, etc.

31. Hesiod says: "They lived like gods, free from worry and fatigue, old age did not afflict them, they rejoiced [in] continual festivity. . . . At their death . . . [they] became benevolent genii, protectors and tutelary guardians of the living." *New Larousse Encyclopedia of Mythology*, rev. ed. (New York: Prometheus Press, Paul Hamlyn, 1968), p. 93.

32. Ibid., p. 319.

33. Gardiner, *Egyptian Grammar*, p. 84.

34. Sir Flinders Petrie, *Prehistoric Egypt* (London: British School of Archaeology in Egypt, 1920).

35. Ibid., pp. 5–6, 47.

36. William C. Hayes, *The Sceptre of Egypt* (New York: Harper, 1953), pp. 14–15; similarly described in G. Brunton and Caton-Thompson, *The Badarian Civilization and Predynastic Remains near Badari* (London: British School of Archaeology in Egypt, and Egyptian Research Account, 1928).

37. James Henry Breasted (1865–1935) in *Development of Religion and Thought in Ancient Egypt* (New York: Scribners, 1912), p. 191.

38. Arnold Joseph Toynbee, *A Study of History*, 10 vols. (London: Oxford University Press, 1934–61).

39. Professor Pitirim A. Sorokin, *Social and Cultural Dynamics*, ed. Kimball Young, 4 vols., American Sociology Series (Boston, San Francisco: American Book, 1937); also in Sorokin, *The Crisis of Our Age* (New York: Dutton, 1946).

40. Henry Frankfort, *Ancient Egyptian Religion* (New York: Harper, 1961), p. 22. Cf. his critique of Breasted, p. vi.

41. E. A. Wallis Budge, "The Doctrine of Eternal Life," in *The Egyptian Book of the Dead* (New York: Dover Publications, 1967), pp. lv–lxxxi.

42. In the Metropolitan Museum of Art in New York. A fairly detailed description is given by Budge in *Egyptian Magic*, including a picture, p. 199.

43. Evans-Wentz, *Tibetan Book of the Dead*, p. 32.

44. Gardiner, *Egyptian Grammar*, p. 501, sign R4, phonetically *htp* (often read as *hotep*).

45. There has been much research on "primeval monotheism," such as P. Schebesta, "Das Problem des Urmonotheismus" (in German), in *Anthropos* (an anthropological periodical) 49 (1954), pp. 3–4. The most widely known is by Professor Wilhelm Schmidt on the origin of the idea of God, *Der Ursprung der Gottsidee*, 12th ed. (Münster, Ger.: 1955). This contains rather comprehensive research with linguistic, anthropological, and other observations. The idea of the one high god in Egypt and all indications for it in ancient times: Thausing, *Sein und Werden*, containing a great many quotes from ancient texts, which also include references to certain feminine aspects.

46. The messianic qualities of Osiris were emphasized by C. Th. Odhner, *The Correspondences of Egypt* (Bryn Athyn, Pa.: Academy Bookroom, 1914), pp. 108ff. About Osiris, see also A. S. Mercatante, *Who's Who in Egyptian Mythology* (New York: Clarkson N. Potter, 1978), p. 114. At the middle phase of Egyptian history, the name Osiris was written with the sign for (human) flesh (Gardiner, *Egyptian Grammar*, p. 467, sign F51).

47. Gardiner, *Egyptian Grammar*, p. 402, sign R8.

48. Ibid., p. 486, sign E27.

49. Ibid., p. 462, sign F9.

50. Ibid., sign F7.

51. Ibid., p. 465, sign F35.

52. Horapollo refers to this—that it also points to the mouth of a good person. *Hieroglyphica*, sects. 2, 4.

Servant of the Lord

Ray Silverman, Ph.D.

> A person is only as a servant and house-steward appointed over the goods of his Lord.
>
> —Emanuel Swedenborg (DLW 333)

The Birth of a Genius

EMANUEL SWEDENBORG HAS OFTEN BEEN DESCRIBED as a towering intellect who mastered all the known sciences of his time. As Robert Ripley put it, in his "Believe It or Not" column, "No single individual in the world's history ever encompassed in himself so great a variety of useful knowledge." Ripley reports on Swedenborg's groundbreaking work in mathematics, geology, chemistry, physics, mineralogy, astronomy, and anatomy. He points out that Swedenborg's original investigations in these areas are "the germs of numerous brilliant discoveries later credited to other investigators."[1] The nebular hypothesis, the first successful sketch of a flying machine, plans for an underwater ship (submarine), the discovery that the brain functions in synchronization with the lungs and has both a right and a left hemisphere with differing functions, the sciences of metallurgy and crystallography—all these find their origin in the mind of a young Swedish genius: Emanuel Swedenborg.

In the years 1709–45 Swedenborg wrote 125 articles, pamphlets, and books, many of which were published at the time, and a few of which, such as his work on the brain, ran well over 1,300 pages.[2] The reader may already be familiar with Swedenborg's achievements. Nevertheless, for those who are not or for the purposes of review, a selected list of titles of early works, chosen to emphasize the diversity and depth of Swedenborg's intellectual pursuits, can be found at the end of this book, as Appendix C.

It is not surprising, then, that Swedenborg would be listed in the *Guinness Book of World Records* as one of the most brilliant individuals who has ever lived, with an IQ estimated at "over 200."[3] His name is included with people such as John Stuart Mill, who began a study of ancient Greek at the age of three, and Mehmed Ali Halici, who recited 6,666 verses from the Koran in six hours. Swedenborg's brilliant ability to penetrate so vastly and so deeply into all areas of human knowledge is aptly summarized by Robert Ripley, who calls him "The Living Encyclopedia."

Swedenborg's Call to Serve as Revelator

There is a difference, however, between being listed as one of the most brilliant men of all times and being called by the Lord to serve as a revelator. What was it about Swedenborg that made him a suitable person for the office of revelator? Was it his extraordinary genius? Some have made that claim. It has been felt that the Lord needed someone exceptionally bright to grasp the depths of the new doctrines that were about to be given to humanity. According to the scholar Alfred Acton:

> A long course of deep and abstract thought had so molded Swedenborg's brain, had so opened and formed the interior organism of its nerve cells wherein the mind performs her operations, that he was gradually initiated into thinking from spiritual light. . . . At last, as his mind and brain became fitly formed, he saw things in the spiritual world.[4]

In this view, much emphasis is placed upon Swedenborg's mind and brain, a brain that had to be developed, formed, and re-formed through years of diligent study and intense

Rev. Dr. RAY SILVERMAN has taught religion, German, and English in the Academy of the New Church schools, has served as curator of the Swedenborgiana Library in Bryn Athyn, Pennsylvania, and has published articles in several denominational periodicals. He received his Ph.D. in English and education from the University of Michigan, Ann Arbor, in 1970. He is currently pastor to the Swedenborg Christian Church in Pittsburgh.

concentration. It would take a most brilliant, highly developed mind to receive the new truths descending from heaven, to understand them, and to record them clearly. Such a mind was Swedenborg's.

Others, however, have emphasized not so much Swedenborg's brilliance as his undaunted zeal for the truth. He is compared to Ulysses in Tennyson's great poem; Ulysses, with an unquenchable thirst to meet and know all of life; Ulysses, who says:

> I cannot rest from travel; I will drink
> Life to the lees . . .
>
> To follow knowledge like a sinking star,
> Beyond the utmost bound of human thought . . .
>
> To strive, to seek, to find, and not to yield.[5]

With an enormous appetite for learning the nature of truth, Swedenborg launched a scientific career almost beyond compare. Long before Kant and Laplace, he originated the nebular hypothesis of the solar system.[6] [For a full discussion of this subject, see Steve Koke's essay "The Search for a Religious Cosmology" elsewhere in this anthology.] At the same time he turned his gaze deep into the earth, studying mineralogy, botany, chemistry, and crystallography. Then, going beyond astrology and geology, he turned to the study of the human anatomy—in a relentless search for the seat of the soul. As one writer puts it, "As a youth he heard the call from the seas, from distant lands, from the realms of nature, to go forth into God's great world and be a seeker of the Truth."[7] He had the feeling that, after a long, dark slumber, the human race was at the dawn of a new awakening. In his introduction to *Dynamics of the Soul's Domain* he writes, "First came the day, and the world was enlightened with the brilliance of genius; then the night, and for ages the human mind lay slumbering in darkness. Now again the dawn is near, and we abound in experience. Haply the progress hence will be to a new day and a second age of genius" (EAK 14).

Was it this great zeal for the truth, this tremendous appetite for knowledge that prepared the way for Swedenborg's call to the office of revelator? It is true that the Lord promises that all who seek shall find; and yet Swedenborg's zeal seems overly self-confident. His intensity is reminiscent of those who strove to build the Tower of Babel, to make a name for themselves, to build an edifice with its head in heaven.[8] Swedenborg wrote, "The time is at hand when we may quit the harbor and sail for the open sea. The materials are ready: shall we not build the edifice? The harvest is ready: shall we not put in the sickle? The produce of the garden is rife and ripe: shall we fail to collect it for use? *Let us enjoy the provided banquet*" (emphasis Silverman's; EAK 14).

"Eat Not So Much"

In raising the question of Swedenborg's call, we have considered a few of his outstanding qualities—qualities that would indeed be necessary for the office he was about to fill. His towering intellect would serve him well, as would his relentless zeal for discovering the truth. And yet, these qualities, in themselves, would not be sufficient. Something more was needed.

That certain "something" was revealed to Swedenborg in April 1745, while he was dining late at an inn. The story is reported by a Mr. Robsahm, who had asked Swedenborg "where and how it was granted him to see and to hear what takes place in the world of spirits, in heaven, and in hell." According to Robsahm, Swedenborg said:

I was in London and dined rather late at the inn where I was in the habit of dining, and where I had my own room. My thoughts were engaged on the subjects we have been discussing. I was hungry, and ate with a good appetite. Towards the close of the meal I noticed a sort of dimness before my eyes: this became denser, and then I saw the floor covered with the most horrid crawling reptiles, such as snakes, frogs, and similar creatures. I was amazed; for I was perfectly conscious, and my thoughts were clear. At last the darkness increased still more; but it disappeared all at once, and then I saw a man sitting in a corner of the room; as I was then alone, I was very much frightened at his words, for he said: "Eat not so much." All became black again before my eyes, but immediately it cleared away, and I found myself alone in the room.

Such an unexpected terror hastened my return home; I did not let the landlord notice anything; but I considered well what had happened, and could not look upon it as a mere matter of chance, or as if it had been produced by a physical cause.

I went home, and during the night the same man revealed himself to me again, but I was not frightened now. He then said that He was the Lord God, the Creator of the world, and the Redeemer, and that He has chosen me to explain to men the spiritual sense of the Scripture, and that He Himself would explain to me what I should write on this subject; that same night also were opened to me, so that I became thoroughly convinced of their reality, the world of spirits, heaven, and hell, and I recognized there many acquaintances of every condition in life. From that day I gave up the study of all worldly science, and laboured in spiritual things, according as the Lord had commanded me to write. Afterwards the Lord opened, daily very often, my bodily eyes, so that, in the middle of the day I could see into the other world, and in a state of perfect wakefulness converse with angels and spirits. (DOC vol. 1, pp. 35–36)

The words "Eat not so much" almost leap forth from the page when regarded in this context. [For a full discussion of this event, see Donald L. Rose's essay, "The Pivotal Change in Swedenborg's Life," elsewhere in this anthology.] Here is the self-confident scientist, who only a few years before boldly proclaimed that the time was at hand to build the edifice and enjoy the banquet. And now he finds himself in an inn, late at night, face to face with the Lord God, the Creator of the Universe. What advice does the Lord have for Swedenborg? "Eat not so much," he says, meaning that Swedenborg should focus his attention less on worldly science. In his eagerness to please, Swedenborg says, "From that day I gave up the study of all worldly science, and laboured in spiritual things, according as the Lord commanded me to write" (DOC vol. 1, p. 36).[9] The command "Eat not so much" was the climax of a long and arduous struggle waged in the recesses of Swedenborg's soul. During that struggle a new interior quality was being forged—a quality more necessary to develop than any other. It was more necessary than all Swedenborg's brilliance; more necessary than all his intense zeal; it was, as Swedenborg was about to learn, the foundation of all human qualities. That certain something was *humility*.

The Birth of Humility

It was not Swedenborg's extraordinary brilliance in itself nor his burning desire to know the truth that qualified him for the office of revelator. While these were valuable qualities, he still lacked a certain depth of humility. While he was alive, Swedenborg never told anyone that it was the gaining of humility that finally prepared him for the office of revelator. Instead, he merely spoke in general terms about the appropriateness of his preparation as a natural scientist. In one of his published works, Swedenborg explained his calling in this manner:

> I was once asked how I from being a philosopher had become a theologian. I replied, "In the same way in which fishermen had been made disciples and apostles by the Lord; and that I also from my earliest youth had been a spiritual fisherman." When asked what was meant by a spiritual fisherman, I replied that by a fisherman in the spiritual sense is meant a person who investigates and teaches natural truths and afterwards spiritual truths in a rational manner. (SBI 20)

In another place Swedenborg says, "By means of the knowledge of natural things I was enabled to reach a state of intelligence, and thus by the Divine mercy of God-Messiah, to serve as an instrument for opening those things which are hidden interiorly in the Word of God-Messiah" (DOC vol. 1, p. 139).

In neither case does Swedenborg refer to the crucial step between his absorption in natural truths and his emergence as a servant of the Lord. That story had been unknown and untold until a remarkable little book was discovered, eighty-

eight years after Swedenborg's death. In this book we learn in detail how Swedenborg gradually acquired the necessary humility to become a revelator for the Lord. This book, which Swedenborg never intended to publish, is now titled *Journal of Dreams*. The book is a collection of journal entries made by Swedenborg during his spiritual awakening of 1744—a time that marked the turning point in his life. It was during this time that Swedenborg came deeply into the meaning of humility, a time when the famous scientist would become an anonymous theologian, signing two dozen volumes of religious writing simply "servant of the Lord."*

In reading the pages of this journal, one becomes aware of Swedenborg's central struggle. It revolved around his intellectual pride. It is hard enough for those of normal intelligence to put aside their conceit, self-love, and pride in their own intelligence. How much more difficult it must have been for a genius like Swedenborg! He writes:

> It came into my thoughts that . . . I ought by no means to attribute anything to myself; but that all is his; although he of grace, imputes to us the same. (JD 60)

> I have now learned this in spiritual things, that there is nothing else but to humble oneself and to desire nothing else, and this with all humility, than the grace of Christ. I attempted of my own to get love, but this is arrogant; for when one has God's grace, one leaves oneself to Christ's good pleasure, and does according to his good pleasure. One is happiest when one is in God's grace. I was obliged with humblest prayers to beg for forgiveness before my conscience could be pacified; for I was still in temptation until this was done. The Holy Spirit taught me this; *but I, with my foolish understanding, left out humility, which is the foundation of all.* (emphasis Silverman's; JD 61)

Here we see a different side of Swedenborg. These are not the words of the brilliant scientist, nor are they the words of the divinely called revelator; they are the confessions of a fallible and penitent human being, groping for divine guidance. Far from the heights of scientific brilliance, he is now in the depths of despair. We feel his anguish as he writes:

> Although I was awake, I could by no means govern myself, but there came a kind of overmastering tendency to throw myself upon my face, to clasp my hands and pray as before; to pray for my unworthiness, and with the deepest humility and reverence to pray for grace; that I as the greatest of sinners, might have the forgiveness of sins. (JD 90)

---

*From 1749 to 1768 Swedenborg published all his religious works anonymously. With the publication of *Conjugial Love*, in 1768 he adds these words to the title page: "Ab Emanuele Swedenborg, Sueco." The words "Emanuel Swedenborg, A Swede" end nineteen years of anonymity, and then, three years later, on the title page of his last published work he writes, "Ab Emanuele Swedenborg, Domini Jesu Christi Servo"—by Emanuel Swedenborg, *Servant of the Lord Jesus Christ.*

It was in the midst of this inner crisis that Swedenborg adopted this motto: "God's will be done; I am thine and not mine" (JD 103). He had learned that humility is the foundation of all. He had come to that point in his life where he was resolved to be led by the Lord alone. He would no longer "eat so much," no longer trust in scientific proofs, no longer try to rely on his natural reason to understand the divine mysteries. No longer would he strive to ascend into the kingdom of God by means of his knowledge of the kingdom of nature. He would believe in his heart what he could not touch with his fingers, or see with his physical eyes. He would trust in the Lord. And so he wrote:

> Happy are they that believe and do not see. . . . How difficult it is for the learned, more difficult than for the unlearned, to come to this faith; and thus to overcome themselves so that they can laugh at themselves. For adoration of their own understanding must in the very first place be plucked up and cast down; which is God's work and not man's. (JD 151)

Swedenborg had come into that state of mind—had developed that interior quality—which is the starting point of all spiritual growth. His former intellectual pride was beginning to die, and something new was being born. He compared himself to a nursing child: "I have now come into the condition that I know nothing and all preconceived notions are taken away from me; which is where learning commences: now namely, first to be a child and thus be nursed into knowledge, as is the case with me now" (JD 267). It is a strange and wonderful thing that this great genius could refer to himself as a man who "knew nothing," and see himself as "a child" who had to be "nursed into knowledge."

Swedenborg's Life as an Allegory

In giving up his intellectual pride, Swedenborg became receptive to the fullness of life that flows in from the Lord. Later, during the time of his profoundest spiritual illumination, he wrote: "Life from the Lord flows only into a humble and submissive heart" (AC 6866). Also: "A state of reception of the Divine and of heaven . . . is a state of humiliation towards God. In proportion as a man can humble himself before the Lord . . . he receives the Divine and is in heaven" (AC 8678 [2]).

Swedenborg's life can be seen as an allegory. He was born with a great gift—a towering intellect—and an equally high level of personal ambition. To the person who takes inordinate pride in his ability to think and reason, there comes a time of great struggle. Swedenborg's struggles with his own intellectual pride, as seen in the *Journal of Dreams*, is a useful allegory—a useful picture of the human intellect unwilling to surrender to the will of God, unwilling to acknowledge that every brilliant thought and benevolent emotion is a gift

from God. To the extent that Swedenborg was willing to make this acknowledgment, the Lord was able to make use of the capabilities with which he had already blessed him.

The story of Swedenborg's life, then, is an allegory reaching beyond the limitations of fact and fiction into the purer realm of spirit. It is the realm where all the great myths have had their origin. It is the story of base metals being turned into gold, the story of the miraculous transformation that takes place when a person's God-given talents become consecrated by acknowledging their source and using them for the glory of God.

In the Old Testament it is the story of Abraham's sacrifice of Isaac.[10] The birth of Isaac, whom Abraham so dearly loved, may be compared to the birth of the finest thoughts in the human mind. They appear to be our own, and yet the moment comes when we must acknowledge their true origin. It is represented in the Word of God as a sacrificial moment: Abraham gives his beloved Isaac back to God on Mount Moriah. It is an analogy of that same sacrifice that must take place in the human mind. It is the moment when it seems that we must surrender our rationality in order to transcend it. Our noblest thoughts are not our own. They are free gifts from God. "No one can receive anything except what is given from heaven."[11] This is extremely difficult for those who have come to believe the Cartesian formula: *Cogito, ergo sum* (I think, therefore I am). As long as intellectual pride is attached to the progeny of our mind—our spiritual "Isaacs"— we shall go on saying to ourselves, "I am this thought; I have thought it; and it is me." Therefore, every person's spiritual journey leads to Mount Moriah, where that archetypal sacrifice is made, where Isaac is given back to God.

It is at this moment that the wondrous transmutation takes place. Isaac is saved. "Do not lay your hand on the lad," says the Angel of the Lord.[12] This transcendent moment has been described in many ways in various religious philosophies. One writer, Ram Dass, puts it like this:

> You are experiencing a unitive link with it [the universe] rather than knowing it through your senses. It is known in the mystic trade as the opening of the third eye. . . . It is very clear that there are ways of knowing that are not knowing either through your senses or through your rational mind.
>
> Whether or not that way of knowing is useful to man is something that we only know as we explore and enter into that realm ourselves, you see. *Now it turns out that what is required to get to the next level of consciousness is to transcend the rational mind* [emphasis Silverman's]. That means to transcend the knower who knows. And that is a very frightening thing when that has been your vehicle for controlling your universe up until that point. And it turns out, of course, that when you do that you end up *with* your rational mind but in the role of a servant rather than a master. We're coming out of that place where we're seeing that we aren't our thinking mind but that it is merely another *servant*, not the master.[13]

The central message is clear and consistent. The human mind, the rational faculty, is not to be regarded as master, but as servant. Thinking is but one of the tools given to us as a part of our humanity. Moreover, our finest thoughts are not even our own, but gifts from God. In states of humility this can be acknowledged. It can be a bitter struggle, for intellectual pride does not die easily, just as it was not easy for Abraham to bring his beloved Isaac to Mount Moriah. The miracle is, however, that in giving up "the rational" we attain to a higher level of rationality; a new level of consciousness dawns in the human mind. We see and understand in new and deeper ways. The lad is not harmed.

In the New Testament it is the story of the disciples and the Lord. Like Abraham, the disciples are called to give something up, to be willing, even, to lay down their lives: "For whoever desires to save his life will lose it, and whoever loses his life for My sake will find it."[14] To acknowledge humbly that our finest thoughts and most benevolent emotions are not our own but gifts from the Lord is a way of giving them back to God. It is a way of saying, "*Cogitat*"— "He thinks"—"Therefore, I am."

Conclusion: A Consecrated Life

For fifty-six years Swedenborg strove to understand the secrets of the universe by means of his own extraordinary powers. From birth, he had been gifted with tremendous intellectual capabilities. He combined these capabilities with an unquenchable thirst to meet and know all of life, and, finally, to discover the very seat of the soul. In his search for the soul he produced voluminous materials and made profound contributions to the world of science and philosophy. But in the world of spirit, he could make no further advance until he discovered the foundation of all spiritual progress—humility. During his religious crisis, beginning around 1744, he came into deeper and deeper states of humility, until he finally acknowledged that everything of life, even his very finest thoughts (his spiritual "Isaacs") were gifts from God.

In his discovery of humility, Swedenborg began to understand the innocence and wisdom of the angels who are closest to the Lord. In describing their wisdom, Swedenborg writes: "They are the wisest of the angels of heaven; since they know that they have nothing of wisdom from themselves, and that acknowledging this is being wise. *They also know that what they know is nothing compared to what they do not know*" (emphasis Silverman's; HH 280). They are wise because they know that "no one can receive anything except what is given from heaven." They are wise because they are like little children in acknowledging that everything they have comes to them from their Heavenly Father. They are wise because they realize that what they know is relatively nothing in comparison to what they do not know—and yet, *they do know something*. The question remains: What do we do with the knowledge that we do possess? How shall we regard it? How shall we use it? "If you wish to be led by Divine Providence," says Swedenborg, "use prudence [the intellect] as a servant" (DP 210). In the allegory of Abraham's life, in the lives of the disciples, and in the life of Swedenborg himself, the intellect had to become a servant rather than a master.

In each case these men were called to make a sacrifice, to give up something they believed to be their own. The word *sacrifice* means to "make sacred or holy" (*sacre* + *ficare*). The individuals who give themselves up to God and lay down their intellectual pride become servants of the Lord. In the process they lose nothing of their original gifts, but rather discover that the miracle of transmutation has taken place. The human has received the Divine. A life has been made holy, consecrated, even as the Lord himself was glorified at what appeared to be the moment of sacrificial death.

And so, in the *Journal of Dreams*, we catch a glimpse of the period of Swedenborg's new birth, the time during which he discovered the "certain something" that would be necessary for the natural scientist to become a spiritual revelator. Retaining all his intellectual power and his undaunted zeal for the truth, he was now able to use these qualities—to consecrate them—in service to God and his neighbor. From the age of fifty-six until his death at the age of eighty-four, he labored diligently in the Lord's vineyard. Though he had let his intellectual pride die, he still retained his towering intellect. Though he had let his personal ambition die, he still retained the desire to serve the Lord with all his heart and with all his mind. He experienced the meaning of the words he would pen years later in the work *Divine Love and Wisdom*: "A person is only as a servant and house-steward appointed over the goods of his Lord" (DLW 333).

Emanuel Swedenborg was born a genius, yet his brilliant mind had to become a servant rather than a master. His life can be seen as an allegory. In Swedenborg we see the archetype of the human intellect made holy—humbly consecrated to the service of God. We hear the refrains of an old Christian hymn:

> *Take my life and let it be*
> *Consecrated Lord to thee . . .*
> *Take my intellect and use*
> *Every power as thou shalt choose . . .*
> *Take my lips and let them be*
> *Filled with messages from thee.*[15]

The real story of Swedenborg's call to the office of revelator is a spiritual one. It is the story of the birth of a servant.

Notes

1. From a cartoon by Robert Ripley in his "Believe It or Not" newspaper column series. It has been reproduced by the Swedenborg Foundation with the special permission of Robert Ripley.

2. This information is gathered from James Hyde, *A Bibliography of the Works of Emanuel Swedenborg: Original and Translated* (London: Swedenborg Society, 1906), pp. 4–109. Swedenborg's study of the brain, e.g., runs to over 1,400 pages. His work called *Principia* is in 2 volumes and comprises over 1,200 pages. Other major works include *Oeconomia Regni Animalis* (Economy of the animal kingdom, or, Dynamics of the soul's domain) in 3 volumes (1,374 pp.), and *Word Explained* (2,012 pp.). James Hyde has estimated that "the whole of Swedenborg's writing amounts to 1,372 pages folio, 10,368 pages quarto, and 7,320 pages octavo, in print, besides 1,688 pages folio, and 7,094 pages quarto, in manuscript, which have never been printed." "Notes and Reviews," *New Church Life* 30 (June 1910), p. 368, quoting from Dr. Wm. E. A. Axon in *New Church Magazine*, (January 1910). In all, this totals 27,842 pages.

3. Norris and Ross McWhirter, *Guinness Book of World Records* (New York: Sterling Publishing, 1977), p. 50.

4. Alfred Acton, *An Introduction to the Word Explained* (Bryn Athyn, Pa.: Academy of the New Church, 1927), p. 19.

5. Alfred Lord Tennyson, "Ulysses" in *Realities of Literature* (Waltham, Mass.: Xerox College Publishing, 1971) pp. 92–93

6. For a discussion of Swedenborg's nebular hypothesis, see also the article by Isaiah Tansley, "Swedenborg as Cosmologist," in *Transactions of the International Swedenborg Congress* (London: Swedenborg Society, 1912), pp. 70–85.

7. Julian K. Smyth, "The Nature of Swedenborg's Illumination," in *Transactions of ISC*, p. 222.

8. Genesis 11:1–9. "Come let us make bricks, and burn them thoroughly. . . . Come let us build ourselves a city and a tower with its top in the heavens, and let us make a name for ourselves." Also, in a letter to the Board of Mines, Swedenborg wrote: "I am influenced interiorly by the desire and longing to produce during my lifetime something real, which may be of use in the general scientific world and also to posterity, and in this way to be useful to and even to please my native country; and if my wishes are realized, *to obtain honour for it*" (emphasis Silverman's; DOC vol. 1, pp. 458–59).

9. Though it is beyond the scope of this aticle, we should mention that there have been other theories that have attempted to explain Swedenborg's illumination. Wilson Van Dusen, e.g., hypothesizes that Swedenborg was an experienced meditator, who entered extremely advanced levels of the meditative and hypnogogic states and then went beyond into trance. Van Dusen claims that "Swedenborg the empirical scientist remained a scientist reporting his findings even when he went within. . . . In a fundamental way he had chosen to examine inner processes in the most direct way possible." See *The Presence of Other Worlds* (New York: Harper & Row, 1974), pp. 33–34. Similarly, Robert Crookall, in his book *Psychic Breathing*, refers to Swedenborg as a pioneer investigator of "breath-change and the 'level' of consciousness." His thesis is that breath-changes can be used to elevate or expand consciousness. He makes special note of Swedenborg's ability to cease breathing while communicating with discarnate souls. *Psychic Breathing* (North Hollywood, Calif.: New Castle, 1985), pp. 14, 38, 55. Another, less flattering view is that of Ping Chong, artistic director of the popular performance *The Angels of Swedenborg*. During the play, a continual message is given to the audience by means of words flashing along a moving sign. The words of the message are "EMANUEL SWEDENBORG B. 1688 D. 1772 STROKE THE LORD HAS GRACIOUSLY OPENED THE SIGHT OF MY SPIRIT. HE HAS THUS RAISED ME INTO HEAVEN AND LOWERED ME INTO HELL AND HAS SHOWN ME VISUALLY WHAT EACH IS LIKE." Does it mean he died of a stroke, or that after having a stroke he experienced other states of consciousness? After the performance in Pittsburgh (November 14, 1986). I asked Mr. Chong about this. His view of the matter was that Swedenborg had spent years and years searching frantically for the soul, relying on his intellect. The "stroke" was a sort of mental breakdown, or spiritual emergence, during which time the more intuitive, instinctual part of the mind could be set free. Chong's closing image of a fictitious Swedenborg touching hands with a playful monkey beautifully represents the reintegration of the intellectual and intuitive faculties. Many people have tried to describe Swedenborg's illumination in many ways; they have sought to discover the roots of this man's wonderful receptivity to such profound and illuminating truths, truths that have been recognized by many as divine revelation. Helen Keller puts it most simply of all. She says that Swedenborg wrote "out of his heart and out of heaven's heart." *My Religion* (New York: Swedenborg Foundation, 1974), p. 104.

10. Genesis 22:1–19.

11. John 3:27.

12. Genesis 22:12.

13. Ram Dass, *The Only Dance There Is* (New York: Anchor Books, 1974), pp. 52–53. Note that while Ram Dass refers to the "transcendence of the rational," he also refers to it as a "servant" rather than a master. This is probably similar to what Swedenborg is getting at when he speaks about "the submission of the rational," as in this passage: "Unless the rational submits itself to the goods and truths of the Lord, then the rational either suffocates, perverts, or rejects the things that flow in, and still more if they flow into the sensual scientifics of the memory. This is meant by the seed falling by the wayside on stony ground. . . . But when the rational submits itself, and believes the Lord, that is, His Word, then the rational is like good ground, into which the seed falls, and bears much fruit" (AC 1940).

14. Matthew 16:25.

15. From the *Service Book and Hymnal*, authorized by the Lutheran Churches Board of Publication (Minneapolis, Minn.: Minneapolis Augsburg Publishing House, 1963), pp. 510–11.

Love: The Ultimate Reality

Lewis Field Hite

Edited and Abridged by William Ross Woofenden, Ph.D.

The original essay (of which this is an edited abridgment) was given by Professor Hite at the International Swedenborg Congress, London, in 1910. A quarter of a century later he had some afterthoughts and wrote a supplementary essay. The full text of both essays was published in 1936 by the Swedenborg Society, London, as no. 3 in their Transaction series, and is still available in that form.

ULTIMATE REALITY is the proper designation of the subject about which philosophy is peculiarly concerned. We may also say at once, God is the ultimate reality, and in doing so, our thoughts pass from the realm of philosophy to that of theology. If, for instance, we should say God is love and wisdom, and add that love and wisdom are the true and only substance and form, we make an assertion that goes to the very depths of metaphysics. If now we note that the point of this teaching is philosophically that substance and form are love and wisdom, rather than that love and wisdom are substance and form, we see that it presents a new view of substance and form.

Again, if we affirm that God is love, we merely repeat Christian tradition; but if we assert that *love is God*, we announce the fundamental thesis of a new revelation—a thesis that gives new significance to the word love, and transforms the theological doctrine that God is the ultimate reality to the philosophical statement that the ultimate reality is love. It seems inevitable, then, that I must, with what light I have from our teachings and from history in general, undertake to say what ultimate reality is as I conceive it.

Early Greek Philosophy

Early Greek philosophy began with the idea of a common background to the body of phenomena, and the term used to designate it was *nature*. This notion of nature as the material background of all the phenomena of the actual world was a permanent and, it would seem, an ineradicable achievement of human thought. It is the ultimate basis of all forms of materialism, and has its origin in the peculiar function of the intellect itself.

It may take the form of Democritean atoms, or the centers of force of Boscovich, or a homogeneous ethereal medium. In all these forms it is the outcome of analysis that has its beginnings in the ordinary operations of the intellect in practical life. Practical life demands stable objects, objects that remain self-identical, unchanged throughout any given operation; it achieves success by selecting or constructing such objects. All our intellectual operations primarily serve our practical life by discovering or by establishing order among such objects. The essence of this intellectual activity consists in detaching from the concrete life the character of permanence. In the course of time, this element of permanence is universalized and made the presupposition of all thought and the basis of all life. Thus universalized, it is what we call nature.

But the process of analysis and abstraction does not stop here. The element of permanence is individualized and located in a system of conceptual objects, giving rise to what we call the world of concepts, in Platonic language the world

LEWIS FIELD HITE was born in 1852 in Virginia and died in his ninety-third year in 1945. After graduating from the University of Virginia in 1882 he taught Latin, Greek, and philosophy in private schools until 1890. He then entered the New Church Theological School and after graduation and ordination was put on the faculty as a teacher of philosophy, a position he retained for the rest of his life. In 1904 he was granted an M.A. degree from Harvard, and in 1910–11 he spent a year abroad, studying at Heidelberg University, the University of Paris, and the College de France. For nearly twenty years he served as president of the Swedenborg Scientific Association and as editor of the *New Church Review*.

of ideas. The further the process of abstraction is carried, and the more the concepts are simplified, the nearer the approach to a mere system of relations in the homogeneous field of empty space. In other words, we are led by this process to a world that takes on more and more the character of a rigid mechanical system. This is precisely the result achieved by the human intellect in the development of Greek philosophy from Thales to Aristotle.

Aristotle

Aristotle's God was the apotheosis of the element of permanence, the unchanging and the unmoved cause of the world. His universe was a static whole, already complete, in which succession and quality were reducible ultimately to bare moments, and time itself was only a one-dimensional and reversible way of taking points in the spread-out field of space. Any critical estimate of Aristotle's philosophy must do justice to the various and complicated human motives that everywhere pervade it, but we must look for the key in the aims and methods of his analysis. A pupil of Plato for twenty years, and, as a consequence, a master of dialectic and of historical movements, his gigantic intellect swept the field of nature and of experience with penetrating insight and marvelous comprehensiveness.

He gathered up, sifted, and recast the results of human thinking, even though already presented by the consummate genius of Plato. The outcome was determined by a single controlling conception, the conception of *subject*. This conception leads back to the nature concept of early Greek philosophy, and now appears under the twofold aspect of material cause and of essence—the universal underlying background of phenomena, what we know as *substance*, the bearer of qualities, activities, changes; in short, the subject of predicates.

Whatever may be the metaphysical value of that which we call substance or thing, we are indebted to Aristotle for the clear and definite conception of it, and we do not have to look far for his motives and methods of procedure. We have seen that the world of practical life, with its concrete objects in all their variety and changes, falls a victim to the processes of analysis and abstraction which are demanded as the necessary conditions of practical success. Stability, plasticity, movability, divisibility, self-identity, and independence are the properties that practical success demands and utilizes; and these are precisely the characters that the intellect discovers, abstracts, and transforms into a conceptual world. No doubt these processes would go on under any conditions where the will and intellect could cooperate, but the supreme agency for promoting the accumulation, preservation, and organization of such experience is the faculty of speech and the use of language. But the development of language itself is due to the intellectual functions of attention, discrimination, selection—in a word, analysis and abstraction.

Language as Symbol

Language is a very simple but effective means of preserving the results of these processes. When a character is once noticed and a name is given it, the name then serves to recall it and so preserve it. Language thus serves practical convenience and acquires practical importance. It is a shorthand method of reproducing and forecasting experience. But it is equally serviceable for intellectual purposes, both as a register and a shorthand method of thought. This dependence of intellect on speech gradually develops a habit that is further cultivated by reading and writing. Ordinary thought is so symbolic that mere words are used in place of conceptions, and systems of word building become themselves objects of construction and reflection.

The result is that we have in due course the science of grammar and that marvelous creation about which the science of grammar revolves—the sentence. The sentence is the unique embodiment of conceptual thought. The subject represents the oneness and changelessness of the concept, and the predicate represents the various qualities and relations of the concept. The two simple elements of the sentence thus acquire metaphysical and logical value.

Thought proceeds, as we have seen, by severing an observed character from the concrete experience in which it is found. This tree is green, that tree is green, and so on indefinitely. Here "tree" stands for the abiding background, and "green" for the constant character. We have various terms for designating this distinction. In grammar it is substantive and adjective; in metaphysics it is thing and quality, substance and form, or substance and attribute; in logic, subject and predicate, term and relation, subject and object. Now, observe that both subject and predicate are concepts, and the concepts are united by a third concept which we call relation. The two concepts in this relation become subject and predicate, and constitute what we call a judgment. The judgment, expressed in words, is the sentence.

This analysis was required to emphasize the fact that thought proceeds with concepts, and language is the product of thought; but thought itself has developed historically as the servant of practical life, and has been controlled by this use. Nevertheless, after having reached a certain stage of development, thought became itself the object of independent interest, and it may be said that Greek philosophy culminated in the triumph of this interest. In other words, Aristotle's logic was the characteristic achievement of Greek philosophy.

Empty Formalism

In the light of the foregoing discussion, we are now able to see that the inevitable outcome of Aristotle's philosophy was empty formalism, a reduction of all concrete experience to abstract conceptions. His analysis of experience stopped with the identification of concepts, and his logic was a formal treatment of concepts in the abstract. It inhered in his undertaking that the further he went in the investigation and treatment of formal thought, the further he left behind him both the concrete experience and the practical life from which he set out. This criticism, however, does not in the least depreciate the value of his achievement. It merely calls attention to its proper character and function in the development of philosophy. Nor does it ignore the fact that Aristotle's conception of reality was far richer than that which the logical outcome of his method indicated.

We need to be reminded that Aristotle was not fully conscious of his task as metaphysician. He accepted in the main the results of early Greek philosophy. He adopted without thoroughgoing criticism the presuppositions of ordinary thought and common sense. He saw in language the natural, characteristic, and fundamental expression of reality, and in the sentence the fundamental constitution of reality. He overlooked the fact that thought is only one of the functions of life, and that it is subservient to life—that it springs out of concrete experience and is developed primarily out of purely practical interests.

Under the requirements of practical and social life, it produces the elements of speech and the form of the sentence. In this way the sentence acquires metaphysical value and, for ordinary thought, determines metaphysical theory. Aristotle unwittingly and uncritically took the grammarian's point of view and made the structure of the sentence the basis of his metaphysics. His logic developed from this starting point. The grammatical subject represented the ultimate reality, and the predicate represented the various states, qualities, and activities of reality. This at once commits us to all the consequences of intellectualism and, in the end, as we have seen, materialism.

One Bright Spot

Subsequent history shows how these consequences were brought out and adhered to. It is unnecessary to trace the course of post-Aristotelian schools, or to point out that the Stoics and the Epicureans, working with Aristotelian conceptions, ended in constructing a purely mechanical universe. The one bright spot in the metaphysics of this period was that created by the transcendent genius of Plotinus, who for the first time in the history of philosophy subjected the nature of thought to systematic and penetrating criticism, and who made out clearly its instrumental and derivative character. As against Aristotle, he denied the ultimate reality of *thought* and affirmed that of *feeling*. Unfortunately he had only Aristotelian terms and concepts to work with, and these were inadequate for the expression of his insight.

Scholasticism

Scholasticism was a revival of Aristotelianism, and moved strictly within Aristotelian metaphysics. Descartes, Spinoza, and Leibniz had the advantage of the new scientific movement; but they, too, accepted as fundamental the subject-predicate metaphysics of Aristotle and tried to build their systems on it. Descartes made a deliberate attempt to turn his back on tradition and make a fresh start, but he very soon fell into the Aristotelian net. The self-assertive, self-certain ego that Augustine had made fundamental in metaphysics Descartes cast into the mold of Aristotle's subject-predicate formula, and proceeded to develop his system in terms of Aristotelian logic and on the lines of familiar tradition. His *res cogitans* [thinking substance] and *res extensa* [extended substance] were simple reaffirmations of the old doctrine of substance; and the two worlds, the spiritual and the material, were merely new editions of our familiar friends, the sensory and supersensory realms of Plato.

Spinoza and Leibniz

Spinoza developed the doctrine of substance in a more strictly systematic way, and for the first time brought out the intellectualistic and materialistic implications of that doctrine.

Leibniz, with the possible exception of Plotinus, the greatest metaphysician since Plato, made some significant alterations in the traditional conception of substance, and by his doctrine of monads freed it in a measure from materialistic implications. But even Leibniz, with all his genius for analysis and reconstruction, fell a victim to intellectualism. His monads turn out in the end to be little more than positions in space. His universe is one in which nothing ever really happens. The monad and the universe that it reflects are what they are: fixed and eternal. Nothing from the outside can affect or change the monad, and there is nothing in the universe that is not already in the monad.

In other words, the ultimately real thing in the universe is the monad and its states, and these states are eternally self-identical and changeless. Whatever may be said of this outcome, Leibniz has the lasting credit of carrying out to the logical conclusion the fundamental conceptions that inhere in any subject-predicate philosophy taken as an ultimate metaphysics.

Every philosophy that makes substance its fundamental category ends, as first Spinoza and after him Leibniz showed, in reducing the universe to states of this substance. The universe is then truly describable by propositions that express only analytical judgments. The so-called synthetic judgments are merely premature and provisional forms of thought, which are convenient for the time being, but which must in the end be set aside and replaced by the analytic. In other words, all characters, qualities, and properties that are expressed by predicates inhere in the subject and are evolved from the subject. These characters, as such, exist eternally in the subject, and our universe falls back into a static, self-identical repose. This follows for the reason that both substance and quality are abstractions and, as such, colorless, changeless, self-identical concepts. Such a universe is the product of abstraction, and was already prefigured in the first attempts of mankind to use intellectual processes in the service of practical life, where distinction, separation, analysis, and reconstruction are necessary for success.

We see from this rapid survey that philosophy chose from the first the intellectualistic trend, that Aristotle forged its fundamental conceptions, and that Spinoza and Leibniz worked these conceptions into their logical consequences.

After Leibniz, philosophy either went off into psychological and epistemological excursions, or became severely self-critical. Criticism found its best expression in the Kantian episode. The constructive efforts of German idealism may occupy us later, as will also the more recent metaphysics of the present day.

Swedenborg's Teaching About Love

It is now time to fix our attention on a figure and a teaching that appeared in the world's intellectual firmament almost without historical associations or historical introduction. This figure was that of Emanuel Swedenborg, and the teaching was his *doctrine of love.*

In spite of his sudden and unique appearance on the world's stage, however, Swedenborg had some historical relations that must be constantly borne in mind; otherwise, we are liable to misread him. The fact that he wrote in neoclassical Latin puts him in the Aristotelian tradition. This gives his language the superficial appearance of abstract conceptualism, and almost mechanical dogmatism, which has misled many casual and especially unsympathetic readers. Nevertheless, we have here the key to his historical position, and it is necessary to acquire a competent knowledge of Aristotle (and to some extent the Aristotelian revival in scholasticism) as a preparation for reading him with critical accuracy.

Effects of the Cartesian Controversy

A more direct relation to history is indicated by the fact that he was educated at Uppsala during the period of the Cartesian controversy, and was thus brought under the spell of the revolutionary spirit and imbued with the fresh intellectual impulses of the age. His frequent references to Aristotle, and his careful study of Wolff, suggest that he was at home in the earliest and latest phases of traditional philosophy. But there is little indication that he ever subjected philosophy in whole or in part to systematic criticism. On the other hand, it seems to have been his habitual method to take the terms and conceptions as he found them, embedded in the language and thought of his day, and use them for his own purposes without caring to keep strictly to their historical meaning. Thus, in a general way we may consider Swedenborg's philosophy as resting, in language at least, rather freely on the influence of scholasticism and common sense—understanding by common sense the popularized results of previous philosophies.

When, therefore, we approach the study of Swedenborg, we must expect to meet the usual mechanical metaphors of ordinary speech and popular science, as well as the technical terms and conceptions of a highly refined philosophical vocabulary. At the same time we must be prepared to see a free use of these as instruments, and be ever careful to interpret them in the light of his own point of view and purpose.

Two Apparently Diverse Tendencies

Our rapid sketch of the history of philosophy has shown us that the notion of ultimate reality has followed two apparently diverse tendencies, the one ending in the atomic theory, and the other in a system of abstract ideas. Around the former have gathered all the interests of materialism, and around the latter the spiritual ideals and aspirations of civilized humanity. But the tendencies are really identical, for the atomic theory is only a convenient stopping place in the process of analysis that, when carried out rigorously, ends in a system of mere positions in space; and this is precisely the outcome of pushing the analysis of ideas to the extreme. It is really due to misconceptions and confusion that idealistic and spiritual interests have centered about a conceptual world. Such a world is as far as possible removed from the actual spiritual world. The spiritual world, like the kingdom of God, is within you. We must therefore turn our backs on any and every form of a conceptual world when we approach Swedenborg for his answer to the question: "What is ultimate reality?"

Swedenborg's Ultimate Reality

Swedenborg's ultimate reality is in the strictest sense spiritual. His spiritual world was made known to him in concrete living experience. The divine nature was revealed to him in the depths of religious feeling and intuition. The world of nature was to him a mirror of the divine and the human. God was to him the perfect type of concrete life, equally removed from Stoic pantheism and from the transcendental, abstract wisdom of Aristotle. Ultimate reality was located by him not in a far-off conceptual region, but was directly sought in the infinite complexity, variety, and richness of experience as it comes.

Already, in his *Principia* [1734], Swedenborg had come to see the futility of attempting to discover reality by processes of analysis. He saw that logical and mathematical entities carry you into a field where analysis breaks down and where the complexities of life again assert themselves as the real background. Again, in his work of the same year, *The Infinite*, although the demands of reason are freely and fully conceded, rational analysis gives place in the end to the direct affirmation of personal life as the properly apprehensible reality. Later [1763], in *Divine Love and Wisdom* 229, we have the definite and explicit statement that analysis does not arrive at any simple entity such as the atom or ultimate particle, but discovers greater and greater complexity.

Not Thought, but Feeling

Indeed, throughout the period of his illumination Swedenborg consistently assigned to rationality as its true function the task of taking what was given to it in spiritual perception, and in this light establishing relations between the various kinds and degrees of life, especially between natural and spiritual life. According to him, the substantive element in life is not thought, but feeling: the elements to which we refer such functions as effort, striving, want, satisfaction, fulfillment, joy, and the like. Life in its first intention is, for reflection, that more or less undifferentiated mass of awareness, that sense of existence, of well-being, of efficiency, of fullness and wholeness which is the common background, source, and fountain of all particulars and of all development.

Swedenborg sums up the situation and points us to the central and fundamental feature of experience in the opening paragraph of *Divine Love and Wisdom*, by the simple formula, "Life is love." This doctrine of life is a new conception in the history of human thought, and philosophically it is the most important of all of the fundamental conceptions that mankind has framed. All of his other great doctrines grow out of it, and it is destined to modify fundamentally the philosophy of the world.

In the beginning of *Divine Love and Wisdom*, and earlier in *Arcana Coelestia* [1749–56], Swedenborg notes the distinguishing mark that separates experience into the twofold aspects of the direct, unreflective, massive on the one hand, and the indirect, reflective, articulate on the other. The former he designates by the term *love*, and makes the critical observation that people have not known what love is, though they have known of its existence, as the use of the word itself testifies. And he explains that people have not known what love is because, when they reflect on it, they always observe some particular state or affection of love, some quality distinguished and selected, and so dissociated from the total mass; or, as we shall say later, externalized and objectified. But of love in its immediacy and wholeness, no idea, mental image, or representation can be formed.

That love is life may be argued from the fact that the word can be used with the names of all the functions of life, as the love of eating, of music, of nature, of God, and so on indefinitely; and, further, it is demonstrated by the simple experiment of taking away all the affections of love, and observing that the activities of life cease.

Thought or Action

Swedenborg further remarks in criticism of the whole course of philosophy down to his day that, for lack of knowing what love is, people have made one or the other of two fundamental mistakes: maintaining either that *thought* is life, or that *action* is life. The former is the view of Aristotelianism and in general of all forms of intellectualism—in short, the view of traditional philosophy; the latter, of all schools of materialism. Swedenborg corrects both of these philosophies by affirming that thought is the first effect of life, action the second effect. He goes on to make a distinction in the grades of thought, and says that, strictly speaking, the first effect of life is the thought or perception of ends or goals. This is inmost thought or the highest degree of thought, while thought of means and thought of results—of accomplished facts—are of relatively lower grade. This passage (DLW 2) is important, not only because of its effective criticism of historic opinion, but because it gives us the key to Swedenborg's philosophical point of view and method. For there is implied in this statement his doctrine of end, cause, and effect—a doctrine that gives us the fundamental conceptions of his metaphysics (DLW 167–72).

We have already seen that scholasticism was the outcome of the recovery and appropriation of Greek thought as presented and transmitted in the works of Aristotle. We have also seen that Aristotle's basic conceptions centered on notions of subject and predicate, or the notion of substance. The notion of substance also plays a large part in Swedenborg's philosophy. Aristotle undertook to interpret early Greek philosophy as a search for causes, and he reduced the conceptions of "cause" to four. But he finally resolved the notion of cause into that of substance. Nevertheless, he set out in his *Metaphysics* to show that the highest and most complete stage of knowledge is the knowledge of causes.

This idea was transmitted to scholasticism and reappears variously in Swedenborg. But both the notion of substance and the notion of cause were used by him concretely in a way that gave them virtually a new meaning, and it is in his doctrine of love that he gives them this concrete meaning.

Substance Identified with Love

In the case of substance, this is done most effectively, perhaps, where he identifies substance with love (DLW 40–46). The point of this teaching is not so much that love is substance as it is that substance is love. In other words, we are not to identify love with the abstract conceptual entity ordinarily termed substance, but rather we are to take the word *substance* with its whole meaning, and apply it to that concrete living experience which we know directly, immediately, and intimately as love.

This doctrine, so interpreted, constitutes a new epoch in the history of philosophy, for according to it we turn our search for reality from the world of abstract conceptions, to the actual, concrete world of living experience. And this experience, in all its fullness and variety, we now call love. The whole body of Swedenborg's teaching, and the philosophy contained in it, is literally an exposition of the nature of love. In this doctrine, love has many aspects: psychological, moral, religious, theological, and metaphysical. Our present purpose limits us specifically to the metaphysical. The proper starting point for the treatment of this aspect is the development of love in the series of end, cause, and effect.

Aristotle, in treating substance as essence, constructed a theory of development in which the two notions of cause, the formal and final, played the chief roles. But this method led him off into the consequences of abstract conceptual and mechanical analysis, where all life was in the end excluded.

Swedenborg adopts the notion of end, but keeps it concrete and living by conceiving it as a present state or affection of love. Any such present state, when made focal to attention and objectified, carries with it the quality and meaning of the love from which it springs, and so is representative of the love. In other words, the love sees its own quality and meaning reflected, revealed, and existent in the state as in a specific instance. When the state or affection, with its quality and meaning, is taken as thus representative, the meaning suggests fulfillment, and this becomes an object of desire, striving, and anticipated satisfaction.

The formation and existence of such states are characteristic of life. The process involves all those functions which correspond to the words *awareness, consciousness, feeling, emotion, effort, striving, longing, change, activity, force, movement,* and a host of others, which are all summed up in the word *love*. All these qualities lie behind the state and seek expression in it; and it belongs to the intimate and constant nature of love to project and *constitute* such states. It is its creative function, a function of self-projection, generation, limitation, definition.

The Role of Fulfillment

To use a gross figure of speech, though one consecrated by Plotinus, love is the total mass of feeling or awareness that bubbles over in those forms of experience we call particular states or affections. To use a figure less materialistic, love is the body of spirit that possesses all the qualities it reveals, and these, as they emerge in distinct consciousness, are observed, are identified as persistent or frequent, and are defined as uniform; receive names, and so become fixed, established, and communicable features of experience. Such qualities come to view out of the depths of love unceasingly and with endless variety. Being present, living, self-conscious, self-identical affections of love, they are its self-representative images, in which the love sees its own longing for self-realization reproduced in the definite striving of the particular affection. In this relation, the affection presents to the love the opportunity for further fulfillment; and as offering such fulfillment, the affection is an end.

The character of achievement is fundamental in the processes of life. Around it cluster innumerable functions that are, as it were, polarized with respect to it. The elements of desire, longing, striving, effort, and the like, are distinguished from those of satisfaction, contentment, enjoyment, realization, fulfillment, achievement, and so on. The latter are set over against and contrasted with the former. In this way the characters of nearness and remoteness arise as contrasting features of experience. Nearness means the feeling of intimacy and immediacy; and these, as properties of the former group, are referred back to the basic, undifferentiated total background that, in the language of our present discourse, we call the active, generating, particularizing love. This reference is made by such words as *I, me, subject, subjective*. On the other hand, the group of characters clustering about the element of fulfillment are more or less dissociated from the primary mass and consolidated into an independent group. The process here involved we denote variously by such words as *project, externalize, objectify*; while of the group thus distinguished and set off, we use, among others, the words *objective* and *object*. Meanwhile, all that we are really doing is simply observing the affections of love and making distinctions in its activities and functions.

One of these functions, inhering in the essence of love and coextensive with its being, is the function variously termed *seeing, perception, awareness, consciousness, thought, wisdom*, and so on, almost indefinitely. Love is throughout and always active and is possessed of this function in the whole and in every detail. It is that function whereby two states of love are mutually present to each other, and share each other's qualities, but at the same time preserve each their own self-identity and also their difference from each other. It is by virtue of this function of *knowing* that the mysterious parting of experience into subjective and objective aspects takes place. The act of knowing is simple and original; it cannot be reduced to lower terms; but the very act itself generates those characters of contrast, otherness, and remoteness which we denote by the words *objectivity* and *object*.

Ends or Goals

With this conception of love let us return to the consideration of ends. An affection, projected and constituted an end with the characters of remoteness, self-identity, and relative independence, is a perceptive mass having perceptive relations with the total love of which it is a present, living, particular state. The total love sees in the *end* the realization of its own purpose, and the end sees in the love the source of its own existence and the conditions of its own fulfillment. The total love strives to fill the end with its own immediate presence, satisfaction, and enjoyment; the end strives to gather into itself all the insights, satisfactions, enjoyments, and activities of the love.

This situation is exemplified in the biological field by the behavior of a unicellular organism, which is ever putting forth parts of its mass in the form of projections. Among the various projections it selects one, and then gradually moves its whole mass into this terminus or end. This is the type of all movement in the organic world. The earthworm extends its forward extremity and then draws the rest of its body toward it, and in this way moves from place to place. More highly organized animals put forward certain parts called limbs, and then draw the body into the new position. In this way bodily movement is effected.

Mental activity is precisely similar in type. The mind, spirit, love, projects a part of its mass in what we call an end or goal. Then it moves into that end, and thus makes the end the new center. This we call making progress, moving to a new position, or fulfilling a purpose. In the case of man, and presumably the higher animals, this mental motion is so coordinated with the bodily functions that it gives rise to bodily movement. In other words, the mind carries the body with it in the accomplishment of purposes. The behavior of a simple cell is thus seen to be typical of the nature and movement of universal life, that is, of universal love. The word *end* is properly used for the terminus of this movement. In Swedenborg's language (DLW 167) it is called an end because it is the end of this movement of the state of love.

End as Idea

We now pass to the second stage of the end. As a state to be reached, the end is an *idea*. It is, as we have seen, a particularized affection of love that has emerged and become disengaged from the immediacy of feeling by the act of attention, and thus set off from love. This whole process is summed up in the word *objectify*. Any state is objectified, made an object, by the mere fact of fixing attention on it. It is thereby distinguished and selected from among the numberless constantly emerging states that occupy the conscious threshold.

An idea, then, is a state of consciousness that is the essence of love in that as a self-projection of the love it retains the qualities of the love; in general, the qualities of feeling and perception. The love is therefore self-represented in the idea. But an idea tends to develop relations to other states of love, whether these be other ideas or mere vague feelings, or more pronounced states, such as emotions, longings, desires. Between the idea and all such states there is mutual reference and participation by virtue of their common ground in the love and their relation to the love as its self-representatives. The mutual relations between the idea and the love as exhibited in the totality of such mediating states constitute the field of articulate consciousness, or, to use the specific term, the field of love's wisdom. In fact, it is perhaps the most fundamental definition of wisdom to say that it is love's self-representative function; for the field of this function is the system of ideas projected as perceptive units from the total love.

When in this field one of these perceptive units is selected as, for the moment or the occasion, the special embodiment of the meaning and purpose of love, this unit then becomes the vehicle of love's fulfillment, and as such is what we have called an end. But, evidently, in the passage to fulfillment, between the stages of want, desire, longing, striving, and that of satisfaction and achievement, there intervenes the field of ideas through which the love and the end cooperate in bringing about the fulfillment. The end selects within the field of ideas those which are referred to in its meaning and which seek embodiment in itself. The love with reference to the end chooses the same ideas as being contained within its purpose.

At this stage the end exists as a system of ideas contained within a single purpose, and organized about the initial stage whose meaning develops into this system. But this second stage of the end, or second end, is constituted of ideas that have the common feature of pointing to a situation in which the organization is complete, the meanings expressed, the desires fulfilled, and the purpose achieved. The affection originally projected and constituted an end is now no longer felt merely as a state to be realized, but the conditions of realization are actually present, and the affection is concretely existent and active in its sought-for context and environment.

The end, therefore, exists successively in three stages: (1) as present affection whose meaning points to a situation to be constructed by the group of ideas and affections in which the meaning would be fulfilled; (2) as the system of ideas included within the meaning of the affection and pointing to the situation in which that meaning would be expressed; and (3) as the completely organized group wherein the affection and its system of ideas are concretely existent and active. In this concrete, active existence we have the fact of fulfillment.

Reviewing the Process

If, now, we review this process, it is evident that the second stage arises, as a development of the first, in a context of elements that first come into the new relation by being selected as included within the meaning of the end; in other words, the end is self-represented in them. But these states in which the end at this stage exists are themselves developed out of the concrete mass of the total love as its self-representatives. They therefore carry with them the qualities of the love seeking effectuation in the end. This relation to fulfillment we call, in common speech, *means*.

Further, it is evident that it is the collection and grouping of these subsidiary ends with reference to the culmination that produces the concrete situation that has been in view from the beginning. This third stage, then, is brought into existence by completing the process of fitting together the relatively dissociated and independent elements of the second stage into the organized context of the initial affection. The result is properly termed a *product*, and the efficiency of the process that leads to the result is expressed by the word *cause*. In ordinary language the relation between these stages, the second and third, is expressed by the terms *cause* and *effect*.

The three stages may be designated respectively *affection, idea, fact*. Affection is the present, immediate element of feeling; idea, the more or less dissociated elements to be grouped; fact, the concrete existence of the affection in its new context, the completely organized group.

This is Swedenborg's doctrine of *end, cause*, and *effect*; and it is a doctrine that grows directly out of his conception of love. With this conception in mind, we see the full significance of such statements as "There are three things which

follow in sequence, called 'first end,' 'intermediate end,' and 'last end.' If any entity is to have real existence, these three must be simultaneously present within it." Again, "The purpose is wholly within the means and wholly within the result as well" (DLW 167–68).

As these three stages of love grow out of its inmost and complete nature, they must belong to it universally.

The Three Processes

The processes of *self-projection, self-representation*, and *self-realization*, which we have found to be the essential characteristics of experience as we directly and most intimately know it in our own personal life, we assume to be characteristic of all experience. If we look at the universe in the light of this view, we see that it is in the strictest sense the process of love. The process of self-projection, self-representation, and self-realization are everywhere going on.

Assuming the truth of the nebular hypothesis, the planets of our solar systems are in origin projected masses of the sun, and in the planets the activities of the sun are reproduced and continued. The earth is everywhere putting up from its mass the bodies of plants. Plants are forever reproducing themselves in the form of seeds; likewise animals. In the mental or spiritual world we see the perpetual processes of putting forth ideas and realizing ideals and ends. *Production, reproduction, action, creation, life* are names for the processes of love.

In short, the universe is love. This being the case, the background of the universe, its core, what we otherwise call its source, first cause, or prime substance, is the total love in its aspect and capacity forming ends of numberless grades of comprehensiveness. The most comprehensive would be the self-represented idea of the universe itself, in which the full nature and whole purpose of love would be expressed. The variety, order, and subordination of ends points to that character of love which can be adequately expressed only in an infinite system, a system in which self-propagation or self-representation is the law.

An Infinity of Infinities

From this point of view love exhibits the character of an infinity of infinities. Among such infinities are the animal and plant series; also such series as the rational and moral life. It is as a member of such series, and as constituting such series, that the individual is a proper function of the universe, and is related to the universe as a whole.

Among the more comprehensive grades of ends, we distinguish the relatively free and the relatively fixed. Self-projected states of love may preserve, according to their meaning and purpose, a separateness and independence that allow only a relatively free context, which is developed largely from its own self-active nature. We call this realm in general the spiritual world. In our present finite life we have something analogous in what we call the ideal world. In either case, the characteristic is self-developing freedom. The total life of the spiritual world is the expression of one purpose, the purpose, namely, to represent and realize particular states of love under relatively free conditions.

But the end thus constituted is pervaded with meanings that point to further perfection. The self-representative and self-realizing nature of love demands greater remoteness, that is, otherness, on the part of its self-projected states. Such states are self-representative in the measure of their relatively independent self-activity. This purpose of love is further fulfilled in those self-identical centers which are organized in relatively stable groups. In this way a further comprehensive end is constituted, which has in view a compact organization of such centers and groups. This region we call the natural world.

The natural world, then, is a second comprehensive end, differing from the end we have called the spiritual world by the fact that it is fulfilled under conditions of greater fixity and uniformity. Thus we have three grades of ends, or three degrees of existence: the divine, the spiritual, and the natural.

The Divine of Love, Wisdom, and Use

The divine is self-represented in the spiritual and, through the spiritual, in the natural. This is the relation of correspondence. It is self-realized in the spiritual and, through the spiritual, in the natural. This is influx. The spiritual and the natural are self-projections of the divine. This is creation.

It would take volumes to work out in detail the various aspects of this doctrine of love; but it is admirably summed up in that remarkable section in *Divine Love and Wisdom* headed: "There are three things in the Lord which are the Lord—divine love, divine wisdom, and divine use" (296). These three are correlated with the three degrees of purpose; or: end, cause, and effect.

We have, in this statement, doctrine about the constitution of the personal life universally, and it is doctrine about the constitution of ultimate reality. According to it, ultimate reality is personal life, and personal life is love. Speaking, then, in the light of history and of doctrine, we may affirm that ultimate reality is love.

New Jerusalem in the World

Inge Jonsson, Ph.D.

Translated by Catherine Djurklou

The article that follows originally appeared as chapter 9 of Inge Jonsson's *Emanuel Swedenborg*, published by Twayne Publishers in 1971, and is reproduced here with minor modifications. It is included in this anthology as an introduction to a scholar whose work is especially relevant for the reader exploring Swedenborg's ideas in the context of European philosophy and theology.

ONE AFTERNOON IN August 1764, Carl Christopher Gjörwell, head of the Royal Library, visited Swedenborg in his house on Hornsgatan in Stockholm. The visitor found him in the garden tending his flowers and was invited to take a stroll and enjoy the splendor of late summer. Gjörwell's errand was to request Swedenborg to present his most recent works to the Royal Library. This request was received very graciously: "Most willingly," Swedenborg answered and added: "Besides, I had intended to send them there, as my purpose in publishing them has been to make them known, and to place them in the hands of intelligent people." As they walked, the kindly and sprightly old man gave the librarian a detailed report on the fundamentals of his theological system interspersed with entertaining glimpses of the spiritual world.[1] Later, in the August issue of his periodical, *Svenska Mercurius*, Gjörwell reported that all Swedenborg's theological works had been received by the Royal Library as a gift from the author.[2]

This idyllic scene is characteristic not only of Swedenborg's friendliness and his sunny nature, documented by many of his contemporaries, but also of the manner in which his ideas were disseminated. Gjörwell's visit occurred a few years after the learned of Stockholm had become aware of the celebrity in their midst, and the librarian himself had spread the word in earlier reports in his publication. In a letter from the beginning of the 1760s, Swedenborg's former assessor colleague, Daniel Tilas, wrote that "the whole town" had recently buzzed with talk about Swedenborg's mystical talents, of which nobody had ever heard: due to the theological censorship in Sweden the great theological volumes had been published abroad and also anonymously (DOC vol. 2, pp. 395–97). It was at about the same time that he began to attract attention abroad, particularly in Germany through Johann August Ernesti's extremely negative criticism and Friedrich Christoph Oetinger's positive and well-informed reviews.[3]

Swedenborg never played the role of a sectarian preacher but relied wholly on his writings, which he, of course, hoped would reach as many qualified readers as possible. Despite the prevailing censorship, he seems to have had no problem in giving away copies of them in Sweden until the last few years, when the consistory in Göteborg held a minor heresy trial of his first real disciples in the country. It was by no means only the Royal Library that received his books, but a long series of the temporal and spiritual leaders of the realm, with whom Swedenborg maintained close relationships. Perhaps the foremost of them all, Anders Johan von Höpken, one of the most brilliant cultural personalities of eighteenth-century Sweden, was fascinated by Swedenborg's theological philosophy and impressed by his intellectual gifts, though doubtful of the value of the descriptions

INGE JONSSON was born in Stockholm in 1928. He graduated from the University of Stockholm in 1961 and has since then held different positions at the same university. In 1973 he was appointed professor of general and comparative literature, in 1978 was dean of the Faculty of History and Philosophy, and is currently president-elect of the university. He is a member of the Royal Swedish Academy of Sciences and the Royal Academy of Letters, History, and Antiquities, as well as of other societies. Among his books may be mentioned *Swedenborgs skapelsedrama* (*Swedenborg's Drama of Creation*) "*De Cultu et amore Dei*" (diss., Stockholm 1961), *Swedenborgs korrespondenslära* (*Swedenborg's Doctrine of Correspondence*) (1969), *Emanuel Swedenborg* (in English, 1971), *Swedenborg* (with Olle Hjern, 1976), *I symbolens hus* (*In the House of the Symbol*) (1983), and *Den sköna lögnen* (*The Beautiful Lie*) (1986).

of the life of the spirits (DOC vol. 2, pp. 405–16).

In attempting to sketch Swedenborg's importance in the history of ideas, it is, of course, essential to differentiate between direct influences, conveyed by various kinds of Swedenborgian societies and congregations, and indirect effects via individual literary works. Obviously the two sometimes coincide, but in general the purpose of the many New Church [Swedenborgian; see Glossary] congregations was to make converts within or without the existing Christian churches, while Swedenborg's influence on belles lettres is in no sense confined to those who wholeheartedly embraced his faith. The earliest effects of his authorship in Sweden can be divided roughly into two groups, which can also be defined geographically. First, we have theological influences in the limited sense of the term, which were concentrated in the dioceses of Göteborg and Skara and which began to be felt at the end of the 1760s. It is true that they caused considerable unrest, even a heresy trial in Göteborg, but in general Swedenborg's rationalistic theology could be accommodated to the accepted doctrines of the Church of Sweden; and it is remarkable how many priests in West Sweden were in sympathy with Swedenborg's teaching in the last decade of the eighteenth century and on into the nineteenth.[4]

The other group had its center in Stockholm with strong ties to the tolerant court of King Gustav III. It was of another type, occult and syncretistic in the sense that Swedenborg's theories were found to provide a rational explanation of all kinds of mysticism, from alchemy to animal magnetism. And it was in Stockholm in the middle of the 1780s that the first Swedish society for the translation and publication of Swedenborg's works was founded, the so-called Exegetic-Philanthropic Society [see Glossary]; it managed to get a few small sections into print before the authorities put their foot down. The ban was effected on the initiative of the church, but strangely enough it was supported by the radical advocates of the Enlightenment. This unholy alliance can be explained by the occult aspect of the society, which made it the target for journalistic attacks, the sharpest and most skillfully worded of which was written by the poet Johan Henric Kellgren.[5] In the eyes of the educated, Swedenborg thus came to be a symbol of folly and befuddled thinking, a stigma that has still not completely disappeared, even though the generation of writers that succeeded him, the young Romantics of the first decades of the nineteenth century, did a great deal to correct Kellgren's profoundly unfair picture.

However, it was outside Sweden's borders that Swedenborg's influence was greatest: this was natural in the light of his own citizenship in the international republic of the learned. The reactions in the nearest major cultural area, the German, appeared at about the same time as the Swedish, in the 1760s; and we have mentioned on several occasions the Swabian theologian F. C. Oetinger as the first example of a perceptive and fascinated reader of Swedenborg. But Oetinger did not determine the German attitude, even though his support resulted in the publication of collections of Swedenborg documents at a very early stage and in the translation of his works. It was a much more powerful spirit that influenced the German image of Swedenborg, namely, Immanuel Kant. Kant must also be given much of the blame for the distortion of Swedenborg's work that arises when the entire emphasis is placed on the conversations with spirits. Kant was one of the first readers of *Arcana Coelestia*, and the experience made him extremely disappointed in the author, to whom he was favorably predisposed. It was in this mood that he wrote his biting attack, the famous *Träume eines Geistersehers* (*Dreams of a Spirit-Seer*, 1766).[6] The tract introduced Kant's accounting with the principles of traditional metaphysics that culminated in *Critique of Pure Reason*: Swedenborg's admirers can thus find some comfort in the circumstance that his negative influence had extraordinary effects.

But Swedenborg's importance to German intellectual evolution is not entirely negative, even though Kant's scornful pamphlet made his admirers cautious and reticent. In a review of Lavater's *Aussichten in die Ewigkeit* in 1773, the young Goethe advised the later-so-famous physiognomist to study Swedenborg—superfluous advice, indeed, because Lavater had been in correspondence with the author of *Arcana*, but it does reflect the reviewer's positive attitude.[7] Despite Kant's one-sided and strangely ill-informed condemnation, Swedenborg became an active force in German tradition and was sometimes even included in it. In his tremendously widely read and discussed book, *Rembrandt als Erzieher* (*Rembrandt as Educator*, 1890), Julius Langbehn wrote that Swedenborg's doctrine of the unity of the organisms corresponds "to the thinking of every truly German spirit": a greater tribute could scarcely have been paid in such a culturally chauvinistic context.[8]

The Exegetic-Philanthropic Society in Stockholm had active relations with a number of occult counterparts in Germany, but its closest prototypes were the Swedenborgian societies founded in England in 1782 and 1783; many personal relationships were established with members, and there were certain transactions with manuscripts and letters in Swedenborg's handwriting. The first independent Swedenborg congregation, the origin of the worldwide New Church, was founded in London at the end of the 1780s, and it is primarily due to the efforts of the English and American societies that Swedenborg's works were translated and his manuscripts published—a magnificent effort, not least when one recalls that the membership has probably never exceeded twenty thousand.[9] In the same decade, Swedenborg was introduced in the United States. On June 2, 1784, the following advertisement appeared in the *Pennsylvania Gazette*, as Marguerite Beck Block tells us in her book on Sweden-borgianism in America:

> For the Sentimentalists. A Discourse on the extraordinary Science of Celestial and Terrestrial Connections and Correspondences, recently revived by the late honorable and learned Emanuel Swedenborg, will be delivered by Mr. James Glen, an humble Pupil and Follower of the said Swedenborg's at 8 o'clock on the evening of Saturday the 5th of June 1784, at Bell's Book-Store, near St. Paul's Church, in Third St., Philadelphia.[10]

The contributions of these enthusiasts led to Swedenborg's becoming a part of the cultural heritage of England and the United States to a far greater extent than in his homeland, and a very long list of prominent readers and disciples could be cited. William Blake was one of the signatories of the conference resolutions in the newly founded London congregation in 1789, and he dedicated mind and heart to his research on Swedenborg during the next few years. But his revolutionary spirit could not subordinate itself to any system, neither Swedenborg's nor, even less, his disciples' interpretations of it. Instead, the most tangible reminiscences of Swedenborg in Blake's poetry are in the form of parody and satire. The very title of his remarkable *The Marriage of Heaven and Hell* (1790) is a critical allusion to *De Coelo et . . . de Inferno . . .* (1758)—known as *Heaven and Hell* in English—which expresses the poet's aversion to Swedenborg's strict distinction between good and evil. The disposition is also a parody of the master: a "Memorable Fancy" concludes every chapter, comparable to Swedenborg's memorabilia. Despite these defiant gestures, Blake received decisive impulses from Swedenborg, not the least concerning the interpretation of the Bible; and his reading of newly translated works such as *Divine Love and Wisdom* and *Divine Providence*—a temperamental reading with pen in hand—aroused his need for a personal stand on problems of decisive importance.[11]

William Blake is admittedly one of the most profoundly original geniuses in the history of literature, but his ambivalent attitude to Swedenborg can nevertheless be regarded as typical of the reactions of the poets. It is hard to find any great writer who accepted Swedenborg without reservation or who involved himself in any New Church congregation. Therefore it is frequently difficult to determine Swedenborg's influence. Henry James, Sr., overcame a severe mental crisis in the middle of the 1840s—a *vastatio* [vastation; see Glossary] in Swedenborg's terminology—as a result of being advised to read Swedenborg; the first works he read were those studied so thoroughly by Blake. This experience made him a faithful though independent disciple for the rest of his life. He published anonymously *The Secret of Swedenborg* and had contacts with Swedenborgian circles. He never joined the New Church, but evolved a personal interpretation of Swedenborg without proselytic aspirations. In the words of Henry James, Jr., "The temple of Swedenborg stood in the centre of our family life." What appears to have been of greatest concern in this temple was the morally activist aspect of the master's teaching, the experience of the creation as an unceasing progression toward the Kingdom of God, the belief that man can help to hasten the achievement of this goal by conquering his egoism and his attachment to the good things of this world. Neither Henry nor William James could share their father's optimism or accept his visionary master, but there is no doubt that they received indelible impressions from the temple in the center of their family. This is particularly noticeable in the older brother, William, who himself experienced a *vastatio* resembling his father's and wrote of it in his great work on the varieties of religious experience.[12]

One of the family's closest friends was the great American author who drew what is perhaps the most important of the many Swedenborg portraits in literature. When Ralph Waldo Emerson published his famous collection of essays, *Representative Men* (1850), he chose Swedenborg to represent mysticism. This essay has become such a standard work for the profane evaluation of Swedenborg that to read it is constantly to meet old acquaintances. Emerson wanted to give an overall picture, in which the scientific period is attributed as much significance as the spiritual, and he was fully aware of the close connection between them. He also reproduced the intellectual milieu in a way that admittedly is not correct in every detail but that nevertheless reduces Swedenborg's originality to reasonable proportions. And he treats the visionary aspect without dramatization, regarding it as an interesting psychical aberration of relative insignificance in a larger context—"to a reader who can make due allowance in the report for the reporter's peculiarities, the results are still instructive, and a more striking testimony to the sublime laws he announced, than any that balanced dullness could afford."[13]

Emerson's principal objection is to Swedenborg's theological system, which in his opinion suppresses the symbolical interpretation of nature and eliminates all true individuality and freedom; we have already encountered similar reservations in Herder at the beginning of the Romantic movement. Even what to Emerson was Swedenborg's greatest strength, namely, his gospel of love, suffers from this theological aridity. Though Emerson obviously read Swedenborg with considerable effort and with many reservations, the result was a tribute to the greatness of the author, generously and gracefully expressed in the conclusion of the essay: Swedenborg has given mankind an intimation of the innermost harmony and bliss of existence, and the circumstance that the radiance of what he had glimpsed had dazzled his own vision is only more powerful evidence of the glory of the drama.

Emerson's essay also opened the door to the world of Swedenborg for many people. For example, it was his fervent admiration for Emerson that led the remarkable Swedish poet and aphorist, Vilhelm Ekelund (1880–1949), to begin to read Swedenborg at the end of 1913. For Ekelund's generation, however, there was a whole series of signposts leading to Swedenborg among the swarm of religious and spiritistic works, which were essential to the change in spiritual climate at the end of the nineteenth century. In the English-speaking world, the poet who expressed this renaissance of mysticism most brilliantly was undoubtedly William Butler Yeats. However, his poetry has such profound and highly ramified roots in the hermetic tradition that it is almost impossible to isolate Swedenborg's influence; but he himself declared in a letter in 1915 that his foremost mystical authorities were Böhme, Blake, and Swedenborg.[14] In the general introduction to his writings as late as 1937 (published posthumously in 1961), he avowed his belief in an "interpenetration of natural and supernatural" and mentioned Irish folklore, spiritism, Swedenborg, and Indian religions as sources of wisdom for future poets.[15] As William York Tindall and others assumed, it was probably Swedenborg's doctrine of correspondence that fascinated Yeats, but it is clear, not least from the many passing allusions, that Yeats was moved by the scenes from the world of spirits, by the visions of the eternally young and eternally loving angels.[16] Just after he received the Nobel Prize in Stockholm in 1923 and was looking at his diploma, which pictures a young man listening to a muse, he immediately thought of Swedenborg; and he wrote in his autobiographical notes: "I was good-looking once like that young man, but my unpracticed verse was full of infirmity, my Muse old as it were; and now I am old and rheumatic, and nothing to look at, but my Muse is young. I am even persuaded that she is like those Angels in Swedenborg's vision, and moves perpetually 'towards the day-spring of her youth.' "[17] It is unlikely that any of Swedenborg's countrymen in that august assemblage would have found the association as natural as Yeats did.

Yeats gained his insight into Swedenborg's spiritualism in the course of his work on Blake's *Prophetic Books*, which he published in 1893; and, as Tindall pointed out, his confrontation with the French symbolists did not change his thinking but confirmed conclusions he had already reached.[18] Other modern poets, however, became interested in Swedenborg through nineteenth-century French literature. When the young hero of Balzac's novel *Louis Lambert*, who has so many characteristics in common with the author, is introduced to Madame de Staël in 1811, he is avidly reading *Heaven and Hell*, and Balzac stresses that in those days it was only Saint-Martin, the renowned Illuminist, and a handful of other men of letters in France who had ever heard of Swedenborg.[19] This may be true of the period in question, but it does not mean that Swedenborg was unknown before that. On the contrary, his message had penetrated the French milieu as early as the 1770s through the intermediary of English and German writers, and many of his spiritual works were translated in whole or in part at an early stage.

However, this early Swedenborgian influx coincided to a great extent with the syncretistic mysticism known in France as Illuminism. The best-known and most important of the mystical societies had its seat in Avignon, where a former librarian of Frederick II, Dom Pernety, among others, developed a form of theosophy in which Swedenborg's heavenly secrets were combined with elements of Catholic mysticism, of hermetic tradition, and of alchemy. The result was a brew that for a time was extremely attractive to numerous magnates during the turbulent years of the Revolution. A disciple of Swedenborg was even a member of the dreaded Committee of Public Safety, and the number of Swedenborg societies in France increased during the first years of the Revolution.[20]

As in Stockholm, the associations with alchemists and hypnotists eventually had disastrous effects on Swedenborg's influence, and the first wave of French Swedenborgianism receded in the 1790s. Meanwhile, a new and more qualified interest in the Swedish visionary developed around 1820, partly as a result of the first complete French translation of his spiritual treatises; and it is to this that we can trace the literary influence of Swedenborg on Victor Hugo, Lamartine, George Sand and—above all—on Balzac.[21] The protagonist in *Louis Lambert* expresses the greatest admiration for Swedenborg's doctrines, which undoubtedly agreed with Balzac's own, at least in the 1830s. Swedenborg's spiritual system came to represent a definitive synthesis of all the religions of history.[22] Thus, Balzac's declaration of allegiance to Swedenborgianism as a religion did not imply a break with the church, but was an expression of his desire for synthesis, his longing for a God for whom the physical and the spiritual are one and the same.

In *Séraphita* (1835) Balzac moved one step further in the direction of Swedenborgianism than *Louis Lambert*.[23] In the latter book, he propounded the concept of unity on a theoretical level, while in the former he gave it poetic form. The hermaphrodite Séraphitus-Séraphita, whose father Balzac identifies as a cousin of Swedenborg himself, is depicted against the background of a magnificent Norwegian fjord, together with three beings, each representing a different attitude: the skeptical priest Becker, his loving and devoted daughter Minna, and the disharmonious romantic Wilfred. The protagonist symbolizes humanity in the stage of becoming angelic, and the theme of the novel is his/her transformation from mortal into angel. The esthetic result of this attempt is questionable, and it is equally doubtful whether the interpretation of Swedenborg is based on a real understanding of his philosophy; but *Séraphita* is unquestionably the most remarkable manifestation of Balzac the mystic. The novel is important in evaluating its author's realism, because it illustrates his belief in the supreme unity, in the spiritual being represented in nature. With his strong physiological and psychological interests, Balzac is a true disciple of Swedenborg in the manner in which he experiences and expresses the conditions of man.[24]

It is also through Balzac that the strongest Swedenborgian impulses were channeled into French tradition and thence disseminated in many directions—we find traces of *Séraphita* everywhere in subsequent literature. It was probably through Balzac that Baudelaire began to read Swedenborg. This resulted in a temporary outburst of enthusiasm, and Swedenborg obviously played a major role in introducing him to mysticism. What primarily fascinated Baudelaire was the notion of correspondence, which became a cornerstone of his aesthetic metaphysics. As Michaud and others pointed out, even though Baudelaire did not actually create an aesthetic system, sensitive readers of his criticism and his poetry could not help discovering how close he came to mysticism in his literary concept of reality; the state of poetic creativity reveals the true reality, provides the contact with ideas and spiritual forces within and beyond the visible phenomena.[25] Passages in one of his Poe essays (1857) reveal unequivocally that Swedenborg helped him to orchestrate the theme:

> It is this admirable, this immortal instinct of the beautiful which makes us consider the earth and its spectacles as a revelation, as something in *correspondence* with Heaven. The insatiable thirst for everything that lies beyond, and that life reveals, is the most living proof of our immortality. It is at the same time by poetry and *through* music that the soul glimpses the splendors beyond the tomb; and when an exquisite poem brings us to the verge of tears, those tears are not the proof of excessive pleasure; they are rather evidence of an aroused melancholy, of a condition of nerves, of a nature which has been exiled amid the imperfect and which would like to take possession immediately, on this very earth, of a revealed paradise.[26]

And it was also Baudelaire who gave classical lyrical expression to the notion of correspondence in the sonnet *Correspondences*:

> *Nature is a temple from which living pillars*
> *Now and then allow disordered phrases to emerge;*
> *Man comes there among forests of symbols*
> *Who observe him as if familiar.*
>
> *Like long echoes that mingle from afar*
> *In a profound and tenebrous unity,*
> *Vast as night and radiance,*
> *So perfumes, colors, sounds correspond.*

FIG. 322. *Honoré de Balzac (1799–1850), chalk sketch by Bertell, n.d.*

FIG. 323. *Charles Pierre Baudelaire (1821–1867)*

There are perfumes fresh as the flesh of infants,
Sweet as oboes, green as prairies,
—And others, corrupt, rich, and triumphant,

Expansive as infinite things:
Amber, bergamot, incense, and musk.
Singing the rapture of spirit and senses.[27]

This exquisite tissue of symbols naturally contains many elements in addition to the idea of correspondence, primarily the idea of concordance between different sensory areas, or synesthesias, and its mood of sensual melancholy is far removed from Swedenborg's mathematical aspirations. It is not bizarre details that Baudelaire borrowed from the master, but Swedenborg's total vision as a poet; and he felt that his function as a disciple was to decode and translate nature's hieroglyphs—an expression he often uses, possibly to associate to Swedenborg's own terminology.

Baudelaire's way of utilizing Swedenborg in his poetic universe became to a great extent the norm for his successors in the symbolist generation. Swedenborg's name is frequently mentioned in the numerous manifestos and declarations of principles—incidentally, the visionary is even encountered in Breton's first surrealistic manifesto in 1924—and it is usually the artistic application of the doctrine of correspondences that is called for. Most striking, however, is that Swedenborg is classified in the hermetical tradition in almost the same way as a century earlier.[28] The explanation is the renaissance of occultism, which occurred in the wake of hypnotic therapy and the psychology of suggestion and which was of central importance in French intellectual life around 1890. The frequent references to Swedenborg do not, however, reflect any profound study of his works, which, of course, differ radically from the efforts of the alchemists, the Rosicrucians, and the spiritualists.

It is nevertheless symptomatic that Strindberg first became a follower of Swedenborg in the full tide of this Parisian occultism and under its direct influence. He himself relates in *Inferno* (1897) how he came to read Balzac's *Séraphita*, an overwhelming experience, even though he had already read it as a young man:

> Indeed, it proved absolutely new to me, and now that my mind was prepared for it I was able to absorb the contents of this extraordinary book. I had never read any of Swedenborg's works (for in his own country—which is also mine—he is accounted a charlatan, a madman with a lubricious imagination), and I was seized with ecstatic admiration as I listened to the voice of this angelic giant of a previous century being interpreted to me by the most profound of all French geniuses.[29]

Strindberg is unquestionably the greatest of Swedenborg's readers among Swedish men of letters (to appreciate him as an artist). There were others who were much better informed on Swedenborg's works than Strindberg, particularly writers belonging to the Romantic movement, and at least one of them adhered periodically to Swedenborgianism, namely, Carl Jonas Love Almqvist (1793–1866). To him Swedenborg's ideas of the lives of the dead, which he made use of in his own scenes from the spiritual world, were tragically decisive in his entire attitude to mankind and to life.[30]

However, none of the Romantic disciples of Swedenborg in Swedish literature have had an international reputation comparable with Strindberg's. According to *Inferno*, it was through the intermediary of *Séraphita* that "Swedenborg revealed himself as a spiritual mentor in my life—in which he has played a tremendous role—and thus, on the anniversary of his death, he presented me with palms—whether of victory or martyrdom who could say?[31] The date was March 29, 1896, but as usual Strindberg dramatized the incident: in reality he probably first became acquainted with Swedenborg twenty years earlier, when he was working at the Royal Library in Stockholm, whose director, Gustaf Klemming, had published the *Journal of Dreams*.[32] Reading Swedenborg's works nevertheless had a decisive effect on the development of the crisis that had plagued Strindberg for several years, a religious crisis that coincided with literary sterility and completely wild scientific speculations. Strindberg's suspiciousness developed during these turbulent years in the direction of clearly pathological delusions of persecution. His encounter with Swedenborg, primarily *Arcana Coelestia*, delivered him of the fear of madness, because he found a way of interpreting his experiences as consequences of the disciplinary activities of the spirits. He applied Swedenborg's term *vastatio*, vastation [see Glossary], to these years of imagined persecution, and he found his situation portrayed in detail in Swedenborg's *Journal of Dreams* and in the accounts of hell in *Arcana*. Swedenborg's postmortem inferno was for Strindberg his own daily life in Paris and in many other places to which he was driven during the miserable years of the mid-1890s.

Swedenborg's doctrine of activity, the doctrine that man must struggle for salvation with his evil nature, was a lifesaver for Strindberg, and he wrote in *Legends* (1898) that Swedenborg "has become my Virgil, who guides me through hell, and I follow him blindly."[33] But as could be expected, Strindberg also felt a need to free himself from this teacher, as he had done with all the other great spirits who had influenced his life and work. In the fragment entitled "Wrestling Jacob," at the end of *Legends*, his book of confession, he attacks the man who had saved him from the madhouse, and he does so in order that his soul should not be injured by the elements in Swedenborg that are too human, too petty:

> So long as Swedenborg in the *Arcana* and the *Apocalypse* treats of revelations, prophecies, interpretations, he has a religious effect upon me, but when in the *Vera [Christiana] Religio* he

begins to reason about dogmas, he becomes a freethinker and Protestant. When he draws the sword of reason, he has himself chosen the weapons, and they are likely to prove bad ones for himself. I wish to have religion as a quiet accompaniment to the monotonous music of life, but here it is a matter of professional religion and pulpit-discussion—in brief, a struggle for power.[34]

What terrified him, therefore, was mainly *Vera Christiana Religio*, and he bid a solemn farewell "with gratitude, as of one who, although with alarming pictures, had frightened me like a child back to God."[35]

This farewell, however, was not definitive. About ten years later when Strindberg published the first volume of *A Blue Book*, he dedicated it to "Emanuel Swedenborg, mentor and master," the superficial reason for this was that Swedenborg's remains were brought home to Sweden from London at the same time. Combined with the teachings of French occultism at the end of the nineteenth century, influences from Swedenborg play a very important part in this strange book of reflections; and according to contemporary notes in the so-called *Occult Diary*, Strindberg was still seeking relief from his own unhappiness in the writings of the visionary. It is clear that the complex, somber sense of life portrayed in Strindberg's later dramas with such extraordinary power had profound roots in the works of Swedenborg.

As a religious body, Emanuel Swedenborg's New Jerusalem has not achieved a large following. Nevertheless, his writings—and even more so his aspirations and the vision on which they are founded—belong to the most remarkable in Western literature. The main purpose of my presentation has been to try to sketch the natural-philosophical background of Swedenborg's development and to indicate its roots in ancient and Christian tradition and its relative agreement with contemporary science. The portrait should have been given clearer contours, but it may nevertheless correspond to my high esteem for its subject: this is confirmed by a host of witnesses infinitely more competent than I. Through his ability to inspire writers who have exerted a major influence on modern literature—Balzac, Baudelaire, Yeats, and, in Swedenborg's ungrateful mother country, Strindberg, Vilhelm Ekelund, Gunnar Ekelöf, and Lars Gyllensten—the scientist and mystic Emanuel Swedenborg is deserving of the place of honor accorded him by Emerson among "Representative Men." And almost two centuries after Swedenborg at last was taken into the world of spirits that he described to us in such detail and in such a fascinating manner, his inspiration is still a stimulus to research, still provokes controversy, and still serves as a source of consolation.

Notes

1. Quoted at length by Cyriel Odhner Sigstedt, *The Swedenborg Epic* (London: Swedenborg Society, 1981), pp. 312–15.

2. Carl Christopher Gjörwell, *Svenska Mercurius* (August 1764), p. 651.

3. Harry Lenhammar, *Tolerans och bekännelstvång* (Toleration and doctrinal unity: A study in Swedish Swedenborgianism 1765–1795), with a summary in English (Uppsala: Acta Universitatis Upsaliensis, 1966), pp. 20–29.

4. Ibid., pp. 40–172, 324–30.

5. Ibid., pp. 175–321, 330–34.

6. Ernst Benz, *F. C. Oertingers und Imanuel Kants Aus ein andersetzung mit der Person und Lehre Emanuel Swedenborgs nach neven Quellen bearbeitet.* (F. C. O.'s and I. K.'s controversy with the character and teachings of Emanuel Swedenborg according to recent sources) (Frankfurt am Main: Vittorio Klostermann, 1947), pp. 235–85 (a thorough study of Swedenborg's early influence in Germany). Cf. Robert Kirven, "Emanuel Swedenborg and the Revolt Against Deism" (Ph.D. diss., Brandeis University, 1965).

7. Ernst Benz, "Swedenborg und Lavater," *Zeitschrift fur Kirchengeschichte*, 1938, pp. 156–57; Kirven, pp. 90–95.

8. Julius Langbehn, *Rembrandt als Erzieher* (Rembrandt as educator), 67–71 ed. (Leipzig: C. L. Hirschfeld, 1922), p. 130; cf. pp. 264, 289. Also, Kirven's examination of Swedenborg's influences in Germany till 1840 is a very valuable contribution; see Kirven, pp. 259–95.

9. George Trobridge, *Swedenborg, Life and Teaching*, 4th rev. ed. (New York: Swedenborg Foundation, 1955), pp. 210–26; Freda G. Griffith, *The Swedenborg Society 1810–1960* (London: Swedenborg Society, 1960); S. C. Eby, *The Story of the Swedenborg Manuscripts* (New York: New-Church Press, 1926).

10. Marguerite Beck Block, *The New Church in the New World: A Study of Swedenborgianism in America* (New York: Henry Holt, 1932), pp. 73–74.

11. H. M. Margoliouth, *William Blake* (Oxford: Oxford University Press, 1951), pp. 10, 74–78. Cf. a penetrating analysis by David V. Erdman, "Blake's Early Swedenborgianism: A Twentieth-Century Legend," *Comparative Literature* 5 (1953), pp. 247–57. See also Harvey F. Bellin and Darrell Ruhl, eds., *Blake and Swedenborg: Opposition Is True Friendship* (New York: Swedenborg Foundation, 1985), passim.

12. Leon Edel, *Henry James*, 2 vols. (London: Rupert Hart-Davis, 1953), vol. 1, pp. 34–36, 38, 47; vol. 2 (1962), pp. 141–42.

13. Ralph Waldo Emerson, *Representative Men* (London: 1901, p. 91; also in *The Complete Works of Ralph Waldo Emerson*, 12 vols. (Boston: Houghton Mifflin, 1903–4), vol. 4.

14. William Butler Yeats, *The Letters of W. B. Yeats*, ed. Allan Wade (London: Rupert Hart-Davis, 1954), p. 592.

15. David R. Clark, "Metaphors for Poetry: W. B. Yeats and the Occult," in *The World of W. B. Yeats: Essays in Perspective*, ed. Robin Skelton and Ann Saddlemeyer (Victoria, Canada: University of Victoria, 1965), pp. 62–63.

16. William York Tindall, "The Symbolism of W. B. Yeats," in *Yeats: A Collection of Critical Essays*, ed. John Unterecker (Englewood Cliffs, N.J.: Prentice-Hall, 1963), p. 46.

17. Willaim Butler Yeats, *Autobiographies* (London: Macmillan, 1955), p. 541.

18. Tindall, pp. 43–51.

19. Honoré de Balzac, *Oeuvres completes de H. de Balzac* (Paris: Michel Levy Frères, 1870), vol. 17, p. 7.

20. Auguste Viatte, *Les Sources occultes du romantisme* (Paris: Librairie Ancienne Honoré Champion, 1928), vol. 1, pp. 80–103. Cf.

Kirven, pp. 217–53. See also K.-E. Sjödén, *Swedenborg en France* (Stockholm: Acta Universitatis Stockholmiensis, 1985), pp. 23–73.

21. Viatte, vol. 2, pp. 248–53; Sjödén, pp. 154–178.

22. Balzac, vol. 17, p. 68.

23. Ibid., pp. 103–236.

24. Cf. René Wellek, *Concepts of Criticism* (New Haven, Conn.: Yale University Press, 1964), pp. 174–75. Cf. Samuel Rogers, *Balzac and the Novel* (Madison, Wis.: University of Wisconsin Press, 1953), pp. 82–91.

25. Guy Michaud, *Message poétique du symbolisme* (Poetic message in symbolism) (Paris: Librairie Nizet, 1951), pp. 67–78.

26. Charles P. Baudelaire, *Oeuvres complétes de Baudelaire* (Complete works of Baudelaire) (Paris: Le Club du meilleur livre, 1955), vol. 1, pp. 628–48. The quoted passage, on p. 645, recurs in his Gautier essay 1859, vol. 2, pp. 94–95. Quoted here from *Baudelaire on Poe*, trans. and ed. Lois and Francis E. Hyslop, Jr. (State College, Pa.: Bald Eagle Press, 1952), pp. 140–41.

27. Translation, from the original French, by Robin Larsen.

28. Guy Michaud, *La Doctrine symboliste* (The symbolic doctrine) (Paris: Librairie Nizet, 1947), pp. 20–22, 40–41, 43.

29. August Strindberg, *Inferno, Alone, and Other Writings by August Strindberg in New Translations*, ed. Evert Sprinchorn, trans. Derek Coltman and Evert Sprinchorn (New York: Anchor Books, 1968), p. 164.

30. Cf. Staffan Björck, "C. J. L. Almqvist: Romantic Radical," *The American-Scandinavian Review* 57, no. 1 (1969), p. 24: "During the second decade of the 1800's he belonged to several societies of this type, in which Swedenborgian thought was united with a worship of the Old Norse—related to the Gothic vogue. . . ."

31. Strindberg, p. 164.

32. Gunnar Brandell, *Strindbergs Infernokris* (Strindberg's inferno crisis) (Stockholm: Albert Bonniers Förlag, 1950), p. 263.

33. August Strindberg, *Legends: Autobiographical Sketches by August Strindberg* (London: 1912), p. 108.

34. Ibid., p. 231.

35. Ibid., p. 233.

Poets with Swedenborgian Connections

Compiled by Alice B. Skinner, Ph.D.

Devotional Verse

"THE FIRST and foremost principle of every religion is the recognition of the divine, and the rules of every religion center in worship—in how the divine is to be revered in order to be accepted" (HH 319).

Poetic statements of faith and worship read something like psalms, expressions of dedication, humility, and aspiration.

"It cannot happen that the Lord is in any angel or person unless that individual in whom the Lord is present in love and wisdom perceives these as his or her own. In this way the Lord is not only accepted, but having been accepted is kept, and is also loved in return" (DLW 115).

"WHOM HAVE I BUT THEE?"

HAVE you any joy
but of God's bestowing?
Have you any refuge
but in Him?
Though the world destroy
does not He remain?
Can He who gave the seed
forget His children's need?
sow in vain?

Oh, be still, be patient,
learn to pray,
and wait for wisdom, knowing
nothing can stop the seed from growing;
nothing of men's devising
can stop the sun from rising,
hinder its course, or speed.

Let Him, uncompromising,
lead each in His own way,
till in the dawn's first whitening
the Truth bursts forth like lightning—
brings day!

ALICE VERY[1]

SELECTION FROM ABT VOGLER

9.

THEREFORE to whom turn I but to thee, the ineffable
  Name?
  Builder and maker, thou, of houses not made with
  hands!
What, have fear of change from thee who art ever the
  same?
  Doubt that thy power can fill the heart that thy
  power expands?
There shall never be one lost good! What was, shall live
  as before;
  The evil is null, is naught, is silence implying sound;
What was good, shall be good, with, for evil, so much
  good more;
  On the earth the broken arcs; in the heaven, a
  perfect round.

10.

All we have willed or hoped or dreamed of good, shall
  exist;
  Not its semblance, but itself; no beauty, nor good,
  nor power

Whose voice has gone forth, but each survives for the
    melodist,
  When eternity affirms the conception of an hour.
The high that proved too high, the heroic for earth too
    hard,
  The passion that left the ground to lose itself in the
    sky,
Are music sent up to God by the lover and the bard;
  Enough that he heard it once: we shall hear it
    by-and-by.

11.

And what is our failure here but a triumph's evidence
  For the fulness of the days? Have we withered or
    agonized?
Why else was the pause prolonged but that singing
    might issue thence?
  Why rushed the discords in, but that harmony should
    be prized?
Sorrow is hard to bear, and doubt is slow to clear,
  Each sufferer says his say, his scheme of the weal
    and woe:
But God has a few of us whom he whispers in the ear;
  The rest may reason and welcome; 'tis we musicians
    know.

ROBERT BROWNING[2]

SELECTION FROM SAUL

"I HAVE gone the whole round of creation: I saw and I
    spoke;
I, a work of God's hand for that purpose, received in
    my brain
And pronounced on the rest of his handwork—returned
    him again
His creation's approval or censure: I spoke as I saw.
I report, as a man may of God's work—all's love, yet
    all's law.
Now I lay down the judgeship he lent me. Each faculty
    tasked
To perceive him, has gained an abyss, where a dewdrop
    was asked.
Have I knowledge? confounded it shrivels at Wisdom
    laid bare.
Have I forethought? how purblind, how blank, to the
    Infinite Care!
Do I task any faculty highest, to image success?
I but open my eyes,—and perfection, no more and no
    less,

In the kind I imagined, full-fronts me, and God is seen
    God
In the star, in the stone, in the flesh, in the soul and
    the clod.
And thus looking within and around me, I ever renew
(With that stoop of the soul which in bending upraises
    it too)
The submission of man's nothing-perfect to God's all-
    complete,
As by each new obeisance in spirit, I climb to his feet.

ROBERT BROWNING[3]

ON READING THE WORD

DAILY as I read
A familiar phrase will
Suddenly drop deep—
As into a well of stored rain,
Resound with new meaning
As it strikes the quiet tension
Of my listening mind,
And send out from its plumbed depths
Concentric circles, degree outreaching degree,
Of pulsing, vibrant life,
The outmost reflected back to its origin
By the very stony walling in
Of my limitations.
Then it lies still again,
No sign of change,
But from henceforth
My spirit will be lifted to a new level
Almost imperceptibly.

CAROLYN A. BLACKMER[4]

THE DIVINE IMAGE

To Mercy Pity Peace and Love,
All pray in their distress:
And to these virtues of delight
Return their thankfulness.

For Mercy Pity Peace and Love,
Is God our father dear:
And Mercy Pity Peace and Love,
Is Man his child and care.

For Mercy has a human heart
Pity, a human face:

And Love, the human form divine,
And Peace, the human dress.

Then every man of every clime,
That prays in his distress,
Prays to the human form divine
Love Mercy Pity Peace.

And all must love the human form,
In heathen, turk or jew.
Where Mercy, Love & Pity dwell
There God is dwelling too.

WILLIAM BLAKE[5]

BALLAD OF THE GOODLY FERE*

(*Simon Zelotes speaketh it somewhile after the Crucifixion*)

HA' we lost the goodliest fere o' all
For the priests and the gallows tree?
Aye, lover he was of brawny men,
O' ships and the open sea.

When they came wi' a host to take Our Man
His smile was good to see,
"First let these go!" quo' our Goodly Fere,
"Or I'll see ye damned," says he.

Aye, he sent us out through the crossed high spears,
And the scorn of his laugh rang free,
"Why took ye not me when I walked about
Alone in the town?" says he.

Oh we drank his "Hale" in the good red wine
When we last made company,
No capon priest was the Goodly Fere
But a man o' men was he.

I ha' seen him drive a hundred men
Wi' a bundle o' cords swung free,
When they took the high and holy house
For their pawn and treasury.

They'll no get him a' in a book I think
Though they write it cunningly;
No mouse of the scrolls was the Goodly Fere
But aye loved the open sea.

If they think they ha' snared our Goodly Fere
They are fools to the last degree.
"I'll go to the feast," quo' our Goodly Fere,
"Though I go to the gallows tree."

*Fere = Mate, Companion

"Ye ha' seen me heal the lame and the blind,
And wake the dead," says he,
"Ye shall see one thing to master all:
'Tis how a brave man dies on the tree."

A son of God was the Goodly Fere
That bade us his brothers be.
I ha' seen him cow a thousand men.
I ha' seen him upon the tree.

He cried no cry when they drave the nails
And the blood gushed hot and free,
The hounds of the crimson sky gave tongue
But never a cry cried he.

I ha' seen him cow a thousand men
On the hills o' Galilee,
They whined as he walked out calm between,
Wi' his eyes like the gray o' the sea.

Like the sea that brooks no voyaging
With the winds unleashed and free,
Like the sea that he cowed at Gennesaret
Wi' twey words spoke' suddenly.

A master of men was the Goodly Fere,
A mate of the wind and sea,
If they think they ha' slain our Goodly Fere
They are fools eternally.

I ha' seen him eat o' the honey-comb
Sin' they nailed him to the tree.

EZRA POUND[6]

THE SECOND POEM
THE NIGHT-WALKER WROTE

OVER all the hilltops
Silence,
Among all the treetops
You feel hardly
A breath moving.
The birds fall silent in the woods.
Simply wait! Soon
You too will be silent.

JOHANN WOLFGANG VON GOETHE[7]

SELECTION FROM AURORA LEIGH

THE creature who stands front-ward to the stars,
The creature who looks inward to himself,
The tool-wright, laughing creature. 'T is enough:
We'll say instead, the inconsequent creature, man,
For that's his specialty. What creature else
Conceives the circle, and then walks the square?
Loves things proved bad, and leaves a thing proved
   good? . . .
Alas, long-suffering and most patient God,
Thou needst be surelier God to bear with us
Than even to have made us! thou aspire, aspire
From henceforth for me! thou who hast thyself
Endured this fleshhood, knowing how as a soaked
And sucking vesture it can drag us down
And choke us in the melancholy Deep,
Sustain me, that with thee I walk these waves,
Resisting!—breathe me upward, thou in me
Aspiring who art the way, the truth, the life,—
That no truth henceforth seem indifferent,
No way to truth laborious, and no life,
Not even this life I live, intolerable!

         'T is impossible
To get at men excepting through their souls,
However open their carnivorous jaws;
And poets get directlier at the soul,
Than any of your oeconomists:—for which
You must not overlook the poet's work
When scheming for the world's necessities.
The soul 's the way. Not even Christ Himself
Can save man else than as He holds man's soul;
And therefore did He come into our flesh,
As some wise hunter creeping on his knees
With a torch, into the blackness of a cave,
To face and quell the beasts there,—take the soul,
And so possess the whole man, body and soul. . . .
We surely made too small a part for God
In these things. What we are, imports us more
Than what we eat; and life, you've granted me,
Develops from within. But innermost
Of the inmost, most interior of the interne,
God claims his own, Divine humanity
Renewing nature,—or the piercingest verse,
Prest in by subtlest poet, still must keep
As much upon the outside of a man
As the very bowl in which he dips his beard.

ELIZABETH BARRETT BROWNING[8]

THE INDIAN UPON GOD

I PASSED along the water's edge below the humid trees,
My spirit rocked in evening light, the rushes round my
   knees,
My spirit rocked in sleep and sighs; and saw the
   moorfowl pace
All dripping on a grassy slope, and saw them cease to
   chase
Each other round in circles, and heard the eldest speak:
Who holds the world between His bill and made us strong or
   weak
Is an undying moorfowl, and He lives beyond the sky.
The rains are from His dripping wing, the moonbeams from
   His eye.
I passed a little further on and heard a lotus talk:
Who made the world and ruleth it, He hangeth on a stalk,
For I am in His image made, and all this tinkling tide
Is but a sliding drop of rain between His petals wide.
A little way within the gloom a roebuck raised his eyes
Brimful of starlight, and he said: *The Stamper of the Skies,*
He is a gentle roebuck; for how else, I pray, could He
Conceive a thing so sad and soft, a gentle thing like me?
I passed a little further on and heard a peacock say:
Who made the grass and made the worms and made my
   feathers gay,
He is a monstrous peacock, and He waveth all the night
His languid tail above us, lit with myriad spots of light.

WILLIAM BUTLER YEATS[9]

BENEDICTION HYMN

THE Lord be with thee in the flush of morn,
  When life springs new, and holiest thoughts are born,
  When earth would draw thee, may the heavenly way
  Shine more and more unto the perfect day.

The Lord be with thee, in the height of noon,
  When hours of action vanish all too soon,
  Through all the heat, the burden and the strife,
  The Lord refresh thee with eternal life.

The Lord be with thee, in the twilight dim,
  The sweet home-coming, and the evening hymn;
  His dews upon thy thirsty soul descend,
  His peace abide with thee, unto the end.

The Lord be with thee thro' the silent night,
  His arms thy refuge, and His face thy light,
  When foes arise, the Lord thy keeper be
  Until the day dawn, and the shadows flee.

MARY ARTEMISIA LATHBURY[10]

Connections of the Poets with Swedenborg

(See earlier sections for information on Very, R. Browning, Blake, Pound, Goethe, E. B. Browning, and Yeats.)

CAROLYN A. BLACKMER (1899–1972), an educator who sometimes wrote poetry, studied and taught in Swedenborgian institutions and was an active New Churchwoman. Information about her is available in the archives at the Swedenborg School of Religion in Newton, Massachusetts, and at Urbana University, Urbana, Ohio.

MARY ARTEMISIA LATHBURY (1841–1913) was known as the Poet Laureate of Chatauqua (New York), where her hymns and devotional poems were favorites. She was the sister of a Swedenborgian minister, Clarence Lathbury, and is thought to have learned about Swedenborg through her brother. Information about her is available at the archives of the Swedenborg School of Religion in Newton, Massachusetts.

Notes for the Poems

1. Alice Very, "Whom Have I But Thee?" in *Write on the Water* (Boston: Branden Press, 1972).
2. Robert Browning, selection from "Abt Vogler" in *An Introduction to the Study of Robert Browning's Poetry*, ed. Hiram Corson (Boston: D. C. Heath, 1901), pp. 274–75.
3. Robert Browning, selection from "Saul," ibid., p. 329.
4. Carolyn A. Blackmer, "On Reading the Word," private collection.
5. William Blake, "The Divine Image," in *Complete Poems*, ed. Alicia Ostriker (Harmondsworth, England: Penguin Books, 1977), p. 111. (The punctuation of this poem varies in different editions of Blake's works.)
6. Ezra Pound, "Ballad of the Goodly Fere," in *Modern American Poetry*, 6th rev. ed., ed. Louis Untermeyer (New York: Harcourt Brace, 1942), pp. 344–45.
7. Johann Wolfgang von Goethe, "The Second Poem the Night-Walker Wrote," trans. Robert Bly, in *News of the Universe*, ed. Robert Bly (San Francisco: Sierra Club Books, 1980), p. 45.
8. Elizabeth Barrett Browning, Selections from "Aurora Leigh" in *Poetical Works* (New York: Dodd, Mead, 1899), pp. 302–3, 332–33.
9. William Butler Yeats, "The Indian upon God," in *Collected Poems*, def. ed. (New York: Macmillan, 1956), p. 13.
10. Mary Artemisia Lathbury, "Benediction Hymn," in *Complete Poems* (Minneapolis: Nunc Licet Press), p. 140.

V
Theoretical
&
Applied Sciences

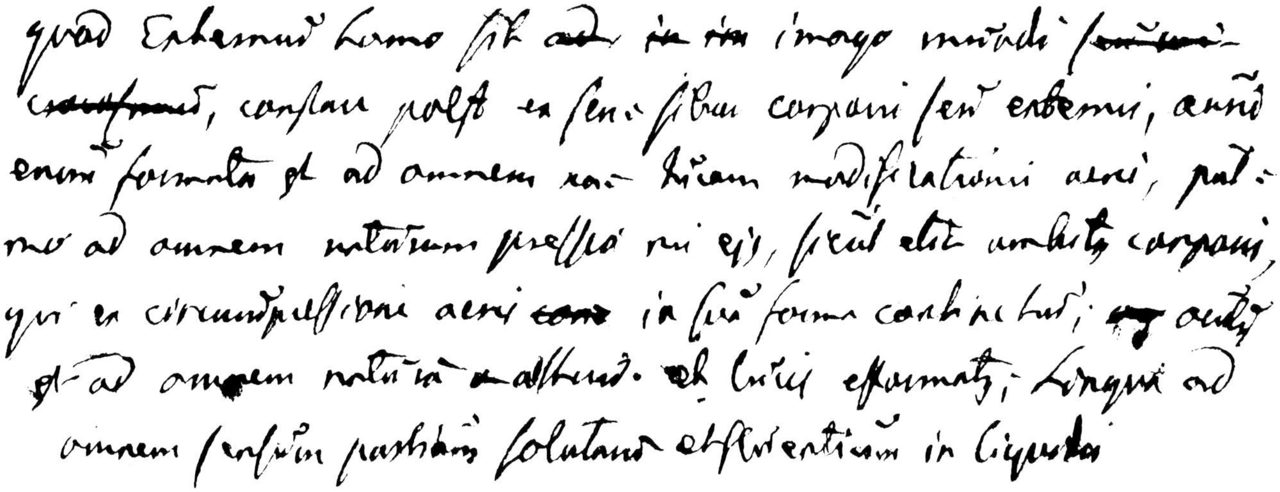

[handwritten manuscript text in Latin]

We can see from the physical or outer senses that the outer person is an image of the world. The ear, after all, is formed [to respond] to every kind of change in the air, the lungs to every change in air pressure—like the whole surface of the body, which is held in its form by the surrounding air pressure. The eye is formed [to respond] to every change in the ether and light, the tongue to sense the elements dissolved and suspended in liquids. . . . (AC 6057)

Science in Swedenborg's Time

Gregory L. Baker, Ph.D.

FIG. 324. *Eighteenth-century astronomer*

GREGORY L. BAKER received his B.S., M.S., and Ph.D. from the University of Toronto, where his graduate work was the study of molecular motions using Nuclear Quadrupole Resonance techniques. Dr. Baker is an associate professor at the College of the Academy of the New Church, and his current interests include deterministic chaos, cosmology, and the history of science.

THE PERIOD ENCOMPASSING Swedenborg's life (1688–1772) is characterized by a degree of scientific vitality and revolution of thought patterns surpassed only in the twentieth century. While Swedenborg's own scientific activity developed over three decades—from about 1710 to the 1740s—much of his work, especially in the physical sciences, rested heavily upon seventeenth- rather than eighteenth-century ideas and modes of thought. Therefore, to understand Swedenborg's contributions in a transitional period, it is important to have some appreciation of the seventeenth-century scientific and intellectual climate.

One important feature of the seventeenth-century intellectual milieu is the fact that scholarship and research were rare commodities in the economy of that time. Public communication did not exist in the pervasive manner we experience today, and therefore society at large was insulated from these advances. For the masses, ignorance and superstition tended to be the rule, and enlightened scientific curiosity was a luxury afforded by few. Nevertheless there were pockets of intellectual activity. Universities in the early-seventeenth century were scattered through Europe. Generally, though, the professors at these institutions tended to concentrate their efforts on classical thought and scholasticism instead of science. With some exceptions, science, especially experimental science, seems to have developed independently of the university structure.

One type of structure supportive of scientific inquiry was the newly developed "academy," or scientific society. These academies began to spring up throughout western Europe.

FIG. 325. *Royal Society House, London*

Notable among the early ones were the Academie des Sciences (1631) in France; the Accademia dei Lincie (1603) of Rome, to which Galileo belonged; and somewhat later, the Royal Society of London, chartered by Charles II in 1662. Sweden's Uppsala University did not have its own academy until 1710. It was in these groups and many others that the new discoveries and theories were presented and argued, often with great vigor and emotion.

What were these new ideas? The novelty lay not so much in particular discoveries as in the modes of thought developed. In somewhat earlier times Francis Bacon (1561–1626) had advocated the empirical method, with its emphasis on the knowledge of nature being firmly grounded in observation. This viewpoint assumes that observations have some sort of absolute truth component, and therefore one finds conflict when observation and religious or philosophical dogma do not coincide. The relative strength of observation versus dogma depended in part upon the religious climate of the geographical location where the natural philosopher resided. While countries such as England and Holland provided a relatively free intellectual climate, others, including Sweden, were not so liberal.

Aside from the debated truth value of the empirical method, there was the seeking of truth through theoretical methods. Two approaches were common. Chronologically first, the rationalistic viewpoint of René Descartes (1596–1650) and the early cosmology of Johannes Kepler (1571–1630) typified an approach that involved the construction of a model universe on the basis of logical thought processes developed from a few first principles. For example, Kepler based his early model of the solar system, which consisted of the five regular solids alternately surrounded by six spheres, on Plato's assumption that "God always geometrizes"[1] and Euclid's statement of the completeness of the set of regular solids. Descartes built an entire model of the world based upon his assumptions of what could exist in the universe. In his *Principia Philosophiae* he proposed vortices that whirl around the sun(s) and fixed stars (Ff), as well as comets (EAM) traveling on a curve.

The other mode of thought that grew to achieve dominance, at least in physical science, was that of mathematical analysis and prediction of nature's actions. Most well known in this connection is the work of Isaac Newton (1642–1727). Newton's mathematical statement of a law of gravity is interesting on several counts. First, the equation itself is not an attempt to state the basic nature of gravity. Rather it is a description or summary of observed phenomena. This represents a departure from the rationalist efforts to achieve total explanation or understanding of the deepest levels of nature. In modern terms we would consider this the process of making the problem manageable. But second, and more far-

FIG. 326. *Johannes Kepler (1571-1630)*

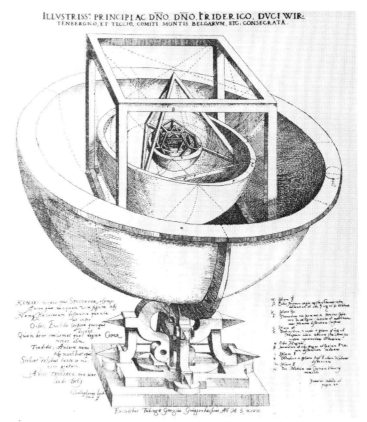

FIG. 327. *Kepler's solids and spheres*

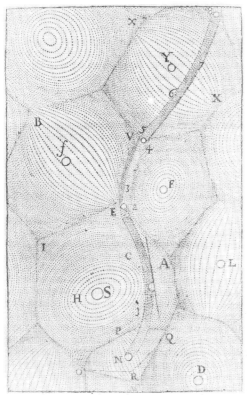

FIG. 328. *Descartes's vortices*

FIG. 329. *René Descartes (1596-1650)*

reaching in its consequences, is the fact that the equation can predict future events with precision. And once there is prediction of nature there is the possibility of control and exploitation. These properties of summarized observation, prediction, and control are the hallmark of modern science.

Swedenborg's life was at the chronological confluence of these influences. Uppsala was somewhat of a scientific back-water, being more concerned with scholasticism than empirical science. In 1649 Queen Kristina had persuaded René Descartes to come to Stockholm to spread his light among the northern intellectuals. (The attempt was short-lived: Descartes died the following year, apparently "as a result of the Swedish Climate and the rigorous schedule demanded by the Queen."[2]) After his formal education, Swedenborg certainly became very aware of the empirical and mathematical methods; yet his preference for the rationalist ap-proach, similar to Descartes's, remained dominant.

With these general considerations in mind, we now turn to a sampling of some of the specific scientific achievements of the seventeenth and early-eighteenth centuries. Through such a survey we hope to provide a picture of the state of science contemporary with Swedenborg.

Mathematics

Mathematics, more than any other science of the time, ex-hibited a continuity of development on many fronts. There-fore the advances here described must not be considered to be new and abrupt beginnings but part of ongoing trends.

We begin with the focus on Descartes's work in what is now called analytic geometry—the application of algebraic methods to geometry and "the translation of algebraic op-

FIG. 330. Queen Kristina Together with the Intellectuals *(including Descartes)*, by *L. M. Dumesnil, 1600s–1700s*

erations into the language of geometry."[3] This work was published as "La Geometrie," one of three appendixes to Descartes's main opus *Discours de la methode* (1637). Because the connections of "La Geometrie" to the larger work was not obvious, later editions often did not include it, an especially ironic fact because this mathematical contribution has had a more lasting effect than his grand cosmological and philosophical schemes. A further irony is the fact that it was analytic geometry that allowed Newton later to show that the Cartesian doctrine of planetary vortices was not correct.

Important as the work on analytic geometry was, the most exciting episode in seventeenth-century mathematics was the development of the calculus. Isaac Newton and Gottfried Wilhelm Leibniz (1646–1716) were the central figures, but many others provided ideas that were precursors and special cases of the subject. Notable among these pioneers was Pierre de Fermat (1601–65), who developed the method for finding the tangent to a curve, which is the principal task of differential calculus. Other workers included Gilles Personne de Roberval (1602–75), Evangelista Torricelli (1608–47), and Blaise Pascal (1623–62), who also built the first mechanical computer and was an early contributor to probability theory.

Newton (1642–1727) and Leibniz are generally considered to share the credit for the development of the calculus. That this common enterprise could have involved two such disparate figures seems hardly possible. Newton, the academician, who spent his years in relative security in England, sensed an absoluteness in space and time, a fixity to God's creation. He came to be honored to such a degree that his funeral was a state occasion. Leibniz, on the other hand, was a wandering diplomat, negotiating the vagaries of European court life. His views of space and time understandably took on a more relativistic character, and again in contrast to Newton, he passed away in poverty and obscurity. These men left a mathematical legacy that affects every part of twentieth-century quantitative science and is responsible for a significant part of the control man now possesses over nature.

Much of the mathematical work of the late-seventeenth and early-eighteenth centuries focused on the further development of the calculus and its applications. This would include the work of the two Bernoulli brothers from Switzerland, Jacques (1654–1705) and Jean (1667–1748), who, incidentally, were from a family that produced about a dozen members who would gain distinction in mathematics and physics. Another contributor to the calculus was Abraham de Moivre (1667–1754), who is even more well known for his basic work in probability theory. His work *Doctrine of Chance*, published in 1718, was filled with problems and probability principles as well as work on life annuities.

This period draws to a close with the advent of work by Leonhard Euler (1707–83); his era marks a new chapter in the history of mathematics.

FIG. 331. *Sir Isaac Newton (1642–1727), by Sir Godfrey Kneller, 1702*

FIG. 332. *Gottfried Wilhelm Leibniz (1646–1716)*

FIG. 333. *Christian Huygens (1629-1695)*

Physics

As in the case of mathematics, physics entered a heroic age during this period. In mechanics, Christian Huygens (1629–95) built on previous work by Galileo (1564–1614) on the impact of bodies, to formulate the conservation laws for energy and momentum. In his *Celestial Worlds Discover'd*, appropriately subtitled *Conjectures concerning the Inhabitants, plants, and productions of the Worlds in the Planets*, Huygens discusses the ring of Saturn and the positions from which the ring will be visible to the inhabitants of that planet. Newton put forward his three laws of motion, which, together with his law of gravity, were used to predict the planetary motion Kepler had observed and codified years earlier. With the publication of Newton's *Principia* (1687), Descartes's mechanical and astronomical ideas began to lose their primacy.

FIG. 334. *Otto von Guericke's atmospheric-pressure experiment*

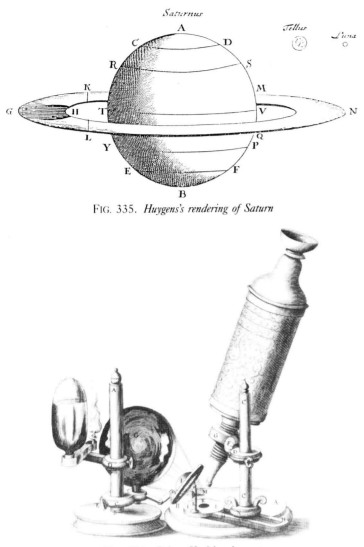

FIG. 335. *Huygens's rendering of Saturn*

FIG. 337. *Newton dispersing sunlight through a prism*

FIG. 336. *Robert Hooke's microscope*

In the study of bulk matter, the dispute over the notion of a vacuum became fashionable. The "horror vacui" was only dispelled when the phenomenon of atmospheric pressure was demonstrated. In Germany, Otto von Guericke (1602–86) became famous for his vacuum experiments and is reputed to have shown that sixteen horses could not separate the evacuated space between two large hemispherical shells. Evangelista Torricelli and Pascal also worked on vacuum pumps and the notion of air having weight. Robert Boyle (1627–91), a founding member of the Royal Society of London, demonstrated his famous theorem of the relationship between pressure and volume for a dilute gas—that the product of pressure and volume is a constant (as every high school chemist now knows).

The field of optics was another area of much advancement during this period. In 1678 Huygens published *Traite de la lumiere*, the first significant treatise on the wave theory of light, and he advanced the principle (now named for him) that from every point on a wave front a new wave is developed.[4] Then he coupled this principle with the existence of a luminiferous ether (a medium for light), a concept vigorously analyzed throughout the nineteenth century. Robert Hooke (1635–1703) should also be associated with the wave theory, especially as he strongly criticized Newton for the latter's corpuscular theory of light.[5] Hooke also invented a microscope, with a light-focusing device (on left) known as the "bull's-eye." Newton's major contribution to the theory of light was his interpretation that a prism's color production indicated that the colors were actual components of the white light, not effects added by the prism. It was also during this period that Olaf Romer (1644–1710) measured the speed of light by observing eclipses of Jupiter's moons at different times of the year. His method was heavily criticized by members of the French Academy, but the English astronomer Edmund Halley (1656–1742) was very supportive.

Along with these developments in optics there were some significant improvements in optical instruments. The grinding of microscope lenses was a developing art in which Swedenborg had participated during his stay in Holland (circa 1713).

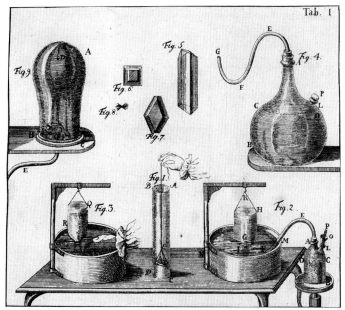

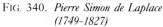

FIG. 338. *One of Torbern Olof Bergman's chemical experiments*

FIG. 339. *Immanuel Kant (1724-1804)*

FIG. 340. *Pierre Simon de Laplace (1749-1827)*

Chemistry

Chemistry in Swedenborg's time was still very much influenced by the traditions and goals of alchemy. Yet some advances were made. Robert Boyle's treatise *Sceptical Chymist* (1661) argued against the classical belief that all matter was composed of earth, air, fire, and water, and suggested that more primitive substances were the main elements. He seemed to think in atomic terms, with his notion of *minima naturalia* as "least things." While these ideas and Boyle's advocacy of the experimental method were advances for modern science, the theory of phlogiston, associated with burning materials (introduced by the Bavarian chemist Georg Ernst Stahl during the eighteenth century), was to sidetrack the analysis of thermodynamic effects for several decades. Chemistry did not really start to move into the modern era until the latter part of the eighteenth century, with the work of Carl Wilhelm Scheele (1772), a Swedish chemist, and Joseph Priestley

(1774), on oxygen. Geographically close to Swedenborg was Torbern Olof Bergman (1735-84) of Uppsala, one of Scheele's teachers and responsible for much work on the effect of carbon in iron, the ingredients of steel for which Sweden is justly famous.

Astronomy

Because of the developments in related sciences and the improvement of the telescope, the intelligent man's concept of the universe was rapidly changing. Newton was the first to build a successful reflecting (mirrored-surface) telescope, in 1668, while Huygens was developing better techniques for grinding lenses. The problem of determining the longitude component of a ship's position was a popular problem for which Swedenborg proposed a practical solution. But it was not implemented until 1759 when an accurate and sturdy chronometer was carried on a voyage to the West Indies.

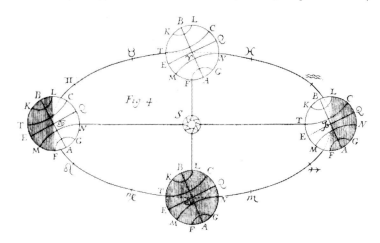

FIG. 341. *David Gregory's theory of Earth's positioning*

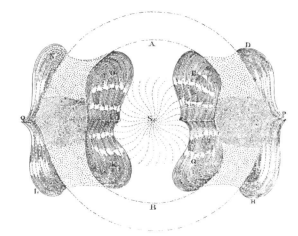

FIG. 342. *Detail from Swedenborg's rendering of planetary evolution*

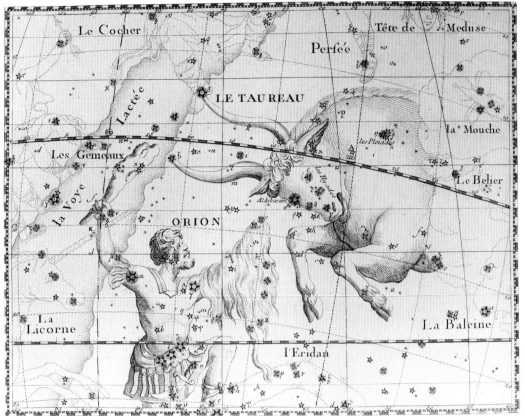

FIG. 343. Le Taureau, *one of John Flamsteed's celestial charts*

Other specific challenges met in that time included a satisfactory theory of tides (1756) and James Bradley's (1692–1762) discovery of stellar aberration resulting from the earth's motion.

Thought about the large-scale features of the universe were also changing rapidly. From Kepler's early cosmology of the solar system there is a gradual evolution, through the application of Newton's mechanical laws, toward a more unified concept of the solar system. The eventual hypothesis of the nebular evolution of the solar system (1754), credited to Kant and Pierre Simon de Laplace (1749–1827), became dominant in the eighteenth century. However, it is interesting to note that a claim for Swedenborg's priority of the nebular hypothesis was later forwarded by Swedish Nobel Prize winner Svante Arrhenius.[6]

Regarding the scope of the universe as a whole—this too was expanding with further discoveries. David Gregory (1661–1708) developed a theory of Earth's positioning and orientation relative to the sun; his and James Gregory's (1638–75) findings are noted by Swedenborg in his *Principia*. John Flamsteed (1646–1719) cataloged the stars and, although astronomer royal at Greenwich, also prepared charts of the heavens under the auspices of the Academie des Sciences. The famous Edmund Halley, and eventually William Herschel (1738–1822), along with the Gregorys and Flamsteed—contributed to the modern view of the universe as consisting of myriads of stars arranged in galaxies and then clusters of galaxies—a kind of "islands of universes" concept, quite different from the primitive views of the early 1600s. Again, this maturation of scientific thought during Swedenborg's era is remarkable.

Biological Science

While the survey of developments in physical science during Swedenborg's time has been severely abridged to give but a flavor, we cannot leave this period without some description, albeit incomplete, of the contemporary progress in biological sciences. Swedenborg became vitally interested in this area as he moved from his studies of the first material points of nature to a search for the natural resting place of the soul.

It is fitting to begin this section by alluding to the work of William Harvey (1578–1657), for although he was of an earlier time, his work on the circulation of the blood was of the more modern genre. He used experimental and mathematical methods to show that the heart had a basic role in the circulatory system. In this way Harvey's work prefigures the biological studies of the late seventeenth and early eighteenth centuries.

Various forays were made into zoology and botany. In botany the ubiquitous Robert Hooke subjected plants to

FIG. 344. *Marcello Malpighi*
(1628-1694)

FIG. 345. *Antoni van Leeuwenhoek*
(1632-1723)

separate environments of air and vacuum, thereby demonstrating that plants needed air to prosper (1665). Nehemiah Grew (1641–1712) showed the sexual nature of plant reproduction (1682), and Marcello Malpighi (1628–94) of Bologna proved that plants absorb nutrients from the soil. During the early-eighteenth century, the study of plants developed significantly with the classification work of the great Swedish botanist Carolus Linnaeus (Carl von Linné) (1707–78). In the area of what we might now call cell biology, Antoni van Leeuwenhoek (1632–1723) used the new technology of the microscope to study organisms in rainwater (1675), and then followed with his discovery in 1677 of spermatozoa and in 1683 of bacteria.

The beginnings of life were a subject of lively debate, with the theory of spontaneous generation being popular in the seventeenth century. There were doubters though, Harvey being one of these. Francesco Redi (1626–99) did some experiments on exposed meat, which tended to disprove spontaneity of growth. But it was not until the eighteenth and nineteenth centuries that the concept of spontaneous generation fully lost currency.

Most advances in biological science came in the areas of anatomy, physiology, and medicine. In his *Elements of Natural Philosophy*, Peter van Musschenbroek devoted a chapter to the subject of sound and illustrated the creation of sound

and its reception by the human ear. Building on the work of Harvey, Malpighi observed the transition of venous blood to arterial blood in the lungs of a frog (1661) and was the first to distinguish red corpuscles and to describe the circulatory and nervous systems in the embryo. (Hooke made the identification of the exposure of blood to air in the lungs with change to the color red.) Olof Rudbeck (1630–1702), one of Swedenborg's teachers at Uppsala, discovered the lymphatic system (1653),[7] and in 1664 Jan Swammerdam (1637–80) identified the lymphatic valves.

Swedenborg has been acclaimed for his work on the brain, *De Cerebro*.[8] Earlier, Thomas Willis's (1621–75) "*Cerebri Anatome*" (1664) contains an account of the central nervous system.

Although the developments in biology during this period were not as "heroic" as in the physical sciences, clearly some very fundamental discoveries were made. Toward the end of this time, in the mid-eighteenth century, Georges Buffon (1708–88) produced a mammoth forty-four-volume treatise on every known aspect of nature, which marked a transition to a new underlying philosophy of biological science. His ideas portend the reductionist emphasis in biology, in which man is "an animal in every material point," and his categorization of all animals according to their utility to man showed a Darwinian emphasis.

Conclusion

Although he did his scientific work in the early eighteenth century, Swedenborg's work rested heavily on seventeenth-century discoveries. The time frame of these scientific gains is particularly marked by a giant leap away from the rationalist approach, especially one based on religious or other "first" principles. The experimental and mathematical methods, the approach to pieces of a problem rather than to the whole, is characteristic of this new method, which in the twentieth century remains the confirmed scientific method. This change of direction in method is one reason an assessment of the value of Swedenborg's scientific work is always a challenge, and it shows the importance of understanding the science of his time, if such an assessment is to be an accurate one.

Acknowledgments

I would like to acknowledge the help of Professor Prescott Rogers with the translation of certain key Latin passages in original works, and I am especially grateful for the help of Mr. David Glenn with the use of the Swedenborgiana collection at the Academy of the New Church.

Notes

1. S. Sambursky, ed., *Physical Thought from the Pre-Socratics to the Quantum Physicists* (New York: PICA Press, 1975), p. 206.
2. Paul Edwards, ed., *Encyclopedia of Philosophy* (New York: Macmillan, 1967), vol. 2, p. 345.
3. Carl C. Boyer, *A History of Mathematics* (New York: Wiley, 1965), p. 370.
4. Florian Cajori, *A History of Physics* (New York: Dover, 1962), p. 88.
5. Ibid., p. 94.
6. Svante Arrhenius, *The Life of the Universe* (London: Harper and Brothers, 1909).
7. Eric Nordenskiöld, *The History of Biology* (New York: Tudor, 1928), p. 187.
8. J. H. Talbot, "Natural Scientist, Neurophysiologist, Theologian," *Journal of American Medical Association* 206 (1986), p. 87.

Swedenborg and the Holographic Paradigm

Michael Talbot

IF EMANUEL SWEDENBORG WERE ALIVE TODAY, it is very likely that he would consider many of the findings of the "new physics" compatible with his own thought. This is surprising, for many of the concepts arrived at by contemporary physics are so foreign to everyday ways of thinking that it is difficult for modern sensibilities to grasp them. That a man born three centuries ago should articulate them in his writings is nothing short of remarkable.

For example, in the Newtonian view of physics, time and space were considered absolute. Even Einstein, who proposed that time was relative and space a malleable something subject to the warping effects of gravity, shied away from the theoretical territory that would have allowed him to postulate the existence of "black holes." It wasn't until the German physicist Karl Schwarzschild calculated what space would look like surrounding a gravitationally collapsed star that the concept of a black hole was given birth and with it the understanding that there could exist regions literally beyond space and time. However, in his writings Swedenborg revealed that he was already quite comfortable with the notion that there existed regions beyond space and time. As he wrote, "I beg you, though, not to muddle your concepts with time and space. To the extent that there is time and space in your concepts as you read what follows, you will not understand it; for the Divine is not in time and space" (DLW 51).[1]

Another assertion of twentieth-century physics that has caused no small amount of dismay among scientists is the discovery that the mere act of observation alters and actually helps create what is perceived in the subatomic landscape. Although it is difficult for most Earthbound minds to fathom, the current view of physics holds that subatomic particles or "quanta" do not really exist until an observer enters the picture and, through the act of observation, somehow imbues them with actuality.

Although this mysterious transaction between the observer and the observed is now an accepted phenomenon of quantum physics, physicists are still in staunch disagreement as to what it implies about the workings of reality. Some refuse to confront the philosophical implications at all, while others assert that it is undeniable evidence that the human consciousness actually reaches out and interacts with physical reality, and again Swedenborg would most assuredly concur. As he stated in *Heaven and Hell*:

> There are people who believe that thoughts and affections do not really reach out around them, but occur within them, because they see their thought processes inside themselves, and not as remote from them; but they are quite wrong. As eyesight has an outreach to remote objects, and is influenced by the pattern of things seen "out there," so too that inner sight which is discernment has an outreach in the spiritual world, even though we do not perceive it. (HH 203)[2]

Swedenborg even foretold the finding that gave quantum physics its name, the discovery that at the subatomic level phenomena in nature cease to be continuous. For the better part of human existence the idea that phenomena in nature are continuous had been accepted as self-evident. After all, this is what our everyday experience tells us. When you turn the spigot on a keg of cider, the cider flows out in a continuous stream, not in discontinuous spurts. Similarly, rivers move along continuously, as do air currents, and when you pedal faster on a bicycle, the bicycle does not accelerate in sporadic lurches, but accelerates smoothly.

It thus came as some surprise to physicists to discover that this was not the case with subatomic phenomena. The first indication of the discontinuous nature of the quantum realm

---

MICHAEL TALBOT graduated from Michigan State University in 1975. He took physics courses on both undergraduate and graduate levels and made extensive studies on his own as well. He has had a lifelong interest in the confluence between science and spirituality and is the author of five books, including *Mysticism and the New Physics* and *Beyond the Quantum: God, Reality, and Consciousness in the New Scientific Revolution.*

was made in 1900 by the German physicist Max Planck. Planck was studying black-body radiation, or the way that nonluminous objects such as iron bars give off light when they are heated to high temperatures. Much to his chagrin, he found that the frequency of radiation given off by such slowly heated objects did not rise continuously, but instead rose in distinct spurts. As he stated later, out of "sheer desperation" he called these discrete spurts of energy "quanta," and thus gave quantum physics its name.[3]

In time it was discovered that many other subatomic phenomena were similarly quantized. For example, although a planet theoretically can occupy any orbit in the solar system, it was found that electrons could only inhabit very specific orbits, or energy levels, around the nucleus of an atom. In short, as science probed deeper into the very small, it was found that although reality appears to be continuous at our level of existence, like a photograph in a magazine, which is composed of so many tiny dots, at the subatomic level reality is discontinuous and granular. (Although it should be noted that, again, the granular appearance of subatomic reality does not actually coalesce into being until an observer enters the picture.) The acceptance of this fact is one of the first lessons that a modern student of physics must acknowledge in order to have any hope of pushing the boundaries of science farther. Or as Swedenborg prophetically wrote:

> A knowledge of levels is like a key for unlocking the causes of things and entering into them. Without this knowledge, one can know hardly anything about the causes of things. In fact, the objects and subjects of each world seem straightforward, as though nothing more were involved than the eye can observe. Yet this, relative to what lies within, is only a minute fraction—most minute. The deeper matters that are not visible cannot be unveiled without a knowledge of levels. We progress from more outward to more inward things, and through these to the inmost, by levels—not by a continuous slope [literally, continuous levels] but by quantum leaps [literally, discrete levels]. (DLW 184)[4]

Such remarkable insights notwithstanding, perhaps the most astonishing foreshadowing of new-physics ideas in Swedenborg's writings are the similarities between his world view and a revolutionary new way of looking at nature known as the "holographic paradigm."

To understand what is meant by the holographic paradigm, it is first necessary to say a few words about holography. Holography is a type of photography that utilizes laser light instead of regular light to create three-dimensional photographs known as "holograms." To make a hologram, a laser is shone on an object and then a second laser beam is bounced off the reflected light of the first. The pattern that results from the intermingling of the two lasers (known as a "pattern of interference") is then recorded on a piece of photographic film. To the naked eye such a pattern is a meaningless swirl.

However, when a laser beam is passed through the film, a three-dimensional image of the original object reappears.

Aside from being three-dimensional, holograms differ from normal photographs in another intriguing way. If you cut a photograph of an apple in half, you will end up with only half an apple in each severed piece. However, if you cut a hologram of an apple in half, each half will still contain a smaller but complete image of the whole apple. In other words, because it is the product of a pattern of interference, the image in a hologram is not localized, but is contained equally in every portion of the whole.

This is an important point, for it illustrates an entirely new way of perceiving and thinking about order. Throughout most of human history we have viewed the universe and the various natural phenomena it contains as functioning like so many machines. To figure out the way something works—whether it be an atom or a blood cell—we have sought to break it down into its respective parts. Such an approach, the belief that a phenomenon can be understood by dismantling it and studying the way its pieces fit together, is known as "mechanism."

What a hologram teaches us is that not everything in the universe is put together like a machine and therefore a mechanistic approach may not always lead us to a greater understanding of a phenomenon. For example, if we try to take apart something that is constructed holographically, we do not get the pieces of which it is made, we only get smaller wholes.

A Holographic Model of the Brain

The principle of holography was first advanced in 1947 by the British physicist Dennis Gabor and was first given substance in the early 1960s with the invention of the laser. However, it wasn't until the middle 1960s that an understanding of holographic ordering started to impact on other areas of science. One branch of science on which it had an influence was brain research, and the man responsible for this thought-provoking marriage of ideas was Stanford neurophysiologist Karl Pribram.

One of the problems Pribram was interested in solving was how and where the brain stores memories. For example, for decades brain researchers had searched for the specific site within the brain where memories were located, but their efforts had all been resoundingly unsuccessful. In fact, experimental evidence seemed to indicate that there was no such specific site (as is borne out by the fact that a head injury, for example, does not make a person forget half of his or her family). In pondering this strange state of affairs Pribram began to realize that memories seem somehow to be spread throughout the whole brain, although he was at a loss to come up with a brain model that might explain how this was possible. It wasn't until he encountered an article on holography that he realized he had found the model he was looking for. Memories were not stored in the brain mechanistically, but holographically. The brain functioned like a hologram.

Moreover, Pribram began to realize that memory storage was not the only problem that became more tractable in light of a holographic model of the brain. Another long-standing neurophysiological puzzle is how the brain is able to translate the ocean of frequencies it receives via our senses (light frequencies, sound frequencies, and so on) into the objective world of our mental constructs. However, once again, this problem becomes far less troublesome in light of a holographic brain model, for encoding and decoding frequencies are precisely what a hologram does best.

Bohm's Implicate Order

Pribram was not the only one musing on the implications of holographic ordering. At about this same time and working halfway around the world, University of London physicist David Bohm was applying the holographic model to yet another natural phenomenon. However, the subject occupying Bohm's thoughts was not the human brain but some of the most fundamental problems of quantum physics.

One of the problems in which Bohm was interested was the seeming ability of subatomic particles to remain in contact with one another regardless of the distance separating them. For example, if you isolate an atom of an extremely unstable substance called "positronium" and allow it to decay (break down into its constituent parts), it will release two "protons," or wave particles of light, in opposite directions. What is unusual about these photons is that no matter how far apart they travel, when they are measured they will always be found to have identical angles of "polarization" (the spatial orientation of a light wave as it travels through space).

This would not present a problem if it weren't for two other factors. The first is that a photon's angle of polarization is one of those features of the subatomic landscape which does not coalesce into reality until an observer enters the picture. In other words, a photon's angle of polarization literally does not exist until it is measured. This seems to indicate that, at the moment they are measured, the photons must somehow signal each other in order to be able to know what angle of polarization to assume. However, experimentation has shown that, even when the photons have been allowed to travel far apart and then are both measured simultaneously, they still have identical angles of polarization. This suggests that, if the photons are communicating with one another, their communication takes place instantaneously, and this does present a problem. According to Einstein's special theory of relativity, no communication or sig-

naling process can travel faster than the speed of light, for if it did, it would break the time barrier and this would open the door on all sorts of unacceptable paradoxes.

In a purely mechanistic universe such a state of affairs presents an unsolvable quandary. However, Bohm began to perceive another way of looking at the phenomenon. What if the photons were not sending signals back and forth at all? What if they always possessed the same angle of polarization, not because they were communicating, but because their separateness was an illusion and at some deeper level of reality they were actually extensions of the same fundamental something?

To illustrate what he was talking about, Bohm came up with the following example. Imagine an aquarium containing a goldfish. Imagine also that there are two television cameras focused on the aquarium, one pointed at the front and one pointed at the side. Finally, imagine that each television camera is connected to a monitor and that you cannot see the aquarium or the fish directly, but are only able to see what takes place in the aquarium by watching the two television monitors. If you did not have a full understanding of what was going on, you might at first assume that what you were watching was really two fish. After all, you would be seeing them from different angles and in different locations.

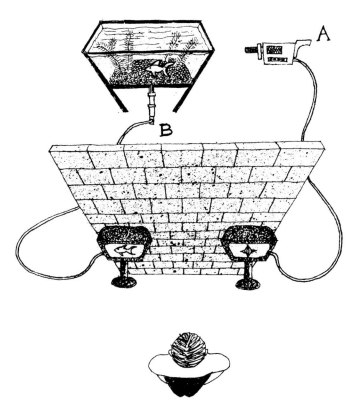

FIG. 346. *Bohm's application of the holographic model. Bohm believed that subatomic particles are ultimately connected, in the same way as are two different images of the same fish when viewed on two separate television monitors. In both cases, the apparent separateness of such images is an illusion.*

However, after a while you would also begin to assume that the two fish were communicating with each other, for as one moved, the other would also make a slightly different but corresponding movement. This, says Bohm, is precisely what is going on between the two photons. At our own level of reality—a level Bohm calls the "explicate order"—the two photons appear to be separate. But at a deeper level of reality—a level Bohm calls the "implicate order"—everything is an unbroken whole and the two photons, like the goldfish above, are actually just different facets of the same fundamental something.

Although Bohm was convinced that he had arrived at an important new insight into the workings of subatomic reality, he realized that his theory did more than just explain the seeming ability of quantum particles to communicate instantaneously over vast tracts of space and time. It indicated that, far from being built like a giant machine, the universe was structured along the lines of quite a different order. At its most fundamental level the cosmos was quite literally a gigantic, multidimensional hologram.

This then is the holographic paradigm, that both the brain and reality itself are holographic, and although many of the implications of this new way of looking at nature may seem new and astonishing, it is a tribute to Swedenborg's visionary genius that they were already a part of his body of ideas. For example, if Bohm is correct and subatomic particles are just different facets of a fundamental unity, this means that, like a hologram at its most basic level, the universe is indivisible and ultimately cannot be broken down into constituent parts. Similarly, in *True Christian Religion* Swedenborg seems to imply that spiritual reality is equally indivisible. As he stated, "[In heaven, no one can pronounce a trinity of persons each of whom separately is God]—the heavenly aura itself, in which their thoughts fly and undulate the way sound does in our air, resists [such pronouncement]" (TCR 173 [2]).[5]

Another aspect of the holographic universe is the infinite interconnectedness of all things. Just as every portion of a hologram contains all of the information of the whole, so would every portion of a holographic universe contain the whole; every subatomic particle would be an extension of every other subatomic particle, and every point in space and time would, at a deeper level, be adjacent to every other point in space and time. Again, throughout his writings Swedenborg frequently seems to refer to the same stupendous interconnectedness of all things. As he wrote, "Nothing unconnected ever occurs, and anything unconnected would instantly perish" (AC 2556e).[6]

As startling as such assertions as the indivisibility and infinite interconnectedness of subatomic reality may seem, two other ideas advanced by the holographic paradigm are even more astounding. The first is Bohm's proposal that in a universe in which subatomic particles are merely facets of a more fundamental unity, objective reality itself must be seen as an illusion of sorts, a projection from a more complex dimension beyond our own. In other words, just as the two fish on the television monitors in the earlier illustration are actually two-dimensional projections of the three-dimensional reality of the aquarium, our own three-dimensional universe must be seen as a projection of a yet more multidimensional level of reality. Put another way, the universe as we perceive it is only one of the images that might be extracted out of Bohm's implicate order—the superhologram that has given our cosmos birth.

As for what other images/realities this superhologram contains, this is an extremely open-ended question. If Bohm is correct in his surmise, it is clear that it contains everything we perceive in reality and more. Because it is the matrix that gives birth to both space and time, it contains the entire recorded past of our universe and its future. Because it is the archetypal or primary reality from which all things spring, it contains every subatomic particle that ever has been or will be; every conceivable energy state and configuration of matter that is possible, from sequoia trees to neutron stars, from maple leaves to gamma rays to human brain cells. In short, it must be seen as the cosmic storehouse of All That Is, the very womb of creation itself. And this is the very least that it contains.

As for what else the superhologram contains, that is a matter on which mere mortals must remain silent, for, as Bohm prudently notes, it is a question that requires a knowledge of things transcendent. However, he does venture to say that we have no reason to assume that it does not contain more, levels of reality not yet even suspected by science and aspects of existence still beyond our most fantastical imaginings. Furthermore, because of the remarkable diversity and richness of the forms put forth by the superhologram and because we live in a universe in which projections of the superhologram are governed by extraordinarily ordered and dependable laws of physics, Bohm feels that whatever its full extent, at the very least it is safe to conclude that this more complex dimension beyond our own is "purposive" and possesses "deep intentionality."[7] Indeed, because it is the wellspring from which our self-awareness is derived and is itself a realm in which all things become indivisible, Bohm feels that the superholographic level of reality should not even be thought of as a material plane. As he states, "It could equally well be called Idealism, Spirit, Consciousness. The separation of the two—matter and spirit—is an abstraction. The ground is always one."[8]

As for how the projections we know as physical reality manage to coalesce out of the superhologram, Bohm sees this as a rich and unending process of enfoldment and unfoldment. In other words, subatomic particles are no more objects moving through space than are the images on a television screen. Rather, what is perceived as movement is actually the result of the continuous appearance and disappearance of the projection, an unending exchange between the two levels of reality.

Again, this radical departure from the mechanistic view of the universe, that the objective world is a projection of a more fundamental and spiritual level of existence, is clearly elucidated in Swedenborg's writings:

> Absolutely everything comes from the first Reality [*Esse*], and the design is so established that the first Reality is present in the derived forms [both] indirectly and directly, just as much in the most remote part of the design, therefore, as in its first part. The actual Divine-True is the only substance; its derivatives are simply successive secondary forms. This also enables us to see that the divine does flow directly into absolutely everything. (AC 7004 [2])[9]

Indeed, Bohm's notion that the objective reality is actually the product of a constant series of enfoldings and unfoldings is mirrored uncannily in Swedenborg's assertion that everything in the universe is the result of two intersecting forces he calls "direct" and "indirect" inflow. As he put it in *Arcana Coelestia*, "There are always two forces which hold anything together in its coherence and its form—a force acting from the outside, and a force acting from within. Where they meet is the thing that is being held together (AC 3628 [3]).[10] Similarly, in *Heaven and Hell* he wrote, "The Lord unites all the heavens by means of a direct and an indirect inflow—by a direct inflow from himself into all the heavens, and by an indirect inflow from one heaven into another" (HH 37).[11]

An Ocean of Frequency

But the most mind-boggling proposal made by the holographic paradigm is the new picture of reality that develops when both Pribram's and Bohm's ideas are considered together. For if the concreteness of the world is but a secondary reality and what is "there" is actually an inchoate ocean of potentiality, and if the brain is a hologram and simply plucks various frequencies out of this ocean and mathematically converts them into images, what becomes of objective reality? Put quite simply, it ceases to exist. As the religions of the East have long upheld, the material world is *maya*, an illusion, and although we may think that we have physical bodies and are moving through a physical domain, this, too, is an illusion. What we really are are "frequency receivers" floating through a kaleidoscopic sea of frequency, and what we extract from this sea and transmogrify into physical reality is but one channel from many beamed to us from a dimension beyond our own.

To support this view further, Pribram points out that studies have shown that our visual systems are also sensitive to sound frequencies. Even the very cells of our bodies are known to respond to a broad range of frequencies that we do not necessarily translate into perceptions. It is suggested that only in the holographic domain of consciousness are these sorted out into those which will be translated into perceptions and those which will not.[12] Thus, in this view it is not the eye that sees, but the holographic domain of consciousness, and again Swedenborg echoes this sentiment:

> The thinking mind flows into the sight, subject to the state imposed on the eyes by the things that are being seen—a state which that mind, further, organizes at will. . . . If our more inward sight were not constantly flowing into our outer or eyesight, this latter could never apprehend or discern any object. For it is the more inward sight that apprehends through the eye what the eye is seeing: it is by no means the eye [that does this], even though it may seem so. We can also determine from this how involved people are in sensory illusions if they believe that their eye sees, when on the contrary it is the sight of their spirit, a more inward sight, that sees through the eye. (AC 1954)[13]

If Bohm and Pribram are correct in their views, even Swedenborg's mystical experiences become more comprehensible. For example, once his spiritual vision had been awakened, Swedenborg reported that he was able actually to see thought. As he wrote in *Arcana Coelestia*:

> I could see solid concepts of thought as though they were surrounded by a kind of wave, and I noticed that this wave was nothing other than the kinds of thing associated with the matter in my memory, and that in this way spirits could see the full thought. But nothing reaches [normal] human sensation except what is in the middle and seems to be solid. (AC 6200)[14]

Such an ability remains unexplainable in terms of our current paradigm of reality, but if the hologram of our brain is only converting a small portion of the frequencies it receives into sensory data, it may be that Swedenborg's spiritual awakening was simply the result of his brain's learning to convert a bit more of the frequencies it was receiving into concrete images. Perhaps he was merely plucking a little more out of the superhologram than most of us do.

Even Swedenborg's concept of "portrayals"—his assertion that the inhabitants of spiritual regions communicate through elaborate sequences of images or pictures—may be explainable in terms of the holographic paradigm. If the apparent concreteness of objective reality is only a partial and fragmented translation of All That Is, it may be that the various spiritual kingdoms Swedenborg witnessed were only deeper levels of the superholographic domain. If this is the case, it may be that the deeper our "frequency receivers" travel into the superhologram, the more freely such frequencies are translated into images. In other words, here in the so-called physical world the holograms of our brains have learned to translate frequencies in a rigid and highly structured manner, and this has caused us to view reality as solid and objective. However, as we drop this misconception and learn to tune into more and more of the superhologram (become spiritually awakened), like children who have grown beyond needing the rigid lines of a coloring book, we may no longer need such rigorously defined parameters and will instead translate the frequencies we receive more loosely and into more flowing shapes and patterns.

In a way, this is perhaps what Swedenborg is getting at when he says that everything in nature has a correspondence with things that exist in the spiritual world, that everything in objective reality is also, in its own way, a portrayal (AC 2999),[15] for in a holographic universe nothing can be seen as truly objective. No matter how concrete our perceptions may seem, they are always the product of a deeper level of reality, a still richer strata of the holographic domain. And the deeper we penetrate into this holographic domain, the greater the spectrum of frequencies that must be translated into portrayals until portrayals or concrete images cease to be able to convey the richness of the information coming through and pure frequency must by necessity predominate. Perhaps this is why Swedenborg found that the language of "angels of the third heaven" appeared to him only as "a streaming of light, containing a perception, from its flame, of the good within it" (AC 3346).[16]

If this is the case, if Swedenborg had become privy to a holographic level of reality, a spiritual dimension that science is only now beginning to rediscover, it is important to realize that all of his descriptions of spiritual regions are also only portrayals. Such an admission is not intended to diminish the magnitude of his mystical experience, but merely to point out that in a holographic universe there can no longer be any distinction between what is symbolic and what is real. All apparent realities possess a deeper symbolic meaning, for all are translations of a deeper and still more fundamental level of order.

In this light, Swedenborg's assertion that each region of heaven corresponds with a different member or organ of the human body and that every human being "is a heaven in miniature" (HH 203)[17] becomes his most holographic concept of all. Viewed as a portrayal, what else can it mean but that the whole is the part and the part is the whole; that like a hologram the cosmos too contains the entire design in every minute portion? Or as Swedenborg so eloquently put it, "The divine is the same in the largest and smallest things" (DLW 77–81).[18]

Notes

1. From *A View from Within*, comp. and trans. George F. Dole (New York: Swedenborg Foundation, 1985) p. 29.
2. Ibid., p. 24.
3. Heinz Pagels, *The Cosmic Code* (New York: Simon & Schuster, 1982), p. 26.
4. From Dole, *View*, p. 29.
5. Ibid., p. 36.
6. Ibid., p. 37.
7. David Bohm and Renée Weber, "Nature as Creativity," *Revision* 5, no. 2 (Fall 1982), p. 40.
8. Ibid.
9. From Dole, *View*, p. 35.
10. Ibid.
11. Ibid.
12. Wiktor Osiatynski, *Contrasts: Soviet and American Thinkers Discuss the Future* (New York: Macmillan, 1984), pp. 70–73.
13. From Dole, *View*, p. 26.
14. Ibid., p. 36.
15. From George F. Dole, *Emanuel Swedenborg: The Universal Human and Soul-Body Interaction* (New York: Paulist Press, 1984), p. 41.
16. Ibid., p. 53.
17. From Dole, *View*, p. 40.
18. Ibid., p. 34.

Carolus Linnaeus

Anja Hübener

FIG. 347. *Carolus Linnaeus (1707-1778), after Alexander Roslin, 1775*

For biographical information on the author, see her other essay, "Academic Uppsala," earlier in this anthology.

CAROLUS LINNAEUS (Carl von Linné) laid the foundations for modern biological thought. As doctor and professor of medicine, he specialized in botany and made major discoveries and observations in a time when botany was still in its infancy. But he was also a versatile scholar, occupying himself successfully with other branches of the natural sciences, such as zoology, geology, and mineralogy. He was one of the brilliant natural scientists who, along with Emanuel Swedenborg, Christopher Polhem, and Anders Celsius, helped place Sweden among the leading nations on the scholarly map of the eighteenth century.

That nature obeys simple laws, that it is resting on a rationality of its own, was to Linnaeus an obvious truth. He spent his life proving this by arranging and classifying each new species he came across. His scientific work is not a subject, but a method. He introduced binomial specific nomenclature, and was responsible for devising precise systems of classification for animals and plants.

Linnaeus was fortunate in that he was born in a time of profound change. After several years of war, the former Swedish empire was starting to develop a new spirit. New life-styles and new ideas found their way into the society. This was a slow process, and one that first became visible in the sciences and in cultural life. It would take some time for the mundane, utilitarian ideal of the Age of Freedom to penetrate these northern latitudes, but the time was ripe for new discoveries and radical reevaluations of old ones.

Holland was already known for its free intellectual climate and was a vital center for science and publishing. This determined Linnaeus's decision to take his degree as doctor of medicine there. This was a crucial move in his career. At the small university at Harderwijk people were immediately taken in by the eager and ambitious young man. He got to know the leading botanists and zoologists, and was exposed to the latest ideas and discoveries in his field. With their help and encouragement, he published no fewer than ten scientific works during his three years in Holland. The major part of these works had already been written during his time as a student in Uppsala, and although composed early in his life, they show a remarkable, systematic genius and an unusual knowledge of all branches of nature. It is clear that Linnaeus's intellectual powers matured early and that he had worked extremely hard and methodically during the eight years of study in Sweden. He says of himself in his amusing and very self-conscious autobiography: "He had thought out everything before his twenty-eighth year."[1]

After receiving his doctor's degree at Harderwijk, Linnaeus was employed by a wealthy Dutch banker, whose botanical garden he arranged and supervised. During this time, he frequently visited Leiden to audit lectures in medicine given by Hermann Boerhaave, the most eminent doctor of his day.

FIG. 348. *Carolus Linnaeus, the "Bridegroom portrait," after J. H. Scheffel, 1739*

FIG. 349. *The botanical garden in Leiden*

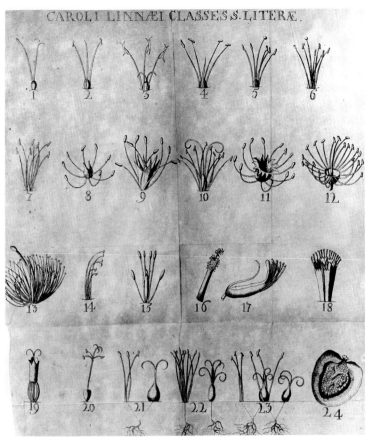

FIG. 350. *Linnaeus's sexual classification of plants*

Systema Naturae, a gigantic survey on nature, which Linnaeus would spend the rest of his life expanding and revising, was the most important of those ten early books. The first edition (1735) contained only ten pages. The twelfth and last authorized version (1766–68) ran to twenty-three hundred pages. It is a work that was never finished. Nor can it be. Scientists are still laboring over an inventory of every living thing on this earth. Today nobody would even dream of undertaking this task alone.

In *Systema Naturae* Linnaeus introduced his sexual system, based on the appearance and number of a plant's reproductive parts. He introduced a method of definition and classification far surpassing any other that was previously known. The system divided the plant kingdom into classes and subclasses, according to the number of stamens and pistils in the flowers. Part of the classification system is still used today, although many of the species have been subdivided or recombined. He also introduced and developed a system of binomial nomenclature, naming both genus and species, for example, *Linnaea borealis* (the twinflower, Linnaeus's favorite flower and named after him), *Iris xiphium, Homo sapiens*.

Botany was Linnaeus's subject par excellence, and his time was devoted to the exploration and research on the world's flora. But *Systema Naturae* attempted to take on the organization of every part of nature's structure, and it contains a classification of the animal and mineral kingdoms as well—a fact sometimes forgotten.

Linnaeus studied minerals in Bergslagen, the major mining district in Sweden, and it is inevitable that he was familiar with Swedenborg's writings on the subject. Swedenborg had published a number of books on geology and mineralogy during his years on the Board of Mines. Geology and mineralogy were important fields with respect to Sweden's economy, and therefore a subject in which rapid development would bring fame and resources to gifted scholars. Johann Gottschalk Wallerius, a scientist and contemporary of Linnaeus, made a thorough systematization of minerals, which was often used internationally as a supplement to Linnaeus's classifications of plants and animals.

Linnaeus made a number of changes in his original classifications of the animal kingdom. But the division into six classes remained: four-footed animals, birds, fish, amphibious animals, insects, and worms. The last class turned out to be an overall heading for all kinds of invertebrates. One of the changes that became permanent was the designation of the term *mammals* instead of "four-footed animals."

According to Linnaeus, the human being should be classified as an animal, and as such *Homo sapiens* heads the table in *Systema Naturae*'s section on the animal kingdom, immediately followed by the monkey. Naturally, placing humans in the same category as the apes was a very radical move in the eighteenth century, and it raised quite a few eyebrows in the still religiously orthodox Sweden. In the following century Charles Darwin would make his entry and carry this thought a considerable step further.

On his return to Sweden, Linnaeus set up a medical practice in Stockholm and became a sought-after society doctor. He soon came in contact with influential circles. One of the leaders of the governing party, the Hats, was Count Carl Gustaf Tessin. His party was planning to set up an academy of science, and Tessin invited Linnaeus to take part in the preliminary work. When the Royal Academy of Sciences was constituted in 1739, Linnaeus was elected its first president. The following year Emanuel Swedenborg was elected a member. This is one of the few recorded instances where Linnaeus's and Swedenborg's paths crossed. But because they were related (Linnaeus married the daughter of Johan Moraeus, who was Swedenborg's cousin, and also his childhood tutor) and moved in the same circles, both academically and socially, it can be assumed that they knew each other and were familiar with each other's writings.

After three years of practicing medicine, Linnaeus was, in 1741, appointed to one of the professorships in medicine at Uppsala University. According to many sources, Linnaeus was one of the most eminent teachers the university has ever had. With him and his colleague Nils Rosén, medicine received new impetus.

FIG. 351. *The Linnaeus Museum, formerly his house, in Uppsala*

FIG. 352. *One of Linnaeus's taxidermied specimens, the rare albino squirrel*

FIG. 353. *Specimen cases containing herbarium sheets, and various animals preserved in alcohol*

FIG. 354. *The lecture room, with one of Linnaeus's medicine chests standing on the table*

FIG. 355. *The study, where Linnaeus wrote many of his botanical treatises*

As was common, his lectures were held in the professor's residence, conveniently located in the botanical garden. Before Linnaeus, the two famous Rudbecks had resided there: Olof Rudbeck, Sr., who founded the botanical garden, and Olof Rudbeck, Jr., Linnaeus's professor and mentor during his years as a student. Not only were the different species and their uses taught, but also Linnaeus's systems and methods. It was not unusual for two hundred to three hundred students to attend his lectures, and Linnaeus proudly tells in his autobiography that frequently part of the group had to listen to him from the hallway. Linnaeus also lectured alfresco, in the countryside around Uppsala. These excursions drew big crowds, and for some time turned botany into something of a popular entertainment for the upper classes. For illustrations, he made use of sheets (paper on which dried plants were mounted) from the herbarium, and of his extensive collection of stuffed and preserved animals. In

Linnaeus's own words, the student could

take delight in seeing with his own eyes the *Rattlesnake* which charms the *Squirrel* . . . the *Spider* which catches birds, the *Scorpion* which emits a deadly sting, the *Didelphis*, which suckles its young inside itself, the fish *Callichtys* which goes overland from one stream to another, the *Aspredo* which chews up food with the movements of its fins, the *Octopus* which clouds the water with black ink, and other even more remarkable things brought hither from a strange world, preserved in bottles, filled with *Spiritu Vini*.[2]

Students came for knowledge, and enthusiasts were permitted to visit, although the botanical garden was closed to the general public. The regulations said: "Respectable folks who wish to see the garden should be allowed so by the gardener, who should always accompany them."[3] Above all, the garden was the place where Linnaeus pursued his own

FIG. 356. *Linnaeus displaying a flower during one of his popular botanical excursions*

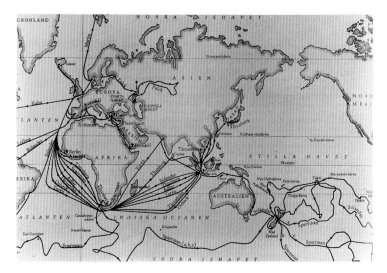

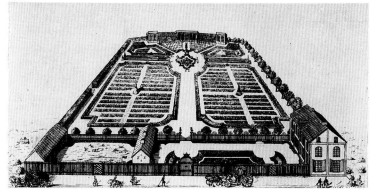

FIG. 357. (left) *The major journeys undertaken by Linnaeus's students, who contributed greatly both to Linnaeus's own studies and to the development of botany as a science*

FIG. 358. *Linnaeus's botanical garden*

research, made new observations, and got inspiration and ideas. "Daily, indeed hourly, I make fresh discoveries in the garden; never do I enter it, but I learn something new."[4] For a great many of the over-seven-thousand descriptions in his work *Species Plantarum* (1753), observations in the garden provided the material. Linnaeus kept extensive diaries of his garden. He noted how leaves and petals settled down for the night, the time of day at which flowers opened, and recorded the date on which different species began to flower.

A team of eager and intellectually outstanding students flocked around Linnaeus, and many of them were later to become prominent scholars in the fields of botany and zoology. They were to travel to all parts of the world, making observations and collecting information on plants and other materials. Some of them accompanied scientific experts on foreign expeditions. Two of Linnaeus's students went with James Cook on his voyages to the South Seas, one conducted a Spanish expedition to South America, and one went on a major Danish expedition to the Arabian countries. From these men, and from an impressive network of correspondence, material streamed into Uppsala to be cataloged and named in the *Systema Naturae*.

Immediately after his appointment as professor of medicine, Linnaeus set out to convince the university of the necessity to extend and reorganize the botanical garden. After acquiring a larger piece of land, Linnaeus and Carl Hårleman, Sweden's foremost architect at the time, planned a garden and orangerie that was in full accord with the ideals of baroque architecture. By the mid-1740s the orangerie and the newly landscaped garden, in the French style, were completed.

The number of plants and flowers cultivated in the garden grew rapidly from a few hundred to about three thousand. Seeds, shoots, and plants were coming in from all over the world. Linnaeus received gifts from several heads of state. Louis XV of France, Catherine II of Russia, and Gustav III of Sweden were among those who gave him their royal support. They were all interested in the development of what would soon become one of Europe's leading botanical gardens. As both the garden and Linnaeus's reputation grew, he was able proudly to declare that his garden included such "plants that none in Europe can equal them, although it is situated in so much colder a climate than gardens in the south."[5]

But as the years passed, Linnaeus found it increasingly difficult to keep up the garden, and it slowly fell into decay. King Gustav III, who had taken great interest in the garden from its start, soon declared it too small and its site unsuitable. Instead, he granted his own palace garden to be developed as a new botanical garden. The old palace garden is now part of the present Uppsala University Botanical Garden, and in the 1920s Linnaeus's garden, in another part of Uppsala, was restored.

The peak of Linnaeus's life came early, and as an old man he seems somewhat bitter. He writes of the world that it is conceited and imperfect, although he found consolation in the harmony and justice of nature. Linnaeus had a sturdy, Carolingian belief in religion. In *Nemesis Divina*, he wrote to his son, "You see confusion around you, as though men never saw nor did they hear. You see the most beauteous lilies choked by weeds. And yet a just god dwells here, giving unto each of us as he deserves."[6] Like many other scientists of his time, working against skepticism and disbelief and aware of the limitations of their knowledge and methods, Linnaeus in his later years gravitated toward a more philosophical and spiritual view of the world.

In this century Linneaus has become more and more appreciated as a writer. The accounts of his five journeys in Sweden, made both during his student years and later, have become classic works of Swedish literature. They are striking descriptions of different parts of the country—Lappland, Dalarna, Öland and Gotland, Västergötland, and Skåne—

FIG. 359. *The orangerie, at one time housing tropical plants, now an administrative building*

FIG. 360. *The "lake pool" in the botanical garden, containing numerous varieties of water lilies*

FIG. 361. Amaranthus caudatus, *commonly called love-lies-bleeding, one of the many flowers cataloged and named by Linnaeus*

FIG. 362. *Statue of Carolus Linnaeus, in the botanical garden*

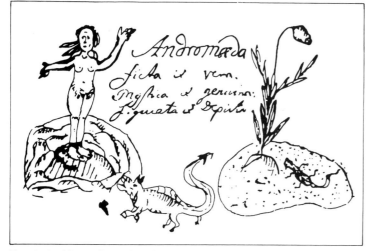

FIG. 363. *Linnaeus's sketch of the flower he named Andromeda, and its mythological background*

with thorough investigations into folklore, economics, geography, and plant and animal life. Linnaeus kept day-to-day records, giving detailed information on historic structures, ancient cult sites, evidence of older cultures, and historic episodes. They are all written in a spontaneous and direct style, uninfluenced by the stereotypes of his age, and express his strong feelings about nature in vivid descriptions of the countryside and its inhabitants.

The first and most important journey was to Lappland, in 1732. Entering an almost unknown region of Sweden, Linnaeus encountered a magnificent nature with many new and fascinating species, and a foreign people with customs and traditions unfamiliar to him. The botanical discoveries he published in *Flora Lapponicum* (1737), but his travel journal, *Iter Lapponicum*, remained unpublished until the nineteenth century. His trip to Lappland proved to be a profound and lasting experience, one that he would often quote in lectures and writings.

Even though his systems and methods of classification have been to some extent revised, Linnaeus remains on the scientific Parnassus as one of the greatest botanists in history. He had a poet's awareness of intrinsic relationships and comprehensive wholes, matched with an ability to embrace a broad spectrum without disregard for detailed knowledge. Linnaeus's fame was built upon a remarkable talent for research and classification, paired with a never-fluctuating belief in the values of his own theories. He was one of the most remarkable scientists Sweden, and the world, have ever known.

FIG. 364. *Linnaeus in Lapp costume, a souvenir from his Lappland journey, by Martin Hoffman, 1737*

Notes

1. Arvid Hjalmar Uggla, *Linnaeus* (Stockholm: Almqvist & Wiksell, 1957), p. 11.
2. Gunnar Broberg, Allan Ellenius, and Bengt Jonsell, *Linnaeus and His Garden* (Uppsala: Swedish Linnaeus Society), p. 27.
3. Ibid., p. 31.
4. Ibid., p. 32.
5. Ibid., p. 29.
6. Ibid., p. 14.

The Search for a Religious Cosmology

Steve Koke

I frame no hypotheses, for whatever is not deduced from the phenomena is to be called an hypothesis; and hypotheses, whether metaphysical or physical, whether of occult qualities or mechanical, have no place in experimental philosophy.

—Sir Isaac Newton, *Principia Mathematica*

The sign that we are willing to be wise, is the desire to know the causes of things, and to investigate the secret and unknown operations of nature. It is for this purpose that each one . . . is eager to acquire a deeper wisdom than merely that which is proffered to him through the medium of the senses.

—Emanuel Swedenborg, *Principia*

SWEDENBORG LIVED AT THE TIME when modern science was finding its soul. He was born one year after Isaac Newton published his *Principia Mathematica* and established the basic concepts of modern physics. Newton's work did not by itself give birth to the science we know; Laplace, Einstein, Bohr, Heisenberg, and others were to complete the birth process. But Newton taught people how to *think* about the world in a new way. His experimental philosophy was destined to influence future scientists to a degree that he did not anticipate, for he saw himself as very much a member of the old school.

Up to Newton's time, theories about the universe were combinations of logic, the few telescopic observations available from a young optical science, and theology. Theology provided facts about God and his creation from revelation. In the absence of firsthand knowledge, there was no other source of comprehensive information about the universe, so eloquently worded convictions about God's purposes were often pitted against each other in an effort to solve all questions with a breakthrough of religious vision. An especially intriguing question was whether any other worlds existed. Aristotle had argued forcefully against the atomist position that there were an infinite number of worlds, or *kosmoi* (one-earth cosmoses, not planets)[1] believing instead that we lived in the only world that God had made, and that we were God's greatest work. Such an idea would have destroyed the unity of a one-world concept, and to medieval thinkers, it would have unseated humanity as the greatest of God's creations.

Later on, other objections to many *kosmoi* were put forward. Should not the Son of God have been born in those other worlds, too? The idea of many incarnations seemed highly objectionable to many thinkers. And why had the Bible not said anything about other worlds? It had to be because there were no others.

In the latter years of the seventeenth century, the concept

STEVE KOKE has had a lifelong interest in the relationship between religion and science. He took his B.A. degree in philosophy in 1964 at San Francisco State College, concentrating on epistemology and philosophy of science. He has written numerous philosophical articles for *The Messenger* and coedited it on two occasions in the early 1960s. Other articles have appeared in various Swedenborgian publications over the last twenty-seven years. He is a life member of the Swedenborg Foundation, a former member of the Board of Managers of the Swedenborg School of Religion, and he participates in a number of scientific organizations.

FIG. 365. *Sir Isaac Newton (1642–1727), by Sir Godfrey Kneller, n.d.*

of *kosmoi* had been replaced long before by the concept of many planets in the same universe, but many thinkers became tired of biblical arguments and their tendency to bog down in speculation. They suggested that the Bible did not forbid the existence of other worlds. Then they introduced a very important change: instead of depending on the Bible for our picture of the universe, we should depend on natural theology. Natural theology was an attempt to read the purposes of God from nature itself. Nature seemed much more able than scripture to show forth the glory of God, for it provided much more direct evidence of what he intended. The hopes of natural theology were grandiose: a new Christianity based on God's works directly consulted.

The natural theologians claimed Newton as one of their own, for Newton was religious and privately believed that God had a role in maintaining order. For example, he believed that his laws could not explain how the planets remained in their orbits; consequently, God had to intervene from time to time to set things back on course. He also could not explain how the solar system began: "I . . . am forced to ascribe it to the counsel and contrivance of a voluntary Agent."[2]

But the truth about Newton's system, if it is considered apart from his personal opinions, is that it did not need a God. Newton had kept his religious beliefs to himself and had worked out his physics with implacable objectivity and logic. That example of intellectual purity inspired others to

dispense with any references to an outside divine force at all, and science eventually became completely detached from religion.

In 1710, Emanuel Swedenborg was a young man of twenty-two. He enthusiastically pursued several scientific interests at the same time and visited London to get instruments and books and to soak in the heady intellectual atmosphere. He made an intensive study of Newton's books and bought telescope tubes and scientific instruments. To a close friend, he wrote, "You encourage me to go on with my studies in science, but it is something that I ought rather to be discouraged in, as I have an immoderate desire for them, especially for astronomy and mechanics."[3]

He also spent time with the astronomer royal of England, the Reverend John Flamsteed, and with Edmund Halley (the discoverer of Halley's comet), discussing astronomy and other scientifc subjects. Halley had played a critical role in the new scientific revolution. Newton was shy; he had developed his ideas as a very private study and had not cared to publish them. After reading his notes, Halley pleaded with Newton to publish them. Finally Newton gave in. If it had not been for Edmund Halley, the history of science, and therefore of many aspects of Western culture, might have been very different.

Swedenborg had hoped to see Newton himself, but the meeting never occurred. He had also expected to be very

FIG. 366. *Edmund Halley (1656–1742)*

impressed with the new science, but he was not. He did not like Newton's theory that space was empty, and he felt that it was wrong to stop thinking scientifically when a phenomenon had been described and formulated into a law. Instead, science should go on to inquire into the ultimate causes of things.[4] As he expressed it in his *Principia* some years later: "The sign that we are willing to be wise, is the desire to know the causes of things, and to investigate the secret and unknown operations of nature. It is for this purpose that each one . . . is eager to acquire a deeper wisdom than merely that which is proffered to him through the medium of the senses" (PRIN vol. 1, p. 2). By this criterion, Newton's science could not reach high enough to be truly enlightening.

"I frame no hypotheses," Newton had said, "for whatever is not deduced from the phenomena is to be called an hypothesis; and hypotheses, whether metaphysical or physical, whether of occult qualities or mechanical, have no place in experimental philosophy."[5] By so saying, he had cleaned up the cluttered halls of the old science, which had engaged in too much theorizing at the expense of the physical evidence. But although Swedenborg agreed on the need for a strongly empirical science, he saw a baby going out with the bathwater—Newton's science was forfeiting its ability to explain truly.

The Longitude Problem

Swedenborg's science was not yet ready to move out into the academic world, for he had not yet decided where he wanted to concentrate his efforts. But his "immoderate" interest in astronomy inspired him to enter a competition for a method of finding longitude at sea. In 1714, a group of sea captains petitioned England's House of Commons for a solution to this problem. The English government then announced an international competition with a prize of twenty thousand pounds sterling. The purpose of the competition was to help international trade. Many European nations were heavily dependent on the exchange of goods by sea, and accurate navigation was a key to their ability to keep up with Europe's rising standard of living. Navigation depends in turn on a special branch of astronomy called "positional astronomy," which concentrates on finding the positions of planets and stars with a very high degree of accuracy. Once the positions of key heavenly bodies are established, the precise locations of ships, cities, and harbors can be determined.

Swedenborg saw in this a clear chance to help Sweden move into modern life and become more competitive. However, he knew nothing of the mathematical theory and procedures that would be required, so he threw himself into positional astronomy and quickly became so expert that he found a solution. The solution was to determine longitude

by referring to the position of the moon. Newton had also arrived at that insight and had tried to work out the details that navigators would need. But nothing could be done without accurate predictions of where the moon would be at a given time. Unfortunately, the moon's motion across the heavens is subject to several influences, and predicting its precise position is one of the most complex problems in astronomy. Newton in fact had confessed that it was the only problem that made his head ache.[6]

Swedenborg was on the right track, but he had launched himself on a long and frustrating quest. Although he was certain that he had the prestigious prize locked up, no one would agree. His theory, *On Finding the Longitude on Land and Sea by Means of the Moon*, was published both inside and outside of Sweden, but it strangely attracted only disinterest or criticism.

The competition was not won until forty years after it was announced. The solution required not only accurate lunar tables, but new mathematical techniques, that had to await invention by Leonhard Euler. Tobias Mayer then worked out the tables that, in 1752, would finally yield the longitude of a ship at sea. Ironically, his tables, which were so long in coming, were not to be the actual solution. The longitude of a ship can also be found by referring to a clock. But up to the time when the competition ended, all clocks were pendulum clocks and would have been completely unreliable at sea; the pitching and tossing of a ship would, of course, violently upset the motion of a pendulum. No sooner had Mayer produced his tables than an English inventor, John Harrison, produced the chronometer. Mayer died, and the twenty-thousand-pound prize was finally divided equally between Harrison and Mayer's widow.[7]

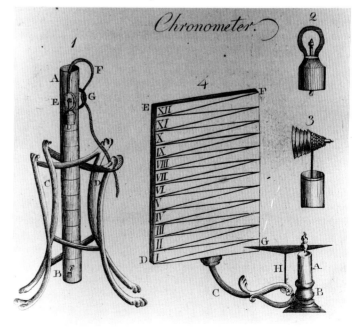

FIG. 367. *An early example (eighteenth century) of a chronometer*

But why did Swedenborg's solution not receive more attention? In her biography, *The Swedenborg Epic,* Cyriel O. Sigstedt quotes Dr. Charles P. Olivier, director of the Flower Observatory:

> The principle of Swedenborg's method of longitude determination seems to be entirely correct. If the two stars are not in the same longitude, the method is still theoretically sound. But the fact that the moon may not be on the ecliptic will make a noticeable error in the solution.[8]

The Universe as an Image of the Infinite

In 1734, Swedenborg published his *Principia,* a general theory about the nature of the universe. Like many modern cosmologists, he began at the level of the extremely small. The material world is built up from simple, dimensionless points that are very like the point in Euclidean geometry. In fact, he believed that Euclidean geometry does indeed describe the world. (Scientists these days believe that it does not, although it is very useful in describing local distances and spaces.) These points were primal expressions of their own origin, what Swedenborg called the Infinite.

Starting with the point in motion, he derived a hierarchy of forms and processes, each stage of which was created by, and was a larger version of, the one that preceded it. All taken together could account for everything in the world.

What is philosophically interesting about the entire scheme is that it is an example of what some philosophers have called *likepartedness.* A philosophy of likepartedness makes an object a collection of smaller versions of itself. Those versions may in turn be made of even smaller versions, and so on, for as many stages as seem necessary. To give a trivial example, a horse may be made up of smaller horses, those of even smaller

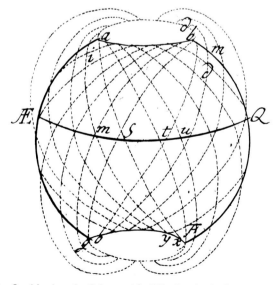

FIG. 368. *Outside view of a finite particle. This drawing by Swedenborg shows how a particle is created by the rapid spiral motions of a more elementary particle. The large globular particle is merely the sum of the motions.*

horses, and so on. Or the strategy may be extended upward: the object is a component of a larger version of itself, and so on. In either case, the part is like the whole, hence the term. Charles A. Whitney, professor of astronomy at Harvard University, finds evidence that likepartedness philosophies were in use in ancient Rome.[9]

The beauty of such a scheme in physics and cosmology is that the origin, or smallest part, by which an object might be explained, is reflected in the form of every larger stage. Thus, an image of the origin is always at hand, preventing long and laborious searches for something entirely different that may in fact never be uncovered and clearly seen. The transparency and simplicity of a likeparted universe promises to clarify ancient and frustrating philosophical questions about its nature and origin. Such a universe is, in fact, just its origin multiplying itself over and over again. In the case of the *Principia,* the Infinite ought to be inferrable from any part of the universe.

The strategy also has enormous aesthetic appeal, for it obeys a traditional rule in science for a well-formed theory— Ockham's razor: "Do not multiply causes unnecessarily." That is, make each cause produce as many of the effects you want to explain as possible. Ideally, only one cause will produce everything. The result of such high efficiency in our thinking is a pretty theory, and scientists have felt that nature, ideally, is pretty, too. Swedenborg's theory obeys the rule ideally.

Swedenborg also seems to have felt that the rational mind proceeds from inference to inference by a recognition of analogous connections between one thing and another. So his hierarchy of forms may even have conformed to the logic of thought itself!

The *Principia* builds its hierarchy of forms and processes out to the stars. Swedenborg anticipated the modern picture of the galaxy by painting the Milky Way as a vast collection of stars wheeling about a common center. It was the ultimate expression of the pattern set up by his tiny fundamental particles. On the way out to the galaxy, however, he offered a "nebular" theory of how the solar system was formed that has become the center of an old but still instructive debate. What is today called "the nebular hypothesis" is the general notion that the solar system was formed from a giant cloud whose matter condensed into the sun and planets.

Most histories of astronomy give Pierre Simon de Laplace, the greatest theorist and mathematician of the late-eighteenth century, the credit for inventing the nebular hypothesis. It is often contended by Swedenborg's students that Swedenborg should have been given credit for the earliest version of it. In fact, they say, Laplace may very well have been inspired either by his exposure to the ideas of Immanuel Kant, who in turn had read Swedenborg's account, or by having read Swedenborg himself.

Let us look at the two contenders. They illustrate some

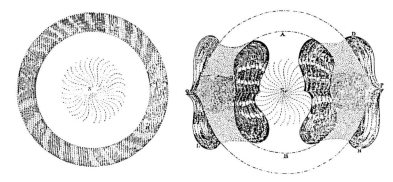 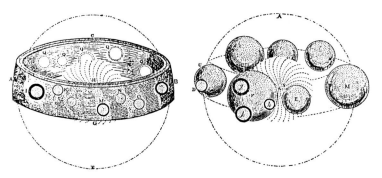

FIG. 369. *Evolution of planets. Swedenborg's drawings show, from left to right, the solar crust surrounding the sun before breakup; the breakup of the crust with some* *parts moving inward and others outward; the gathering of planetary material after the crust collapses into a zone; and the final emergence of individual planetary bodies.*

of the critical changes that science was undergoing at the time.

Swedenborg's hypothesis begins with a mature sun already in place. The sun is at the center of a vortex, a kind of whirlpool in the ether. In time the sun develops a dense crust. But the crust is forced outward by the centrifugal force of the sun's rotation. The crust moves out along the sun's equator into a large, flat ring. Forced to occupy more and more space, it thins until it breaks apart. The pieces then collapse upon themselves like drops of water in midair and become spheres. Some of these spheres continue to move about the sun, but others move out in long, oval orbits, and still others fall into orbits about the larger ones. They become planets, comets, and satellites (PRIN vol. 2, pp. 251–72).

Laplace introduced his nebular hypothesis in a more complex but tentative argument in his book, *The System of the World*. First published in 1796, it went through six editions before Laplace was satisfied with it. He died in 1827, but he had already reviewed the proofs for the sixth edition, which finally appeared in 1835.

Laplace presented not only the theory but also the logic by which he had worked it out. He had been intrigued by some mysterious patterns in the solar system: all of the planets, he said, were for some reason in the same plane; that plane was very near the sun's equatorial plane; they all moved in the same direction around the sun; and they all rotated on their axes in the same direction. In addition, the moons rotated in the same direction around their planets. The entire remarkable picture demanded a systematic explanation.

> The chances are four million to one that this arrangement is not haphazard. . . . Thus we must believe, with at least that much confidence, that a primitive cause has directed the motions of the planets, particularly if we consider that the inclinations of most of the motions are much less than a quarter circle.[10]

Laplace arrived at the following explanation. Unlike Swedenborg, who begins with a philosophical plan, he begins with a telescopic observation.

During the primitive state we suppose for the sun, it resembled the nebulae which the telescope shows to be composed of a nucleus surrounded by a nebulosity. By condensing on the surface of the nucleus, such a nebulosity is being transformed into a star. By extension, one can imagine an earlier state, preceded itself by other states, in which the nucleus was diffuse and less luminous. Thus, one arrives, by tracing back as far as possible, at a nebulosity so diffused that its existence would only be suspected with difficulty.[11]

This enormously distended cloud contracts by gravity toward a relatively dense center. As more and more material pours into the central region, that center becomes the sun. But shreds of cloud are left behind in the form of rings, and these eventually gather themselves into planets.

Now, how much do these theories have in common? The differences would be enormous from a physicist's point of view. Swedenborg has the planets form from a disk that originates in the sun, moves out from it, and breaks up, while Laplace depicts just the opposite process, a contracting nebular cloud that forms the sun and the planets in a sweeping inward motion. The physics of the two processes must solve entirely different sets of problems.

Furthermore, the sun in Swedenborg's system is a vast image of one of his most fundamental particles, and is in a similar way a seed of all subsequent physical creations. The planets are born from the sun as his tiniest "finites" are born from their "actives." His nebular hypothesis is therefore merely one stage in the growth of a hierarchy of similar forms in the *Principia*'s vast likepartedness scheme. That means that the fate of the hypothesis is dependent from the start on the fate of the system. Of course, the hypothesis could be proven true independently, but then one would have to wonder if that was not merely an elaborate coincidence, for the origin or inspiration of a hypothesis determines its character and integrity as much as does its content. Scientists have been reluctant to accept an idea as significant unless it is the result of evidence and remains close to it. A lucky hit doesn't count. Laplace's theory is, on the other hand, inspired entirely by observations.

But what is most dramatic is that Laplace's theory contradicts Swedenborg's system in principle. In Swedenborg's system, everything must evolve from the inside out, and the sun is the required cause of everything around it. In Laplace's system, the solar system is created from the outside in, and the planets and sun are both formed by the original cloud; thus, the sun and planets begin as siblings.*

Therefore a difference exists not only in physical details between the two hypotheses: they are opposed to each other in spirit. So one must ask whether the tendency to link the two theories just because both use a nebular medium represents a significant judgment about them. Even the one overall similarity—the nebular medium—is not free of doubt, for it is not clear that Swedenborg includes a nebular cloud at all. The word *nebular* comes from the nebulous patches of light astronomers saw in the night sky. It is still used to denote a very low-density cloud. Swedenborg does not use the term, and his "dense crust" suggests something much more substantial that is not clearly cloudlike even in its distended stage.

The two theories actually belong to two different scientific traditions, and the old question "Why is Swedenborg's theory not included in more histories of science?" may best be answered from this point of view: the entire controversy is an illustration of what happens when a "paradigm shift"—a complete change in the concept of how science is to be pursued—takes place between one thinker's work and another's. In the course of such a shift, even the meanings of basic terms may change. To see this a little more clearly, let us empathize a bit with the beleaguered historians in this case. Including Swedenborg in the history of the nebular hypothesis seems to be a matter of judgment for two reasons:

First, historians of science typically start with the very useful and interesting intention of clarifying the present. Why is Western science the way it is? What got us to this point? Researching a book then becomes a search for roots, and the most logical way to uncover those roots is to trace events backward until one gets to a likely starting point, then tell the story forward. Consequently, anything that does not lie on the line of succession has a good chance of being bypassed, *even though* it is in some more general sense an

*One should be aware of a confusing use of language in discussions of nebular theories. Laplace, in the previous quote, calls the original nebular cloud "the sun" as soon as it develops a nucleus. Other commentators have done the same thing. The problem is that a nebular mass that is in the process of contracting into a sun and planets is not clearly a nebular cloud or a sun and planets. Calling the contracting cloud "the sun" can then convey the misleading impression that Laplace's theory is like Swedenborg's, a theory in which the sun creates the planets from its own material. The two theories are not so similar, and I have tried to preserve a sense of their differentness by not referring to a sun until it has been fully formed.

event in science. This is the most likely fate of any scientific movement whose values and methods have not remained a significant force in our own time.

Second, the meaning of the term *nebular hypothesis* has undoubtedly shifted to reflect current ideas. Scientists have never observed a nebular cloud emerge from a sun. But they have seen suns emerge from nebular clouds, and they are confident that the same clouds produce planets as well. The term *nebular hypothesis* in a scientist's working vocabulary tends to refer only to theories that are actually proving themselves out or are in line with current expectations. Scientific ideas are required to remain close to the evidence for them, and that produces a tendency for the evidence to color the terminology. With the current terminology in mind, historians may not think that *nebular hypothesis* leads to a meaningful discussion if one must bring in everything that has ever borne the name.

The result is an apparent rejection, by many historians, of Swedenborg's work. But it is not rejection so much as a judgment about what would better explain our time in the terms of our time.

Still, one has to admit that scientists are not known for their fondness for religions and mystical experience, and it is therefore possible that Swedenborg's theological work seemed to them to cast a shadow on his scientific work. That has been a strong suspicion among many of Swedenborg's students. But there is a problem here: only those scientists who knew of both sides of this complex man but had somehow missed the sequence in which these sides asserted themselves would have tried to dismiss his scientific work because of his revelatory claims. Swedenborg was a scientist first and introduced his nebular hypothesis in 1734; he did not become a theologian until 1745. Consequently, the later appearance of any apparent religious irrationality in his life would have condemned his scientific work retroactively. Despite their feelings about theologians and mystical experience, most scientists would consider that illogical. That type of rejection is probably the least likely to last two full centuries.

Obviously, there has been an informal but dramatic controversy between Swedenborg and many scientists, even of his own time, over the proper relationship between guiding principles about the universe and immediate findings. We have seen Swedenborg at work with high philosophical principles; but after the midpoint of the century he looked to a radically different source for his guiding ideas.

The Universe as a Nursery for Humanity

In 1758, Swedenborg published *Earths in the Universe*. It contained the astonishing claim that he had conversed with people in the spiritual world who had inhabited other planets.

The material had appeared in his *Arcana Coelestia,* but it was now available under its own title with a few changes in organization and wording.

It consisted of four parts: an opening chapter presenting arguments for the existence of human life everywhere in the universe, a set of chapters describing life on the moon and on each of the planets in the solar system, an explanation of the reasons that the Lord was born on this planet and not on another, and a final set of chapters on five inhabited planets in other solar systems.

Every star, Swedenborg said, is a sun, and every sun has planets. Each planet is an "earth" and an earth has no purpose other than to serve as a nursery for the human race. This picture supported a grand cosmological principle: the Divine Being created the universe for no other purpose than to form an angelic heaven from the human race "wherein the Divine may dwell with angels and men" (EU 4). The universe was typically described by other thinkers of the period as a creation by God for humanity or for some collection of intelligent species; there they stopped. Only Swedenborg seems to have formulated a vision of the universe as an instrument of the *relationship* between God and humanity.

The planets are inhabited by people who look very much like us. There are minor differences in some cases; for example, the people of Mars have dark skin in roughly the same area in which we have facial hair, and the people of the moon look very much like dwarfs. The planets are physically similar to Earth, with soil-covered surfaces and a full complement of plants, trees, and animals, none of which is at all so bizarre as the mental creations of science-fiction writers and evolutionary theorists.

Swedenborg described life as we know it, and he thereby created a number of problems for modern readers. We have been schooled to believe that a different planet, with a different size, a different distance from the sun, and a generally different chemistry, must of necessity give birth to strange forms of life. Even in Swedenborg's time, which was before Darwin's theory of evolution appeared, writers commonly put fantastic creatures on the moon and planets. Swedenborg's account supports his general theological insight that the human form is not just the utilitarian result of different physical conditions; instead, it is a representation of understanding and will, intellect and emotion, themselves. With his doctrine that physical forms reflect the spiritual forces that they contain, the human form becomes the standard for intelligent life everywhere. And if nature reflects these spiritual forces in more highly specialized ways, even the animals and plants of other planets will look familiar.

That seems incredible now, but it must be noticed that the definition of *human* is open-ended in Swedenborg's system. There are infinite ways in which the same form can vary. All that is definitely excluded is a complete departure from the basic form with its one head, two eyes, nose, a mouth below, two arms, two legs, and so on. Within that framework there can be many variations. In fact, Swedenborg makes an interesting observation in the chapter on the inhabitants of Jupiter—they are better-looking than we are. Lest we think that Swedenborg surreptitiously makes *our* form the standard for the universe, we are only a variation on the standard ourselves.

All planetary cultures other than our own are technologically primitive and do not even possess the art of writing. Astronomy and the other sciences do not exist elsewhere. Instead of astronomy, there is a kind of mythology in which the stars are typically regarded as the abodes of angels. That was also an early belief here.

In Swedenborg's time, the atmosphere in the sciences was very encouraging to ideas such as these. As we have seen, a long and sometimes bitter debate over the existence of other worlds had raged since Aristotle, and it was resolved, for the time being, only at the end of the seventeenth century in favor of many inhabited worlds. *Earths in the Universe* was astonishing only in its claim that Swedenborg had spoken personally to other beings. Swedenborg's arguments that all planets were inhabited were repetitions, sometimes with a minor difference or two, of arguments that went back a century or more. In these arguments Swedenborg evidently tries only to remind his readers of the strength of the other-worlds philosophy. It was the dominant viewpoint of the time and a convenient way to prepare the reader for his revelatory experiences.

Today, however, the book has become an enigma. As planetary astronomy evolved through the nineteenth and twentieth centuries, it developed an almost morose tendency to bad news: the planets Swedenborg had described so charmingly were probably barren. Then, in the last half of the twentieth century, the exploration of the solar system exploded with the invention of the space probe. In the most active period, from October 11, 1958, the date of the launch of *Pioneer 1* toward the moon, to September 14, 1978, the launch date of *Venera 12,* a Soviet spacecraft destined for Venus, sixty-nine space probes from the United States and the Soviet Union were sent into space. In the meantime, six manned *Apollo* flights put a total of twelve men on the moon's surface. Important advances in Earth-based astronomy also took place. Radar astronomy actually anticipated the discovery of the Venus probes that the surface of Venus was extremely hot, and infrared astronomy and X-ray astronomy probed deep into planetary atmospheres and the nature of distant stars.

All that adventurous activity was disastrous for Swedenborg's vision of the solar system. Now the other planets do not look as though they were ever intended to support life. We cannot even claim to be surrounded by planets that once were occupied but failed their people in some way, for the solar system is not yet very old, and too many defunct planets would compromise Swedenborg's principle that the universe is a nursery for the human race.

But this is also a time of confusion, a time when questions need to be reformulated, a mountain of new data geared to old questions reviewed, and new perspectives generated. We have opened the exploration of the solar system, but the result has been something like the opening of Fibber McGee's closet. In the future we can expect more revealing patterns, more overall enlightenment. But we cannot expect inhabitants, especially of the kind that Swedenborg described:

What has happened?

That will probably remain one of the most interesting questions for Swedenborg's students. But we can take a look, here, at some suggestive facts.

First, Swedenborg's picture of the solar system fits very comfortably into the culture and the philosophical expectations of the eighteenth century. As we have mentioned, its arguments are those of the then-current other-worlds debate. Its concepts do not try to revise any basic concepts and imagery already in use. The idea that one could communicate with the spiritual world was a radical claim, but the solar system that Swedenborg explored was the classical solar system then in place in the sciences. As we now know, it was incomplete; Uranus, Neptune, and Pluto, far beyond Saturn, the most distant planet of antiquity, were still to be discovered. Swedenborg anticipates no new discoveries about the solar system.

Neither did the angels have a more advanced view of things. In *Earths in the Universe*, Swedenborg describes the picture of the solar system that angels and spirits shared with each other (EU 42). It, too, only goes out to Saturn. Evidently, the angels know no more about the solar system than we do at any given time; and that in turn suggests that they get their astronomy from us.

Now, if they get their astronomy from us, then their picture of the planets cannot contain more accurate information than the state of *our* knowledge would allow. Not very much was known about the other planets in the eighteenth century, and the possibility therefore arises that *Earths in the Universe* was strongly influenced by miscues and omissions in eighteenth-century astronomy. It is ironic that Uranus, the first planet to be discovered beyond Saturn, was found in 1781; if Swedenborg had lived only nine more years, he would undoubtedly have made some interesting additional comments on the solar system.

It is sometimes suggested that the planets were misidentified. That is, Swedenborg's spiritual-world encounters with the former inhabitants of other planets were genuine, but the planets from which they were supposed to have come were not correctly identified. That turns out to be a very arguable thesis. Swedenborg tells us that the planets cannot be seen in the spiritual world. And because they had not developed the sciences, the inhabitants could not have told him where their planets were.

Consequently, there was no other astronomy on the scene than that of eighteenth-century Earth. In fact, the inhabitants of other planets undoubtedly did not even know what a planet was, for the concept of a planet is an artifact of a fairly well developed astronomy. The idea is only a few hundred years old, and we were able to formulate it only after some struggle with old scientific ideas and cosmologies.

There is positive evidence of planetary misidentification. For example, Swedenborg reports that the Jovian day was only six hours long. However, Jean Dominique Cassini, one of the most famous astronomers of the seventeenth century, had measured the length of Jupiter's day through the telescope; it was a little short of ten hours, which is very close to the modern figure. Swedenborg may have wondered what to do with the discrepancy, for when he was a young man he had admired Cassini. The six-hour figure appears in his private *Spiritual Diary*, but not in any of the works that he published (SD 583).

In another suggestive case, Swedenborg asked the inhabitants of Saturn about their spectacular ring system. They replied that they did not see rings, but a snowy light "in various directions." In the *Arcana*'s account, there is an earlier passage in which the light is described as a great nocturnal light that some Saturnians believed was the Lord. Swedenborg attributes the entire display to the rings aided by Saturn's moons (AC 8951–52; see also EU 104).

Some of the details are vague; one does not always know just what was seen. But in general, the entire phenomenon seems open to other interpretations. We now know that the rings lie in Saturn's equatorial plane and at least would not appear to move. As the planet rotated on its axis and carried its inhabitants on around, an observer would always be at the same distance north or south of the ring plane at any time of the day. The rings would therefore always appear in an unvarying shape and position above the horizon. The rings are also not visible at night; the vast shadow of Saturn darkens them (and some of the moons) on the night side. Another explanation may work just as well: a brilliant aurora.

What is especially arresting is that Christian Huygens described the position of the rings and the planet's shadow as early as the late-seventeenth century. Swedenborg may have felt, nevertheless, that the observation by the Saturnians remained highly suggestive. For whatever reason, he decided to publish it.

We can extend the list of examples, but for our purposes here, it is enough just to be suggestive. Swedenborg seems to have found people in the spiritual world who came from planets that were similar to ours in some respects, but that in other respects were different—fully as if they were actually located elsewhere.

Furthermore, he describes none of his planets as having a characteristic we know to be unique to it.

Because some of his information was not in full agreement even with good eighteenth-century observations, Swedenborg must have sensed that his thesis was not working as smoothly as he would have hoped. But at the time there was no other way to think about life in the universe. The concept had to be based on astronomy, and there is usually no more than one astronomy available at any one time. We can take a different position today *only* because another astronomy has arisen and forced the issue for us.

Also, some writers have pointed out that Swedenborg was an honest reporter. Inge Jonsson (professor in the Department of the History of Ideas and Science at the University of Uppsala), in his biography *Emanuel Swedenborg,* points out Swedenborg's "scientific lack of prejudice," which "allowed him to present undaunted the most absurd information about the lunar spirits."[12] That is a thoughtful observation, for it suggests that Swedenborg felt more obligated to transmit the ideas and experiences that came to him than to be analytical about them.

Nevertheless, he may have made sure that the uncertain elements of the subject would not be too influential. The portentous identities of the planets are actually inactive. That is, nothing depends on Mars being Mars rather than some other planet. The names of the planets thus do no philosophical work; they fill out a picture, but to no significant effect. Furthermore, the angels had a complete philosophy about the solar system; its meaning is buried in the partially described imagery of paragraph 42 (EU). Swedenborg surprisingly spends no time with it, though, and seems to have deliberately scrambled the order of the chapters themselves. He may not have wanted his readers to race into generalizations with which he did not feel secure himself.

Each planet thus stands alone, a completely individual case, as if it really could have been anywhere. Elsewhere in his theological works, the subject of other planets and the universal spiritual world is almost never mentioned.

Earths in the Universe seems to have functioned as an elaborate feedback system for the eighteenth century. It took that culture's picture of the solar system, infused it with spiritual contents, and reflected it back to the culture. That endowed the eighteenth century with a stronger vision of our place in the universe (even if only a few people read the book) and redefined humanity as a presence throughout the universe. That was a sharp departure from the common idea that other planets contained only strange forms of life, and it is still a challenging concept. The book is also a reminder

that religious cosmologies as such may be, for whatever reason, subject to the current state of the sciences.

Some Final Comments

Swedenborg's criticism of modern science is devastating: Unless one can stand somewhere above the universe, nothing in it can be explained. What one ends up with is a kind of reasoning that is "continuous with effects." That is, the universe is the realm of effects, and their causes are above the universe in some realm of spiritual or "First Principles." Newton's science, limited to the realm of effects, could only explain one natural phenomenon in terms of another. In fact, it is a rule in modern science that everything has a natural explanation. Yet, that seems to mean that nature herself must be without an explanation.

As we have seen, Swedenborg tried to overcome such limitations by working, first, from philosophical principles in the *Principia.* The result is so well integrated with itself that it is virtually a work of art. But the sciences later came up with some different results. In *Earths in the Universe,* Swedenborg tried his top-down approach again, this time utilizing the spiritual world as his starting point. But again, a later science came up with a dissenting picture.

It is difficult not to see a fundamental wisdom in Swedenborg's elevated starting points. Significantly, his method was to use his principles and spiritual insights to infuse meaning into the *current* scientific view of the universe. His spiritual experiences did not include any scientific revelations; the only view of the universe that he could build upon at any time in his life was that of eighteenth-century science. Even the angels seemed to reflect it back to him. That had two important consequences.

First, he had to be both empirical, or dependent on current observations, and highly principled and philosophical. In a way often avoided by modern scientists, he was the "compleat scientist," who saw no limit to the resources that a cosmologist could use to develop a satisfying understanding of the universe.

But, second, his approach was necessarily dependent on the accuracy of the science at hand. If that science had errors of omission or erroneous ideas, the religious cosmology that even the best principles inspire would be limited and unable to survive the next revolution in scientific ideas.

Nevertheless, it is difficult to avoid this problem, for science always uses all that we know to tell us what kind of universe we live in. Future changes in science, therefore, cannot be predicted, for *the universe always seems to conform precisely to the current scientific picture of it*. As has been mentioned, it is only because we have seen some very surprising revolutions take place in astronomy since Swedenborg's time that we can even consider an alternative to Swedenborg's view of the solar system.

It seems that the search for a religious cosmology will always entail taking risks. Swedenborg seems to have done so, perhaps in order to present a complete viewpoint to the eighteenth century. The fact that science grows and changes forces us to see that the quest for a religious cosmology may have to be renewed in every century. But what we gain from our cosmologies is a very revealing look at the best knowledge and spiritual insight that our time has acquired.

Notes

1. Steven J. Dick, *Plurality of Worlds: The Origins of the Extraterrestrial Life Debate from Deocritus to Kant* (Cambridge, Eng.: Cambridge University Press, 1982), pp. 12–22.

2. Sir Isaac Newton to Richard Bentley, in Charles A. Whitney, *The Discovery of Our Galaxy* (New York: Alfred A. Knopf, 1971), p. 52.

3. Cyriel O. Sigsted, *The Swedenborg Epic* (New

4. Inge Jonsson, *Emanuel Swedenborg,* trans. Catherine Djurklou (New York: Twayne Publishers, 1971), p. 30.

5. Sir Isaac Newton, *Mathematical Principles of Natural Philosophy* (1687), trans. Andrew Motte, Great Books of the Western World, vol. 34 (Chicago: *Encyclopaedia Britannica*, 1952), p. 371.

York: Bookman Associates, 1952), p. 21.

6. Fred Hoyle, *Astronomy* (New York: Crescent Books, n.d.), p. 144.

7. Ibid., pp. 142–45.

8. Sigstedt, p. 331.

9. Whitney, p. 73.

10. Laplace as quoted in Whitney, p. 140.

11. Whitney, p. 145.

12. Jonsson, p. 148.

Homeopathy and the
Swedenborgian Perspective

FIG. 370. *Samuel Hahnemann (1755-1843)*

In this section we have included the briefest of introductions to what has proved to be an immense topic, worthy of a book in its own right: the similarity and actual connection between the ideas of Emanuel Swedenborg and Samuel Hahnemann, founder of the healing science called homeopathy.

Such a connection would have been far easier to make during the nineteenth century, when many more people were conversant with both philosophers and put them to use in their daily lives. For example, in the homes of R. W. Emerson or the James family, and throughout New England's intellectual culture, during discussions of why homeopathy should work as well as it does, seemingly in defiance of materialistic reality, Swedenborg's spiritual cosmology would frequently be drawn upon as providing an explanatory framework.

Our major article was solicited from Elinore Peebles, who grew up in such a household and was steeped in both homeopathic and Swedenborgian philosophies from an early age. Her biographical as well as scholarly perspective helps to underline the connection we are exploring.

To add some theoretical depth to our topic we requested a brief article from Dr. Edward C. Whitmont, a Jungian analyst and one of the foremost theorists of homeopathy in the world today. The selection included is from an unpublished paper and a preface penned by him. He is the author of *Psyche and Substance*, an influential book that helps to lay a theoretical groundwork for an energy-based concept of health and healing that also accords with the discoveries of modern physics.

To lend a realistic flavor of how a practicing homeopath works, we have a brief outline by Richard Moskowitz, M.D., a well-respected New England homeopath who is familiar with Swedenborgian thought, and who has contributed a brief but coherent outline entitled, "What Is Homeopathy?"

Lastly, the reader who wishes to learn more about homeopathy is referred to relevant books and publications as well as addresses of associations for contemporary homeopathy, and suppliers of homeopathic remedies.

Part 1
Homeopathy and the New Church

Elinore Peebles

THERE ARE MANY POINTS OF SIMILARITY between Emanuel Swedenborg, the religious reformer, and Samuel Hahnemann, the medical rebel. Both had almost unlimited curiosity and intellectual capacity as well as spiritual vision, and they were both dedicated to the service of humankind—Swedenborg in his quest for the true meaning of our life on earth and our spiritual growth through "regeneration" [see Glossary], and Hahnemann in his search for an understanding and cure of disease. Each had a permanent impact on later religious and medical thinking. Swedenborg's writings have challenged and modified the dogmatic theology of the past, and Hahnemann broke the grip of the ineffective and often lethal medical practice of his day.

My earliest recollection of hearing of a possible relationship between homeopathy and the New Church [Swedenborgian; see Glossary] takes me back to my seventh year, when I began to sit in on Sunday afternoon gatherings of several local homeopathic physicians who met in my father's office to prepare medicines and compare notes on their cases. Of the five who got together more or less regularly, three were Swedenborgians, so they were well qualified to compare the two disciplines. Quite early I was conditioned to accept this connection as a fact of life, and throughout adolescence I made a real nuisance of myself on the subject, until one day a visiting relative said, "Listen to my dear cousin, a good

Swedenborgian and Hahnemannian! To hear her, you'd have to believe homeopathy could raise the dead."

After that, I acquired some discretion and came to agree with Constantine Hering, the "Father of American Homeopathy," who formulated "Hering's Law"* and who is said to have written in 1850, "While there is good reason why Swedenborgians might prefer homeopathic treatment, there is none at all that all homeopaths be Swedenborgians."[1] He felt that the science did not need to prove itself by religious doctrine and should not try to do so. Nevertheless, as a member of the Philadelphia New Church, he was always ready to discuss the philosophical similarities, as were many of his colleagues.

There are several interesting pamphlets on this subject in the library of the Swedenborg School of Religion in Newton, Massachusetts. One in particular, *A Defense of Homeopathy against its New Church Assailants*,[2] is of particular interest. Hering contributed to it, as did Richard de Charms. Dr. William Holcombe (who later became a member of the Cincinnati New Church) took the negative position very forcefully, writing that he had been an allopathic physician for

---

*Hahnemann taught, and Hering agreed, that in the curative process, symptoms move directionally, from within → out, from above → below, so that illness moves from more to less vital parts of the whole organism as healing takes place.

ELINORE PEEBLES, born April 28, 1897, is the daughter of the well-known homeopathic physician Charles Cutting. From early childhood she had one ambition: to follow in her father's profession. Listening at his feet and accompanying him sometimes on his rounds, she absorbed the principles of homeopathy from the time she was about seven. After leaving the Waltham New Church School in 1913, family circumstances interdicted her desire to enter the medical profession, and the premature death of Dr. Cutting left Elinore, at an early age, to seek employment to help support the family. Though she gave up all thought of college and professional training, Mrs. Peebles became one of this country's most knowledgeable students of the history, theories, and practice of homeopathy. She was married to Waldo Cutler Peebles, who was active in both homeopathy and the New Church and who published a number of essays and articles on Swedenborg. All her adult life, Mrs. Peebles has been active in the homeopathic lay movement, especially in her home area of Massachusetts. She has received awards from both the Swedenborgian church and the American Institute of Homeopathy for her outstanding work and support.

many years and expected to remain one for the rest of his life. However, in 1851 he became a homeopathic physician, writing with equal force for its defense and, according to his biography, became so thoroughly converted that he is known as the "Father of Southern Homeopathy." Dr. Holcombe was later a member of the Cincinnati New Church.

Constantine Hering was assigned by the medical association to expose this medical heresy called "homeopathy," but he had to leave Germany when his investigations led him to study it more deeply and finally to practice the very science he was supposed to discredit. He very prudently removed to America. De Charms tells us that Hering, a Lutheran, had been charged by a Lutheran clergyman with "casting out devils by Beelzebub, the prince of devils, as a homeopathist."[3]

Many years ago, when I first became interested in this subject, I was surprised to discover the great number of homeopathic physicians who were what I would call "unchurched Swedenborgians." For, although only a minority were active church members, a great many more believed that familiarity with Swedenborg's writings was helpful in practicing their homeotherapeutics.

In writing about homeopathy, especially for those who may know little about it, it seems logical to start by introducing the founder of the science. Samuel Hahnemann was born in Meissen, Germany, in 1755, the oldest child in a large and poverty-stricken family. His father, a porcelain worker, seems to have recognized special qualities in this son. He encouraged his interest in nature, gave him "lessons in thinking," taught him to look for reasons in all things, and supported his wish to become a physician.

Hahnemann worked his way through two years of premedical studies by teaching German and French to a wealthy Greek, and by translating books from English into German; with some financial difficulty he put himself through his two final years at Erlangen University. When he graduated in 1779 and started to practice, in addition to his native German he knew, according to William Harvey King,[4] Latin, Greek, English, Hebrew, Syriac, Italian, Arabic, and Spanish. He also had some knowledge of Chaldean and some writers add Sanskrit.* Becoming increasingly unhappy with the drastic medical treatments then in vogue, and fearful of hurting rather than helping the sick, he temporarily gave up the practice of medicine and moved to chemistry, a newly developing science. By 1784 Hahnemann was well known as a teacher of chemistry, as well as for his original and sometimes daring experiments.

It was during this professional interlude that he got a com-

mission to translate into German the Materia Medica of the Scottish physician William Cullen. In this work he found what seemed to him a fanciful discussion of the way Peruvian bark (cinchona) worked in treating malaria. So Hahnemann decided to experiment by taking a dose of this drug himself; and he discovered—to his great astonishment—that it produced in him the symptoms of malaria. Hahnemann was so impressed that he then began to experiment with other drugs. He found that, in each case, a drug would induce in a healthy subject symptoms of a disease that it would cure in a sick subject.

Certain now that he had found a safe method of treating illness, he set out on a path from which he never deviated. He called this new medical technique "homeopathy" (from the Greek, "similar suffering") and adopted as his motto, *Similia similibus curantur* ("Let likes be cured by likes"—or, popularly, "Like cures like"). Hahnemann's later research into medical history turned up some references to this same theory or principle, in writings of Hindu sages (ca. 2000 B.C.) down through Hippocrates (ca. 460 B.C.).*

It was not long before Hahnemann discovered why the theory of similars had not prevailed. He first experimented by giving small doses of medicinal substances to healthy family members and friends who volunteered to be tested, and recording their reactions in terms of symptoms produced. He then prescribed the appropriate medicine to patients whose symptoms matched those that had been caused in the healthy person. Most of the drugs used were more or less poisonous, and Hahnemann knew that the body would try to excrete them as rapidly as possible. But when he diluted them to a point where they could be tolerated, he found that, although patients sometimes felt better for a short time, they were not cured, and the disease was still active when the substance was withdrawn.

Pursuing his basic premise, he continued to experiment, and discovered quite by accident that when a phial containing a diluted drug was struck sharply against a hard surface (which he called "succussion") and the contents then administered to healthy persons (Hahnemann called such persons "provers"), the drug, although no longer poisonous in its dilute form, had developed a much wider range of action. He pursued this process in a series: first he added one part of the crude drug to nine parts of a diluent and then subjected the container to succussion. He called the resulting dilution a "1× potency." He then diluted one part of this mixture with nine parts of a diluent and, after succussion, he got what he called a "2× potency." Continuing this process, he reached a 30× potency, in which no trace of the original drug was detectable. However, its medicinal qualities remained, greatly

---

*Swedenborg too was to become a great scholar of languages, mastering Greek and Latin, Hebrew, English, French, German, Italian, and probably Dutch.

*The "Law of Similars," oddly enough, seemed to surface during periods when religious philosophy and medicine were combined, and seemed to go underground during periods of materialistic philosophy.[5]

enhanced. (Originally done laboriously by hand, succussion is now done by sophisticated machines, and the energy can be increased by the thousands.)

Recent research in England suggests that as the dilutions increase, the molecular pattern remains the same but the latent energy increases. Attempts are now being made to find out what kind of energy is involved and why it increases.

There is a great deal more to be discovered about why homeopathy works as it does. Much of it is methodology. Doctors often differ in practice, but almost all agree on its three basic principles: the *similia* approach to illness, and either the single smallest dose or few repetitions of the indicated remedy. Most homeopathically prepared medicines are from natural sources in the animal, vegetable, and mineral kingdoms. Hahnemann taught that all things in nature are living entities and that it is necessary to develop medicinal substances beyond their material state and to tap their immaterial power (he called it "spirit-life" power) to deal with disease, which he believed had an immaterial cause before the visible material symptoms appeared.

Nowhere in Hahnemann's voluminous writings (and I have read all that have been translated) does he mention Swedenborg or make any direct reference to his writings. But in many paragraphs throughout the six editions of his *Organon of Medicine* he equates physical health with spiritual health. In his analysis of chronic diseases, which he considered an expression of evils inherited from hereditary sources, his treatment is directed toward eliminating or modifying their destructive force, so that their impact may be less in future generations. In fact, the homeopathic emphasis on constitutional treatment from infancy is directed to that end.*

In Hahnemann's letters and other writings one can see his gradual shift from a purely physiological approach to the causes of disease, toward a more spiritual causality. In the first edition of his *Organon* he refers to a "healing principle in man, the essence of which is not known."[6] His search for a beyond-the-visible corrective action of remedies continued throughout his later years, and throughout his writings his belief that there exists in diseases an immaterial, spiritlike force is evident. He called this the "vital *dynamis*," which must be met by a similar but different vital force in the medicine.

Swedenborg wrote in *Divine Love and Wisdom*, "All animals, large and small, have their source in something spiritual on that lowest level called 'actual.'" Also, "Both the animal kingdom and the vegetable kingdom have their source from a spiritual inflow" (DLW 346). This seems to suggest a relationship between Swedenborg's teachings and those of

Hahnemann, and may be one reason some Swedenborgians have preferred homeopathic treatment in illness. Hahnemann writes:

> Our vital force, as a spirit-like *dynamis*, cannot be attacked by injurious external influences on the healthy organism otherwise than in a spirit-like way, and in like manner all such morbid derangements [diseases] cannot be removed from it by the physician in any other way than by spirit-like powers in the medicinal substance acting on our spirit-like force.[7]

Again in *Divine Love and Wisdom* we find: "People are born into all kinds of evil as a result of hereditary defect, and these evils dwell in the outmost reaches. This defect is not removed unless the higher levels are opened" (DLW 432).

Hahnemann divided diseases into three classes: (1) those that belong to the individual and his or her surroundings, developed by his or her situation; (2) constitutional inheritance to which we are particularly susceptible; and (3) diseases that flow from the solidarity of the race, that is, concrete spheres of evil, epidemics, and contagions that come and go, visiting their destructive powers on persons who had not originated them and are therefore in no way spiritually responsible for their influence. It is the second and third of these types, he says, that must be met on the dynamic plane to remove their effects from the organism.

Hahnemann recognized that in addition to the spiritual *dynamis*, which was designed by a "beneficent Creator" to channel the influences intended to keep the body in balance, there must be a corresponding physical system (1) through which health could be maintained, and (2) whose highly individual manifestations were spread throughout the entire physical body.

It seems likely that Hahnemann was describing the immune system, which normally responds immediately to remove the material effects of "morbific" (disease causing) influences. But he also suggested that it only works as it is intended if the corresponding spiritual influence is in order. Because often this is not the case, help provided by the medicines may be needed.

In the sixteenth century an English physician wrote that "our bodies cannot be hurt by corrupt and infective causes except there be in them a certain matter apt to receive it, else if one were sick, all would be sick."[8] And on the contemporary scene, the late Dr. René Dubos, a microbiologist at the Rockefeller Institute for Medical Research, said in a frank examination of the entire germ theory of disease that "man always harbors a host of potentially dangerous microbes and has in his tissues everything required for their life. Most of them will probably remain dormant but some will eventually proliferate despite the presence of specific antibodies if the body's normal physiology is upset."[9] He postulated a

---

*Homeopaths distinguish between constitutional (long-term, or chronic) illnesses, prescribing high-potency remedies; and acute illnesses, often (though not always) prescribing lower-potency doses, repeated more frequently.

FIG. 371. *James Tyler Kent (1849–1916)*

state of biological equilibrium between people and microbes that is rendered unstable by any shift from the normal—emotional, nutritional, environmental, or from excessively vigorous treatment with drugs.

James Tyler Kent* put a number of Hahnemann's scattered statements together and found that the explanation of the apparent inability of the spiritlike *dynamis* always to hold the material organism in balance (suggesting that in a time long ago this presumably had been possible) must be that throughout many generations mankind has allowed evils and falsities to creep in, making it too difficult to keep the good influences in the ascendancy. Over and over he reminds us that health flows from the spiritual to the physical, that is, from the innermost to the outermost and from above downward. Swedenborg said the same thing in *Arcana Coelestia*, stating that "influx" [see Glossary] always moves from internals to externals (AC 6322).

Kent further condenses the sense of several paragraphs in different editions of the *Organon* into the following:

Falsities which interfere with harmonious influx are shown in the physical organism by their natural correspondences, and these are the symptoms which tell us which medicine

*James Tyler Kent was a renowned nineteenth-century physician, as well as a writer and professor of the Materia Medica and an outstanding teacher of homeopathy. Kent was an avid reader of Swedenborg, and his writing is full of Swedenborgian thought (see "Supplemental Readings," at the end of this section on homeopathy).

will remove them and permit the immaterial vital force which permeates all parts of the body to be receptive again to heavenly influences. Therefore, obedience to spiritual and natural laws is the absolute condition to health in both soul and body. Every deviation may bring spiritual and natural disease.[10]

Kent tells us that Hahnemann believed there were three degrees in the dynamis and that all objects in the natural world correspond to them. Swedenborg puts it this way: "The whole natural world corresponds to the spiritual world" (HH 89). Hahnemann's philosophical writings show a partial understanding of Swedenborg's doctrine of the Universal Human (*Maximus Homo* [see Glossary]) although he does not use either term. He speaks, rather, of every person's being a representative of the "collective spiritual man," and believed that every part of an individual has its natural correspondence with this spiritual representative human.

Swedenborg says in *Arcana Coelestia* that the true principle of cure is the divine love brought by the Lord's humanity and life of divine truth to infernal spirits in the bodies of people, so as to cause them to recede. He adds, "But this is no hindrance to a person's being healed naturally, for divine providence concurs with such means of healing" (AC 5712).

Hahnemann differentiates between the slow process of healing or inhibiting the progress of (1) chronic diseases, and that of dealing with (2) diseases on the natural plane that do not disturb the spiritual force so profoundly. The former must be met and overcome as far as possible on the spiritual plane by immaterial forces, developed by potentization [dilution and succussion]; the latter by lower potencies of medical substances, but still by an immaterial force. Kent felt that the course of homeopathic treatment of chronic diseases as discussed by Hahnemann was analogous to the regeneration process as described by Swedenborg. Not long ago, in the *British Homeopathic Journal*, a Dr. Twentyman wrote, "One took it that Kent was a pure Hahnemannian, but of course he was not. He was a synthesis of Hahnemann and Swedenborg."[11]

A few years ago, researchers in England concluded that Hahnemann's infinitesimal doses were energy, although it was not clear what kind or how it developed. In his *Organon*, Hahnemann states, "The doctrine of divisibility of matter teaches us that energy is never divided to the point where it would cease to be something and would share all the properties of the whole."[12] Swedenborg, in *Conjugial Love*, wrote: "Everything divided is more and more multiple, and not more and more simple; for when divided again and again, it approaches nearer and nearer to the infinite in which are all things infinitely" (CL 329). And in *True Christian Religion*: "This coincides with the wisdom of the ancients, according to which all things and each are divisible to eternity" (TCR 33).

There is no record of Hahnemann's ever having been affiliated with any church organization, but he called his labors a "God-given philosophy."[12] His writings show a firm belief in the correspondence of natural with spiritual things. His system of medicine is certainly developed from that premise.

Like Swedenborg, Hahnemann was a totally dedicated man. Nevertheless, when he died in Paris at the age of eighty-eight, he was disillusioned and disappointed, and unable to accept the fact that his long years of research and logical reasoning were rejected or derided by so many of his contemporaries.

Today, despite its founder's disillusionment, homeopathy is practiced and respected in many countries throughout the world. However, in the United States, where a materialistic and mechanistic approach has dominated medicine since the early 1900s, homeopathy has until recently been generally ignored.

On the organizational level, the history of the Swedenborgian church has been similar. Almost until the end of the nineteenth century there were many New Church societies and groups of receivers all over the country. During the same period there were homeopathic medical schools and hospitals in almost every state. In the latter part of the nineteenth century, there were seventy thousand practicing homeopathic physicians and several million homeopathic patients. Both homeopathy and Swedenborgianism began losing ground numerically in the early-twentieth century, a trend that has continued until just recently. Now there is a ground swell of interest in homeopathy all over the country, and also new signs of change and outreach among Swedenborgians. Perhaps our culture is going through a reawakening to the spiritual dimension.

Informed Swedenborgians have traditionally found little difficulty in accepting a medical philosophy based on the immaterial and invisible activating force of the spirit. Kent's interpretation of it and his analysis of the spiritual correspondences that exist between homeopathic medical substances and the organs of the body is well worth reading [see "Supplemental Readings," at the end of this section on homeopathy]. It has often been said that he believed Swedenborg's science of correspondences to be in harmony with what he had learned throughout the years and was a help in evaluating the effects of prescriptions.[13]

We can illustrate this by citing just one example of Swedenborg's explanation of the correspondence between the gold (the metal) and the human heart. In his language of correspondence, gold corresponds to love. He says: "Heart in the Word signifies will and also the good of love. Hence it is that the affections are ascribed to the heart, although they are not in it or from it" (HH 95). Some years ago research at the Massachusetts Institute of Technology affirmed the possible affinity of certain metals for certain organs. They noted that a considerable percentage of gold is found in the heart, and not a trace of it in any other organ. Homeopaths use potentized aurum (gold) in the treatment of some heart conditions. [See also Edward Whitmont's article "Homeopathy and Archetypal Meaning" in the following pages.]

There are many more similarities in the writings of Swedenborg and Hahnemann, and anyone inclined to compare them further cannot fail to be interested. I have found myself sometimes startled by the correspondence. How did this happen? Was it through apprehension of a common underlying truth to things, or a traceable connection? We know that the two men never met but that Hahnemann was in touch with and may have prescribed for both Johann Wolfgang von Goethe and Heinrich Heine, who were familiar with and moved by the spiritual side of Swedenborgian philosophy. Over the years many people have tried to find the answer, but unless or until some untranslated letters or other papers come to light, an actual documentable connection will remain a mystery.

At this point, however, we are safe in saying that each man in his own way drew from similar perceptions of deep spiritual realities pervading the entire universe. For those whose approach to life continues to include spiritual realities, a highly developed spiritual philosophy may be drawn from the one, and a coherent approach to health and healing from the other. Swedenborg and Hahnemann both must figure as important guides and sources of inspiration as our century seeks to rediscover its spiritual roots.

Notes

1. Constantine Hering, in Richard de Charms, *Homeopathy and the New Church*, pamphlet in library of the Swedenborg School of Religion, Newton, Mass.
2. Richard de Charms, *A Defense of Homeopathy against its New Church Assailants* (Philadelphia: New Jerusalem Press, 1854).
3. Ibid, p. 6.
4. William Harvey King, *The History of Homeopathy and Its Institutions* (New York: Lewis, 1905), vol. 1, p. 24.
5. See Elinore C. Peebles, *The Place of Homeopathy in Modern Medicine* (Homeopathic Information Service of the American Institute for Homeopathy).
6. Samuel Hahnemann, *Organon of the Art of Healing*, trans. R. E. Dudgeon, 1st ed. (Philadelphia: Hahnemann Publishing Society, 1810).
7. Ibid., trans. William Boericke, M.D., 6th ed. (Philadelphia: Boericke & Tafel, 1922), p. 103.
8. *British Homeopathic Journal.*
9. Taken from a speech by René Dubos, M. D.
(later appearing in the *British Homeopathic Journal*), in which he quotes a 1552 essay by John Caius.
10. James Tyler Kent, M.D., *Lectures on Homeopathic Philosophy* (Lancaster, Pa.: Examiner Printing House, 1900).
11. *British Homeopathic Journal* (July–October 1956), p. 260.
12. Hahnemann, *Organon*, Dudgeon ed., p. 301.
13. Thomas L. Bradford, *Life and Letters of Hahnemann* (Philadelphia: Boericke & Tafel, 1895).

Part 2
Homeopathy and Archetypal Meaning

Edward C. Whitmont, M.D.

HOMEOPATHY USES SPECIALLY PREPARED "potentized," namely, essentially dematerialized, substance derivatives for the treatment of illness. They are prescribed on the basis of the "Law of Similars."*

In this system substances are "proven," that is, tested for their effects on human beings, by "provers" of average physical health.† Those symptoms that are elicited by a majority of provers are considered to express the characteristic pathogenetic effects of that particular substance. When the symptom complex of any spontaneous illness is compared with the artificial symptom complexes produced by the "provings," there often will be found an extraordinarily close resemblance between disease picture and proving picture. And the drug whose symptomatology represents the closest resemblance to the symptom complex of the sick person, the "simillium," has been found clinically to be the most successful means for the healing of this condition, when it is administered in "potentized" form. In contradistinction to the allopathic method, this healing effect is holistic and not organ limited; it affects the whole person constitutionally and psychosomatically in the sense of reordering and integrating, even though it is often preceded by therapeutic regressions and healing crises. Accordingly, the similarity that leads to the therapeutic choice also has to be expressive of the total complex pattern of personality and illness dynamic, not merely of isolated symptoms. The term "genius" of a substance or remedy has been used in homeopathic writing to denote the sense of a *gestalt* core, which would be representative of the "essence-pattern" shared by patient and medicine.

Imagine a condition of dammed-up grief, worry, or anxiety in an overdisciplined and overly responsible and repressed person. A condition may ensue that is characterized by depressive irritability, brooding listlessness, hopelessness, in more extreme forms, suicide or substance addiction. Organic expressions may range from headaches and hypertensive states to chronic indigestion, biliary disorders, and disturbances of the heart function and circulation.[1]

Such a state is duplicated, often to minute details, in a person who "proves" gold in a suitable assimilable form. Regardless of external exciting factors, the gold prover becomes subject to depression and anxiety; to brooding, pessimistic, hopeless and suicidal moods; and may develop a craving for alcohol or other mind-altering substances. Physically, the gold proving produces circulatory and cardiac pathology, as well as digestive, biliary, and rheumatoid disorders. Most significantly, people of stature, power, responsibility, and discipline are more likely to respond to gold with symptoms in the proving experiment and with therapeutic response when ill.

Rounding out our example, we may remember that the symbolic range of the gold archetype as we know it from alchemy includes not only the principles of individuation and indestructible value, but also, on the more secular level, power, wealth, and security, as well as the solar principle and the heart, the "sun" of the organism, from which "radiates" the circulation.

Because every existing substance is both potentially productive of pathology (in a proving or poisoning) and healing, when used on the basis of symptom similarity, we can see

---

*In my own experience I have found this system to be not only highly effective but also, by and large, vastly superior as well as safer than the standard "allopathic" approach to the prescribing of drugs.

†In a proving, the substance to be tested is introduced, "introjected," as it were, into the organism in repeated doses until symptoms appear. These symptoms show the ways in which the particular substance affects (in the case of the proving, unbalances) organismic functioning. Nontoxic, or presumably inert, substances are proven in "potentized" (diluted and succussed), dematerialized form; in this way they also exhibit definite effects.

EDWARD C. WHITMONT, M.D., is a Jungian analyst and practicing homeopath. He is director of studies at the C. G. Jung Institute in New York and author of *Psyche and Substance,* a book about homeopathy, as well as *The Symbolic Quest* and *Return of the Goddess.*

that the whole range of human functional patterns is mirrored in macrocosmic fields of form that are embodied in mineral, plant, and animal substances. Their healing essences can be activated and connected with on the basis of symbolic likeness or similarity. Just as "wolfness" is assimilated through the enacting of the wolf ceremony or meditation of wolf power, so the solar principle embodied in gold and heart can be assimilated through the potentized, dematerialized preparation (and probably meditation) of gold. Weakness, fear of death, and the need for bravery that yet may be lacking are responses to feeling threatened or unbalanced by wolf being; they are the wolf pathology, as it were. Cardiac or circulatory disorder, depression, loss of value ensue through being unbalanced by the gold or solar archetype.

The experimental and clinical evidence of homeopathy makes it quite evident that what we call health and illness are mutually inclusive of one another. They are changing faces of one and the same entity, two sides of the same coin: the individual constitutional state, or archetypal form pattern. The same dynamic fields inherent in the various substances call forth illness as well as health.

These fields are, moreover, intrinsic to the very organismic process, our own as well as the planet's. The dynamic of every existing substance, whether it be mineral, plant, or animal, hence every constituent of our bodies as well as of the universe in which we live, is able to call forth illness patterns in its own likeness (as in a "proving") and of healing through that likeness when used in therapeutic dosage. The tendency to illness is "built in" to physical existence. Illness is an aspect of being alive, an aspect of the constitutional inherency of a particular person. But so is healing. They both are elements of the *"principium individuationis,"* the urge to individuation; and this in quite specific psychosomatic terms.[2]

Notes

1. E. Weiss and S. English, *Psychosomatic Medicine* (Philadelphia: 1949), pp. 339, 347, 430.
2. Concluding paragraphs from the Preface to Catherine R. Coulter, *Portraits of Homeopathic Medicines* (Berkeley, Calif.: Homeopathic Educational Service, and Washington, D.C.: National Center for Homeopathy, 1986).

Part 3
What Is Homeopathy?

Richard Moskowitz, M.D.

HOMEOPATHY IS A METHOD of treating the sick, developed by Samuel Hahnemann, M.D. (1755–1843), an eminent German physician and professor of pharmacology.

The Law of Similars

In a series of experiments from 1792 onward, Hahnemann proved (1) that medicines regularly *produce* in healthy people the same symptoms that they cure in the sick; and (2) that the medicine that produces symptoms most *similar* to those of the illness as a whole initiates a genuinely *curative* response, which completes itself spontaneously, without any further assistance.

Hahnemann understood these experiments to mean that the symptomatic expressions of illness already represent the *attempt* of the organism to heal itself, and that the similar remedy acts by *reinforcing* that attempt in some way.

Hahnemann also showed that true *cure* involves a *concerted* response of the whole organism, because the similar remedy acts only if it is correctly chosen, if its essential similarity to the illness somehow renders the patient abnormally *sensitive* to it. Otherwise, the minuteness of the dose makes it likely that little or nothing will happen—an important safety feature.

The Classical Method

Classical homeopathy, as it is practiced today, includes the following elements:

1. Each remedy is given in small doses to healthy volunteers, and the full range of physical, mental, and emotional responses to it are carefully recorded.
2. Each patient is interviewed at length, and all the signs and symptoms of the illness to be treated are noted in detail.
3. The patient is given that *one* remedy that produces a *total symptom-picture* most nearly like the patient's own.
4. The remedy is given until a curative reaction occurs, and then stopped for as long as the reaction lasts.
5. The patient is instructed to avoid coffee, camphor, herbal or conventional drugs, and dental work, and to limit the use of tea, menthol, tobacco, alcohol, marijuana, etc., as much as possible.
6. The remedies, which are mostly of natural origin (herbs, minerals, animal poisons, etc.), are specially diluted and refined, both to minimize the risk of toxicity and to enhance the depth and completeness of their action.

The Interview

The homeopathic interview is necessarily detailed and intimate, because it looks beyond the abstract "disease entity" to the illness as a unique set of lived responses of the *patient*. Special attention must be paid to the most unusual or idiosyncratic features of the case, which are often ignored during a traditional physician's diagnostic work-up, even by the patient himself.

Homeopathy: Pros and Cons

Homeopathic remedies are safe and economical, simple to use, and act very gently as a rule, with very few side effects. The cure, when it occurs, is prompt, thorough, and long-lasting, and does not require repeated doses of medication. By utilizing the innate healing power of the patient, it helps the patient to assume more responsibility for his or her own health.

On the other hand, it is an *art*, requiring many years of study and practice to master, such that even a qualified practitioner may have to try several remedies before a correct one is found. Moreover, we do not really understand how the dilute remedies act, so that we cannot always predict

Dr. RICHARD MOSKOWITZ did his undergraduate work at Harvard, where he was elected to Phi Beta Kappa, and received his M.D. from New York University in 1963. He has been practicing classical homeopathy more or less exclusively since 1974.

exactly how a given patient will respond to them. Finally, the remedies are somewhat delicate, and may be inactivated or antidoted rather easily.

When to Consider Homeopathy

Although *any* patient may (or may not) respond to it, the following are some situations in which homeopathic treatment is *most likely* to be successful, or should at least be *considered* before resorting to something more drastic, or after standard methods have failed.

1. *Functional complaints*, with little or no tissue damage, such as simple dysmenorrhea, constipation, headache, insomnia, anxiety, etc.
2. *Conditions for which no specific treatment is available*, such as viral illnesses; to promote wound healing after major trauma or surgery; and crippling diseases, such as multiple sclerosis, emphysema, etc., where great benefit may be obtained and very little harm can be done.
3. *Conditions for which elective surgery is indicated*, such as fibroids, varicose veins, gallstones, ulcers, cysts, abscesses, etc., as long as immediate operation is not required and the surgery can always be performed later if necessary.
4. *Conditions for which the standard drugs would have to be taken over prolonged periods of time*, such as recurrent bacterial infections (otitis, mastitis, pelvic inflammatory disease, etc.); allergies (eczema, hay fever, asthma, etc.); and even severe chronic diseases (epilepsy, ulcerative colitis, systemis lupus erythmatosis, etc.), short of irreversible tissue damage or chronic drug dependence.
5. *Conditions in which the standard medications have not worked or the patient refuses to take them*, including even incurable or terminal cases, in which only palliation is possible.

Homeopathy tends to be much *less* suitable for severe chronic cases with established dependence on conventional drugs, especially corticosteroids, antipsychotic drugs, and anticonvulsants, where it would be dangerous or harmful to withdraw them.

Supplemental Readings in Homeopathy

Boerick, William. *Homeopathic Materia Medica.* New Delhi, India: B. Jain, 1979.

Bradford, Thomas. *Life and Letters of Samuel Hahnemann.* Philadelphia: Boericke & Tafel, 1895.

Hahnemann, Samuel. *Organon of Medicine.* Translated by C. Wesselhoeft, M.D. Philadelphia: Boericke & Tafel, 1917; paperback edition Los Angeles: Tarcher, 1982.

Kent, J. J. *Lectures on Homeopathic Philosophy.* Chicago: Ehrhart & Karl, 1954.

King, William Harvey. *The History of Homeopathy and Its Institutions in America.* 4 vols. New York: Lewis, 1905.

Stephenson, James, M.D. "Homeopathic Philosophy"; "Homeopathic Pharmacognosy, Pharmacy, and Pharmacodynamics"; "Homeopathic Pharmacotherapy"; "Homeopathic Research." Series of 4 talks given at Boston University Faculty Club, 1958. Pamphlets may be available from the Homeopathic Information Service at the National Center for Homeopathy (address under "Suppliers").

Transactions of the American Institute of Homeopathy. Chicago: Stevenson & Foster, 1884; or from AIH (address under "Suppliers").

Tyler, M. L. *Homeopathic Drug Pictures.* Essex, Eng.: C. W. Daniel, 1952.

Vithoulkas, George. *The Science of Homeopathy.* New York: Grove Press, 1980.

Whitmont, Edward. *Psyche and Substance: Essays on Homeopathy in the Light of Jungian Psychology.* Richmond, Calif.: North Atlantic Books, 1980.

Suppliers of Medicines, Publications, and/or Information

BOERICKE & TAFEL, 1101 Arch St., Philadelphia, PA 19107 (medicines).

JOHN A. BORNEMAN & SONS, 1208 Amosland Rd., Norwood, PA 19074 (books and medicines).

HOMEOPATHIC EDUCATIONAL SERVICE, 2124 Kittredge St., Berkeley, CA 94704.

INTERNATIONAL FOUNDATION FOR HOMEOPATHY, 4 Sherman Ave., Fairfax, CA 94930.

NATIONAL CENTER FOR HOMEOPATHY, and AMERICAN INSTITUTE OF HOMEOPATHY, 1500 Massachusetts Ave., NW, Suite 41, Washington, DC 20005.

Mining and Engineering in Swedenborg's Time

Erland J. Brock, Ph.D.

FIG. 372. *Mine workings—heating a rock face*

ERLAND BROCK, born in 1932 at Adelaide, South Australia, was educated at King's College and the University of Adelaide. After completing his B.A. Honors degree in geography and geology, he was employed as a mining geologist with the Consolidated Zinc Corporation during 1957–58. Following a year abroad, he returned to the University of Adelaide, receiving his M.A. Taking up employment at the Academy of the New Church in 1964, he is now professor of science in the college, teaching chemistry, geography, and history and philosophy of science. In 1981 he received his Ph.D. Erland is a contributor to geological journals, and is editor of, and contributor to, *The New Philosophy*, journal of the Swedenborg Scientific Association. His current research interests are in the history of geology and epistemology. He and his wife, June, live in Bryn Athyn, where they raised their six children.

WHEN HUMANKIND MADE THE CHANGE from nomadic pastoralist or hunter and gatherer to sedentary agriculturalist — the change we call the Neolithic Revolution — a whole new set of physical challenges arose. Centered as it was on permanent villages and towns, the new economic and social order created many needs, such as for buildings, roadways, port facilities, and the materials for their construction. The response to these demands built into the growing culture what we now call engineering.

The seventeenth and eighteenth centuries represent a period in time that witnessed changes as far-reaching for humankind as those wrought by the Neolithic Revolution, for the new ways of thought embodied in modern science were taking hold, and coupled with the Industrial Revolution, were beginning to launch humankind into the modern industrial era. And now we find added to the age-old guides of intuition, common sense, aping the ways of nature, and trial and error, new insights from applying scientific principles established through experimental science.

Pictorial representation of engineering and mining prac-tices was an important part of the literature of the day. Beyond illustrating the written text, the diagrams were often the only means of describing the methods employed for accomplishing a particular task. The accompanying selections here illustrate methods employed to meet a variety of needs, needs that ancient and modern people alike encountered, and that were often addressed in remarkably similar ways, as historian Martin Jensen has observed in reference to the practices of the seventeenth and eighteenth centuries compared to those of today.[1]

In the context of this pictorial essay, it is noteworthy that Assessor Emanuel Swedenborg followed in the footsteps of his revered countryman Christopher Polhem, of whom Abraham Wolf said, "He was one of the first engineers to combine scientific study with wide engineering experience and mechanical instinct."[2] And from an examination of Swedenborg's own life and works, it is clear that he shared with his mentor a strong desire to further the well-being of his native land by his inventions and application of scientific principles to meeting the practical needs of the state.

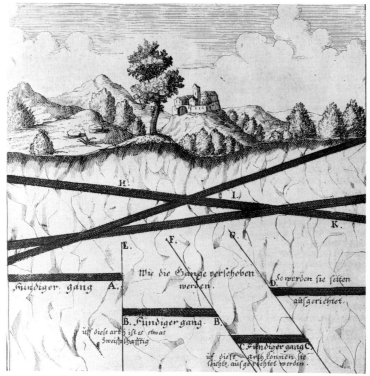

FIG. 373. *Underground veins of ore and their emplacement*

In a picturesque portrayal of mine workings in the late-seventeenth century, the process of heating a rock face to weaken the rock is shown on the preceding page. The miner in the foreground appears to be repairing his wheelbarrow, while the one near the top of the ladder is taking a safety precaution by testing the roof for partially dislodged rock.

This rare early geologic cross section depicts veins of ore or intruded igneous rock. The faulted vein *ABCD* displaced along the fault planes (not so recognized then) *E*, *F*, and *G*, lies below undeformed veins above. The artist was here unwittingly representing a geological sequence of events involving the emplacement of the lower vein, its subsequent faulting (in what had to be more than one phase of disturbance), and then the younger emplacement of the veins *H*, *I*, and *K*, all unaffected by the disturbance that faulted the lower vein.

FIG. 374. *Mine surveyor with plumb lines*

Once the disposition of an ore body has been established as well as possible from the surface geology, and the engineer or mine operator has established how he shall proceed, it is necessary for a surveyor to keep track of the operation. A surveyor uses frame, plumb lines, and cords of known length, to establish the depth of shaft and/or length of tunnel necessary for the intersection of these.

Prior to the use of explosives, mining was done with a pick, sometimes aided by a hammer. After fires were lit at the rock face to weaken it, the heated rock (at *E*) was then doused with water. This process had serious disadvantages. Combustion consumed the oxygen (not so understood in the early eighteenth century) and produced smoke and noxious fumes. For illumination, whale oil was commonly used. At the bottom of the drawing and in the enlarged detail, a miner with a lamp, covering his face from the smoke and fumes, follows the men hauling ore to a hoisting station.

FIG. 375. *Mine workings—heating, hammering, and hauling*

FIG. 375 detail. *Miner shielding face*

FIG. 376. *Mine ventilation with bellows and wind traps*

The problem of providing ventilation for mines was met in a variety of ways, some of which are shown here. Bellows were commonly used, often operated by manpower (*B*). Where the mine's location permitted it, ventilation shafts at elevated sites were mounted with devices for trapping wind and funneling it into the mine. The device labeled *A* in this drawing is an example. It is fixed but designed to trap the wind from whatever direction it blew. The smoke rising in the background may be from fires lit in ventilation shafts to increase the updraft.

A method for removing mine water involved the use of a paternoster-work bailing device, so named because the disks are reminiscent of the large Lord's Prayer beads of a rosary. It consists of regularly spaced wooden disks (*F*), which engage the forks (*E*) on the driving axle. The disks mechanically lift the water up the tube *G*. As an alternative, leather spheres stuffed with horsehair were used instead of wooden disks.

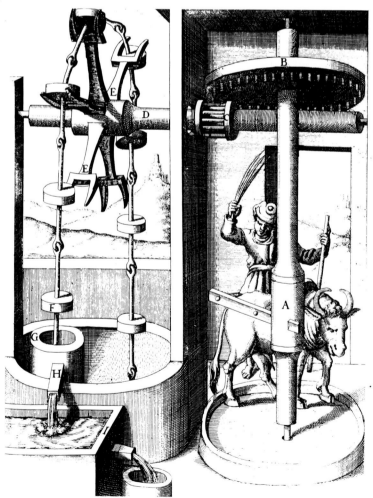

FIG. 377. *Paternoster-work bailing device*

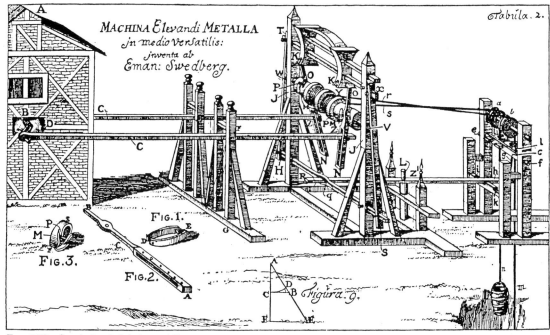

FIG. 378. *Swedenborg's hoisting machine*

This hoisting machine was invented by Swedenborg for use at mines. It is power-driven by a water wheel to which is attached a crank (*B*), which in turn is connected to the hoist by connecting rods. (*C*). The back-and-forth movement of the rod causes the shafts *ON* to rock, and this in turn engages a ratchet wheel ("*Fig. 3*" within this picture), and causes the axle drum *VW* to rotate, thereby raising or lowering buckets. One direction of rotation of the water wheel can either raise or lower the bucket—depending on how the ratchets are set on the axle.

Prior to the development of technology, animals and men, wind and water provided the necessary power. Here, horses provide the means for hoisting the ore from the mine.

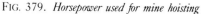

FIG. 379. *Horsepower used for mine hoisting*

FIG. 380. *Eighteenth-century blast furnace*

The term *metallurgy* embraces the various processes employed in winning metals from ore minerals. It therefore included the separation of the ore from unwanted minerals ("gangue"), called ore dressing; the smelting of the ore to obtain the metal in crude form; and the refining of the metal. Furnaces were used for these latter two processes. Forced-air furnaces—"blast" furnaces—were commonly employed. Fuel, ore, and flux such as lime may be fed in at the top, allowing for continuous operation. The forced-air intake, and cellar permitting the tapping of the furnace, are clearly shown.

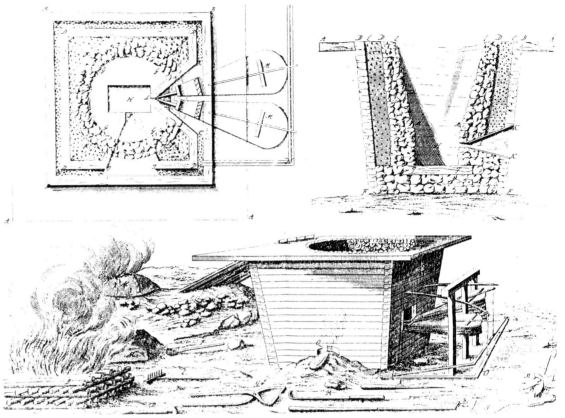

FIG. 381. *Swedenborg's rendering of blast furnaces for iron manufacture*

The export of copper and iron was important to the economy of Sweden in the eighteenth century. As assessor of mines, Swedenborg was deeply involved with the mining industry. Aside from his inventions related to mining, he wrote several treatises that relate to this aspect of his life: *De Sale Communi* (*On Common Salt*), *De Ferro* (*Treatise on Iron*), and *De Cupro* (*Treatise on Copper*), the latter two works being volumes 2 and 3 of his famed *Opera Philosophica et Mineralia*. These three drawings are from *De Ferro*, and portray in plan, elevation, and perspective views a blast furnace for obtaining iron from its ore.

Smelters at work are here engaged in the smelting of ores of gold, silver, and copper. Smelters often wore hooded garments to protect them from the heat of the furnace fires. Furnaces *A* and *B* each have a forehearth into which the metal from the furnace may flow when the smelter breaks open the taphole *C*, as shown. Nearby lies a dipping pot (*F*) and a pile of charcoal, a measured quantity of which is being carried by the worker (*G*) to fuel the furnaces. In this kind of furnace the ore and fuel are in direct contact, in contrast with the reverbatory furnace in which the ore or metal is in crucibles that have hot gases flowing over them.

FIG. 382. *Smelters working at furnaces*

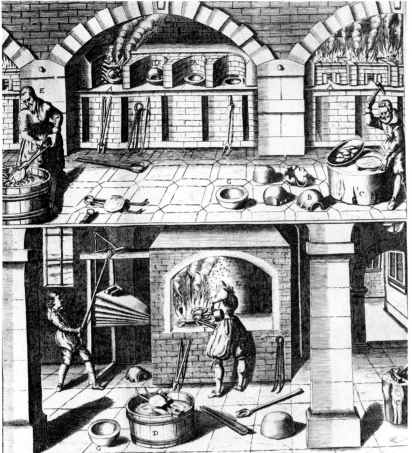

FIG. 383. *Metal foundry*

Once metal had been won from its ore and refined, it could then be used for the production of serviceable items. Some operations in a metal foundry are here graphically displayed.

After iron was refined, it could then be used for one or another of the multitude of uses we have found for it. This drawing displays the verve with which the workers are operating a water-powered rolling mill. The hot slabs were first rolled thinner, then passed through the second roller, which imparted corrugations to the iron sheet, shown also being packed against the wall.

FIG. 384. *Water-powered iron-rolling mill*

Energy sources are crucial to the operation and survival of civilizations. Indeed, their rise and fall is closely related to energy supplies. Stone structures such as the Great Pyramids, Stonehenge, and the Great Wall of China evoke a special fascination; but on a less-dramatic scale, the use of stone for buildings required great manpower and ingenuity, both in obtaining it, transporting it to the building site, and in putting it in place. Here the transport of a huge fifty-ton stone slab from Meudon to Louvre, a distance of two miles, is depicted. It is being towed by means of winches *R* and *S*.

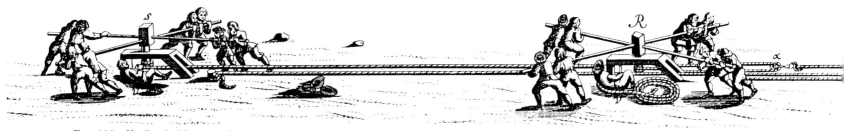

FIG. 385. *Hauling building stone by means of manpower and winches*

The advent of the steam engine had a profound effect on technology. It overcame difficulties associated with other sources of power: the uncertainties of wind power, and the geographical restrictions in the use of water power, for examples. In addition, it could be used in a variety of circumstances. Here the steam engine is shown in its application of raising water. Steam is generated in the boiler (*B*) and passes into the receiver (*A*). Here it is condensed by the intake of a small amount of water through pipe *IM*, creating a vacuum. Well water is drawn up the pipe *HZ* into the receiver by the suction, and then forced up the pipe *EE* to the receiver above by steam pressure.

In this pictorial commentary on wind power, we have an example of the newly developing modern scientific mode of explanation of natural phenomena. In this case, "*Fig. 1*" shows solar input greater at the equator than at higher latitudes, this being the cause of the generation of wind via density differences of the air: lower at the equator, higher at higher latitudes. The top left drawing depicts an anemometer, an instrument to measure wind speed. "*Fig. 2*" shows windmill construction.

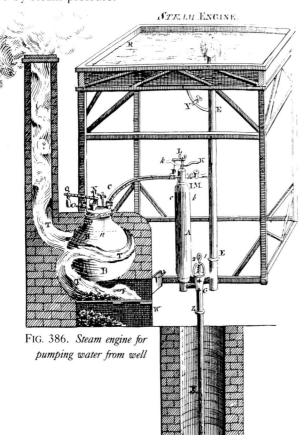

FIG. 386. *Steam engine for pumping water from well*

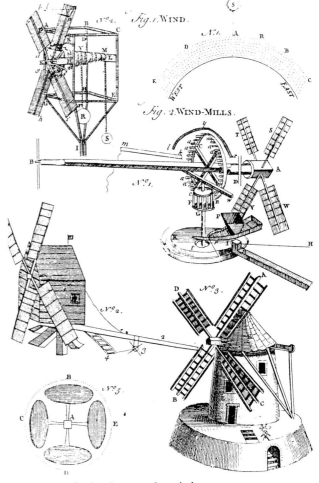

FIG. 387. *Devices for generating wind power*

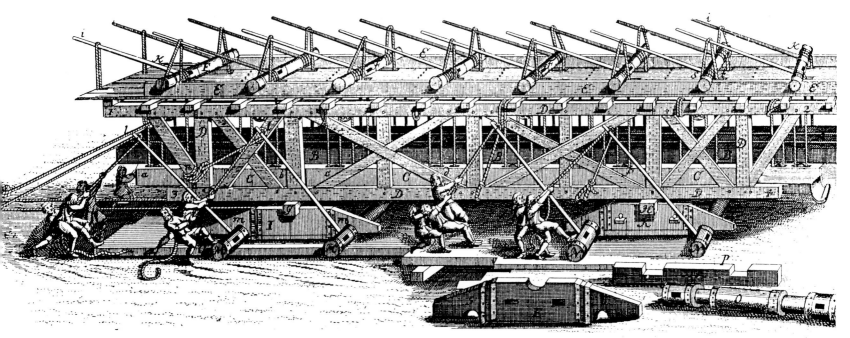

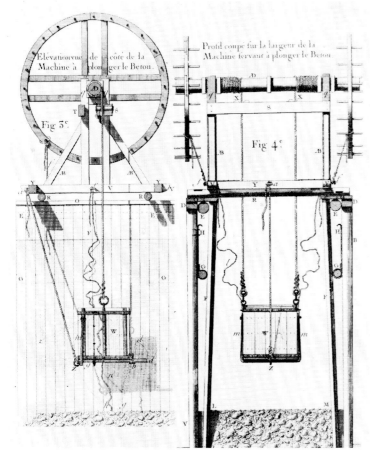

FIG. 388. *Mole construction for protecting harbors*

Harbors and harbor facilities have played a vital role in the development of European and Mediterranean culture since ancient times. Harbors often required protection from storm waves, and for this, massive structures called moles were built. How this could be done is indicated here. "*Fig. 4*" on the illustration shows, in section, the sheet piling (*F*) between which the concrete is poured; it is lowered in the 27-cubic-foot "kibble" (*W*) by the winch (*AD*). The mixture of mortar and stone is lowered to the sea bottom, a door (*Zb*) is opened, and the concrete flows out. This layer is covered by one of stones, and the concrete/stone layering is continued until the desired elevation is attained. "*Fig. 3*" shows an elevation view of the operation at right angle to "*Fig. 4*."

In bridge building, "cofferdams" were used to construct the bridge supports. The cofferdam shown here is constructed of tongue-and-grooved piles, and provided water-free working space for the construction of foundations for bridges and other structures underwater. The workmen are shown bailing out the water prior to the construction of the foundations.

FIG. 389. *Cofferdam construction*

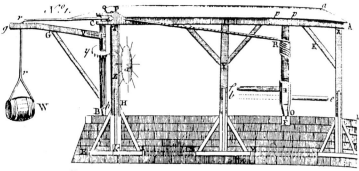

FIG. 390. *Wharf crane*

Cranes served the crucial function of the transfer of goods. The upright shaft is fixed by iron collars at the top and bottom, and goods are raised and lowered by means of the capstan (*P*). The gibbet (*GVB*) allows goods to be brought from above the ship or barge to the wharf.

This manpowered pile driver, used to build cofferdams and bridges, operated synchronously with twenty or so men on each ram. A "volley" of twenty-five to thirty strokes took about three minutes to execute.

With harbors often located at river mouths, silting is a constant problem. Dredging in the eighteenth century, as now, was regularly done to keep the shipping channels open. This is an elevation view of the dredger used at Toulon.

FIG. 391. *Synchronous pile drivers*

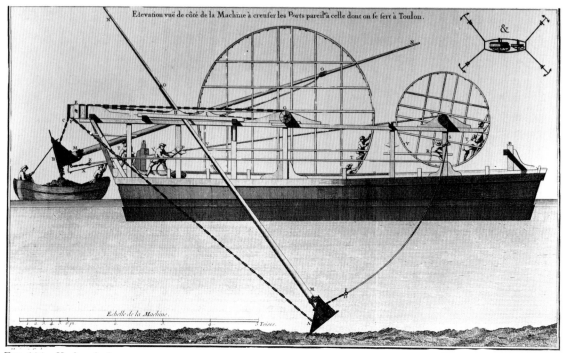

FIG. 392. *Harbor dredger*

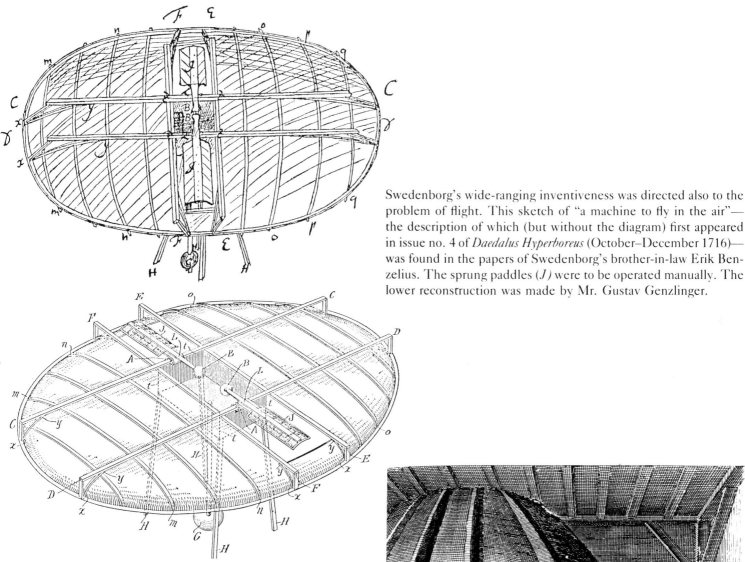

Swedenborg's wide-ranging inventiveness was directed also to the problem of flight. This sketch of "a machine to fly in the air"—the description of which (but without the diagram) first appeared in issue no. 4 of *Daedalus Hyperboreus* (October–December 1716)—was found in the papers of Swedenborg's brother-in-law Erik Benzelius. The sprung paddles (*J*) were to be operated manually. The lower reconstruction was made by Mr. Gustav Genzlinger.

FIG. 393. *Two sketches of Swedenborg's aircraft*

A little reflection draws our attention to the importance of glass. When we think of the Renaissance, stained glass windows of the magnificent cathedrals of Europe come to mind. As with all other aspects of the materials of culture, a wealth of technology lies behind the finished product. Here we catch a glimpse of what was involved in the production of glass from its raw materials. Furnaces played the primary role. In the first furnace on the right, the "calcar," sand and potash, are converted to "frit," or crude glass. This is used in the glass furnace, where frit is converted into the desired glass by the addition of particular substances. Then the glass is cooled ("annealed") in the cooling furnace, above the glass furnace.

FIG. 394. *Glass furnace and glassmakers at work*

Ground glass in the form of lenses was instrumental in bringing about the dramatic shift in humankind's world view represented by the so-called scientific revolution, for it was through lenses that Galileo discerned the unevenness of the moon's surface and observed the phases of Venus, thereby challenging the established cosmology derived from Greek science. But ground glass also served more mundane functions, too. Here workers are shown making plate glass. The glass from the furnace is fixed to a table; upon this is spread grinding sands and water; and upon this is another glass plate; in turn a plank and wheel are attached, which can be moved back and forth or around, thus providing the necessary movement. In the background two workers are shown doing the final polishing.

The eighteenth-century preoccupation and fascination with refinement and adornment created a demand for fine silk (among many other things). A weaver is shown operating his loom in the production of silk ribbon.

FIG. 395. *Grinding and polishing plate glass*

FIG. 396. *Silk weaving loom*

Acknowledgments

The author wishes to acknowledge the help of Mr. David B. Glenn, archivist and Swedenborgian librarian at the Academy of the New Church, Bryn Athyn, Pennsylvania, and of Kirsten Gyllenhaal (Mrs. E. Edward Gyllenhaal), research assistant, also of Bryn Athyn, in preparing this contribution.

Notes

1. Martin Jensen, *Civil Engineering Around 1700* (Copenhagen: Danish Technical Press, 1969).
2. A. Wolf, *A History of Science Technology, and Philosophy in the Eighteenth Century*, 2nd ed. (London: Allan & Unwin, 1952), p. 635.

The Soul and the Abyss of Nature

Stephen Larsen, Ph.D.

> In the human body Nature has gathered together and poured forth the whole of her art and science. . . . the longer one dwells on them, the more numerous are the marvels and hidden mysteries brought to light; and though thrice the age of Nestor was his, yet other mysteries remain. . . . Nature is an *abyss*, as it were, and nought remains but *amazement*.
>
> —Swedenborg, *Rational Psychology*

This essay first appeared in condensed form in the introductory issue (Winter 1985) of *Chrysalis*, the journal of the Swedenborg Foundation.

WITH THE PASSAGE ABOVE, Emanuel Swedenborg began his detailed and scientifically precocious book, *Rational Psychology*. This work, however, was but one chapter in his lifelong quest: the search for proof of the soul's reality. Theologians of the eighteenth century assumed that the soul's existence needed no proof beyond scriptural authority. But during the European Enlightenment empirical scientists investigating the natural world struggled to reconcile the nakedness and sheer factuality of their findings with their religious belief systems. To many it seemed the more deeply one looked into the Abyss of Nature, the more one saw only more nature, not theophany.

We may imagine that the truly intelligent and sensitive minds of the time were poised in a kind of awful tension between indoctrinated beliefs thought to be indisputable and the contradictory but equally indisputable revelations of science. For some, the solution was "compartmentalization"—a kind of voluntary schizophrenia that did not try to reconcile the opposites. But for certain minds incapable of such cognitive segregation, the paradox energized the major quest of their lives—their personal myths. This was true for such men as Descartes, Kant, and Newton. And so it was for Swedenborg. These men were among the first to grapple with great questions still abroad today: Is the universe as we know it (even the very minds with which we know it) the vast unfoldment of a Divine Plan, or is it the outcome of complex accidents? Is what we call "mind" merely an epiphenomenon of matter? Is the brain itself the soul? Does soul exist apart from matter?

Since the European Enlightenment the Western imagination has increasingly referred questions about such intangibles as the soul to physical process. That "good old-time religion" called *animism* by the anthropologists, in which nature was permeated by and ultimately reducible to spirit, yielded, in historically discernible stages, to science's "secular religion," in which all spirituality is seen as just one of nature's more persistent and seductive illusions. If this seems like a catastrophe (and it is from the viewpoint of soul), it must be remembered that in the eighteenth century it was a downright relief for many to separate science from religion and the claustrophobic God-concept of the clergy, whose own all-seeing eye seemed constantly to look for the theological implications of any fact or finding. (Discovering any such implications, the various medieval mechanisms wielded by church or state would bring the issue to some kind of conclusion.) The historically later materialistic determinism and logical positivism, which would come to dominate the scientific weltanschauung, was merely the opposite swing of the pendulum.[1]

But Swedenborg's proof of the soul was not to be in the theological style, so acceptable at the time, and as might have been expected of a proper bishop's son. After all, the pulpit is a good place from which to persuade lots of other people about your beliefs. But this somewhat shy, profoundly intellectual young man preferred something else throughout his life: he wanted to peer deeply into the Abyss

---

For biographical information, see Stephen Larsen's other essay in this anthology, "Swedenborg and the Visionary Tradition."

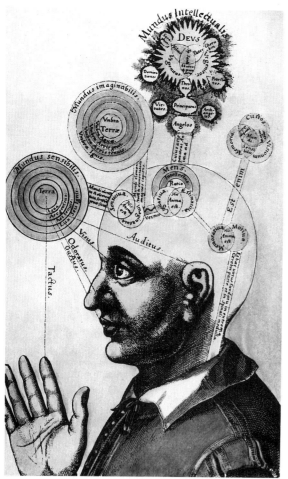

FIG. 397. *Human mental abilities classified in terms of God
and the universe, from an alchemical text, 1617*

of Nature, even if it meant putting a stress on his own soul,
and taking the risk of losing in those unencountered depths
the religion of his fathers, especially its shallower aspects.
He chose the unknown, the left-hand path of science.

The number of fields Swedenborg set out to master was
rather astonishing, yet somewhat more possible in the eighteenth century than it would be in modern times. He studied
geology, mineralogy, and chemistry, which seemed to connect logically to his work as assessor for the Swedish Board
of Mines. He made groundbreaking discoveries in crystallography. But he also insisted on studying mathematics,
physics, astronomy. He proposed a cosmological theory, the
"nebular hypothesis" that history has ascribed to the later
work of Kant and Laplace. He speculated that the basis of
all matter was energy or motion in the form of gyres—an
unpopular idea in a time that still embraced Democritus's
idea of atoms as hard irreducible bits of matter.[2]

Demanding as these studies were, they were merely preparatory to the central task that began to consume Swedenborg in his middle years:

> I have undertaken to search out with all possible zeal what
> the soul is, and what the body, and what the intercourse

between them, and also what the state of the soul is when
in the body, and what her state after the life of the body. . . . I
finally discerned that no other course lay open save that which
leads through the anatomy of the soul's organic body, it being
there that she carries on her sports and completes her course.
I have pursued this anatomy solely for the purpose of searching out the soul. If I should thereby have supplied anything
of use to the anatomical and medical world, it would give
me pleasure, but the pleasure would be greater if I should
have thrown light on the search for the soul.[3]

It may be hard for modern folk to imagine the life of a
well-to-do intellectual aristocrat who spent the most useful
years of his life searching for the soul. But no mere dilettante
was he, though he delighted in his study—days, months,
and years of poring over, in a meticulous and dedicated way,
the anatomical research available at the time. He decided to
eschew, for himself, the way of the scalpel, though he visited
many of the famous anatomical theaters in Paris and elsewhere. Dissection was still profoundly stigmatized, but
Swedenborg avoided it probably not out of mere conformity
nor squeamishness, but rather to exercise the full potential
of his specialty—a uniquely intuitive way of reasoning about
how things worked from a study of their structure.*

He felt that if he conducted the research himself, making
original discoveries, he would go on a kind of "ego trip,"
that would lead him away from the truth of the matter

> . . . and to originate the whole series of inductive arguments
> from my particular discovery alone; and consequently to be
> incapacitated to view and comprehend the idea of universals
> in individuals and of individuals under universals. . . . I
> therefore laid aside my instruments, and restraining my desire
> for making observations, determined rather to rely on the
> researches of others than trust to my own.[4]

We see here a methodological stance that Swedenborg
promised to take as he worked. His method included introspective or phenomenological elements as well as inductive ones. He found that great discoveries are intoxicating
and subtly bend the mind of the researcher to confirm and
support them. (Similarly, is this not why modern psychologists use "double-blind" studies and other control measures
to be sure that the researcher does not, even unconsciously,
bias the results?)

We know that Swedenborg read widely and deeply in the
anatomical work of his time—Leeuwenhoek (1632–1723),
Malpighi (1628–1694), Willis (1622–1675), Vieussens (1641–
1716), and Boerhaave (1668–1738), among others—before

---

*In many branches of science we find what is called the "structural-
functionalist" debate. Is it better to define something by what it *is* or what
it *does*? Swedenborg's speciality was to infer function from structure. This
derived from a unique sense of causality based on theological relation of
end, cause, and effect.

synthesizing his own novel theories. And the question is, Did he go beyond what a simply well-read scholar of physiology of his time could have known? In order to answer this satisfactorily, we move now to look at some specifics of psychology and neuroanatomy and to examine them in the context of a philosophy of nature and of the spirit (one of the main themes of this essay).

A common belief prevalent in the seventeenth century—and held by no lesser person than Descartes—was that the "seat of the soul" was the pineal gland. There was little evidence to support this. The brain was the abode, or "control room," for a kind of independent entity that flitted around, mysteriously activating this or that control. Even through the nineteenth century, the soul was often graphically depicted in this role as a *homunculus*, a little anthropomorphic being, the ghost, if you will, in the machine.

Swedenborg's view was no such nursery tale. He assumed from the start the very thing that has led modern materialistic psychology to reject the soul—that all of mind's many capacities are indeed precisely mirrored in the physical structure of the brain. Swedenborg is often cited as the first person specifically to assign to the gray matter of the cerebral cortex the locus of voluntary activity, both receiving sensory information and originating motor activity. (The prevailing view at his time was that the cortex was a kind of gland that nourished the cerebral medulla [white matter] but had no role in mental life.) Swedenborg not only studied anatomical charts from dissection but also compared them to accounts of psychological impairments caused by specific damage to parts of the brain (aphasias), as do modern neuropsychologists. From these comparisons he postulated the cortex as the seat of voluntary and conscious mental life, and then even described accurately the upside-down distorted "homunculus" of the sensory and motor areas of the cortex.

He asserted that the cerebral cortex and the cortical elements form the seat for the activity of the soul, and are ordered into departments according to the various functions. The "cortical elements" Swedenborg mentions, to which he attached great importance, resemble the neuron, or nerve cell (then still undiscovered). He found it necessary to postulate such minute units, each like a tiny brain, which he called "cerebellula," each with the ability to make the little decisions that add up to the larger mental processes of which we are aware. Swedenborg also thought the area of the frontal lobes was especially important in the higher mental functions.

The almost-uncanny correctness of some of these early speculations, as confirmed by subsequent research, excited much interest in certain scholarly circles. In 1910 a world congress of scientific scholars, anatomists, and neuropsychologists assembled in London to testify about Swedenborg's achievements in the scientists' own specific areas of

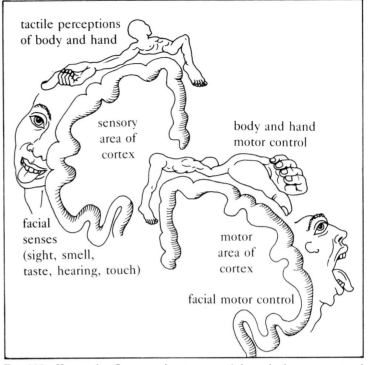

FIG. 398. *Homunculus. Sensory and motor areas of the cerebral cortex correspond to parts of the body.*

expertise. Professor Max Neuburger of Vienna cited Swedenborg as

> . . . an example of how at times a gifted, speculatively endowed theorizer may, from neglected, empirical material, draw conclusions which reach to the very heart of the subject, and penetrate much deeper into its nature than do the soulless deductions of the correct representatives of the "exact sciences."[5]

Neuburger also cited among Swedenborg's premonitory discoveries the nature of the cerebrospinal fluid, the role of the spinal cord as a decision-making rather than merely transmissive organ, the sychronization of brain rhythms to rate of respiration, assigning the pituitary as master gland of the ductless system (Swedenborg calls it the "chemical laboratory of the brain"), and the importance of the ductless (endocrine) glands in behavior.

Gustave Retzius, a distinguished Swedish scholar, described him as ". . . a deep and unprejudiced anatomical thinker."[6] And J. J. Garth Wilkinson,* an influential nineteenth-century English scholar and translator of Swedenborg's scientific works, reported to the 1910 congress that Swedenborg's inductions worked so precisely because, first, he had read and studied so much scientific literature, and, second, he assumed there was no difference between the

---

*J. J. Garth Wilkinson, along with A. Clissold and R. Tafel, was an early translator of Swedenborg's scientific works. He was also involved in the early connection between Swedenborg and homeopathy, and was a friend of Henry James, Sr.

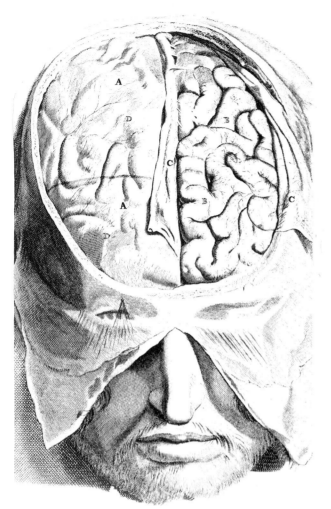

FIG. 399. *View of the gross meninx, from Bidloo's 1685 text. Swedenborg rejected dissection as a method but referred to the work of other anatomists (in* Cerebrum*), among them, Bidloo.*

structural minutiae of the brain and the functional precision of the Divine Plan that formed it. Swedenborg made little compromise with the paradoxes and seeming contradictions between science and religion; instead, they provoked him to further synthetic or inductive efforts. For him the physical complexities of the brain did not "explain away" the soul but were its precise physical manifestation.

Among the most important of his informing values and methodological discoveries were (1) to assume that psychological events indeed correspond to neurological structures, without allowing this to devaluate or disprove the existence of the soul; (2) further, to assume a purposefulness and intelligence in nature that bespeaks its secret affiliation with spirit (the increasingly precise revelations of brain's relation to mind evoked in him only spiritual wonder, not spiritual disillusionment); (3) to assume that structure exists fundamentally for the sake of function; the end of things is as important as the beginning; the flow of the universe is to be understood teleologically (as to its ends) as well as causally,

(as in determinism); (4) to avoid getting caught in approaches based on monolithic points of view, or in basing deductions on evidence from a single source; he would compare structural observations from neuroanatomy with other sources, for example, animal experiments, and observations of psychological alterations of human subjects with brain damage (much as modern neuropsychologists do).

Swedenborg's original notion of correspondences, later more fully developed as a theory in his theological period, holds that nature is the symbolic manifestation of spirit or psyche. The world as we experience it is but a shadow of inconceivable spiritual realities, which it nonetheless prefigures in its intricacies and vital creativity. In this way Swedenborg avoided the whole pitfall of "parallelism"—mind and body operating as two totally separate processes—which was to occupy the learned academies for two more centuries.[7] For Swedenborg, soul was to be neither a thing apart from nature nor a mere emanation of it, but the very same thing existing on a different degree of reality from its body-sheath.

Elucidating this principle of correspondences, he claimed, ever and again, that there is nothing in the world of nature that does not correspond to something in the world of spirit. The realities hover next to each other, an existential hair's-breadth apart, what he calls a "discrete degree" [see Glossary]. In the secular mode of consciousness, all we see in the Abyss of Nature is physical process. But make the shift to what the *philosophia perennis* has identified as sacred awareness, and we experience the abyss as filled with spiritual mystery, as Rudolf Otto called it, the *mysterium tremendum et fascinans.* Perhaps William Blake captured it most exquisitely and simply in "Auguries of Innocence":

> *To see the world in a grain of sand,*
> *And heaven in a wildflower;*
> *Hold infinity in the palm of your hand,*
> *And eternity in an hour*

It was in this mood that our eighteenth-century anatomist must often have dwelt, perhaps unconsciously before his mid-life revelation, but consciously and continually thereafter.

Through the nineteenth and into the twentieth centuries, as neuropsychologists sought "models" for explaining the functioning of the brain and nervous system, their attention seemed irresistibly drawn in another direction from this imagery of rapture, specifically, more and more to the new wonder of the age—the machine. This movement may have reached its peak in the late-nineteenth and early-twentieth centuries. For example, in the classification system for mental illnesses, still largely in use at the present day, psychiatrist Emil Kraepelin fully assumed that organic causes would be discovered for every psychological abnormality (types of organic lesions, or microorganisms [germ theory] for each specific disease). In psychology, Pavlov in the Soviet Union and Watson in the United States tried to establish the mechanical bases for all behavior, to be understood through conditioned reflexes (classical conditioning) and operant responses (reinforcement theory).

The logical extension of this line of reasoning led to psychosurgery—the belief that mental and emotional illnesses or something like chronic criminal behavior could be cured by extirpating parts of the brain. An example of this is the infamous "prefrontal lobotomy" developed by a Portuguese doctor Antonio Egaz Moniz. (The soul-destroying quality of not just the operation but its whole underlying value system is shown forth in counterpolemics such as Ken Kesey's *One Flew over the Cuckoo's Nest*; he clearly portrays the operation as a crime against humanity.)

But also in the late-nineteenth century another kind of countermovement began, also in psychiatry. This perspective began to show the opposite of "mind as a mere emanation of matter." Sigmund Freud, though trained as a neurologist, began to use Breuer's "talking cure" to find the psychological roots not only of mental but even physical illnesses. Examples are the (seeming) physical symptoms of hysteria, in which problems such as blindness, paralysis, or anesthesia are shown to be without organic cause (Freud became a specialist in these cases); or psychosomatic illness in which real physical impairments such as stomach ulcers, asthma, and hypertension are shown to have psychological (psychogenic) causes.

Further developments along this line have led to the modern technology of biofeedback. Paradoxically, this approach uses machines to show the mind to be anything but mechanical. The electronic machines such as electroencephalographs (EEGs) or electromyographs (EMGs) feed back information about the body's state to its "consciousness." This simple consciousness or awareness of what is going on allows us to control aspects of our functioning previously thought to be involuntary and uncontrollable. In reporting a brilliant experiment (of the 1960s) showing that people could learn to control units as small as the firing of a single muscle cell, neurophysiologist J. V. Basmajian said, "We are going to have to bring that exiled factor, *the will*, back into our equation."[8]

Most recently neuropsychologist Karl Pribram has developed a model of brain functioning that is to the machine model as Einsteinian physics is to Newtonian. He calls it the *holographic* model, because it most resembles the new technology of the hologram. Pribram used the very realities that frustrate psychosurgeons as a starting point for his investigations. Though we know indeed that specific functions are carried out in equally specific parts of the brain, there is no simple isomorphism between mental events and brain locale. An example is memories, which remain after portions

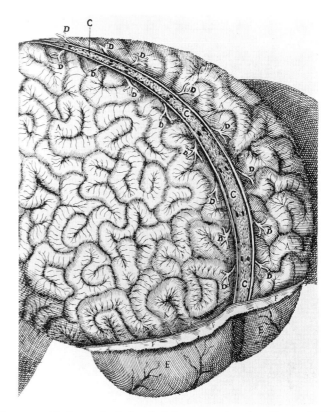

FIG. 400. *The human brain bared of the gross meninx, from Vieussens's 1716 text, also referred to by Swedenborg*

of the brain in which they presumably were stored have been destroyed. In some animal experiments, whole areas of the brain were covered with crosshatched lesions, and still the memories "stored there" remained intact. Pribram began to reason that memories and behaviors might be stored throughout the brain, in much the same way as each piece of a hologram contains the whole image.[9]

It is not difficult to connect the *hol* of *holographic* to *holistic* and find a philosophical resonance.* Holistic health is reminding us that our well-being is determined by the totality of our relationship to the world. It is not very successful, either physically or psychologically, to single out a particular part of the body as "pathological" and remove it surgically. If this seems to work as a drastic intervention in some cases of illness, we should remember that this method has virtually no promise as a technique of health maintenance, and in fact constitutes the very dismemberment that "preventive medicine" aims to avoid. *Iatrogenic* illness (that which is caused by physicians) seems to result from intervening in the ecology of human health with such unilateral measures.

In psychology we have similar approaches, based on the medical model, which suppress a symptom without asking

---

*Holistic philosophy, which resembles Gestalt psychology in its presuppositions about the importance of the "wholeness" of things being more than the sum of its parts, was derived from the ideas of General Jan Smuts, first a Dutch, later a South African philosopher and politician.

what then happens to it (certain aspects of behavior modification). And even the psychoanalytic schools, which warn the behaviorist of "symptom substitution" (a piece of psyche is not to be so easily removed, but may surface, as with physics's law of "conservation of energy," in some new form), themselves use a kind of excavation model for getting rid of old neuroses (dig them out with the precise tools of analysis).

Freud was fond of hydrological models for psyche: reservoirs of libido, the "pressures" accumulated by suppression and repression of id. Unquestionably such a model has heuristic value; but when held unconsciously as well as deployed intentionally as metaphor, it bends the whole value and orientation of the theorist's model to its mold. Philosopher of science Thomas Kuhn hypothesized in *The Structure of Scientific Revolutions* that such models, or "paradigms," are resistant to change, becoming as entrenched as theologies; and subtly determine values, inferences, and ways of formulating scientific questions.

As I was writing this paper I received my latest copy of *Brain/Mind Bulletin*, a periodical that covers the current scientific research in the areas of neurophysiology and consciousness. The journal cited material further supporting the holographic theory and showing that our mental life seems to be less the simply computerlike results of neuron activity, or of mechanical conditioned reflexes, and more the result of intersecting patterns of wave-form activities. In the terms of physics, consciousness behaves more like "waves" than "particles." (The perennial dilemma of quantum "mechanics": Is light made up of waves or particles; or do we agree to accept the paradox—somehow, both?)

The journal says:

> The brain's neural networks appear more flexible and self-organizing than was previously believed. Experiments at the University of California reinforce new theories about dynamic, nonlinear brain action—and raise new questions about the validity of current research assumptions.[10]

Theoretically "brain waves" were discovered only in this century with the advent of electronics technology and the EEG, which reads summaries of brain-wave rhythms arriving at the surface of the scalp and assigns them frequency categories based on Hz, or cycles per second, and designated by Greek letters: *delta*, 0–4 Hz (dreamless sleep), *theta*, 4–8 Hz ("twilight" or threshold states), *alpha*, 8–13 Hz (relaxed attention), and *beta*, 13–22 Hz (mental effort, problem solving, or anxiety).

At one point in his anatomical researches, Swedenborg became excited by an idea he intuited but could not prove—that the energy of the brain proceeded by what he called "tremulations," a vibratory kind of propagation. This seems to me uncannily close not only to brain-wave theory but to

the holographic model as well, in which the real form of our consciousness is an energy resembling light. The "spectrum of consciousness" (also the title of a book by Ken Wilber) is as colorful an event as a rainbow, spanning heaven and earth. I think here of Owen Barfield's image of the soul as rainbow. [See also the Roberts Avens essay, elsewhere in this anthology, for further comparison.] Here, the brain is an organ not unlike a prism or crystal (a symbolic theme so important in shamanism) which diffracts the clear light of unconditioned consciousness into a personal spectrum of awareness.

If the implications of the holographic model are enormous for brain research, they are more so for cognitive and introspective psychology. We need a model that includes transparency, depth, imagery, feeling tone, shades of meaning, and the possibility of many meanings in a single image, as we find in dreams. We need to accommodate creativity, visionary capacity, and the spiritual dimension. The holographic model provides a metaphor based on the transformations of light,* more appropriate than machinery metaphors (based on the transformations of matter) to address the "visionary" abilities of human beings, the very abilities that so easily make the mechanistic models fall flat.

It is interesting to note that Swedenborg discovered even more from his later phenomenological (introspective) researches than his scientific ones, though there can be no question that his anatomy lessons informed his speculations on the nature of soul and spiritual reality.

Another article in my issue of *Brain/Mind Bulletin* carries a subtitle: "Transcending in Meditators Linked to Suspended Breath. . . ." The article describes what a team at Harvard found in a study of 73 elderly people:

> TM and mindfulness programs appear effective in increasing cognitive flexibility alertness and health in the elderly. . . . The TM group showed greater improvement in cognitive tasks and behavioral flexibility. The mindfulness group showed more inner directedness.[11]

Swedenborg had practiced introspective meditation involving altered respiration since early childhood, a topic studied in another article by me in this anthology [see "Swedenborg and the Visionary Tradition"]. He noted that in holding the breaths, thought almost seems stilled. It was in these states of profound concentration, that he discovered, for example, the differential functioning of the cerebral hemispheres. While in a state of yogic stillness he observed that thoughts flow into the left hemisphere, and feelings into the right. Modern psychology has verified that the left hemisphere is the specialist in cognitive, linear mentation, and that the right is the specialist in "holistic" processing—faces,

---

*"Enlightenment" becomes a metaphor for a breakthrough in consciousness in many traditions. See my essay "Swedenborg and the Visionary Tradition," earlier in this anthology.

places, mental imagery, and music. The right has a feeling, valuing tone, which provides a different modality of comprehension than the information-processing mode of the left, as when you extract a different meaning from a person's facial expression than what they are saying verbally. (Carl Jung postulated *feeling* as a rational or valuing function equal in importance to *thinking*.)

Swedenborg was to systematize this dual functioning of mental life into one of the great themes of his later spiritual psychology—the dialogue and interaction of *will* and *understanding*, or *intention* and *discernment* (in Dole's translation) in the human soul. As psychologists have shown, it is virtually impossible to have an experience without an accompanying feeling tone. How inappropriate to portray human life in only cognitive or affective terms; it is clearly always both. When we feel without thinking, or think without feeling, we are one-sided and less than human. True human life is a dialogue between the two, an intersection of two overlapping wave fronts, which provide texture and complexity to our lives. (That is why I have such trouble with the psychosurgical "split-brain" operation, where, as a cure for radical epilepsy, the intervening channel of the *corpus callosum* is severed. The person's true humanity depends upon thinking and feeling in interplay.) We cannot talk about whether we "like" a work of art, understand a play or a poem without the simultaneous presence of both dimensions.

Recently Dr. George Dole, the eminent Swedenborg scholar and translator, has begun to spell out the psychospiritual implications of the holographic model, taking off in his own direction from Pribram and physicist David Bohm, as well as Swedenborg. (See Dole's essay "An Image of God in a Mirror," elsewhere in this anthology.) He writes, "We can visualize [the] sea of human thought as an immensely complex field of overlapping waves, with each of us located at some unique point in it. There is no pattern that is simply self-generated: every pattern is the result of a confluence of causes."[12] Put another way, are we indeed dreams in the mind of God? And are we ourselves, body and soul, holographic images and likenesses of him/her?

We know that we may resonate with all human beings, and not only understand them but also resonate with empathy (as if we were they). In other cases we may shake our heads sadly and say we don't understand them (as if we certainly *should*), and we may resonate with revulsion, as if their very way of being human caused a cringing within our own humanity. Swedenborg was ahead of us here, too. As Dole translates him:

It does seem as though the divine were not the same in one person as in another—that it were different in an elderly person than in an infant. But this appearance is deceptive. The person is a recipient, and the recipient or recipient vessel may vary. A wise person is a recipient of divine love and divine wisdom more aptly and therefore more fully than a simple person, and an elderly person who is also wise more than an infant or child. Still the divine is the same in the one as it is in the other. (DLW 78)

Swedenborg's interior perceptions led him to a holistic and spiritual view of the universe worthy of the deepest insights of Taoism, as well as Sankhya and Buddhist philosophy. We are not at all parts of a mindless whole, but a whole that is itself unconditioned mind (the *purusha* of Sankhya).

I submit that not only did Swedenborg's yogic practices keep him cognitively alert and in good health in the second half of life, but aided his unique intuition and special kind of metaphysical vision. At one point he even "saw" his mental life holographically, saying that when he thought, he could see solid concepts of thought as though they were

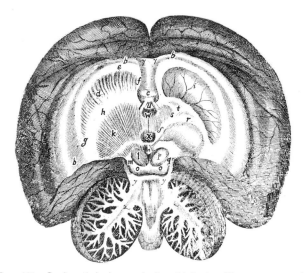

FIG. 401. *Section of the human brain with its lotuslike symmetry and complexity, from Willis's 1672 text, which Swedenborg examined*

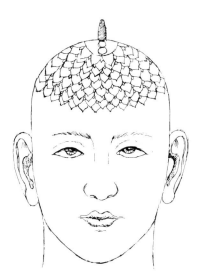

FIG. 402. *Lotus of a Thousand Petals, or* Sahasrāra, *soul image and jewel of consciousness as represented in a yogic text*

surrounded by a kind of wave. Elsewhere, as Dole quotes him, "There are always two forces which hold anything together in its coherence and its form—a force acting from the outside, and a force acting from within. Where they meet is the thing that is being held together . . ." (AC 3628 [3]).

And what is that thing that is "held together" by waves of divine energy? It is nothing less than the soul: neither wholly spirit nor only matter, neither beast nor angel, neither only feeling nor merely thinking, neither just sensation nor intuition; always more than just its heredity and its experiences. There in the overlap of the waves, including the very "wave" which searches for it, it is "the lotus of a thousand petals," in which the jewel of consciousness sits: the human soul.

Notes

1. The Swedish King Karl XI was to rule that "The doctrines of the Christian faith may not be subjected to philosophical criticism, but for the rest, philosophy shall be free, in practice and discussion." From Cyriel Odhner Sigstedt, *The Swedenborg Epic* (New York: Bookman, 1952), p. 9.

2. The nebular hypothesis in which Swedenborg ascribed the origins of the planets to the solar mass was later embraced by Kant and Laplace. See Swedenborg's *Principia*.

3. Quoted from Harold F. Pitcairn, *A Concordance of Subjects Treated in Swedenborg's "Rational Psychology"* (Bryn Athyn, Pa.: Swedenborg Scientific Association, 1960), n. 1.

4. Quoted from Martin Ramstrom's article in The Swedenborg Society, *Transactions of the International Swedenborg Congress, London, July 1910* (London: Swedenborg Society, 1910), p. 57.

5. Ibid.

6. Ibid.

7. Theorists have asked: Are mind and brain the same, or parallel processes functioning on different levels of existence? Is mind a mere *epiphenomenon* of matter? See discussion on "The Mind-Body Problem" in John Beloff, *The Existence of Mind* (New York: Citadel Press, 1962), p. 22.

8. Basmajian's major contribution has been to show that without being able to specify exactly *how*, subjects in his experiments were able to control the activity of single cells (using biofeedback, which showed a characteristic profile of the firing of a single muscle cell). This was previously considered well outside the realm of possibility. See J. V. Basmajian, *Muscles Alive* (Baltimore, Md.: Williams and Wilkins, 1967).

9. Karl Pribram, interviewed by Daniel Goleman, "Holographic Memory," *Psychology Today*, February 1979. See also Pribram, "The Neurophysiology of Remembering," *Scientific American* 220, no. 1 (1969); and "Problems Concerning the Structure of Consciousness," in *Consciousness and the Brain: A Scientific and Philosophical Inquiry*, ed. Gordon Globus et. al. (New York: Plenum Press, 1976).

10. *Brain/Mind Bulletin: Frontiers of Research, Theory, and Practice* 9, no. 17 (October 1984). (Marilyn Ferguson, ed., Interface Press, Box 42211, 47 N. Figueroa St., Los Angeles, CA 90042).

11. Ibid., p. 2.

12. Dole quotes are by permission of the author from as-yet-unpublished manuscripts: George F. Dole, "An Outline of a Holographic Psychology"; and "Fryeburg Lectures: Implications of the Holographic Model."

Poets with Swedenborgian Connections

Compiled by Alice B. Skinner, Ph.D.

Life Beyond

WHAT IS IT to die? The poetic imagination describes some possibilities. Yeats asks, "What's dying but a second wind?" Baudelaire anticipates that lovers will lose the warm feeling of "two / torches reflecting . . . double fires," while the poor will have access to a "mystic granary" and a welcoming inn. Goethe contrasts the experiences of a boy about to enter the spiritual world, and his father who remains tied to the natural world.

TOM O'ROUGHLEY

"THOUGH logic choppers rule the town,
And every man and maid and boy
Has marked a distant object down,
An aimless joy is a pure joy,"
Or so did Tom O'Roughley say
That saw the surges running by,
"And wisdom is a butterfly
And not a gloomy bird of prey.

"If little planned is little sinned
But little need the grave distress.
What's dying but a second wind?
How but in zig-zag wantonness
Could trumpeter Michael be so brave?"
Or something of that sort he said,
"And if my dearest friend were dead
I'd dance a measure on his grave."

WILLIAM BUTLER YEATS[1]

THE DEATH OF THE POOR

WHAT else consoles? It is the remedy
and the preventive too, the one escape
that like a stupefying draught of wine
gives us the heart to get through one more day;

sure on the dim horizon shines one light
that never fails, in spite of storm and cold—
the famous inn all guidebooks recommend
where we can count on lodging for the Night.

Angel of Death, in your transforming hands
the straw we lie on turns to softest down,
our sleep is sound, our dreams are ecstasy!

Here is the mystic granary of heaven,
purse of the poor and our inheritance,
the open gateway to the unknown God!

CHARLES PIERRE BAUDELAIRE[2]

THE DEATH OF LOVERS

WE shall have richly scented beds—
couches deep as graves, and rare
flowers on the shelves will bloom
for us beneath a lovelier sky.

Emulously spending their last
warmth, our hearts will be as two
torches reflecting their double fires
in the twin mirrors of our minds.

One evening, rose and mystic blue,
we shall exchange a single glance,
a long sigh heavy with farewells;

and then an Angel, unlocking doors,
will come, loyal and gay, to bring
the tarnished mirrors back to life.

CHARLES PIERRE BAUDELAIRE[3]

⁓

THE INVISIBLE KING

WHO rides at night, who rides so late?
The father rides on, his child in his arms.
His arms are curled and firm round the boy,
He keeps him from falling, he keeps him warm.

"My boy, why is it you hide your face?"
"Dad, over there do you see the King?
The Invisible King with ermine and staff?"
"Dear boy, what you see is a rolling mist."

"Hey there, my boy, come along with me!
I have the neatest games you'll ever see.
On the shore my daisies blow in a line.
My mother has shirts all golden and fine."

"Dad, is it true you don't hear at all
The little gifts the King is offering me?"
"Calm down, my boy, no need for all this—
It's dry oak leaves making noise in the wind."

"Child, good child, do you want to go?
My daughters will care and wait on you so.
The great circle dance they do every night,
They'll sing and dance and tuck you in tight."

"Dad, it worries me that you don't see
The Daughters there at that ugly spot."
"I see the spot very clearly, my boy—
An old gray willow, that's all there is."

"Your body is slim, and I love you.
Come now, or seize you is what I'll do."
"Dad listen, please Dad, he's got hold of me!
He's done something bad to me, he has!"

The terrified father rides wilder and wilder;
The boy is now groaning as he sits slumped over;
In grief and fear at last the father got home.
The boy lay dead in the father's arms.

JOHANN WOLFGANG VON GOETHE[4]

⁓

When we cross from the natural world into the spiritual, which happens when we die, we take with us everything that is ours, everything personal, except our earthly bodies. This has been demonstrated to me by an abundance of experience. For when we enter the spiritual world or the life after death, we are in a body as we were in the world. There is no obvious difference, because we neither feel nor see any difference. But this body is spiritual, separated and purified from earthly things; and when the spiritual touches and sees the spiritual, it is just the same as when the natural touches and sees the natural. (HH 461)

Oscar Milosz anticipates a continuation of the sights and sounds and smells known in this world, but finds, despite darkness, "Love . . . rising like an inner sun."

NOVEMBER SYMPHONY

IT will be exactly as in this life. The same room.
—Yes, my child, the same. At daybreak, time's bird in
    the foliage
Pale as a corpse: then the servants rise
And you hear the frozen, hollow noise of buckets

At the fountain. O terrible, terrible youth! Empty heart!
It will be exactly as in this life. There will be
Poor voices, wintry voices of old neighborhoods,
The glazier with his singsong call,

The bent grandmother who beneath a dirty bonnet
Calls out the names of fishes, and the man in the blue
    apron
Who spits into his barrow-worn hand
And roars who knows what, like the Angel of
    Judgement.

It will be exactly as in this life. The same table,
The Bible, Goethe, the ink and its odour of time,
Paper, the white woman who reads thought,
The pen, the portrait. My child, my child!

It will be exactly as in this life! The same garden,
Deep, deep, thick, dark. And towards midday
People will delight to be united there
Who never knew each other and who knew

Only this: that they must dress
As for a celebration and go, without love, without light,
Alone into the night of those who have disappeared.
It will be exactly as in this life. The same avenue:

And (in the autumn afternoon) at the bend of the
    avenue,
Where the beautiful path descends timidly like a
    woman

Going to gather flowers of convalescence—listen, my
    child,—
We shall meet each other, as we once did here.

And you, you have forgotten the color your dress was
    then;
But I have only known a few moments of happiness.
You will be clothed in pale violet, beautiful sorrow!
And the flowers in your hat will be sad and small

And I won't know their name: because I have known
    the name
Of only a single, small, sad flower in my life, the
    forget-me-not,
The orphan flower, the old sleeper in ravines of the
    land
Of Hide-and-Seek. Yes, yes, deep heart! as in this life.

And the dark path will be there, damp
With an echo of waterfalls. And I shall speak to you
Of the city on the water and of the Rabbi of Bacharach
And of Florentine Nights. The low, crumbling wall

Will also be there, where the odour drowsed
Of old, old rains, and a leprous herb,
Cold and oily, will shake its hollow flowers there
In the silent stream.

OSCAR V. de L. MILOSZ[5]

UNFINISHED SYMPHONY

YOU scarcely knew me down there, under the sun of
    chastisement
That unites men's shadows, never their souls,
On the earth where the hearts of benumbed men
Travel alone through the darks and terrors, without
    knowing their destined land.

It was long ago—listen, bitter love of the other world—
It was far, far away—hearken to me, sister of this
    present world—
In the North of our birth, where scent from the primal
    past ascends
From the large water-lilies of the lakes, a waft of
    fabulous engulfed orchards.

Far from our archipelagoes of ruins, lianas and harps,
Far from our fortunate mountains.
—There was a lamp and a sound of hatchets in the
    haze
I remember,

And I was alone in the house you never knew,
The house of childhood, the dumb, dark house,

Deep in the leafy parks wherein the chill bird of
    morning
Softly sang for the love of the long-since dead, in the
    sombre dew.

It was there, in those vast drowsily windowed rooms
That the ancestor of our family line once lived,
And it was there that my father, his long journeys done,
Went back to die.

I was alone and, I remember,
It was the season when the wind of our native lands
Bears with it a breath of wolves, sedges and rotting flax
And sings old child-snatcher's lays in the ruins of the
    night.

2

The last evening had come and with it fever,
Sleeplessness and fear. And I could not recall my name.
The guard had no doubt gone to the priest's house
For the lantern no longer stood on the footstool.

All our old servants were dead; their children
Had emigrated; I was a stranger
In the slanting house
Of my childhood.

The smell of that silence was just like that of corn
Found in a tomb; and no doubt you know
That moss of the mute places, sister of the buried
And colored like a full moon low over Memphis.

For a long while I had travelled the world with my
    restless
Brother: and had lain awake with anguish
In all the inns of this world. Now, there I was,
Whiteheaded as our brother cloud. And there was no-
    one left.

A footstep's echo, the old mouse's scuttering would
    have been sweet to me,
For what was eating my heart out made no sound.
I was like the garret's lamp at daybreak,
Like the portrait in the album of the prostitute.

Family and friends were dead. You, my sister, you were
    further
Away than the halo with which in bright January
The snow's mother crowns herself. And you scarcely
    knew me.
When you spoke, you trembled to hear the voice of my
    heart,

But you had met me only one single time,
In the strange light of the gaudy lamps
Among the night flowers, and there were gilded
    courtiers there

And I bade farewell only to your reflection in the
    mirror.

Solitude was awaiting me with the echo
In the sombre gallery. A child was there
With a lantern and the key
To a graveyard. The winter of the streets

Breathed a wretched odor into my face.
I believed myself followed by my weeping youth;
But beneath the lamp with my Hyperion on her knees
Old age was seated; and she did not raise her head.

3

Hearken to me, my earthly sister. It was the old blue
    room
Of the house of my childhood.
There was I born.
It was also there

That long ago I beheld, at the festal Eve gathering,
My first Christmas tree, that dead tree turned into an
    angel
Emerged from the deep, harsh forest,
Emerged all lit up from the ancient depths

Of the frozen forest and proceeding all by itself,
King of the snowy swamps, with its repentant and
    sanctified
Will-o'-the-wisps, in the beautiful silent and white
    countryside:
And behold the refulgent windows of the house of the
    well-behaved child.

Such olden far-off days! so beautiful, so pure! it was the
    same
Room, but forever cold, but dumb and gray.
It seemed to have lost all recollection
Of the hearth and the cricket of long-ago evenings.

There were no relatives, friends or servants there any
    more!
There were only old age, silence and the lamp.
Old age lulled my heart as a maddened mother would a
    dead child,
Silence no longer loved me. The lamp went out.

But under the weight of the Mountain of darkness
I felt that Love was rising like an inner sun
Over the olden lands of memory and that I was flying
Far, far away, as I used to once in my sleeper's travels.

4

—"This is the third day."—And I suddenly shivered,
    for the voice

Came from my heart. It was the voice of my life.
—"This is the third day."—And I slept no more but
    knew that the time
Had come for the morning prayer. But I was tired

And I thought of the things I should see once more; for
    there
Was the alluring archipelago and the isle of the Center,
The misty, the pure, that vanished long ago
With the coral tomb of my youth

And fell half-asleep at the feet of the lava cyclops. And
    before me
On the hill, there was the ornamental fountain with
The lianas of Eden and the velvets of decay
On the steps worn by the moon's feet, and there, on
    the right,

In the glorious glade in the midst of the grove
The ruins colored like the sun! and there, not a single
    secret
Passage! for in this desert solitude I have strayed
With speechless love, beneath the midnight snow. I
    know

Where to find the darkest mulberries; the tall grass
In which the stricken statue has hidden its face
Is my friend and the lizards have long known
That I am a messenger of peace, that it never thunders

In the cloud of my shadow. Everything here loves me
For everything has seen me suffer.—"This is the third
    day.
Arise, I am thy sleeper of Memphis,
Thy death in the land of death, thy life in the land of
    life.

The most wise, the well-deserved". . .

OSCAR V. de L. MILOSZ[6]

"Our first state after death is like this state in the world,
because we are at that point similarly involved in external
concerns. Face, speech, and personality are similar, and
so therefore are moral and civil behavior. . . . So the one
is carried over into the other, and death is only a crossing"
(HH 491f).

Vachel Lindsay imagines the arrival in heaven of General Booth, the founder of the Salvation Army, still leading
boldly and looking like "the chief / Eagle countenance in
sharp relief, / Beard a-flying, air of high command / Unabated in that holy land."

GENERAL WILLIAM BOOTH
ENTERS INTO HEAVEN

(To be sung to the tune of "The Blood of the Lamb"
with indicated instruments)

I

(Bass drum beaten loudly.)

Booth led boldly with his big bass drum—
(Are you washed in the blood of the Lamb?)
The Saints smiled gravely and they said: "He's come."
(Are you washed in the blood of the Lamb?)
Walking lepers followed, rank on rank,
Lurching bravos from the ditches dank,
Drabs from the alleyways and drug fiends pale—
Minds still passion-ridden, soul-powers frail:—
Vermin-eaten saints with moldy breath,
Unwashed legions with the ways of Death—
(Are you washed in the blood of the Lamb?)

(Banjos.)

Every slum had sent its half-a-score
The round world over. (Booth had groaned for more.)
Every banner that the wide world flies
Bloomed with glory and transcendent dyes.
Big-voiced lasses made their banjos bang,
Tranced, fanatical they shrieked and sang:—
"Are you washed in the blood of the Lamb?"
Hallelujah. It was queer to see
Bull-necked convicts with that land make free.
Loons with trumpets blowed a blare, blare, blare
On, on upward thro' the golden air!
(Are you washed in the blood of the Lamb?)

II

(Bass drum slower and softer.)

Booth died blind and still by faith he trod,
Eyes still dazzled by the ways of God.
Booth led boldly, and he looked the chief,
Eagle countenance in sharp relief,
Beard a-flying, air of high command
Unabated in that holy land.

(Sweet flute music.)

Jesus came from out the court-house door,
Stretched his hands above the passing poor.
Booth saw not, but led his queer ones there
Round and round the mighty court-house square.
Yet in an instant all that blear review
Marched on spotless, clad in raiment new.
The lame were straightened, withered limbs uncurled
And blind eyes opened on a new, sweet world.

(Bass drum louder.)

Drabs and vixens in a flash made whole!

Gone was the weasel-head, the snout, the jowl!
Sages and sibyls now, and athletes clean,
Rulers of empires, and of forests green!

(Grand chorus of all instruments.
Tambourines to the foreground.)

The hosts were sandalled, and their wings were fire!
(Are you washed in the blood of the Lamb?)
But their noise played havoc with the angel-choir.
(Are you washed in the blood of the Lamb?)
Oh, shout Salvation! It was good to see
Kings and Princes by the Lamb set free.
The banjos rattled and the tambourines
Jin-jing-jingled in the hands of Queens.

(Reverently sung, no instruments.)

And when Booth halted by the curb for prayer
He saw his Master thro' the flag-filled air.
Christ came gently with a robe and crown
For Booth the soldier, while the throng knelt down.
He saw King Jesus. They were face to face,
And he knelt a-weeping in that holy place.
Are you washed in the blood of the Lamb?

VACHEL LINDSAY[7]

"The relationship of heaven to hell and of hell to heaven
is like that between two opposite [forces] which are acting
against each other, from whose action and reaction there
results a balance in which all events take place. . ." (HH
536).

Czeslaw Milosz and Baudelaire envision some facets of
hell and heaven.

ON THE OTHER SIDE

Some hells present an appearance like the ruins of houses and cities after
conflagrations, in which infernal spirits dwell and hide themselves. In
the milder hells there is an appearance of rude huts, in some cases
contiguous in the form of a city with lanes and streets.

—Emanuel Swedenborg

FALLING, I caught the curtain,
Its velvet was the last thing I could feel on earth
As I slid to the floor, howling: aah! aaah!

To the very end I could not believe that I too must . . .
Like everyone.

Then I trod in wheel-ruts
on an ill-paved road. Wooden shacks,
A lame tenement house in a field of weeds.
Potato-patches fenced in with barbed wire.
They played as-if-cards, I smelled as-if-cabbage,

There was as-if-vodka, as-if-dirt, as-if-time.
I said: "See here . . . ," but they shrugged their
    shoulders,
Or averted their eyes. This land knew nothing of
    surprise.
Nor of flowers. Dry geraniums in tin cans,
A deception of greenery coated with sticky dust.
Nor of the future. Gramophones played,
Repeating endlessly things which had never been.
Conversations repeated things which had never been.
So that no one should guess where he was, or why.
I saw hungry dogs lengthening and shortening their
    muzzles,
And changing from mongrels, to greyhounds, then
    dachshunds,
As if to signify they were perhaps not quite dogs.
Huge flocks of crows, freezing in mid-air,
Exploded under the clouds . . .

CZESLAW MILOSZ[8]

THE LID

WHEREVER he goes—on land or out to sea,
under a flaming sun or a frozen sky—
servant of Jesus, Aphrodite's slave,
Midas in splendor, mendicant in rags,

city-mouse, country-mouse, anchored or adrift,
whether his wits are vacuous or keen,
man lives in terror of the Mystery
and casts a trembling glance above his head

to heaven—Heavens! the vault that walls him in,
illuminated ceiling of a music-hall
where every walk-on treads a bloody board;

the hermit's hope, the libertine's despair—
the Sky! black lid of that enormous pot
in which innumerable generations boil.

CHARLES PIERRE BAUDELAIRE[9]

". . . from angels . . . so much love flows forth that you would think they are nothing but love. It flows from their whole body, so that their body seems radiant and clear because of the light that comes from it . . ." (AC 6135[3]).

ON ANGELS

ALL was taken away from you: white dresses,
wings, even existence.
Yet I believe you,
messengers.

There, where the world is turned inside out,
a heavy fabric embroidered with stars and beasts,
you stroll, inspecting the trustworthy seams.

Short is your stay here:
now and then at a matinal hour, if the sky is clear,
in a melody repeated by a bird,
or in the smell of apples at the close of day
when the light makes the orchards magic.

They say somebody has invented you
but to me this does not sound convincing
for humans invented themselves as well.

The voice—no doubt it is a valid proof,
as it can belong only to radiant creatures,
weightless and winged (after all, why not?),
girdled with the lightning.

I have heard that voice many a time when asleep
and, what is strange, I understood more or less
an order or an appeal in an unearthly tongue:

day draws near
another one
do what you can.

CZESLAW MILOSZ[10]

Connections of the Poets with Swedenborg

(See earlier sections for information on Yeats, Baudelaire, Goethe, O. Milosz, and Lindsay.

CZESLAW MILOSZ (1911–   ), winner of the Nobel Prize for literature in 1980, became acquainted with the writings of Swedenborg through his cousin, Oscar V. de L. Milosz. Czeslaw Milosz's thoughtful reading of Swedenborg is documented in *The Land of Ulro*, a summary of his spiritual and intellectual pilgrimage.

Source

Czeslaw Milosz. *The Land of Ulro*. Translated by Louis Iribarne. New York: Farrar, Straus, Giroux, 1984.

Notes for the Poems

1. William Butler Yeats, "Tom O'Roughley," in *Collected Poems*, def. ed. (New York: Macmillan, 1956), p. 139.
2. Charles Pierre Baudelaire, "The Death of the Poor," in *Les Fleurs du Mal*, trans. Richard Howard (Boston: David R. Godine, 1982), pp. 149–50.
3. Charles Pierre Baudelaire, "The Death of Lovers" in ibid. p. 149.
4. Johann Wolfgang von Goethe, "The Invisible King," trans. Robert Bly, in *News of the Universe*, ed. Robert Bly (San Francisco: Sierra Club Books, 1980), p. 67.
5. O. V. de L. Milosz, "November Symphony," in *The Noble Traveller: The Life and Writings of O. V. de L. Milosz*, ed. and trans. Christopher Bamford (West Stockbridge, Mass.: Lindisfarne Press, 1985), pp. 117–19.
6. O. V. de L. Milosz, "Unfinished Symphony," trans. David Gascoyne, in ibid., pp. 121–27.
7. Vachel Lindsay, "General William Booth Enters into Heaven," in *Collected Poems* (New York: Macmillan, 1925), pp. 123–25.
8. Czeslaw Milosz, "On the Other Side," in *Selected Poems*, rev. ed. (New York: Ecco Press, 1980), pp. 99–100.
9. Charles Pierre Baudelaire, "The Lid," in *Les Fleurs du Mal*, p. 175.
10. Czeslaw Milosz, "On Angels," in *Selected Poems*, p. 112.

Reference

Appendix A
Key Concepts in the Theology of Emanuel Swedenborg

George F. Dole, Ph.D.

IN PARAGRAPH 172 OF *True Christian Religion*, Swedenborg wrote, "Anyone who reads the Athanasian Creed with open eyes can see that nothing less than a trinity of gods was understood by the participants in the Council of Nicea, who brought forth that creed like a stillborn infant." Yet beginning at paragraph 55 of *Doctrine of the Lord*, he had written a section to demonstrate "that the import of the Athanasian faith is in accord with the truth, if only we understand the 'trinity of persons' to mean the trinity of person that exists in the Lord." This contrast may serve to suggest the subtlety of the difference between Swedenborg's theology and traditional Christian theology; and it may also serve to introduce two of his key concepts underlying the others.

In regard to the subtlety, Swedenborg was well aware of the limitations of language. If his expositions sometimes seem to proceed at a snail's pace by reason of repetitiveness, this may be ascribed to a sense of need to carry his context with him. It bears witness also to his strong sense of the relatedness of all his concepts, to his love of detail, and to his insistence on looking at everything from all sides.

The underlying key concepts this contrast introduces may help define the subtlety. The first is the concept of "*distinguishable oneness*." For example, while the form and the substance of an object can usefully be distinguished from each other, they cannot be separated from each other in fact. In precisely similar fashion, Swedenborg held that love, wisdom, and action can usefully be distinguished from each other, but cannot be separated from each other in fact. This principle he extended to all of reality, insisting that nothing exists in isolation, and particularly that the divine is essentially one in the special sense that it is wholly present everywhere and always, in an infinite number of distinguishable forms. (DLW 14, 77–81)

The second underlying key concept that may help define the subtlety is that of the *reality of spirit*. For Swedenborg, there is nothing vague or amorphous about spirit. It was substantial, crisp and clear, and potent. Angels are in human form, with marvelously acute senses including touch, experiencing themselves and their environment as solid. By comparison, the physical world is cloudy, ambiguous, and sluggish. (AC 6724, 7270; DLW 40)

With these most basic premises in mind, then, we may look at some more specific concepts.

GOD

God is the absolute "distinguishable one," both within and transcending all space and all time, by nature incapable of being less than wholly present. The fundamental nature of the universe is therefore coherent at all times and in all places: the same fundamental laws apply, as indeed science, either intuitively or of necessity, assumes. (DLW 23, 27)

To grasp the nature of that infinite oneness, we may distinguish the primary features of infinite love, wisdom, and power—love being wholly ineffective without wisdom, wisdom inert without love, and power the wholly natural result of their oneness. God is one in the essential sense that there is no conflict within the divine: love does not bid one course of action, with wisdom counseling another. (DLW 28)

Love is intrinsically personal, and God is therefore the essential and only person, the definition of "human." There is no other source of life, which is in its essence love. We have been created not "out of nothing," but quite literally "out of love," since love is by nature self-giving and self-expressive. We are in that sense differentiated from the divine but never separated (again "distinguishably one"); we are recipients of being rather than beings. We differ from each other not in the presence of the divine within us, but in our acceptance of or receptivity to the divine. (DLW 11, 4)

OUR HUMANITY

This is not, however, the way we experience ourselves most of the time. We are apparently self-contained and self-sustaining, characterized essentially by particular purposes and particular ways of understanding ourselves and our world. This appearance is God's intentional gift of freedom and rationality, which are designed to enable us to accept the divine willingly and, therefore, are capable of being used to reject it. (CL 444; DLW 264)

The physical world is the arena in which we choose to accept or to reject. Its ambiguity is essential to this purpose, enabling us to convince ourselves that we are self-sustaining in fact, to focus on our distinguishability to the exclusion of our oneness. If we so choose, we voluntarily forfeit the unitive power of love and thereby set ourselves against the fundamental nature of reality. (HH 528)

This manifests itself in isolation and hostility, both internal and external. That is, we develop a delight in conflict with others, and our own loves and thoughts are in conflict with each other. Our satisfaction comes only at the expense of others, which is inherently unworkable. (HH 553)

By contrast, if we choose to accept the divine, we necessarily recognize its presence in others. We are drawn into relationships that combine a sense of oneness and a sense of individuality, relationships that are inherently workable because they are mutually fulfilling. For Swedenborg, then, evil is not evil simply because it violates arbitrary laws, but because it is intrinsically and inevitably self-defeating. (AC 6135[3])

LOVE

Swedenborg sees love as the fundamental energy and substance of human beings, with wisdom as its means. Ultimately, we will believe what we want to believe and understand what we want to understand. Our purposes, rather than our knowledge, determine our character. (DP 195[2]; DLW 40ff.)

Swedenborg distinguishes a hierarchy of loves: love of the Lord, love of others, love of the world, and love of self. When these are in this order of priority, all are necessary and good. Love of self or of the world becomes harmful only when it dominates the higher loves rather than serving them. In practical terms, this means that Swedenborgian theology provides no warrant for asceticism or "renunciation of the world," but rather values all moments of genuine joy. (AC 8850)

This affirmative stance is particularly clear in his treatment of marriage. He sees marriage as offering an opportunity for the most complete uniting of love and wisdom, so that the fully married couple is "distinguishably one" with no hint of domination on either side. (AC 10168–70)

HUMAN PROCESS

From birth, the dominant mode of our sensitivity seems to be self-sensitivity, with relatively rare moments of spontaneous empathy. This entails a radically distorted view of reality, giving each individual the impression of being the only one with live feelings and thoughts. This is rationally indefensible, and for this reason our egocentricity has an Achilles' heel that is specifically vulnerable to rationality. (AC 6323)

The further consequence of this is that our feelings and our thoughts—our "love" and our "wisdom"—unlike God's, are often in conflict. We can see mentally what we do not feel, and we have the freedom to follow that sight rather than our feelings. To the extent that we do so, we gradually become conscious of our latent "other-sensitivity." In one of Swedenborg's images, we open the way for the Lord's presence within us to flow through into our consciousness. This results in increasing oneness within us as well as with others. (AC 2694[2])

It must be stressed that this process of growth is seen to require an active life in the world. The primary agent of change is constructive activity; and the disciplines of private study, self-examination, or meditation are effective only as they focus on such activity. Again, this is consistent with Swedenborg's emphasis on wholeness: the individual is not fulfilled by neglecting a whole level of being. (HH 475)

REVELATION

It is axiomatic for Swedenborg that we cannot lift ourselves by our own bootstraps. If it seems that we can, it is because God is constantly providing us with the resources for change. Granting the premise that rationality is a primary agent in this change, revelation emerges as a primary form of divine aid; and in Swedenborg's thought, the Bible is the central revelation. He finds it to be essentially a parable, a literal story embodying a spiritual one. This conviction was so strong that he regarded the heart of his mission as the disclosing of the spiritual meaning of the Word. (AC 10632[4])

He came to see the Bible not as a compendium of theological propositions or proof-texts, but as a coherent story. The process of growth noted in the preceding section involves a lifelong task, which proceeds in an orderly fashion from more physical interests to more spiritual ones. The underlying order of that process is reflected in the biblical story under the primary image of the establishment of the Lord's kingdom. The literal story moves from an initial vague promise through many vicissitudes to the successful founding of an earthly empire. When this proves inadequate, the incarnation translates the hope into one of a spiritual kingdom, the "kingdom of heaven," which is at last prophetically realized in the descent of the holy city. (AC 3304[3])

In precisely analogous fashion, we can progress from our first vague "dreams of glory" through experience to the establishment of self-identity, can realize the inadequacy of that outward appearance, and can become conscious participants in the vibrant world of spiritual love, wisdom, and activity. (AC 92)

It may be added that just as the ambiguity of the physical world supports our freedom, the ambiguities of the Bible leave us free to interpret it in many ways. This, for Swedenborg, is not at all a liability, but a loving and wise provision of its ultimate author. (AC 3769)

CORRESPONDENCE

In the process of spiritual realization, the ambiguities of the world and of the Bible become increasingly resolved. The central concept in that resolution is the concept of "correspondence" or "responsiveness." The divine, as the source of all, works most directly through the spiritual realm into the physical, and while the divine nature is progressively obscured by the growing unresponsiveness of these successive realms, it is never obliterated. (AC 3223)

Swedenborg therefore sees the physical world as the result of spiritual causes, a result that reflects those causes, albeit dimly at times. The growth of deeper consciousness brings an understanding of this relationship. Laws of nature are seen as reflections of spiritual laws; physical entities and events are seen as results and therefore images of spiritual ones. The effort toward establishing an earthly kingdom is an appropriate prelude to the establishment of a heavenly one because the underlying principles are the same in each case. The instances are "distinguishable" in level, one being internal to the other, and "one" in principle. (AC 5173[2])

UNIVERSALITY

To return for a moment to the first paragraph of this treatment, there is one respect in which the difference between Swedenborgian and traditional Christian theology emerges with no subtlety whatever. That is, Swedenborg insists that the Lord is effectively present in all religions, with the result that "the good" of all religions are saved. He speaks far more affirmatively, in fact, about Gentiles than about Christians. For him, a god who did not provide at least the means of salvation to everyone must be unloving, unwise, or ineffective. (DP 326[9]f.)

Yet there is no hesitation in his insistence that the incarnation was the turning point of all history, and that genuine Christianity is therefore the most perfect of religions. Perhaps the most straightforward way to explain this apparent paradox is to state that in Christianity we see most clearly the God who is active everywhere. It is a distortion of that religion itself to claim that salvation is for Christians alone. (DP 322[4]f.)

IMMORTALITY

Seeing spirit as substantial and structured, Swedenborg sees people as essentially spiritual beings, whose bodies are primarily means of usefulness in a physical environment. For him, it is in fact preoccupation with the physical that blinds us to the reality of spirit. So on the one hand, progress toward oneness entails growing spiritual awareness, and on the other, death results primarily in a shift in the level of consciousness. (AC 8939[2])

The spiritual world is, by comparison with the physical, unambiguous. This provides the essential mechanism of judgment—disclosure, or the loss of the ability to dissemble. Swedenborg's heaven is simply the voluntary community of people who care about each other, and his hell is simply the voluntary association of people who care about only themselves. God enables all individuals to associate with their likes; and the only torments of hell are the inevitable results of the utter impracticality of evil. (HH 421f.)

The choice after death is not necessarily instantaneous. Swedenborg describes a "World of Spirits" between heaven and hell, where the newly deceased gradually lose their ability to dissemble and resolve any remaining indecisions. (HH 499ff.)

MAXIMUS HOMO

Because the trinity of love, wisdom, and power is characteristic of the divine, it is characteristic of all reality; and because that trinity is intensely personal, the human form is pervasive. Swedenborg sees it as the form of the individual almost as a matter of course. He also sees it as the form of any group of people united by mutual love and understanding. He therefore refers to heaven in its entirety as the *Maximus Homo*, the "greatest person" or "Universal Human," and goes into some detail about the spiritual functions corresponding to the various members and organs of the human body. (AC 4302[3])

INCARNATION

As noted, Swedenborg regards the incarnation as the central event of human history. In his view, the human race declined from a primal state of innocence, becoming progressively more materialistic, until the only way it could be reached was through the physical presence of deity. In the Christ, Swedenborg sees God as assuming our own fallen nature and transforming it by the process of conflict between the divine best and the human worst within him. This experience precisely parallels our own inner conflicts, and his life is therefore the model for our own. (AC 3061[2])

The virgin birth, in this understanding, is essential for two reasons. First, there must be a physical mother to transmit the fallen nature: for Swedenborg, an "immaculate conception," conception by a *sinless* mother, would have been quite pointless and ineffective. Second, there needed to be within that fallen nature a capacity for the infinite acceptance of the divine. Without the first, Jesus' life is irrelevant to ours; without the second, it is ineffective. (AC 2288)

Jesus is then seen as having grown as we do, knowing doubt, selfishness, and all the distortions of humanity we can experience in ourselves. His life is the perfect exemplar of the process of transformation which is our own hope, and which, as already noted, is imaged in the biblical story. He was in a very special sense "the Word made flesh" and the fulfillment of scripture. The passion of the cross was not a propitiation, but a final trial, a final self-giving. By refusing to override human anger by miraculous means, Jesus took the last step into perfect, loving wholeness; and because that wholeness was complete, the resurrection included even his physical body. (TCR 105)

CONCLUSIONS

Swedenborg's theology calls for the fullest development of the individual emotionally, intellectually, and behaviorally. It values open and profound love, clear and free thinking, and faithful activity. It relates these qualities directly to the nature of reality, thereby avoiding any system of arbitrary rewards and punishments. Above all, it points toward an individual and collective oneness in which differences are not divisive but consistently enrich the whole. (AC 9613)

Appendix B
Distributors of Swedenborgian Literature

THE FOLLOWING list of distributors includes worldwide publishing houses, schools, and libraries from which books, pamphlets, and other materials may be ordered.

Swedenborg Lending Library and
Enquiry Center
4 Shirley Road
Roseville 2069
Sydney, New South Wales
AUSTRALIA

Church of the Good Shepherd
Margaret Avenue & Queen Street North
N2H 2H7 Kitchener, Ontario
CANADA

The Swedenborg Society and the New
Church Press, Ltd.
20 Bloomsbury Way
W.C. 1A 2TH, London
ENGLAND

New Church Book Depot
34 John Dalton Street
M2 6LE, Manchester
ENGLAND

The New Church College Book
Department
25 Radcliffe New Road
M26 9LS, Manchester
ENGLAND

New Church Society
Swedenborg & Worldwide Publications
David Arul
5/23 Sevenwells St.
St. Thomas Mt., Madras-16
INDIA

Rev. Yuzo Noda
1-15-13 Akasutsumi
Setagaya-Ku
Tokyo
JAPAN

Swedenborg Society of China
James Wang Sum, Honorary Secretary
Central Post Office Box 1063
Tokyo
JAPAN

The New Jerusalem Church Library
17 George Street
Paisley
SCOTLAND

The New Church of Southern Africa
Rev. Obed S. D. Mooki
Mooki Memorial College
Box 1, Orlando
Johannesburg
SOUTH AFRICA

Agence des Publications de la Nouvelle
Église et Cercle
21, rue Caroline
Lausanne
SWITZERLAND

Swedenborg Verlag
Appolostrasse 2
8032 Zurich
SWITZERLAND

UNITED STATES:

New Church Book Room
1010 South Flower Street
Suite 404
Los Angeles, CA 90015

Wayfarers Chapel
Portuguese Bend
Palos Verdes, CA 90015

Swedenborg Library
2107 Lyon Street
San Francisco, CA 94115

New Church Library
1611 16th Street, NW
Washington, DC 20009

New Church Book Room
Pennsylvania Avenue & Broom Street
Wilmington, DE 19806

New Church Book Room
825 West Mercer's Fernery Road
DeLand, FL 32720

Swedenborg Library
Massachusetts New Church Union
79 Newbury Street
Boston, MA 02116

General Convention Office
48 Sargent Street
Newton, MA 02158

Swedenborg School of Religion
48 Sargent Street
Newton, MA 02158

Virginia Street Church Library
170 Virginia Street
St. Paul, MN 55102

Swedenborg Foundation, Inc.
139 East 23rd Street
New York, NY 10010

Urbana College Library
Urbana, OH 43078

Academy of the New Church
General Church of the New Jerusalem
    Office
Cairncrest
Bryn Athyn, PA 19009

General Church Press
Box 278
Bryn Athyn, PA 19009

Swedenborg Scientific Association
Box 11
654 Dale Road
Bryn Athyn, PA 19009

Swedenborg Book Center, Inc.
American New Church Tract and
    Publication Society
2129 Chestnut Street
Philadelphia, PA 19103

Stone House Book Room
16244 Cleveland Street
Redmond, WA 98052

Appendix C

Selected Chronology of Swedenborg's Early Works

FROM 1709 to 1745 Emanuel Swedenborg published 125 articles, pamphlets, and books. The following selected list of scientific and philosophic works has been compiled by Ray Silverman to indicate the diversity and depth of Swedenborg's writing during this time period. A more complete bibliography of his major works can be found later in this reference section. The abbreviations after some titles listed here are those used throughout this book and can be found in the key at the beginning of the Bibliography of Swedenborg's Works.

1709   Selected Sentences from L. Annaeus Seneca and Publius Syrus Mimus with Annotations by Erasmus and Greek Version by Joseph Scaliger (graduate thesis)

1714   The Elevation of Weights by the Aid of Water and the Portable Siphon

1714   A Universal Musical Instrument, by the Aid of Which the Most Unskilled in Music Can Play All Kinds of Harmonies That Are Found in the Score

1714   A Method of Ascertaining the Inclinations and Affections of Men's Minds

1717   A New Theory Concerning the Earth's Stoppage

1719   New Hints for the Discovery of Mines, or a Certain Undiscovered Knack by Which to Find out Mines and Treasures Which Are Hidden Deeply in the Earth

1719   Information on Docks, Sluices, and Salt-works

1720   First Principles of Natural Things Deduced from Experiments and Geometry, or from Posteriori and Priori Reasonings

1721   New Observations and Discoveries Respecting Iron and Fire

1721   A New Method of Finding the Longitudes of Places, on Land, or at Sea, by Lunar Observations

1722   The Magnet and Its Different Properties; An Elucidation of a Law of Hydrostatics

1724   On the Extraction of Silver from Copper

1733   A General Comparison of the Ontology and Cosmology of Christian Wolff with the Principles of Natural Things

1734   New Attempts Toward a Philosophical Explanation of the Elementary World

1734   Outlines of a Philosophical Argument on the Infinite, and the Final Cause of Creation . . . (INF)

1738–40   Three Transactions on the Cerebrum (CER)

1739   The Muscles in General

1739   The Way to a Knowledge of the Soul

1740   Economy of the Animal Kingdom

1741   An Introduction to Rational Psychology (part 7 of AK)

1743–44   The Brain, Considered Anatomically, Physiologically and Philosophically

1744   A Hieroglyphic Key to Natural and Spiritual Arcana by Way of Representations and Correspondences (KEY)

1745   A History of Creation

Glossary of Swedenborgian Terms

Compiled by William Ross Woofenden, Ph.D.

IN USING THIS GLOSSARY, the reader should be aware of a few clarifying points.

Because Swedenborg wrote in Latin, most of the terms contained herein are not his terms but word choices made by his English translators. In compiling this list I have tried always to go back to the original meanings that the author had in mind, so far as that is possible.

This glossary was compiled independently and without access to the texts of most of the essays in this anthology. Therefore it is possible that some terms defined here may not appear in any of the articles, and that there may be omissions of items that perhaps should have been included. Because of the publication demands of compiling an anthology by more than forty authors and editors, text and glossary were not intended to be mutually inclusive.

George F. Dole and John Elliott, named in some of the following entries, are two contemporary scholars actively engaged in doing new translations of Swedenborg's theological works.

ADSCITITIOUS
Sometimes translated "adventitious," additional, added externally.

AFFECTION OF TRUTH FROM GOOD
A precise definition of "charity," that love of truth that results in useful actions, formed from good in the individual.

AFFLUX
A flowing to or toward. The mode by which the Lord controls the evil. Good and truth can only flow to, but not into, them, and thus govern them from without rather than from within. This use is in sharp contrast to the mode called "influx" (q.v.).

ANCIENT CHURCH
The religion of the biblical people of ancient times represented by Noah and his descendants.

ANGEL
A person in heaven. In Swedenborg's theology all angels are people who have lived in the natural world first and then entered heaven after death. He rejects the concept of angels as a separate class of creation.

ANIMA
The human soul, in its various traditional meanings: viz., that part of a person that lives after death. Pre-dating Jung, Swedenborg's use of *anima* carries none of the specifically feminine attributes Jung assigns to the word.

ANIMAL KINGDOM, ECONOMY OF THE
A poor translation of the title of Swedenborg's 1740 work *Oeconomia Regni Animalis*, which deals with the "dynamics of the domain of the human soul."

ANIMAL SPIRIT
In the notion of Galen, one of the three body spirits. Used by Swedenborg to mean a purer kind of blood, translated by Dole in DLW 423 as "soul-spirit."

ANIMUS
Sometimes translated "disposition," this refers in general to the mind (or to the lower level of the mind if used in contrast to *anima*), one's temperament or personality.

APPROPRIATE
Never used by Swedenborg as an adjective, but as a verb, meaning to take possession of or to claim as one's own.

ARCANA
Secrets, things hidden. Singular: arcanum. In the phrase, or title of the work by that name, *arcana coelestia:* "heavenly secrets."

AS OF SELF
As if by one's own power, seemingly on one's own. A critical concept in Swedenborg's theology: one is to act "as if" self-powered, but at the same time to acknowledge that all power to act comes from God.

ASSESSOR
In 1716 Swedenborg was appointed "Extraordinary Assessor" to the Royal College of Mines," i.e., he was named an associate member of the Swedish Board of Mines. He became a full member (assessor) in 1724.

BEING [ENS]
Used infrequently by Swedenborg, to mean an entity or distinguishable thing, also used in the phrase *ens rationis* to mean a purely mental construction. Contrast this with *esse*, the "soul" or essential nature of a thing.

BEING [ESSE]
The essential quality of a thing, reality itself, God's fundamental essence, i.e., divine love.

BOARD OF MINES
Sometimes called the Royal College of Mines; the governmental board that controlled the vital mining industry of Sweden. Swedenborg served as a member of this board (see *assessor* above).

CHARITY

In common usage this word generally means relief of material want. Our author uses it to mean a spirit of caring, of disinterested service, a heartfelt delight in doing good to one's neighbor without any thought of recompense.

CHASTE

In common usage, innocent, pure, celibate. Used by Swedenborg to mean having a pure and clean attitude toward sex, predicated only of those who are married. True marriage love is said to be "chastity itself."

CHURCH

Even this common word is used in an unusual sense, to mean neither the spiritual life alone nor any one denomination or institution, but a realization of spiritual life either in an institution or an individual. A spiritual person is thus a "church."

CHURCH OF THE NEW JERUSALEM

The most generally used name of those churches that draw their essential interpretation of Christian doctrine from the theological writings of Emanuel Swedenborg. Often simply "New Church" (q.v.).

COGNITIONS

Sometimes translated "knowledges," it is used to mean facts organized into ideas, or deeper levels of knowing. Elliott retains it in his new version of *Arcana Coelestia*, defining it as "items of knowledge relating to interior things."

COLLATERAL GOOD

A degree of goodness between natural and spiritual goodness, resembling each in part but being essentially a natural love of spiritual things, thus not genuine goodness but related to it.

CONATUS

Often rendered as "endeavor," it generally refers to the energy behind actions. It can be a life attitude or mind set, a constant impulse to strive for particular goals.

CONJUGIAL

A word coined by an early translator to reflect Swedenborg's preference for the spelling *conjugialis* (instead of *conjugalis*). It refers to things belonging to marriage and the love married partners have for each other. Generally used positively.

CONNATE

Meaning literally "existing from birth," it is sometimes used to refer to negative hereditary tendencies. It is also often used as synonymous with "innate," i.e., inborn, congenital.

CONNUBIAL

Relating to marriage, but generally used in a negative sense or concerning merely external things associated with marriage. Used of the mating of birds and animals.

CONSCIENCE MONGERS

Overly conscientious people, people who are hypercritical of others.

CONSUMPTION OF THE AGE

Identifiable with the erroneous King James Bible phrase "end of the world," this refers to the end or close of an age or era.

CONTAINANT

A word made up by some early translator of Swedenborg, also rendered "continent" (not in the usual sense), it refers to a container or receptacle, sometimes metaphorically, as in stating that the mind is a "containant" of ideas.

CONTINENT

See *containant*.

CONTINUOUS DEGREES

Levels or gradations, as from cold to warm, dark to light. Also called "degrees of breadth" or "horizontal levels."

CORPOREAL

Often used as a substantive, to mean a bodily part or the part of the mind attached to the body. Bodily, physical, preoccupied with sensations and physical pleasures.

CORRESPONDENCE

A concept basic to Swedenborgianism, correspondence is both a causal and a functional relation between God and all lower degrees of life. It is the law or mode of divine inflow into all of creation.

CORRESPONDENCES

Things or entities that respond, match, agree, or are analogous to each other, as that the heat and light of the sun correspond to God's love and wisdom. Thus heat and love, light and wisdom are correspondences.

DEVIL

"The Devil" for Swedenborg means the totality of the hells. A devil is an evil person after death. When contrasted with a "satan" (q.v.), satans intellectually confirm lusts of evils in themselves, devils will to live them.

DISCRETE DEGREES

Distinct levels, one higher than the other, as in the relationships of end, cause, effect. Also called vertical levels, degrees of altitude, and degrees of height.

DISTINCTLY ONE

Oneness for Swedenborg is unity of purpose, not simplicity. Love and truth, e.g., cannot exist separately in act, but still are distinguishable in their oneness, thus are "distinctly" or, better, "distinguishably one."

DIVINE HUMAN

The central idea in the theology of the New Church, this term applies to the Lord Jesus Christ after glorification of his human, thus divine love in human form—"all the fullness of Deity living in bodily form" (Colossians 2:9).

DIVINE NATURAL

The natural or lowest level of the inner nature or mind of Jesus glorified or made divine.

DIVINE PROCEEDING

The Divine in the act of proceeding, thus the qualities of God emanating from him, equatable with the Holy Spirit.

EFFLUX

Output, a flowing out. The good and truth that flow into persons from God should in turn flow out into the world in the form of acts of love to the neighbor. God's universal law is that influx is always according to efflux.

END, CAUSE, EFFECT

Used in the philosophical sense of goal or purpose, *end* is the love or intention of the will, *cause* is the means through understanding to achieve the purpose, *effect* is the resulting action, speech, sensation, or production thus achieved.

ENS RATIONIS

A purely mental construction, something existing only in the mind. Roughly equivalent in some contexts to will-o'-the-wisp or *ignis fatuus*. See *being (ens)*.

EVIL

Evil, regarded in itself, is severance from good or disordered good, disunion from God and opposition to the Lord and heaven. Thus evil in a person is hell within that person.

EXEGETIC-PHILANTHROPIC SOCIETY

The first organization in Sweden devoted to promoting Swedenborg's doctrines, formed in 1786 by a group that included von Höpken, the Nordenskiölds, and Wadström. Although short-lived, it had some 150 members.

EXINANITION

An emptying out of the spirit, a state of spiritual desolation. With the Lord it was a state of humility in which his human was seemingly separated from the divine within. Cf. *vastation*.

FALLACY

A deceptive appearance. Least significant are fallacies of the senses (such as that the sun "rises"). Worse are those derived from one's lower nature, being falsities that become conjoined with evil, due to lack of faith on the part of the person.

FALSITY OF EVIL

Also called "falsity from evil," a false idea or distortion of truth caused by an evil desire.

FORM

Used in its philosophic sense of organization, or an organic receptacle in which an essence appears. It does not relate to shape but to the order, disposition, arrangement, and relation of the parts of an entity. Closely allied to function or use.

GENII

Swedenborg's term for evil spirits of the worst kind, acting malevolently on a person's will, twisting desires to evil purposes. Contrasted with those evil spirits who strive to make truth appear as falsity and vice versa.

GENIUS

A person's disposition or character type; the talent, inclination, quality, or spirit of a person or group of persons.

GLORIFICATION

The process by which the Lord Jesus Christ gradually put off the merely human things of all planes of his being and made them divine. Also used to mean the establishment of a divine consciousness in the Lord's mind, so that he became life itself.

GOOD

Used to mean goodness or a good thing, it is generally defined as the affection of thinking and acting according to divine order. Thus it is a quality of love to the Lord and the neighbor involving use. Good in a person is relative to God's divine good.

GOOD OF TRUTH

A state reached by truth in an individual in which it expresses itself in acts of love, whereby the truth becomes good. It is also called spiritual good.

GRAND MAN

A less-acceptable translation of the Latin *Maximus Homo* ("greatest person"), now translated by Dole as the "Universal Human" (q.v.).

GYMNASIUM

In common European usage, a secondary school. Swedenborg uses it to refer to schools or gatherings in the spiritual world where the members of groups discuss ideas and exercise their minds.

HEREDITARY EVIL

Although often used without apparent qualification by Swedenborg, he in fact rejects the traditional view and insists that we inherit not actual evil but tendencies toward evil, which we may either confirm and adopt, or refuse and reject as adults.

HISTORICAL FAITH

"Faith" based only on tradition or on the beliefs of others, thus not truly faith at all but only the appearance of faith.

HUMAN DIVINE

Swedenborg's the "Divine Human," denoting the incarnation of God in Jesus, was transposed by Blake to suggest our own potential to realize the divine image.

HUMILIATION

Not used in the modern sense of embarrassment, but to mean a state of humility, in which a person acknowledges that any good or truth that seems to be one's own is really the Lord's within the person. Also used of the Lord in his states of spiritual emptiness.

IN

Often used in the sense of "engaged in" or "in a condition or state." Thus we read of a person being "in good," or "in an affection of good," etc., meaning in a state of goodness or in a state in which one loves doing that which is good.

INFLUX

Meaning inflow or input or influence, this term is used to describe the fundamental concept that all power to act flows into all of creation from God constantly and unceasingly.

INSINUATE

Used in the basic Latin meaning as introducing or instilling something subtly, rather than openly. To assign to an interior position without the recipient's being fully aware of the process.

INTERCOURSE

An older translation of *commercium*, meaning interaction, association between persons or things. Used also to refer to how a person's soul and body communicate and generally interact.

ITERATED MARRIAGES

Repeated marriages, remarriage.

JEALOUSY [ZELOTYPIA]

Used by Swedenborg only in one chapter of *Conjugial Love*, to mean love of protecting what is precious, especially marriage love. He admits there is a wrong jealousy, but his emphasis is on the positive side. He calls it the zeal of zeals—the true type of zeal.

LIMBUS

Also translated "envelope" or "border;" used to mean a border drawn from nature and retained after death (in some form not clearly delineated) to give one fixity, stability, and permanence in the spiritual world. According to Swedenborg, a person's limbus is "a skinlike case for the spiritual body which a spirit or angel inhabits" (DLW 257). It comprises the "walls of the spirit" of that particular individual—limits, boundaries, or psychic walls unique to that person, never to be fully duplicated in another.

LOWER EARTH

In Swedenborg's detailed description of the spiritual world, the lower earth is a region below or inferior to the world of spirits but above or superior to hell.

MAN [*HOMO, VIR*]

Latin has two words for "man": *homo*, a person (male or female), humankind, the Lord as essential person; and *vir*: a male human being.

MAXIMUS HOMO

See *Grand Man* and *Universal Human*.

MEDIA

Often singular: medium. Means, things that go between. An intermediary that derives something from each of two entities and has the effect that as a person draws near to one, the other becomes subordinate.

MEMORABLE RELATIONS

Also memorabilia, memorable occurrences. Stories or accounts of otherworld experiences that Swedenborg appended to or interspersed in chapters of his late works.

MERIT, MERITORIOUS

The connotation of these words in common usage is generally positive. In Swedenborg's use they almost always mean merit-seeking, expecting a reward of money or prestige (merit) for any seemingly charitable or kindly action.

MODIFICATION

Used in some of the pretheological works as a concept that connotes all the modes of communication throughout nature. The idea was incorporated into and subsumed in the later doctrine or concept of *correspondences* (q.v.).

MOST ANCIENT CHURCH

Often capitalized (as a proper name) this term refers to the earliest prehistoric culture as it related to the divine. Linked symbolically with the Genesis accounts of creation and the Garden of Eden.

NATURALIST

Used only in the pejorative sense of a person who believes in nature instead of in God, i.e., a materialist. Naturalism, similarly, is defined as belief in nature as the source of all religious concepts.

NATURAL MAN

Not generally used to mean the total person, although it can mean a person whose interests are mainly worldly. More often it refers to the lowest level of the human mind in any individual.

NEIGHBOR

Not at all confined to "the person next door," the distinctive idea is that good from the Lord is the neighbor, and each person is neighbor in the degree in which he or she receives that good. The Lord, the church, one's country, etc., are all neighbor.

NEW CHURCH (1)

Used in general of any new state of God-human relations, also used to refer to a church era that will acknowledge and worship the Lord alone, hold his Word holy, love divine truths, and reject faith separated from charity.

NEW CHURCH (2)

The popular identifying name of any organized religious group that adheres to the doctrines found in the theological writings of Swedenborg. An individual member of such groups is often called a New Churchman or New Churchwoman (see *Church of the New Jerusalem*).

NEW JERUSALEM

The symbolic city described in the Bible in the last chapters of the book of Revelation. It was early adopted by Swedenborgians to identify their church with the church signified or symbolized by the heavenly city.

OWN

Used by some translators to render both *suus* and *proprium* (q.v.)— in the latter case as if it were a noun. Own refers to self, living from and for self; sense or feeling of selfhood; a necessary illusion of self-guidance in human regeneration.

PELLICACY

From *pellex* (a concubine or mistress); state of keeping or living with a mistress.

PERMISSIONS

Identified by Swedenborg as a part of divine providence, permissions or tolerations are things allowed or tolerated but not necessarily desired by God. Not to tolerate such undesirable actions would infringe on human freedom.

PROPRIUM

This feeling of selfhood, in addition to its basic meaning, has many variant senses, as proprium that is angelic, diabolical, human, divine, infernal, intellectual, voluntary, etc. In its negative usages it often means very much the same as pride. See *own*.

PURE INTELLECT

In the pretheological work *Rational Psychology*, Swedenborg defines this as a faculty that gives persons the power to think and reason, and that also governs all the processes of the organic body with an intuitive wisdom derived from God.

RATIOCINATION

Often unfortunately translated "reasoning," this refers to the process of drawing false inferences, of false reasoning, to a false inference or deduction. Very close in meaning to the contemporary psychological connotation of "rationalizing."

REFORMATION

Used to describe a part of the process of regeneration, this involves putting one's outward life in order. One is led by truth to good in a state of obedience in which truth predominates. It is preparation to receive a new will from the Lord.

REGENERATION

In a broad sense, the entire process of rebirth. In a restricted sense, that part of the process that follows reformation, being chiefly the forming of a new will in the person by the Lord. Also, rarely the goal of the process.

RELIGIOSITY
Used to describe an external or superstitious belief system, a sort of religion that has no depth of inner commitment on the part of its adherents.

REMAINS
Impressions of love and truth deeply implanted in a person by the Lord in ways unknown and "remaining" with the person from infancy through the rest of life, serving as a basis for rebirth. Also translated "remnants" or "remnant states."

REMNANT STATES
See *remains*.

REPENTANCE
The first stage in rebirth, involving confessing sins to God, praying that they be forgiven, followed by a sincere effort to lead a new life according to precepts of true charity and faith.

REPRESENTATIVE
A natural object, a person, or an action used to symbolize a spiritual idea, or that spiritual idea itself. Also the presentation of an idea in visible form in the spiritual world.

ROYAL COLLEGE OF MINES
See *Board of Mines*.

RULING LOVE
The strongest love in a person that dominates his or her life. Four possible ruling loves are named: love of (1) God, (2) neighbor, (3) self, and (4) the world. Only 1 and 2 are considered acceptable ruling loves for a regenerating person.

SATAN
An evil spirit who intellectually confirms lusts of evil. Also used as a name of "the evil one" (even though Swedenborg did not believe in one prime devil or prince of darkness.) See *devil*.

SCIENTIFICS
Knowledges, facts, data. See *scientific truths*.

SCIENTIFIC TRUTHS
A poor translation, because the term seldom refers to "science" as we know it, but to facts, data, truths gained from the study of nature and from the literal sense of scripture.

SCORTATORY
Descriptive of promiscuous sexual behavior, harlotry, or whoredom. A "scortatory marriage," for instance, would be one in which the partners feel free to commit adultery.

SENSUOUS
Also sensual, sensory, and sense-oriented (of people). Not exclusively sexual in connotation, but characterized by concentration on the senses in general, apprehended by the senses. The lowest of the planes of the natural degree of the mind.

SERIES
Connected sequence, train of thought. In the pretheological works the terms *series and society* and *series and degrees* referred to hypotheses later subsumed in the theological concept of degrees.

SIGNIFICATIVE
Something that carries or points to a spiritual meaning. Having a special meaning, significant. Used at times in distinction to *representatives* and *correspondences* (q.v.).

SOCIETY
Association with a group of people, a group of people living together, a community, a group of spirits or angels in the other world. Also often used by Swedenborgians to refer to their local church organization or congregation.

SPIRIT WORLD
A term referring in general to the other world or abode of persons after death. Not to be confused with the World of Spirits, Swedenborg's name for the first state one enters after death, midway between heaven and hell.

STORGE
A word borrowed from Greek meaning love for infants, especially the love felt for them by their parents. Also translated "parental love" and "parental affection."

SUBJECT
In addition to its common usages, also used in the philosophical sense of that which underlies an activity or kind of behavior. Charity, e.g., must have a "subject," i.e., a personality that embodies, feels, and exercises charity.

TEMPTATION
Not used in the sense of allurement or an impulse to do wrong, it refers to an assault on a person's ruling love, which tries and tests the person; an inner conflict that both reveals one's character and offers opportunity to strengthen it.

THEOSOPHICAL
Used by early followers of Swedenborg as part of the name of a society to promote his ideas, but soon dropped due to the negative connotations that *theosophy* took on. Madame Blavatsky, e.g., founded the journal *The Theosophist*, which became identified as fostering belief in reincarnation, spiritism, and occult sciences. Many of her so-called miracles were shown to be fraudulent. The term *theosophical* is still used by some European writers to refer to Swedenborg's theological ideas.

TRANSFLUX
Flowing through, flowing throughout. Also used negatively to refer to how good from the Lord flows through some persons without effect, as water flows through a sieve. Such persons are said to be without conscience.

TRUE
In an absolute sense, the true is the form and means of divine love. In a relative sense, it is the perceiving and effecting function of individual human love.

TRUTH OF FAITH
A true idea that is part of one's faith, but that has not yet been put to use in the life. It is used in contrast to the "good of faith," which is the goodness that comes from living one's beliefs.

TRUTH OF GOOD
Of this phrase our author once suggested as alternative wording the "wisdom of love," noting that wisdom is unattainable unless

one has a love or desire to be wise. The wisdom that can result from this love is the "truth of good."

ULTIMATE

Last in sequence, lowest, most external, final, most remote. Not used by Swedenborg to mean "greatest" (as for instance, in the title of Lewis Hite's article "Love: The Ultimate Reality").

UNIVERSAL CHURCH

Also "the church universal," referring to the church as it exists everywhere, transcending church organizations. A truly ecumenical concept, referring to sincere persons of faith of every world religion.

UNIVERSAL HUMAN

Dole's translation of *Maximus Homo*. Refers to the entire heavens as the "body" of the Lord, or the Lord's kingdom, including heaven and the church on earth. Sometimes used to mean the Lord himself (see *Divine Human*).

USE

Useful activity, a function that serves a purpose; often synonymous with good. It regularly implies service where there is a real desire to serve. Thus a "good of use" is a purpose, attitude, or deed that has this appropriate content or motive.

VASTATION

A state of desolation, a consummation, an emptying out. It is used of the process in the world of spirits whereby external evils and falsities are removed from the good, and hypocritical goods and mere knowledges are removed from the evil.

VESSEL

An individual person is said to be a "vessel" that receives life from God, not as a mere container but as an organic form that reacts with or against any influx impinging on it.

WILL AND UNDERSTANDING

Also "intentionality and discernment," "the voluntary and the intellectual." These are the two comprehensive aspects or faculties of human personality. Will includes all volitional functions and serves as receptor and reactor to divine influences. Understanding includes all discriminating functions and serves as that which instructs the will and executes its intents.

Bibliography of Swedenborg's Works

Compiled and Annotated by
William Ross Woofenden, Ph.D.

EMANUEL SWEDENBORG BEGAN TO WRITE and publish at the age of twelve. He continued to do so for seventy years. Much of what he wrote he left unpublished. His followers, however, in the course of the years, have made a well-nigh heroic attempt to edit, translate, and publish *every* known manuscript that came from Swedenborg's pen, often without any apparent regard to their relative significance. This effort has in no sense been coordinated, and there is a great deal of overlap and duplication of posthumously published works. Nor has there been any consistency in the choice of English titles for his works.

This bibliography, although not exhaustive, includes all works of Swedenborg (whether published by the author or published posthumously) that are relevant to the articles in this anthology, as well as a few major commentaries and documentary collections of his works. Following all titles are the abbreviations (in brackets) of the titles used consistently in this book. Authors of the essays may have cited passages from different editions of Swedenborg's works, but paragraph numbers or volume and page numbers should coincide between editions.

Publication data is provided for most entries, followed by annotations that clarify the content of and differences between editions. Cross-references are included to guide the reader from and to various translations and editions of the same work, for example, from the Latin title to one or more of the English titles used by translators. English editions cited are usually the versions preferred by the editors of this volume and currently or most recently in print.

In addition to the publications included here, there is also a short selected list of Swedenborg's early works compiled by Ray Silverman in Appendix C.

Key to Abbreviations of Swedenborg's Works

Abbrev.	Titles of Works
[9Q]	Nine Questions, Questiones Novem de Trinitate
[AC]	Arcana Coelestia, Heavenly Arcana, Heavenly Secrets
[AE]	Apocalypse Explained, Apocalypsis Explicata
[AK]	Animal Kingdom, Regnum Animale, Soul's Domain
[AR]	Apocalypse Revealed, Apocalypsis Revelata
[ATH]	Athanasian Creed, De Athanasii Symbolo
[BE]	Brief Exposition, Summary Exposition, Summaria Expositio Doctrinae Novae Ecclesiae
[BRAIN]	Brain (1743–44), De Cerebro (Brain)
[CAN]	Canons of the New Church, Canones Novae Ecclesiae
[CB]	Camena Borea, Northern Muse
[CER]	Cerebrum (1738–40), De Cerebro (Cerebrum)
[CHAR]	Charity, Doctrine of Charity, Doctrina Novae Hierosolymae de Charitate
[CHEM]	Chemistry, Principles of Chemistry, Prodromus Principiorum Rerum Naturalium
[CLJ]	Continuation on the Last Judgment, Continuatio de Ultimo Judicio
[CL]	Marriage Love, Marital Love, Conjugial Love, Delitiae Sapientia de Amore Conjugiali
[CONJ]	On Marriage, De Conjugio
[COP]	Treatise on Copper, De Cupro et Orichalco, On Copper and Brass, Swedenborg's Treatise on Copper

[COR]	Coronis, Appendix to True Christian Religion, Coronis seu Appendix ad Veram Christianam Religionem
[CS]	On Common Salt, De Sale Communi
[DAED]	Northern Inventor, Daedalus Hyperboreus
[DLDW]	On the Divine Love and on the Divine Wisdom, Doctrine of Uses, De Devina Amore, et de Divina Sapientia
[DLW]	Divine Love and Wisdom, Sapientia Angelica de Divino Amore et Divina Sapientia
[DOC]	Documents on Swedenborg, Tafel Documents
[DP]	Divine Providence, Sapientia Angelica de Divina Providentia
[DV]	De Verbo, Sacred Scripture or Word of the Lord from Experience
[EAK]	Economy of the Animal Kingdom, Oeconomia Regni Animalis, Dynamics of the Soul's Domain
[EU]	Earths in the Universe, De Telluribus in Mundo Nostro Solari
[FA]	Festivus Applausus in Caroli XII in Pomeraniam suam adventum
[FAITH]	Doctrine of Faith, Doctrina Novae Hierosolymae de Fide
[FD]	Four Doctrines, Four Leading Doctrines (Lord, Holy Scripture, Life, Faith)
[FIBRE]	Fibre, De Fibra, EAK Transaction III
[GEN]	Human Genitalia, Generation, De Generatione
[HH]	Heaven and Hell, De Coelo et . . . de Inferno
[HW]	Height of Water, Om Wattnens Hogd
[INDEX]	Bible Index, Index Biblicus
[INF]	The Infinite, On the Infinite and Final Cause of Creation, Prodromus Philosophiae Ratiocinantis de Infinito
[INV]	Invitation to the New Church, *Invitatio ad Novam Ecclesiam*
[IRON]	Treatise on Iron, De Ferro
[JD]	Journal of Dreams, Dream Book, Drömmar, Swedenborg's Journal of Dreams
[KEY]	Hieroglyphic Key, Clavis Hieroglyphica
[L PRIN]	Lesser Principia, First Principles, [Minor] Principia
[L&M]	Letters and Memorials of Emanuel Swedenborg, Acton's Letters and Memorials of Swedenborg
[LIFE]	Doctrine of Life, Doctrina Vitae pro Nova Hierosolyma ex Praeceptis Decalogi
[LJP]	Last Judgment (Posthumous)
[LJ]	Last Judgment (and Babylon Destroyed), De Ultimo Judicio et de Babylonia Destructa
[LORD]	Doctrine of the Lord, Doctrina Novae Hierosolyma de Domino
[MES]	Messiah About to Come
[MISC]	Miscellaneous Observations on Physical Sciences, Miscellanea Observata circa Res Naturales
[MOT]	Motion and Position of the Earth and Planets
[MT]	Modest Thoughts on the Deflation and Inflation of Swedish Coinage, Offörgripelige tanckar om swenska myntets förnedring och förhögning
[MT2]	Offörgripelige tanckar om myntets ophöjande och nedsättjande
[MTW]	Miscellaneous Theological Works
[NJHD]	New Jerusalem and Its Heavenly Doctrine, De Nova Hierosolyma et ejus Doctrina Celesti, Heavenly Doctrine
[OM]	Opera Minora
[ONT]	Ontology, Ontologia
[OPEM]	Philosophical and Metallurgical Works, Opera Philosophica et Mineralia (Principia, De Ferro, De Cupro)
[OP]	Opera Poetica
[OQ]	Opera Quaedam
[PHIL]	A Philosopher's Note Book
[PP]	Prophets and Psalms, Summaria Expositio Sensu Interni . . . Propheticorum ac Psalmorum
[PRIN]	Principia, Principia Rerum Naturalium
[PSY]	Psychological Transactions
[RP]	Rational Psychology; De Anima; Psychologia Rationalis; The Soul, or Rational Psychology
[SBI]	Soul-Body Interaction, Influx, Intercourse Between Soul and Body, De Commercio Animae et Corporis
[SC]	Scripture Confirmations, Dicta Probantia
[SD]	Spiritual Diary, Memorabilia, Experientiae Spirituales
[SENSE]	Five Senses, De Sensu Communi
[SPT]	Scientific and Philosophical Treatises
[SS]	Doctrine of Sacred Scripture, Doctrine of Holy Scripture, Doctrina Novae Hierosolymae de Scriptura Sacra
[STW]	Small Theological Works
[TCR]	True Christian Religion, Vera Christiana Religio
[TREM]	Tremulation, On Tremulation
[WE]	Word Explained, Explicatio in Verbum Historicum Veteris Testamenti, Adversaria
[WH]	White Horse, De Equo Albo, de quo in Apocalypsi
[WLG]	Worship and Love of God, De Cultu et Amore Dei

List of Works

Acton's Letters and Memorials of Swedenborg [L&M]. See *Letters and Memorials of Emanuel Swedenborg.*

Adversaria [WE]. *Adversaria in Libros Veteris Testamenti.* Edited by J. F. I. Tafel. 4 vols. Tübingen, Germany: Verlagsexpedition; and London: William Newbery, 1842–54. See *Word Explained.*

Animal Kingdom [AK]. Translated by J. J. G. Wilkinson. 2 vols. London: William Newbery, 1843. Reprint. Bryn Athyn, Pa.: Swedenborg Scientific Association, 1960. See *Regnum Animale.*

A poor translation of the title of Swedenborg's 1744–45 work *Regnum Animale*, which deals with the domain of the human soul. Though it has never been published under this title, the preferred English translation is *Soul's Domain.* This was the last of a series of works on the natural sciences before the author commenced his labors as a theologian.

Apocalypse Explained [AE]. A posthumous publication. Translation revised by J. Whitehead. 6 vols. New York: Swedenborg Foundation, 1911. Several reprints. See *Apocalypsis Explicata.*

Apocalypsis Explicata [AE]. *Apocalypsis Explicata secundum Sensum Spiritualem, ubi revelantur arcana, quae ibi praedicta, et hactenus recondita fuerunt.* Edited and published by R. Hindmarsh. 4 vols. London: 1785–89.

On the title page of the manuscript is written, "London, 1759," indicating the author's original intent to publish this work. Both first-draft and clean-copy manuscripts exist of the work up to the treatment of Revelation 19. But the work was never completed. For more details, see *Apocalypsis Revelata.*

Apocalypse Revealed [AR]. Translated by F. Coulson. 2 vols. London: Swedenborg Society, 1970. See *Apocalypsis Revelata.*

A detailed unfolding of the inner sense of the book of Revelation. There is an author's preface, followed by his summary of Catholic and Protestant doctrines. This is the first of the late works in which Swedenborg appended so-called "memorable relations" or "memorable occurrences" to the explications of the chapters of Revelation. In 1765 he had stopped writing in his *Spiritual Diary*—a work that contained much material similar to these descriptions of otherworld events—and now in this 1766 work (and all subsequent publications) he included accounts of such happenings. In a letter written to his friend Dr. Gabriel Beyer in April 1766, he recommended that the doctor read these passages first.

Apocalypsis Revelata [AR]. *Apocalypsis Revelata, in qua deteguntur arcana quae ibi praedicta sunt, et hactenus recondita latuerunt.* Amsterdam: 1766.

This is the last of the works that Swedenborg published anonymously. There is some difference of opinion as to whether this is, as its most recent translator F. Coulson, says, "a condensed and modified version" of the earlier incomplete work. *Apocalypse Explained*, or a completely new and independent explication of the last book of the Bible. The weight of evidence seems to be with the latter view. Unlike the earlier work, this one is openly addressed to the Christian world, and thus marks an apparently new attitude on the part of the author as to where the New Church proclaimed in his writings was to have its origin.

Appendix to True Christian Religion [COR]. See *Coronis.*

Arcana Coelestia [AC]. *Arcana Coelestia, quae in Scriptura Sacra, seu Verbo Domini sunt, detecta. . . .* 8 vols. London: John Lewis, 1749–56.

For details as to the printing and publishing of this multivolume work in its original Latin, see J. Hyde's *Bibliography of Swedenborg's Works* listed in the Select Bibliography of this book. Facsimiles of the title pages of the first Latin edition and variant readings in the drafts of these title pages where they occur in the autograph will be found in *An Appendix to Arcana Caelestia* (*sic*), published in London by the Swedenborg Society, 1973. Details as to the contents of the entire work will be found in the next entry.

Arcana Coelestia [AC]. *Arcana Coelestia, the Heavenly Arcana Contained in the Holy Scripture or Word of the Lord Unfolded, Beginning with the Book of Genesis.* Translation revised and edited by J. F. Potts. 12 vols. New York: American Swedenborg Printing and Publishing Society (predecessor to Swedenborg Foundation), 1905–10. Many reprints.

This is the edition currently kept in print in the United States. The Swedenborg Society, in London, also keeps another revision in print and is in the process of publishing a new translation by J. Elliott. In 1987 (when this bibliography was prepared) only the first 4 volumes were in print.

This largest of Swedenborg's works explains in detail the inner or spiritual meaning of the books of Genesis and Exodus. Between chapters the author added a wide variety of essays on doctrinal subjects as well as a number of articles descriptive of his otherworld experience. Some of the topics are continued from chapter to chapter. These interchapter articles were later abstracted, rewritten, and published in five smaller works.

This work has also been published as *Heavenly Arcana* and *Heavenly Secrets.* These sets have long been out of print.

Athanasian Creed [ATH]. A posthumous publication. Translated by D. Harley. Latin-English edition. London: Swedenborg Society, 1954.

The original manuscript of this fragmentary work is lost. A copy made by A. Nordenskiöld is held by the Swedenborg Society. This work is an incomplete commentary on the creed of Athanasius. It was first published in Stockholm in 1869.

Bible Index [INDEX]. See *Index Biblicus.*

Brain (1743–44). [BRAIN]. *The Brain, Considered Anatomically, Physiologically and Philosophically.* A posthumous publication. Edited, translated, and annotated by R. L. Tafel. 2 vols. London: Swedenborg Society, 1882, 1887. Vol. 1 reprinted 1934.

Tafel planned a 4-volume work, but only 2 volumes were completed. Volume 1 is mainly on the cerebrum, volume 2 on the pituitary gland, cerebellum, and medulla oblongata. In addition to the portions of Swedenborg's manuscript printed here, the editor has introduced many citations from "modern authorities," i.e., 19th-century anatomists. The editor's preface gives an extensive analysis of the contents.

The unpublished portion of the English translation of the original manuscript is in typescript in the library of the Academy of the New Church, Bryn Athyn, Pa.

Brief Exposition [BE]. *Brief Exposition of the Doctrine of the New Church, Signified by the New Jerusalem in [the Book of] Revelation.* Translated by R. Stanley. London: Swedenborg Society, 1952.

First published in Latin in 1769, as *Summaria Expositio* (q.v.), this small work is described in the opening paragraph as a preliminary sketch of a larger work to follow, viz., *Vera Christiana Religio* (1771). See translator's preface for more information.

Camena Borea [CB]. *Camena Borea cum heroum et heroidum factis ludens: sive fabellae Ovidianis similes sub variis nominibus.* Greifswald, Germany: D. B. Starck, 1715. Eng. trans.: *Northern Muse.*

A set of 22 Latin fables. In a letter to his brother-in-law dated 4 April 1715, Swedenborg described them as "fables like Ovid's, in which are concealed the deeds of certain kings and magnates, and other events." No English edition has been published.

Canones Novae Ecclesiae [CAN]. *Canones Novae Ecclesiae seu Integra Theologia Novae Ecclesiae.* A posthumous publication. Published in *Opera Minora.* Edited by S. H. Worcester. New York: American Swedenborg Printing and Publishing Society, 1906. See *Canons of the New Church.*

Canons of the New Church [CAN]. Translated by F. Coulson. London: Swedenborg Society, 1954.

Written probably in 1769 and left by Swedenborg among his manuscripts, the original is now lost. An incomplete work, it was written as a preparation for *Vera Christiana Religio*, covering the same ground as the first three chapters of that work. This edition has had paragraph numbers added by the translator. See his editorial note for more information.

Cerebrum (1738–40) [CER]. *Three Transactions on the Cerebrum.* Translated by A. Acton. A posthumous publication. 3 vols. Philadelphia: Swedenborg Scientific Association, 1938–40.

See table of contents and translator's preface for full details as to the subject matter of this work and how it fits into the total corpus of Swedenborg's treatises on the brain.

Charity [CHAR]. A posthumous publication. Translated by F. Coulson. London: Swedenborg Society, 1947.

Written in 1766, *Charity* was left among Swedenborg's manuscripts. This edition has the advantage for the reader of using the paragraph numbering adopted by Potts in his *Swedenborg Concordance.* At least three other numbering schemes had been devised, leading Potts to include a full page "key" cross-referencing the various versions. The 1931 version of W. Wunsch is worth noting, although it omits paragraph numbers entirely.

Chemistry [CHEM]. *Some Specimens of a Work on the Principles of Chemistry, with Other Treatises.* Translated by C. E. Strutt. London: William Newbery, 1847. Reprint 1976 by Swedenborg Scientific Association, Bryn Athyn, Pa. See *Prodromus Principiorum Rerum Naturalium.*

Strutt notes in his introduction that this is a translation of three Latin treatises published at Amsterdam in 1721. His assessment of the contents of the first treatise, however, was challenged by Lewis Hite in his 1929 presidential address to the Swedenborg Scientific Association. See the text of that address in *New Philosophy* 32, nos. 1–4, pp. 8–18.

Clavis Hieroglyphica [KEY]. *Clavis Hieroglyphica Arcanorum Naturalium et Spiritualium per viam Representationum et Correspondentiarum.* A posthumous publication. London: R. Hindmarsh, 1784. See *Hieroglyphic Key.*

Conjugial Love [CL]. *The Delights of Wisdom Concerning Conjugial Love, After Which Follows the Pleasures of Insanity Concerning Scortatory Love.* Translated by A. Acton. London: Swedenborg Society, 1953. See *De Amore Conjugiali, Marriage Love, Marital Love.*

This edition is listed here mainly because it is the most recent translation. There is no agreement as to which is the "best title" or "best translation" of this work. This work has also been issued under this title for many years by the Swedenborg Foundation, but it is an edited version of S. Warren's 1907 translation, which he originally titled *Marriage Love* (q.v.).

This is the first of the theological works published with the author's name on the title page. See *De Amore Conjugiali* for more details.

Continuatio de Ultimo Judicio [CLJ]. *Continuatio de Ultimo Judicio, et de Mundo Spirituali.* Amsterdam: 1763. See *Continuation on the Last Judgment.*

Continuation on the Last Judgment [CLJ]. *Continuation Concerning the Last Judgment, and Concerning the Spiritual World.* Translated by D. Harley. London: Swedenborg Society, 1961. Bound with *Last Judgment and Babylon Destroyed* (q.v.).

This is the last of six works published in Amsterdam in 1763. Paragraph 2 says, "The reason for a Continuation concerning the Last Judgment is chiefly that it may be known what was the state of the world and of the Church before the last judgment, and what the state of the world and of the Church has been after it; also, to describe how the last judgment was effected on the Reformed."

Copper and Brass [COP]. *Swedenborg's Treatise on Copper and Brass.* Translated by A. Searle. 3 vols. London: Swedenborg Society, and British Non-Ferrous Metals Research Association, 1938. See *De Cupro et Orichalco (Opera Philosophia et Mineralia,* vol. 3).

Coronis [COR]. *Coronis or Appendix to True Christian Religion.* A posthumous publication. Edited and revised by J. Buss. London: Swedenborg Society, 1931. Reprinted 1966.

This is the last work of the author and was still incomplete when he was seized with his last illness. It deals mainly with the several church eras described elsewhere by Swedenborg. This separate work should not be confused with the "Supplement" (*Coronis*) that is a part of the published work *True Christian Religion*.

Coronis seu Appendix ad Veram Christianam Religionem [COR]. A posthumous publication. In *Opera Minora*. Edited by S. Worcester. New York: American Swedenborg Printing and Publishing Society, 1906. See *Coronis*.

Daedalus Hyperboreus [DAED]. 6 issues. Uppsala, Sweden: J. Werner, 1716–18. English translation: *Northern Inventor*.

This is the first scientific journal published in Sweden, and the present Society of Sciences in Uppsala regards it as the first of its proceedings. Only six issues were produced, in Swedish, except no. 5, which was in Swedish and Latin. Facsimile copies are in volume 1 of *Swedenborg Archives*, edited by A. Stroh, published in Stockholm by the editor, 1918. Portions have been translated into English. For details see Hyde, *Bibliography of Swedenborg's Works*, and *Additions to Hyde's Bibliography*, edited by A. S. Wainscot, published in London by the Swedenborg Society, 1967.

De Amore Conjugiali [CL]. *Delitiae Sapientiae de Amore Conjugiali, post quas sequuntur voluptates insanie de Amore scortatorio*. Ab Emanuele Swedenborg, Sueco. Amsterdam: 1768. See *Conjugial Love, Marriage Love, Marital Love*.

All of the theological works of Swedenborg from 1749 through 1766 were published anonymously. This work is the first to have the author's name on the title page ("by Emanuel Swedenborg, a Swede"). At the back of the volume he appended a list of "theological books hitherto published by me" (for more details, see *Studia Swedenborgiana*, vol. 5, no. 4). This disclosure later led to a heresy trial at Göteborg (see, listed in the Select Bibliography, Sigstedt, *Swedenborg Epic*, chap. 41).

De Anima [RP]. *Opusculum de Anima*. A posthumous publication. Edited by J. F. I. Tafel. Tübingen, Germany: Verlagsexpedition; and London: William Newbery, 1849. See *Rational Psychology*.

Identified by the editor as part 7 of the *Regnum Animale* series. See *Rational Psychology* for more details about the contents and English editions of this work.

De Athanasii Symbolo [ATH]. See *Athanasian Creed*.

De Cerebro [BRAIN]. See *Brain* (1743–44).

De Cerebro [CER]. See *Cerebrum* (1738–40).

De Coelo . . . et de Inferno [HH]. *De Coelo et ejus mirabilibus, et de Inferno, ex auditis et visis*. London: 1758. See *Heaven and Hell*.

De Commercio Animae et Corporis [SBI]. London: 1769. Also called *Intercourse Between Soul and Body*. See *Soul-Body Interaction, Influx*.

De Conjugio [CONJ]. A posthumous publication. Edited by J. F.

I. Tafel. Tubingen, Germany: Verlagsexpedition; and London: Swedenborg Society, 1860. See *On Marriage*.

De Cultu et Amore Dei [WLG]. Pts. 1 and 2. London: 1745. See *Worship and Love of God*.

The Latin manuscript of part 3, left incomplete by the author, was reproduced in Stockholm, 1780 in the *Photolithograph Manuscripts*, volume 7, and the *Photostats*, codex 51, in Academy of the New Church Library, Bryn Athyn, Pa., 1930.

De Cupro et Orichalco [COP]. Vol. 3 of OPEM (q.v.). Dresden and Leipzig: F. Hekel, 1734. Also called *Treatise on Copper and Brass*. See *Copper and Brass, Swedenborg's Treatise on Copper and Brass*.

The full title of this large work is *Regnum subterraneum sive minerale de cupro et orichalco, deque modus liquationum cupri per Europam passim in usum receptis; de secretione ejus ab argento; de conversione in orichalcum, inque metalla diversi generis; de lapide calaminari; de zinco; de vena cupri et probatione ejus; pariter de chymicis praeparatis, et cum cupro factis experimentis . . . etc., etc.* The English translation of this title also serves as an adequate summary of the contents: "The subterranean or mineral kingdom in respect to copper and brass, and the methods of smelting copper which are in use in various parts of Europe; further its separation from silver and its conversion into brass and metals of various kinds; respecting calamine, zinc, and various methods of assaying copper ore; likewise respecting the various chemical preparations and experiments made with copper," etc.

De Divina Amore, et de Divina Sapientia [DLDW]. A posthumous publication. Issued in *Apocalypsis Explicata*, vol 5. New York: American Swedenborg Printing and Publishing Society, 1900. Also called *Doctrine of Uses*. See *On the Divine Love and on the Divine Wisdom*.

De Equo Albo, de quo in Apocalypsi [WH]. *De Equo Albo, de quo in Apocalypsi, cap: xix. Et dein de Verbo et ejus sensu spirituali seu interno, ex Arcanis Coelestibus*. London: J. Lewis, 1758. See *White Horse*.

De Ferro [IRON]. Vol. 2 of *Opera Philosophica et Mineralia* (q.v.). Dresden and Leipzig: F. Hekel, 1734.

The full title of this large work is *Regnum subterraneum sive minerale de ferro deque modis liquationum ferri per Europam passim in usum receptis; deque conversione ferri crudi in chalybem; de vena ferri et probatione ejus; pariter de chymicis praeparatis et cum ferro et victriolo ejus factis experimentis . . . etc., etc. Cum figuris aeneis.*

The English translation of this title also serves as an adequate summary of the contents: "The subterranean or mineral kingdom in respect to iron and the methods of smelting it which are in use in various parts of Europe; further the method of converting crude iron into steel; the various methods of assaying iron ore, and likewise the chemical preparations and experiments made with iron and its vitriol . . . With copper plates."

The chapter on converting iron into steel was translated into

French and printed in Strasbourg in 1737: "Traduction de quelques chapitres tires due livre de Mr. Swedenborg, sur la maniere de convertir le fer crud ou de fonte en acier, en divers lieux," in *Traite sur l'Acier d'Alsace, ou l'art de convertir le fer de fonte en acier*, published by chez Jean Renauld Dulsecker.

A Swedish excerpt was published by Peter Jöransson Nyström in Stockholm in 1753: "Utdrag af någre Herr Assessor Svedenborgs Anmärkningar, om Ståhl, öfwersatte från Fransöskan," in *Tractat om Ståhltilkwärkning i Alsas. Eller Konsten, at af Tackjärn tilkwärka Ståhl*.

The whole of part 1 was translated into French and published in *Descriptions des arts et metiers*, vol. 1, in Paris, 1762. It was included as the fourth part of a section on forges and iron furnaces: "Traite du fer, par M. Swedenborg; traduit du Latin par M. Bouchu." There is a copy in the library of the British Museum.

In 1923 Wahlström & Widstrand of Stockholm published a 455-page Swedish translation of the entire work on iron: *Mineralriket av Emanuel Swedenborg, Assessor i Kungl. Svenska Bergscollegium, om järnet. . . .* Edited by Hj. Sjögren. Copies are in the Academy of the New Church Library at Bryn Athyn, Pa., and the library of the Swedenborg School of Religion, Newton, Mass.

De Fibra [FIBRE]. *Oeconomia Regni Animalis in transactions divisa, quarum haec tertia de Fibra, de Tunica Arachnoidea, et de Morbis Fibrarum agit, anatomice, physice, et philosophice perlustrata*. A posthumous publication. Edited by J. J. G. Wilkinson. London: William Newbery, 1847. Also called *Economy of the Animal Kingdom, Transaction III*.

De Generatione [GEN]. *Opusculum de Generatione, de Partibus Genitalibus utriusque Sexus, et de Formatione Foetus in Utero*. A posthumous publication. Edited by J. F. I. Tafel. Tübingen, Germany: Verlagsexpedition; and London: William Newbery, 1849. See *Generation*.

Delitiae Sapientia de Amore Conjugiali [CL]. See *De Amore Conjugiali*.

De Nova Hierosolyma et ejus Doctrina Celesti [NJHD]. London: John Lewis, 1758. Also called *Heavenly Doctrine*. See *New Jerusalem and Its Heavenly Doctrine*.

De Sale Communi [CS]. *De Sale Communi, hoc est de sale fossili vel gemmeo, marino et fontano*. A posthumous publication. Edited by A. Acton. Philadelphia: Swedenborg Scientific Association, 1910. See *On Common Salt*.

De Sensu Communi [SENSE]. *De Carotidibus, de Sensu Olfactus, Auditis, et Visus, de Sensatione et Affectione in Genere, ac de Intellectu et ejus operatione agit*. A posthumous publication. Edited by J. F. I. Tafel. Tubingen, Germany: Verlagsexpedition; and London: William Newbery, 1848. See *Five Senses*.

De Telluribus in Mundo Nostro Solari [EU]. *De Telluribus in Mundo Nostra Solari quae vocantur Planetae, et de telluribus in coelo astrifero, deque illarum incolis, tum de spiritibus et angelis ibi; ex auditis et visis*. London: J. Lewis, 1758. See *Earths in the Universe*.

De Ultimo Judicio [LJ]. *De Ultimo Judicio et de Babylonia Destructa: ita quod omnia, quae in Apocalypsi praedicta sunt, hodie impleta sint*. London: John Lewis, 1758. See *Last Judgment*.

De Verbo [DV]. *De Scriptura Sacra seu Verbo Domini, ab experientia*. A posthumous publication. Reproduced in *Photolithograph Manuscripts*, vol. 8. Stockholm: 1780; also in *Photostats*, codex 12. Bryn Athyn, Pa.: Academy of the New Church Library. See *Sacred Scripture or Word of the Lord from Experience*.

Dicta Probantia [SC]. *Dicta Probantia Veteris et Novi Testamenti collecta et breviter explicata*. A posthumous publication. Edited by J. F. I. Tafel. Tübingen, Germany: Verlagsexpedition, 1845. See *Scripture Confirmations*.

Divine Love and Wisdom [DLW]. Translated by G. Dole. New York: Swedenborg Foundation, 1986. See *Sapientia Angelica de Divino Amore et Divina Sapientia*.

The translator describes this work as being "literally cosmic in its scope." The ground it covers is summarized by the five chapters listed in the table of contents: (1) "The Creator," (2) "The Means of Creation," (3) "The Structure of Creation," (4) "The Method of Creation," and (5) "The Goal of Creation."

Divine Providence [DP]. Translated by W. Wunsch. New York: Swedenborg Foundation, 1963. Several reprints.

This work is the sequel to *Divine Love and Wisdom* and deals with how God governs his creation. It is based in part on a doctrinal treatise interwoven in late paragraphs of *Apocalypse Explained*, from para. 1135 to para. 1194. This material has also been abstracted and published separately in several forms.

The published work first defines divine providence and then states its goal and outlook. The various laws under which providence works are dealt with, after which a rationale is given for why evil is permitted. The work ends with a charming anecdote, a discussion between Swedenborg and some spirits from hell. Prefaced by the words "Excuse the addition of what follows to fill the rest of the sheet," it is not directly related to the text of the book. See *Sapientia Angelica de Divina Providentia*.

Doctrina Novae Hierosolyma de Charitate [CHAR]. A posthumous publication. Edited by S. Worcester. In *Opera Minora*. New York: American Swedenborg Printing and Publishing Society, 1906. See *Charity*.

Doctrina Novae Hierosolyma de Domino [LORD]. Amsterdam: 1763. See *Doctrine of the Lord*.

Doctrina Novae Hierosolyma de Fide [FAITH]. Amsterdam: 1763. See *Doctrine of Faith*.

Doctrina Novae Hierosolyma de Scriptura Sacra [SS]. Amsterdam: 1763. See *Doctrine of Sacred Scripture, Doctrine of Holy Scripture*.

Doctrina Vitae pro Nova Hierosolyma ex Praeceptis Decalogi [LIFE]. See *Doctrine of Life*.

Doctrine of Charity [CHAR]. See *Charity*.

Doctrine of Faith [FAITH]. Translated and edited by J. Potts. In *Four Doctrines*. New York: Swedenborg Foundation, 1904. Many reprints. See *Doctrine Novae Hierosolymae de Fide*.

Faith is first defined as "an internal acknowledgment of truth," and then it is noted that only those in a state of charity, i.e., living a life of love to the Lord and the neighbor, are able to have such an acknowledgment.

Doctrine of Holy Scripture [SS]. Translated and edited by J. Potts. In *Four Doctrines*. New York: Swedenborg Foundation, 1904. Many reprints. Also often published as *Doctrine of Sacred Scripture* (q.v.). See *Doctrina Novae Hierosolyma de Scriptura Sacra*.

The fundamental relationship between the holy scripture found in the Bible and true Christian religion is carefully dealt with in considerable detail. Closely related treatments are also found in *White Horse* and *True Christian Religion*.

Doctrine of Life [LIFE]. Translated and edited by J. Potts. In *Four Doctrines*. New York: Swedenborg Foundation, 1904. Many reprints. See *Doctrina Vitae pro Nova Hierosolyma ex Praeceptis Decalogi*.

Beginning with one of the most frequently cited sayings of Swedenborg, "All religion has relation to life, and the life of religion is to do good," this work goes on to define what is involved in "doing good," and how this is intimately related to observing the laws of the decalog, understood on several levels of depth.

Doctrine of the Lord [LORD]. Translated and edited by J. Potts. In *Four Doctrines*. New York: Swedenborg Foundation, 1904. Many reprints. See *Doctrina Novae Hierosolyma de Domino*.

See the author's preface, where—still keeping his anonymity—Swedenborg names earlier works he has published, and then gives a forecast of works to follow. The actual works published do not agree in all details with the proposed list found there. Some of the most radically new theology of the author is set forth in this work, redefining most of the traditional beliefs and concepts respecting Jesus. Very strong emphasis on scripture verification of these new ideas is found throughout this work. For a quite different treatment of this topic, see the opening chapters of *True Christian Religion*.

Doctrine of Sacred Scripture [SS]. Edited by W. Dick. London: Swedenborg Society, 1954. See *Doctrine of Holy Scripture*, *Doctrina Novae Hierosolyma de Scriptura Sacra*.

Doctrine of Uses [DLDW]. See *On the Divine Love and on the Divine Wisdom*, and *De Divina Amore, et de Divina Sapientia*.

Documents on Swedenborg [DOC]. *Documents Concerning the Life and Character of Emanuel Swedenborg*. Collected, translated, and annotated by R. L. Tafel. 2 vols. bound as 3. London: Swedenborg Society, 1875, 1877.

Although not a publication of Swedenborg, this set contains many letters and other documents by and about Swedenborg, in English translation, and has become a standard reference work. Its main sections are (1) General biographical notices; (2) Swedenborg's ancestry and family genealogy; (3) his letters, 1709–47; (4) documents on his private property; (5) his official life on the Board of Mines; 1717–47; (6) his public life as a member of the House of Nobles; (7) as a man of science; (8) his travels and diaries up to 1744; (9) his letters, 1749–72; (10) testimony of contemporaries on his life and character, 1747–72; (11) anecdotes and miscellaneous documents; (12) documents relating to his published and unpublished writings; and (13) appendix. There are copious notes to both volumes.

Dream Book [JD]. Also called *Drömmar*. See *Journal of Dreams*, *Swedenborg's Journal of Dreams*.

Drömmar [JD]. Also called *Dream Book*. See *Journal of Dreams*, *Swedenborg's Journal of Dreams*.

Dynamics of the Soul's Domain [EAK]. See *Economy of the Animal Kingdom*.

Economy of the Animal Kingdom, Transaction III [FIBRE]. See *De Fibra, Fibre*.

Earths in the Universe [EU]. Translated by J. Whitehead. In *Miscellaneous Theological Works*. New York: Swedenborg Foundation, 1915. Many reprints.

This small work contains the substance of articles appended to the chapters on Exodus in *Arcana Coelestia*. One section from the earlier work is omitted. This has become one of the most controversial works of the author, as it asserts that he met in the spiritual world former inhabitants of several of the other planets in our solar system and Earth's moon. For some of the theories of how to account for this, see *Studia Swedenborgiana* 2, nos. 1, 2, and 4.

Economy of the Animal Kingdom [EAK]. Translated by A. Clissold. 2 vols. London: W. Newbery, 1845. Reprints New York: New Church Press, 1903; and Philadelphia: Swedenborg Scientific Association, 1955. See *Oeconomia Regni Animalis*.

In all issues of this work, chapter 8 of volume 1 is bound at the beginning of volume 2, causing some problems for scholars. The English title is misleading, and is better translated according to its subject, *Dynamics of the Soul's Domain*. It is a study of both human physiology and psychology, a part of the author's avowed search for the "seat" of the soul.

Experientiae Spirituales [SD]. See *Spiritual Diary*, *Memorabilia*.

Explicatio in Verbum Historicum Veteris Testamenti [WE]. A posthumous publication. Edited by J. F. I. Tafel. Tubingen, Germany: 1842–47. See *Adversaria*, *Word Explained*.

Festivus Applausus in Caroli XII in Pomeraniam suam adventum [FA]. Edited, with introduction, translation, and commentary by H. Helander. Uppsala, Sweden: Acta Universitatis Upsaliensis, Studia Latina Upsaliensia, 1985.

This panegyric was written as a tribute to the return from exile of Karl XII, and published at Greifswald in 1714 or 1715. G. Dole notes in his *Messenger* review of this work (September 1986) that "Swedenborg was only one of many who wrote extravagant compositions celebrating the king's spectacular return." Later he adds, "The present edition is extraordinarily informative. . . . It is well organized, written, and indexed, and has a valuable bibliography."

Fibre [FIBRE]. *Economy of the Animal Kingdom, Transaction III: Medullary Fibre of the Brain and Nerve Fibre of the Body, Arachnoid Tunic, Diseases of the Fibre.* Translated and edited by A. Acton. Philadelphia: Swedenborg Scientific Association, 1918. Reprint 1976. See *De Fibra*.

Of special interest in this work is a 30-page section appended to chapter 16 subtitled by the editor, "The Doctrine of Forms." It is a critical part of the author's development of his causal theory. For a brief summary of this doctrine, see W. R. Woofenden's, Ph.D. dissertation "Swedenborg's Philosophy of Causality," St. Louis University, 1970, pp. 50–54.

First Principles [L PRIN]. See *Lesser Principia*, *[Minor] Principia*.

Five Senses [SENSE]. A posthumous publication. Translated by E. Price. Philadelphia: Swedenborg Scientific Association, 1914. See *De Sensu Communi*.

In the translator's preface it is noted that this work "gives every internal evidence of having been written at the utmost speed merely as memoranda. . . ." It was first printed serially in *New Philosophy*, 1900–1912.

Four Doctrines [FD]. *The Four Doctrines, with the Nine Questions, Containing I. The Doctrine of the New Jerusalem Concerning the Lord, Followed by the Nine Questions Relating to the Lord, the Trinity, and the Holy Spirit. II. The Doctrine of the New Jerusalem Concerning the Holy Scripture. III. The Doctrine of Life for the New Jerusalem from the Ten Commandments. IV. The Doctrine of the New Jerusalem Concerning Faith.* Translated and edited by J. Potts. New York: Swedenborg Foundation, 1946. Many reprints. Also published as *Four Leading Doctrines*. See *Doctrine of the Lord, Doctrine of the Holy Scripture, Doctrine of Sacred Scripture, Doctrine of Life, Doctrine of Faith*.

Four Leading Doctrines [FD]. See *Four Doctrines*.

Generation [GEN]. *The Generative Organs, Considered Anatomically, Physically, and Philosophically.* A posthumous publication. Translated by J. J. G. Wilkinson. London: William Newbery, 1852. See *De Generatione*.

A second edition was later published titled *The Animal Kingdom, Considered Anatomically, Physically and Philosophically, Parts 4 and 5. The Organs of Generation, and the Formation of the Foetus in the Womb, After Which Follow Chapters on the Breasts and the Periosteum.* Edited and translated by A. Acton. Philadelphia: Boericke & Tafel, 1912. Reprinted Bryn Athyn, Pa.: Academy of the New Church, 1928; and Bryn Athyn, Pa.: Swedenborg Scientific Association, 1976.

Heaven and Hell [HH]. Translated and revised by G. Dole. New York: Swedenborg Foundation, 1979. Several reprints. See *De Coelo . . . et de Inferno*.

This work, originally published in Latin in London in 1758, has had at least twenty distinct translations or revisions of translations since it first appeared in English in 1778. It is without doubt the most frequently published of all of Swedenborg's works. The 1976 version by Dole, revised by him in 1979, was the first completely fresh translation of the work done since J. Ager's 1900 version.

Following a brief preface by the author, the contents are (1) "Heaven," (2) "The World of Spirits," (3) "Hell." In the original edition, the author included copious citations from his *Arcana Coelestia*. In most paperback editions (including Dole's) these have been omitted. An English reader wishing to see the complete text of this work should consult one of the hardcover editions published by either the Swedenborg Foundation, New York, or the Swedenborg Society, London.

Heavenly Arcana [AC]. See *Arcana Coelestia*.

Heavenly Doctrine [NJHD]. See *New Jerusalem and Its Heavenly Doctrine, De Nova Hierosolyma et ejus Doctrina Coelesti*.

Heavenly Secrets [AC]. See *Arcana Coelestia*.

Height of Water [HW]. *On the Height of Water and the Strong Tides in the Primeval World: Proofs from Sweden.* Translated from the Swedish by J. Rosenquist and revised by A. Stroh. Bryn Athyn, Pa.: Swedenborg Scientific Association, 1908. In *Scientific and Philosophical Treatises*, pt. 1, no. 1 (q.v.). For more details on the contents of this short work, see Introduction in vol. 1 of *Opera Quaedam*, which contains *Om Watnens Hogd. . . .*

Hieroglyphic Key [KEY]. *A Hieroglyphic Key to Natural and Spiritual Arcana by way of Representations and Correspondences.* A posthumous publication. Translated and edited by A. Acton. In *Psychological Transactions and Other Posthumous Tracts*, 2nd ed. Bryn Athyn, Pa.: Swedenborg Scientific Association, 1984, pp. 157–94. See *Clavis Hieroglyphica*.

The word *hieroglyphic* in the title of this work is used to mean "something with a hidden meaning." In this work, written in 1744, the author is not addressing the question of deciphering ancient Egyptian writing, although in the so-called "appendix" to his 1758 treatise *White Horse*, written in 1769, Swedenborg did offer to interpret the Egyptian hieroglyphics, presuming they would yield to his system of correspondences. There is no record that he actually attempted to do this deciphering. See *Letters and Memorials of Emanuel Swedenborg*, vol. 2, pp. 684–86, for more details.

This work comprises 21 "Examples," dealing with such topics as motion, energy, inertia, the sun, harmony, etc., and their symbolic meanings.

Human Genitalia [GEN]. See *Generation*.

Index Biblicus [INDEX]. *Emanuelis Swedenborgii Index biblicus, sive Thesaurus Bibliorum emblematicus et allegoricus.* A posthumous publication. 4 vols. Vols. 1–3 edited by J. F. I. Tafel, vol. 4 edited by A. Kahl. London: Swedenborg Society, 1859–68. English translation: *Bible Index*.

This 4-volume set, although based on Swedenborg's own *Bible Index*, was considerably enlarged and rearranged by Tafel and Kahl. In volumes 1–3, Tafel added quotations from published works, such as *Arcana Coelestia*, thus greatly enlarging the work. In volume 4, Kahl arranged the alphabetical entries from *debilis* through *hortus* in the order of the books of the Bible, from Genesis to Revelation. But from *hostis* through *zona* he followed the order in which he found the entries in the manuscript.

The Infinite [INF]. *The Infinite and the Final Cause of Creation*. Translated with introductory remarks by J. J. G. Wilkinson, with a new introduction by L. Hite. London: Swedenborg Society, 1902. Reprinted 1908, 1915. Also in the same volume is *The Intercourse between the Soul and the Body: Outlines of a Philosophical Argument*. See *Prodromus Philosophiae Ratiocinantis de Infinito*. . . .

Both the introductory remarks by Wilkinson from the original 1847 edition and the new introduction by Hite give the reader valuable insights into the development of Swedenborg's metaphysical views. At the same time it should be noted that F. Sewall, in his review of this work in *New Philosophy*, April 1903, disagrees strongly with some of Wilkinson's stated views. In this treatise dedicated to his brother-in-law Erik Benzelius, the author makes this statement in his preface: "Philosophy, if it be truly rational, can never be contrary to revelation."

From internal and other evidence, it would seem that Swedenborg composed this work in as little as a month's time in 1734 while seeing his large 3-volume work, *Opera Philosophia et Mineralia*, through the press.

Influx [SBI]. Translated by T. Hartley. London: 1770. See *Soul-Body Interaction, De Commercio Animae et Corporis*.

Several translations and many printings of this short work have been done, the first English edition appearing while the author was still alive. It was originally titled *A Theosophic Lucubration on the Nature of Influx, as It Respects the Communication and Operations of Soul and Body*. The most recent English edition appeared in the Paulist Press volume on Swedenborg in their extensive series, "The Classics of Western Spirituality." See *Soul-Body Interaction*.

The author states in the opening paragraph that "there are three opinions and traditions—three hypotheses—about the interaction of soul and body, or the way one works in the other and with the other. The first is called 'physical inflow,' the second 'spiritual inflow,' and the third 'preestablished harmony.' " Later he notes that "there can be no fourth opinion. . . ." His thesis is that spiritual inflow is "based on order and its laws" and his argument supports that view. His "solution" to the mind-body problem, however, may well constitute the most singularly unique methodology yet found to cope with this time-honored philosophic problem: conducting a lottery, in which the piece of paper on which had been written "spiritual inflow" was drawn!

Intercourse Between the Soul and Body [SBI]. See *Soul-Body Interaction, Influx, De Commercio Animae et Corporis*.

Invitatio ad Novam Ecclesiam [INV]. A posthumous publication. In *Opera Minora*, edited by S. Worcester. New York: American Swedenborg Printing and Publishing Society, 1906. See *Invitation to the New Church*.

Invitation to the New Church [INV]. A posthumous publication. In *Posthumous Theological Works* 1, translated by J. Whitehead. New York: Swedenborg Foundation, 1914. Several reprints.

This fragmentary work is part of the last work projected by Swedenborg. It was probably intended to be part of *Coronis*. The autograph manuscript is lost, but a copy made by or under the direction of A. Nordenskiöld is in the library of the Swedenborg Society, London.

Journal of Dreams [JD]. A posthumous publication. Edited from the Swedish by G. Klemming, translated by J. J. G. Wilkinson, edited by W. Woofenden. New York: Swedenborg Foundation, 1977. Also called *Dream Book, Drömmar*. See *Swedenborg's Journal of Dreams*.

This was a private diary kept by Swedenborg during parts of 1743 and 1744. See the preface for details about the publication history of this unusual work. See also W. Van Dusen's introductory essay, "Swedenborg's Journey Within," and also his much more extensive commentary on this journal in the 1986 publication, *Swedenborg's Journal of Dreams* (q.v.).

Last Judgment (Posthumous) [LJP]. In *Posthumous Theological Works* 1, edited by J. Whitehead. New York: Swedenborg Foundation, 1914. Several reprints.

This draft, probably written in 1762 in preparation for the published work *Continuation on the Last Judgment* (q.v.), deals briefly with a number of other related topics in addition to the specific topic of judgment. In the section on "the spiritual world," Swedenborg records talks he says he had in that realm with Leibniz, Wolff, and Newton.

Last Judgment (and Babylon Destroyed) [LJ]. Translated by D. Harley. London: Swedenborg Society, 1961. See *De Ultimo Judicio et de Babylonia Destructa*.

This is the most recent translation of this work originally published in 1758, being one of the five works of the author to appear that year. This work broke new ground theologically by its claim that the long-expected Last Judgment predicted in the Bible had already taken place in the spiritual world by the time this work was published. So far as this editor knows, this remains to the present day a uniquely Swedenborgian belief.

This work has been published in English and other languages many times. As is generally true of Swedenborg's works, paragraph numbers are uniform in all editions.

Lesser Principia [L PRIN]. Also called *First Principles*. See *[Minor] Principia*.

Although never published under this title, this work has frequently been referred to as *Lesser Principia*. In *New Philosophy* 2, 1899, pp. 17–20, 23–26, there is an English summary of the contents of the work.

Both R. L. Tafel in *Documents on Swedenborg* (vol. 2, p. 899) and Hyde in his *Bibliography of Swedenborg's Works* date this work at 1720. Tafel bases his dating on a hypothesis that its contents is closely related to that of the 1721 publication *Chemistry*. L.

Hite, however, disagrees (see *New Philosophy*, 1929, pp. 13–14). A. Stroh, in *Opera Quaedam*, volume 3, page 327, states that after Hyde's work had been published he and Hyde came to an agreement that the true date of composition is probably 1729. Wainscot, in his 1967 *Addenda to Hyde* was apparently unaware of this and therefore put his additional entries under the incorrect date of 1720.

Letters and Memorials of Emanuel Swedenborg [L&M]. Translated and edited by A. Acton. 2 vols. Bryn Athyn, Pa.: Swedenborg Scientific Association, 1948, 1955.

Although, like R. L. Tafel's *Documents*, this is not a work of Swedenborg, it is another indispensable reference work for Swedenborgian scholars, being the most complete collection of Swedenborg's letters, memoranda, and records of his travels, in chronological order, ever assembled.

Unlike Tafel, who undertook to edit Swedenborg's letters into standard English (where the language of the original was cryptic or anything but "standard"), Acton, in his translating, endeavored "to retain, so far as possible, the style and flavor of the originals." Acton has also included extensive commentary and many informative footnotes.

Marital Love [CL]. Translated by W. Wunsch. New York: Swedenborg Publishing Association, 1938. Some reprints. See *Conjugial Love*, *De Amore Conjugiale*, *Marriage Love*.

Marriage Love [CL]. See *Conjugial Love*, *De Amore Conjugiale*, and *Marital Love*. Translated by S. Warren. Rotch edition. Boston and New York: Houghton Mifflin, 1907.

Memorabilia [SD]. A posthumous publication. Tubingen, Germany: Verlagsexpedition; and London: William Newbery, 1844 (vol. 1, pt. 1) and 1845 (vol. 2, pt. 1). See *Spiritual Diary*.

Although this work has regularly been referred to in recent years as *Spiritual Diary*, early drafts and editions, both in Latin and English, refer to it in part as *Memorabilia*. R. L. Tafel, in *Documents*, also uses this title. The reader should not confuse this designation with the so-called "memorable relations" or "memorable occurrences" included by Swedenborg in his late works, as these, also, are referred to from time to time as "memorabilia."

Messiah About to Come [MES]. *Concerning the Messiah About to Come and Concerning the Kingdom of God and the Last Judgment*. A posthumous publication. Translated and edited by A. Acton. Bryn Athyn, Pa.: Academy of the New Church, 1949.

See the translator's preface for details about this fragmentary work. It consists mainly of passages from the Bible on the predicted Second Coming and Last Judgment.

[*Minor*] *Principia* [L PRIN]. A posthumous publication. Translated by I. Tansley. London: Swedenborg Society, 1913. See *First Principles*, *Lesser Principia*.

This translation was first published in volume 2 of *Principia*. Although, so far as this editor knows, this is the only English version of this work ever published, it should be noted that it received a very detailed negative review, which challenged among other things the competence of the translator. See the entry under *Principia* for more details.

Miscellanea Observata circa Res Naturales [MISC]. Leipzig, Germany: 1722. See *Miscellaneous Observations on Physical Sciences*.

Miscellaneous Observations on Physical Sciences [MISC]. Translated by C. Strutt. London: William Newbery, 1847. Reprint Bryn Athyn, Pa.: Swedenborg Scientific Association, 1976. See *Miscellanea Observata*. . . .

This work was first published by Swedenborg in Leipzig in 1722, to which was added a fourth part published the same year at Schiffbeck. The English edition contains all four parts. See translator's preface for full details.

Miscellaneous Theological Works [MTW]. Translated by J. Whitehead. New York: Swedenborg Foundation, 1928. Reprints.

This volume contains the following short works: *New Jerusalem and Its Heavenly Doctrine, Brief Exposition, Intercourse Between Soul and Body, White Horse, Appendix to White Horse, Last Judgment, Continuation on Last Judgment*. (See the separate listings of most of these works for more detail.)

Modest Thoughts on the Deflation and Inflation of Swedish Coinage. [MT]. Translated by A. Acton and B. Boyesen. Edited by G. Dole. In *Studia Swedenborgiana* 6, no. 2. See *Offörgripelige tanckar om swenska myntets förnedring och förhögning*.

This is the first English version of this early work to be published.

For more details see *Offörgripelige tanckar om myntets uphöhjande och nedsättjande* [MT2].

Motion and Position of the Earth and Planets [MOT]. *The Motion & Position of the Earth & Planets: in Which Are Some Conclusive Proofs That the Earth's Course Decreases in Rapidity, Being Now Slower Than Heretofore, Making Winter and Summer Days and Nights Longer in Respect of Time Than Formerly*. Translated by D. May. London: James Speirs, 1900. Reprinted London: Swedenborg Society, 1915.

This short work was written in Swedish in 1718 and published in 1719 at Skara. At that time the author seemed to have been influenced by biblical literalism regarding the flood as well as by the conjecture that Sweden might be the mythological lost Atlantis.

New Jerusalem and Its Heavenly Doctrine [NJHD]. Translated by J. Whitehead. In *Miscellaneous Theological Works* (q.v.). See *De Nova Hierosolyma et ejus Doctrina Celesti*.

The contents of this work, first published in Latin in 1758, was rewritten largely from articles prefixed to the chapters on Exodus in *Arcana Coelestia*, titled "Doctrine of Charity," and "Doctrine of Charity and Faith." It also includes extensive citations directly from *Arcana*.

It has also been published separately as a booklet, omitting the *Arcana* citations. In 1938, as a 250th anniversary edition, it was published simultaneously in this abridged form in nineteen languages.

Nine Questions [9Q]. *Nine Questions Chiefly Relating to the Lord, the Trinity, and the Holy Spirit, Proposed by the Rev. Thomas Hartley to Emanuel Swedenborg, with his Answers.* Translated and edited by J. Potts. In *Four Doctrines* (q.v.).

This short work was first published in the original Latin in London by R. Hindmarsh in 1785. It seems likely that it was written after the publication of *True Christian Religion.* The translator states that the reasons for placing it immediately after the *Doctrine of the Lord* are self-evident.

Northern Inventor [DAED]. See *Daedalus Hyperboreus.*

Northern Muse [CB]. See *Camena Borea.*

Oeconomia Regni Animalis [EAK]. Amsterdam: 1740. See *Economy of the Animal Kingdom.*

Oförgripelige tanckar om swenska myntets förnedring och förhögning. [MT]. Stockholm, Joh. Hinr. Werner, 1722. See *Modest Thoughts on the Deflation and Inflation of Swedish Coinage.*

Copy in the library of the Massachusetts New Church Union, Boston.

Oförgripelige tanckar om myntets uphöjande och nedsättjande, utgifne på trycket år 1722, men nu på fleres begäran å nyo tryckte, tillika med någre i anledning deraf författade oförgripelige reflexioner om myntets förhållande i äldre och senare tider, samt grunden til wäxel-coursens stigande, och på hwad sätt den så för kronan som en hwar enskildt deraf flytande förlust måtte kunna hjelpas och rättas utan myntets widare förändring, med mera. [MT2]. Uppsala, Sweden: Joh. Edman, Kongl. Acad. Boktyckare, 1771. (Modest Thoughts on the Inflation and Deflation of Money, published by the press in 1722, but now, by request of several persons, printed anew, together with some modest reflections on the state of money in older and more recent times; also the reason for the rising rate of exchange, and by what means its current loss for both the Crown and individuals can be relieved and rectified without further rate changes in 1771, etc.)

This work included a reprint of the original memorandum, about a dozen pages, plus more than 50 pages of comments. The reissue of the work immediately after Gustav III came to the throne was clearly intended to help deal with the financial crisis the country then faced. Gustav, however, sought a temporary solution by borrowing from some Dutch bankers. It was not until 1772 that the Riksdag made a serious attempt to institute currency reform.

Om Wattnens Hogd . . . [HW]. Uppsala: 1719. See *Height of Water.*

On Copper and Brass [COP]. See *Copper and Brass, De Cupro et Orichalco.*

On Common Salt [CS]. A posthumous publication. Translated by M. David. In *New Philosophy,* the quarterly journal of the Swedenborg Scientific Association. Four installments have appeared to date in vols. 86–88, 1983–85. See *De Sale Communi.*

The full title of this work is, "On Common Salt, That is on Mined or Crystal, Sea or Spring Salt." It is expected that the SSA will publish the entire work separately after the serial publication.

On Marriage [CONJ]. A posthumous publication. In *Posthumous Theological Works 2.* See *De Conjugio.*

This is an incomplete draft, left in manuscript by the author. It was probably written in preparation for *Conjugial Love.* In addition to this draft, two indexes of either projected or lost works on marriage have been found. All are in *Posthumous Theological Works 2.*

On the Divine Love and on the Divine Wisdom [DLDW]. A posthumous publication. Translated by E. Mongredien. London: Swedenborg Society, 1963. See *De Divina Amore, et de Divina Sapientia.*

Although this work comprises what were two separate manuscripts, consecutive paragraph numbers have been added to this British version, making it practical to refer to it as a single work. It was earlier published in this form under the title *Doctrine of Uses.*

In the Swedenborg Foundation's American standard edition, this material appears in the back of volume 6 of *Apocalypse Explained,* but without the paragraph numbers. There is little doubt that this is a first draft of one of the works published in 1763, *Divine Love and Wisdom.*

On the Infinite and Final Cause of Creation [INF]. See *The Infinite, Prodromus Philosophiae Ratiocinantis de Infinito.*

Ontologia [ONT]. See *Ontology.*

Ontology [ONT]. *Ontology, or the Significance of Philosophical Terms.* A posthumous publication. Translated and edited by A. Acton. Boston: Massachusetts New Church Union, 1901. Reprinted Bryn Athyn, Pa.: Swedenborg Scientific Association, 1964.

This incomplete work consists of a series of quotations by various authors involving philosophic terms, along with Swedenborg's comments.

On Tremulation [TREM]. Translated from the Swedish by C. Odhner. Boston: Massachusetts New Church Union, 1899. Reprinted Bryn Athyn, Pa.: Swedenborg Scientific Association, 1976. Also called *Tremulation.*

This work is a conflation of two parts of what may have been intended to be a single work. The first part, titled, "A Proof That Our Vital Essence Consists for the Most Part of Small Vibrations, That Is, of Tremulations," was published in *Daedalus Hyperboreus* (1716–18). The English version incorporates both this short article and the extant portions of a larger work titled, "Anatomy of Our Most Subtle Nature, Showing That Our Moving and Living Force Consists of Vibrations." This paper was sent to Benzelius in parts, of which only chapters 1–6 and 13 are preserved. This portion fills 48 closely written quarto pages. The treatise was read and discussed in the Society of Sciences, Uppsala. A copy, which is now lost, was also handed by the author to the board of health.

Opera Minora [OM]. A posthumous publication. Editor's Preface by S. Worcester, 1885. New York: American Swedenborg Printing and Publishing Society, 1906. Eng. trans.: *Minor Works.*.

This collection contains the following small works: *New Jerusalem and Its Heavenly Doctrine, Charity, Indexes to Conjugial Love, Canons of the New Church, Coronis*, and *Invitation to the New Church*. See individual entries for more information.

Opera Philosophica et Mineralia [OPEM]. 3 vols. Dresden and Leipzig: Friedrich Hekel, 1734. The three volumes are popularly identified as (1) *Principia*, (2) *De Ferro*, and (3) *De Cupro et Orichalco* (q.v.). Eng. trans.: *Philosophical and Metallurgical Works*.

Opera Poetica [OP]. Uppsala, Sweden: Uppsala University, 1910. Eng. trans.: *Poetical Works*.

In 1910, in connection with the Swedenborg Congress in London, and in connection with the 1908 removal of Swedenborg's remains to the cathedral in Uppsala, the original texts of a number of Swedenborg's earlier works, long out of print, were republished. This volume issued by the University of Uppsala contains all the known poems of the author, in their original Latin or Swedish. See *New Philosophy*, April 1920, for more details.

Opera Quaedam [OQ]. *Opera Quaedam aut Inedita aut Obsoleta de Rebus Naturalibus, nunc edita sub auspiciis Regiae Academiae Scientarum Suecicae*. Edited by A. Stroh. 3 vols. Volume 1, *Geologica et Epistolae*. Preface by G. Retzius, introduction by A. Nathorst. Volume 2, *Cosmologica*. Introduction by S. Arrhenius. Volume 3, *Miscellanea*. Preface, introduction, and notes by A. Stroh. Stockholm: Ex Officina Aftonbladet, 1907, 1908, 1911.

This large 3-volume set, published under the auspices of the Royal Swedish Academy of Sciences, constituting the most complete collection of Swedenborg's works on geology, chemistry, physics, mechanics, and cosmology ever printed, was originally intended to be part of an imposing plan to put in print all of the author's scientific and philosophic works, including both works published by Swedenborg and works left by him in manuscript. The project was never completed, due in part to the failing health of the editor, A. Stroh. Nevertheless, this set deserves to be better known and more widely used.

Note: the intended appendix to volume 1, although listed in the table of contents, is not found in the volume and may never have been published. The reader is referred to the detailed tables of contents of all 3 volumes for information as to the contents of this work.

A Philosopher's Note Book [PHIL]. *Excerpts from Philosophical Writers and from the Sacred Scriptures on a Variety of Philosophical Subjects; Together with Some Reflections, and Sundry Notes and Memoranda*. A posthumous publication. Translated and edited by A. Acton. Philadelphia: Swedenborg Scientific Association, 1931. Reprinted 1976.

The title of this work was given to it by the translator. Its contents comprise an extensive series of notes on philosophical and theological words and terms, probably written in 1741. Many pages are filled with comparative studies of the concepts involved in such words as *good, truth, imagination, memory*, etc., as defined by Plato, Aristotle, Augustine, Leibniz, Descartes, and many more. This editor has sometimes called this work "Swedenborg's Do-It-Yourself Crash Course in Philosophy." It was the result of a relatively brief period of intensive study and note taking, and could be considered an early attempt at exegesis—a task that would occupy much of his time in later years.

Philosophical and Metallurgical Works [OPEM]. See *Opera Philosophica et Mineralia*.

Poetical Works [OP]. See *Opera Poetica*.

Posthumous Theological Works, volume 1 [PTW 1]. Edited by J. Whitehead. New York: Swedenborg Foundation, 1914. Reprints.

In addition to a number of minor works and letters, this volume contains *Coronis, Invitation to the New Church, Canons*, and *Last Judgment (Posthumous)*. See separate entries on these works for more information.

Posthumous Theological Works, volume 2 [PTW 2]. Edited by J. Whitehead. New York: Swedenborg Foundation, 1928. Reprints.

This volume contains *Prophets and Psalms, Scripture Confirmations, On Marriage*, a short tract on the decalog, two indexes for lost works on marriage, a brief bibliography of Swedenborg's works, and an index of publications (long out of date) of the Swedenborg Foundation. See separate entries on these works for more information.

Principia [PRIN]. *The Principia; or, the First Principles of Natural Things, Being New Attempts Toward a Philosophical Explanation of the Elementary World*. Translated by A. Clissold. 2 Vols. London: William Newbery, 1846. Reprinted Bryn Athyn, Pa.: Swedenborg Scientific Association, 1976.

The first complete English translation of this work was this one done by August Clissold. *Principia* was volume 1 of *Opera Philosophica et Mineralia*. Included in the appendix are translations of the prefaces to the companion works on iron and copper.

A second complete English version of this work, translated by J. R. Rendell and I. Tansley, was published by the Swedenborg Society, London, in 1912. Nearly half of volume 2 is devoted to a translation of the so-called *Lesser* [*Minor*] *Principia* (q.v.).

The appearance of this new edition was noted editorially in *New Philosophy*, July 1912, extending hearty congratulations to the publisher but at the same time calling attention to some strong initial adverse criticism of the inclusion of some comments by Frank W. Very and Sir. W. F. Barrett that were construed to be negative.

Then, a year later, in the July 1913 issue of *New Philosophy*, Alfred Acton devoted half the issue to a scathingly negative review of this edition, challenging the claim that it was a new translation, calling attention in detail to many "ignorant and ludicrous blunders," and concluding: ". . . we must give wholesale and well-nigh unqualified condemnation to the publication."

Then, to come full circle, in the October 1919 edition of *New Philosophy*, there is an article by Ernest Pfeiffer, "A Few Notes on Clissold's Translation of *The Principia*," in which he notes that while "it is true that the 'revised' edition published in London in 1912 is much worse than that by Clissold, London 1846 . . . it must also be said that very many of the erroneous renderings have been copied from Clissold." He then goes on to detail, in several pages, portions of Clissold's work with which he disagrees. *Caveat lector!* The decision by the Swedenborg Scientific Association to reprint this first English version rather than the Swedenborg Society's 1912 version of Rendell and Tansley was based in large part on the thoroughly negative review of the latter version by A. Acton. (See related comment under the entry for [*Minor*] *Principia*.)

Principia Rerum Naturalium [PRIN]. *Principia rerum naturalium sive novorum tentaminum phaenomena mundi elementaris philosophice explicandi.* Cum figuris aeneis. (First principles of natural things, or new attempts to explain philosophically the primordial world. With copper plates.) See *Principia, Opera Philosophica et Mineralia.*

A facsimile edition, photographically reduced in size, was published in 1954 by the Swedenborg Institut, Basel.

Principles of Chemistry [CHEM]. See *Chemistry*.

Prodromus Philosophiae Ratiocinantis de Infinito . . . [INF]. Dresden and Leipzig: 1734. See *The Infinite*.

Prodromus Principiorum Rerum Naturalium [CHEM]. Amsterdam: 1721. See *Chemistry*.

Prophets and Psalms [PP]. *Summaries of the Internal Sense of the Prophets and Psalms, also of Genesis 1-16.* A posthumous publication. Translation edited by A. Clapham. London: Swedenborg Society, 1960.

This brief work was probably written in 1761. It has appeared in many editions and several languages. In addition to the summaries of the inner sense, the author has keyed most entries to a numbered list of topics relating to the Lord's coming, his experiences, and their effect on the state of the church.

The American standard edition, in *Posthumous Theological Works* 2, translated by E. Schreck in 1900, has added to the text a preface, introduction, index of words and subjects, and index of scripture passages, nearly doubling the size of the work.

Psychologia Rationalis [RP]. See *De Anima, Rational Psychology*.

Psychological Transactions and Other Posthumous Tracts, 1734–1744 [PSY]. Translated and edited by A. Acton. 2nd ed., rev. Bryn Athyn, Pa.: Swedenborg Scientific Association, 1984.

See the foreword for new data about several of the short works in this volume, information that has come to light since the first edition was published in 1920 (reprinted unchanged in 1955).

The main works included are the *Psychological Transactions, Hieroglyphic Key*, and *Correspondences and Representations*. The extensive indexes have been corrected in this edition.

Quaestiones Novem de Trinitate [9Q]. See *Nine Questions*.

Rational Psychology [RP]. A posthumous publication. Translated by N. Rogers and A. Acton, edited by A. Acton. Philadelphia: Swedenborg Scientific Association, 1950.

The first English edition, translated by F. Sewall and titled *The Soul, or Rational Psychology*, was published in 1886 and reprinted in 1900. In the course of preparing to publish a new edition, Acton discovered that what he had previously thought to be "Psychological Transaction 6" was instead the missing beginning of *Rational Psychology*. This textual correction, together with other editorial changes, made the older edition obsolete.

Although this version has not become the accepted one, there remains some difference of opinion among Swedenborgians as to how relevant this psychology is to that of the theological period.

Regnum Animale [AK]. *Regnum Animale, Anatomice, Physice, et Philophice Perlustratum.* The Hague: 1744. See *Animal Kingdom*.

Sacred Scripture or Word of the Lord from Experience [DV]. A posthumous publication. Edited and translated by J. Whitehead. In *Posthumous Theological Works* 1.

Swedenborg made use of this fragmentary work, together with articles on the Word in *Apocalypse Explained*, paras. 1065–89 when he wrote and published *Doctrine of the Sacred Scripture*.

Sapientia Angelica de Divina Providentia [DP]. Amsterdam: 1764. See *Divine Providence*.

Sapientia Angelica de Divino Amore et Divina Sapientia [DLW]. Amsterdam: 1763. See *Divine Love and Wisdom*.

Scientific and Philosophical Treatises [SPT]. Edited by A. Stroh. Bryn Athyn, Pa.: Swedenborg Scientific Association, 1905, 1908.

Part 1 (in 2 fasicles) is on chemistry, geology, physics, and cosmology. Part 2 is on anatomy, physiology, psychology, and philosophy. These are small works, letters, and memoranda, mostly unpublished, dating from 1717 to 1740. At least two of the papers included by Stroh were later discovered to have been copied by Swedenborg from the works of others: "On the Causes of Things" (probably by Polhem) and "Observations on the Human Body" (according to Acton—see his preface to *Cerebrum*, volume 1, pp. xv–xvi—by C. F. Richtern).

Scripture Confirmations [SC]. A posthumous publication. In *Posthumous Theological Works* 2. Edited by J. Whitehead. See *Dicta Probantia*.

This small work consists of a collection of Bible passages arranged under subject headings as a reference work for the use of the author. It was probably compiled in 1769 and contains many passages from the book of Acts and from the Epistles—a number of which were used by Swedenborg in *True Christian Religion*.

Small Theological Works [STW]. *Small Theological Works and Letters of Emanuel Swedenborg*, Latin-English, edited by J. Elliott. London: Swedenborg Society, 1975.

The stated purpose of this volume is to make more readily available a number of short documents in both their original language and in English translation. Most of the works here have been published in the United States in other volumes.

The Soul, or Rational Psychology [RP]. See *Rational Psychology*.

Soul-Body Interaction [SBI]. Translated by G. Dole. New York: Paulist Press, 1984. See *Influx, De Commercio Animae et Corporis*.

Soul's Domain [AK]. See *Animal Kingdom*.

Spiritual Diary [SD]. A posthumous publication. Translated by G. Bush, J. Smithson, and J. Buss. 5 vols. London: James Speirs, 1883–1902.

A new translation of volume 1 by W. H. Acton and A. W. Acton was published by the Swedenborg Society, London, in 1962, reprinted in 1977. Volumes 2–5 were reprinted in 1978 by the Swedenborg Foundation, New York, and the Academy of the New Church, Bryn Athyn, Pa. The original English version of volume 1 has gone out of print.

In Acton's volume 1, the subtitle reads: *Records and Notes Made by Emanuel Swedenborg Between 1746 and 1765 from His Experiences in the Spiritual World.*

The subject matter of this large work is too varied to lend itself to being summarized. It seems quite likely that Swedenborg (who indexed the work) drew on it frequently for examples to be included in his published works from 1749 through 1764. In all the works he published after 1765 (1766–71) he included material similar to much of the data in this work, identifying these accounts as "memorable relations" or "memorable occurrences."

Summaria Expositio Doctrinae Novae Ecclesiae [BE]. Amsterdam: 1769. See *Brief Exposition*.

Summaria Expositio Sensu Interni . . . Propheticorum ac Psalmorum [PP]. See *Prophets and Psalms*.

Summary Exposition (of the Doctrine of the New Church) [BE]. See *Brief Exposition*.

Swedenborg's Journal of Dreams [JD]. Commentary by W. Van Dusen. Edited from the original Swedish by G. E. Klemming. Translated into English in 1860 by J. J. G. Wilkinson. Edited by W. R. Woofenden. New York: Swedenborg Foundation, 1986. See *Journal of Dreams*.

The text of this edition is the same as that in *Journal of Dreams*, which was first printed serially in *Studia Swedenborgiana* 1, nos. 1–4, 1974–75. When the Swedenborg Foundation reprinted this version in 1977, they included a valuable introductory essay by Van Dusen. Now, in this 1986 publication, Van Dusen has greatly expanded his commentary on this intimate diary kept by Swedenborg in the crucial years 1743–44.

Swedenborg's Treatise On Copper and Brass [COP]. Translated by A. H. Searle. 3 vols. London: London Swedenborg Society and the British Non-Ferrous Metals Research Association, 1938. Copies of this duplicated typescript are in the library of the Swedenborg Society, London; the Academy of the New Church Library, Bryn Athyn, Pa.: and the library of the Swedenborg School of Religion, Newton, Mass.

Tafel Documents [DOC]. See *Documents on Swedenborg*.

Treatise on Copper and Brass [COP]. See *Copper and Brass, De Cupro et Orichalco, Swedenborg's Treatise on Copper and Brass*.

Treatise on Iron [IRON]. See *De Ferro*.

Tremulation [TREM]. See *On Tremulation*.

True Christian Religion [TCR]. *The True Christian Religion Containing the Universal Theology of the New Church Foretold by the Lord in Daniel 7:13–14 and in Revelation 21:1–2.* Translated by J. Ager. New York: Swedenborg Foundation, 1915. Reprints.

The basic topics covered in the fourteen chapters of this final summary work are: (1) God the Creator, (2) the Lord the Redeemer, (3) the Holy Spirit, (4) sacred scripture, (5) decalog, (6) faith, (7) charity, (8) free will, (9) repentance, (10) reformation and regeneration, (11) imputation, (12) baptism, (13) Holy Supper, (14) end of the age. There is a supplement with many particulars about the spiritual world.

The Swedenborg Society, London, has commissioned a new translation of this work by John Chadwick, with the intention of publishing it by 1988 for the tricentenary celebration of Swedenborg's birth.

Vera Christiana Religio [TCR]. *Vera Christiana Religio, continens universam Theologiam Novae Ecclesiae, a Domino apud Danielem cap. vii. 13, 14, et in Apocalypsi cap. xxi. 1, 2, praedicta. Ab Emanuele Swedenborg, Domini Jesus Christi servo.* Amsterdam: 1771. See *True Christian Religion*.

White Horse [WH]. *White Horse of the Apocalypse.* Translation edited by B. Willmott. London: Swedenborg Society, 1954. See *De Equo Albo, de quo in Apocalypsi*.

This short work was one of five published by Swedenborg in 1758. It was drawn for the most part from *Arcana Coelestia* (see paras. 2760–63) and rewritten. Its theme is that of the spiritual sense of the Word.

Word Explained [WE]. A posthumous publication. Translated and edited by A. Acton. 10 vols. Bryn Athyn, Pa.: Academy of the New Church, 1927–51. See *Adversaria*.

This extensive but tentative effort of Swedenborg at scripture interpretation predates his full illumination and was composed mainly during 1746 and 1747. Although there is some internal evidence of intent to publish, the author left the work in manuscript. It was first published in Latin by J. F. I. Tafel, 1842–54.

Acton has renumbered the paragraphs in his English version consecutively through the whole work. He has furnished a cross-reference key at the bottoms of pages in later volumes to the numbering system in Tafel's Latin edition.

Volume 1 is not a part of the work but is Acton's extended introduction to it. Volume 10 is a volume indexing the entire work.

Worship and Love of God [WLG]. Translated and edited by A. Stroh and F. Sewall. Boston: Massachusetts New Church Union, Rotch edition, 1914. See *De Cultu et Amore Dei*.

This was the last work Swedenborg published before commencing on the theological period of his life and the writing and printing of his theological works. It is written in the form of a fable or creation drama. Being poetic in style it is unlike any of the author's other works (except his early poems).

The chief characters are Supreme Love or the Only Begotten, the heavenly Intelligences or guardians, the First-begotten or Adam, the Mother-Soul and her daughter Intelligences and Wisdoms, the Spouse of Adam, and the Prince of this World.

In 1961, Inge Jonsson wrote and had accepted as a thesis at Stockholm University a study of this work of Swedenborg.

Select Bibliography

Compiled and Annotated by
William Ross Woofenden, Ph.D.

DURING THE PAST TWO HUNDRED YEARS, since the first group of readers of Swedenborg set up a separate Christian church organization in London, England, followers of the Swedish scientist, philosopher, and seer have produced a massive body of publications collateral to or in some way inspired by the lifetime literary works of this remarkable man. At best, in this bibliography I can call the readers' attention to some of the reference works that deal in some detail with this enormous output of printed matter. Included in this bibliography you will also find a few reference works not by Swedenborgians, but which nevertheless shed light on the thought world of Swedenborg's time.

Most disciples of Swedenborg have been attracted to his religious writings. Others have simply admired him as a significant contributor to world thought on a wide variety of subjects. He has been called the last of the universal scholars. John Ruskin once wrote, "The greatest thing a human soul ever does in this world is to *see* something, and tell what it *saw* in a plain way. Hundreds of people can talk for one who can think, but thousands can think for one who can see. To see clearly is poetry, prophecy, and religion, all in one." Swedenborgians have tended to identify their mentor as a seer, thus defined.

Reference Works

ACTON, ALFRED, ed., comp., and trans. *Letters and Memorials of Emanuel Swedenborg*. 2 vols. Bryn Athyn, Pa.: Swedenborg Scientific Association, 1948, 1955.

See the annotation for this important work in the main Swedenborg Bibliography.

————. *The Mechanical Inventions of Emanuel Swedenborg*. Philadelphia: Swedenborg Scientific Association, 1939.

This 50-page booklet comprises all that is known concerning Swedenborg's mechanical inventions, giving the descriptions in Swedenborg's own words, together with one or two supplementary descriptions, reproductions of Swedenborg's original sketches, and a few additional drawings. See *New Philosophy* January 1940 for more details.

BLACKMER, FRANKLIN, ed. and comp. *A Bibliography of Publications by Swedenborgians*. Boston: Massachusetts New Church Union, 1977.

This paperback volume of 380 pages was published under the auspices of the Trustees of the Lydia S. Rotch Legacy and is subtitled, *A Handbook on New Church Libraries*. The preface indicates that the compilation is based mainly on the collections in the Swedenborg Society, London, the Swedenborg School of Religion, Newton, Mass., the Academy of the New Church, Bryn Athyn, Pa., and Urbana College, Urbana, Ohio.

The three major sections of the work are comprised of (1) check list of collaterals, alphabetical by author; (2) periodicals published under Swedenborgian auspices; and (3) works by or about Swedenborg. It claims to be comprehensive though not exhaustive.

The work is marred by the mechanical design and composition, being photocopied from typescript, with a number of handwritten emendations and strike-outs. The fact that some pages are vertical and others horizontal is a further distraction.

DOLE, GEORGE F., comp. and trans. *A View from Within*. New York: Swedenborg Foundation, 1985.

This 140-page paperback is subtitled, *A Compendium of Swedenborg's Theological Thought*. Following a brief biographical sketch of Swedenborg, the book comprises 10 sections of carefully chosen passages from the theological works, translated into eminently readable contemporary English. It is an excellent brief introduction to the main features of Swedenborg's religious thought.

HYDE, JAMES, comp. and ed. *A Bibliography of the Works of Emanuel Swedenborg, Original and Translated*. London: Swedenborg Society, 1906.

This basic reference work was eight years in preparation. The editor states in the preface that "the main object of the book has been to gather into one volume, and thus facilitate reference to, the bibliographical data of all Swedenborg's works, or attempted works, printed or unprinted, as well in their original as in their translated forms, in all editions of each, so arranged that while the reader has in one view the history of Swedenborg's literary life, he may also easily follow each distinct work through its versions and editions, or even re-impressions of the same edition."

The main bibliography comprises 600 pages. An appendix lists and describes Swedenborg's extant manuscripts, composite volumes, biographies of the author, and portraits of Swedenborg. There are three indexes: of books, of persons and institutions, and of places.

In 1967, the Swedenborg Society issued in mimeograph format a supplement to this bibliography, prepared by A. S. Wainscot. Although it is a very welcome update of Hyde's work, the reader should know that this addenda volume is completely dependent on the original work, having no table of contents, no index, nor any helps for the reader. The additions to Hyde's identifying numbers follow a scheme adopted by the library of the Swedenborg Society and therefore do not agree with numbering schemes devised by other Swedenborgian libraries.

JUDAH, J. STILLSON. *The History and Philosophy of the Metaphysical Movements in America*. Philadelphia: Westminster Press, 1967.

The chapters in this carefully researched work deal with: (1) "The Mirror of American Culture"; (2) "Spiritualism"; (3) "Theosophy and Its Allies"; (4) "Phineas P. Quimby and Warren Felt Evans"; (5) "New Thought"; (6) "The Divine Science Church"; (7) "The Church of Religious Science"; (8) "The Unity School of Christianity"; (9) "Christian Science"; (10) "The Church and Health."

Although the author in no way implies or states that Swedenborg and his writings should in any sense be classified as part of the "metaphysical movement," or as the basis of a "cult," he shows time and again that Swedenborgian philosophy has been fundamental in shaping the thought patterns of practically every subdivision of metaphysical religious thought in America.

MERCER, L. P. *Review of the World's Religious Congresses of the World's Congress Auxiliary of the World's Columbian Exposition, Chicago, 1893*. Chicago and New York: Rand, McNally, 1893.

A major part of the World's Columbian Exposition was the religious congress, featuring papers by representatives of Hinduism, orthodox Christianity, liberal Christianity, Buddhism, Judaism, Mohammedanism, Roman Catholicism, the Greek church, Japanese Criticism and Appeal, the Brahmo-Somaj, and the New Christianity [Swedenborgianism].

Mercer was a member of the general committee for the World's Religious Congresses and published two books concerning the proceedings (this and next entry).

————, ed. *The New Jerusalem in the World's Religious Congresses of 1893*. Chicago: Western New-Church Union, 1894.

The first section of this book discusses the parliament of religion in general and includes the papers given by Swedenborgians to the general meetings. The second section deals with the separate Swedenborgian sessions and reproduces all the papers presented. The topic subdivisions were (1) the origin and nature of the New Church; (2) its doctrines, the true basis of a universal faith and charity; (3) the planting of the New Church; (4) the future of the New Church; and (5) woman in the New Church.

ODHNER, CARL T. *Annals of the New Church, with a Chronological Account of the Life of Emanuel Swedenborg*. Vol. 1, 1688–1850. Bryn Athyn, Pa.: Academy of the New Church, 1898.

This important reference work first traces details of Swedenborg's life year by year, outlining, in addition to biographical data, contemporary events that affected his life. Publications listed in this section are, for the most part, those of Swedenborg. In entries after 1772 (the year of Swedenborg's death), the general format remains the same, but publications are wide ranging, and events annotated are gradually more global in scope. There is an extensive index to the entire work.

ODHNER, CARL T., and WHITEHEAD, WILLIAM. *Annals of the New Church*. Edited by Morley D. Rich. Vol. 2, 1851–90. Bryn Athyn, Pa.: General Church of the New Jerusalem, 1976.

Although on the one hand one must applaud the appearance of this second volume, published seventy-eight years after the first volume, one must at the same time express profound regret at the publication format. The pages are photoreduced from a typescript, with paper cover and plastic spine binding. A number of the typing errors—but not all, by any means—have been hand corrected. For example, page 1 has four listings for a periodical abbreviated "Med.," but this periodical (*The Medium*) was omitted from the list of abbreviations. There is no index.

POTTS, JOHN F., comp., ed., trans. *Swedenborg Concordance: A Complete Work of Reference to the Theological Writings of Emanuel Swedenborg; Based on the Original Latin Writings of the Author*. 6 vols. London: Swedenborg Society, 1888–1902. Reprints.

One of the hazards of compiling a work of this size is exhibited on the title page of volume 1, which states that it is "in four volumes." In fact, it was issued in fascicles over a fourteen-year period and has always been bound in 6 volumes. The introduction states that the compiler had already devoted "between thirteen and fourteen years" to the task before publication began.

This work is without rival as a primary reference work for all scholars of Swedenborg's theological writings. The volumes average over 900 pages each, and—in addition to the main alphabetical concordance—the set includes a wealth of valuable data, both in the frontmatter of volume 1 and the backmatter of volume 6. Careful students will thoroughly familiarize themselves with this material.

Potts (who also translated and edited a number of Swedenborg's complete works) has used his own translations of all entries in this work. One should note that in later years he radically changed his mind about the choice of a number of English renderings of the original Latin. Thus, e.g., in the *Concordance* one finds an entry for the English term *scientific truth*, whereas in the translator's preface of his version of *Arcana Coelestia* (Swedenborg Foundation, 1905–10 standard edition) we find that Potts has by this time coined the term *memory-knowledge* to translate the same Latin; further, in this preface he is quite intolerant of those who exhibit the "lamentable ignorance" of rendering *scientia* and *scientifica* as "science" and "scientifics"!

Because this concordance has been so universally used as a basic reference work by Swedenborgians worldwide, it is probably not unfair to attribute to it much "in-house," or arcane, terminology (what has been called, with some justification, "Swedenborgese").

Note: In 1980 the General Church Press, Bryn Athyn, Pa., issued a slim hardcover volume compiled by Donald L. Rose titled *Additions to the Swedenborg Concordance.*

RAMSTROM, MARTIN. *Emanuel Swedenborg's Investigations in Natural Science and the Basis for His Statements Concerning the Functions of the Brain.* Uppsala, Sweden: University of Uppsala, 1910.

At the time this work was written, Ramstrom was professor of anatomy at Uppsala University. In his conclusion to this monograph he says in part "that it was in truth a *work of genius* to search out of such chaos the guiding threads which were concealed within . . ."

He also gave a related paper the same year at the International Swedenborg Congress, London, titled, "Swedenborg on the Cerebral Cortex as the Seat of Psychic Activity," published in *Transactions of the International Swedenborg Congress.* London: Swedenborg Society, 1910.

SEARLE, A. H., ed. *General Index to Swedenborg's Scripture Quotations.* 2nd edition. London: Swedenborg Society, 1954.

To one whose primary interest is in Swedenborg's exegesis of sacred scripture, this is an invaluable reference work.

The first edition of this work, published in 1883, was based on an earlier work, *Index generale des passages de la Divine Parole, cites dan les ecrits d'Emmanuel Swedenborg,* compiled by J. F. E. Le Boys des Guays and published in Paris, 1859. This latter work had prefatory material in French, German, and English. One of its distinctive features was a system of symbols indicating whether the passage was cited or simply referred to, and—most importantly—whether or not Swedenborg gave any interpretation of the inner sense of the particular scripture passage.

When Searle prepared his edition, he eliminated most of these helpful references, distinguishing only between passages actually quoted and passages simply referred to. Although several editorial improvements were made in the second edition, one in search of help in scripture interpretation must still look up *all* references to be sure of having fully researched any given passage.

TAFEL, RUDOLPH L., ed., comp, trans. *Documents Concerning the Life and Character of Emanuel Swedenborg.* 2 vols. London: Swedenborg Society, 1875, 1877.

See the annotation to this critical reference work in the main Bibliography of Swedenborg's Works.

WARREN, SAMUEL M., ed. *A Compendium of the Theological Writings of Emanuel Swedenborg.* New York: Swedenborg Foundation, 1979.

This compilation has a long history dating back to its predecessor, compiled and published by W. Fernald in 1853. The first edition of Warren's version was issued in 1875 in London, and there have been many reprints. It has the advantage (for some) of much more extensive citations on a very broad range of topics than most of the compendiums of Swedenborg's works (such as

Dole's, q.v.), but has the disadvantage (for some) of being in the English of the last century.

WHITEHEAD, WILLIAM, comp. vol. 1. Whitehead, William, and Rich, Morley, comp. vol. 2. *Annals of the General Church of the New Jerusalem.* 2 vols. Bryn Athyn, Pa.: General Church of the New Jerusalem, 1976.

Edited by Morley Rich, this 2-volume set has the same mechanical format as volume 2 of *Annals of the New Church* (see Odhner and Whitehead).

The preface notes that this set begins a chronicle of the Academy of the New Church (1876), later organized as the General Church of the New Jerusalem (1897). Thus the general title of the work refers to the church organization. Volume 1 is in 2 parts: (1) the Academy (1876–96), and (2) the General Church (1897–1937). Volume 2 deals with the General Church from 1938 to 1976.

WOOFENDEN, WILLIAM ROSS. *Swedenborg Researcher's Manual.* Bryn Athyn, Pa.: Swedenborg Scientific Association, 1988.

It is with the express encouragement of the editor of this anthology that this entry has been included. Although at the time this pictorial anthology is going to press my research manual is not yet published, it is my definite intent to see that it is in print early in 1988. It is anticipated that several other publishers of Swedenborgian literature will be co-publishers.

The idea of a 1-volume research manual for writers of academic theses and other serious scholars of Swedenborg and Swedenborgianism grew out of this editor's own frustrations while he was preparing his own Ph.D. dissertation (Swedenborg's Philosophy of Causality," St. Louis University, 1970).

In addition to the usual frontmatter and extensive cross-indexes, the main sections will be: (1) an annotated chronological bibliography of Swedenborg's complete lifetime literary output; (2) a selected, annotated bibliography of collateral literature; (3) a glossary of Swedenborgian terms cross-referenced to contemporary scholarly terms in several disciplines; (4) a summary of selected key concepts found in Swedenborg; (5) locations, listings, and detailed descriptions of major documentary collections of Swedenborgiana worldwide.

Biographies

ACTON, ALFRED. *The Life of Emanuel Swedenborg: A Study of the Documentary Sources of His Biography, Covering the Period of His Preparation, 1688–1744.* Edited by B. Briscoe, foreword by H. Odhner. Bryn Athyn, Pa.: Academy of the New Church, 1958.

This work, based on the so-called "Green Books" (Academy Collection of Swedenborg Documents [ACSD]), is a valuable reference work because of its comprehensiveness. It had been Dr. Acton's intent to put together a biography this fully detailed of the whole of Swedenborg's life, but the work was left unfinished at Acton's death in 1956.

The table of contents is extensive and arranged chronologically, serving also, to a reasonable degree, as an index. Entries are well documented. It is, however, a rare work, as only one hundred copies were made of the typescript.

BENZ, ERNST. *Emanuel Swedenborg: Naturforscher und Seher.* Edited by F. Horn. 2nd ed., rev. Zurich: Swedenborg Verlag, 1969.

This German biography of Swedenborg, originally published in 1948, is a thorough and scholarly work by a non-Swedenborgian. Dr. Horn, who was a student of Benz at Marburg University, revised and updated the study with the full consent of the author. To date it has not been translated and published in English.

JONSSON, INGE. *Emanuel Swedenborg.* Translated from the Swedish by Catherine Djurklou. New York: Twayne Publishers, 1971.

This is the third major work on Swedenborg by Dr. Jonsson, professor of literature at Stockholm University. One is his Ph.D. dissertation, a study of Swedenborg's *Worship and Love of God.* Another is a treatise on Swedenborg's concept of correspondence. But only this work, *Emanuel Swedenborg*, has been translated and published in English.

Only the first chapter of this work is, strictly speaking, a biography. The major part of the book focuses on the thought content of Swedenborg's writings. This scholar's keenest assessment of our author's work is that of his scientific and philosophical works. He seems less familiar with the theological ideas. The closing chapter, "New Jerusalem in the World," traces some of the channels of Swedenborg's influence on European literature up to the present, and is included in this anthology (q.v.).

KINGSLAKE, BRIAN. *A Swedenborg Scrapbook.* London: Seminar Books, 1986.

This small, attractive, fully illustrated paperback is well written and can easily be read in one sitting. The author notes that it is not intended to take the place of any of the many full biographies available, but "to shine a spotlight on a number of selected aspects and incidents of Swedenborg's life" that Kingslake found particularly interesting and to comment on them. Most of the book, he explains, is nonchronological, "a kind of literary montage."

LAMM, MARTIN. *Swedenborg. En studie öfver hans utveckling till mystiker och andeskadare.* Stockholm: Hugo Geber, 1915.

This biography is, in the opinion of Inge Jonsson, "still the most important monograph on Swedenborg." It was translated into German and published in Leipzig in 1922, and into French and published in Paris in 1936. A typescript in English translation is in the library of the Swedenborg School of Religion, Newton, Mass.

In this study, Lamm tries to demonstrate that there is a logical and consistent line of thought development in Swedenborg from his earliest childhood experiences to his most mature theological statements. This would seem to be the sort of positive approach that any Swedenborgian should applaud. But what is perhaps most remarkable about this work, among biographies of Swedenborg, is that in this author's opinion, otherworld experience is quite irrelevant to the conclusions reached: for Lamm, Swedenborg's claim that his theological concepts were largely based

on such experiences is simply something for those interested in the paranormal to investigate.

SIGSTEDT, CYRIEL O. *The Swedenborg Epic: The Life and Works of Emanuel Swedenborg.* New York: Bookman Associates, 1952. Reprint. London: Swedenborg Society, 1981.

Mrs. Sigstedt was for a number of years secretary to Alfred Stroh while he was painstakingly investigating archives in Sweden in search of further data on Swedenborg's life. She realized that enough new material had been uncovered that a new biography needed to be written. Failing to find anyone else to do it, she took on the task herself, producing what must be judged to be the most complete, most thoroughly documented biography to date.

The reprint edition has an errata sheet, correcting a number of errors. Most of these are minor in nature.

TOKSVIG, SIGNE. *Emanuel Swedenborg: Scientist and Mystic.* New Haven, Conn: Yale University Press, 1948. Reprinted, with a new introduction by Brian Kingslake. New York: Swedenborg Foundation, 1983.

Toksvig, a skillful writer who published other biographies, seemed to be fascinated by psychic phenomena. Thus, her main interest in this work apparently was to demonstrate her thesis that Swedenborg was a mystic—an identification that many of his followers have been unwilling to accept. She was only secondarily interested in him as a scientist, and least of all was her interest in his mature lifework as a theologian.

Thus, although engagingly written and easily read, it is a biography with a number of strong biases, and, in the opinion of some, with many errors in fact. It was widely reviewed in the press. For instance, *The New York Times* devoted half a page to it in its book-review section. And of course all Swedenborgian periodicals reviewed it. With these latter the mood ranged from cautious delight to profound disappointment.

For a detailed analysis to the major criticisms of this work, see *Studia Swedenborgiana* 5, no. 3.

VAN DUSEN, WILSON. *The Presence of Other Worlds: The Psychological/Spiritual Findings of Emanuel Swedenborg.* New York: Harper & Row, 1974. Several reprints.

This popular work by a clinical psychologist is not a biography in the usual sense of the word: all the facts or events of Swedenborg's life are gathered together in chapter 1. The main body of the work is a psychological study of Swedenborgian ideas and their significance in personal lives. There is strong emphasis on the "inner world" and on the symbolic nature of existence itself.

It is very well written and provides absorbing reading. The author is clearly a dedicated admirer of Swedenborg and his works.

WORCESTER, BENJAMIN. *The Life and Mission of Emanuel Swedenborg.* Boston: Roberts Brothers, 1883. Reprints.

In Hyde's 1906 *Bibliography*, over one hundred biographies or biographical sketches of Swedenborg are listed, including this one. Worcester's work, in the opinion of this editor, is one of the best written of the older biographies—accurate, thorough, and well researched and documented. It has an extensive index.

Current Periodicals

Since the first Swedenborgian organization came into existence over two hundred years ago, partisans of various aspects of Swedenborg's thought have founded and published dozens and dozens of periodicals, some short-lived, some incredibly long-lived. What follows here is a select list of currently published periodicals, chosen because of their wide circulation, scholarly content, and/or excellence of production. Many other useful and valuable reference-resource periodicals, past and present, not mentioned here, can be found in Swedenborgian and other libraries around the world. Addresses of these libraries and the organizations that publish the following periodicals can be found in Appendix B of this book.

Chrysalis. Quarterly journal of the Swedenborg Foundation. New York.

This handsomely produced journal is a new outreach effort, with a prestigious editorial staff. Each issue centers on a theme, such as "In Search of the Soul," "The Holy City," and "Wise Woman: A Human Process."

Lifeline. A monthly journal of the New Church. Manchester, England: General Conference of the New Church.

This unpretentious illustrated monthly magazine is the official journal of the British General Conference Church [Swedenborgian]. It prints news of the church, study materials, essays, and sermons. It has a regular section for young readers.

The Messenger. Official publication of the General Convention of Swedenborgian Churches in the United States and Canada.

This long-lived monthly journal has had many format changes over the years. The present version has a carefully chosen color illustration on the cover of each issue. Its contents include news of the church, articles widely varied in content, pictures of personnel and events, reviews, departments called "Women Communicating" and "Opinion," as well as statistical data.

The New Age. The official journal of the New Church in Australia. Wahroonga, New South Wales.

The journal is published monthly (or at times bimonthly) for the Swedenborgian church in Australia. It contains news of the church, articles of general interest to church people, sermons, book reviews, etc. There is a special insert with local news.

New Church Life. A monthly magazine devoted to the teachings revealed through Emanuel Swedenborg. Bryn Athyn, Pa.: General Church of the New Jerusalem.

This long-lived journal has had some format changes. It prints sermons, articles on theological topics, editorials, communica-

tions, church news, announcements, and information on General Church places of worship.

The New-Church Magazine. New series. A quarterly journal published by the Committee of Ministers of the General Conference of the New Church, sponsored by the New Church College. Manchester, England.

This new series is a thin, inexpensively produced typescript magazine with articles largely of scholarly interest. Its long-lived predecessor was a normally printed, saddle-stitched journal that discontinued publication in 1983. The present edition is being edited by a number of ministers of the conference, in turn.

New Philosophy. The quarterly journal of the Swedenborg Scientific Association. Bryn Athyn, Pa.

This journal has been continuously published since 1898. In 1900 it became the official journal of the Association. The Association was founded for the preservation, translation, publication, and distribution of the scientific and philosophical works of Emanuel Swedenborg.

Many of the early works of Swedenborg now in print were originally published serially in this journal. In recent years, articles of a theological nature have also been published.

Offene Tore: Beitrage zum Neuen Christlichen Zeitalter (Open gates: Contributions to the new Christian age). Zurich: Swedenborg Verlag.

This quarterly journal has been published for German-speaking Swedenborgians since 1957. The editor, a gifted linguist, often translates scholarly articles from other periodicals into German for inclusion here.

Studia Swedenborgiana. An occasional journal published by the Swedenborg School of Religion. Newton, Mass.

This journal, founded in 1974, has generally been published at the rate of 2 issues per year. It has featured from the start new translations of Swedenborg's works, which have been published later in book form. Its statement of purpose notes that it is "devoted to philosophical and theological concepts found in, or related to, the writings of Emanuel Swedenborg. Its aim is to serve as an international forum of scholarly and critical thought, contemporary as well as retrospective."

The Swedenborg Society Magazine. Published by the Swedenborg Society. London, England.

The first issue of this newest of the publications listed in this bibliography appeared in April 1986. It is not clear at this time how frequently it will be published. The editor states that he hopes the magazine will foster "that particular spirit of enquiry inspired by the Writings of Swedenborg." The early issues have comprised only a dozen or so pages each.

List of Figures

Compiled and Annotated
by Robin Larsen, Ph.D.

Information provided in entries of this figure list include the caption or shortened form, and where it differs, complete title of work; artist's full name (entries on graphic art often include artist of original work as well as engraver or print-maker); artist's dates, where available (birth and death dates appear at first reference within an essay); medium and date of artwork or, where appropriate, publishing information; source of reproduction or permission-granting institution, and/or repository of original artwork.

The materials collected by Virginia Branston for this volume are so extensive and so integral to the Swedenborg Image Archive that any attempt to distinguish them by specific credits would be impractical. However, certain photographs were donated personally to Mrs. Branston by her friends and associates in Sweden, and these have been so designated in the following figure list.

In this list, the Academy of the New Church refers to collections at Glencairn Museum and the Swedenborg Library, Bryn Athyn, Pennsylvania. The Swedenborg School of Religion is in Newton, Massachusetts. The Swedenborg Image Archive is located at the Swedenborg Foundation, New York City. Under the auspices of Sweden's Nationalmuseum, Stockholm, Svenska Porträttarkivet includes numerous other public and private collections, among them the extensive portrait museum at Gripsholm Castle. The H. W. Janson Photographic Archive is administered by the Fine Arts Department, College of Arts and Science, New York University.

HALF TITLE. Emanuel Swedenborg at his writing desk. Torsten Schonberg (1882–1950s?), crayon drawing, 1930. Swedenborg Image Archive. Torsten Schonberg was a Swedish painter and engraver, one of a number of artists commissioned by Swedish authorities to produce a series of portraits of Sweden's great men for the Stockholm World's Fair, 1930. The original is in the collection of the Nationalmuseum.

FRONTISPIECE. *Emanuel Swedenborg*, with *Apocalypse Revealed*. Pehr Krafft, the Elder (1724–1793), oil on canvas, ca. 1768. Swedenborg Image Archive (R. Larsen photo, 1986, from a fair copy made in 1870, which can be seen at the offices of the Swedenborg Foundation, New York). There were two Krafft families of distinction among painters: The Swedish family included Pehr, the Elder, and his son of the same name, who studied with the French master Jacques-Louis David (1748–1825). Unrelated to the Swedish painters, David von Krafft (1655–1724) was born in Hamburg and emigrated to Sweden (cf. fig. 53). Pehr Krafft, the Elder's, original portrait was presented by Swedenborg to his friend Count von Höpken; it later came into the possession of Count C. Gyldenstolpe, who presented it to Svenska Porträttarkivet, under whose auspices it presently hangs in Gripsholm Castle. Several scholars have noted its resemblance to the Brander portrait of the same period (cf. fig. 63), and suggested that one may have influenced the other.

A Pictorial Biography

FIG. 1. *Emanuel Swedenborg*. By an unidentified artist, undated drawing in charcoal with white highlights, probably 1900s. Courtesy of the Swedenborg School of Religion (R. Larsen photo, 1982). Apparently drawn from the steel-plate engraving by William Cooke, 1804, which was a copy after the "assessor portrait" by J. W. Stör, 1734 (cf. fig. 91).

FIG. 2. *Emanuel Swedenborg* in his nineteenth year. By an unidentified artist, oil painting, ca. 1707. Courtesy of the collection of Adolf Stroh (Lennart Fornander photo).

Ancestry & Birth

FIG. 3. *Jesper Swedberg*. Johan S. Salmson (1799–1859), lithograph, n.d. Swedenborg Image Archive. Possibly from a drawing made in 1734.

FIG. 4. *Sveden*. Sigurd Erixon, (1700s–1800s), oil painting on canvas, 1819. Linnémuseet, Uppsala. Executed in the workshop of Magistrate Nils Asplund, Falun.

FIG. 5. Guest cottage at Svedens Gård. Swedenborg Image Archive (Dély photo, Falun, probably 1908, collected by Virginia Branston).

FIG. 6. Linnaeus marriage room. Swedenborg Image Archive (Dély photo, Falun, probably 1908, collected by Virginia Branston).

FIG. 7. Cupboard in Linnaeus's marriage room. Swedenborg Image Archive (S. & R. Larsen photo, 1983, by permission of Mrs. Lilly Westin).

FIG. 8. *The Death of Absalom*. Berndt Hakonson Svedin (1700s), wall painting in the guest cottage at Svedens Gård, ca. 1700. Swedenborg Image Archive. B. H. Svedin was a painter of Falun known to have been active after 1732 when he worked in several churches.

FIG. 9. *Falu Koppargruva*. Count Erik Dahlberg (1625–1703), engraving from *Svecia Antiqua et Hodierna*. 1716. Swedenborg Image Archive. A valuable source of period views is Dahlberg's pictorial survey of Swedish historical sites and structures commissioned by the government in 1661 and first published in 1716. (It may be noticed that some engravings published in this volume are dated as early as 1661 while others carry the later date.)

FIG. 10. Stora Kopparberg purchase deed, 1288. Stora Kopparbergs Bergslags AB, Falun.

FIG. 11. Miners at work. Pehr Hilleström (1732–1816), oil on canvas, 1788. Stora Kopparbergs Bergslags AB, Falun.

FIG. 12. Sara Behm Swedberg. By an unidentified artist, oil painting, 1692. Svenska Porträttarkivet.

FIG. 13. Stockholm viewed from the west. Count Erik Dahlberg (1625–1703), engraving from *Svecia Antiqua et Hodierna*, 1716. Swedenborg Image Archive.

FIG. 14. *Borggården*. Count Erik Dahlberg, engraving from *Svecia Antiqua et Modierna*. 1716. Swedenborg Image Archive.

FIG. 15. Chancel of Royal Chapel. Count Erik Dahlberg, engraving from *Svecia Antiqua et Hodierna*, 1694. Antikvarisk-Topografiska Arkivet, Stockholm.

FIG. 16. Jakobs Kyrka. By an unidentified artist whose signature resembles Fr. Arrelius, engraving, 1700s. Stockholms Stadsmuseum. Jakobs Kyrka was begun by the Flemish master builder Willem Boy in the 1500s, mostly completed in the 1600s by Hans Ferster; the tower was added in 1730s by royal architects Göran Josua A. Adelcrantz (1668–1789) and Carl Hårleman (1700–1753).

FIG. 17. Base of baptismal font; putti, or cherub. Jost Schutz (d. 1674), oak, with painted flesh tones, 1643. Antikvarisk-Topografiska Arkivet, Stockholm.

FIG. 18. Baptismal plate. J. Jäger (1600s–1700s), silver, ca. 1660. Stockholms Stadsmuseum.

Childhood & Education at Uppsala

FIG. 19. Uppsala Cathedral, aerial view. Uppsala Touristinformation. Founded by sanction of King Valdemar ca. 1260, consecrated by Archbishop Olof Larsson in 1435. Scandinavia's largest cathedral, it

has not yet been identified by Svenska Porträttarkivet. Possibly painted at the same time as the 1707 portrait of Swedenborg (cf. fig. 2). Scheffel's own birthdate calls into question this attribution.

FIG. 65. Starbo. Wooden dwelling, 1600s–1700s. Swedenborg Image Archive (photo early 1900s, collected by Virginia Branston).

FIG. 66. Tiled stove at Starbo. Possibly designed and/or built by Swedenborg in the mid-1700s. Swedenborg Image Archive (photo early 1900s, collected by Virginia Branston).

FIG. 67. *Skinnskatteberg*. Ulrik Thersner (1779–1828), engraving, 1854. Nordiska Museet, Stockholm.

FIG. 68. Axmar. Masonry dwelling, 1600s–1700s. Swedenborg Image Archive (photo early 1900s, collected by Virginia Branston).

FIG. 69. Mynttorget. By an unidentified artist, etching, 1700s. Stockholms Stadsmuseum.

FIG. 70. Island of Riddarholmen (the Knights' Island). Swedenborg Image Archive (Daniel Fitzpatrick photo, 1986). Burial place of many Swedish kings since A.D. 1290, and site of the Wrangel Palace, formerly a royal residence.

Travels & Foreign Studies in Metallurgy Metallurgy

MAP. Swedenborg's second and third European journeys. Drawn by Nancy Crompton, 1987, after maps researched by M. Elizabeth M. Hallowell. Swedenborg Image Archive.

FIG. 71. *Copenhagen*. Johann Balthasar Probst (1673–1750), engraving, 1700s. Royal Danish Ministry for Foreign Affairs (Danish Information Office, New York).

FIG. 72. *Hamburg, View from Harbor*. By an unidentified artist, woodblock, 1700s. Archiv für Kunst und Geschichte, Berlin.

FIG. 73. *Comédie Précédente*. J. De Geyer (1700s), engraving, probably from a book by Fouquet, 1700s. Courtesy Consulate General of the Netherlands, New York.

FIG. 74. Pieterskerk in Leiden. Swedenborg Image Archive (S. & R. Larsen photo). St. Pieterskerk dates from the Middle Ages.

FIG. 75. View of the Hague (*Vue de l'entrée de la Haye régardant de la Maison des Pauvres ver l'Eghse Neuve*). By an unidentified artist, engraving, 1700s. Courtesy Consulate General of the Netherlands, New York. In the background is the New Church (1654), where Spinoza lies buried. In the 1600s the city became a refuge for those fleeing religious persecution.

FIG. 76. Aachen. Courtesy of the German Information Center, New York. Aachen, or Aix-la-Chapelle, was a Roman spa and later the favorite residence of Charlemagne. Its cathedral retains Charlemagne's Palatine Chapel (A.D. 790–805), and the later choir (1355). It is still an industrial and coal-mining center.

FIG. 77. Cologne, view with cathedral. Anton Woensam (b. ca. 1500, d. 1541), woodcut, 1531. Courtesy of the German Information Center, New York.

FIG. 78. Cologne Cathedral, with Hohenzollern Bridge across the Rhine River. Courtesy of the German Information Center, New York. Cologne Cathedral was begun in 1248 and completed in the 1800s.

FIG. 79. Altenburg, tin-rolling mill. Archiv für Kunst

FIG. 80. Altenburg Caverns, tin mine. Archiv für Kunst und Geschichte, Berlin (photo early 1900s).

FIG. 81. Leipzig city plan. Matthäus Merian, the Elder (1593–1650), copperplate from *Topographia*, 1642–88. Archiv für Kunst und Geschichte, Berlin. Merian was a Swiss engraver and bookseller who ran a noted publishing house in Frankfurt. He is best known for his perspective views of European cities, castles, etc., in the sixteen-volume *Topographia*, with text by Austrian Martin Zeiller. Merian also published alchemical works, among them Michael Maier's *Atlanta Fugiens*, 1617 (cf. fig. 198) and possibly editions of several other works cited in Larsen, "Swedenborg and the Visionary Tradition" (see the anthology). His sons Matthäus, the Younger (1621–1687), and Kaspar (1627–1686), and his daughter Anna Maria Sibylla Graff (1647–1717), were all significant painters and engravers. Anna Maria is particularly known for her illustrated works on natural science, especially her studies of insect and plant life in Surinam.

Author & Philosopher

FIG. 82. Riddarhuset. Simon de la Valée and Justus Vingboons, masonry, 1653–1674 (cf. fig. 60). Svenska Institutet, Stockholm.

FIG. 83. Cogging machine. Designed and perhaps constructed by Emanuel Swedenborg under the direction of Christopher Polhem, probably at the Stjärnsund factory, ca. 1717–30. Swedenborg Image Archive (S. & R. Larsen photo, 1983, by permission of Tekniska Museet, Stockholm).

FIG. 84. *Kristina Maria Steuch*. Georg Engelhardt Schröder (1684–1750), oil painting, ca. 1730. Svenska Porträttarkivet.

FIG. 85. *Elisabet H. Stierncrona*. Georg Engelhardt Schröder, painting, ca. 1735. Svenska Porträttarkivet.

FIG. 86. Gamla Stan, Prästgatan. Swedenborg Image Archive (Daniel Fitzpatrick photo, 1987).

FIG. 87. Berlin city plan. Johan Bernhard Schultz (d. 1695), copperplate, 1688. Archiv für Kunst und Geschichte, Berlin. The artist's name is more commonly spelled Schulz; he is known to have worked in Berlin after 1685 as an engraver of currency.

FIG. 88. Dresden, Grossen Garde (*Platz der Grossen Garde, auf einer seiten das Gewandt-Haus, auf der anderen Unser Lieben Frauen Kirch zu Dresden*). Johann Balthasar Probst (1673–1750), copperplate, 1700s. Archiv für Kunst und Geschichte, Berlin.

FIG. 89. Saurian fossil. Engraved plate from Emanuel Swedenborg, *De Cupro et Orichalco*, 1734. Swedenborg Image Archive (S. & R. Larsen photo, 1983).

FIG. 90. Leipzig, Peters Vorstadt (*Esplanade in der Peters Vorstadt zu Leipzig*). By an unidentified artist, copperplate, ca. 1770. Archiv für Kunst und Geschichte, Berlin.

FIG. 91. *Emanuel Swedenborg* as assessor of mines. Johann-Martin Bernigeroth, the Younger (1703–1767), engraved frontispiece to *Principia*, Leipzig, 1734. Swedenborg Image Archive. Bernigeroth, or Berningroth, was the name of a family of engravers who worked in Leipzig. J.-M. Bernigeroth was especially noted for his portraits; as was Johann Wilhem Stör, a portraitist active in Nuremberg 1725–55. Hyde (see Select Bibliography) suggests a drawing may have been made from life by Stör when

Swedenborg was in Nuremberg; Bernigeroth would have engraved it later, possibly also having met Swedenborg in person when he came to Leipzig to oversee the printing of *Principia*. Because it originated with a sitting, this would be one of the more important Swedenborg portraits (cf. figs. 2, 126, 135, and the note on Brander, fig. 63).

FIG. 92. Varnhem Cloister, view of apse and spire from southeast. Masonry and timber, 1673. Swedenborg Image Archive (S. & R. Larsen photo, 1983).

FIG. 93. Varnhem Cloister, view through transept. Masonry and timber, 1673. Swedenborg Image Archive (S. & R. Larsen photo, 1983).

FIG. 94. Jesper Swedberg's crypt. Masonry, 1735. Swedenborg Image Archive (S. & R. Larsen photo, 1983).

Search for the Soul

FIG. 95. Amsterdam, view of Old Quarter. Swedenborg Image Archive (S. & R. Larsen photo, 1983).

FIG. 96. Windmill near Amsterdam. Swedenborg Image Archive (S. & R. Larsen photo, 1983).

FIG. 97. Swedenborg's inlaid table. Hardwood, ca. 1739. Stockholms Stadsmuseum.

FIG. 98. L'Observatoire Nationale. Probably Gabrielle Perelle (1638–1695), engraving, late 1600s. Swedenborg Image Archive. The artist could also be Adam Perelle (1603–1677), father of Gabrielle.

FIG. 99. View of Paris from Notre Dame. Construction of cathedral begun under direction of Maurice de Sully (ca. 1120–1196), masonry with lead roofing, 1163–1245. Swedenborg Image Archive (S. & R. Larsen photo, 1976). De Sully was the bishop of Paris who made the decision to begin building the cathedral.

FIG. 100. Teatro Regio. Pietro Domenico Oliviero, the Elder (1679–1755), oil painting, probably early 1700s. Museo Civico, Torino (Turin).

FIG. 101. *The Doge in the Bucintoro Departing for the Lido to Perform the Ceremony of the Marriage of the Sea on Ascension Day*. Giovanni-Battista Brustoloni (b. ca. 1726), engraving, 1738(?). Metropolitan Museum of Art, New York. Brustoloni (also spelled Brostoloni) was a Veronese engraver.

FIG. 102. University of Padua. After a drawing possibly by Antonio Bellucci (1654–1726), engraving, 1600s–1700s. Museo Civico, Padua. The name on the engraving appears to be Bellucco, but Bellucci was an Italian painter and engraver who traveled widely and left a large body of work. He was followed by his son Giambattista, who was active in the early 1700s.

FIG. 103. *Theatrum Anatomicum*, University of Padua. By an unidentified artist, engraving, 1600s. Museo Civico, Padua.

FIG. 104. *Cognoscenti in the Uffizi*. John Zoffany (1733–1810), painting, 1779. Courtesy of Her Royal Majesty, Queen Elizabeth of England.

FIG. 105. Colosseum. Giovanni Battista Piranesi (1720–1778), engraving, 1700s. Gabinetto Nazionale delle Stampa, Rome.

FIG. 106. *Vatican Library*. Francesco Bartolozzi (b. ca. 1725–27, d. 1815), after a drawing by Faustino Bocchi (1659–1722), engraving, 1700s. Swedenborg Image Archive (collected by Virginia Branston). Bartolozzi was a Florentine painter and engraver who died in Lisbon. Bocchi (also spelled Boccasi) was an Italian painter of battles and fantasies, who is

I. Arts & Letters

etching from *Jerusalem*, 1804–20. Houghton Library, Harvard University.

FIG. 146. *When the Morning Stars Sang Together*. . . . William Blake, watercolor, ca. 1805–10. Pierpont Morgan Library, New York.

FIG. 147. Frontispiece from *Jerusalem*. William Blake white-line etching colored with watercolor, 1804–20. Courtesy of the collection of Mr. and Mrs. Paul Mellon.

FIG. 148. *Leviathan*. William Blake, facsimile drawing, after the relief etching in *The Marriage of Heaven and Hell*, 1790–93. Swedenborg Image Archive.

FIG. 149. Frontispiece from *For the Sexes . . . (What is Man!)*. William Blake, engraving from *For the Sexes: The Gates of Paradise*, ca. 1818. Lessing J. Rosenwald Collection, Library of Congress, Washington, D.C. Originally a small book of engravings entitled *For Children: The Gates of Paradise* (1793), this series was reworked by Blake in 1818 and reissued under the title *For the Sexes*. . . .

FIG. 150. *At length for hatching ripe*. . . . William Blake, engraving from *For the Sexes: The Gates of Paradise*, ca. 1818 (cf. fig. 149). Lessing J. Rosenwald Collection, Library of Congress, Washington, D.C.

FIG. 151. *William*. William Blake, relief etching, self-portrait from *Milton, a Poem in 2 Books*, 1804–08. Lessing J. Rosenwald Collection, Library of Congress, Washington, D.C.

FIG. 152. Title page from *Jerusalem*. William Blake, relief etching colored with watercolor, 1804–20. Courtesy of the collection of Mr. and Mrs. Paul Mellon.

FIG. 153. Los at forge with a spectre. William Blake, relief etching from *Jerusalem*, 1804–20. Courtesy of the collection of Mr. and Mrs. Paul Mellon.

FIG. 154. Los (detail). William Blake, relief etching from *The (First) Book of Urizen*, 1794. Lessing J. Rosenwald Collection, Library of Congress, Washington, D.C.

FIG. 155. Jerusalem and Vala. William Blake, relief etching from *Jerusalem*, 1804–20. Courtesy of the collection of Mr. and Mrs. Paul Mellon.

FIG. 156. Title page from *The (First) Book of Urizen*. William Blake, relief etching, painted with watercolor and gold, from *The (First) Book of Urizen*, 1794. Lessing J. Rosenwald Collection, Library of Congress, Washington, D.C.

FIG. 157. *The Ancient of Days* (Urizen). William Blake, Relief etching, color printed and painted with watercolor, frontispiece from *Europe a Prophecy*, 1794. Whitworth Art Gallery, University of Manchester, Eng. Etched in 1794, but also printed and sold as a single color print at other times.

FIG. 158. Urizen as skeleton. William Blake, relief etching, color printed and painted with watercolor, from *The (First) Book of Urizen*, 1794. Lessing J. Rosenwald Collection, Library of Congress, Washington, D.C.

FIG. 159. Albion on a hill. William Blake, relief etching from *Jerusalem*, 1804–20. Courtesy of the collection of Mr. and Mrs. Paul Mellon.

FIG. 160. *Thine Is the Kingdom*. John Flaxman (1755–1826), plaster relief, early 1800s. Swedenborg Image Archive (R. Larsen photo, 1983, by permission of the Academy of the New Church).

FIG. 161. *Prometheus Sarcophagus*. Nancy Crompton, rendering of an anonymous marble sarcophagus of ca. A.D. 100. Swedenborg Image Archive.

FIG. 162. *Animation of Adam*. Nancy Crompton, rendering of an anonymous Venetian mosaic, probably A.D. 500–800. Swedenborg Image Archive.

FIG. 163. *Dormition*. Nancy Crompton, rendering of an anonymous relief in ivory, Byzantine, probably late A.D. 900s. Swedenborg Image Archive.

FIG. 164. *The Burial of Count d'Orgaz*. El Greco (1540–1614), painting, 1586–88. Scala/Art Resource, New York.

FIG. 165. Papal tomb design. Bartolommeo Bandinelli (1493–1560), drawing, early 1500s. Rhode Island School of Design, Providence.

FIG. 166. Tomb of Mrs. Engelbach. Landolin Ohmacht (1760–1834), marble relief, 1796. Museum für Kunst und Gewerbe, Hamburg.

FIG. 167. Tomb of Sarah Morley. John Flaxman, marble relief, 1784. Courtauld Institute of Art, Conway Library, London, courtesy of Fred R. Crossley and Maurice H. Ridgway.

FIG. 168. *Deliver Us from Evil*. John Flaxman, plaster relief, early 1800s. Swedenborg Image Archive (R. Larsen photo, 1983, by permission of the Academy of the New Church).

FIG. 169. Tomb of Ann Neufville and F. Dwarris. John Bacon (1740–1799), marble relief, 1798. Courtauld Institute of Art, Conway Library, London, courtesy of Fred R. Crossley and Maurice H. Ridgway. There were two eminent sculptors in this family, John Bacon, Sr., and Jr. (1777–1859), both members of the Royal Academy.

FIG. 170. Memorial to Admiral Richard Kempenfelt. John Bacon, marble relief, 1782. Courtauld Institute of Art, Conway Library, London, courtesy of Fred R. Crossley and Maurice H. Ridgway. This sculpture was attributed to John Bacon, Jr., but his dates seem to preclude this (cf. fig. 169).

FIG. 171. Tomb of Mrs. Montagu. Sir Joseph-Edgar Boehm (1834–1890), marble relief, 1871. Courtauld Institute of Art, Conway Library, London, courtesy of Fred R. Crossley and Maurice H. Ridgway.

FIG. 172. Tomb of Susanna Forcart. Anonymous, marble relief, 1820s. H. W. Janson Photographic Archive.

FIG. 173. Tomb of Louise Faureau. Mlle. Félicie de Fauveau (1799–1886), marble relief, 1858. H. W. Janson Photographic Archive. De Fauveau was born in Florence of Breton parents; her father was a French diplomat in residence in Italy. She was a Romantic sculptor of considerable note in her time.

FIG. 174. Monument to Baroness Chandoir. Bertel Thorvaldsen (1768–1844), marble relief, 1818. H. W. Janson Photographic Archive. Thorvaldsen (sometimes spelled Thorwaldsen in English reference works) was a distinguished Danish sculptor whose work has had a wide influence in Europe and America.

FIG. 175. Tomb of Angela Colognesi. Anonymous, marble relief, 1864. H. W. Janson Photographic Archive.

FIG. 176. Tomb of Ruffa family. Anonymous, marble relief, 1800s. H. W. Janson Photographic Archive.

FIG. 177. Monument to G. Solari. Federico Fabiani (active by ca. 1835), marble relief, 1901. H. W. Janson Photographic Archive.

FIG. 178. Tomb of Giuseppe Benedetto Badaracco. G. Moreno (1800s), marble relief, 1878. H. W. Janson Photographic Archive.

FIG. 179. Crypt of Gnecco-Garibaldi. A. Rota (1800s),

marble relief, 1882. H. W. Janson Photographic Archive.

FIG. 180. Tomb of J. M. Pelton. Anonymous, cast-iron relief, late 1800s–early 1900s. H. W. Janson Photographic Archive (Pattie C. Slattery photo, ca. 1976).

FIG. 181. Soul guided by angel. Anonymous, marble relief, probably late 1800s–early 1900s. H. W. Janson Photographic Archive.

FIG. 182. Tomb of Trowbridge twins. Anonymous, marble relief, 1849. H. W. Janson Photographic Archive.

FIG. 183. Tomb of Jane Trowbridge. Anonymous, marble relief, 1850. H. W. Janson Photographic Archive.

FIG. 184. Ralph Waldo Emerson. Engraved plate from William Cullen Bryant, ed. (1794–1878), *A New Library of Poetry and Song*, vol. 3, New York, 1880s. Courtesy of the collection of Harvey Bellin.

FIG. 185. *Brook Farm*. Josiah Wolcott (1800s), oil painting, ca. 1844. Massachusetts Historical Society, Boston.

FIG. 186. G. E. Klemming. Johan August Strindberg (1849–1912), sketch from Strindberg's diary, *Ockulta dagboken*, 1896–1908. Kungliga Biblioteket, Stockholm.

FIG. 187. *August Strindberg*. Edvard Munch (1863–1944), lithograph, 1896. Munch-Museet, Oslo.

FIG. 188. G. E. Klemming "in a cloud." Johan August Strindberg, sketch from Strindberg's diary, *Ockulta dagboken*, 1896–1908. Kungliga Biblioteket, Stockholm.

FIG. 189. Johan August Strindberg. Courtesy of the collection of Göran Stockenström (photo 1896).

FIG. 190. The Stranger and The Doctor. Ingmar Bergman, director, *Til Damascus*, pt. II, Stockholm, 1974. Kungliga Dramatiska Teatern, Stockholm.

FIG. 191. The Confessor and the Stranger. Ingmar Bergman, director, *Til Damascus*, pt. I and II, Stockholm, 1974. Kungliga Dramatiska Teatern, Stockholm.

FIG. 192. Fedor Dostoevsky. By an unidentified artist, engraving, n.d. Bettman Archive, New York.

FIG. 193. *Voyage of the Magi*. Anonymous Byzantine mosaic. Scala/Art Resource, New York.

II. *Social Issues & Psychology*

SECTION TITLE. Excerpt from photoreproduction of Swedenborg's original manuscript of *Apocalypse Explained*, para. 1112. Trans. George F. Dole. Swedenborgii Autographa Ed. Photolith. X, *Apocalypsis Explicata*, vol. II, p. 1079.

FIG. 194. Libavius's monument. Engraved plate from A. Libavius, *Alchymia*, "Commentarium," pt. II, Frankfurt, 1606. Owlcliff Associates.

FIG. 195. Internal levels of the vision quest. Diagram, 1972. Owlcliff Associates.

FIG. 196. Yogasana with chakras. Redrawn by Nancy Crompton after adaptation by Robin Larsen, 1978. Swedenborg Image Archive.

FIG. 197. Initiation on a mountaintop. Redrawn by Robin Larsen after Arthur E. Waite, *The Hermetic Museum Restored and Enlarged* (1893), translation of Lambspringk, *Musaeum Hermeticum Reformatum et Amplificatum* (1678), 1978. Owlcliff Associates.

FIG. 198. The king revived by the wolf, or dog. Re-

duced by William Le Baron Jenney (1832–1907) in his Home Insurance Company Building (Chicago, 1883–85).

FIG. 229. Masonic Temple. Daniel H. Burnham, steel frame and masonry, 1890–92. Chicago Historical Society.

FIG. 230. Monadnock Building. Daniel H. Burnham, solid masonry, 1889–92. Chicago Historical Society. Burnham and Root's original construction was a narrow, unornamented masonry building sixteen stories tall, which occupied one-half block on Dearborn Street. The last and highest American skyscraper to rely entirely upon masonry bearing walls, it has been admired as the final statement of its kind. A later addition was designed by Holabird and Roche (1893), continuing the building to Van Buren Street; this uses steel-frame construction.

FIG. 231. Flatiron Building. Daniel H. Burnham, steel frame and masonry, 1903. Granger Collection, New York.

FIG. 232. White City (The World's Columbian Exposition, 1893). Daniel H. Burnham, steel frame and masonry, 1893. Chicago Historical Society. The World's Columbian Exposition is also known as the Chicago World's Fair, 1893. The White City was a masonry structure in the lightest sense of the word: It consisted of a steel skeleton covered by a skin of plaster and glass. The use of plaster gave a substantial appearance to the completed "city," yet made it possible for Burnham's crews to build it in one and one-half years.

FIG. 233. City center plan, Chicago. Irving Fisher, overlay on drawing by Daniel H. Burnham, 1909. Avery Library, Columbia University.

FIG. 234. Proposed Field Museum. Daniel H. Burnham, drawing, 1908. Field Museum of Natural History, Chicago.

FIG. 235. Field Museum of Natural History. Daniel H. Burnham, steel frame and masonry, 1920. Field Museum of Natural History, Chicago.

FIG. 236. Pentagonal Civic Center Plaza. Jules Guerin, watercolor rendering of the site designed by Daniel H. Burnham, 1909. Avery Library, Columbia University.

FIG. 237. Regional plan, Chicago. Daniel H. Burnham, drawing, 1909. Avery Library, Columbia University, New York.

III. The Man & His World

SECTION TITLE. Excerpt from photoreproduction of Swedenborg's original manuscript of *Spiritual Diary*, para. 4165. Trans. George F. Dole. *Diarium Spirituale*, vol. II., p. 98.

FIG. 238. *Violin Player*. Pehr Hilleström (1733–1816), oil painting, 1700s. Nordiska Museet, Stockholm.

FIG. 239. Storage building at Julita Gård. Timber, probably 1600s–1700s. Swedenborg Image Archive (S. & R. Larsen photo, 1983). The farm site was established in the early 1100s; building continued through the 1700s.

FIG. 240. Wall painting in the farmhouse at Julita Gård. Mural painting on plaster, 1600s–1700s. Swedenborg Image Archive (S. & R. Larsen photo, 1983).

FIG. 241. Bishop's coach at Brunnsbo Kungsgård. Leather, cast iron, and wood, 1700s. Swedenborg

Image Archive (S. & R. Larsen photo, 1983).

FIG. 242. Midsummer pole at Svedens Gård. Swedenborg Image Archive (S. & R. Larsen photo, 1983).

FIG. 243. *Midsummer Eve at Munkbron in Stockholm.* Elias Martin (1739–1818), hand-tinted etching, late 1700s. Kungliga Biblioteket, Stockholm, Riddarhuset can be seen in the background.

FIG. 244. View of the farm at Julita Gård. Timber, 1600s–1700s (cf. fig. 239). Swedenborg Image Archive (S. & R. Larsen photo, 1983).

FIG. 245. Mine manager's house and grounds. Masonry manor house, probably 1600s–1700s. Stora Kopparbergs Bergslags AB, Falun (photo early 1900s, collected by Virginia Branston).

FIG. 246. Miner's cottage. Timber, probably 1700s. Stora Kopparbergs Bergslags AB, Falun (photo early 1900s, collected by Virginia Branston).

FIG. 247. *Stockholm from Kungsholmen.* Elias Martin (1739–1818), aquatint, 1700s. Kungliga Biblioteket, Stockholm.

FIG. 248. Carl Bellman drawing a mangle. Johann Gottlob Bruselle (1700s), wash drawing from Carl Michael Bellman (1740–1795), *Tjälvesta-breven*, 1790–96. Kungliga Biblioteket, Stockholm. The Tjälvesta letters include drawings by a number of eighteenth-century artists.

FIG. 249. *Grinding Coffee.* Pehr Hilleström (1733–1816), oil painting, 1778. Nordiska Museet, Stockholm.

FIG. 250. Sailors. Elias Martin, watercolor, probably late 1700s. Kungliga Biblioteket, Stockholm.

FIG. 251. *Carpenter in His Workshop.* Pehr Hilleström, oil painting, probably late 1700s. Nordiska Museet, Stockholm.

FIG. 252. *Harvest.* Pehr Hilleström, oil painting, 1778. Nordiska Museet, Stockholm.

FIG. 253. *Open Pit Mine.* C. G. Gillberg (1774–1855), watercolor, early 1800s. Nordiska Museet, Stockholm.

FIG. 254. Miners at work in the Falun copper mine. Pehr Hilleström, oil painting, 1781. Järnkontoret, Stockholm.

FIG. 255. *Iron Weigh-house.* Elias Martin, wash drawing, 1700s. Kungliga Biblioteket, Stockholm.

FIG. 256. Olof Rudbeck and family. By an unidentified artist, drawing from *Rudbeck Studier. Festskrifter vid Uppsala Universitets Minnesfest av 300-Årsminnet av Olof Rudbecks Födelse* (Rudbeck Studies: Commemorative Publication of Uppsala University's Celebration of the 300th Anniversary of Olof Rudbeck's Birth) (1930), 1680s. Uppsala Universitetsbibliotek.

FIG. 257. Musical group in eighteenth-century salon. Pehr Hilleström, oil painting, 1776. Nordiska Museet, Stockholm.

FIG. 258. *Cardgame at State Secretary Schröderheim's Home.* Pehr Hilleström, oil on canvas, ca. 1782. Nationalmuseum, Stockholm.

FIG. 259. Ball at Gröna Lund amusement park. By an unidentified artist, lithograph after a drawing by Elis Chiewitz (1784–1839), 1829. Nordiska Museet, Stockholm. The artist's name is also spelled Chevitz.

FIG. 260. Celebration at unveiling of monument to Carl Bellman. Carl Gustaf Hjalmar Mörner (1794–1837), lithograph, 1829. Kungliga Biblioteket, Stockholm.

FIG. 261. Drottningholm Theater. Carl Fredrik Adelcrantz (1716–1796), 1762–66. Drottningholms Tea-

termuseum, Stockholm. The "Palace on the Lake" (Drottningholm) replaced an earlier palace built by Willem Boy (cf. fig. 16), begun in 1597 for Johan III as a present for his queen, Katarina Jagiellonica. After it burned down in 1661, the present palace was built under the patronage of Queen Hedvig Eleonora, consort of Karl X. Nicodemus Tessin, the Elder (1615–1681), designed the palace and began its construction in 1662; it was completed by his son, Nicodemus Tessin, the Younger (1654–1728), around 1700. Theatrical events were staged in several parts of the palace until Queen Lovisa Ulrika built her theater (ca. 1754), which burned in 1762 and was replaced by the present theater.

FIG. 262. Assassination of Gustav III. A. W. Kusner (1700s–1800s), copper engraving, after 1792. Kungliga Biblioteket, Stockholm.

FIG. 263. Olof Rudbeck. Engraved frontispiece from Olof Rudbeck, the Elder (1630–1702), *Atlantica*, 1675. Swedenborg Image Archive (S. & R. Larsen photo, 1983).

FIG. 264. St. Erik's Square. By an unidentified artist, colored engraving, 1700s. Swedenborg Image Archive.

FIG. 265. View of Uppsala with the cathedral, the university, and the castle. Count Erik Dahlberg (1625–1703), engraving, 1716 (cf. fig. 9). Uppsala Universitetsbibliotek.

FIG. 266. Academia Carolina. Engraved plate from J. B. Busser, *Utkast till Beskrifning af Uppsala* (Draft for a Description of Uppsala), 1769. Uppsala Universitetsbibliotek.

FIG. 267. Stora Torget. By an unidentified artist, engraving, 1700s. Uppsala Universitetsbibliotek.

FIG. 268. An eighteenth-century student in fashionable dress. By an unidentified artist, engraving, 1700s. Swedenborg Image Archive.

FIG. 269. Entrance hall of the Västmanland-Dala Nation. Swedenborg School of Religion (photo 1918, collected by Virginia Branston).

FIG. 270. Academia Gustaviana. Johan Silfverling, engraving, 1700s. Swedenborg Image Archive. The original Gustavianum was built by Dutch master-builder Casper Panten, 1622–25. It was named after King Gustavus Adolphus, whose endowments of estates, books, and funds made possible the expansion of Uppsala University in the 1600s. After 1650 Olof Rudbeck (cf. fig. 21) supervised the restoration of the Gustavianum and added the Anatomical Theater with its cupola. Carl Hårleman again restored the Gustavianum in the mid-1700s (cf. fig. 16).

FIG. 271. Consistorium. Engraved plate from J. B. Busser, *Utkast till Beskrifning af Uppsala*, 1769. Uppsala Universitetsbibliotek.

FIG. 272. Observatorium. Engraved plate from J. B. Busser, *Utkast till Beskrifning af Uppsala*, 1769. Uppsala Universitetsbibliotek.

FIG. 273. Laboratorium Chemicum. Engraved plate from J. B. Busser, *Utkast till Beskrifning af Uppsala*, 1769. Uppsala Universitetsbibliotek.

FIG. 274. Olof Rudbeck's botanical garden. Engraved plate from Olof Rudbeck, the Elder (1630–1702), *Atlantica*, 1679. Uppsala Universitetsbibliotek.

FIG. 275. Exercitiegården. J. Härstedt (1755–1810), watercolor, 1782. Uppsala Universitetsbibliotek.

FIG. 276. Seventeenth-century houses in Uppsala. J. Härstedt, watercolor, 1700s. Uppsala Universitetsbibliotek.

IV. Religion & Philosophy

probably Middle Kingdom period, 2065 (?) B.C. Rosicrucian Egyptian Museum, San Jose, California (J. Chapman photo). (The museum in San Jose houses what is considered the best Egyptian collection west of the Mississippi). Osiris is not only judge in the afterlife, but also god of resurrection and eternal life.

FIG. 321. *Judgment of the Soul in the Other World*. Tomb with wall painting, 2065 (?) B.C. Rosicrucian Egyptian Museum, San Jose, California (J. Chapman photo).

FIG. 322. Honoré de Balzac. Reine Bertelle (?) (1900s), chalk sketch, n.d. Bettman Archive, New York. Bettman Archive spells the artist's name Bertell.

FIG. 323. Charles Pierre Baudelaire. Bettman Archive, New York.

V. *Theoretical & Applied Sciences*

SECTION TITLE. Excerpt from photoreproduction of Swedenborg's original manuscript of *Arcana Coelestia*, para. 6057. Trans. George F. Dole. Emanuelis Swedenborgii Autographa Ed. Phototypica, tom. XI, *Arcana Coelestia*, vol. II, p. 1005.

FIG. 324. Astronomer. J. G. Soibler (1700s), engraving, 1726, Courtesy of the Academy of the New Church (Diane Fehon photo, 1987).

FIG. 325. Royal Society House. By an unidentified artist, engraving, probably late 1700s. British Museum, London.

FIG. 326. Johannes Kepler. By an unidentified artist, painting, 1656. Bettman Archive, New York.

FIG. 327. Kepler's solids and spheres. By an unidentified artist, engraving, ca. 1596. Bettman Archive, New York.

FIG. 328. Descartes's vortices. Engraving from René Descartes (1596–1650), *Principia Philosophiae*, Amsterdam, 1656. Courtesy of the Academy of the New Church (Diane Fehon photo, 1987).

FIG. 329. René Descartes. Engraving, frontispiece from René Descartes, *Principia Philosophiae*, Amsterdam, 1656. Courtesy of the Academy of the New Church (Diane Fehon photo, 1987).

FIG. 330. *Queen Kristina Together with the Intellectuals*. Louis-Michel Dumesnil (b. 1680), oil painting, 1600s–1700s. Svenska Porträttarkivet.

FIG. 331. Sir Isaac Newton. Sir Godfrey Kneller (1647–1723), oil on canvas, 1702. Granger Collection, New York. Kneller was born Gottfried Kniller, in Germany; he emigrated to England, where he became a successful portrait painter, a member of the Royal Academy, and was knighted.

FIG. 332. Gottfried Wilhelm Leibniz. Engraving from Leibniz (1646–1716), *Tentamina Theodicaeae de Bonitate Dei Libertate Hominis et Origine Mali*, 1739. Courtesy of the Academy of the New Church (Diane Fehon photo, 1987).

FIG. 333. Christian Huygens. Engraving from Huygens (1629–1695), *Opera Varia*, vol. 1, 1724. Courtesy of the Academy of the New Church (Diane Fehon photo, 1987).

FIG. 334. Atmospheric-pressure experiment. Engraving from Otto von Guericke (1602–1686), *Experimenta Nova Magdeburgica de Vacuo Spatis*, 1672. Courtesy of the Academy of the New Church (Diane Fehon photo, 1987).

FIG. 335. Rendering of Saturn. Engraving from Christian Huygens (1629–1695), *The Celestial Worlds Discovered or Conjectures Concerning the Inhabitants, Plants and Productions of the Worlds in the Planets*, 1722. Courtesy of the Academy of the New Church (Diane Fehon photo, 1987).

FIG. 336. Robert Hooke's microscope. Engraving from Robert Hooke (1635–1703), *Micrographia, or some Physiological Descriptions of Minute Bodies made by Magnifying Glasses with Observations and Inquiries thereupon*, printed by John Martyn & James Alleatry, Printers to the Royal Society, 1665. Courtesy of the Academy of the New Church (Diane Fehon photo, 1987).

FIG. 337. Newton with prism. By an unidentified artist, colored engraving, 1800s. Granger Collection, New York.

FIG. 338. One of Bergman's experiments. By an unidentified artist, engraving, 1788. Uppsala Universitetsbibliotek.

FIG. 339. Immanuel Kant. Karl Barth (1886–1968), engraving, n.d. Bettman Archive, New York.

FIG. 340. Pierre Simon de Laplace. Engraving, frontispiece from *Exposition du Systeme due Monde*, 4th ed., Paris, 1813. Courtesy of the Academy of the New Church (Diane Fehon photo, 1987).

FIG. 341. Theory of Earth's positioning. Engraving from *Astronomiae Physicae & Geometricae Elementa*, 1726, David Gregory (1661–1708). Courtesy of the Academy of the New Church (Diane Fehon photo, 1987).

FIG. 342. Planetary evolution. Emanuel Swedenborg, engraving from *Principia*, 1734. Swedenborg Image Archive.

FIG. 343. *Le Taureau*. Engraving from *Atlas Celeste*, 2nd ed., Paris, 1776, John Flamsteed (1646–1719). Courtesy of the Academy of the New Church (Diane Fehon photo, 1987).

FIG. 344. Marcello Malpighi. Engraving, frontispiece from *Opera Posthuma*, 1687. Courtesy of the Academy of the New Church (Diane Fehon photo, 1987).

FIG. 345. Antoni van Leeuwenhoek. Engraving from van Leeuwenhoek, *Select Works*, trans. from Dutch and Latin eds., London, 1798. Granger Collection, New York.

FIG. 346. Application of the holographic model. Michael Talbot, pen and ink drawing, 1980s. Courtesy of the collection of Michael Talbot.

FIG. 347. Carolus Linnaeus. After Alexander Roslin (1718–1793), painting, 1775. Linnean Society, London.

FIG. 348. Carolus Linnaeus. After Johan H. Scheffel (1690–1781), painting, 1739. Linnean Society, London.

FIG. 349. The botanical garden in Leiden. Engraved plate from Hermann Boerhaave (1668–1738), *Index Plantarum*, 1710. Linnean Society, London. Boerhaave was a Dutch physician, professor at Leiden, author of important medical books; he is considered the founder of the modern system of clinical instruction.

FIG. 350. Sexual classification of plants. George-Dyonis Ehret (1710–1770), engraving, 1735. Engraved plate from Carolus Linnaeus (1707–1778), *Systema Naturae*, 1st ed., 1735. Courtesy of Svenska Linné-Sällskapet, Uppsala.

FIG. 351. Linnaeus Museum, formerly his house. Designed by Olof Rudbeck, the Elder (1630–1702), late 1600s. Swedenborg Image Archive (S. & R. Larsen photo, 1983, by permission of Linnémuseet). Rudbeck held the chair of medicine and botany at Uppsala University, which passed to his son, Olof, the Younger, and then to Linnaeus; each in turn occupied the house, which is now the Linnémuseet, Uppsala.

FIG. 352. Albino squirrel. Courtesy of Linnémuseet, Uppsala. Collected by Carolus Linnaeus.

FIG. 353. Specimen cases, in Linnaeus Museum (cf. fig. 356). Swedenborg Image Archive (S. & R. Larsen photo, 1983, by permission of Linnémuseet, Uppsala).

FIG. 354. Linnaeus's lecture room, in Linnaeus Museum (cf. fig. 356). Courtesy of Linnémuseet, Uppsala.

FIG. 355. Linnaeus's study, in Linnaeus Museum (cf. fig. 356). Courtesy of Linnémuseet, Uppsala.

FIG. 356. Linnaeus displaying a flower. Gustaf Henrik Brusewitz (1812–1899), lithograph, published in *Svenska Familje-Journalen*, 1860s. Linnean Society, London.

FIG. 357. Major journeys undertaken by Linnaeus's students. Professor Robert Fries, drawing, 1951. Courtesy of Svenska Linné-Sällskapet, Uppsala.

FIG. 358. Linnaeus's botanical garden (*Horti Upsaliensis Prospectus*). Engraved plate from Carolus Linnaeus, *Hortus Upsaliensis*, 1745. Uppsala Universitetsbibliotek.

FIG. 359. The orangerie. Designed by Carolus Linnaeus, 1700s. Swedenborg Image Archive (S. & R. Larsen photo, 1983, by permission of Linnémuseet). The orangerie stands at the back of Linnaeus's garden, Linneémuseet.

FIG. 360. "Lake pool" with water lilies. Designed by Carolus Linnaeus, 1700s. Swedenborg Image Archive (S. & R. Larsen photo, 1983, by permission of Linnémuseet).

FIG. 361. *Amaranthus caudatus*. Swedenborg Image Archive (S. & R. Larsen photo, 1983, by permission of Linnémuseet). These flowers are in Linnaeus's garden, Linnémuseet.

FIG. 362. Statue of Carolus Linnaeus. Carl Eldh (1873–1954), bronze, 1900s. Swedenborg Image Archive (S. & R. Larsen, 1983, by permission of Linnémuseet). Sculpture in the Linnaeus garden, Linnémuseet; Eldh has also done several portraits of Strindberg.

FIG. 363. Andromeda. Carolus Linnaeus, drawing, 1732. Courtesy of Svenska Linné-Sällskapet, Uppsala. Sketch of the Andromeda flower from *Iter Lapponicum*, 1732, Linnaeus's diary of his Lappland travels.

FIG. 364. Linnaeus in Lapp costume. Martin Hoffman (1700s), oil on canvas, 1737. Swedenborg Image Archive (S. & R. Larsen photo, 1983, by permission of Linnémuseet). Hoffman was a German painter working in Holland; he may have illustrated some of Linnaeus's work, and painted this portrait while Linnaeus was in Holland.

FIG. 365. Sir Isaac Newton. Sir Godfrey Kneller (1646–1723), painting, n.d. (cf. fig. 331). Bettman Archive, New York.

FIG. 366. Edmund Halley. By an unidentified artist, engraving, n.d. Bettman Archive, New York.

FIG. 367. Chronometer. By an unidentified artist, engraving, 1700s. Courtesy of the Academy of the New Church (Diane Fehon photo, 1987).

FIG. 368. Outside view of a finite particle. Engraving from Emanuel Swedenborg, *Principia*, 1734. Swed-

Index